Essentials of School Neuropsychological Assessment

Essentials of Psychological Assessment Series
Series Editors, Alan S. Kaufman and Nadeen L. Kaufman

Essentials

of School

Neuropsychological

Assessment

Second Edition

Daniel C. Miller

John Wiley & Sons, Inc.

WILEY

Cover Design: John Wiley & Sons, Inc.
Cover Image: © Greg Kuchik/Getty Images

This book is printed on acid-free paper. ⊗

Copyright © 2013 by John Wiley & Sons, Inc. All rights reserved.

Published by John Wiley & Sons, Inc., Hoboken, New Jersey.

Published simultaneously in Canada.

This publication is designed to provide accurate and authoritative information in regard to the subject matter covered. It is sold with the understanding that the publisher is not engaged in rendering professional services. If legal, accounting, medical, psychological, or any other expert assistance is required, the services of a competent professional person should be sought.

Designations used by companies to distinguish their products are often claimed as trademarks. In all instances where John Wiley & Sons, Inc. is aware of a claim, the product names appear in initial capital or all capital letters. Readers, however, should contact the appropriate companies for more complete information regarding trademarks and registration.

For general information on our other products and services, please contact our Customer Care Department within the United States at (800) 762-2974, outside the United States at (317) 572-3993 or fax (317) 572-4002.

Wiley publishes in a variety of print and electronic formats and by print-on-demand. Some material included with standard print versions of this book may not be included in e-books or in print-on-demand. If this book refers to media such as a CD or DVD that is not included in the version you purchased, you may download this material at http://booksupport.wiley.com. For more information about Wiley products, visit www.wiley.com.

Library of Congress Cataloging-in-Publication Data
Miller, Daniel C. (Daniel Carlton), 1956-
Essentials of school neuropsychological assessment [electronic resource]/Daniel C. Miller.—2nd ed.
1 online resource.
  Includes bibliographical references and index.
  Description based on print version record and CIP data provided by publisher; resource not viewed.
  ISBN 978-1-118-17584-2 (paper/cd)
  ISBN 978-1-118-41931-1 (ebk)
  ISBN 978-1-118-42107-9 (ebk)
  ISBN 978-1-118-43376-8 (ebk)
  1. Neuropsychological tests for children. 2. Pediatric neuropsychology. 3. School psychology.
4. School children—Mental health services. 5. Behavioral assessment of children. I. Title.
  RJ486.6
  618.928—dc23   2012028393

Printed in the United States of America

10 9 8 7 6 5 4 3 2 1

To my loving wife, Michie, who for 26 years has been my
best friend and best supporter, and to my parents,
Roger Carlton Miller and Mary Jane Miller.

CONTENTS

FOREWORD

The *Essentials of School Neuropsychological Assessment* by Daniel C. Miller is yet one more excellent addition to the Wiley *Essentials* series. Over the years, the *Essentials* series, designed and edited by Alan and Nadeen Kaufman, has provided a valuable avenue for the dissemination of information across many specialties in psychology. Each book is a concise, well-written, up-to-date, and practical resource. These "little" books may be small in size, yet they consist of a synthesis of huge amounts of information. They are relatively little in cost, yet they provide referenced materials that are used in everyday practice over and over again. It is hard not to own an *Essentials* book that does not look dog-eared and well worn!

From experience, I know that it is not easy to write these seemingly easy-to-read books. Parsimony is the rule of thumb during manuscript preparation, and the author(s) struggles with the synthesis of vast quantities of information sifted down into small tables, "Don't Forget" boxes, and streamlined chapters that give all the constituent parts of a subject while not losing the big picture. *Essentials* authors try to be fair and represent the subject matter objectively and with substantial evidence. They take great pains to give practical, evidence-based guidance that translates quickly into everyday practice. In this instance, I am delighted to say that Daniel C. Miller has managed to provide us in this second edition another typical *Essentials* book!

In the 1960s and 1970s, when school psychology was formed as a field of practice, little was known about brain-behavior relationships compared to today. School psychology practitioners had to assemble quickly after the passage of the first laws that guaranteed children with special needs rights to a free appropriate public education. Researchers struggled with vague technology to document what was going on in the brain. In kind, school psychologists struggled with their duty to bring science down to the everyday level of the classroom. The gap between the laboratory and the classroom was wide indeed.

As technology improved in the 1980s and 1990s researchers were able to observe the brain processing information with increasingly clearer media and the natural progression of applying the information began in earnest. Studies investigating dyslexia, attention deficit-hyperactivity disorder, and autism (to name a few) gave us direct inroads into understanding the physical processes that underlined the behaviors that we were seeing in the classroom. In turn, the following first decade of the century witnessed direct remediative attempts that were based in concrete imaging neuroscience. Work by eminent researchers, such as Sally Shaywitz, Bob Schultz, Ami Klin, Peg Semrud-Clikeman, Erin Bigler, and many others, showed serious and powerful attempts to bring laboratory findings directly into clinical practice. Interventions that were previously based on theory and speculation were now becoming interventions based on concrete attempts to encourage neural plasticity and all of the benefits of strength models of remediation. Therefore the gap between science and practice has been steadily decreasing and school psychology practitioners are finding themselves in the middle of new information that must be translated into practice.

In the first edition of the *Essentials of School Neuropsychology* we acknowledged that there was "a movement afoot in school psychology to include neuropsychological assessment principles into everyday practice" and that this movement did not evolve as a strong reactionary force loudly proclaiming its right to be heard, but more as "a reflection of practitioners trying to keep up with the advances of modern science." Some five years later, there is evidence that this quiet and serious grassroots movement is strong and continuing to strengthen as research on neuropsychological aspects of autism, traumatic brain injury, and specific learning disabilities are common in school psychology journals and trade publications. Indeed, the demise of the discrepancy model of learning disability identification has given way to powerful and theoretically based methods of determining cognitive strengths and weaknesses as they relate to academic skills. The latter requires inquiry into brain-behavior relationships and cements school psychology's commitment to translating neuroscientific knowledge to the individual level in the classroom.

How does the school psychologist keep up? What kind of information is needed in today's workplace? This quiet movement of applying neuropsychological information into school psychology practice is starting to crystallize. Leaders in the field are recognizing the need for training and school psychology training programs across the country are enhancing their curriculums to include courses on neuroanatomy, neuropsychological assessment, consultation, and competencies in medical liaison activities. Indeed, school psychology doctoral programs that have a strong emphasis on pediatric neuropsychology are now becoming common as the grassroots movement for continuing education grows.

There is enough established activity and interest in school neuropsychology for some authors to suggest that the time for a specialty within school psychology has come. The issues surrounding credentialing and competencies for such a specialty are quite complex, but regardless of the outcome of such issues, *the fact that the ethical demand for school psychologists to be aware of and to incorporate scientific information into everyday practice will remain.* Efforts to codify and express practice guidelines, such as those found in this book are needed at this time to direct and assist school psychologists in navigating their way in the future. It is not possible to wait for all issues to be resolved before applying new knowledge: That day may never come. After all, as a child stands before us today, we are charged to bring everything that we have and know to help him or her meet the demands of everyday living in the real world—not in a clinical setting, not in a hospital or rehabilitation center, but in a real classroom where most of the children have few problems and can easily perform learning and social tasks that sometimes seem insurmountable to the children we serve.

Daniel C. Miller's *Essentials of School Neuropsychological Assessment—Second Edition* is an important book. It provides us with clear and concise guidance on how to bring neuropsychological information and research into our non-clinical settings. This second edition merges the theoretical application of neuropsychological principles with the Cattell-Horn-Carroll model, which will hopefully assist with translating information to educational personnel in the school system. The second edition also provides supplementary information that is designed to have an immediate practical application. Clinicians can use the Neuropsychological Processing Concerns Checklist for Children and Youth immediately. The sample school neuropsychology report shell is also available. Dr. Miller also has updated the tables of numerous new tests and assessment measures to reflect a commitment to using the best tools of the trade within a practical model. All in all, the additions to the second edition are abundant and happily reflect the passion and strength of progress in the past 5 years.

The guidance in this book is not elementary; it is complex and requires much effort on the part of the reader to assimilate and translate into everyday practice. Dr. Miller emphasizes the need for formal training, appropriate supervision, and ongoing education. He also infuses the text with an exceptional level of competency, enthusiasm, and excitement for the subject matter that is contagious and motivating. This second edition is a welcome addition to the school psychologist's library and, like the first edition, is destined to become dog-eared and well worn!

Elaine Fletcher-Janzen, EdD, NCSP, ABPdN
Chicago School of Professional Psychology
Chicago, Illinois
June, 2012

SERIES PREFACE

I n the *Essentials of Psychological Assessment* series, we have attempted to provide the reader with books that deliver key practical information in the most efficient and accessible style. The series features instruments in a variety of domains, such as cognition, personality, education, and neuropsychology. For the experienced clinician, books in the series offer a concise yet thorough way to master utilization of the continuously evolving supply of new and revised instruments, as well as a convenient method for keeping up-to-date on the tried-and-true measures. The novice finds here a prioritized assembly of all the information and techniques that must be at one's fingertips to begin the complicated process of individual psychological diagnosis.

Wherever feasible, visual shortcuts to highlight key points are utilized alongside systematic, step-by-step guidelines. Chapters are focused and succinct. Topics are targeted for an easy understanding of the essentials of administration, scoring, interpretation, and clinical application. Theory and research are continually woven into the fabric of each book, but always to enhance clinical inference, never to sidetrack or overwhelm. We have long been advocates of "intelligent" testing—the notion that a profile of test scores is meaningless unless it is brought to life by the clinical observations and astute detective work of knowledgeable examiners. Test profiles must be used to make a difference in the child's or adult's life, or why bother to test? We want this series to help our readers become the best intelligent testers they can be.

The *Essentials of School Neuropsychological Assessment—Second Edition* provides clinicians with a thoroughly updated practical guide on how to integrate neuropsychological assessment into educational practice. The author, a world leader in the emerging specialty of school neuropsychology, provides a useful review of the history of adult and pediatric clinical neuropsychology and paints a careful picture of the emerging specialization of this rapidly growing field. The book features a list of professional organizations, training requirements, and professional resources, such as books and journals, that relate to school neuropsychology. The author provides an updated, state-of-the-art conceptual framework that can be used to guide practitioners who are interested in conducting school neuropsychological assessments. The current version of the school neuropsychological model (SNP) explained in this second edition is a further integration of Cattell-Horn-Carroll (CHC) Theory with neuropsychological theories. This Integrated SNP/CHC Model is described thoroughly and systematically with a chapter on each component. The author provides a comprehensive case study that illustrates how the school neuropsychological conceptual model can be operationalized and the reader is provided with a step-by-step interpretation guide for making sense of divergent data. The second edition of this book contains a supplemental CD that is filled with copies of rating forms, sample case studies, and a sample report shell template. We believe that *Essentials of School Neuropsychological Assessment— Second Edition* is a vital resource for all mental health care providers who work with children and who are interested in integrating neuropsychological principles into educational practice.

Alan S. Kaufman, PhD, and Nadeen L. Kaufman, EdD,
Series Editors
Yale Child Study Center, School of Medicine

ACKNOWLEDGMENTS

I would like to acknowledge several people in my life for their support and contributions. First and foremost, I want to thank my wife, Michie. She has been my best friend and primary editor for the past 26 years. I also want to thank my parents, Roger Carlton Miller and Mary Jane Miller. I got the writing gene from my father, the newspaper columnist and playwright. I got the attention to detail and patience from my mother. Thank you both for the nurturing guidance and support throughout the years.

For the first time in 23 years, I got some time off from the university to work on this book. Special thanks to my dean, Ann Staton, to the associate provost, Michael Stankey, and to the provost and vice president for academic affairs, Robert Neely, for their support of my release time. Also, thank you to Dr. Shannon Rich for stepping in as department chair in my absence.

Thank you to Bill Benson for doing the brain illustrations for the book and thank you Elaine Fletcher-Janzen for writing the Foreword to the book. Thank you to my colleague, Denise Maricle, who graciously edited early versions of the book and offered insights on ways to improve the content. Thank you to Glenda Peters, my administrative assistant at TWU, who helped "hold down the office" in my leave and who has been a good friend over the many years.

Thank you to several of my colleagues who contributed case studies to the supplemental CD. Thank you to my colleagues whom I have had the pleasure to work with in the School Neuropsychology Post-Graduate Training Program since 2002. I continue to be inspired by your professionalism and passionate commitment to school neuropsychology. Special thanks to Marquita Flemming, my senior editor at John Wiley & Sons, and her staff, for making the editorial process run smoothly for this second edition.

Finally, I want to thank the school psychologists I have taught or influenced over the past 20-plus years to integrate neuropsychological principles into their professional practices. Your collective commitment to providing high-quality services to children and their families is the inspiration that keeps me working hard.

Chapter One

THE EMERGING SPECIALIZATION OF SCHOOL NEUROPSYCHOLOGY

This first chapter reviews the major reasons why there is an interest in the emerging specialization of school neuropsychology, including the acknowledgment of the neurobiological bases of childhood learning and behavioral disorders, the increased number of children with chronic medical conditions that affect school performance, the increased use of medications with school-age children, the increase in the number of children with severe behavioral and emotional challenges, and the increased emphasis on the identification of processing disorders in children with specific learning disabilities. The chapter also reviews the need for providing neuropsychological assessment and consultation services within the schools. A definition of school neuropsychology is provided and the roles and functions of a school neuropsychologist are outlined. Finally, lists of the recent school neuropsychological publications and scholarly journals, that publish school neuropsychology research are presented.

REASONS WHY THERE IS A GROWING INTEREST IN SCHOOL NEUROPSYCHOLOGY

There are several reasons why there is a growing interest in school neuropsychology, including: (1) the wealth of research on the neurobiological bases of childhood learning and behavioral disorders; (2) the increased numbers of children in the schools with medical conditions that affect their school performance; (3) the increased use of medications prescribed to children; (4) the increase in the incidence rate of children who had serious educational and behavioral problems; and (5) the increased emphasis on the identification of processing disorders within children diagnosed with a specific learning disability. These reasons will be covered in more detail in this section of the chapter.

Recognition of the Neurobiological Bases of Childhood Learning and Behavioral Disorders

The interest in the biological bases of human behavior is not new to the school psychology profession, but it is becoming more relevant to the current generation of school psychologists. Some of the seasoned veterans or psychology historians suggest that there has always been an interest in the biological bases of behaviors. In fact, the "nature versus nurture" debate is as old as the psychology profession. Some major theorists in our shared past, such as B. F. Skinner and John B. Watson, were strict behaviorists. They believed that observable behavior was the only essential element that needed to be considered in human behavior. The curriculum-based measurement/assessment approach touted by many practitioners today has its theoretical roots in behaviorism.

> **DON'T FORGET**
> ....
> Many parents and educators are looking to school psychologists for answers as to why a student is not achieving at grade level or is behaving in socially inappropriate ways, rather than merely receiving a special education diagnosis.

In the late 1950s, researchers came to realize that the behaviorist approaches could not "explain complex mental functions such as language and other perceptual functions" (Gazzaniga, Ivry, & Mangun, 2002, p. 21), and this still holds true today. On the opposite end of the theoretical spectrum were the cognitive psychologists such as George Miller, Noam Chomsky, and Michael Posner, who believed that brain function needed to be considered in understanding human behaviors. Starting in the 1970s and continuing through today, the cognitive psychologists were tremendously aided by the development of neuroimaging techniques. Magnetic resonance imaging (MRI), positron emission tomography (PET), and functional MRI (fMRI) are all useful tools in validating or helping to refine theoretical models of cognition developed by cognitive psychologists.

It is important to acknowledge that the integration of neuropsychological principles into educational practice got off to a rough start. Practitioners who entered the field prior to the 1970s may remember Doman and Delcato's perceptual-motor training (R. Doman, Spitz, Zucman, Delacato, & G. Doman, 1960) for children with "minimal brain dysfunction" or tests such as the *Illinois Test of Psycholinguistic Abilities* (S. Kirk, McCarthy, & W. Kirk, 1968). These approaches may have had good face validity, but they did not accurately show treatment efficacy for either perceptual-motor deficits or language deficits. These early missteps in integrating neuropsychological principles into educational practice only reinforced the rising role of behaviorism in school psychology (Hynd & Reynolds, 2005).

Some contemporary and influential scholars still cite inadequate findings on the early process assessment approach in the 1970s as the basis for current legislative changes to the definition of a specific learning disability (Reschly, Hosp, & Schmied, 2003). Unfortunately, these influential scholars seem to have omitted an impressive body of empirical research in the past 30-plus years that supports the biological bases to the majority of childhood disorders.

CAUTION

A chief concern among school neuropsychologists is the increased emphasis in these federal laws and national reports on behavioral techniques at the expense of the role that individual differences in cognitive processes play in the child's learning.

After passage of Public Law 94–142 in the 1970s, researchers began to investigate the neurobiological bases of learning disabilities and behavioral disorders (Obrzut & Hynd, 1996). The past 40 years have yielded substantial evidence for the biological bases of behavior. There is strong neurobiological evidence for attention deficit hyperactivity disorders (see Hale et al., 2010, for a review), reading disorders (see Feifer, 2010, for a review), written language disorders (see Berninger, 2010, for a review), mathematics disorders (see Maricle, Psimas-Fraser, Muenke, & Miller, 2010, for a review), pervasive developmental disorders (see Bauman & Kemper, 2005; Dooley, 2010, for reviews), autism spectrum disorders (see Lang, 2010, for a review), and Asperger's disorder (see DeOrnellas, Hood, & Novales, 2010, for a review). See D. Miller (2010) for a comprehensive review of the neurobiological correlates to common childhood developmental disorders, academic disabilities, and processing disorders. School psychologists who want to translate this brain-behavior research into practice are increasingly interested in applying neuropsychological principles into their professional practice.

Increased Number of Children with Medical Conditions That Affect School Performance

An increasing number of children in the schools are affected with known or suspected neurological conditions. Unfortunately, many of these children rarely have their educational needs addressed. Accurate developmental histories may not be available to reflect early developmental concerns, medical conditions, or genetic predispositions.

As an example, if you were to walk into a neonatal intensive care unit, you would find many infants who were born prematurely and with very low birth weight. Many of these infants are so small that you might hold them in the palm of your hand. These infants often spend the first several months of their lives hooked up to ventilators and a mass of other medical monitors. Researchers have been increasingly interested in the potential negative academic and behavioral consequences of these premature and low-birth-weight babies as they reach school age and beyond (see Colaluca & Ensign, 2010; Dooley, 2010, for reviews).

When a school neuropsychologist reviews the cumulative record of a child referred for special education services, it is not uncommon to find a positive history of birth trauma or neonatal risk factors. Although there has been no noticeable decrease in the number of low-birth-weight infants born each year, advancement in quality neonatal intensive care has resulted in an increased survival rate. Whereas in the recent past, low-birth-weight and premature infants faced a high mortality rate, more of these at-risk infants are surviving early neurological insults. The premature birth rate in the United States rose by more than one third from the early 1980s through 2006; however, the upward trend has finally reversed based on 2007 and 2008 data (J. A. Martin, Osterman, & Sutton, 2010). Martin and colleagues reported that in 2008, 12.3% of all live births were preterm, or premature. In addition to prematurity and low-birth-weight, Rapid Reference 1.1 lists several other major medical influences on school neuropsychology.

Despite this high perinatal mortality rate (741 per 100,000; Miniño, 2011), there has been an improvement in the overall survival of low-birth-weight infants, most likely associated with advanced technology (Meadow, Lee, Lin, & Lantos, 2004). Interestingly, the actual cause of preterm birth remains somewhat elusive. While there are definite risk factors (e.g., African American ethnicity, low socioeconomic status, substance abuse, and poor maternal nutrition), there is essentially no one known identifiable cause (Slattery & Morrison, 2002). A review of the literature reveals that low-birth-weight infants are at risk for neurosensory, cognitive/neuropsychological, behavioral, and school/academic difficulties (Colaluca & Ensign, 2010; Dooley, 2010; Litt, Taylor, Klein, & Hack, 1995; Riccio, Sullivan, & Cohen, 2010).

Modern medical advances have also had an impact on the lives of children with other medical conditions such as cancer, AIDS, demyelinating diseases, traumatic brain injuries, and more rare medical diseases and conditions. The rate of chronic health conditions among children in the United States increased from 12.8% in 1994 to 26.6% in 2006 (Van Cleave, Gortmaker, & Perrin, 2010). Kline, Silver, and Russell (2001) reported that within the population of chronically ill children, 30% to 40% have school-related problems (see Colaluca & Ensign, 2010, for a review). The majority of these children would qualify

≋ *Rapid Reference 1.1*

Increased Medical Influences on School Neuropsychology

- More children are surviving birth traumas and other major medical illnesses with known correlates to later academic and behavioral concerns.
- Children and adolescents with traumatic brain injury present unique challenges to educators.
- There has been a tremendous increase in the number of children who are prescribed medications to control mood and behavioral disorders.
- There has been an increased number of research studies illuminating neuropsychological deficits associated with chronic illnesses such as asthma, diabetes, and heart disease.
- There has been an increased discovery of the limitations of clinical treatment for neurological disorders such as autism in school-based settings.

under the Individuals With Disabilities Education Act (IDEA) category of *other health impaired* (OHI). These health problems and their treatments can cause secondary academic and behavioral problems that could also lead to classification under other IDEA categories (e.g., *specific learning disabilities, serious emotional disturbance*).

In the early 1990s, a child with a head injury would move from an acute care hospital setting, where the physical and medical needs were met, to an intermediate rehabilitation setting for a few months, where cognitive rehabilitation took place (D. Miller, 2004). Today it is typical for a child to forego any formal cognitive rehabilitation and return to school soon after he or she is medically stabilized. During the past 10 to 15 years, managed health care has led to a reduction in cognitive rehabilitation services offered to children and youth with traumatic brain injuries (TBIs). In defense of the managed health care industry, the literature on the effectiveness of cognitive rehabilitation with children has been sparse (Slomine & Locascio, 2009). Despite the fact that TBI and OHI have been disability classifications for decades, school personnel are not often prepared to educate children with, or recovering from, severe and chronic illnesses, including TBI. Children and adolescents with TBI require specialized treatment and monitoring different from other special education classifications (see Morrison, 2010, for a review). Due to uneven spontaneous recovery of brain function and continued developmental changes, the clinical manifestation of TBI is constantly changing and requires frequent monitoring. Unlike some disabilities that require only 3-year reevaluations, children with TBI need frequent monitoring for changes in academic, behavioral, adaptive, and social-emotional functioning

(Morrison, 2010). School neuropsychologists can play a major role in being the liaisons between the school and the medical community, developing transitional/reentry plans for school-age children returning to school after injury or insult, assisting with IEP development and monitoring, and general case management (see Prout, Cline, & Prout, 2010, for a review).

Increased Use of Medications with School-Age Children

There has been a dramatic increase in the number of school-age children taking psychotropic medications. Patel (2005) examined the prevalence rates of antipsychotic use in children and adolescents from 1996 to 2001 across three Medicaid states (Ohio, Texas, and California) and one private managed care organization. The prevalence of atypical antipsychotic use increased dramatically (Ohio Medicaid: 1.4 to 13.1 per 1,000; Texas Medicaid: 2.5 to 14.9; California Medi-Cal: 0.3 to 6.2; and, Managed Care Organization: 0.4 to 2.7). Disruptive behavioral disorders were most commonly associated with antipsychotic prescriptions. Medicaid Medical Directors Learning Network and Rutgers Center for Education and Research on Mental Health Therapeutics (2010) examined antipsychotic medication use in Medicaid children and adolescents across 16 states. The study found that in 2007, 1.7% of Medicaid children and adolescents received antipsychotic prescriptions, which represents a 10% increase from comparable data in 2004.

Another disturbing trend with school-age children is the multiple types of medications prescribed without apparent regard for the potential drug interactions and adverse side effects. Zonfrillo, Penn, and Leonard (2005) reviewed the research studies published from 1994 to 2004 regarding the practice of prescribing multiple medications to treat mental conditions in children and adolescents. The results suggested that there was a marked increase in the use of multiple medications (or polypharmacy) with children, despite a lack of research in this area. Constantine, Boaz, and Tandon (2010) reported similar finding based on trends between 2002 and 2007.

School neuropsychologists are not physicians, but they can provide information about how psychotropic medication used to treat common problems like depression, anxiety, and attentional processing disorders can affect learning and behavior. There is a wealth of information available about medication interactions and potential side effects on the Internet. Questions concerning the interactions and long-term consequences of polypharmacy and the neuropsychological effects of medications are currently being researched.

Increase in the Number of Challenging Educational and Behavioral Issues in the Schools

School psychologists note that there appear to be more children today, than 10 to 20 years ago, who are exhibiting severe behavioral, social-emotional, and academic problems. There is evidence to support that consensus. In the *Report of the Surgeon General's Conference on Children's Mental Health: A National Action Agenda* (2000), it was reported that there are approximately 6 to 9 million U.S. children and adolescents with serious emotional disturbances, which accounts for 9% to 13% of all children. Unfortunately, many children with diagnosable mental disorders do not receive services. The *Report of the Surgeon General on Children's Mental Health: A National Action Agenda* (U.S. Department of Health and Human Services, 2001) indicated that approximately 70% of children and adolescents who are in need of treatment do not receive services. Many of the serious emotional disturbances experienced by children such as depression, anxiety-related disorders, and ADHD all have known or suspected neurological etiology. Therefore, many children with known or suspected neurological impairments who exhibit symptoms of mental health problems are not identified, or are identified and not receiving services.

Another major concern in educational practice is inaccurate diagnoses and placements of children and adolescents with known or suspected neurological impairments. Neurologically impaired children are often mislabeled as seriously emotionally disturbed or learning disabled. These diagnoses and subsequent educational and behavioral interventions do not address underlying neuro-psychological dysfunction. Misdiagnosis or misclassification can lead to serious consequences in a child's lifetime. Lewis et al. (1988) evaluated 14 juveniles incarcerated in four U.S. states using comprehensive psychiatric, neurological, neuropsychological, and educational evaluations. The results were alarming. Nine of the 14 juveniles had symptoms consistent with major neurological impairment, 7 suffered from psychotic disorders that preceded incarceration, 7 showed symptoms of significant organic brain dysfunction on neuropsychological testing, and only 2 had Full Scale IQ scores above 90.

From a prevention and early intervention perspective, it seems to make sense that children with known or suspected neurological disorders must be educated appropriately. Too often, educators treat only the symptoms and not the under-lying problems. Even though the classification of TBI has been in the IDEA law since 1990, many educators and school psychologists are ill equipped to deal with the special needs of this population.

School psychologists are also working with more children who have survived major medical insults and children who are taking more medications that affect learning and behavior. The effects of changing educational law, policies, and practices on the emerging specialization of school neuropsychology have been reviewed in this section of the chapter. In the next section, the reasons for neuropsychological assessment to be in included in the schools are reviewed.

Increased Emphasis on the Identification of Processing Disorders in Specific Learning Disabled Children

In the most recent version of the Individuals with Disabilities Act of 2004 (U.S. Department of Education, 2004), the definition of a Specific Learning Disability (SLD) includes language that stated:

"[A] disorder in one or more of the basic psychological processes involved in the understanding or in using language, spoken or written, that may manifest itself in an imperfect ability to listen, think, speak, read, write, spell, or do mathematical calculations, including conditions such as perceptual disabilities, brain injury, minimal brain dysfunction, dyslexia, and developmental aphasia" but does not include " . . . learning problems that are primarily the result of visual, hearing, or motor disabilities, or intellectual disability, or emotional disturbance, or of environmental, cultural, or economic disadvantage." (34 C.F.R. § 300.8(c)(10))

By requiring an assessment specialist to rule out exclusions such as intellectual disability or perceptual limitations as the causal factors for an SLD, the SLD definition encourages the assessment specialist to determine the reasons why there is a learning delay. The assessment specialist, who is a school neuropsychologist, brings a unique set of skills to bear on the need to identify the underlying neurological deficits that could explain the presence of an SLD. School neuropsychologists have a more sophisticated set of testing instruments that they are trained to use that will help address the neurocognitive strengths and weaknesses of an SLD child and increase the likelihood of academic improvement through targeted, evidence-based interventions.

IDEA 2004 allowed states to move away from the use of discrepancy models for the identification of an SLD. One of the approved approaches for SLD identification is the assessment of processing strengths and weaknesses to determine the underlying causes for an SLD. With this change in the federal law, many assessment specialist practitioners, including school psychologists, have the need to enhance their professional skills. School psychologists trained in how to integrate neuropsychological principles into their professional practice are uniquely qualified to assess processing strengths and weaknesses in SLD children.

THE NEED FOR NEUROPSYCHOLOGICAL ASSESSMENT IN THE SCHOOLS

This section of the chapter attempts to answer the question, why is there a need for neuropsychological assessment in the schools? The reasons for having access to more neuropsychological assessments accessible in the schools include: (1) the limited access to pediatric neuropsychological services in general; (2) the limited usefulness of some neuropsychological reports; and (3) the unique contributions of school neuropsychological assessments in making diagnoses and linking evidence-based interventions.

Access to Neuropsychological Services in the Schools

Access to neuropsychological services both inside and outside of the schools is often limited. Due to a supply-and-demand problem, even if a school district locates a neuropsychologist to evaluate a child, the evaluation may be costly and there may be a long wait time to have it completed. Access to neuropsychological services is even more difficult, if not impossible, in rural portions of the country where there are often no neuropsychologists.

In an ideal world, each school district would have access to a pediatric neuropsychologist who would write reports that were both informative and educationally relevant and who would consult regularly with educators and parents. Across the country, clinical neuropsychologists are more plentiful than pediatric neuropsychologists, but most clinical neuropsychologists are trained to work with adult populations, not school-age children. A pediatric neuropsychologist would typically be found working in a hospital or rehabilitation setting with severely impaired children and generally would not have time for school-based assessments. Therefore, access to neuropsychological services from a clinical neuropsychologist for school-age children is often difficult.

DON'T FORGET

Access to clinical and pediatric neuropsychologists is often difficult or impossible in some portions of the country. At a minimum, school psychologists need to enhance their knowledge base about the biological bases of behavior.

Limited Usefulness of Some Neuropsychological Reports

Educators may have experienced sitting in an IEP meeting where a parent brings in a report from a neuropsychologist consultant. Too frequently, neuropsychological reports from outside consultants are filled with diagnostic conclusions and much test

> **DON'T FORGET**
> ....
> The delivery of neuropsychological services in the schools is more than completing comprehensive assessments. Overseeing the implementation of the evidence-based interventions is crucial.

data, but lack prescriptive recommendations that would be useful interventions in educational settings. Pelletier, Hiemenz, and Shapirio (2004) refer to this report as a "pin the tail on a lesion" type of report. In these cases, the expensive report that the parent brings to the school is frequently filed in the child's educational folder as educationally irrelevant and the experience becomes frustrating for all parties concerned.

Historically, neuropsychologists come from clinical psychology doctoral programs and have been trained in clinical psychopathology models of assessment and intervention for adults. These practitioners are often not familiar with educational laws such as IDEA, NCLB, and Section 504 of the Rehabilitation Act or with the organization and operation of schools in general. Hurewitz and Kerr (2011) stated, "because neuropsychologists may provide reports for treatment, school programming, legal disputes, or any combination thereof, it is important that they are familiar with the school programming process and the unique litigation procedures available for children with disabilities in special education" (2011, p. 1058). Fletcher-Janzen (2005) presented a chart showing a clear comparison of the differences between neuropsychologists that practice in the schools and neuropsychologists that practice in private agencies. School neuropsychologists have the advantage of working with children with whom they have a long educational history and multiple opportunities for assessment and intervention progress monitoring. Comparatively, pediatric neuropsychologists typically only see children outside of the school setting for a brief period of time (e.g., during a hospital stay) and are not able to observe the child in the natural school setting, nor to follow up on the effectiveness of their recommended interventions.

Also clinical neuropsychologists may not understand that a clinical report with a *DSM* diagnosis does not always equate to a child's need for special education services. There is an obvious need for more cross training between school psychologists and clinical neuropsychologists (pediatric neuropsychologists included). To best help the child, clinical neuropsychologists must learn which diagnoses and educational interventions are useful to school districts (Hurewitz & Kerr,

> **DON'T FORGET**
> ....
> School psychologists are ideal candidates to broaden their competencies in neuropsychology because they are increasingly being held accountable for evidence of success or failure of interventions.

2011). School psychologists with training in neuropsychology can play a role in consulting with clinical neuropsychologists to help determine services needed by the school districts.

Keeping in mind the limited access to neuropsychologists and the documented needs of children with known or suspected neurological conditions in the schools, we turn our attention to the approximately 35,000 school psychologists in the United States who have direct access to children. Miller (2004, 2007, 2010) pointed out that many of the new cognitive abilities tests and tests of memory and learning that are routinely used by school psychologists have strong theoretical foundations in neuropsychological theory. At a minimum, all school psychologists will have to improve their knowledge base about neuropsychological theories if they are going to appropriately interpret these new tests. The advantage of having a school psychologist trained in integrating neuropsychological principles into practice is that the end product of all services delivered by the school psychologist will be generally more pragmatic for the school and the child. However as D. Miller (2004, 2007, 2010) pointed out, although a school neuropsychologist writes an insightful report and makes practical, evidence-based recommendations, there is no guarantee that the recommendations will be implemented. A major role of a neuropsychologist, whether an external consultant or an internal school psychologist with neuropsychology expertise, is to help teachers implement the educational recommendations using their consultation skills, instructional design knowledge, and program evaluation skills. An excellent neuropsychological evaluation filed away in the child's cumulative folder will benefit neither the school nor the child.

The Unique Contribution of School Neuropsychological Assessments

In Chapter 6, the differences among psychoeducational, psychological, and school neuropsychological assessments are discussed. In general, neuropsychological assessments are the most comprehensive of the three types and often encompass both the psychoeducational and psychological components. What makes school neuropsychological assessments unique is the inclusion of more in-depth assessment of individual neurocognitive constructs such as sensory-motor functions, attentional processing, learning and memory, and executive functions.

School neuropsychological assessments are useful for:

- Identifying processing deficits in a child that could adversely affect educational attainment and developing remedial and/or compensatory strategies to maximize the child's learning potential.

- Describing a profile of a child's neurocognitive strengths and weaknesses and relating that information to the child's learning and behavior in the school and home environments.
- Determining whether changes in learning or behavior are associated with neurological disease, psychological conditions, neurodevelopmental disorders, or non-neurological conditions.
- Monitoring educational progress over time in children, particularly in children with severe neuropsychological insults such as traumatic brain injury.
- Providing comprehensive assessment data that will increase the likelihood of success with evidence-based interventions.

Summary of the Need for School Neuropsychological Assessment in the Schools

There is a documented need for neuropsychological services within the schools. However, finding a neuropsychologist with an understanding of developmental issues and the rules and regulations that guide educational practice is difficult. Traditional reports written by clinical neuropsychologists are often not useful in the schools. These reports tend to be too long and cumbersome, often describe the tests more than the child, and often have recommendations not relevant for most school-based learning environments. In addition, clinical neuropsychologists are not in a position to be held accountable for evidence of the success or failure of interventions. School psychologists, on the other hand, are directly responsible for outcomes and therefore are close at hand on a daily basis to see the interventions through to fruition. School psychologists are ideal candidates to broaden their competencies in neuropsychology to better serve educators, children, and their families.

DEFINITION OF SCHOOL NEUROPSYCHOLOGY

Miller, along with two colleagues, wrote the following definition of school neuropsychology for a series of training workshops:

> School neuropsychology requires the integration of neuropsychological and educational principles to the assessment and intervention processes with infants, children, and adolescents to facilitate learning and behavior within the school and family systems. School neuropsychologists also play an important role in curriculum development, classroom design, and the integration of differentiated instruction that is based on brain-behavior

principles in order to provide an optimal learning environment for every child. (D. Miller, DeFina, & Lang, 2004)

In order to discuss some of the associated implications, this definition will be broken down into smaller components.

"School neuropsychology requires the integration of neuropsychological and educational principles . . ." The blend between educational and neuropsychological foundations is an essential knowledge base for school neuropsychologists.

"[T]o the assessment and intervention processes with infants, children, and adolescents . . ." School neuropsychology is not limited to assessment and diagnosis. Linking assessment with evidence-based interventions is an important focus for school psychologists and school neuropsychologists. Also, school neuropsychologists are trained to work with infants and school-age children.

"[T]o facilitate learning and behavior within the school and family systems." School neuropsychologists are trained to work with children and adolescents within the context of their school and home environments. Learning and behavioral problems do not stop at the end of the school day. Family involvement is crucial in affecting positive behavioral and academic change in a child.

"School neuropsychologists also play an important role in curriculum development, classroom design, and the integration of differentiated instruction that is based on brain-behavior principles in order to provide an optimal learning environment for every child." School psychologists and school neuropsychologists are trained as consultants to the learning environment, linking instructional design, curriculum development, and differential assessment to research-based interventions. School neuropsychologists are uniquely trained to apply brain-based research principles to enhance the educational environment.

ROLES AND FUNCTIONS OF A SCHOOL NEUROPSYCHOLOGIST

George Hynd (1981) is credited as being the first school psychologist to advocate for doctoral school psychologists to be trained in clinical neuropsychology. Hynd suggested that a doctoral-level school psychologist with training in neuropsychology:

- Interprets the results of neuropsychological assessment and develops strategies of intervention.
- Presents recommendations for remediation based on knowledge of scientifically validated interventions.
- Consults with curriculum specialists in designing approaches to instruction that more adequately reflect what is known about neuropsychological development.

DON'T FORGET

··

The roles and functions for school neuropsychologists suggested by Hynd in 1981 are still relevant today.

- Acts as an organizational liaison with the medical community, coordinating and evaluating medically based interventions.
- Conducts inservice workshops for educational personnel, parents, and others on the neuropsychological basis of development and learning.
- Conducts both basic and applied educational research investigating the efficacy of neuropsychologically based interventions and consultation in the schools.

More recently, Crespi and Cooke (2003, pp. 98–99) posed that training in neuropsychology can:

- Facilitate teacher and parent education/consultation.
- Assist in developing neuropsychologically informed special education decisions.
- Enhance referral use for neuropsychological services.
- Increase the ability to comprehend articles that have relied on neuropsychological concepts and methods in attempts to understand the etiology and behavioral or educational consequences of childhood developmental disorders.
- Protect against more simplistic and inaccurate habits (i.e., specific localization of brain functions or dysfunctions based on performance on a single psychological measure).
- Serve as a bridge between clinically based neuropsychologists and school-based psychologists in providing an interpretative explanation of specific results and recommendations.
- Provide a theoretical framework that appreciates the value of multidimensional batteries and the inherent complexities and difficulties of making inferences about brain integrity.

Rapid Reference 1.2 summarizes the various roles and functions of a school neuropsychologist.

LIST OF RECENT SCHOOL NEUROPSYCHOLOGY BOOKS

Rapid Reference 1.3 lists some of the major school neuropsychology books that have been published in recent years. The vast majority of the authors of the school

=== *Rapid Reference 1.2*

Roles and Functions of a School Neuropsychologist

- Provide neuropsychological assessment and intervention services to schools for students with known or suspected neurological conditions.
- Assist in the interpretation of neuropsychological findings from outside consultants or medical records.
- Seek to integrate current brain research into educational practice.
- Provide educational interventions that have a basis in the neuropsychological or educational literature.
- Act as a liaison between the school and the medical community for transitional planning for TBI and other health-impaired children and adolescents.
- Consult with curriculum specialists in designing approaches to instruction that more adequately reflect what is known about brain-behavior relationships.
- Conduct inservice training for educators and parents about the neuropsychological factors that relate to common childhood disorders.
- Engage in evidence-based research to test for the efficacy of neuropsychologically based interventions.

neuropsychology resource books cited in Rapid Reference 1.3 are school psychologists.

LIST OF JOURNALS THAT PUBLISH SCHOOL NEUROPSYCHOLOGICAL RESEARCH

Rapid Reference 1.4 presents a list of journals most relevant to school neuropsychology. Rapid Reference 1.4 also presents a tabulation of the number of published articles related to pediatric/school neuropsychology in each of these journals from 1991 to 2012. These figures were derived by initially going to the online PsycInfo database and searching peer-reviewed journal articles that contained the word "neuropsychology" with age ranges including preschool through adolescence. The numbers of articles that match these criteria are presented in Rapid Reference 1.4. Despite the certain biological bases of all developmental disorders, school psychologists interested in reading original research on topics related to school neuropsychology must go beyond the traditional school psychology journals (e.g., *School Psychology Review*—The official journal of the National Association of School Psychologists, or the *School Psychology Quarterly*—the official

≋ *Rapid Reference 1.3*

Major School Neuropsychology Publications (most recent to oldest)

Barkley, R. A. (2012). *Executive functions: What are they, how they work, and why they evolved.* New York, NY: Guilford Press.

Davis, A. S. (Ed.). (2011). *Handbook of pediatric neuropsychology.* New York, NY: Springer.

Anderson, V., & Yeates, K. O. (Eds.). (2010). *Pediatric traumatic brain injury: New frontiers in clinical and translational research.* New York, NY: Cambridge University Press.

Dawson, P., & Guare, R. (2010). *Executive skills in children and adolescents: A practical guide to assessment and intervention* (2nd ed.). New York, NY: Guilford Press.

Dehn, M. J. (2010). *Long-term memory problems in children and adolescents: Assessment, intervention, and effective instruction.* Hoboken, NJ: Wiley.

Goldstein, S., & Reynolds, C. R. (Eds.). (2010). *Handbook of neurodevelopmental and genetic disorders in children* (2nd ed.). New York, NY: Guilford Press.

Kemp, S. L., & Korkman, M. (2010). *Essentials of the NEPSY-II assessment.* Hoboken, NJ: Wiley.

Koziol, L. F., & Budding, D. E. (2010). *Subcortical structures and cognition: Implications for neuropsychological assessment.* New York, NY: Springer.

Meltzer, L. (2010). *Promoting executive function in the classroom (what works for special-needs learners).* New York, NY: Guilford Press.

Miller, D. C. (Ed.). (2010). *Best practices in school neuropsychology: Guidelines for effective practice, assessment, and evidence-based intervention.* Hoboken, NJ: Wiley.

Riccio, C. A., Sullivan, J. R., & Cohen, M. J. (2010). *Neuropsychological assessment and intervention for childhood and adolescent disorders.* Hoboken, NJ: Wiley.

Christo, C., Davis, J., & Brock, S. E. (2009). *Identifying, assessing, and treating dyslexia at school.* New York, NY: Springer.

McCloskey, G., Perkins, L. A., & Diviner, B. V. (2009). *Assessment and intervention for executive function difficulties.* Florence, KY: Routledge.

Petersen, R. L., Yeates, K. O., Ris, M. D., Taylor, H. G., & Pennington, B. F. (2009). *Pediatric neuropsychology, Research, theory, and practice* (2nd ed.). New York, NY: Guilford Press.

Semrud-Clikeman, M., & Teeter-Ellison, P. A. (2009). *Child neuropsychology: Assessment and interventions for neurodevelopmental disorders* (2nd ed.). New York, NY: Springer.

Apps, J. N., Newby, R. F., & Roberts, L. W. (2008). *Pediatric neuropsychology case studies: From the exceptional to the commonplace.* New York, NY: Springer.

Castillo, C. L. (Ed.). (2008). *Children with complex medical issues in schools: Neuropsychological descriptions and interventions.* New York, NY: Springer.

Dehn, M. J. (2008). *Working memory and academic learning: Assessment and intervention.* Hoboken, NJ: Wiley.

Fletcher-Janzen, E., & Reynolds, C. R. (Eds.). (2008). *Neuropsychological perspectives on learning disabilities in the era of RTI: Recommendations for diagnosis and intervention.* Hoboken, NJ: Wiley.

Mody, M., & Sullivan, E. R. (Eds.). (2008). *Brain, behavior, and learning in language and reading disorders.* New York, NY: Guilford Press.

Reed, J., & Warner-Rigers, J. (Eds.). (2008). *Child neuropsychology: Concepts, theory, and practice.* New York, NY: Wiley-Blackwell.

Reynolds, C. R., & Fletcher-Janzen, E. (Eds.). (2008). *Handbook of clinical child neuropsychology* (3rd ed.). New York, NY: Plenum Press.

Feifer, S. G., & Della Toffalo, D. A. (2007). *Integrating RTI with cognitive neuropsychology: A scientific approach to reading.* Middletown, MD: School Neuropsych Press.

Miller, D. C. (2007). *Essentials of school neuropsychological assessment.* Hoboken, NJ: Wiley.

Dehn, M. J. (2006). *Essentials of processing assessment.* Hoboken, NJ: Wiley.

Feifer, S. G., & DeFina, P. A. (2005). *The neuropsychology of mathematics: Diagnosis and intervention.* Middletown, MD: School Neuropsych Press.

Baron, I. S. (2004). *Neuropsychological evaluation of the child.* New York, NY: Oxford University Press.

Dewey, D., & Tupper, D. E. (2004). *Developmental motor disorders: A neuropsychological perspective.* New York, NY: Guilford Press.

Hale, J. B., & Fiorello, C. A. (2004). *School neuropsychology: A practitioner's handbook.* New York, NY: Guilford Press.

Shaywitz, S. (2003). *Overcoming dyslexia: A new and complete science-based program for reading problems at any level.* New York, NY: Knopf.

Berninger, V. W., & Richards, T. L. (2002). *Brain literacy for educators and psychologists.* New York, NY: Academic Press.

Eslinger, P. J. (Ed.). (2002). *Neuropsychological interventions.* New York, NY: Guilford Press.

Feifer, S. G., & DeFina, P. A. (2002). *The neuropsychology of written language disorders: Diagnosis and intervention.* Middletown, MD: School Neuropsych Press.

Semrud-Clikeman, M. (2001). *Traumatic brain injury in children and adolescents.* New York, NY: Guilford Press.

Goldstein, S., & Reynolds, C. R. (Eds.). (1999). *Neurodevelopmental and genetic disorders in children.* New York, NY: Guilford Press.

Siantz-Tyler, J., & Mira, M. P. (1999). *Traumatic brain injury in children and adolescents: A sourcebook for teachers and other school personnel.* Austin, TX: Pro-Ed.

≡ Rapid Reference 1.4

Journals Relevant to School Neuropsychology[1]

Journal	Number of Articles (1991–2012) Related to School/Pediatric Neuropsychology Issues
Developmental Neuropsychology	502
Child Neuropsychology[2]	407
Journal of Clinical and Experimental Neuropsychology	277
Archives of Clinical Neuropsychology	214
Neuropsychology	194
Applied Neuropsychology	91
Journal of the International Neuropsychological Society	57
Cognitive and Behavioral Neurology	55
Journal of Child Psychology and Psychiatry	38
Aging, Neuropsychology, and Cognition	36
Journal of Cognitive Neuroscience	32
Clinical Neuropsychologist	27
Neuropsychology Review	14
Journal of Intellectual Disability Research	12
Developmental Psychology	10
Brain Impairment	5
International Journal of Developmental Neuroscience	5
Mind, Brain, and Education[3]	4
Journal of Psychoeducational Assessment	4
Psychology in the Schools	4
Psychological Assessment	3
School Psychology Review	1
School Psychology Quarterly	0

[1] Through May 11, 2012.
[2] The Child Neuropsychology journal was introduced in 1995.
[3] Mind, Brain, and Education was introduced in 2007.

journal of the American Psychological Association's Division 16—School Psychology). These two school psychology journals have published only one original school/pediatric neuropsychology article in the past 21 years, compared to 1,594 original peer-reviewed journal articles published in the top five journals associated with neuropsychology. School neuropsychology professional practice issues and research are currently published across a broad spectrum of journals, with the majority in neuropsychology journals.

CHAPTER SUMMARY

The understanding and respect for the biological bases of behavior has been a part of the field of psychology since its inception. The increased interest in applying neuropsychological principles into the practice of school psychology and educational settings has been a direct result of many factors including:

- The growth in pediatric/child neuropsychological research.
- Advances in neuropsychological theories applied to assessment.
- Advances in functional and structural brain imaging techniques.
- Limitations of clinical applications in school settings.
- Increased use of medications by children and youth and their potential side effects on cognitive processing.
- Advances in understanding the neurocognitive effects of traumatic brain injury, common neurodevelopmental disorders, and chronic illness.

There continues to be interest in school neuropsychology because school psychologists work every day with children who have known or suspected neurodevelopmental disorders. With the increased emphasis on implementing and monitoring the effectiveness of evidence-based interventions, school psychologists are under pressure to provide the best assessment-intervention linkage as quickly as possible. School psychologists and educators need to know the documented neuropsychological correlates to common neurodevelopmental disorders to prescribe and monitor the most effective interventions. The past two decades, in particular, have been an exciting time for school psychologists interested in learning more about neuropsychology and how to apply that knowledge base to helping children, their families, and educators. School psychologists have more assessment tools today that are psychometrically sound and theoretically based than ever before. The challenge for all of education, school psychology as a discipline, and school neuropsychology as an emerging specialization is to increase research that validates the linkage between assessment data and the prescriptive interventions that have been shown to be the most effective.

School neuropsychology has its roots firmly planted in the historical foundations of clinical neuropsychology and school psychology. These historical influences on the emerging specialization of school neuropsychology are the focus of Chapter 2.

TEST YOURSELF

1. The 1970s catalyst for researchers to investigate the neurobiological bases of learning disabilities and behavioral disorders was:
a. Passage of *No Child Left Behind* legislation
b. Doman Delcato's perceptual-motor training
c. Passage of P.L. 94–142
d. The *Illinois Test of Psycholinguistic Abilities*

2. True or False? More children are surviving birth traumas and medical illnesses with known correlates to later academic and behavioral concerns.

3. What term is associated with children who are taking multiple medications, without full consideration of the potential drug interaction side effects?
a. Polypharmacy
b. Substance abuse
c. Combined drug treatment
d. Multipharmacy

4. In what year did traumatic brain injury become part of IDEA?
a. 1976
b. 1990
c. 1997
d. 2004

5. Who is credited as being the first school psychologist to advocate for doctoral school psychologists to be trained in clinical neuropsychology?
a. Alfred Binet
b. Cecil Reynolds
c. David Wechsler
d. George Hynd

6. True or False? A major role of a school neuropsychologist is to identify processing deficits in children that could adversely affect educational attainment and develop remedial and/or compensatory strategies to maximize the children's learning potential.

7. All of the following could be a typical role of a school neuropsychologist, except one—which one?
a. Seek to integrate current brain research into educational practice.

b. Administer CBM measures exclusively without regard to individual differences.
c. Provide educational interventions that have a basis in the neuro-psychological or educational literature.
d. Act as a liaison between the school and the medical community for transitional planning for TBI and other health-impaired children and adolescents.

Answers: 1. c; 2. true; 3. a; 4. b; 5. d; 6. true; 7. b

Chapter Two

HISTORICAL INFLUENCES OF CLINICAL NEUROPSYCHOLOGY AND SCHOOL PSYCHOLOGY

This chapter focuses on how the fields of clinical neuropsychology and school psychology along with educational policies and law have influenced the emerging specialization of school neuropsychology. The chapter ends with a review of the major historical events and landmark publications (e.g., books and tests) that have been a part of the rapid advances in school neuropsychology.

HISTORICAL INFLUENCES OF CLINICAL NEUROPSYCHOLOGY ON SCHOOL NEUROPSYCHOLOGY

To understand and appreciate the emerging specialty of school neuropsychology, one must review the influences of adult clinical neuropsychology, pediatric neuropsychology, school psychology, and education in general (see Figure 2.1). Several authors (Hartlage, Asken, & Hornsby, 1987; Rourke, 1982) have reviewed the history of adult clinical neuropsychology. Rourke labeled the first three historical stages of clinical neuropsychology as (1) the *single test approach stage*, (2) the *test battery/lesion specification stage*, and (3) the *functional profile stage*. This author has labeled current trends in neuropsychology as the *integrative and predictive stage*. These stages are reviewed in the next few sections of this chapter.

Single Test Approach Stage

Modern adult clinical neuropsychology has its origins in the mid-19th century researchers (e.g., Broca, 1865, as cited in von Bronin, 1960; Jackson, 1874, as cited in Taylor, 1932) who studied localization of brain functions. Despite the early emphasis on localization of brain functions, such as Broca's and Wernicke's areas,

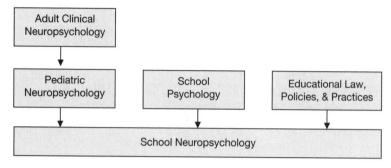

Figure 2.1. Historical Influences on School Neuropsychology

> **CAUTION**
>
> The single test approach did not differentiate brain injured from non-brain-injured children with sufficient validity.

early adult clinical neuropsychology in the United States focused on global brain function and dysfunction.

The single test approach dominated the practice of adult clinical neuropsychology from 1900 to 1950. One goal of practitioners during this period was to differentiate patients with brain damage from other groups using a single measure. Practitioners were taught to look for signs of overall "organicity" or brain dysfunction using single tests such as the *Bender Visual-Motor Gestalt*, *Benton Visual Retention*, or the *Memory for Designs* tests.

An analogy to the *single test approach* is the example of baking a cake. If your mother taught you how to bake a cake, she probably told you to stick a toothpick into the center of the cake to see if the cake was completely baked. In other words, you generalize from a single sample to the rest of the cake. If the toothpick comes out clean, then the rest of the cake is assumed to be baked all the way through (see Figure 2.2). The "single sample" toothpick works well in generalizing to the rest of the cake.

However, if we conceptualize the cake as being the construct of brain organicity (see Figure 2.2), a single test does not generalize well to overall brain function.

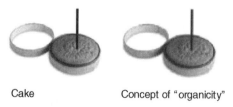

Cake   Concept of "organicity"

Figure 2.2. Analogy of Baking a Cake

For example, a child's poor performance on the *Bender Visual-Motor Gestalt* test could be a result of multiple factors rather than an indicator of organicity, or overall brain functioning. Poor performance on the *Bender Gestalt* could be a result of poor visual-motor coordination, motor awkwardness, poor visual-spatial skills, poor motivation, or poor fine motor coordination, and so on. In current school psychology practice, there are still some practitioners who refer to signs of organicity being observed in single samples of assessment; however, this approach has not differentiated brain-injured from non-brain-injured children with sufficient validity (Rourke, 1982).

Test Battery/Lesion Specification Stage

As neuropsychological measurement increased in sophistication, clinicians and researchers determined that taking multiple samples of the same construct led to a better measurement of the construct of brain organicity or dysfunction. Therefore, in the cake pan analogy, in which the cake is the construct of organicity, that construct would be better measured by taking samples from several "locations" or cognitive processes such as visual-spatial abilities, executive functions, attentional skills, memory and learning functions, and so on. Test batteries that measured a variety of neuropsychological constructs were developed to alleviate some of the concerns of using a single test to predict neuropsychological dysfunction.

In the 1940s, World War II played a major role in reshaping clinical neuropsychology. The war created a large number of soldiers who became patients with severe concussive and penetrating head injures (Hartlage, Asken, & Hornsby, 1987). During this period, clinical psychology was also emerging as a profession, and a host of practitioners became available to evaluate patients with brain injuries. From the 1940s through the 1970s, several major neuropsychological test batteries were developed and widely used by clinicians. The principle role of the clinical neuropsychologist during this period was to administer neuropsychological batteries of tests to determine the source of possible brain dysfunction(s). The contributions of Ward Halstead, Ralph Reitan, Alexander Luria, Edith Kaplan, and colleagues are reviewed in this section.

Halstead and Reitan's Contributions to Clinical Neuropsychology

Ward Halstead was a prominent researcher and practitioner who published a monograph in 1947 that related the observations made on hundreds of patients with frontal lobe damage (see Halstead, 1952). Halstead's approach to assessment was largely atheoretical and designed to maximize the hit-rate in differentiating brain-injured patients from normal controls.

One of Halstead's students, Ralph Reitan, expanded the Halstead neuro-psychological test battery and verified its use with lateralizing brain dysfunction (Reitan, 1955), lateralized motor deficits (Reed & Reitan, 1969), temporal lobe damage (Reitan, 1955), abstraction ability (Reitan, 1959), dysphasia (Reitan, 1960), and sensorimotor functions (Reitan, 1971). The *Halstead-Reitan Neuropsychological Test Battery* (HRNTB; Reitan, 1955; Reitan & Davidson, 1974; Reitan & Wolfson, 1993), as it became known, has been widely used in adult clinical neuropsychology practice.

The normative database for the adult version of the HRNTB has been updated (Heaton, Grant, & Matthews, 1991), which makes it still clinically useful with adults. While the Halstead-Reitan tests were assembled into a battery, the *single test approach stage* that dominated the early field is still somewhat evident. For example, on the *Halstead-Reitan's Aphasia Screening* test, a child is labeled *dyslexic* if only one item is failed. As in the *single test approach stage*, this is a questionable practice because there are multiple explanations for poor performance on a particular item rather than ascribing a neuropsychological condition.

Luria's Contributions to Clinical Neuropsychology

Alexander Luria was a Russian neuropsychologist who spent more than 40 years evaluating the psychological and behavioral effects of brain-injured adults. Although Luria and Halstead were contemporaries, they took a different approach to understanding brain-behavior relationships. Whereas, Halstead (and subsequently Reitan) used a *quantitative* approach to differentiate brain-injured individuals from controls, Luria heavily emphasized the *qualitative* observations of the error patterns of patients. He summarized his theoretical and clinical observations in two influential books, *Higher Cortical Functions in Man* (Luria, 1973, 1980) and *The Working Brain* (Luria, 1966).

Luria's original method relied on detailed clinical insight and informal hypothesis testing. U.S. clinicians were suspicious of Luria's approach because it did not have the standardization of procedures and established psychometric properties that they were growing accustomed to with other instruments. Anne-Lise Christensen, an apprentice of Luria, originally standardized some of Luria's stimulus materials in the 1960s. In the 1970s, an English version of the test was standardized by Charles Golden, a Nebraska neuropsychologist, along with Thomas Hammeke and Arnold Purish. Golden and his colleagues administered the original Luria items to hundreds of neurologically impaired and nonimpaired adults. They then used discriminant function analyses to determine which test items differentiated the normal controls from the brain-injured patients. Their research produced the first version of the *Luria-Nebraska Neuropsychological*

Battery (LNNB; Golden, Hammeke, & Purish, 1978), which was revised in 1986 (Golden, 1986).

Kaplan and Colleague's Contributions to Clinical Neuropsychology

In the 1960s and 1970s, a group of clinicians and researchers (e.g., Norman Geschwind, Harold Goodglass, Nelson Butters, and Heinz Warner; see Hebben & Milberg, 2009) in the Boston area investigated variations in cognitive processes across clinical populations but did not use either the HRNTB or the LNNB. Instead, this group used a flexible test battery designed to answer the referral question. This approach was named the Boston Process Approach in 1986 (Milberg, Hebben, & Kaplan, 1996) and has been called the *Boston Hypothesis Testing Approach* (Semrud-Clikeman & Teeter-Ellison, 2009). The basic tenet of this approach to neuropsychological assessment was the idea that how a person arrives at an answer on a test is as important as the test score itself. This emphasis on qualitative behaviors and hypothesis testing has some similarities to the original Lurian clinical method, but the Boston Process Approach uses standardized tests.

> **DON'T FORGET**
> ....
> Luria's conceptualization of "functional systems" within the brain has served as the theoretical foundation for several current tests (e.g., *Das-Naglieri Cognitive Assessment System*: Naglieri & Das, 1997; *Kaufman Assessment Battery the Children—Second Edition*: A. Kaufman & Kaufman, 2004; *NEPSY-II*: Korkman, Kirk, & Kemp, 2007).

The principle of "testing the limits," by asking individuals questions beyond the ceiling levels or by modifying the questions, is a hallmark of this approach. Edith Kaplan was one of the principle advocates for this approach to assessment. Many of the "process oriented" approaches originally advocated by these clinicians and researchers have become part of current assessment techniques.

Early Neuropsychological Test Batteries for Children

While adult clinical neuropsychologists were moving away from fixed batteries of assessment to more flexible batteries of assessment by the end of the 1990s, pediatric neuropsychologists had few assessment tools from which to choose. This section reviews the history of pediatric neuropsychology and its influence on school neuropsychology.

First Neuropsychological Test Battery for Children. In the 1960s, pediatric neuropsychology emerged as a subspecialization within the broader field of clinical neuropsychology. Initially, many of the early neuropsychological test batteries developed for children were downward extensions of adult test batteries. Ernhart, Graham, and Eichman (1963) were credited as being the first researchers to apply

> **CAUTION**
> ·······························
> The Halstead-Reitan tests for children should not be used in clinical practice today. A better practice for practitioners would be to use the *Dean-Woodcock Neuropsychological Battery* (Dean & Woodcock, 2003), which includes many of the original Halstead-Reitan tests but is based on a more recent broad-based, restandardized population.

a battery of tests to assess developmental outcomes in children with brain injuries. They found that brain-damaged children manifested deficits on multiple verbal and conceptual measures, as well as on multiple perceptual measures. They reported that no single measure yielded a satisfactory discrimination of brain-damaged children, whereas the use of the whole battery did. This was consistent with the idea that multiple measures are better discriminators of brain function/dysfunction than a single sample of behavior.

Halstead-Reitan Tests for Children. In the 1970s, a downward extension of the adult HRNTB was developed for children in the 9- to 14-year-old range called the *Halstead-Reitan Neuropsychological Test Battery for Older Children* (HRNTB-OC; Reitan & Davidson, 1974; Reitan & Wolfson, 1992).

A version of the test was also developed for children ages 5 to 8 called the *Reitan-Indiana Neuropsychological Test Battery* (RINTB; Reitan & Wolfson, 1985). See Reitan and Wolfson (1992) for an expanded description of the HRNTB-OC and RINTB tests, and see Johnson and D'Amato (2011) and Semrud-Clikeman and Teeter-Ellison (2009) for reviews of the HRNTB and RINTB clinical research studies. Semrud-Clikeman and Teeter-Ellison pointed out that the Halstead-Reitan tests for children must be used with caution. Concerns about the HRNTB-OC and RINTB tests include: insufficient norms (Leckliter & Forster, 1994), covariance with intelligence, inability to distinguish psychiatric from neurological conditions in children, and the inability of the tests to localize dysfunction or to predict recovery after a brain insult or injury.

Several researchers have compiled HRNTB-OC and RINTB normative data sets for children since their initial publications (see Baron, 2004, for consolidated norms for most of the Halstead-Reitan tests for children). Rather than using the original Halstead-Reitan tests for children based on a synthesized collection of normative data that may be up to 40-plus years old, it is recommended that practitioners use the *Dean-Woodcock Neuropsychological Battery* (DWSMB; Dean & Woodcock, 2003). The DWSMB incorporated many of the Halstead-Reitan tests when it restandardized the tests using a broad-based national sample. The DWSMB is also co-normed with the *Woodcock-Johnson III Tests of Cognitive Abilities* (Woodcock, McGrew, & Mather, 2001, 2007a). The DWSMB is discussed in a later section of this book.

Luria-Nebraska Neuropsychological Battery: Children's Revision. After the *Luria-Nebraska Neuropsychological Battery* for adults was introduced in 1978, Golden and his colleagues started working on a revision. In 1986, the revised *Luria-Nebraska Neuropsychological Battery* for adults was published along with a separate *Luria- Nebraska Neuropsychological Battery: Children's Revision* (LNNB-CR; Golden, 1986). The LNNB-CR was designed to evaluate a wide range of skills aimed at assessing the neuropsychological processes of children ages 8 through 12.

Golden (1997) reported that he and his colleagues spent nearly a decade, from the mid-1980s to the mid-1990s working on the LNNB-III that would integrate the child and adult versions; but the test has never been published. Therefore, practitioners who use the LNNB-CR must rely on standardization sample norms that come from samples collected in the 1980s. Please refer to Golden (2011) for an expanded description of the LNNB-CR tests, and see Golden (2011) and Semrud-Clikeman and Teeter-Ellison (2009) for an extensive review of the LNNB-CR clinical research studies. Some studies found the LNNB-CR was useful in discriminating LD (learning disabled) from non-LD children, but little research has been done on the effectiveness of the test in discriminating neurologically impaired children from nonclinical groups.

A major concern about both the Halstead-Reitan and the Luria-Nebraska tests for children is that conceptually both instruments are downward extensions of adult models. These early fixed batteries treated children as miniature adults and did not take into consideration the developmental variations of childhood.

In summary, the focus of the test battery/lesion specification stage was to develop multiple neuropsychological measures within a test battery that when viewed together were useful predictors of brain dysfunction. The fixed-battery approach by its definition was restrictive. The tests served as gross indicators of brain function or dysfunction but were not useful in localization or in developing prescriptive interventions. The need to move beyond assessment only for the sake of diagnosis to a model of assessment that linked to prescriptive interventions laid the foundation for the next stage in clinical neuropsychology, called the *functional profile stage.*

Functional Profile Stage

Rourke (1982) referred to the first two stages in the history of clinical neuro-psychology (single test approach and the test battery/lesion specification) as *static* stages. Starting in the late 1970s, three major factors influenced the evolution of neuropsychology: (1) pediatric neuropsychologists started to question the downward extension of adult models applied to children, (2) neuropsychologists in general started to question the validity of neuropsychological test batteries to localize brain lesions, and (3) noninvasive neurodiagnostic methods (e.g., CAT, MRI, PET scans) began to replace neuropsychological tests for making inferences regarding brain lesions. With the evolution of neuroimaging techniques, neuropsychologists no longer used test batteries to determine localization of the sites of possible brain dysfunction. CAT and MRI scans provide detailed views of the structure of the brain, while early PET scans provided both structural and functional information about the brain. During this period, neuropsychologists shifted the focus of their reports away from brain localization issues to identifying a functional profile of an individual's strengths and weaknesses. The neuropsychologist's goal became to differentiate between spared and impaired abilities.

Rourke (1982) referred to this functional profile stage as the *cognitive stage*. Rourke's implication was that the functional profile stage put the principles of cognitive psychology back into the practice of neuropsychology. Rather than administer a fixed battery of tests and indicate the presence or absence of a suspected lesion, the neuropsychologists of the 1980s and beyond were asked to comprehensively assess the cognitive processes of the individual.

One cannot help but draw a parallel between the shift from the fixed battery/brain localization stage to the functional profile stage in clinical neuropsychology and the current state of school psychology specific learning disabilities (SLD) identification practices. Rapid Reference 2.1 highlights these similarities. During the fixed battery stage, the assessment tools themselves made clinical neuropsychologists become more like technicians rather than clinicians. The test results were clear-cut, indicating either the presence or the absence of brain dysfunction. Many aspects of school psychology practice between the 1980s and the 2000s relied too heavily on using fixed methods (e.g., discrepancy formulas) to indicate the presence or absence of specific learning disabilities. When the field of neuropsychology made the shift to valuing a more functional assessment of the individual's strengths and weaknesses and linking that information to prescriptive interventions, neuropsychologists were at a disadvantage because there were no new testing instruments that addressed this reconceptualization.

School psychology is in a much more favorable position than clinical neuropsychology was in the 1980s because since the 1990s there has been a steady increase in assessment

DON'T FORGET

With recent changes to federal education laws, school psychologists are uniquely poised to put the practice of "psychology" back into the practice of school psychology, more specifically integrating the principles of cognitive psychology and neuropsychology.

≣ *Rapid Reference 2.1*

Parallels between the shift in neuropsychology from a fixed-battery stage to a functional profile stage and present day school psychology practice.

Neuropsychology	School Psychology
• "Repsychologizing" of the field through emphasis on cognitive strengths and weaknesses.	• Deemphasis on SLD discrepancy formulas and reemphasis on processing deficits.
• Few new tests in the 1980s that addressed the reconceptualization.	• Many new assessment measures and intervention techniques designed to address processing deficits.

tools designed to address functional strengths and weaknesses and make prescriptive linkages. School psychologists are on the cusp of putting the practice of "psychology" back into the practice of school psychology, or more specifically, integrating the principles of cognitive psychology and neuropsychology into school psychology.

So the functional profile stage of neuropsychology reemphasized the "repsychologizing" of neuropsychology by emphasizing the psychological aspects of neurological insults and anomalies and identifying the functional strengths and weaknesses of individuals. Although this stage of development represented a shift in the goals of neuropsychological assessment, there were no dramatic changes or innovations in the types of tests and measures being used. The "state of the art" of clinical neuropsychological assessments during this period was still the three major approaches: the Halstead-Reitan, the Lurian perspective, and the Boston Process Approach.

For the sake of continuity, let's return to the analogy of the cake pan. If we continue to use the analogy that the cake represents the construct of organicity, or overall brain function, neuropsychologists in the functional profile stage would continue to advocate for taking multiple samples of behavior (or tests). However, the emphasis would shift from prediction of "organicity" to an analysis of the relationships between the performances on the behavioral samples (i.e., did the "cake" samples show differences between the sample sites?).

Integrative and Predictive Stage

The *integrative and predictive stage* is a term used by this author to describe the period of the early 1990s to present time. During this period, many multidisciplinary changes have influenced school neuropsychology. Many of these changes are related to advances in how the brain influences learning and behavior. The rapid explosion of research related to brain-behavior relationships resulted in the U.S. Congress declaring the 1990s as the "Decade of the Brain."

School neuropsychologists are ultimately interested in how to reliably and validly assess neurocognitive functions. Accurate assessment is essential for accurate diagnoses and strengthening prescriptive interventions. The multidisciplinary advances since the 1990s that have influenced the practice of school psychology and the specialty of school neuropsychology include: development of tests specifically designed for children, advancement of neuroimaging techniques, theoretical advancement, influences of a cross-battery approach, influences of a process-assessment approach, and the professional focus on ecological validity and linking assessment data with evidence-based interventions.

Development of Neuropsychological Tests Specifically Designed for Children

Prior to the integrative stage, if a researcher wanted to develop a new test that measured visual short-term memory, as an example, the courses of action were clear. The researcher would develop a set of items, administer them to a broad-based sample, validate the psychometric properties of the test, and then publish the test. A common method for establishing the validity of that new test would have been to correlate it with an existing test that purported to measure the same construct. If the two tests correlated, the researcher indicated that the new test was a valid measure of the construct being tested. Today, the test developer is faced with a new set of challenges. A new test must still adhere to psychometric rigor, but it is also important for the test to fit within a theoretical frame of reference, report both quantitative and qualitative samples of behavior, be ecologically valid, and have some linkages to evidence-based interventions. This push for integration of all of these attributes is also an important feature of the integrative and predictive stage.

One of the hallmark features of the integrative and predictive stage is that neuropsychological tests developed for children in this period were not downward extensions of adult models. The newer neuropsychological batteries for children and stand-alone tests of neuropsychological processes (reviewed in Chapter 7) were specifically designed for and standardized on children. The *Test of Memory and Learning* (TOMAL; Reynolds & Bigler, 1994) was one of the first examples of a neuropsychological test designed specifically for school-age children. Test authors in the 1990s and beyond have provided school neuropsychologists with a rich array of assessment tools that were developed specifically for school-age children.

Influences of Brain Imaging Studies on Learning and Behavior
The TOMAL (Reynolds & Bigler, 1994) was also one of the first measures that used CT scans to validate the constructs being measured. Increasingly, neuroimaging techniques such as functional MRI scans (fMRI) are being used to validate neuropsychological instruments that report to measure certain cognitive processes. In addition, functional imaging techniques are opening the "windows of the mind" to allow us to peek into the brains of children while they are performing basic cognitive functions. In a more recent and exciting application, researchers such as Shaywitz (2003) and Odegard, Ring, Smith, Biggan, and Black (2008) have started to use functional imaging techniques to evaluate the effects of specific reading interventions. In the future, neuropsychological test development and validation will include neuroimaging studies.

Influences of the Process Assessment Approach
One of the legacies of the Boston Process Approach has been the inclusion of qualitative aspects of a child's performance within new tests. Practitioners and researchers have recognized the importance of both the quantitative and qualitative aspects of a child's performance. The emphasis on the qualitative behaviors is part of a broader process assessment approach. The process assessment approach assists school neuropsychologists in determining the strategies a child uses to solve a particular task. Test authors and their publishers have excelled in recent years in establishing base rates for common qualitative behaviors. For example, a test with such data included in the standardization will allow a practitioner to make statements such as "Asking for repetitions 10 times on the verbally presented material occurred with such frequency in only 3% to 10% of other 5-year-olds in the standardization sample." The qualitative information can provide useful clues to interventions. See Rapid Reference 2.2 for a list of assessment instruments that have included qualitative components.

Emphasis on Ecologically Valid Assessment
As practitioners, we have attempted to administer standardized assessments to children in school closets or gymnasium stages only to later question if those test results mirror the child's actual level of abilities or achievement. This is an issue of ecological and predictive validity, which has been discussed in the literature (Chaytor & Schmitter-Edgecombe, 2003; Sbordone, 1996). Improving the ecological validity of our assessment approaches was one of the goals of the Futures in School Psychology Conference in 2002 (Harrison et al., 2004).

In the integrative and predictive stage of neuropsychology, there has been, and is, an increased emphasis on relating assessment findings to an individual's everyday functioning. Sbordone (1996) defines ecological validity as "the

≡ Rapid Reference 2.2

Tests With an Increased Emphasis on the Qualitative Aspects of Performance
- Luria-Nebraska Neuropsychological Battery—Children's Revision (Golden, 1986).
- Naglieri-Das Cognitive Assessment System (Naglieri & Das, 1997).
- NEPSY (Korkman, Kirk, & Kemp, 1997).
- Wechsler Intelligence Scale for Children—Third Edition, as a Process Instrument (Kaplan, Fein, Kramer, Delis, & Morris, 1999).
- Delis-Kaplan Executive Function System (Delis, Kaplan, & Kramer, 2001).
- Wechsler Intelligence Scale for Children—Fourth Edition Integrated (Wechsler, 2004a).
- NEPSY-II (Korkman, Kirk, & Kemp, 2007).

functional and predictive relationship between the patient's performance on a set of neuropsychological tests and the patient's behavior in a variety of real-world settings" (p. 16). As in the functional stage of neuropsychology, the emphasis on assessment today is more on the prescriptive recommendations rather than on the diagnostic conclusions within a report. In recent years, greater emphasis has been placed on the fields of clinical neuropsychology, school psychology, and the emerging specialty area of school neuropsychology to demonstrate predictive validity of assessment techniques. Parents and educators want to know how well the child will perform in the future, based on current assessment data. This is especially true of using current assessment data to predict performance on high-stakes competency-based accountability testing for *No Child Left Behind Act of 2001* (NCLB) compliance. If we must continue to use high-stakes assessment, there will always be a percentage of students who fail to reach the cutoff scores. School neuropsychologists can provide valuable assessment services to children who are failing competency-based tests by linking the assessment results to individualized remedial interventions.

Let's return to the cake pan analogy one last time. If we consider the cake pan analogous to the concept of "organicity" or brain function/dysfunction, neuro-psychologists in the current integrative and predictive stage would continue to advocate for taking multiple samples of behavior (i.e., multiple toothpick probes into the cake). However, in the past stages, all of the samples of behavior were based on behavioral test samples; that is what we would actually see on the toothpick after it is stuck in the cake. Today in clinical practice and research there is a cross-disciplinary approach to understanding brain functioning with integrated functional imaging techniques, advancements in test development, and inclusion of qualitative analyses of test performance. These multiple samples of any construct such as organicity must also strive to be ecologically valid and have good predictive validity; that is, we have to take the temperature of the cake using the probe (i.e., the toothpick) and analyze the contents adhering to the toothpick by using technology and other tests that provide qualitative, chemical, physiological, and functional information. Future researchers will continue to advance the knowledge base in all disciplines such as education, psychology (including neuropsychology), school psychology, functional neuroanatomy, biochemistry, electrophysiology, and genetics. The knowledge gleaned from these fields will reshape the ways in which we practice.

Summary of the Historical Influences of Clinical and Pediatric Neuropsychology on School Neuropsychology

Rapid Reference 2.3 presents a review of the historical stages in clinical and pediatric neuropsychology and the major focus of each stage. The influences of clinical neuropsychology and pediatric neuropsychology on the emerging specialty of school neuropsychology have been reviewed. The next section shifts the focus to the history of school psychology and its influence on school neuropsychology.

≡ Rapid Reference 2.3

Historical Stages of Neuropsychological Assessment

Stage	Focus of Stage
• Single test approach (1900–1950)	• Emphasized using a single test (e.g., *Bender Visual-Motor Gestalt*) to predict brain dysfunction.
• Test battery/lesion specification (1940–1980s)	• Emphasized using a battery of tests to predict brain dysfunction.
• Functional profile (1970–2000)	• Deemphasized localization of brain "lesions" and emphasized the identification of impaired and spared abilities.
• Integrative and predictive (1990–present)	• Current view of neuropsychology with an emphasis on cross-battery, multidimensional, and ecologically valid assessments.

HISTORICAL INFLUENCES OF SCHOOL PSYCHOLOGY ON SCHOOL NEUROPSYCHOLOGY

This section of the chapter will address some of the historical influences of school psychology on the emerging specialization of school neuropsychology, including: (1) the influences of federal education laws and national task force reports; (2) the continued expansion of theoretical frames of reference; (3) the influences of cross-battery assessment; and (4) the national educational mandate to link assessment to prescriptive interventions. Each of these influences on school neuropsychology is discussed in more detail.

Influences of Federal Education Laws and National Task Force Reports

Since 2000, there have been several key pieces of federal legislation and national task force reports that have influenced the practice of school psychology and the emerging movement toward school neuropsychology for years to come. Rapid Reference 2.4 outlines those recent federal laws and task force reports.

≡ *Rapid Reference 2.4*

Recent Federal Legislation and National Task Force Reports Influencing the Practice of School Neuropsychology

- No Child Left Behind (NCLB) Act of 2001.
- *Rethinking Special Education for a New Century* (Finn, Rotherham, & Hokanson, 2001). Report for the Thomas B. Fordham Foundation and the Progressive Policy Institute.
- *A New Era: Revitalizing Special Education for Children and Their Families*. Report of the President's Commission on Excellence in Special Education (2002).
- *Minority Students in Special and Gifted Education—Report for the National Research Council*. (Donovan & Cross, 2002).
- Learning Disabilities Roundtable Report (2002).
- *And Miles to Go. . . : State SLD Requirements and Authoritative Recommendations*. Report to the National Center for Learning Disabilities (Reschly, Hosp, & Schmied, 2003).
- Learning Disabilities Roundtable Report (2004).
- Individuals with Disabilities Education Improvement Act (IDEA) of 2004.
- *White Paper on Evaluation, Identification, and Eligibility Criteria for Students with Specific Learning Disabilities* (Hale et al., 2010a, 2010b). Learning Disabilities Association of America. Pittsburgh, PA.

• *Memorandum to State Directors of Special Education—A Response to Intervention (RTI) Process Cannot Be Used to Delay-Deny an Evaluation for Eligibility under the Individuals with Disabilities Act (IDEA)* (January, 2011). United States Department of Education—Office of Special Education and Rehabilitative Services.

The *No Child Left Behind Act of 2001* (NCLB) and the *Education Improvement Act of 2004* (IDEA) were not designed to be mutually exclusive. Together, these laws envision a seamless system of supports in both general and special education based on evidence-based instruction (Kovaleski & Prasse, 2005). Both laws emphasize scientifically based instruction, curriculum, and interventions; early identification of learning problems (i.e., reading); ongoing monitoring of annual yearly progress (AYP); designing and implementing remedial and individualized interventions for those who do not respond to the general curriculum; and inclusion of students in a single, statewide accountability system (Kovaleski & Prasse, 2005).

A chief concern among school neuropsychologists is the increased emphasis in these federal laws and national reports on behavioral techniques at the apparent expense of the role that individual differences in cognitive processes play in the child's learning.

DON'T FORGET

A chief concern among school neuropsychologists is the increased emphasis in these federal laws and national reports on behavioral techniques at the apparent expense of the role that individual differences in cognitive processes play in the child's learning.

NCLB placed emphasis on early intervention, particularly with reading problems, state-wide accountability requirements, and alternatives for parents to move their child from a failing school. The NCLB changes have had a profound impact upon public education. After the passage of NCLB in 2001, the focus shifted to what was, and was not, working in special education. The *Rethinking Special Education for a New Century* (Finn et al., 2001) report for the Thomas B. Fordham Foundation and the Progressive Policy Institute and the *Report of the President's Commission on Excellence in Special Education* (2002) focused clearly on the problems with the operationalization of the specific learning disabled (SLD) classification. The identified problems with SLD identification included:

• Too many students were being identified as SLD as compared to other disabilities.

- There was an overrepresentation of minorities identified as SLD (reiterated in the *Overrepresentation of Minorities in Special Education Report* by Donovan & Cross, 2002).
- The widespread use of the discrepancy model required a "wait-to-fail" approach, resulting in identification much too late in the educational process.
- Current identification methods were too costly and often identified the wrong students.

In 2002, the Office of Special Education Programs within the U.S. Department of Education sponsored a Learning Disabilities Roundtable discussion. Ten stakeholder organizations, including the National Association of School Psychologists (NASP), participated in this event and issued a final report entitled, *Specific Learning Disabilities: Finding Common Ground* (Learning Disabilities Roundtable, 2002). There were several key portions in the consensus statements that are relevant to school neuropsychologists:

- The concept of Specific Learning Disabilities (SLD) is valid and supported by strong converging evidence.
- Specific learning disabilities are neurologically based and intrinsic to the individual (and the statutory definition of SLD should be maintained in IDEA reauthorization).
- Individuals with SLD show intra-individual differences in skills and abilities.
- The ability-achievement discrepancy formula should not be used for determining eligibility.
- Decisions regarding eligibility for special education services must draw from information collected from a comprehensive evaluation using multiple methods and sources in gathering relevant information.

The 2002 Learning Disabilities Roundtable consensus report was not without critics. In the 2003 report for the National Center for Learning Disabilities, *And Miles to Go. . . : State SLD Requirements and Authoritative Recommendations*, Reschly and colleagues expressed a few concerns about the Roundtable report and provided some useful survey data about SLD identification practices across states. Reschly et al. (2003) expressed a concern that:

> The LD Roundtable participants did not recommend changes in the IDEA definition of SLD, although the National Joint Committee on Learning Disabilities (NJCLD) formulated an SLD definition in 1988 that did not mention psychological process disorders (Hammill, 1990). It is likely that

this was not a mere oversight, but more likely a conscious effort to focus on the most pressing issues, elimination of the ability-achievement discrepancy and development of a reasonable set of alternative procedures. (p. 7)

Members of the Learning Disabilities Roundtable have reported to this author that when the Roundtable reconvenes, the definition of SLD will be a topic of discussion. Despite years of empirical evidence, which proves that learning disabilities are a result of neuropsychological deficits, some key educational policy makers remain unconvinced.

In the reauthorization of the IDEA (2004) law and subsequent 2006 Federal Regulation (34 CFR § 300.307–309) the long-standing definition of SLD remained the same. The IDEA law and regulations provided states the option of not using a discrepancy-based formula for the identification of specific learning disabilities. As an alternative to the discrepancy-based formula identification method, a response-to-intervention (RTI) model is being suggested. The inclusion of RTI as an allowable option for SLD identification has generated the most controversy (see Flanagan & Alfonso, 2011, for a comprehensive review). Concerns have been expressed that districts that have adopted an RTI-only model would have students that are determined to have an SLD by default after repeated failures to respond to evidence-based interventions. In 2011, the U.S. Department of Education's Office of Special Education and Rehabilitation Services released a Memorandum to State Directors of Special Education indicating that a Response to Intervention (RTI) process cannot be used to delay-deny an evaluation for eligibility under IDEA.

It is important to remember that under IDEA 2004, RTI is only one component of the process to identify children with specific learning disabilities in need of special education and related services. Determining why a child has not responded to research-based interventions requires a comprehensive evaluation. The RTI process does not replace the need for a comprehensive evaluation. The IDEA law also requires the use of a variety of assessment tools and the use of any single measure or assessment as the sole criterion for determining SLD is *not permitted*. Finally, the IDEA law requires that assessments must not be discriminatory based on race or culture. The 2004 reauthorization of IDEA also opened the door to other methods of SLD identification besides the ability achievement discrepancies in the identification of SLD, including a process-oriented, school neuropsychological approach.

In 2010, the Learning Disabilities Association of America released a *White Paper on Evaluation, Identification, and Eligibility Criteria for Students with Specific Learning Disabilities*, which was subsequently published (Hale et. al., 2010a). The five conclusions of this white paper are:

1. The SLD definition should be maintained and the statutory requirements in SLD identification procedures should be strengthened.
2. Neither ability-achievement discrepancy analysis nor failure to respond to intervention alone is sufficient for SLD identification.
3. A "third method" approach that identifies a pattern of psychological processing strengths and weaknesses, and achievement deficits consistent with this pattern of processing weaknesses, makes the most empirical and clinical sense.
4. An empirically validated RTI model could be used to prevent learning problems, but comprehensive evaluations should occur for SLD identification purposes, and children with SLD need individualized interventions based on specific learning needs, not merely more intense interventions.
5. Assessment of cognitive and neuropsychological processes should be used for both SLD identification and intervention purposes.

In this book, the author is advocating for a process assessment approach for evaluating children with neurocognitive processing disorders (e.g., ADHD, SLD, TBI).

Expansion of Theoretical Frames of Reference

From the early 1900s through the mid-1980s, the theoretical frames of reference for classifying human cognitive abilities were limited to one-factor (verbal) or two-factor (verbal and visual-spatial) solutions. The theoretical models of intelligence increased dramatically just prior to the start of the integrative and predictive stage of neuropsychology in the 1990s. See Flanagan and Harrison (2012) for a comprehensive review of the contemporary theories of intelligence, including: Carroll's Three-Stratum Theory of Cognitive Abilities, Gardner's Theory of Multiple Intelligences, the Cattell-Horn Fluid-Crystallized (*Gf-Gc*) theory, and the Luria-Das Model of Information Processing.

> **DON'T FORGET**
> ....
> Current state-of-the-art practice demands that assessments have a theoretical foundation to aid in test interpretation.

The current state of the art of school psychology and school neuropsychology demands that assessment of cognitive abilities have a strong theoretical foundation. The strong theoretical foundation also facilitates the interpretation of the test data within a theoretical frame of reference. For example, the advanced and integrated Carroll-Horn-Cattell theory served as the theoretical foundation for the *Woodcock-Johnson Third Edition Tests of Cognitive Abilities* (Woodcock, McGrew, & Mather, 2001, 2007a), while the Luria-Das Model of Information Processing served as the theoretical model of the *Naglieri-Das Cognitive Assessment System* (Naglieri & Das, 1997) and the *Kaufman Assessment Battery for Children—Second Edition* (A. Kaufman & N. Kaufman, 2004).

Influences of the Cross-Battery Approach

An outgrowth of the advances in our theoretical conceptualization of cognitive abilities is the cross-battery approach. In constructing a school-based neuropsychological assessment to answer a particular referral question, a school neuropsychologist may need to draw subtests from multiple test batteries. This is essentially a cross-battery approach. At the foundation of the cross-battery approach, Carroll (1983, 1993) and Horn (1988, 1994) conducted several factor analytical studies across multiple measures of intelligence, which yielded a taxonomy of broad cognitive abilities. See Horn and Blankson (2012) for an updated review of *Gf-Gc* theory and Schneider and McGrew (2012) for an updated review of the CHC model of intelligence. Woodcock (1990) was one of the first to suggest that pulling measures from one or more intellectual test batteries during a single assessment would provide a broader measure of cognitive abilities. The cross-battery approach was expanded as a means of bridging a gap between modern theories of the structure of intelligence and current practice of assessing those cognitive abilities (Flanagan, Alfonso, & Ortiz, 2012).

Mandate to Link Assessment Results with Evidence-Based Interventions

In the grand scheme of things, the field of school psychology is relatively young. Within the past 100 years, the field has become better at developing and validating theoretical constructs and approaches to assessment. However, the field is lagging in the area of empirically validated interventions. School psychologists have many "cookbook" resources that provide recommendations based on common academic or behavioral problems. Review of the literature shows there is little solid evidence for many of the recommendations that are consistently made by practitioners. As a result of the recent legislative changes, there is an added emphasis in education on identifying methods that work.

Having stated the need for evidence-based interventions, where does the field proceed? Questions need to be answered, such as "What constitutes an evidence-based intervention?" Kratochwill and Shernoff (2004) suggested that an intervention could be considered *evidence-based* if its application to practice was clearly specified and if it demonstrated efficacy when implemented into practice. Several joint task forces across professional organizations have been working on establishing guidelines for evidence-based practice research. This line of research is crucial to the credibility of school psychology and the school neuropsychology specialty. Gone are the days of assessing a student only for an educational classification. Clearly lawmakers, educators, teachers, and parents are demanding assessment that guides intervention.

There are challenges to conducting evidence-based research in the schools. Obtaining permission to conduct applied research in the schools has become increasingly difficult because administrators, teachers, and parents are concerned with "time on task" and maximizing the classroom time spent on preparing for high-stakes, competency-based exams. Evidence-based research may have the best chance of getting into the schools if the results can be shown to help improve test performance on statewide competency exams.

SUMMARY OF HISTORICAL INFLUENCES OF SCHOOL PSYCHOLOGY ON SCHOOL NEUROPSYCHOLOGY

In summary, school psychologists have been interested in applying neuro-psychological principles since the early 1980s. Since then, there has been an explosion of research that provides support for the biological bases of learning and behavior. Within the past 20 years there has been a resurgence of interest in school neuropsychology due to the convergence of several factors. First, federal legislation such as NCLB and the 2004 reauthorization of IDEA have caused school psychologists to critically evaluate their service delivery models. Old models, such as using the ability-achievement discrepancy model for the identification of SLD, have proven to be ineffective (Flanagan & Alfonzo, 2011; Flanagan, Alfonso, Mascolo, & Soleto-Dynega, 2012). There is a conceptual tug-of-war taking place as the school psychology profession struggles to come to terms with all of the systemic changes in education: on one side the strict behaviorists (the curriculum-based assessment advocates), who discount the value of individualized assessment of cognitive abilities, and on the other side the school psychologists and school neuro-psychologists, who advocate for a more individualized process-based assessment to guide interventions.

HISTORY OF SCHOOL NEUROPSYCHOLOGY

The history of school neuropsychology is still emerging as a specialty area. Rapid Reference 2.5 presents some of the historical events and major publications in the emerging specialization of school neuropsychology.

≡ *Rapid Reference 2.5*

Historical Events and Major Publications in School Neuropsychology

1963	Emhardt and Graham published the first neuropsychological test battery for children.
1974	*Halstead-Reitan Neuropsychological Test Battery for Older Children* test published (Reitan & Davidson, 1974).
1976	P.L. 94–142—The Education of All Handicapped Children Act—is passed by the United States Congress.
1981	Neuropsychology as a specialty area in school psychology first appeared in publication in the *Journal of School Psychology*.
1981	*Neuropsychological Assessment of the School-Aged Child: Issues and Procedures* (Hynd & Obrzut, 1981) book published.
1983	*Child Neuropsychology: An Introduction to Theory, Research, and Clinical Practice* (Rourke, Bakker, Fisk, & Strang, 1983) book published.
1986	*Luria-Nebraska Neuropsychological Battery: Children's Revision* test published (Golden, 1986).
1986	*Child Neuropsychology: Volume 1—Theory and Research* (Obrzut & Hynd, 1986a) book published.
1986	*Child Neuropsychology: Volume 2—Clinical Practice* (Obrzut & Hynd, 1986b) book published.
1986	*Neuropsychological Assessment and Intervention With Children and Adolescents* (Hartlage & Telzrow, 1986) book published.
1988	*Pediatric Neuropsychology* (Hynd & Willis, 1988) book published.
1988	*Fundamentals of Clinical Child Neuropsychology* (Novick & Arnold, 1988) book published.
1988	*Assessment Issues in Clinical Neuropsychology* (Tramontana & Hooper, 1988) book published.
Late 1980s	Neuropsychology Special Interest Group formed in the National Association of School Psychologists.
1989	First edition of the *Handbook of Clinical Child Neuropsychology* (Reynolds & Fletcher-Janzen, 1989) book published.
1990	*IDEA* reauthorized and traumatic brain injury was included as a disability.

(continued)

≡ *Rapid Reference 2.5 continued*

1990s	Several tests of memory and learning specifically designed for school-age children were published; e.g., *Wide Range Assessment of Memory and Learning: WRAML* (Sheslow & Adams, 1990, 2003); *Test of Memory and Learning: TOMAL* (Reynolds & Bigler, 1994); and *Children's Memory Scale: CMS* (Cohen, 1997).
1992	*Advances in Child Neuropsychology—Volume 1* (Tramontana & Hooper, 1992) book published.
1995	*Child Neuropsychology* journal published first issue.
1996	*Neuropsychological Foundations of Learning Disabilities: A Handbook of Issues, Methods, and Practice* (Obrzut & Hynd, 1996) book published.
1996	*Pediatric Neuropsychology: Interfacing Assessment and Treatment for Rehabilitation* (Batchelor & Dean, 1996) book published.
1997	*Child Neuropsychology: Assessment and Interventions for Neurodevelopmental Disorders* (Teeter & Semrud-Clikeman, 1997) book published.
1997	Second edition of the *Handbook of Clinical Child Neuropsychology* (Reynolds & Fletcher-Janzen, 1997) book published.
1997	*NEPSY* test published (Korkman, Kirk, & Kemp, 1997).
1999	American Board of School Neuropsychology (ABSNP) established.
2000	*Pediatric Neuropsychology: Research, Theory, and Practice* (Yeates, Ris, & Taylor, 2000) book published.
2000	*The Neuropsychology of Reading Disorders: Diagnosis and Intervention* (Feifer & DeFina, 2000) book published.
2002	*The Neuropsychology of Written Language Disorders: Diagnosis and Intervention* (Feifer & DeFina, 2002) book published.
2002	*Brain Literacy for Educators and Psychologists* (Berninger & Richards, 2002) published.
2003	*Overcoming Dyslexia: A New and Complete Science-Based Program for Reading Problems at Any Level* (Shaywitz, 2003) book published.
2004	*Neuropsychological Evaluation of the Child* (Baron, 2004) book published.
2004	*School Neuropsychology: A Practitioner's Handbook* (Hale & Fiorello, 2004) book published.
2004	The annual theme for the year and the NASP convention was "Mind Matters: All Children Can Learn."
2004	*Brainstorming: Using Neuropsychology in the Schools* (Jiron, 2004) resource book published.
2004	*IDEA* reauthorized—discrepancy formula-based methods of identifying specific learning disabilities deemphasized—opens door to a more process assessment approach in identifying all children with special needs.
2005	*The Neuropsychology of Mathematics: Diagnosis and Intervention* (Feifer & DeFina, 2005) book published.

2005	*Handbook of School Neuropsychology* (D'Amato, Fletcher-Janzen, & Reynolds, 2005) book published.
2006	First national conference for school neuropsychologists held in Dallas, Texas.
2007	NEPSY-II published (Korkman, Kirk, & Kemp, 2007).
2007	First edition of the *Essentials of School Neuropsychological Assessment* (D. Miller, 2007) book published.
2008	*Working Memory and Academic Learning: Assessment and Intervention* (Dehn, 2008) book published.
2008	*Neuropsychological Perspectives on Learning Disabilities in the Era of RTI: Recommendations for Diagnosis and Intervention* (Fletcher-Janzen & Reynolds, 2008) book published.
2008	*Children with Complex Medical Issues in Schools: Neuropsychological Descriptions and Interventions* (Castillo, 2008) book published.
2008	Third edition of the *Handbook of Clinical Child Neuropsychology* (Reynolds & Fletcher-Janzen, 2008) book published.
2009	*Assessment and Intervention for Executive Function Difficulties* (McCloskey, Perkins, & Diviner, 2009) book published.
2009	*Emotional Disorders: A Neuropsychological, Psychopharmacological, and Educational Perspective* (Feifer & Rattan, 2009) book published.
2009	*Pediatric Neuropsychology, Second Edition: Research, Theory, and Practice* (Petersen, Yeates, Ris, Taylor, & Pennington, 2009) book published.
2009	*Child Neuropsychology: Assessment and Interventions for Neurodevelopmental Disorders—Second Edition* (Semrud-Clikeman & Teeter-Ellison, 2009).
2010	*Long-Term Memory Problems in Children and Adolescents: Assessment, Intervention, and Effective Instruction* (Dehn, 2010).
2010	*Neuropsychological Assessment and Intervention for Childhood and Adolescent Disorders* (Riccio, Sullivan, & Cohen, 2010) book published.
2010	*Best Practices in School Neuropsychology: Guidelines for Effective Practice, Assessment, and Evidence-Based Interventions* (D. Miller, 2010) book published.
2011	*Handbook of Pediatric Neuropsychology* (Davis, 2011) book published.
2011	The fifth national school neuropsychology conference held in Dallas, Texas.

The 1960s

As previously mentioned in the history of clinical neuropsychology, Ernhardt, Graham, and Eichman published the first neuropsychological test battery for children in 1963.

The 1970s

The *Halstead-Reitan Neuropsychological Test Battery for Older Children* was published in 1974. In 1976, P.L. 94–142—The Education for All Handicapped Children Act—was passed by the U.S. Congress.

The 1980s

George Hynd (1981) was first to refer to neuropsychology as a specialty area in doctoral school psychology. A clinical and pediatric neuropsychology literature review places Hynd's first mention of this potential specialty within the *test battery/ lesion specification stage* shortly after the publication of the *Halstead-Reitan Neuropsychological Test Battery for Older Children*.

The first textbook for practitioners was called *Neuropsychological Assessment of the School-Aged Child: Issues and Procedures* (Hynd & Obrzut, 1981). In the 1981 book, Marion Selz, an early researcher of the Halstead-Reitan tests for children, wrote a chapter on the test battery. Charles Golden also wrote a chapter on the early development of the *Luria-Nebraska Neuropsychological Battery—Children's Revision* that was later published in 1986.

Several school neuropsychology textbooks published in the mid-to-late 1980s were used for a number of years in many graduate neuropsychology classes (Hartlage & Telzrow, 1986; Hynd & Willis, 1988; Novick & Arnold, 1988; Obrzut & Hynd, 1986a, 1986b; Reynolds & Fletcher-Janzen, 1989; Rourke et al., 1983; Tramontana & Hooper, 1988). In the late 1980s, neuropsychology had gained such a following within the school psychology community that a special interest group was formed within the National Association of School Psychologists.

The 1990s

The federal IDEA legislation was reauthorized in 1990 and included traumatic brain injury as a handicapping condition for the first time. The 1990s was the decade that test authors and test publishers provided school neuropsychology practitioners with a set of new assessment tools specifically designed for the assessment of memory and learning in school-age children (e.g., WRAML, TOMAL, CMS) and with complete cognitive or neuropsychological test batteries (e.g., CAS, NEPSY, WISC-III PI).

In the 1990s and through the year 2000, several books were published by school psychologists related to school neuropsychology (see Obrzut & Hynd, 1991; Reynolds & Fletcher-Janzen, 1997; Teeter & Semrud-Clikeman, 1997) and pediatric neuropsychology (see Batchelor & Dean, 1996; Tramontana & Hooper, 1992; Yeates, Ris, & Taylor, 2000). In 1995, the *Child Neuropsychology* journal published its first issue. This journal has become an important outlet for research related to school neuropsychology and pediatric neuropsychology.

In 1999, the American Board of School Neuropsychology (ABSNP) was established. The ABSNP started issuing diplomate certificates in school neuropsychology based on peer-review case studies and objective written examinations.

The 2000s

During this decade many more scholarly resources became available to practitioners. In 2000, 2002, and 2005, Steven Feifer and Philip DeFina, two school psychologists/neuropsychologists published three informative books: *The Neuropsychology of Reading Disorders, The Neuropsychology of Written Language Disorders,* and *The Neuropsychology of Mathematics,* respectively. In 2007, Steven Feifer and Douglas Della Toffalo wrote *Integrating RTI With Cognitive Neuropsychology: A Scientific Approach to Reading.*

In 2002, Virginia Berninger, a trainer of school psychologists, and Todd Richards, a neuroscientist, wrote a book called *Brain Literacy for Educators and Psychologists* designed to bridge the gap between brain-behavior research and education.

In 2003, Sally Shaywitz, a physician, wrote an influential book called *Overcoming Dyslexia.* She was the keynote speaker at the 2004 NASP Convention in Dallas, Texas.

In 2004, three school neuropsychology books were published: Ida Sue Baron, a clinical neuropsychologist, wrote the *Neuropsychological Evaluation of the Child*; two school psychologists, James B. Hale and Catherine A. Fiorello, wrote *School Neuropsychology: A Practitioner's Handbook*; and Colleen Jiron, a school psychologist and pediatric neuropsychologist, wrote *Brainstorming: Using Neuropsychology in the Schools.*

In 2005, Rick D'Amato, Elaine Fletcher-Janzen, and Cecil Reynolds served as editors for the first publication of the *School Neuropsychology Handbook.*

In 2006, the first national School Neuropsychology conference was held in Dallas, Texas.

In 2007, the first edition of the *Essentials of School Neuropsychological Assessment* and the NEPSY-II were published.

In 2008, four influential school neuropsychological books were published: Milton Dehn wrote *Working Memory and Academic Learning: Assessment and Intervention*; Elaine Fletcher-Janzen and Cecil Reynolds wrote a timely and influential book called *Neuropsychological Perspectives on Learning Disabilities in the Era of RTI: Recommendations for Diagnosis and Intervention*; Christine Castillo, a pediatric neuropsychologist wrote *Children With Complex Medical Issues in Schools: Neuropsychological Descriptions and Interventions*; and Reynolds and Fletcher-Janzen edited the third edition of the *Handbook of Clinical Child Neuropsychology*.

In 2009, four more school neuropsychological books were published: George McCloskey wrote a book called *Assessment and Intervention for Executive Function Difficulties;* Feifer and Rattan wrote a book called *Emotional Disorders: A Neuropsychological, Psychopharmacological, and Educational Perspective*; Petersen and colleagues wrote *Pediatric Neuropsychology—Second Edition: Research, Theory, and Practice*; and Semrud-Clikeman and Teeter-Ellison wrote *Child Neuropsychology: Assessment and Interventions for Neurodevelopmental Disorders—Second Edition.*

The 2010s

In 2010, Milton Dehn wrote *Long-Term Memory Problems in Children and Adolescents: Assessment, Intervention, and Effective Instruction* and Riccio and her colleagues wrote *Neuropsychological Assessment and Intervention for Childhood and Adolescent Disorders.* This author edited a comprehensive book called *Best Practices in School Neuropsychology: Guidelines for Effective Practice, Assessment, and Evidence-Based Interventions.*

In 2011, Andrew Davis edited a comprehensive book on pediatric neuropsychology called the *Handbook of Pediatric Neuropsychology.* In July 2011, the fifth annual school neuropsychology summer institute was held in Dallas, Texas.

CHAPTER SUMMARY

Chapter 2 presents the history of the interest in school neuropsychology with its influences heavily entrenched in clinical neuropsychology, school psychology, and educational policies and law. In Chapter 3, training and credentialing issues for school neuropsychology are discussed, along with a proposed set of training standards and a model program of study.

🐟 TEST YOURSELF 🐟

I. **Using the Bender Visual-Motor Gestalt test to predict overall brain dysfunction would be an example of what stage in the history of clinical neuropsychology?**
   a. The integrative and predictive stage.
   b. The functional profile stage.

c. The single test approach stage.

d. The test battery/lesion specification stage.

2. **According to the author, what is the principal reason why the Halstead-Reitan tests for children and the Luria-Nebraska Neuropsychological Battery—Children's Revision are not suitable for current clinical use?**

   a. Neither test has been shown to differentiate brain-injured from normal controls.

   b. Neither test has collected contemporary broad-based normative data.

   c. Neither test has a strong theoretical basis.

   d. Neither test is empirically designed.

3. **True or False? George Hynd was the first person to refer to neuropsychology as a specialty area in doctoral school psychology.**

4. **Luria's conceptualization of "functional systems" within the brain has served as the theoretical foundation for several current tests including all of the following except one. Which one?**

   a. Naglieri-Das Cognitive Assessment System

   b. Kaufman Assessment Battery the Children—Second Edition

   c. NEPSY-II

   d. Test of Memory and Learning—Second Edition

5. **True or False? Current state-of-the-art practice demands that assessments have a theoretical foundation to aid in test interpretation.**

6. **What stage in the history of clinical neuropsychology deemphasized localization of brain "lesions" and emphasized the identification of impaired and spared abilities?**

   a. The integrative and predictive stage.

   b. The functional profile stage.

   c. The single test approach stage.

   d. The test battery/lesion specification stage.

7. **True or False? According to IDEA (2004), a response-to-intervention model is required for the identification of a specific learning disability.**

Answers: 1. c; 2. b; 3. true; 4. d; 5. true; 6. b; 7. false

Chapter Three

TRAINING AND CREDENTIALING IN SCHOOL NEUROPSYCHOLOGY

T his chapter focuses on training and credentialing standards and a proposed model curriculum to train school neuropsychologists.

HOW DOES THE INTEGRATION OF NEUROPSYCHOLOGICAL PRINCIPLES FIT WITHIN THE BROADER FIELD OF SCHOOL PSYCHOLOGY?

The following four questions are posed to the reader:

1. Is the integration of neuropsychological principles into the practice of school psychology an expansion of basic neuropsychological training received at the specialist level?
2. Is school neuropsychology a specialty within the broader field of school psychology?
3. Is school neuropsychology an emerging and unique specialization, separate from but related to school psychology and pediatric neuropsychology?
4. Is the integration of neuropsychological principles into the practice of school psychology an expansion of training received at the doctoral level?

These four questions represent different levels of classification of school neuropsychology based on current practice. The first question suggests that school neuropsychology may be a focused area of interest for some school psychology practitioners. Many practitioners attend, as often as possible, continuing education workshops that relate to neuropsychological topics. There is a tremendous interest in any topic related to school neuropsychology at each annual National Association of School Psychologists (NASP) and American Psychological Association (APA) conventions and annual state

DON'T FORGET

··

School neuropsychology is quickly becoming a specialty within school psychology even though it has not been formally recognized by the school psychology professional organizations.

school psychology association conferences. This level of practice is considered a baseline entry into school neuropsychology and only implies interest in the school neuropsychology field, not *competency* in school neuropsychology.

The second question suggests that school neuropsychology is a specialty area within the broader field of school psychology. Currently, NASP does not recognize specialties within the field of school psychology. Hynd and Reynolds (2005) emphatically stated in the *Handbook of School Neuropsychology* that, "the time for development of specializations in school psychology has come" (p. 12). This author endorses that sentiment as well (D. Miller, DeOrnellas, & Maricle, 2008; D. Miller, Maricle, & DeOrnellas, 2009) recognizing that there is still controversy in the school psychology profession over this subject (Pelletier, Hiemenz, & Shapiro, 2004).

The body of specialized school psychology knowledge has grown exponentially in recent years. We truly live in the information age. The training requirements for entry-level school psychology practitioners have increased dramatically since the early 1990s. Trainers of school psychologists do their best to train entry-level and advanced practitioners in a variety of roles and functions including data-based problem solving, assessment, consultation, counseling, crisis intervention, and research. Most school psychology curriculums at the specialist level have a class that covers the biological bases of behavior; but there is no in-depth exposure to neuropsychology. School psychology trainers often feel that they only have enough time to introduce specialist-level students to the broad array of roles and functions available to them as practitioners. Increased specializations in areas such as school neuropsychology must occur either through organized, competency-based postgraduate certification programs or through doctoral school psychology programs that offer specialization in school neuropsychology.

Many graduates of school psychology graduate programs (specialist or doctoral levels) report that they quickly choose an area of specialization once they graduate. Some graduates become "specialists" in autism assessment and interventions; others are "specialists" in early childhood assessment, adolescent psychopathology, curriculum-based measurement consultants, and so on. The point is that the field of school psychology has become so rich in knowledge that practitioners often seek a specialization. These specializations already taking place within our field are a result of both individual interest and the need for more in-depth knowledge and training in narrower areas of knowledge and practice.

Currently, the movement of integrating neuropsychological principles into school psychology practice is naturally evolving into a specialty within the broader field of school psychology. The question that arises with the specialization topic is: What constitutes specialization? Taking one course on how to administer a popular neuropsychological battery certainly does not constitute specialization; specializing in school neuropsychology does require minimum levels of training in identified competencies.

The third statement suggests that school neuropsychology is an emerging and unique specialization, separate from but related to school psychology and pediatric neuropsychology. This may be the long-range status of school neuropsychology some years from now, but school neuropsychology is probably best viewed as an area of interest for practicing school psychologists or, at best, as an emerging subspecialty area within the broader field of school psychology.

Finally, the fourth statement suggests that training in school neuropsychology could be an area of specialization within a doctoral school psychology program. Given the increased complexity of school psychology and the requirement for supervised practice, a convincing argument could be made for school neuropsychology training to be at the postspecialist level.

TRAINING AND CREDENTIALING STANDARDS

This section of the chapter deals with training and credentialing standards that relate to the emerging specialization of school neuropsychology. A review of what constitutes competency as defined by the major specialty certification boards is presented.

What Constitutes Competency?

In larger school districts with multiple school psychologists, the practitioners often, by choice or demand, "specialize" into niches of interest and expertise. For example, one or more school psychologists are identified as experts in such diverse areas as autism spectrum disorders, early childhood assessment/interventions, or neuropsychological assessment/interventions. The question that arises is: What constitutes competency within a specialty area? Competency is often defined by training standards that are set by professional organizations.

DON'T FORGET

Not all referrals for comprehensive assessments need a full neuropsychological evaluation.

When school psychologists are trained to understand, appreciate, and utilize neuropsychological principles in their practice, there is a misconception that they are only trained to administer and interpret neuropsychological test batteries. In fact, not all referrals for special education would benefit from a complete neuropsychological assessment. Neuropsychological assessments are time consuming and not viable for many practitioners with heavy caseloads (D. Miller, 2010).

When school psychologists receive advanced training in neuropsychology, they often report that their perceptions of children are unequivocally changed. The practice of school neuropsychology is largely a qualitative understanding of brain-behavior relationships and how those relationships are manifested in behavior and learning. A competent school neuropsychologist with a solid understanding of brain-behavior relationships can recognize neuropsychological conditions based on observing the child in the normal course of daily activities. A competent school neuropsychologist could conduct a neuropsychological examination of a child using a set of Legos^{TM}. Neuropsychological tests are tools, but knowing how to use those tests does not make a practitioner a school neuropsychologist. A school neuropsychologist is not someone who went to a workshop and knows how to administer the latest and greatest neuropsychological test battery. A school neuropsychologist knows how to interpret any data from a neuropsychological perspective, whether from an educational, psychological, or neuropsychological report, and correlates it with behavior in order to recommend educationally relevant interventions.

Competency is often loosely defined in many professions, particularly as it relates to postgraduate CEU training. For example, in school psychology when a new version of a cognitive abilities test becomes available, a practitioner goes to a 3-hour workshop on how to administer and interpret that new instrument. Does that make the practitioner competent to use that new test? The answer should be no. Competency must involve supervised practice and feedback on performance during the acquisition of a new skill. A better approach would be to have the basic 3-hour training; send the practitioner off to a daily job to practice the new test; and then return at a later date for small group supervision to review competencies gained in administering and interpreting the new test. If the practitioner demonstrated

DON'T FORGET

....

Learning to administer a new neuropsychological test battery does not mean that one can practice as a school neuropsychologist. The school neuropsychology specialty area must involve supervised, competency-based training.

evidence of mastery of the new test, then that new test could be confidently integrated into practice. If the practitioner could not demonstrate mastery of the new test, additional time for supervised practice should be mandated. This model of competency-based workshop and training should be used more often in the ever changing and often technically and theoretically complex field of school psychology.

Crespi and Cooke (2003) posed several questions related to a specialization in neuropsychology that have sparked a debate in the profession (see Lange, 2005; Pelletier et al., 2004). One of the questions posed by Crespi and Cooke (2003) was "What constitutes appropriate education and training for the school psychologist interested in practicing as a neuropsychologist?" The terms *psychologist* and *neuropsychologist* are protected terms in many states by Psychology Licensing Acts. In most states, if a practitioner wants to be called a psychologist, he/she most probably will be required to have a doctorate in psychology and be licensed as a psychologist. Licensure as a psychologist in most states is generic. In other words, a doctoral psychologist trained in the specialties of clinical or school neuropsychology, or industrial/organization psychology can be uniformly licensed as a psychologist. The title *neuropsychologist* is usually not regulated by state licensing acts, but rather is regulated by the level of attained professional experience and training. Unfortunately, there are too many practitioners who claim expertise in neuropsychology when they have had only minimal training in the area (Shordone & Saul, 2000).

The American Psychological Association (APA) has consistently taken the position that a doctorate is the entry level of training for clinical neuropsychology, including the subspecialization of pediatric neuropsychology. In 1987, a joint task force representing the International Neuropsychological Society (INS) and APA's Division 40 (Clinical Neuropsychology) published the first formal guidelines for the education, training, and credentialing of clinical neuropsychologists (*Report of the INS-Division 40 Task Force on Education, Accreditation, and Credentialing*, 1987). These standards were most recently updated in 1997 by an interorganizational group of neuropsychologists at a conference held in Houston, Texas. The consensus report of the "Houston Conference" reiterated the doctorate as the entry level of training for clinical neuropsychology.

The APA's Division 40 and the National Academy of Neuropsychologists (NAN) have adopted similar guidelines for the definition of a clinical neuropsychologist (Division 40, 1989; Weinstein, 2001). Both organizations state that a clinical neuropsychologist is a doctoral-level service provider of diagnostic and intervention services who has demonstrated competencies in the following:

- Successful completion of systematic didactic and experiential training in neuropsychology and neuroscience at a regionally accredited university.
- Two or more years of appropriate supervised training applying neuropsychological services in a clinical setting.
- Licensing and certification to provide psychological services to the public by the laws of the state or province in which he or she practices.
- Review by one's peers as a test of these competencies.

To be prepared as a clinical neuropsychologist, most training takes place within PhD or PsyD clinical psychology programs. Most clinical neuropsychology training programs have an adult focus, with few programs offering a pediatric track. There are several doctoral school psychology programs that offer a specialization in school neuropsychology (e.g., Texas Woman's University, Texas A&M, University of Texas, Ball State University, University of Northern Colorado).

Specialty Certification in Adult and Pediatric Clinical Neuropsychology

At the doctoral level of clinical neuropsychology there are two specialty boards that certify clinical neuropsychologists: the American Board of Clinical Neuropsychology (ABCN) and the American Board of Professional Neuropsychology (ABN). The American Board of Professional Psychology (ABPP) formally recognized the ABCN in 1984, while the ABN remains autonomous. Each of these boards requires a doctoral degree from a regionally accredited university, current licensure as a psychologist, at least 3 years of supervised experience in neuropsychology, and rigorous review of work samples. All three boards require an objective written exam and an oral exam. It is clear from the definitions as set forth by the APA, the International Neuropsychological Society (INS), the National Academy of Neuropsychologists (NAN), and the doctoral specialty boards that a clinical neuropsychologist is defined as a doctoral level psychologist with specific training, supervised experience, and demonstrated competency in neuropsychology.

Recognizing the subspecialization in pediatric neuropsychology within the broader field of clinical neuropsychology remains unclear and somewhat controversial in some professional circles. In 1996, a group of pediatric neuropsychologists expressed concern that neither the ABCN nor the ABN provided board examinations that were sufficient to the task of assessing the unique skills set of pediatric neuropsychologists, and a third certification board was formed and called the *American Board of Pediatric Neuropsychology* (ABPdN).

The ABPdN was reorganized in 2004 and in 2007 it submitted an application to the ABPP to become officially recognized as a member, but the application was denied. The ABPdN application for membership to the ABPP was denied in part because Baron, Wills, Rey-Casserly, Armstrong, and Westerveld (2011) pointed out that the ABCN board examination process already had multiple procedural steps in place to assess for pediatric neuropsychology competency. The ABPdN remains a relatively small board in comparison to the ABCN and ABN.

In 2007, the ABN recognized the increased subspecialization within clinical neuropsychology by creating an Added Qualifications Certificate, in addition to the generic board certification credential. Initially, the ABN recognized peer review and additional examination in the areas of child and adolescent neuropsychology, forensic neuropsychology, geriatric neuropsychology, and rehabilitation neuropsychology. Unfortunately, the Added Qualifications Certificate in child and adolescent neuropsychology was dropped as an option by the ABN in 2010.

Although 40.7% of the ABCN Diplomate respondents to the 2010 *Clinical Neuropsychologist/American Academy of Clinical Neuropsychologist Salary Survey* (Sweet, Meyer, Nelson, & Moberg, 2011) serve pediatric patients in their practice, formal recognition of pediatric neuropsychology as a subspecialty has not come to fruition (Baron et al., 2011). However, doctoral level psychologists who are interested in pediatric neuropsychology, and are licensed as psychologists with documented expertise in clinical neuropsychology, have several options to choose from when it comes to board certification.

Specialty Certification in School Neuropsychology

So where does the practice of school neuropsychology fit, or does it fit at all? The American Board of School Neuropsychology (ABSNP) was incorporated in 1999 in response to the need for setting some standards of practice for those school psychologists who claim competency in school neuropsychology. The purpose of the ABSNP is to promote the active involvement of school psychologists in training and application of neuropsychological principles to the individuals they serve. The ABSNP does require that applicants for the Diplomate in School Neuropsychology be certified or licensed school psychologists, or licensed psychologists with specialization in school neuropsychology, or ABPP Diplomates in School Psychology. See Rapid Reference 3.1 for a comparison of the requirements of the specialty boards in adult and pediatric neuropsychology and school neuropsychology.

⟍ Rapid Reference 3.1

Requirements for Specialty Certification Boards in Neuropsychology and School Neuropsychology

Requirement	ABCN[a]	ABN[b]	ABPdN[c]	ABSNP[d]
Completed doctorate in psychology	Yes[e]	Yes	Yes	No[f]
Completed specialist-level training (60+ hour) in School Psychology	n/a	n/a	n/a	Yes
Completion of an APA[g], CPA[h], or APPIC[i] listed internship	No	No	Yes	No
Completion of a 1,200-hour internship with at least 600 hours in the schools	No	No	No	Yes
Licensed as a psychologist	Yes	Yes	Yes	No
State-certified or licensed as a school psychologist or a NCSP[j] or ABPP[k] Board Certified in School Psychology	No	No	No	Yes
3 years of experience[l]	Yes	Yes	Yes	Yes
2 years postdoctoral residency[m]	Yes	No	Yes	No
Minimum 500 hours each of the past 5 years providing neuropsychological services	No	Yes	No	No
Documentation of approved ongoing CEU workshops	No	Yes	No	Yes
Objective written exam	Yes	Yes	Yes	Yes
Work samples peer-reviewed	Yes	Yes	Yes	Yes
Oral exam	Yes	Yes	Yes	Yes
Number of board-certified individuals as of 1999	444[n]	217[n]	Not Known	10[o]
Number of board-certified individuals as of 10/25/06[p]	562	197	40	197

Number of board-certified individuals as of 10/25/08[q]	632	283	41	354
Number of board-certified individuals as of 10/25/12[r]	864	323	73	490
Percentage change in a 3-year period	36.7%	14.1%	78.0%	38.4%

[a]ABCN stands for the American Board of Clinical Neuropsychology.
[b]ABN stands for the American Board of Professional Neuropsychology.
[c]ABPdN stands for the American Board of Pediatric Neuropsychology.
[d]ABSNP stands for the American Board of School Neuropsychology.
[e]For persons receiving a doctorate after 1/1/2005, the training program must have conformed with the Houston Conference Guidelines (Hannay et al., 1998).
[f]A doctorate in psychology (school or clinical) with a specialization in neuropsychology is recognized but not required. ABPP Board Certified in School Psychology is also recognized.
[g]APA stands for the American Psychological Association.
[h]CPA stands for the Canadian Psychological Association.
[i]APPIC stands for the Association of Psychology Postdoctoral and Internship Centers.
[j]NCSP stands for Nationally Certified School Psychologist.
[k]ABPP stands for the American Board of Professional Psychology.
[l]The ABCN board will accept 3 years of experience, including 1 year predoctoral, for candidates who received their doctorate between 1/1/90 and 1/1/05.
[m]The ABCN board requires that candidates who received their doctorate after 1/1/05 must document a 2-year postdoctoral residency (a requirement consistent with the Houston Conference Training Standards: Hannay et al., 1998).
[n]As cited in Rohling, Lees-Haley, Langhinrichsen-Rohling, & Williamson, 2003.
[o]Review of historical records from the ABSNP.
[p]Cited in D. Miller (2007, p. 46). Includes board-certified professionals from both United States and Canada.
[q]Cited in D. Miller (2010, p. 30). Includes board-certified professionals from both United States and Canada.
[r]Data retrieved from certification board websites or through personal communication with their respective offices on 10/25/12.

When a potential candidate for specialty certification is considering which board to apply to, the following factors should be considered:

- Does the Diplomate or Board Certification credential applied for reflect the practitioner's past and current training and professional experiences? For example, a clinical psychologist who was trained in neuropsychology would most probably apply for the ABCN or ABN Diplomate; whereas a school psychologist with expertise in applying neuropsychological principles to the school setting would probably consider the ABSNP Diplomate or recertify in clinical psychology and pursue the ABCN or ABN.

- Does the Diplomate credential or Board Certification applied for reflect the clinical populations with which the practitioner typically works? An adult clinical neuropsychologist may have a difficult time getting board certified as a pediatric neuropsychologist or a school neuropsychologist. The potential applicant to a diplomate board should read the entrance requirements carefully and talk to other practitioners who have recently completed the credentialing process and ask for advice.
- What are the implications, if any, for practice within a particular state after the receipt of a Diplomate or Board Certification credential? Generally, the Diplomate credential is an endorsement of a professional's expertise in the area of neuropsychology and not necessarily a license to practice in that area of expertise. An applicant for a Diplomate in neuropsychology must be aware of current licensing laws within the state(s) of practice.

PROPOSED PROFESSIONAL GUIDELINES TO TRAIN SCHOOL NEUROPSYCHOLOGISTS

Currently, there are no professional standards or guidelines for the practice of school neuropsychology. The National Association of School Psychologists (NASP) has a set of training standards (NASP, 2010) but as previously mentioned, NASP does not endorse specialties within the field of school psychology. D. Miller (2007, 2010) proposed a set of professional guidelines to train school neuropsychologists (see Rapid Reference 3.2). If the training guidelines presented by Shapiro and Ziegler (1997) for pediatric neuropsychologists are compared to the training guidelines presented by this author, there are some noticeable differences. The author would argue that training guidelines for pediatric neuropsychologists and school neuropsychologists may have some conceptual overlap, but the guidelines should be inherently different. The training guidelines for pediatric neuropsychologists emphasize more medical aspects of neuropsychology such as neurophysiology, neurochemistry, basic knowledge of imaging techniques, and cognitive and medical rehabilitation in hospital settings. The school neuropsychology training guidelines, as presented in the next section, emphasize the theories, assessment, and interventions with the various neurodevelopmental processing systems (e.g., attention, memory, executive functions) within the context of an educational environment.

≡ *Rapid Reference 3.2*

Proposed Training Guidelines for School Neuropsychologists

A school neuropsychologist must first have a clear professional identity as a school psychologist. The school neuropsychologist:

- Must be trained at the specialist or doctoral level (preferred) in school psychology from a regionally accredited university.
- Must have completed a minimum 1,200-hour internship, of which 600 hours must be in the school setting.
- Must be state credentialed (certified or licensed) as a school psychologist or equivalent title, or be certified as a Nationally Certified School Psychologist (NCSP), or hold a Diplomate in School Psychology from the American Board of Professional Psychology (ABPP).
- Should have a minimum of 3 years of experience working as a school psychologist before seeking to add the school neuropsychology specialization.

In addition to the entry-level credentials as just outlined, the school neuropsychologist must have a documented knowledge base and competencies in the following areas:

- Functional neuroanatomy.
- History of clinical neuropsychology, pediatric neuropsychology, and school neuropsychology.
- Major theoretical approaches to understanding cognitive processing and brain behavior relationships related to learning and behavior.
- Professional issues in school neuropsychology.
- Neuropsychological disorder nomenclature.
- Conceptual model for school neuropsychology assessment.
- Specific theories of, assessment of, and interventions with:
  - Sensory-motor functions
  - Attention functions
  - Visual-spatial functions
  - Language functions
  - Memory and learning functions
  - Executive functions
  - Cognitive efficiency, cognitive fluency, and processing speed functions
  - General cognitive abilities
- Genetic and neurodevelopmental disorders.
- Childhood and adolescent clinical syndromes and related neuropsychological deficits.
- Neuropsychopharmacology.
- Neuropsychological intervention techniques

(continued)

≡ *Rapid Reference 3.2 continued*

- Professional ethics and professional competencies (i.e., report-writing skills, history taking, and record review).
- Competency-based supervised experiences, specifically in school neuropsychology (minimum of 500 hours).
- Continuing education requirements (minimum of 6 CEU hours per year).

DON'T FORGET

Specialization in school neuropsychology at the doctoral level is preferred. The school psychologist at the specialist level must investigate the *limitations* of practice with national, state, and local credentialing agencies before deciding on the type of training program and board certification.

The entry-level skills and competencies of a school neuropsychologist should first meet the specialist-level training standards as set forth by NASP (2010; *Standards for Graduate Preparation of School Psychologists, 2010*).

Therefore, it is assumed that a school psychologist trained to become a school neuropsychologist would already have a base knowledge of psychological and educational principles gained as part of their specialist or doctoral-level of training (e.g., child psychopathology, diagnosis/intervention, special education law, professional ethics). Specialization in school neuropsychology at the doctoral level is the preferred model of training; however, some specialist-level school psychologists will seek out formal training in this area as well.

These proposed guidelines for the training of school neuropsychologists are expanded in more detail in Rapid Reference 3.3.

Functional Neuroanatomy

School neuropsychologists must have a knowledge base of functional neuroanatomy. In the school setting it is more important for the school neuropsychologist to know functional neuroanatomy over structural neuroanatomy. School neuropsychologists must also become more familiar with neuroimaging techniques such as functional magnetic resonance imaging (fMRI) and diffusion tensor imaging (DTI), which will increasingly be used in research and clinical practice to study childhood neurodevelopmental disorders (Miller & DeFina, 2010; Noggle, Horwitz, & Davis, 2011).

≡ Rapid Reference 3.3

Model Doctoral School Neuropsychology Curriculum

Area of Focus	Possible Class Title
• Functional neuroanatomy.	Functional Neuroanatomy, Advanced Behavioral Neuroscience, Advanced Neurophysiology (3-semester-hour class)
• History of clinical neuropsychology, pediatric neuropsychology, and school neuropsychology.	School Neuropsychology I, Neuropsychological Assessment I (3-semester-hour class)
• Professional ethics.	
• Major theoretical approaches and professional issues.	
• Conceptual model for school neuropsychology.	
• Neuropsychological disorder nomenclature.	
• Theories of, assessment of, and interventions with:	
▪ Sensory-motor functions	
▪ Attentional processes	
▪ Visual-spatial processes	
▪ Language functions	
• Report writing.	
• Supervised practice (minimum 50 hours).	
• Theories of, assessment of, and interventions with:	School Neuropsychology II, Neuropsychological Assessment II (3-semester-hour class)
▪ Learning and memory functions.	
▪ Executive functions.	
▪ Speed and efficiency of cognitive processes.	
▪ Social-emotional functions.	
• Childhood/adolescent clinical syndromes and related neuropsychological deficits.	
• Report writing (reinforced).	
• Professional ethics (reinforced).	
• Supervised practice (minimum 50 hours).	

(continued)

≡ *Rapid Reference 3.3 continued*

• Genetic and neurodevelopmental disorders.	Genetic and Neurodevelopmental Disorders (3-semester-hour class)
• Neuropsychopharmacology.	Neuropsychopharmacology (3-semester-hour class)
• Neuropsychological intervention techniques.	Neuropsychological Intervention Techniques- or Neurocognitive Intervention Techniques (3-semester-hour class)
• Competency-based supervised experiences (minimum of 225 hours, preferred 500 hours).	Supervised Practicum (3-semester-hour class)
• Internship hours (minimum of 600 hours in school neuropsychology experiences).	Internship (6- to 8-semester-hour classes)
Total hours:	27 to 29 hours of concentrated study in school neuropsychology

Source: Adapted from the School Psychology Doctoral Training Program at Texas Woman's University, Denton, Texas.

History of Clinical, Pediatric, and School Neuropsychology

To appreciate the current state of professional practice in the field, it is important for school neuropsychologists to review and appreciate the contributions of other related fields to the emerging school neuropsychology specialty.

Major Theoretical Approaches in School Neuropsychology

Many of the theoretical foundations of the newest cognitive abilities tests are based on neuropsychological theories (e.g., Lurian theory, process assessment approach). School neuropsychologists need to understand the major theoretical approaches related to the field.

Professional Issues in School Neuropsychology

School neuropsychologists need to be aware of professional issues within the field (e.g., the debate over the use of the title school neuropsychologist, current practice trends).

Neuropsychological Disorder Nomenclature

School neuropsychologists are frequently called on to *translate* medical records or previous outside neuropsychological reports to educators and parents. It is crucial that school neuropsychologists know and can appropriately use the neuropsychological nomenclature (e.g., knowing the meaning of unilateral neglect).

Conceptual Model for School Neuropsychological Assessment

School neuropsychologists must be taught a conceptual model to use in their neuropsychological assessments and interventions. Miller's school neuropsychology conceptual model (2007, 2010, 2012) is presented and illustrated in later chapters of this book.

Specific Theories of, Assessment of, and Interventions With:
- Sensory-motor functions
- Attentional processes
- Visual-spatial processes
- Language functions
- Learning and memory functions
- Executive functions
- Speed and efficiency of cognitive processes
- Broad indicators of general intellectual functioning
- Academic achievement
- Social-emotional functions
- Adaptive behaviors

School neuropsychologists need to know the specific theoretical models that apply to the processes and functions listed above and their relationship to manifestations in learning problems and in making differential diagnosis with the data. They also need to be proficient in the best assessment instruments designed to measure these individual constructs. The school neuropsychologist needs to know which empirically validated interventions can be linked with the assessment data to maximize the educational opportunities for students and to demonstrate the efficacy of the interventions used to address the learning problems.

Genetic and Neurodevelopmental Disorders

School neuropsychologists need to understand the low-incidence genetic and neurodevelopmental disorders found in some children. They need to be able to recognize characteristics associated with genetic and neurodevelopmental disorders in children and the related neuropsychological correlates. Often, children identified with a low-incidence disorder will require supplemental medical services, and the school neuropsychologist along with the school nurse may be the first to recognize the characteristic symptoms.

Childhood and Adolescent Clinical Syndromes and Related Neuropsychological Deficits

School neuropsychologists must be familiar with the research related to the known or suspected neuropsychological correlates of common childhood disorders (e.g., ADHD, Tourette's, pervasive developmental disorder) and empirically validated interventions in a school setting.

Neuropsychopharmacology

As reported in Chapter 1, children and adolescents are increasingly being administered medications. School neuropsychologists need to understand the mechanism of drug actions on brain neurochemistry. They also need to know the medications used to treat common childhood disorders and the potential side effects in order to consult effectively with medical and health personnel, parents, and educators.

Neuropsychological Evidence-Based Interventions

School neuropsychologists must be proficient in linking evidenced-based interventions to their assessment data. They also must monitor the implementation of their recommendations and evaluate the interventions for effectiveness.

Professional Ethics and Professional Competencies

School neuropsychologists must understand, appreciate, and integrate professional ethics into their daily practice. School neuropsychologists must gain proficiency in skills such as integrative report writing, history taking, record review, and clinical interviewing.

Competency-Based Supervised Experiences

Miller stated "Mastering the knowledge base of school neuropsychology is not sufficient to claim competency in school neuropsychology. Supervised experience where the knowledge base can be applied to real-world experiences is a basic requirement of formal training in school neuropsychology" (D. Miller, 2010, p. 35). A school psychologist cannot become a school neuropsychologist without competency-based supervised experiences. Individual supervision or a "grand rounds" group type of supervision must be incorporated into a training program to ensure that the trainee is getting practice and quality feedback on emerging skills before putting those skills into actual practice. It is recommended that the school neuropsychologist have a minimum of 500 hours of supervised, field-based experiences.

Continuing Education Requirements

A school neuropsychologist must be committed to lifelong learning. School neuropsychology is an emerging field. New resources (e.g., books, tests, and interventions) are becoming available on a regular basis and school neuropsychologists must maintain their professional skills. The ABNSP requires that Diplomates in School Neuropsychology obtain a minimum of 6 hours of continuing education (CE) credit annually in order to maintain their Diplomate status. Other organizations also require CEs or CEUs to renew certification or licensure. For example, NASP requires 75 continuing professional development units every 3 years for renewal of the NCSP credential. Rapid Reference 3.3 presents a doctoral school neuropsychology curriculum that was modeled after the School Psychology Doctoral Program at Texas Woman's University, Denton, Texas.

CHAPTER SUMMARY

This chapter discusses the need for training and credentialing models for practitioners with advanced graduate degrees and presents a proposed model curriculum to train school neuropsychologists. The increased interest in school neuropsychology and the demand for more training will undoubtedly help shape credentialing issues in the future. School psychologists and educators are fundamentally interested in helping children learn in the schools and providing targeted interventions as needed. As basic research in cognitive neuroscience and neuropsychology becomes more readily translated into educational practice, there will be a need to define what constitutes competency for practitioners who want to apply this knowledge base with school-age children and youth.

▰ TEST YOURSELF ▰

1. **Which area of training is more likely to be present in a pediatric neuropsychology program as opposed to a school neuropsychology training program?**
   a. Functional neuroanatomy
   b. Professional ethics
   c. Genetic and neurodevelopmental disorders
   d. Medical aspects of neuropsychology

2. **According to the author, all of the following constitute competency to provide school-based neuropsychological services except one. Which one?**
   a. Take a couple of CEU workshops on the latest neuropsychology instruments.
   b. Complete a doctoral program with an emphasis in school neuropsychology.
   c. Become a Diplomate in School Neuropsychology from the ABSNP.
   d. Complete a postgraduate, competency-based certification program with a strong supervised component.

3. **Which of the neuropsychology credentialing boards is affiliated with the American Board of Professional Psychology?**
   a. American Board of School Neuropsychology
   b. American Board of Clinical Neuropsychology
   c. American Board of Professional Neuropsychology
   d. American Board of Pediatric Neuropsychology

4. **True or False? All of the certification boards in neuropsychology require passing an objective written exam.**

5. **Which of the neuropsychology credentialing boards does not currently require a doctorate in psychology?**
   a. American Board of School Neuropsychology
   b. American Board of Clinical Neuropsychology
   c. American Board of Professional Neuropsychology
   d. American Board of Pediatric Neuropsychology

6. **True or False? There is an adopted national set of training standards for school neuropsychology.**

7. **True or False? A school neuropsychologist must be committed to lifelong learning.**

Answers: 1. d; 2. a; 3. b; 4. true; 5. a; 6. false; 7. true

Chapter Four

WHEN TO REFER FOR A SCHOOL NEUROPSYCHOLOGICAL ASSESSMENT

This chapter begins with a review of the common referral reasons for a school neuropsychological evaluation. The reasons for referral for a school neuropsychological evaluation covered in this chapter include children with known or suspected neurological disorders (e.g., traumatic brain injury, acquired brain injury), children with neuromuscular diseases (e.g., cerebral palsy, muscular dystrophy), brain tumors, central nervous system infection or compromise, children with neurodevelopmental risk factors (e.g., prenatal exposure to drugs and/or alcohol, low birth weight and/or prematurity), students returning to school after a head injury, students with a documented rapid drop in academic achievement that cannot be explained by social-emotional or environmental causes, students who are not responding to interventions, children with suspected processing weaknesses, and students with significant scatter in psychoeducational test performance. This chapter concludes with a discussion on the consideration of students with special needs.

COMMON REFERRAL REASONS FOR A SCHOOL NEUROPSYCHOLOGICAL EVALUATION

When a student is experiencing learning or behavioral difficulties, it is uncommon to start with a neuropsychological evaluation. The next section of this chapter discusses where neuropsychological assessment fits within a hierarchical model of assessment. A school neuropsychological assessment should be requested when one of the referral questions listed in Rapid Reference 4.1 is under consideration.

This chapter is intended to be a basic review of childhood medical disorders that warrant neuropsychological evaluations. For more comprehensive reviews on the neuropsychological assessment of childhood disorders see the publications listed in Rapid Reference 4.2.

≡ *Rapid Reference 4.1*

Common Referral Reasons for a School Neuropsychological Evaluation
- A student who is not responding to multiple intervention strategies.
- A student with evidence of processing deficiencies on a psychoeducational evaluation.
- A student with a valid large scatter in psychoeducational test performance.
- A student with a known or suspected neurological disorder.
- A student with a history of a neurodevelopmental risk factor.
- A student returning to school after a head injury or neurological insult.
- A student who has a dramatic drop in achievement that cannot be explained.

Children with a Known or Suspected Neurological Disorder

Children and adolescents with known or suspected neurological disorders may not always have clear or readily accessible developmental and medical histories. A thorough record review and gathering a developmental history from the caregiver are important steps in uncovering any past neurological

≡ *Rapid Reference 4.2*

Additional Resources for Research Related to Neuropsychological Correlates of Childhood Medical Disorders

Castillo, C. L. (Ed.). (2008). *Children with complex medical issues in schools: Neuropsychological descriptions and interventions.* New York, NY: Springer.

Colaluca, B., & Ensign, J. (2010). Assessment and intervention with chronically ill children. In D. C. Miller (Ed.), *Best practices in school neuropsychology: Guidelines for effective practice, assessment, and evidence-based intervention* (pp. 693–736). Hoboken, NJ: Wiley.

Davis, A. S. (2011). *Handbook of pediatric neuropsychology.* New York, NY: Springer.

Goldstein, S., & Reynolds, C. R. (Eds.). (2010). *Handbook of neurodevelopmental and genetic disorders in children* (2nd ed.). New York, NY: Guilford Press.

Riccio, C. A., Sullivan, J. R., & Cohen, M. J. (2010). *Neuropsychological assessment and intervention for childhood and adolescent disorders.* Hoboken, NJ: Wiley.

Semrud-Clikeman, M., & Teeter-Ellison, P. A. (2009). *Child neuropsychology: Assessment and interventions for neurodevelopmental disorders* (2nd ed.). New York, NY: Springer.

traumas. However, uncovering evidence of neurological trauma or risk factors may be difficult in families that are reluctant to share information about past childhood abuse or neglect, or from families where the child is adopted or being raised by a relative or in foster care.

DON'T FORGET

....

It is not uncommon for children who suffer a brain injury or insult to appear to recover and function normally, only to have learning and/or behavioral problems surface later on as their brains mature.

If a student has a positive history for neurological trauma or insult (see examples later) or the school neuropsychologist, parents, or educators suspect a positive, but undocumented, history of neuropsychological trauma or insult, the student is probably a viable candidate for a school neuropsychological evaluation. The only caveat to consider before referring a student for a school neuropsychological evaluation is that the student must be experiencing some form of academic or behavioral difficulties. Some children have a positive history of a head injury but are not experiencing any academic or behavioral difficulties. Children that fall into this category should be marked for monitoring. Monitoring children and youth who have a positive history of neurological insults (e.g., traumatic brain injury) is important because these children may be showing adequate annual yearly progress currently, but they are at risk for future learning and behavioral problems. It is not uncommon for children who experience a head injury at a young age to "look all right" and function normally for a period of time, but later experience learning or behavioral deficits as their brains mature and the academic demands of school become increasingly more difficult.

Children with Past or Recent Head Injuries Who Are Having Academic or Behavioral Difficulties

"Traumatic brain injury (TBI), also called acquired brain injury or simply head injury, occurs when a sudden trauma causes damage to the brain" (National Institute of Neurological Disorders and Stroke website, http://www.ninds.nih.gov/disorders/tbi/tbi.htm). TBI is usually the result of the skull suddenly hitting an object or the skull is hit by an object with blunt force. A closed head injury happens when the skull is not penetrated but the force of the blow causes damage. An open head injury happens when an object pierces the skull and enters brain tissue. TBI is classified as mild, moderate, or severe, depending on the extent of the brain damage. Mild TBI symptoms include no loss of consciousness or loss of consciousness for only a few seconds or minutes, headache, confusion, lightheadedness, dizziness, blurred vision or tired eyes, ringing in the ears, bad taste in the mouth, fatigue or lethargy, a change in sleep patterns, behavioral or mood changes, and trouble with memory, concentration, attention, or thinking (Semrud-Clikeman, 2001).

A student with moderate to severe TBI will likely show all of the same symptoms of a mild TBI but also include a headache that only gets worse or does not go away, repeated vomiting or nausea, convulsions or seizures, an inability to awaken from sleep, dilation of one or both pupils of the eyes, slurred speech, weakness or numbness in the extremities, loss of coordination, and increased confusion, restlessness, or agitation (National Institute of Neurological Disorders and Stroke website, http://www.ninds.nih.gov/disorders/tbi/tbi.htm).

The neuropsychological consequences of TBI have been extensively investigated by researchers (see Morrison, 2010, for a review). Like many of the disorders or traumas to the brain, developmental factors play a major role in the loss of function, course of recovery, and manifestation of the TBI symptoms acutely and later on in the life of a student. Research has not supported long-term neurocognitive deficits associated with mild head injuries (Anderson & Yeates, 2007). However, neurocognitive deficits are associated with moderate-to-severe TBI including problem solving, learning and memory, and attention and concentration (Yeates et al., 2007).

> # DON'T FORGET
> ··
> TBI has been associated with deficits in various domains including:
> • Alertness and orientation
> • Attention and concentration
> • Intellectual functioning
> • Language skills
> • Academic achievement
> • Adaptive behavior and behavioral adjustment

When TBI children are experiencing academic and behavioral difficulties, they are often misclassified or misdiagnosed as having a different disability other than TBI such as specific learning disability, mental retardation, or severe emotional disturbance (Morrison, 2010). As Morrison points out, practitioners that work with TBI children and adolescents must remember that the first few years after a TBI hold the most potential for functional change and remediation. A student with a history of a TBI should be monitored for behavioral or academic difficulties. Furthermore, children with TBI may need to be reevaluated more frequently than every 3 years, as is standard with most special education children. Keep in mind that damage to the same part of the brain can lead to an overall pattern of deficits that look different from one student to another. This is because of the differences in the secondary deficits related to axonal shearing, swelling of the brain, infections, and so on.

Children with a History of Acquired or Congenital Brain Damage

In this section, the neuropsychological correlates to acquired or congential brain damage such as anoxia, brain tumors, encephalitis, genetic abnormalities, meningitis, neurofibromatosis, seizure disorders, and sickle cell disease and other cerebrovascular diseases will be presented.

Anoxia

Anoxia is an absence of oxygen supply to organ tissues, including the brain. Hypoxia is a decreased supply of oxygen to organ tissues. Anoxia and hypoxia can be caused by a variety of factors including near drowning, strangulation, smoke or carbon dioxide inhalation, and poisoning. Anoxia/hypoxia can cause loss of consciousness, coma, seizures, or even death. The prognosis for anoxia/hypoxia is dependent on how quickly the student's respiratory and cardiovascular systems can be supported and the extent of the injuries. Anoxia or hypoxia may cause irreparable harm to a student. If the student does recover from anoxia/hypoxia, a variety of psychological and neurological symptoms may appear, last for a while, and may then disappear. These symptoms may include mental confusion, personality regression, parietal lobe syndromes, amnesia, hallucinations, and memory loss (National Institute of Neurological Disorders and Stroke website, http://www.ninds.nih.gov/disorders/anoxia/anoxia.htm). Hypoxia is frequently associated with birth trauma resulting in respiratory distress during labor and delivery. Colaluca and Ensign (2010) report that even relatively minor birth hypoxia may result in significant cognitive impairments including selective and sustained attention, receptive vocabulary in preschoolers, emergent math skills, overall cognitive and academic functioning, and social skills.

Brain Tumors

Rapid Reference 4.3 presents the types and characteristics of childhood brain tumors. Brain tumors can be small and focal, or spread across large areas (invasive). Brain tumors can be noncancerous (benign) or cancerous (malignant) in nature. Brain tumors can destroy brain cells as they grow, as well as cause damage to the brain in secondary ways. Brain tumors can cause inflammation or swelling of the surrounding tissue and overall brain. Brain tumors are classified according to a variety of factors including their size, location, common characteristics, and treatment outcomes. The effects of brain

≡ Rapid Reference 4.3

Common Childhood Brain Tumors

Tumor type	Characteristics	Incident rate
• Cerebellar astrocytoma	• Usually benign, cystic, and slow growing. • Signs usually include clumsiness of one hand, stumbling to one side, headache, and vomiting. • Typical treatment is surgical removal of the tumor. • The cure rate varies, depending on the ability of the tumor to be completely removed by surgery, the tumor type, and the response to other therapies.	• Accounts for about 20% of pediatric brain tumors (peak age is 5 to 8 years old).
• Medulloblastoma	• Signs include headache, vomiting, uncoordinated movements, and lethargy. • Can spread (metastasize) along the spinal cord. • Surgical removal alone does not cure medullablastoma. Radiation therapy or chemotherapy are often used with surgery. • If the cancer returns, it is usually within the first 5 years of therapy.	• The most common pediatric malignant brain tumor (10% to 20% of all pediatric brain tumors). • Occurs more frequently in boys than in girls. Peak age is about 5 years old. Most occur before 10 years.
• Ependymoma	• Tumor growth rates vary. • Tumors are located in the ventricles of the brain and obstruct the flow of cerebrospinal fluid (CSF).	• Accounts for 8% to 10% of pediatric brain tumors.

- Signs include headache, vomiting, and uncoordinated movements.

- Single or combination therapy includes surgery, radiation therapy, and chemotherapy.

- The cure rate varies, depending on the ability of the tumor to be completely removed by surgery, the tumor type, and the response to other therapies if needed.

- Brainstem glioma

  - Tumor of the pons and medulla occurs almost exclusively in children.

  - May grow to very large size before symptoms are present.

  - Signs include double vision, facial weakness, difficulty walking, vomiting.

  - Surgical removal is usually not possible due to the location of the tumor.

  - Radiation therapy and chemotherapy are used to shrink the tumor size and prolong life.

  - Five-year survival rate is low.

  - Accounts for 10% to 15% of primary brain tumors in children; average age is about 6 years old.

- Craniopharyngioma

  - Tumor located near the pituitary stalk.

  - Often close to vital structure, making surgical removal difficult.

  - Signs include vision changes, headache, weight gain, and endocrine changes.

  - Rare, less than 10% of childhood brain tumors; average age is about 7 to 12 years old.

(continued)

≋ Rapid Reference 4.3 continued

....

- Treated with surgery, radiation therapy, or a combination. There is some controversy over the optimal approach to therapy for craniopharyngioma.
- Survival and cure rates are favorable, though endocrine dysfunction may persist as well as the effects of radiation on cognition (thinking ability).

Source: National Institutes of Health http://www.nlm.nih.gov/medlineplus/ency/article/000768.htm

tumors and their treatment can cause a wide range of neurocognitive deficits (see Begyn & Castillo, 2010, for a review). Once the student is medically stabilized and has returned to school, it is important for the school neuropsychologist to establish a baseline profile of the student's neurocognitive strengths and weaknesses. It is equally important to regularly monitor the changes in the student's profile of strengths and weaknesses as the student's brain heals. The functional profile across all dimensions of neuropsychological functioning is important to document and monitor for appropriate intervention planning and implementation. If a school neuropsychologist suspects that a student may have the symptoms of a brain tumor, a referral to a neurologist should be strongly encouraged. Symptoms such as unusual increased irritability, lethargy, diplopia (double vision), vomiting, headaches, or unexplained changes in personality and behavior may all be associated with a possible brain tumor (Begyn & Castillo, 2010).

Encephalitis

Encephalitis refers to an inflammation of the brain usually caused by viruses that occur perinatally or postnatally (Semrud-Clikeman & Teeter-Ellison, 2009). Acute symptoms include fever, altered consciousness, seizures, disorientation, and memory loss (Colaluca & Ensign, 2010). Encephalitis is classified according to the type of onset as acute, subacute, or chronic. There is a lack of published research on the neuropsychological effects of encephalitis; however, intellectual disability, irritability and lability, seizures, hypertonia, and cranial nerve involvement are seen in more severely infected children.

Genetic Abnormalities

It is beyond the scope of this book to cover all of the genetic abnormalities that can affect neuropsychological processes. These disorders include, but are not limited to, disorders such as Down Syndrome, Fragile X, Williams Syndrome, Angelman Syndrome, Prader-Willi Syndrome, Turner's Syndrome, Klinefelter Syndrome, and Noonan Syndrome. The neurocognitive deficits associated with these disorders are reviewed by Goldstein and Reynolds (2010) and Riccio, Sullivan, and Cohen (2010).

Meningitis

Meningitis is an inflammation of the lining around the brain and spinal cord that is relatively common in children and can be life-threatening (Anderson & Taylor, 2000). Early symptoms of meningitis include severe headache, stiff neck, dislike of bright lights, fever/vomiting, drowsiness and less responsive to stimuli, vacant stares, rash anywhere on the body, and possible seizures (Meningitis Research Foundation website, http://www.meningitis.org). Baraff, Lee, and Schriger (1993) conducted a meta-analysis of 19 studies that examined the neuropsychological deficits associated with meningitis. They found that 16% of the children who had meningitis also had major long-term deficits including total deafness (11%), bilateral severe or profound hearing loss (5%), mental retardation (6%), spasticity or paresis (4%), and seizure disorders (4%). Methodological problems across studies have made it difficult to document the neuropsychological problems or deficits associated with meningitis (see Colaluca & Ensign, 2010, for a review). The neuropsychological deficits related to meningitis seem to be a function of developmental variables. As an example, gross motor skills appear to be impaired after discharge from acute hospital care, whereas fine motor incoordination, visual-perceptual deficits, and language deficits may become evident when the child starts preschool and be more readily recognized.

Neurofibromatosis

Neurofibromatosis is a rare disorder classified as a neurocutaneous syndrome. There are two forms of neurofibromatosis: NF1 and NF2. NF1 occurs more frequently in children; whereas NF2 does not. NF1 is characterized by spots of skin pigmentation that look like birthmarks, or benign tumors on or under the skin, benign tumors in the iris of the eye, focal lesions in various parts of the brain, and freckles in unexposed body areas such as the armpits (NINDS, 2012). NF2 is characterized by a slow-growing tumor in the eighth cranial nerve and is more rare. NF2 symptoms include hearing loss, poor balance, headaches, and ringing in the ears (NINDS).

Visual-spatial impairment is considered to be one of the major neuro-cognitive deficits in children with NF1 (Billingsley et al., 2004). Cutting, Clements, Lightman, Yerby-Hammack, and Denckla (2004) reported that children with NF1 had neurocognitive deficits in language, motor, and visual-motor areas. For a more complete review of neurofibromatosis see Moore and Frost (2011), Riccio et al. (2010), or Semrud-Clikeman and Teeter-Ellison (2009).

Seizure Disorders

Seizure disorders can occur throughout childhood and are typically caused by metabolic disorders, hypoxia, head injury, tumors, high fevers, or other congenital problems (Semrud-Clikeman & Teeter-Ellison, 2009). Pinpointing the cause of a seizure can be difficult and may reflect a more serious neurological condition or secondary characteristic of an illness. Up to 70% of all seizure disorders have no known cause and are labeled as *idiopathic* (Freeman, Vining, & Pillas, 2002). In children, the diagnosis of seizure disorders is complicated by clinical manifestations, which are age-dependent and differ substantially from seizure disorders in adults. More than 50% of all seizure disorders begin before the age of 25 and many start in early childhood (Freeman et al., 2002).

The term *epilepsy* is used to describe chronic conditions that involve seizures that affect a wide variety of neuropsychological processes; whereas, seizures refer to *individual episodes.* Seizures interfere with the child's normal brain functions. They can produce sudden changes in consciousness, movement, or sensation. Untreated seizures can lead to an overall dampening of neurocognitive functions and lower achievement (Youngman, Riccio, & Wicker, 2010).

Rapid Reference 4.4 presents the list of the major types of seizures and associated neuropsychological deficits.

Occasionally tonic-clonic seizures persist for long periods of time in a condition called *status epilepticus*, which results in hospitalization. There are other epilepsy syndromes that affect children such as juvenile myoclonic epilepsy, benign rolandic epilepsy, infantile spasms, Lennox-Gastaut syndrome, Rasmussen's syndrome, Landau-Kleffner syndrome, and progressive myoclonic epilepsy (see Youngman et al., 2010, for a review of these seizure disorders). Seizure disorders can affect all of the neurocognitive processing areas, see comprehensive reviews by Salpekar et al. (2011), Semrud-Clikeman and Teeter-Ellison (2009), or Riccio et al. (2010).

Sickle Cell Disease and Other Cerebrovascular Diseases

Cerebrovascular diseases represent a group of vascular disorders that cause brain damage. Some cerebrovascular disorders result in stroke and are sometimes

≡ *Rapid Reference 4.4*

....

Types of Seizures

Type	Characteristics
	Partial Seizures
Simple partial seizures	• Affects movement that starts with jerking in the fingers or toes and progresses to one whole side of the body.
	• Sensations usually occur on one side of body. May cause things to look, smell, taste, sound, or feel different.
	• Child stays aware of surroundings.
Complex partial seizures	• Alters consciousness. Child will be unaware of what is happening during seizure.
	• Often starts with a blank stare, followed by oral movements such as chewing, then repeated movements that seem out of place (e.g., lip smacking, hair twirling, or hand patting).
Secondarily generalized	• Seizures start as partial seizures and become generalized seizures.
	Generalized Seizures
Absence seizures	• Previously known as *petit mal* seizures.
	• Seizures are brief staring spells often misdiagnosed as ADHD-Inattentive Type. Staring spells may occur more than 100 times in a day.
	• Distinctive EEG wave pattern used in diagnosis.
Myoclonic seizures	• Brief involuntary muscle jerks involving the limbs or trunk.
	• May occur as a single seizure or in a cluster.
Clonic seizures	• Jerking of all limbs without prior stiffening.
Tonic seizures	• Stiffness with sudden muscle contractions.
Atonic seizures	• Sudden loss of muscle tone causing child to become floppy and drop to ground.
Tonic-clonic seizures	• Previously known as grand mal seizures.
	• Often called a convulsion.
	• Loss of consciousness occurs.
	• Begins with a sudden cry, fall, bodily stiffness; followed by jerking movements due to muscles tensing (clonic) and then relaxing (atonic) repeatedly.

Sources: Salpekar, Berl, and Kenealy (2011); Semrud-Clikeman and Teeter-Ellison (2009); Riccio, Sullivan, and Cohen (2010); and Youngman, Riccio, and Wicker (2010).

referred to as cerebrovascular accidents (CVAs). Children who experience a CVA as a result of a wide variety of etiologies often have significant and permanent neuropsychological impairments. These impairments include deficits in intellectual functioning, language, attention, verbal learning and memory, visual-spatial processing, and processing speed (Colaluca & Ensign, 2010; Riccio et al., 2010).

Sickle cell disease (SCD) is a group of genetically transmitted blood disorders that results in chronic anemia. SCD has a high incidence rate in African Americans (Wang, 2007). Neuropsychological deficits associated with SCD include motor functioning and language in young children and a decline in IQ in older children, and generalized difficulties with attention, working memory, and with reading and math across age ranges (Colaluca & Ensign, 2010).

Children with Neuromuscular Diseases

In this section of the chapter, the neuropsychological correlates to childhood neuromuscular diseases such as cerebral palsy and muscular dystrophy will be presented.

Cerebral Palsy
Cerebral palsy (CP) is a term used to describe a heterogeneous group of chronic movement disorders. CP is not a disease. CP is not caused by disturbances in the muscles or nerves, but rather caused by faulty development in the brain structures that help control movement and posture (pyramidal or extrapyramidal tracts). CP is characterized by:

> [A]n inability to fully control motor function, particularly muscle control and coordination. Depending on which areas of the brain have been damaged, one or more of the following may occur: muscle tightness or spasticity; involuntary movement; disturbance in gait or mobility, difficulty in swallowing and problems with speech. In addition, the following may occur: abnormal sensation and perception; impairment of sight, hearing or speech; seizures; and/or mental retardation. Other problems that may arise are difficulties in feeding, bladder and bowel control, problems with breathing because of postural difficulties, skin disorders because of pressure sores, and learning disabilities." (United Cerebral Palsy website, http://www.ucp.org)

CP is generally classified into four subtypes: spastic, athetoid or dyskinetic, ataxic, or mixed. The neuropsychological correlates to CP have not been fully investigated. Semrud-Clikeman and Teeter-Ellison (2009) reviewed the literature on the neuropsychological functioning associated with CP. They found several studies that suggested that children with spastic CP appear to be characterized by specific impairments in visual-perceptual-motor functioning with children achieving lower performance on nonverbal IQs than verbal IQs. Children diagnosed with some form of CP should be administered a school neuropsychological assessment battery to determine baseline levels of functioning, particularly in the areas of sensory-motor, visual-spatial, and academic achievement.

Muscular Dystrophy Disorders

Congenital muscular dystrophy (CMD) refers to a group of disorders in which infants evidence muscle weakness at birth or shortly thereafter. CMD is generally classified into one of six subtypes: Myotonic Muscular Dystrophy (MMD) (aka Steinert's Disease), Duchenne Muscular Dystrophy (DMD) (aka Pseudo-hypertrophic), Becker Muscular Dystrophy (BMD), Limb-Girdle Muscular Dystrophy (LGMD), Facioscapulohumeral Muscular Dystrophy (FSH or FSHD) (aka Landouzy-Dejerine), and Spinal Muscular Atrophy (SMA) (Blondis, 2004). CMD affects all muscle groups and onset begins at or near birth. The progression varies with the subtype with many being slowly progressive and some may shorten the lifespan. Severe mental retardation is often associated with CMD that has structural brain changes. The effects of pure CMD on cognitive abilities are variable (Blondis, 2004).

The infant form of MMD affects a wide variety of muscle groups and is associated with mental retardation, while the juvenile form is associated with learning disabilities before onset of motor problems (Blondis, 2004). ADHD and anxiety disorders are also present in children with MMD. The progression of MMD is slow, often spanning 50 to 60 years.

The DMD subtype of CMD affects the proximal muscle groups and the mean IQ of children with DMD appears to be 85 with a skewed distribution to the left (lower than normal). The age of onset for DMD is early childhood to about 2 to 6 years of age. Children with DMD have neuropsychological deficits in verbal fluency, reading, phonological processing, receptive and expressive language, verbal learning and attention, and working memory and survival is rare beyond the early 30s (Blondis, 2004).

The BMD and LGMD subtypes of CMD mainly affect the limb girdle and proximal muscle groups. The age of onset for both of these subtypes of CMD is adolescence or adulthood. Limited studies suggest that children with BMD have low average verbal and nonverbal IQs, while children with LGMD have a wider range of IQ scores. Children with either of these subtypes of CMD typically survive into mid- to late adulthood (Blondis, 2004).

The FSH or FSHD subtype of CMD initially affects proximal and then later distal muscle groups but does not have an onset until age 20 or later. There are no known neuropsychological correlates to this subtype of CMD (Blondis, 2004). Finally, the SMA subtype of CMD affects proximal muscles, starts in childhood, with symptoms progressing slowly into adulthood. Like the FSH/FSHD subtype, there are no known neuropsychological correlates (Blondis, 2004).

Children with Central Nervous System Infection or Compromise

In this section of the chapter, the neuropsychological correlates of childhood central nervous system infections will be presented. These common central nervous infections or compromises include asthma, end-stage renal disease, HIV/AIDS, juvenile diabetes, leukemia, and spina bifida or hydrocephalus.

Asthma

The Centers for Disease Control and Prevention (CDC) estimated that 9.6 million children (13.1%) less than 18 years of age have been diagnosed with asthma at some point in their lives (2007), making asthma the most prevalent health condition in children. One direct negative consequence of asthma is the increased number of absences that often result in academic deficiencies. Medications such as Albuterol[TM] can have side effects that alter the child's arousal and attention levels, memory, motor steadiness, and visual-spatial planning (see Donnelly, 2005, for a review). Recent research has suggested that these neuropsychological deficits may be overstated and only affect children with the most severe forms of asthma (Colaluca & Ensign, 2010). A school neuropsychologist should be aware of children with a positive history for asthma and help educators and parents be aware of any potential negative side effects the medication may have on the child's behavior and learning.

End-Stage Renal Disease

Renal failure in children can be caused by a variety of disorders or abnormalities, including trauma to the kidneys, hypoxia, infections, drug toxicity, and immunological disorders (Fennell, 2000). Colaluca and Ensign (2010) reviewed the literature and found that renal failure is associated with the following neuropsychological problems: intellectual impairments (lower performance and full scale IQs), developmental delays in infants (motor and mental), memory disorders (impaired short-term memory and verbal learning problems), attentional dysfunction (impaired immediate span, slower reaction times, errors of impulsivity and inattention on tests of vigilance), and visuospatial and visuoconstructional problems (impaired two-dimensional construction, and impaired two-dimensional copying). School neuropsychologists can be helpful in monitoring educational progress and providing the student emotional support in dealing with the consequences of the disease.

HIV/AIDS

Human immunodeficiency virus (HIV) infection and the acquired immune deficiency syndrome (AIDS) in children are primarily due to the transmission of the virus from HIV-positive mothers to their children (Dhurat, Manglani, Sharma, & Shah, 2000). Allen, Jesse, and Forsyth (2011) pointed out that while HIV in adults affects a fully mature and myelinated nervous system, this is not the case in the developing brains of children, thus making them more vulnerable. In a review of the literature, Pulsifer and Aylward (2000) found that children with AIDS frequently had abnormal motor functions at a young age (less than 12 months), but these abnormalities decreased with age. In preschool-age children with AIDS, research has found high correlations with progressive encephalopathy, increased developmental delays or loss of developmental milestones, and signs of pyramidal motor dysfunctions. Cognitive decline is seen in children with AIDS as in all other immunological abnormalities (Jeremy et al., 2005; Pulsifer & Aylward, 2000). Specific cognitive deficits associated with AIDS in children can include fine and gross motor development (Pearson et al., 2000), attention and executive functioning (Schneider & Walsh, 2008), visual scanning, verbal and nonverbal memory, expressive and receptive language, and psychomotor speed (Pulsifer & Aylward, 2000). Academic deficits in children with AIDS have been found in the areas of mathematics (Pearson et al., 2000) and in writing (Fundarò et al., 1998). Compounding the potential deficits associated with the HIV virus, the medical treatment for AIDS can also cause significant cognitive deficits. A child with AIDS could qualify for special education services, as needed, under the Other Health Impaired category. School neuropsychologists may be asked to assess or consult on a child with AIDS to help address some of the potentially related cognitive and behavioral deficits.

Juvenile Diabetes

Insulin-dependent diabetes mellitus (IDDM) is a common childhood auto-immune disease. The disease destroys the cells within the pancreas that are essential to produce insulin. Children with this disease must take daily injections of insulin. Rovet (2000) reported that there are both transient and permanent effects of diabetes on the brain associated with too much or too little glucose or insulin. Children with diabetes might have associated neurocognitive deficits in the areas of visual-motor, memory, and attention (see Riccio et al., 2010, for a review). Rovet found that the age of onset of IDDM will vary the associated neurocognitive deficits. According to Rovet's research, visual-spatial abilities appear to be more adversely affected by early-onset diabetes, and language, memory, and attention seem to be more adversely affected by late-onset diabetes. School neuropsychologists should be aware of children in their schools who have been diagnosed with IDDM and monitor their educational progress carefully.

Leukemia

Acute lymphoblastic leukemia (ALL) is the most common malignancy in children (see Waber & Mullenix, 2000, for a review). Current treatment of ALL has resulted in a remission success rate of more than 70%. The most common treatments used to treat ALL are chemotherapy and radiation. These treatments carry with them associated toxicity to the entire central nervous system, especially in younger children. The role of the pediatric neuropsychologist is to help oncologists determine the extent of the neurobehavioral outcomes related to the medical treatment. Espy et al. (2001) investigated the long-term outcomes of ALL children at 2, 3, and 4 years postchemotherapy. Modest deficits were noted in arithmetic, visual-motor integration, and verbal fluency. Donnelly (2005) noted that some important roles of a school neuropsychologist in working with ALL children would be monitoring educational performance, providing feedback, and helping the child with ALL to maintain a sense of self-efficacy and a continued connection to the school environment.

Spina Bifida and Hydrocephalus

Spina bifida occurs as a result of the neuronal tube failing to fuse early in the course of gestation (3 to 6 weeks). The neuropsychological deficits associated with spina bifida, are in part, influenced by the level of the lesion within the spinal cord; the higher the lesion, the more impairment (Colaluca & Ensign, 2010). Hydrocephalus is a medical condition that is characterized by the ventricles of the brain overfilling with cerebrospinal fluid, resulting in increased intracranial pressure (Fletcher, Dennis, & Northrup, 2000). Hydrocephalus is not a disease by itself, but rather a symptom of some other physiological disorder (e.g., tumors, infections, or trauma to the brain). Early onset hydrocephalus occurs in children within the first year of life as a result of congenital or perinatal disorders (Fletcher et al., 2000). The increased cranial pressure in the brain can cause increased head size, and lasting damage to the brain tissue as it gets compressed and squeezed against the skull. A common treatment for children with hydrocephalus is surgical implantation of a shunt to drain the extra cerebrospinal fluid into the abdominal cavity. Children with early onset hydrocephalus have been found to have deficits in both fine and gross motor coordination, visual-motor and visual-spatial processes, some language delays, problem-solving skills and focused attention (Colaluca & Ensign, 2010; Fletcher et al., 2000; Loveday & Edginton, 2011). If a preschool or elementary-age child had a history of early onset hydrocephalus, a school neuropsychologist would be encouraged to monitor the potential deficit areas listed above.

Children with Neurodevelopmental Risk Factors

See Riccio et al., (2010) for a detailed review of the literature related to the effects of prenatal exposure to neurotoxins. Neurodevelopmental risk factors include prenatal exposure to drugs and alcohol, and low birth weight and prematurity. The neuropsychological deficits associated with these risk factors are discussed in this section. See Horton Jr., Soper, McHale, and Doig (2011) for a review of the neuropsychological correlates related to exposure to other drugs such as opiates/heroin, inhalants or solvents, and hallucinogens such as ACID or Ecstasy. Methamphetamine (Meth) use in children and youth has become a serious problem, as well as babies being born addicted to prescription and street drugs. There appears to be a serious lack of available research on the effects of these types of substance abuse within pediatric populations.

Alcohol Exposure

Fetal alcohol syndrome disorder (FASD) is a broad classification of disorders associated with prenatal exposure of varying degrees. It includes Fetal Alcohol Syndrome (FAS), Fetal Alcohol Effects (FAE), and Partial Fetal Alcohol Syndrome (PFAS) (Streissguth & O'Malley, 2000). Vaurio, Crocker, and Mattson (2011) reviewed the literature on the neuropsychological correlates associated with FASDs. They found that children with FASD had relative strengths in auditory attention, verbal retention, and basic language functions. However, the FASD children had relative weaknesses in overall general intellectual ability, executive functions, visual attention, verbal and nonverbal learning, motor functions, externalizing behaviors, and adaptive behaviors.

Cocaine Exposure

Frank, Augustyn, Knight, Pell, and Zuckerman (2001) reviewed the literature on the effects of prenatal exposure to *cocaine*. Contrary to popular belief that prenatal exposure to cocaine must lead to severe neurodevelopmental and neurobehavioral disturbances, the research does not support this myth, or at best the research findings are mixed (Horton et al., 2011). Any behavioral or neurodevelopmental effects observed in children exposed to cocaine is probably due to the child's exposure to other concurrent substances during pregnancy (e.g., nicotine, marijuana, or alcohol) or to maternal neglect or abuse.

Environmental Toxin Exposure

A teratogen is a substance that adversely affects normal development. The effects of exposure to a teratogen vary depending upon the time of exposure to the fetus, the amount of exposure, the duration of the exposure, and the genetic vulnerability of the mother and fetus to the teratogen. There has been a dramatic increase in prenatal and childhood exposure to environmental toxins during the past few decades (Arnstein & Brown, 2005). Toxin exposure to polychlorinated biphenyls (PCBs), methylmercury, and lead can lead to known neurodevelopmental problems. For further review of various teratogens and their relative impact on neurodevelopment, refer to Colaluca and Ensign (2010).

Nicotine Exposure

According to Martin et al. (2003), 11.4% of pregnant women continued to smoke during their pregnancies. Smoking during pregnancy causes the fetus to be exposed to *carbon dioxide and nicotine* along with multiple other chemicals. Causal links have been made between smoking and infertility, miscarriages, still births, and low-birth-weight babies (Olds, 1997). Olds conducted a meta-analysis of the research related to the long-term neurobehavioral effects of nicotine on children. He found that when studies controlled for the effects of prenatal alcohol exposure and the quality of parental caregiving, maternal nicotine use was related to conduct and attention problems in children. See Colaluca and Ensign (2010) for a more thorough review of the neuropsychological consequences of nicotine exposure.

Low Birth Weight and Prematurity

Low birth weight in infants has been associated with developmental delays, attention problems, behavioral difficulties, academic failure, and cognitive impairment. Delays in cognitive and motor functioning can be found in children with a history of low birth weight as early as 18 to 24 months (Dooley, 2005). Riccio et al. (2010) provided an extensive review of the low-birth-weight literature and identified many short-term and long-term neuropsychological deficits. School neuropsychologists should consider conducting a broad-based assessment with children who have a positive history of low birth weight to determine a profile of their strengths and weaknesses.

Marijuana Exposure

Fried and Simon (2001) reviewed the literature on the neurodevelopmental and neurobehavioral effects of *marijuana use* during pregnancy. Similar to smoking, the fetus is exposed to carbon dioxide when the mother smokes, as well as the chemical THC that is specific to marijuana. Fried and Simon's examination of the literature concluded there was no evidence that prenatal marijuana use adversely affects the course of the pregnancy or early development; however, prenatal marijuana use may be associated with later neurocognitive difficulties. Specifically, Fried and Simon (2001) found support for a linkage between maternal marijuana use and later deficits in executive functions within the offspring. Goldschmidt, Richardson, Cornelius, and Day (2004) found that regular prenatal exposure to marijuana used by mothers resulted in 10-year-old children having lower achievement scores in reading and spelling. Horton Jr. et al. (2011) suggests that additional research is needed to clarify the extent of any long-term effects of prenatal exposure to marijuana.

Students Returning to School After a Head Injury

School neuropsychologists are in a unique position to facilitate a smooth transition from the hospital setting back to the school setting for a child or adolescent recovering from a TBI or other neurological conditions, which resulted in hospitalization. In addition, school neuropsychologists are increasingly getting involved in monitoring athletes for sports-related concussions (Webbe & Salinas, 2011). Regardless of the cause of a student's neurologic injury, it is important for the school district to have a plan in place for students who are coming back to the school after medical recovery.

For example, typically the school discovers that a student has sustained a TBI, if or when the teacher or principal is notified by the parent, or in high-profile car accidents when school personnel see all of the details on the evening news. When the school finds out about a student who has been hospitalized for a TBI, the Special Education Director should be notified. Ideally, there should be a TBI team in place within the district or region that can be contacted as well. The TBI team should be composed of a school neuropsychologist (or school psychologist), a speech and language pathologist, an occupational therapist, a school nurse, and a curriculum specialist (e.g., teacher, homebound instructor). Other specialized personnel such as adaptive physical therapists and mobility specialists can be called on as needed and if they are available to the school district. The function of the TBI team is to interface with the hospital or medical setting and plan for the acute and long-term educational needs of the student.

Initially, the medical needs of the student take precedent. As the student's medical condition becomes stabilized and the student regains mental capacities, the school will need to provide some educational services. As the student recovers from the TBI, the educational services may range from homebound instruction to full reintegration into the regular classroom. The school-based TBI team needs to be a part of the decision-making process related to the child's educational needs as soon as possible. If the school-based TBI team can get involved early, the student should benefit from coordinated medical-home-school interventions. Rapid Reference 4.5 highlights some of the roles that a school-based TBI team can play in the student's course of recovery. See Prout, Cline, and Prout (2010) or Semrud-Clikeman (2001) for more detailed reviews of how school neuropsychologists can help with a TBI student coming back to school. Keep in mind that many of these same principles for school reentry could be applied to any student returning to school after hospitalization for a neurological illness.

≡ Rapid Reference 4.5

Possible Roles of School-Based TBI Teams

Stage	Possible Functions
• Initial identification of the TBI child	• Provide counseling support to the school friends of the TBI student.
	• Provide the hospital with educational records on parental/guardian release of information.
• Medical treatment planning at the hospital	• Attend the case staffing at the hospital to monitor the therapies received by the student (e.g., speech therapy, physical therapy) with the awareness that those therapies may need to be picked up by the school at a later stage of recovery.
	• Plan for the educational needs of the student as the student becomes medically stabilized.
	• Provide regular updates to the school personnel (e.g., Special Education Director, principal, and teachers).
• Prior to hospital discharge	• Arrange a home visit with the hospital rehabilitation personnel and the school-based TBI team to assess the physical layout of the home, any architectural barriers, and any potential hazards that would interfere with the student's discharge to the home.

	• Assess the school's physical layout, any architectural barriers, and any potential hazards that would interfere with the student's reintegration into the school.
	• Determine the need for in-service training, consultation, and/or peer preparation for the school staff and students and deliver appropriate education and counseling.
	• In conjunction with the hospital social worker and rehabilitation personnel, prepare the family for the reentry process.
	• Obtain medical records for educational programming upon appropriate release of the medical records by the parent/guardian.
	• Establish a follow-up schedule and postdischarge set of contacts.
	• Conduct a school neuropsychological evaluation to determine the educational needs of the student.
• School reentry	• Put any special education or educational modifications in place and monitor regularly.
	• Coordinate the home/school/agency service delivery.
	• Monitor the educational progress of the student regularly and adjust the IEP goals as needed.

Students Who Have a Documented Rapid Drop in Academic Achievement That Cannot Be Explained by Social-Emotional or Environmental Causes

If a school neuropsychologist receives a referral for a student who has a sudden drop in academic achievement along with symptoms of lethargy, headaches, increased irritability, diplopia (double vision), vomiting, or unexplained changes in personality and behavior, that child must be carefully evaluated. It must be determined if the student is experimenting with drugs or is overly medicated. Other possible explanations for this unusual behavior must be explored such as acute social-emotional changes or environmental causes. It is important to note that some aggressive brain tumors can cause a sudden change in academic performance, as well as an undiagnosed seizure disorder. If a school neuropsychologist suspects that the child has a neurological condition, first refer the child to a neurologist for a medical evaluation before proceeding with the assessment.

Students Not Responding to Repeated Evidence-Based Interventions

Recent federal educational laws such as No Child Left Behind (NCLB; 2001) and IDEA (2004) have placed an emphasis on early interventions using evidence-based instructional methods. If a student does not respond to multiple interventions, a student may be referred for a comprehensive evaluation by a multidisciplinary team to determine eligibility for special education and related services. What constitutes a comprehensive, multifactored evaluation will vary based on the referral question(s). In Chapter 6, the differences between psychoeducational and neuropsychological evaluation will be presented.

The purpose of a school neuropsychological evaluation is to determine if there are neurocognitive explanations for a student's poor response to prior intervention (s) and to align new interventions with the neurocognitive assessment data. A school neuropsychological assessment, if conducted properly, can provide educators with a rationale for a targeted, prescriptive intervention that will likely succeed. For example, if the student has difficulty with reading due to a poor grasp of phonological skills, early intervention and remedial strategies to teach phono-logical processing should be tried. However, after a period of time during which the student has not shown adequate academic progress in reading, further assessment is needed to help guide alternative interventions.

Children with Suspected Processing Weaknesses

Typically, students with learning problems are administered a psychoeducational evaluation prior to a school neuropsychological evaluation. As an example, if students achieve low scores on the long-term memory cluster on the WJIII-COG (Wood-cock, McGrew, & Mather, 2001, 2007a) or low Working Memory Index scores on the WISC-IV (Wechsler, 2003), then additional neuropsychological testing may be warranted. It is important to evaluate the relative strengths and weaknesses of students compared to their own scores (i.e., ipsative comparisons) and evaluate the students' scores relative to a norming group. Generally, a processing weakness is defined as an ipsative score of at least 1.5 standard deviations below the average of their other test scores and at least 1 standard deviation below the mean for a standardization group (e.g., standard score of 85 or lower). Some general interpre-tative guidelines are presented in Chapter 8. The purpose of a school neuro-psychological assessment with children who have suspected processing weaknesses is to establish, confirm, or deny the existence of any processing deficits, discuss the potential impact those deficits may have on the learning potential of the child, and link appropriate educational interventions to the assessment data (see Dehn, 2006, for a thorough review of processing assessment).

Students with Significant Scatter in Psychoeducational Test Performance

Children sometimes have an unusually large and significant range of performance on traditional psychoeducational measures. An example would be a student who obtains standard scores on the WJII-COG ranging from 65 to 115, which is an occurrence obtained by 1% or less of children their age. If an examiner has confidence that the student put forth good effort and motivation while obtaining these scores, then the student is probably a good candidate for a school neuro-psychological evaluation. The purpose of the school neuropsychological evaluation would then be to tease out specific neurocognitive strengths and weaknesses, and to develop an intervention plan consistent with the unique learning profile of the student.

CONSIDERATION OF STUDENTS WITH SPECIAL NEEDS

This section of the chapter discusses what considerations should be made when assessing students with special needs. These accommodations include: modification of the testing materials or standardizes instructions, and recognizing the influences of cultural, social-economic, and environmental factors on test results.

Modification of the Testing Materials and Standard Administration Instructions

Every effort should be made to administer tests following standardized instructions. However, a major part of the process assessment approach is testing the limits. After the test has been administered in a standardized manner, the examiner may "test the limits" by asking individuals questions beyond the ceiling levels or modifying the questions to see if the child's performance will improve. The WISC-IV Integrated (Wechsler et al., 2004a) is an example of a test that has standardized the testing of the limits concept. The WISC-IV Integrated is discussed in Chapter 7. The scores from the standardized administration should always be reported. Scores generated from a modified administration may be reported if the examiner clearly reports how the test instructions or materials were modified. Scores from a modified administration should not replace scores from a standardized administration.

Many of the neuropsychological tests designed for school-age children assume that the child's motor and sensory functions are intact (Hebben & Milberg, 2009). When a child's motor functions (e.g., cerebral palsy, muscular dystrophy) or sensory functions (e.g., vision, hearing) are impaired, it becomes a challenge for the school neuropsychologist to assess the child. Ideally, if test modifications are needed for a particular child, the school neuropsychologist should first determine if there is a standardized test available to meet the child's needs. If customized modifications to the testing materials are made by the examiner to elicit a behavioral sample, the characteristic of these modifications must be reported. For example, to assess the receptive language skills in a visually impaired child, visual stimuli may need to be enlarged, or visual stimuli may need to be avoided altogether. Rapid Reference 4.6 presents some possible test modifications for children with special needs.

≡ Rapid Reference 4.6

Possible Test Battery Modification for Students with Special Needs

Testing Students with Visual Impairments
- Administer verbal portions of standardized tests.
- Administer nonverbal tests that require spatial manipulation and problem solving but not sight.
- Administer a standardized or criterion-referenced test specifically designed to evaluate visually impaired students.

Testing Students with Hearing Impairments
- Have an interpreter use American Sign Language if possible for verbal tasks.
- Substitute written language for oral language.
- Give directions through pantomime, signing, or gesture.
- Use standardized nonverbal tests (e.g., *Universal Nonverbal Intelligence Test* [UNIT], Bracken & McCallum, 1998).

Testing Students with Expressive Language Impairments
- Establish that an adequate output channel exists (e.g., pointing).
- Document expressive language deficits on standardized tests (e.g., NEPSY-II: Korkman, Kirk, & Kemp, 2007).
- Use nonverbal tests.
- Give directions through pantomime and gesture.

Testing Students with Motor Impairments
- Assess overall cognitive ability with verbal and motor-free tasks.
- Avoid speeded motor tasks.
- Test motor abilities without time constraints

Source: Adapted from Hebben and Milberg, 2009, p. 90.

Recognizing the Influences of Cultural, Social-Economic, and Environmental Factors

It is assumed that neuropsychological constructs such as sensory-motor functions, attention, memory, and executive functions are universal across cultures, class, and race. It is the measurement of these neuropsychological constructs across cultures that represents the real challenge. The majority of neuropsychological tests are "conceived and standardized within the matrix of Western culture" (Nell, 2000, p. 3). There are two major barriers in the assessment of children from non-Westernized cultures: language differences and acculturation. When a 7-year-old child, who has recently come to the United States from Mexico, performs poorly on a test of intelligence, both the poor understanding of the English language and the poor knowledge of the U.S. culture may be contributing factors to the child's poor performance. Additionally, most nationally norm-referenced tests were not standardized on students outside of the United States.

There are many languages spoken in the United States. For example, when most people think about Texas they would say that English and Spanish are the primary languages spoken. They would be correct, but, as an example, there are 70 different languages spoken in the homes of Dallas Independent School District students (Dallas Independent School District website). Ardila, Roselli, and Puente (1994) noted that a common solution to assessing a child whose primary language is not English is to use translations of the tests. There are few foreign language neuropsychological tests designed for children. Rapid Reference 4.7 lists a sample of the tests that are available in a foreign language, which can be used, in neuropsychological assessment.

Another approach to the lack of foreign language translations of neuropsychological tests is to use a translator to assist with the administration. There are three problems with using translators: (1) some of the concepts in the English version of the test are not directly translatable into a foreign language; (2) there is no guarantee that the translator will not embellish or alter the meaning of the question or the student's response via translation; and (3) even if a translator is used, most of the neuropsychological tests lack appropriate normative samples for different cultures (Ortiz, Ochoa, & Dynda, 2012). Even more problematic is the lack of appropriate norms for individuals from different countries. Translated tests that are still using primarily white, American norm groups may result in inaccurate scores (Ortiz et al., 2012). Rhodes (2000) developed a practical guide for using interpreters in a school setting that is relevant to school neuropsychologists.

≡ *Rapid Reference 4.7*

....

Selected Foreign Language Translated Neuropsychological Tests

Test	What It Measures
• *Batería III Woodcock-Muñoz* (Woodcock, Muñoz-Sandoval, McGrew, & Mather, 2005).	The WJIII-Cognitive and Achievement Batteries translated into Spanish; ages 2 to 90+ years.
• *Battelle Developmental Inventory— Second Edition* (Newborg, 2005).	Personal-social, adaptive, motor, communication, and cognitive development in children birth to 7 to 11 years. Spanish version available.
• *Bilingual Verbal Ability Tests— Normative Update* (BVAT-NU: Muñoz-Sandoval, Cummins, Alvarado, Ruef, & Schrank, 2005).	Assesses the total knowledge of a bilingual individual using a combination of two languages for ages 5 to 90+ years. Norms available in 17 languages plus English.
• *CELF-4 Spanish* (Wiig, Secord, & Semel, 2006).	A comprehensive language assessment for Spanish speakers ages 5 to 21 years.
• *Dean-Woodcock Neuropsychological Battery* (Dean & Woodcock, 2003).	Directions for the test are available in Spanish for ages 4 to adult.
• *Expressive One-Word Picture Vocabulary Test, 2000 Edition— Spanish-Bilingual Edition* (EOWPVT-SBE: 2000a).	Verbal expression of language for children who are bilingual in English and Spanish for ages 4–0 to 12–11 years.
• *Preschool Language Scale—Fourth Edition (PLS-4)—Spanish Edition* (Zimmerman, Steiner, & Pond, 2002).	Receptive and expressive language skills in young children ages birth through 6 years, 11 months.
• *Receptive One-Word Picture Vocabulary Test, 2000 Edition— Spanish-Bilingual Edition* (ROWPVT-SBE: 2000b).	Receptive vocabulary for children bilingual in English and Spanish, ages 4 to 12 years.
• *Test de Vocabulario en Imágenes Peabody* (TVIP: Dunn, Lugo, Padilla, & Dunn, 1986).	Receptive vocabulary for Spanish-speaking and bilingual students ages 2–6 to 17–11 years.
• *Test of Phonological Awareness in Spanish* (TPAS: Riccio, Imhoff, Hasbrouck, & Davis, 2004).	Phonological awareness in Spanish-speaking children ages 4–0 to 10–11 years.
• *WISC-IV Spanish* (Wechster, 2004b).	The Spanish version of the WISC-IV for ages 6–0 to 16–11 years.
• *Woodcock-Muñoz Language Survey—Revised* (Woodcock, Muñoz-Sandoval, Ruef, & Alvarado, 2005).	Establishes language proficiency level in English or Spanish in measures of reading, writing, listening, and comprehension for ages 2 to 90+ years.

The other major barrier in the assessment of children from non-Westernized cultures is acculturation. Acculturation is defined as "the change in cultural patterns that result from the direct and continuous firsthand contact of different cultural groups" (Pontón & Leon-Carrión, 2001). Acculturation may be best conceptualized as a cluster of interrelated variables including "language, values, beliefs, attitudes, gender roles, psychological frames of references, skills, media preferences, leisure activities, observance of holidays, and cultural identity" (Felix-Ortiz, Newcomb, & Myers, 1994, as cited in Pontón & Leon-Carrión, p. 40).

Given the ever-growing culturally diverse populations with which school neuropsychologists are being asked to work, there are some possible approaches to assessment. Nell (2000) recommended that neuropsychologists should use a core test battery for cross-cultural assessment. The specific cognitive constructs that he recommended to be assessed in children are visuomotor abilities, visuopraxis, stimulus resistance, working memory, auditory memory (immediate, delayed, and recognition), visual memory (immediate and delayed), and language. Nell provided descriptions of the various tests that could be used to measure each one of these cognitive domains.

Remember that the practice of school neuropsychology is largely a qualitative understanding of brain-behavior relationships and how those relationships are manifested in behavior and learning. Neuropsychological tests are tools to aid in assessing brain-behavior functions but they are not our only tools. Hess and Rhodes (2005) suggest that, given the scarcity of neuropsychological measures for culturally and linguistically diverse children, the clinical interview may be the best source of information. The neuropsychological assessment of culturally and linguistically diverse populations will continue to be a challenge for practitioners. Researchers, test authors, and publishers are encouraged to develop new measures that are ecologically valid and reliable for use with multiple populations.

CHAPTER SUMMARY

This chapter reviews the common referral reasons for a school neuropsychological evaluation. The chapter concludes with a discussion on potential modifications for special needs children and recognizing the influences of cultural, social-economic, and environmental factors on school neuropsychological assessment. In the next chapter, Chapter 5, a conceptual model for school neuropsychological assessment is presented.

✎ TEST YOURSELF ✎

1. **All of the following are valid reasons for a neuropsychological evaluation except which one?**
   a. A student returning to school after a head injury.
   b. A student with a valid large scatter in psychoeducational test performance.
   c. A mentally retarded child.
   d. A student who is not responding to multiple intervention strategies.

2. **Which of the following refers to a decreased oxygen supply to the brain?**
   a. Anoxia
   b. Repoxia
   c. Dyspoxia
   d. Hypoxia

3. **True or False? It is not uncommon for children who suffer a brain injury to appear to recover and function normally, only to have learning and/or behavioral problems surface later on as their brains mature.**

4. **Which subtype of cerebral palsy (CP) affects 70% to 80% of CP patients with the symptoms of muscles stiffly and permanently contracted?**
   a. Spastic cerebral palsy
   b. Ataxic cerebral palsy
   c. Mixed cerebral palsy
   d. Dyskinetic cerebral palsy

5. **What is the most common type of malignant brain tumor in children?**
   a. Cerebellar astrocytoma
   b. Medulloblastoma
   c. Ependymoma
   d. Brainstem glioma

6. **True or false? Cocaine exposure prenatally leads to serious neurodevelopmental and neurobehavioral disturbances.**

7. **According to the research, the long-term neuropsychological deficits associated with acute lymphoblastic leukemia are:**
   a. Modest deficits in reading, written language, and verbal immediate memory.
   b. Severe deficits in social skills, expressive language, and fine motor coordination.
   c. Modest deficits in arithmetic, visual-motor integration, and verbal fluency.
   d. Severe deficits in spelling, reading, and written language.

8. **The juvenile form of this muscular dystrophy is associated with learning disabilities before onset of motor problems. ADHD and anxiety disorders may also be present.**
   a. Congenital Muscular Dystrophy
   b. Myotonic Muscular Dystrophy
   c. Duchenne Muscular Dystrophy
   d. Becker Muscular Dystrophy

Answers: 1. c; 2. d; 3. true; 4. a; 5. b; 6. false; 7. c; 8. b

Chapter Five

AN INTEGRATED MODEL FOR SCHOOL NEUROPSYCHOLOGY ASSESSMENT

This chapter begins with a review of school neuropsychology conceptual models previously reported in the literature. A proposed *Levels of Assessment Model* illustrates where neuropsychological assessment fits within a broader range of assessment. Finally, the evolution of a comprehensive model for school neuropsychological assessment is presented along with a rationale for each of the components.

PRIOR MODELS OF SCHOOL NEUROPSYCHOLOGICAL ASSESSMENT

Two contemporary models have been proposed in the literature for conceptualizing school neuropsychology: the Transactional Model and the Cognitive Hypothesis Testing Model. A transactional model of child clinical neuropsychology was proposed by Teeter and Semrud-Clikeman (1997; Semrud-Clikeman & Teeter-Ellison, 2009). In this model, the authors recognize the importance of both genetic and environmental factors in the development and maturation of the central nervous system. The model also illustrates the bidirectional influence of the subcortical and cortical regions of the brain on various neurocognitive functions. Neurocognitive functions were said to form the foundations for intelligence or cognitive abilities, which in turn influence academic, behavior, and social functions. The basic tenets of the transactional neuropsychological paradigm were the appreciation of the neuropsychological correlates of psychiatric, neurodevelopmental, and acquired disorders of childhood; the understanding of the neurodevelopmental course of those disorders; and a recognition of the importance of moderating variables (e.g., cognitive, social, and behavioral) on the overall adjustment of children who have neurodevelopmental disorders. The rationale for this transactional model of child clinical neuropsychology is consistent with the integrative stage of neuropsychology that was reviewed in Chapter 2.

Hale and Fiorello (2004) proposed a Cognitive Hypothesis-Testing (CHT) Model. See Fiorello, Hale, and Wycoff (2012) for an updated discussion of the model. The authors combine two approaches into their model: (1) individual psychoeducational assessment, and (2) intervention development and monitoring, using both behavioral interventions and problem-solving consultation. Inherent in their model is a respect for assessing the child's behavior within the confines of their environment and for assessing the influences of the neuropsychological constraints on the child's behavior. The authors advocate using behavioral analyses to track intervention progress and they stress the importance of single-subject designs. However, unlike the strict behaviorists that advocate for behavioral assessment and monitoring exclusively, Hale and Fiorello also recognized the importance of using information about the child's cognitive functioning in forming appropriate and effective interventions.

The baseline component of the CHT Model is the stated need for school psychologists to engage in more indirect service delivery, such as consultation and serving on prereferral intervention teams. Hale and Fiorello's advocacy for an indirect service delivery model that relies on problem-solving techniques is consistent with the positions taken by the national school psychology organizations for almost 20 years. An indirect service delivery model has become paramount in recent years because of the increasing shortage of school psychologists (D. Miller & Palomares, 2000). With the recent reauthorization of IDEA 2004 and the potential adoption of a response-to-intervention model for special education, the school psychology field may finally have a stronger push for utilizing prereferral intervention teams and an evidence-based problem solving approach.

The CHT Model has four component parts: theory, hypothesis, data collection, and interpretation. Hale and Fiorello (2004) proposed that once a child is referred for a psychoeducational or school neuropsychological evaluation there are up to 13 steps in a CHT evaluation. Figure 5.1 illustrates the CHT Model. Hale and Fiorello pointed out that the majority of psychoeducational evaluations stop at Step 5 in the model. Recent federal mandates, such as NCLB of 2001 and IDEA of 2004, will require educators to implement Steps 9 through 13, which is consistent with the Tier I and II levels of a response to intervention model.

A key component of the CHT Model, particularly the assessment component, is the analysis of the neurocognitive demands/solution strategies required to perform a given task (Fiorello et al., 2012). To generate hypotheses about

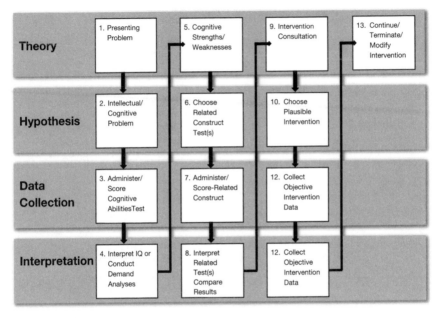

Figure 5.1. The Cognitive Hypothesis Testing (CHT) Model

Source: Adapted from Hale and Fiorello, 2004.

why a particular student performed poorly or well on any given task, the examiner must understand the neurocognitive demands/solution strategies for successful performance on the task. An examiner can obtain this information in several ways. First, the examiner can access the promotional literature about the test from the test publishers and read what the test is reported to measure. Second, the examiner can read the test manual to evaluate the test's construct validity: Does the test measure what it reports to measure? Third, the examiner can read the research literature about the test to see how it can be used with clinical populations and how it relates to similar measures. Fourth, further training in school neuropsychology provides the examiner a greater understanding of the neuropsychology constructs vital for the development of reading, math, writing, and spelling. The second and third methods stated above are the most reliable methods for obtaining the demand characteristics of a particular test.

The CHT Model relies heavily on Lurian and process-oriented approaches to neuropsychological assessment. In the CHT Model, if a global deficit is observed in a student's assessment data, a reason for the global deficit is hypothesized and

≡ Rapid Reference 5.1

Comparison of Two School/Pediatric Neuropsychology Models

Model	Principle Tenets
Transactional model of child clinical neuropsychology (Semrud-Clikeman & Teeter-Ellison, 2009; Teeter & Semrud-Clikeman, 1997)	• Neuropsychological correlates of psychiatric, neurodevelopmental, and acquired disorders of childhood appreciated. • Neurodevelopmental course of those disorders understood. • Importance of the moderating variables on the overall adjustment of children who have neurodevelopmental disorders recognized.
Cognitive Hypothesis-Testing (CHT) Model (Fiorello et al., 2012; Hale & Fiorello, 2004)	• Assess children's behavior within the confines of their environment. • Assess the influences of the neuropsychological constraints on the child's behavior. • Employ an indirect consultation model and problem-solving approach model. • Identify the demand characteristics/solution strategies required for successful task completion. • Conduct systematic hypothesis testing.

then further tested for specific deficits. This approach is consistent with the Lurian and process-oriented approaches. In this section of the chapter, two previously formulated theories on how to approach school neuropsychology are reviewed. Rapid Reference 5.1 presents a comparison of the basic tenets of these two theories of school/pediatric neuropsychology. In the next sections a levels of assessment model and a conceptual model for school neuropsychological assessment will be presented. These models adhere to many of the same tenets of the transactional model and the CHT Model.

LEVELS OF ASSESSMENT MODEL

It is uncommon for a student to be referred for a neuropsychological evaluation without some prior history of formal or informal assessment. Typically,

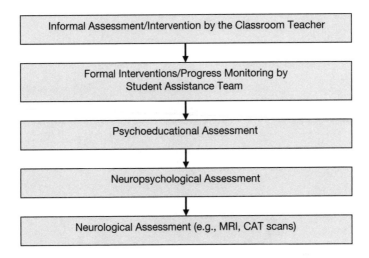

Figure 5.2. Levels of Assessment Model

Source: From D. C. Miller, 2007, *Essentials of School Neuropsychological Assessment*, p. 93. Copyright © 2007 by John Wiley & Sons, Inc.

neuropsychological evaluations fall within a levels of assessment model. See Figure 5.2 for an illustration of the levels of assessment model.

When a student is evidencing signs of a learning problem (e.g., poor acquisition of reading skills), the first step in the assessment model is to identify the extent of the problem. The classroom teacher may try a variety of educationally sound teaching techniques to remediate the identified academic deficiency. The student's parent(s)/guardian(s) may be informed of these interventions and deficit skill levels through normal means (e.g., grades/report cards, parent-teacher conferences). At this level of intervention, the teacher may choose to use a variety of informal measures to assess the student's current skill levels. These assessments are typically criterion-referenced tests to determine skill strengths and weaknesses. This level of assessment and intervention would fall within the first tier of the Response-to-Intervention (RTI) Model (see Figure 5.3).

If a student failed to respond to a series of research-based interventions, the prereferral intervention team may choose to refer the student for a psychoeducational assessment. The purposes of the psychoeducational assessment may be twofold: (1) identify strengths and weaknesses that may be used to target prescriptive interventions, and (2) qualify the student for special education services. A traditional psychoeducational assessment may include a measure of

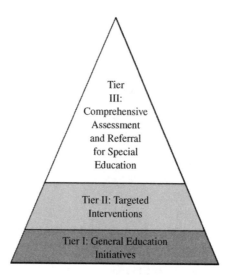

Figure 5.3. Illustration of the Traditional Response-to-Intervention (RTI) Model

Source: From D. C. Miller (Ed.), 2010, *Best Practices in School Neuropsychology: Guidelines for Effective Practice, Assessment, and Evidence-Based Assessment* (p. 93). Copyright © 2010 by John Wiley & Sons, Inc.

intellectual/cognitive functioning, a measure of academic functioning, and perhaps a measure of visual-motor functioning and a social-emotional screener.

When a student fails to respond to special education services or if there is a suspected neurological basis for the student's learning difficulties, the student may be referred for a neuropsychological evaluation. A neuropsychological assessment is more thorough than a psychoeducational assessment (see Chapter 6 for a discussion of the differences between psychoeducational, psychological, and neuropsychological assessments). The purpose of the neuropsychological evaluation is typically not to qualify a student for special education services, except in the case of traumatic brain injury, but rather to provide educators and parents with a comprehensive overview of the student's neurocognitive strengths and weaknesses that may be used to tailor instructional strategies. The psychoeducational and neuropsychological assessments would fall within the third tier of the RTI model (see Figure 5.3).

There are times after a school neuropsychological (school-based) or pediatric neuropsychological (private practice-based) evaluation has been conducted when the student is referred to a neurologist for a consultation. For example, if the student is experiencing a rapid decline in global or specific cognitive functions that cannot be explained by social-emotional or environmental factors, a referral to a neurologist may be warranted. The student may be evidencing signs of a brain tumor or other degenerative neurological disease.

This levels of assessment model is not an invariant sequence, meaning that the only way a student could get referred for a neurological consultation would be to first pass through all of the other levels of assessment. As an example, if a student has suspected seizures, a referral to a neurologist is recommended immediately without other formal assessments. Another example is referring a student for a neuro-psychological evaluation if there is a suspected head injury. The farther a student progresses down the levels of assessment model, there are additional costs in terms of money and time. Knowing when—and when not to—refer for additional assess-ments is a major role that school neuropsychologists can play in the schools to maximize the benefits for children that really need the additional evaluations.

SCHOOL NEUROPSYCHOLOGICAL ASSESSMENT MODEL OVERVIEW

This section of the chapter provides a review of the changes to the school neuropsychological conceptual model between 2007 and 2012 and introduces the new Integrated SNP/CHC Model.

School Neuropsychological Conceptual Model (2007–2012)

Figure 5.4 illustrates a conceptual model for school neuropsychological assess-ment (D. Miller, 2007, 2010, 2012; D. Miller & Maricle, 2012). Miller introduced the school neuropsychological conceptual model (SNP Model) as a way of organizing school-age, cross-battery assessment data based on the underlying principle neuropsychological constructs being measured. The three purposes of the SNP Model are: (1) to facilitate clinical interpretation by providing an organizational framework for the assessment data; (2) to strengthen the linkage between assessment and evidence-based interventions; and (3) to provide a common frame of reference for evaluating the effects of neurodeve-lopmental disorders on neurocognitive processes (D. Miller, 2012). The complete SNP Model includes the integration of academic achievement and social-emotional functioning with the major neuropsychological assessment components (see D. Miller, 2007, 2010, 2012; D. Miller & Maricle, 2012, for reviews).

The SNP Model represents a synthesis of several theoretical and clinical approaches including: Lurian theory (Luria, 1966, 1973), a process-oriented

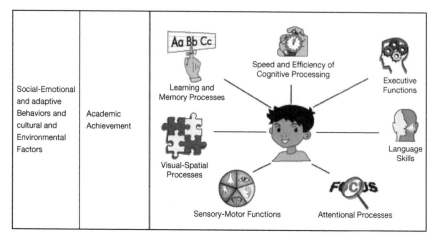

Figure 5.4. Conceptual Model for School Neuropsychological Assessment

Source: D. Miller, 2012; D. Miller and Maricle, 2012.

approach to assessment (Milberg et al., 2009), neuropsychological theories (e.g., Mirsky's theory of attention; Mirsky, 1996), the cross-battery assessment approach (Flanagan, Alfonso, & Ortiz, 2012), and Cattell-Horn-Carroll (CHC) Theory (McGrew, 2005). In the initial development of the SNP Model, CHC Theory and cross-battery assessment were used to classify the subtests from the major tests of cognitive abilities into broad classifications. However, these theoretical models did not adequately address other important neurocognitive processes such as sensori-motor functions, attentional processes, working memory, and executive functions (D. Miller, 2012). Therefore, the SNP Model integrated additional neuro-psychological theories such as Mirsky's theory of attention (Mirsky, 1996) and Baddeley and Hitch's (1974) theory of working memory (Baddeley, 2000). The SNP Model was also heavily influenced by Kaplan's process-oriented approach (Milberg et al., 2009), which resulted in the inclusion of qualitative, as well as quantitative assessment data. Recognizing what strategies individuals employ during performance on any given task is as important, if not more so, than the test score itself; and was inherent in the SNP Model (D. Miller, 2012).

The SNP Model also follows a Lurian approach in which an individual's neurocognitive strengths and weakness are systematically determined by varying the input, processing, and output demands across a variety of tasks (see Fiorello et al., 2012; Hale & Fiorello, 2004 for a discussion of what is called *conducting demand characteristics analyses*). As an example, it is not sufficient to say a student has an attentional processing problem and stop at that broad diagnostic level. The SNP Model emphasizes the need to further define the type of attentional deficit(s) the student may be experiencing such as a shifting, sustained, or selective attention deficit. Narrowing down to greater neurocognitive processing specificity in assessment for each of the broad SNP classifications will lead to more refined prescriptive remediations, accommodations, and interventions (D. Miller, 2012).

Once the classification schema for the SNP Model was created, individual tests from the major instruments used in the assessment of pediatric cognition, academic achievement, neuropsychological functioning, attention, learning, and memory were classified into the SNP Model using a variety of techniques (see subsequent chapters for specific examples). Published correlational and factorial data were used to group tests together that were shown to measure similar neuropsychological processes or functions. When such data were not available, tests were classified into the SNP Model based on what the authors reported the tests were designed to measure. Recent factorial analyses of more than 900 clinical cases (see preliminary results in D. Miller, 2012) further helped refine the SNP Model as it is presented in this chapter. The SNP Model continues to be refined and evolve based on ongoing research.

The 2012 SNP Model (see Rapid Reference 5.2) consists of seven *broad classifications* representing basic neurocognitive functions and processes, including sensorimotor functions, attentional processes, visual-spatial processes, language functions, learning and memory, executive functions, and speed and efficiency of cognitive processing. D. Miller (2012) noted that within the SNP Model, all of these broad classifications except for speed and efficiency of cognitive processing could be further subdivided into what he referred to as *second-order classifications*. As an example, sensorimotor tasks (*broad classification*) could be further subdivided into the second order classifications of lateral preference, sensory functions, fine motor functions, gross motor functions, visual scanning, and qualitative behaviors. These second-order classifications could be further subdivided into *third-order classifications*. As an example, the second order classification of sensory functions could be further subdivided into the third order classifications of auditory and visual acuity, and tactile sensation and perception. See Rapid Reference 5.2 for the full delineation of the broad classifications broken down by second- and third-order classifications in the 2012 version of the SNP Model.

≡ *Rapid Reference 5.2*

School Neuropsychology Conceptual Model Classifications

Broad Cassifications	Second-Order Classifications	Third-Order Classifications
Sensorimotor functions	• Lateral preference	
	• Sensory functions	• Auditory and visual acuity
		• Tactile sensation and perception
	• Fine motor functions	• Coordinated finger/hand movements
		• Psychomotor speed and accuracy
		• Visual-motor copying skills
	• Gross motor functions	• Balance
		• Coordination
	• Qualitative behaviors	
Attentional processes	• Selective/focused attention	• Auditory selective/focused attention
		• Visual selective/focused attention
	• Sustained attention	• Auditory sustained attention
		• Visual sustained attention
		• Auditory and visual sustained attention
	• Shifting attention	• Verbal shifting attention
		• Visual shifting attention
		• Verbal and visual shifting attention
	• Attentional capacity	• Memory for numbers, letters, or visual sequences
		• Memory for words and sentences
		• Memory for stories
	• Qualitative behaviors	
	• Behavioral rating scales	
Visuospatial processes	• Visual spatial perception	• Visual discrimination and spatial localization
		• Visual-motor constructions
		• Visual-motor integration error analyses

		• Qualitative behaviors
	• Visual spatial reasoning	• Recognizing spatial configurations
		• Visual gestalt closure
		• Visuospatial analyses with and without mental rotations
	• Visual scanning/tracking	• Direct measures
		• Indirect measures
		• Qualitative behaviors
Language functions	• Sound discrimination	
	• Auditory/phonological processing	
	• Oral expression	• Oral motor production
		• Vocabulary knowledge
		• Verbal fluency (rapid automatized naming)
		• Qualitative behaviors
	• Receptive language	• Receptive language with verbal response
		• Receptive language with nonverbal motor response
		• Qualitative behaviors
Learning and memory processes	• Rate of new learning	• Verbal learning
		• Visual learning
		• Paired associative learning
	• Immediate verbal memory	• Letter recall (no contextual cues)
		• Number recall (no contextual cues)
		• Word recall (no contextual cues)
		• Sentence recall (contextual cues)
		• Story recall (contextual cues)
	• Delayed verbal memory	• Recall with contextual cues
		• Recall without contextual cues
		• Verbal recognition
	• Immediate visual memory	• Abstract designs, spatial locations, or visual sequences with motor response (no contextual cues)

(continued)

⟨ *Rapid Reference 5.2 continued*

		• Faces, objects, or pictures with verbal or pointing response (no contextual cues)
		• Visual digit span with verbal response (no contextual cues)
		• Picture/symbolic (with contextual cues)
	• Delayed visual memory	• Recall without contextual cues
		• Recall with contextual cues
		• Visual recognition
		• Qualitative behaviors
	• Verbal-visual associative learning and recall	• Verbal-visual associative learning
		• Verbal-visual associative delayed recall
	• Working memory	• Verbal working memory
		• Visual working memory
		• Qualitative behaviors
	• Semantic memory	
Executive functions	• Concept recognition and generation	• Concept recognition
		• Concept generation
	• Problem solving, fluid reasoning, and planning	• Verbal problem solving, fluid reasoning, and planning
		• Visual problem solving, fluid reasoning, and planning
	• Response inhibition	• Verbal response inhibition
		• Motoric response inhibition
	• Retrieval fluency	• Verbal retrieval fluency
		• Nonverbal retrieval fluency
	• Qualitative behaviors	
	• Behavioral Rating Scales	
Speed and efficiency of cognitive processing	• Speed efficiency	
	• Speed efficiency with accuracy	
	• Qualitative behaviors	

Reading achievement	• Basic reading skills	• Phonological decoding
		• Orthographic coding
		• Morphological/syntactic coding
	• Reading comprehension skills	
	• Reading fluency	• Rapid phonological decoding
		• Rapid morphological decoding
Written language achievement	• Written expression	
	• Expository composition	
	• Writing fluency	
	• Orthographic spelling	
	• Handwriting skills	
	• Qualitative behaviors	
Mathematics achievement	• Oral counting	
	• Fact retrieval	
	• Mathematical calculations	
	• Mathematical reasoning	
	• Mathematical fluency	
	• Qualitative behaviors	

Source: D. Miller, 2012; D. Miller and Maricle, 2012.

Integrated SNP/CHC Model

As previously stated, one of the goals of the SNP Model was to facilitate clinical interpretation by providing an organizational framework for the assessment data. As the SNP Model was refined through 2012, there were several lingering questions related to the organizational framework of the model. For example, attentional processes were designated as a separate broad classification, when in fact, attentional processes permeate almost every other process and function described in the SNP Model. This is also the case for the speed and efficiency of processing and working memory. All three of these: (1) attention, (2) processing speed, and (3) working memory act as *facilitators* to enhance the performance of other cognitive functions. It can be argued that these three processes do not work in isolation per se, but are cognitive facilitators. One of the major changes to the SNP Model is the creation of a broad classification called *facilitators/inhibitors*, which was initially referred to in an information-processing model by Dean and Woodcock (1999).

In 2010, Flanagan, Alfonso, Ortiz, and Dynda wrote a groundbreaking chapter in this author's edited book, *Best Practices in School Neuropsychology*. They presented the major tests of cognitive processing along with several other major pediatric neuropsychological measures and classified each of the subtests from these measures using the Lurian Block nomenclature, the SNP Model nomenclature, and the CHC Theory nomenclature. They referred to this as an integrated framework based on psychometric, neuropsychological, and Lurian perspectives.

In 2012, Schneider and McGrew wrote:

> The most active CHC "spillover" has been in the area of neuropsychological assessment. . . . It is our opinion that CHC-based neuropsychological assessment holds great potential. Much clinical lore within the field of neuropsychological assessment is tied to specific tests from specific batteries. CHC theory has the potential to help neuropsychologists generalize their interpretations beyond specific test batteries and give them greater theoretical unity. (p. 109)

In updating the SNP Model, one of Miller's goals was to provide a greater integration with some of the CHC theoretical classifications. This effort was based on current psychometric research (Flanagan, Alfonso, & Ortiz, 2012; Horn & Blankson, 2012; Keith & Reynolds, 2012; Schneider & McGrew, 2012; Schrank & Wendling, 2012) and ongoing discussions with the CHC theorists and cross-battery researchers. The constructs or processes that were contained in the 2012 and earlier versions of the SNP Model have not changed in the modified version of the model, but how they are classified in the newly updated *Integrated SNP/CHC Model* has been updated based on current psychometric and theoretical research.

One major change in the Integrated SNP/CHC Model is conceptualizing the model as encompassing four major classifications: (1) basic sensorimotor functions, (2) facilitators and inhibitors for cognitive processes and acquired knowledge skills, (3) basic cognitive processes, and (4) acquired knowledge (see Figure 5.5). All four of these broad classifications are influenced by each other and by social-emotional, cultural, and environmental factors.

Basic sensorimotor functions within the Integrated SNP/CHC Model include sensory, fine motor,

DON'T FORGET

The Integrated SNP/CHC Model encompasses four major classifications:

1. Basic sensorimotor functions
2. Facilitators and inhibitors
3. Basic cognitive processes
4. Acquired knowledge

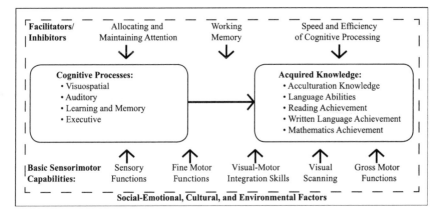

Figure 5.5. Integrated SNP/CHC Model

visual-motor integration, visual scanning, and gross motor functions. These sensorimotor motor functions are the basic building blocks for higher-order cognitive processes and influence the acquisition of acquired knowledge.

Another fundamental change to the Integrated SNP/CHC Model is the reduction in the number of what is considered to be a cognitive process. In previous versions of the SNP Model (D. Miller, 2007, 2010, 2012; D. Miller & Maricle, 2012), attention, language, and processing speed were all considered to be cognitive processes. As a result of reclassifications within the model, the only remaining cognitive processes are visuospatial, auditory, learning and memory, and executive.

The Integrated SNP/CHC Model includes a broad classification called *facilitators/inhibitors*, which includes three board categories: (1) allocating and maintaining attention, (2) working memory, and (3) speed, fluency, and efficiency of processing. The concept of facilitators/inhibitors used in this model is much broader than the types of facilitators/inhibitors described in Dean and Woodcock's (1999) information-processing model. They included external factors such as sensory-motor deficits and internal factors such as motivation, fatigue, and behavioral style as examples of facilitators and inhibitors.

The facilitators/inhibitors described in the Integrated SNP/CHC Model influence both cognitive processes and acquired knowledge. Let's consider the following example. Think of a student attempting to solve a story problem. For the student to initially encode an auditorially presented story problem, the student must focus attentional resources on the task at hand (a facilitator). Depending on the length of the story problem, the student may have to utilize sustained attention (a facilitator) to maintain focus. The student also has to not pay attention to the extraneous details in the story or to any other distractors in the environment or internal distractors (an inhibitor). In story problems, the student must figure out what elements to extract and then manipulate to solve the problem, which requires working memory and reasoning skills (a facilitator). Story problems are generally thought of as a mathematical reasoning task, but attempting to solve a story problem also requires a combination of facilitators and inhibitors to accomplish the task. The facilitators/inhibitors brought to bear on the wide variety of capacities to perceive, feel, think, or act, will vary based on the neurocognitive demands of the processes (McCloskey, Perkins, & Diviner, 2009).

Within the broad classification of speed, fluency, and efficiency of processing facilitators/inhibitors four second-order classifications were created: (1) performance fluency, (2) retrieval fluency, (3) acquired knowledge fluency, and (4) fluency and accuracy. Measures of performance fluency do not require any memory retrieval and principally are designed to measure automaticity of processing. Performance fluency has five third-order classifications: (1) psychomotor fluency, (2) perceptual fluency, (3) figural fluency, (4) naming fluency, and (5) oral motor fluency. These constructs are described in greater detail in Chapter 15.

Measures of retrieval fluency were reclassified from a second-order classification under the broad classification of learning and memory to a second-order classification under the broad classification of speed, fluency, and efficiency of processing facilitators/inhibitors. The principle focus of retrieval fluency is not the memory demand per se, but the fluency of the retrieval from memory.

Academic fluency measures such as reading fluency, writing fluency, and mathematics fluency were all reclassified from their respective academic acquired knowledge areas to the second-order classification of acquired knowledge fluency within the broad classification of speed, fluency, and efficiency of processing facilitators/inhibitors.

The classification of working memory within CHC theory or the SNP model remains debatable. Schneider and McGrew (2012) pointed out that "many of us use the term 'working memory capacity' to refer to the superordinate category of *Gsm*, whereas others use it to refer to a narrow ability within *Gsm*" (p. 116). Working memory tasks involve processes of attentional control and memory functions working together to help facilitate other cognitive processes and acquired knowledge. In the Integrated SNP/CHC Model, Miller reclassified working memory from a second-order classification under the broad classification of learning and memory to a broad classification of working memory facilitators/inhibitors (see Chapter 14 for further discussion).

Here are six additional examples of further CHC theory integration into the SNP Model:

1. Reclassifying psychomotor speed and accuracy as an example of psychomotor fluency (third-order classification) within the second-order classification of performance fluency, which is a part of the broad classification of speed, fluency, and efficiency of processing facilitators/inhibitors (Schneider & McGrew, 2012).

2. Reclassifying oral and receptive language skills from the broad classification of language functions, an implied cognitive process, to a new broad classification of language abilities, a part of acquired knowledge (Mather & Wendling, 2012).

3. Reclassifying semantic memory from the learning and memory broad classification to a broad classification called acculturation knowledge (a term used by Horn & Blankson, 2012, to refer to Gc), part of acquired knowledge.

4. Expanding the construct of speed and efficiency of processing modeled, in part, on McGrew's hypothesized speed hierarchy (McGrew & Evans, 2004; Schneider & McGrew, 2012). Further discussion of the cognitive facilitator called *speed and efficiency of processing* and the related second- and third-order classifications are presented in Chapter 15.

5. Including planning, inductive reasoning, sequential reasoning, and quantitative reasoning as second-order classifications of executive functions (Schneider & McGrew, 2012).

6. Reclassifying shifting attention form attentional processes to executive functions, specifically with a second-order classification called *cognitive flexibility* or *set shifting.*

The broad classifications and second- and third-order subclassifications of the Integrated SNP/CHC Model are presented in Rapid Reference 5.3. The corresponding CHC broad and narrow abilities are cross-referenced to the SNP model classifications in Rapid Reference 5.3 based on the current CHC classifications referenced in Horn and Blankson (2012) and Schneider and McGrew (2012). Current CHC theory still does not adequately classify all of the basic neuropsychological constructs. Recent expansion of the CHC theory by Schneider and McGrew (2012) has included narrow abilities for sensori-motor functions such as tactile abilities (Gh), kinesthetic abilities (Gk), and olfactory abilities (OM). Narrow abilities have also been identified for fine

≡ Rapid Reference 5.3

Integrated SNP/CHC Model Classifications

Broad Cassifications	Second-Order Classifications	Third-Order Classifications
Basic Sensorimotor Functions		
Sensorimotor functions	• Lateral preference	
	• Sensory functions	• Auditory and visual acuity
		• Tactile sensation and perception (Tactile abilities: Gh)
		• Kinesthetic sensation and perception (Kinesthetic abilities: Gk)
		• Olfactory sensation and perception (Olfactory memory: OM)
	• Fine motor functions	• Coordinated finger/hand movements (Finger dexterity: P2 and Manual dexterity: P1)
	• Visual-motor integration skills	
	• Visual scanning	• Direct measures
		• Indirect measures
		• Qualitative behaviors
	• Gross motor functions (Psychomotor abilities: Gp)	• Balance (Gross body equilibrium: P4)
		• Coordination (Control precision: P8)
	• Qualitative behaviors	
Cognitive Processes		
Visuospatial processes (Visual processing: Gv)	• Visual spatial perception	• Visual discrimination and spatial localization (Spatial orientation: S)
		• Visual-motor constructions (Visualization: Vz and Manual dexterity: P1)
		• Qualitative behaviors

		• Visual spatial reasoning	• Recognizing spatial configurations (*Flexibility of closure: CF*)
			• Visual gestalt closure (*Closure speed: CS*)
			• Visuospatial analyses with and without mental rotations (*Speeded rotation: SR* and *Visualization: Vz*)

Auditory processes (*Auditory processing: Ga*)

Sound discrimination (*Speech sound discrimination: U3*)

Auditory/phonological processing (*Phonetic coding: PC*)

Learning and memory processes (*Short-term memory: Gsm, and long-term memory: Glr*)

• Rate of new learning

• Verbal learning (*Free recall memory: M6*)

• Visual learning (*Free recall memory: M6*)

• Paired associative learning (*Associative Memory: Ma*)

• Immediate verbal memory (*Short-term memory: Gsm, and auditory processing: Ga*)

• Letter recall (no contextual cues) (*Memory span: MS*)

• Number recall (no contextual cues) (*Memory span: MS*)

• Word recall (no contextual cues) (*Memory span: MS*)

• Sentence recall (contextual cues) (*Memory span: MS*)

• Story recall (contextual cues) (*Meaningful memory: MM*)

• Immediate visual memory (*Short-term memory: Gsm, and visual processing: Gv*)

• Abstract designs, spatial locations, or visual sequences with motor response (no contextual cues)

(continued)

≡ Rapid Reference 5.3 continued

		• Faces, objects, or pictures with verbal or pointing response (no contextual cues) (*Visual memory: MV*)
		• Visual digit span with verbal response (no contextual cues)
		• Picture/symbolic (with contextual cues)
	• Delayed verbal memory (*Long-term storage and retrieval: Glr*)	• Free recall without contextual cues (*Free recall memory: M6*)
		• Free recall with contextual cues (*Meaningful memory: MM*)
		• Verbal recognition
	• Delayed visual memory (*Long-term storage and retrieval: Glr*)	• Free recall without contextual cues (*Free recall memory: M6*)
		• Free recall with contextual cues (*Meaningful memory: MM*)
		• Visual recognition
		• Qualitative behaviors
	• Verbal-visual associative learning and recall (*Associative memory: MA*)	• Verbal-visual associative learning
		• Verbal-visual associative delayed recall
Executive processes (*Fluid reasoning: Gf*)	• Cognitive flexibility (set shifting)	• Verbal set shifting
		• Visual set shifting
		• Verbal and visual set shifting
	• Concept formation	• Concept recognition
		• Concept generation
	• Problem solving, planning, and reasoning	• Planning (*Spatial scanning: SS*)
		• Deductive and inductive reasoning (*Induction: I*)

		• Sequential reasoning (*General sequential reasoning: RG*)
		• Quantitative reasoning (*RQ*)
	• Response inhibition	• Verbal response inhibition
		• Motoric response inhibition
	• Qualitative behaviors	
	• Behavioral/emotional regulation	

Facilitators and Inhibitors

Allocating and maintaining attention facilitators/inhibitors:	• Selective/focused attention	• Auditory selective/focused attention
		• Visual selective/focused attention
(Attention/ Concentration: AC)	• Sustained attention	• Auditory sustained attention
		• Visual sustained attention
		• Auditory and visual sustained attention
	• Attentional capacity	• Memory for numbers, letters, or visual sequences (*Memory span: MS*)
		• Memory for words and sentences (*Memory span: MS*)
		• Memory for stories (*Meaningful memory: MM*)
	• Qualitative behaviors	
Working memory facilitators/inhibitors: (Attentional Control: WM)	• Verbal working memory	
	• Visual working memory	
	• Qualitative behaviors	

(continued)

≡ *Rapid Reference 5.3 continued*

Speed, fluency, and efficiency of processing facilitators/inhibitors	• Performance fluency (*Processing speed: Gs*)	• Psychomotor fluency (*Psychomotor speed: Gps and Movement time: MT*)
		• Perceptual fluency (*Perceptual speed: P*)
		• Figural fluency (*Figural fluency: FF*)
		• Naming fluency (*Naming facility: NA*)
		• Rate-of-test-taking fluency (*R9*)
		• Oral motor fluency (*Speed of articulation: PT and Movement time: MT*)
	• Retrieval fluency	• Word fluency (*Word fluency: FW and Ideational fluency: FI*)
		• Semantic fluency
	• Acquired knowledge fluency	• Reading fluency: Rapid phonological decoding (*Reading speed: RS*)
		• Reading fluency: Rapid morphological decoding
		• Writing fluency (*Writing speed: WS*)
		• Mathematics fluency (*Number facility: N*)
	• Fluency and accuracy	

Acquired Knowledge (*Gc*)

Acculturation knowledge	• Semantic memory (*Comprehension-Knowledge: Gc*)	• Verbal comprehension (*Lexical knowledge: VL and Language development: LD*)
		• General information (*General verbal information: KO*)
		• Domain-specific knowledge (*Domain-specific knowledge: Gkn*)
Language abilities (*Language development: LD*)	• Oral expression (*Communication ability: CM*)	• Vocabulary knowledge (*Lexical knowledge: VL*)

	• Qualitative behaviors	
	• Receptive language (*Listening ability: LS and auditory comprehension: ACV*)	• Receptive language with verbal response
		• Receptive language with nonverbal response
	• Qualitative behaviors	
Reading achievement (*Reading and writing: Grw*)	• Basic reading decoding skills (*RD*)	• Phonological decoding (*Reading decoding: RD*)
		• Orthographic coding
		• Morphological/syntactic coding
	• Reading comprehension skills (*Reading comprehension: RC*)	
Written language achievement (*Reading and writing: Grw*)	• Written expression (*Writing ability: WA*)	
	• Expository composition	
	• Orthographic spelling (*Spelling ability: SG*)	
	• Knowledge of mechanics of writing (*English usage: EU*)	
	• Handwriting	
	• Qualitative behaviors	
Mathematics achievement (*Quantitative knowledge: Gq*)	• Oral counting	
	• Fact retrieval	
	• Mathematical calculations (*Mathematical achievement: A3*)	
	• Mathematical reasoning (*Mathematical knowledge: KM and Quantitative reasoning: RQ*)	
	• Quantitative knowledge (*Gq*)	
	• Qualitative behaviors	

Note: The labels in parentheses relate to CHC broad or narrow abilities (Horn & Blankson, 2012; Schneider & McGrew, 2012).

motor functions such as finger dexterity (*P2*), and manual dexterity (*PI*); and for gross motor functions such as gross motor equilibrium (*P4*) and control precision (*P8*). CHC theorists have not yet identified narrow abilities for visual-motor integration skills and visual scanning.

Within the broad classification of learning and memory, CHC theory does not provide the specificity needed for classification. Specifically, within the neuropsychology realm, distinctions are made between free recall of information versus recognition. Recognition memory is not addressed in CHC theory. CHC theory also does not address in detail attention. From a neuropsychological point of view, it is important to determine the type of attentional processing difficulty a student may be experiencing such as selective/focused, sustained, shifting, or attentional capacity. In the *Woodcock-Johnson III Tests of Cognitive Abilities* (Woodcock, McGrew, & Mather, 2001, 2007a) a clinical cluster score was included called *Broad Attention* and included a conceptualization of attention that mirrored the SNP Model. However, there are no narrow abilities identified for these attentional facilitators and inhibitors.

Finally, CHC theory does not define narrow abilities for several written language achievement skills such as expository composition and handwriting that are operationalized by Berninger (2007b) on the *Process Assessment for the Learner—Second Edition: Diagnostics for Reading and Writing*. Nor does CHC theory define narrow abilities for several mathematics achievement skills such as oral counting and fact retrieval that are operationalized by Berninger (2007a) on the *Process Assessment for the Learner—Second Edition: Diagnostics for Math*.

Each of the areas within the Integrated SNP/CHC Model will be further defined and refined in other chapters; however, a brief overview is provided here. *Sensorimotor functions* serve as the essential building blocks for all other higher order cognitive processes. *Sensory functions* include baseline assessments of vision, hearing, and touch. Motor functions include baseline assessments of fine and gross motor skills, visual-motor integration, visual scanning, and balance and coordination. An examiner does not want to attribute a poor performance on a higher order cognitive task to a cognitive process such as auditory short-term memory, if the true reason for the poor performance is poor auditory acuity. Chapter 10 reviews sensory-motor functions.

The cognitive processes considered next in the SNP model are *visuospatial* and *auditory processes*. Visual-spatial skills are subdivided into the following areas: visual-spatial perception and visual spatial reasoning. *Auditory processes* are subdivided into the following areas: sound discrimination and auditory/pho-nological processing. Chapter 11 reviews both visuospatial and auditory processes.

Learning and memory is dependent on sensory-motor functions, attentional processes, visuospatial processing, and auditory processes. In Chapter 12, learning and memory will be conceptually divided into four major classifications: rate of learning, immediate memory, long-term (delayed) memory, and associative memory and learning.

Executive processes serve as the command and control center for the other cognitive processes. In Chapter 13, executive functions are classified into the broad classifications of cognitive flexibility or set shifting, concept formation, problem solving or reasoning, response inhibition, qualitative behaviors, and behavioral and emotional regulation.

In Chapter 14, the attention and working memory facilitators/inhibitors are discussed. Attention is not a unitary construct. It is important for a school neuropsychologist to understand how *attentional processes* can be subdivided into selective/focused attention, sustained attention, and attentional capacity components. Working memory can be subdivided into verbal working memory and visual working memory.

In Chapter 15, the speed, fluency, and efficiency of processing facilitators/inhibitors is discussed. This cognitive facilitator is subdivided into five second-order classifications: performance fluency, retrieval fluency, acquired knowledge fluency, the influence of fluency on performance accuracy, and qualitative behaviors that relate to speed and efficiency of processing.

In Chapter 16, the broad classifications of acculturation knowledge and language abilities that are part of acquired knowledge are discussed. In Chapter 17, the other achievement areas with acquired knowledge, such as reading, writing, and mathematics, are discussed.

The final consideration that must be made in interpreting any assessment results with the SNP Model are the contributions made by the student's social-emotional, environmental, and cultural factors. It is imperative that a learning difficulty or behavioral problem not be attributable to a processing disorder if one or more of these other factors (e.g., social-emotional, environmental, or cultural) are deemed to be the root cause of the student's current difficulties.

CHAPTER SUMMARY

In this chapter several school neuropsychology conceptual models are reviewed. A comprehensive model for school neuropsychological assessment is presented with a rationale for each component of the model. In subsequent chapters of this book, each of the major processing areas of the school neuropsychological model is examined in greater detail.

🦫 TEST YOURSELF 🦫

1. **The basic tenets of which model are: the appreciation of the neuropsychological correlates of psychiatric, neurodevelopmental, and acquired disorders of childhood; the understanding of the neurodevelopmental course of those disorders; and a recognition of the importance of the moderating variables (e.g., cognitive, social and behavioral) on the overall adjustment of children who have neurodevelopmental disorders?**
   a. Transactional model of child clinical neuropsychology.
   b. Cognitive hypothesis-testing (CHT) model.
   c. School neuropsychology conceptual model.
   d. None of the above.

2. **Which of the theoretical models combines two approaches: (1) individual psychoeducational assessment and (2) intervention development and monitoring, using both behavioral interventions and problem-solving consultation?**
   a. Transactional model of child clinical neuropsychology.
   b. Cognitive hypothesis-testing (CHT) model.
   c. School neuropsychology conceptual model.
   d. None of the above.

3. **A key component of the CHT model is the analysis of the neurocognitive demands required to perform a given task. This is called:**
   a. Conducting a factorial analysis.
   b. Conducting a behavioral analysis.
   c. Conducting a demand analysis.
   d. Conducting a task analysis.

4. **One of the major changes to the Integrated SNP/CHC Model is the inclusion of what broad classification(s)?**
   a. Cognitive facilitators for attention.
   b. Cognitive facilitators for working memory.
   c. Cognitive facilitators for speed and efficiency of processing.
   d. All of the above.

5. **According to the SNP Model, which two functions or processes lay the foundations for all other higher order processes?**
   a. Memory and learning.
   b. Visual spatial processes and language processes.
   c. Executive functions and speed of cognitive processes.
   d. Sensory motor functions and attentional processes.

6. The SNP Model is heavily influenced by all of the following except one. Which one?

a. A process-oriented approach to assessment.
b. A cognitive-behavioral approach to assessment.
c. Cross-battery assessment.
d. CHC Theory.

Answers: 1. a; 2. b; 3. c; 4. d; 5. d; 6. b

Chapter Six

SCHOOL NEUROPSYCHOLOGY REPORT WRITING

I n Chapter 5 a model for school neuropsychological assessment is presented and Chapters 10 through 17 define and operationalize each of the sub-components of the conceptual model. This chapter illustrates how the assessment model can be integrated into a school neuropsychological report. Some principles of neuropsychological assessment and report writing are presented first in this chapter. Secondly, the essential elements of a comprehensive neuropsychological report are reviewed (e.g., identifying information, reason for referral, background information). Please note that not all children require a comprehensive school neuropsychological assessment. The actual neuropsychological domains measured in a particular evaluation varies based on the referral question(s) and the history of the student. However, in this chapter, the components of the entire model are illustrated for instructional purposes.

BASIC PRINCIPLES OF SCHOOL NEUROPSYCHOLOGICAL ASSESSMENT AND REPORT WRITING

Writing a useful school neuropsychological assessment report takes practice. This section of the chapter reviews a set of basic principles for writing a school neuropsychological report.

Why Are School Neuropsychological Evaluations Lengthy?

Traditional psychoeducational or psychological reports are not as comprehensive as neuropsychological reports. Rapid Reference 6.1 presents the common components of psychoeducational, psychological, and neuropsychological assessments. Psychoeducational assessment typically includes measures of cognitive and academic functioning at a minimum, and perhaps a measure of

DON'T FORGET

The ultimate goal of a good neuropsychological evaluation should be to identify the student's neurocognitive strengths and weaknesses and link that information to prescriptive interventions that will maximize the student's learning potential.

visual-motor integration. Psychoeducational assessments conducted by an assessment specialist (e.g., school psychologist, educational diagnostician) generally provide data to determine eligibility for IDEA disabilities (e.g., mental retardation and specific learning disability classifications). Because the primary goals of both a psychological and psychoeducational report are to assist schools with eligibility decisions, these types of assessments often yield limited information for making prescriptive interventions. Psychological assessment within the schools typically includes measures of personality and psychopathology (e.g., depression, anxiety, conduct, hyperactivity/inattention scales). Psychological evaluations conducted in the schools are usually completed to determine eligibility for the IDEA Emotional Disturbance classification.

≡ Rapid Reference 6.1

Typical Components Across Psychoeducational, Psychological, and Neuropsychological Assessments

	Psychoeducational	Psychological	Neuropsychological
Record review	X	X	X
Developmental history	X	X	X
Clinical interviews	O	X	X
Intellectual	X	X	X
Academic functioning	X	X	X
Personality assessment	—	X	O
Psychopathology	—	X	O
Adaptive behavior	O	O	O
Visual-motor skills	O	—	X
Sensory-motor skills	—	—	X
Attentional processes	O	—	X

Visual-spatial	X	X	X
Verbal processes	X	X	X
Memory/learning	O	—	X
Executive processes	O	—	X
Rate of processing	O	—	X
X: typically used; O: optional; —: not typically used			

Neuropsychological evaluations are more comprehensive and may include assessments of sensorimotor functions, attention, memory and learning, and executive functions. The inclusion of these more specific cognitive processing domains in a comprehensive neuropsychological assessment, by default, requires a longer written report.

Armengol, Kaplan, and Moes (2001) suggest that there are three factors that may dictate the length of the neuropsychological report: (1) the nature of the exam, (2) efficiency, and (3) expectations or purpose. If the test battery includes only a neuropsychological screener as compared to a comprehensive assessment, the length of the report will vary. Armengol et al. (2001) suggest that some busy clinicians may not have the luxury of writing long reports due to lack of time. The expectations and purpose of the evaluation will help determine the length of the report as well. The report may be lengthy if the evaluation is to determine both eligibility for special education services and provide evidence for prescriptive interventions.

An important principle to remember is that a long report does not necessarily make it better. A list of do's and don'ts for neuropsychological report writing is presented in Rapid Reference 6.2. The rationale for these best practices and poor practices are discussed in the remainder of this chapter. Keep in mind that the

≡ Rapid Reference 6.2

Tips for School Neuropsychological Report Writing

Neuropsychological Report "Do's"	Neuropsychological Report "Don'ts"
• Administer a battery of tests comprehensive enough to answer the referral question(s).	• Ignore the referral question. • Overtest the student, only for the sake of testing. *(continued)*

Rapid Reference 6.2 continued

- Discuss the validity of the assessment and any interpretation cautions as needed.
- Interpret the various assessment results throughout the report to support the final diagnostic conclusions.
- Avoid medical and educational jargon.
- Provide data to support the diagnostic conclusions and related recommendations within the report.
- Organize the report into sections to aid the reader.
- Use tables, charts, and figures to illustrate multiple data.
- Integrate the presenting concerns from the referral source(s) with the current assessment results.
- List the tests administered to aid in a reevaluation.
- Discuss the student's strengths first, then the weaknesses, in the summary section of the report.
- Interpret the results within the student's developmental, social-emotional, cultural, and environmental backgrounds.
- Answer the referral question(s).
- Link the diagnostic conclusions with evidence-based, prescriptive interventions.
- Always provide educational recommendations for the home and school, and, where applicable, the student and outside agency personnel.
- Hierarchically arrange the recommendations from the most important first to the least important last.

- Ignore the assessment validity section of the report.
- Write a report in a pure linear fashion with the results of test 1, 2, . . . X.
- Write a report that reads like a summary section with no supporting evidence for the conclusions. At a minimum include a data sheet at the end of the report.
- Provide much assessment data but do not put it in the context of the student's developmental, social-emotional, cultural, and environmental background.
- Introduce new information in the summary section of the report.
- Overemphasize the presence of brain lesions or dysfunctions.
- Include a *DSM* diagnosis only and assume that will qualify a student for special education services.
- Conclude the report with a diagnosis only.
- Provide a long list of recommendations that are not organized by home or school, or by neurocognitive areas.
- Describe the tests but not the student.

ultimate goal of a good neuropsychological evaluation is to identify the student's neurocognitive strengths and weaknesses and to link that information to prescriptive interventions that maximize the student's learning potential.

Linear Versus Integrative Report Writing Styles

School psychologists often write psychoeducational and psychological reports in a linear manner. The background information and observations of the child are reported, the results of Test 1, Test 2, . . . Test X, then the examiner writes a summary section and makes recommendations based on the results of the evaluation. The reader of a linear report must wait until the end of the report to see how all of these data relate to each other to help explain the student's current academic or behavioral difficulties.

It is recommended that school neuropsychological evaluations not be written in a purely linear fashion. This is due, in part, to the fact that many of the neurocognitive processes measured are not factorially pure. A particular test may require a student to use sustained attentional skills as well as verbal memory processes. The intertwined and cognitively complex neurocognitive tasks that comprise many of the current tests require a more integrative approach to report writing.

A truly integrated report requires more effort, critical thinking skills, and problem solving on the part of the report writer. It is recommended, at a minimum, that the report writer relate the elements of the assessment together as the report is being written. For example, after the background information is presented and it is reported that the student has a history of attention problems, confirm or not confirm that positive history of attention problems based on the classroom observations. In many ways, the examiner is like a "cognitive detective" who constantly searches for clues in the test results to build a case that best explains the student's academic or behavioral difficulties. Likewise, if a student performs poorly on a test that measures attention, the examiner should relate that back to the background information and behavioral observations. Continue to "weave a tapestry" of the supporting evidence of your diagnostic conclusions. Reports that suddenly suggest a diagnosis of ADHD, for example, in the summary section, yet provide no supportive evidence throughout the report for that diagnosis, are not credible.

Avoiding the Use of Jargon

The report writer has a responsibility to try to communicate complex information in a meaningful way to parents and educators. Several key

> # CAUTION
>
> ....
>
> Avoid using medical and educational jargon in a report. A teacher might find the statement that "Johnny suffered a subarachnoid hemorrhage" interesting but not know what to do with the information to better educate Johnny.

reminders are important. First, try to avoid professional jargon in the report. Parents and often educators will not understand the medical jargon that is often associated with school neuropsychological cases. When reporting medical jargon from an outside evaluation that is part of the student's relevant background information, it is appropriate to quote the medical terminology, diagnosis, or procedure.

However, it is then imperative that the school neuropsychologist defines, in lay terms, that medical jargon. For example, a student's medical records might indicate, "He suffered a subarachnoid hemorrhage as a result of the head injury." A good practice is to report the medical finding and then put in parentheses a definition. Using the example above, the report could read: "He suffered a subarachnoid hemorrhage . . . (bleeding under the outer membrane of the brain) . . . as a result of the head injury." Jargon is not limited to medical terminology. Educators have a whole set of acronyms that we use when communicating with each other. Parents will not readily understand a statement in a report such as: "Johnny was initially referred for a CIA by his parents. The IEP team will consider the LRE for placement including possible placements within the LEAP, SBU, Resource, Content Mastery, or continuing regular classroom placement. EYP will also be considered in order to maximize his AYP." School neuropsychologists should minimize or avoid the use of educational and medical jargon. If complex language is used, define it in the report so the reader will be able to better understand what is being communicated.

Including or Not Including Data in a Report

The issue of including data in neuropsychological reports has been debated in the field (see Armengol et al., 2001; Freides, 1993, 1995; Matarazzo, 1995; Naugle & McSweeney, 1996). Some neuropsychologist practitioners write reports that read like summary sections. In these reports there is no data to support their diagnostic conclusions or recommendations. It is almost as if the practitioner is saying "Trust me, my conclusions do not need to be justified because I am the expert." These types of reports are generally of little use to a school district that is trying to integrate those test results with their own test results to help the student. By excluding data from a report it makes it nearly impossible for another knowledgeable practitioner to come to the same diagnostic conclusions, or to compare test results from a reevaluation. At a minimum, get in the practice of including a data sheet at the end of the report as an attachment. That way other practitioners can review the data on their own. Also there is a legal consideration. Unfortunately, we live in a litigious age. If a school neuropsychologist provides testimony in court about a written report, the data used to reach the diagnostic conclusions will be paramount. Finally, there is a pragmatic reason why data should be included in a report. School psychologists often have heavy caseloads and the cases have a tendency to "run together" after a while. When sitting in an Individual Education Program (IEP) meeting reviewing the report with the student's parents and educators, the data helps reframe the rationale for your diagnostic conclusions and recommendations.

"A Picture Is Worth a Thousand Words"

Consistent with the idea that school neuropsychologists need to avoid the use of jargon in their report writing, they should also seek methods that clearly communicate complex data to the report reader as quickly and efficiently as possible. Visual charting of data and the use of figures to convey trends in data can be very useful.

Charts that present data that share a common construct, but come from different test batteries, can be a useful method (see example in Figure 6.1). Graphs can also be useful in presenting data that can illustrate strengths and weaknesses clearly. Figure 6.2 illustrates to the report reader how a student's learning curve compares to his or her same-age peers.

Describing the Child's Performance, Not Just Test Scores

An occupational hazard that occurs when new professionals are learning how to write up a school neuropsychological evaluation is an overfocus on what the tests are measuring and an underfocus on describing the student's performance on tests. In an effort to minimize the description of every test administered in the narrative of the written report, it is recommended that when the test data is reported in the table, include a brief description of what the test was designed to measure (see Figure 6.1 for an example). By reporting your test results in a tabular format with test descriptions this will minimize the need to describe in the narrative what the test was designed to measure. Rather, the narrative should focus on how the student approached the tests, why particular tests were easier than others, and why particular tests were more difficult than others.

Fine-Motor Functions							
Instrument – Subtest: Description	Well Below Expected Level	Below Expected Level	Slightly Below Expected Level	At Expected Level	Slightly Above Expected Level	Above Expected Level	Well Above Expected Level
Coordinated Finger/Hand Movements							
DWSMB – Mime Movements: Following commands (e.g., "Show me how you would brush your teeth").						105	
KABC-II – Hand Movements: Producing a sequence of motor acts with dominant hand.				100			
WRAVMA – Pegboard: Inserting as many pegs as possible, within 90 seconds, into a waffled pegboard.				95			

Figure 6.1. An Example of Charting Data

Note: Dean-Woodcock Sensory Motor Battery (DWSMB) W scores can be translated into standard scores using the free scoring software that may be downloaded from this site: http://www.woodcock-munoz-foundation.org/press/dwnr.html — note that the standard score conversion is a truncated distribution of scores and average scores are designated as a standard score of 100+.

When it is obvious that a student used an uncommon strategy or process to complete a particular test, that unique behavior should be mentioned in the report narrative. For example, if a test was designed to measure verbal working memory yet the student only used immediate verbal memory, the overall results of the test could change and not be measuring what the test was designed to measure. Also when several tests are administered to a student and all of the tests are designed to measure a similar neurocognitive process, yet the results are variable; the school neuropsychologist must attempt to explain the disparity in the scores. Conducting demand analyses of the tasks (e.g., the input, processing, and output) will help generate hypotheses about why the student's performance was variable. Sometimes non-neuropsychological factors such as fatigue, motivation, or poor attitude may explain the variability in test performance as well.

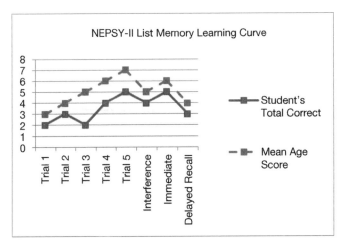

Figure 6.2. Example of a Report Graph

Figure 6.3 presents an example of the sensorimotor section of a report. This is a good example of how the school neuropsychologist brings to life for the reader how the child performed these tasks and most importantly what would be the instructional implications for the pattern of these strengths and weaknesses.

Relate the Child's Test Performance to Real-World Examples

The goal of any school neuropsychological assessment should not only be to report a set of test scores and come up with a diagnosis. The goal of a school neuropsychological assessment is to take samples of behavior to determine a student's functional strengths and weaknesses and relate that information to actual classroom behaviors. Reporting to the classroom teacher that "Johnny has a fine-motor weakness" will probably not do Johnny any good. However, reporting that Johnny has difficulty copying and producing shapes and letters on paper due to an identified fine-motor coordination deficiency would help the teacher understand how a processing deficit would manifest itself in the classroom. The final step in the process would be to provide evidence-based remediation

DON'T FORGET

The goal of a school neuropsychological assessment is to take samples of behavior to determine a child's functional strengths and weaknesses and to relate that information to actual classroom behaviors.

Instrument – Subtest: Description	Well Below Expected Level	Below Expected Level	Slightly Below Expected Level	At Expected Level	Slightly Above Expected Level	Above Expected Level	Well Above Expected Level
Coordinated Finger/Hand Movements							
NEPSY-II – Fingertip Tapping Dominant Hand Combined: Dominant hand completion time for two fine-motor tasks.				(11)			
NEPSY-II – Fingertip Tapping Nondominant Hand Combined: Nondominant hand completion time for two fine-motor tasks.				(11)			
NEPSY-II – Imitating Hand Positions: Imitating hand positions shown by examiner.				(8)			
• With Dominant Hand						>75	
• With Nondominant Hand			11–25				
NEPSY-II – Visuomotor Precision Combined: Tracing a path from start to finish quickly and while trying to stay within the lines.				(10)			
• **Total Completion Time:** Slower completion time = lower scaled score				(8)			
• **Total Errors:** More errors = lower % rank			51–75				
• **Pencil Lift Total:** More lifts = lower % rank		6–10					

Figure 6.3. An Example of a Well-Written Sensorimotor Section of a Report

Visual-Motor Copying Skills							
Beery Visual Motor Integration Total: Copying simple to complex designs on paper.					96		
• **Visual Perception:** Visual perception aspects of the task.						117	
• **Motor Coordination:** Motor coordination aspects of the task.			87				
NEPSY-II – Design Copying General Score: Copying simple to complex designs on paper.						>75	
• **Design Copying Process Motor:** This score represents the motor output portion of the overall score.					(10)		

Figure 6.3. (Continued)

Note: Standard scores appear in normal font. Scaled scores appear in (parentheses). Percentile ranks of any kind appear in *italics*.

Written Report Narrative: The majority of Peter's scores on tasks measuring fine-motor coordination were at an expected level for his age. Basic coordination through finger tapping was adequate and equal in both hands. On increasingly more complex imitation of motor sequences, Peter's performance was slightly below an expected level. On this task, he sometimes struggled to initially coordinate the movement, so he slowed his pace to obtain accuracy. At other times, he had difficulty with maintaining the sequence of movements in a repetitive manner. Complex coordination can impact daily tasks, such as buttoning and using eating utensils, which are reported by his parents as challenging for Peter. When asked to imitate hand positions, Peter's performance was considerably stronger when using his dominant, right hand than when using his left hand, as he tended to transpose the position of his fingers on his left hand for the more complex items. When required to trace a path within a given visual framework, his completion time and accuracy were at an expected level for his age, but Peter frequently lifted his pencil in order to maintain accuracy to stay within the lines upon changing directions. He was highly determined to stay within the track and occasionally used his nondominant hand in an attempt to avoid lifting the pencil from the page (in order to follow the rules), while adjusting the grip of his dominant hand. Thus, pencil control for forming letters and maintaining alignment with handwriting is challenging. When asked to copy shapes (e.g., Design Copy and VMI), Peter demonstrated an excellent ability to perceive the overall design; however, fine-motor challenges with coordination impacted the precision of his designs, as he tended to overshoot forming corners and connections between shapes, as well as unintentionally made extraneous marks on the page. While considered adequate for his age, Peter's motor skills are a relative weakness for him. This can result in frustration, as Peter may have a specific vision for how he wants a design or letter to appear, but lacks advanced motor skills to reproduce the image on paper to his precise specifications.

strategies to improve Johnny's fine-motor coordination difficulties and/or to develop some compensatory strategies to bypass Johnny's processing difficulties. Figure 6.3 presents a school neuropsychological report narrative for the sensori-motor section of the report and is an example of relating the student's test performance to real classroom behaviors.

COMPONENTS OF A SCHOOL NEUROPSYCHOLOGICAL REPORT

This section of the chapter will review the components of a school neuro-psychological report. Organizing a report into sections will aid the clinician in explaining and the report recipient in understanding the results of neuro-psychological findings.

What to Title the Report?

Report titles are often linked to the credentials of the examiner. If the examiner has competency in school neuropsychology, the report could be titled "School Neuro-psychological Evaluation." Other titles could be used based on the examiner's qualifications including: "Neurocognitive Evaluation," or the traditional "Psycho-educational Evaluation." Report titles may be regulated by practice acts within a particular state. Practitioners are urged to know the limits of the practice acts within their states.

Organizing the Report

Rapid Reference 6.3 presents a suggested list of major report headers for a school neuropsychological report. The rationale for each of these report sections is presented in the remainder of this chapter.

Identifying Information

Typically psychoeducational and school neuropsychological reports contain the following identifying information on the front page of the report:

- Name of student
- Date of birth and age of student
- School name and grade placement of student
- Name of parents/guardians
- Primary language spoken at home
- Name of examiner
- Dates of testing
- Date of report

≡ Rapid Reference 6.3

Suggested Overall Organization of the School Neuropsychology Report
- Identifying information
- Reason for referral
- Background information
- Current assessment instruments and procedures
- Test observations and related assessment validity
- Evaluation results
- Summary
- Diagnostic impressions
- Intervention strategies and recommendations

This identifying information is important to establish the child about whom this report is written, when in the life of the student the evaluation was conducted, and by whom the evaluation was conducted.

Reason for Referral

One of the most important sections of a school neuropsychological report is the reason(s) for referral. It is important to clarify the reasons for referral and the expected outcomes from all parties involved. In this section of the report, identify the person(s) making the referral (e.g., teacher, parent, guidance counselor, or private practitioner). It is crucial to document the referral source, because this is the principle audience for the written report. List the questions to be answered by the current evaluation. A referral question such as: What is causing a student to have reading problems and what interventions would work best for this particular student? is much better than a referral question that states: Is the student learning disabled in reading? It is imperative that the referral questions are answered by the end of the evaluation and are clearly stated in the report.

Background Information

Background information may be generally obtained from two sources: (1) a review of the student's educational records and (2) clinical interviews with the parent(s)/guardian(s), the student's current teacher(s), and the student, as age appropriate. A student's cumulative record or educational file is often a "treasure trove" of information that is essential to understanding the history and extent of the presenting problem(s). Fletcher-Janzen (2005) suggests that the student's educational records should be reviewed specifically for information related to absences from school, history of chronic illnesses, evidence of events that could have induced psychological trauma, evidence of events that could reflect neurotoxin exposure, and any assessments or diagnoses that the student might have received in the past.

A thorough clinical interview with the student's parent(s)/guardian(s) is crucial to fully understanding the student. Potential explanations or insights into the causal factors of the student's current presenting problems may often be found in the student's background information. The time spent in reviewing the student's educational records and interviewing the student's parent(s)/guardian(s) and teacher(s) is as important as assessing the student directly.

It is good practice to divide this section of the report into subsections. When a reader of the report wants to retrieve a detail from the report related to the birth history, it is easier to find that information if this section is subdivided by background information topics.

The following subsections are recommended with some example questions:

- Family history
  - With whom does the student live?
  - How many brothers and sisters does the student have?
  - Is the student adopted or living with a stepparent or other relative?
  - What is the principle language spoken at home?
  - What cultural factors in this student's life play a role in the student's achievement and behavior at school, in the home, and in the community?
  - Have there been any major family stressors in the past year?
  - Are the parents/guardians employed and if so, in what occupations?
  - Does the family have any major socioecomomic limitations that could impede following the report recommendations?
- Birth and developmental history
  - Was the student exposed to any prenatal toxins (e.g., alcohol, lead)?
  - Did the mother receive adequate prenatal care?
  - Was the pregnancy carried full term?
  - What was the birth weight of the student?
  - Were there any complications during pregnancy or delivery?
  - Did the student achieve developmental milestones within normal age limits?
- Health history
  - Does the student have a history of any major illnesses?
  - What is the status of the student's weight, height, sight, and hearing?
  - Has the student experienced any ear infections or hearing problems?
  - Has the student taken any medications, and if so, name of drug and dosage?

- Is there a history of neurological problems (e.g., seizures, head injury, high fever)?
- Is there a positive family history on either or both sides of the biological family for health-related problems?
- Is the student right- or left-handed?
- How many days of school has the student missed each year, on average?
- Social history
  - In which social activities does the student engage?
  - Does this student have many friends?
  - Describe the types of friends this student has and the activities in which they engage.
  - Does this student engage in any organized sporting activities?
- Educational history
  - How many schools has the student attended?
  - Has the student been retained?
  - Has the student received any special education services?
  - What is the history of the student's educational performance? Have there been any dramatic changes in the student's school performance in the past year?
  - Does the student like school?
  - What are the student's best subjects in school?
  - What school subjects are the most challenging for this student?
  - What specific academic or behavioral interventions has the student received?
- Previous test results
  - Review the major highlights of any prior test results.
  - Be sure to mention changes in placement, diagnosis of a psychological disorder or special education classification, and interventions that were implemented.
  - Do not restate the entire content of a prior report in this section. Report only the highlights of previous testing. The reader can read the prior report for more information as needed.
  - If the same test was administered previously, it might be helpful to report those scores in this section or in the later section of the report to illustrate changes in scores over time.

Information about the child's family, birth and developmental, health, educational, and social histories may be obtained by using a structured developmental history (e.g., *BASC-2 Structured Developmental History*, Reynolds & Kamphaus, 2004).

Current Assessment Instruments and Procedures

In this section of the report, the school neuropsychologist lists the names of the current assessment instruments and the procedures used. As a rule of thumb, list the procedures used or tests administered first to last from the top down. For example, "Record Review" is often the first procedure used in an evaluation so it can be listed first. The developmental/clinical interview with the parent/guardian is used next, followed by classroom observation, and then a detailed list of the names of the tests administered. It is a good practice to list the name of the test and then abbreviate it. The abbreviation for the test can be used thereafter in the report. For example, the *Behavior Assessment System for Children—Second Edition: Teacher Rating Scale* (BASC-2 TRS: Reynolds & Kamphaus, 2009).

By listing the name of a test in this section, it implies that the examiner administered the test in its entirety. If only a portion of the test was administered put "Selected Subtests" after the name of the test. Also if the examiner did not administer the test him/herself put "as administered by . . ." after the name of the test. For example, it is common practice to integrate the results of a speech and language evaluation that was administered by the speech and language pathologist into a school neuropsychological report; however, credit must be given to the person who administered the test for legal and ethical reasons.

Related to the Do's and Don'ts of Neuropsychological Report Writing presented in Rapid Reference 6.2, limit the number of procedures and tests to only those needed to answer the referral question. Before starting an evaluation, it is appropriate to design a test battery to fully answer the referral question(s). *The Neuropsychological Processing Concerns Checklist for Children and Youth—Third Edition* (D. Miller, 2012; see supplemental CD) may be used to select the assessment tools needed to address the identified areas of concern. Keep in mind that the planned test battery may need to change as the assessment progresses. For example, the student may perform poorly on a test that measures visual-spatial processing and the examiner may want to add an additional test to the battery to further explore that neurocognitive area of functioning.

DON'T FORGET

Do not get "locked into" a fixed battery approach. Plan the test battery based on the referral question(s), but expand or eliminate tests based on the student's actual test performance. Be flexible!

To have this flexible battery approach to assessment, the examiner needs to score and minimally interpret the test results as soon as possible. For example, if the student is administered the *Woodcock-Johnson III Tests of Cognitive Abilities* (Woodcock, McGrew, & Mather, 2001, 2007a), and no short-term or long-term memory problems are evident; it may not be necessary to administer a battery of memory and learning tests (e.g., *Wide Range Assessment of Memory and Learning—Second Edition*: WRAML-2; Sheslow & Adams, 2003), even though the WRAML-2 was part of the initially planned assessment battery. A flexible battery based on the referral question and the subsequent performance on the tests is best practice.

Test Observations and Related Assessment Validity

In this section of the report, the examiner reports test observations such as level of conversational proficiency, level of cooperation, level of activity, level of attention and concentration, level of self-confidence, style of responding (e.g., impulsive or reflective), and response to challenging tasks (see the *Woodcock-Johnson III Tests of Cognitive Abilities* test session observations checklist on the cover of the *Test Record Booklet* as an example: Woodcock et al., 2001, 2007a). In addition, any overt pathognomonic signs, such as excessively large or excessively small handwriting, are reported.

The old adage "garbage in and garbage out" applies here. The school neuropsychologist can construct a thorough test battery and administer it to a student. However, the results could be meaningless or questionable if the child does not cooperate, puts forth poor effort, or is distracted during the examination. Armengol et al. (2001) suggested numerous factors that could compromise the test validity and reliability, including:

> [D]iminished attention, effort, or motivation; capacity to understand and remember test instructions (e.g., cultural, linguistic, academic, or intellectual limitations); physical limitations; affective or anxiety disorders; personality problems (e.g., hostility, paranoia), or other distracting conditions (e.g., pain, sleep deprivation, illnesses); and any suspicions of malingering, exaggeration of deficits, or other deliberate or subconscious attempts by the patient to manipulate the results of the examination. (p. 99)

When the validity of the assessment results is in question, the examiner includes statements in this section such as "the results of test 'x' must be interpreted with caution because . . . " Or if the results appear valid, the examiner makes a statement such as "these results appear to be an accurate reflection of that [name of student's] current levels of functioning."

Another useful statement to add to a school neuropsychological assessment report that uses a variety of assessment techniques is:

> The reader is reminded that these results are compiled from tests that were not normed from the same sample; however, test results have been

integrated with data from other sources including review of records, interview, observations, other test results and work samples to ensure ecological validity. Standardization was followed for all administrations. No single test or procedure was used as the sole determining criteria for eligibility or educational planning. Unless otherwise noted these results are considered a valid estimate of [insert student's name] demonstrated skills and abilities at this point in time (D. Miller, 2012b).

Evaluation Results

Standardizing the test descriptors. When interpreting a battery of test results for a parent or an educator, the descriptors of a child's performance level (e.g., average, above average, below average) vary widely across test instruments. For example a standard score of 84 is labeled as "below average" on some tests and "slightly below average" on other tests. In an effort to make the test results easier to comprehend for parents and educators, it is recommended that a common set of performance level descriptors be used for all tests scores. The exception to this classification schema is tests that use a truncated t-score distribution to indicate psycho-pathology (e.g., BASC-II scores). Those tests use descriptors such as average, at-risk, and clinically significant. It is recommended that those types of tests keep these descriptors intact.

It is recommended that the classification labels for all tests administered, with those exceptions mentioned above, be reported according to the scale shown in Figure 6.4.

If the NESPY-II is administered as part of the assessment battery, use the scale as shown in Figure 6.5 to account for the differences in how the NEPSY-II test results are classified.

Standard Score	Scaled Score	Percentile Rank	Normative Classification
> 129	> 15	> 98%	Superior
121–129	15	92–98	Well Above Expected
111–120	13–14	76–91	Above Expected
90–110	8–12	25–75	At Expected
80–89	6–7	9–24	Slightly Below Expected
70–79	4–5	2–8	Below Expected
< 70	1–3	< 2	Well Below Expected

Figure 6.4. Standardized Test Score Descriptors

Standard Score	Scaled Score	% Rank	Normative Classification	Proficiency Classification	NEPSY-II Scaled Score	NEPSY-II % Rank	Normative Classification	Proficiency Classification
>129	>15	>98%	Superior	Markedly Advanced	13–19	>75	Above Expected	Very Proficient to Markedly Advanced
121–129	15	92–98	Well Above Expected	Advanced				
111–120	13–14	76–91	Above Expected	Very Proficient				
90–110	8–12	25–75	At Expected	Proficient	8–12	26–75	At Expected	Proficient
80–89	6–7	9–24	Slightly Below Expected	Inefficient	6–7	11–25	Slightly Below Expected	Inefficient
70–79	4–5	2–8	Below Expected	Deficient	4–5	3–10	Below Expected	Deficient
<70	1–3	<2	Well Below Expected	Markedly Deficient	1–3	≤2	Well Below Expected	Markedly Deficient

Figure 6.5. Standardized Test Score Descriptors If the NEPSY-II Is Administered

145

≡ Rapid Reference 6.4

Suggested Report Headers for the Evaluation Results Section of a School Neuropsychological Report

I. Classroom Observations

II. Basic Sensorimotor Functions

III. Cognitive Processes: Visuospatial

IV. Cognitive Processes: Auditory/Phonological

V. Cognitive Processes: Learning and Memory

VI. Cognitive Processes: Executive

VII. Facilitators/Inhibitors: Allocating and Maintaining Attention

VIII. Facilitators/Inhibitors: Working Memory

IX. Facilitators/Inhibitors: Speed, Fluency, and Efficiency of Processing

X. Acquired Knowledge: Acculturation Knowledge

XI. Acquired Knowledge: Language Abilities

XII. Acquired Knowledge: Reading Achievement

XIII. Acquired Knowledge: Written Language Achievement

XIV. Acquired Knowledge: Mathematics Achievement

XV. Social-Emotional Functioning and Adaptive Behaviors

Notice that the classification ranges in Figures 6.4 and 6.5 are not based on the standard deviation unit of 15 with an average standard score falling within the range of 85 to 115. The classification ranges were based initially on those used by the NEPSY-II, which reflect better precision for those scores that fall below the mean.

Organizing the evaluation results section of the report. Rapid Reference 6.4 presents a list of suggested report headers for the evaluation results section of the school neuropsychological report. It is suggested that the evaluation results section of the report be organized following the conceptual model of school neuro-psychological assessment presented in the Chapter 5. Lichtenberger, Mather, Kaufman, and Kaufman (2004) refer to this type of organization as an "ability by ability" way to organize a report.

Classroom observations do involve an evaluation of the student's behavior within the natural environment. Typically, practitioners are encouraged to observe the student across multiple settings including structured and un-structured academic activities and structured and unstructured nonacademic activities (e.g., lunch, recess, walking down the hall). It is best practice to try to observe the student before he or she knows that an evaluation will be taking place.

In most psychoeducational reports, the results of the general intellectual functioning scores are reported first in the test results section. Too much emphasis has been placed on global measures of intelligence while ignoring or de-emphasizing the subcomponents of cognitive processing such as attention, memory, and executive functions. In a school neuropsychological report, it is suggested that the subcomponents of cognitive processing be reported first and given the priority of focus.

In all of the evaluation results sections except the classroom observations section, it is suggested that the remaining sections be further subdivided into three areas:

1. *Presenting concerns*—A list of the presenting concerns relevant to the area being assessed. If a concern is expressed, state it in terms of severity (mild, moderate, or severe). Also try to get the perspective from both the parent(s)/guardian(s) and one or more teachers, depending on the student's age.

2. *Current levels of functioning*—The test results are presented relevant to the area being assessed. This section may need to be subdivided (see Rapid Reference 6.5).

3. *Summary of results*—This section should address how the presenting concerns relate to the current levels of functioning.

In addition to the developmental history information reported in the background information section of the report, a school neuropsychologist gathers information regarding the current presenting concerns about the student. The presenting concerns information are ideally obtained from both a teacher and the student's parent(s)/guardian(s). On the supplemental CD, there is a checklist that can be used to gather information on the presenting concerns. The checklist is called the *Neuropsychological Processing Concerns Checklist for School-Aged Children & Youth—Third Edition* (NPCC-3: D. Miller, 2012a). The NPCC-3 is available in English and Spanish. The checklist was designed to mirror the areas assessed in the school neuropsychological conceptual model that are presented in this book. See Figure 6.6 for an example of a completed NPCC-3 rating form completed by a Mother (M) and a Teacher (T) for the Attention Problems section of the scale.

In some report writing models, all of the presenting concerns are listed in the beginning of the report, often within the background information section. The problem with this approach is that it forces the reader to keep flipping

Attention Problems	Mild	Moderate	Severe
Selective or Sustained Attention Difficulties			
• Seems to get overwhelmed with difficult tasks.		M, T	
• Difficulty paying attention for a long period of time.	M	T	
• Seems to lose place in an academic task (e.g., reading, writing, math).	M	T	
• Mind appears to go blank or loses train of thought.		M, T	
• Inattentive to details or makes careless mistakes.		M	T
Shifting or Divided Attention Difficulties			
• Gets stuck on one activity (e.g., playing video games).		M, T	
• Does not seem to hear anything else while watching TV.		M	T
• Difficulty transitioning from one activity to another.	M	T	

Figure 6.6. An Example of a Completed NPCC-3 by a Mother (M) and a Teacher (T) for the Attention Problems Section of the Scale

back to the previous section of the report to compare the presenting concerns with the current assessment findings. Putting both the presenting concerns and the current assessment results in the same section leads to better integration of the information.

For each of the neurocognitive functions or processes (Sections II–VIII) there are subcomponents that may or may not be addressed in the report based on the referral question(s). Rapid Reference 6.5 provides a more detailed list of the subcomponents that can be considered for inclusion in the report.

≡ Rapid Reference 6.5

Expanded Report Headers for the Evaluation Results Section of a School Neuropsychological Report

I. Classroom Observations
II. Basic Sensorimotor Functions
   1. Presenting concerns
   2. Current levels of functioning
     • Lateral preference
     • Sensory functions
      ▪ Auditory and visual acuity
      ▪ Tactile sensation and perception

- Kinesthetic sensation and perception
- Olfactory sensation and perception
- Fine-motor functions
  - Coordinated finger/hand movements
- Visual-motor integration skills
- Visual scanning
  - Direct measures
  - Indirect measures
  - Qualitative behaviors
- Gross motor functions
  - Balance
  - Coordination
- Qualitative behaviors
3. Summary of sensorimotor functions

Cognitive Processes

III. Visuospatial Processes
  1. Presenting concerns
  2. Current levels of functioning
     - Visual spatial perception
       - Visual discrimination and spatial location
       - Visual-motor constructions
       - Qualitative behaviors
     - Visual spatial reasoning
       - Recognizing spatial configurations
       - Visual gestalt closure
       - Visuospatial analyses with and without mental rotations
  3. Summary of visuomotor processes
IV. Auditory Processes
  1. Presenting concerns
  2. Current levels of functioning
     - Sound discrimination
     - Auditory/phonological processing
  3. Summary of auditory processes
V. Learning and Memory Processes
  1. Presenting concerns
  2. Current levels of functioning
     - Overall learning and memory index scores
     - Rate of learning
       - Verbal learning

(continued)

≡ *Rapid Reference 6.5 continued*

....

- Visual learning
- Paired associative learning
- Verbal immediate versus visual immediate memory
  - Immediate verbal memory
    □ Letter or number recall (no contextual cues)
    □ Word recall (no contextual cues)
    □ Sentence recall (contextual cues)
    □ Story recall (contextual cues)
  - Immediate visual memory
    □ Abstract designs with motor response (no contextual cues)
    □ Abstract designs with verbal response (no contextual cues)
    □ Faces with verbal or pointing response (no contextual cues)
    □ Objects or pictures with verbal or pointing responses (no contextual cues)
    □ Spatial locations with motor response (no contextual cues)
    □ Visual digit span with verbal response (no contextual cues)
    □ Visual sequences imitation with motor response (no contextual cues)
    □ Picture or symbolic (with contextual cues)
- Delayed memory: Recall versus recognition
  - Delayed verbal memory
    □ Delayed verbal recall (without context)
    □ Delayed verbal recall (with context)
    □ Delayed verbal recognition (without context)
    □ Delayed verbal recognition (with context)
  - Delayed visual memory
    □ Delayed visual recall (without context)
    □ Delayed visual recall (with context)
    □ Delayed visual recognition (without context)
    □ Delayed visual recognition (with context)
    □ Qualitative behaviors
- Verbal-visual associative learning and recall
  - Verbal-visual associative learning
  - Verbal-visual delayed associative memory
3. Summary of learning and memory processes
VI. Executive Functions
  1. Presenting concerns
  2. Current levels of functioning
     - Cognitive flexibility or set shifting

- Verbal set shifting
  - Visual set shifting
  - Verbal and visual set shifting
- Concept formation
  - Concept recognition
  - Concept generation
- Planning
- Deductive and inductive reasoning
- Sequential reasoning
- Quantitative reasoning
- Response inhibition
  - Verbal response inhibition
  - Visual response inhibition
- Qualitative behaviors
- Behavioral and emotional regulation
  3. Summary of executive functions

Facilitators/Inhibitors

VII. Allocating and Maintaining Attentional Resources Facilitators/Inhibitors
  1. Presenting concerns
  2. Current levels of functioning
  - Selective/focused and sustained attention
    - Auditory selective/focused and sustained attention
    - Visual selective/focused and sustained attention
  - Attentional capacity
    - Attentional capacity for numbers or letters with verbal response
    - Attentional capacity for visual sequential patterns with motor response
    - Attentional capacity for words and sentences (increased meaning) with verbal response
    - Attentional capacity for stories (even more contextual meaning) with verbal response
    - Qualitative behaviors of attention
    - Behavioral ratings of attention and hyperactivity
  3. Summary of attentional facilitators/inhibitors

VIII. Working Memory Facilitators/Inhibitors
  1. Presenting concerns
  2. Current levels of functioning
  - Verbal working memory
  - Visual working memory
  3. Summary of working memory processes

(continued)

≡ *Rapid Reference 6.5 continued*

IX Speed, Fluency, and Efficiency of Processing Facilitators/Inhibitors
1. Presenting concerns
2. Current levels of functioning
   - Performance fluency
     - Psychomotor fluency
     - Perceptual fluency
     - Figural fluency
     - Naming fluency
   - Retrieval fluency
     - Word fluency
     - Semantic fluency
   - Acquired knowledge fluency
     - Reading fluency: Rapid phonological decoding
     - Reading fluency: Rapid morphological decoding
     - Writing fluency
     - Mathematics fluency
   - Fluency and accuracy
   - Qualitative behaviors
3. Summary of speed and efficiency of processing

Acquired Knowledge

X. Acculturation Knowledge
1. Presenting concerns
2. Current levels of functioning
   - Semantic memory
     - Verbal comprehension
     - General information
3. Summary of acculturation knowledge

XI. Language Abilities
1. Presenting concerns
2. Current levels of functioning
   - Oral expression
     - Oral motor production
     - Vocabulary knowledge
     - Qualitative behaviors
   - Receptive language
     - Receptive language with a verbal response
     - Receptive language with a nonverbal response

- Qualitative behaviors
  3. Summary of language abilities
XII. Reading Achievement
  1. Presenting concerns
  2. Current levels of functioning
  - Basic reading skills
    - Phonological decoding
    - Orthographic coding
    - Morphological/syntactic coding
  - Reading comprehension skills
  3. Summary of reading achievement abilities
XIII. Written Language Achievement
  1. Presenting concerns
  2. Current levels of functioning
  - Written expression
  - Expository composition
  - Orthographic spelling
  - Handwriting skills
  - Qualitative behaviors
  3. Summary of written language achievement abilities
XIV. Mathematics Achievement
  1. Presenting concerns
  2. Current levels of functioning
  - Oral counting
  - Fact retrieval
  - Mathematical calculations
  - Mathematical reasoning
  - Qualitative behaviors
  3. Summary of mathematics achievement abilities
XV. Social-Emotional Functioning and Adaptive Behaviors
  1. Presenting concerns
  2. Current levels of functioning
  - Social-emotional rating scales
  - Social-emotional test results
  - Social-emotional qualitative behaviors
  - Adaptive behavior rating scales
  - Processing concerns checklists
  3. Summary of social-emotional functioning

These subcomponents reflect the second-order classifications within the school neuropsychology assessment model (see Chapter 5). After the basic cognitive processes are presented, the overall general intellectual functioning scores are presented along with the current levels of academic achievement. Social-emotional functioning and adaptive behaviors are reported last.

Summary Section

The summary section of a school neuropsychological report is a review of the major findings of the evaluation. Keep in mind that some educators and outside consultants working with the student may read only the summary section of the report. Be careful to note that this is not a section of the report that repeats verbatim prior sections of the report (Lichtenberger et al., 2004). Also, it is not an appropriate practice to introduce new content in the summary section that has not been introduced elsewhere in the report. For example, the revelation that, "Johnny had a head injury prior to the evaluation," is information that should not be introduced for the first time in this section of the report. Review the reason(s) for referral, the highlights of the background information, and test results. This is an ideal place in the report to restate the referral question(s) and answer directly based on the interpretation of the current assessment data.

It is suggested that when reviewing the test results, discuss the student's strengths first, followed by the student's weaknesses. By the time a student gets to a neuropsychological evaluation, the student may have been evaluated multiple times. Too often evaluations focus on what a student cannot do for special education qualification purposes while de-emphasizing the strengths of the student. Lead with the student's strengths in the summary section and the parent might continue to read more optimistically through the next section that describes the student's weaknesses.

In the summary section, it is important to interpret the results within the student's developmental, social-emotional, cultural, and environmental backgrounds. For example, be careful not to suggest neuropsychological deficits that are actually caused by an overall dampening of neurocognitive processing due to social-emotional trauma, or dysfunction, or cultural factors.

DON'T FORGET

When writing the summary section of the report, lead with the child's strengths before presenting the areas of concern.

Diagnostic Impressions

Should the presence or absence of a brain lesion/dysfunction be suggested in a school neuropsychology report? A school neuropsychologist needs to know about brain physiology and should know how to recognize signs of brain dysfunction. However, too often neuropsychological reports from outside consultants to the schools proclaim diagnostic statements such as "Johnny has a right parietal lesion." Although Johnny's teacher might find that diagnosis fascinating, she or he probably does not know what to do to better educate Johnny based on that information. Statements like that also scare the parent(s) senselessly. It is best if the clinical/school neuropsychologist describes the constellations of deficits and/or strengths associated with a right parietal lobe dysfunction and then in the next section of the report suggest prescriptive interventions that target the deficit areas. It is probably best practice never to use the word *lesion* in a school neuro-psychological report, or to refer to specific anatomical locations of the brain unless previously noted by the medical community. Lesion is a word best used by a physician who has direct access to neuroimaging tools such as MRI or CAT scans. As a school neuropsychologist interested in measuring and describing functional strengths and weaknesses, a better word to describe a neuropsychological deficit is *dysfunction*.

Should a Diagnostic Statistical Manual (DSM) *diagnosis be used in the report?* In some states and local school districts, school psychologists are expressly forbidden to use a *DSM-IV TR* diagnosis in their reports. A good rule of thumb is whether the report will be used by outside practitioners (e.g., psychologist, counselor, speech pathologist) that rely on third-party reimbursement for their fees. The private practitioner will appreciate the school neuropsychologist com-municating with them in a common language (i.e., the *DSM-IV TR* diagnosis) (Lichtenberger et al., 2004). The school neuropsychologist must still use the language of IDEA to determine eligibility for special education services. A *DSM-IV TR* diagnosis alone does not qualify a student for IDEA special education services. This is a misunderstanding that many private practitioners have about writing diagnostic statements in reports based on the *DSM-IV TR* exclusively.

Finally, it is imperative that school neuropsychological reports not simply end with a diagnosis of the student. It would be a waste of the student's time and effort to participate in a comprehensive school neuropsychological evaluation only to come away with a diagnosis or set of diagnoses.

Intervention Strategies and Recommendations

Organization of the intervention strategies and recommendations section. The real value of a school neuropsychological assessment is to target interventions that capitalize on a student's strengths and to work to improve the student's weaknesses. A dubious practice that is used by some practitioners is to provide a long list of recommendations and not have them listed in any organized manner. Parents and teachers want to prioritize the top interventions they can provide to help the student. Too many recommendations in a report overwhelm the reader and it runs the risk that none of the recommendations are followed. Another critical consideration in making recommendations is to use those intervention strategies that have a proven effectiveness and are most appropriate to provide in the home or academic environments.

Lichtenberger et al. (2004) suggests that the reasons that recommendations are not followed are because:

> [T]he recommendations are too vague, not shared with appropriate personnel, too complex, too lengthy, inappropriate for the person's age or ability levels, not understood by the person responsible for implementation, impossible to implement in the setting, too time-consuming, and rejected by the client or student. (p. 162)

A good practice is to divide the recommendations section into a *minimum* of two parts: recommendations for school and recommendations for home. It is also a good practice to add a section entitled "Recommendations for the Student." The student is obviously the focus of the home and school recommendations and needs to be an active participant in recommendations as well, particularly as the student reaches middle childhood and adolescence. An additional section may be warranted that is entitled "Recommendations for the Outside Consultant or Agency." This section contains recommendations for agency or private mental health professionals, educational consultants, or physicians who end up reading the report.

Each of the recommendations sections are further subdivided into the areas that need to be addressed. For example, if the current assessment found that the student had poor processing speed, then make recommendations for what the parent(s), school personnel, student (if applicable), and agency personnel (if applicable) can do to help improve the student's processing speed. It is suggested that within each section that addresses a particular processing deficit or concern, that the report writer hierarchically arrange the recommendations from the most important to the least important. The report writer can ask the question: "If the parent could only do one thing different to help this student, what would that be?" Make sure that recommendation is at the top of the list. Try to stay within the limit of five or fewer recommendations for each area.

Remediation versus compensation issues. A question that has been debated for a long time in education is how long an intervention lasts before it is determined to be ineffective and the decision is made to try another intervention.

Our profession is grappling with this issue currently as a Response to Intervention (RTI) model is implemented. Within the RTI model the second tier consists of targeted interventions. It is within this tier that questions about the length and the methods of the intervention need to be addressed before reassessment and further prescription of intervention is deemed necessary.

The issue of remediation versus compensation can be looked at more broadly, as well. For example, Fletcher and Lyon (1998) reviewed the research on the remediation of reading disorder and found that remediation of reading skills in students past the fourth grade is difficult. Thus, in the area of reading, there appears to be a critical period in which basic reading skills (e.g., phonological awareness and decoding) must be taught. If it is discovered that an 8-year-old does not have good phonological decoding skills, then intensive remedial strategies can be targeted at the problem. However, if a 14-year-old has still not acquired basic phonological decoding skills, then the focus of the intervention needs to be more compensatory then remedial. In this case the 14-year-old student might benefit from learning a whole word as he sees it in space; therefore, new vocabulary words may be learned using flash cards. A basic rule of thumb for reading, as well as many other academic skills, is that more "bottom-up" strategies should be explored in the early years, and more "top-down" strategies in the later years. These "top-down" or metacognitive strategies are often more compensatory in nature. At some point, calculators replace an inability to perform manual mathematical calculations and word processors replace an inability to write grammatically correct sentences without spelling errors.

In summary, the recommendations that are made in a school neuropsychological report are organized and prioritized to aid the reader. Recommendations are based on intervention strategies that have a research base of effectiveness. And finally, recommendations are tailored in such a way that the student's strengths help compensate for their weaknesses. School neuropsychological evaluations can provide educators and parents a wealth of information that can be used to improve educational quality for students.

CHAPTER SUMMARY

In this chapter, a model for a school neuropsychological report is presented that follows the school neuropsychological assessment model. As a reminder, not every school neuropsychological assessment is as thorough as the school neuropsychological report outline implies. The referral question and the student's profile of strengths and weaknesses, and the available clinician's time all dictate the thoroughness of the report.

TEST YOURSELF

1. **True or False? The comprehensive model described in this chapter needs to be used for each student who needs a school neuropsychological evaluation.**

2. **The title of a school neuropsychological report should be:**
   a. School Neuropsychological Evaluation
   b. It depends on the rules of practice within the state.
   c. Neurocognitive Assessment
   d. Neuropsychological Evaluation

3. **True or False? If a school neuropsychologist must use jargon in a report, it is best practice to define the jargon in terms a lay person understands.**

4. **School neuropsychologists should consider using a *DSM-IV* diagnosis in their reports when:**
   a. School neuropsychologists should never use a *DSM-IV* diagnosis in their report.
   b. If the school neuropsychologist wants to qualify the student as Severe Emotionally Disturbed under IDEA.
   c. The report will be used by the classroom teacher to craft a set of educationally relevant interventions.
   d. The report will be used by a specialist outside of the school district such as a private practitioner or agency personnel and the district allows the use of the *DSM-IV* diagnoses.

5. **True or False? Introducing new information into the summary section of the report is acceptable practice.**

6. **Which of the referral questions below is stated in the most complete way?**
   a. Is Johnny learning disabled?
   b. What is causing Johnny to have reading problems and what interventions would work best for him?"
   c. Is Johnny dyslexic?
   d. Is Johnny reading disabled?

7. **Which of the following reasons are good reasons for including data in the school neuropsychological report?**
   a. The examiner who evaluates the student years later will have something to compare the current results to.
   b. The data will provide support for the diagnostic conclusions and related educational recommendations.
   c. The data will help the examiner reconstruct the reasoning behind the diagnostic conclusions made in the report.
   d. All of the above are good reasons to include data in the report.

Answers: 1. false; 2. b; 3. true; 4. d; 5. false; 6. b; 7. d

Chapter Seven

MAJOR SCHOOL NEUROPSYCHOLOGICAL TEST BATTERIES FOR CHILDREN

Prior to the 1990s, practitioners interested in conducting neuropsychological assessments with a pediatric population were limited to the Halstead-Reitan or Luria-Nebraska Batteries, as reviewed in Chapter 2. Currently there are three major test batteries designed to assess neuropsychological functioning in school-age children: the NEPSY-II, the WISC-IV Integrated and the Delis-Kaplan Executive Functions System (D-KEFS). This chapter provides an overview of these three test batteries.

NEPSY-II: A DEVELOPMENTAL NEUROPSYCHOLOGICAL ASSESSMENT

The NEPSY (Korkman, Kirk, & Kemp, 1997) was the first neuropsychological test battery specifically designed for children ages 3 to 12. The NEPSY-II (Korkman, Kirk, & Kemp, 2007) has some major differences from the NEPSY. A significant, beneficial change is the upward extension of the test to 16 years 11 months. The NEPSY-II also includes new subtests and has removed the domain scores.

Marit Korkman originally developed the first version of the test in Finland in the 1980s. The NEPSY was expanded and restandardized on a large sample of U.S. children based on the 1995 U.S. census data. Likewise, the NEPSY-II was expanded and restandardized on a sample of U.S. children based on the 2000 U.S. census data. The NEPSY-II is based on Lurian theory and has a strong process-oriented approach embedded in the tests. Data obtained from the NEPSY-II are interpreted in both a quantitative and qualitative manner.

The NEPSY-II tests have four purposes:

1. To assess the effects of damage to the brain regardless of whether the reasons for that damage are known or not.

2. To use in long-term follow-up of children with acquired or congenital brain damage or dysfunction.
3. To identify patterns of deficiencies in children that are consistent with the research on neurodevelopmental disorders.
4. To identify strengths and weaknesses that can be directly linked to prescriptive interventions. (Kemp & Korkman, 2010)

The NEPSY-II batteries assess six functional domains: Attention/Executive Functions, Language, Sensorimotor, Visuospatial, Memory and Learning, and Social Perception. Rapid Reference 7.1 shows the NEPSY-II subtests for each of the six functional domains.

≡ Rapid Reference 7.1

NEPSY-II Subtests by Domain

Subtest	Age Range	Description
Measures of Attention/Executive Functioning		
Animal sorting	7–16	Assesses the ability to formulate basic concepts, sort those concepts into categories, and shift set from between categories.
Auditory attention and response set	Part 1: 5–16 Part 2: 7–16	The subtest has two parts. The first part, Auditory Attention, assesses selective and sustained auditory attention. The second part, Response Set, maintains the selective and sustained attention requirements of Part 1 and adds a shifting attention component.
Clocks	7–16	Assesses planning and organization, visuospatial skills, and the concept of time in relation to analogue clocks.
Design fluency	5–12	Assesses the ability to generate unique designs by connecting dots presented in either a structured or a random array.
Inhibition	5–16	A timed test that assesses the ability to inhibit automatic responses in favor of novel responses.
Statue	3–6	Assesses motor persistence and inhibition.

Measures of Language

Body part naming and identification	3–4	Assesses confrontational naming, name recognition, and basic components of expressive and receptive language.
Comprehension of instructions	3–16	Assesses the ability to perceive, process, and execute oral instructions of increasing syntactic complexity.
Oromotor sequences	3–12	Assesses oromotor production.
Phonological processing	3–16	The test has two parts; Part 1, Word Segment Recognition, requires identifying words from segments. Part 2, Phonological Segmentation, requires reorganization of phonemes to form new words.
Repetition of nonsense words	5–12	Assesses phonological encoding and decoding.
Speeded naming	3–16	Assesses rapid access to and production of names of colors, shapes, letters, numbers, or sizes.
Word generation	3–16	Assesses the ability to generate words within specific semantic or phonemic categories.

Measures of Memory and Learning

List memory, list memory delayed	7–12	Assesses immediate and delayed recall, rate of learning, the role of interference, and retention after interference.
Memory for designs, memory for designs delayed	Immediate: 3–16 Delayed: 5–16	Assesses immediate and delayed spatial memory for novel visual material.
Memory for faces, memory for faces delayed	5–16	Assesses immediate and delayed visual memory of facial features, as well as face discrimination and recognition.
Memory for names, memory for names delayed	5–16	Assesses verbal-visual associative immediate learning and delayed recall.
Narrative memory	3–16	Assesses narrative memory under free recall, cued recall, and recognition conditions.
Sentence repetition	3–6	Assesses the ability to repeat sentences of increasing complexity and length.

(continued)

≡ Rapid Reference 7.1 continued

....

| Word list interference | 7–16 | Assesses verbal working memory, repetition, and word recall following interference. |

Measures of Sensorimotor Functioning

Fingertip tapping	5–16	The subtest has two parts. Part 1 assesses finger dexterity and motor speed. Part 2 assesses rapid motor programming.
Imitating hand positions	3–12	Assesses the ability to imitate hand/finger positions.
Manual motor sequences	3–12	Assesses the ability to imitate a series of rhythmic movement sequences using one or both hands.
Visuomotor precision	3–12	Assesses graphomotor speed and accuracy.

Measures of Social Perception

| Affect recognition | 3–16 | Assesses the ability to recognize emotional affect from photographs of children's faces. |
| Theory of mind | 3–16 | Assesses the ability to understand mental functions such as belief, intention, deception, emotion, imagination, and pretending, as well as the ability to understand how emotion relates to social context and to recognize the appropriate affect given various social contexts. |

Measures of Visuospatial Processing

Arrows	5–16	Assesses the ability to judge line orientation.
Block construction	3–16	A timed subtest that assesses the visuospatial and visuomotor ability to reproduce 3-dimensional constructions from models or 2-dimensional drawings.
Design copying	3–16	Assesses the ability to copy 2-dimensional geometric figures.
Geometric puzzles	3–6	Assesses mental rotation, visuospatial analysis, and attention to detail.
Picture puzzles	7–16	Assesses visual discrimination, spatial localization, and visual scanning, as well as the ability to deconstruct a picture into its parts and recognize part-to-whole relationships.

Route finding	5–12	Assesses knowledge of visual spatial relations and directionality, as well as the ability to use this knowledge to transfer a route from a simple schematic map to a more complex one.

Source: Adapted from Kemp and Korkman (2010).

Administration Choices with the NEPSY-II

It should be first pointed out that not all of the NEPSY-II tests are suitable for all ages between 3 and 16 years. There are two record forms that may be used: one for children ages 3 to 4, and the other for children ages 5 to 16. The NEPSY-II tests in each protocol are alphabetically arranged by test name but should not be administered in sequential order like other tests.

There are four types of assessment batteries that an examiner can choose from: (1) a full assessment of all age appropriate tests; (2) a general referral battery; (3) a diagnostic referral battery; or (4) selective assessment.

> **DON'T FORGET**
>
> The NEPSY-II has four types of assessment batteries:
> 1. Full Assessment
> 2. General Referral Battery
> 3. Diagnostic Referral Battery
> 4. Selective Assessment

Full Assessment

The full assessment uses all of the subtests that are age appropriate across all six domains. When time permits and a thorough neuropsychological assessment is warranted, the full assessment battery may be chosen as the administration option. Students who may warrant the full assessment battery option would be those with:

- Severe brain damage or dysfunction.
- Notable neurodevelopmental risk factors such as prenatal exposure to drugs or alcohol.
- A severe learning or behavioral problem that has been monitored for multiple years.
- Severe medical treatments that may effect the central nervous system such as radiation treatments for cancer, or neurosurgeries to treat seizure disorders.

For all of the conditions above, the purpose of the full assessment is to establish a comprehensive profile of the student's neurocognitive strengths and weaknesses

≡ *Rapid Reference 7.2*

NEPSY-II Tests in the General Referral Battery

Domain	Ages 3–4	Ages 5–16
Attention/executive functions	Statue	Statue (ages 5–6)
		Auditory attention and response set inhibition
Language	Comprehension of instructions	Comprehension of instructions
	Speeded naming	Speeded naming
Sensorimotor	Visuomotor precision	Visuomotor precision (ages 5–12)
Visuospatial	Design copying	Design copying
	Geometric puzzles	Geometric puzzles
Memory/learning	Narrative memory	Narrative memory
		Memory for faces/memory for faces delayed
		Word list interference (ages 7–16)

Source: Adapted from Korkman, Kirk, and Kemp (2007).

and use that information to tailor evidence-based interventions (Kemp & Korkman, 2010).

General Referral Battery

The general referral battery is a subset of all of the NEPSY-II tests but it still taps into five of the six core domains (see Rapid Reference 7.2). The general referral battery does not include subtests from the Social Perception domain, which is typically reserved for suspected autism disorders. The general referral battery is often recommended as the starting point for most school-based referrals, particularly when the referral questions are unclear or when multiple problems are cited (Kemp & Korkman, 2010).

Diagnostic Referral Batteries

The NEPSY-II introduced eight Diagnostic Referral Batteries designed to address specific presenting problems (Korkman, Kirk, & Kemp, 2007). The subtests selected in these batteries were selected based on: (a) the largest effect sizes in scores

> ### ≡ *Rapid Reference 7.3*
>
> *NEPSY-II Diagnostic Referral Batteries*
> 1. Learning Differences—Reading
> 2. Learning Differences—Mathematics
> 3. Attention/Concentration
> 4. Behavior Management
> 5. Language Delays/Disorders
> 6. Perceptual-Motor Delays/Disorders
> 7. Social Perception
> 8. School Readiness

within a clinical group as compared to a matched normative sample; and (b) clinical experience and the known neurocognitive deficits associated with these clinical groups based on the literature (Kemp & Korkman, 2010). Rapid Reference 7.3 shows the eight diagnostic referral batteries.

The compilation of NEPSY-II subtests contained within each Diagnostic Referral Battery are different because they reflect which neurocognitive processes are predictive of specific types of clinical syndromes. The neurocognitive processes that predict, or are related to, a student with a reading disorder will be different from those neurocognitive processing deficits associated with a student with social perception difficulties.

Rapid Reference 7.4 provides an example of how the NEPSY-II subtests change based on which Diagnostic Referral Battery is chosen. Use caution when selecting a specific Diagnostic Referral Battery and making the assumption that the presenting problems will fall within that single category. It is not uncommon for children to have multiple learning problems that will cut across these diagnostic categories. When in doubt, start with the General Referral Battery and add supplemental subtests that relate to the stated referral concerns.

Selective Assessment Batteries

Selected subtests from the NEPSY-II may also be used as part of a cross-battery assessment. Since the NEPSY-II tests are not subject to order effects, individual subtests may be selected for administration based on the referral question(s). The selection and interpretation of an individual NEPSY-II subtest or subtests as part of a broader comprehensive assessment battery

≡ Rapid Reference 7.4

An Example of NEPSY-II Tests Based on Two Different Diagnostic Referral Batteries

Domain	Learning Differences— Reading	Perceptual-Motor Delays/Disorders
Attention/executive functions	Auditory attention and response set (ages 5–16) Inhibition (ages 5–16) Statue (ages 3–6)	Auditory attention and response set (ages 5–16) Clocks (ages 7–16) Design fluency (ages 5–12) Statue (ages 3–6)
Language	Comprehension of instructions (ages 3–16) Oromotor sequences (ages 3–12) Phonological processing (ages 3–16) Speeded naming (ages 3–16)	Oromotor sequences (ages 3–12)
Sensorimotor	Manual motor sequences (ages 3–12)	Finger tapping (ages 5–16) Imitating hand positions (ages 3–12) Manual motor sequences (ages 3–12) Visuomotor precision (ages 3–12)
Visuospatial	Design copying (ages 3–16) Picture puzzles (ages 7–16)	Block construction (ages 3–16) Design copying (ages 3–16) Geometric puzzles (ages 3–16)
Memory/learning	Memory of names/delayed (ages 5–16) Word list interference (ages 7–16)	Memory for designs/memory for designs delayed (ages 3–16)
Social perception	Not applicable	Affect recognition (optional) (ages 3–16)

Source: Adapted from Korkman, Kirk, and Kemp (2007).

depends on the knowledge and expertise of the school neuropsychologist. Kemp and Korkman (2010) pointed out that when only a few selected subtests from the NEPSY-II are added to a routine test of cognitive abilities that does not warrant being called a neuropsychological assessment.

Order of Subtest Administration

Once an examiner has chosen which NEPSY-II subtests to administer, the order of the subtests must be determined. The order of the subtests is dependent on several factors including the ability of the child to sustain interest in the tasks, the time lapse between the immediate and delayed memory tasks must be accounted for, and some common sense principles such as not starting with subtests that will be especially difficult based on the referral questions should be considered. When planning the order of the subtest administration, do not take a break between the immediate and delayed memory subtests and do not intersperse other types of memory tests in the immediate to delayed recall interval to minimize any potential interference effects.

Types of Scores Generated

The sheer number of scores generated by the NEPSY-II can be at first overwhelming even for the most experienced school neuropsychologists. Rapid Reference 7.5 presents the types of scores generated by the NEPSY-II.

≡ Rapid Reference 7.5

....

Scores Generated by the NEPSY-II

Scaled scores	These scores are normalized and corrected by age and have a mean of 10 with a standard deviation of 3.
Percentile rank ranges	These scores are normalized and corrected by age and are expressed as a percentile score. The NEPSY-II groups these percentile ranks into ranges that correspond to the following classifications: ≤ 2, well below expected level; 3–10, below expected; 11–25, slightly below expected; 26–75, at expected level; > 75 above expected level.
Cumulative percentages (base rates)	These scores represent the cumulative percentages of the standardization sample or one of the clinical validation groups used to construct the diagnostic

(continued)

⩵ *Rapid Reference 7.5 continued*

	referral batteries. They are descriptive base rates and are not actual percentile ranks. As an example, a base of 26 would be interpreted as "26% of the same-age children obtained the same score or lower."
Combined scores	The combined score integrates two standardized scores from the same subtest. For example, a combined score might be a synthesis of a completion time score and a score that reflects the number of correct items. Hooper (2010) questioned the clinical utility and validity of the combined scores and this author agrees. The combined score is only valid when there is no significant difference between the two scores that are used to form the combined score; otherwise, the individual scores must be interpreted in isolation.
Contrast scores	A contrast score takes the difference between two scores and creates a norm-based value to determine the statistical and clinical significance between the performance on those two measures.
Process scores	Process scores allow the clinician to evaluate subtle aspects of a student's performance on a particular task. For example, examining the number of novel sort and repeated sort errors made on the Animal Sorting test.
Qualitative behavioral observations	When a child engages in a qualitative behavior such as asking for repetitions on verbal tasks, occurrences or absence of these behaviors are recorded and base rates can be determined with comparisons made to the same age group within the standardization sample.

Reporting NEPSY-II Scores Within the SNP Model

As reported in Chapter 6, it is suggested that within a school neuro-psychological assessment report, test results should not be reported in a pure linear fashion. The NEPSY-II is organized in such a way that it makes it easier to report the results based on the six functional domains. However, many of the NEPSY-II tests have subscores and process scores that may involve neurocognitive processes other than the principle processing domain in which the test is categorized. As an example, the Inhibition test has three conditions: (1) inhibition naming, (2) the inhibition portion of the test, and (3) a switching (shifting) attention portion of the test. The test is categorized as an Attention and Executive Functions test. Within the SNP Model, the first part of the test, the naming portion, is a simple task that requires the child to name shapes rapidly and this subscore is reported in the Speed, Fluency, and Efficiency of Processing Facilitator/Inhibitor (Broad Classification), Performance Fluency (second-order classification), and Naming Fluency (third-order classification) section of the school neuropsychological report.

The second part of the Inhibition test requires the child to inhibit the natural tendency to name the shape and requires the child to name an alternative shape, so a circle is called a *square* and a square is called a *circle*. This subscore from the test is reported under the Executive Process (Broad Classification)—Response Inhibition (second-order classification)—Verbal Response Inhibition (third-order classification) section of the school neuropsychological report.

The third part of the Inhibition test requires the child to name the actual shape for some items then switch to naming the alternate shape based on a prescribed rule. This subscore of the test is reported in the Executive Process (Broad Classification)—Cognitive Flexibility (second-order classification)—Verbal Cognitive Flexibility (third-order classification) section of the school neuropsychological report.

In Chapters 10 through 17, the NEPSY-II scores are reclassified according to the Broad Classification, second-order classifications, and third-order classifications of the SNP Model, as appropriate. The NEPSY-II is a valuable assessment tool for school neuropsychologists but the test requires practice to administer and score and requires careful consideration of how to interpret the wide variety of the scores that are generated.

WECHSLER INTELLIGENCE SCALE FOR CHILDREN—FOURTH EDITION INTEGRATED

The WISC-IV Integrated (Wechsler et al., 2004a) reflects the revision of the WISC-IV (Wechsler, 2003) and the updated process assessment approach tasks and procedures originally used in the *WISC-III as a Processing Instrument* (WISC-PI: Kaplan, Fein, Kramer, Delis, & Morris, 1999). Figure 7.1 shows the framework of the WISC-IV Integrated test structure. The WISC-IV yields a Full Scale score, which is composed of four indices: Verbal Comprehension, Perceptual Reasoning, Working Memory, and Processing Speed. Each index has core subtests and at least one supplemental subtest.

DON'T FORGET
....
The WISC-IV Integrated tests are not routinely administered to all children. The tests are intended to be used on an as needed basis to aid in the clinical interpretation of the WISC-IV test results.

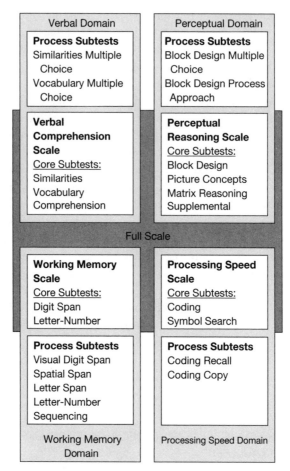

Figure 7.1. The WISC-IV Integrated Test Framework

Source: Adapted from Wechsler et al., 2004.

The WISC-IV Integrated may be purchased as a supplement to the stand-alone WISC-IV kit. The stand-alone version of the WISC-IV Integrated incorporates the process assessment approach into one manual and record form and a combined set of stimulus booklets (Prifitera, Saklofske, & Weiss, 2005). There are 15 process subtests on the WISC-IV Integrated. Some of the WISC-IV Integrated subtests help clinicians to better understand the cognitive processes that are involved in the performance of the core or supplemental WISC-IV tests (Design Multiple Choice, Block Design Process Approach, Coding Copy), while other subtests from the WISC-IV Integrated modify the input modality or item content to better understand the cognitive processes that are involved in the performance of the core of supplemental WISC-IV tests (Elithorn Mazes, Visual Digit Span, Spatial Span, Letter Span, Letter-Number Sequencing Process Approach) (Flanagan & Kaufman, 2009). Another important feature of the WISC-IV Integrated is the coding of qualitative observations during assessment. An example of a qualitative observation is the number of times a child asks for repetitions on the Arithmetic subtest. The frequency of these qualitative behaviors has been translated into norm-referenced base rates and may be used for clinical interpretation.

The WISC-IV Integrated subtests are not routinely administered to all children. McCloskey and Maerlender (2005) pointed out that the process subtests are intended to be used on an as-needed basis. For example, if a child performs poorly on the WISC-IV Vocabulary subtest, the examiner may want to "test the limits" and administer the WISC-IV Integrated Vocabulary Multiple Choice subtest. The Vocabulary Multiple Choice subtest from the WISC-IV Integrated is designed to measure word knowledge and verbal concept formation, as is the Vocabulary subtest on the WISC-IV. The difference between the two measures is that the multiple-choice format decreases the demands for verbal expression and memory retrieval (Wechsler et al., 2004). The memory demands shift from a recall memory task (WISC-IV Vocabulary) to a recognition memory task (WISC-IV Integrated Vocabulary Multiple Choice). The WISC-IV Integrated process subtests are reviewed based on where they are conceptually located in the test framework (see Figure 7.1).

Verbal Comprehension Process Subtests

This section of the chapter reviews the WISC-IV Integrated subtests that are designed to measure verbal comprehension.

Similarities Multiple Choice, Vocabulary Multiple Choice, Picture Vocabulary Multiple Choice, Comprehension Multiple Choice, and Information Multiple Choice

Each of these subtests falls under the Verbal domain. These subtests use the same content as used on the WISC-IV version of the test, except the response format is changed from free-recall to recognition. The goal of these subtests was to decrease the demands for verbal expression and memory retrieval. An example would be a Vocabulary item that asked the child "What is a banana?"; whereas, on the Vocabulary Multiple Choice subtest, the question would be: "Is a banana: (a) vegetable, (b) mineral, (c) fruit, (d) meat."

Generally, when the multiple choice scaled score is greater than the WISC-IV scaled score it supports the hypothesis that the child may have difficulty with retrieval of verbal concepts if external prompts or cues are not available. If the WISC-IV scaled score is higher than the multiple choice scaled score, it may indicate that "the child may have difficulty rejecting salient but conceptually lower-level distracters, or impulsively chooses responses without careful consideration of options" (Wechsler et al., 2004, p. 189).

Perceptual Reasoning Process Subtests

Block Design No Time Bonus

On the WISC-IV Block Design subtest, the child gets a higher scaled score if the designs are completed quickly. If a child has a processing speed deficit, a low score on Block Design may, in part, be due to the slow processing speed. The examiner may "test the limits" of the Block Design subtest by administering the test again but without the time bonus. If a child obtains a higher scaled score on Block Design with No Time Bonus compared to the Block Design subtest, then factors such as slow processing speed, poor visual-perceptual processing, weak motor skills, or slow rates of cognitive processing could account for the difference between the two scores.

Block Design Multiple Choice

This subtest is designed to measure visual-perceptual and perceptual-organizational skills while removing the motor planning and execution demands placed on the WISC-IV Block Design subtest. On the WISC-IV Block Design subtest, the child is shown a 2-dimensional picture of a block design and is asked to construct the design using 3-dimensional blocks. On the Block Design Multiple Choice subtest, the child is shown a 2-dimensional design and must choose from four response options within a specified time limit. The multiple-choice format of the test decreases the motor response demands and relies more on visual-spatial processing. The Block Design Multiple Choice subtest also includes a section in which the child is shown a 3-dimensional design and must choose from four response options within a specified time limit. This version of the test requires more mental imaging. The Block Design Multiple Choice subtest can be administered in timed and untimed conditions to test for the negative influences of processing speed, motor skills, and so on. (Wechsler et al., 2004).

Block Design Process Approach

For each item of this subtest, the child is presented more blocks than needed to construct the block design. Part of the task is for the child to figure out the number of blocks needed to complete the task. The child is presented with a 2-dimensional picture of a block design and asked to construct the design using the correct number of blocks. If the child does not construct the block design correctly within the time limits, a grid overlay is placed over the stimulus picture of the block design to provide additional visual cues for the child. Performance across the two conditions, no grid and grid as needed, are combined to form the test score. A child who has difficulties processing global details will often have an improved performance with the presence of the grid overlay (Wechsler et al., 2004). The types of errors made during the construction of the block designs are also recorded by the examiner and evaluated qualitatively.

Elithorn Mazes

On this subtest, the child is presented with a maze in the response booklet and is instructed to draw a path through a specified number of dots to move from the bottom to the top of the maze. The test is administered in two conditions, timed and untimed. The test is designed to measure "scanning ability, visual and motor sequential processing, planning, organization, motor execution, and ability to inhibit impulsive responses" (Wechsler et al., 2004). The examiner is instructed to record the time it takes the child to make the first move (i.e., latency time), which is a reflection of an impulsive or reflective style of processing. Low scores on this test may be due to a variety of factors including: poor comprehension of the instructions, poor planning and execution, impulsivity, slow processing speed, poor graphomotor speed, obsessive-compulsive tendencies, and so on. (Wechsler et al.).

Working Memory Process Subtests

This section of the chapter reviews the WISC-IV Integrated subtests, which are designed to measure working memory.

Visual Digit Span

On the WISC-IV Digit Span subtest, the child is presented with a set of digits with increasing length and asked to recall them in the exact order presented by the examiner. On the Visual Digit Span subtest, the length of the digit spans are the same but the digit sets are presented visually rather than verbally. The child is instructed to repeat the numbers in the same order in which they were presented. Visual Digit Span is principally a measure of visual short-term memory. This subtest does not have a backward repetition condition, like the WISC-IV Digit Span subtest, which would be a more direct measure of working memory.

Spatial Span

The Spatial Span subtest is designed to be a nonverbal analog to the WISC-IV Digit Span subtest. The child is presented with a board that has a series of raised blocks attached to it. The examiner touches the blocks one at a time in a sequence and asks the child to then touch the blocks in the same order. The task is divided into two trials: Spatial Span Forward (measuring visual short-term memory) and Spatial Span Backward (measuring visual-spatial working memory).

Letter Span

This subtest is a variation of the WISC-IV Digit Span subtest. The Letter Span subtest uses letter strings of the same span length rather than numbers. The subtest does include both rhyming (i.e., t, g, e) and nonrhyming (i.e., g, r, s) letter strings. Performance on this subtest may be compared to performance on the Digit Span subtest "as a means of assessing the differences between auditory encoding skills and auditory-verbal processing of letters versus numbers" (Wechsler et al., 2004).

Letter-Number Sequencing Process Approach

This subtest is similar to the WISC-IV Letter-Number Sequencing subtest. Both versions measure sequencing ability, mental manipulation, attention, short-term auditory memory, working memory, visuospatial imaging, and processing speed (Wechsler et al., 2004a). On the Letter-Number Sequencing Process Approach, the child is read a sequence of letters and numbers, some of which contain an embedded word. The child is instructed to first recall the letters from the original list in alphabetical order, followed by the numbers in ascending order. The embedded word placed in some trials is designed to provide a memory cue that reduces the demands placed on auditory working memory.

Arithmetic Process Approach

This subtest contains the same items as the WISC-IV Arithmetic subtest, but rather than presenting the math problems verbally, the items are presented in different formats. In Part A, the math problem is read to the child while the child looks at the same item in writing on a page. In Part B, the child is given the same problems to solve with the addition of paper and pencil to assist in calculations. The pairing of the visual–verbal presentation of items and the use of paper and pencil help decrease the demands on attention and working memory (Wechsler et al., 2004).

Written Arithmetic

This subtest uses the same problems as in the Arithmetic and Arithmetic Process Approach subtests, but the problems are taken out of the story problem format and put in a mathematical calculation format. The subtest is timed. This subtest is designed to measure numerical reasoning ability while reducing the demands placed on attention and language processing skills.

Processing Speed Process Subtests

This section of the chapter reviews the WISC-IV Integrated subtests which are designed to measure processing speed.

Coding Recall

The purpose of this subtest is to measure the amount of incidental learning that occurred after Coding B is administered. The subtest contains three parts. Part A (Cued Symbol Recall) shows the child the numbers that were part of the number–symbol associations learned in Coding B, and the child is asked to recall and fill in the symbols that were paired with the numbers. On Part B (Free Symbol Recall), the child is asked to write as many symbols as he or she can remember on a blank space in the Response Booklet. On Part C (Cued Digit Recall), the child is shown the symbols that were part of the symbol–number associations learned on Coding B, and the child is asked to recall and fill in the numbers that were paired with the symbols. Each of the parts of the subtest is timed. No standard scores are generated for the Coding Recall subtest. The results are evaluated qualitatively and interpreted in terms of the relative frequency within the normative population (Wechsler et al., 2004).

Coding Copy

The purpose of this subtest is to remove the paired associative learning part of the Coding B subtest and solely evaluate the child's graphomotor speed and accuracy. The child is presented with a page full of the same symbols used in the Coding B subtest and is instructed to copy each one in the square below as quickly as possible. Poor performance on the Coding B test may be due to poor graphomotor speed. This subtest helps to isolate the contributions of graphomotor speed and accuracy to the overall Coding B performance (Wechsler et al., 2004).

Reporting WISC-IV Integrated Scores Within the SNP Model

Similar to the NEPSY-II test scores previously discussed in this chapter, the WISC-IV Integrated test scores should not be reported all together in one section of a school neuropsychological report, but should be reported within the SNP

Model domains and subclassifications based on the principle neurocognitive demands of the tasks.

In Chapters 10 through 16, the WISC-IV Integrated scores are reclassified according to the Broad Classification, second-order classifications, and third-order classifications of the SNP Model, as appropriate. The WISC-IV Integrated is a valuable addition to the WISC-IV and affords school neuropsychologists the opportunity to systematically test the limits for low performing WISC-IV scores.

DELIS-KAPLAN EXECUTIVE FUNCTION SYSTEM (D-KEFS)

The D-KEFS (Delis, Kaplan, & Kramer, 2001) is a comprehensive battery of tests that measure skills associated with executive functioning. All of the subsets may be administered to children aged 8 to adults aged 89, except for the Proverbs Test, which can be administered to ages 16 to 89. The D-KEFS subtests are presented in Rapid Reference 7.6. Practitioners who are familiar with the neuropsychology

---

≡ *Rapid Reference 7.6*

D-KEFS Executive Function System (D-KEFS) Tests

- *Trail-Making Test*—A visual-motor task designed to measure flexibility in thinking.
- *Verbal Fluency*—Assesses the ability to quickly produce verbal responses in accordance with a set of rules.
- *Design Fluency*—The production of as many differing designs as possible using a series of dots and rules as a guide within a delineated time period
- *Color-Word Interference Test*—Measures the inhibition of the natural inclination to respond in a certain way in order to respond in accordance with a set of defined rules.
- *Card Sorting Test*—Measures concept generation and recognition using a set of cards.
- *Word Context Test*—Requires the individual to discover the meanings of a made-up word based on its use in five clue sentences, which progressively provide more detailed information about the target word's meaning.
- *Twenty Questions*—Requires the individual to identify a target stimulus from an array of pictures by asking questions in a yes/no format.
- *Tower Test*—Measures visual attention, visual-spatial skills, spatial planning, rule learning, inhibition, and the establishment and maintenance of cognitive set.
- *Proverbs Test*—Assesses the ability to interpret pithy, concrete phrases that convey deeper, abstract meaning.

field recognize these tests. For example, the Trail-Making Test has its origins with the Halstead-Reitan Neuropsychological Battery (HRNTB: Reitan & Davidson, 1974; Reitan & Wolfson, 1993); the Color-Word Test is similar to the *Stroop Color-Word Test* (Lowe & Mitterer, 1982) that measures the Stroop Effect (Stroop, 1935); and the Tower Test originally designed by Simon (1975).

The fundamental differences and advantages of the D-KEFS over the previous versions of these tests are (1) the updated normative sample, and (2) the integration of a process-assessment approach into each test. The goal of the process assessment approach is to generate hypotheses or possible explanations for poor performance on a test. The approach uses a "testing of the limits" or a subtle variation of the presentation content. For example, if a task requires sequential processing with a motor output, then poor performance on the task could be caused by one or the other, or both, of the neurocognitive processes. Using a process assessment approach, two additional trials would be added to the task, one that isolated the contribution of the motor output and another that isolated the contribution of the sequential processing.

The D-KEFS is a valuable contribution to the field but it needs to be used with caution until a body of research emerges on its clinical efficacy. Baron (2004) warned that "data are still needed to confirm its sensitivity and specificity across diagnostic groups and with normal subjects" (p. 233). The D-KEFS is best suited for an experienced school neuropsychologist. The test produces a large amount of quantitative data that can be overwhelming to a new user of the test. It is also important to recognize that while the test is marketed as a test of executive functions, the tests are stand-alone measures of different aspects of executive functions and are not interchangeable. The tests also measure other interdependent neurocognitive processes such as processing speed and cognitive efficiency, memory and learning, visual-spatial processing, sensory-motor functions, and language functions. Examples of the interrelated neurocognitive demands of these tasks will be addressed in the Chapter 8.

Reporting D-KEFS Scores Within the SNP Model

Similar to the NEPSY-II and WISC-IV Integrated test scores previously discussed in this chapter, the D-KEFS test scores should not be reported all together in one section of a school neuropsychological report, but should be reported within the SNP Model domains and subclassifications based on the principle neurocognitive demands of the tasks.

In Chapters 10 through 16, the D-KEFS scores will be reclassified according to the broad classification, second-order classification, and third-order classification of the SNP Model, as appropriate. The D-KEFS is a valuable assessment tool for school neuropsychologists but the test requires practice to administer and score and careful consideration of how to interpret the wide variety of the process-related scores that are generated.

CHAPTER SUMMARY

In this chapter the NEPSY-II, WISC-IV Integrated, and D-KEFS used for school neuropsychological assessment are reviewed. These three tests are chosen for review because they often serve as part of a core assessment for school neuropsychologists.

 TEST YOURSELF

1. **True or False? The NEPSY-II is standardized on a sample of children ages 3–0 to 16–11.**

2. **The Clocks test on the NEPSY-II is classified in what domain according to the test authors?**
   a. Attention/Executive Functions
   b. Language Functions
   c. Sensorimotor Functions
   d. Visuospatial Processing

3. **All of the following diagnostic referral batteries are part of the NEPSY-II except for one. Which one?**
   a. Behavior Management
   b. Perceptual-Motor Delays/Disorders
   c. Traumatic Brain Injured
   d. School Readiness

4. **On the WISC-IV Integrated, all of the tests below have a multiple-choice version of the WISC-IV test except for one. Which one?**
   a. Similarities
   b. Vocabulary
   c. Block Design
   d. Coding

5. What WISC-IV Integrated test does not appear on the WISC-IV in an alternate form?

a. Elithorn Mazes
b. Similarities
c. Vocabulary
d. Coding

6. What test battery was designed specifically to test for executive functions across the life span?

a. NEPSY
b. D-KEFS
c. WISC-IV Integrated
d. WJIII-COG

Answers: 1. true; 2. b; 3. c; 4. d; 5. a; 6. d

Chapter Eight

CLINICAL INTERPRETATION GUIDELINES

I n this chapter, a set of clinical interpretation guidelines for school neuropsychologists is presented. The chapter is divided into three sections. The first section presents some guidelines related to selecting a test or test battery. Topics in this first section include case conceptualization, relating the assessment to the referral question(s), adopting a flexible approach to assessment, understanding the neurocognitive demands of assessment measures, understanding the role of "brief" and behavioral rating measures, and knowing when to stop testing. The clinical interpretation guidelines that are discussed in this chapter are outlined in Rapid Reference 8.1.

The second section of this chapter presents some guidelines related to data interpretation and analyses. Topics in the second section include the importance of asking children about the strategies they used to approach tasks, cautions about self-fulfilling prophecies, over- and underinterpretations of the results, integrating reported problems with observation and assessment data, and the introduction of a depth of processing interpretation model. The final section of the chapter provides two examples of clinical interpretation.

SELECTING A TEST OR ASSESSMENT BATTERY

This section of the chapter reviews the basic principles of selecting a test or an assessment battery that relates to the referral question(s). Choosing a test or a set of tests starts with case conceptualization and ends with being knowledgeable of a wide variety of assessment instruments so a flexible test battery can be assembled.

Case Conceptualization

Ideally, the clinician does not want to overtest or undertest a student, but choose the optimal amount of assessment for the student. Advances in our knowledge base related to the known neuropsychological deficits associated with common

⇛ Rapid Reference 8.1

Clinical Interpretation Guidelines for School Neuropsychologists
- Relate the assessment to the referral question(s).
- Adopt a flexible approach to assessment.
- Understand the neurocognitive demands of any given task.
- Remember that two or more tasks that report to measure the same construct may or may not.
- Don't forget to ask children how they approach the tasks.
- Understand the role of "brief" measures and behavioral rating scales.
- Get a feel for what constitutes the right amount of testing. Avoid over- or undertesting.
- Integrate reported learning and/or behavior problems with observable behavior and assessment data.
- Use a "vector analysis" to confirm hypotheses about the assessment data.
- Avoid underinterpretations and overinterpretations of the assessment data.
- Be cautious with a student who appears to be following self-fulfilling prophecies.
- Appreciate the multiple causes of behavior.
- Implement a depth of processing interpretation model.

neurodevelopmental disorders serve as a starting point when assembling test batteries. Test publishers and authors have done a better job of providing practitioners with suggested diagnostic batteries for various clinical groups based on validation studies (e.g., NEPSY-II).

To improve efficiency and accuracy of assessment, it behooves the school neuropsychologist to be familiar with the known neuropsychological correlates of common childhood disorders, which helps the clinician assemble a targeted assessment battery. Books such as the *Handbook of Pediatric Neuropsychology* (Davis, 2011), *Essentials of School Neuropsychological Assessment: Guidelines for Effective Practice, Assessment, and Evidence-Based Interventions* (D. Miller, 2010), *Neuropsychological Assessment and Intervention for Childhood and Adolescent Disorders* (Riccio, Sullivan, & Cohen, 2010) all provide updated literature reviews on what neuropsychological processes are impaired and spared in childhood

DON'T FORGET

The "art form" behind good clinical practice is knowing which assessment instruments to choose to ultimately answer referral questions and to provide useful information that helps guide prescriptive interventions.

neurodevelopmental disorders. It is important for school neuropsychologists to continue to update their own knowledge base on the current research in the field of school and pediatric neuropsychology.

Once a research-based test battery is administered, the patterns of student test performances are related back to the neuropsychological literature to determine if the patterns match the neurodevelopmental disorder(s) being assessed. School neuropsychologists need to have the cognitive flexibility to modify the assessment battery to address additional neuropsychological processing concerns that may not have been anticipated at the start of the evaluation but emerge as the initial test results are interpreted.

Relating the Assessment to the Referral Question(s)

Make sure to select a test or battery of tests designed to answer the referral question (s). For example, if the referral question is: "Why can't Johnny read?" it would be best practice to have some tests of phonological awareness, auditory processing, and reading achievement in the test battery. Some school psychologists and related educational assessment personnel rely on one assessment battery to answer all referral questions. Practitioners need to be trained to administer a wide variety of assessment instruments or components of instruments and ideally should have access to those instruments within the schools.

Adopting a Flexible Approach to Assessment

Assessment specialists (e.g., school neuropsychologists, school psychologists, educational diagnosticians, psychometrists) should be flexible during the assessment process itself. In the example earlier, the referral question is: "Why can't Johnny read?" An assessment specialist could plan an evaluation to address the potential phonological and auditory processing causes of a reading problem, only to find significant short-term memory problems and poor processing speed during the course of the evaluation. If a particular processing disorder is suspected as a result of observations of children during testing or based on samples of their test performance, the assessment specialist needs to alter the assessment battery and further explore those suspected deficit areas. In some states, the assessment

CAUTION

Some assessment specialists only rely on one fixed assessment battery to answer all referral questions. Assessment specialists need to select assessment instruments that have constructs related to the referral question(s).

must be preplanned and agreed to by the parent(s)/guardian(s). In these cases, it may be necessary to go back to the parties of the informed consent and ask to broaden the scope of the assessment to further explore the suspected processing deficits.

Understanding the Neurocognitive Demands of the Assessment Measures

It is important for school neuropsychologists to understand the neurocognitive demands of a particular test. Any time samples of behavior are taken on a test, the test may be measuring several abilities. Test publishers and test authors generally attempt to make tests/subtests as factorially pure as possible during test construction. However, it is not uncommon for a particular test to measure more than one neurocognitive process: referred to here as primary and secondary abilities. An example would be the WJIII-COG Numbers Reversed Test (Woodcock, McGrew, & Mather, 2001, 2007a) that requires attentional capacity and working memory.

Figure 8.1 illustrates the conceptual variables that are measured by a particular test. Anytime a sample of behavior is taken there is also error variance included in the measure. Sources of error variance include environmental factors (e.g., noise in the testing room), examiner variables (e.g., administration errors), and student moderator variables (e.g., the student not feeling well on the day of testing). These sources of error variance can invalidate the interpretation of the test score.

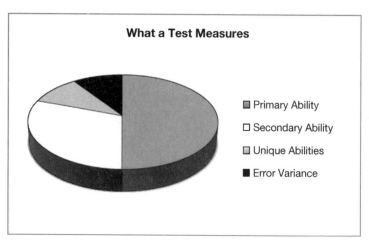

Figure 8.1. Conceptual Variables Measures by Any Test

If students achieve a low score on the WISC-IV Block Design (Wechsler, 2003) subtest because they were extremely distracted and did not put forth good effort, the low performance should not be attributed to poor visual-motor constructional skills. Observed or suspected samples of error variance should be noted in the Assessment Validity section of the report, with the inclusion of a statement that those results should be interpreted with caution or not interpreted at all.

To interpret the results of any given test, the school neuropsychologist should understand the neurocognitive demands required by the test. The first step in determining what a test is measuring is to read the test manual and review the technical properties of the test. Look at the intercorrelations of the subtests within a given battery of tests and any reported correlations with other tests that report to measure the same construct. Test technical manuals are often the best source of information to aide in test interpretation. Many of the major tests used by school neuropsychologists also have supplemental interpretative guides, such as those included in the *Essentials Series* published by John Wiley & Sons, Inc. Finally, it is important to read the research studies related to the test as published in the research. Studies that validate the test with various clinical populations and replicate the reliability and validity of the test should be reviewed.

Tests Reporting to Measure the Same Construct Sometimes Measure Something Different

A common misconception of practitioners is to assume that two tests that have the same process or skill in their title must measure the same construct. For example, on the surface it would make sense that the WISC-IV Processing Speed Index (Wechsler, 2003) and the WJIII-COG Processing Speed Cluster scores would measure the same construct. However, if the neurocognitive demands of each subtest are carefully considered, there appear to be differences on how processing speed is being measured. Floyd, Bergeron, McCormack, Anderson, and Hargrove-Owens (2005) examined six samples of children and adults who completed two or more intelligence tests. They found that some of the constructs, such as processing speed, have low levels of exchangeability among tests. A school neuropsychologist must remain current with the ongoing professional research in the field. As a professional specialty, we have had a tremendous increase in the number of assessment tools at our disposal in recent years, and we are only beginning to understand how these instruments relate to each other in a cross-battery assessment approach.

Understand the Role of "Brief" Measures

> # CAUTION
> ....
> Brief measures of intelligence,
> achievement, or behavioral constructs
> should be viewed as screeners only
> and are not substitutes for a more
> comprehensive test battery.

In some states, there has been a tremendous burden placed on school psychologists to be the sole assessment specialist for determining special education eligibility. This testing pressure, coupled with the ever-increasing shortage of school psychologists across the country, has placed practitioners in an untenable position. School psychologists often do not have the luxury of spending many hours conducting an in-depth evaluation for a child because they have so many more children waiting to be tested. Recognizing this dilemma in practice, there have been tests introduced on the market that are designed to shorten the administration time. For example, there are brief intelligence tests, brief achievement tests, and brief behavioral rating scales, all of which are designed to save the examiner time. Some cautions seem warranted here.

In Chapter 2, the Single Test Approach characterizing the early neuropsychology practice is reviewed. Remember the goal in the early history of neuropsychology was to use a single measure (e.g., the Bender Visual-Motor Gestalt Test) to characterize the overall integrity of brain functioning. The Single Test Approach did not work well and was abandoned in favor of using multiple measures. We know that the reliability of a measure increases when there are multiple items within a given test. Conversely, the reliability of a measure decreased when there are fewer items within a given test. Brief measures of intelligence, achievement, or behavioral constructs, should be viewed as screeners only and are not substitutes for a more comprehensive test battery. Some students may only need the screener, while other students need more in-depth assessment.

Understand the Role of Behavioral Rating Scales

Assessment specialists in the schools have access to a variety of behavioral rating scales that may be based on self-report, or the parent(s) or teacher(s) evaluation of the student. There are behavioral ratings for ADHD, generalized and specific behavioral and personality disorders, and specific cognitive functions (e.g., executive functioning). As an example, let's examine a behavioral rating of executive functioning that is completed by the student's parents. The important concept to remember is that the behavioral rating is the parent's perception of the child's executive functioning and not actual samples of the child's executive functioning. Some practitioners rely only on behavioral ratings in their evaluation of the child and do not include direct samples of the child's behavior. It would not be the best professional practice to assume that a child has a working memory deficit based solely on the parent's endorsement of a child's working memory problems. Behavioral rating scales are excellent means of generating hypotheses about the potential cause of a student's current learning or behavioral difficulties

> **CAUTION**
>
> Behavioral rating scales are excellent means of generating hypotheses about the potential cause of a student's current learning or behavioral difficulties and may be useful in determining a comprehensive testing approach, but this use represents a starting point, not a stopping point.

and may be useful in determining a comprehensive testing approach, but only as a starting point, not a stopping point. Furthermore, if behavioral rating measures are used, a general rule should be a minimum of two samples of behavior collected in two different domains by two different raters.

When Is Enough, Enough, in Terms of Testing?

Jerome is referred for a school neuropsychological evaluation due to a suspected processing deficit in the area of working memory. The school neuropsychologist, administers Jerome a subtest that measures his memory for digits backward. Jerome achieved an average score on this subtest so Alicia concludes that Jerome has no working memory problems. What is wrong with this example?

In the example, the school neuropsychologist does not have enough assessment data to determine whether Jerome has a working memory problem. Jerome may have achieved an average score on a memory for digits backward task because of the small chucks of information to be manipulated in memory. Jerome may have difficulties with visual working memory, or with working memory of more complicated verbal stimuli. In Chapters 10 through 17, the basic cognitive processes and achievement areas are subdivided into classifications for assessment purposes. To conduct a thorough evaluation, the school neuropsychologist should fully explore the suspected deficit area(s). As a general rule of thumb, it is good practice to administer two tests that purport to measure the same suspected deficit area as a means of verifying the deficit.

Historically in the practice of neuropsychology it was common to

> **DON'T FORGET**
>
> One hour of assessment that specifically addresses the referral question(s) is much better than 6 hours of assessment that is only partially related to the referral question(s).

administer a single measure, such as the drawing of a Greek Cross, and to conclude that the child had constructive dyspraxia based on poor performance. A more valid professional practice would be to administer the Greek Cross test and another measure of visuospatial processing to validate the hypothesis of poor visuospatial constructive skills. Additional guidelines for data interpretation and analyses are presented in the next section. A final point must be made about overassessment. Assessment for the sake of assessment is never good practice. One hour of assessment that specifically addresses the referral question (s) is much better than 6 hours of assessment that is only partially related to the referral question(s).

DATA ANALYSES AND INTERPRETATIONS

This section of the chapter details the best practices in data analyses and clinical interpretations. Both quantitative and qualitative data are important to consider in the overall clinical picture of the student.

Ask How the Child Approached the Tasks

In Chapter 2, Historical Influences of Clinical Neuropsychology and School Psychology, the contributions of the Boston Process Approach were reviewed in the context of the history of neuropsychology. The basic tenet of this approach to neuropsychological assessment was the idea that how a student arrives at an answer on a test is equally as important as the test score itself. Too often assessment specialists are so concerned about administering a test in a standardized manner that they forget that a student, with a dynamic thinking brain, is sitting in front of them. It is important to administer the test in a standardized manner, but it is equally important to use the testing session to discuss the samples of behavior with the student. After administering a test to a student in a standardized manner, ask the student what was easy and what was hard for the student to perform. Ask the student what could have been done to make harder tasks easier, and vice versa. Students often have excellent "metacognitive" awareness of their own cognitive strengths and weaknesses and they have identified compensatory methods for their own perceived or actual neurocognitive weaknesses. A school neuropsychologist often looks to "test the limits" to best answer the referral questions.

DON'T FORGET

Too often assessment specialists are so concerned about administering a test in a standardized manner that they forget that a student with a dynamic thinking brain is sitting in front of them.

Be Careful of Self-Fulfilling Prophecies

A school neuropsychologist was evaluating Tonika and she was asked to perform a list-learning memory task. Tonika became very agitated and upset and she indicated that she could not attempt this task because it was too difficult for her and she was "not any good at these kinds of tests." The school neuropsychologist asked Tonika why she thought she could not perform this kind of task. Tonika told the school neuropsychologist that when she was last evaluated she had been administered a similar test and she performed poorly. The test examiner at that time indicated to her that this was a weak area for her and she should avoid tasks in her schooling that involved memorizing verbal material. The current school neuropsychologist explained the demands of the task, calmed Tonika by listening to her concerns, and told her to try her best on the task. Tonika performed the task and achieved an average score.

What does the vignette above tell us? Tonika had convinced herself, or had been convinced by a previous examiner, that she could not perform verbal memory tasks. Sometimes students develop these self-fulfilling prophecies about their learning and behavior that can actually disrupt their true potential. In cases like these, it is a good idea to stop the testing, calm the student, explain the demands of the test, indicate that good effort is what is important on the task, and then administer the test. It is important to treat the student as a partner in discovering his or her neurocognitive strengths and weaknesses. Students need to be debriefed by the examiner at the conclusion of the evaluation about the results. Too frequently, students referred for a school neuropsychological evaluation have been told for years that they did not do well, discounting their strengths and developmental changes. Students need to be told about their neurocognitive strengths and taught methods to use those strengths to work around their neurocognitive limitations.

Integrating Reported Problems with Observable Behavior and Assessment Data

How often have assessment specialists (e.g., educational diagnosticians, school psychologists, school neuropsychologists) been relegated to a confined space (e.g., a supply closet, or a stage in the auditorium) within a public school to test a child? The generalizability of any test results obtained in these situations should be suspect, at best. Ideally, assessment specialists should take samples of behavior in a variety of settings (e.g., classroom observations, parents or teachers perceptions of the child's learning and/or behavioral problems, standardized measures) that relate to the child's everyday environment. In the conceptual school neuropsychological model outlined in this book, it is suggested that concerns of parents and teachers about the child's learning should be integrated within the current assessment findings. The *Neuropsychological Processing Concerns Checklist for School-Aged Children & Youth—Third Edition* (Miller, 2012, see the supplemental CD), provides a standardized method of collecting concerns about a child's cognitive processing.

Look for Confirming Trends in Data

School neuropsychologists are urged to use a "vector analysis" approach in their clinical interpretations of data. Figure 8.2 illustrates a "vector analysis" approach

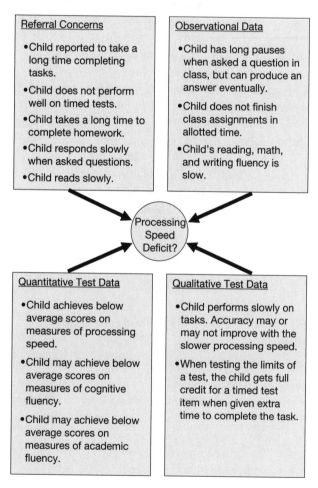

Figure 8.2. A Vector Analysis Model for Clinical Interpretation

for a suspected processing speed deficit. Referral concerns, observational data, quantitative and qualitative data must be integrated in order to confirm suspected processing deficits.

In the example presented in Figure 8.2, the data from the four sources converge to support the diagnostic conclusion of a processing speed deficit. Sometimes, the four sources of data do not converge, but rather offer disparate views. The most common form of disagreement is that referral behaviors and classroom observations do not always match the quantitative and qualitative test data. This occurs because educators and parents may misidentify behavioral symptoms and relate those behaviors to the wrong neurocognitive areas. For example, a child may appear to not be "paying attention" in the classroom and referred for attentional processing deficits. After a school neuropsychological evaluation, those behaviors may be explained by the child's poor auditory processing, and not attentional deficits, as originally suspected. The school neuropsychologist must try to align the four sources of information to support the diagnostic conclusions made in the written report.

As mentioned in the previous section, the school neuropsychologist must look for confirming trends in the data. In the earlier example there is not 100% agreement in four samples of behavior that report to measure the same construct. Remember to evaluate the neurocognitive demands of the tasks. Look for similarities on the three tasks on which the child performed well and look for some neurocognitive demand differences on the one task performed poorly. The school neuropsychologist would not want to indicate a universal processing deficit in reading based on the earlier example. When doing a task analysis of the tests administered, one reading test in which the child performed poorly may use nonsense words that must be read while the other tests used real words. Be cautious of "false positives" that may be due to noncognitive factors (e.g., fatigue, poor motivation).

Avoid Underinterpretation of the Data

Clifford is suspected of having problems with his memory. He constantly forgets to turn in assignments and he does not seem to remember what he is taught from one day to another. He is administered the WISC-IV and he achieves an average score on the Working Memory Index. The school neuropsychologist indicates in the report that Clifford does not have a memory problem. Is this interpretation correct?

When using a limited battery of tests, do not assume that an average score is indicative of across-the-board average skills. For a referral question area, it is a best practice to administer several measures to prove or disprove the suspected weakness. In the example above, Clifford may have memory problems that relate to long-term memory rather than working memory. As discussed in Chapter 12, Learning and Memory Cognitive Processes, there are many subcomponents of memory that need to be assessed when a memory-processing deficit is suspected. In this case, concluding that Clifford has no problems in the area of memory based on one sample of behavior is an underinterpretation of the data.

Depth of Processing Interpretation Model

It is proposed that school neuropsychologists use a *depth of processing model* (see Figure 8.3) to aid in the clinical interpretation of data. This model has five levels of interpretation. At each level, the school neuropsychologist must consider the noncognitive (e.g., fatigue, poor motivation), environmental, or cultural factors that influence performance on any given test. Also, the school neuropsychologist must consider the linkage between the assessment data and evidence-based interventions at each level.

Level I of the model interprets only the global indices or factors of a test. To effectively interpret the data at this level, the assessment specialist must have knowledge of measurement theory, as well as ethical and legal use of assessment data. The first clinical interpretation case example provided in the next section illustrates why using only Level I interpretations can mask important neuro-cognitive deficits.

Level II of the model extends interpretation to the subtest scores. Statistically significant and clinically relevant differences between subtests must be interpreted. A practitioner operating at this level must have an understanding of the technical manuals that describe the intercorrelations of the subtests and the external construct validity of the measures.

Level III of the interpretative model takes into consideration the qualitative behaviors and their relationship to the quantitative scores. Qualitative behaviors are reported as *base rates* by some test publishers (e.g., what was the percentage of children at a particular age level that engaged in a qualitative behavior). To understand the importance of qualitative behaviors, the assessment specialist must have a good working knowledge of soft neuropsychological signs, be able to analyze the neurocognitive demands of any given task, and be able to look for patterns of qualitative behaviors across tasks. A useful technique to investigate the qualitative behaviors is to interview the child about the strategies used in completion of the tasks. Children's metacognitive awareness of their own cognitive processes can be very insightful and useful to the school neuropsychologist.

Level IV of the interpretative model moves beyond the standardized test score results to refine the diagnoses. For example, if a child achieves a standard score of

Level	Focus of Analyses	Needed Knowledge Base (cumulative from one level to the next)
I	Global Index/Factor Scores Only	• Measurement theory (e.g., standardization, reliability, validity). • Ethical and legal principles of assessment.
II	Addition of subtest analyses (e.g., individual subtest and intra-subtest variability)	• Incidence of intra-subtest variability (e.g., technical manual data). • Difference between clinical and statistical significance.
III	Qualitative performance data, supplemental scores, process data, etc.	• Base rates of qualitative performance data. • Neurocognitive demand of each task and the qualitative demands typically elicited. • Interviewing techniques to measure the student's metacognitive awareness of the strategies employed during task performance.
IV	Error analysis, informal samples, testing the limits, etc.	• Evaluation of the patterns of errors within and across subtests and in work samples (e.g., signs of dysnomia). • Linkage of criterion-referenced and curriculum-based measures with standardized measures. • How to test-the-limits after standardized administration.
V	Neuropsychological interpretation of data.	• Theoretical bases of the assessment instrument. • Construct validity of the test and components. • Functional neuroanatomy.

Consideration of noncognitive factors (e.g., motivation, fatigue), environmental, cultural factors that contribute to performance as each level.

Evidence-based interventions

Figure 8.3. Levels of Processing Interpretative Model for School Neuropsychologists

78 (100 is the mean and 15 is the standard deviation) on a measure of reading accuracy, one can safely conclude that the child is below expected levels for a comparable child his or her age in reading accuracy. However, the standard score itself does not reveal the nature of the reading decoding problem. At this stage of the assessment, the school neuropsychologist should conduct an error analysis of the reading decoding errors to see if there is a pattern of errors that would suggest a particular subtype of reading disorder. Other techniques used may include informal reading samples from a classroom reader, or testing the limits of standardized testing to determine if the child can perform a task when the instructions, methods, or materials are modified.

Level V of the interpretative model requires the school neuropsychologist to be able to understand the neurocognitive demands of any given cognitive task. To accomplish this goal, the school neuropsychologist must have a good knowledge base of the theories used to construct and validate assessment instruments, the

═══ *Rapid Reference 8.2*

NEPSY-II Auditory Attention and Response Set Interpretative Examples

Test Scores	1	2	3	4	5
Part 1: Measures of Selective/Focused and Sustained Attention					
Auditory attention combined total: Selectively responding to auditory target words while ignoring auditory nontarget words over time.	(8)	(6)	(4)	(10)	(6)
Total commission errors: Responding to nontarget words that were to be ignored (more errors = lower % rank).	3–10	26–75	≤ 2	26–75	26–75
Total correct: Responding correctly to target words (more correct = higher scaled score).	(10)	(5)	(5)	(10)	(7)
Total omission errors: Missing target words (more errors = lower % rank).	25–75	3–10	3–10	26–75	3–10
Total inhibitory errors: Ignoring distracter words (more errors = lower % rank).	3–10	26–75	26–75	26–75	3–10

Part 2: Measures of Selective/Focused, Sustained, and Shifting Attention

Response set combined total: Added shifting of attention while selectively responding to auditory target words while ignoring auditory nontarget words over time.	(9)	(7)	(5)	(6)	(10)
Total commission errors: Responding to nontarget words that were to be ignored (more errors = lower % rank).	11–25	26–75	3–10	26–75	26–75
Total correct: Responding correctly to target words (more correct = higher scaled score).	(11)	(6)	(6)	(7)	(10)
Total omission errors: Missing target words (more errors = lower % rank).	25–75	3–10	3–10	3–10	26–75
Total inhibitory errors: Ignoring distracter words (more errors = lower % rank).	11–25	26–75	26–75	3–10	26–75
Qualitative Behaviors					
Inattentive/distracted off-task behaviors	No	Yes 23%	No	No	No
Out of seat/physical movement in seat off-task behaviors	No	Yes 14%	No	No	No

construct validity of tests, and a good knowledge of neuropsychological theories and research.

At each level of assessment, the school neuropsychologist must consider potential influences on performance other than neurocognitive processes including: noncognitive factors (e.g., motivation, fatigue), environmental, and cultural factors. A practitioner operating at each stage of the interpretative model takes the data and develops prescriptive interventions that are linked to the assessment data. Finally, the assessment data at each level should be linked to prescriptive and evidence-based interventions. It can be argued that at each increased interpretative level, as the assessment data becomes more precise, the prescriptive interventions should become more targeted and educationally relevant.

In the next section two examples of data from case studies are presented to illustrate either the Levels of Processing Interpretative Model for School Neuropsychologists or the multiple causes of test behaviors.

CLINICAL INTERPRETATION EXAMPLES

In Rapid Reference 8.2, five sets of test scores are presented from the NEPSY-II's (Korkman, Kirk, & Kemp, 2007) Auditory Attention and Response Set (AARS) test. This test is presented as an example to illustrate that reporting only one test score may not be enough to fully explain a student's performance on a test. For the reader not familiar with the AARS test, a quick review is needed. The AARS test is divided into two parts: (1) Auditory Attention, and (2) Response Set. For each part of the test, the student has a stimulus booklet page in front of them with four colored circles: black, red, yellow, and blue. After a brief practice period for each part, the student listens to a CD recording of an examiner reading one word per second over an extended period of time.

On the Auditory Attention part of the test, the student is instructed to touch, as quickly as possible, the red circle on the page after the word "red" is spoken. The student is taught to ignore all other color words. On the Response Set part of the test, the task becomes more difficult because the student is instructed to touch, as quickly as possible, the yellow circle when the word "red" is spoken, touch the red circle when the word "yellow" is spoken, and touch the blue circle when the word "blue" is spoken. The "red" and "yellow" word prompts require students to switch their cognitive set while the "blue" word prompt requires students to maintain an expected cognitive set.

For a correct response to a stimulus word to occur, the student has 2 seconds to touch the correct circle. A Combined Total score is calculated based on the total number of commission errors and total number of correct responses. The total number of omission errors (not touching the red circle within 2 seconds) and inhibitory errors (touching another color circle in response to the corresponding color word when instructed not to) are also recorded.

AARS Example 1—Too Many Commission and Inhibitory Errors Across Both Parts of the Test

The different levels of interpretation are illustrated in this first example.

Level 1 Analysis—Interpreting Global Scores

In this example, the student achieved a scaled score of 8 (10 is average with a standard deviation of 3) on the Auditory Attention Combined Score and a scaled score of 9 on the Response Set portion of the test. Some inexperienced clinicians may only present these two scores in a report and draw the incorrect diagnostic conclusion that the student did not have any performance difficulties on this task.

Level 2 Analysis—Interpreting Subtest Scores

The interaction between the four AARS test scores, total correct, commission errors, omission errors, and inhibitory errors, for each part of the test must be interpreted to fully understand how a student performed on this test. In this example on the Auditory Attention part of the test, the student achieved an average score for the total number correct (scaled score = 10) and paid attention throughout the tasks as reflected by an average score for the total omission errors (average percentile rank range of 25% to 75%). However, the student made many commission and inhibitory errors on the Auditory Attention part of the test. The student achieved below expected level percentile rank range scores (3% to 10%) for both the number of commission and inhibitory errors. These low scores reflect an impulsive response style without paying attention to the specific rules of the task; in this case, only touching the red circle in response to the word "red" while ignoring all other stimuli. This same impulsive style of responding while not maintaining the rules of the task was also evident in the Response Set portion of the test.

Level 3 Analysis—Interpreting Qualitative Behaviors

The AARS test yields two qualitative behaviors: (1) the number of times the student was inattentive/distracted or engaging in off-task behaviors, and (2) the number of times the student was out of the seat, or engaged in extraneous physical movements and was off task. In this first example, while the student did show an impulsive response style, no qualitative behaviors were noted. If the qualitative behaviors were noted in this first example, a diagnosis of ADHD Predominantly Hyperactive-Impulsive Type could be considered. Since these qualitative behaviors were not exhibited in this example, the clinician would want to rule out that the student fully understood the task (receptive language issues) or that the student was being oppositional or overly compliant (a behavioral issue), or that the student lost the cognitive set of what the task directions were (an executive dysfunction).

Level 4 Analysis—Error Analysis and Integration With Other Assessment Data

The student's performance on the AARS must be interpreted in light of the referral question, background information, formal and informal observations, and other assessment data. Determining if the student's impulsive response style was due to receptive language, behavioral issues, or executive dysfunction requires the clinician to integrate informal and formal data about the student (the vector analyses previously discussed in this chapter).

Level 5 Analyses—Understanding the Neurocognitive Demands of the Test

The Auditory Attention portion of the AARS requires the student to selectively focus attention on target stimuli while selectively ignoring nontarget stimuli. This portion of the test also requires sustaining attention over a prolonged period of time and response inhibition. The Response Set portion of the AARS requires all of these same attentional processes and the additional component of shifting attention or cognitive flexibility (e.g., touching the red circle in response to the word "yellow" or vice versa). Beyond these primary neurocognitive processes that are required to successfully perform this task, the test also requires, receptive language input and minimal fine motor coordination output. Non-neurocognitive factors of the student such as motivation, fatigue, and attitude may also factor into the overall test performance.

AARS Example 2—Student Distracted During the Test Causing Many Omission Errors, Few Correct, and Few Commission Errors

For the Example 2 AARS scores, the student achieved an Auditory Attention Combined Total scaled score of 6 on the Auditory Attention portion of the test and a scaled score of 7 on the Response Set portion of the test, both of which are in the slightly below average range of functioning (Level 1 analysis). For both portions of the test, the student had a low number of correct responses, a high number of omissions, and few commission errors. Behaviorally, the student frequently became distracted throughout each section of the test and did not respond to the stimuli items, which resulted in the low number correct and the high number of omissions. Commission errors were low because the student was not responding to anything including making errors (Level 2 analysis). The student did have both qualitative behaviors present: inattentive and hyperactive behaviors. The NEPSY-II provides base rates for these qualitative behaviors. In this example, only 23% of children the same age exhibited the same amount of inattentive/distracted off-task behaviors and only 14% of the children the same age exhibited the same amount of out of seat hyperactive behaviors (Level 3 analysis). The scores alone do not provide enough detail about the student's behavior during the test. The examiner would need to report the child's distractibility during the test in order to appropriately interpret the test results and integrate those results in light of the other case study data (Level 4 analyses). The neurocognitive demands of the test remain the same as outlined in Example 1 (Level 5 analyses).

AARS Example 3—Student With Slow Processing Speed Resulting in Many Omission Errors, Few Correct, and a High Number of Commission Errors

On the AARS test, the student has 2 seconds to touch a color circle in response to a stimulus prompt. Children with slow processing speed correctly touch the correct colored circle in response to the corresponding prompt but they do so outside of the 2-second window. As a result of this time delay in responding, the number of correct items is low and since the correct responses occurred late they count as commission errors. Students with this type of score pattern will not necessarily have the qualitative behaviors of inattention or hyperactivity, but rather just a slow response time. The clinician in these types of cases should look for confirmatory evidence of slow processing speed in other parts of the assessment.

AARS Example 4—Average Performance on Auditory Attention but Weaker Performance on Response Set

In this example, the addition of the shifting attention requirement is most probably the cause of the weaker performance on the Response Set portion of the test. The clinician should look for other evidence of a shifting attention deficit in the student from other assessment data, background information, and behavioral observations.

AARS Example 5—Weaker Performance of Auditory Attention and Stronger Performance on Response Set

In this example, the student performed better on the more challenging Response Set portion of the test. When this profile emerges it usually is indicative that the student was bored on the first part of the test and did not put forth good effort. However, when the task became more challenging, and perhaps more interesting, the student was able to marshal the cognitive resources needed to complete the task. Again, the clinician should look for other confirmatory evidence of this type of response style across other samples of behavior.

A danger in interpretation of any assessment data is not fully interpreting the results. In these AARS examples, if a clinician were to stop interpreting the test data at the first level, the full picture of how the student performed the tasks would be lost. Test authors and publishers have included supplemental and qualitative behaviors as part of their test batteries to reveal a more complete clinical picture of the student's performance.

In the next case study example, test data from the D-KEFS Trail-Making Test (Delis, Kaplan, & Kramer, 2001) is used to make the point about the potential multiple contributors of test behaviors.

Interpretative Example 2—Performance on the D-KEFS Trail-Making Test

As reported in Chapter 14, Attention and Working Memory Facilitators/Inhibitors, the Trail Making Test (TMT) is widely used by practitioners because it is sensitive to overall brain dysfunction; however, it does not reliably localize brain dysfunction. The TMT test is thought to measure alternating and sustained visual attention, sequencing, psychomotor speed, cognitive flexibility, and inhibition-disinhibition. The D-KEFS version of the TMT (D-KEFS-TMT: Delis et al., 2001) sought to address some of these interpretative limitations by including five conditions (see Rapid Reference 8.3).

In Rapid Reference 8.3, the primary and secondary constructs for each of the D-KEFS trail-making test scores are presented. For example, in Condition 1—

≡ *Rapid Reference 8.3*

The D-KEFS Trail-Making Test Scores

Score	Primary Measure Conditions	Secondary Measures
Condition 1—Visual scanning	• Visual scanning • Visual attention	• Motor functions
Condition 2—Number sequencing	• Basic numeric sequential processing	• Visual scanning • Visual attention • Motor functions
Condition 3—Letter sequencing	• Letter sequential processing	• Visual scanning • Visual attention • Motor functions
Condition 4—Number-letter sequencing	• Shifting attention/ cognitive flexibility/ divided attention	• Visual scanning • Visual attention • Motor functions • Sequential processing
Condition 5—Motor speed	• Motor functions	• Visual scanning • Visual attention

Contrast Scores

Condition 4 versus Condition 1	Contribution of visual scanning and attention to the performance on Condition 4.
Condition 4 versus Condition 2	Contribution of number sequencing to the performance on Condition 4.
Condition 4 versus Condition 3	Contribution of letter sequencing to the performance on Condition 4.
Condition 4 versus Condition 2 + 3	Contribution of sequential processing in general to the performance on Condition 4.
Condition 4 versus Condition 5	Contribution of motor output to the performance on Condition 4.

Visual Scanning, visual scanning and visual attention are the principle constructs being measured. On this task, the child is asked to find all of the number 3s on the page and put a mark with a pen/pencil on them as quickly as possible. The task does require a minimal motor response but that is not the principle construct being measured. Condition 4—Number-Letter Switching represents the major part of the test. All of the other conditions and contrast scores were designed to help interpret the child's performance on the number-letter switching condition. Figure 8.4 illustrates the contribution of conditions and contrast scores to the understanding of the number-letter switching condition.

The D-KEFS Condition 4 is considered a classic measure of executive functioning; however, as shown in Rapid Reference 8.4 there are multiple reasons that can be hypothesized for poor performance on this part of the test. The possible explanations for poor performance on the D-KEFS-TMT are organized according to the conceptual school neuropsychological model.

Sensory-Motor Deficits

Motor Impairment

- Look at the D-KEFS-TMT Condition 5—Motor Speed to determine if that is a significantly low score.
- Look at the Condition 4 (Number-Letter Switching) versus Condition 5 (Motor Speed) contrast score.
- Look to other measures to confirm motor impairment (e.g., Dean-Woodcock Neuropsychological Battery, WISC-IV Coding, NEPSY Visual-Motor Precision, WRAVMA Pegboard). See Rapid References 10.5 to 10.10 for a list of other measures of sensorimotor functions.

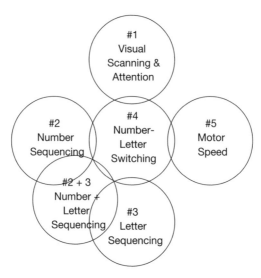

Figure 8.4. Conceptual Interpretative Model of the D-KEFS Trail-Making Test. Poor Performance on Condition #4—Number-Letter Switching May Be Attributable to Poor Performance on Any One or More of the Other Conditions

Attentional Processing Deficits The child must allocate attentional resources to complete the D-KEFS-TMT. Poor performance on Condition 4—Number-Letter Switching may be caused by poor selective/focused attention, sustained attention, shifting attention, or attentional capacity. The examiner should look at other tests of attention to verify hypotheses about which attentional processes could be causing poor performance on the D-KEFS-TMT. See Rapid References 14.4 to 14.8 for a list of other measures of attentional facilitators/inhibitors.

Visual-Spatial Processing Deficits The child must be able to visually scan the visual stimuli on the D-KEFS-TMT. Poor performance on all of the test conditions may be caused by poor visual scanning abilities. Some children may perform poorly on any test that has a visual component because of poor attention to visual detail.

- Examine the D-KEFS-TMT Condition 1—Visual Scanning to determine if that is a significantly low score.
- Examine the Condition 4 (Number-Letter Switching) versus Condition 1 (Visual Scanning) contrast score.
- Examine other measures to confirm visual scanning deficits (see Rapid Reference 10.9 for a list of comparison tests).

≡ *Rapid Reference 8.4*

....

Possible Explanations for Poor Performance of the D-KEFS Trail-Making Test

Possible cause of poor performance	D-KEFS Trail-Making Condition				
	1	2	3	4	5
Sensory motor deficits:					
• Poor motor speed	√	√	√	√	√
Attentional processing deficits:					
• Poor selective/focused attention	√	√	√	√	√
• Failure to maintain cognitive set: distractibility/sustained attention	√	√	√	√	√
• Poor shifting of attention				√	
• Poor divided attention				√	
• Poor attentional capacity	√	√	√	√	
Visual-spatial processing deficits:					
• Poor visual-scanning	√	√	√	√	√
Language deficits:					
• Failure to maintain cognitive set: poor comprehension of instructions	√	√	√	√	√
Memory and learning deficits:					
• Poor working memory				√	
Executive function deficits:					
• Poor cognitive flexibility				√	
• Poor set-shifting				√	
Speed and efficiency of cognitive processing deficits:					
• Poor processing speed	√	√	√	√	√
Intellectual/academic deficits					
• Poor generalized intellectual skills	√	√	√	√	√
• Poor number processing	√	√		√	
• Poor letter processing	√		√	√	
• Poor generalized sequencing skills		√	√	√	
Noncognitive (cultural, social, or environmental) factor deficits:					
• Noncognitive factors (e.g., poor effort)	√	√	√	√	√

Language Deficits To successfully accomplish the D-KEFS-TMT, the child must be able to comprehend the oral instructions that are administered by the examiner. Failure to comprehend the instructions could be a reason for poor performance on each of the D-KEFS-TMT conditions. The examiner should review the child's performance on other measures of receptive language for confirmatory evidence. See Rapid Reference 16.9 for a list of other measures of receptive language.

Learning and Memory Deficits Condition 4—Number-Letter Switching on the D-KEFS-TMT requires some aspects of working memory. The child must maintain the number and letter sequencing in his or her head while alternating back and forth between their proper sequences (e.g., 1-A-2-B-3-C . . .). If the examiner thinks that poor working memory is the cause of poor performance on Condition 4 of the D-KEFS-TMT, then the examiner should review other samples of working memory to support or refute that hypothesis. See Rapid Reference 14.9 for a list of other measures of working memory.

Executive Function Deficits Condition 4 of the D-KEFS-TMT requires the student to use some executive functioning processes such as set shifting, which is a measure of cognitive flexibility. The examiner should evaluate the contrast scores on the D-KEFS-TMT to determine if the student is exhibiting disproportionate impairment in cognitive flexibility relative to the other four baseline conditions (Delis et al., 2001). If a problem of cognitive flexibility is suspected, the examiner should review other measures of executive processing to support or refute that hypothesis. See Rapid Reference 13.10 to 13.11 for a list of other measures of executive functioning.

Speed and Efficiency of Cognitive Processing Deficits Because scores for each of the conditions on the D-KEFS-TMT are based on completion time, the test is indirectly measuring processing speed. Similar to each of the other areas, if the examiner suspects that poor performance on the D-KEFS-TMT is a result of poor processing speed, this hypothesis should be verified or refuted by looking at other measures of processing speed. See Rapid Reference 15.3 to 15.10 for a list of other measures of speed and efficiency of cognitive processing.

Intellectual/Academic Deficits If students have limited intellectual ability (e.g., full scale IQs less than 70) then poor performance on the D-KEFS-TMT may be a function of poor overall cognitive capabilities. The examiner needs to verify this hypothesis by reviewing the results of measures of cognitive processing.

Noncognitive Factors Sometimes there is no definitive neurocognitive explanation for why a child performed poorly on a task. Other noncognitive factors such as lack of effort or motivation, fatigue, pain avoidance, or emotional problems (e.g., lethargy due to depression, oppositional behaviors, cultural factors, medications) may be the reason for poor performance on a task. The following is a partial list of noncognitive factors that can cause or contribute to poor performance on a test:

Readiness/motivational states: If fatigue is a possible cause of poor performance, do not include those results and readminister them at another time (test the limits) when the student is not so tired. It is probably best practice to report both test scores (fatigued and nonfatigued) in the report. A dubious practice is to administer a lengthy test battery to a student, with few if any breaks, and then equate poor performance at the end of the session with true neurocognitive deficits. In this example, the deficits may or may not be real, but one must rule out the effects of fatigue as well.

Psychological factors: Review the reasons for referral and the background information provided by the student's teacher(s) and parent(s). Look for clues related to the noncognitive factors that could explain poor test performance. A student that has been diagnosed with major depression and has been prescribed an antidepression medication may appear lethargic and undermotivated. The psychological state of the student is an important consideration when interpreting neuropsychological results.

Acculturation is an important factor to consider as a noncognitive factor. If English is not the child's primary language, or if the child has recently arrived in the United States, acculturation may be a major contributing factor to poor test performance. Consider the need for using neuropsychological measures translated into a foreign language (see Rapid Reference 4.6).

Environmental factors (e.g., Maslow's 1943 Hierarchy of Needs—A student who is hungry or fearing for his or her safety will not perform well on testing). If noncognitive factors are causing poor performance consider invaliding the test results or use strong qualifiers in the "Assessment Validity" section of the report. The purpose of this second case study is not to frustrate the aspiring or seasoned school neuropsychologist, but to make them aware of the multiple explanations for human behavior. The sciences of psychology, school psychology, and school neuropsychology are still relatively young with the body of knowledge related to each rapidly expanding discipline or subspecialty area. A well-trained school neuropsychologist must be able to use data from multiple sources to generate and test hypotheses about a student's profile of neurocognitive strengths and weaknesses.

CHAPTER SUMMARY

In this chapter, a set of clinical interpretation guidelines for school neuropsychologists was presented. The guidelines included the importance of relating the assessment to the referral question(s), adopting a flexible approach to assessment, understanding the neurocognitive demands of assessment measures, understanding the role of "brief" and behavioral rating measures, and knowing when to stop testing. The second section of this chapter presented some guidelines related to data interpretation and analyses. These guidelines included the importance of asking children about the strategies they used to approach tasks, cautions about self-fulfilling prophesies, cautions about over- and underinterpretations of the results, integrating reported problems with observation and assessment data, and the introduction of a *Levels of Processing Interpretative Model for School Neuropsychologists.*

TEST YOURSELF

1. **True or False? Most assessment specialists (e.g., school psychologists, educational diagnosticians, psychometrists) within the schools will stop at Level IV in their data analyses.**

2. **What is the term used to describe a child that believes he or she cannot perform well on a given task, even though there may be evidence to indicate that the child should perform well on the task?**
   a. Low self-esteem
   b. Major depression
   c. Confabulation
   d. Self-fulfilling prophecy

3. **Level III of the Levels of Processing Interpretative Model for School Neuropsychologists is related to analyzing?**
   a. Error analysis, informal samples, testing the limits, and so on.
   b. Qualitative performance data, supplemental scores, process data, and so on.
   c. Global Index/Factor Scores Only
   d. Neuropsychological interpretation of the data

4. **True or False? To apply a neuropsychological perspective to assessment data, a practitioner needs to understand brain-behavior relationships, theories of brain function, and the construct validity of the instruments used in evaluations.**

5. **In the case study Example #2, poor performance on the D-KEFS Trail-Making Test, Condition #4 (Number-Letter Switching) may be attributable to all of the following except?**
   a. Poor visual scanning
   b. Poor attentional processing skills

c. Poor long-term memory
d. Poor motivation

6. Level I of the Levels of Processing Interpretative Model for School Neuropsychologists is related to analyzing?

   a. Error analysis, informal samples, testing the limits, and so on.
   b. Qualitative performance data, supplemental scores, process data, and so on.
   c. Global Index/Factor Scores Only
   d. Neuropsychological interpretation of the data.

7. Level V of the Levels of Processing Interpretative Model for School Neuropsychologists is related to analyzing?

   a. Error analysis, informal samples, testing the limits, and so on.
   b. Qualitative performance data, supplemental scores, process data, and so on.
   c. Global Index/Factor Scores Only
   d. Neuropsychological interpretation of the data.

Answers: 1. false; 2. d; 3. b; 4. true; 5. c; 6. a; 7. d

Chapter Nine

CASE STUDY ILLUSTRATION

In this chapter a comprehensive school neuropsychological report is presented, which illustrates the component parts of the Integrated SNP/CHC Model. The case study is of a 16-year 7-month old male in high school who is being diagnosed with a nonverbal learning disability as a result of this evaluation.

SCHOOL NEUROPSYCHOLOGICAL EVALUATION

Identifying Information

Name of Student: John Doe
Age: 16 years 7 mos.
School: No Name High School
Parents: Mr. and Mrs. John Doe

Date of Birth: 05/02/1999
Ethnicity of Student: Caucasian
Grade: 10
Home Language: English

Reason for Referral

John's current language arts teacher expressed concerns regarding John's reading progress and difficulties with understanding and following certain directions/instructions. John struggles with reading words and understanding content, despite a strong work ethic and good effort. The special education teachers have followed up with skills testing using the READ 180 and Wilson Reading programs. Scores on these measures were very low, with John earning a 0% on the READ 180 Skills Survey. The teacher indicated that she has never had a student score a 0%. John's grades are very good, but are not reflective of having met grade level standards. Given John's continuing struggles with progressing academically, further investigation into possible neuropsychological contributors was deemed warranted.

Background Information

Family History

John is an only child living with both biological parents. The family has always lived in the surrounding metropolitan area. Mr. Doe is a plumber for an independent contractor with 2 years of college. Mrs. Doe earned her GED and she reported receiving special education services through junior high for difficulties with reading. Mrs. Doe has been a cafeteria worker for the school district for a number of years. The family is reportedly well adjusted with both parents and John confirmed a close relationship. According to his parents, John is rarely a discipline problem at home. His strengths are his level of patience and his willingness to try hard. Parents perceive his areas of difficulty being his lack of concentration and fine motor skills related to school. Parents also reported that John's mind frequently seems to wander.

Birth and Developmental History

John was born 1 month premature with low birth weight (4 lbs. 7oz.) and was jaundiced. He spent his first 10 days in the hospital due to an undeveloped sucking reflex and being fed with a tube, which continued for 4 days after going home. He crawled at 8 and a half months, walked at 13 months and was potty trained by 3 years of age. Parents reported that he had good gross motor skills, but experienced difficulties with fine motor skills, especially handwriting.

Health History

John suffered from high fevers (at times 104 degrees) as a toddler, and had ear infections and sinus headaches as a child. The frequency of the high fevers was not reported. No other illnesses were reported. John is nearsighted and has been wearing glasses since second grade. He takes no medications. There is a family history of diabetes, heart problems, and cancer.

Educational History

John has attended school in the No Name School District since beginning kindergarten. He attended one elementary school for grades Kindergarten through third grade, including a third grade retention. He was enrolled at a different elementary school in the district in fourth grade. The usual progression of schools through fifth and sixth grades and junior high was achieved. He received special education services beginning in first grade in the resource room for language arts and math. In junior high and high school, a special education study skills class was added. He also received speech/language therapy and occupational therapy until these services were discontinued in upper elementary grades. Currently four of seven of John's classes are in special education. Historically, teachers have reported that John has a tendency to become frustrated and will shut down for extended periods of time when he is upset. He is, and has been, a conscientious student, attempting to do his best. John typically seems to rush through tasks, appearing to be unaware of the quality of his work. This also is descriptive of his current approach to completing tasks when he does not know answers or is unsure as to how to proceed. His performance is much improved when he slows down with teacher-assisted cueing. John is intent on obtaining the credits needed to graduate with a regular high school diploma.

Educational Interventions (Response to Interventions)

John has been receiving special education services. These were READ 180 in eighth grade, Language Exclamation in ninth grade, repeating Level C of READ 180 during the first semester of the school year, and is currently placed in Wilson Reading and Step-Up-To-Writing programs. He is currently receiving math instruction in a Basic Math Class in the resource room, which addresses skills at a third to fourth grade equivalent. READ 180 was discontinued after achievement testing was conducted and indicated that the program did not match his auditory/verbal learning strengths. Even in special education, students progress through a predetermined schedule of classes, even if the grade is 1 percentage point above failing. If a class is failed, the student repeats that class. John has received accommodations from his regular education classes, which include extended time for assignment completion and test taking, having tests read aloud in a separate, quiet location such as the resource room, frequent comprehension checks, and the provision of class notes after effort has been demonstrated.

Previous Testing Results

A comprehensive school evaluation was last conducted when John was 9 years 8 months old and in his second year of third grade. The evaluation consisted of ability, achievement, speech/language, and perceptual motor assessment. Cognitive assessment yielded a significant difference between verbal and nonverbal ability on the *Wechsler Intelligence Scale for Children—Third Edition* (Verbal Comprehension Index = 92; Perceptual Organization Index = 56; Freedom from Distractibility = 72). Achievement testing with the *Woodcock Johnson Test of Achievement-III* showed academic skills to approximate grade expectancies in word identification, math calculation, and spelling. Areas of difficulty included reading comprehension, written expression, and math word problem solving. After results of this evaluation were obtained, additional assessment in reading was requested by John's parents. The reading subtests of the *Wechsler Individual Achievement Test-II* (WIAT-II) yielded scores significantly below grade expectancies and were deemed to be an underestimate of his true skill levels because he reportedly did not try as hard as he could have. Both receptive and expressive language skills were significantly delayed, as were fine motor skills. It was hypothesized that his performance was better on novel language tasks because his attention was more focused. The Child Study Committee (CSC) determined that additional information was needed to assist in determining eligibility for special education.

A neuropsychological evaluation by a clinical neuropsychologist was subsequently contracted for and conducted a few months later while John was still 9 years old. The NEPSY (first edition) yielded the following categorical results: Attention SS = 70; Language SS = 60; Sensorimotor SS = 57; Visual Spatial SS = 52; Memory SS = 61. Scores reflected his struggle with visual-spatial information, as well as difficulty dealing with complex verbal information. The clinical neuropsychologist made the following *DSM-IV* diagnoses:

Axis I   ADHD—Inattentive type
Learning Disorder associated with nonverbal learning disability
Axis II   Borderline intellectual functioning
Axis III   History of ear infections, high fevers
Axis IV   Learning problems

Current Assessment Instruments and Procedures

- Record Review, Parent Interview, Teacher Reports, Student Interview, & Classroom Observations.
- Conners Comprehensive Behavior Rating Scales (Conner's CBRS)
- Delis-Kaplan Executive Function System (D-KEFS)—Selected Subtests
- Developmental Test of Neuropsychological Assessment—Second Edition (NEPSY-2)
- Neuropsychological Processing Concerns Checklist for School Age Children and Youth—Second Edition (NPCC-2)
- Test of Memory and Learning—Second Edition (TOMAL-2)
- Woodcock-Johnson III, Tests of Achievement (WJIII-ACH) Normative Update
- Woodcock-Johnson III, Tests of Cognitive Abilities (WJIII-COG) Normative Update

Assessment Validity

At one point during the administration of the WJIII-ACH, testing was discontinued because it appeared that John was not putting forth optimal effort. This was based on his consistent approach to problem solving where he would rush through all items appearing not to give any thought to answers he provided. He was able to answer the beginning items of subtests; however, his rapid pace of responding did not vary as items increased in difficulty, answering all items without regard to whether his responses were related to the test items. It was explained to him that testing would resume later and the reason for stopping was to attempt to obtain valid results. He was informed that in no way was this meant to be punitive. Teachers and parent reported that John was upset about this for the entire day, remaining upset after he came home from school. On checking with teachers it was revealed that John frequently rushes through work and will slow down only when prompted, which does not consistently result in improved performance. After resuming testing the following day, John made an initial attempt to be more reflective, but this did not last throughout the remainder of testing. It appeared that John placed more value on rapidly completing the entirety of a task, rather than risking not completing a task by taking his time and examining his responses. Given the input from teachers, his behavior is not likely to have adversely affected test results.

Evaluation Results

Performance levels for all tests administered will be reported according to the following scale:

I. Classroom Observations

John was observed in his U.S. History class. It is a full class that includes the classroom teacher, the English Language Learner (ELL) teacher, a special education aide, and two ELL aides. There was much talking and commotion in the class, as well as a great deal of off-task behavior from several students. The CNN Student News Clip was shown at the beginning of the class. John, sitting in the front desk of one of five short rows facing the center of the room, was scribbling, coloring on paper, and only occasionally watching the clip when something appeared to spark his interest. He did not immediately begin working on his map, as directed by the teacher, after the clip ended, but neither did most of the other students. John accomplished little during the class period, because he spent the majority of the time soliciting help from both the teacher and the special education aide. He did attempt to complete a part of his map for a few minutes immediately following each individualized explanation. John frequently rubbed his head and eyes in apparent frustration and confusion. At one point he talked with his teacher about leaving out part of the assignment

Table 9.1.

STANDARD SCORE	SCALED SCORE	% RANK	NORMATIVE CLASSIFICATION	PROFICIENCY CLASSIFICATION	NEPSY-II SCALED SCORE	NEPSY-II % RANK	NORMATIVE CLASSIFICATION	PROFICIENCY CLASSIFICATION
> 129	> 16	> 98%	Superior	Markedly advanced	13–19	> 75	Above expected	Very proficient to markedly advanced
121–129	15	92–98	Well above expected	Advanced				
111–120	13–14	76–91	Above expected	Very proficient				
90–110	8–12	25–75	At expected	Proficient	8–12	26–75	At expected	Proficient
80–89	6–7	9–24	Slightly below expected	Inefficient	6–7	11–25	Slightly below expected	Inefficient

and was told that he would receive only partial credit, but also that the information would be needed for the upcoming test the following week. Class notes were disseminated to several students, including John who mentioned to the teacher and the aide that he had lost previous notes.

The teacher indicated that John does not understand concepts and needs everything to be explained to him. If it were not for the special education aide, he would be totally lost. John does leave the room to take tests and to have them read aloud for him. John expressed great frustration with the noise level in the class and how it interferes with his concentration. He mostly does not understand the information that is presented.

II. Basic Sensorimotor Functions

Sensory functions encompass our ability to process visual, auditory, kinesthetic, and olfactory information. Dysfunction in any single sensory system can have a dramatic effect on a student's learning capabilities and behavioral regulation. **Motor functions** encompass both fine motor skills (e.g., picking up or manipulating small objects, holding a pencil correctly, buttoning a button) and gross

Table 9.2.

Sensorimotor Functions	Mild	Moderate	Severe
Auditory Functioning			
• Does not like loud noises.	P	T	
Motor Functions	**Mild**	**Moderate**	**Severe**
Motor functioning **Circle right (R), left (L) or both right and left (B) as applicable**			
• Poor fine motor skills (e.g., using a pencil). (L)		P T	

motor skills (e.g., walking in a balanced and coordinated manner, running, jumping, riding a bike).

Presenting concerns. The *Neuropsychological Processing Concerns Checklist for School-Aged Children & Youth—Second Edition* (NPCC-2) was completed by Mr. Doe [parent] and John's special education teacher. Current Sensory presenting concerns on the NPCC were as follows (T = teacher, P = parent):

John's teacher reported that he will isolate himself from peers in the classroom when working independently, especially when there is much chatter and commotion occurring. Mr. Doe noted that John has fewer noise interferences at home. John enjoys hunting and is around guns frequently, which reportedly does not bother him. It is only when he needs to concentrate on academic tasks that he requires less noise according to his father. Both parent and teacher perceive fine motor skills, especially as related to handwriting, to be a moderate difficulty.

Current levels of functioning. On the NEPSY-II Design Copying subtest John was asked to copy a number of increasingly more detailed and complex designs in a box beneath each design. He drew each design rapidly appearing not to take particular care as to the appearance of the designs. The low Design Copying Process Motor score indicates that difficulties with motor control interfere with accuracy of drawing. Poor fine motor coordination also adversely affects the accuracy of his graphomotor output. John commented that copying the designs was hard, especially as the designs became more detailed. He appeared to have little concern for the quality of his drawings as evidenced by lines that were not straight and crowding of details within the boundaries of designs. This impulsive approach to task completion has been noted on other tasks, as well as for completion of assignments in the classroom. Although he was able to recognize the overall configuration of the designs his difficulties with fine motor skills appear to impact

Table 9.3. Sensorimotor Functions

Instrument—Subtest: Description	Well Below Expected Level	Below Expected Level	Slightly Below Expected Level	At Expected Level	Above Expected Level	Well Above Expected Level	Superior
Visual-Motor Integration Skills							
NEPSY-II—Design copying general score: Copying simple to complex designs on paper.		*2–5*					
NEPSY-II—Design copy process total: The fine motor contribution to the overall visual-motor task.	(1)						
• **Design copying process motor:** This score represents the motor output portion of the overall score.	(3)						
• **Design copying process global:** Ability to recognize the overall configuration of the design.	(1)						
• **Design copying process local:** Ability to recognize details of the design.	(3)						
Visual Scanning/Tracking: Direct Measure							
D-KEFS—Trail making condition 1 (visual scanning): Marking all the Number 3s on a page as quickly as possible.					(10)		
Visual Scanning/Tracking: Indirect Measures							
NEPSY-II—Picture puzzles total: A large picture divided by a grid with four smaller pictures taken from sections of the larger picture is presented. The student identifies the location on the grid of the larger picture from which each of the smaller pictures was taken.	(1)						

Note: Standard scores appear in normal font. Scaled scores appear in (parentheses). Percentile ranks of any kind appear in *italics*.

his ability to correctly reproduce them. He did not consistently connect lines within designs and shapes were disproportionately drawn with regard to dimension and location indicating poor visuospatial ability. His speed of production may also have negatively impacted the quality of his drawings. These results have implications for his poor handwriting skills in relation to letter formation and spacing between letters and words. Consequently, copying from the board or book to paper will likely be difficult, as will expressing his thoughts or ideas on paper.

John does well when there are limited stimuli for which he needs to perform an operation, such as in Trail Making Condition 1. However, as detail and spatial orientation are added, visual scanning becomes far more difficult, and his ability to discern detail becomes impaired. In the classroom, finding information in passages with small print, or completing many math problems on a page could be overwhelming for John.

Sensorimotor functioning summary. John's father and the resource room teacher noted that noise interferences for John are directly proportional to the amount of work completion evidenced. Handwriting is an area of concern for both parties. Test results substantiate these concerns with regard to the speed and accuracy of motor output. As the complexity and amount of material increases the accuracy of his reproductions decreases. Legibility of handwriting or production of maps, for example, will be adversely affected with the increase of material required to be written or drawn. He will also require more time to complete tasks requiring increased amount of material. John will perform better when auditory distractions are minimized or when he is able to work in a quiet location away from noise in the regular classroom environment.

III. Cognitive Processes: Visuospatial Processes

For the purposes of this report, visual-spatial processes include *visual spatial perception* and *visual spatial reasoning*.

Presenting concerns. On the *Neuropsychological Processing Concerns Checklist for School-Aged Children & Youth—Second Edition* (NPCC-2) John's father and teacher reported the following concerns. John's father has ongoing concerns regarding John's handwriting, which the father relates to his perception that John experiences difficulty in copying notes from the board. He indicated that John tries to copy notes from the board quickly, which interferes with legibility. John's teacher sees mild difficulties here, primarily because he is given copies of notes allowing him to copy notes from the board at a more comfortable pace and reducing any stress related to being able to get down everything he needs to copy. Drawing and activities with puzzles are not a priority at school and thus are not observed. Both parent and teacher have concerns with handwriting legibility.

Table 9.4. Visuospatial Perception

Instrument—Subtest: Description	Well Below Expected Level	Below Expected Level	Slightly Below Expected Level	At Expected Level	Above Expected Level	Well Above Expected Level	Superior
Visual Discrimination and Spatial Localization							
NEPSY-II—Arrows total: Two arrows from many are chosen by letter label, which are thought to point to the center of the target.	(1)						
NEPSY-II—Picture puzzles total: A large picture divided by a grid with four smaller pictures taken from sections of the larger picture is presented. The student identifies the location on the grid of the larger picture from which each of the smaller pictures was taken.	(1)						

Note: Standard scores appear in normal font. Scaled scores appear in (parentheses). Percentile rank ranges appear in *italics*.

Current levels of functioning. John required repetition of the directions for the Arrows task, and even after three repetitions, he demonstrated limited reflection responding almost immediately with each presentation. He was required to find two lines from an array of lines, which pointed to the middle of a circle. Despite his seemingly impulsive approach, he was generally able to accurately identify one of the two lines. His low score does suggest poor visuospatial skills in judging line orientation. John's struggle with identifying geometric shapes requiring some degree of mental rotation is a weakness. Again, he was generally able to identify one of two required responses, despite demonstrating little reflection. Sustained attention and attentional capacity were problematic, since he quickly lost interest in this task. Part/whole visual perception and separating figure from ground within pictures is problematic. This was evidenced by his low score on Picture Puzzles where he was shown pictures of objects and landscapes then asked to correctly position specified parts of these on a grid. John did not enjoy this task, and as the details within the pictures increased he began to indiscriminately and inaccurately choose places on the grid. His performance here appears to be related to difficulties with attentional capacity

Table 9.5. Visuospatial Reasoning

Instrument—Subtest: Description	Well Below Expected Level	Below Expected Level	Slightly Below Expected Level	At Expected Level	Above Expected Level	Well Above Expected Level	Superior
Recognizing Spatial Configurations							
WJIII-COG—Spatial relations: Identify two or more pieces that go together to form a complete target shape.	60						
Visuospatial Analyses with and without Mental Rotations							
NEPSY-II—Geometric puzzles total: A picture of a large grid containing several shapes is presented, then the student matches two shapes outside of the grid to two shapes within the grid.	(1)						

Note: Standard scores appear in normal font. Scaled scores appear in (parentheses). Percentile rank ranges appear in *italics*.

as well as cognitive overload. John does experience difficulty in perceiving connections between parts when removed from a whole.

Summary of visual-spatial functioning. Visual perception appears to be intact for John; however, as visual complexities increase he experiences difficulty in perceiving and recalling details, which ultimately leads to problems with correct spatial positioning. Although he strives to maintain speed, the degree of accuracy suffers. There was little difference between his visual perception with and without motor involvement, although the fact that he was often able to recognize one of the required two correct responses on subtests requiring this, suggests that perceptual flexibility may be limited. Difficulties with spatial positioning may be influential here, which has implications for his difficulties in recreating details within designs. Not only will legibility of handwriting be problematic due to incorrect letter formation, but reading comprehension and written expression will likely be adversely affected, as well. John will have difficulties finding information in text to answer questions. The act of handwriting will become laborious causing him to focus more effort on putting words on paper, rather than on the content of what he writes.

Table 9.6. Auditory/Phonological Processing

Instrument—Subtest: Description	Well Below Expected Level	Below Expected Level	Slightly Below Expected Level	At Expected Level	Above Expected Level	Well Above Expected Level	Superior
WJIII-ACH NU—Sound awareness: Rhyming, deletion, substitution, and reversal of phonemes.						124	
WJIII-COG NU—Incomplete words: Listening to a word with one or more missing phonemes and then identifying the whole word.				103			
WJIII-COG NU—Sound blending: Blending sounds to form a whole word.					118		

Note: Standard scores appear in normal font. Scaled scores appear in (parentheses). Percentile rank ranges appear in *italics.*

III. Cognitive Processes: Auditory Processing

We live in a highly verbal society; therefore, language skills are necessary for successful academic and behavioral functioning in school-age children.

Presenting concerns. On the *Neuropsychological Processing Concerns Checklist for School-Aged Children & Youth—Second Edition* (NPCC-2) John's father and teacher did not report any concerns in this area.

Current levels of functioning. John's major strength is his knowledge of letter sounds and letter combinations for forming whole words. His skills are above expected level in these areas. John does prefer to read aloud, or whisper to himself as he reads because he recognizes words more readily if he hears that his pronunciations sound like words he knows. Allowing him to do this in the classroom by providing a study carrel or seating at a distance away from other students will facilitate more accurate reading of passages.

Summary of language functioning. Phonological processing is an outstanding strength for John, especially for sound awareness and sound blending.

Table 9.7. Memory and Learning Functions

	Mild	Moderate	Severe
General learning efficiency			
• Difficulty learning verbal information.		T	P
• Difficulty learning visual information.	T		
• Difficulty integrating verbal and visual information.	T		
Long-term memory difficulties			
• Forgets where personal items or school work were left.	T		
• Forgets to turn in homework assignments.	T P		
• Forgets what happened days or weeks ago.			T

III. Cognitive Processes: Learning and Memory

Presenting concerns. On the *Neuropsychological Processing Concerns Checklist for School-Aged Children & Youth—Second Edition* (NPCC-2) John's father and teacher reported significant concerns regarding Memory and Learning functions.

Many concerns were noted by John's teachers regarding memory and learning functions, with fewer, although severe concerns, also noted by John's father. Difficulties with long-term memory impact his recollection of math facts and procedures, forgetting details of events, which occurred in the past, and forgetting to turn in assignments. Although he is noted to have difficulty with both, John's teacher indicates that he struggles more with learning verbal information than with visual information. Integrating verbal and visual information is mildly difficult for John according to his teacher.

Current levels of functioning

1. Overall memory index scores. The assessment data indicates that there is a similar development between verbal and nonverbal memory indices. John is better able to recall information immediately after presentation, than he is able to recall the same information after a time delay. This suggests that many verbal repetitions and information presented in sequence will facilitate recall. This requires a higher order of cognitive processing and integration. Associative memory is a relative strength for John and helps to explain how he remembers any type of information. Associations provide a cognitive link, whether visual or

Table 9.8. TOMAL-2 Memory Indices

Index	Well Below Expected Level	Below Expected Level	Slightly Below Expected Level	At Expected Level	Above Expected Level	Well Above Expected Level	Superior
Verbal memory index		76					
Nonverbal memory index		74					
Verbal delayed recall index	66						
Composite memory index		75					
Supplemental indices							
Sequential recall index			83				
Free recall index	58						
Associative recall index			82				
Learning index		70					

Note: Standard scores appear in normal font. Scaled scores appear in (parentheses). Percentile rank ran.es appear in *italics*.

verbal that aids in retrieval. In contrast, the Free Recall Index represents his struggle to consolidate information into memory when there are no links provided. Because memory is a pervasive weakness for John, his Learning Index is below expected level. He will require the presentation of smaller chunks of information over an extended period of time.

2. *Rate of learning*

Figure 9.1 illustrates the benefit that John received from verbal reminders of words he forgot when recalling a list of twelve words over eight trials. He did not recall as many words as subjects in the normative sample for his age. His rate of learning was relatively comparable to that for the normative sample with a gradual upward slope, indicating benefit from reminders. By Trial 6 John had reached attentional capacity and he was able to recall only one more word without reminders as he had for Trial 1. His learning rate is slow, but steady until he reaches cognitive overload at which point his learning rate decreases. John demonstrates this in the classroom when he can encode information to a certain point, then reaches his limits. Frequent breaks may refresh his ability to benefit from instruction over an extended period of time.

Table 9.9. Rate of Learning

Instrument—Subtest: Description	Well Below Expected Level	Below Expected Level	Slightly Below Expected Level	At Expected Level	Above Expected Level	Well Above Expected Level	Superior
Verbal Learning							
TOMAL-2—Word selective reminding: Learning a list of words then repeating it, and then only reminded of words left out.	(5)						

Note: Standard scores appear in normal font. Scaled scores appear in (parentheses). Percentile rank ranges appear in *italics*.

3. Verbal immediate versus visual immediate memory. John struggles with both verbal and visual immediate memory, with or without context. Recalling factual information appears to be more problematic than fictional information, perhaps due to the interest level, or to the ability to better comprehend that which is presented. The more information presented the less he seems able to recall. The combination of visual, verbal, and motor associations may account for his average score for manual imitation. In the classroom, information to be remembered should be presented in smaller chunks. Using a multisensory presentation and presenting information in more than one way may also facilitate immediate memory.

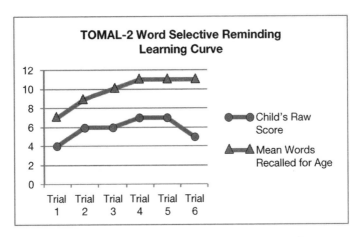

Figure 9.1. TOMAL-2 Word Selective Reminding Learning Curve

Table 9.10. Immediate Verbal Memory

Instrument—Subtest: Description	Well Below Expected Level	Below Expected Level	Slightly Below Expected Level	At Expected Level	Above Expected Level	Well Above Expected Level	Superior
Letter Recall (No Contextual Cues)							
TOMAL-2—Letters forward: Repeating a string of letters spoken by the examiner.			(7)				
Number Recall (No Contextual Cues)							
TOMAL-2—Digits forward: Repeating a string of digits spoken by the examiner.		(5)					
Word Recall (No Contextual Cues)							
TOMAL-2—Word selective reminding: Learning a list of words then repeating it, and then only reminded of words left out.		(5)					
Story Recall (With Contextual Cues)							
NEPSY-II—Narrative memory free recall: Details recalled from verbally presented stories.	(2)						
• NEPSY-II—Narrative memory recognition: Details recognized from verbally presented stories.		(4)					
• NEPSY-II—Narrative memory free and cued recall: Details recalled freely and with cues from verbally presented stories.		(4)					
TOMAL-2—Memory for stories: Details recalled from verbally presented stories.			(7)				

WJIII-ACH—Story recall: Details recalled from verbally presented stories.		79					
Immediate Visual Memory							
Abstract Designs With Verbal Response (No Contextual Cues)							
TOMAL-2—Abstract visual memory: Recalling geometric designs when order is not important.	(1)						
TOMAL-2—Visual sequential memory: Recalling a sequence of geometric designs.		(6)					
Faces with Verbal or Pointing Response (No Contextual Cues)							
TOMAL-2—Facial memory: Recognition and identification of faces.		(4)					
Spatial Locations with Motor Response (No Contextual Cues)							
TOMAL-2—Memory for locations: Remembering the locations of dots on a page.		(6)					
TOMAL-2—Visual selective reminding: Learning a pattern of dots then repeating it, and then only reminded of the dots left out.		(6)					
Visual Sequences Imitation with Motor Response (No Contextual Cues)							
TOMAL-2—Manual imitations: Copying the examiner's precise sequence of taps on the table.			(9)				

Note: Standard scores appear in normal font. Scaled scores appear in (parentheses). Percentile ranks of any kind appear in *italics*.

4. *Delayed memory: Recall versus recognition.*

There is little difference between verbal immediate and delayed memory recall. A strength was demonstrated when John imitated hand movements presented by the examiner. The auditory association of the hand movements tapped on the table with the presence of gross motor functioning may provide an association for recall. Abstract visual immediate memory is well below expected level suggesting that he may be better able to recall more concrete information. He does not benefit from

Table 9.11. Delayed Memory

Instrument—Subtest: Description	Well Below Expected Level	Below Expected Level	Slightly Below Expected Level	At Expected Level	Above Expected Level	Well Above Expected Level	Superior
Verbal Delayed Recall (Without Context)							
TOMAL-2—Word selective reminding delayed: Delayed recall of the words learned in the Word selective reminding task.		(5)					
Verbal Delayed Recall (With Context)							
TOMAL-2—Memory for stories delayed: Delayed recall of story details.			(3)				

Note: Standard scores appear in normal font. Scaled scores appear in (parentheses). Percentile ranks of any kind appear in *italics.*

added context, placement of objects on a page, or sequenced information. Recall is facilitated when John needs to recall smaller chunks of information. Delayed memory is below expected level. Neither consistently provided reminders, nor added context, assist with information retrieval. Immediate and delayed memory deficits will be most noticeable when John takes tests requiring him to recall greater amounts of information presented over time. Performance will be enhanced if smaller chunks of material are presented over a shorter amount of time.

5. *Verbal-visual associative learning and recall.* John struggled with associating symbols for words in the absence of seeing the words to "read" sentences. He required many reminders of the words that the symbols represented as he progressed from sentence to sentence. The repetition did not appear to be of benefit. He performed somewhat better when there was a resemblance of the symbol to the word, such as for horse. His ability to recall the associated words with the symbols diminished as sentences increased in length. Combining visual and verbal associations appears to create confusion for John. There were numerous errors on delayed recall as well, but he did remember many of the "words" representing the symbols. He may have difficulty with reading words that are spelled differently, but sound the same. Recalling phonetically irregular words may be difficult, as well.

Summary of memory functioning. These results present a comparison between the contributing factors of verbal and visual associations for assisting John with

Table 9.12. Verbal-Visual Associative Learning and Recall

Instrument—Subtest: Description	Well Below Expected Level	Below Expected Level	Slightly Below Expected Level	At Expected Level	Above Expected Level	Well Above Expected Level	Superior
Verbal-Visual Associative Learning							
TOMAL-2—Object recall: Recalling names associated with pictures.			(4)				
TOMAL-2—Paired recall: Recalling a list of paired words when the first word is provided by the examiner.				(7)			
WJIII-COG—Visual-auditory learning: Learning visual-verbal associations and then recalling them.		71					
Verbal-Visual Associative Delayed Recall							
WJIII-COG—Visual-auditory learning delayed: Recalling, after a delay, visual-verbal associations.		*4*					

Note: Standard scores appear in normal font. Scaled scores appear in (parentheses). Percentile ranks of any kind appear in *italics*.

understanding information presented to best consolidate that information into memory. He appears to be better able to attach meaning through words than through visuospatial processing. John is very much aware of difficulties with memory as evidenced by the following analogy which he volunteered: "I can't hardly remember the information . . . it's there for a few seconds . . . it's like the nickel with the dot in front of the zero in front of the five. That's how long it lasts then it's gone." This suggests that John is unable to remember information long enough to progress academically in any area at the same rate as his peers. Each aspect of memory assessed is below expected level and will significantly impact his ability to progress at a traditional rate to acquire credits for graduation. Teacher and parent concerns emphasize his need for repetition and reminders. He has trouble remembering multiple steps for problem solving and forgets details of past events. They do agree that verbal memory is stronger than visual memory.

IV. Cognitive Processes: Executive Functions

Executive functioning can be conceptualized into four broad areas: concept formation, problem solving and reasoning, qualitative behaviors, and behavioral/emotional regulation. Each of these broad areas has some relationship to the frontal lobes of the brain.

Presenting concerns. On the *Neuropsychological Processing Concerns Checklist for School-Aged Children & Youth—Second Edition* (NPCC-2) John's father and teacher noted the following behaviors:

Many concerns are noted by John's teacher regarding his difficulties with learning new concepts, learning from prior mistakes, organizational skills, time management, task initiation, impulsivity, irritability when frustrated and lack of common sense. John's father noted fewer concerns, but indicated that at home John has a set routine, and has parental guidance for most activities. John's ability to shift attention from one activity to another, although less problematic, has implications for difficulties in learning from prior experience.

Current Levels of Functioning

1. Cognitive flexibility or set shifting. On the D-KEFS Verbal Fluency test, John was able to produce only a few words that switched between two semantic categories, but he was able to switch the limited words he did produce. On the NEPSY-II Inhibition test, John was not able to switch between the natural inclination to name a circle a "circle" rather than call it a "square" and vice versa. On the D-KEFS Trail-Making test, his ability to switch between letters and numbers was poor due to limited letter sequencing abilities and limited motor output fluency.

The low score for response set total correct reflects poor sustained attention during high cognitive load and multitasking in working memory. This suggests greater difficulties with the ability to shift attentional focus. As the cognitive requirements increase, John becomes more impulsive with his responding and attends less to stimulus content. John experiences difficulty with more complex mental processes. John will benefit from explicit instruction for one concept at a time.

2. Problem solving and reasoning. John's ability to identify, categorize, and determine rules for problem solving (inductive reasoning) and to analyze puzzles using symbolic formulations to determine missing parts (deductive reasoning) was very poor. John did not appear to understand the nature of Analysis/

Table 9.13. Executive Functions

	Mild	Moderate	Severe
Shifting or divided attention difficulties			
• Gets stuck on one activity (e.g., playing video games).	T		
• Difficulty transitioning from one activity to another.	T		
Planning difficulties			
• Difficulty making plans.	T		
• Quickly becomes frustrated and gives up easily.			T
• Difficulty sticking to a plan of action.	T		
Problem solving and organizing difficulties			
• Difficulty solving problems that a younger child can do.	T		
• Difficulty learning new concepts or activities.	P	T	
• Makes the same kinds of errors over and over, even after corrections.	P	T	
Behavioral/emotional regulation			
• Demonstrates signs of overactivity (hyperactivity).	T		
• Does not seem to think before acting.	P T		
• Difficulty following rules.	T		
• Demonstrates signs of irritability.	P	T	
• Lack of common sense or judgment.	T		

Synthesis and he impulsively provided any response. John tends to sacrifice accuracy for speed resulting in inefficient processing of information. Despite completing academic tasks rapidly, John will likely exhibit a lack understanding for content.

3. Response inhibition. John was focused primarily on showing how quickly he could complete the inhibition tasks. He commented that the tasks would be

Table 9.14. Shifting Attention

Instrument—Subtest: Description	Well Below Expected Level	Below Expected Level	Slightly Below Expected Level	At Expected Level	Above Expected Level	Well Above Expected Level	Superior
Verbal Shifting Attention							
D-KEFS—Color-word interference condition 4—Inhibition/switching: Child switches back and forth between naming the dissonant ink colors and reading the words.				(7)			
D-KEFS—Verbal fluency condition 3—Category switching: Total correct responses: Switching between verbalizing fruits and pieces of furniture.			(6)				
• **Verbal fluency condition 3—Category switching total switching accuracy:** The correct number of switches between verbal categories.						100	
NEPSY-II—Inhibition: Switching combined: Rapidly and accurately name shapes while switching cognitive sets.	(3)						
• **Switching total completion time:** How quickly the task was completed (slower time = lower scaled score).		(4)					
• **Switching total errors:** Total errors made on the task (more errors = lower % rank).			2–5				
• **Switching uncorrected errors:** Errors with no attempt to correct (more errors = lower % rank).	< 2						
• **Switching self-corrected errors:** Errors that were self-corrected (more self-corrections = lower % rank).				51–75			

Visual Shifting Attention						
D-KEFS—Trails condition 4—Number-letter switching: A psychomotor task which requires switching between number and letter sequences (e.g., 1-A-2-B . . .).	(2)					
• **Trail-making condition 1 (visual scanning):** All of the number 3s on a page are marked as quickly as possible.				(10)		
• **Trail-making condition 2 (number sequencing):** Quickly connecting lines between consecutive numbers.				(11)		
• **Trail-making condition 3 (letter sequencing):** Quickly connecting lines between sequential letters.	(1)					
• **Trail-making conditions 2 and 3 combined:** Time taken across number and letter trials.		(6)				
• **Trail making condition 5—Motor speed:** Tracing a dotted line as quickly as possible.		(6)				
Verbal and Visual Shifting Attention						
NEPSY-II—AARS—Response set combined score: Added shifting of attention while selectively responding to auditory target words while ignoring auditory nontarget words over time.		(5)				
• **Response set total commission errors:** Responding to nontarget words that were to be ignored.			*11–25*			
• **Response set total correct:** Responding correctly to target words.		*2–5*				
• **Response set total omission errors:** Missing target words.			*11–25*			
• **Response set total inhibitory errors:** Ignoring distracter words.				*26–50*		

Note: Standard scores appear in normal font. Scaled scores appear in (parentheses). Percentile ranks of any kind appear in *italics*.

Table 9.15. Problem Solving, Planning, and Reasoning

Instrument—Subtest: Description	Well Below Expected Level	Below Expected Level	Slightly Below Expected Level	At Expected Level	Above Expected Level	Well Above Expected Level	Superior
Inductive Reasoning							
WJIII-COG—Concept formation: Categorical reasoning and inductive logic.		71					
Sequential Reasoning							
WJIII-COG—Analysis/synthesis: General sequential (deductive) reasoning.		53					

Note: Standard scores appear in normal font. Scaled scores appear in (parentheses). Percentile ranks of any kind appear in *italics*.

easy, because he did not have to read anything. His low scores are generally reflective of uncorrected errors. It was as if he had built up a momentum and just "plowed through" as quickly as he could. On the Inhibition tasks he self-corrected only two errors. He made considerably more errors when required to switch between naming shapes/arrow directions to indicating the opposite of these. He demonstrated impulsive responding, and poor self-monitoring. His performance was better on the Color-Word Naming Inhibition task, seeming to be more focused on the accuracy of his responses. Cognitive flexibility appears to be an area of difficulty. John's teacher and observations during testing indicate that John has a tendency to rush through tasks often, which does result in incorrect answers and limited understanding of concepts.

Summary of executive functioning. John appears to be more reflective and takes more time to examine components of tasks when there are fewer cognitive demands. He responds rapidly and impulsively when overwhelmed with complex tasks, causing him to rush through things just to be done. He is more concerned with finishing an activity without regard to how well it is completed or whether he has understood how to do it or what knowledge can be gained. He does not take the time to plan strategies for problem solving and quickly becomes frustrated when expected to think things through. Visual and auditory distracters interfere

Table 9.16. Response Inhibition

Instrument—Subtest: Description	Well Below Expected Level	Below Expected Level	Slightly Below Expected Level	At Expected Level	Above Expected Level	Well Above Expected Level	Superior
Verbal Response Inhibition							
D-KEFS—Color-word naming condition 3 (inhibition): Rapidly naming the color of the ink a color word ("red") is printed in. An inhibitory task.			(7)				
NEPSY-II—Inhibition combined: Rapidly and accurately naming the opposite names of shapes (e.g., "circle" for "square").	(3)						
• **Inhibition total completion time:** How quickly the task was completed.	(3)						
• **Inhibition total errors:** Total errors made on the task.	(3)						
• **Inhibition uncorrected errors:** Errors with no attempt to correct.	< 2						
• **Inhibition self-corrected errors:** Errors that were self-corrected.			*11–25*				

Note: Standard scores appear in normal font. Scaled scores appear in (parentheses). Percentile ranks of any kind appear in *italics*.

with remembering directions once he encounters difficulty, which also inhibits retrieval of information from memory. He does not learn from previous errors, such that he cannot generate different strategies for solving the same problem. His mind tends to wander, as indicated by parents as being historically problematic. He has trouble organizing his thoughts and his time in relation to developing a plan for completing tasks with accuracy. John would benefit from being taught self- monitoring techniques to include more focus on information processing speed rather than task completion speed.

V. Cognitive Facilitators: Allocating and Maintaining Attention

Attention is a complex and multifaceted construct used when an individual must focus on certain stimuli for information processing. To regulate thinking and to complete tasks of daily living such as schoolwork, it is necessary to be able to attend to both auditory and visual stimuli in the environment. Attention can be viewed as a facilitator for all other higher-order processing. In other words, if attention is compromised it can adversely affect the other cognitive processes of language, memory, visuospatial skills, and so on. Attention can be divided into four subareas: selective/focused attention, shifting attention, sustained attention, and attentional capacity. The test results will be reported broken down into those subtypes of attentional processing.

Selective/focused attention refers to the ability to pay attention to relevant information while ignoring irrelevant information. An example of selective/focused attention would be the child's ability to pay attention to only the classroom teacher when there is the noise and the visual distracters of the classroom to ignore. *Shifting attention* refers to the ability to maintain mental flexibility in order to shift from one task to another. Some children get stuck "in one gear" and cannot easily change from one activity to another. Completing a math worksheet that has both addition and subtraction problems on the same page requires the child to shift attention between the addition and subtraction problems. *Sustained attention* refers to the ability to maintain an attention span over a prolonged period of time. *Attentional capacity* refers to the child's ability to recall information ranging from small chunks (e.g., a string of numbers or letters), to larger chunks of information (e.g., list of unrelated words or sentences of increasing length and complexity), and to even larger semantically complex chunks of information (e.g., memory for stories).

Presenting concerns. The *Neuropsychological Processing Concerns Checklist for School-Aged Children & Youth—Second Edition* (NPCC-2) John's father and his special education teacher reported that John experiences difficulties with all aspects of attention. Perceptions of the degree of difficulty that John experiences are illustrated in the chart below.

John's teacher appears to have more concerns regarding all aspects of attention as defined in the introduction to this section. Each aspect of attention is required for academic and social success. John is perceived to be distracted by environmental sensory stimuli. This was particularly evident during the classroom observation in his history class. He demonstrates a short attention span and loses track of what is being discussed or may not know where to read when called on. Only John's teacher noted moderate concerns with his ability to pay attention to more than one thing at a time, such as taking notes while listening for key concepts as teachers lecture. Finally, attentional capacity is viewed by both parent and teacher as being a

Table 9.17. Attention Problems

	Mild	Moderate	Severe
Selective or sustained attention difficulties			
• Seems to get overwhelmed with difficult tasks.		T	P
• Difficulty paying attention for a long period of time.	P	T	
• Seems to lose place in an academic task (e.g., reading, writing, math).		T	
• Mind appears to go blank or loses train of thought.		T P	
• Inattentive to details or makes careless mistakes.		P T	

significant area of difficulty. He becomes tired and overwhelmed when information to be learned or retrieved from memory requires effort. As John commented in relation to completing certain tasks during testing, "my brain hurts."

Current levels of functioning.
1. Selective/focused and sustained attention.

John did appear to enjoy the tasks comprising each of these subtests. Auditory selective and sustained attention appears to be a relative strength for John when the tasks are reduced to one or two requirements. He needed to point to color shapes in a specified sequence presented verbally. He did well despite the addition of distracters added to the directions. He performed similarly on a task requiring him to peruse a number of small pictures on a page and to circle as many of a particular pair of pictures as he could find within a time limit. With both tasks the objective was clear; the motor output was minimal, requiring only pointing and circling pictures with a pencil. There was minimal environmental noise to interfere with concentration. John made few errors and only twice looked up from the auditory attention tasks on the NEPSY II. The novelty of the Auditory Attention task was interesting and challenging for him contributing to his ability to focus and sustain attention for a limited amount of time.

His performance on the Pair Cancellation subtest where he was required to circle as quickly as possible, all of the pairs of a ball and a puppy occurring together did contain several errors. John finished three seconds before the three minutes allotted was concluded, but he had five omission errors. There were no incorrect pairs circled.

Table 9.18. Selective/Focused and Sustained Attention

Instrument—Subtest: Description	Selective	Sustained	Well Below Expected Level	Below Expected Level	Slightly Below Expected Level	At Expected Level	Above Expected Level	Well Above Expected Level	Superior
Auditory Selective/Focused and Sustained Attention									
NEPSY-II—Auditory attention combined: Selectively responding to auditory target words while ignoring auditory nontarget words over time.	X	X				(8)			
• **Auditory attention commission errors:** Responding to nontarget words that were to be ignored.	X	X				*26–50*			
• **Auditory attention total correct:** Responding correctly to target words.	X	X			*11–25*				
• **Auditory attention total omission errors:** Missing target words.	X	X			*11–25*				
• **Auditory attention total inhibitory errors:** Ignoring distracter words.	X					*26–50*			
Visual Selective/Focused and Sustained Attention									
WJIII-COG—Pair cancellation: Matching target stimuli from a large visual array under time constraints.		X				82			

Note: Standard scores appear in normal font. Scaled scores appear in (parentheses). Percentile ranks of any kind appear in *italics*.

2. Attentional capacity.

John's attentional capacity is diminished as the cognitive load increases. The addition of more information that needs to be retrieved appears to interfere with his ability to recall details. As noted by his parents and teacher, he tends to become overwhelmed with tasks containing too many details. He consequently avoids tasks that require a great deal of mental effort. Analogies or stories provided to assist with recalling information may be more interfering for him unless the content is brief and specifically related to the information. He will require much repetition to consolidate information into memory.

Summary of the cognitive facilitator of attentional processing. Auditory attention is an area of strength for John as long as environmental distractions and motor output are minimized. His speed and accuracy of responses is average to

Table 9.19. Attentional Capacity

Instrument—Subtest: Description	Well Below Expected Level	Below Expected Level	Slightly Below Expected Level	At Expected Level	Above Expected Level	Well Above Expected Level	Superior
Memory for Numbers, Letters, or Visual Sequences							
TOMAL-2—Digits forward: Repeating auditorially presented digits of increasing length.		(5)					
TOMAL-2—Letters forward: Repeating auditorially presented letters of increasing length.			(8)				
Attentional Capacity for Stories (With Contextual Meaning)							
NEPSY-II—Narrative memory free recall: Recalling verbally presented story details.	(2)						
TOMAL-2—Memory for stories: Recalling verbally presented story details.		(5)					
WJIII-ACH—Story recall: Recalling verbally presented story details.		79					

Note: Standard scores appear in normal font. Scaled scores appear in (parentheses). Percentile ranks of any kind appear in *italics*.

slightly below average given these conditions. The visual attention required for pair cancellation demonstrates a relative strength in focused and selective attention when auditory distracters are eliminated. Auditory working memory is also a relative strength in the absence of distracters, although as the cognitive load increases he makes more errors. As John reaches his attentional capacity limits, his focused, selective, and sustained attention diminishes. These factors relate to parent and teacher concerns regarding the increase of errors when auditory distractions increase, as well as difficulties in paying attention for long periods of time when cognitive load increases. The hyperactive behaviors noted by his parent and teacher are related to cognitive inattention more so than an acting out behavioral inattention. John will tend to rush through tasks in an effort to "fake good." He will do this to look like he has understood what is required, but he has difficulty sustaining attention due to stretching his attentional capacity. His ability to retrieve information will be impaired as well.

VI. Cognitive Facilitators: Working Memory

Working memory is the active manipulation of information that is being held in immediate memory or information recalled from long-term memory. Working memory is classified as a cognitive facilitator because it is used frequently to help process higher order cognitive and academic tasks. Working memory can be measured using verbal or visual stimuli.

Presenting concerns. On the *Neuropsychological Processing Concerns Checklist for School-Aged Children & Youth—Second Edition* (NPCC-2) John's father and teacher reported significant concerns regarding Memory and Learning functions.

With regard to working memory, John requires many repetitions to follow directions, forgets information right after being presented, and has trouble remembering multistep directions. He does not remember steps involved with completing tasks, such as solving a math problem, and has trouble with summarizing narrative information.

Current levels of functioning.

Summary of the cognitive facilitator of working memory. John was less engaged in the tasks for the TOMAL-2. By this time he was beginning to tire of being tested. He immediately responded with a string of numbers after hearing them, but generally the numbers did not include the actual numbers. Consequently, results of the TOMAL-2 are not a valid measure of his verbal working memory. He was more attentive for the WJIII-COG: Numbers Reversed, but errors began when a series of five numbers was presented for recall. He could only recall four numbers out of sequence. In contrast, despite the increased cognitive load, John's attention was well focused for Auditory Working Memory. He was able

Table 9.20. Learning and Memory Functions

	Mild	Moderate	Severe
Working memory difficulties			
• Frequently asks for repetitions of instructions/explanations.		T	
• Trouble following multiple step directions.		P	T
• Loses track of steps/forgets what they are doing amid task.			T P
• Loses place in the middle of solving a math problem.		P	T
• Loses train of thought while writing.	P		T
• Trouble summarizing narrative or text material.			T P

Table 9.21. Working Memory

Instrument—Subtest: Description	Well Below Expected Level	Below Expected Level	Slightly Below Expected Level	At Expected Level	Above Expected Level	Well Above Expected Level	Superior
Verbal Working Memory							
TOMAL-2—Digits backward: Repeating number strings in reverse order that were spoken by the examiner.		(5)					
TOMAL-2—Letters backward: Repeating letter strings in reverse order that were spoken by the examiner.		(4)					
WJIII-COG—Numbers reversed: Repeating number strings in reverse order that were spoken by the examiner.			82				
WJIII-COG—Auditory working memory: Repeating the name of the objects in sequential order, followed by the numbers in sequential order, after listening to an audio recording of a series of names of both objects and digits.			86				

Note: Standard scores appear in normal font. Scaled scores appear in (parentheses). Percentile ranks of any kind appear in *italics.*

to separate the words from the numbers and to repeat them backward in sequence. His performance was sporadic, in that he would correctly repeat the words, not the numbers or would miss two items of a shorter series of numbers and correctly repeat a longer series. This suggests that there may be some kind of association that is unique to John to assist with recalling numbers and words in reverse order. This may be due to focused and sustained attention. When presented with vocabulary words, or states and capitals to be remembered, his working memory would be facilitated if unique references are also provided, or if a mnemonic approach to memory is employed.

VII. Cognitive Facilitators: Speed, Fluency, and Efficiency of Processing

Another cognitive facilitator that is frequently utilized in cognitive processes that are more automatic is speed, fluency, and efficiency of cognitive processing. This cognitive facilitator can be subdivided into four subcomponents: performance fluency (automatic processing of stimuli with no memory requirement), retrieval fluency (efficiency of memory retrieval), acquired knowledge fluency (rapid reading, writing, and math), and accuracy as a function of fluency or processing speed.

Presenting concerns. On the *Neuropsychological Processing Concerns Checklist for School-Aged Children & Youth—Second Edition* (NPCC-2), John's father and teacher reported significant concerns regarding Memory and Learning functions.

Table 9.22. Speed and Efficiency of Cognitive Processing

	Mild	Moderate	Severe
Processing speed and fluency difficulties			
• Takes longer to complete tasks than others the same age.		T P	
• Slow reading that makes comprehension difficult.		P	T
• Homework takes too long to complete.		T	
• Requires extra time to complete tests.			T P
• Responds slowly when asked questions.	P	T	
Processing speed with accuracy difficulties			
• Does well on timed tests.			T
• Difficulty recalling information accurately and quickly.		T	P
Academic fluency			
• Slow and deliberate reader.		T	
• Takes a long time to write.	T		

John's father and teacher have significant concerns regarding the extended amount of time that John requires to complete assignments when effort is applied. He requires extra time for test taking, especially since he wants to do well. He is perceived as having a great deal of difficulty with reading, stumbling over words and needing to reread passages due to not getting the gist of what he reads the first time. Answers are not readily available when asked questions and he needs extra "think time." Parent concern is mostly that he needs the extra time in order to obtain good grades.

Current levels of functioning.
1. Performance fluency.

Results for the verbal fluency section are consistent with John's tendency to rush through tasks while being unaware of errors. Automaticity of naming letters and colors in isolation is a relative strength, however, when inhibitory and switching conditions are added his cognitive efficiency is slowed and error rates significantly increase. His speed of task completion slowed significantly when cognitive load increased, such that there appears to be difficulty with processing speed, which adversely affects verbal fluency. John's attention was well focused during these subtests, with good adherence to following directions. John may have difficulty with math computation of mixed problems on a given assignment due to difficulties in noticing a change in signs. He will require extended time when new concepts are introduced which requires the assimilation of new information with previously learned information.

2. Retrieval fluency.

John demonstrates relative strengths for both verbal and nonverbal retrieval. As noted in his performance on other tasks, he tends to do well when he is provided with limited amounts of information, as in generating lists of words beginning with a specified letter or category or in generating designs based on only one type of dot.

His slightly lower score on Verbal Fluency Condition 2 may reflect a higher order thinking process in that he needed to cluster words into a category as opposed to just naming unrelated words beginning with a designated letter. Nonetheless, there was little difference between his ability to quickly produce words and designs. It is also apparent, however, that his speed of production slows when he is required to focus on a task when distracters are added. An example of this in the classroom might be when he is performing a math fluency task. He will likely perform better on a page of all addition problems than on a page with mixed operations. John showed little forethought in completing the fluency tasks; however, this appears to have been a benefit since he was able to more rapidly complete the task. On the Decision Speed test, John made no errors while matching two pictures within a row belonging to a category; however, he completion speed was slow.

Table 9.23. Performance Fluency

Instrument—Subtest: Description	Well Below Expected Level	Below Expected Level	Slightly Below Expected Level	At Expected Level	Above Expected Level	Well Above Expected Level	Superior
Perceptual Fluency							
WJIII-COG—Visual matching: Rapidly matching two numbers on a row.		73					
Figural Fluency							
D-KEFS—Design fluency condition 1 (filled dots): Connects filled dots to create as many different designs as possible in 60 seconds.				(6)			
D-KEFS—Design fluency condition 2 (empty dots): Connects empty dots to create as many different designs as possible in 60 seconds.					(8)		
• Design fluency structured array				(7)			
• Design fluency random array			(5)				
Naming Fluency (Rapid Automatized Naming)							
D-KEFS—Color-word interference condition 1 (color naming): Naming the color of colored squares rapidly.				(7)			
D-KEFS—Color-word interference condition 2 (word reading): Naming color words (e.g., "red") rapidly.				(8)			
NEPSY-II—Inhibition: Naming combined: Rapidly and accurately name shapes.	(2)						

• **Naming total completion time:** How quickly the task was completed.	(3)				
• **Naming total errors:** Total errors made on the task.		*2–5*			
• **Naming uncorrected errors:** Errors with no attempt to correct.	*< 2*				
• **Naming self-corrected errors:** Errors that were self-corrected.				*51–75*	
NEPSY-II—Speeded naming combined scaled: Rapidly naming attributes of objects or a series of numbers and letters.		(5)			
• **Speeded naming total completion time:** How quickly the task was completed.			(7)		
• **Speeded naming total correct:** How accurately the task was completed.		*2–5*			
• **Speeded naming total self-corrected errors:** Awareness of errors made on the task with self-correction.				*51–75*	
WJIII-COG—Rapid picture naming: Rapidly naming common pictures.		73			

Note: Standard scores appear in normal font. Scaled scores appear in (parentheses). Percentile ranks of any kind appear in *italics.*

3. Acquired knowledge fluency.

All of the acquired knowledge fluency measures were below expected level for a student his age. Writing fluency was low in part because he did not apply capitalization or punctuation consistently in his sentences. Many items were not complete sentences and words were incorrectly utilized to form sentences.

4. Accuracy as a function of fluency.

Completion time scores by themselves are not always accurate predictors of processing speed because sometime a student slows down to improve accuracy. The number of errors in combination with the task completion time must be interpreted

Table 9.24. Retrieval Fluency

Instrument—Subtest: Description	Well Below Expected Level	Below Expected Level	Slightly Below Expected Level	At Expected Level	Above Expected Level	Well Above Expected Level	Superior
Word Fluency							
D-KEFS—Verbal Fluency— Condition 1 (letter fluency): Naming as many words within a time limit that start with a specific letter.				(9)			
Semantic Fluency							
D-KEFS—Verbal Fluency— Condition 2 (category fluency): Naming as many words within a time limit that all fall in the same category (e.g., fruits).			(7)				
WJIII-COG—Decision speed: Rapidly matching two pictures in a row that belong in the same category.		76					

Note: Standard scores appear in normal font. Scaled scores appear in (parentheses). Percentile ranks of any kind appear in *italics*.

in tandem. Despite John's slowing down, his accuracy did not improve across multiple measures, which is usually indicative of low ability in the tested area.

Summary of speed, fluency, and efficiency of cognitive processing. Processing speed is an area of difficulty for John regardless of the academic or cognitive task; however, it would appear that when the cognitive load increases cognitive efficiency becomes significantly impaired. This would be apparent in his need for extended time in taking tests and completing assignments, as well as in utilizing short-term memory to respond to questions about material just reviewed.

VIII. Acquired Knowledge
Acquired knowledge is different from cognitive processes or cognitive facilitators. Acquired knowledge is the learning of useful information (acculturation knowledge), development of language abilities, especially vocabulary, and learning academic skills associated with reading, writing, and mathematics.

Table 9.25. Acquired Knowledge Fluency

Instrument—Subtest: Decription	RPI	Well Below Expected Level	Below Expected Level	Slightly Below Expected Level	At Expected Level	Above Expected Level	Well Above Expected Level	Superior
Reading fluency: Rapidly reading short, simple sentences and circles yes or no if they make sense over a 3-minute interval.	25/90		71					
Writing fluency: Producing, in writing, simple sentences that are legible.	17/90	61						
Math fluency: Solving simple math problems quickly.	57/90	68						

Note: Standard scores appear in normal font. Scaled scores appear in (parentheses). Percentile ranks of any kind appear in *italics*.

Current levels of functioning.
1. *Acculturation knowledge.*
Retrieval of encyclopedic information is low due to initial problems with encoding the information. The score for Verbal Comprehensions is elevated due to John's more accurate performance on the Picture Vocabulary subtest (one of four components of the subtest). His knowledge of synonyms, antonyms, and verbal analogies was weak. His approach to providing answers for General Information was rushed, with answers frequently unrelated to the items. He provided an answer to each item, but accuracy was poor. It is apparent that this is an area of difficulty.

2. *Language abilities.*
On each one of these subtests John did well on initial items. Based on this performance he did understand the directions and maintained cognitive set throughout for both the Understanding Directions and the Comprehension of Instructions subtests. Understanding Directions required John to point to pictured objects in a given order delivered orally on a cassette recording. He made increasingly more errors as the number of pictures to which he was required to point in sequence increased. He was unable to remember each of the directions. He did well with understanding and following directions on Comprehension of Instructions. There were fewer directions to recall, as in the former subtest, which contributed to more

Table 9.26. Semantic Memory

Instrument—Subtest: Description	Well Below Expected Level	Below Expected Level	Slightly Below Expected Level	At Expected Level	Above Expected Level	Well Above Expected Level	Superior
Verbal Comprehension							
WJIII-COG—Verbal comprehension: Four parts (picture vocabulary, synonyms, antonyms, and verbal analogies) that measures semantic memory.			82				
General Information							
WJIII-COG—General information: Depth of verbal knowledge based on "where" and "what" questions.		72					

Note: Standard scores appear in normal font. Scaled scores appear in (parentheses). Percentile ranks of any kind appear in *italics.*

accurate performance. Two errors appeared to be due to vocabulary interference. In one item he was directed to "point to the shape that is diagonal to . . . " and in another item directions were to "point to a shape adjacent to . . . ". He did not appear to know the meanings of diagonal or adjacent. Another error was due to starting on the left rather than the right as stipulated in the directions, although he accurately followed the remainder of the directions. With Oral Comprehension he again started out well, but as the difficulty of items increased he began to give any answer, many of which were unrelated to the specific item. He was unable to retrieve the appropriate word to complete passages, which were read to him. Both parent and teacher noted difficulties with John finding the right words, and in having trouble understanding verbal directions. These results indicate that as long as John has few directions to follow containing vocabulary that he understands, he will do well.

3. *Academic achievement*.

***Presenting concerns*.** On the *Neuropsychological Processing Concerns Checklist for School-Aged Children & Youth—Second Edition* (NPCC-2) John's father and teacher reported significant concerns regarding academic achievement. Many concerns in all

Table 9.27. Language Abilities

Instrument—Subtest: Description	Well Below Expected Level	Below Expected Level	Slightly Below Expected Level	At Expected Level	Above Expected Level	Well Above Expected Level	Superior
Vocabulary Knowledge							
WJIII-ACH—Picture vocabulary: Naming pictured objects.		80					
Receptive Language							
NEPSY-II—Comprehension of instructions total: Respond quickly to verbal instructions of increasing complexity.				(8)			
WJIII-ACH—Oral comprehension: Listening to passages and then orally providing a one-word response to fill in a missing last word.		78					
WJIII-ACH—Understanding directions: Pointing to various objects in a picture after listening to a sequence of recorded instructions.		77					

Note: Standard scores appear in normal font. Scaled scores appear in (parentheses). Percentile ranks of any kind appear in *italics.*

aspects of John's academic functioning were noted by both parents and teachers, but concerns were most severe related to John's understanding of math concepts. He often overlooks signs in math problems, does not know math facts, and "forgets" how to do basic borrowing and carrying. He seems unable to make sense of story problems. Handwriting is frequently difficult to decipher, especially when John is distracted or disinterested. Letter formation is large with excessive spacing between words. Vocabulary, spelling and grammar are significant areas of difficulty. John has trouble transferring his thoughts to paper. John's teacher reports that spelling is a relative strength for familiar words. John dislikes reading due to struggles with understanding what he reads and recalling detail from passages read. He also has difficulty with word identification, which causes reading to be slow and laborious.

Table 9.28. Academic Functions: Reading

	Mild	Moderate	Severe
Reading decoding difficulties			
• Over relies on sounding out most words when reading, even familiar words.		T	P
Reading comprehension difficulties			
• Difficulty understanding what is read.			T P
• Difficulty identifying main elements of a story.			P
• Appears distracted while reading.	P	T	
• Misses important details while reading.		P	T
Reading: Attitudinal issues			
• Avoids reading activities.	P	T	
• Appears anxious/uptight/nervous while reading.	P	T	
• Shows no interest in reading for information or pleasure.		T	P

Current levels of functioning.

Summary of acquired knowledge. John's acculturation knowledge is weak for someone his age. He is having difficulty storing new long-term memories into his encyclopedic knowledge. John also has some difficulties with oral expression and receptive language skills. John struggles in all aspects of achievement. Although below expected level, he has relative strengths in sounding out letter combinations and in reading words in isolation. Reading fluency is similarly developed. He relied heavily on his fingers and touch-point math for figuring problems on the math calculation subtest. Effort did not appear to be focused with some opposition observed when he refused to show his work despite several requests for him to do so. He wrote words rapidly on the spelling subtest and did not finish several words because he was uncertain of the correct spelling. John's handwriting was difficult to read with large letter formation and inconsistent spacing between words. He wrote very rapidly. Oral reading consisted of omitted words and miscalled words. He did not pay attention to punctuation within sentences while reading. When queried about incorrect responses for providing missing words within sentences, he would not admit that his answers did not make sense, and made no attempt to provide a different answer.

Table 9.29. Academic Functions: Writing

	Mild	Moderate	Severe
Writing: Spatial production difficulties			
• Demonstrates uneven spacing between words and letters.	P		T
• Trouble staying on the lines.			T
• Others have difficulty reading what the child has written.			T
• Trouble forming letters and words.	T	P	
• Writes overly large letters and words.			T
Writing: Expressive language difficulties			
• Limited vocabulary for age; uses lots of easy words.	P		T
• Difficulty putting ideas into words.	P	T	
• Uses simple sentence structure and lacks variety.			T
• Produces poor spelling in writing.			T P
• Poor grammar in writing.			T P
Writing: Graphomotor output difficulties			
• Difficulty holding the pencil or pen correctly.	T		
• Presses too soft with the pencil/pen while writing.	T		
• Shows preference for printing over cursive writing.			T
• Has trouble coming up with topics to write about.	T		
Writing: Attitudinal issues			
• Avoids writing activities.		T	P
• Appears anxious/uptight/nervous while writing.	T P		

IX. Social-Emotional Functioning and Adaptive Behaviors

Presenting concerns. John's language arts teacher from the previous school year expressed concerns about the lack of progress that John had demonstrated in reading. This was corroborated by the READ 180 skill testing on which he earned a 0%. Parents were less concerned about this because his grades were very good due to his excellent effort. John's parents and teacher have noted difficulties with math concepts. Again, his grades are good because of his good work ethic and placement in a special education math class. Parent noted, however, that John

Table 9.30. Academic Functions: Mathematics

	Mild	Moderate	Severe
Mathematical computational and procedural difficulties			
• Forgets what steps to take when solving math problems (e.g., carrying in addition or borrowing in subtraction).			T P
• Makes careless mistakes while solving math problems.			T P
• Does not always pay attention to the math problem signs.			T
Mathematics: Verbal difficulties			
• Difficulty with retrieval of basic math facts.			T P
• Difficulty solving story problems.			T
Attitudes toward mathematics			
• Appears anxious/uptight/nervous when working with math.	T		
• Avoids math activities.	T		

tends to internalize anything he perceives as criticism and worries excessively about this for extended periods of time. His current resource room teacher has noted that John has a tendency to "wear his heart on his sleeve."

Current levels of functioning. Each *Conner's Comprehensive Behavior Rating Scales* (CBRS) was rated with four responses (not true at all, just a little true, pretty much true, and very much true). Raw scores obtained are converted to T-Scores for interpretation. T-Scores have a mean (average) of 50. In general, higher T-Scores are associated with a greater number and/or frequency of reported problems. Caution: Please note that T-score cutoffs are guidelines only and may vary depending on the context of assessment. T-scores from 57 to 63 should be considered borderline and of special note because the assessor must decide (based on other information and knowledge of the youth) whether the concerns in the associated area warrant clinical intervention.

1. CBRS Content Scales: Detailed Scores. The following tables summarize the results of the teacher's and parent's assessment (F = father and T = teacher).

The Response Scale Analysis revealed no overly positive or negative response styles, nor was there an indication of an inconsistent response style, thus substantiating the validity of these results. Both parent and teacher ratings on the CBRS Rating Scales concurred regarding significant problems with learning

Table 9.31. Academic Achievement

Instrument—Subtest: Description	RPI	Well Below Expected Level	Below Expected Level	Slightly Below Expected Level	At Expected Level	Above Expected Level	Well Above Expected Level	Superior
Basic Reading Skills								
WJIII-ACH—Letter-word identification: Reading words in isolation.	22/90			81				
WJIII-ACH—Word attack: Reading phonetically regular nonsense words orally.	37/90			81				
Reading Comprehension								
WJIII-ACH—Passage comprehension: Reading a passage silently and provides the missing word.	27/90	66						
WJIII-ACH—Reading vocabulary: Orally producing synonyms, antonyms, or verbal analogies	10/90	63						
Written Expression								
WJIII-ACH—Writing samples: Producing meaningful written sentences.	33/90	62						
Mathematical Calculations								
WJIII-ACH—Calculations: Performing a variety of math calculations.	7/90	57						
Mathematical Reasoning								
WJIII-ACH—Applied problems: Analyzing and solving practical math problems.	0/90	45						

Note: Standard scores appear in normal font. Scaled scores appear in (parentheses). Percentile ranks of any kind appear in *italics*.

Table 9.32.

T-Score	Guideline
70+	Very elevated score (Many more concerns than are typically reported)
60–69	High average score (Slightly more concerns than are typically reported)
40–59	Average score (Typical levels of concern)
< 40	Low score (Fewer concerns than are typically reported)

and understanding material specific to reading, written expression and math. Both raters also had scores in the high average range for social anxiety. This is mainly in relation to the anxiety experienced as a result of excessive and prolonged worrying when he perceives certain events as criticism. This adversely affects concentration until he resolves the issue for himself. John's teacher's perception is that John is somewhat shy, becoming quiet and reserved during interactions around those with whom he does not yet feel comfortable. Mr. Doe's high average score for hyperactivity/impulsivity is mostly related to John's worrying tendencies and the fact that he will often impulsively make comments not appropriate to the situation when he feels anxious. There are no physical manifestations such as fidgeting or moving around in his seat.

2. DSM-IV-TR symptom scales. The following table summarizes the results of the parent's and teacher's assessment with respect to the *DSM-IV-TR* symptom scales (other than the ADHD scales reported in the Attention section of this chapter), and provides general information about how he compares to the normative group.

John's parent and teacher ratings indicate no problems with conduct disorder or oppositional defiant disorder. John's father does indicate that John can be stubborn at home. It is sometimes difficult to convince him to look at situations from another point of view. After time and persuasion, John can be convinced to change his perceptions or to go forth without judgment. His teacher also notes a degree of stubbornness in John, but she describes him as cooperative, hardworking, striving to do his best.

These results indicate that John's teacher has observed significantly more behaviors related to ADHD Inattentive Type than has either John or his father. The behavioral raters noted that John had difficulties with failure to pay attention to details or with making careless mistakes. Parent and teacher ratings agreed that John often has difficulty organizing tasks and activities. Teacher ratings further endorsed John's difficulties with sustaining attention to task, often appearing not to listen

Table 9.33. Conners Comprehensive Behavior Rating Scales (CBRS)

Content Scales	Low Score <40 T	Average Score 40–59 T	High Average Score 60–69 T	Very Elevated Score 70 T+
Hyperactivity/impulsivity: High activity levels, may be restless, may have difficulty being quiet.			F, T	
Emotional distress: Worries a lot (including possible social and/or separation anxieties), may show signs of depression or may have physical complaints; may have rumination.		F, T		
Upsetting thoughts/physical symptoms (ED subscale): Has upsetting thoughts and/or ruminations. May complain about physical symptoms; may show signs of depression.		F, T		
Worrying (CRBS-P) (ED subscale): Worries a lot, including anticipatory and social worries. May experience inappropriate guilt.			T	F
Social problems: Socially awkward, may be shy; may have difficulty with friendships, poor social connections, limited conversational skills; may have poor social reciprocity.			F	T
Social anxiety (CRBS-T) (ED subscale): Worries about social and performance situations; worries about what others think.			F, T	
Defiant/aggressive behaviors: May be argumentative; may defy requests from adults; may have poor control of anger or may lose temper; may be physically and/or verbally aggressive; may show violence, bullying, and destructive tendencies; may seem uncaring.		F	T	
Academic difficulties (AD): Total: Problems with learning and/or understanding academic material. Poor academic performance.				F, T

Language (AD subscale): Problems with reading, writing, and/or language skills.				F, T
Math (AD subscale): Problems with math.				F, T
Hyperactivity/impulsivity: High activity levels, may be restless, may have difficulty being quiet.		T	F	
Perfectionistic and compulsive behaviors: Rigid, inflexible. Has repetitive behaviors. May become "stuck" on a behavior or idea at times. May be overly concerned with cleanliness.	F	T		
Violence potential: At risk for acting violently.	F, T			
Physical symptoms: Complains about aches, pains, or feeling sick; may have sleep or weight/appetite issues.	F	T		

when spoken to directly; often has difficulty with organizing tasks; is distracted by outside stimuli and forgetful in daily activities. The teacher also observes that John avoids, dislikes, or is reluctant to engage in tasks that require sustained mental effort (such as schoolwork or homework). Parent and teacher ratings yield scores in the high average range specific to fidgeting or squirming in his seat, he appears to be restless or to act impulsively. Perception of the teacher was that John often interrupts or intrudes on others as in butting into conversations.

John's low scores suggest significant deficits in social perception. Deficits in Theory of Mind reflect problems with taking the perspective of others into

Table 9.34. Conners Comprehensive Behavior Rating Scales (CBRS): *DSM-IV TR* Symptom Scales

DSM-IV-TR Symptom Scales	Low Score < 40 T	Average Score 40–59 T	High Average Score 60–69 T	Very Elevated Score 70 T+
Conduct disorder	T	F (2)		
Oppositional defiant disorder		F, T		
ADHD predominantly inattentive type			F (2), T (4)	

Table 9.35. Social Perception

Instrument—Subtest: Description	Well Below Expected Level	Below Expected Level	Slightly Below Expected Level	At Expected Level	Above Expected Level	Well Above Expected Level	Superior
NEPSY-II—Affect recognition total	2						
• Total happy errors			*11–25*				
• Total sad errors			*11–25*				
• Total neutral errors		*6–10*					
• Total fear errors		*2–5*					
• Total angry errors	*>2*						
• Total disgust errors	*<2*						
NEPSY-II—Theory of mind total	*<2*						

Note: Standard scores appear in normal font. Scaled scores appear in (parentheses). Percentile ranks of any kind appear in *italics.*

account or understanding the intentions of others. As a result, he may misinterpret remarks or comments from others intended to be joking or playful, attaching a negative connotation instead. Misperceptions here likely contribute to his feelings of anxiety and worry when he believes that he has been criticized or discounted. Both parent and teacher have noted his stubbornness in letting go of perceived slights. John put little thought into his answers on this subtest, and at times responded according to aspects in the pictures associated with the items. Reflection related to the feelings of the characters in the pictures appeared to be somewhat lacking.

John was less than enthusiastic about completing this subtest, but complied nonetheless. He indicated that it was difficult to see much of a difference between many of the pictures. This was particularly true of the pictures portraying neutral expressions. He tended to attribute "sad" or "disgust" to these, expressing some confusion about what a neutral expression should look like. His ability to identify the expressions of anger, fear, and disgust was poor. These results are indicative of his tendencies to misinterpret the motives of others for which he often holds grudges for extended periods of time. Support is given to the teacher's concern that John exhibits some social anxiety and difficulties with social reciprocity. The Total Affect Recognition Score does not, however, represent the variance among all scores, nor does it reflect the relative strength for recognizing happy and sad expressions.

Summary of social-emotional functioning. John's parents and his teacher acknowledge and praise John's conscientious work ethic. He is, in general, as well behaved as other students his age and in some instances more so. Concerns from both parent and teacher primarily involve John's struggles with learning and understanding academic material, especially in relation to reading and math. He does tend to worry excessively and for extended periods of time when he perceives that he has been criticized or slighted. Both parent and teacher note that he can be stubborn, but after a period of time can be dissuaded from his original perception. John does have some difficulty with taking the perspective of others into account and may often misunderstand the intent of comments or actions of others. Accurate identification of the emotions and expressions of others is also problematic.

Summary

A neuropsychological evaluation was conducted in 2003 during John's second year in third grade after completion of a comprehensive school reevaluation. Results at that time showed verbal ability to be significantly stronger than nonverbal ability. Academic strengths included word calling, spelling, and math calculation, with reading comprehension, written expression, and math word problem solving being areas of difficulty. Receptive and expressive language skills and visual motor skills were also areas of difficulty. NEPSY results from the 2003 neuropsychological evaluation confirmed deficits in language, sensorimotor, visual spatial abilities, memory, and attention areas.

Based on the current assessment results, John's overall relative strengths include above expected levels for processing of limited units of letters, numbers, and words with accompanying limited numbers of operations to be performed when information is presented verbally. Phonological processing skills are well above expected levels. Reading comprehension and spelling (based on work samples and teacher report) are relative strengths at slightly below expected levels. Working memory for smaller chunks of information is also a relative strength.

There are major interferences of cognitive inattention, especially for sustained attention and attentional capacity. Cognitive overload resulting from visuospatial difficulties and executive functioning problems interfere with acquiring and remembering information. Memory is a significant weakness with areas of difficulty indicated for both immediate and delayed memory. John has difficulty processing complex verbal and visual information, resulting in slow processing speed. Weaknesses in each of these areas contribute to inconsistent progress in reading comprehension. Verbal immediate memory is stronger, which allows John to use his strong phonological processing skills for reading words, but does not contribute to knowledge of word meanings within the context of passages read. His struggles with visual/spatial information and dealing with complex verbal information interfere with consistent progress in reading. John demonstrates difficulties with perspective taking and accurately interpreting the emotional intent of others.

Diagnostic Impressions

Assessment results indicate that John's attention processes are impaired in relation to his ability to focus and sustain attention when cognitive overload is reached. Although he appears to be able to shift attention between categories of information or activities, he has great difficulty in processing the information presented for learning. Visual spatial processing is a significant weakness. Memory is a pervasive weakness that adversely affects the acquisition and learning of new material, as well as the retrieval and application of new concepts. Processing speed and cognitive efficiency are below expected levels.

John's pattern of performance is characteristic of many aspects of a Nonverbal Learning Disability (NVLD) and ADHD—Inattentive Type. The description of John's strengths and weaknesses are characteristics of NVLD. Deficits in selective, sustained attention, shifting attention and attentional capacity are problematic relative to ADHD. Educational eligibility for special education services does not include a NVLD; however, John will continue to meet criteria for a learning disability in reading, math and written expression, as well as for an Attention Deficit Disorder.

Intervention Strategies and Recommendations

Recommendations for Instruction at School

Understanding and Following Directions

1. John requires multiple steps in moving from simple to complex instruction. He will learn best by a verbal step-by-step presentation.
2. Use language to clarify questions, and to explain and interpret written information.

3. Due to his difficulties with visualizing and integrating information, he may be more successful when he attempts to memorize verbatim small chunks of verbally presented material.
4. Stress smaller chunks of information to be learned rather than everything at once.
5. Avoid jargon, double meaning words, sarcasm, and nicknames and teasing.

Strategies for Improving Attention
1. Assist John in developing coping skills to deal with attentional capacity. Noise levels in a confined area have proven to be extremely distracting for him, consider placement in another class, or allow a change in seating arrangements.
2. Allow John to take open book tests and evaluate him on the basis of portfolios and other alternative means of assessing knowledge and skill.
3. Attempt to avoid visual distractions in the classroom.
4. John could be allowed to wear headphones to reduce or eliminate noise in the classroom when he is trying to focus.

Math Accommodations
1. It would be beneficial to capitalize on John's stronger verbal skills in teaching math rules and operations. Write out rules for a particular operation, and allow him to use this "cheat sheet" as a reference to solve problems.
2. For math, use real-life examples with extensive verbal explanations, and hands-on experiences.
3. For computational math difficulties have John write out math problems on graph paper or ruled leaf paper held sideways to form columns to provide spatial structure.

Ways to Lessen John's Anxiety
1. Students with NVLD are frequently prone to anxiety. Individual counseling would be helpful to teach John some anxiety management techniques.
2. Students with NVLD often have poor social skills due to difficulties with recognizing nonverbal communication cues. John would benefit from some social skills training to help him lessen his social anxiety.

Recommendations for Instruction at Home

Assisting With Academic Progress

1. Establish proper working conditions and timing arrangements for optimal consolidation of information into memory (e.g., try to pick a study place that is used consistently).
2. It would be beneficial for John if parents would review homework completed, pointing out errors and encouraging John to correct these errors before turning in the assignments.

Increase Self-Awareness

1. Parents could make sure that John receives any counseling, therapies, and/or medications that may be needed to treat any other problems or medical conditions he may have.
2. Reassure John that he is valued for who he is. It may be tricky to help him improve social skills, while at the same time nurturing his confidence to hold on to his unique individuality.

Recommendations for the Student

1. John should engage in intermittent self-testing and self-monitoring using checklists to indicate stages of completion.
2. John should liberally use underlining and rereading of underlined material.
3. John should acquire the habit of maintaining "to do lists" and assignment books, checking off completed items.
4. John should review material for a test just before sleeping, and then engage in morning self-testing (perhaps with the assistance of parents) before going to school.
5. With teacher guidance, John should break down lengthy assignments into smaller chunks.
6. John should engage in self-talk (verbal mediation) to compensate for visual spatial difficulties.

Seymore Children, PhD, ABSNP
School Neuropsychologist

COMMENTS FROM THE AUTHOR

This was an actual case study. The names and background information have been modified to protect the identity of the student. The diagnoses of NVLD and ADHD-Inattentive Type seem appropriate; however, there is an established set of known neuropsychological deficits associated with NVLD and to be more thorough, the case study could have included some additional assessments (see Rapid Reference 9.1).

≡ Rapid Reference 9.1

Verified Known NVLD Symptoms in the Case Study Illustration

Known NVLD Deficit Area	Verified in Case Study	Possible Additional Assessment
• Bilateral tactile-perceptual deficits	No	NEPSY-II Manual Motor Sequences or equivalent
• Complex psychomotor deficits	Yes	
• Poor visual attention	Partially	CAS Number Detection and Receptive Attention
• Poor prosody and pragmatics	Partially through observation	Complete speech and language evaluation
• Poor visual memory and memory in general	Yes	
• Poor nonverbal problem solving	Yes	
• Poor concept formation	Yes	
• Poor social judgment	Yes	
• Poor social perception	Partially	NEPSY II: Affect Recognition
• Internalizing problems	Yes	
• Poor comprehension/better decoding	Yes	
• Good spelling skills	No	Spelling test from an achievement battery
• Poor handwriting	Yes	
• Poor math calculations	Yes	
• Poor processing speed	Yes	

Chapter Ten

SENSORIMOTOR FUNCTIONS

One of the unique components of a school neuropsychological evaluation compared to a psychoeducational evaluation is the inclusion of the assessment of sensory-perceptual and motor functions. In the school neuropsychological conceptual model, the sensory-motor functions serve as a baseline for all of the higher-order processes (e.g., visual-spatial processing, language skills, memory and learning). For example, if basic auditory discrimination skills are impaired, then the higher-order skill of sound blending, a basic skill for reading, may be compromised. A school neuropsychologist should routinely investigate whether higher-order processing deficits (e.g., verbal working memory) are caused by underlying deficits in sensorimotor problems. In this chapter, sensory and motor functions are defined, the neuro-anatomy of each is described, and the common tests used to assess sensorimotor functions are presented.

SENSORY FUNCTIONS

Jimmy does not like to wear long pants, even in the winter. He says that the fabric on his skin makes him feel "itchy." Jimmy is also a picky eater. He will not eat foods that have a certain texture. Finally, Jimmy likes to play with his fingers over and over again as a means of stimulating his senses. Jimmy is experiencing some symptoms of sensory dysfunction.

Definitions

Sensory Processing Disorder (SPD) is an umbrella term used to cover a variety of neurological disabilities that interfere with the normal ability to use sensory information to function smoothly in daily life (Kranowitz, 2005). Sensory functions encompass our ability to process visual, auditory, kinesthetic, and olfactory information. Dysfunction in any one sensory system can have a dramatic effect on a child's learning capabilities and behavioral regulation. Sensory dysfunction can be manifested in multiple ways. Some children are *overstimulated* by sensory input to the point that sensory input may be painful. An example would be a child who is hypersensitive to touch. A light brush against the child's skin could feel as if the skin has been set on fire. Other children are *understimulated* by sensory input, which can be dangerous. For example, a child falls while roller-skating and injures herself but does not respond to the pain of the injury and returns to the activity. In addition, other children are *sensation seekers*, sometimes to the exclusion of all other activities. For example, some children chew on their shirt sleeves excessively to the point that their mouths are chapped and bleeding.

Sensory discrimination is also an important part of the overall sensory functions. A child with poor tactile sensory discrimination may have difficulty holding a pencil and producing legible writing. A child with poor auditory discrimination may have difficulty acquiring reading and language skills. The sensory systems of the body also interact with motor functions. Children with *sensory-motor integration* problems may have difficulties with balance, movement, using both sides of the body in a unified fashion, and confusion over right versus left sided movements.

Neuroanatomy of Sensory Functions

The primary visual cortex, *regulating the sense of sight*, is located in the striate cortex of the occipital lobe. The retina, located at the back of the eye, transmits information via the optic nerve. Before reaching higher cortical regions of the brain, the optic nerve splits into two parts. The temporal (lateral) part continues its path to higher cortical regions on the same side of the body. The nasal (medial) part continues its path to higher cortical regions by crossing over to the opposite side of the body at the optic chiasm. The temporal and nasal portions of the optic nerve terminate in the lateral geniculate nuclei or the pulvinar nucleus of the thalamus and the superior colliculus of the midbrain. The visual information then travels from the lateral geniculate nuclei to terminate in the primary visual area of the occipital lobe (see Figure 10.1).

The primary auditory cortex, regulating the *sense of hearing*, is located in the superior part of the temporal lobe and buried within the sylvian fissure. The cochlea is the auditory sense organ in the inner ear. Projections from the cochlea pass through the subcortical relays of the medial geniculate of the thalamus, and then onto the supratemporal cortex (see Figure 10.1).

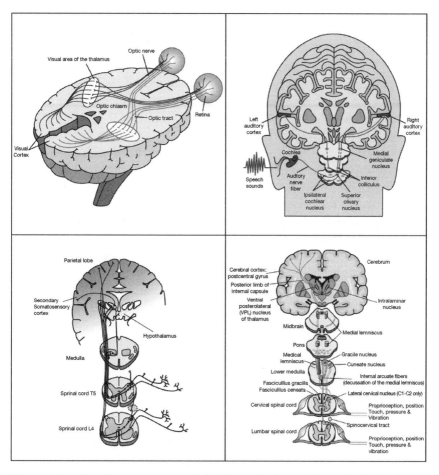

Figure 10.1. The Neuroanatomy of the Visual Pathway (Upper Left); Auditory Pathway (Upper Right); Anterolateral System for Pain and Temperature Sense (Bottom Left); and the Dorsal Column-Medial Lemniscal System for Touch, Proprioception, and Movement (Bottom Right).

The primary somatosensory cortex, *regulating the sense of touch, pain, temperature*, and *limb proprioception (limb position)*, is located in the post-central gyrus. There are two pathways for somatosensory information: the anterolateral system for pain and temperature sense (see Figure 10.1), and the dorsal column-medial lemniscal system for touch, proprioception, and movement (see Figure 10.1).

Vision, hearing, and touch, all have contralateral projections in the brain. This means that if a child has a defect in a right-sided sense organ, the deficit will show as damage in the left side of the brain that controls that sense organ. The sense of smell is the only sense organ that does not have a contralateral projection to the brain. The primary olfactory cortex, regulating the *sense of smell*, is located in the ventral region of the anterior temporal lobe. A secondary area for olfaction is located in the lateral parts of the orbitofrontal cortex (Sobel et al., 1998). Due to the unilateral projections of smell, a left-sided lesion in the right ventral region of the temporal lobe will produce a severe deficit when an odor is smelled in the right nostril. The sense of smell is the only sense not processed by the thalamus, but goes directly to the cortex. Also, the anterior portion of the insular cortex (insula) is a crucial brain region receiving input from all the senses as well as limbic regions, and is thought to integrate information for the perception of pain, as well as fear avoidance.

Damage along the sensory pathways can cause a variety of impairments. Some of the neuropsychological terms associated with sensory impairments are presented in Rapid Reference 10.1. These terms are used by physicians in medical records to describe neuropsychological deficits in children. It is important that school neuropsychologists understand the terminology but it is recommended that use of these terms be minimized in school neuropsychological reports (see the "Avoiding the Use of Jargon" section in Chapter 6).

MOTOR FUNCTIONS

Michelle is a third grader. Her least favorite subject is gym class and she hates to go outside on the playground at recess. In gym class, Michelle does not perform well on the gross motor tasks compared to her peers (e.g., running). On the playground, Michelle has tried to play hopscotch and tag with her friends but she is clumsy and her peers have started to make fun of her. Recently, Michelle has begun to play by herself on the playground and she has started to develop physiological complaints (e.g., stomachaches, headaches) to avoid gym class. Michelle's gross motor deficiencies are causing her to experience some anxiety-related disorders and social isolation.

Definitions

Disorders of motor functions have been historically assigned many labels including: sensory-integrative dysfunction, perceptuomotor dysfunction, developmental dyspraxia, minimal brain dysfunction, visuomotor difficulties, clumsy child

≣ Rapid Reference 10.1

Neuropsychological Terms Associated With Sensory Impairments

- *Achromatopsia*—A rare disorder in which color is not recognized.
- *Ageusia*—Loss of the sense of taste.
- *Anosmia*—Impaired sense of smell.
- *Asterognosia*—Inability to recognize an object on the basis of its three-dimensionality through palpation (aka tactile agnosia/dysnosia).
- *Auditory agnosia*—Inability to recognize auditory stimuli.
- *Autotopagnosia*—Disturbed body scheme that manifests itself by the inability to identify the parts of one's body.
- *Barognosia*—Inability to estimate weight when objects are placed in the affected hand.
- *Finger agnosia*—Inability to recognize a sensory stimulus via the fingers.
- *Graphestheia*—Difficulty recognizing shapes or letters written on the hand.
- *Hemianopia*—A loss of vision for one half of the visual field of either one or both eyes.
- *Hypesthesia*—Decreased desensitivity to stimulation.
- *Kinesthesia*—The conscious awareness of joint position and body movement in space.
- *Pallinopsia*—Visual perseveration of a stimulus no longer present.
- *Parosmia*—An abnormal sense of smell.
- *Proprioception*—The unconscious awareness of sensations coming from one's muscles and joints that helps regulate our position in 3-dimensional space.
- *Tactile defensiveness*—The tendency to react negatively to unexpected, light touches.
- *Tactile localization disorder*—The inability to localize a stimulus on the skin.
- *Two-point discrimination disorder*—The inability to discriminate between sensations arising from a single touch versus two simultaneous and nearby touches.
- *Visual agnosia*—Inability to recognize visual stimuli (e.g., signs or pictures).

Sources: Ayd, 1995; Loring, 1999.

syndrome, and motor-learning difficulties (Ball, 2002). The *Diagnostic and Statistical Manual of Mental Disorders—Fourth Edition, Text Revision* (American Psychiatric Association, 2000) includes the diagnostic criteria for developmental coordination disorders (DCD). Children with DCD are characterized as being "clumsy" or "awkward." Children with DCD exhibit motor coordination that is substantially below expected levels compared to same-age peers and measured cognitive capabilities. The essential feature of DCD is a marked impairment in the development of motor coordination. These children have marked delays in reaching developmental motor milestones (e.g., crawling, walking, sitting) and have difficulty mastering other gross motor tasks such as catching a ball or jumping and mastering fine motor tasks such as tying shoelaces, or buttoning a shirt. Children with DCD may appear clumsy, have poor handwriting, and demonstrate poor performance in sports.

Prevalence of DCD has been estimated to be as high as 6% for children in the age range of 5 to 11 years (American Psychiatric Association, 2000). The etiology or prognosis of DCD is still not clear. The diagnosis of DCD can only be made when there is significant interference with daily living or academic achievement and it is not due to a medical condition such as cerebral palsy, hemiplegia, or muscular dystrophy. Children with DCD often have developmental delays in other areas, such as expressive and receptive language in isolation or combined, or in phonological processing. DCD is often comorbid with attention deficit-hyperactivity disorder, conduct disorder, and pervasive developmental disorder (Hertza & Estes, 2011).

Neuroanatomy of Motor Functions

The frontal regions of the cortex are involved in planning movements. The frontal region receives information about what is happening (the ventral stream terminating in the inferior temporal cortex) and where it is happening (the dorsal stream terminating in the posterior parietal lobe). Carlson (2010) noted that because the parietal lobes contain spatial information (perception of space and location of limbs), the connections between the parietal and frontal lobes are important in controlling both locomotion and hand movements. Figure 10.2 illustrates the interconnections of multisystems that help to regulate motor activity. The premotor cortex helps regulate preprogrammed or sequential motor responses and is involved in learning and executing complex movements. The primary motor cortex helps to regulate the motor movements of our body. Finally, the cerebellum, the brain structure that lies at the back of the head about the brain stem, plays an important role in motor coordination.

There are two semi-independent neural systems that help regulate motor activity in humans: the pyramidal system and the extrapyramidal system. The pyramidal system "is the executive system responsible for the initiation of voluntary skilled movements involving rapid and precise control of the extremities" (Tupper & Sondell, 2004, pp. 16–17). The pyramidal system is composed of the precentral motor cortex, the corticospinal tract and its connections to the

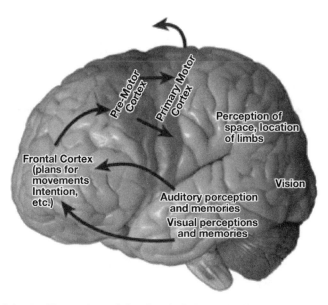

Figure 10.2. An Illustration of the Cortical Control of Movement

spinal motor neurons. Subcortical brain structures such as the cerebellum, basal ganglia, the red nucleus and substantia niagra regions of the brain stem form the extrapyramidal system. The extrapyramidal system helps regulate motor coordination and maintain posture. Rapid Reference 10.2 presents some of the common neuropsychological terms associated with motor disorders. Examples of pyramidal motor disorders include cerebral palsy, diplegia, paraplegia, hemiparesis, and hemiplegia. Examples of extrapyramidal motor disorders include: choreas, dystonias, postural disruptions, tics, and Tourette's syndrome.

When to Assess Sensorimotor Functions

When planning a neuropsychological assessment it is important to know when to include a sensory-motor component to the testing battery based on the referral question(s) and the suspected disability. Sensory deficits have been associated with autism spectrum disorders, attention-deficit hyperactivity disorder, learning disabilities, dyslexia, nonverbal learning disorder, genetic disorders (e.g., Down Syndrome), nongenetic disabilities (e.g., Fetal Alcohol Syndrome or Fetal Alcohol Effects), or psychological disorders (e.g., obsessive-compulsive disorder) (Kranowitz, 2005). See D. Miller (2010) for a review of the most common neurodevelopmental disorders with known sensorimotor deficits.

≡ *Rapid Reference 10.2*

Neuropsychological Terms Associated With Motor Impairments

- *Apraxia*—Inability to plan and execute a learned voluntary movement smoothly, not due to muscle weakness or failure to understand directions.
- *Asterixis*—A motor disturbance characterized by a rapid, sporadic limb contraction followed by a slower return to extension.
- *Ataxia*—Incoordination of movement, usually due to disease of sensory or cerebellar pathways.
- *Chorea*—Involuntary performance of fragments of movement, for example, suddenly raise arm, flex, extend, abduct, adduct, fragments of purposeful movement (usually associated with degeneration of the basal ganglia).
- *Clonus*—Rapid repetitive alternating muscle contraction and relaxation.
- *Constructional apraxia*—Inability to assemble, build, draw, or copy accurately, not due to apraxia of simple movements.
- *Diplegia*—A form of cerebral palsy primarily affecting the legs.
- *Dysphagia*—An impaired ability to chew or swallow food or liquid.
- *Dystonia*—Characterized by involuntary muscle contractions, which force certain parts of the body into abnormal, sometimes painful, movements or postures.
- *Graphomotor apraxia*—Inability to draw and write despite normal capacity to hold a writing instrument.
- *Hemiparesis*—Weakness on one side of the body.
- *Hemiplegia*—Paralysis of one half of body due to lesion leading to complete interruption of contralateral pyramidal tract.
- *Hypotonia*—Absent or decreased muscle tone.
- *Ideational apraxia*—Inability to perform gestures based on verbal command.
- *Monoplegia*—Paralysis of one upper limb or lower limb due to cortical damage.
- *Optic ataxia*—Can recognize objects but cannot use visual information to guide their action.
- *Paraplegia*—Paralysis of two lower limbs due to interrupted nerve supply.
- *Quadraplegia*—All four limbs are paralyzed.
- *Spasticity*—A condition in which certain muscles are continuously contracted.
- *Tics*—A sudden, rapid, repetitive motor movement or vocalization. Tics can include eye blinking, repeated throat clearing or sniffing, arm thrusting, kicking movements, shoulder shrugging or jumping.
- *Tourette's Syndrome*—Characterized by repeated and involuntary body movements (tics).

Sources: Ayd, 1995; Loring, 1999.

Identifying Sensorimotor Concerns

It is suggested that the *Neuropsychological Processing Concerns Checklist for Children and Youth—Third Edition* (NPCC-3: D. Miller, 2012a) be completed by the parent/guardian and at least one teacher of the student being referred for a comprehensive assessment (see supplemental CD for the complete NPCC-3). The questions on the NPCC-3 that pertain to sensorimotor functions are shown in Rapid Reference 10.3. For each behavior listed on the NPCC-3, the rater is

≡ *Rapid Reference 10.3*

Sensorimotor Items From the Neuropsychological Processing Concerns Checklist for Children and Youth—Third Edition (NPCC-3: Miller, 2012a)

Basic sensory deficits:
- Difficulty with pitch discrimination (tone deaf).
- Difficulty with simple sound discrimination.
- Known or suspected hearing acuity problems.
- Difficulty identifying basic colors (color blind).
- Difficulty smelling or tasting foods.
- Less sensitive to pain and changes in temperature.
- Complains of loss of sensation (e.g., numbness).

Motor functioning difficulties:
- Muscle weakness or paralysis.
- Muscle tightness or spasticity.
- Clumsy or awkward body movements.
- Walking or posture difficulties.

Visual spatial and visual motor functioning difficulties:
- Difficulties with drawing or copying.
- Difficulties with fine motor skills (e.g., using a pencil).

Neurologically related sensorimotor symptoms:
- Displays odd movements (e.g., hand flapping, toe walking).
- Displays involuntary or repetitive movements.
- Ignores one side of the page while drawing or reading.
- Difficulty with dressing (e.g., buttoning and zippering).

Sensory sensitivity issues:
- Does not like loud noises.
- Overly sensitive to touch, light, or noise.

instructed to put a check mark in the "Not Observed" column if the behavior has not been observed in the past 6 months for this child. If the behavior has been observed during the past 6 months, the rater is instructed to put a check mark in one of the three columns marked Mild (behavior occasionally observed), Moderate (behavior frequently observed), or Severe (behavior almost always observed).

The purpose of the NPCC-3 is to provide school neuropsychologists or other assessment specialists with specific examples of recently exhibited behaviors of the child or adolescent. These behaviors, either endorsed or not endorsed by caregivers and/or teachers, help assessment specialists assemble a testing battery to address the stated concerns. For example, if none of the sensorimotor items are observed by the caretaker(s) and/or teacher(s), the school neuropsychologist or other assessment specialists may choose not to include tests of sensorimotor functions in the assessment battery. However, if many of the basic sensory deficit items are endorsed by the raters, additional physiological examinations of the basic sensory systems may be warranted, such as a follow-up thorough visual examination or hearing examination. If many of the motor functioning items are endorsed, particularly at moderate or severe ratings, an assessment and/ or consultation with a physical or occupational therapist may be warranted as part of the assessment plan. Finally, if many of the neurologically related sensorimotor symptoms or sensory sensitivity issues are endorsed, particularly at moderate or severe ratings, the assessment plan should include tools for differential diagnosis of autism spectrum disorders.

Assessing Sensorimotor Functions

Rapid Reference 10.4 restates the second- and third-order classifications of sensorimotor functions within the integrated SNP/CHC Model. Tests designed to measure these second- and third-order classifications of sensorimotor functions are presented in this section of the chapter.

Assessing Lateral Preference

Many of the sensory and motor tests require the examiner to know the student's lateral dominance or preference. The *Dean-Woodcock Sensory-Motor Battery* (DWSMB: Dean & Woodcock, 2003) has a Lateral Preference test. This test should be administered first in a sensorimotor assessment to establish the child's lateral preference. Lateral preference is not just limited to handedness, but also includes eye and foot preference (e.g., which eye is preferred to look through a telescope, or which foot would be used to kick a football).

≣ Rapid Reference 10.4

Integrated SNP/CHC Model Classifications of Sensorimotor Functions

Broad Classifications	Second-Order Classifications	Third-Order Classifications
Sensorimotor functions	• Lateral preference	
	• Sensory functions	• Auditory and visual acuity
		• Tactile sensation and perception
		• Kinesthetic sensation and perception
		• Olfactory sensation and perception
	• Fine motor functions	• Coordinated finger/hand movements
	• Visual-motor integration skills	
	• Visual scanning	• Direct measures
		• Indirect measures
		• Qualitative behaviors
	• Gross motor functions	• Balance
		• Coordination
	• Qualitative behaviors	

Assessing Sensory Functions

The following section presents the tests designed to measure the sensory functions of: auditory and visual acuity, and tactile, kinesthetic, and olfactory sensation and perception.

Tests of Auditory and Visual Acuity. If a student has visual acuity problems, a more thorough visual examination by an optometrist or ophthalmologist, preferably a developmental ophthalmologist, may be warranted. Likewise, when a student has more serious known or suspected hearing problems, a more thorough audiological examination by an audiologist may be warranted. Rapid Reference 10.5 presents some common tests of auditory and visual acuity that may be administered as part of a comprehensive school neuropsychological assessment battery.

≡ Rapid Reference 10.5

Tests of Auditory and Visual Acuity

Test–Subtest: Description	Age/Grade Range	Publisher
DWSMB—Auditory Acuity: A basic auditory test (right, left, both).	4 to 90 years	Riverside
DWSMB—Near Point Visual Acuity: Measures near-point vision in each eye (right and left).		
DWSMB—Visual Confrontation: Measures visual field perception (right, left, and both).		

See Appendix for the full names of the tests and their references.

Basic hearing and vision problems can have a pervasive negative impact on a student's classroom performance. A student with visual acuity problems may not be able to see information presented in the front of the classroom or may have difficulties seeing information close up in printed materials. A student with hearing problems may appear to be disengaged in classroom activities or not paying attention and may have difficulty comprehending and following verbally presented information and/or directions. Students with auditory and visual acuity problems should not be administered higher-order cognitive tasks that require verbal and visual inputs or processing.

Tests of Tactile Sensation and Perception. Rapid Reference 10.6 presents tests that are designed to measure tactile sensation and perception. The tests referenced in Rapid Reference 10.6 are designed to measure proprioception processes with the somatosensory strip area of the brain. Students with tactile sensation and perception deficiencies may have difficulty with fine motor activities such as applying the correct pressure to a pencil or pen when writing or being able to recognize objects based on touch. Tactile sensation and perception deficiencies may also cause students to be either hyposensitive or hypersensitive to touch, light, or sound sensations.

Assessing Fine Motor Functions

The following section presents the tests designed to measure the fine motor functions related to coordinated finger/hand movements.

≡ Rapid Reference 10.6

Tests of Tactile Sensation and Perception

Test–Subtest: Description	Age/Grade Range	Publisher
DWSMB—Finger Identification: While blindfolded, identifying the finger that is touched (right and left).	4 to 90 years	Riverside
DWSMB—Object Identification: While blindfolded, identifying common objects by touch (right and left).		
DWSMB—Palm Writing: While blindfolded, recognizing a number or letter traced on palm by the examiner (right and left).		
DWSMB—Simultaneous Localization: While blindfolded, identifying the hand, cheek, or both that is touched (hands: right, left, and both; hand and cheek: right, left, and both).		
PAL-II RW—Finger Localization: Ability to point to the finger touched by the examiner's pencil behind a shield.	K to 6th grade	Pearson
PAL-II RW—Finger Recognition: Ability to give the number of the finger on a hand map that corresponds to the finger touched by the examiner.		
PAL-II M—Fingertip Writing Total: Ability to integrate kinesthetic-sensory input (touch) and abstract symbols without visual cues.		

See Appendix for the full names of the tests and their references.

Tests of Coordinated Finger/Hand Movements. Rapid Reference 10.7 presents tests that are designed to measure coordinated finger or hand movements. Students with poor coordinated finger and hand movements will often have difficulty with tasks requiring coordinated motor output, including fine motor tasks such as buttoning buttons, using a zipper, picking up or manipulating objects, copying 2-dimensional drawings, and/or constructing 3-dimensional objects with hands.

≡ Rapid Reference 10.7

Tests of Coordinated Finger/Hand Movements

Test–Subtest: Description	Age/Grade Range	Publisher
DWSMB—Coordination: Touching the end of nose with the index finger then touches the examiner's index finger as it moves across field of vision or touching the back of the hand then the front of the same hand to the thigh quickly (finger-to-nose: right and left; hand-to-thigh: right and left).	4 to 90 years	Riverside
DWSMB—Finger Tapping: Measuring the speed of fine-motor movement for the index finger of each hand over five trials (dominant and non-dominant hands).		
DWSMB—Left-Right Movements: Making purposeful left-right motor movements upon command.		
DWSMB—Mime Movements: Following commands (e.g., "Show me how you would brush your teeth").		
KABC-II—Hand Movements: Producing a sequence of motor acts with dominant hand.	3 to 18 years	Pearson
NEPSY-II—Fingertip Tapping: Dominant and nondominant hand completion times for two fine motor tasks.	5 to 16 years	Pearson
NEPSY-II—Imitating Hand Positions: Imitating hand positions shown by examiner with dominant and nondominant hands.	3 to 12 years	
NEPSY-II—Manual Motor Sequences: Sequencing motor acts with dominant hand.	3 to 12 years	
WRAVMA—Pegboard: Inserting as many pegs as possible, within 90 seconds, into a waffled pegboard.	3 to 17 years	PAR

See Appendix for the full names of the tests and their references.

Assessing Visual-Motor Integration Skills

There are a wide variety of visual-motor copying tasks available for school neuro-psychologists. Rapid Reference 10.8 presents tests that are designed to measure 2-dimensional visual-motor copying skills. Students with visual-motor copying deficiencies will have difficulty with writing and drawing activities in the classroom.

≡ Rapid Reference 10.8

Tests of Visual-Motor Copying Skills

Test–Subtest: Description	Age/Grade Range	Publisher
Beery VMI—Total Test:	2 to 100 years	Pearson
Copying simple to complex designs on paper.		
• **Visual Perception:**		
Visual perception aspects of the task.		
• **Motor Coordination:**		
Motor coordination aspects of the task.		
Bender II—Copy:	3 to 85+ years	Riverside
Copying 2-dimensional geometric figures.		
• **Motor Test:**		
Motor coordination aspects of the task.		
• **Perception Test:**		
Visual perception aspects of the task.		
DWSMB—Construction:	4 to 90 years	Riverside
Drawing figures (cross and clock).		
DAS-II—Copying:	2–6 to 8–11 years	Pearson
Copying 2-dimensional geometric figures.		
NEPSY-II—Design Copying General Score:	3 to 16 years	Pearson
Copying simple to complex designs on paper.		
• **Process Motor:**		
This score represents the motor output portion of the overall score.		
• **Process Global:**		
Ability to recognize the overall configuration of the design.		

(continued)

≡ *Rapid Reference 10.8 continued*

- **Process Local:**
  Ability to recognize details of the design.

ECFT—Copy Score: Copying an abstract design on paper.	6 years through adult	Western Psychological Services
WMS-IV—Visual Reproduction II Copy: Copying a design on paper.	16 to 90 years	Pearson
WRAVMA—Drawing: Coping designs that are arranged in order of increasing difficulty.	3 to 17 years	PAR

See Appendix for the full names of the tests and their references.

Assessing Visual Scanning

Children with significant visual scanning deficits often have difficulty with reading, writing, performing paper-and-pencil tasks, and telling time (Diller et al., 1974). Tests of sustained attention (described in Chapter 11), as well as other tests that measure processing speed (described in Chapter 16), require visual scanning. Examples of several visual scanning tests are described in this section. Rapid Reference 10.9 presents a list of common tests of visual scanning/tracking for school-age children.

Children with visual scanning or tracking problems often have difficulties with reading words on a line, or writing text on a straight line, or efficiently searching for a key piece of information embedded within a visual array of data. Lining up mathematical operations may be a difficult challenge for students with visual scanning problems. A referral to a developmental ophthalmologist may be warranted for specific visual scanning remedial exercises.

Qualitative Behaviors of Visual Scanning/Tracking. On the WISC-IV Integrated (Wechsler et al., 2004a), the Cancellation test provides two process scores: Cancellation Random Search Strategy and Cancellation Structured (Organized) Search Strategy. Each of these scores generates a base rate or cumulative percentage of children in the same age range that use one of the two types of search strategies. This is useful information to consider when interpreting the performance on the Cancellation test.

≡ *Rapid Reference 10.9*

Tests of Visual Scanning/Tracking

Test–Subtest: Description	Age/Grade Range	Publisher
Direct Measure of Visual Scanning/Tracking		
D-KEFS—Trail-Making Condition 1 (Visual Scanning): Marking all of the number 3s on a page as quickly as possible.	8–0 to 89–11 years	Pearson
Indirect Measures of Visual Scanning/Tracking		
NEPSY-II—Picture Puzzles Total: A large picture divided by a grid with four smaller pictures taken from sections of the larger picture is presented. The student identifies the location on the grid of the larger picture from which each of the smaller pictures was taken.	7 to 16 years	Pearson
WISC-IV—Cancellation: Marking target pictures within a visual set of pictures in a specified time period.	6–0 to 16–11 years	Pearson
WISC-IV—Coding: Symbols that are paired with simple geometric shapes or numbers are copied within a specified time limit.	6–0 to 16–11 years	Pearson
WISC-IV—Symbol Search: Visual scanning a group of stimuli to match target symbols.		
WNV—Coding: Copying symbols paired with geometric shapes or numbers within a time limit.	4–0 to 21–11 years	Pearson
WJIII-COG NU—Decision Speed: Rapidly matching two pictures in a row that belong in the same category.	2–0 to 90+ years	Riverside
WJIII-COG NU—Pair Cancellation: Matching target stimuli from a large visual array under time constraints.		
WJIII-COG NU—Visual Matching: Rapidly matching two numbers on a row.		

See Appendix for the full names of the tests and their references.

≡ Rapid Reference 10.10

Tests of Gross Motor Functions

Test–Subtest: Description	Age/Grade Range	Publisher
DWSMB—Gait and Station: Walking using three gaits—free walking, heel-to-toe, and hopping.	4 to 90 years	Riverside
DWSMB—Romberg: Maintaining balance with feet together, standing toe-to-heel, and standing on one foot, without visual cues.	4 to 90 years	Riverside

See Appendix for the full names of the tests and their references.

Assessing Gross Motor Functions

There are several tests available to school neuropsychologists to assess gross motor functions within the areas of balance and gross motor coordination. If serious gross motor coordination problems are known or suspected, the school neuropsychologist should consider referring the student to a physical therapist for a thorough assessment.

Rapid Reference 10.10 presents tests that are designed to measure gross motor coordination. Students with poor gross motor skills present a wide variety of clinical symptoms that vary with the child's age (see Hertza & Estes, 2011, for a review). Young children may appear clumsy and uncoordinated and have frequent falls and poor posture. School-age children will have difficulties with handwriting and poor participation in sports. Adolescents will have difficulty with driving, self-grooming, and poor motor dexterity, which could affect future career choices.

Qualitative Behaviors of Sensorimotor Functions

One of the major advantages of the NEPSY-II (see Chapter 7 for a discussion of the NEPSY-II) is the inclusion of base rates for qualitative behaviors based on either age norms or one of the clinical diagnostic groups. Rapid Reference 10.11 presents qualitative measures related to sensorimotor functions. As an example, if a child used visual guidance to facilitate performance on the NEPSY-II's Fingertip Taping Test, the percentage of other children the same age (the base rate) that used visual guidance is provided by the test publisher. As an added feature, the test publisher also provides the qualitative

≡ Rapid Reference 10.11

NEPSY-II (Korkman, Kirk, & Kemp, 2007) Qualitative Behaviors Related to Sensorimotor Functions

Fingertip tapping

- **Visual guidance:** Looking at fingers during the performance of task.
- **Incorrect position:** Wrong position of fingers.
- **Posturing:** Finger/hand on opposite side extended stiffly.
- **Mirroring:** Fingers on opposite side move involuntarily.
- **Overflow:** The lips or mouth move involuntarily.

Imitating hand positions

- **Mirroring:** Fingers on opposite side move involuntarily.
- **Other hand helps:** The child uses the other hand to help model the position.

Manual motor sequences

- **Rate change:** Variable speed and tempo during performance of task.
- **Overflow:** The lips or mouth move involuntarily.
- **Perseveration:** Movement continues for 3 to 4 sequences after being told to stop.
- **Loss of asymmetrical movement:** Loss of one side dominance on task.
- **Body movement:** Extraneous whole body movements in conjunction with the movement sequences.
- **Forceful tapping:** Tapping becomes louder during the production of the movement tasks.

Visuomotor precision

- **Pencil lift total:** Sum of the pencil lifts (a rule violation).
- **Quality of pencil grip:** Percentage of standardization sample with a specific type of pencil grip.

behavior base rates for each of the clinical diagnostic groups. These base rates provide the clinician the opportunity to make statements such as "Mary used visual guidance to help her perform the fingertip tapping test on the NEPSY-II. Only 14% of other children Mary's age used this compensatory strategy; however, 35% of the children within the Attention Deficit Hyperactivity Disorder diagnostic group used this compensatory strategy." The occurrence of qualitative behaviors, such as motor overflow, provides insights into the neuroanatomical functions of an individual. As an example, fingertip tapping should only elicit a precise activation of the motor strip area associated with finger control. However, when the individual produces mouth and tongue movements during the performance of a fingertip tapping task, this motor overflow is caused by broader areas of the motor strip being activated than what is typically observed.

CHAPTER SUMMARY

In this chapter, the terminology, neuroanatomy, and major assessment instruments associated with sensory-motor functioning were reviewed. Sensory-motor functions lay a foundation for all other higher order processes and should be systematically assessed by a school neuropsychologist. Sensory-motor dysfunctions are observed in many common developmental disorders.

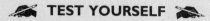

TEST YOURSELF

1. **True or False? *Sensory Processing Disorder* is an umbrella term used to cover a variety of neurological disabilities that interfere with the normal ability to use sensory information to function smoothly in daily life.**

2. **Which of the neuropsychological terms below means the unconscious awareness of sensations coming from one's muscles and joints?**
   a. Graphestheia
   b. Visual agnosia
   c. Proprioception
   d. Asterognosia

3. **All of the following are types of subtypes of sensory processing difficulties except one, which one?**
   a. Understimulated
   b. Sensation seekers
   c. Overstimulated
   d. Hypervigilance

4. **True or False? The pyramidal and extrapyramidal neural systems help regulate motor activity in humans.**

5. **What neuropsychological term means an inability to assemble, build, draw, or copy accurately, not due to apraxia of simple movements?**
   a. Constructional apraxia
   b. Ataxia
   c. Dystonia
   d. Clonus

6. Which one of the following sensory-motor batteries is typically administered by an occupational therapist?

    a. Wide Range Assessment of Visual Motor Abilities
    b. Sensory Integration and Praxis Tests
    c. Dean-Woodcock Sensory-Motor Battery
    d. Beery-Butkencia Developmental Test of Visual-Motor Integration

7. The inability to perform gestures based on verbal command is called?

    a. Ideational apraxia
    b. Dysphagia
    c. Constructional apraxia
    d. Ataxia

Answers: 1. true; 2. c; 3. d; 4. true; 5. a; 6. b; 7. a

Chapter Eleven

VISUOSPATIAL AND AUDITORY COGNITIVE PROCESSES

VISUOSPATIAL PROCESSES

Much of what is learned in school has either a visuospatial or auditory basis. Visuospatial skills and auditory processing skills are essential for a child to achieve academic success. Visual perceptual skills play a major role in the development of a child's handwriting skills and academic fluency. The school neuropsychologist should include measures of visuospatial processes in any comprehensive school neuropsychological evaluation. In this chapter, the neuropsychology of visuospatial and auditory processes are reviewed, subcomponents of visuospatial functions are defined, the neuroanatomy of visuospatial functions are described, and the common tests used to assess visuospatial functions are presented.

Subcomponents Associated With Visuospatial Processing

Visuospatial processing is a broad cognitive process that encompasses many subcomponents. Many of the visuospatial subcomponents involve other cognitive processes such as attention, sensory-motor, memory, and executive functions. Any neurocognitive task that uses visual stimuli involves a certain degree of visual processing. Some neurocognitive tasks require visual attention to detail, as in a visual sustained attention task (e.g., WJIII-COG Pair Cancellation: Woodcock et al., 2001, 2007a). Other neurocognitive tasks require visual-motor integration (e.g., *Beery-Buketenica Developmental Test of Visual-Motor Integration*: Beery, Buktenica, & Beery, 2010; *Wide Range Assessment of Visual Motor Abilities*: Adams & Sheslow, 1995), visual-motor planning (e.g., WJIII-COG Planning: Woodcock et al., 2001, 2007a; *WISC-IV Integrated* Elithorn Mazes: Wechsler, 2004a), visual memory (e.g., *Children Memory*

⚋ Rapid Reference 11.1

Visuospatial Processing Subcomponents

Subcomponent	Where Covered in Conceptual Model
• Visual attention	• Allocating and maintaining attention facilitators/inhibitors
• Visual-motor integration	• Covered under sensory-motor functions
• Visual-motor planning	• Covered under executive processes
• Visual (spatial) memory	• Covered under learning and memory processes
• Visual spatial perception	• Covered in this section
• Visual spatial reasoning	• Covered in this section
• Visual scanning/ tracking	• Covered under sensory-motor functions

Scale Dot Localization: Cohen, 1997; *Wide Range Assessment of Memory and Learning—Second Edition* Design Memory: Sheslow & Adams, 2003), visual perception with a motor response (e.g., *Kaufman Assessment Battery for Children—Second Edition* Triangles: A. Kaufman & N. Kaufman, 2004), visuospatial reasoning (e.g., WJIII-COG Spatial Relations Woodcock et al., 2001, 2007a), visual perception without a motor response (e.g., NEPSY-II Arrows: Korkman et al., 2007), visual perceptual organization (e.g., *Extended Complex Figure Test*: Fastenau, 1996), visual perceptual reasoning (e.g., WISC-IV Block Design: Wechsler, 2003), and visual scanning or tracking (e.g., D-KEFS: Trail Making Test [Condition 1]: Delis, Kramer, & Kaplan, 2001).

Rapid Reference 11.1 lists the subcomponents associated with visuospatial processing and indicates the areas in the Integrated SNP/CHC Model where the subcomponents are covered.

Neuroanatomy of Visuospatial Processes

This section reviews the neuroanatomy of the visuospatial processes including the primary visual pathway, the dorsal and ventral pathways, the areas of the brain activated during visual object recognition, and the areas of the brain activated during face recognition.

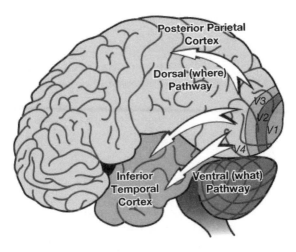

Figure 11.1. The Dorsal and Ventral Streams

Primary Visual Pathway

Visual perception is distributed across two distinct subsystems (Gazzaniga, Ivry, & Mangun, 2002). Ninety percent of the optic nerve axons terminate in the lateral geniculate nuclei of the thalamus, the relay station of the brain. The remaining 10% of the optic nerve axons terminate at other subcortical structures, including the superior colliculus of the midbrain and the pulvinar nucleus of the thalamus. The final axonal pathway leaves the lateral geniculate nuclei and terminates in the primary visual cortex of the occipital lobe (see Figure 11.1).

The primary visual cortex within the occipital lobe has many specialized areas. Visual perception appears to involve a "divide and conquer" strategy (Gazzaniga et al., 2002). While each of the visual areas within the primary visual cortex help to provide a visual map of the external world, some neuronal areas are sensitive to variations in color, others to movement, etc. The specialized visual areas provide distributed and specialized analyses that are integrated into perceptual wholes at higher levels of processing.

The Dorsal and Ventral Pathways

The outputs from the primary visual cortex follow two general pathways: the superior longitudinal fasciculus and the inferior longitudinal fasciculus. The superior longitudinal fasciculus fibers terminate in the posterior parietal cortex and the inferior longitudinal fasciculus fibers terminate in the inferior temporal cortex. Ungerleider and Mishkin (1982) proposed that the ventral or occipital-parietal pathway (superior longitudinal fasciculus) is specialized for object perception and object recognition. Ungerleider and Mishkin (1982) refer to the occipital-parietal pathway as the "where" pathway, where an object is relative to different objects. The dorsal or occipital-temporal pathway (inferior longitudinal fasciculus) is specialized for spatial perception (see Figure 11.1). Ungerleider and Mishkin (1982) refer to the occipital-temporal pathway as the "what" pathway, as in what we are looking at.

Both the "what" and the "where" aspects of visual perception are important. We need to recognize what we are looking at and know where it is.

Visual Object Recognition

The common neuropsychological terms associated with visuospatial impairments are presented in Rapid Reference 11.2. The label *visual agnosia* is used to describe a child who has difficulty recognizing visually presented objects. A child with visual agnosia will not be able to identify a pencil based on sight alone, but may be able to quickly identify the pencil when it is placed in the child's hand. *Apperceptive agnosia* is a subtype of visual agnosia in which failures in object recognition are linked to problems with visual perceptual processing. However, *associative agnosia* is used to describe a child who has normal visual representations but cannot use that

---

≡ Rapid Reference 11.2

Neuropsychological Terms Associated With Visuospatial Impairments

- *Apperceptive agnosia*—A form of visual agnosia in which the deficit is caused by impaired visual perception.
- *Associative agnosia*—A failure of visual object recognition that cannot be attributed to perceptual abilities.
- *Astereopsis*—Inability to perceive the depth of objects.
- *Color agnosia*—Inability to appreciate differences between colors or to relate colors to objects in the presence of intact color vision.
- *Integrative agnosia*—A failure in integrating the parts of an object into a coherent whole.
- *Pantomime agnosia*—Inability to comprehend pantomimes, even when the ability to copy them remains intact.
- *Prosopagnosia*—Impaired face recognition.
- *Simultanagnosia*—Impaired recognition of the meaning of whole pictures or objects, but intact ability to describe the parts of the pictures/objects.
- *Visual agnosia*—Impaired ability to recognize visual information.

Sources: Ayd, 1995; Loring, 1999.

information to recognize an object. Warrington (1985) proposed a two-stage, neuroanatomical model of object recognition. Warrington proposed that visual processing would initially be bilateral and involve both occipital cortices. Next, perceptual categorization within the right parietal hemisphere is employed. Perceptual inputs are aligned with visually stored representations of objects. This stage is thought to be presemantic, in that a child may be able to recognize two pictures that illustrate the same object without having to name the object or describe its function. The second stage of object recognition, according to Warrington's model, is semantic categorization within the left hemisphere. In the second stage, visual information is linked to knowledge in long-term memory concerning the name and function of the object (e.g., *Woodcock-Johnson III Tests of Achievement:* Picture Vocabulary). Warrington found that adults with lesions in their right hemisphere were more likely to demonstrate characteristics of apperceptive agnosia and adults with lesions in their left hemispheres were more likely to demonstrate characteristics of associative agnosia.

Face Recognition

An important subset of object recognition is face recognition. We can be walking down the street and meet an old friend from high school and instantly recognize their face. The inferior temporal lobe, specifically the fusiform gyrus, is involved in recognizing objects, especially faces (see Figure 11.2). When a face is recognized in the fusiform gyrus, the information is transmitted to the frontal lobes for processing. *Prosopagnosia* is a term used to describe the inability to

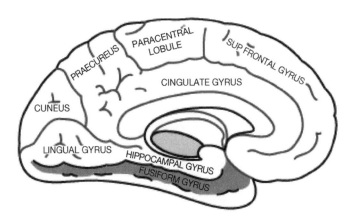

Figure 11.2. The Fusiform Gyrus Involved in Recognizing Objects, Particularly Faces

recognize faces, which is a socially disabling disorder. Prosopagnosia rarely occurs with unilateral, left lesions. It is more likely associated with bilateral lesions caused by multiple stokes, head injury, encephalitis, or poisoning (Gazzaniga et al., 2002) or right hemispheric lesions that include the ventral regions of the occipital and temporal lobes (DeRenzi, Perani, Carlesimo, Silveri, & Fazio, 1994).

We live in a multimodal society where learning requires both intact auditory and visual processing skills. When a child is experiencing a visuospatial processing disorder it can severely impact the child's learning potential and their social functioning. Reading and math both rely heavily on the use of symbols (e.g., letters for reading and numbers and signs for math) and accurate visual perception is important. Writing also has a large visuospatial component. Students with visual perception problems may have difficulties with directionality, letter and number reversals, spacing problems in writing, visually discriminating shapes from a whiteboard, recognizing missing details within a partial visual object (visual closure), and so on. A child with visual perception difficulties may also have related social problems because of difficulties recognizing facial expressions and emotions in others. Some visual problems may just be related to an acuity problem and can be addressed by a visual exam and possible glasses or contacts. Other visual problems may be perceptual in nature and require a more thorough examination by and intervention from a developmental ophthalmologist.

Identifying Visuospatial Processing Concerns

It is suggested that the *Neuropsychological Processing Concerns Checklist for Children and Youth—Third Edition* (NPCC-3: Miller, 2012a) be completed by the parent/ guardian and at least one teacher of the student being referred for a comprehensive assessment (see the supplemental CD for the complete NPCC-3). The questions on the NPCC-3 that pertain to visuospatial problems are shown in Rapid Reference 11.3. Note that these items are contained with the Sensorimotor

---

≡ Rapid Reference 11.3

Visuospatial Items From the Neuropsychological Processing Concerns Checklist for Children and Youth—Third Edition (NPCC-3: Miller, 2012a)

- Confusion with directions (e.g., gets lost easily).
- Shows right-left confusion or directions (up-down).
- Difficulties with putting puzzles together.

section of the NPPC. Any endorsed items in the moderate to severe range should be followed up with formal assessment measures in the school neuro-psychological assessment.

Assessing Visuospatial Processes

Rapid Reference 11.4 restates the second- and third-order classifications of visuospatial processes within the Integrated SNP/CHC Model. Tests designed to measure these second- and third-order classifications of visuospatial processes are presented in this section.

Tests of Visuospatial Perception

The second-order classification of visuospatial perception separates the tasks into two categories: tests that require visual discrimination and spatial localization, and tests that require visual-motor constructions. Rapid Reference 11.5 presents a list of common tests of visuospatial perception for school-age children.

The Block Design test from the WISC-IV (Wechsler, 2003) is classified under Visual Spatial Perception (second-order classification) and Visual-Motor Construction (third-order classification). When considering a student's performance on the Block Design test, it is important to consider differences in performance when completion time is not considered (the Block Design No Time Bonus score). The WISC-IV Integrated (Wechsler et al., 2004a) provides variations of

≡ *Rapid Reference 11.4*

Integrated SNP/CHC Model Classifications of Visuospatial Processes

Broad Classifications	Second-Order Classifications	Third-Order Classifications
Visuospatial processes	• Visual spatial perception	• Visual discrimination and spatial localization
		• Visual-motor constructions
		• Qualitative behaviors
	• Visual spatial reasoning	• Recognizing spatial configurations
		• Visual gestalt closure
		• Visuospatial analyses with and without mental rotations

≡ Rapid Reference 11.5

Tests of Visuospatial Perception

Test–Subtest: Description	Age/Grade Range	Publisher
Visual Discrimination and Spatial Localization		
NEPSY-II—Arrows Total: Two arrows from many are chosen by letter label, which are thought to point to the center of the target.	5 to 16 years	Pearson
NEPSY-II—Picture Puzzles Total: A large picture divided by a grid with four smaller pictures taken from sections of the larger picture is presented. The student identifies the location on the grid of the larger picture from which each of the smaller pictures was taken.	7 to 16 years	
NEPSY-II—Route Finding Total: A schematic map with a target house is presented and the student is asked to find that house in a larger map with other houses and streets.	5 to 12 years	
TVPS-3—Visual Discrimination: Matching a target design among a set of designs on the same page.	4–0 to 18–11 years	Academic Therapy Publications
Visual-Motor Constructions		
DAS-II—Pattern Construction: Imitating constructions made by the examiner with wooden blocks, color tiles, or patterned cubes.	2–6 to 17–11 years	Pearson
KABC-II—Triangles: Re-creating shapes that were modeled by examiner.	3–0 to 18–0 years	
NEPSY-II—Block Construction total: Reproducing 3-dimensional constructions from models or 2-dimensional drawings under time constraints.	3 to 16 years	

WISC-IV—Block Design:	6 to 16–11 years
Re-creation of a constructed model or a picture of a block design within a specified time limit.	
WNV—Object Assembly:	4–0 to 21–11 years
Putting puzzle pieces together to form a meaningful whole.	

See Appendix for the full names of the tests and their references.

Block Design to test the limits and to isolate reasons for poor performance on the test. WISC-IV Integrated scores such as the Block Design Process Approach, Block Design Multiple Choice, and Block Design Multiple Choice No Time Bonus should all be administered and interpreted when a student achieves a low score on the WISC-IV Block Design test relative to performance on other cognitive measures.

Qualitative Behaviors of Visuospatial Perception

On the WISC-IV Integrated (Wechsler et al., 2004a), the Block Design subtest has a set of qualitative scores that aid in the clinical interpretation of the test. These qualitative scores are calculated as base rates comparing a student's performance to their same aged peers. These score are listed in Rapid Reference 11.6.

Tests of Visuospatial Reasoning

The second-order classification of visuospatial reasoning separates the tasks into three categories: tests that require recognition of spatial configurations, tests that require visual gestalt closure, and tests that require visuospatial analyses with and without mental rotations. Rapid Reference 11.7 presents a list of common tests of visuospatial reasoning for school-age children.

Visuospatial reasoning skills are required in the discrimination of letters, numbers, and words. Mathematical reasoning skills requiring estimates of quantity and certainly geometry rely heavily on visuospatial reasoning.

Auditory Processes

Samuel is a poor reader. He has difficulty sounding out words. If he is able to read a word, it is because he has memorized what the word looks like rather than sounding it out. As a result of his poor phonological processing skills, his reading fluency and reading comprehension are also weak.

≡ Rapid Reference 11.6

Qualitative Behaviors for WISC-IV Integrated: Block Design

- *Partial Score Part A:* Percentage of same-age peers that received a partial score on the task that required the student to select the correct number of blocks to construct block designs that match a model presented on a page (global details).
- *Partial Score Part B:* Percentage of same-age peers that received a partial score on the readministration of failed Part A items using a grid overlay (specific details).
- *En Route Break in Configuration—Part A:* Percentage of same-age peers that violated the rules of correct block placement or no rotation on Part A during the construction.
- *En Route Break in Configuration—Part B:* Percentage of same-age peers that violated the rules of correct block placement or no rotation on Part B during the construction.
- *Break in Final Configuration—Part A:* Percentage of same-age peers that violated the rules of correct block placement or no rotation on Part A at the completion of the construction.
- *Break in Final Configuration—Part B:* Percentage of same-age peers that violated the rules of correct block placement or no rotation on Part B at the completion of the construction.
- *Extra Block Construction—Part A:* Percentage of the same-age peers that used an extra block in the Part A construction.
- *Extra Block Construction—Part B:* Percentage of the same-age peers that used an extra block in the Part B construction.

≡ Rapid Reference 11.7

Tests of Visuospatial Reasoning

Test–Subtest: Description	Age/Grade Range	Publisher
Recognizing Spatial Configurations		
DAS-II—Matching Letter-Like Forms: Multiple-choice matching of shapes that are similar to letters.	2–6 to 8–11 years	Pearson
KABC-II—Block Counting: Counting 3-dimensional cubes.	3 to 18 years	Pearson

TVPS-3—Spatial Relationships: Choosing one design that is different from the rest.	4 to 18–11 years	Academic Therapy Publication
WJIII-COG NU—Spatial Relations: Identify two or more pieces that go together to form a complete target shape.	2–0 to 90+ years	Riverside

Visual Gestalt Closure

KABC-II—Gestalt Closure: Figuring out what a picture is when it has been partially erased or obscured.	3 to 18 years	Pearson
RIAS—What's Missing: Naming a missing part of a visual picture.	3 to 94 years	PAR
TVPS-3—Visual Closure: Matching an incomplete pattern with a completed design.	4 to 18–11 years	Academic Therapy Publication
TVPS-3—Visual Figure-Ground: Finding one design among many within a complex background.		
WISC-IV—Picture Completion: Naming a missing part of a visual picture.	6 to 16–11 years	Pearson
WJIII-COG DS—Visual Closure: Verbally naming a drawing or picture that has been altered in some way.	2–0 to 90+ years	Riverside

Visuospatial Analyses with and without Mental Rotations

NEPSY-II—Geometric Puzzles total: A picture of a large grid containing several shapes is presented, then the student matches two shapes outside of the grid to two shapes within the grid.	3 to 16 years	Pearson
SB5—Nonverbal Visuospatial Processing: Ability to identify, analyze, and mentally rotate or assemble visual images, geometric shapes, or natural objects occurring in spatial arrangements.	2 to 85+ years	Riverside
TVPS-3—Form Constancy: Finding a design embedded within another object.	4 to 18–11 years	Academic Therapy Publication

(continued)

≡ Rapid Reference 11.7 continued

WRAVMA—Matching: Looking at a visual "standard" and select the option that "goes best" with it.	3 to 17 years	Pearson
WJIII-COG DS—Block Rotation: Ability to select the two sets of blocks that are rotated versions of the target pattern.	2–0 to 90+ years	Riverside

See Appendix for the full names of the tests and their references.

We live in a language-rich society where verbal skills are often valued above nonverbal skills. The basic building blocks of language are basic sound discrimination and auditory processing skills. When a first or second grader is still struggling with basic sound discrimination such as knowing words that sound alike or rhyme, the clinician should evaluate the student's basic sound discrimination skills. Sometimes a child has acquired basic sound discrimination but has difficulty manipulating phonemes such as blending sounds to form words or identifying missing phonemes to complete whole words. These auditory processing skills along with the ability to discriminate sounds are basic building blocks for the acquisition of reading. When delays occur in acquiring these basic skills, a referral for criterion-referenced or norm-referenced assessment is probably warranted.

Neuroanatomy of Auditory Processes

The ears receive sound waves that travel into the ear canal where they vibrate the eardrum. As the eardrum vibrates, it moves tiny bones in the middle ear, which in turn carry the vibrations through the fluid filled cochlea. Inside the cochlea a series of tiny hairs called cilia vibrate and are attached to the cochlear nerve. It is the movements of the cilia that stimulate the cochlear nerve and send signals to the brain. The ear receives auditory input but the brain hears.

Figure 11.3 illustrates the auditory pathway from the ear to the primary auditory cortex. The cochlear nerve passes through the medulla in the brainstem and then to the inferior colliculus. The auditory pathway divides so input from each ear can ultimately be received and processed in each hemisphere. The auditory pathway is then processed through the thalamus, the sensory relay station of the brain, and onto the auditory cortex. The auditory cortex is responsible for phonological processing, by allowing us to recognize words by the way they sound.

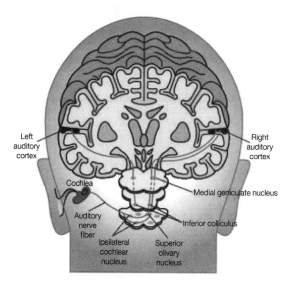

Figure 11.3. Neuroanatomy of Hearing

Identifying Auditory Processing Concerns

It is suggested that the *Neuropsychological Processing Concerns Checklist for Children and Youth—Third Edition* (NPCC-3: Miller, 2012a) be completed by the parent/guardian and at least one teacher of the student being referred for a comprehensive assessment (see the supplemental CD for the complete NPCC-3). The questions on the NPCC-3 that pertain to auditory processing problems are shown in Rapid Reference 11.8. Any endorsed items in the moderate to severe range should be followed up with formal assessment measures in the school neuropsychological assessment.

≡ Rapid Reference 11.8

....

Auditory Processing Items From the Neuropsychological Processing Concerns Checklist for Children and Youth—Third Edition (NPCC-3: Miller, 2012a)

Phonological/auditory processing difficulties:
- Difficulty with sound discrimination.
- Difficulty with blending of sounds to form words.
- Difficulty with rhyming activities.
- Omits sounds when reading or speaking.
- Substitutes sounds when reading or speaking.

≡ Rapid Reference 11.9

Integrated SNP/CHC Model Classifications of Auditory Processes

Broad Classifications	Second-Order Classifications	Third-Order Classifications
Auditory processes	• Sound discrimination • Auditory/phonological processing	

Assessing Auditory Processing

Rapid Reference 11.9 restates the second- and third-order classifications of language processes within the Integrated SNP/CHC Model. Tests designed to measure these second- and third-order classifications of auditory processes are presented in this section.

Tests of Basic Sound Discrimination

Rapid Reference 11.10 lists the Sound Patterns—Music and Sound Patterns—Voice tests from *The Diagnostic Supplement to the Woodcock-Johnson III Tests of Cognitive Abilities* (WJIII-COG DS: Woodcock, McGrew, Mather, & Schrank, 2003, 2007) that were designed to measure basic sound discrimination skills.

≡ Rapid Reference 11.10

Tests of Sound Discrimination

Test–Subtest: Description	Age/Grade Range	Publisher
WJIII-COG DS—Sound Patterns—Music: Determining if musical sounds presented in a pair are the same or different.	2–0 to 90+ years	Riverside
WJIII-COG DS—Sound Patterns—Voice: Determining if human speech sounds presented in a pair are the same or different.		

See Appendix for the full names of the tests and their references.

A speech and language pathologist has access to other tests that are designed to measure sound discrimination and the student should be referred for a speech and language assessment when deficits in this area are suspected. A student with deficits in basic sound discrimination will have difficulty learning to read using a phonological approach.

Tests of Auditory/Phonological Processing

Rapid Reference 11.11 lists the major tests at the disposal of a school neuropsychologist that are designed to assess auditory and/or phonological processing. This listing only includes tests that are typically used by school psychologists and school neuropsychologists. There are many other tests from the speech and language assessment batteries that are also designed to measure auditory and/or phonological processing.

≡ Rapid Reference 11.11

Tests of Auditory/Phonological Processing

Test–Subtest: Description	Age/Grade Range	Publisher
CTOPP—Blending Words: Listening to words in small parts and blending the parts together to make a whole word.	5–0 to 24–11 years	PRO-ED
CTOPP—Elision: Omitting a phoneme from a word to create a new word.		
CTOPP—Sound Matching: Choosing a word that contains a target sound.	5–0 to 6–11 years	
DAS-II—Phonological Processing: Rhyming, blending sounds, deleting sounds, and identifying the individual sounds in words.	5–0 to 12–11 years	Pearson
DTAP—Composite Auditory Perception Index: Overall performance on various auditory perception tasks.	6–0 to 18–11 years	PRO-ED
KTEA-II—Phonological Awareness: Manipulation of sounds (e.g., rhyming, blending).	4–6 to 25 years	Pearson
NEPSY-II—Phonological Processing: Part 1: Word segment recognition Part 2: Phonological segmentation	3 to 16 years	

(continued)

⟰ *Rapid Reference 11.11 continued*

PAL-II RW—Phonological Coding Scores: Ability to segment spoken words into units that are related to units of written words.	Grades K to 6	
TAPS-3—Phonological Blending: Ability to synthesize a word when given the individual phonemes.	4 to 18–11 years	Academic Therapy Publications
TAPS-3—Phonological Segmentation: Ability to manipulate phonemes in words.		
TAPS-3—Word Discrimination: Ability to discern phonological differences and similarities in word pairs.		
TOPA-2+ Kindergarten Edition—Initial Sound Same: Marking which of three words begins with the same sound as a target word.	Kindergarten	PRO-ED
TOPA-2+ Kindergarten Edition— Initial Sound Different: Marking which of three words begins with a different first sound than the other three.		
TOPA-2+ Early Elementary Edition—Ending Sound Same: Identify which of three words ends with the same sound as a target word.	First–second grades	
TOPA-2+ Early Elementary Edition—Ending Sound Different: Marking which of a group of four words ends in a different sound than the others.		
TOPAS—Incomplete Words: Ability to discern a missing phoneme from a spoken word.	Grades K to 3+	
TOPAS—Phoneme Deletion: Ability to repeat a word, then say the word with a certain phoneme missing.		
TOPAS—Rhyming: Ability to complete a sentence with a word that is both semantically correct and rhymes with another word.		

TOPAS—Sound Sequencing:
Ability to sequence a set of color blocks
that correspond to a speech sound.

TPAS—Composite Score: 4–0 to 10–11
Overall measure of phonological   years
awareness in Spanish-speaking children.

- **TPAS—Initial Sounds:**
  Determining if a second word begins
  with the same sound as a target
  word.

- **TPAS—Final Sounds:**
  Determining if a second word ends
  with the same sound as a target
  word.

- **TPAS—Rhyming Words:**
  Determining if a second word rhymes
  or sounds like the target word.

- **TPAS—Deletions:**
  Repeating a specific word while
  leaving out a syllable or sound at the
  beginning, middle, or end of the
  word.

WJIII-ACH NU—Sound Awareness: 2–0 to 90+   Riverside
Rhyming, deletion, substitution, and   years
reversal of phonemes.

**WJIII-COG NU—Incomplete
Words:**
Listening to a word with one or more
missing phonemes and then identifying the
whole word.

WJIII-COG NU—Sound Blending:
Blending sounds to form a whole word.

See Appendix for the full names of the tests and their references.

On the Developmental Test of Auditory Perception (DTAP: Reynolds, Voress, & Pearson, 2008) there is an overall composite score that reflects overall auditory perception abilities; however, there are four separate indices that should be reported and interpreted as well. According to Reynolds et al. (2008), the Language Perception Index in an indicator of more left temporal lobe processing of language (Reynolds et al., 2008). The Non-Language

Perception Index is an indicator of more right temporal lobe processing of language. The Background Noise Perception Index measures the ability to accurately perceive a target set of sounds in the presence of background noise, and the No Background Noise Perception Index measures the ability to accurately perceive a target set of sounds in the presence of no back-ground noise.

On the *Process Assessment of the Learner—Second Edition: Diagnostics for Reading and Writing* (PAL-II RW: Berninger, 2007b) the Phonological Coding test is designed to measure ability to segment spoken words into units that are related to units of written words. The test yields a composite score but also generates separate scores for the ability to segment words into phonemes (Phonemes), ability to analyze and generate rhymes for spoken words (Rhyming), understanding of rhymes in syllables (Rimes), and ability to segment spoken words into syllables (Syllables). Performance on these subtests should also be examined beyond the composite score.

Students with deficits in auditory/phonological processing have difficulties with reading acquisition that is taught using purely phonological instruction. Students with severe deficits in this area may have to learn how to read based on memorizing the whole word visually rather than applying a sounding out, phonetic approach to reading.

CHAPTER SUMMARY

In this chapter, the terminology, neuroanatomy, and major assessment measures associated with visuospatial and auditory processes were reviewed. Visuospatial processes have a strong influence on academic achievement (e.g., handwriting, math, and reading fluency) and should be systematically assessed by a school neuropsychologist. Auditory processes serve as the foundation for reading and language skills and need to be assessed by the school neuropsychologist, particularly in young children. Visuospatial and auditory processing disorders are observed in many common developmental disorders.

🐟 TEST YOURSELF 🐟

I. **What term means an impaired ability to recognize visual information?**
   a. Simultanagnosia
   b. Astereopsis
   c. Prosopagnosia
   d. Visual agnosia

2. What term means impaired face recognition?

   a. Simultanagnosia
   b. Astereopsis
   c. Prosopagnosia
   d. Visual agnosia

3. True or False? Ungerleider and Mishkin refer to occipital-parietal pathway as the "where" pathway.

4. What part of the brain is responsible for processing hearing?

   a. Temporal lobes
   b. Frontal lobes
   c. Parietal lobes
   d. Occipital lobes

5. True or False? The KABC-II Block Counting subtest is an example of a visuospatial reasoning test.

6. Which of the tests below is an example of a visual gestalt closure type of task?

   a. NEPSY-II—Arrows total
   b. WISC-IV—Picture completion
   c. DAS-II—Pattern construction
   d. KABC-II—Triangles

Answers: 1. d; 2. c; 3. true; 4. a; 5. true; 6. b

Chapter Twelve

LEARNING AND MEMORY COGNITIVE PROCESSES

I n this chapter learning and memory processes are defined, theories of learning and memory are reviewed, the neuroanatomy of learning and memory are described, and the common tests used to assess learning and memory within the school neuropsychological assessment model are presented.

THEORIES OF LEARNING AND MEMORY

Learning is defined as the process of acquiring new information, and *memory* is defined as the persistence of learning that can be assessed at a later time (Squire, 1987). Learning and memory are typically conceptualized into three hypothetical stages: encoding, storage, and retrieval. *Encoding* is the processing of incoming information to be stored. *Storage* is the result of acquisition and consolidation that creates and maintains a permanent memory trace. *Retrieval* is the conscious recall or recognition of previously learned and stored memories. When a student is suspected of having a memory problem, the school neuropsychologist will try to determine, among other things, if the memory problems are a function of encoding, storage, retrieval, or a combination of the three.

Atkinson and Shiffrin (1968) proposed a modal model of memory, consisting of sensory memory, short-term memory, and long-term memory. These categories of memory will be discussed in greater detail in the following sections.

Sensory Memory

Sensory memory has a high capacity for information, but has a short life of just a few milliseconds. Visual sensory memory is referred to as *iconic memory* or an *iconic store*, and verbal sensory memory is referred to as *echoic memory*. Sensory memories are like background noise in our memory systems. If we do not attend to the sensory memory traces, they decay rapidly. A classic example of a sensory memory is the "cocktail party effect." If you are at a cocktail party talking to a friend, you are paying attention to that conversation. The background conversations are being processed in sensory memory but you are not attending to those conversations. Someone across the room suddenly mentions your name in the middle of their conversation and you shift your attention to that conversation to hear what that person is saying about you. We can extract information from sensory memory if we attend to it quickly. In this example, our spoken name would be otherwise lost had we not attended to it. Sensory memory is an interesting basic part of memory, but it is not a construct that is measured directly by school neuropsychologists.

Short-Term Memory

Leticia is a third grader. She frequently does not seem to remember things right after information is presented. She frequently asks to have something repeated and she has trouble taking notes. Leticia is experiencing difficulties with her short-term memory.

Unlike sensory memory that has a high capacity and short duration, *short-term memory* has a limited capacity and a long duration based on continual rehearsal. Short-term memory is associated with retention over seconds to minutes. An example would be a telephone number given to you by a friend. As long as you mentally rehearse the number verbally in your head, you can conceivably continue to hold that telephone number in short-term memory. However, as soon as you are the slightest bit distracted, the telephone number is lost to conscious memory. The capacity of short-term memory has been shown to be seven bits or chunks of information, plus or minus two (G. Miller, 1994).

Long-Term Memory

Adrienne is a fifth grader. She has trouble remembering to turn in her homework assignments even when they are completed. Adrienne can perform well on a daily quiz over a content area, but then she performs poorly on a more comprehensive exam. She has difficulty answering questions about factual information. Adrienne is evidencing signs of long-term memory deficits.

Long-term memory is measured in days or years. Long-term memory represents near permanent memory storage. Cognitive psychologists have conceptualized two distinct subdivisions of long-term memory: *declarative memory* and *nondeclarative memory*. Declarative memory refers to "knowledge that we have conscious access to, including personal and world knowledge"

(Gazzaniga, Ivry, & Magun, 2002, p. 312). Declarative memory can be further subdivided into *episodic memory*, our autobiographical memories, and *semantic memory*, our knowledge of basic facts. The major tests of memory, learning, and intelligence do measure semantic memory. Episodic or autobiographical memory is difficult to measure because it is personal and lacks objective verification. In severe cases of memory loss due to trauma or disease, episodic or autobiographical memory can be informally assessed using a clinical interview and verified by a third party (e.g., parents).

Nondeclarative memory refers to "knowledge that we have no conscious access to, such as motor and cognitive skills (procedural knowledge), perceptual priming, and simple learned behaviors that derive from conditioning, habituation, or sensitization (Gazzaniga et al., 2002, p. 314). The only nondeclarative memory that may be included in a school neuropsychological assessment is procedural memory. Procedural memory involves the learning of a variety of motor skills such as riding a bike, or cognitive skills such as knowing to start reading from left to right. The disruption of procedural memories may be questioned in a clinical interview or directly observed by the school neuropsychologist.

Evidence for and against the Modal Model of Memory

The *serial-order position effect* provides support for the distinction between short-term and long-term memory. The serial-order position effect is observed using a list-learning task. A distinct pattern for the number of correctly identified words emerges when a group of individuals are presented with a list of words and asked to recall those words. Some students are better at recalling words at the beginning of the list, a *primacy effect*, whereas other students perform best when recalling words at the end of the list, a *recency effect*. The primary effect is thought to be reflective of long-term memory and the recency effect is thought to reflect short-term memory.

Atkinson and Shiffrin's (1968) proposed modal model of memory held widespread appeal for decades. However, experimental and theoretical evidence does not support the modal model of memory. The modal model of memory proposed that rehearsal was the key factor in transferring information from sensory memory to short-term memory and from short-term memory to long-term memory. Researchers have found that other factors besides rehearsal seem to influence long-term memory. Craik and Lockhart (1972) illustrated that the more meaningfully a stimulus item was processed the more it was consolidated and stored in long-term memory. This is called the *levels of processing model.*

Gazzaniga and his colleagues (2002) reviewed several case studies of patients with brain damage. In these case studies, the patients were not able to form new short-term memories, yet they were able to form new long-term memories. These case studies suggested that short-term memory was not the absolute "gateway" to forming long-term memories.

A CONCEPTUAL MODEL OF LEARNING AND MEMORY FOR SCHOOL NEUROPSYCHOLOGISTS

Rapid Reference 12.1 presents the classification of learning and memory within a conceptual school neuropsychological assessment model. Immediate memory is typically assessed using verbal or visual modalities. Likewise, long-term or delayed memory is typically assessed using verbal or visual modalities. Within the long-term memory area, it is also possible to assess for any differences between free recall and recognition using either modality.

Rapid Reference 12.1

Classification of Tests of Learning and Memory

Classification	Definitions
• Verbal immediate memory	• The capacity to maintain verbal information in conscious awareness.
• Visual immediate memory	• The capacity to maintain visual information in conscious awareness.

• Verbal (delayed) long-term memory
   • Verbal learning
   • Verbal delayed recall
   • Verbal delayed recognition
	• Retention of verbal information for prolonged, perhaps indefinite periods of time.

• Visual (delayed) long-term memory
   • Visual learning
   • Visual delayed recall
   • Visual delayed recognition
	• Retention of visual information for prolonged, perhaps indefinite periods of time.

• Verbal-visual associative learning and memory	• Learning and retention of associated verbal and visual stimuli for prolonged periods of time.

Verbal-visual associative learning and memory is another construct frequently assessed. Associative learning and memory tasks pair verbal and visual information (e.g., the WJIII-COG Visual-Auditory Learning subtest). The final two common learning and memory constructs that are frequently assessed are working memory (ability to perform complex mental operations on material placed in immediate memory) and semantic memory (knowledge of basic facts).

A conceptual model of learning and memory for school neuropsychologists is illustrated in Figure 12.1. The conceptual model first subdivides learning and memory into three divisions: immediate memory, working memory, and long-term memory. Immediate memory is further subdivided into verbal immediate memory, visual immediate memory, and verbal-visual associative learning. Performance comparisons can be made between verbal and visual immediate memory, as designated by the two-way arrow on Figure 12.1. Clearly, immediate memory is contingent on attentional factors as well.

Within the verbal and visual immediate memory areas, these constructs are often measured with stimuli that range from simple to complex. For example, for verbal immediate memory, some tasks may measure immediate memory for numbers and letters, and then shift to memory for words, then sentences, and finally stories. Performance that increases or decreases, as a function of the changes in the semantic loading of the test, should be considered in the overall interpretation of verbal immediate learning and memory. Similar semantic loading changes in visual immediate memory tasks may be a part of a learning and memory test as well and should be interpreted as needed.

Verbal-visual associative learning requires pairing verbal and visual stimuli in active learning tasks. For younger students, the ability to name colors, pictures, numbers, and shapes, all require pairing visual stimuli with a verbal label. These verbal-visual associative learning tasks may involve an immediate learning component and a delayed recall and recognition component. The immediate learning component falls under the immediate memory category and the delayed associative memory falls under the long-term memory category.

Long-term memory can be divided into four categories: delayed associative memory, semantic memory, verbal long-term learning and memory, and visual long-term memory. Delayed associative memory is the amount of verbal-visual associative stimuli remembered after a delay and can be compared to the performance on verbal-visual associative learning.

Long-term memory can also be classified as verbal long-term memory or visual long-term memory. Each of these long-term memory components may be further subdivided into indices of learning, measures of delayed free recall, and delayed recognition. Indices of learning are generally total scores of learning

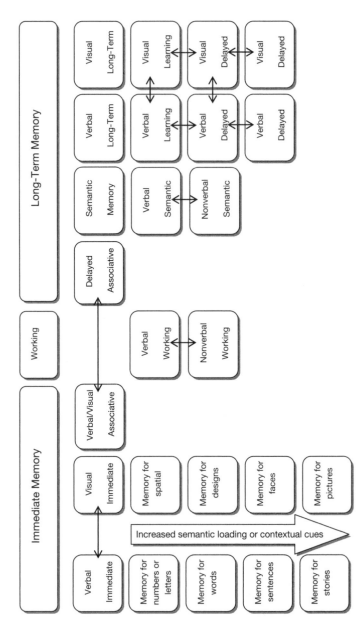

Figure 12.1. Conceptual Model of Learning and Memory for School Neuropsychology (D. Miller, 2007)

verbal or visual information over repeated trials. Delayed free recall is the amount of verbal or visual information remembered after a period of elapsed time (from minutes, to hours, to days). Delayed recognition is the amount of verbal or visual information remembered after a period of elapsed time and when provided with multiple-choice cues. Multiple performance comparisons may be made across these constructs (e.g., verbal versus visual learning, verbal versus visual delayed recall, verbal versus visual delayed recognition). Students with strong delayed recognition memories probably would perform best with multiple-choice types of examinations. Delayed free recall versus delayed recognition is also an interesting comparison. A deficit in recognition memory as compared to free recall is a better indicator of a memory disorder and poor recognition often suggests more severe impairment (Gazzaniga et al., 2002). Inclusion of a recognition trial, along with free recall, increases the sensitivity of a memory test.

NEUROANATOMY OF LEARNING AND MEMORY PROCESSES

Much of what we know today about the neuroanatomy of learning and memory comes from the study of patients with memory impairments, comparative animal research, and functional imaging techniques (Miller, Maricle, & Mortimer, 2010). Converging evidence from these sources indicates that the *medial temporal lobe* (primarily the hippocampus and secondarily the amygdala) and the *midline diencephalon* (the dorsomedial nucleus of the thalamus) are essential brain structures for the learning and retention of new information. These structures permit the storage of information until consolidation is complete. Damage to the medial temporal lobe does not wipe out most declarative memories, but rather prevents new long-term memories from being formed. These anatomical sites are not the storage sites of memory but rather the brain regions that are essential for consolidation of new memories into long-term memory. The amygdala seems to play a role in emotional memory. *Flashbulb memories* of highly emotional memories (e.g., events from 9/11) would involve the amygdala and the hippocampus working in tandem to form new, emotionally charged long-term memories.

Damage to the temporal lobe in areas besides the hippocampus can produce severe retrograde amnesia (loss of previous memories), while the ability to form new memories remains intact. The prefrontal cortex is involved with the encoding and retrieval of information. Neuroimaging studies have revealed that episodic retrieval seems to activate the right prefrontal cortex while semantic retrieval activates the left prefrontal cortex (see Gazzaniga et al., 2002, for a review). Jonides et al., (2000) found that there were functional changes in the prefrontal cortex in adult subjects with poor working memory. Neuroimaging studies have shown that the prefrontal cortex is activated during verbal working memory (Awh et al., 1996) and nonverbal working memory (Jonides et al., 1993).

Summary of Learning and Memory Processes

Learning and memory form the foundation for what education is all about. A school neuropsychological evaluation must include assessment of both the subcomponents of learning and memory. There are many neuropsychological terms associated with learning and memory with which school neuropsychologists should become familiar (see Rapid Reference 12.2).

≡ Rapid Reference 12.2

Neuropsychological Terms Associated with Learning and Memory

- *Anterograde amnesia*—The inability to learn and recall new information.
- *Anterograde memory*—The ability to learn and recall new information.
- *Autobiographical memory*—An aspect of episodic or declarative memory related to the recollection of personal memories.
- *Central executive*—Responsible for selection, initiation, and termination of processing routines (e.g., encoding, storage, and retrieval).
- *Color amnesia*—Loss of knowledge about color even with intact color vision and color perception.
- *Declarative (explicit) memory*—Memories for experiences, facts, or events that can be consciously recalled.
- *Echoic memory*—Sensory memory for auditory material that has a relatively large capacity but short duration.
- *Elaboration*—A memory process in which the products of initial encoding are enriched by further processing.
- *Encoding*—The process by which the cognitive system builds up a stimulus representation to place into memory.
- *Episodic memory*—Memory that is content-specific and often autobiographical.
- *Flashbulb memory*—A vivid memory of the circumstance surrounding shocking or emotionally charged news.
- *Focal retrograde amnesia*—Severe and lasting retrograde amnesia that occurs with relatively new learning ability preserved.
- *Forgetting (memory decay)*—The loss of information over time. Often calculated in neuropsychological assessment by subtracting delayed recall from immediate recall.
- *Free recall*—Memory retrieval without the aid of external cues.

- *Iconic memory*—Sensory memory for visual material that has a relatively large capacity but short duration.
- *Immediate memory*—The capacity to maintain information in conscious awareness.
- *Incidental learning*—Learning that occurs without conscious effort.
- *Learning*—The process of acquiring new information.
- *Learning curve*—A graph frequently used in memory tests to plot out the number of correctly recalled words over a number of trials.
- *Long-term memory*—The retention of information for prolonged, perhaps indefinite periods of time.
- *Memory span*—The amount of information that can be repeated immediately with complete accuracy. Memory span is assumed to be a measure of short-term memory capacity.
- *Metamemory*—Knowledge about the nature and contents of one's own memory.
- *Mnemonic*—Techniques for improving one's own memory.
- *Nondeclarative (implicit) memory*—A range of memory types in which performance is altered without conscious mediation (e.g., procedural memory, priming, and classical conditioning).
- *Paired-associate learning*—A memory task that assesses the ability to learn the relationship between paired stimuli (e.g., ice cream).
- *Phonological loop*—A temporary storage system for acoustic and speech-based information in working memory.
- *Practice effects*—Improved performance on a second trial of the same test.
- *Primacy effect*—The tendency for words presented earlier in a list to be more easily recalled during a free recall task.
- *Priming*—A form of nondeclarative memory in which prior exposure to a stimulus exerts an effect on subsequent stimulus detection or identification.
- *Proactive inhibition*—Decreased learning of new information as a result of learning something in the past.
- *Procedural memory*—A type of nondeclarative memory for skills that are not verbalized or consciously analyzed (e.g., tying one's shoes).
- *Prospective memory*—Memory for plans, appointments, and actions anticipated to occur in the future.
- *Recency effect*—The tendency to recall the last few words presented in a list-learning task during free recall.
- *Recognition*—Memory that is assessed by presenting material shown earlier with new items not previous presented.
- *Retention*—The amount of information persisting over time.
- *Retroactive inhibition*—Impairment in recall of previously learned materials due to newly learned material.
- *Retrograde amnesia*—The inability to recall information that was previously learned or stored.

(continued)

≡ *Rapid Reference 12.2 continued*

- *Retrograde memory*—The ability to recall information that was previously learned or stored.
- *Semantic memory*—Memory that is context-free, reflecting general knowledge of symbols, concepts, and the rules for manipulating them.
- *Sensory memory*—The first stage of memory processing in which a perceptual record is stored.
- *Serial learning*—Any learning task in which items to be learned are presented over multiple trials.
- *Serial position effect*—The tendency to recall items presented at the beginning (primacy effect) and end (recency effect) of a list of words in a free recall task.
- *Short-term memory*—Retention of information over brief periods.
- *Topographical amnesia*—Specific loss of memory for places.
- *Visuospatial sketchpad*—Allows manipulation of visuospatial information in working memory.
- *Working memory*—A limited capacity memory system that provides temporary storage to manipulate information for complex cognitive tasks such as learning and reasoning.

Sources: Ayd, 1995; Loring, 1999.

WHEN TO ASSESS FOR LEARNING AND MEMORY PROCESSES

"In the school environment, the rapid acquisition and long-term retention of facts and concepts is fundamental to success" (Dehn, 2010, p. 3). From a school neuropsychological perspective, the question should not be when to assess for learning and memory functions, but when would you not assess for those functions. The acquisition of new knowledge and the subsequent storage and retrieval of that knowledge is the foundation of what we strive to accomplish in education.

A challenge for school neuropsychologists is to determine if a student's memory difficulties can be attributed to problems with initial encoding, inefficient storage, or poor retrieval strategies, or a combination of all three. Poor encoding is often attributable to not paying attention to the stimuli to be learned, due to distractibility. Poor encoding of verbal information may also be attributable to poor receptive language skills. If a child cannot understand verbal information, that information will not be encoded into memory.

A child may initially encode information but not store that information in an efficient manner. Information may be stored incorrectly based on how something sounds; a phonemic encoding error (e.g., the word "bat" is stored as "hat") or information may be stored inaccurately based on a semantic encoding error (e.g., the word "car" is stored as the word "truck").

The majority of current memory tests focus on retrieval of newly learned information. The school neuropsychologist must infer where the breakpoints occur in the memory process based on how well a child recalls newly learned material (immediate memory) or how well information is remembered over time (delayed recall or recognition and long-term memory). If a child shows little to no evidence of learning new material, such as a list of words over repeated trials, distractibility, poor attentional skills, and/or poor receptive language skills must be ruled out. Potential storage and/or retrieval problems can be suggested based on the types of errors made during retrieval (e.g., phonological or semantic errors).

IDENTIFYING LEARNING AND MEMORY CONCERNS

It is suggested that the *Neuropsychological Processing Concerns Checklist for Children and Youth—Third Edition* (NPCC-3: D. Miller, 2012a) be completed by the parent/guardian and at least one teacher of the student being referred for a comprehensive assessment (see the supplemental CD for the complete NPCC-3). The questions on the NPCC-3 that pertain to learning and memory difficulties are shown in Rapid Reference 12.3. Any endorsed items in the moderate to severe

---

≡ *Rapid Reference 12.3*

Learning and Memory Items from the Neuropsychological Processing Concerns Checklist for Children and Youth—Third Edition *(NPCC-3: Miller, 2012a)*

General learning efficiency:
- Difficulty learning new verbal information.
- Difficulty learning new visual information.
- Difficulty integrating verbal and visual information.

Long-term memory difficulties:
- Forgets where personal items or school work were left.
- Forgets to turn in homework assignments.
- Forgets what happens days or weeks ago.
- Does well on daily assignments but does not do well on end of the week quizzes.
- Limited knowledge of basic facts for places, events, and people.

range should be followed up with formal assessment measures in the school neuropsychological assessment. The major tests of learning and memory for school-age children are reviewed in the next section.

ASSESSING LEARNING AND MEMORY

Rapid Reference 12.4 restates the second- and third-order classifications of learning and memory processes within the Integrated SNP/CHC Model. The next section of this chapter describes the major stand-alone test batteries of learning and memory followed by a cross-battery listing of tests designed to measure each of the second and third order learning and memory classifications in the Integrated SNP/CHC Model.

≡ *Rapid Reference 12.4*

Integrated SNP/CHC Model Classifications of Learning and Memory Processes

Broad Classifications	Second-Order Classifications	Third-Order Classifications
Learning and memory processes	• Rate of new learning	• Verbal learning • Visual learning
	• Immediate verbal memory	• Letter recall (no contextual cues) • Number recall (no contextual cues) • Word recall (no contextual cues) • Sentence recall (contextual cues) • Story recall (contextual cues)
	• Delayed verbal memory	• Recall with contextual cues • Recall without contextual cues • Verbal recognition • Qualitative behaviors
	• Immediate visual memory	• Abstract designs, spatial locations, or visual sequences with motor response (no contextual cues) • Faces, objects, or pictures with verbal or pointing response (no contextual cues)

		• Visual digit span with verbal response (no contextual cues)
		• Picture or symbolic (with contextual cues)
• Delayed visual memory		• Recall without contextual cues
		• Recall with contextual cues
		• Visual recognition
		• Qualitative behaviors
• Verbal-visual associative learning and recall		• Verbal-visual associative learning
		• Verbal-visual associative delayed recall

STAND-ALONE TESTS OF LEARNING AND MEMORY

The major tests of learning and memory can be divided into two categories: (1) stand-alone tests (e.g., *Children's Memory Scale*), or (2) learning and memory tests embedded within test batteries (e.g., WJIII-COG Long-term Retrieval Cluster and related subtests). Rapid Reference 12.5 lists the major stand-alone tests of learning and memory for school-age children and youth.

≡ *Rapid Reference 12.5*

Major Tests of Learning and Memory

Test	Age Range	Publisher
• *California Verbal Learning Test—Children's Version* (CVLT-C)	5 to 16 years	Pearson
• *Children's Auditory Verbal Learning Test-2* (CAVLT-2)	7 to 17 years	PAR
• *Children's Memory Scale* (CMS)	5 to 16 years	Pearson
• *Test of Memory and Learning—Second Edition* (TOMAL-2)	5 to 59–11 years	PRO-ED
• *Wechsler Memory Scale—Fourth Edition* (WMS-IV)	16–90.11 years	Pearson
• *Wide Range Assessment of Memory and Learning—Second Edition* (WRAML2)	5 to 90 years	PAR

California Verbal Learning Test—Children's Version (CVLT-C)

The CVLT-C (Delis, Kramer, Kaplan, & Ober, 1994) is designed to measure verbal immediate and delayed learning and memory. The CVLT-C was standardized on children ages 5 to 16 and takes approximately 30 minutes to administer. On this test, the examiner reads one of two shopping lists to the child. The child is instructed to recall as many items from the list as possible. The test is structured in such a way that the scores are generated for correct responses across trials, recall errors (perseverations or intrusions), short- and long-delayed free recall, short- and long-delayed cued recall, and semantic cluster indices (the degree to which the child may favor a semantic strategy in recalling a list).

Children's Auditory Verbal Learning Test22 (CAVLT-2)

The CAVLT-2 (Talley, 1994) is similar to the CVLT-C and yields measures of immediate memory span, level of learning, immediate recall, delayed recall, recognition accuracy, and total intrusions. The CAVLT-2 scores for each trial may be obtained and base rate tables are included for standard score comparisons.

Children's Memory Scale (CMS)

The CMS "is a comprehensive learning and memory assessment instrument designed to evaluate learning and memory functioning in individuals ages 5 through 16 years" (Cohen, 1997, p. 1). The three core domains measured by the CMS are: (1) auditory/verbal learning and memory, (2) visual/nonverbal learning and memory, and (3) attention/concentration. The core battery can be administered in approximately 35 minutes, and a supplemental set of subtests will add approximately 15 minutes to the total administration time. In terms of the school neuropsychology conceptual model, the attention/concentration subtests are covered within Chapter 14.

Test of Memory and Learning—Second Edition (TOMAL-2)

The TOMAL-2 (Reynolds & Voress, 2007) is a comprehensive memory battery designed for children ages 5 through adults up to 59 years, 11 months. The TOMAL-2 is composed of eight core subtests divided into a Verbal Memory Scale and a Nonverbal Memory Scale. The test generates a Composite

Memory Scale. The TOMAL-2 has two delayed recall tasks that yield a Delayed Recall Index based on the delayed recall of both verbal and nonverbal information learned on the first four subtests. The test also includes six supplemental subtests, which are used in combination with the core subtests to generate supplemental indices for a Verbal Delayed Recall Index, Learning Index, Attention and Concentration Index, Sequential Memory Index, Free Recall Index, and an Associate Recall Index.

Wechsler Memory Scale—Fourth Edition (WMS-IV)

The WMS-IV (Wechsler, 2009b) is an individually administered battery designed to measure learning and memory in individuals ages 16 to 90 years. The test has two distinct batteries: the Adult Battery for ages 16 to 69, and the Older Adult Battery for ages 65 to 90. The focus in this book is on the Adult Battery only.

The WMS-IV Adult Battery has seven subtests, with six of the seven considered primary and one considered to be optional. The primary subtests are: Logical Memory, Verbal Paired Associates, Designs, Visual Reproduction, Spatial Addition, and Symbol Span. The optional subtest is the Brief Cognitive Status Exam. Five index scores are derived from the primary subtests including: Auditory Memory, Visual Memory, Visual Working Memory, Immediate Memory, and Delayed Memory. The WMS-IV also provides additional process scores which aid in clinical interpretation.

Wide Range Assessment of Memory and Learning—Second Edition (WRAML2)

The WRAML2 (Sheslow & Adams, 2003) is a comprehensive test of learning and memory designed for children ages 5 to 17 years. The WRAML2 consists of six core subtests that yield the Verbal Memory Index, the Visual Memory Index, and the Attention/Concentration Index. These three indices combine to form a General Memory Index. The WRAML also includes indices for comparing recognition versus recall. There are two delayed verbal free recall subtests, a Verbal Recognition Index, and a Visual Recognition Index. The WRAML also includes a Working Memory Index that encompasses both verbal and visual working memory subtests.

The subtests from each of these stand-alone memory and learning tests are individually reported in the Integrated SNP/CHC Model based on which aspect of learning and memory is being assessed.

ASSESSING THE RATE OF NEW LEARNING

The acquisition of newly learned information is frequently assessed by school neuropsychologists. Many of the major stand-alone tests of memory include tests that require the student to learn content (e.g., words, word pairs, location of a pattern of dots on a page) over repeated trials. Rapid Reference 12.6 presents a list of tests designed to measure the rate of new learning.

≡ Rapid Reference 12.6

Tests of New Learning Rate

Test–Subtest: Description	Age/Grade Range	Publisher
Verbal Learning		
CMS—Word Lists—Learning: Learning a list of words over repeated trials.	5–0 to 16–11 years	Pearson
CMS—Word Pairs—Learning: Recalling a word that had been previously associated with another word.		
CVLT-C—Learning Slope: The average number of new words per trial across five trials.	5–0 to 16–11 years	
NEPSY-II—List Memory Learning Effect: The number of correctly recalled words on the last trial minus the number of correctly recalled words on the first trial.	7–0 to 12 years	
NEPSY-II—List Memory Interference Effect: Recalling a second list of words after the first list is presented.		
TOMAL-2—Word Selective Reminding: Recalling a list of words over repeated trials but only being reminded of the words not recalled each time.	6–0 to 59–11 years	PRO-ED
WRAML2—Verbal Learning: Learning a list of words over repeated trials.	5–0 to 90 years	PAR

Visual Learning		
CMS—Dot Locations Learning:	5–0 to 16–11 years	Pearson
Number of correctly recalled dots on a grid over three trials.		
CMS—Dot Locations Total:		
Number of correctly identified dots on a grid over three learning trails and one short delayed recall condition.		

See Appendix for the full names of the tests and their references.

An index of learning is calculated differently across tests. Some tests total the number of correctly identified stimuli over repeated trials as an indicator of overall learning (e.g., WRAML2 Verbal Learning). Other tests with repeated trials subtract the number of correctly identified stimuli on the last learning trial from the number of correctly identified stimuli on the first learning trial (e.g., NEPSY-II List Memory Learning Effect). The majority of these types of tests have repeated trials of the same stimuli and the student is instructed to recall as many as possible of the stimuli each time. On one test, the Word Selective Reminding test from the TOMAL-2, the student is only reminded of the words not recalled on each trial, yet expected to recall as many as possible of the words on the list in each trial. When interpreting cross-battery assessment results within this section, the school neuropsychologist must consider the subtle differences in how the test scores are derived and how different task requirements may affect the test scores.

List learning tests should be a regular part of most neuropsychological test batteries and the student's learning curve across trials should be compared to the learning curve of the student's same aged peers. Figure 12.2 illustrates three different learning curves from children all the same age: Student #1, Student #2, and the average correct scores for same aged-peers. The average learning curve for the same-age peers shows a steady increase in the number of correctly identified words from a repeated list-learning task. Student #1 shows a pattern of performance frequently seen in children with ADHD. For Student #1, the number correct on the first trial of the task is below average but the number correct does improve with repeated exposure to the same list of words. The lower number of correctly recalled words in this example is due to initial distractibility, but the pattern of performance does suggest that the student will learn with repeated exposure to the same material.

The learning curve of Student #2 indicates that the student did not benefit from repeated exposure to the same material and was incapable of learning the

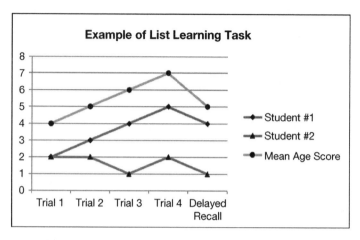

Figure 12.2. Example of List Learning Curves

content. Student #2 may have an auditory processing disorder and has difficulty learning verbally presented information. Repeated exposure to verbal material is not an advisable instructional strategy for Student #2. The school neuropsychologist evaluates Student #2's visual learning skills to see if that mode of learning is best.

It is important to analyze what types of errors are made during the recall of a serial list of words. Intrusion errors are words that are recalled that were not part of the original list. Phonological errors are recalled words that sound like the originally presented words (e.g., "*far*" for "*car*"). Semantic errors are recalled words that are similar in meaning to the originally presented words (e.g., "*truck*" for "*car*"). Sometimes students recall nonlist words that are neither phonological or semantic error types, which could be indicative of more serious learning and memory problems. In a repeated list-learning task, students who make intrusion errors often repeat the same intrusion errors over and over again despite the repetition of the list of the words.

ASSESSING IMMEDIATE VERBAL MEMORY

Rapid Reference 12.7 presents the major tests designed to measure immediate verbal memory across five third-order classifications. In the SNP Model, immediate verbal memory is a second-order classification within the broad classification of learning and memory functions. Immediate verbal memory is subdivided further into third-order classifications of: (1) letter recall

≋ Rapid Reference 12.7

....

Tests of Immediate Verbal Memory

Test–Subtest: Description	Age/Grade Range	Publisher
Letter Recall (No Contextual Cues)		
TOMAL-2—Letters Forward: Repeating a string of letters spoken by the examiner.	6–0 to 59–11 years	PRO-ED
WISC-IV Integrated—Letter Span–Rhyming: Repeating auditorially presented letters of increasing length which rhyme	6–1 to 16–11 years	Pearson
WISC-IV Integrated—Letter Span–Nonrhyming: Repeating auditorially presented letters of increasing length that do not rhyme		
Number Recall (No Contextual Cues)		
CMS—Numbers Forward: Repeating increasingly long series of digits.	5–0 to 16–11 years	Pearson
DAS-II—Recall of Digits Forward: Repeating increasingly long series of digits.	6–0 to 18–11 years	Pearson
KABC-II—Number Recall: Repeating a string of digits spoken by the examiner.	3 to 18 years	Pearson
TAPS-3—Number Memory Forward: Repeating a string of digits spoken by the examiner.	4 to 18–11 years	Academic Therapy Publications
TOMAL-2—Digits Forward: Repeating a string of digits spoken by the examiner.	6–0 to 59–11 years	PRO-ED
WISC-IV—Digits Forward: Repeating a string of digits spoken by the examiner.	6–0 to 16–11 years	Pearson
Word Recall (No Contextual Cues)		
CAS—Word Series: Recall of words from a verbally presented list.	5–0 to 17–11 years	PRO-ED

(continued)

≡ Rapid Reference 12.7 continued

CVLT-C—Level of Immediate Recall: 5–0 to 16–11 years   Pearson

Recall of words from a verbally presented list across five trials (List A) or an additional trial of a new list of words (List B).

CVLT-C—Learning Strategies:

The type of strategy used to facilitate learning the list of words across multiple trials.

CVLT-C—List A Short-Delay Free Recall:

Immediate recall of words on a list after multiple learning trials.

CVLT-C—List A Short-Cued Free Recall:

Immediate recognition of words contained on a list after multiple learning trials.

CMS—Word Lists Total: 5–0 to 16–11 years

Learning a list of unrelated words over multiple trials.

CMS—Word Pairs Immediate Recall:

Recalling word pairs over three trials.

KABC-II—Word Order (without Color Interference):   3 to 18 years

Touching a series of silhouettes of common objects in the same order as touched by the examiner.

KABC-II—Word Order (with Color Interference):

Same as the Word Order task with an added interference task (naming colors) between trials.

NEPSY-II—Word List Interference Repetition: 7 to 16 years

Repeating an initial string of unrelated words.

TAPS-3—Word Memory: 4 to 18–11 years   Academic Therapy Publications

Ability to retain and manipulate simple sequences of auditory information.

TOMAL-2—Word Selective Reminding:	6–0 to 59–11 years	PRO-ED
Learning a list of words then repeating it, and then only reminded of words left out.		
WJIII-COG DS—Memory for Words:	2–0 to 90+ years	Riverside
Repeating a list of unrelated words in the correct sequence.		

Sentence Recall (Contextual Cues)

NEPSY-II—Sentence Repetition:	3 to 6 years	Pearson
Immediate recall of sentences of increasing length and complexity.		
TAPS-3—Sentence Memory:	4 to 18–11 years	Academic Therapy Publications
Memory for sentences of increasing length and complexity.		
WRAML2—Sentence Memory:	5–0 to 90+ years	PAR
Memory for sentences of increasing length and complexity.		
WJIII-COG DS—Memory for Sentences:	2–0 to 90+ years	Riverside
Memory for sentences of increasing length and complexity.		

Story Recall (Contextual Cues)

CMS—Stories Immediate:	5–0 to 16–11 years	Pearson
Details recalled from verbally presented stories.		
CMS—Stories Immediate Thematic:		
General themes recalled from verbally presented stories.		
NEPSY-II—Narrative Memory-Free Recall:	3 to 16 years	
Details recalled from verbally presented stories.		
RIAS—Verbal Memory:	3 to 94 years	PAR
Details recalled from verbally presented sentences and stories.		
TOMAL-2—Memory for Stories:	6–0 to 59–11 years	PRO-ED
Details recalled from verbally presented stories.		
WMS-IV—Logical Memory I:	16 to 90 years	Pearson
Details recalled from verbally presented stories.		

(continued)

===== *Rapid Reference 12.7 continued*

WRAML2—Story Memory:
Details recalled from verbally presented stories.

5–0 to 90+ years

PAR

WJIII-ACH NU—Story Recall:
Details recalled from verbally presented stories.

2–0 to 90+ years

Riverside

See Appendix for the full names of the tests and their references.

(no contextual cues), (2) number recall (no contextual cues), (3) word recall (no contextual cues), (4) sentence recall (contextual cues), and (5) story recall (contextual cues).

The *California Verbal Learning Test: Children's Version* (CVLT-C: Delis et al., 1994) has several scores listed within the Word Recall (no contextual cues) third-order classification. The Level of Immediate Recall actually contains multiple scores designed to measure recall of words from a verbally presented list across five trials (List A) or an additional trial of a new list of words (List B). The multiple scores include: List A Total Trials 1–5, List A Trial 1 Free Recall, List A Trial 5 Free Recall, List B Free Recall, Percent Recall Consistency, Perseveration Errors, and Free-Recall Intrusions. Each of these scores needs to be considered in the interpretation of the test.

The CVLT-C also has several scores subsumed under the category of Learning Strategies, including: Semantic-Cluster Ratio, Serial-Cluster Ratio, Percent of the Total Recall from Primacy Region, Percent of the Total Recall from Middle Region, and Percent of the Total Recall from Recency Region. Interpretation of these scores will determine the influence of the serial-order position effect on the word recall.

The NEPSY-II (Korkman, Kirk, & Kemp, 2007) Narrative Memory-Free Recall score is categorized within the Story Recall (contextual cues) third-order classification. The test has two subscores, Narrative Memory Recognition and Narrative Memory Free and Cued Recall, which need to be considered in the interpretation of the overall test score. The subscores help the clinician determine if there are beneficial effects of cued recall versus relying solely on free recall.

The Story Memory test from the WRAML2 (Sheslow & Adams, 2003) includes a total score and two subscores: Verbatim Total and Gist Total. The Verbatim Total is a measure of the exact story details recalled and the Gist Total score measures the recall of general details. These scores provide some insight into whether the student is a wholistic or "big picture" thinker or a detail-oriented thinker.

The clinician should evaluate the performance of the student across multiple levels of immediate verbal memory to determine if the inclusion of contextual cues makes a difference in facilitating or hindering recall. Some students are able to recall small chunks of verbal information easily such as memory for digits but quickly become overwhelmed when the cognitive load increases. Other students seem to need the added contextual cues to facilitate encoding and retrieval.

ASSESSING IMMEDIATE VISUAL MEMORY

In the Integrated SNP/CHC Model, immediate visual memory is a second-order classification within the broad classification of learning and memory functions. Immediate visual memory is subdivided further into eight third-order classifications of: (1) abstract designs with motor response (no contextual cues), (2) abstract designs with verbal response (no contextual cues), (3) faces with verbal or pointing responses (no contextual cues), (4) objects or pictures with verbal or pointing response (no contextual cues), (5) spatial locations with motor response (no contextual cues), (6) visual digit span with verbal response (no contextual cues), (7) visual sequential imitation with motor response (no contextual cues), and (8) picture or symbolic (contextual cues). Rapid Reference 12.8 presents the major tests designed to measure immediate visual memory across these eight third order classifications.

The NEPSY-II (Korkman et al., 2007) Memory for Designs test is categorized within the Abstract Designs with Motor Response third-order classification. The test requires the student to place elements of an abstract design into a grid after briefly looking at an abstract design. The test has two subscores that are important to consider in interpretation: A Content score and a Spatial score. The Content score reflects an accurate placement of a design piece into the proper position based on visual immediate memory. The Spatial score reflects a design piece placed in a position based on spatial memory alone but the piece does not match the exact piece originally seen in that position. The WMS-IV Designs I (2009b) subtest has the same types of supplemental scores as the NEPSY-II Memory for Designs test. The only other supplemental score within these tests that needs to be considered in overall interpretation is the Picture Memory test from the WRAML2 (Sheslow & Adams, 2003), which includes a score for the number of commission errors made on the performance of the test.

≋ Rapid Reference 12.8

Tests of Immediate Visual Memory

Test–Subtest: Description	Age/Grade Range	Publisher
Abstract Designs with Motor Response (No Contextual Cues)		
Bender Visual-Motor Gestalt Test—Recall:	3–0 to 85+ years	Pearson
Drawing copies of abstract, geometric designs from memory.		
CAS—Figure Memory:	5–0 to 17–11 years	PRO-ED
Tracing a geometric figure embedded within a more complex pattern after initial exposure to the geometric figure.		
DAS-II—Recall of Designs:	6–0 to 18–11 years	Pearson
Drawing copies of abstract, geometric designs from memory.		
NEPSY-II—Memory for Designs Total:	3 to 16 years	
Placing elements of an abstract design into a grid after briefly looking at an abstract design.		
WMS-IV—Designs I:	16 to 90 years	
Placing elements of an abstract design into a grid after briefly looking at an abstract design.		
WMS-IV—Visual Reproduction I:		
Drawing a set of five designs that were presented one at a time.		
WNV—Recognition:	4–0 to 21–11 years	
Identifying previously seen pictures embedded in a set of similar pictures.		
WRAML2—Design Memory:	5–0 to 90+ years	PAR
Redraw geometric shapes in proper locations after brief visual exposure.		
Abstract Designs with Verbal Response (No Contextual Cues)		
TOMAL-2—Abstract Visual Memory:	6–0 to 59–11 years	PRO-ED
Recalling geometric designs when order is not important.		

TOMAL-2—Visual Sequential Memory:

Recalling a sequence of geometric designs.

TVPS-3—Sequential Memory: Identifying a previously seen design sequence embedded in a set of similar design sequences designs.	4 to 18–11 years	Academic Therapy Publications

TVPS-3—Visual Memory:

Identifying previously seen abstract designs embedded in a set of similar abstract designs.

Faces with Verbal or Pointing Response (No Contextual Cues)

CMS—Faces Immediate Recall: Remembering faces.	5–0 to 16–11 years	Pearson
KABC-II—Face Recognition: Attending to photographs of faces briefly then picking the same photograph of faces in slightly different poses.	3 to 18 years	
NEPSY-II—Memory for Faces Immediate Recall: Picking out faces from many faces that were previously seen.	5 to 16 years	
TOMAL-2—Facial Memory: Recognition and identification of faces.	6–0 to 18–11 years	PRO-ED

Objects/Pictures with Verbal or Pointing Response (No Contextual Cues)

DAS-II—Recognition of Picture: Recalling a set of pictures previously seen.	6–0 to 18–11 years	Pearson
UNIT—Object Memory: Identifying common objects shown in a first set of pictures now embedded with many other pictures of common objects.	5–0 to 17–11 years	Riverside
RIAS—Nonverbal Memory: Identifying previously seen pictures embedded in a set of similar pictures.	3 to 94 years	PAR
WISC-IV Integrated—Coding Recall: Immediate recall of the coding subtest shapes and numbers.	6–1 to 16–11 years	Pearson

(continued)

≡ *Rapid Reference 12.8 continued*

WJIII-COG NU—Picture Recognition:	2–0 to 90+ years	Riverside
Identifying previously seen pictures embedded in a set of similar pictures.		

Spatial Locations with Motor Response (No Contextual Cues)

CMS—Dot Locations Short Delayed Recall:	5–0 to 16–11 years	Pearson
Immediate recall of the location of dots on a grid after multiple learning trials.		
CMS—Picture Locations:		
Immediate recall of the location of pictures on a grid.		
TOMAL-2—Memory for Locations:	6–0 to 59–11 years	PRO-ED
Remembering the locations of dots on a page.		
TOMAL-2—Visual Selective Reminding:		
Learning a pattern of dots then repeating it, and then only reminded of the dots left out.		
UNIT—Spatial Memory:	5–0 to 17–11 years	Riverside
Recreating a previously seen pattern of colored dots using colored chips on a grid.		
WISC-IV Integrated—Spatial Span Forward:	6–1 to 16–11 years	Pearson
Touching a sequence of blocks that was shown by the examiner.		

Visual Digit Span with Verbal Response (No Contextual Cues)

WISC-IV Integrated—Visual Digit Span:	6–1 to 16–11 years	Pearson
Recalling numbers orally in the same sequence as shown in a visual sequence of numbers.		

Visual Sequences Imitation with Motor Response (No Contextual Cues)

KABC-II—Hand Movements:	3 to 18 years	Pearson
Copying the examiner's precise sequence of taps on the table.		
TOMAL-2—Manual Imitations:	6–0 to 59–11 years	PRO-ED
Copying the examiner's precise sequence of taps on the table.		

Picture or Symbolic (with Contextual Cues)		
CMS—Family Pictures Immediate: Remembering the locations of family members in a picture.	5–0 to 16–11 years	Pearson
UNIT—Symbolic Memory: Re-creating a sequence of pictures of people.	5–0 to 17–11 years	Riverside
WRAML2—Picture Memory: Detecting changes in specific features or details after brief visual exposure to original scenes.	5–0 to 90+ years	PAR

See Appendix for the full names of the tests and their references.

The clinician should evaluate student performance across multiple measures of immediate visual memory to determine if there is variability based on the type of stimuli to be remembered (e.g., abstract designs, faces, pictures, objects, spatial locations) or the type of response (verbal or motoric). Poor visual memory skills can affect sight word reading, writing production, and visual-spatial aspects of mathematics. Poor visual memory skills can also affect social-emotional skills such as face recognition and recall.

ASSESSING DELAYED VERBAL MEMORY

In the Integrated SNP/CHC Model, delayed verbal memory is a second-order classification within the broad classification of learning and memory functions. The third-order classifications are similar to the ones found in the immediate verbal memory second-order classifications including (1) delayed verbal recall with no contextual cues, (2) delayed verbal recall with contextual cues, (3) delayed verbal recognition with no contextual cues, and (4) delayed verbal recognition with contextual cues. Rapid Reference 12.9 presents the major tests designed to measure delayed verbal recall and recognition memory across these four third-order classifications.

Delayed verbal memory is often assessed using two conditions: (1) free recall, where the student recalls details freely without any cues, or (2) recognition recall, where the student is provided with partial cues to aid in the recall of previously learned material. If a student is able to freely recall details from previously learned material, testing formats in the classroom such as fill in the blank or essays will be appropriate. However, if a student is not able to freely recall details yet recall

≡ Rapid Reference 12.9

Tests of Delayed Verbal Memory

Test–Subtest: Description	Age/Grade Range	Publisher
Delayed Verbal Recall (without Context)		
CVLT-C—List a Long-Delay Free Recall: Long-delay (after 20 minutes) recall of the List A words after multiple learning trials.	5–0 to 16–11 years	Pearson
CMS—Word Lists Delayed Recall: Delayed recall of unrelated words previously learned.	5–0 to 16–11 years	
CMS—Word Pairs Long-Delayed Recall: Delayed recall of word pairs previously learned.		
NEPSY-II—List Memory-Delayed Effect: The number of correctly recalled words on Trial 5 minus the number of correctly recalled words on the delayed recall trial.	7 to 12 years	
TOMAL-2—Word Selective Reminding Delayed: Delayed recall of the words learned in the word selective reminding task.	5–0 to 59–11 years	PRO-ED
WRAML2—Verbal Learning Delayed Recall: Number of correct words recalled from list after delay.	5–0 to 90 years	PAR
Delayed Verbal Recall (with Context)		
CMS—Stories-Delayed Recall: Delayed recall of story details.	5–0 to 16–11 years	Pearson
CMS—Stories-Delayed Thematic: Delayed recall of story themes.		
TOMAL-2—Memory for Stories Delayed: Delayed recall of story details.	5–0 to 59–11 years	PRO-ED
WMS-IV—Logical Memory II: Delayed free recall of story details.	16 to 90 years	Pearson
WRAML2—Story Memory-Delayed Recall: Number of correct story details recalled after delay.	5–0 to 90 years	PAR

WJIII-ACH NU—Story Recall Delayed: Delayed recall of story details.	2–0 to 90+ years	Riverside
Delayed Verbal Recognition (Without Context)		
CMS—Word Lists Delayed Recognition: Delayed recognition of words contained within the previously learned list of words.	5–0 to 90 years	PAR
CMS—Word Pairs Delayed Recognition: Delayed recognition of previously learned word pairs.		
CVLT-C—Short- and Long-Delay Cued Recall: Short-delay cued recall of the List A words and long-delay (after 20 minutes) recall of the List A words after multiple learning trials.	5–0 to 16–11 years	Pearson
WMS-IV—Logical Memory II Recognition: Delayed recognition of story details.	16 to 90 years	Pearson
WRAML2—Verbal Learning Recognition: Number of words correctly recognized as being on the original learned list of words.	5–0 to 90 years	PAR
Delayed Verbal Recognition (With Context)		
CMS—Stories Delayed Recognition: Recognize details of a story after a delay.	5–0 to 90 years	PAR
WRAML2—Story Memory-Delayed Recognition: Number of story details recalled with additional multiple-choice cues.	5–0 to 90 years	PAR

See Appendix for the full names of the tests and their references.

improves substantially when partial cues are presented, a multiple-choice format of testing in the classroom may be more appropriate.

On the CVLT-C (Delis et al., 1994) the Short- and Long-Delay Cued Recall portion of the test generates multiple scores: List A Short-Delay Cued Recall, List A Long-Delay Cued Recall, Correct Recognition Hits (the number of List A words endorsed as correct on the recognition trial), Cued-Recall Intrusions (the number of recalled words not on the original list), Discriminability Index (a measure of overall recognition performance that takes into consideration both correct and incorrect responses), False-Positive Rate (endorsing a word as being on the original list of words when it was not present), and Response Bias (a tendency to overrespond with too many "yes" or "no" responses on the recognition trial). A well-trained clinician would consider all of these scores in the overall interpretation of the CVLT-C Short and Long-Delay Cued Recall performance.

The only other supplemental score within these tests that needs to be considered in overall interpretation is the Verbal Learning Recognition test from the WRAML2 (Sheslow & Adams, 2003), which includes a score for the number of Semantic Errors and the number of Phonological Errors made on the performance of the test. Semantic and phonological errors give insight into the types of encoding or retrieval errors made by a student.

ASSESSING DELAYED VISUAL MEMORY

In the Integrated SNP/CHC Model, delayed visual memory is a second-order classification within the broad classification of learning and memory functions. The third-order classifications are similar to the ones found in the immediate visual memory second-order classifications including (1) delayed visual recall without contextual cues, (2) delayed visual recall with contextual cues, (3) delayed visual recognition without contextual cues, and (4) delayed visual recognition with contextual cues. Similar to delayed verbal memory, delayed visual memory is also often assessed using free recall and recognition conditions. Rapid Reference 12.10 presents a list of the major tests designed to measure delayed visual free and recognition recall.

The NEPSY-II (Korkman et al., 2007) Memory for Designs-Delayed Total test score has two subscores that are important to consider in interpretation: a Delayed Content score and a Delayed Spatial score. The interpretation of these scores is similar to the immediate memory version of the scores. The WMS-IV Designs II subtest has similar supplemental process scores including: Content, Spatial, and Recognition. The WMS-IV Visual Representation II subtest has supplemental process scores for Delayed Recognition and Copy (reported under Visual-Motor Integration Skills in the Sensorimotor section).

Long-term memory plays a major role in the acquisition and retrieval of new learning. Some students have good immediate memory but are not able to store that content into long-term memory. This could be due to forgetting content over time or a true neurological deficit in the ability to create memory traces. Occasionally, students will have poor immediate memory but obtain average scores for long-term retrieval. This generally indicates that the student needed extra time to process the information to be learned and once that information was encoded and stored in long-term memory it became more readily accessible. See *Long-Term Memory Problems in Children and Adolescents: Assessment,*

≡ Rapid Reference 12.10

Tests of Delayed Visual Memory

Test–Subtest: Description	Age/Grade Range	Publisher
Delayed Visual Recall without Contextual Cues		
CMS—Dot Locations Long Delayed: Delayed recall of the location of dots on a grid.	5–0 to 90 years	PAR
CMS—Faces Delayed: Delayed recall of faces.		
NEPSY-II—Memory for Faces Delayed: Delayed recall of previously learned target faces.	5–0 to 16–0 years	Pearson
NEPSY-II—Memory for Designs Delayed Total: Delayed recall of the abstract designs.		
WMS-IV—Designs II: Delayed recall of spatial and visual memory with free recall and recognition tasks.	16 to 90 years	
WMS-IV—Visual Reproduction II: Delayed visual-spatial memory with free recall and recognition tasks.		
Delayed Visual Recall with Contextual Cues		
CMS—Family Pictures Delayed Recall: Delayed recall of the locations of family members in a picture.	5–0 to 90 years	PAR
Delayed Visual Recognition without Contextual Cues		
WRAML2—Design Memory Recognition: Correctly identifying designs that appeared in the original stimuli.	5–0 to 90 years	PAR
Delayed Visual Recognition with Contextual Cues		
WRAML2—Picture Memory Recognition: Correctly identifying portions of pictures that appeared in the original stimuli.	5–0 to 90 years	PAR

See Appendix for the full names of the tests and their references.

≡ *Rapid Reference 12.11*

Qualitative Behaviors for the WISC-IV Integrated: Coding

- Cued symbol recall:
    Percentage of same age peers correctly recalling which symbol goes with which number.
- Free symbol recall:
    Percentage of same age peers correctly recalling the symbols from Coding B with no regard to the associated number.
- Cued digit recall:
    Percentage of same age peers correctly recalling the numbers from paired associates in Coding B.

Intervention, and Effective Instruction by Dehn (2010) for a thorough review of the literature.

Qualitative Behaviors for Delayed Visual Memory

On the WISC-IV Integrated (Wechsler et al., 2004), the Coding subtest has a set of qualitative scores that aid in the clinical interpretation of the test. These qualitative scores are calculated as base rates comparing a student's performance to their same aged peers. These score are listed in Rapid Reference 12.11.

ASSESSING VERBAL-VISUAL ASSOCIATIVE LEARNING AND RECALL

In the Integrated SNP/CNC Model, verbal-visual associative learning and recall is a second-order classification within the broad classification of learning and memory functions. Verbal-visual associative learning and recall is subdivided further into third-order classifications of (1) verbal-visual associative learning, and (2) verbal-visual associative recall. Each of the verbal-visual associative learning and recall tasks involve learning to associate a visual stimulus (e.g., picture or face) with a verbal label. Many of the tasks involve an immediate learning and recall portion and a delayed recall portion. Rapid Reference 12.12 presents a list of the major tests designed to measure verbal-visual associative learning and recall.

Assessing verbal-visual associative learning is often overlooked; however, it is an important aspect of learning and memory. Verbal-visual associative learning plays

≡ *Rapid Reference 12.12*

Tests of Verbal-Visual Associative Learning and Recall

Test–Subtest: Description	Age/Grade Range	Publisher
Verbal-Visual Associative Learning		
DAS-II—Recall of Object—Immediate:	2–6 to 8–11 years	Pearson
Naming pictures from memory over repeated trials.		
KABC-II—Atlantis:	3–0 to 18–0 years	
Learning visual-verbal associations and then recalling them.		
KABC-II—Rebus:		
Learning new information in the form of symbols and words.		
NEPSY-II—Memory for Names Total:	5 to 16 years	
Recalling names associated with faces over repeated trials.		
TOMAL-2—Object Recall:	5–0 to 59–11 years	PRO-ED
Recalling names associated with pictures.		
TOMAL-2—Paired Recall:		
Recalling a learned word paired with a first word provided by the examiner.		
WMS-IV—Verbal Paired Associates I:	16 to 90 years	Pearson
Recalling a learned word paired with a first word provided by the examiner.		
WRAML-2—Sound Symbol:	5 to 8 years	PAR
Remembering the unique sound associated with a unique nonsense shape.		
WJIII-COG NU—Visual-Auditory Learning:	2–0 to 90+ years	Riverside
Learning visual-verbal associations and then recalling them.		
WJIII-COG DS—Memory for Names:		
Ability to learn associations between unfamiliar auditory and visual stimuli.		
Verbal-Visual Associative Delayed Recall		
DAS-II—Recall of Objects—Delayed:	2–6 to 8–11 years	Pearson
Recalling the names of the pictures after a delay in time.		

(continued)

≡ Rapid Reference 12.12 continued

KABC-II—Atlantis Delayed: Recalling visual-verbal associations after a delay. **KABC-II—Rebus Delayed:** Recalling associations between symbols and words after a delay.	3–0 to 18–0 years	
NEPSY-II—Memory for Names Delayed: Recalling names associated with faces after a delay.	5 to 16 years	
WMS-IV—Verbal Paired Associates II Free Recall: Delayed free recall of a learned word pair.	16 to 90 years	
WMS-IV—Verbal Paired Associates II Recognition: Delayed recognition of a learned word pair.		
WRAML-2—Sound-Symbol Delayed Recall: Remembering the unique sound associated with a unique nonsense shape after a period of delay.	5 to 8 years	PAR
WJIII-COG NU—Visual-Auditory Learning Delayed: Recalling visual-verbal associations after a delay. **WJIII-COG DS—Memory for Names—Delayed:** Ability to recall the previously learned associations between unfamiliar auditory and visual stimuli.	2–0 to 90+ years	Riverside

See Appendix for the full names of the tests and their references.

a major role in the early stages of reading acquisition. For the automaticity of reading to develop, a child must learn sound-symbol associations. Verbal-visual associative learning is the cognitive process that facilitates verbal fluency in reading.

CHAPTER SUMMARY

In this chapter the theories, terminology, neuroanatomy, and major tests associated with learning and memory functioning were reviewed. Learning and memory processes are essential elements in education and must be systematically evaluated by a school neuropsychologist. Learning and memory disorders are observed in many common developmental disorders.

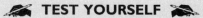 TEST YOURSELF

1. **What type of memory is verbal and has a very short life of just a few milliseconds?**
   a. Verbal long-term memory
   b. Echoic sensory memory
   c. Verbal short-term memory
   d. Iconic sensory memory

2. **Long-term memory can be conceptually divided into two distinct subdivisions. What are they called?**
   a. Episodic and semantic memory
   b. Echoic and iconic memory
   c. Declarative and nondeclarative memory
   d. Primacy and recency effect

3. **True or False? The serial-order position effect lends support to the distinction between short- and long-term memory.**

4. **Baddeley and colleagues initially proposed a 3-part working memory system that contained a central executive system that regulated which two subordinate subsystems?**
   a. Visuospatial sketchpad and phonological loop
   b. Short-term and long-term memory
   c. Episodic and semantic memory
   d. Iconic and echoic memory

5. **What is the type of memory that is related to the recollection of personal memories?**
   a. Episodic memory
   b. Anterograde memory
   c. Nondeclarative memory
   d. Autobiographical memory

6. **What term is used to describe memory retrieval without the aid of external cues?**
   a. Recognition
   b. Free recall
   c. Learning
   d. Incidental learning

7. **What part of the brain is responsible for the consolidation of memory from immediate- to long-term memory?**
   a. Hypothalamus
   b. Amygdala
   c. Hippocampus
   d. Pituitary gland

Answers: 1. b; 2. c; 3. true; 4. a; 5. d; 6. b; 7. c

Chapter Thirteen

EXECUTIVE FUNCTIONS

Executive functions encompass many behaviors ranging from initiation responses, maintenance and cessation of actions, abstract and conceptual thinking, and the ability to plan and organize behavior towards a goal (Stirling, 2002). This chapter reviews (1) the terms associated with executive functions; (2) the neuroanatomy of executive functions; (3) the major tests associated with executive functions; and (4) the behavioral rating scales designed to measure executive functions.

WHAT ARE EXECUTIVE FUNCTIONS?

In the popular press, executive functions are often referred to as the *brain boss* that guides all behavior and basic definitions of executive functions often associate the frontal lobes as the primary source of these functions (McCloskey, Perkins, & Divner, 2009). Despite the fact that many executive functions are related to frontal lobe functioning there is not a single frontal lobe syndrome that has a point-by-point correspondence to an executive functioning homunculus (Stuss & Alexander, 2000).

Barkley 2012b) defines executive functions as:

> [T]he use of self-directed actions so as to choose goals and to select, enact, and sustain actions across time toward those goals usually in the context of others often relying on social and cultural means for the maximization of one's long-term welfare as the person defines that to be. (p. 176)

McCloskey et al. (2009) propose that executive functions are a set of directive capacities that facilitate a person's ability to engage in purposeful processing of perceptions, emotions, thoughts, and actions. Executive functions can be thought of as facilitators that guide other cognitive processing. These facilitators include attentional control, goal-directed behaviors, behavioral regulation,

≡ Rapid Reference 13.1

Terms Associated With Executive Functions

- Abstract reasoning
- Anticipation
- Attentional control
- Behavioral initiation/productivity
- Behavioral regulation
- Common sense
- Concept formation
- Creativity
- Estimation
- Fluency (verbal and nonverbal)
- Goal setting

- Hypothesis generation
- Inhibition of impulsiveness
- Mental flexibility
- Organization
- Planning
- Problem solving
- Rule learning
- Self-control
- Self-monitoring
- Set formation and maintenance
- Set shifting
- Working memory

Source: Adapted from Baron (2004), p. 134.

organizational skills, planning, and problem-solving strategies. Some examples of terms researchers and practitioners use to describe executive functioning are presented in Rapid Reference 13.1.

McCloskey's model of executive functions outlines five tiers of executive capacity including: self-activation, self-regulation, self-realization and determination, self-generation, and trans-self integration (see McCloskey et al., 2009). McCloskey's model of executive functions (McCloskey et al., 2009) initially identified 23 different self-regulation executive functions and the list has expanded to 32 self-regulation executive functions (McCloskey & Wasserman, 2012). See Rapid Reference 13.2 for a brief description of the 32 self-regulation executive function capacities.

From a theoretical standpoint, McCloskey's conceptualization of executive functions is very broad and seems to encompass many areas within the Integrated SNP/CHC Model. From an assessment standpoint, current assessment instruments designed to measure executive functions do not include the degree of specificity that McCloskey and his colleagues have postulated. Within the Integrated SNP/CHC Model, executive functions encompass cognitive flexibility or set shifting, concept formation, problem solving or reasoning, and response inhibition.

≡ *Rapid Reference 13.2*

Brief Description of McCloskey's 32 Self-Regulation Executive Function Capabilities

Attention cluster

- *Perceive/aware*—Cueing the taking in of information from the external environment (e.g., seeing, hearing, touching), cueing awareness of the need to tune to thoughts and/or feelings, body position in space and body movements.

- *Focus/select*—Cueing attention to the most relevant specifics of a given environment, situation, or content while downgrading or ignoring the less relevant elements.

- *Sustain*—Cueing sustained engagement of the processes involved in perceiving, feeling, thinking, or acting for as long as a situation requires.

Engagement cluster

- *Initiate*—Cueing the initial engagement of perceiving, feeling, thinking, or acting.

- *Energize*—Cueing the application of energy and effort into perceiving, feeling, thinking and acting.

- *Inhibit*—Cueing resistance to, or suppression of, urges to perceive, feel, think, or act.

- *Stop*—Cueing the immediate cessation of perceiving, feeling, thinking, or acting.

- *Interrupt*—Cueing the brief interruption of perceiving, feeling, thinking, or acting.

- *Flexible*—Cueing the realization and acceptance of the need to change perceptions, feelings, thoughts, or actions based on the situation at hand.

- *Shift*—Cueing the transition from one perception, feeling, thought, or action to another without difficulty.

Optimization cluster

- *Modulate*—Cueing changes in the amount and intensity of mental energy invested in perceiving, feeling, thinking, and acting. For example, can effectively adjust voice volume, activity level, reactions to sights and sounds.

- *Monitor*—Cueing the use of routines to check on the accuracy of perceptions, emotions, thoughts, or actions.

- *Correct*—Cueing the correction of errors of perception, emotion, thought, or action based on feedback from internal or external sources.

- *Balance*—Cueing the establishment of balance when perceiving, feeling, thinking, or acting to enhance or improve experiencing, learning, or performing. Cueing the sensing of the trade-off between opposing processes or states (e.g., pattern versus detail; speed versus accuracy; humor versus seriousness) to maintain a balance.

Evaluation/solution cluster

- *Gauge*—Cues the "sizing up" of the demands of a task to know the perceptions, emotions, thoughts, or actions needed to effectively engage the task or situation.

- *Anticipate/foresee*—Cues the anticipation of conditions or events in the very near future, such as the consequences of one's own perceptions, feelings, thoughts, and/ or actions.

- *Estimate time*—Cues the use of an internal time sense to determine how long something will take to complete, or how much time is still left in a specific period of time.

(continued)

Rapid Reference 13.2 continued

- *Analyze*—Cues the close examination of perceptions, feelings, thoughts, or actions to obtain a greater understanding of a problem or situation.

- *Associate*—Cues the activation of the resources needed to make the proper associations among perceptions, feelings, thoughts, and actions appropriate for the situation at hand.

- *Generate*—Cues the activation of the resources needed to carry out novel problem-solving routines.

- *Organize*—Cues the use of routines for sorting, sequencing, or otherwise arranging perceptions, feelings, thoughts, and/or actions, to enhance or improve the efficiency of experiencing, learning, or performing.

- *Plan* (short term)—Cues for the specification of a series of perceptions, feelings, thoughts, and/or actions that, if carried out, would be most likely to produce a desired outcome in the very near future (within minutes to within several hours).

- *Evaluate/compare*—Cues the making of comparisons among, or the evaluation of the adequacy of, perceptions, feelings, thoughts, or actions.

- *Choose/decide*—Cues for the making of a choice or the rendering of a decision.

Efficiency cluster

- *Sense time*—Cues for the monitoring of the passage of time (recognizes the need for having an internal sense of how long they have been perceiving, feeling, thinking or acting).

- *Pace*—Cues for the regulation of the rate at which perceptions, feelings, thoughts, and actions are experienced or performed.

- *Sequence*—Cues for the ordering of a series of perceptions, feelings, thoughts, and/or actions, especially in cases where automated routines are being accessed or are initially being developed.

- *Execute*—Cues for the activation of well-known series of perceptions, feelings, thoughts, and/or actions, especially in cases where automated routines have been practiced and used frequently.

Memory cluster

- *Hold*—Cues the holding onto of specific perceptions, feelings, thoughts, and actions for a brief period of time.

- *Manipulate*—Cues for the manipulation of perceptions, feelings, thoughts, or actions as they are being held in mind.

- *Store*—Cues the storing of specific perceptions, feelings, thoughts, and actions so that they can be retrieved as needed at a later time.

- *Retrieve*—Cues for the retrieval of previously stored information about perceptions, feelings, thoughts, and actions.

Source: Self-Regulation Executive Function Definitions. Copyright © 2012 George McCloskey, PhD Reprinted with permission.

NEUROANATOMY OF EXECUTIVE FUNCTIONS

Historically, executive functions have been viewed to be synonymous with frontal lobe involvement. While the frontal and prefrontal lobes do play major roles in executive functioning, there are excitatory and inhibitory pathways that start in subcortical regions of the brain (e.g., the basal ganglia and thalamus) and project to the frontal cortex and vice versa. Alexander, DeLong, and Strick (1986) introduced the idea that there is a parallel but segregated set of frontal-subcortical (FSC) circuits that influence both movement and behavior.

A five-circuit scheme has been generally accepted in the literature (Lichter & Cummings, 2001); and more recently a seven-circuit scheme has been suggested (Middleton & Strick, 2001). These FSC circuits can be divided into seven general categories: skeletomotor, oculomotor, dorsolateral prefrontal, lateral orbitofrontal, ventromedial orbitofrontal, anterior cingulate, and inferotemporal/posterior parietal. The lateral and ventromedial orbitofrontal circuits are discussed together in this section.

Two of the circuits appear to be related to the control of movement: the skeletomotor circuit (body movements) and the oculomotor circuit (eye movements). The skeletomotor circuit is related to premotor, supplementary motor, and primary motor output functions of the brain. Hale and Fiorello (2004) suggested that evaluation of a student's handwriting would be an appropriate ecological validity check of the integrity of the skeletomotor circuit. The oculomotor circuit is related to the frontal eye fields and helps regulate visual scanning. Hale and Fiorello (2004) suggest that oculomotor functioning could be measured by the student's performance on word tracking and visual scanning. The function of the inferior-temporal/posterior parietal circuit has not been clearly articulated in the literature but may be related to the working memory functions of the frontal lobes.

The three remaining FSC circuits all appear to be associated with executive functions and are of the most interest to school neuropsychologists. The locations of the major frontal-subcortical circuits that help regulate behavior are illustrated in Figure 13.1.

Dorsolateral Prefrontal Circuit

Tonika is having trouble at school and at home. Her symptoms are varied but always seem to come down to a few difficulties. Tonika has poor organizational skills. She is always losing her school papers and she never knows when assignments are due in class. Tonika seems to have trouble remembering things

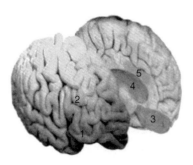

1. Orbitofrontal (lateral)
2. Dorsolateral prefrontal
3. Orbitofrontal (ventromedial)
4. Limbic System
5. Anterior Cingulate

Figure 13.1. The Locations of the Major Frontal-Subcortical Circuits That Help Regulate Behavior Relative to the Location of the Limbic System

as well. When working on an assignment at school she performs well, but when presented with the same assignment later she cannot remember what she is supposed to do. Tonika also has problems focusing her attention for prolonged periods of time. Tonika is experiencing many of the symptoms associated with damage or dysfunction in the dorsolateral prefrontal regions of her brain.

The major functions attributable to all seven FSC circuits are presented in Rapid Reference 13.3.

≡ Rapid Reference 13.3

The Major Functions of the Frontal-Subcortical Circuits

Frontal-Subcortical Circuits	Major Functions
Skeletomotor circuit	Regulates large and fine muscle movements.
Oculomotor circuit	Regulates eye movements.
Dorsolateral prefrontal circuit	The "Executor of the Brain" regulates: • Anticipation • Goal selection • Planning • Monitoring • Use of feedback in task performance • Focusing and sustaining attention

- Generating hypotheses
- Maintaining or shifting sets
- Verbal and design fluency
- Visual-spatial search strategies
- Constructional strategies on learning and copying tasks
- Motor programming disturbances

Orbitofrontal circuit	• Integration of emotional information into contextually appropriate behavioral responses
	• Integration of emotional functions with the internal states of the child
Anterior cingulate circuit	• Motivational mechanisms (e.g., apathy)
	• Behavioral initiation responses
	• Creativity and concept formation
	• Allocation of attentional resources
Inferior/temporal posterior parietal circuit	• Working memory

The dorsolateral prefrontal circuit serves as the principle "executor of the brain." As shown in Rapid Reference 13.3, the dorsolateral prefrontal circuit regulates multiple executive functions, ranging from planning and maintaining organizational strategies, implementing efficient memory search strategies, sustaining the instructional demands of a task, having the cognitive flexibility to shift sets, and regulating complex motor programming output. Therefore, the dorsolateral prefrontal cortex primarily regulates most cognitive executive functioning skills, which are critical to the execution of a goal-directed academic task in school. The neuropsychological deficits associated with damage to the dorsolateral prefrontal circuit are presented in Rapid Reference 13.4. The majority of neuropsychological and cognitive tests activate the dorsolateral prefrontal circuit (Ardila, 2008).

Orbitofrontal Circuit

In the history of neuropsychology, the classic case study of Phineas Gage illustrates the functions of the orbitofrontal circuit. Phineas Gage was a railroad worker in the 1800s, when as a result of an accident, an iron rod blew through his left eye socket and out the top of his head. Phineas Gage survived the accident

≡ Rapid Reference 13.4

Neurocognitive Deficits Associated With Damage or Dysfunction in the Dorsolateral Prefrontal Circuit

- Decreased verbal retrieval
- Decreased nonverbal retrieval
- Abnormal motor programming
- Impaired set shifting
- Reduced learning and memory retrieval
- Disruptions in working memory
- Poor organizational skills
- Poor constructional strategies in copying
- Poor problem solving, goal selection, planning, monitoring, and use of feedback in task performance.
- Difficulty focusing and sustaining attention.
- Difficulty generating hypotheses.

but he had marked personality changes as a result of the destruction of the orbitofrontal region of his brain. Before the accident, Phineas was described as a capable foreman with a well-balanced mind. After the accident, Phineas showed no empathy for anyone else, he was quick to make plans but slow to follow through on those plans, he was often crude, socially inappropriate, impatient, and obstinate.

A summary of the neurocognitive deficits associated with damage or dysfunction to the orbitofrontal circuit is presented in Rapid Reference 13.5. "The orbitofrontal circuit mediates empathic, civil, and socially appropriate behaviors; personality change is the hallmark of orbitofrontal dysfunction" (Chow & Cummings, 1999, p. 6). The orbitofrontal circuit regulates our abilities to inhibit, evaluate, and act on social and emotional decision-making. The orbitofrontal circuit is also involved in cognitive and affective functions such as assessing emotional significance of events, anticipating rewards and punishments, adjusting behaviors to adapt to changes in rule contingencies, and inhibiting inappropriate behaviors. Damage to the orbitofrontal circuit seems to disconnect the frontal monitoring systems from the emotional responses of the limbic system, resulting in behavioral disinhibition (Lichter & Cummings, 2001). Obsessive-compulsive symptoms also seem to be associated with damage to the orbitofrontal circuit (Lichter & Cummings, 2001).

≡ Rapid Reference 13.5

Neurocognitive Deficits Associated With Damage or Dysfunction in the Orbitofrontal Circuit

- Impulsivity
- Antisocial behavior
- Inappropriate feelings under normal circumstances (e.g., inappropriate laughter or crying)
- Irritability
- Tactlessness
- Undue familiarity
- Reduced empathy

There also seems to be some specific hemispheric deficits associated with orbitofrontal damage. Right orbitofrontal damage seems to produce greater disinhibition and loss of socially appropriate behaviors than damage to the left orbitofrontal region (Miller, Chang, Mena, Boone, & Lesser, 1993). Left orbitofrontal damage seems to produce some disinhibition, poor judgment, and irresponsibility toward responsibilities at home and at school (Meyers, Berman, Scheibel, & Lesser, 1993). Students who consistently blurt out answers in class or continually say inappropriate comments in social situations, or lash out at classmates when they walk by, may have some damage or dysfunction associated with the orbitofrontal regions of the brain.

Anterior Cingulate Circuit

Jose is 16 years old. Over the past year or so, he has become increasingly apathetic and lethargic. He shows no motivation at school or at home. Jose only speaks when he is spoken to. He seems to be content sitting in a chair picking at his fingers and hands. Jose's symptoms are consistent with damage or dysfunction to the anterior cingulate portion of his brain.

A summary of the neurocognitive deficits associated with damage or dysfunction to the anterior cingulate circuit is presented in Rapid Reference 13.6. The anterior cingulate circuit regulates motivational mechanisms. Apathy is the common behavioral manifestation to damage in the anterior cingulate region of the brain. A condition called *akinetic mutism* is often present when there is bilateral damage to the anterior cingulate. "Akinetic mutism represents a wakeful state of profound apathy, with indifference to pain, thirst, or hunger; absence of motor or

≡ Rapid Reference 13.6

Neurocognitive Deficits Associated With Damage or Dysfunction in the Anterior Cingulate Circuit

- Apathy
- Limited spontaneous speech
- Indifference to pain, thirst, or hunger (in severe cases)
- Obsessive-compulsive characteristics
- Poor response inhibition (impulsive)
- Poor creativity or generation of new concepts
- Poor allocation of attentional resources

psychic initiative, manifested by lack of spontaneous movement; absent verbalization; and failure to respond to questions or commands" (Lichter & Cummings, 2001, p. 13). Similar to the orbitofrontal circuit, obsessive-compulsive symptoms seem to be associated with damage to the anterior cingulate circuit as well (Lichter & Cummings, 2001).

On neuropsychological measures, the most pronounced deficit associated with damage to the anterior cingulate is the failure of response inhibition. For example, on the NEPSY-II Inhibition test, when the child is to name a "square" in lieu of a "circle" or vice versa, this would be difficult for a child with damage to the anterior cingulate. Children with damage to the anterior cingulate may also show deficits in creative thought processes and generating new concepts (Miller & Cummings, 1999). Finally, the anterior cingulate has been hypothesized to operate as an executive attention system (Posner, 1994; Posner & Raichle, 1994). The anterior cingulate allocates attentional resources to other parts of the brain to ensure that a particular task is handled most efficiently. In brain imaging studies using PET scans, blood flow increases in the anterior cingulate when tasks become difficult (e.g., incongruent Stroop trial compared to congruent Stroop trial or on divided attention tasks) (see Gazzaniga, Ivry, & Mangrum, 2002, for review).

Rapid Reference 13.7 lists some common neuropsychological terms used to describe impairments in executive functioning.

WHEN TO ASSESS FOR EXECUTIVE FUNCTIONS

Deficits in some or all of these executive functions have been associated with more than one neurodevelopmental disorder including: attention-deficit hyperactivity

≡ Rapid Reference 13.7

Neuropsychological Terms Associated With Impairments in Executive Functioning

- *Abulia*—Lack of initiation or drive.
- *Anterior cingulate syndrome*—Symptoms consist of reduced spontaneous activity (increased apathy, do not speak spontaneously, eat and drink only if fed, show little to no emotion, and may be incontinent).
- *Dorsolateral frontal syndrome*—Symptoms consist of difficulty with generating hypotheses, cognitive flexibility, shifting of cognitive sets, reduced verbal or design fluency, poor organizational strategies for learning, constructional strategies for copying complex designs, and motor programming deficits.
- *Echopraxia*—Pathological copying of another person's speech. Associated with frontal lobe disorders.
- *Emotional lability*—Abnormal variability in emotional expression characterized by repetitive and abrupt shifts in affect. Often seen after damage to the orbitofrontal regions of the frontal lobes.
- *Initiation deficit*—The failure to act, or behavior requiring extensive cueing, despite a demonstrated ability to perform the desired behavior. Child may be able to describe the intended action but not be able to initiate the action. Characteristic of damage to the anterior cingulate region of the frontal lobes.
- *Orbitofrontal syndrome*—Characterized by prominent personality changes including: emotional lability, impulsivity, irritability, becoming more outspoken and less worried, and occasionally showing imitation and utilization behaviors.
- *Perseveration*—A tendency to repeat the same response over and over, even when it is shown to be inappropriate. Perseveration may involve motor acts, speech, or ideas.
- *Utilization behavior*—The tendency to grasp and use objects within reach regardless of whether they are related to the current task. An example would be a child feeling compelled to start hammering when handed a hammer. This behavior is thought to arise from an enslavement to the environment and is associated with bilateral frontal lobe damage.

Sources: Ayd, 1995; Loring, 1999.

disorder, Tourette's syndrome, obsessive-compulsive disorder, and schizophrenia. The relationships between these executive dysfunction disorders are not yet clearly understood and make differential diagnosis difficult (Maricle, Johnson, & Avirett, 2010). Given the fact that the majority of cognitive processes described in this book use some combination of executive facilitators it is suggested that screening for executive functions be included in all assessments. See Miller (2010) for a review of the common neurodevelopmental disorders, which have evidenced executive dysfunctions.

IDENTIFYING EXECUTIVE DYSFUNCTION CONCERNS

It is suggested that the *Neuropsychological Processing Concerns Checklist for Children and Youth—Third Edition* (NPCC-3: 2012a) be completed by the parent/guardian and at least one teacher of the student being referred for a comprehensive assessment (see the supplemental CD for the complete NPCC-3). The questions on the NPCC-3 that pertain to executive function difficulties are shown in Rapid Reference 13.8. Any endorsed items in the moderate to severe range should be followed up with formal assessment measures in the school neuropsychological assessment.

⇶ Rapid Reference 13.8

Executive Function Items From the Neuropsychological Processing Concerns Checklist for Children and Youth—Third Edition (NPCC-3: Miller, 2012a)

Flexibility in thinking difficulties:
- Gets stuck on one activity (e.g., playing video games).
- Does not seem to hear anything else while watching TV.
- Difficulty transitioning from one activity to another.

Planning difficulties:
- Difficulty with making plans.
- Quickly becomes frustrated and gives up easily.
- Difficulty figuring out how to start a complex task.
- Difficulty sticking to a plan of action.

Problem solving and organizing difficulties:
- Difficulty solving problems that a younger child can do.
- Difficulty learning new concepts or activities.
- Makes the same kinds of errors over and over, even after corrections.
- Frequently loses track of possessions.

Behavioral/emotional regulation difficulties:
- Demonstrates signs of over activity (hyperactivity).
- Does not seem to think before acting.
- Difficulty following rules.
- Demonstrates signs of irritability.
- Lacks common sense or judgment.
- Cannot empathize with the feelings of others.

ASSESSING EXECUTIVE FUNCTIONS

Behavioral samples of executive functioning come from four primary sources:

1. *Comprehensive test batteries designed to measure executive functioning* [e.g., Delis-Kaplan Executive Function System (D-KEFS: Delis, Kaplan, & Kramer, 2001)];
2. *Comprehensive test batteries designed to measure all major neuropsychological processes including executive functions* [e.g., NEPSY-II: Korkman, Kirk, & Kemp, 2007];
3. *Tests of cognitive functions* [e.g., Woodcock-Johnson III Tests of Cognitive Ability (WJIII-COG: Woodcock, McGrew, & Mather, 2001, 2007a)]; and
4. *Stand-alone tests that were designed to measure executive functions* [e.g., Wisconsin Card Sorting Test (Heaton, 1981)].

It is important to note that traditional cognitive abilities tests do not measure executive functioning skills. In fact, the examiner often provides a "surrogate" executive functioning role during the evaluation by telling the child what to do when, allocating enough time to complete each task, reinforcing sustained effort, and assisting the child to refocus their attention when distracted. Still, there are certain components within cognitive test batteries that attempt to tease out various aspects of executive functioning skills (e.g., measures of planning, reasoning, concept generation). Tests from cognitive instruments designed to measure executive functions will be reported in the second- and third-order classifications of the SNP Model in the sections below.

Rapid Reference 13.9 restates the second- and third-order classifications of executive functions within the Integrated SNP/CHC Model. Tests designed to measure these second- and third-order classifications of executive functions are presented in this section.

Assessing Cognitive Flexibility or Set Shifting

The second-order classification of cognitive flexibility or set shifting separates the tasks based on the modality of the input demands, either verbal or visual, or verbal and visual combined. Rapid Reference 13.10 presents tests that measure verbal, visual, or verbal and visual aspects of cognitive flexibility.

Within the verbal cognitive flexibility tasks, it is important to note that the fourth condition of the Color-Word Test on the Delis-Kaplan Executive Function System (D-KEFS: Delis et al., 2001) measures verbal inhibition

≡ Rapid Reference 13.9

Integrated SNP/CHC Model Classifications of Executive Functions

Broad Classifications	Second-Order Classifications	Third-Order Classifications
Executive functions	• Cognitive flexibility (set shifting)	• Verbal set shifting • Visual set shifting • Verbal and visual set shifting
	• Concept formation	• Concept recognition • Concept generation

	• Problem solving, planning, and reasoning	• Planning
		• Deductive and inductive reasoning
		  • Verbal deductive and inductive reasoning
		  • Visual deductive and inductive reasoning
		• Sequential reasoning
		• Quantitative reasoning

	• Response inhibition	• Verbal response inhibition • Motoric response inhibition
	• Qualitative behaviors • Behavioral rating scales	

≡ Rapid Reference 13.10

Tests of Cognitive Flexibility

Test–Subtest: Description	Age/Grade Range	Publisher
Verbal Cognitive Flexibility		
D-KEFS—Color-Word Interference—Condition 4 (Inhibition/Switching): Completion time as the child rapidly switches back and forth between naming the dissonant ink colors and reading the words.	8–0 to 89–11 years	Pearson

D-KEFS—Verbal Fluency Condition 3—Category Switching: Total Correct Responses: Switching between verbalizing fruits and pieces of furniture.

NEPSY-II—Inhibition Condition 3 (Switching): Rapidly and accurately name shapes while switching cognitive sets.

5 to 16 years

Visual Cognitive Flexibility

D-KEFS—Design Fluency Condition 3—Switching: Switching between connecting solid dots and empty dots.

8–0 to 89–11 years

Pearson

D-KEFS—Trail-Making Condition 4—Number-Letter Switching:

A psychomotor task that requires switching between number and letter sequences (e.g., 1-A-2-B . . .).

TEA-Ch—Creature Counting Total Correct: Ability to follow a path and count up or down depending on the direction of the arrows along the path.

6 to 15–11 years

Pearson

WCST—Perseveration Responses:

Responses that involve getting stuck on the correct response from a previously learned rule.

6–5 to 89 years

PAR

Verbal and Visual Cognitive Flexibility

NEPSY-II—AARS—Response Set:

Added shifting of attention while selectively responding to auditory target words and ignoring auditory nontarget words over time.

7 to 16 years

Pearson

PAL-II RW and PAL-II M—RAS Word and Digit Total Time:

The time taken to rapidly name a mixture of words and digits.

Grades K to 6

PAL-II RW and M—RAS Words and Digits Rate Change: The incidence rate of changing the speed of reading the words and digits.

Grades K to 6

PAL-II RW and M—RAS Words and Digits Total Errors: The total number of errors when rapidly reading the mixture of words and digits.

(continued)

≋ Rapid Reference 13.10 continued

TEA-Ch—Opposite Worlds—Same World Total: Ability to follow a path filled with the digits 1 and 2 while saying "1" when seeing a 1 and "2" when seeing a 2.	6 to 15–11 years	
TEA-Ch—Opposite Worlds—Opposite World Total: Ability to follow a path filled with the digits 1 and 2 while saying "1" when seeing a 2 and "2" when seeing a 1.		
WJIII-COG NU—Auditory Attention: Listening to a word while seeing four pictures and then pointing to the picture of the word that was spoken amid increasingly loud background noise.	2 to 80+ years	Riverside

See Appendix for the full names of the tests and their references.

and switching of attention. The D-KEFS Color-Word Test includes scores for total completion time and the total number of switching (or shifting attention) errors. Likewise, the third condition of the Verbal Fluency test on the D-KEFS includes scores for the total number of correct responses and the total number of correct switches between verbal categories of words retrieved. Finally, the third part of the Inhibition test on the NEPSY-II (Korkman et al., 2007) measures verbal cognitive flexibility and includes a Switching Combined score that is a composite score derived from the Total Completion Time score and the Total Number of Errors score. There are also supplemental scores for the Total Number of Uncorrected Errors and the Total Number of Self-Corrected Errors. It is important for the school neuro-psychologist to analyze and report these subscores to accurately describe the performance of a student on each test, respectively.

Condition 4 (Number-Letter Switching) of the D-KEFS's Trail-Making Test is reported in the visual cognitive flexibility section. When a student achieves a low score on this test, the clinician will need to examine and possibly report the scores from the other conditions on the Trail-Making Test, which measure visual scanning (Condition 1), number sequencing (Condition 2), letter sequencing (Condition 3), and motor speed (Condition 5). See a discussion of how to interpret these scores in Chapter 8.

Creature Counting from the TEA-Ch has a total correct and a timing score, which should both be considered when interpreting the test results. Likewise, the Wisconsin Card Sorting Test (WCST) yields scores for the percent of persever-ation responses, the number of perseveration errors, and the percentage of perseveration errors; all of which should be considered in test interpretation.

Within the verbal and visual cognitive flexibility tasks, the Response Set portion (Part 2) of the Auditory Attention and Response Set test on the NEPSY-II measures aspects of both auditory and visual selective/focused, sus-tained, and shifting of cognitive set. This test includes several scores, which should all be interpreted and reported. Response Set (Part 2 of the test) scores include Response Set Combined, a composite of the Commission Errors and Total Correct scores, and supplemental scores of Total Omission Errors and Total Inhibitory Errors. A school neuropsychologist needs to fully understand how the student's performance on this task influences these scores (see Chapter 8 for an interpretative example). Students with cognitive flexibility deficits have difficulty with transitioning from one activity in the classroom to another. They have a tendency to perseverate, or get stuck, doing one task and have difficulty letting go of that task to start a new one.

Assessing Concept Formation

Tests designed to measure concept formation are presented in Rapid Refer-ence 13.11. It is important to make a distinction between concept recognition and

≋ Rapid Reference 13.11

Tests of Concept Recognition and Generation

Test–Subtest: Description	Age/Grade Range	Publisher
Concept Recognition		
Boehm-3—Preschool: Measures the child's ability to identify basic concepts.	3–0 to 5–11 years	Pearson
Boehm-3—Grades K to 2: Measures the child's ability to identify basic concepts.	Grades K–2	
CTONI-2—Geometric Categories: Categorical classification using geometric designs.	6–0 to 89–11 years	PRO-ED
CTONI-2—Pictorial Categories: Categorical classification using pictures of familiar objects.		

(continued)

⫸ *Rapid Reference 13.11 continued*

DAS-II—Early Number Concepts:
Oral math questions with illustrations.

2–6 to
8–11 years

Pearson

DAS-II—Picture Similarities:
Multiple-choice matching of pictures on the basis
of relationships.

DAS-II—Verbal Similarities:
Explaining how three things or concepts go together.

5 to
17–11 years

**D-KEFS—Sorting Test—Combined
Conditions 1 + 2 Description:**
Accuracy in describing sorts either completed by
self or by the examiner.

8 to
89–11 years

**D-KEFS—Twenty Questions Initial
Abstraction:**
Level of abstract reasoning in the first questions asked.

**D-KEFS—Twenty Questions Total
Questions Asked:**
The fewer the questions asked the better.

**D-KEFS—Twenty Questions Total
Weighted Achievement:**
This score is used only if the child guesses
the correct answer quickly.

WISC-IV—Similarities:
Describing how two words that represent
common objects or concepts are similar.

6–0 to
16–11 years

**WISC-IV Integrated—Similarities
Multiple-Choice:**
A multiple-choice version of the Similarities
subtest, which lowers the verbal and memory
demands of the task.

6–1 to
16–11 years

Concept Generation

**D-KEFS—Sorting test—Condition 1
(free sorting) Confirmed Correct Sorts:**
The number of confirmed correct sorts made on
the two card sets.

8 to 89–11
years

Pearson

NEPSY-II—Animal Sorting Combined:
A combination of the number of correct sorts and
the number of errors. Measures initiation, cognitive
flexibility, self-monitoring, and conceptual knowledge.

7 to 16
years

See Appendix for the full names of the tests and their references.

concept generation. Concept recognition provides a measure of the underlying reasoning and concept formation skills. Tests that measure concept recognition may involve classification of pictures or objects based on a common concept or describing a common characteristic that two words share. Another example of concept recognition is the ability to verbally describe common attributes used to sort stimuli into conceptual groupings.

Concept generation is the ability to classify objects into conceptual groupings that share a common characteristic; however, no verbal justification or rationale used for sorting the objects is required. Some students achieve an average score on concept generation tasks because their sorts are correct by chance only; however, on tasks that require the additional step of describing the rationale for sorting, as in many concept recognition tasks, they are not always able to perform as well.

The D-KEFS Sorting Test (Delis et al., 2001) includes measures of both concept generation and recognition and is the most thorough of all of the concept recognition and generation measures. The D-KEFS Sorting Test includes four additional measures that should be included in the interpretation of the overall performance on the test including: Free Sorting Description (Condition 1), Sort Recognition Description (Condition 2), Combined Conditions $1 + 2$ Description (verbal rules), and Combined Conditions $1 + 2$ (perceptual rules).

In the classroom, concept recognition plays an important role in learning. When presented with new information an efficient learner must try to relate that new information to previous learning. In Piagetian terms this was described as assimilation and accommodation. If the new information can be categorically or semantically related to previous learning it is assimilated into our memory stores. If the new information is unique to our semantic classifications we must accommodate that information by modifying or creating a new way of storage. Concept recognition facilitates the storage and retrieval of information. Concept generation also plays an important role in learning. However, concept generation is a more active process of seeing the similarities in objects or concepts or words and being able to identify those shared similarities. Concept generation is concept recognition put into action.

Assessing Problem Solving, Planning, and Reasoning

The second-order classification of problem solving, planning, and reasoning separates the tasks into the third-order classifications of planning, deductive and inductive reasoning, sequential reasoning, and quantitative reasoning.

≡ Rapid Reference 13.12

....

Tests of Planning

Test–Subtest: Description	Age/Grade Range	Publisher
CAS—Planned Connections: Quickly connecting number and letter sequences.	2–0 to 90+ years	Riverside
KABC-II—Rover: Moving a toy dog through a maze in an efficient manner.	3–0 to 18–0 years	Pearson
UNIT—Mazes: Tracing a path through mazes.	5–0 to 17–11 years	Riverside
WISC-IV Integrated—Elithorn Mazes: Tracing a path through mazes as quickly as possible.	6–1 to 16–11 years	Pearson
WISC-IV Integrated—Elithorn Mazes: No Time Bonus: The Elithorn mazes task with no completion time bonus.		
WJIII-COG NU—Planning: Measures the mental control process in determining, selecting, and applying solutions to problems using forethought.	2–0 to 90+ years	Riverside

See Appendix for the full names of the tests and their references.

Tests of Planning

Tests designed to measure planning are presented in Rapid Reference 13.12.

Tests of Deductive and Inductive Reasoning

Tests designed to measure deductive and inductive reasoning are presented in Rapid Reference 13.13.

The D-KEFS measures (Delis et al., 2001) all have additional processing scores that aid in the clinical interpretation of the test. For example, the Word Context test has a global score for the total consecutive correct but also yields scores for the number of repeated incorrect responses and the consistently correct ratio. The Proverbs test yields a total achievement score based on free inquiry but also provides the clinician with separate scores for common and uncommon proverbs and scores for accuracy only and abstraction only. The Proverbs test also yields a total achievement score based on multiple choice and process scores for common and uncommon proverbs, total correct abstract or concrete responses, and total incorrect phonemic or unrelated choices.

≡ Rapid Reference 13.13

Tests of Deductive and Inductive Reasoning

Test–Subtest: Description	Age/Grade Range	Publisher
Verbal Deductive and Inductive Reasoning		
D-KEFS—Proverbs Total Achievement: Free Inquiry: Knowledge of verbal proverbs.	16–0 to 89–11 years	Pearson
D-KEFS—Proverbs Total Achievement: Multiple Choice: Recognition of verbal proverbs.		
D-KEFS—Word Context Total Consecutively Correct: Verbal abstract deductive reasoning.	8–0 to 89–11 years	
RIAS—Guess What: Deduction of object or concept being described with a set of 2–4 clues.	3 to 94 years	PAR
RIAS—Verbal Reasoning: Competing sentences to form verbal analogies.		
SB5—Verbal Fluid Reasoning: Ability to solve novel problems presented in words and sentences.	2 to 85+ years	Riverside
TAPS-3—Auditory Reasoning: Understanding jokes, riddles, inferences, and abstractions.	4 to 18–11 years	Academic Therapy Publications
WISC-IV—Comprehension: Answering questions based on understanding of general principles and social situations.	6–0 to 16–11 years	Pearson
WISC-IV Integrated—Comprehension Multiple Choice: A multiple-choice version of the Comprehension subtest. Lesser verbal and recall memory demands.	6–1 to 16–11 years	
WISC-IV—Word Reasoning: Identifying an object, word, or concept with incremental clues.	6–0 to 16–11 years	
Visual Deductive and Inductive Reasoning		
CAS—Nonverbal Matrices: Comprehend the relationships among the parts of a visual matrix and choose the best of six options.	2–0 to 90+ years	Riverside

(continued)

≡ Rapid Reference 13.13 continued

CTONI-2—Geometric Analogies: Completing nonverbal analogies using geometric designs.	6–0 to 89–11 years	PRO-ED
CTONI-2—Pictorial Analogies: Completing nonverbal analogies using pictures of familiar objects.		
D-KEFS—Tower Total Achievement: Overall quality of tower building within time limits.	8–0 to 89–11 years	Pearson
DAS-II—Matrices: Solving visual puzzles.	2–6 to 17–11 years	
NEPSY-II—Clocks: Recognizing time on analog clocks, and constructing clock faces.	7 to 16 years	
RIAS—Odd-Item Out: Designating one item out of many visual objects that does not match the remainder of the objects.	3 to 94 years	PAR
SB5—Nonverbal Fluid Reasoning: Ability to solve novel problems presented in pictures and figures.	2 to 85+ years	Riverside
UNIT—Analogic Reasoning: Completing a matrix analogies task using common objects.	5–0 to 17–11 years	Riverside
UNIT—Cube Design: Completing a 3-dimensional block design.		
WISC-IV—Matrix Reasoning: Completing a missing portion of a picture matrix.	6–0 to 16–11 years	Pearson
WISC-IV—Picture Concepts: Choosing one picture from among two or three rows of pictures to form a group with a common characteristic.		
WNV—Matrices: Completing a missing portion of a picture matrix.	4–0 to 21–11 years	
WCST—Total Number of Errors: Number of errors made in categorizing cards.	6–5 to 89 years	PAR
WJIII-COG NU—Concept Formation: Categorical reasoning and inductive logic.	2–0 to 90+ years	Riverside

See Appendix for the full names of the tests and their references.

On the *Wisconsin Card Sorting Test* (Heaton, Chelune, Talley, Kay, & Curtiss, 1993) the primary score generated is the total number of errors. However, the test also provides the clinician with supplemental scores, which will aid in clinical interpretation, including percentage of total errors, total number of nonperseverative errors, percentage of perseverative errors, percentage of conceptual level responses, and a learning to learn score.

Tests of Sequential Reasoning
Tests designed to measure sequential reasoning are presented in Rapid Reference 13.14.

Tests of Quantitative Reasoning
Tests designed to measure quantitative reasoning are presented in Rapid Reference 13.15.

≡ Rapid Reference 13.14

Tests of Sequential Reasoning

Test–Subtest: Description	Age/Grade Range	Publisher
CTONI-2—Geometric Sequences: Sequential reasoning using geometric designs.	6–0 to 89–11 years	PRO-ED
CTONI-2—Pictorial Sequences: Sequential reasoning using pictures of familiar objects.		
KABC-II—Pattern Reasoning: Selecting a pattern that completes a logical, linear pattern.	3–0 to 18–0 years	Pearson
KABC-II—Story Completion: Selecting a scene that completes a complete story sequence.		
WNV—Picture Arrangement: Rearrange a set of pictures to tell a story that makes sense.	4–0 to 21–11 years	
WJIII-COG NU—Analysis/Synthesis: General sequential (deductive) reasoning.	2–0 to 90+ years	Riverside

See Appendix for the full names of the tests and their references.

≡ Rapid Reference 13.15

Tests of Quantitative Reasoning

Test–Subtest: Description	Age/Grade Range	Publisher
DAS-II—Sequential and Quantitative Reasoning: Figuring out sequential patterns in pictures or geometric figures, or common rules in numerical relationships.	5–0 to 17–11 years	Pearson
WJIII-COG DS—Number Matrices: Ability to analyze the relationship among numbers and identify the missing number.	2–0 to 90+ years	Riverside
WJIII-COG DS—Number Series: Ability to determine a numerical pattern and provide the missing number in a series.		

See Appendix for the full names of the tests and their references.

Problem solving, fluid reasoning, and planning are processes that help students be active learners. These processes help students to make complex choices and decisions, understand the interconnections between subject matter, learn to identify and ask significant questions that help clarify differing points of view which lead to better solutions, and framing, analyzing, and synthesizing information to solve problems and answer questions. Problem solving skills are especially important in learning the procedural steps and reasoning required in mathematics.

ASSESSING RESPONSE INHIBITION

A distinction needs to be made between cognitive and behavioral response inhibition. If a child has difficulty controlling his or her impulse to lash out at another child sitting nearby, this would be an example of a behavioral response inhibition control problem. In this section, cognitive response inhibition is the focus. An example of a cognitive response inhibition task is the classic Stroop effect when a student is asked to look at a series of color words ("red," "green," and "blue") and inhibit the natural tendency to read the word itself rather than naming the color of the ink in which the word is printed. For example, the student sees the word "red" printed in green ink and is instructed to say "green." Response inhibition requires vigilance to rules, patience, and impulse control, attributes that many students struggle with in an educational environment.

≡ Rapid Reference 13.16

Tests of Response Inhibition

Test–Subtest: Description	Age/Grade Range	Publisher
Verbal Response Inhibition		
CAS—Expressive Attention: Rapidly naming animals or color words with varying degrees of stimulus distraction.	5–0 to 17–11 years	PRO-ED
D-KEFS—Color-Word Interference Condition 3 (Inhibition): Time taken to rapidly name the color of the ink a color word ("red") is printed in.	8–0 to 89–11 years	Pearson
NEPSY-II—Inhibition (Condition 2) Combined: Rapidly and accurately naming the opposite names of shapes (e.g., "circle" for "square").	5 to 16 years	
Motoric Response Inhibition		
NEPSY-II—Statue Total: Maintaining a body position during distractions.	3 to 6 years	Pearson
TEA-Ch—Walk Don't Walk: Marking a line on a printed pathway only in response to a target tone.	6 to 15–11 years	

See Appendix for the full names of the tests and their references.

Tests designed to measure verbal and visual response inhibition are presented in Rapid Reference 13.16. The major scores for these tests are listed but some of the measures yield supplemental scores, which will aid in clinical interpretation. For example, the third condition of the Color-Word Interference test on the D-KEFS (Delis et al., 2001) is the classic inhibition portion of the test and generates a total score based on the amount of time required to complete the task. A supplemental score is generated for the total number of uncorrected and corrected errors made on the task. This supplemental score for errors is important to consider in the interpretation of the test, because completion time may be very slow due to poor processing speed or due to the high number of self-corrected errors made during the performance of the task.

On the second condition of the NEPSY-II Inhibition test (Korkman et al., 2007), the students are shown pictures of circles and squares or up and down arrows. On this condition students are asked to say "circle" every time they see a square and say "square" every time they see a circle, and the same alternative labels for up and down arrows. The test yields a total score, which combines the effects of completion time and errors. It is important for the clinician to analyze the supplemental scores on this test, which include separate scores for completion time and total errors. The interplay between speed and accuracy has important clinical implications and may be masked by the total combined score. Two additional scores provide greater interpretative precision for analyzing the errors by examining a supplemental score for the total number of uncorrected errors versus the total number of self-corrected errors.

On the NEPSY-II Statue test (Korkman et al., 2007), students are asked to stand with their eyes closed and pretend to hold a flag while the examiner provides distractions. The task measures the student's ability to inhibit motoric responses. The test yields a total score and supplemental scores for the number of body movement inhibitory errors, eye opening inhibitory errors, and vocalization inhibitory errors. These supplemental scores will provide additional insight to the clinician about the types of errors made in a motoric response inhibition task.

Qualitative Behaviors of Executive Functions

Several tests such as the D-KEFS (Delis et al., 2001) and NEPSY-II (Korkman et al., 2007) have provided clinicians with normative information that quantifies qualitative behaviors. The qualitative behaviors that relate to executive functions are presented in Rapid Reference 13.17.

≡ *Rapid Reference 13.17*

Qualitative Behaviors Related to Executive Functions
Set-loss errors (failure to maintain the directions):
- D-KEFS: Design Fluency: Total Set-Loss Designs
- D-KEFS: Sorting Test Condition 1 Set-Loss Sorts
- D-KEFS: Trail-Making Test: Condition 2—Number Sequencing Set-Loss Errors
- D-KEFS: Trail-Making Test: Condition 3—Letter Sequencing Set-Loss Errors
- D-KEFS: Trail-Making Test: Condition 4—Number-Letter Switching Set-Loss Errors
- D-KEFS: Twenty Questions: Set-Loss Questions
- D-KEFS: Verbal Fluency: Set-Loss Errors
- D-KEFS: Verbal Fluency: Percent Set-Loss Errors

- D-KEFS: Word Context: Total Correct-to-Incorrect Errors
- WCST: Failure to Maintain Set

Repetition errors (close together = perseveration, far apart = memory weakness):

- D-KEFS: Design Fluency: Total Repeated Designs
- D-KEFS: Proverbs Repeated Responses
- D-KEFS: Sorting Test Condition 1 Repeated Sorts
- D-KEFS: Sorting Test Combined Repeated Descriptions
  - Condition 1: Free Sorting Repeated Descriptions
  - Condition 2: Sort Recognition Repeated Descriptions
- D-KEFS: Twenty Questions: Repeated Questions
- D-KEFS: Verbal Fluency: Repetition Errors
- D-KEFS: Verbal Fluency: Percent Repetition Errors
- D-KEFS: Word Context Repeated Incorrect Responses

Corrected errors (good self-monitoring):

- D-KEFS: Color-Word Interference Test: Condition 3—Inhibition Corrected Errors
- D-KEFS: Color-Word Interference Test: Condition 4—Inhibition/Switching Corrected Errors

Uncorrected errors (poor self-monitoring):

- D-KEFS: Color-Word Interference Test: Condition 3—Inhibition Uncorrected Errors
- D-KEFS: Color-Word Interference Test: Condition 4—Inhibition/Switching Uncorrected Errors

Omission errors:

- D-KEFS: Trail-Making Test: Condition 1—Visual Scanning Omission Errors

Commission errors:

- D-KEFS: Trail-Making Test: Condition 1—Visual Scanning Commission Errors

Sequencing errors:

- D-KEFS: Trail-Making Test: Condition 2—Number Sequencing: Sequencing Errors
- D-KEFS: Trail-Making Test: Condition 3—Letter Sequencing: Sequencing Errors
- D-KEFS: Trail-Making Test: Condition 4—Number-Letter Switching: Sequencing Errors

Time-discontinuation errors:

- D-KEFS: Trail-Making Test: Condition 2—Number Sequencing: Time Discontinuation Errors
- D-KEFS: Trail-Making Test: Condition 3—Letter Sequencing: Time Discontinuation Errors

(continued)

≡ *Rapid Reference 13.17 continued*

- D-KEFS: Trail-Making Test: Condition 4—Number-Letter Switching: Time Discontinuation Errors
- D-KEFS: Trail-Making Test: Condition 5—Motor Speed: Time Discontinuation Errors

initiating behaviors (reflective or impulsive):

- D-KEFS: Tower Mean First-Move Time
- D-KEFS: Verbal Fluency First 15" Interval Correct
- D-KEFS: Verbal Fluency Second 15" Interval Correct
- D-KEFS: Verbal Fluency Third 15" Interval Correct
- D-KEFS: Verbal Fluency Fourth 15" Interval Correct
- WCST: Trials to Complete First Category

Rule violations during task performance (impulsive response style or oppositional response style):

- D-KEFS: Tower Total Rule Violations
- D-KEFS: Tower Rule Violations-Per-Item Ratio
- NEPSY-II: Memory for Designs and Memory for Designs Delayed

Total attempted items:

- D-KEFS: Design Fluency: Total Attempted Designs
- D-KEFS: Sorting Test: Condition 1 Attempted Sorts

Percent accuracy:

- D-KEFS: Design Fluency Percent Design Accuracy
- D-KEFS: Sorting Test: Condition 1 Percent Sorting Accuracy

See Appendix for the full names of the tests and their references.

Interpreting Set-Loss Errors (Failure to Maintain the Directions)

Set-loss errors are quantified on several of the D-KEFS tests (Delis et al., 2001) and the Wisconsin Cart Sorting Test (Heaton et al., 1993; see Rapid Reference 13.16). A trained school neuropsychologist can look for signs of set-loss errors on other instruments as well. Set-loss errors occur when a student loses track of the task requirements. A student may have accurate performance on practice test items; however, during the actual test performance set-loss errors occur. When interpreting set-loss errors, make sure that the student's receptive language skills and sustained attention skills are intact. Set-loss errors may be indicative of a student's inability to maintain the cognitive set or task requirements due to a high level of distractibility or failure to fully comprehend the task requirements (Delis et al., 2001). In the classroom, a student with frequent set-loss errors may appear lost or confused in the middle of assignments and would require frequent redirection or reminder of the task requirements.

Interpreting Repetition Errors

Repetition errors are quantified on several of the D-KEFS tests (Delis et al., 2001; see Rapid Reference 13.17). Repetition errors occur when answers are repeated on a task despite explicit instructions asking the student not to repeat answers. Repetition errors may be attributable to poor receptive language skills, in that, the student did not understand the directions in the first place. If receptive language is intact, the examiner should evaluate the proximity of the repetition errors. If the same answers are repeated close together, it is characterized as a perseveration error (an executive dysfunction). If the same answers are repeated far apart it is characterized as a working memory problem.

Interpreting Corrected Versus Uncorrected Errors

Corrected errors are better than uncorrected errors. A corrected error indicates that a student is using an executive function called *self-monitoring* and catches some or all errors as they occur. Uncorrected errors indicate that the student has poor self-monitoring skills. Self-corrected errors are recorded and norm-referenced on the D-KEFS Color-Word Test (Delis et al., 2001) (see Rapid Reference 13.17).

Self-monitoring skills can be taught to students and it is an important executive skill, which encourages students to check their work before turning in assignments (see Dawson & Guare, 2010, or Metzler, 2010, for some instructional strategies for teaching self-monitoring). It is important for the school neuropsychologist to keep in mind that many tests measure completion time and accuracy rate. If a student has many self-corrections during a test, completion time will be slower than normal. It is important to consider the interaction between completion time and accuracy when interpreting the overall test scores. A student who has slow completion time and few self-corrected errors is a qualitatively different type of student than one who has slow completion time with a high number of self-corrected errors.

Interpreting Omission and Commission Errors

On the D-KEFS Trail-Making Test (Delis et al., 2001), the omission and commission errors are norm-referenced for the first condition of the test that requires visual scanning. Omission errors generally reflect an impulsive or careless response style (Delis et al., 2001). Commission errors are rare and may indicate a marked impairment in either the student's ability to sustain attention or a failure to maintain a cognitive set.

Interpreting Sequencing Errors

On the D-KEFS Trail-Making Test (Delis et al., 2001), Condition 2 requires number sequencing and Condition 3 requires letter sequencing. If a student has difficulty finding stimuli in the correct sequence, this may reflect a fundamental sequential processing deficit.

Interpreting Time Discontinuation Errors, Initiating Behaviors, Rule Violations, Total Attempted Items, and Percent Accuracy

The total number of attempted items is recorded and norm-referenced for the D-KEFS Design Fluency and Sort Test—Condition 1 (Delis et al., 2001: see Rapid Reference 13.17). Poor problem solving or poor concept generation will result in a low score on total attempted items. A low score may indicate poor effort due to poor motivation or a total lack of the cognitive skills or processes being measured.

The percent accuracy score is usually interpreted in conjunction with the total number of attempted items. Some students will try to complete very few designs, but the designs that they do construct reflect set-loss errors. Other students will attempt an average number of items but the percent correct is low, which indicates good initiation but poor problem solving or concept generation.

Measures That Use Feedback During Task Performance

Being able to modify one's performance based on feedback during learning has some regulatory components that are controlled by the frontal lobes. The tests that measure the use of feedback during task performance generally fall under the category of active learning. Tests such as the Category Test (Boll, 1993) and the WCST (Heaton et al., 1993) are active learning tasks. Children must learn to modify their cognitive sets based on the feedback of the examiner during the task performance. Other tests that require the use of feedback during the performance of the task include the D-KEFS: Twenty Questions (Delis et al., 2001), and the WJIII-COG: Analysis-Synthesis, Concept Formation, and Visual-Auditory Learning tests (Woodcock et al., 2001, 2007a). These tests are covered in other parts of the book. The D-KEFS tests were reviewed earlier in this chapter.

Summary of Behavioral Measures of Executive Functions

The proceeding section of this chapter has reviewed the common behavioral tests for measuring deficits in executive functioning. The tests of executive function are categorized into measures of concept generation, problem solving, planning, reasoning, and qualitative behaviors. The next section of this chapter reviews an indirect method of gathering information about a child's executive functioning, through behavioral rating scales.

Behavioral Rating Scales of Executive Functions

There are several new rating scales for evaluating executive functions in children and adolescents that were being published just prior to the release of this book. These new executive function rating scales include: the *Barkley Deficits in Executive Functioning Scale: Children and Adolescents* (BDEFS: CA; 2012a), *Delis-Rating of Executive Functions* (D-REF; Delis, 2012), and the *Comprehensive Executive Function Inventory* (CEFI; Naglieri & Goldstein. 2012). It was not possible to review these rating scales for this book, but clinicians are encouraged to investigate the clinical utility of these instruments. The *Behavior Rating Inventory of Executive Function* (BRIEF) is reviewed in this section.

Behavior Rating Inventory of Executive Function (BRIEF) Scales

The BRIEF is an indirect method of gathering information about a child's executive functioning (see Rapid Reference 13.18). The BRIEF uses a questionnaire format that is completed by parents, teachers, day care providers, or the adolescent, based on the version of the test. The BRIEF is published in several versions including: the BRIEF (Gioia, Isquith, Guy, & Kenworthy, 2000) designed for children ages 5 to 18 years; the BRIEF-Preschool Version (BRIEF-P: Gioia, Espy, & Isquith, 2003) designed for preschool children 2-5 to 11 years; and the BRIEF—Self-Report Version (BRIEF-SR: Guy, Isquith, & Gioia, 2004) designed for adolescents ages 11 to 18 years.

The BRIEF has two empirically validated factor scales: the Behavioral Regulation Index and the Metacognition Index. Rapid Reference 13.18 shows the BRIEF factor scales and the subtests that load on them for the version of the test. The Behavioral Regulation Index "represents a child's ability to shift cognitive set and modulate emotions and behavior via appropriate inhibitory control" (Gioia et al., 2000, p. 20). The Behavioral Regulation Index is a factor score for both the BRIEF and BRIEF-SR versions. For the Preschool Version of the test, the Behavioral Regulation Index is split into two factors labeled the Flexibility Scale and the Inhibitory Self-Control Scale.

The Metacognition Index "represents the child's ability to initiate, plan, organize, and sustain future-oriented problem-solving in working memory" (Gioia et al., 2000, p. 20). The Metacognition Index is a factor score for both the BRIEF and BRIEF-SR versions of the test, although subtests used to derive

≡ Rapid Reference 13.18

The Behavior Rating Inventory of Executive Function

	BRIEF	BRIEF-P	BRIEF-SR
Age ranges	5 to 18 years	2 to 5–11 years	11 to 18 years
Raters	Parent or teacher	Parent, teacher, or day care provider	Adolescent self-report
Behavioral regulation scale	X X	X X	X X
Flexibility scale			
Inhibitory self-control			
Inhibit	X	X X	X
Shift	X	X X	X
Emotional control	X	X X X	X
Metacognition scale	X X		X X
emergent metacognition scale		X	
Initiate	X		
Working memory	X	X X	X
Plan/organize	X	X X	X
Organization of materials	X		
Monitor	X		X
Task completion			X
Global executive composite	X	X	X
Validity scales:			
Negativity scale	X	X	X
Inconsistency scale	X	X	X

each of the indices differ between versions. The BRIEF-P has a slightly different factor structure that was labeled the Emerging Metacognition Scale.

Each version of the BRIEF has two validity scales: negativity and inconsistency. "The Negativity scale measures the extent to which the respondent answers selected BRIEF items in an unusually negative manner relative to the clinical samples" (Gioia et al., 2000, p. 14). The BRIEF should be viewed as a screener for executive functions in children and youth and not as a replacement for direct measures. An external rater's assessment of a child's executive functioning may or may not be equivalent to actual behavioral samples of the child's executive functioning.

CHAPTER SUMMARY

In this chapter, the terminology, neuroanatomy, major behavioral tests, and rating scales associated with executive functioning were reviewed. Executive functions play a major role in regulating purposeful behavior and should be systematically assessed by a school neuropsychologist. Executive dysfunctions are observed in many common developmental disorders.

 TEST YOURSELF

1. **All of the terms below are associated with executive functions except which one?**
   a. Tactile perception
   b. Self-monitoring
   c. Planning
   d. Abstract reasoning

2. **Which one of the following frontal-subcortical circuits is not involved with the regulation of behavior?**
   a. Dorsolateral prefrontal circuit
   b. Oculomotor circuit
   c. Orbitofrontal circuit
   d. Anterior cingulate circuit

3. **Which of the frontal-subcortical circuits helps regulate socially appropriate behaviors under normal circumstances?**
   a. Oculomotor circuit
   b. Anterior cingulate circuit
   c. Dorsolateral prefrontal circuit
   d. Orbitofrontal circuit

4. **Damage to the frontal-subcortical circuit can cause decreased retrieval fluency, poor organizational skills, poor planning, impaired set shifting, and so on. What frontal-subcortical circuit seems to be impaired?**
   a. Orbitofrontal circuit
   b. Anterior cingulate circuit
   c. Dorsolateral prefrontal circuit
   d. Oculomotor circuit

5. **True or False? Phineas Gage was a railroad worker who sustained a head injury to his orbitofrontal region of the brain.**

6. A tendency to repeat the same response over and over again, even when shown it to be inappropriate is referred to as?

a. Initiation deficit
b. Perseveration
c. Utilization behavior
d. Echopraxia

7. True or False? The Wisconsin Card Sorting Test is typically associated with measuring retrieval fluency.

8. Which of the tests below measures a child's executive functioning using a rating scale completed by either the parent or teacher?

a. D-KEFS
b. WCST
c. BRIEF
d. Stroop Color-Word Test

Answers: 1. a; 2. b; 3. d; 4. c; 5. true; 6. b; 7. False; 8. c

Chapter Fourteen

ATTENTION AND WORKING MEMORY FACILITATORS/INHIBITORS

I n this chapter, the facilitators/inhibitors of attention and working memory are defined, their neuroanatomy are described, and the common tests used to assess attention and working memory are presented.

In the SNP Model (D. Miller, 2007, 2010, 2012; D. Miller & Maricle, 2012), attention processes and executive functions are separated into two broad classifications; whereas, Korkman, Kirk, and Kemp (2007) combine attention and executive functions into a single domain on the NEPSY-II. The process of allocating sufficient attentional resources to perform a given mental operation or the process of shifting attentional focus from one activity to another can also be viewed as an executive facilitator. Likewise, working memory was classified within the SNP Model under the broad classification of Learning and Memory but may also be viewed as a facilitator/inhibitor. In the updated Integrated SNP/CHC Model presented in Chapter 5, some of the processes and functions originally classified as executive functions have been reclassified as facilitators/inhibitors.

ALLOCATING AND MAINTAINING ATTENTION FACILITATORS/INHIBITORS

In addition to sensory-motor functions, attentional processes serve as a baseline for all of the higher-order processes (e.g., visual-spatial processing, language skills, memory and learning). For example, a verbal list-learning task can be contaminated by a child's poor ability to pay attention. Difficulties with attention are often a symptom of other underlying neurological disabilities. Attentional processing disorders are common in children who have compromised brain functioning as a result of neurodevelopmental disorders, exposure to environmental toxins, traumatic and acquired brain injuries, and so on. Approximately 9.5% or 5.4 million children, 4 to 17 years of age, have been diagnosed with ADHD, as of 2007 (Centers for Disease Control and Prevention, 2010).

Unfortunately, too many children are misdiagnosed as having Attention-Deficit Hyperactivity Disorder (ADHD) without a satisfactory evaluation to determine the root cause of the inattention, the type of attention deficit, and the proper course of treatment. Consequently, the true disability often goes undiagnosed, misdiagnosed, or untreated.

The *Diagnostic and Statistical Manual of Mental Disorders—Fourth Edition— Text Revision* (American Psychiatric Association, 2000) classifies ADHD within four subtypes: 314.01—ADHD, Combined Subtype; 314.00—Predominantly Inattentive Type; 314.01 ADHD, Predominantly Hyperactive-Impulsive Type; and 314.9—ADHD Not Otherwise Specified (NOS). Unfortunately, these four *DSM-IV* ADHD diagnoses do not address the neuropsychological subtypes of attention that have been documented in the literature.

Theories of Attention

Mirsky and his colleagues (Mirsky, 1987, 1996; Mirsky, Anthony, Duncan, Ahearn, & Kellam, 1991; Mirsky & Duncan, 2001) conducted a factor analysis of neuropsychological tests, each of which measured some aspect of attention. The data were based on more than 600 subjects including many subjects with clinical disorders of attention. Based on the factor analysis, Mirsky and his colleagues proposed a taxonomy of attention functions including *focus/execute*, *sustain* and *stabilize*, *shift*, and *encode*. This Mirsky model of attention has been applied to several clinical populations [e.g., Barkley, 1996; Block, 2002; Burden, Jacobson, Sokol, & Jacobson, 2005 (children with fetal alcohol exposure); Ewing-Cobbs et al., 1998; Kavros et al., 2008 (children rolandic epilepsy); Leffard, 2009; Loss, Yeates, & Enrile, 1998 (children with myelomenigocele); McDiarmid, 2003 (children with lead exposure); Mirsky, Pascualvaca, Duncan, & French, 1999; Thaler, Allen, Park, McMurray, & Mayfield, 2010 (children with traumatic brain injury); Wolfe, 2006 (children with ADHD)].

Mirsky's *focus/execute*, *sustain*, and *shift* subcomponents have endured in the neuropsychological literature, some with different names. Posner and Peterson (1990) theorized the existence of three attentional systems: *orienting*, *selection*, and *alerting or sustained attention*. The orienting system lies in the posterior regions of the brain, directs spatial attention, and is implicated in neglect syndromes (the failure to attend to stimuli presented in the hemispace contralateral to a brain lesion that cannot be attributed to primary sensory or motor deficits; Loring, 1999). The selection system in the Posner and Peterson model is similar to Mirsky's focus/execute attention functions. The third Posner and Peterson attentional system, alerting or sustained attention, is comparable to Mirsky's sustained attention function.

Mirsky's *stability* subcomponent was related to the variability of reaction time to the target stimuli on a Continuous Performance Test. Mirsky's *encode* component described the abilities required to perform the Digit Span and Arithmetic subtests of the Wechsler Adult Intelligence Scale—Revised (WAIS-R: Wechsler, 1981). The tasks that loaded on the encode component of attention all required a memory capacity to hold information briefly in store while performing some action or cognitive operation on it. In recent literature, this encode subcomponent would be considered to measure working memory.

See Baron (2004) for a more thorough review of theories of attention. The attentional processing labels that have been adopted for the Integrated SNP/CHC Model are selective/focused, sustained, and capacity. Each of these subcomponents of attention are discussed in more detail in the next sections.

Selective/Focused Attention

Johnny is sitting in a classroom and is supposed to be paying attention to the teacher for a lesson. The classroom environment is filled with potential distracters including Mary sitting next him tapping her pencil on her desk, the rich colored bulletin boards posted on the wall, and the lack of air-conditioning on that particular day. Johnny has some potential internal distracters to deal with as well, including the uncomfortable chair he is sitting in that is hurting his back, the hungry feeling he has in his stomach because he forgot to eat breakfast, or the loose Band-Aid on his finger. Johnny's ability to choose to pay attention to the teacher and ignore the potential external and internal distracters requires selective or focused attention.

Mirsky and colleagues (Mirsky, 1987, 1996; Mirsky & Duncan, 2001; Mirsky et al., 1991) refer to the ability to scan an array of stimuli and selectively respond as *focus/execute*. *Focused attention* is the perceptual ability to scan a stimulus array, while the *execute component* is the ability to make a response. Mirsky and his colleagues were unable to separate the focusing aspect from the executed response component, so they used the term *focus/execute* to describe this subtype of attention. An interchangeable term used in the neuropsychology literature for focus-execute is *selective attention*. Selective attention is defined as "the ability to maintain a cognitive set in the presence of background "noise" or distraction" (Baron, 2004, p. 222). An example of a neuropsychological test that measures selective attention is the Stroop Color-Word Test (SCWT). On SCWT, the child is presented with a list of color words (e.g., red, blue, green) that are printed in different colors of ink (e.g., the word "red" printed in green ink or the word "green" printed in blue ink). The child is asked to *selectively attend* to the color of the ink that the word is printed in and name that color, while ignoring the name of the color word itself.

Sustained Attention

Nisha is at home and she is trying to watch a television show with her mother. Nisha is able to watch the first 5 minutes of the show but she quickly loses interest and moves on to another activity. According to her mother, Nisha "flits" from one activity to another because she cannot maintain her attentional focus for prolonged periods of time. Nisha is experiencing difficulty with her sustained attention.

Mirsky and his colleagues (Mirsky, 1987, 1996; Mirsky & Duncan, 2001; Mirsky et al., 1991) refer to the ability to stay on task in a vigilant manner for a prolonged period of time as *sustained attention*. In a sense, sustained attention is applying selective attention or vigilance over a prolonged period of time. A classic sustained attention task is the Continuous Performance Test (CPT) in which the child is asked to attend to a "target" event (e.g., pressing a counter when an "X" is followed by an "O") while ignoring all other events over a prolonged period of time.

Attentional Capacity

Tonya can attend to small bits of information but she quickly becomes overwhelmed if too much information is presented to her at once. Tonya may be experiencing problems with attentional capacity.

Mirsky and his colleagues (Mirsky, 1987, 1996; Mirsky & Duncan, 2001; Mirsky et al., 1991) did not find a subcomponent of attention called *attentional capacity* because the neuropsychological tasks that were factor analyzed did not require those skills. Attentional capacity has a direct relationship with the cognitive capacity or load required on memory tasks (Miller & Maricle, 2012). As the length of the stimuli to be recalled increases, as in digits or letters, and as the semantic loading increases from words to sentences, to stories, there are concurrent changes in the attentional demands of the tasks. A typical test that measures attentional capacity is a digit span test, in which the child is asked to recall digits of increasing length. Other tests that measure attentional capacity are tests that measure memory for words, memory for sentences, or memory for stories. All of these tests obviously have a strong memory component, but they also require attentional skills.

Neuroanatomy of Attentional Processes

The neuroanatomy of attention includes the subcortical portions of the brain (e.g., the reticular activating system) that help regulate and maintain arousal, to higher cortical regions (e.g., prefrontal lobes and anterior cingulate cortex) that help allocate attentional resources, selectively attend, and regulate response inhibition. The frontal-subcortical pathways that help regulate attention are also involved in regulating executive functions (see a broader review on this circuit in Chapter 13). Mirsky and his colleagues (1991, 1996) believed that the brain structures involved with the regulation of *selective/focused attention* were the superior temporal cortex, the inferior parietal cortex, and the corpus striatum structures (including the caudate, putamen, and globus pallidus) (see Figure 14.1). Posner and Peterson (1990) believed selective attention was linked to the functions of the anterior cingulate and the supplemental motor areas (see Figure 14.2). Mirsky and his colleagues believed the brain structures involved with regulating *sustained attention* were the subcortical rostral midbrain structures (including the tectum, mesopontine, reticular formation, and midline and reticular thalamic nuclei) (see Figure 14.1). Posner and Peterson believed sustained attention was regulated by the right side of the brain, particularly the anterior, prefrontal regions (see Figure 14.2). Mirsky and his colleagues believed the dorsolateral prefrontal cortex and the anterior cingulate gyrus were the brain structures involved with *shifting attention* (see Figure 14.1).

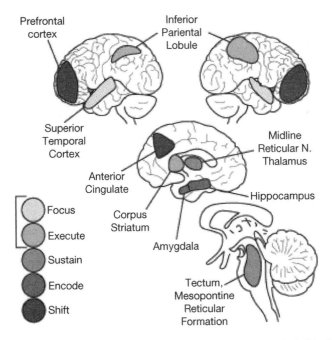

Figure 14.1. Neuroanatomical Regions Associated with Mirsky's Model of Attention

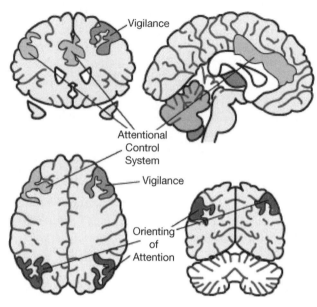

Figure 14.2. The Neural Network of Attention According to Posner (1994). This Model Highlights Brain Regions That are Involved in the Attentional Control System, Orienting of Attention, and Vigilance

Casey, Tottenham, and Fossella (2002) used functional magnetic resonance imaging (fMRI) to measure the brain activation and localization that occurred during the performance of a go/no go task in a sample of normal children and adults. Go/no go tasks are designed to measure response inhibition (e.g., Knock and Tap subtest on the NEPSY-II; Korkman et al., 1997). Casey and colleagues found performance on the go/no go task produced activation in the orbitofrontal, dorsolateral, and right anterior cingulate cortex. The orbitofrontal and right anterior cingulate cortex areas were significantly correlated with behavioral performance and the activation of the dorsolateral cortex was much higher in children than adults. Perhaps some of the variability in linking specific attentional processes with specific neuroanatomical structures may be attributed to differences in neuroimaging techniques, adult versus child populations, and tasks that require more "bottom-up" versus "top-down" attentional processes. Rapid Reference 14.1 presents some neuropsychological terms associated with attention deficits.

It is important to remember that attention is not a unitary process and that it serves as a baseline function for all other higher-order processes. Consistent with the current literature in the field, the Integrated SNP/CHC Model conceptualizes

≡ Rapid Reference 14.1

Neuropsychological Terms Associated with Attention Impairments

- *Divided attention*—The ability to attend to more than one stimulus at a time.
- *Hemispatial neglect/inattention*—Frequently used to describe a milder form of neglect.
- *Neglect*—The failure to respond to visual, auditory, or tactile stimuli presented in the hemispace contralateral to a brain lesion that cannot be attributed to primary sensory or motor deficits.
- *Unilateral neglect*—The tendency to ignore information presented in the hemispace contralateral to a cerebral lesion.

Sources: Ayd, 1995; Loring, 1999.

attention in the subdomains of selective/focused attention, sustained attention, and attentional capacity. Many neuroimaging studies support the frontal-subcortical bases of attention, though precise anatomical locations of specific attentional subtypes have shown varying results.

Since Mirsky's research in the early 1990s, the neuroanatomical structures that play a role in attention have been of particular focus to researchers using a variety of neuroimaging and neurosurgical techniques and evaluation of clinical populations (e.g., ADHD; see Hale, Reddy et al., 2010, for a thorough review). Reductions in volume and/or hypoactive regions within the right prefrontal, globus pallidus, caudate nucleus, and cerebellar regions of the brain have been found in ADHD populations (Castellanos et al., 2002; Durston, 2003; Rubia et al., 1999; Vaidya et al., 1998; Valera, Faraone, Murray, & Seidman, 2007). Other neuroimaging studies with ADHD samples have also implicated deficiencies in the frontal-subcortical, and possibly limbic regions (Benson, 1991; Heilman, Voeller, & Nadeau, 1991; Zametkin et al., 1990; Zametkin et al., 1993). Neuroimaging studies have shown the right prefrontal regions of the brain being activated during tasks that require sustained attention (Lewin et al., 1996; Pardo, Pardo, Janer, & Raichle, 1991).

When to Assess Attentional Processes

Attentional processing deficits are common in a wide variety of neurodevelopmental disorders beyond ADHD. Since attentional processing is such an important basic function that permeates all other higher-order cognitive processes, it is important to include some basic attentional processing measures in a school neuropsychological battery to verify the integrity of attention.

Identifying Attentional Processing Concerns

It is suggested that the *Neuropsychological Processing Concerns Checklist for Children and Youth—Third Edition* (NPCC-3: Miller, 2012a) be completed by the parent/guardian and at least one teacher of the student being referred for a comprehensive assessment (see the supplemental CD for the complete NPCC-3). The questions on the NPCC-3 that pertain to attention problems are shown in Rapid Reference 14.2. Any endorsed items in the moderate to severe range should be followed up with formal assessment measures in the school neuropsychological assessment.

Assessing Attentional Processes

Rapid Reference 14.3 restates the second- and third-order classifications of attentional facilitators/inhibitors within the Integrated SNP/CHC Model. Tests designed to measure these second- and third-order classifications of attentional facilitators/inhibitors are presented in this section.

Tests of Selective/Focused and Sustained Attention

The second-order classification of selective/focused and sustained attention facilitators/inhibitors separates the tasks based on the modality of the input demands, either verbal or visual. Ideally, tests designed to measure selective/focused attention would be different from tests designed to measure sustained attention; however, this is the exception instead of the rule. Many of the tests designed to measure attention co-mingle the two types of attention. Some tests, such as continuous performance tests are specifically designed to measure sustained attention and these tests are discussed in the next section. Rapid Reference 14.4 presents tests that measure aspects of either selective/focused attention, or sustained attention, or both.

≡ Rapid Reference 14.2

Attention Items From the Neuropsychological Processing Concerns Checklist for Children and Youth—Third Edition (NPCC-3: D. Miller, 2012a)

Selective or sustained attention difficulties:
- Seems to get overwhelmed with difficult tasks.
- Difficulty paying attention for a long period of time.
- Seems to lose place in an academic task (e.g., reading, writing, math).
- Mind appears to go blank or loses train of thought.
- Inattentive to details or makes careless mistakes.

≡ Rapid Reference 14.3

Integrated SNP/CHC Model Classifications of Attentional Facilitators/Inhibitors

Broad classifications	Second-Order Classifications	Third-Order Classifications
Allocating and maintaining attention facilitators/ inhibitors	Selective/focused attention	• Auditory selective/focused attention • Visual selective/focused attention
	Sustained attention	• Auditory sustained attention • Visual sustained attention • Auditory and visual sustained attention
	Attentional capacity	• Memory for numbers, letters, or visual sequences • Memory for words and sentences • Memory for stories
	Qualitative behaviors	
	Behavioral rating scales	

≡ Rapid Reference 14.4

Tests of Selective/Focused and Sustained Attentional Facilitators/ Inhibitors

Test–Subtest: Description	Selective	Sustained	Age/ Grade Range	Publisher
Auditory Selective/Focused and Sustained Attention				
NEPSY-II—Auditory Attention: Selectively responding to auditory target words while ignoring auditory nontarget words over time.	X	X	5 to 16 years	Pearson

(continued)

⇶ Rapid Reference 14.4 continued

TEA-Ch—Code Transmission: Listening to a series of numbers and recalling the number heard just prior to two fives being heard together.			X	6 to 15–11 years	
TEA-Ch—Score! Keeping count of "scoring sounds."		X			
TEA-Ch—Score DT: Keeping count of "scoring sounds" from an audiotape with the presence of an auditory distracter.		X			
Visual Selective/Focused and Sustained Attention					
CAS—Number Detection: Quickly finding target numbers within a visual array.	X			5 to 17–11 years	PRO-ED
CAS—Receptive Attention: Quickly finding target letters within a visual array.	X				
TEA-Ch—Map Mission: Searching a map to find as many target symbols as possible in one minute.	X			6 to 15–11 years	Pearson
TEA-Ch—Sky Search Attention Score: Quickly finding as many "target" spaceships as possible on paper filled with target and nontarget ships.	X				
TEA-Ch—Sky Search Dual Task (DT): Combines two tasks of finding spaceships and counting score sounds.	X	X			
WJIII-COG NU—Pair Cancellation: Matching target stimuli from a large visual array under time constraints.		X		2 to 80+ years	Riverside

See Appendix for the full names of the tests and their references.

The Auditory Attention portion of the Auditory Attention and Response Set test on the NEPSY-II (Korkman et al., 2007) measures aspects of both auditory selective/focused attention and sustained attention and includes several scores, which should all be interpreted and reported. Auditory Attention (Part 1 of the test) scores include: Auditory Attention Combined, a composite of the Commission Errors and Total Correct scores, and supplemental scores of Total Omission Errors and Total Inhibitory Errors. A school neuropsychologist needs to fully understand how the student's performance on this task influences these scores (see Chapter 8 for an interpretative example).

The *Test of Everyday Attention for Children* (TEA-Ch: Manly, Robertson, Anderson, & Nimmo-Smith, 1999) is a stand-alone measure of attention that is modeled after Mirsky's conceptualization of attention. One of the concerns about using the TEA-Ch in clinical practice in the United States is the fact the test was standardized on only 293 Australian children. However, the latent factor structure of the TEA-Ch has been shown to be the same as the Australian standardization sample with a sample of Chinese children (Chan, Wang, Ye, Leung, & Mok, 2008) and a stratified sample of children from the United States (Belloni, 2011). In regard to the SNP Model, the Sky Search test from the TEA-Ch includes a composite score, separate scores for the number of correctly identified targets, and a score for the processing time per target. These scores should be reported and interpreted separately in light of the student's performance on the overall task.

Continuous Performance Tests

Riccio, Reynolds, and Lowe (2001) provide a comprehensive review and comparison of the continuous performance tests. The continuous performance test (CPT) was originally designed to be a measure of vigilance or sustained attention, whereby the subject is asked to respond to a target event repeatedly over time while ignoring distracter or nontarget events. Riccio, Reynolds, Lowe, and Moore (2002) reported that while CPT performance does seem to reflect attentional disturbances, the various versions of the test do not discriminate particular disorders well (e.g., ADHD). Rapid Reference 14.5 presents some of the commonly used CPT tests. The methods used to administer the CPT vary tremendously. Some CPT tests are computer administered; others use a stand-alone electronic device, and others are paper-and-pencil versions. Some of the CPT tests use only an auditory mode of processing.

Students with selective/focused attention deficits will have difficulties determining what is relevant in their learning environments and what can be ignored. Children with ADHD frequently have difficulty with selective/focused attention, which leads to distractibility, inefficiency in learning, and uneven performance.

≡ Rapid Reference 14.5

Continuous Performance Tests

Test Name	Modality	Age Range	Publisher
• Auditory Continuous Performance Test (ACPT: Keith, 1994)	Auditory	6 to 11–11 years	Pearson
• Conners' Continuous Performance Test II Version 5 (Connors & MHS Staff, 2004a)	Visual	6 years to Adult	Multihealth Systems (MHS)
• Conners' Continuous Performance Test for Windows®: Kiddie Version (Connors & MHS Staff, 2004b)	Visual	4 to 5 years	MHS
• Gordon Diagnostic System (Gordon, 1983; Gordon, McClure, & Alyward, 1996)	Auditory only Visual only auditory and visual	4 to 16 years	Gordon Systems
• Integrated Visual and Auditory Continuous Performance Test (IVA+Plus: Sandford & Turner, 1993–2006)	Auditory and visual	6 to 96 years	BrainTrain
• Test of Variables of Attention (T.O.V.A.: Greenberg & Waldman, 1993)	Auditory only Visual only	6 to 16 years	The TOVA Company

Students with sustained attention or vigilance deficits, have difficulty maintaining their attentional focus in the classroom. These children may be able to initially focus on the relevant task at hand, but quickly lose that focus.

Tests of Attentional Capacity

The second-order classification of attentional capacity separates the tasks based on the cognitive load of the tasks. These same tasks measure aspects of learning and memory but in this interpretative section, the focus is on how does changing the level of semantic meaning or contextual cues and increasing the length of stimuli to be learned affect the student's capacity to pay attention to the respective task. Attentional capacity is examined as a function of learning a series of numbers or letters of increasing length, or learning visual sequential patterns of increasing length, or recalling word strings or sentences of increasing lengths, or finally recalling content from stories with increasing semantic cues. Rapid Reference 14.6 presents tests that measure attentional capacity based on these third-order classifications.

≡ Rapid Reference 14.6

Tests of Attentional Capacity

Test–Subtest: Description	Age/Grade Range	Publisher
Attentional Capacity for Numbers or Letters with Verbal Response		
DAS-II—Recall of Digits Forward: Repeating a series of digits of increasing length.	2–6 to 17–11 years	Pearson
KABC-II—Number Recall: Repeating auditorially presented digits of increasing length.	3 to 18 years	
TOMAL-2—Digits Forward: Repeating auditorially presented digits of increasing length.	5 to 59–11 years	PRO-ED
TOMAL-2—Letters Forward: Repeating auditorially presented letters of increasing length.		
WRAML2—Number/Letter: Repeating auditorially presented number/letter strings of increasing length.	5 to 90 years	PAR
WISC-IV—Digits Forward: Repeating auditorially presented digits of increasing length.	6 to 16–11 years	Pearson
WISC-IV Integrated—Letter Span— Rhyming: Repeating auditorially presented letters of increasing length that rhyme.	6–1 to 16–11 years	
WISC-IV Integrated—Letter Span— Nonrhyming: Repeating auditorially presented letters of increasing length that do not rhyme.		
WISC-IV Integrated—Visual Digit Span: Repeating visually presented digits of increasing length.		
Attentional Capacity for Visual Sequential Patterns with Motor Response		
WISC-IV Integrated—Spatial Span Forward: Repeating visually presented motoric sequences of increasing length.	6–1 to 16–11 years	Pearson
WRAML2—Finger Windows: Using a finger to repeat a visual pattern of increasing length.	5 to 90 years	PAR
Attentional Capacity for Words and Sentences (Increased Meaning) with Verbal Response		
CAS—Word Series: Recall of words from a verbally presented list.	5–0 to 17–11 years	PRO-ED
KABC-II—Word Order (without Color Interference): Touching pictures in sequential order based on the order spoken by the examiner.	3 to 18 years	Pearson

(continued)

≡ Rapid Reference 14.6 continued

NEPSY-II—Sentence Repetition: Repeating sentences of increased length and complexity.	3 to 6 years	
WRAML2—Sentence Memory: Repeating sentences of increased length and complexity.	5 to 90 years	PAR
WJIII-COG DS—Memory for Sentences: Memory for sentences of increasing length and complexity.	2 to 90+ years	Riverside
WJIII-COG NU—Memory for Words: Repeating lists of unrelated words in correct sequence.	2 to 90+ years	

Attentional Capacity for Stories (Even More Contextual Meaning) with Verbal Response

CMS—Stories Immediate: Recalling verbally presented story details.	5 to 16–11 years	Pearson
NEPSY-II—Narrative Memory Free Recall: Recalling verbally presented story details.	3 to 16 years	
TOMAL-2—Memory for Stories: Recalling verbally presented story details.	5 to 59–11 years	PRO-ED
WRAML2—Story Memory: Recalling verbally presented story details.	5 to 90 years	PAR
WJIII-ACH NU—Story Recall: Recalling verbally presented story details.	2 to 90+ years	Riverside

See Appendix for the full names of the tests and their references.

The patterns of performance that a clinician looks for across the attentional capacity tasks are:

- Does the student perform well when recalling short strings of information (e.g., digit recall) but performance drops significantly when too many strings of numbers are presented?
- Does the student's performance worsen as words, sentences, and finally stories are presented? In other words, as the semantic cues increase does that cause information overload?
- Does the student not perform well on the simple digit or letter recall tasks but performs much better as the semantic cues are increased from words, to sentences, to stories?

Some children need the added contextual cues and increased meaning to capture and maintain their attentional focus; whereas, other children (particularly children with ADHD) shut down their learning when too much information is presented.

Qualitative Behaviors of Attention

On the NEPSY-II, the frequency of two qualitative behaviors such as inattentive/distracted off-task behaviors and out of seat/physical movements are recorded and base rates compared to the student's same age group or to one of the clinical validation sample groups can be generated. These base rates provide the clinician the opportunity to make statements such as "Alice exhibited out of seat/physical movements in her seat on the Auditory Attention and Response Set test of the NEPSY-II. Only 14% of other children Alice's age engaged in this level of out of seat behaviors; however, 35% of the children within the Attention Deficit Hyperactivity Disorder diagnostic group had this same level of out-of-seat behaviors."

Behavioral Rating Scales of Attention

Following an integrative style of report writing, any behavioral rating of attention and/or hyperactivity is reported in the attentional processing section of the report since those behaviors are related to attention. The remainder of behavioral rating scales, which measure psychological concerns such as depression, conduct disorders, and anxiety, are reported in the social-emotional section of the report.

There are multiple behavioral rating scales for assessing ADHD and attentional processing disorders, including, but not limited to:

- ACTeRS: *ADHD-H Comprehensive Teacher's Rating Scale* (2nd ed.) [Teacher, Parent, and Self-Report Forms] (Ullmann, Sleator, & Sprague, 1991; Ullman, Sleator, Sprague, & Meritech Staff, 1996).
- ADDES/ADDES-S: *Attention Deficit Disorders Evaluation Scale Third Edition/Attention Deficit Disorders Evaluation Scale: Secondary-Age* (McCarney, 2004a, 2004b). Available in English or Spanish.
- ADHD-SRS: *ADHD Symptoms Rating Scale.* Available in English or Spanish. (Holland, Gimpel, & Merrell, 1998).
- ADHD-SC4: *ADHD Symptoms Checklist—4* (Gadow & Sprafkin, 1997).
- ADHDT: *Attention Deficit Hyperactivity Disorder Test* (Gilliam, 1995).
- BASC-2: *Behavior Assessment System for Children* (2nd ed.) (Reynolds & Kamphaus, 2009).
- CBRS: *Conners Comprehensive Behavior Rating Scales* (Conners, 2008a).
- Conners 3: *Conners* (3rd ed.) (Conners, 2008b).

- CBCL/6–18; TRF; YSR: *Child Behavior Checklist* (CBCL), *Teacher Rater Form* (TRF), and *Youth Self Report* (YSR) (Achenbach, 2007a, 2007b, 2007c).

There are other behavioral rating scales that assess attention within a broader context. The BASC-2, Conners-3, CBCL/6–8; TRF, & YSR, *Brown Attention-Deficit Disorder Scales for Adolescents and Adults* (BADDS: Brown, 1996), the *Brown Attention-Deficit Disorder Scales for Children and Adolescents* (BADDS: Brown, 2001), and the *Clinical Assessment of Attention Deficit–Child* (CAT-C: Bracken & Boatwright, 2005) are all examples of rating scales for attention within a broader context.

WORKING MEMORY FACILITATORS/INHIBITORS

Timothy is 12 years old and has a history of uneven academic progress. He has recently been having trouble with mathematics, reading, and writing. His teachers observe that he seems to lose track of what he is doing in the middle of math problems. When he tries to write he seems to lose track of what he was trying to communicate. Timothy seems to understand what he reads and he has good accuracy, but he has difficulty summarizing the overall content of a chapter or section in a book. Timothy is experiencing the symptoms that are consistent with a working memory deficit.

"The concept of working memory was developed to address the various short-comings in the short-term memory concept as expressed in the modal model" (Gazzaniga et al., 2002, p. 311). *Working memory* is "a memory system that underpins our capacity to "keep things in mind' when performing complex tasks" (Baddeley, Eysenck, & Anderson, 2008, p. 9). Information placed in working memory may come from sensory memory, short-term memory, or from long-term memory. The key component of a working memory task is the requirement for active manipulation of the information. Working memory has been shown to be a required cognitive process for components of reading, mathematics, and writing achievement in children (Evans, Floyd, McGrew, & LeForgee, 2002; see Dehn, 2008, for a review).

Baddeley and colleagues (Baddeley, 1986, 1995; Baddeley & Hitch, 1974) originally proposed a three-part working memory system that contains a *central executive* control system that regulates two subordinate subsystems: the *visuospatial sketchpad* and the *phonological loop*.

The central executive system is a command and control center that presides over the interactions between the two subordinate systems and long-term memory (Gazzaniga et al., 2002). Norman and Shallice (1980) referred to the central executive system as the supervisory attentional system (SAS). The phonological loop is thought to be responsible for the temporary storage of speech-like information (Baddeley et al., 2008). The visuospatial sketchpad is thought to be responsible for temporary maintenance of visual and spatial information (Baddeley et al., 2008).

In 2000, Baddeley (2000) made two major changes in the working memory model. The first change was the assumed linkage between the phonological and visuospatial subsystems to long-term memory. The long-term memory and phonological loop linkage allows for the acquisition of language. The long-term memory and visuospatial sketchpad allows for the acquisition of visual-spatial information.

The second change to Baddeley and Hitch's original working memory model (1974), was the inclusion of the episodic buffer (Baddeley, 2000). The episodic buffer is assumed to be a system of storage that can hold a limited amount (four chunks) of information. The information within the episodic buffer is thought to be multidimensional in nature, meaning that information from our senses, emotions, and memory stores are all combined. As a result of this multi-dimensional storage of information, the episodic buffer can act as a link between the phonological loop and the visuospatial sketchpad with input from long-term memory and from our perceptual processing. The episodic buffer is theorized by Baddeley (2000) to be the site of a mental workspace that assists in performing complex cognitive activities. See Figure 14.3 for an illustration of Baddeley's current model of working memory.

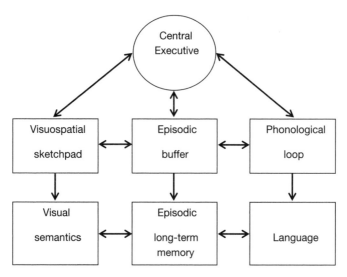

Figure 14.3. Baddeley's Current Model of Working Memory (2000)

Neuroanatomy of Working Memory

There is neuroanatomical evidence for Baddeley's working memory model. Patients with left supramarginal gyrus (temporal-parietal gradient) lesions have deficits in phonological working memory. The rehearsal process of the phonological loop involves areas of the left premotor region. Therefore, the phonological working memory system is thought to involve the lateral frontal, superior temporal, and inferior parietal regions of the brain (Gazzaniga et al., 2002).

Damage to the parietal-occipital region of either hemisphere will produce deficits in the visuospatial sketchpad, but damage to the right parietal-occipital region will produce even greater deficits (Gazzaniga et al., 2002). Children with lesions or damage to the right parietal-occipital region would have great difficulty performing a task like the *WISC-IV Integrated* (Wechsler et al., 2004) Spatial Span test, in which the child has to touch blocks on a board following the same sequence as the examiner.

Identifying Working Memory Concerns

It is suggested that the *Neuropsychological Processing Concerns Checklist for Children and Youth—Third Edition* (NPCC-3: Miller, 2012a) be completed by the parent/guardian and at least one teacher of the student being referred for a comprehensive assessment (see the supplemental CD for the complete NPCC-3). The questions on the NPCC-3 that pertain to working memory difficulties are shown in Rapid Reference 14.7. Any endorsed items in the moderate-to-severe range should

≡ *Rapid Reference 14.7*

Working Memory Items from the Neuropsychological Processing Concerns Checklist for Children and Youth—Third Edition (NPCC-3: D. Miller, 2012a)

Working memory difficulties:

- Frequently asks for repetitions of instructions/explanations.
- Trouble following multiple step directions.
- Loses track of steps/forgets what they are doing amid task.
- Loses place in the middle of solving a math problem.
- Loses train of thought while writing.
- Trouble summarizing narrative or text material.
- Trouble remembering facts or procedures in mathematics.

≡ Rapid Reference 14.8

Integrated SNP/CHC Model Classifications of Working Memory Facilitator/Inhibitor

Broad Classifications	Second-Order Classifications	Third-Order Classifications
Working memory facilitator/inhibitor	• Working memory	• Verbal working memory • Visual working memory • Qualitative behaviors

be followed up with formal assessment measures in the school neuropsychological assessment. The major tests of working memory for school-age children are reviewed in the next section.

Assessing Working Memory

Rapid Reference 14.8 restates the second- and third-order classifications of learning and memory processes within the Integrated SNP/CHC Model. The next section of this chapter describes the major stand-alone test batteries of learning and memory followed by a cross-battery listing of tests designed to measure each on the second and third order learning and memory classifications in the Integrated SNP/CHC Model.

In the Integrated SNP/CHC Model, working memory is classified within the broad classification of Working Memory Facilitator/Inhibitor. Working memory is subdivided further into third-order classifications of (1) verbal working memory, and (2) visual working memory. Working memory has a major impact on many aspects of academic achievement (see *Working Memory and Academic Learning: Assessment and Intervention,* Dehn, 2008, for a thorough review). Rapid Reference 14.9 presents a list of the major tests designed to measure either verbal or visual working memory.

Qualitative Behaviors of Working Memory

On the WISC-IV (Wechsler, 2003) and *WISC-IV Integrated* (Wechsler et al., 2004), the Working Memory subtests have a set of qualitative scores that are calculated as base rates comparing a student's performance to their same aged peers (see Rapid Reference 14.10).

≡ Rapid Reference 14.9

Tests of Working Memory Facilitators/Inhibitors

Test– Subtest: Description	Age/ Grade Range	Publisher
Verbal Working Memory		
CMS—Numbers Backward: Repeating number strings previously spoken by examiner in reverse order.	5–0 to 16–11 years	Pearson
CMS—Sequences: Ability to manipulate and sequence verbal information quickly.		
DAS-II—Recall of Digits Backward: Repeating number strings previously spoken by examiner in reverse order.	2–6 to 17–11 years	
DAS-II—Recall of Sequential Order: Sequencing, from highest to lowest, increasingly long sequences of words.		
KABC-II—Word Order (with Color Interference): Touching pictures in sequential order based on the order spoken by the examiner.	3 to 18 years	
NEPSY-II—Word List Interference Recall: Repeating an initial string of unrelated words after a second interference list of unrelated words is presented.	7 to 16 years	
PAL-II M—Numeric Coding Total: Ability to code written numerals into working memory accurately and quickly.	K to 6 grades	
PAL-II M—Quantitative Working Memory: Ability to store numbers and perform quantitative operations on them in working memory.		
PAL-II RW—Letters + Words: Ability to store and manipulate letters or words in working memory.		
PAL-II RW—Sentences: Listening + Sentences: Ability to manipulate sentences in working memory.		
SB5—Verbal Working Memory: Ability to store verbal information in short-term memory and then sort or transform that information.	2 to 85+ years	Riverside

TAPS-3—Number Memory Reversed: Repeating number strings previously spoken by examiner in reverse order.	4 to 18–11 years	Academic Therapy Publications
TOMAL-2—Digits Backward: Repeating number strings previously spoken by examiner in reverse order.	5 to 59–11 years	PRO-ED
TOMAL-2—Letters Backward: Repeating letter strings previously spoken by examiner in reverse order.		
WISC-IV—Arithmetic: Mentally solving orally presented arithmetic problems within time limits.	6–0 to 16–11 years	Pearson
WISC-IV—Digit Span Backward: Repeating number strings previously spoken by examiner in reverse order.		
WISC-IV—Letter-Number Sequencing: Recalling numbers in ascending order and letters in alphabetical order after listening to a sequence of numbers and letters spoken by the examiner.		
WJIII-COG NU—Auditory Working Memory: Repeating the name of the objects in sequential order, followed by the numbers in sequential order, after listening to an audio recording of a series of names of both objects and digits.	2–0 to 90+ years	Riverside
WJIII-COG NU—Numbers Reversed: Repeating number strings in reverse order that were spoken by the examiner.		
WRAML-2—Verbal Working Memory: Three levels of difficulty, which requires reordering of words to some stimulus property (e.g., word order, size of object).	5–0 to 90 years	PAR
Visual Working Memory		
PAL-II M—Spatial Working Memory: Ability to locate objects in a 2-dimensional visual array and code their quantity.	K to 6 Grades	Pearson
SB5—Nonverbal Working Memory: Ability to store nonverbal information in short-term memory and then sort or transform that information.	2 to 85+ years	Riverside

(continued)

≡ Rapid Reference 14.9 continued

WISC-IV Integrated—Spatial Span Backward: Touching a sequence of blocks that was shown by the examiner in reverse order. — 6–1 to 16–11 years — Pearson

WMS-IV—Spatial Addition: Adding or subtracting the location of circles based on a set of rules. — 16 to 90 years

WMS-IV—Symbol Span: Selecting symbols from an array in the same order previously presented.

WNV—Spatial Span: Touching a sequence of blocks that was shown by the examiner in forward to reverse order. — 4–0 to 21–11 years

WRAML-2—Symbolic Working Memory: I Pointing to number strings recalled or number letter strings. — 5 to 90 years — PAR

See Appendix for the full names of the tests and their references.

≡ Rapid Reference 14.10

Qualitative Behaviors for the WISC-IV and WISC-IV Integrated: Working Memory

- Longest digit span forward versus backward:
    Percentage of same age peers with a better verbal immediate memory (digits forward) compared to verbal working memory (digits backward).
    - Longest digit span forward:
        Percentage of same age peers who achieved this number of the longest digit span forward (verbal immediate memory).
    - Longest digit span backward:
        Percentage of same age peers who achieved this number of the longest digit span backward (verbal working memory).
- Longest visual digit span:
    Percentage of same age peers who achieved this number of the longest visual digit span (visual immediate memory).

- Longest spatial span forward versus backward:
    Percentage of same age peers with a better visual immediate memory (spatial span forward) compared to visual working memory (spatial span backward).
    - Longest spatial span forward:
        Percentage of same age peers who achieved this number of the longest spatial span forward (visual immediate memory).
    - Longest spatial span backward:
        Percentage of same age peers who achieved this number of the longest spatial span backward (visual working memory).
- Longest letter span nonrhyming versus rhyming:
    Percentage of same age peers whose encoding is better for nonrhyming letters compared to rhyming letters.
    - Longest letter span nonrhyming:
        Percentage of same age peers who achieved this number of the longest non-rhyming letter spans (verbal immediate memory).
    - Longest letter span rhyming:
        Percentage of same age peers who achieved this number of the longest rhyming letter spans (verbal immediate memory).
- Longest letter-number sequence versus process approach:
    Percentage of same age peers who achieved a higher number of the longest letter-number sequences (verbal immediate memory) compared to the number of the longest letter-number sequences using a process approach (verbal working memory).
    - Longest letter-number sequence:
        Percentage of same age peers who achieved this number of the longest letter-number sequences (verbal immediate memory).
    - Longest letter-number sequence process approach:
        Percentage of same age peers who achieved this number of the longest letter-number sequences using a process approach (verbal working memory).

CHAPTER SUMMARY

In this chapter the theories, terminology, neuroanatomy, and major tests associated with the cognitive facilitators/inhibitors of attention and working memory were reviewed. Attention and working memory help facilitate many essential elements in education and must be systematically evaluated by a school neuropsychologist. Attention and working memory deficits are observed in many common developmental disorders.

TEST YOURSELF

1. Mirsky's model of attention includes all of the following except:
  a. Encoding
  b. Orienting
  c. Sustained
  d. Focus/selective

2. Jimmy has trouble paying attention in class because he is distracted by other things going on in the classroom (e.g., noises made by the air conditioner). What subcomponent of attention is Jimmy probably having the most trouble with?
  a. Sustained attention
  b. Shifting attention
  c. Attentional capacity
  d. Selective/focused attention

3. True or False? Neuroimaging studies have shown that the right prefrontal region of the brain helps regulate sustained attention.

4. Baddeley and colleagues initially proposed a three-part working memory system that contained a central executive system that regulated which two subordinate subsystems?
  a. Visuospatial sketchpad and phonological loop
  b. Short-term and long-term memory
  c. Episodic and semantic memory
  d. Iconic and echoic memory

5. What is the name of the test battery for children that measures attention based on Mirsky's model?
  a. Test of Everyday Attention for Children
  b. Wisconsin Card Sorting Test
  c. NEPSY-II
  d. Das-Naglieri Cognitive Assessment System

6. What type of memory has a limited capacity and provides temporary storage to manipulate information for complex cognitive tasks such as learning and reasoning?
  a. Long-term memory
  b. Short-term memory
  c. Working memory
  d. Sensory memory

Answers: 1. b; 2. d; 3. true; 4. d; 5. d; 6. c

Chapter Fifteen

SPEED, FLUENCY, AND EFFICIENCY OF PROCESSING FACILITATORS/INHIBITORS

Speed and efficiency of information processing constructs are not as clearly defined and agreed upon by researchers as the other processes that have already been discussed in previous chapters. This chapter reviews the definitions of the speed of information processing constructs, presents the theoretical neuroanatomical bases for the constructs, and reviews the common tests used to assess these constructs.

PROCESSING SPEED DEFINITION

Juan's teachers are always prompting him to get his work turned in on time. Juan is generally accurate in his seatwork but it takes him longer than his classmates to complete assignments. Juan also has trouble with the rate of his reading. He often takes so long to read a passage that by the time he gets to the end, he has forgotten what he has read. Juan is experiencing problems with his speed and efficiency of cognitive processing.

Measures of processing speed have been explicitly included in two of the mainstream tests of intelligence since the late 1980s (*Wechsler Intelligence Scale for Childre—Third Edition*: WISC-III: Wechsler, 1991; *Woodcock-Johnson Revised Tests of Cognitive Ability*: WJ-R COG: Woodcock & Johnson, 1989). The processing speed construct has remained in the updated versions of each test as well (WISC-IV: Wechsler, 2003; WJIII-COG: Woodcock, McGrew, & Mather, 2001, 2007a).

However, not all processing speed tests measure the same construct (Feldmann, Kelly, & Diehl, 2004; Floyd, Evans, & McGrew, 2003), which has led to interpretation confusion for clinicians. Motor speed (aka psychomotor skill, graphomotor speed, or paper-and-pencil skill) and number facility (skill in dealing with numbers ranging from number recognition, counting, to simple mathematical computations) have been hypothesized to be contributors to an individual's performance on processing speed measures (Feldmann et al., 2004; Floyd et al., 2003).

Feldman et al. (2004) examined the relationship between five measures of processing speed: (1) WISC-III Coding, (2) WISC-III Symbol Search, (3) WJR Visual Matching, (4) WJR Cross Out, and (5) Differential Ability Scale—Second Edition's (DAS-II; Elliott, 2007) Speed of Information Processing. Feldmann and colleagues (2004) found that Motor Speed accounted for small (7% to 17%) but significant amounts of variance on all five processing speed tests. Number Facility was found to account for 14% of the variance for the WJR Visual Matching and the DAS-II Speed of Information Processing tests and 8% of the variance for the WISC-III Symbol Search subtest.

As children develop, they process information more rapidly (Kail & Miller, 2006). Processing speed deficits have been found in clinical populations of children, including ADHD (e.g., Fuggetta, 2006); youth diagnosed as having Bipolar Disorder (Doyle et al., 2005); children exposed prenatally to alcohol (e.g., Burden, Jacobson, & Jacobson, 2005); and children with reading disabilities (Willcutt, Pennington, Olson, Chhabildas, & Hulslander, 2005).

Following the Cattell-Horn-Carroll (CHC) model, processing speed (*Gs*) measures the speed with which an individual performs simple cognitive tasks (Schrank, Miller, Wendling, & Woodcock, 2010). The tasks used to measure processing speed typically are timed on a fixed interval and require little in the way of complex thinking or cognitive processing. Schneider and McGrew (2012) point out that processing speed is not that crucial during the initial learning phases of a task, but becomes "an important predictor of skilled performance once people know how to do a task" (p. 119). Processing speed is of special importance to consider when students have already learned a particular task or skill and the difference in speed with which they perform that task or skill is being measured. For example, two children could each have good reading decoding skills, yet one child is a slow and methodical reader and the other child reads very quickly.

MODELS OF PROCESSING SPEED

Processing speed may be best conceptualized as a broad construct containing several specific or narrow abilities based on item content (Carroll, 1993). Carroll found replicated evidence that processing speed is composed of mutually exclusive narrower abilities such as movement time, reaction time, correct decision speed, incorrect decision speed, perceptual speed, short-time retrieval speed, and retrieval fluency. Horn and Blankson (2012) note that speed is related to reaction time, decision making, perception, and problem solving in almost all of the abilities that are involved with what is widely considered as human intelligence. They suggest that although there are certainly different types of processing speed, there is not a unified general factor for the speediness of thinking. Processing speed has been shown to improve in children through adolescence and with practice (Kail, 2007).

Based on the synthesis of multiple exploratory and confirmatory factor analytic studies, McGrew (2005) and McGrew and Evans (2004) concluded that processing speed (*Gs*) might be best represented as a set of hierarchically organized speed taxonomy. Schneider and McGrew (2012) modified the aforementioned hierarchical model of processing speed to include a hypothesized general *g* factor of speed and composed of the broad factors of cognitive speed, decision speed, and psychomotor speed. These broad factors included constructs of perceptual speed, rate of test taking, reaction time, movement time, and retrieval fluency.

In the current conceptualization of the Integrated SNP/CHC Model, speed, fluency, and efficiency of processing is classified as a type of facilitator/inhibitor. As previously stated, almost all cognitive and behavioral tasks require some aspect of processing speed to increase the automaticity of responses. However, fast processing speed is not always a desired outcome as evidenced by the child who rushes through an assignment to get it done, but makes multiple errors in completing the task. The interplay between speed, efficiency, fluency, and accuracy must be considered in evaluating the facilitating and inhibiting influences of processing speed. A child may consciously choose to slow down speed of processing to improve accuracy which is more desirable than the alternative, but that may be a compensatory strategy on the part of the child and not indicative of a processing speed deficit per se.

The broad classification of speed, fluency, and efficiency of processing facilitators/inhibitors is conceptualized to be composed of four second-order classifications: performance fluency, retrieval fluency, acquired knowledge fluency, and fluency and accuracy (see Figure 15.1). Performance fluency is defined as the ability to quickly perform simple, repetitive tasks. Retrieval fluency is defined as how quickly information can be retrieved from long-term memory. Performance fluency tasks do not require accessing previously learned or stored information; whereas, retrieval fluency requires quick access to long-term memory.

Acquired knowledge fluency relates to the automaticity of academic achievement including reading fluency, writing fluency, and mathematic fluency. The final second-order classification within the speed and efficiency of processing area is fluency as it relates to accuracy. Processing speed must be interpreted within the context of performance accuracy. For example, a student that rushes through a task while making many errors is qualitatively different from a child who slows down completion of a task to improve accuracy. The third-order classifications related to each of the second-order classifications are discussed in the following sections.

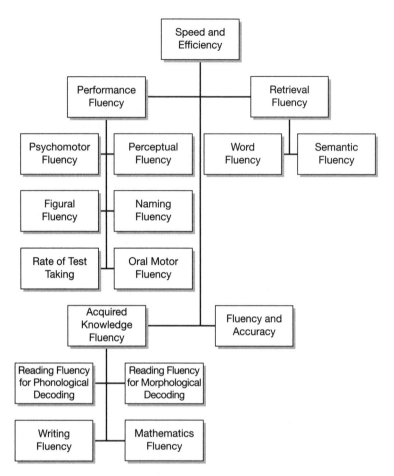

Figure 15.1. Miller's Integrated Speed, Fluency, and Efficiency Model

NEUROANATOMY OF SPEED, FLUENCY, AND EFFICIENCY OF PROCESSING

The neuroanatomical bases of speed, fluency, and efficiency of processing are not fully understood. The neuroanatomy of speed of information processing is thought to have a close relationship with the brain's myelination (Kail, 2000). Myelination is the formation of the myelin sheath around a nerve fiber. Myelin makes up the white matter within the brain. A myelinated pathway within the brain will produce more efficient and faster processing.

Clinical syndromes in children and adults, which adversely affect speed of processing, give us some insight into the brain mechanisms that help regulate efficiency and speed within the brain. Children with head injuries that caused axonal shearing (tearing of the myelin sheath over the axons) show deficits in processing speed and reading fluency (Barnes, Dennis, & Wilkinson, 1999). Speed of visual searches in children ages 6 to 17 years were reported to change as a function of increases in parietal white matter (Mabbott, Laughlin, Noseworthy, Rockel, & Bouffett, 2005). In addition, children treated with radiation for acute lymphoblastic leukemia (ALL) have secondary damage to myelin and as a result have slower processing speeds (Cousins, Ungerer, Crawford, & Stevens, 1991; Schatz, Kramer, Ablin, & Matthay, 2000, 2004).

Most processing speed tests for younger children involve rapid and automatic naming of colors, numbers, familiar pictures, and letters. This type of visual-verbal learning is often mediated by the ventral stream, a neural pathway connecting the visual centers of the brain in the occipital lobe with the verbal centers of the brain in the temporal lobe. Tests requiring students to rapidly look at a visual stimulus and attach a verbal label are, in essence, measuring the integrity of the ventral stream.

WHEN TO ASSESS FOR SPEED, FLUENCY, AND EFFICIENCY OF PROCESSING

Students who are experiencing difficulties with school assignments or homework completion in a reasonable period of time are probably candidates to be assessed for processing speed deficits. Other possible signs of processing speed deficits include difficulty understanding lengthy directions or lectures, difficulty with complex mathematical calculations, difficulty on timed tests, and difficulty with tasks that involve coordinated eye-hand skills. Fluency deficits are manifested by slow oral speech, or academic fluency for reading, writing, and math. Retrieval deficits are manifested by difficulty bringing information out of long-term memory for current use.

If this author was granted permission to change the IDEA law for the identification of children with special needs, several changes would be appropriate; however, the inclusion of processing speed as a specific learning disability would be paramount. Many children have neuropsychological deficits that are caused by physiological damage or degradation of the white matter tracts in the brain, which results in processing speed deficits (see Davis & Broitman, 2011, and Yalof & McGrath, 2010, for reviews of neuropsychological deficits associated with nonverbal learning disabilities and other white matter diseases). At a minimum, these children certainly need to have educational accommodations made for their slow processing speed, with the most common sense one being extended time for task completion.

IDENTIFYING SPEED, FLUENCY, AND EFFICIENCY OF PROCESSING DEFICITS

It is suggested that the *Neuropsychological Processing Concerns Checklist for Children and Youth—Third Edition* (NPCC-3; D. Miller, 2012a) be completed by the parent/guardian and at least one teacher of the student being referred for a comprehensive assessment (see the supplemental CD for the complete NPCC-3). The questions on the NPCC-3 that pertain to speed and efficiency of cognitive processing difficulties are shown in Rapid Reference 15.1. Any endorsed items in the moderate to severe range should be followed up with formal assessment measures in the school neuropsychological assessment.

≡ *Rapid Reference 15.1*

Speed, Fluency, and Efficiency of Cognitive Processing Items from the Neuropsychological Processing Concerns Checklist for Children and Youth—Third Edition (NPCC-3: Miller, 2012a)

Processing speed and fluency difficulties:

- Takes longer to complete tasks than others the same age.
- Homework takes too long to complete.
- Requires extra time to complete tests.
- Responds slowly when asked questions.

Processing speed and accuracy difficulties:

- Does not do well on timed tests.
- Difficulty recalling information accurately and quickly.

Reading fluency difficulties:

- Has a limited reading vocabulary.
- Slow reading that makes reading comprehension poor.
- Difficulty reading quickly and accurately.
- Slow and deliberate reader.
- Difficulty using appropriate phrasing and expression while reading.

Writing fluency difficulties:

- Takes a long time to write even simple sentences.
- Develops an organized sequence in writing that is easy to follow.
- Maintains a clear and sustained focus on the main writing topic.

Mathematics fluency difficulties:

- Takes a long time to solve simple math problems.
- Difficulty pulling basic math facts out of memory quickly.

ASSESSING SPEED AND EFFICIENCY OF COGNITIVE PROCESSING

Rapid Reference 15.2 restates the second- and third-order classifications of speed and efficiency of processing within the Integrated SNP/CHC Model. Tests designed to measure these second- and third-order classifications of speed and efficiency of processing are presented in this section.

Assessing Performance Fluency

As previously defined, performance fluency is the ability to quickly perform simple, repetitive tasks. Performance fluency tasks do not require any memory retrieval. The tasks in this area are all related to overlearned, automatic processing. The second-order classification of performance fluency has several third-order

≡ *Rapid Reference 15.2*

Integrated SNP/CHC Model Classifications of Speed and Efficiency of Cognitive Processing

Broad Classifications	Second-Order Classifications	Third-Order Classifications
Speed, fluency and efficiency of processing facilitators/inhibitors	• Performance fluency	• Psychomotor fluency
		• Perceptual fluency
		• Figural fluency
		• Naming fluency
		• Rate of test-taking fluency
		• Oral motor fluency
	• Retrieval fluency	• Word fluency
		• Semantic fluency
	• Acquired knowledge fluency	• Reading fluency: Rapid phonological decoding
		• Reading fluency: Rapid morphological decoding
		• Writing fluency
		• Mathematics fluency
	• Fluency and accuracy	

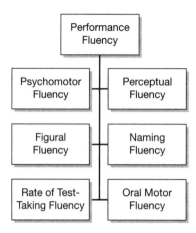

Figure 15.2. Third-Order Classifications of Performance Fluency

classifications including psychomotor fluency, perceptual fluency, figural fluency, naming fluency, rate of test-taking fluency, and oral motor fluency (see Figure 15.2).

Tests of Psychomotor Fluency

The demands of a psychomotor fluency task require rapid motor output. In CHC nomenclature, psychomotor fluency is a measure of psychomotor speed (*Gps*) and movement time (*MT*). An example of this kind of task would be keeping a pencil line moving through a maze as quickly as possible. Students with psychomotor speed and accuracy deficiencies take longer to complete assignments with motor output demands. The interplay between speed and accuracy is discussed in more detail later in this chapter. Some students sacrifice accuracy for speed while others slow down to be more accurate. Ideally, students will be sufficiently fast and accurate instead of slow and inaccurate. Rapid Reference 15.3 presents a list of tests designed to measure the third-order classification of psychomotor fluency.

The Visuomotor Precision test on the NEPSY-II (Korkman et al., 2007) yields an overall combined score and this is often the only score reported by some clinicians. The test also yields three additional measures that should be interpreted as well. These additional scores are for the total completion time, the total number of errors, and the total number of pencil lifts (a rule violation). The overall combined score is a combination of the total completion time and the total number of errors and may be misleading depending on the individual scores for the total completion time and total number of errors, respectively. The clinician needs to examine the interplay between completion time and errors.

≡ Rapid Reference 15.3

Tests of Performance Fluency: Psychomotor Fluency

Test–Subtest: Description	Age/Grade Range	Publisher
D-KEFS—Trail-Making Condition 5—Motor Speed: Tracing a dotted line as quickly as possible.	8 to 89 years	Pearson
NEPSY-II—Visuomotor Precision: Tracing a path from start to finish quickly and while trying to stay within the lines.	3 to 12 years	
WISC-IV Integrated—Coding Copy: Rapidly and accurately copying symbols.	6–1 to 16–11 years	

See Appendix for the full names of the tests and their references.

A student who is slow and accurate does better than a student who is slow and inaccurate or fast and inaccurate. The number of pencil lifts is a measure of how well the student can follow a set of rules and is reflective of self-monitoring, a behavioral executive function. Students with psychomotor fluency deficits will have difficulty with writing fluency in general, and experience difficulty with accurately copying information from a projected computer screen, whiteboard, or blackboard in the front of a classroom.

Tests of Perceptual Fluency and Rate of Test Taking
Perceptual speed or fluency (*P*) is defined as the ability to quickly distinguish similar but different visual patterns and maintain attention under timed conditions (Horn & Blankson, 2012). Rate of Test Taking (*R9*) is a narrow ability within the CHC nomenclature and relates to the perform of tests that are relatively easy or those that require very simple decisions (Horn & Blankson, 2012). On several of the major tests of cognitive abilities there are tests that are designed to measure perceptual fluency or rate of test taking in isolation and other tests require both aspects. Rapid Reference 15.4 presents a list of tests designed to measure the third order classification of perceptual fluency and/or rate of test taking fluency.

Tests of Figural Fluency
Figural fluency refers to the ability to connect dots with unique line patterns while following discrete rules. Difficulty with figural fluency has been associated with right dorsolateral prefrontal circuit damage or dysfunction (Baldo, Shimamura, Delis, Kramer, & Kaplan, 2001). On the D-KEFS Design Fluency test (Delis

≡ *Rapid Reference 15.4*

Tests of Performance Fluency: Perceptual Fluency and Rate of Test Taking

Test–Subtest: Description	Perceptual Fluency	Rate or Test Taking	Age/ Grade Range	Publisher
CAS—Matching Numbers: Underlining the two numbers in each row that are the same.	X	X	2–0 to 90+ years	PRO-ED
CAS—Planned Codes: Quickly filling in the appropriate codes in empty boxes beneath each letter from a corresponding legend.		X	5–0 to 17–11 years	
DAS-II—Speed of Informational Processing: Marking a target figure or number contained within a row of similar objects or numbers.	X		6–0 to 18–11 years	Pearson
WISC-IV— Cancellation: Marking target pictures within a visual set of pictures in a specified time period.	X	X	6 to 16 years	
WISC-IV—Coding: Copying symbols paired with geometric shapes or numbers within a time limit.		X	4 to 16 years	
WISC-IV—Symbol Search: Scanning a search group and marking the presence or absence of a target symbol or symbols within a time limit.	X	X	4 to 89 years	
WNV—Coding: Copying symbols paired with geometric shapes or numbers within a time limit.		X	4 to 21 years	

WJIII-COG DS— **Cross Out:** Rapidly scanning a row of 19 drawings and marking the 5 that match a target drawing.	X		4–0 to 90+ years	Riverside
WJIII-COG NU— **Visual Matching:** Rapidly matching two numbers on a row.	X	X	2–0 to 90+ years	

See Appendix for the full names of the tests and their references.

et al., 2001) a total score is generated for the total number of correct responses across conditions 1 (filled dots) and condition 2 (empty dots). Supplemental scores are also generated for each of the conditions separately to aid in clinical interpretation. Rapid Reference 15.5 presents a list of tests designed to measure the third order classification of figural fluency.

Tests of Naming Fluency (Rapid Automatized Naming)

Rapid Reference 15.6 presents a list of commonly used measures of naming fluency, or what is often referred to as rapid automatized naming (RAN). These tasks require the student to rapidly name common objects, colors, words, or letters as quickly as possible. Naming fluency or RAN tests are frequently used for diagnosing reading disabilities in children.

Naming fluency tests require efficient processing speed and accuracy. Several of these measures (KTEA-II: A. Kaufman & Kaufman, 2005; CTOPP: Wagner, Torgesen, & Rashotte, 1999) only include completion time as a measure of verbal fluency. Other

≡ Rapid Reference 15.5

Tests of Figural Fluency

Test– Subtest: Description	Age/Grade Range	Publisher
D-KEFS—Design Fluency: Total Correct **Condition 1 + 2:** The total number correct across Conditions 1 and 2.	8–0 to 89–11 years	Pearson
NEPSY-II—Design Fluency Total: Connecting dots with unique line patterns.	3 to 16 years	

See Appendix for the full names of the tests and their references.

⟰ Rapid Reference 15.6

Tests of Naming Fluency

Test–Subtest: Description	Age/Grade Range	Publisher
CTOPP—Rapid Digit Naming: Naming numbers on a page as quickly as possible.	7–0 to 24–11 years	PRO-ED
CTOPP—Rapid Letter Naming: Naming letters on a page as quickly as possible.		
CTOPP—Rapid Color Naming: Naming colors on a page as quickly as possible.	5–0 to 24–11 years	
CTOPP—Rapid Object Naming: Naming objects on a page as quickly as possible.		
DAS-II—Rapid Naming: Naming colors or pictures as quickly as possible.	5–0 to 17–11 years	Pearson
D-KEFS—Color-Word Interference Condition 1 (Color Naming): Time taken to name the color of colored squares rapidly.	8 to 89–11 years	
D-KEFS—Color-Word Interference Condition 2 (Word Reading): Time taken to name color words (e.g., "red") rapidly.		
KTEA-II—Naming Facility (RAN): Naming objects, colors, and letters quickly.	4–6 to 25 years	
NEPSY-II—Inhibition: Naming: Rapidly and accurately naming shapes.	5 to 16 years	
NEPSY-II—Speeded Naming Combined: Rapidly naming attributes of objects or a series of numbers and letters.	3 to 16 years	
PAL-II M—RAN Digits and Double Digits: Total time required to rapidly read single and double digits.	Grades K to 6	
PAL-II RW—RAN Letters + Letter Groups + Words: Total time required to rapidly read letters, letter groups, and words.		
RAN/RAS—Rapid Automatized Naming Objects: Correctly identifying pictures of objects as rapidly as possible.	5 to 18–11 years	PAR
RAN/RAS—Rapid Automatized Naming Colors: Correctly identifying color names as rapidly as possible.		
RAN/RAS—Rapid Automatized Naming Letters: Correctly identifying letters by name as rapidly as possible.		

RAN/RAS—Rapid Alternating Switching Letters and Numbers: Correctly identifying letters and numbers as rapidly as possible.		
RAN/RAS—Rapid Alternating Switching Letters, Numbers, and Colors: Correctly identifying letters, numbers, and colors as rapidly as possible.	5 to 18–11 years	
WJIII-COG NU—Rapid Picture Naming: Quickly naming pictures of common objects across a row of five objects.	2–0 to 90+ years	Riverside

See Appendix for the full names of the tests and their references.

measures in this area, discussed below, include supplemental scores to help the clinician parse out the contributions of processing speed, accuracy, and the role self-corrected errors play in the interpretation of the results.

On the first condition of the D-KEFS's Color-Word Interference test (Delis et al., 2001), the student is asked to name the color of a series of squares as quickly as possible. This condition of the Color-Word Interference test generates a score for the total completion time and a separate score for the number of errors. It is important for a clinician to choose a test that provides this level of detail because it allows for the analysis of the completion time as a function of accuracy. Some students will slow down the task in order to improve accuracy, which can be a good compensatory skill. Other students will exhibit signs of impulsivity and rush through the task with above average completion times but make many errors along the way. The second condition of the Color-Word Interference test, in which the student has to read color words (e.g., *red, blue, green*) as quickly as possible, also includes scores for completion time and the number of errors.

Another factor that needs to be considered in interpreting these naming fluency tests relates to the self-corrected or uncorrected errors made during the performance of the tasks. The NEPSY-II (Korkman et al., 2007) has two tests that are classified in this section that provide greater specificity for clinical interpretation: the first condition of the Inhibition test, the Naming portion, and the Speeded Naming test. On the Naming portion of the Inhibition test, the student is required to name common shapes as quickly as possible. The principle score is completion time on this task; however, students are allowed to self-correct items as the test is administered but the timing continues during those self-corrections. A student with slow completion time and a high number of uncorrected errors is very different from a student with slow completion due to a high number of self-corrected errors. Self-corrected errors are a sign of an executive function skill called self-monitoring which is better than a student not being aware of the fact that errors are being made on the tasks.

The *Process Assessment of the Learner—Second Edition: Diagnostics for Math* (PAL-II M; Berninger, 2007a) contains RAN tests for single and double digits, and yields scores for both completion time and the total number of errors. Likewise, the PAL-II RW (Berninger, 2007b) contains RAN tests for letters, letter groups, and words, and yields scores for both completion time and the total number of errors. If a clinician suspects naming fluency deficiencies in a student, it is recommended that the clinician choose one of the tests that provide additional scores beyond completion time, such as the number of errors and types of errors.

Tests of Oral Fluency

Rapid Reference 15.7 presents a list of commonly used measures of oral motor fluency. Many of the tests that measure oral motor fluency require the student to repeat words that are not real words but require the application of phonological rules. Students with deficits in this area should be referred to a speech and language therapist for a thorough evaluation.

≡ Rapid Reference 15.7

Tests of Oral Motor Fluency

Test–Subtest: Description	Age/Grade Range	Publisher
CAS—Sentence Repetition: Repeating nonsense sentences.	5–0 to 17–11 years	PRO-ED
CAS—Speech Rate/Sentence Questions: Repeating a three word series of high imagery, single or double syllable words in order, 10 times in a row.		
CTOPP—Segmenting Words: Repeating a word then saying it one sound at a time.	7–0 to 24–11 years	
CTOPP—Segmenting Nonwords: Listening to nonwords, repeats each nonword, then says it one sound at a time.		
DWSMB—Expressive Speech: Repeating groups of successively more difficult words and phrases.	4 to 90 years	Riverside
KTEA-II—Oral Expression: Performing specific speaking tasks in the context of real-life scenarios.	4–6 to 25 years	Pearson

NEPSY-II—Oral Motor Sequences Total: Repetition of articulatory sequences like tongue twisters.	3 to 12 years	
NEPSY-II—Repetition of Nonsense Words Total: Repetition of nonsense words.	5 to 12 years	
OWLS-II—Oral Expression: Answering questions, completing sentences, or generating sentences in response to oral or verbal stimuli.	3 to 21 years	Western Psychological Services
PAL-II RW—Oral Motor Planning Total Time: Time taken to plan the production of alternating syllables compared to repeatedly producing the same syllables.	Grades K to 6	Pearson
PAL-II RW—Oral Motor Planning Errors Total: Total errors in the production of alternating syllables compared to repeatedly producing the same syllables.		
WIAT-III—Oral Expression: Naming concepts, words, or repeating sentences.	4–0 to 50–11 years	

See Appendix for the full names of the tests and their references.

On the NEPSY-II Oromotor Sequences test (Korkman et al., 2007), clinicians are provided with three process scores that aid in clinical interpretation: oral motor hypotonia, rate change, and stable misarticulations. Base rates can be established for each of these scores. Oral motor hypotonia refers to poor muscle tone, which could affect the oral production of speech. Rate change refers to the variability in the rate of the motor output response. Stable misarticulations are not counted as errors on the Oromotor Sequences test but are noted by the clinician. If these behaviors are observed or inferred by the clinician, the student should be referred to a speech and language pathologist for a thorough evaluation.

Assessing Retrieval Fluency

Retrieval fluency tasks require a student to recall as quickly as possible words that start with a particular letter or words that can be categorized within a particular semantic category (e.g., examples of furniture). The performance fluency measures previously discussed do not require memory skills to complete those fairly automatic tasks; whereas, the retrieval fluency tasks combine speed of retrieval and memory recall. Schrank and Wendling (2012) pointed out that the WJIII-COG Retrieval Fluency test does not measure the encoding and storage elements of memory, but rather emphasizes the rate or automaticity of retrieval.

The memory component of these tasks is important and must be considered in the overall interpretation of the results; however, for purposes of classification within the Integrated SNP/CHC Model, the emphasis is placed on the speed of retrieval for retrieval fluency tasks.

Tests designed to measure retrieval fluency are presented in Rapid Reference 15.8. Difficulty with verbal retrieval fluency has been associated with left dorsolateral prefrontal circuit damage or dysfunction (Butler, Rorsman, Hill & Tuma, 1993) and/or damage or dysfunction to the striatum (Stuss et al., 1998).

≡ Rapid Reference 15.8

Tests of Retrieval Fluency

Test–Subtest: Description	Age/Grade Range	Publisher
Word Fluency		
D-KEFS—Verbal Fluency—Condition 1 (Letter Fluency): Naming as many words within a time limit that start with a specific letter.	8–0 to 89–11 years	Pearson
NEPSY-II—Word Generation Initial Letter Total: Words recalled quickly that start with a particular letter.	3 to 16 years	
Semantic Fluency		
D-KEFS—Verbal Fluency—Condition 2 (Category Fluency): Naming as many words within a time limit that all fall in the same category (e.g., fruits).	8–0 to 89–11 years	Pearson
KTEA-II—Associational Fluency: Naming words quickly that belong to a semantic category to start with the same letter.	4–6 to 25 years	
NEPSY-II—Word Generation Semantic Total: Words recalled quickly that fit into a category.	3 to 16 years	
WJIII-COG NU—Decision Speed: Rapidly matching two pictures in a row that belong in the same category.	2–0 to 90+ years	Riverside
Word and Semantic Fluency		
WJIII-COG NU—Retrieval Fluency: Naming words as quickly as possible that start with a particular letter or fit in the same category (e.g., animals).	2–0 to 90+ years	Riverside

See Appendix for the full names of the tests and their references.

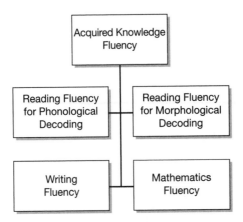

Figure 15.3. Third-Order Classifications of Acquired Knowledge Fluency

Students with retrieval fluency deficits may exhibit difficulties with finding the right words to say in oral and written expressions.

Assessing Acquired Knowledge Fluency

Within the Integrated SNP/CHC Model, acquired knowledge fluency is designed as a second order classification within the broad classification of speed, fluency, and efficiency of processing facilitators/inhibitors. Figure 15.3 illustrates the third-order classifications of acquired knowledge fluency. These academic fluency measures represent the automaticity of processing for rapid reading, writing, and solving math problems. These academic fluency measures are classified as facilitators/inhibitors because that is how they function. For example, reading fluency is important because it allows the reader to maintain an even flow of comprehension. Therefore, good reading fluency facilitates reading comprehension and poor reading fluency inhibits reading comprehension. The same logic applies to writing and math fluency.

Tests of Reading Fluency

With the revision of IDEA in 2004 (U.S. Department of Education, 2004), reading fluency was added as a type of specific learning disability. The major academic test publishers have included a variety of reading fluency measures. Rapid Reference 15.9 presents a list of the tests designed to measure the third order classifications of reading fluency.

Typically, students with poor reading fluency will have poor decoding skills, which slows down the automaticity of reading and thus adversely affects reading comprehension. Many achievement tests include measures of reading fluency

≡ Rapid Reference 15.9

....

Tests of Reading Fluency

Test–Subtest: Description	Age/Grade Range	Publisher
Reading Fluency: Rapid Phonological Decoding		
GORT-5—Rate: The amount of time taken to read a story.	6–0 to 23 years	PRO-ED
GORT-5—Fluency: Rate and Accuracy Scores combined.		
KTEA-II—Decoding Fluency: Quickly applying decoding nonsense words.	4–6 to 25 years	Pearson
KTEA-II—Word Recognition Fluency: Reading isolated words quickly.		
PAL-II RW—Pseudoword Decoding Fluency Total Correct at 60 Seconds: Number of words accurately decoded after 60 seconds.	Grades K to 6	
TOSWRF—Silent Word Reading Fluency: Ability to properly segment letters into words rapidly.	6–6 to 17–11 years	PRO-ED
WIAT-III—Oral Reading Fluency: Reading passages aloud and then orally responding to comprehension questions.	Grades 1 to 12	Pearson
WJIII COG NU—Reading Fluency: Rapidly reading short, simple sentences and circling yes or no if they make sense over a 3-minute interval.	2–0 to 90+ years	Riverside
Reading Fluency: Rapid Morphological Decoding		
PAL-II RW—Morphological Decoding Composite: Quickly and accurately pronouncing words when different suffixes are added to the same word base.	Grades K to 6	Pearson
• **PAL-II RW—Find the True Fixes:** Ability to differentiate spelling patterns that are and are not prefixes and suffices.		
• **PAL-II RW—Morphological Decoding Fluency Accuracy:** Number correct of pronounced words in which the base word is modified with different suffixes.		
• **PAL-II RW—Morphological Decoding Fluency:** Quickly pronouncing words when different suffixes are added to the same word base.		
PAL-II RW—Sentence Sense Fluency: Ability to quickly coordinate silent word-recognition and sentence comprehension when reading for meaning under timed conditions.		

See Appendix for the full names of the tests and their references.

based on rapid phonological decoding. The *Process Assessment of the Learner: Diagnostic Assessment for Reading and Writing* (PAL-II RW; Berninger, 2007b) includes a measure of rapid phonological decoding as a measure of reading fluency, but also adds a measure of rapid morphological decoding. Morphological decoding fluency measures the ability to read words orally and to distinguish between common initial spelling patterns that do and do not serve as morphemes, or prefixes to a base word (e.g., take, taken, taking). Berninger (2007b) also included a test on the PAL-II RW called *Sentence Sense Fluency*, which measures silent reading fluency. The Sentence Sense Fluency test assesses the ability to integrate word decoding with sentence-level comprehension. When reading fluency skills are a deficit area for a student and the clinician wants to thoroughly assess this area, the PAL-II RW is recommended.

Tests of Writing Fluency

Although writing fluency is not yet recognized as a specific learning disability in IDEA, it is an important skill to be assessed. Rapid Reference 15.10 presents a list of the tests designed to measure the third-order classification of writing fluency. Writing fluency represents the automaticity of writing, which can be adversely affected by a variety of deficiencies such as poor graphomotor output or poor language abilities. The subtypes of written language disorders are discussed in Chapter 17.

≡ Rapid Reference 15.10

Tests of Writing Fluency

Test–Subtest: Description	Age/Grade Range	Publisher
PAL-II RW—Narrative Compositional Fluency: • **Narrative Compositional Fluency Total Number of Words:** Total number of words written across items. • **Narrative Compositional Fluency Total Correctly Spelled Words:** Total number of correctly spelled words written across items.	Grades K to 6	Pearson
WIAT-III—Alphabet Writing Fluency: Ability to write the letters of the alphabet quickly.	Grades Pre-K to 3	
WJII ACH NU—Writing Fluency: Producing, in writing, simple sentences that are legible.	2–0 to 90+ years	Riverside

See Appendix for the full names of the tests and their references.

Tests of Mathematics Fluency

Mathematics fluency is also not yet recognized as a specific learning disability in IDEA, yet it is also an important skill to be assessed. Mathematics fluency represents the automaticity of completing math problems quickly and efficiently. There are many reasons why mathematics fluency can be disrupted. The various subtypes of math disabilities are discussed in Chapter 17. Rapid Reference 15.11 presents a list of the tests designed to measure the third-order classification of mathematics fluency.

Assessing Fluency with Accuracy

An important measure to consider in a school neuropsychological evaluation is the interaction between fluency and accuracy. Anytime a test requires the examiner to record completion time, processing speed is indirectly being measured. Typically, tests that measure completion time also provide a measure of performance accuracy. Figure 15.4 presents a list of processing speed tests

≡ Rapid Reference 15.11

Tests of Mathematics Fluency

Test—Subtest: Description	Age/Grade Range	Publisher
PAL-II M—Numerical Writing: Ability to write numerals both legibly and automatically.	Grades K to 6	Pearson
• **Automatic Legible Numeral Writing at 15 Seconds:** The sum of legible numerals written in 15 seconds.		
• **Legible Numeral Writing:** The sum of legible numerals written in 3 minutes.		
• **Total Time:** Total completion time required to complete writing of 26 numerals.		
WIAT-III—Math Fluency—Addition: Solving simple addition problems quickly.	Grades 1 to 12	
WIAT-III—Math Fluency—Subtraction: Solving simple subtraction problems quickly.		
WIAT-III—Math Fluency—Multiplication: Solving simple multiplication problems quickly.	Grades 3 to 12	
WJII ACH NU—Math Fluency: Solving simple math problems quickly.	2–0 to 90+ years	Riverside

See Appendix for the full names of the tests and their references.

Tests	Average to Low Number of Errors				High Number of Errors			
	Fast Completion Time	Average Completion Time	Slow Completion Time		Fast Completion Time	Average Completion Time	Slow Completion Time	
D-KEFS Color-Word Interference Test: Color Naming								
D-KEFS Color-Word Interference Test: Word Reading								
D-KEFS Color-Word Interference Test: Inhibition Condition								
D-KEFS Color-Word Interference Test: Inhibition/Switching Condition								
NEPSY-II Speeded Naming								
NEPSY-II Visual-Motor Precision								
NEPSY-II Inhibition: Naming								
NEPSY-II Inhibition: Inhibition								
NEPSY-II Inhibition: Switching								
PAL-II RW: RAS Words and Digits								
TEA-Ch Sky Search: # Correct & Time Per Target								
TEA-Ch Creature Counting: # Correct & Timing Score								

Figure 15.4. A Chart for Analyzing the Interaction Between Completion Time and Accuracy

	Low Number of Errors	High Number of Errors
Fast completion time	Indicates that the child has excellent processing speed and accuracy.	Reflective of impulsive behaviors.
Average completion time	Indicates a child with good inhibitory skills.	The child is attempting to balance speed with control but lacks the inhibitory skills to keep his or her error rate within normal limits.
Slow completion time	Indicates that the child may have chosen to slow down to increase accuracy or may have slow processing speed.	Indicates that despite the child slowing down accuracy did not improve; usually indicative of low ability in the tested area.

Figure 15.5. Interpretation of the Completion Time—Accuracy Interaction

from the D-KEFS and NEPSY-II that record completion time. The tests are presented in a table that provides a method of evaluating the interaction between completion time and accuracy.

The clinician is encouraged to put an X in the box that describes the performance of the student on any of these administered measures. See the chart in Figure 15.5 for an interpretation guide based on the profile of scores. Interpreting below average completion time with a high number of errors is more complex. The examiner needs to know the neurocognitive demands of the respective task to generate a hypothesis for the poor performance. For example, on the Speeded Naming subtest, slow but inaccurate work may reflect a word retrieval problem or an oromotor articulation problem. The examiner needs to look to other portions of the NEPSY-II test results and reported educational history to verify the causes of some slow and inaccurate task performances.

CHAPTER SUMMARY

In this chapter the facilitators/inhibitors of speed, fluency, and efficiency of processing were reviewed. Measures of performance fluency, retrieval fluency, acquired knowledge fluency, and the interaction between fluency and accuracy are all related to the automaticity and efficiency of processing. When these measures are impaired it may be due to an overall speed of information processing deficit or may be related to an underlying processing deficit (e.g., visual-spatial weakness) or skill deficit (e.g., phonological decoding). The clinician needs to conduct a thorough school neuropsychological evaluation to ascertain the reasons for deficits in these speed, fluency, and efficiency of processing areas.

🐟 TEST YOURSELF 🐟

1. All of the following are examples of second order classifications of performance fluency, except one. Which one?

a. Perceptual fluency
b. Naming fluency
c. Semantic fluency
d. Psychomotor fluency

2. What part of neuroanatomy is most closely related to the speed of information processing?

a. The brain's myelination
b. The corpus collosum
c. The frontal lobes
d. The cerebellum

3. True or False? Measuring rapid phonological decoding skills is the only method of measuring reading fluency.

4. Which of the performance fluency measures has been found to be a good predictor of reading disabilities?

a. Psychomotor fluency
b. Naming fluency (rapid automatized naming)
c. Figural fluency
d. Perceptual fluency

5. With the NEPSY-II's assessment of oral fluency, there is a qualitative behavior that measures muscle tone that could affect the oral production of speech. What is that qualitative behavior called?

a. Stable misarticulations
b. Stuttering
c. Confabulations
d. Oral motor hypotonia

6. True or False? Difficulty with verbal retrieval fluency has been associated with left dorsolateral prefrontal circuit damage or dysfunction.

7. Which test provides a broader assessment of reading fluency beyond just rapid phonological decoding?

a. KTEA-II
b. WJIII ACH NU
c. PAL-II RW
d. WIAT-III

Answers: 1. c; 2. a; 3. false; 4. b; 5. d; 6. true; 7. c

Chapter Sixteen

ACQUIRED KNOWLEDGE

Acculturation Knowledge and Language Abilities

Comprehension-Knowledge (*Gc*), Domain-Specific Knowledge (*Gkn*), Reading and Writing (*Grw*), and Quantitative Knowledge (*Gq*) are all classified as acquired knowledge within CHC theory because "they all involve the acquisition of useful knowledge and understanding of important domains of human functioning" and all of "these factors represent information stored in long-term memory" (Schneider & McGrew, 2012, p. 122). This chapter reviews two components of acquired knowledge; acculturation knowledge and language abilities. The next chapter reviews the academic achievement areas within acquired knowledge.

ACCULTURATION KNOWLEDGE

The term *acculturation knowledge* was used by Horn and Blankson (2012) to describe *Gc* and is synonymous with the label *comprehension-knowledge.* In the Integrated SNP/CHC Model, the label acculturation knowledge was used as a broad classification. The term *semantic memory*, first used by Miller (2007) in the original SNP Model, is a second-order classification within acculturation knowledge. Semantic memory has three third-order classifications within the Integrated SNP/CHC Model: verbal comprehension, general information, and domain-specific knowledge. In CHC nomenclature, semantic memory is a measure of comprehension-knowledge (*Gc*), verbal comprehension measures lexical knowledge (*VL*), and language development (*LD*), general information measures, general verbal information (*KO*), and domain-specific knowledge measures that same label (*Gkn*).

When to Assess Semantic Memory

Semantic memory is encyclopedic information retrieved from long-term memory storage. Young children, ages 4 to 6 with learning and memory difficulties, may initially appear to have average to slightly below average scores on measures of semantic memory. Early measures of semantic memory are largely dependent on information that most children learn through watching television. However, when learning and memory problems persist into middle childhood and adolescence, semantic memory scores often drop significantly because the student is not able to acquire new information to add to his or her encyclopedic knowledge base. Children who are not yet fully acculturated into our society may also achieve low scores on measures of semantic memory, not due to poor semantic memory, but due to lack of acculturation. Generally when there are concerns about a student's long-term memory, it is good clinical practice to assess the student's semantic memory.

Assessing Semantic Memory

Rapid Reference 16.1 restates the second- and third-order classifications of semantic memory within the Integrated SNP/CHC Model. Tests designed to measure these second- and third-order classifications of semantic memory are presented in this section.

In terms of the neuroanatomy associated with semantic memory, these processes are severely impaired by damage to the anterolateral temporal lobe (Levy, Bayley, & Squire, 2004). Rapid Reference 16.2 presents a list of the major tests designed to measure semantic memory.

⟰ Rapid Reference 16.1

Integrated SNP/CHC Model Classifications of Acquired Knowledge: Acculturation Knowledge

Broad Classifications	Second-Order Classifications	Third-Order Classifications
Acculturation knowledge	• Semantic memory	• Verbal comprehension • General information • Domain-specific knowledge

≡ Rapid Reference 16.2

....

Tests of Semantic Memory

Test–Subtest: Description	Age/Grade Range	Publisher
Verbal Comprehension		
KABC-II—Riddles: Pointing or naming a concrete or abstract verbal concept based on verbal characteristics (riddles) provided by the examiner.	3 to 18 years	Pearson
WJIII-COG NU—Verbal Comprehension: Four parts (Picture Vocabulary, Synonyms, Antonyms, and Verbal Analogies) that measures semantic memory.	2–0 to 90+ years	Riverside
WJIII-COG DS—Bilingual Verbal Comprehension: Four parts (Picture Vocabulary, Synonyms, Antonyms, and Verbal Analogies) that measure semantic memory in Spanish.		
General Information		
KABC-II—Verbal Knowledge: Selecting one picture that corresponds to a vocabulary word or answering a general question.	3 to 18 years	Pearson
SB-V—Nonverbal Knowledge: Ability to recall from the accumulated fund of nonverbal general information.	2 to 85+ years	Riverside
SB-V—Verbal Knowledge: Ability to recall from the accumulated fund of verbal general information.		
WISC-IV—Information: Answering questions about a wide range of general knowledge topics.	6–0 to 16–11 years	Pearson
WJIII-COG NU—General Information: Depth of verbal knowledge based on "where" and "what" questions.	2–0 to 90+ years	Riverside
Domain-Specific Knowledge		
WJIII-ACH NU—Academic Knowledge: Knowledge of basic academic areas (e.g., science, humanities).	2–0 to 90+ years	Riverside

See Appendix for the full names of the tests and their references.

LANGUAGE ABILITIES

Much of what is learned in school has a language basis. Language enables us to share our experiences with each other and pass our knowledge gained from those experiences onto the next generation (Carlson, 2010). Language skills are essential for a child to achieve academic success. Language development (*LD*) is considered to be a narrow ability within *Gc* in CHC Theory (Schneider & McGrew, 2012). Within the Integrated SNP/CHC Model, language abilities are viewed as a separate but equal broad classification of acquired knowledge.

Neuroanatomy of Language

This section of the chapter reviews the neuroanatomy of language functions, including the lateralization of language, the areas of the brain which are activated during oral expression and receptive language, and the right hemispheric involvement in language functions.

Lateralization of Language

Language skills are lateralized in the left side of the brain in 90% of the total population (Carlson, 2010). Knecht et al., (2001) found that left-hemispheric speech is dominant in 96% of healthy, right-handed people; 85% of ambidextrous people, and 73% of left-handed people. Vikingstad et al., (2004) reported that if the left hemisphere is malformed or damaged early in development, then the right hemisphere might take over language functions. While the left hemisphere plays a major role in the production and understanding of language, the right hemisphere plays a role in the spatial aspect of language.

Oral Expression

Virginia has difficulty producing oral language. Her speech could be characterized as slow, laborious, and nonfluent. Virginia can understand what others say to her much better than she can produce language. Virginia also has some moderate articulation problems and she experiences difficulty in finding the right word to say. Virginia exhibits symptoms of a type of disorder called expressive aphasia.

Much of what we know about the neuropsychology of language stems from the study of patients with *aphasia*. Aphasia is a deficit in the ability to produce or understand language caused by some form of brain damage or dysfunction. In 1861, Paul Broca was the first practitioner to notice damage to the inferior prefrontal cortex of the left hemisphere in postmortem examinations of the brains of patients who had expressive aphasias. This area became known as *Broca's area*. More recent research has suggested that damage to Broca's area alone does not produce expressive aphasia. For expressive aphasia to occur, damage must extend to brain tissue surrounding Broca's area within the frontal lobe and to underlying subcortical white matter (Naeser, Palumbo, Helm-Estabrooks, Stiassny-Eder, & Albert, 1989). Also lesions within the head of the caudate nucleus within the basal ganglia can produce Broca-like aphasia (Damasio, Eslinger, & Adams, 1984). Lesions within the left precentral gyrus of the insula, located on the anterior wall of the cerebral hemisphere, directly behind the temporal lobe have been found to cause *apraxia of speech*, an impairment in the ability to program movements of the lips, tongue, and throat for the production of speech (Dronkers, 1996).

Broca's aphasia is characterized by slow, laborious, and nonfluent speech. Children with Broca's aphasia, or expressive aphasia, can comprehend speech much better than they can produce it. Broca's aphasia has several common deficits associated with it including: poor programming of oromotor movements used to produce speech, agrammatism, anomia, and articulation difficulties (Carlson, 2010). *Agrammatism* refers to a child's difficulty or inability to produce a grammatical or intelligible sentence. *Anomia* refers to word finding difficulty. Anomia is often characteristic of many forms of aphasia but it is very apparent in expressive or Broca's aphasia. *Articulation difficulties* are often observed in children with expressive or Broca's aphasia. Children have trouble pronouncing words and many alter the sequence of the sounds (Carlson, 2010).

Receptive Language or Listening Comprehension

Justin has difficulty producing understandable oral language. He even has difficulty repeating oral directions. When he writes, his words often consist of letter combinations that look like real words, but are in fact nonsense words. Justin exhibits symptoms of a type of disorder called receptive aphasia.

In 1874, Carl Wernicke identified another area of the brain that was damaged in clinical patients with aphasia. This additional language area was located in the left temporal lobe, posterior to the primary auditory cortex in an area known as the planum temporale. This area became known as *Wernicke's area* and damage to this area became known as *Wernicke's aphasia*. Wernicke's aphasia is characterized by poor speech comprehension and fluent but meaningless speech, also referred to as *word salad* (Carlson, 2010). Wernicke also discussed the importance of the pathway that connected Broca's and Wernicke's areas called the *arcuate fasciculus*. Damage to the arcuate fasciculus can cause a third type of aphasia, which he called *conduction aphasia*. Wernicke suggested that patients with damage to the arcuate fasciculus would have intact comprehension and spontaneous speech but would have difficulty repeating words they had just heard.

Language comprehension difficulties, such as the inability to understand the meaning of words and the inability to express thoughts in meaningful speech, appear to involve the cortical associational areas immediately surrounding Wernicke's area. These areas are often referred to collectively as the posterior language area (Carlson, 2010). The posterior language area plays a major role in interchanging information between the auditory representation of words and the meaning of these words, stored as memories in the rest of the sensory association cortex (Carlson, 2010). A fourth type of aphasia occurs when the damage to the language system is isolated to Wernicke's area alone and does not extend to the posterior language area. This type of aphasia is known as *transcortical sensory aphasia*. Children with transcortical aphasia can repeat what others say to them, but they can neither comprehend the meaning of what they hear, nor produce meaningful speech on their own (Carlson, 2010).

Rapid Reference 16.3 summarizes the various forms of aphasias, their neuroanatomical bases, and their associated characteristics. Figure 16.1 illustrates the major brain structures involved with expressive and receptive language.

≣ *Rapid Reference 16.3*

Summary of Aphasias

Type of Aphasia	Brain Regions Involved	Characteristics
Expressive aphasias		
• Broca's (expressive) aphasia	• Inferior prefrontal cortex of the left hemisphere (Broca's area). • Head of the caudate nucleus in the basal ganglia. • Subcortical white matter below Broca's area and surrounding cortical areas.	• Slow, laborious, and nonfluent speech. • Comprehends speech much better than produces it.
• Apraxia of speech	• Left precentral gyrus of the insula.	• Impairment in the ability to program movements of the lips, tongue, and throat for the production of speech.
Receptive aphasias		
• Wernicke's aphasia	• Left temporal lobe just posterior to the primary auditory cortex in an area known as the *planum temporale* (Wernicke's area).	• Poor speech comprehension and fluent but meaningless speech.

• Conduction aphasia	• Damage to the arcuate fasciculus pathway connecting frontal and posterior language areas.	• Intact comprehension and spontaneous speech but would have difficulty repeating words that they had just heard.
• Transcortical sensory aphasia	• Damage to Wernicke's area alone, isolating it from the posterior language areas.	• Can repeat what others say to them, but they cannot comprehend the meaning of what they hear nor produce meaningful speech on their own.

Right Hemispheric Language Involvement

Although the various forms of language disorders described above seem to have a left hemispheric focus, the right hemisphere does appear to play a role in language as well. Our oral language usually has a cadence or rhythm to it. Our speech also contains intonations and changes in pitch and volume. Finally, our speech contains hints of our emotional states. The rhythmic, emotional, and melodic aspects of speech are referred to as *prosody of speech*. Prosody is the use of changes in intonation and emphasis to convey meaning in speech besides that specified by the particular words (Carlson, 2010). Prosody appears to be a right hemispheric function. Rapid Reference 16.4 provides a list of neuropsychological terms associated with language impairments.

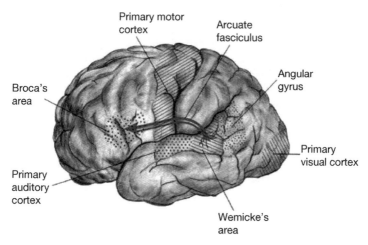

Figure 16.1. Wernicke-Geschwind Model of Language

≡ *Rapid Reference 16.4*

Neuropsychological Terms Associated With Language Impairments

- *Anomia*—Inability to find the correct word or name objects.
- *Amusia*—Inability to process music.
- *Aphasia*—Impairment of some aspect of language not due to defects in speech or hearing organs, but due to brain impairment.
  - *Broca's aphasia*—Nonfluent aphasia characterized by effortful, often agrammatic speech production.
  - *Conduction aphasia*—Fluent aphasia with severely impaired repetition but relatively preserved language comprehension.
  - *Expressive aphasia*—Nonfluent output is the prominent feature.
  - *Global aphasia*—Involves the complete loss of all linguistic functions including fluency, comprehension, repetition, reading, and writing.
  - *Mixed aphasia*—Aphasia with both expressive and receptive deficits.
  - *Receptive aphasia*—Impaired comprehension is the prominent feature.
  - *Transcortical motor aphasia*—Impaired expressive aphasia, similar to Broca's aphasia except for preserved repetition.
  - *Transcortical sensory aphasia*—Fluent aphasia in which language comprehension is severely impaired but repetition is relatively preserved. Similar to Wernicke's aphasia except that repetition is preserved.
  - *Wernicke's aphasia*—Receptive language and repetitions are severely impaired.
- *Aprosodia*—Impairment in the prosody or melodic component of speech.
- *Auditory agnosia*—Impaired ability to recognize sounds despite normal hearing.
- *Circumlocution*—Discourse that begins with a specific subject, wanders to various other subjects, and then returns to the original topic.
- *Color anomia*—A loss of color naming ability.
- *Coprolalia*—Vocal tic consisting of either a vulgarity or its initial phoneme.
- *Dysarthria*—Difficulty with pronunciation due to weakness or poor coordination of the muscles of lips, tongue, jaw, and so on.
- *Dysnomia*—Difficulty finding the correct word.
- *Mental lexicon*—A mental store of information about words.
- *Orthographic representation*—A visual-based storage of a word.
- *Phonological representation*—A sound-based storage of a word.
- *Prosody*—The inflections and intonations of speech.

Sources: Ayd, 1995; Loring, 1999.

When to Assess for Language Abilities

The most common entry for a child into special education services is related to language delays, which are often associated with articulation difficulties. Language disorders are different from articulation disorders and encompass oral expressive skills and receptive language skills. When a student is having severe oral expressive or receptive language difficulties a referral for additional formal assessment to help guide targeted interventions is probably warranted. It is also important to refer students suspected of having ADHD for a thorough language evaluation to rule out an auditory or receptive language disorder. Often students with auditory processing difficulties look to the untrained observer as if they are not paying attention and get misdiagnosed as ADHD—Inattentive Type.

Language deficits have been shown to be related to a wide variety of neurodevelopmental disorders including autism (Lang, 2010), nonspecific developmental delays (Dooley, 2010), externalizing disorders (Jiron, 2010), internalizing disorders (J. Miller, 2010), deaf and hard of hearing (Metz, Miller, & Thomas-Presswood, 2010), reading disabilities (Feifer, 2010), written language disabilities (Berninger, 2010), some types of math disabilities (Maricle, Psimas-Fraser, Muenke, & Miller, 2010), some chronically ill disorders (see Colaluca & Ensign, 2010, for a review), some types of brain tumors (see Begyn & Castillo, 2010, for a review), some types of seizure disorders (see Youngman, Riccio, & Wicker, 2010, for a review), and some types of traumatic brain injury (see Morrison, 2010, for a review).

Identifying Language Ability Concerns

It is suggested that the *Neuropsychological Processing Concerns Checklist for Children and Youth—Third Edition* (NPCC-3; Miller, 2012a) be completed by the parent/ guardian and at least one teacher of the student being referred for a comprehensive assessment (see the supplemental CD for the complete NPCC-3). The questions on the NPCC-3 that pertain to language problems are shown in Rapid Reference 16.5. Any endorsed items in the moderate to severe range should be followed up with formal assessment measures in the school neuropsychological assessment.

Assessing Language Abilities: Oral Expression

Rapid Reference 16.6 restates the second- and third-order classifications of language processes within the Integrated SNP/CHC Model. Tests designed to measure these second- and third-order classifications of language abilities are presented in this section.

≡ *Rapid Reference 16.5*

Language Ability Items from the Neuropsychological Processing Concerns Checklist for Children and Youth—Third Edition (NPCC-3; Miller, 2012a)

Oral expression difficulties:

- Slow labored speech.
- Limited amount of speech.
- Distorts sounds (e.g., slurring, stuttering).
- Difficulty finding the right word to say.

Receptive language difficulties:

- Trouble understanding what others are saying.
- Does not do well with verbal directions.
- Loses track of what he/she was told to do.
- Does not follow conversations well.

Tests of Oral Expression: Vocabulary Knowledge

Rapid Reference 16.7 presents a list of commonly used measures of vocabulary knowledge. Vocabulary tests are difficult to categorize in the SNP Model because they can measure multiple cognitive processes and may be influenced by environmental and cultural factors. Many of the vocabulary tests require the student to name pictures of common objects or to define word meanings. All of these tests in Rapid Reference 16.8 require an oral response of some kind, which

≡ *Rapid Reference 16.6*

Integrated SNP/CHC Model Classifications of Acquired Knowledge: Language Abilities

Broad Classifications	Second-Order Classifications	Third-Order Classifications
Language abilities	• Oral expression	• Vocabulary knowledge
		• Qualitative behaviors
	• Receptive language	• Receptive language with verbal response.
		• Receptive language with nonverbal response qualitative behaviors

≡ Rapid Reference 16.7

Tests of Vocabulary Knowledge and Retrieval

Test–Subtest: Description	Age/Grade Range	Publisher
CREVT-2—Expressive Vocabulary: Ability to define a word spoken by the examiner.	4 to 89–11 years	PRO-ED
DAS-II—Naming Vocabulary: Naming pictures.	2–6 to 8–11 years	Pearson
DAS-II—Word Definitions: Explaining the meaning of each word.		
DWSMB—Naming Pictures of Objects: Measures knowledge of semantic labels for pictures of common objects.	4 to 90 years	Riverside
EOWPVT-4: Ability to name objects, actions, or concepts illustrated in pictures.	2 to 80+ years	Academic Therapy Publications
EOWPVT-SBE—English Expressive language: Naming in English colored pictures on common objects, actions, or concepts.	2 to 80+ years	
EOWPVT-SBE—Spanish Expressive language: Naming in Spanish colored pictures on common objects, actions, or concepts.		
EVT-2: Ability to define vocabulary words.	2–6 to 90+ years	Pearson
KABC-II—Expressive Vocabulary: Naming pictures.	3 to 18 years	
NEPSY-II—Body Part Naming Total: Naming of body parts.	3 to 4 years	
SPELT-P 2: Assesses expressive vocabulary related to everyday situations and objects.	3–0 to 5–11 years	Janelle Publications
SPELT-3: Assesses expressive vocabulary related to everyday situations and objects.	4–0 to 9–11 years	
WIAT-III—Oral Expression (Expressive Vocabulary): Naming the concept shown in a picture or saying words from a given category and repeating sentences.	4 to 50–11 years	Pearson
WISC-IV—Vocabulary: Naming pictures that are displayed in the stimulus book or giving definitions for words that the examiner reads aloud.	6 to 16–11	

(continued)

≡ *Rapid Reference 16.7*

WISC-IV Integrated—Vocabulary **Multiple Choice:** A multiple-choice version of the Vocabulary subtest. Lesser verbal and recall memory demands.	6–1 to16–11 years	
WISC-IV Integrated—Picture Vocabulary **Multiple Choice:** Same items as the WISC-IV Vocabulary test except with reduced memory and verbal expression demands.		
WJIII-ACH NU—Picture Vocabulary: Recognize and name pictured objects.	2–0 to 90+ years	Riverside

See Appendix for the full names of the tests and their references.

is why these tests are classified as a subclassification of oral expression. However, the trained examiner needs to be aware that a student may have a limited vocabulary due to being raised in a verbally impoverished environment with lack of educational opportunity. In these cases, the clinician would not want to attribute poor vocabulary skills to an oral expressive disorder.

Poor performance on measures of vocabulary may also be due to retrieval deficits. The student may exhibit signs of anomia, or word retrieval difficulties, on these types of tasks. For example, a student may be shown a picture of a rose and asked to name it. The student proceeds to say "it has petals, you smell it, it is red," but cannot come up with the name "rose. "Poor vocabulary knowledge could be related to poor initial encoding of the word (an memory deficit) or poor retrieval of the word (an executive function), rather than an oral expressive deficit. Clinicians need to interpret the student's performance on these vocabulary tests carefully and interpret the results in light of the types of errors made on the tests.

Oral Expression Qualitative Behaviors

The Oromotor Sequences test on the NEPSY-II (Korkman et al., 2007) provides the clinician with three supplemental qualitative behaviors to aid in interpretation: oral motor hypotonia, rate change, and stable misarticulations. The Oromotor Sequences test requires the student to repeat a set of tongue twisters orally. Oral hypotonia is a qualitative behavior that reflects low muscle tone, which affects the oral motor production of speech. If the student performing the task changes the rate of speech multiple times, the qualitative behavior of rate change is noted. Stable misarticulations are noted on this test as well as on the NEPSY-II's Repetition of Nonsense Words test. All of these qualitative behaviors are represented as cumulative percentile ranks, which reflect the percentage of students in a normative sample, typically based on the student's age, that also had one of the qualitative behaviors. If only a small percentage ($\leq$ 10%) of students the same age exhibited any of these qualitative behaviors, a referral to a speech and language pathologist may be warranted.

The Twenty Questions test on the D-KEFS (Delis et al., 2001) measures the ability to efficiently ask yes/no questions to search for a correct answer. The Spatial Questions qualitative score from the Twenty Questions test reflects the number of yes/no questions asked by the student in an attempt to eliminate objects based on their location on the stimulus page (e.g., "Is it in the bottom two rows?"). Asking a spatial question, rather than a verbal question on this test is highly unusual with only 2.7% of the normative sample asked these kinds of spatial questions (Delis et al., 2001). A high number of spatial questions could indicate an oral language deficit such as developmental or acquired aphasia. A student with a high number of spatial questions asked may or may not have intact problem-solving skills but the verbal expression deficits are interfering with the normal performance of the task. Students with this type of response style may try to approach the majority of learning tasks using visual strategies, while avoiding verbal strategies.

Assessing Language Abilities: Receptive Language

Rapid Reference 16.8 presented a list of commonly used measures of receptive language or measures of listening comprehension. Receptive language tests can be subclassified based on the output demands of the task, either verbal response or nonverbal, motoric response. These tasks require the student to listen to orally presented content and then answer questions or view visual stimuli and point to various aspect of the stimuli based on verbal prompts.

As previously mentioned in this chapter, children with receptive language deficiencies are often misdiagnosed with ADHD-Inattentive type. Differential diagnosis for ADHD and Auditory Processing Disorder is very important. Children with receptive language difficulties will look like they are not paying attention when, in fact, they are just having difficulty processing language.

Qualitative Behaviors for Receptive Language

Asking for a repetition of verbally presented material is a qualitative behavior on several NEPSY-II tests including Comprehension of Instructions, Phonological Processing, Sentence Repetition, and Word List Interference. These asking for repetitions qualitative behaviors are represented as cumulative percentile ranks,

≡ Rapid Reference 16.8

Tests of Receptive Language

Test–Subtest: Description	Age/Grade Range	Publisher
Receptive Language with Verbal Response		
CAS—Sentence Questions: Responding to content from verbally read sentences.	5–0 to 17–11 years	PRO-ED
KTEA-II—Listening Comprehension: Listening to passages and then responding to questions.	6–0 to 18–11 years	Pearson
ROWPVT-4: Ability to match verbally or by pointing a word spoken by the examiner to a picture of an object, action, or concept.	2–0 to 80+ years	Academic Therapy Publications
ROWPVT-SBE—English Receptive Language: Ability to match verbally or by pointing a spoken English word by the examiner to a picture of an object, action, or concept.	4–0 to 12–0 years	
ROWPVT-SBE—Spanish Receptive Language: Ability to match verbally or by pointing a spoken Spanish word by the examiner to a picture of an object, action, or concept.		
TAPS-3—Auditory Comprehension: Listening to an oral passage and then answering questions.	4 to 18–11 years	
WIAT-III—Listening Comprehension: Listening to a word and pointing to a picture that illustrates the word, then listening to passages and answering questions about each one.	4–0 to 50–11 years	Pearson
WJIII-ACH NU—Oral Comprehension: Listening to passages and then orally providing a one-word response to fill in a missing last word.	2–0 to 90+ years	Riverside
WJII ACH NU—Understanding Directions: Listening to a sequence of audio instructions then following them.		

Receptive Language with Nonverbal Motor Response		
CAS—Verbal-Spatial Relations: Matching a spatial configuration of objects to a verbal description.	5–0 to 17–11 years	PRO-ED
CREVT-2—Receptive Vocabulary: Pointing to one of four pictures that corresponds to a spoken word.	4 to 89–11 years	
DAS-II—Verbal Comprehension: Following oral instructions to point to or move pictures and toys.	6–0 to 18–11 years	Pearson
NEPSY-II—Body Part Identification Total: Pointing to body parts on self on command.	3 to 4 years	
NEPSY-II—Comprehension of Instructions Total: Respond quickly to verbal instructions of increasing complexity.	3 to 16 years	
OWLS-II—Listening Comprehension: Pointing to a picture that matches the corresponding word spoken by the examiner.	3 to 21 years	Western Psychological Services
PPVT-IV—Total Score: Pointing to one of four pictures that corresponds to a spoken word.	2–6 to 90+ years	Pearson
WJIII-ACH NU—Understanding Directions: Pointing to various objects in a picture after listening to a sequence of recorded instructions.	2–0 to 90+ years	Riverside

See Appendix for the full names of the tests and their references.

which reflect the percentage of students in a normative sample, typically based on the student's age, that also had one of the qualitative behaviors. If only a small percentage ($\leq$ 10%) of students the same age exhibited any of these qualitative behaviors, a referral to a speech and language pathologist may be warranted.

Tests for Speech and Language Pathologists

Brief descriptions of the following tests were included in this section (see Rapid Reference 16.9), even though school neuropsychologists probably will not administer them. This is not a complete list of all of the assessments available for speech and language pathologists. Speech and language pathologists will typically administer these tests to school-age children but school neuropsychologists need to be

≡ Rapid Reference 16.9

Tests of Speech and Language Functions Typically Administered by Speech and Language Pathologists

Test	What Is Measured	Age Range
• *Comprehensive Assessment of Spoken Language* (CASL; Carrow-Woolfolk, 1999)	• Language processing skills (comprehension, expression, and retrieval) • Language structure (lexical/semantic, syntactic, supralinguistic, and pragmatic)	3 to 21 years
• *Clinical Evaluation of Language Fundamentals— Fourth Edition* (CELF-4; Semel, Wiig, & Secord, 2003)	• Receptive language • Expressive language • Language Structure • Language Content • Language Content and Memory • Working Memory	5 to 21 years
• *Goldman-Fristoe Test of Articulation 2* (Goldman & Fristoe, 2000)	• Articulation of consonant sounds	2–21 to 11 years
• *KLPA-2: Khan-Lewis Phonological Analysis— Second Edition* (KLPA-2; Khan & Lewis, 2002)	• Phonological processes	2 to 21 years
• *Lindamood Auditory Conceptualization Test* (LAC-3; P. C. Lindamood & P. Lindamood, 2004)	• Ability to perceive and conceptualize speech sounds using a visual medium	5–0 to 18–11 years
• *Test of Word Finding— Second Edition* (TWF-2; German, 2000)	• Expressive word finding	4–0 to 12–11 years
• *Test of Early Language Development—Third Edition* (TELD-3; Hresko, Reid, & Hammill, 1999)	• Receptive language • Expressive language	2 to 7–11 years
• *Test of Language Development (Primary)— Third Edition* (TOLD-3; Hammill & Newcomer, 1997b)	• Expressive language	4–0 to 8–11 years

• *Test of Language Development (Intermediate)—Third Edition* (TOLD-3; Hammill & Newcomer, 1997a)	• Expressive language	8–0 to 12–11 years
• *Utah Test of Language Development* (Mecham, 2003)	• Expressive language	3–0 to 9–11 years

familiar with what the tests are measuring and when to refer a child for a particular assessment. School neuropsychologists need to work collaboratively with speech and language pathologists in planning their respective assessments to avoid overlap and to maximize the opportunities to answer the referral question(s).

CHAPTER SUMMARY

In this chapter two broad classification types of acquired knowledge, acculturation knowledge and language abilities were reviewed. The neuroanatomy of language functions is reviewed along with a discussion of when to assess for language abilities. As mentioned in the chapter, much of what is taught in schools has a language basis. School neuropsychologists should work in collaboration with the speech and language pathologist to evaluate for expressive and receptive language disorders as warranted.

🐾 TEST YOURSELF 🐾

1. **Examples of third-order classifications of semantic memory include all of the following except for one. Which one?**
   a. Procedural memory
   b. Verbal comprehension
   c. General information
   d. Domain-specific knowledge

2. **Language skills are lateralized in the left hemisphere for approximately what percentage of all people?**
   a. 65%
   b. 70%
   c. 80%
   d. 90%

3. **What type of aphasia is characterized by slow, laborious, and nonfluent speech?**
   a. Wernicke's aphasia
   b. Broca's aphasia
   c. Conduction aphasia
   d. Transcortical Sensory Aphasia

4. **What type of aphasia is characterized by intact comprehension and spontaneous speech but difficulty with repeating words?**
   a. Wernicke's aphasia
   b. Broca's aphasia
   c. Conduction aphasia
   d. Transcortical Sensory Aphasia

5. **True or False? Prosody of speech is a right hemispheric function.**

6. **What term is used to describe the inability to find the correct word or difficulty in naming objects?**
   a. Anomia
   b. Amusia
   c. Aphasia
   d. Aprosodia

7. **Which one of the following speech and language batteries is most likely to be administered by a speech and language pathologist?**
   a. WJIII-ACH Oral Expression and Listening Comprehension Cluster subtests
   b. *Clinical Evaluation of Language Fundamentals—Fourth Edition* (CELF-4)
   c. NEPSY-II Language Domain subtests
   d. *Kaufman Test of Educational Achievement—Second Edition* (KTEA-II)

8. **What term is used to describe difficulty with pronunciation due to weakness or poor coordination of the muscles of lips, tongue, jaw, and so on?**
   a. Dysarthria
   b. Dysnomia
   c. Aphasia
   d. Circumlocution

Answers: 1. a; 2. d; 3. b; 4. c; 5. true; 6. a; 7. b; 8. a

Chapter Seventeen

ACQUIRED KNOWLEDGE

Academic Achievement

C hapters 10 through 13 present information about essential cognitive elements required for success in school and in life, ranging from baseline sensory-motor functions to higher-order executive functions. Chapters 14 and 15 review the cognitive facilitators/inhibitors, which influence cognitive processes and measures of acquired knowledge. In Chapter 16, the acquired knowledge skills of acculturation knowledge and language abilities are presented. In this chapter, the acquired knowledge areas of reading, writing, and mathematics achievement are discussed.

Academic achievement is often the "measuring stick" used by school personnel to determine a child's progress in school. Academic achievement is closely related to a student's profile of cognitive strengths and weaknesses. A school neuropsychologist must include measures of academic achievement in an assessment battery, but the interpretation must move beyond looking at standard scores alone.

This chapter reviews (1) when to assess for academic functioning; (2) a glossary of neuropsychological terms used for academic disorders; (3) the neuropsychology of reading disorders; (4) the neuropsychology of written language disorders; (5) the neuropsychology of mathematics; and (6) a listing of the common achievement tests subdivided by academic area.

WHEN TO ASSESS FOR ACADEMIC FUNCTIONING

The National Center for Education Statistics (U.S. Department of Education, 2011) reported that in the 2008 to 2009 academic year, 5% of total enrollments of children in public schools were classified as having a specific learning disability (SLD). The prevalence rate for reading and writing disabilities appears to be between 2% and 8% of school-age children. About 7% of school-age children have a specific learning disability in mathematics (Geary, Hoard, & Bailey, 2011). These prevalence rates are estimates of students with significant problems in reading, writing, or mathematics to warrant a SLD diagnosis, but does not include a larger number of students who struggle with these academic areas on a daily basis, but to a lesser degree than those with SLD. With so many children experiencing academic difficulties, the school neuropsychologist must be able to correctly identify the disabilities associated with these disorders and make appropriate prescriptive educational recommendations. Proper identification of children with reading, writing, and mathematics disabilities requires the school neuropsychologist to understand the neuropsychological terms associated with academic impairments (see Rapid Reference 17.1), and the characteristics of the subtypes associated with each of the academic areas. Proper identification of the neuropsychological subtypes of reading, writing, and mathematics disabilities cannot be determined by administering an individual achievement test alone. A school neuropsychologist must do error analyses, miscue analyses, and evaluate qualitative behaviors to fully understand the type of academic problems a child may be experiencing. The next few sections of this chapter review the disability subtypes associated with reading, writing, and mathematics.

READING DISORDERS

Tyron is in the second grade and he has difficulty reading. Tyron can read familiar words but he has difficulty reading unfamiliar words or pronounceable nonwords. He had a tendency to over rely on the visual representation of words because of his difficulty sounding out words. His reading comprehension is poor, particularly when there are many words in the passages that he does not recognize.

Tyron has a subtype of reading disorder called *dysphonetic dyslexia*, which is one of several types of reading problems that children may experience. This section of the chapter reviews the relationship between reading and language disorders, the neuro-anatomical circuitry of reading, and the subtypes associated with reading disorders.

Neuroanatomical Circuitry of Reading

Shaywitz (2003) and S. Shaywitz and Shaywitz (2005) reviewed several major studies that used functional brain imaging techniques (e.g., fMRI) to study reading in efficient and inefficient readers. The studies revealed two slower and more inefficient pathways used by the dyslexic readers and one quicker pathway used by skilled readers. When a child reads a word, the visual image of the word is

≡ Rapid Reference 17.1

Neuropsychological Terms Associated With Academic Impairments

- Acalculia—Inability to perform mathematic computations.
- Agraphia—An acquired difficulty in writing or spelling.
  - Central agraphia—A spelling disorder in both written and oral spelling that is related to linguistic disturbance and not to motor or sensory systems that support spelling.
- Alexia—Inability to read.
  - Acquired alexia—Loss of reading ability due to some form of brain trauma.
  - Alexia with agraphia—Inability to read and write.
  - Pure alexia—Sometimes referred to as word blindness or alexia without agraphia.
- Dyscalculia—Difficulty with mathematics.
- Dysgraphia—Difficulty with written language.
- Dyslexia—Difficulty with reading.
  - Deep dyslexia—Reliance on visual and semantic cues. Reading abstract words is difficult because of impaired phonological processing. Semantic errors are the hallmark of this disorder (e.g., "food" for "dinner").
  - Developmental dyslexia—A reading disorder present from birth and not acquired.
  - Dysphonetic dyslexia—Difficulty with reading because of poor phonological skills. Having an overreliance on visual cues.
  - Mixed dyslexia—Poor reading because of an overreliance on semantic cues. Auditory and visual processing of reading is impaired.
  - Surface dyslexia—Poor reading because of difficulty recognizing symbols of language. Having an overreliance on auditory cues.

Sources: Ayd, 1995; Loring, 1999.

projected to the primary visual cortex of the *right occipital lobe*. Information about the visual features of the word (e.g., the lines and curves that make up the letters) is processed within the occipital lobe. Next, the brain needs to transform the letters into sounds of language, and ultimately attach meaning to those sounds. The visual feature information of the word processed within the occipital lobe is passed onto one of two different brain pathways: an upper pathway, called the *dorsal stream*, emanates from the left *parieto-temporal region* and a lower pathway called the *ventral stream* is at the junction of the occipital and temporal lobes, the *occipito-temporal area*.

The parieto-temporal system is essential for phonetic decoding in reading: initially analyzing a word, pulling it apart by phonemes, and linking the letters to sounds. Specific brain regions that are activated in the parieto-temporal region include the *angular gyrus* and the *supramarginal gyrus*. Children learning to read initially use the parieto-temporal system almost exclusively.

As children become more skilled at reading, the occipito-temporal pathway becomes more active. The *insular cortex* also has been implicated with automatically recognizing words in print, and along with the occipito-temporal pathway, plays a key role in reading fluency. The occipito-temporal pathway uses a whole-word approach to reading. Words are automatically recognized by sight in the occipito-temporal system and do not need to be deconstructed phonetically as in the parieto-temporal system. When the occipito-temporal region of the brain is activated, an exact neural form of the word is retrieved along with the word's spelling, pronunciation, and meaning. Therefore, the occipito-temporal region allows reading to become more fluent and automatic because words are recalled quickly by sight rather than relying on sounding out words every time they are read. Figure 17.1 illustrates a model of reading then speaking a word based on either the parieto-temporal or the occipito-temporal pathways in the brain.

There is a third reading pathway in the brain for reading that lies in the frontal region associated with Broca's area. This pathway also helps with the phonemic decoding of words, and like the parieto-temporal pathway is not as efficient as the occipito-temporal pathway. The inferior frontal gyrus around Broca's area appears to be the end point for the brain's inner articulation system. In summary, three pathways for processing reading have been identified, with two relying on phonemic decoding and one relying on a whole-word processing approach.

Good readers show a consistent pattern of activation in the back of the brain with less activation in the front pathways; whereas, inefficient readers or children with dyslexia have shown the opposite pattern (Shaywitz, 2003; S. Shaywitz & Shaywitz, 2005). Children with dyslexia show two distinct patterns. First, dyslexics can activate all three brain pathways required for reading individually, but they have trouble activating them simultaneously (Feifer, 2010, 2011). Second, dyslexics often show an overactivation in Broca's area while reading. Using the frontal system as a guide, a dyslexic reader can form sound structures of words and can subvocalize the words as they are being read. These compensatory strategies can aid a dyslexic reader to sound out words, but the fluency and automaticity that is regulated by the posterior systems remains elusive. In an exciting line of research, Shaywitz (2003) and S. Shaywitz and Shaywitz (2005) reported several fMRI studies that showed how early intervention and effective reading instruction helps develop the posterior, automatic reading system of the brain.

In summary, there appears to be compelling evidence that skilled readers activate the quicker, more rapid and automatic pathways to decipher words in

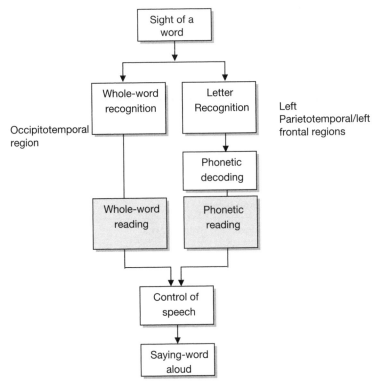

Figure 17.1. A Model of Reading a Word Aloud Following a Whole-Word or Phonetic Approach

Source: Adapted from Carlson (2010).

print (McCandliss & Noble, 2003; Owen, Borowsky, & Sarty, 2004; S. Shaywitz, 2003). This pathway is primarily situated in the posterior portions of the brain, along the interface of the occipital and temporal lobes, in a brain region called the *fusiform gyrus.* Conversely, dyslexics do not activate these selfsame pathways, but instead rely on different pathways, forged in part by compensatory mechanisms, which are slower and less efficient, to assist with word recognition skills (S. Shaywitz & Shaywitz, 2005). These slower pathways, which over rely on breaking down each word into its phonological core, are referred to as the dorsal stream. The quicker, automatic pathway, which processes words at the lexical level, is sometimes referred to as the *ventral stream.* This pathway may have further assistance from yet another brain region, the insular cortex, when automatically processing unusual spellings of words, which tend to be common in the English language (Owen et al., 2004).

Subtypes of Reading Disorders

There are several classification schemas for naming the subtypes of reading disorders. For the purposes of the school neuropsychological assessment model, the following reading subtypes are discussed: pure alexia, phonological dyslexia, surface dyslexia, spelling or word-form dyslexia, direct dyslexia, and semantic dyslexia. An overview of these reading disorder subtypes is presented in Rapid Reference 17.2.

≡ Rapid Reference 17.2

Subtypes of Reading Disorders

Reading Disorder Subtype	Symptoms
• Pure alexia	• A perceptual disorder in which the child has difficulty with visual input. • Also referred to as *word blindness* or *alexia without agraphia.* • Limited writing capability if writing skills were present prior to an acquired pure alexia.
• Phonological dyslexia	• Good whole-word reading. • Poor phonetic reading. • Overrely on memorizing a whole word as seen in space rather than phonetic decoding.
• Surface dyslexia	• Good phonetic reading. • Poor whole-word reading.
• Spelling/word-form/mixed dyslexia	• Poor whole-word reading. • Poor phonetic reading. • Can read words letter-by-letter.
• Direct dyslexia	• Good phonetic reading. • Good whole-word reading. • Poor reading comprehension.
• Semantic dyslexia	• Rely on visual and semantic cues in reading. • Make semantic errors in reading (e.g., "food" for "dinner"). • May have trouble reading function words (e.g., "of," "an," "not,").

Pure alexia, also referred to as *word blindness* or *alexia without graphia*, is a perceptual disorder that prevents a child from reading. Pure alexia is caused by lesions in the visual pathways that prevent visual information from reaching the extrastriate cortex within the occipital lobe (Carlson, 2010). Children with pure alexia cannot read, but they can recognize words that are spelled aloud to them, if the word was previously learned. Children with pure alexia cannot use either the whole-word or phonetic approaches to read because they are not getting the initial visual information to process. However, if a child has previously learned to read and write and has acquired pure alexia due to some type of brain damage, the child will be able to write some, even in the absence of reading.

Phonological dyslexia, also referred to as *dysphonetic dyslexia*, is a reading disorder in which a person can read familiar words but has difficulty reading unfamiliar words or pronounceable non-words (Carlson, 2010). A model that illustrates the phonological dyslexia impairment is shown in Figure 17.2. Phonological reading is required when a reader is presented with a nonsense word or a new word that is not yet learned. Children with phonological dyslexia overrely on memorizing whole words as they are visualized in space because they cannot phonetically sound out the word.

Surface dyslexia, also referred to as *dyseidetic dyslexia*, is a reading disorder in which a person can read words phonetically but has difficulty reading irregularly spelled words by the whole-word method (Carlson, 2010). The term *surface* is used because children with this type of disorder make errors based only on what the word looks like on the "surface" rather than related to the word meanings. Surface dyslexia is usually caused by a lesion within the left temporal lobe (Patterson & Ralph, 1999). Children with surface dyslexia have difficulty memorizing a whole word, which makes them over rely on phonetically sounding out almost every word. Over relying on phonetic decoding slows down reading fluency and can adversely affect reading comprehension. Children with surface dyslexia often can read words that have regular spelling (e.g., bat, fist, chin), but they have difficulty with reading words with irregular spelling (e.g., pint, yacht). A model of surface dyslexia impairment is illustrated in Figure 17.3.

Spelling or word-form dyslexia, also known as *mixed dyslexia*, is a reading disorder in which the ability to read a word using a whole word or phonetic approach is disrupted but the visual pathways remain intact. Although a child with word form dyslexia cannot recognize words as a whole or sound them out phonetically, individual letters can be recognized. The child reads words by reading the letters individually (e.g., c-a-t, for *cat*). A model of word form dyslexia impairment is illustrated in Figure 17.4.

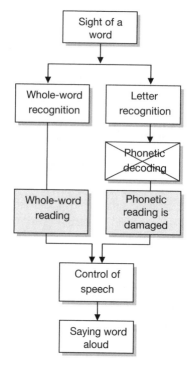

Figure 17.2. A Reading Model Showing Phonological Dyslexia. Phonetic Reading Is Damaged While Whole-Word Reading Remains Intact

Source: Adapted from Carlson (2010).

Direct dyslexia is a language disorder caused by brain damage in which the person can read words aloud without understanding them (Carlson, 2010). In Chapter 16, a type of aphasia, transcortical sensory aphasia, was described, in which a child can repeat what others say to the child, but can comprehend neither the meaning of what they hear, nor produce meaningful speech on his or her own. Direct dyslexia is similar to transcortical sensory aphasia; however, in direct dyslexia the words are written in text not spoken (Carlson, 2010).

Semantic dyslexia, also known as *deep dyslexia*, is a reading disorder in which the hallmark feature is making semantic errors (e.g., *food* for *dinner*)

DON'T FORGET

....

Dyslexia Subtype ====> *Relies On:*

- Phonological dyslexia   Visual cues
- Surface dyslexia   Auditory cues
- Spelling dyslexia   Individual letters
- Direct dyslexia   All cues
- Semantic dyslexia   Visual and semantic cues

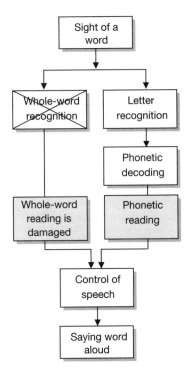

Figure 17.3. A Reading Model Showing Surface Dyslexia. Whole-Word Reading Is Damaged While Phonemic Reading Remains Intact

Source: Adapted from Carlson (2010).

during reading (Feifer, 2010, 2011). Children with semantic dyslexia rely heavily on visual and semantic cues during reading, while minimizing phonetic decoding. Reading abstract words is difficult because of the impaired phonetic decoding and difficulty conjuring up a visual image of the word.

It is important for a school neuropsychologist to identify the reading disorder subtype that a poor reader is experiencing because the ultimate effectiveness of any intervention(s) will be dependent on matching the reading subtype with the proper intervention. See Feifer (2010) and Mather and Wendling (2012) for subtype based reading interventions.

Identifying Reading Achievement Concerns

It is suggested that the *Neuropsychological Processing Concerns Checklist for Children and Youth—Third Edition* (NPCC-3: Miller, 2012a) be completed

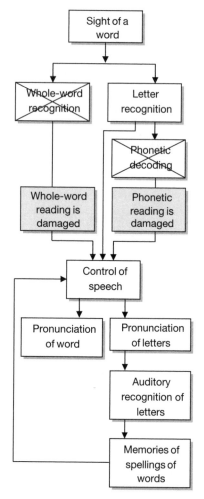

Figure 17.4. A Reading Model Showing Spelling or Word-Finding Dyslexia. Whole Word and Phonetic Reading Are Damaged. The Child Must Pronounce the Letters, Recognize the Words, and Then Say Them

Source: Adapted from Carlson (2010).

by the parent/guardian and at least one teacher of the student being referred for a comprehensive assessment (see the supplemental CD for the complete NPCC-3). The questions on the NPCC-3 that pertain to reading problems are shown in Rapid Reference 17.3. Any endorsed items in the moderate to

≡ *Rapid Reference 17.3*

Reading Achievement Items From the Neuropsychological Processing Concerns Checklist for Children and Youth—Third Edition (NPCC-3: Miller, 2012a)

Reading decoding difficulties:

- Over relies on sounding out most words when reading; even familiar words.
- Over relies on memorizing what words look like rather than sounding them out.
- Substitutes words that sound like the target word (e.g., reading "pear" for "bear").
- Substitutes words that mean the same as the word being read, but not the word itself (e.g., reading "truck" for "car").

Reading comprehension difficulties:

- Difficulty understanding what is read.
- Difficulty identifying main elements of a story.
- Appears distracted while reading.
- Misses important details while reading.

Attitudinal issues:

- Avoids reading activities.
- Appears anxious/uptight/nervous while reading.
- Shows no interest in reading for information or pleasure.

severe range should be followed up with formal assessment measures in the school neuropsychological assessment.

Assessing Reading Achievement

Rapid Reference 17.4 restates the second- and third-order classifications of reading processes within the Integrated SNP/CHC Model. Tests designed to measure these second- and third-order classifications of reading achievement are presented in Rapid Reference 17.5.

WRITTEN LANGUAGE DISORDERS

David has difficulty spelling words that are new to him. He does well in copying words or writing words told to him by his teacher. Peter has trouble with written expression as well but his difficulties with writing are different. Peter has difficulties with putting writing on paper. He is a very slow writer and seems to have trouble sequencing the proper motor acts to write successfully. Both David and Peter have written language disorders but they represent two

≡ Rapid Reference 17.4

SNP Model Classifications of Reading Achievement

Broad Classifications	Second-Order Classifications	Third-Order Classifications
Acquired Knowledge: Reading achievement	• Basic reading skills	• Phonological decoding • Orthographic coding • Morphological/syntactic coding
	• Reading comprehension skills	

≡ Rapid Reference 17.5

Tests of Reading Achievement

Test–Subtest: Description	Age/Grade Range	Publisher
Basic Reading Skills: Phonological Decoding		
GORT-5—Accuracy: Ability to pronounce each word in the story correctly.	6–0 to 18–11 years	Pearson
KTEA-II—Letter and Word Recognition: Identifying letters and pronouncing words of gradually increasing difficulty.	4–6 to 25 years	
KTEA-II—Nonsense Word Decoding: Application of phonics and structural analytic skills to decode made-up words.		
PAL-II RW—Pseudoword Decoding Accuracy: Ability to phonologically decode pseudowords.	Grades K to 6	
TOWRE-2—Reading Efficiency Index: An overall indicator of reading efficiency.	6 to 24–11 years	PRO-ED
WIAT-III—Early Reading Skills: Basic letter identification and phonemic awareness skills.	Grades Pre-K to 3	Pearson
WIAT-III—Pseudoword Decoding: Ability to phonologically decode pseudowords.	Grades 1 to 12	

WIAT-III—Word Reading:

Reading words in isolation.

WJIII ACH NU—Letter-Word Identification:

Reading words in isolation.

2–0 to 90+ years | Riverside

WJIII ACH NU—Word Attack:

Reading phonetically regular nonsense words orally.

WIST—Sound-Symbol Knowledge:

Ability to produce the appropriate sounds associated with specific letters.

7–0 to 18–11 years | PRO-ED

WIST—Word Identification:

Ability to read words aloud accurately.

Basic Reading Skills: Orthographic Coding

PAL-II RW—Orthographic Coding:

Ability to code whole words into memory and then relate units of these words to corresponding units.

Grades K to 6 | Pearson

- **Expressive Coding:**
  Ability to code whole written words into memory and then reproduce the words in whole or part in writing,

- **Receptive Coding:**
  Ability to code whole written words into memory and then to segment each word into units of different sizes.

Basic Reading Skills: Morphological/Syntactic Coding

PAL-II RW—Morphological/Syntactical Coding Composite:

Assesses knowledge of word structure that conveys meaning, especially suffixes that code meaning and part of speech.

Grades K to 6 | Pearson

- **Are They Related?**
  Ability to understand morphemes that are presented both orally and in writing.

- **Does It Fit?**
  Ability to understand morphemes and syntax (parts of speech) when presented both orally and in writing.

- **Sentence Structure:**
  Ability to understand morphemes and syntax (parts of speech) when presented both orally and in writing.

(continued)

≡ Rapid Reference 17.5 continued

Reading Comprehension Skills

GORT-5—Comprehension: Appropriateness of responses to questions about the content of each story read.	6–0 to 18–11 years	Pearson
KTEA-II—Reading Comprehension: Different levels of tasks designed to measure reading comprehension.	4–6 to 25 years	
WIAT-III—Reading Comprehension: Reading passages aloud or silently under untimed conditions, then answering open-ended questions about each one.	Grades 1 to 12	
WJIII ACH NU—Passage Comprehension: Reading a passage silently and providing the missing word.	2–0 to 90+ years	Riverside
WJIII ACH NU—Reading Vocabulary: Orally producing synonyms, antonyms, or verbal analogies.		
PAL-II RW—Sentence Sense Accuracy: Ability to coordinate silent word recognition and sentence comprehension when reading for meaning under timed conditions.	Grades K to 6	Pearson

See Appendix for the full names of the tests and their references.

different subtypes: phonological dysgraphia for David, and ideational dysgraphia for Peter.

The writing process is very complex and involves the coordination between language, thought and motor acts (Mather & Wendling, 2011). This section of the chapter reviews the subtypes associated with writing disorders, reviews the neuroanatomical circuitry of writing, and presents the major tests of written language that fit within the Integrated SNP/CHC Model.

Subtypes of Written Language Disorders

There are three types of writing disorders: one involves an inability to spell words; the other two involve difficulties with motor control. Rapid Reference 17.6 presents the common subtypes of written language disorders classified as *aphasic*

≡ *Rapid Reference 17.6*

Subtypes of Written Language Disorders

Writing Disorder Subtype	Symptoms
Dyslexic Dysgraphia (Language-Based Disorder)	
• Phonological dysgraphia	• Characterized by impaired phonetic decoding.
	• Spelling of unfamiliar words, nonwords, and phonetically irregular words is impaired.
	• Good skills in copying words, writing from dictation, and spelling relatively familiar words.
• Orthographic dysgraphia	• Characterized by an overreliance on phonetics, cannot visually recall words.
	• Can spell phonetically regular words.
	• Has difficulty spelling phonetically irregular spelled words.
	• Poor lexical representations of words.
	• Poor knowledge of the idiosyncratic properties of words.
• Mixed dysgraphia	• Inability to recall letter formations.
	• Inconsistent spelling skills.
	• Phonological and orthographic errors.
	• Cannot sequence letters accurately in words.
• Semantic/syntactic (direct) dysgraphia	• Can write dictated words.
	• Cannot understand written words.
	• Lack of understanding of the implicit rules of grammar.
Apraxic Dysgraphia (Nonlanguage Based)	
• Ideomotor dysgraphia	• Failure to carry out a motor act or gesture in response to a verbal command.
	• Intact comprehension and motor skills but they do not work together.
• Ideational dysgraphia	• Poor sequential motor processing.
	• Slow writing output.
	• Can copy.
	• Mild difficulty with dictation.
	• Cannot write well spontaneously.
• Constructional dyspraxia	• Visuospatial difficulty.
	• Cannot copy.

(continued)

≡ *Rapid Reference 17.6 continued*

Mechanical Dysgraphia

- Motor dysgraphia
  - No cognitive dysfunction related to writing.
  - Poor penmanship.
  - Writing deficits caused by mechanical problems with hands only (e.g., stiffness, tremors, poor fine motor skills).

Source: Adapted from Feifer and DeFina (2002).

dyslexic disorders (language-based), *apraxic dysgraphia* (nonlanguage based), and *mechanical dysgraphia*.

Dyslexic Dysgraphias

Phonological dysgraphia is a writing disorder in which the person cannot sound out words and write them phonetically (Carlson, 2010). Children with phonological dysgraphia have difficulty with spelling unfamiliar words, nonwords, or phonetically irregular words because their phonetic decoding skills are impaired. They can write relatively familiar words by visually imagining them. Children with phonological dysgraphia can also copy words and write from dictation.

Orthographic dysgraphia is a disorder of visually based writing (Carlson, 2010). Children with this subtype of writing disorder over rely on sounding out words, thus they can spell phonetically regular words but not phonetically irregular ones. Children with orthographic dysgraphia can only sound out a word because they cannot visually remember the whole word. As a result, children with this writing disorder can spell regular words and they can write pronounceable nonsense words. They do however have difficulties spelling irregular words (*half* becomes *haff, said* becomes *sed*). Children with orthographic dyslexia are also at-risk for poor handwriting and orthographic spelling and may have difficulty processing serial finger movements (Berninger, 2010).

Mixed dysgraphia is a writing disorder characterized by the inability to sequence letters accurately in words, the inability to recall letter formations properly, and inconsistent spelling skills (Feifer & Defina, 2002). Children with this writing disorder can copy written text and they can form letters correctly. However, children with mixed dysgraphia make phonological errors in spelling and orthographic errors based on faulty sequential arrangement of letters (e.g., *advantage* is misspelled as *advangate*).

Semantic/syntactic (direct) dysgraphia is characterized by a lack of understanding of the implicit rules of grammar that help guide how words and phrases are combined (Feifer & DeFina, 2002). In the reading disorders section of this chapter, direct dyslexia is characterized as being able to read aloud but not understand what is read. Semantic/syntactic or direct dysgraphia is similar in that children with this disorder can write words that are dictated to them but they cannot understand those words (Carlson, 2010).

Apraxic Dysgraphias

The term *apraxia* refers to a variety of motor skill deficits in which the child has little control over skilled motor movement. By definition, the motor difficulties are not a result of paralysis, paresis, or lack of comprehension. Writing problems can be caused by poor motor control that adversely affects the movements of the pen or pencil when forming letters and words.

Ideomotor dysgraphia is the failure to carry out a motor act or gesture in response to a verbal command. A child with ideomotor dysgraphia will have intact comprehension and the necessary motor skills to perform a motor response, but the connection between the understanding of a verbal command and the motor act is impaired. Ideomotor dysgraphia is generally associated with left inferior parietal lobe or left supplementary motor cortex area lesions, or a lesion of the corpus callosum.

Ideational dysgraphia is an inability to perform a series of gestures due to a loss of plan of action (ideation) for movement. Children with ideational dysgraphia have trouble with planning a written assignment and organizing their thoughts in a sequential manner. Children with this writing disorder can perform motor acts in isolation and on command but cannot string a series of motor acts together. Therefore, a child might be able to construct the letter "b" in isolation, though have difficulty writing the same letter within the context of the word "ball." For children with this disorder, writing is slow and laborious and characterized by frequent erasures, or self-corrections (Feifer & DeFina, 2002).

Constructional dyspraxia is "an inability to produce and/or modulate written language production due to deficits with the spatial constraints of letter and word production" (Feifer & DeFina, 2002, p. 79). Most written language processes involve left hemispheric functioning, but the visual-spatial aspect of writing (e.g., staying within the lines, maintaining a horizontal plane in a sentence, starting at the top of the page and writing from left to right) is a right hemispheric function. Poor handwriting skills are often related to the failure to obey spatial constraints coupled with a lack of consistency.

Mechanical Dysgraphia

Motor dysgraphia does not have any cognitive (language or nonlanguage) based impairment that can be linked to a writing impairment. Rather the writing problems stem from a difficulty with motor output. Motor dysgraphia can cause the child to hold a pen or pencil incorrectly and to apply the wrong type of pressure to the writing instrument. Motor dysgraphia is usually associated with mechanical problems of the hands (e.g., stiffness, tremors, poor fine motor skills). An occupational therapist can serve as an excellent resource for assessments and interventions for children with motor dysgraphia (see Chapter 10 for a list of assessments).

Handwriting and Spelling

In IDEA (U.S. Department of Education. 2004), written expression is one of the eight areas of eligibility for a specific learning disability (SLD). Difficulties with spelling and handwriting are often symptomatic of a writing disorder but are not sufficient alone for a diagnosis of a SLD (Mather & Wendling, 2011). Berninger (2010) pointed out that the IDEA written expression SLD criteria is based on qualifying children for special education services and not on evidence-based differential diagnoses. Fayol, Zorman, and Lété (2009) found that individuals with dysgraphia almost always have difficulties with handwriting with or without related spelling problems. Therefore, while handwriting and spelling deficits will not by themselves qualify a student for special education services school neuropsychologists should not ignore them.

Motor output problems in writing can include a poorly developed pencil grip, illegible writing, or stopping writing due to fatigue (Mather & Wendling, 2011). Berninger (2010) suggests that aspects of legibility, automaticity, speed, and sustained writing over time should be assessed as subcomponents of handwriting. The *Process Assessment for the Learner—Second Edition: Diagnostics for Reading and Writing* (PAL-2 RW: Berninger, 2007b) was specifically designed to measure all three subcomponents of handwriting. Berninger and Wolf (2009) have developed specific lesson plans for the treatment of dysgraphia, including handwriting.

Spelling has a strong relationship to sound-symbol associations. As in reading, some children over rely on sounding out words when spelling and have not learned to memorize the whole word visually. Children with this type of spelling problem have difficulty spelling irregular words. Other children over rely on the orthographic representations of spelling words and cannot apply phonetic rules to assist them in spelling. A student with poor spelling may have limited written expression, as they choose only familiar, and often simpler words in writing (Mather & Wendling, 2011).

Neuroanatomical Circuitry of Writing

Benson and Geschwind (1985) suggested that phonological dysgraphia is caused by damage to the superior temporal lobe, whereas surface (orthographic) dysgraphia is caused by damage to the inferior parietal lobe. More recent functional imaging studies and postmortem studies of patients with known brain lesions have found that the posterior inferior temporal cortex is involved with both phonological dysgraphia and surface (orthographic) dysgraphia (Carlson, 2010). Specifically, the anterior portion of the supramarginal gyrus seems to be impaired or dysfunctional in individuals with phonological dysgraphia.

Mixed dysgraphia seems to involve dysfunction within the left inferior parietal lobe. Also because of the planning and sequential organization needed for proper letter sequencing, there may be some prefrontal cortex impairment in children with mixed dysgraphia. The motor aspects of writing involve the dorsal parietal lobe, the premotor cortex, and the primary motor cortex (Carlson, 2010).

Identifying Written Language Achievement Concerns

It is suggested that the *Neuropsychological Processing Concerns Checklist for Children and Youth—Third Edition* (NPCC-3: Miller, 2012a) be completed by the parent/guardian and at least one teacher of the student being referred for a comprehensive assessment (see the supplemental CD for the complete NPCC-3). The questions on the NPCC-3 that pertain to written language problems are shown in Rapid Reference 17.7. Any endorsed items in the moderate to severe range should be followed up with formal assessment measures in the school neuropsychological assessment.

Assessing Written Language Achievement

Rapid Reference 17.8 restates the second- and third-order classifications of written language processes within the Integrated SNP/CHC Model. Tests designed to

≡ Rapid Reference 17.7

....

Written Language Achievement Items From the Neuropsychological Processing Concerns Checklist for Children and Youth—Third Edition (NPCC-3: Miller, 2012a)

Spatial production functions:
- Demonstrates uneven spacing between words and letters.
- Trouble staying on the horizontal lines.
- Others have difficulty reading what the child has written.
- Trouble forming letters and words.
- Writes overly large letters and words.

Expressive language functions:
- Limited vocabulary for age; uses lots of easy words.
- Difficulty putting ideas into words.
- Uses simple sentence structure and lacks variety.
- Produces poor spelling in writing.
- Poor grammar in writing.

Graphomotor output functions:
- Difficulty holding the pencil or pen correctly.
- Presses too soft with the pencil/pen while writing.
- Writes overly small letters and words.
- Presses too hard with the pencil/pen while writing.
- Shows preference for printing over cursive writing.

Attitudinal issues:
- Avoids writing activities.
- Appears anxious/uptight/nervous while writing.
- Shows no interest in writing activities.

measure these second- and third-order classifications of written language achievement are presented in Rapid Reference 17.9.

Qualitative Behaviors of Writing

The PAL-II RW (Berninger, 2007b) provides several qualitative behaviors from the writing subtests, including: alignment on baseline, letter sizing, overall consistency of sizing, and process observations for expository note taking and report writing. All of these qualitative behaviors are scored as base rates, or the percentage of same-age peers that evidence these types of behaviors. These process scores aid in clinical interpretation.

≡ Rapid Reference 17.8

SNP Model Classifications of Written Language Achievement

Broad Classifications	Second-Order Classifications	Third-Order Classifications
Acquired Knowledge: Written language achievement	• Written expression • Expository composition • Orthographic spelling • Handwriting skills • Qualitative behaviors	

≡ Rapid Reference 17.9

Tests of Written Language Achievement

Test–Subtest: Description	Age/Grade Range	Publisher
Written Expression		
KTEA-II—Written Expression: Measures writing skills at all levels.	4–6 to 25 years	Pearson
OWLS-II—Written Expression: The examiner presents oral, written, and pictorial prompts, and examinees write their responses in a booklet.	6–0 to 21–11 years	PRO-ED
WIAT-III—Written Expression: Measures writing skills at all levels.	Grades K to 12	
WJIII ACH NU—Written Expression: Measures writing skills at all levels.	2–0 to 90+ years	Riverside
Expository Composition		
PAL-II RW—Expository Note Taking and Report Writing: Ability to take notes for up to 5 minutes after reading some text, plan a composition, and compose a report.	Grades K to 6	Pearson

(continued)

≡ Rapid Reference 17.9 continued

PAL-II—Cross-Genre Compositional and Expository Writing:

A composite score based on the total number of words, correctly spelled words, and complete sentences in writing samples.

WIAT-III—Sentence Composition: Combining information from two or three sentences into single sentences that mean the same thing, then writing meaningful sentences that use specific words.	Grades 1 to 12	
WIAT-III—Essay Composition: Writing an essay within a 10-minute time limit.	Grades 3 to 12	
WJIII ACH NU—Writing Samples: Producing meaningful written sentences.	2–0 to 90+ years	Riverside

Orthographic Spelling

KTEA-II—Spelling: Writing words from dictation.	4–6 to 25 years	Pearson
PAL-II RW—Orthographic Spelling: Measures word choice accuracy and fluency in spelling.	Grades K to 6	
TOC—Orthographic Ability: Measures orthographic abilities in reading and writing.	PRO-ED	
• **Sign and Symbols:** Ability to identify a series of signs and symbols.	6 to 7 years	
• **Grapheme Matching:** Ability to identify two of five objects in a row that are identical.	6 to 7 years	
• **Homophone Choice:** Ability to choose the correct spelling of a word from several choices related to a visual picture of that word.	6 to 12 years	
• **Conventions:** Understanding of basic English usage conventions.	8 to 17 years	
• **Punctuation:** Ability to apply the correct punctuation in sentences.	6 to 17 years	
• **Abbreviations:** Ability to write what each abbreviation means.	8 to 17 years	

- **Spelling Speed:**   8 to 17 years
  Spelling fluency.
- **Letter Choice:**   8 to 17 years
  Ability to write in missing letters in words.
- **Word Scramble:**   8 to 17 years
  Ability to unscramble letters to form words.
- **Spelling Accuracy:**   8 to 17 years
  Accuracy of spelling.
- **Sight Spelling:**   8 to 17 years
  Ability to listen to a spoken word and
  fill in the missing letter or letters.
- **Word Choice:**   13 to 17 years
  Ability to listen to a spoken word and
  circle the correct spelling of that word
  from several choices.

WIAT-III—Spelling: Grades K to 12   Pearson

Writing single words that are dictated
within the context of a sentence.

WIST—Spelling: 7–0 to 18–11 years   PRO-ED

Ability to spell words from dictation.

Handwriting Skills

PAL-II RW—Alphabet Writing: Grades K to 6   Pearson

The automatic printing of lowercase
letters in alphabetical order from
memory.

PAL-II RW—Copying a Sentence (Task A):

Ability to copy a sentence containing all
letters of the alphabet.

PAL-II RW—Copying a Paragraph (Task B):

Ability to sustain copying a paragraph.

PAL-II RW—Handwriting Errors:

Quantifies handwriting errors such as
reversals, inversions, omissions.

See Appendix for the full names of the tests and their references.

MATHEMATICS DISORDERS

Patrice has difficulty with math. She has trouble with correctly aligning a column of numbers and even with the visual perception of numbers. She is able to remember basic math facts and has no trouble reading numbers. Patrice has a subtype of mathematics disorder called *visual-spatial dyscalculia.*

The neuropsychology of mathematics was not as widely researched nor was as much attention paid to it as reading and writing until recent years. In 2008, the National Mathematics Advisory Panel (U.S. Department of Education, 2008) stressed the importance of mathematics education in industrialized nations such as the United States. This section of the chapter reviews the subtypes associated with mathematics disorders, reviews the neuroanatomical circuitry of mathematics, and presents the major tests of mathematics that fit with the Integrated SNP/CHC Model.

Definitions

Acalculia is the neuropsychological term that means an acquired disturbance of computational ability associated with impairment in both the ability to read and write numbers (Loring, 1999). Dyscalculia, not the same as acalculia, is defined as a specific neurological-disorder affecting a person's ability to understand and/or manipulate numbers. Acalculia/dyscalculia are very rare and are generally seen in children with head injuries or other neurological insults. Hale and Fiorello (2004) pointed out that the likelihood of finding a "pure" dyscalculia in children is rare.

Subtypes of Mathematics Disorders and Neural Substrate

The neuropsychological explanations and neuroimaging evidence for subtypes of mathematics disorders is still evolving and lacks consensus (Maricle, Psimas-Fraser, Muenke, & Miller, 2010). Geary (1993, 2003) and Mazzocco (2001) suggested three subtypes of dyscalculia: semantic, procedural, and visuo-spatial. Wilson and Dehaene (2007) identified three subtypes of dyscalculia in adults, which were verified by lesion evidence and neuroimaging studies. These three dyscalculia subtypes included: number sense, verbal-symbolic, and spatial attention. Wilson and Dehaene (2007) pointed out that these same subtypes might not be present in children during developmental acquisition of mathematics. They suggested that in children there could be several other subtypes of dyscalculia including:

- A deficit in verbal symbolic representation of numbers
- A deficit in executive function.
- A deficit in spatial attention.

Hale, Fiorello, Dumont et al. (2008) examined the neuropsychological processing differences among typical children and children with a math specific learning disability on the Differential Ability Scales—Second Edition (Elliott, 2007). Hale, Fiorello, Miller et al. (2008) examined similar math and nonmath disabled children on the WISC-IV (Wechsler, 2004a) and the WIAT-II (Wechsler, 2001). These authors described five developmental subtypes of dyscalculia:

1. Numeric Quantitative Knowledge
2. Dyscalculia/Gerstmann Syndrome
3. Mild Executive/Working Memory
4. Fluid/Quantitative Reasoning
5. Nonverbal Learning Disability/Right Hemisphere

The deficits and strengths of these dyscalculia subtypes, along with their neural substrates, are presented in Rapid Reference 17.10.

≣ *Rapid Reference 17.10*

Subtypes of Mathematics Disorders and Related Neural Substrate

Math Disorder Subtype	Symptoms	Neural Substrate

• Number Sense Dyscalculia (Wilson & Dehaene, 2007) or Numerical-Quantitative Knowledge (Hale, Fiorello, Dumont et al., 2008; Hale, Fiorello, Miller et al., 2008)	• Deficits in:
	  ▪ Understanding the meaning of numbers
	  ▪ Comparison and approximation of dots
	  ▪ Numerical comparison, addition, and subtraction
	  ▪ Automatic activation of quantity from number words and digits
	• Strengths in:
	  ▪ Counting
	  ▪ Fact retrieval
		• Horizontal intraparietal sulcus within the parietal cortex

• Verbal-Symbolic Dyscalculia (Wilson & Dehaene, 2007) or Dyscalculia-Gerstmann Syndrome	• Deficits in:
	  ▪ Counting
	  ▪ Rapid number identification
		• Left angular gyrus
		• Inferior frontal and/or temporal language areas

(continued)

☰ *Rapid Reference 17.10 continued*

(Hale, Fiorello, Dumont et al., 2008; Hale, Fiorello, Miller et al., 2008)	▪ Retrieval of stored facts
	▪ Addition and multiplication facts
	▪ Numerical reasoning
	▪ Possible coexisting reading/writing difficulties
	• Strengths in:
	  ▪ Number qualities
	  ▪ Comparisons between numbers
	  ▪ Understanding basic concepts
	  ▪ Visual Spatial skills
		• Left basal ganglia

• Visual-Spatial Dyscalculia
(Geary, 1993, 2003; Mazzocco, 2001; Wilson & Dehaene, 2007)
	• Deficits in:
	  ▪ Aligning a column of numbers
	  ▪ Visual perception of numbers
	  ▪ Spatial attributes (e.g., size, location)
	  ▪ Magnitude comparisons
	• Strengths in:
	  ▪ Retrieval of stored facts
	  ▪ Reading numbers
	  ▪ Math algorithms
	  ▪ Verbal strategies
		• Posterior superior parietal lobe

• Executive Memory Dysfunction
(Wilson & Dehaene, 2007) or Mild Executive/Working Memory Dysfunction
(Hale, Fiorello, Dumont et al., 2008; Hale, Fiorello, Miller et al., 2008)
	• Deficits in:
	  ▪ Fact retrieval
	  ▪ Strategies and procedure usage
	• Strengths in:
	  ▪ Numerical operations
	  ▪ Math reasoning
		• Frontal-striatal dysfunction

Number Sense or Numerical Quantitative Knowledge Dyscalculia

Hale, Fiorello, Miller et al. (2008) referred to this subtype of mathematics as numerical quantitative knowledge dyscalculia, which describes similar symptomology as Wilson and Dehaene's (2007) number sense dyscalculia. Number sense seems to be an implicit and possibly inherent ability in children (Butterworth & Reigosa, 2007). Number sense is the "understanding of the exact quantity of small collections of objects and of symbols (e.g., Arabic numerals) that represent these quantities . . . , and of the approximate magnitude of larger quantities" (Geary, Hoard, & Bailey, 2011, p. 46). The ability to determine the quantity of small sets of items without counting is called *subitizing*. There is evidence that children with specific learning disabilities in mathematics have deficits in both subitizing and the ability to represent approximate quantities (Geary, Hoard, Nugent, & Byrd-Craven, 2008). The neural substrate for number sense is the horizontal intra-parietal sulcus (HIPS) within the parietal cortex.

Some clinicians believe that deficits in mathematics equate to a nonverbal specific learning disability (Maricle et al., 2010). Hale, Fiorello, Miller, et al. (2008) found that a group of mathematics SLD children performed below average on the Digits Forward, Arithmetic, and Processing Speed tests of the WISC-IV. Hale and his colleagues pointed out that these scores suggest that some children with deficiencies in mathematics have comorbid language, writing, and reading SLDs.

Verbal-Symbolic Dyscalculia or Dyscalculia-Gerstmann Syndrome

Verbal-Symbolic Dyscalculia was a mathematics subtype identified by Wilson and Dehaene (2007). Hale and his colleagues (Hale, Fiorello, Dumont, et al., 2008; Hale, Fiorello, Miller, et al., 2008) have used the label Dyscalculia-Gerstmann Syndrome to describe similar mathematic deficiencies. Children with this subtype of dyscalculia have difficulty with the verbal representations of numbers and use of language-based procedures for the retrieval of arithmetic facts.

Children with verbal dyscalculia have difficulties with counting and rapid number identification, and difficulties retrieving or recalling previously learned math facts. Verbal dyscalculia often coexists with reading and spelling difficulties because of the generalized language processing deficits (von Aster, 2000). Children with verbal dyscalculia are still able to appreciate numeric qualities, understand mathematical concepts, or make comparisons between numbers.

Dyscalculia-Gerstmann Syndrome is a neurological impairment that is associated with damage or dysfunction in the left parietal lobe, specifically within the regions of the angular gyrus, left inferior frontal, and/or temporal language areas, or the left basal ganglia (Maricle et al., 2010). Hale, Fiorello, Miller, et al. (2008) found that children with this subtype of dyscalculia achieved low scores on the

Information, Arithmetic, Block Design, Picture Completion, and the Processing Speed subtests on the WISC-IV. This pattern of low scores suggested that children with this mathematics subtype had generalized left hemispheric deficits that can co-occur with reading disorders.

Visual-Spatial Dyscalculia

Visual-spatial dyscalculia is characterized by poor column alignment, difficulties with place values, and not paying attention to the mathematical operational signs (e.g., adding all problems, including subtraction problems [Hale & Fiorello, 2004]). Visual-spatial dyscalculia is often associated with Rourke's (1994) classification of nonverbal learning disabilities. The constellation of symptoms associated with visual-spatial dyscalculia includes poor visual-spatial, organization, psychomotor, tactile-perceptual, and concept formation skills. In other words, these children have trouble thinking in pictures, which is often required for more abstract types of mathematical problem solving such as geometry. However, children with visual-spatial dyscalculia have good rote, automatic, and verbal skills. Visual-spatial dyscalculia is due to dysfunction within the posterior superior parietal lobe (Wilson & Dehaene, 2007).

Executive Memory or a Mild Executive/Working Memory Dysfunction

Hale and Fiorello (2004) suggest there might be two separate visual-spatial dyscalculia subtypes: one involving right posterior area deficit that causes visual-spatial problems of poor alignment and attention to detail (visual-spatial dyscalculia as described above), and one involving the right frontal area that disrupts problem solving skills and novel concept formation. Wilson and Dehaene (2007) refer to this subtype of mathematics as *Executive Memory Dysfunction*. Hale, Fiorello, Miller, et al. (2008) include executive dysfunction as well as working memory deficits to explain this subtype of mathematics disorder and label it as mild executive/working memory dysfunction.

Children with executive functions and working memory deficits do well on numerical operations and math reasoning. Hale, Fiorello, Miller et al. (2008) report that children with these processing deficits achieved low scores on Information, Digits Backwards, Arithmetic, and Matrix Reasoning. Typically, children with this subtype have only mild deficits in math compared to the other subtypes. Frontal-striatal dysfunction is the neural substrate for this math subtype.

Identifying Mathematics Achievement Concerns

It is suggested that the *Neuropsychological Processing Concerns Checklist for Children and Youth—Third Edition* (NPCC-3; D. Miller, 2012a) be completed

≡ Rapid Reference 17.11

Mathematics Achievement Items From the Neuropsychological Processing Concerns Checklist for Children and Youth—Third Edition (NPCC-3; Miller, 2012a)

Computational and procedural difficulties:

- Forgets what steps to take when solving math problems (e.g., carrying in addition or borrowing in subtraction).
- Makes computational errors.
- Slow in solving math problems.
- Makes careless mistakes while solving math problems.
- Does not always pay attention to the math problems signs.

Visual-spatial difficulties:

- Difficulty aligning a column of numbers.
- Difficulty understanding spatial attributes such as size and location of numbers.
- Difficulty recognizing visual differences in magnitude (e.g., which group of objects has more items than another group).

Verbal difficulties:

- Difficulty with retrieval of basic math facts.
- Difficulty solving story problems.
- Difficulty with counting.
- Slow in number identification.

Attitudinal issues:

- Avoids math activities.
- Appears anxious/uptight/nervous when working with math.
- Shows no interest in math.

by the parent/guardian and at least one teacher of the student being referred for a comprehensive assessment (see the supplemental CD for the complete NPCC-3). The questions on the NPCC-3 that pertain to math problems are shown in Rapid Reference 17.11. Any endorsed items in the moderate to severe range should be followed up with formal assessment measures in the school neuropsychological assessment.

Assessing Mathematics Achievement

Rapid Reference 17.12 restates the second- and third-order classifications of mathematics processes within the Integrated SNP/CHC Model. Tests designed to

≡ *Rapid Reference 17.12*

SNP Model Classifications of Written Language Achievement

Broad Classifications	Second-Order Classifications	Third-Order Classifications
Acquired Knowledge: Mathematics achievement	• Oral counting • Fact retrieval • Mathematical calculations • Mathematical reasoning • Qualitative behaviors	

measure these second- and third-order classifications of mathematics achievement are presented in this section. Tests designed to measure these second- and third-order classifications of mathematical achievement are presented in Rapid Reference 17.13.

≡ *Rapid Reference 17.13*

Tests of Mathematic Achievement

Test–Subtest: Description	Age/Grade Range	Publisher
Oral Counting		
PAL-II M—Oral Counting: Ability to orally produce numbers along the internal number line.	Grades K to 6	Pearson
Fact Retrieval		
PAL-II M—Fact Retrieval: The accuracy and speed in retrieving basic math facts, depending on different combinations of input and output modes.	Grades K to 6	Pearson
Mathematical Calculations		
KTEA-II—Math Computation: Performing a variety of math calculations.	4–6 to 25 years	Pearson
KeyMath3—Operations: Written and mental computation skills.	4–6 to 21–11 years	

PAL-II M—Computation Operations Composite: Evaluation of the visual-spatial and temporal-sequential processes underlying the student's application of computational algorithms.	Grades K to 6	
PAL-II M—Place Value Composite: Evaluation of understanding of the place value concept when representing numbers orally and in writing.	Grades K to 6	
PAL-II M—Part-Whole Relationship Composite: Evaluation of the understanding of the relationships between relative and absolute size of parts of wholes, fractions and mixed numbers, and the measurement system of time.	Grades K to 6	
WIAT-III—Numerical Operations: Performing a variety of math calculations.	Grades K to 12	
WJIII ACH NU—Calculations: Performing a variety of math calculations.	2–0 to 90+ years	Riverside
Mathematical Reasoning		
KeyMath3—Applications: Ability to identify the key elements of math problems and the operations and strategies necessary to solve problems.	4–6 to 21–11 years	Pearson
KeyMath3—Basic Concepts: Conceptual understanding of basic math concepts.		
KTEA-II—Math Concepts and Applications: Analyzing and solving practical math problems.	4–6 to 25 years	
PAL-II M—Finding the Bug: Ability to detect computational or fact retrieval errors.	Grades K to 6	
PAL-II M—Multistep Problem Solving: Ability to understand the question a math word problem is asking and to plan the calculation steps necessary to solve it.		
SB5—Nonverbal Quantitative Reasoning: Ability to solve nonverbal problems with numbers or numerical concepts.	2 to 85+ years	Riverside
SB5—Verbal Quantitative Reasoning: Ability to solve verbal problems with numbers or numerical concepts.		

(continued)

≡ *Rapid Reference 17.13 continued*

WIAT-III—Math Problem Solving:	Grades	Pearson
Analyzing and solving practical math problems.	K to 12	
WJIII ACH NU—Applied Problems:	2–0 to 90+	Riverside
Analyzing and solving practical math problems.	years	
WJIII ACH NU—Quantitative Concepts:		
Measures mathematical knowledge and quantitative reasoning.		

See Appendix for the full names of the tests and their references.

Qualitative Behaviors of Mathematics

The PAL-II M (Berninger, 2007a) provides qualitative behaviors for numeral writing errors. These qualitative behaviors are scored as base rates, or the percentage of same-age peers that evidence these types of behaviors. These process scores aid in clinical interpretation.

CHAPTER SUMMARY

In this chapter the theories, terminology, neuroanatomy, and major tests associated with the academic achievement areas are reviewed. The neuropsychological aspects of reading, writing, and mathematics were presented along with the major achievement tests designed to measure those academic areas. Achievement deficits are observed in many common developmental disorders, thus academic achievement measures are typically included in the majority of school neuropsychological assessments. For more comprehensive reviews of achievement tests see Naglieri and Goldstein (2009) or Flanagan, Ortiz, Alfonso, and Mascolo (2006). For a review of evidence-based academic interventions see Wendling and Mather (2009).

> **DON'T FORGET**
>
> A major contribution of a neuropsychological perspective in assessment is the ability to subtype disorders of reading, writing, and mathematics, which can lead to more targeted, evidence-based interventions.

A major contribution of a neuropsychological perspective in assessment is the ability to subtype disorders of reading, writing, and mathematics, which can lead to more targeted, evidence-based interventions. School neuropsychologists are trained not to stop at a generic diagnosis of a reading disorder, but to specify through differential diagnosis, the potential subtype of a reading disorder. The same principle applies to the identification of specific learning disabilities in writing and mathematics. Ongoing research is needed to continue to validate the linkage between the efficacy of prescriptive interventions based on specific subtypes of reading, writing, and mathematics.

 TEST YOURSELF

1. **What subtype of a reading disorder is characterized by overreliance on memorizing a whole word as seen in space rather than phonetic decoding?**
   a. Pure alexia
   b. Phonological dyslexia
   c. Surface dyslexia
   d. Direct dyslexia

2. **What subtype of a reading disorder is characterized by an overreliance on visual and semantic cues and frequent semantic errors during reading?**
   a. Semantic dyslexia
   b. Direct dyslexia
   c. Mixed dysgraphia
   d. Direct dysgraphia

3. **What subtype of a written language disorder is characterized by an inability or difficulty with sequencing letters accurately in words?**
   a. Phonological dysgraphia
   b. Surface dysgraphia
   c. Mixed dysgraphia
   d. Direct dysgraphia

4. **What subtype of a written language disorder does not involve a cognitive component but results in poor penmanship?**
   a. Phonological dysgraphia
   b. Surface dysgraphia
   c. Mixed dysgraphia
   d. Motor dysgraphia

5. **What subtype of a mathematics disorder results in difficulties with poor alignment of number columns?**
   a. Visual-spatial dyscalculia
   b. Semantic-memory dyscalculia
   c. Procedural dyscalculia
   d. Verbal-symbolic dyscalculia

6. What subtype of a mathematics disorder is associated with dysfunction or damage with the horizontal intraparietal sulcus within the parietal cortex?

a. Visual-spatial dyscalculia
b. Number sense dyscalculia
c. Verbal-symbolic dyscalculia
d. Executive memory dysfunction

Answers: 1. b; 2. a; 3. c; 4. d; 5. a; 6. b

Chapter Eighteen

FUTURE DIRECTIONS OF SCHOOL NEUROPSYCHOLOGICAL ASSESSMENT

"Prediction is difficult, especially about the future!" This quote has been attributed to a wide variety of people including Yogi Berra, the baseball player and manager, Neils Bohr, a Nobel laureate physicist, and Mark Twain, a humorist. The purpose of this chapter is to humbly peek into the near future, perhaps 5 to 10 years from now, and speculate about the future of school neuropsychology. This chapter discusses the need for the continued refinement of the school neuropsychological conceptual model, the emergence of neuroeducation and role of school psychologists and school neuropsychologists, the influences of neuroimaging on the practice of school neuropsychology, future trends in school neuropsychological assessment, and finally training issues.

CONTINUED REFINEMENT OF THE SCHOOL NEUROPSYCHOLOGY CONCEPTUAL MODEL

The school neuropsychological conceptual model has been updated regularly in tandem with the evolution of the overall field of school neuropsychology. As the theoretical foundations for neuropsychological constructs are validated over time, the school neuropsychological conceptual model will continue to evolve. As an example, CHC theory has served as the theoretical foundation for several major tests of cognitive functions and this theory continues to be refined. As cited previously in this book, Schneider and McGrew (2012) stated:

> The most active CHC "spillover" has been in the area of neuropsychological assessment. . . . It is our opinion that CHC-based neuropsychological assessment holds great potential. . . . However, more CHC-organized factor-analytic studies of joint neuropsychological and CHC-validated batteries are needed before such a synthesis is possible. . . . Even more crucial are studies that describe the functioning

of the brain (e.g., with functional magnetic resonance imaging) during performance on validated tests of CHC abilities. (p. 109)

In this book, an attempt is made to further integrate CHC theory with the school neuropsychological conceptual model. This Integrated SNP/CHC Model needs to be validated over the coming years using a variety of statistical techniques including factor analytic studies and structural equation modeling.

A challenge for researchers and theorists is to strive for a common set of nomenclature for research and applied practice. It would be ideal if there could be a consensus established for what constitutes a cognitive process, versus a cognitive function, versus a cognitive skill, and so on. If the field of school psychology is going to embrace the notion of cognitive processing deficits being the basis for specific learning disabilities and other neurodevelopmental disorders, better clarity in the terminology we use as a discipline should be a goal for our profession.

Another challenge for school psychology and school neuropsychology remains the continued validation of assessment data with evidence-based interventions. School neuropsychologists can identify subtypes of reading, writing, and mathematics disabilities based on a fairly high degree of scientific rigor. However, the same degree of scientific rigor is not yet established for the treatment efficacy of the prescriptive interventions that are often recommended based on these neuropsychological subtypes. For the field of school neuropsychology to legitimately progress as a subspecialization in psychology, continued validation research is warranted.

NEUROEDUCATION AND SCHOOL NEUROPSYCHOLOGY

Since the early part of the 21st century, there has been a growing interest in translating brain research into applied practice. "Neuroscientific research has been integrated in most of the industries of the world (e.g., medicine, manufacturing, business practices); however, the application of neuroscientific knowledge into educational practice is lagging" (Maricle, Miller, Hale, & Johnson, 2012). Bruer (2008) referred to brain-based education as an emerging discipline and labeled it as *"neuroeducation."* Neuroeducation emphasizes the focus of education on transdisciplinary connections (Battro, Fischer, & Léna, 2008a; 2008b). Fischer, Gaowami, and Geake (2010) referred to this integration of neuropsychology and education as "educational neuroscience", which they defined as "a new field that brings together biology, cognitive neuroscience, developmental science, and education to investigate brain and genetic bases of learning and teaching" (p. 68).

School psychologists are the only professional educators within the schools who have formal training in psychology. School psychologists should be a part of neuroeducation or educational neuroscience as it becomes more mainstream, but practitioners will need to enhance their professional skills in neuropsychology and broaden their knowledge base in the biological bases of behavior. School neuro-psychologists, already training in the biological bases of behavior, are uniquely poised to be a part of this next revolution in education. The need to place more emphasis on the biological bases of behavior in school psychology training programs will be discussed in the final section of this chapter.

With the emergence of neuroeducation, some researchers warn school-based practitioners to exercise caution in overgeneralizing brain research into educational practice (Miller & DeFina, 2010). It is easy to state the claim that "research shows", which potentially misleads the public (Bruer, 1997). Swanson (2008) stated that:

> Although correlational research between brain and behavior has a long history in the field of specific learning disabilities (SLD), there is a gap in the application of this research to instruction. Recent work with the advent of fMRI procedures and treatment outcomes is beginning to bridge this gap. However, the bridge between brain studies and education is not well developed (e.g., Bruer, 1997). Knowing precisely which brain centers are activated over time and how they are associated with instruction is rudimentary. (p. 30)

School neuropsychologists have an ethical and professional responsibility to keep abreast of the emerging research in several fields including school psychology, neuropsychology, and neuroscience. It is recognized that this is becoming no easy task with the explosion of empirically based research in each one of these fields. However, it does fall on the school neuropsychologist to endorse or recommend only those assessment techniques and interventions, which have proven to be valid and effective.

NEUROIMAGING AND SCHOOL NEUROPSYCHOLOGY

On a 10-year horizon, if not sooner, neuroimaging techniques will help reshape the practice of school neuropsychology. Advances in neuroimaging techniques have allowed cognitive neuroscientists a window into brain functions (Miller & DeFina, 2010). Through the use of functional neuroimaging, one can look not only at brain structure but also can also examine cognitive functions. As neuroimaging becomes more accessible, it will be more routinely used as a tool to validate what neuropsychological tests were designed to measure (Miller, 2008). Reynolds (2008) speculated that neuroimaging could help school neuropsychologists by creating functional profiles for children that would predict the presence or absence of learning disorders and guide us toward specific interventions. Finally an exciting application of neuroimaging, is to measure brain functioning pre- and postintervention as a means of verifying the effectiveness of the intervention. See Miller and DeFina (2010) for a review of the major neuroimaging techniques (e.g., magnetic resonance imaging) and their potential applications to assessing everyday neurodevelopmental disorders.

FUTURE TRENDS IN SCHOOL NEUROPSYCHOLOGICAL ASSESSMENT

This section of the chapter will present some of the future trends in school neuropsychological assessment, including advances in computerized assessment and the inclusion of more qualitative assessment data to aid clinicians in interpretation.

Computerized Assessment

The test publishing industry has not kept up with the rapid advances in personal computing technologies. It is important to realize that from a business standpoint, the field of school psychology is relatively small. With a market base of approximately 35,000 school psychology practitioners, test publishers have to make sure that their investments in product development will be sufficiently profitable.

Another limiting factor in the transitioning to computerized assessment has been the forced choice of which software platform for application development (Widows^{TM} or Macintosh OS^{TM}). In the past it has been very expensive to develop and maintain product software for two or more platforms. With the advent of Cloud computing, where the software program is stored on the servers and accessible to any users through the Internet, the underlying programming issue becomes a moot point.

The future of computerized neuropsychological assessment is promising. Practitioners of the near future may not have to treat their personal vehicles as a test library and continually cart test kits in and out of schools. Instead, practitioners may carry a computer or tablet that presents stimulus items directly on a screen and allows students to respond. Responses to stimulus items could be captured through touch by a finger, through a stylist for a written response, or through voice-recognition.

There are several advantages of computerized assessment. The first advantage is the increased standardization of assessment. Directions for tests could be recorded and presented to the examinee, thus reducing examiner errors. Computerized assessment would also allow for the collection of additional test measurements such as the average time the examinee took to respond to items on a test. Finally, computerized assessment would create opportunities to capture assessment data across multiple users for research purposes. With paper-and-pencil assessments it can take years to collect samples of sufficient size for small clinical groups. With computerized assessment, all data collected on clinical samples could be synthesized and provided back to clinicians in a broad-based dynamic normative database. There are obvious privacy issues that would need to be worked out, but computerized assessment holds the promise of providing clinicians more reliable and valid assessment data in the future.

Need for More Base Rates for Qualitative Behaviors

When school psychologists are trained in graduate school as to how to conduct individualized assessment, so much emphasis is placed on the standardization of the test directions and procedures. Sometimes, new and existing practitioners are so concerned about administering the directions in a standardized manner that they forget to observe the behavior of the student who is sitting in front of them. When faced with any cognitive or academic task, a student must engage in the proper cognitive processes and apply the proper skills to successfully complete the task. Although the test score itself is an important measure of the student's performance, equally important are the strategies employed by the student to accomplish tasks. This notion is at the heart of the process approach to assessment, which is an integral part of school neuropsychology. Test publishers in recent years have started to provide clinicians with base rate data for some qualitative behaviors that students exhibit during test performance (e.g., asking for repetitions). These data are highly valuable to supplement a clinician's interpretation of test performance and overall response style of a student. Test publishers are hopefully going to provide such quantification of qualitative behaviors in future editions of the major tests used in clinical practice.

TRAINING ISSUES IN SCHOOL NEUROPSYCHOLOGICAL ASSESSMENT

Maricle, Miller, Hale, and Johnson (2012) state several reasons why school psychology training programs should recognize the importance of the biological bases of behavior, including:

(1) increased knowledge of the biological bases of neurodevelopmental disorders; (2) integration of neuropsychological constructs into school psychological assessment tools; (3) the current controversy surrounding the identification of specific learning disabilities; (4) the emerging fields of educational neuroscience and social neuroscience; and (5) the potential encroachment of other specialties into the traditional practice of school psychology (p. 71).

As this author and others (Castillo, 2008; Goldstein & Reynolds, 2010; Hale & Fiorello, 2004; Maricle, Miller et al., 2012; Miller, 2010; Riccio, Sullivan, & Cohen, 2010; Semrud-Clikeman & Teeter-Ellison, 2009) have pointed out, there is strong neurobiological evidence and known neuropsychological correlates of childhood disorders including specific learning disabilities, attention deficit hyperactivity disorder, autism spectrum disorders, internalizing and externalizing disorders, acquired neurological disorders, and genetic disorders affecting learning and behavior. School psychology training programs need to find methods of infusing this knowledge base into their curriculum to ensure that future practitioners will be adequately prepared.

Within the past decade, neuropsychological constructs such as executive functions, working memory, and processing speed have all appeared in mainstream school psychology practice. These neuropsychological constructs have been shown to play a major role in education. School psychology training programs need to emphasize the theoretical foundations and clinical applications of these neuropsychological constructs (Maricle, Miller et al., 2012).

For the identification of specific learning disabilities, a third method using a neuropsychological approach is allowable under IDEA and emerging into practice (Flanagan & Alfonso, 2011; Flanagan, Alfonso, Mascolo, & Sotelo-Dynega, 2012; Hale et al., 2010a, 2010b). School psychology trainers need to incorporate these methodologies into the training of their students.

Finally, the point needs to be made that if school psychologists do not become better trained to assess and treat the neuropsychological manifestations of common neurodevelopmental disorders, other professionals will come into the schools to meet that growing need. Hurewitz and Kerr (2011) stated that evaluations for special education have the basic elements of a forensic reporting "because the evaluation may be used, in part, to affix the rights and privileges of individuals, such as educational placement, reimbursement for services or school tuition, or removal from school for disciplinary infractions" (p. 1059). They noted "as the mandates for compliance with federal and state educational requirements have grown more complex, and in some cases integrated concepts of disability gleaned from research in cognitive psychology and neuropsychology, there has been a call for an increase in the application of neuropsychological methods" (p. 1059). Maricle, Miller, and colleagues concur with the statement that advances within cognitive psychology and neuropsychology are reshaping how we should view the identification and treatment of disabilities; however, they believe that school psychologists should take the lead role in the translation of brain research, cognitive neuroscience, and neuropsychological research related to neurodevelopmental disabilities into educational practice.

CHAPTER SUMMARY

In this chapter an attempt is made to make some predictions about potential influences on the future of school neuropsychology. The school neuropsychological conceptual model continues to evolve based on validation research and advances in theory. General educators are growing increasingly interested in translating brain research into educational practice and school psychologists training in the integration of neuropsychological principles into their practice will be uniquely prepared to contribute to this new educational effort. Computerized assessment will become more mainstream in years to come, which will be beneficial to school neuropsychology practice, and the type of clinical data provided to clinicians will increase in sophistication. Finally, the rationale for why school psychology training programs need to make sure that the biological bases of behavior is emphasized are highlighted.

🪶 TEST YOURSELF 🪶

1. **True or False? According to the author, it would be ideal if there could be a consensus established for what constitutes a cognitive process, versus a cognitive function, versus a cognitive skill, and so on.**

2. **What term(s) have been used to describe the emerging integration of neuroscience and education?**

   a. Neuroeducation
   b. Educational neuroscience
   c. Neither a nor b
   d. Both a and b

3. All of the following are benefits of computerized assessment except for one. Which one?

a. Easier portability
b. Easier accessibility
c. Increased privacy protection
d. Access to additional performance measures

4. True or False? Clinicians do not see much value in the base rates provided by test publishers for qualitative behaviors.

5. Neuroimaging in the future will be used for what?

a. Monitoring the effectiveness of interventions
b. Creating functional profiles that would predict the absence or presence of learning disorders
c. Validation of neurocognitive constructs being measured by tests
d. All of the above

Answers: 1. true; 2. d; 3. c; 4. false; 5. d

Appendix

Referenced Tests, Abbreviations, and Publishers

Test Abbreviation	Test Name	Citation
BASC-2	*Behavior Assessment System for Children—Second Edition*	Reynolds & Kamphaus, 2009
Beery VMI	*Beery-Buktenica Developmental Test of Visual-Motor Integration—Sixth Edition*	Beery, Buktenica, and Beery, 2010
Bender II	*Bender Visual-Motor Gestalt Test—Second Edition*	Brannigan and Decker, 2003
Boehm-3	*Boehm Test of Basic Concepts—Third Edition*	Boehm, 2000
Boehm-3 Preschool	*Boehm Test of Basic Concepts—Third Edition Preschool*	Boehm, 2001
CAS	*Das-Naglieri Cognitive Assessment System*	Naglieri and Das, 1997
CAVLT-2	*Children's Auditory Verbal Learning Test—2*	Talley, 1994
CMS	*Children's Memory Scale*	Cohen, 1997
CREVT-2	*Comprehensive Receptive and Expressive Vocabulary Test—Second Edition*	Wallace and Hammill, 2002
CTONI-2	*Comprehensive Test of Nonverbal Intelligence—Second Edition*	Hammill, Pearson, and Wiederholt, 2009
CTOPP	*Comprehensive Test of Phonological Processing*	Wagner, Torgesen, and Rashotte, 1999
CVLT-C	*California Verbal Learning Test—Children's Version*	Delis, Kramer, Kaplan, and Ober, 1994
DAS-II	*Differential Ability Scales—Second Edition*	Elliott, 2007

(continued)

(Continued)

Test Abbreviation	Test Name	Citation
DWSMB	*Dean-Woodcock Sensory-Motor Battery*	Dean and Woodcock, 2003
D-KEFS	*Delis-Kaplan Executive Function System*	Delis, Kaplan, and Kramer, 2001
DTAP	*Developmental Test of Auditory Perception*	Reynolds, Voress, and Pearson, 2008
ECFT	*Extended Complex Figure Test*	Fastenau, 1996
EOWPVT-4	*Expressive One-Word Picture Vocabulary Test—Fourth Edition*	Brownell, 2010a
EOWPVT-SBE	*Expressive One-Word Picture Vocabulary Test: Spanish-Bilingual Edition*	Brownell, 2000a
EVT-2	*Expressive Vocabulary Test—Second Edition*	Williams, 2006
GORT-5	*Gray Oral Reading Test—Fifth Edition*	Wiederholt and Bryant, 2012
KABC-II	*Kaufman Assessment Battery for Children—Second Edition*	A. Kaufman and Kaufman, 2004
KeyMath3	*KeyMath3 Diagnostic Assessment*	Connolly, 2011
KTEA-II	*Kaufman Test of Educational Achievement—Second Edition*	A. Kaufman and Kaufman, 2004
NEPSY-II	*NEPSY-II: A Developmental Neuropsychological Assessment*	Korkman, Kirk, and Kemp, 2007
OWLS-II	*Oral and Written Language Scales—Second Edition*	Carrow-Woolfolk, 2011
PAL-2 M	*Process Assessment of the Learner: Diagnostics for Math*	Berninger, 2007a
PAL-2 RW	*Process Assessment of the Learner: Diagnostics for Reading and Writing*	Berninger, 2007b
PPVT-IV	*Peabody Picture Vocabulary Test—Fourth Edition*	L. Dunn and Dunn, 2006
RAN/RAS	*Rapid Automatized Naming and Rapid Alternating Stimulus Tests*	Wolf and Denckla, 2005
RIAS	*Reynolds Intellectual Assessment Scales*	Reynolds and Kamphaus, 2003

(Continued)

Test Abbreviation	Test Name	Citation
ROWPVT-4	*Receptive One-Word Picture Vocabulary Test—Fourth Edition*	Brownell, 2010b
ROWPVT-SBE	*Receptive One-Word Picture Vocabulary Test: Spanish—Bilingual Edition*	Brownell, 2000
SB5	*Stanford-Binet Intelligence Scales—Fifth Edition*	Roid, 2003
SPELT-P 2	*Structured Photographic Expressive Language Test—Preschool 2*	Dawson, Stout, Eyer, Tattersall, Fonkalsrud, and Croley, 2005
SPELT-3	*Structured Photographic Expressive Language Test 3*	Dawson, Stout, and Eyer, 2003
TAPS-3	*Test of Auditory Processing Skills—3*	Martin and Brownell, 2005
TEA-Ch	*Test of Everyday Attention for Children*	Manly, Robertson, Anderson, and Nimmo-Smith, 1999
TOC	*Test of Orthographic Competence*	Mather, Roberts, Hammill, and Allen, 2008
TOMAL-2	*Test of Memory and Learning—Second Edition*	Reynolds and Voress, 2007
TOPA-2+ KE	*Test of Phonological Awareness—Second Edition Plus—Kindergarten Edition*	Torgensen and Bryant, 2004
TOPA-2+ EEE	*Test of Phonological Awareness—Second Edition Plus—Early Elementary Edition*	Torgensen and Bryant, 2004
TOPAS	*Test of Phonological Awareness Skills*	Newcomer and Barenbaum, 2003
TOSWRF	*Test of Silent Word Reading Fluency*	Mather, Hammill, Allen, and Roberts, 2004
TOWRE	*Test of Word Reading Efficiency—Second Edition*	Torgensen, Wagner, and Rashote, 2012
TPAS	*Test of Phonological Awareness in Spanish*	Riccio, Imhoff, Hasbrouck, and Davis, 2004

(continued)

(Continued)

Test Abbreviation	Test Name	Citation
TVPS-3	*Test of Visual Perceptual Skills*	Martin, 2006
UNIT	*Universal Nonverbal Intelligence Test*	Bracken and McCallum, 1998
WCST	*Wisconsin Card Sorting Test*	Heaton, Chelune, Talley, Kay, and Curtiss, 1993
WIAT-II	*Wechsler Individual Achievement Test—Second Edition*	Wechsler, 2001
WIAT-III	*Wechsler Individual Achievement Test—Third Edition*	Wechsler, 2009a
WISC-IV	*Wechsler Intelligence Scale for Children—Fourth Edition*	Wechsler, 2004
WISC-IV Integrated	*Wechsler Intelligence Scale for Children—Fourth Edition Integrated*	Wechsler et al., 2004
WMS-IV	*Wechsler Memory Scale—Fourth Edition*	Wechsler, 2009b
WIST	*Word Identification and Spelling Test*	Wilson and Fenton, 2004
WNV	*Wechsler Nonverbal Scale of Ability*	Wechsler and Naglieri, 2006
WRAML2	*Wide Range Assessment of Memory and Learning—Second Edition*	Sheslow and Adams, 2003
WRAVMA	*Wide Range Assessment of Visual-Motor Abilities*	Adams and Sheslow, 1995
WJIII-ACH NU	*Woodcock-Johnson III Tests of Achievement—Normative Update*	Woodcock, McGrew, and Mather, 2001, 2007b
WJIII-COG NU	*Woodcock-Johnson III Tests of Cognitive Abilities—Normative Update*	Woodcock, McGrew, and Mather, 2001, 2007a
WJIII-COG DS	*The Diagnostic Supplement to the Woodcock-Johnson III Tests of Cognitive Abilities*	Woodcock, McGrew, Mather, and Schrank, 2003, 2007

References

A new era: Revitalizing special education for children and their families. (2002). Report of the Presidents Commission on Excellence in Special Education: Author. Washington, DC: U.S. Department of Education, Author.

Achenbach, T. (2007a). *Child behavior checklist.* Burlington, VT: ASEBA.

Achenbach, T. (2007b). *Teacher rater form.* Burlington, VT: ASEBA.

Achenbach, T. (2007c). *Youth self report.* Burlington, VT: ASEBA.

Adams, W., & Sheslow, D. (1995). *Wide range assessment of visual motor abilities.* Odessa, FL: Psychological Assessment.

Alexander, G. E., DeLong, M. R., & Strick, P. L. (1986). Parallel organization of functionally segregated circuits linking the basal ganglia and cortex. *Annual Review of Neuroscience, 9,* 357–381.

Allen, A. B., Jesse, M. T., & Forsyth, B. (2011). Pediatric HIV/AIDS. In A. S. Davis (Ed.), *Handbook of pediatric neuropsychology* (pp. 865–876). New York, NY: Springer.

American Psychiatric Association. (2000). *Diagnostic and statistical manual of mental disorders: DSM-IV-TR.* Washington, DC: American Psychiatric Association.

Anderson, V. A., & Taylor, H. G. (2000). Meningitis. In K. O. Yeates, M. D. Ris, & H. G. Taylor (Eds.), *Pediatric neuropsychology: Research, theory, and practice* (pp. 117–148). New York, NY: Guilford Press.

Anderson, V., & Yeates, K. O. (2007). New frontiers in pediatric traumatic brain injury. *Developmental Neurorehabilitation, 10,* 269–270.

Apps, J. N., Newby, R. F., & Roberts, L. W. (2008). *Pediatric neuropsychology case studies: From the exceptional to the commonplace.* New York, NY: Springer.

Ardila, A. (2008). On the evolutionary origins of executive functions. *Brain and Cognition, 68*(1), 92–99.

Ardila, A., Roselli, M., & Puente, A. E. (1994). *Neuropsychological evaluation of the Spanish speaker.* New York, NY: Plenum Press.

Armengol, C. G., Kaplan, E., & Moes, E. J. (2001). *The consumer-oriented neuropsychological report.* Lutz, FL: Psychological Assessment Resources.

Arnstein, L. M., & Brown, R. T. (2005). Providing neuropsychological services to children exposed prenatally and perinatally to neurotoxins and deprivation. In D. C. D'Amato, E. Fletcher-Janzen, & C. R. Reynolds. (Eds.), *Handbook of school neuropsychology* (pp. 574–595). Hoboken, NJ: Wiley.

Atkinson, R. C., & Shiffrin, R. M. (1968). Human memory: A proposed system and its control processes. In K. W. Spence & J. T. Spence (Eds.), *The psychology of learning and motivation* (Vol. 2, pp. 89–195). New York, NY: Academic Press.

Awh, E., Jonides, J. J., Smith, E. E., Schumacher, E. H., Koeppe, R. A., & Katz, S. (1996). Dissociation of storage and rehearsal in verbal working memory: Evidence from positron emission tomography. *Psychological Science, 7,* 25–31.

Ayd, F. J. (1995). *Lexicon of psychiatry, neurology, and the neurosciences.* Baltimore, MD: Williams & Williams.

Baddeley, A. (1986). *Working memory.* New York, NY: Oxford University Press.

Baddeley, A. (1995). Working memory. In M. S. Gazzaniga (Ed.), *The cognitive neurosciences* (pp. 755–764). Cambridge, MA: MIT Press.

Baddeley, A. (2000). The episodic buffer: A new component of working memory? *Trends in Cognitive Sciences, 4*(11), 417–423.

Baddeley, A., Eysenck, M. W., & Anderson, M. C. (2008). *Memory*. New York, NY: Psychology Press.

Baddeley, A., & Hitch, G. (1974). Working memory. In G. H. Bower (Ed.), *The psychology of learning and motivation* (Vol. 8, pp. 47–89). New York, NY: Academic Press.

Baldo, J. V., Shimamura, A. P., Delis, D. C., Kramer, J., & Kaplan, E. (2001). Verbal and design fluency in patients with frontal lobe lesions. *Journal of the International Neuropsychological Society, 7*, 586–596.

Ball, M. F. (2002). *Developmental coordination disorder: Hints and tips for activities of daily living*. Philadelphia, PA: Kingsley.

Baraff, L. J., Lee, S. I., & Schriger, D. L. (1993). Outcomes of bacterial meningitis in children: A meta-analysis. *Pediatric Infectious Disease Journal, 12*, 389–394.

Barkley, R. A. (1996). Critical issues in research on attention. In G. R. Lyon & N. A. Krasnegor (Eds.), *Attention, memory, and executive function* (pp. 45–56). Baltimore, MD: Brookes.

Barkley, R. A. (2012a). *Barkley deficits in executive functioning scale: Children and adolescents*. New York, NY: Guilford Press.

Barkley, R. A. (2012b). *Executive functions: What are they, how they work, and why they evolved*. New York, NY: Guilford Press.

Barnes, M. A., Dennis, M., & Wilkinson, M. (1999). Reading after closed head injury in childhood: Effects on accuracy, fluency, and comprehension. *Developmental Neuropsychology, 15*, 1–24.

Baron, I. S. (2004). *Neuropsychological evaluation of the child*. New York, NY: Oxford University Press.

Baron, I. S., Wills, K., Rey-Casserly, C., Armstrong, K., & Westerveld, M. (2011). Pediatric neuropsychology: Toward subspecialty designation. *Clinical Neuropsychologist, 25*(6), 1075–1086.

Batchelor, E. S., Jr., & Dean, R. S. (1996). *Pediatric neuropsychology: Interfacing assessment and treatment for rehabilitation*. Boston: Allyn & Bacon.

Battro, A. M., Fischer, K. W., & Léna, P. J. (2008a). *The educated brain: Essays in neuroeducation*. New York, NY: Cambridge University Press.

Battro, A. M., Fischer, K. W., & Léna, P. J. (2008b). Introduction: Mind, brain, and education in theory and practice. In A. M. Battro, K. W. Fischer, & P. J. Léna (Eds.), *The educated brain: Essays in neuroeducation* (pp. 3–19). New York, NY: Cambridge University Press.

Bauman, M. L., & Kemper, T. L. (Eds.). (2005). *The neurobiology of autism*. Baltimore, MD: Johns Hopkins University Press.

Beery, K. E., Buktenica, N. A., & Beery, N. A. (2010). *Beery-Buktenica developmental test of visual-motor integration* (6th ed). San Antonio, TX: Pearson.

Begyn, E., & Castillo, C. L. (2010). Assessing and intervening with children with brain tumor. In D. C. Miller (Ed.), *Best practices in school neuropsychology: Guidelines for effective practice, assessment, and evidence-based intervention* (pp. 737–765). Hoboken, NJ: Wiley.

Belloni, K. C. (2011). *A confirmatory factor analytic comparison of the test of everyday attention for children*. Unpublished doctoral dissertation. Texas Woman's University, Denton, Texas.

Benson, D. F. (1991). The role of frontal dysfunction in attention deficit hyperactivity disorder. *Child Neurology, 6*, 9–12.

Benson, D.-F., & Geschwind, N. (1985). Aphasia and related disorders: A clinical perspective. In M.-M. Mesulam (Ed.), *Principles of behavioral neurology* (pp. 193–238), Philadelphia, PA: Davis.

Berninger, V. W. (2007a). *Process assessment for the learner—Second edition: Diagnostics for math*. San Antonio, TX: Pearson.

Berninger, V. W. (2007b). *Process assessment for the learner—Second edition: Diagnostics for reading and writing.* San Antonio, TX: Pearson.

Berninger, V. W. (2010). Assessment and intervention with children with written language disorders. In D. C. Miller (Ed.), *Best practices in school neuropsychology: Guidelines for effective practice, assessment, and evidence-based intervention* (pp. 507–520). Hoboken, NJ: Wiley.

Berninger, V. W., & Richards, T. L. (2002). *Brain literacy for educators and psychologists.* New York, NY: Academic Press.

Berninger, V. W., & Wolf, B. J. (2009). *Teaching students with dyslexia and dysgraphia: Lessons from teaching and science.* Baltimore, MD: Brooks.

Billingsley, R. L., Jackson, E. F., Slopis, J. M., Swank, P. R., Mahankali, S., & Moore, B. D. (2004). Functional MRI of visual-spatial processing in neurofibromatosis, type I. *Neuropsychologia, 42,* 395–404.

Block, G. W. (2002). Diagnostic subgroups and neuropsychological attention deficits in fetal alcohol syndrome. *Dissertation Abstracts International: Section B: The Sciences and Engineering, 62*(11-B), 5362.

Blondis, T. A. (2004). Neurodevelopmental motor disorders. In D. Dewey & D. E. Topper (Eds.), *Developmental motor disorders: A neuropsychological perspective* (pp. 113–136). New York, NY: Guilford Press.

Boehm, A. E. (2000). *Boehm test of basic concepts* (3rd ed.). San Antonio, TX: Harcourt.

Boehm, A. E. (2001). *Boehm test of basic concepts* (3rd ed . *preschool*). San Antonio, TX: Harcourt.

Boll, T. (1993). *The children's category test.* San Antonio, TX: Harcourt.

Bracken, B. A., & Boatwright, B. S. (2005). *Clinical assessment of attention deficit—Child.* Odessa, FL: Psychological Assessment.

Bracken, B. A., & McCallum, R. S. (1998). *Universal nonverbal intelligence test.* Itasca, IL: Riverside.

Brannigan, G. G., & Decker, S. L. (2003). *Bender visual-motor gestalt test* (2nd ed.). Itasca, IL: Riverside.

Brown, T. E. (1996). *Brown attention-deficit disorder scales for adolescents and adults.* San Antonio, TX: Harcourt.

Brown, T. E. (2001). *Brown attention-deficit disorder scales for children and adolescents.* San Antonio, TX: Harcourt.

Brownell, R. (Ed.). (2000a). *Expressive one-word picture vocabulary test: Spanish-bilingual edition.* Novato, CA: Academic Therapy.

Brownell, R. (Ed.). (2000b). *Receptive one-word picture vocabulary test: Spanish-bilingual edition.* Novato, CA: Academic Therapy.

Brownell, R. (Ed.). (2010a). *Expressive one-word picture vocabulary test, fourth edition.* Novato, CA: Academic Therapy.

Brownell, R. (Ed.). (2010b). *Receptive one-word picture vocabulary test, fourth edition.* Novato, CA: Academic Therapy.

Bruer, J. T. (1997). Education and the brain. *Educational Researcher, 26,* 4–16.

Bruer, J. Y. (2008). Building bridges in neuroeducation. In A. M. Battro, K. W. Fischer, & P. J. Léna (Eds.), *The educated brain: Essays in neuroeducation* (pp. 43–58). New York, NY: Cambridge University Press.

Burden, M. J., Jacobson, S. W., & Jacobson, J. L. (2005). Relation of prenatal alcohol exposure to cognitive processing speed and efficiency in childhood. *Alcoholism: Clinical and Experimental Research, 29,* 1473–1483.

Burden, M. J., Jacobson, S. W., Sokol, R. J., & Jacobson, J. L. (2005). Effects of prenatal alcohol exposure on attention and working memory at 7.5 years of age. *Alcoholism: Clinical and Experimental Research, 29*(3), 443–452.

Butler, R. W., Rorsman, I., Hill., J., & Tuma, R. (1993). The effects of frontal brain impairment on fluency: Simple and complex paridigms. *Neuropsychology, 7,* 519–529.

Butterworth, B., & Reigosa, V. (2007). Information processing deficits in dyscalculia. In D. B. Berch & M.M.M. Mazzocco (Eds.), *Why is math so hard for some children? The nature and origins of mathematical learning difficulties and disabilities* (pp. 65–81). Baltimore, MD: Brookes.

Carlson, N. R. (2010). *Physiology of behavior* (10th ed.). New York, NY: Allyn & Bacon.

Carroll, J. B. (1983). Studying individual differences in cognitive abilities: Through and beyond factor analysis. In R. F. Dillon (Ed.), *Individual differences in cognition* (Col. 1, pp. 1–33). New York, NY: Academic Press.

Carroll, J. B. (1993). *Human cognitive abilities: A survey of factor-analytic studies.* Cambridge, UK: Cambridge University Press.

Carrow-Woolfolk, E. (1999). *Comprehensive assessment of spoken language.* Austin, TX: PRO-ED.

Carrow-Woolfolk, E. (2011). *Oral and written language scales* (2nd ed.). San Antonio: Pearson.

Casey, B. J., Tottenham, N., & Fossella, J. (2002). Clinical, imaging, lesion, and genetic approaches toward a model of cognitive control. *Developmental Psychobiology, 40,* 237–254.

Castellanos, F. X., Lee, P. P., Sharp, W., Jeffries, N. O., Greenstein, D. K., Clasen, L. S., et al. (2002). Developmental trajectories of brain volume abnormalities in children with attention-deficit hyperactivity disorder. *Journal of American Medical Association, 288,* 1740–1748.

Castillo, C. L. (Ed.). (2008). *Children with complex medical issues in schools: Neuropsychological descriptions and interventions.* New York, NY: Springer.

Centers for Disease Control and Prevention. (2007). *National health 7. Interview survey data. Table 1–1, lifetime asthma population estimates—In thousands—By age, United States: National health interview survey, 2007.* Atlanta, Georgia.

Centers for Disease Control and Prevention. (2010). Increasing prevalence of parent-reported attention deficit/hyperactivity disorder among children—United States, 2003 and 2007. *Morbidity and Mortality Weekly Report, 59*(4), 1439–1443.

Chan, R.C.K., Wang, L., Ye, J., Leung, W.W.Y., & Mok, M.Y.K. (2008). A psychometric study of the test of everyday attention for children in the Chinese setting. *Archives of Clinical Neuropsychology, 23,* 455–466.

Chaytor, N., & Schmitter-Edgecombe, M. (2003). The ecological validity of neuropsychological tests: A review of the literature on everyday cognitive skills. *Neuropsychology Review, 13,* 181–197.

Chow, T. W., & Cummings, J. L. (1999). Frontal-subcortical circuits. In B. L. Miller & J. L. Cummings (Eds.), *The human frontal lobes: Functions and disorders* (pp. 3–26). New York, NY: Guilford Press.

Cohen, M. J. (1997). *Children's memory scale.* San Antonio, TX: Harcourt.

Colaluca, B., & Ensign, J. (2010). Assessment and intervention with chronically ill children. In D. C. Miller (Ed.), *Best practices in school neuropsychology: Guidelines for effective practice, assessment, and evidence-based intervention* (pp. 693–736). Hoboken, NJ: Wiley.

Conners, C. K. (2008a). *Conners comprehensive behavior rating scales.* North Tonawanda, NY: Multihealth Systems.

Conners, C. K. (2008b). *Conners* (3rd ed.). North Tonawanda, NY: Multihealth Systems.

Conners, C. K., & Multihealth Systems Staff. (2004a). *Conners' continuous performance test II version 5 for windows (CPT II V.5).* North Tonawanda, NY: Multihealth Systems.

Conners, C. K., & Multihealth Systems Staff. (2004b). *Conners' kiddie continuous performance test.* North Tonawanda, NY: Multihealth Systems.

Connolly, A. J. (2011). *KeyMath3 diagnostic assessment.* San Antonio, TX: Harcourt.

Constantine, R. J., Boaz, T., & Tandon, B. (2010). Antipsychotic polypharmacy in children and adolescents in the fee-for-service component of a large scale Medicaid state. *Clinical Therapeutics, 32*(5), 949–959.

Cousins, P., Ungerer, J. A., Crawford, J. A., & Stevens, M. M. (1991). Cognitive effects of childhood leukemia therapy: A case for four specific deficits. *Journal of Pediatric Psychology, 16*, 475–488.

Craik, F.I.M., & Lockhart, R. S. (1972). Levels of processing: A framework for memory research. *Journal of Learning and Verbal Behaviors, 11*, 671–684.

Crespi, T. D., & Cooke, D. T. (2003). Specialization in neuropsychology: Contemporary concerns and considerations for school psychology. *School Psychologist, 57*, 97–100.

Cutting, L. E., Clements, A. M., Lightman, A. D., Yerby-Hammack, P. D., & Denckla, M. B. (2004). Cognitive profiles of neurofibromatosis type I: Rethinking nonverbal learning disabilities. *Learning Disabilities Research & Practice, 19*, 155–165.

Dallas Independent School District website. Retrieved from http://www.dallasisd.org/inside_disd/

Damasio, H., Eslinger, P., & Adams, H. P. (1984). Aphasia following basal ganglia lesions: New evidence. *Seminar in Neurology, 4*, 151–161.

D'Amato, R. C., Fletcher-Janzen, E., & Reynolds, C. R. (Eds.). (2005). *Handbook of school neuropsychology.* Hoboken, NJ: Wiley.

Davis, A. S. (2011). *Handbook of pediatric neuropsychology.* New York, NY: Springer.

Davis, J. M., & Broitman, J. (2011). *Nonverbal learning disabilities in children: Bridging the gap between science and practice.* New York, NY: Springer.

Dawson, J., Stout, C., & Eyer, J. (2003). *Structured photographic expressive language test—3.* DeKalb, IL: Janelle.

Dawson, J., Stout, C., Eyer, J., Tattersall, P., Fonkalsrud, J., & Croley, K. (2005). *Structured photographic expressive language test—Preschool 2* DeKalb, IL: Janelle.

Dawson, P., & Guare, R. (2010). *Executive skills in the children and adolescents, second edition: A practical guide to assessment and intervention.* New York, NY: Guilford Press.

Dean, R. S., & Woodcock, R. W. (1999). *The WJ-R and Bateria-R in neuropsychological assessment* (Research Report No. 3). Itasca, IL: Riverside.

Dean, R. S., & Woodcock, R. W. (2003). *Dean-Woodcock neuropsychological battery.* Itasca, IL: Riverside.

Dehn, M. J. (2006). *Essentials of processing assessment.* Hoboken, NJ: Wiley.

Dehn, M. J. (2008). *Working memory and academic learning: Assessment and intervention.* Hoboken, NJ: Wiley.

Dehn, M. J. (2010). *Long-term memory problems in children and adolescents: Assessment, intervention, and effective instruction.* Hoboken, NJ: Wiley.

Delis, D. (2012). *Delis-rating of executive function.* San Antonio, TX: Pearson.

Delis, D., Kaplan, E., & Kramer, J. H. (2001). *Delis-Kaplan executive function system examiner's manual.* San Antonio, TX: Psychological Corporation.

Delis, D. C., Kramer, J. H., Kaplan, E., & Ober, B. A. (1994). *California verbal learning test: Children's version.* San Antonio, TX: Harcourt.

DeOrnellas, K., Hood, J., & Novales, B. (2010). Assessment and intervention with children with reading disorders. In D. C. Miller (Ed.), *Best practices in school neuropsychology: Guidelines for effective practice, assessment, and evidence-based intervention* (pp. 305–328). Hoboken, NJ: Wiley.

DeRenzi, E., Perani, D., Carlesimo, G. A., Silveri, M. C., & Fazio, F. (1994). Prosopagnosia can be associated with damage confined to the right hemisphere—An MRI and PET study and a review of the literature. *Neuropsychologia, 32*, 893–902.

Dewey, D., & Tupper, D. E. (2004). *Developmental motor disorders: A neuropsychological perspective.* New York, NY: Guilford Press.

Dhurat, R., Manglani, M., Sharma, R., & Shah, N. K. (2000). Clinical spectrum of HIV infection. *Indian Pediatrics, 37*, 831–836.

Diller, L., Ben-Yishay, Y., Gerstman, L. J., et al. (1974). *Studies in cognition and rehabilitation in hemiplegia.* (Rehabilitation Monograph 50). New York, NY: New York University Medical Center Institute of Rehabilitation Medicine.

Division 40. (1989). Definition of a clinical neuropsychologist. *Clinical Neuropsychologist, 3,* 22.

Doman, R. J., Spitz, E. B., Zucman, E., Delacato, C. H., & Doman, G. (1960). Children with severe brain injuries. Neurological organization in terms of mobility. *JAMA, 174,* 257–262.

Donnelly, J. P. (2005). Providing neuropsychological services to learners with chronic illness. In D. C. D'Amato, E. Fletcher-Janzen, & C. R. Reynolds. (Eds.), *Handbook of school neuropsychology* (pp. 511–532). Hoboken, NJ: Wiley.

Donovan, M. S., & Cross, C. T. (Eds.). (2002). *Minority students in special and gifted education.* Washington, DC: National Academies Press.

Dooley, C. B. (2005). The behavioral and developmental outcome of extremely low birth weight infants: A focus on emotional regulation. (Doctoral Dissertation, Texas Woman's University, 2005). *Dissertations Abstracts International, 66,* 1755.

Dooley, C. B. (2010). Assessment and intervention with children with developmental delays. In D. C. Miller (Ed.), *Best practices in school neuropsychology: Guidelines for effective practice, assessment, and evidence-based intervention* (pp. 329–358). Hoboken, NJ: Wiley.

Doyle, A. E., Wilens, T. E., Kwon, A., Seidman, L. J., Faraone, S. V., Fried, R., . . . Biederman, J. (2005). Neuropsychological functioning in youth with bipolar disorder. *Biological Psychiatry, 58,* 540–548.

Dronkers, N.F.A. (1996). A new brain region for coordinating speech articulation. *Nature, 384,* 159–161.

Dunn, L. M., & Dunn, L. M. (2006). *Peabody Picture Vocabulary Test* (4th ed.). Minneapolis, MN: Pearson.

Dunn, L. M., Lugo, D. E., Padilla, E. R., & Dunn, L. M. (1986). *Test de Vocabulario en Imágenes Peabody.* Minneapolis, MN: Pearson.

Durston, S. A. (2003). A review of the biological bases of ADHD: What have we learned from imaging studies? *Mental Retardation and Developmental Disabilities Research Reviews, 9,* 184–195.

Elliott, C. D. (2007). *Differential ability scales* (2nd ed.). San Antonio, TX: Pearson.

Ernhart, C. B., Graham, F. K., & Eichman, P. L. (1963). Brain injury in the preschool child: Some developmental considerations II. Comparison of brain injured and normal children. *Psychological Monographs, 77* (11, Whole No. 574), 17–33.

Eslinger, P. J. (Ed.). (2002). *Neuropsychological interventions.* New York, NY: Guilford Press.

Espy, K. A., Moore, I. M., Kaufmann, P. M., Kramer, J. H., Matthay, K., & Hutter, J. J. (2001). Chemotherapeutic CNS prophylaxis and neuropsychologic change in children with acute lymphoblastic leukemia: A prospective study. *Journal of Pediatric Psychology, 26,* 1–9.

Evans, J. J., Floyd, R. G., McGrew, K. S., & Leforgee, M. H. (2002). The relations between measures of Cattell-Horn-Carroll (CHC) cognitive abilities and reading achievement during childhood and adolescence. *School Psychology Review, 31,* 246–262.

Ewing-Cobbs, L., Prasad, M., Fletcher, J. M., Levin, H. S., Miner, M. E., & Eisenberg, H. M. (1998). Attention after pediatric traumatic brain injury: A multidimensional assessment. *Child Neuropsychology, 4,* 81–86.

Fastenau, P. (1996). *Extended complex figure test.* Los Angeles, CA: Western Psychological Services.

Fayol, M., Zorman, M., & Lété, B. (2009). Associations and dissociations in reading and spelling French: Unexpectedly poor and good spellers. *BJEP monograph series II, 6—Teaching and learning writing, 1,* 63–75.

Feifer, S. G. (2010). Assessment and intervention with children with reading disorders. In D. C. Miller (Ed.), *Best practices in school neuropsychology: Guidelines for effective practice, assessment, and evidence-based intervention* (pp. 483–506). Hoboken, NJ: Wiley.

Feifer, S. G. (2011). How SLD manifests in reading. In D. P. Flanagan & V. C. Alfonso (Eds.), *Essentials of specific learning disabilities identification* (pp. 21–41). Hoboken, NJ: Wiley.

Feifer, S. G., & DeFina, P. A. (2000). *The neuropsychology of reading disorders: Diagnosis and intervention*. Middletown, MD: School Neuropsych Press.

Feifer, S. G., & DeFina, P. A. (2002). *The neuropsychology of written language disorders: Diagnosis and intervention*. Middletown, MD: School Neuropsych Press.

Feifer, S. G., & DeFina, P. A. (2005). *The neuropsychology of mathematics disorders: Diagnosis and intervention*. Middletown, MD: School Neuropsych Press.

Feifer, S. G., & Della Toffalo, D. A. (2007). *Integrating RTI with cognitive neuropsychology: A scientific approach to reading*. Middletown, MD: School Neuropsych Press.

Feifer, S. G., & Rattan, G. (2009). *Emotional disorders: A neuropsychological, psychopharmacological, and educational perspective*. Middletown, MD: School Neuropsych Press.

Feldmann, G. M., Kelly, R. M., & Diehl, V. A. (2004). An interpretative analysis of five commonly used processing speed measures. *Journal of Psychoeducational Assessment, 22*, 151–163.

Fennell, E. B. (2000). End-stage renal disease. In K. O. Yeates, M. D. Ris, & H. G. Taylor (Eds.), *Pediatric neuropsychology: Research, theory, and practice* (pp. 366–380). New York, NY: Guilford Press.

Finn, C. E., Rotherham, A. J., & Hokanson, C. R. (Eds.). (2001). *Rethinking special education for a new century*. Washington, DC: Thomas B. Fordham Foundation and the Progressive Policy Institute.

Fiorello, C. A., Hale, J. B., & Wycoff, K. L. (2012). Cognitive hypothesis testing. In D. P. Flanagan & P. L. Harrison (Eds.), *Contemporary intellectual assessment: Theories, tests, and issues* (pp. 484–496). New York, NY: Guilford Press.

Fischer, K. W., Gaowami, U., & Geake, J. (2010). The future of educational neuroscience. *Mind, Brain, and Education, 4*(2), 68–80.

Flanagan, D. P., & Alfonzo, V. C. (2011). *Essentials of specific learning disability identification*. Hoboken, NJ: Wiley.

Flanagan, D. P., Alfonso, V. C., Mascolo, J. T., & Sotelo-Dynega, M. (2012). Use of ability tests in the identification of specific learning disabilities within the context of an operational definition. In D. P. Flanagan & P. L. Harrison (Eds.), *Contemporary intellectual assessment: Theories, tests, and issues* (pp. 643–669). New York, NY: Guilford Press.

Flanagan, D. P., Alfonso, V. C., & Ortiz, S. O. (2012). The cross-battery assessment approach. In D. P. Flanagan & P. L. Harrison (Eds.), *Contemporary intellectual assessment: Theories, tests, and issues* (pp. 459–483). New York, NY: Guilford Press.

Flanagan, D. P., Alfonso, V. C., Ortiz, S. O., & Dynda, A. M. (2010). Integrating cognitive assessment in school neuropsychological evaluations. In D. C. Miller (Ed.), *Best practices in school neuropsychology: Guidelines for effective practice, assessment, and evidence-based intervention* (pp. 101–140). Hoboken, NJ: Wiley.

Flanagan, D. P., & Harrison, P. L. (2012). *Contemporary intellectual assessment: Theories, tests, and issues* (3rd ed.). New York, NY: Guilford Press.

Flanagan, D. P., & Kaufman, A. S. (2009). *Essentials of WISC-IV assessment* (2nd ed.). New York, NY: Wiley.

Flanagan, D. P., Ortiz, S. O., Alfonso, V. C., & Mascolo, J. T. (2006). *The achievement test desk reference (ATDR): Comprehensive assessment and learning disabilities*. Boston, MA: Allyn & Bacon.

Fletcher-Janzen, E. (2005). The school neuropsychological examination. In D. C. D'Amato, E. Fletcher-Janzen, & C. R. Reynolds. (Eds.), *Handbook of school neuropsychology* (pp. 172–212). Hoboken, NJ: Wiley.

Fletcher-Janzen, E., & Reynolds, C. R. (Eds.). (2008). *Neuropsychological perspectives on learning disabilities in the era of RTI: Recommendations for diagnosis and intervention*. Hoboken, NJ: Wiley.

Fletcher, J. M., Dennis, M., & Northrup, H. (2000). Hydrocephalus. In K. O. Yeates, M. D. Ris, & H. G. Taylor (Eds.), *Pediatric neuropsychology: Research, theory, and practice* (pp. 25–46). New York, NY: Guilford Press.

Fletcher, J. M., & Lyon, G. R. (1998). Reading: A research-based approach. In W. Evers (Ed.), *What's wrong in America's classrooms* (pp. 49–90). Stanford, CA: Hoover Institute Press.

Floyd, R. G., Bergeron, R., McCormack, A. C., Anderson, J. L., & Hargrove-Owens, G. L. (2005). Are Cattell-Horn-Carroll broad ability composite scores exchangeable across batteries? *School Psychology Review, 34,* 329–357.

Floyd, R. G., Evans, J. J., & McGrew, K. S. (2003). Relations between measures of Cattell-Horn-Carroll (CHC) cognitive abilities and mathematics achievement across the school-age years. *Psychology in the Schools, 40,* 155–171.

Frank, D. A., Augustyn, M., Knight, W. G., Pell, T., & Zuckerman, B. (2001). Growth, development, and behavior in early childhood following prenatal cocaine exposure. *Journal of the American Medical Association, 285,* 1613–1625.

Freeman, J. M., Vining, E.P.G., & Pillas, D. J. (2002). *Seizures and epilepsy in childhood: A guide* (3rd ed.). Baltimore, MD: Johns Hopkins University Press.

Freides, D. (1993). Proposed standard of professional practice: Neuropsychological reports display all quantitative data. *Clinical Neuropsychologist, 7,* 234–235.

Freides, D. (1995). Interpretations are more benign than data? *Clinical Neuropsychologist, 9,* 248.

Fried, P. A., & Simon, A. M. (2001). A literature review of the consequences of prenatal marijuana exposure: An emerging theme of a deficiency of executive function. *Neurotoxicology and Teratology, 23,* 1–11.

Fuggetta, G. P. (2006). Impairment of executive functions in boys with attention deficit/hyperactivity disorder. *Child Neuropsychology, 12,* 1–21.

Fundarò, C., Miccinesi, N., Baldieri, N. F., Genovese, O., Rendeli, C., & Segni, G. (1998). Cognitive impairment in school-age children with asymptomatic HIV infection. *AIDS Patient Care and STDs, 12*(2), 135–140.

Gadow, K. D., & Spraflin, J. (1997). *ADHD symptom checklist-4.* Odessa, FL: Psychological Assessment Resources.

Gazzaniga, M. S., Ivry, R. B., & Mangun, G. R. (2002). *Cognitive neuroscience: The biology of the mind* (2nd ed.). New York, NY: Norton.

Geary, D. C. (1993). Mathematical disabilities: Cognitive, neuropsychological, and genetic components. *Psychological Bulletin, 114,* 345–352.

Geary, D. C. (2003). Learning disabilities in arithmetic: Problem solving differences and cognitive deficits. In H. L. Swanson, K. Harris, & S. Graham (Eds.), *Handbook of learning disabilities* (pp. 199–212). New York, NY: Guilford Press.

Geary, D. C., Hoard, M. K., & Bailey, D. H. (2011). How SLD manifests in mathematics. In D. P. Flanagan, & V. C. Alfonso (Eds.), *Essentials of specific learning disability identification* (pp. 43–64). Hoboken, NJ: Wiley.

Geary, D. C., Hoard, M. K., Nugent, L., & Byrd-Craven, J. (2008). Development of number line representations in children with mathematical learning disability. *Developmental Neuropsychology, 33,* 277–299.

German, D. J. (2000). *Test of word finding* (2nd ed.). Austin, TX: PRO-ED.

Gilliam, J. E. (1995). *Attention deficit/hyperactivity disorder test.* Austin, TX: PRO-ED.

Gioia, G. A., Espy, K. A., & Isquith, P. K. (2003). *Behavior rating inventory of executive function—Preschool version.* Odessa, FL: Psychological Assessment.

Gioia, G. A., Isquith, P. K., Guy, S. C., & Kenworthy, L. (2000). *Behavior rating inventory of executive function professional manual.* Odessa, FL: Psychological Assessment.

Golden, C. J. (1986). *Manual for the Luria-Nebraska neuropsychological battery: Children's revision.* Los Angeles, CA: Western Psychological Services.

Golden, C. J. (1997). The Nebraska neuropsychological children's battery. In C. R. Reynolds & E. Fletcher-Janzen (Eds.), *Handbook of clinical child neuropsychology* (2nd ed., pp. 237–251). New York, NY: Plenum Press.

Golden, C. J. (2011). The Luria-Nebraska neuropsychological children's battery. In A. S. Davis (Ed.), *Handbook of pediatric neuropsychology* (pp. 367–378). New York, NY: Springer.

Golden, C. J., Hammeke, T. A., & Purish, A. D. (1978). Diagnostic validity of a standardized neuropsychological battery derived from Luria's neuropsychological tests. *Journal of Consulting and Clinical Psychology, 46,* 1258–1265.

Goldman, R. & Fristoe, M. (2000). *Goldman-Fristoe test of articulation 2.* Bloomington, MN: Pearson.

Goldschmidt, L., Richardson, G. A., Cornelius, M. D., & Day, N. L. (2004). Prenatal marijuana and alcohol exposure and academic achievement at age 10. *Neurotoxicology and Teratology, 26,* 521–532.

Goldstein, S., & Reynolds, C. R. (Eds.). (2010). *Handbook of neurodevelopmental and genetic disorders in children* (2nd ed.). New York, NY: Guilford Press.

Gordon, M. (1983). *The Gordon diagnostic system.* Dewitt, NY: Gordon.

Gordon, M., McClure, F. D., & Aylward, G. P. (1996). *Gordon diagnostic system interpretative guide* (3rd ed.). DeWitt, NY: Gordon.

Greenberg, L. M., & Waldman, I. D. (1993). Developmental normative data on the test of variables of attention (T.O.V.A.). *Journal of Child Psychology and Psychiatry, 34,* 1019–1030.

Guy, S. C., Isquith, P. K., & Gioia, G. A. (2004). *Behavior rating inventory of executive function—Self-report version.* Odessa, FL: Psychological Assessment Resources.

Hale, J. B., Alfonso, V., Berninger, V., Bracken, C., Christo, C., Clark, E., et al. (2010a). *White paper on evaluation, identification, and eligibility criteria for students with specific learning disabilities.* Learning Disabilities Association of American. Pittsburgh, Pennsylvania.

Hale, J. B., Alfonso, V., Berninger, V., Bracken, C., Christo, C., Clark, E., et al. (2010b). Critical issues in response-to-intervention, comprehensive evaluation, and specific learning disabilities identification and intervention: An expert white paper consensus. *Learning Disability Quarterly, 33*(1), 223–236.

Hale, J. B., & Fiorello, C. A. (2004). *School neuropsychology: A practitioner's handbook.* New York, NY: Guilford Press.

Hale, J. B., Fiorello, C. A., Dumont, R., Willis, J. O., Rackley, C., & Elliott, C. (2008). Differential ability scales—Second Edition: (Neuro)Psychological predictors of math performance for typical children and children with math disabilities. *Psychology in the Schools, 45,* 838–858.

Hale, J. B., Fiorello, C. A., Miller, J. A., Wenrich, K., Teodori, A., & Henzel, J. N. (2008). WISC-IV interpretation for specific learning disabilities identification and intervention: A cognitive hypothesis testing approach. In A. Prifitera, D. H. Saklofske, & L. Weiss (Eds.), *WISC-IV clinical assessment and intervention* (2nd ed., pp. 109–171). New York, NY: Elsevier.

Hale, J. B., Reddy, L. A., Wilcox, G., McLaughlin, A., Hain, L., Stern, A., . . . Eusebio, E. (2010). Assessment and intervention practices for children with ADHD and other frontal-striatal circuit disorders. In D. C. Miller (Ed.), *Best practices in school neuropsychology: Guidelines for effective practice, assessment, and evidence-based intervention* (pp. 225–280). Hoboken, NJ: Wiley.

Halstead, W. (1952). The frontal lobes and the highest integrating capacities of man. *Halstead papers, M175,* 26 Akron, OH: Archives of the History of American Psychology.

Hammill, D. D. (1990). On defining learning disabilities: An emerging consensus. *Journal of Learning Disabilities, 23,* 74–84.

Hammill, D., & Newcomer, P. (1997a). *Test of language development (intermediate)* (3rd ed.). Austin, TX: PRO-ED.

Hammill, D., & Newcomer, P. (1997b). *Test of language development (primary)* (3rd ed.). Austin, TX: PRO-ED.

Hammill, D., Pearson, N. A., & Wiederholt, J. L. (2009). *Comprehensive test of nonverbal intelligence* (2nd ed.). Austin, TX: PRO-ED.

Hannay, H. J., Bieliauskas, L. A., Crosson, B. A., Hammeke, T. A., Hamsher, K. S., & Koffler, S. P. (1998). Proceedings: The Houston conference on specialty education and training in clinical neuropsychology. *Archives in Clinical Neuropsychology Special Issue, 13,* 157–250.

Harrison, P., Cummings, J., Dawson, M., Short, R., Gorin, S., & Palomares, R. (2004). Responding to the needs of children, families, and schools: The 2002 conference on the future of school psychology. *School Psychology Review, 33,* 12–33.

Hartlage, L. C., Asken, M. J., & Hornsby, J. L. (Eds.). (1987). *Essentials of neuropsychological assessment.* New York, NY: Springer.

Hartlage, L. C., & Telzrow, C. F. (1986). *Neuropsychological assessment and intervention with children and adolescents.* Sarasota, FL: Professional Resource Exchange.

Heaton, R. K. (1981). *Wisconsin card sorting test manual.* Odessa, FL: Psychological Assessment Resources.

Heaton, R. K., Chelune, G. J., Talley, J. L., Kay, G., & Curtiss, G. (1993). *Wisconsin card sorting test manual.* Odessa, FL: Psychological Assessment Resources.

Heaton, R. K., Grant, I., & Matthews, C. G. (1991). *Comprehensive norms for expanded Halstead-Reitan battery: Demographic corrections, research findings, and clinical applications.* Odessa, FL: Psychological Assessment Resources.

Hebben, N., & Milberg, W. (2009). *Essentials of neuropsychological assessment* (2nd ed.). Hoboken, NJ: Wiley.

Heilman, K. M., Voeller, K.K.S., & Nadeau, S. E. (1991). A possible pathophysiological substrate of attention deficit hyperactivity disorder. *Journal of Child Neurology, 6,* 76–81.

Hertza, J., & Estes, B. (2001). Developmental dyspraxia and developmental coordination disorder (pp. 593–602). In A. S. Davis (Ed.), *Handbook of pediatric neuropsychology.* New York, NY: Springer.

Hess, R. S., & Rhodes, R. L. (2005). Providing neuropsychological services to culturally and linguistically diverse learners. In D. C. D'Amato, E. Fletcher-Janzen, & C. R. Reynolds (Eds.), *Handbook of school neuropsychology* (pp. 637–660). Hoboken, NJ: Wiley.

Holland, M. L., Gimpel, G. A., & Merrell, K. W. (1998). *ADHD symptoms rating scale.* Odessa FL: Psychological Assessment Resources.

Hooper, S. R. (2010). Strengths and weaknesses of the NEPSY-II. In S. Kemp & M. Korkman (Eds.), *Essentials of NEPSY-II assessment* (pp. 227–249). Hoboken, NJ: Wiley.

Horn, J. L. (1988). Thinking about human abilities. In J. R. Nesselroade & R. B. Cattell (Eds.), *Handbook of multivariate psychology* (Rev. ed., pp. 645–685). New York, NY: Academic Press.

Horn, J. L. (1994). Theory of fluid and crystallized intelligence. In R. J. Sternberg (Ed.), *Encyclopedia of human intelligence* (pp. 443–451). New York, NY: MacMillan.

Horn, J. L., & Blankson, A. N. (2012). Foundations for better understanding of cognitive abilities. In D. P. Flanagan & P. L. Harrison (Eds.), *Contemporary intellectual assessment: Theories, tests, and issues* (pp. 73–98). New York, NY: Guilford Press.

Horton Jr., A. M., Soper, H. V., McHale, T., & Doig, H. M. (2011). Pediatric neuropsychology of substance abuse (pp. 943–954). In A. S. Davis (Ed.), *Handbook of pediatric neuropsychology.* New York, NY: Springer.

Hresko, W. P., Reid, D. K., & Hammill, D. D. (1999). *Test of early language development* (3rd ed.). Austin, TXPRO-ED.

Hurewitz, F., & Kerr, S. (2011). The role of the independent neuropsychologist in special education. *Clinical Neuropsychologist, 25*(6), 1058–1074.

Hynd, G. W. (1981). Training the school psychologist in neuropsychology: Perspectives, issues, and models. In G. W. Hynd & J. E. Obrzut (Eds.), *Neuropsychological assessment of the school-aged child* (pp. 379–404). New York, NY: Allyn & Bacon.

Hynd, G. W., & Obrzut, J. E. (1981). School neuropsychology. *Journal of School Psychology, 19,* 45–50.

Hynd, G. W., & Reynolds, C. R. (2005). School neuropsychology: The evolution of a specialty in school psychology. In D. C. D'Amato, E. Fletcher-Janzen, & C. R. Reynolds (Eds.), *Handbook of school neuropsychology* (pp. 3–14). Hoboken, NJ: Wiley.

Hynd, G. W., & Willis, W. G. (1988). *Pediatric neuropsychology.* New York, NY: Grune & Stratton.

Jeremy, R. J., Kim, S., Nozyce, M., Nachman, S., McIntosh, K., Pelton, S. I., et al. (2005). Neuropsychological functioning and viral load in stable antiretroviral therapy-experienced HIV-infected children. *Pediatrics, 115*(2), 380–387.

Jiron, C. (2004). *Brainstorming: Using neuropsychology in the schools.* Los Angeles, CA: Western Psychological Services.

Jiron, C. (2010). Assessing and intervening with children with externalizing disorders. In D. C. Miller (Ed.), *Best practices in school neuropsychology: Guidelines for effective practice, assessment, and evidence-based intervention* (pp. 359–386). Hoboken, NJ: Wiley.

Johnson, J. A., & D'Amato, R. C. (2011). Examining and using the Halstead-Reitan neuropsychological test battery: Is it our future or our past? In A. S. Davis (Ed.), *Handbook of pediatric neuropsychology* (pp. 353–365). New York, NY: Springer.

Jonides, J. J., Marshuetz, C., Smith, E. E., Reuter-Lorenz, P. A., Koeppe, R. A., & Hartley, A. (2000). Age differences in behavior and PET activation reveal differences in interference resolution in verbal working memory. *Journal of Cognitive Neuroscience, 12,* 188–625.

Jonides, J. J., Smith, E. E., Koeppe, R. A., Awh, E., Minoshima, S., & Mintun, M. A. (1993). Spatial working memory in humans revealed by PET. *Nature, 363,* 623–625.

Kail, R. (2000). Speed of information processing: Developmental change and links to intelligence. *School Psychology Review, 38,* 51–61.

Kail, R. V. (2007). Speed of processing in childhood and adolescence: Nature, consequences, and implications for understanding atypical development. In J. DeLuca & J. H. Kalmar (Eds.), *Information processing speed in clinical applications* (pp. 101–123). New York, NY: Taylor & Francis.

Kail, R. V., & Miller, C. A. (2006). Developmental change in processing speed: Domain specificity and stability during childhood and adolescence. *Journal of Cognition and Development, 7,* 119–137.

Kaplan, E., Fein, D., Kramer, J., Delis D., & Morris, R. (1999). *WISC-III PI manual.* San Antonio. TX: Psychological Corporation.

Kaufman, A. S., & Kaufman, N. L. (2004). *Kaufman assessment battery for children* (2nd ed.). Circle Pines, MN: American Guidance.

Kaufman, A. S., & Kaufman, N. L. (2005). *Kaufman test of educational achievement* (2nd ed.). Circle Pines, MN: American Guidance Service.

Kavros, P. M., Clarke, T., Strug, L. J., Halperin, J. M., Dorta, N. J., & Pal, D. K. (2008). Attention impairment in rolandic epilepsy: Systematic review. *Epilepsia, 49*(9), 1570–1580.

Keith, R. W. (1994). *Auditory continuous performance test examiner's manual.* San Antonio, TX: Harcourt.

Keith, T. Z., & Reynolds, M. R. (2012). Using confirmatory factor analysis to aid in understanding the constructs measured by intelligence tests. In D. P. Flanagan & P. L. Harrison (Eds.), *Contemporary intellectual assessment: Theories, tests, and issues* (pp. 758–799). New York, NY: Guilford Press.

Kemp, S., & Korkman, M. (2010). *Essentials of the NEPSY-II assessment.* Hoboken, NJ: Wiley.

Khan, N. & Lewis, L. (2002). *Khan-Lewis phonological analysis* (2nd ed.). Bloomington, MN: Pearson.

Kirk, S. A., McCarthy, J. J., & Kirk, W. D. (1968). *Illinois test of psycholinguistic abilities* (Rev. ed.). Urbana, IL: University of Illinois Press.

Kline, F. M., Silver, L. B., & Russell, S. C. (2001). *The educator's guide to medical issues in the classroom.* Baltimore, MD: Brookes.

Knecht, S., Drager, B., Deppe, M., Bobe, L., Lohmann, H., Floel, A., . . . Henningsen, H. (2001). Handedness and hemispheric language dominance in healthy humans. *Brain 2000, 123,* 2512–2518.

Korkman, M., Kirk, U., & Kemp, S. (1997). *NEPSY: A developmental neuropsychological assessment.* San Antonio, TX: Psychological Corporation.

Korkman, M., Kirk, U., & Kemp, S. (2007). *NEPSY-II: A developmental neuropsychological assessment.* San Antonio, TX: Psychological Corporation.

Kovaleski, J. F., & Prasse, D. (2005, March). Response to intervention (RTI): Considerations for identification and instructional reform. In D. C. Miller (Chair), *President's special strand: Assessment that informs effective instruction and intervention.* Symposium conducted at the meeting of the National Association of School Psychologists, Atlanta, Georgia.

Koziol, L. F., & Budding, D. E. (2010). *Subcortical structures and cognition: Implications for neuropsychological assessment.* New York, NY: Springer.

Kranowitz, C. S. (2005). *The out-of-sync child.* New York, NY: Penguin.

Kratochwill, T., & Shernoff, E. (2004). Evidence-based practice: Promoting evidence-based interventions in school psychology. *School Psychology Review, 33,* 34–48.

Lang, M. J. (2010). Assessment and intervention with children with autism spectrum disorders. In D. C. Miller (Ed.), *Best practices in school neuropsychology: Guidelines for effective practice, assessment, and evidence-based intervention* (pp. 281–304). Hoboken, NJ: Wiley.

Lange, S. M. (2005). School neuropsychology redux: Empirical versus arbitrary conclusions. *School Psychologist, 58,* 113–115.

Learning Disabilities Roundtable. (2002). *Specific learning disabilities: Finding common ground.* Washington, DC: U.S. Department of Education. Division of Research to Practice. Office of Special Education Program.

Learning Disabilities Roundtable. (2004). *Comments and recommendations on the regulatory issues under the individual with disabilities education improvement act of 2004.* Available at http://www.nasponline.org/advocacy/2004LDRoundtableRecsTransmittal.pdf

Leckliter, I. N., & Forster, A. A. (1994). The Halstead-Reitan neuropsychological test battery for older children. A need for new standardization. *Developmental Neuropsychology, 10,* 455–471.

Leffard, S. A. (2009). Working memory deficits in children: Contributions of executive control processes and symptoms of ADHD. *Dissertation Abstracts International: Section B; The Sciences and Engineering, 69*(7–8), 4430.

Levy, D. A., Bayley, P. J., & Squire, L. R. (2004). The anatomy of semantic knowledge: Medial vs. lateral temporal lobe. *Proceedings of the National Academy of Sciences of the United States of America, 101*(17), 6710–6715.

Lewin, J. S., Friedman, L., Wu, D., Miller, D. A., Thompson, L. A., Klein, S. K. et al. (1996). Cortical localization of human sustained attention: Detection with functional MR using a visual vigilance paradigm. *Journal of Computer Assisted Tomography, 20,* 695–701.

Lewis, D. O., Pincus, J. H., Bard, B., Richardson, E., et al. (1988). Neuropsychiatric, psychoeducational, and family characteristics of 14 juveniles condemned to death in the United States. *American Journal of Psychiatry, 145,* 584–589.

Lichtenberger, E. O., Mather, N., Kaufman, N. L., & Kaufman, A. S. (2004). *Essentials of assessment report writing.* Hoboken, NJ: Wiley.

Lichter, D. G., & Cummings, J. L. (2001). Introduction and overview. In D. G. Lichter & J. L. Cummings (Eds.), *Frontal-subcortical circuits in psychiatric and neurological disorders* (pp. 1–43). New York, NY: Guilford Press.

Lindamood, P. C., & Lindamood, P. (2004). *Lindamood auditory conceptualization test.* Austin, TX: PRO-ED.

Litt, J., Taylor, H. G., Klein, N., & Hack, M. (1995). Learning disabilities in children with very low birth weight: Prevalence, neuropsychological correlates, and educational interventions. *Journal of Learning Disabilities, 38*, 130–141.

Loring, D. W. (1999). *INS dictionary of neuropsychology*. New York, NY: Oxford University Press.

Loss, N., Yeates, K. O., & Enrile, B. G. (1998). Attention in children with myelomeningocele. *Child Neuropsychology, 4*, 7–20.

Loveday, C., & Edginton, T. (2011). Spina bifida and hyprocephalus. In A. S. Davis (Ed.), *Handbook of pediatric neuropsychology* (pp. 769–783). New York, NY: Springer.

Lowe, D. G., & Mitterer, J. O. (1982). Selective and divided attention in a Stroop task. *Canadian Journal of Psychology, 36*, 684–700.

Luria, A. R. (1966). *The working brain: An introduction to neuropsychology*. New York, NY: Basic Books.

Luria, A. R. (1973). *Higher cortical function in man*. New York, NY: Basic Books.

Luria, A. R. (1980). *Higher cortical functions in man* (2nd ed.). New York, NY: Basic Books.

Mabbott, D. J., Laughlin, S., Noseworthy, M., Rockel, C., & Bouffett, E. (2005). *Age related changes in DTI measures of white matter and processing speed.* Paper presented at the annual meeting of the Organization for Human Brain Mapping. Toronto, Canada.

Manly, T., Robertson, I. H., Anderson, V., & Nimmo-Smith, I. (1999). *Test of everyday attention for children (TEA-Ch) manual.* San Antonio, TX: Harcourt.

Maricle, D. E., Johnson, W., & Avirett, E. (2010). Assessing and intervening in children with executive function disorders. In D. C. Miller (Ed.), *Best practices in school neuropsychology: Guidelines for effective practice, assessment, and evidence-based intervention* (pp. 599–640). Hoboken, NJ: Wiley.

Maricle, D., Miller, D. C., Hale, J. B., & Johnson, W. L. (2012). Let's not lose sight of the importance of the biological bases of behavior. *Trainer's Forum. 31*(1), 71–84.

Maricle, D. E., Psimas-Fraser, L., Muenke, R. C., & Miller, D. C. (2010). Assessment and intervention with children with math disorders. In D. C. Miller (Ed.), *Best practices in school neuropsychology: Guidelines for effective practice, assessment, and evidence-based intervention* (pp. 521–550). Hoboken, NJ: Wiley.

Martin, J. A., Hamilton, B. E., Sutton, P. D., Ventura, S. J., Menacker, F., & Minson, M. L. (2003). Births: Final data for 2002. *National Vital Statistics Reports, 5210.* Hyattsville, MD: National Center for Health Statistics.

Martin, J. A., Osterman, M.J.K., & Sutton, P. D. (2010). Are preterm births on the decline in the United States? Recent data from the national vital statistics system. *NCHS Data Brief, No. 39*, 1–8.

Martin, N. (2006). *Test of visual perceptual skills—3.* Novato, CA: Academic Therapy.

Martin, N., & Brownell, R. (2005). *Test of auditory processing skills—3.* Novato, CA: Academic Therapy.

Maslow, A. H. (1943). A theory of human motivation. *Psychological Review, 50*(4), 370–396.

Matarazzo, R. G. (1995). Psychological report standards in neuropsychology. *Clinical Neuropsychologist, 9*, 249–250.

Mather, N., Hammill, D. D., Allen, E. A., & Roberts, R. (2004). *Test of silent word reading fluency.* Austin, TX: PRO-ED.

Mather, N., Roberts, R., Hammill, D. D., & Allen, E. A. (2008). *Test of orthographic competence.* Austin, TX: PRO-ED.

Mather, N., & Wendling, B. J. (2011). How SLD manifests in writing. In D. P. Flanagan & V. C. Alfonso (Eds.), *Essentials of specific learning disabilities identification* (pp. 65–88). Hoboken, NJ: Wiley.

Mather, N., & Wendling, B. J. (2012). *Essentials of dyslexia assessment and intervention.* Hoboken, NJ: Wiley.

Mazzocco, M.M.M. (2001). Math learning disability and math LD subtypes: Evidence from studies of turner syndrome, fragile X syndrome, and neurofibromatosis type 1. *Journal of Learning Disabilities, 34,* 520–533.

McCandliss, B. D., & Noble, K. G. (2003). The development of reading impairment: A cognitive neuroscience model. *Mental Retardation and Developmental Disabilities, 9,* 196–205.

McCarney, S. B. (2004a). *Attention deficit disorders evaluation scale* (3rd ed.). Columbia, MO: Hawthorne.

McCarney, S. B. (2004b). *Attention deficit disorders evaluation scale: Secondary-age student.* Columbia, MO: Hawthorne.

McCloskey, G., & Maerlender, A. (2005). The WISC-IV integrated. In A. Prifitera, D. H. Saklofske, & L. G. Weiss (Eds.), *WISC-IV clinical use and interpretation: Scientist-Practitioner perspectives* (pp. 101–149). New York, NY: Elsevier Academic Press.

McCloskey, G., Perkins, L. A., & Diviner, B. V. (2009). *Assessment and intervention for executive function difficulties.* Florence, KY: Routledge.

McCloskey, G., & Wasserman, J. (2012). *Essentials of executive function assessment.* Hoboken, NJ: Wiley.

McDiarmid, M. D. (2003). The relation between low-lead exposure and attention in preschool children. *Dissertation Abstracts International: Section B: The Sciences and Engineering, 69*(9-B), 4395.

McGrew, K. S. (2005). The Cattell-Horn-Carroll theory of cognitive abilities. In D. P. Flanagan & P. L. Harrison (Eds.), *Contemporary intellectual assessment* (2nd ed. , pp. 136–181). New York, NY: Guilford Press.

McGrew, K. S., & Evans, J. (2004). *Carroll human cognitive abilities project: Research report No. 2. Internal and external factorial extensions to the Cattell-Horn-Carroll (CHC) theory of cognitive abilities: A review of factor analytic research since Carroll seminal 1993 treatise.* St. Cloud, MN: Institute for Applied Psychometrics.

Meadow, W., Lee, G., Lin, K., & Lantos, J. (2004). Changes in mortality for extremely low birth weight infants in the 1990s: Implications for treatment decisions and resource use. *Pediatrics, 113*(5), 1223–1229.

Mecham, M. J. (2003). *Utah test of language development.* Austin, TX: PRO-ED.

Medicaid Medical Directors Learning Network and Rutgers Center for Education and Research on Mental Health Therapeutics. (2010). Antipsychotic medication use in medicaid children and adolescents: Report and resource guide from a 16-state study. *MMDLN/Rutgers CERTs Publication #1,* 1–4.

Meningitis research foundation website. Retrieved from http://www.meningitis.org

Metritech Staff. (1998). *ACTeRS self report.* Champaign, IL: Metritech.

Metz, K., Miller, M., & Thomas-Presswood, T. N. (2010). Assessing children who are deaf or hard of hearing. In D. C. Miller (Ed.), *Best practices in school neuropsychology: Guidelines for effective practice, assessment, and evidence-based intervention* (pp. 419–463). Hoboken, NJ: Wiley.

Metzler, L. A. (2010). *Promoting executive functions in the classroom (what works with special-needs learners).* New York, NY: Guilford Press.

Meyers, C. A., Berman, S. A., Scheibel, R. S., & Lesser, I. M. (1993). Case report: Acquired antisocial personality disorder associated with unilateral left orbital frontal lobe damage. *Journal of Psychiatry and Neuroscience, 17,* 121–125.

Middleton, F. A., & Strick, P. l. (2001). A revised neuroanatomy of frontal-subcortical circuits. In D. G. Lichter & J. L. Cummings (Eds.), *Frontal-subcortical circuits in psychiatric and neurological disorders* (pp. 44–58). New York, NY: Guilford Press.

Milberg, W. P., Hebben, N., & Kaplan, E. (2009). The Boston process approach to neuropsychological assessment. In I. Grant & K. M. Adams (Eds.),

Neuropsychological assessment of neuropsychiatric disorders (3rd ed., pp. 42–65). NY: Oxford University Press.

Milberg, W. P., Hebben, N., & Kaplan, E. (1996). The Boston process approach to neuropsychological assessment. In I. Grant & K. M. Adams (Eds.), *Neuropsychological assessment of neuropsychiatric disorders* (2nd ed., pp. 58–80). NY: Oxford University Press.

Miller, B. L., Chang, L., Mena, I., Boone, K., & Lesser, I. M. (1993). Progressive right frontotemporal degeneration: Clinical, neuropsychological and SPECT characteristics. *Dementia, 4*, 204–213.

Miller, B. L., & Cummings, J. L. (1999). *The human frontal lobes: Functions and Disorders*. New York, NY: Guilford Press.

Miller, D. C. (2004). Neuropsychological assessment in the schools. In C. Spielberger (Ed.), *Encyclopedia of applied psychology* (Vol. 2, pp. 657–664). San Diego, CA: Academic Press.

Miller, D. C. (2007). *Essentials of school neuropsychological assessment*. Hoboken, NJ: Wiley.

Miller, D. C. (Ed.). (2010). *Best practices in school neuropsychology: Guidelines for effective practice, assessment, and evidence-based intervention*. Hoboken, NJ: Wiley.

Miller, D. C. (2011). *Neuropsychological processing concerns checklist for children and youth* (2nd ed.). Hickory Creek, TX: KIDS.

Miller, D. C. (2012a). *Neuropsychological processing concerns checklist for children and youth* (3rd ed.). Hickory Creek, TX: KIDS.

Miller, D. C. (2012b). *School neuropsychological report shell: Version 19.0*. Hickory Creek, TX: KIDS, Inc.

Miller, D. C., & DeFina, P. A. (2010). The application of neuroscience to the practice of school neuropsychology. In D. C. Miller (Ed.), *Best practices in school neuropsychology: Guidelines for effective practice, assessment, and evidence-based intervention* (pp. 141–157). Hoboken, NJ: Wiley.

Miller, D. C., DeFina, P. A., & Lang, M. J. (2004). Working definition of school neuropsychology. In D. C. Miller (Ed.), *The neuropsychology of reading and writing disabilities*. Chicago, IL: 1st Annual National Association of School Psychologists' Summer Workshop.

Miller, D. C., DeOrnellas, K., & Maricle, D. (2008). The time for recognizing subspecialties in school has come. *Communique, 37*(5), *Bethesda*, MD: National Association of School Psychologists.

Miller, D. C., & Maricle, D. (2012). The emergence of neuropsychological constructs into tests of intelligence and cognitive abilities. In D. P. Flanagan & P. L. Harrison (Eds.), *Contemporary intellectual assessment: Theories, tests, and issues* (pp. 800–819). New York, NY: Guilford Press.

Miller, D. C., Maricle, D., & DeOrnellas, K. (2009). A follow-up survey to the question: Is it time for our organization to recognize subspecialties within school psychology? *Communique, 38* (5), Bethesda, MD: National Association of School Psychologists.

Miller, D. C., Maricle, D., & Mortimer, J. (2010). Memory tests in pediatric neuropsychology. In A. S. Davis (Ed.), *Handbook of pediatric neuropsychology* (pp. 275–291). New York, NY: Springer.

Miller, D. C., & Palomares, R. (2000, March). Growth in school psychology: A necessary blueprint. *Communiqué, 28*, 1, 6–7.

Miller, G. (1994). The magical number seven, plus or minus two: Some limits on our capacity for processing information. *Psychological Review, 101*, 343–352.

Miller, J. A. (2010). Assessing and intervening with children with internalizing disorders. In D. C. Miller (Ed.), *Best practices in school neuropsychology: Guidelines for effective practice, assessment, and evidence-based intervention* (pp. 387–417). Hoboken, NJ: Wiley.

Miniño, A. M. (2011). Death in the United States, 2009. *NCHS Data Brief, No. 64*, 1–8.

Mirsky, A. F. (1987). Behavioral and psychophysiological markers of disordered attention. *Environmental Health Perspectives, 74*, 191–199.

Mirsky, A. F. (1996). Disorders of attention: A neuropsychological perspective. In G. R. Lyon & N. A. Krasnegor (Eds.), *Attention, memory and executive function* (pp. 71–95). Baltimore, MD: Brookes.

Mirsky, A. F., Anthony, B. J., Duncan, C. C., Ahearn, M. B., & Kellam, S. G. (1991). Analysis of the elements of attention: A neuropsychological approach. *Neuropsychology Review, 2,* 109–145.

Mirsky, A. F., & Duncan, C. C. (2001). A nosology of disorders of attention. *Annuals of New York Academy of Sciences, 931,* 17–32.

Mirsky, A. F., Pascualvaca, D. M., Duncan, C. C., & French, L. M. (1999). A model of attention and its relation to ADHD. *Mental Retardation and Developmental Disabilities, 5,* 169–176.

Mody, M., & Sullivan, E. R. (Eds.). (2008). *Brain, behavior, and learning in language and reading disorders.* New York, NY: Guilford Press.

Moore, B. D., & Frost, M. K. (2011). Neurofibromatosis type 1: From gene to classroom. In A. S. Davis (Ed.), *Handbook of pediatric neuropsychology* (pp. 821–831). New York, NY: Springer.

Morrison, J. R. (2010). Assessing and intervening with children with traumatic brain injury. In D. C. Miller (Ed.), *Best practices in school neuropsychology: Guidelines for effective practice, assessment, and evidence-based intervention* (pp. 793–816). Hoboken, NJ: Wiley.

Muñoz-Sandoval, A. F., Cummins, J., Alvarado, C. G., Ruef, M. L., & Schrank, F. A. (2005). *Bilingual verbal ability tests (BVAT) normative update.* Itasca, IL: Riverside.

Naeser, M. A., Palumbo, C. L., Helm-Estabrooks, N., Stiassny-Eder, D., & Albert, M. L. (1989). Severe nonfluency in aphasia: Role of the medial subcallosal fasiculus and other white matter pathways in recovery of spontaneous speech. *Brain, 112,* 1–38.

Naglieri, J., & Das, J. P. (1997). *Das-Naglieri cognitive assessment system.* Itasca, IL: Riverside.

Naglieri, J. A., & Goldstein, S. (2012). *Comprehensive executive function inventory.* North Tonawanda, NY: Multihealth Systems.

Naglieri, J. A., & Goldstein, S. (Eds.). (2009). *Practitioner's guide to assessing intelligence and achievement.* Hoboken, NJ: Wiley.

National Association of School Psychologists. (2010). *Standards for graduate preparation of school psychologists, 2010.* Bethesda, MD.

National Institutes of Health: Medline Plus—Medical encyclopedia: Brain tumor—Children. Retrieved from http://www.nlm.nih.gov/medlineplus/ency/article/000768.htm

National Institute of Neurological Disorders and Stroke. (2012, May). NINDS neurofibromatosis information page. Retrieved from http://www.ninds.nih.gov/disorders/neurofibromatosis/neurofibromatosis.htm

National Mathematics Advisory Panel. (2008). *Foundations for success: The final report of the national mathematics advisory panel.* Washington, DC: U.S. Department of Education. Retrieved from www2.ed.gov/about/bdscomm/list/mathpanel/report/final-report.pdf

Naugle, R. I., & McSweeney, A. J. (1996). More thoughts on the practice of routinely appending raw data to reports: Response to Freides and Matarazzo. *Clinical Neuropsychologist, 10,* 313–314.

Nell, V. (2000). *Cross-cultural neuropsychological assessment: Theory and practice.* Mahwah, NJ: Erlbaum.

Newborg, J. (2005). *Battelle developmental inventory* (2nd ed.). Itasca, IL: Riverside.

Newcomer, P., & Barenbaum, E. (2003). *Test of phonological awareness skills.* Austin, TX: PRO-ED.

No Child Left Behind Act of 2001 (Pub. L. No. 107–110). *Most recent set of amendments to the elementary and secondary education act of 1965.* Available at http://www.nochildleftbehind.gov/

Noggle, C. A., Horwitz, J. L., & Davis, A. S. (2011). Neuroimaging and pediatric neuropsychology: Implications for clinical practice. In A. S. Davis (Ed.), *Handbook of pediatric neuropsychology* (pp. 1065–1076). New York, NY: Springer.

Norman, D., & Shallice, T. (1980). *Attention to action: Willed and automatic control of behavior.* Center for Human Information Processing Report 99. La Jolla: University of California, San Diego.

Novick, B. Z., & Arnold, M. M. (1988). *Fundamentals of clinical child neuropsychology.* Philadelphia, PA: Grune & Stratton.

Obrzut, J. E., & Hynd, G. W. (1986a). *Child neuropsychology Volume 1—Theory and research.* San Diego, CA: Academic Press.

Obrzut, J. E., & Hynd, G. W. (1986b). *Child neuropsychology Volume 2—Clinical practice.* San Diego, CA: Academic Press.

Obrzut, J. E., & Hynd, G. W. (1996). *Neuropsychological foundations of learning disabilities: A handbook of issues, methods, and practice.* New York, NY: Academic Press.

Odegard, T. N., Ring, J., Smith, S., Biggan, J., & Black, J. (2008). Differentiating neural response to intervention in children with developmental dyslexia. *Annuals of Dyslexia, 58*(1), 1–14.

Olds, D. (1997). Tobacco exposure and impaired development: A review of the evidence. *Mental Retardation and Developmental Disabilities, 3,* 257–269.

Ortiz, S. O., Ochoa, S. H., & Dynda, A. M. (2012). Testing with culturally and linguistically diverse populations: Moving beyond the verbal-performance dichotomy into evidence-based practice. In D. P. Flanagan & P. L. Harrison (Eds.), *Contemporary intellectual assessment: Theories, tests, and issues* (pp. 526–552). New York, NY: Guilford Press.

Owen, W. J., Borowsky, R., & Sarty, G. E. (2004). FMRI of two measures of phonological processing in visual word recognition: Ecological validity matters. *Brain and Language, 90,* 40–46.

Pardo, J. V., Pardo, P., Janer, K., & Raichle, M. E. (1991). Localization of a human system for sustained attention by positron emission tomography. *Nature, 349,* 61–64.

Patel, N. C. (2005). Antipsychotic use in children and adolescents from 1996 to 2001: Epidemiology, prescribing practices, and relationships with service utilization. *Dissertation Abstracts International: Section B: The Sciences & Engineering, 65*(8-B), 3942.

Patterson, K., & Ralph, M.A.L. (1999). Selective disorders of reading? *Current Opinion in Neurobiology, 36,* 767–776.

Pearson, D. A., McGrath, N. M., Nozyce, M., Nichols, S. L., Raskino, C., Brouwers, P., et al. (2000). Predicting HIV disease progression in children using measures of neuropsychological and neurological functioning. *Pediatrics, 10*(6). Available at www.pediatrics.org/cgi/content/full/106/6/e76

Pelletier, S.L.F., Hiemenz, J. R., & Shapiro, M. B. (2004). The application of neuropsychology in the schools should not be called school neuropsychology: A rejoinder to Crespi and Cooke. *School Psychologist, 58,* 17–24.

Petersen, R. L., Yeates, K. O., Ris, M. D., Taylor, H. G., & Pennington, B. F. (2009). *Pediatric neuropsychology, second edition: Research, theory, and practice.* New York, NY: Guilford Press.

Posner, M. (1994). Attention: The mechanisms of consciousness. *Proceedings of the National Academy of Science U.S.A., 91,* 7398–7403.

Posner, M. I., & Peterson, S. E. (1990). The attention system of the human brain. *Annual Review of Neuroscience, 13,* 25–42.

Posner, M. I., & Raichle, M. E. (1994). *Images of mind.* New York, NY: Freeman.

Pontón, M. O., & Leon-Carrión, J. (2001). *Neuropsychology and the Hispanic patient: A clinical handbook.* Mahwah, NJ: Lawrence Erlbaum Associates, Inc.

Prifitera, A., Saklofske, D. H., & Weiss, L. G. (2005). *WISC-IV clinical use and interpretation: Scientist-practitioner perspectives.* New York, NY: Elsevier Academic Press.

Prout, H. T., Cline, G. D., & Prout, S. M. (2010). School re-entry for children recovering from neurological conditions. In D. C. Miller (Ed.), *Best practices in school neuropsychology: Guidelines for effective practice, assessment, and evidence-based intervention* (pp. 207–224). Hoboken, NJ: Wiley.

Pulsifer, M. B., & Aylward, E. H. (2000). Human immunodeficiency virus. In K. O. Yeates, M. D. Ris, & H. G. Taylor (Eds.), *Pediatric neuropsychology: Research, theory, and practice* (pp. 381–402). New York, NY: Guilford Press.

Reed, J. C., & Reitan, R. M. (1969). Verbal and performance difference among brain injured children with lateralized motor deficits. *Perceptual and Motor Skills, 29,* 747–752.

Reed, J., & Warner-Rigers, J. (Eds.). (2008). *Child neuropsychology: Concepts, theory, and practice.* New York, NY: Wiley-Blackwell.

Reitan, R. M. (1955). Discussion: Symposium on the temporal lobe. *Archives of Neurology and Psychiatry, 74,* 569–570.

Reitan, R. M. (1959). Impairment of abstraction ability in brain damage: Quantitative versus qualitative changes. *Journal of Psychology, 48,* 97–102.

Reitan, R. M. (1960). The significance of dysphasia for intelligence and adaptive abilities. *Journal of Psychology, 56,* 355–376.

Reitan, R. M. (1971). Sensorimotor functions in brain-damaged and normal children of early school age. *Perceptual and Motor Skills, 32,* 655–664.

Reitan, R. M., & Davidson, L. A. (Eds.). (1974). *Clinical neuropsychology: Current status and applications.* Washington, DC: Winston.

Reitan, R. M., & Wolfson, D. (1985). *The Halstead-Reitan neuropsychological test battery: Theory and clinical interpretation.* Tucson, AZ: Neuropsychological Press.

Reitan, R. M., & Wolfson, D. (1992). *Neuropsychological evaluation of older children.* Tucson, AZ: Neuropsychology Press.

Reitan, R. M., & Wolfson, D. (1993). *The Halstead-Reitan neuropsychological test battery: Theory and clinical interpretation* (2nd ed.). Tucson, AZ: Neuropsychology Press.

Report of the INS-Division 40 Task Force on Education, Accreditation, and Credentialing. (1987). Guidelines for doctoral training programs in clinical neuropsychology. *Clinical Neuropsychologist, 1,* 29–34.

Report of the surgeon general's conference on children's mental health: A national action agenda. (2000). Washington, DC: U.S. Public Health Service, Department of Health and Human Services.

Reschly, D. J., Hosp, J. L., & Schmied, C. M. (2003). *And miles to go . . . : State SLD requirements and authoritative recommendations.* Report to the National Research Center on Learning Disabilities. Retrieved from http://www.nrcld.org/html/research/states/MilestoGo.pdf

Reynolds, C. R. (2008). RTI, neuroscience, and sense: Chaos in the diagnosis and treatment of learning disabilities. In E. Fletcher-Janzen & C. R. Reynolds (Eds.), *Neuropsychological perspectives on learning disabilities in the era of RTI* (pp. 14–27). Hoboken, NJ: Wiley.

Reynolds, C. R., & Bigler, E. D. (1994). *Test of memory and learning: Examiner's manual.* Austin, TX: PRO-ED.

Reynolds, C. R., & Fletcher-Janzen, E. (Eds.). (1989). *Handbook of clinical child neuropsychology.* New York, NY: Plenum Press.

Reynolds, C. R., & Fletcher-Janzen, E. (Eds.). (1997). *Handbook of clinical child neuropsychology* (2nd ed.). New York, NY: Plenum Press.

Reynolds, C. R., & Fletcher-Janzen, E. (Eds.). (2008). *Handbook of clinical child neuropsychology* (3rd ed.). New York, NY: Plenum Press.

Reynolds, C. R., & Kamphaus, R. W. (2003). *Reynolds intellectual assessment scales.* Lutz, FL: PAR.

Reynolds, C. R., & Kamphaus, R. W. (2004). *BASC-2 structured developmental history.* Circle Pines, MN: American Guidance.

Reynolds, C. R., & Kamphaus, R. W. (2009). *Behavior assessment system for children* (2nd ed.). San Antonio, TX: Pearson.

Reynolds, C. R., & Voress, J. K. (2007). *Test of memory and learning* (2nd ed.). Austin, TX: PRO-ED.

Reynolds, C. R., Voress, J. K., & Pearson, N. A. (2008). *Developmental test of auditory perception.* Austin: TX: PRO-ED.

Rhodes, R. L. (2000). Legal and professional issues in the use of interpreters: A fact sheet for school psychologists. *Communiqué, 29*(1), 28.

Riccio, C. A., Imhoff, B., Hasbrouck, J. E., & Davis, G. N. (2004). *Test of phonological awareness in Spanish.* Austin, TX: PRO-ED.

Riccio, C. A., Reynolds, C. R., & Lowe, P. A. (2001). *Clinical applications of continuous performance tests: Measuring attention and impulsive responding in children and adolescents.* Hoboken, NJ: Wiley.

Riccio, C. A., Reynolds, C. R., Lowe, P. A., & Moore, J. J. (2002). The continuous performance test: A window on the neural substrates for attention? *Archives of Clinical Neuropsychology, 17*, 235–272.

Riccio, C. A., Sullivan, J. R., & Cohen, M. J. (2010). *Neuropsychological assessment and intervention for childhood and adolescent disorders.* Hoboken, NJ: Wiley.

Rohling, M. L., Lees-Haley, P. R., Langhinrichsen-Rohling, J., & Williamson, D. J. (2003). A statistical analysis of board certification in clinical neuropsychology. *Archives of Clinical Neuropsychology, 18*, 331–352.

Roid, G. H. (2003). *Stanford-Binet intelligence scales: Fifth edition.* Itasca, IL: Riverside.

Rourke, B. P. (1982). Central processing deficits in children: Toward a developmental neuropsychological model. *Journal of Clinical Neuropsychology, 4*, 1–18.

Rourke, B. P. (1994). Neuropsychological assessment of children with learning disabilities. In G. R. Lyon (Ed.), *Frames of reference for the assessment of learning disabilities* (pp. 475–509). Baltimore, MD: Brookes.

Rourke, B. P. (Ed.). (1995). *Syndrome of nonverbal learning disabilities: Neurodevelopmental manifestations.* New York, NY: Guilford Press.

Rourke, B. P., Bakker, D. J., Fisk, J. L., & Strang, J. D. (1983). *Child neuropsychology: An introduction to theory, research, and clinical practice.* New York, NY: Guilford Press.

Rovet, J. F. (2000). Diabetes. In K. O. Yeates, M. D. Ris, & H. G. Taylor (Eds.), *Pediatric neuropsychology: Research, theory, and practice* (pp. 336–365). New York, NY: Guilford Press.

Rubia, K., Overmeyer, S. O., Taylor, E., Brammer, M., Williams, S.C.R., Simmons, A., et al. (1999). Hypofrontality in attention deficit hyperactivity disorder during higher order motor control: A study with functional MRI. *American Journal of Psychiatry, 156*, 891–896.

Salpekar, J., Berl, M., & Kenealy, L. (2011). Seizure disorders. In A. S. Davis (Ed.), *Handbook of pediatric neuropsychology* (pp. 932–942x). New York, NY: Springer.

Sandford, J. A., & Turner, A. (1993 –2006). *Integrated visual and auditory continuous performance test.* Richmond, VA: BrainTrain.

Sbordone, R. J. (1996). Ecological validity: Some critical issues for the neuropsychologist. In R. Sbordone & C. Long (Eds.), *Ecological validity of neuropsychological tests* (pp. 301–314). Delay Beach, FL: GR Press/St. Lucie Press.

Schatz, J., Kramer, J. H., Ablin, A., & Matthay, K. K. (2000). Processing speed, working memory, and IQ: A developmental model of cognitive deficits following cranial radiation therapy. *Neuropsychology, 14*, 189–200.

Schatz, J., Kramer, J. H., Ablin, A., & Matthay, K. K. (2004). Visual attention in long-term survivors of leukemia receiving cranial radiation therapy. *Journal of the International Nueropsychological Society, 10*, 211–220.

Schneider, J. C., & Walsh, K. S. (2008). HIV/AIDS. In C. L. Castillo (Ed.), *Children with complex medical issues in schools* (pp. 253–277). New York, NY: Springer.

Schneider, W. J., & McGrew, K. S. (2012). The Cattell-Horn-Carroll model of intelligence. In D. P. Flanagan & P. L. Harrison (Eds.), *Contemporary intellectual assessment: Theories, tests, and issues* (pp. 99–144). New York, NY: Guilford Press.

Schrank, F. A., Miller, D. C., Wendling, B. J., & Woodcock, R. W. (2010). *Essentials of WJ III cognitive abilities assessment.* Hoboken, NJ: Wiley.

Schrank, F. A., & Wendling, B. J. (2012). The Woodcock-Johnson III normative update. In D. P. Flanagan & P. L. Harrison (Eds.), *Contemporary intellectual assessment: Theories, tests, and issues* (pp. 297–335). New York, NY: Guilford Press.

Semel, E., Wiig, E. H., & Secord, W. A. (2003). *Clinical evaluation of language fundamentals* (4th ed.). San Antonio, TX: Harcourt.

Semrud-Clikeman, M. (2001). *Traumatic brain injury in children and adolescents*. New York, NY: Guilford Press.

Semrud-Clikeman, M., & Teeter-Ellison, P. A. (2009). *Child neuropsychology: Assessment and interventions for neurodevelopmental disorders* (2nd ed.). New York, NY: Springer.

Shapiro, E. G., & Ziegler, R. (1997). Training issues in pediatric neuropsychology. *Child Neuropsychology, 3,* 227–229.

Shaywitz, S. (2003). *Overcoming dyslexia: A new and complete science-based program for reading problems at any level*. New York, NY: Knopf.

Shaywitz, S., & Shaywitz, B. (2005). Dyslexia: Specific reading disability. *Biological Psychiatry, 57,* 1301–1309.

Sheslow, D., & Adams, W. (1990). *Wide range assessment of memory and learning*. Wilmington, DE: Wide Range.

Sheslow, D., & Adams, W. (2003). *Wide range assessment of memory and learning* (2nd ed.). Wilmington, DE: Wide Range.

Shordone, R. J., & Saul, R. E. (2000). *Neuropsychology for health care professionals and attorneys*. New York, NY: CRC Press.

Schrank, F. A., Miller, D. C., Wendling, B. J., & Woodcock, R. W. (2010). *Essentials of WJ III cognitive abilities assessment*. Hoboken, NJ: Wiley.

Siantz-Tyler, J., & Mira, M. P. (1999). *Traumatic brain injury in children and adolescents: A sourcebook for teachers and other school personnel*. Austin, TX: PRO-ED.

Simon, H. A. (1975). The functional equivalence of problem solving skills. *Cognitive Psychology, 7,* 268–288.

Slattery, S. L., & Morrison, J. J. (2002). Preterm delivery. *Lancet, 360,* 1489–1497.

Slomine, B., & Locascio, G. (2009). Cognitive rehabilitation for children with acquired brain injury. *Developmental Disabilities Research Reviews, 15,* 133–143.

Sobel, N., Prabhalaran, V., Desmond, J. E., Glover, G. H., Goode, R. L., Sullivan, E. V., & Gabrielli, J. D. (1998). Sniffing and smelling: Separate subsystems in the human olfactory cortex. *Nature, 392,* 282–286.

Squire, L. R. (1987). *Memory and brain*. New York, NY: Oxford University Press.

Stirling, J. (2002). *Introducing neuropsychology*. New York, NY: Psychology Press.

Streissguth, A., & O'Malley, K. (2000). Neuropsychiatric implications and long-term consequences of fetal alcohol spectrum disorders. *Seminars in Clinical Neuropsychiatry, 5,* 177–190.

Stroop, J. R. (1935). Studies of interference in serial verbal reactions. *Journal of Experimental Psychology, 18,* 643–662.

Stuss, D. T., & Alexander, M. P. (2000). Executive functions and the frontal lobes: A conceptual view. *Psychological Research, 63,* 289–298.

Stuss, D. T., Alexander, M. P., Hamer, L., Palumbo, C., Dempster, R., Binns, M., et al. (1998). The effects of focal anterior and posterior brain lesions on verbal fluency. *Journal of the International Neuropsychological Society, 4,* 265–278.

Swanson, H. L. (2008). Neuroscience and RTI: A complementary role. In E. Fletcher-Janzen & C. R. Reynolds (Eds.), *Neuropsychological perspectives on learning disabilities in the era of RTI* (pp. 28–53). Hoboken, NJ: Wiley.

Sweet, J. J., Meyer, D. G., Nelson, N. W., & Moberg, P. J. (2011). The TCN/AACN 2010 "salary survey": Professional practices, briefs, and incomes of U.S. neuropsychologists. *Clinical Neuropsychologist, 25*(1), 12–61.

Talley, J. L. (1994). *Children auditory verbal learning test—2*. Lutz, FL: PAR.

Taylor, J. (Ed.). (1932). *Selected writing of John Hughlings Jackson* (Vol. II). London, UK: Hodder and Stoughton.

Teeter, P. A., & Semrud-Clikeman, M. (1997). *Child neuropsychology: Assessment and interventions for neurodevelopmental disorders*. Boston, MA: Allyn & Bacon.

Thaler, N. S., Allen, D. N., Park, B. S., McMurray, J. C., & Mayfield, J. (2010). Attention processing abnormalities in children with traumatic brain injury and attention-deficit hyperactivity disorder: Differential impairment of component processes. *Journal of Clinical and Experimental Psychology, 32*(9), 929–936.

Torgensen, J. K., & Bryant, B. R. (2004). *Test of phonological awareness—Second edition: Plus*. Austin, TX: PRO-ED.

Torgensen, J. K., Wagner, R. K., & Rashotte, C. A. (2011). *Test of word reading efficiency* (2nd ed.). Austin, TX: PRO-ED.

Tupper, D. E., & Sondell, S. K. (2004). Motor disorders and neuropsychological development: A historical appreciation. In D. Dewey & D. E. Tupper (Eds.), *Developmental motor disorders: A neuropsychological perspective* (pp. 3–25). New York, NY: Guilford Press.

Tramontana, M. G., & Hooper, S. R. (Eds.). (1988). *Assessment issues in clinical neuropsychology*. New York, NY: Plenum Press.

Tramontana, M. G., & Hooper, S. R. (Eds.). (1992). *Advances in child neuropsychology* (Vol. 1) New York, NY: Springer-Verlag.

Ullmann, R. K., Sleator, E. K., & Sprague, R. L. (1991). *ADD-H: Comprehensive teacher's rating scale* (2nd ed.). Champaign, IL: Metritech.

Ullmann, R. K., Sleator, E. K., Sprague, R. L. & Metritech Staff. (1996). *ADD-H: comprehensive teacher's rating scale: Parent form*. Champaign, IL: Metritech.

Ungerleider, L. G., & Mishkin, M. (1982). Two cortical visual systems. In D. J. Engle, M. A. Goodale, & R. J. Mansfield (Eds.), *Analysis of visual behavior* (pp. 549–586). Cambridge, MA: MIT Press.

United Cerebral Palsy Press Room. (n.d.). *What is cerebral palsy?* Retrieved from http://www. ucp.org/ucp_generaldoc.cfm/1/9/37/37–37/447

U.S. Department of Education. (2004). *Individuals with disabilities education improvement act of 2004, 108–466*. *Federal Register, 70*, 35802–35803.

U.S. Department of Education. (2008). *Foundations of Success: The Final Report of the National Mathematics Advisory Panel*. Retrieved fromhttp://www.ed.gov/about/bdscomm/list/ mathpanel/index.html.

U.S. Department of Education, National Center for Education Statistics. (2011). *Digest of education statistics, 2010* (NCES 2011–015), Chapter 2.

U.S. Department of Education, Office of Special Education and Rehabilitative Services. (2011, January). *Memorandum to state directors of special education—A response to intervention (RTI) process cannot be used to delay-deny an evaluation for eligibility under the Individuals with Disabilities Act (IDEA)*.

U.S. Department of Health and Human Services. U.S. Public Health Services. (2001). *Report of the surgeon general's conference on children's mental health: A national action agenda*. Washington, DC.

Vaidya, C. J., Austin, G., Kirkorian, G., Ridlehuber, H. W., Desmond, J. E., Glover, G. H., et al. (1998). Selective effects of methylphenidate in attention deficit hyperactivity disorder: A functional magnetic resonance study. *Proceedings of the National Academy of Sciences, 95*, 14494–14499.

Valera, E. M., Faraone, S. V., Murray, K. E., & Seidman, L. J. (2007). Meta-analysis of structural findings in attention-deficit/hyperactivity disorder. *Biological Psychiatry, 61*, 1361–1369.

Van Cleave, J., Gortmaker, S. L., & Perrin, J. M. (2010). Dynamics of obesity and chronic health conditions among children and youth. *Journal of the American Medical Association, 303*(7), 623–630.

Vaurio, L., Crocker, N., & Mattson, S. N. (2011). Fetal alcohol spectrum disorders. In A. S. Davis (Ed.), *Handbook of pediatric neuropsychology* (pp. 877–886). New York, NY: Springer.

Vikingstad, E. M., Cao, Y., Thomas, A. J., Johnson, A. F., Malik, G. M., & Welch, K.M.A. (2004). Language hemispheric dominance in patients with congenital lesions of eloquent brain. *Neurosurgery, 47*, 562–570.

von Aster, M. (2000). Developmental cognitive neuropsychology of number processing and calculation: Varieties of developmental dyscalculia. *European Child and Adolescent Psychiatry, 11*, 41–57.

von Bronin, G. (Trans.). (1960). *Some papers on the cerebral cortex.* Springfield, IL: Thomas. (Original work published 1865)

Waber, D. H., & Mullenex, P. J. (2000). Acute lymphobalstic leukemia. In K. O. Yeates, M. D. Ris, & H. G. Taylor (Eds.), *Pediatric neuropsychology: Research, theory, and practice* (pp. 300–319). New York, NY: Guilford Press.

Wagner, R., Torgesen, J., & Rashotte, C. (1999). *Comprehensive test of phonological processing.* Minneapolis, MN: Pearson.

Wallace, G., & Hammill, D. D. (2002). *Comprehensive receptive and expressive vocabulary test.* Austin, TX: PRO-ED.

Wang, W. (2007). Central nervous system complications of sickle cell disease in children: An overview. *Child Neuropsychology, 13*, 103–119.

Warrington, E. K. (1985). Agnosia: The impairment of object recognition. In P. J. Vinken, G. W. Bruyn, & H. L. Klawans (Eds.), *Handbook of clinical neurology* (pp. 333–349). New York, NY: Elsevier.

Webbe, F. M., & Salinas, C. M. (2011). Sport neuropsychology for children. In A. S. Davis (Ed.), *Handbook of pediatric neuropsychology* (pp. 1095–1110). New York, NY: Springer.

Wechsler, D. (1981). *Wechsler adult intelligence scale—Revised: Manual.* New York, NY: Psychological Corporation.

Wechsler, D. (1991). *Wechsler intelligence scale for children* (3rd ed.). San Antonio, TX: Harcourt.

Wechsler, D. (2001). *Wechsler individual achievement test* (2nd ed.). San Antonio, TX: Harcourt.

Wechsler, D. (2003). *Wechsler intelligence scale for children* (4th ed.). San Antonio, TX: Harcourt.

Wechsler, D. (2004a). *Wechsler intelligence scale for children* (4th ed . integrated). San Antonio, TX: Harcourt.

Wechsler, D. (2004b). *WISC-IV Spanish.* San Antonio, TX: Harcourt.

Wechsler, D. (2009a). *Wechsler individual achievement test* (3rd ed.). San Antonio, TX: Harcourt.

Wechsler, D. (2009b). *Wechsler memory scale* (4th ed.). San Antonio, TX: Harcourt.

Wechsler, D., Kaplan, E., Fein, D., Morris, E., Kramer, J. H., Maerlender, A., & Delis, D. C. (2004). *The Wechsler intelligence scale for children—Fourth edition integrated technical and interpretive manual.* San Antonio, TX: Harcourt.

Wechsler, D., & Naglieri, J. (2006). *Wechsler nonverbal scale of ability.* San Antonio, TX: Harcourt.

Weinstein, C. (2001). For your information: Definition of a clinical neuropsychologist— Official position of the National Academy of Neuropsychology (Draft). *Massachusetts Neuropsychological Society Newsletter, 11*, 9.

Wiederholt, J. L., & Bryant, B. R. (2012). *Gray oral reading tests* (5th ed.). Austin, TX: PRO-ED.

Wiig, E. H., Secord, W. A., & Semel, E. (2006). *CELF-4 Spanish.* San Antonio, TX: Harcourt.

Willcutt, E. G., Pennington, B. F., Olson, R. K., Chhabildas, N., & Hulslander, J. (2005). Neuropsychological analyses of comorbidity between reading disability and attention deficit hyperactivity disorder: In search of the common deficit. *Developmental Neuropsychology, 27,* 35–78.

Williams, K. T. (2006). *Expressive vocabulary test* (2nd ed.). Bloomington, MN: Pearson.

Wilson, A. J., & Dehaene, S. (2007). Number sense and developmental dyscalculia. In D. Coch, G. Dawson, & K. W. Fischwer (Eds.), *Human behavior, learning, and the developing brain: Atypical development* (pp. 212–238). New York, NY: Guilford Press.

Wilson, B., & Fenton, R. (2004). *Word identification and spelling test.* Austin, TX: PRO-ED.

Wolf, M., & Denckla, M. B. (2005). *Rapid automatized naming and rapid alternating stimulus tests.* Austin, TX: PRO-ED.

Wolfe, M. E. (2006). Executive function processes: Inhibition, working memory, planning and attention in children and youth with attention deficit hyperactivity disorder. *Dissertation Abstracts International: Section B: The Sciences and Engineering, 66*(12-B), 6940.

Woodcock, R. W. (1990). Theoretical foundation of the WJ-R measures of cognitive ability. *Journal of Psychoeducational Assessment, 8,* 231–258.

Woodcock, R. W., & Johnson, M. B. (1989). *Woodcock-Johnson psychoeducational battery* (Rev.). Chicago, IL: Riverside.

Woodcock, R. W., McGrew, K. S., & Mather, N. (2001, 2007a). *Woodcock-Johnson III tests of cognitive abilities.* Itasca, IL: Riverside.

Woodcock, R. W., McGrew, K. S., & Mather, N. (2001, 2007b). *Woodcock-Johnson III tests of achievement.* Itasca, IL: Riverside.

Woodcock, R. W., McGrew, K. S., Mather, N., & Schrank, F. A. (2003, 2007). *The diagnostic supplement to the Woodcock-Johnson III tests of cognitive abilities.* Itasca, IL: Riverside.

Woodcock, R. W., Muñoz-Sandoval, A. F., McGrew, K. S., & Mather, N. (2005). *Bateróa III Woodcock-Muñoz.* Itasca, IL: Riverside.

Woodcock, R. W., Muñoz-Sandoval, A. F., Ruef, M. L., & Alcardo, C. G. (2005). *Woodcock-Muñoz language survey* (Rev.). Itasca, IL: Riverside.

Yalof, J., & McGrath, M. C. (2010). Assessing and intervening with children with nonverbal learning disabilities. In D. C. Miller (Ed.), *Best practices in school neuropsychology: Guidelines for effective practice, assessment, and evidence-based intervention* (pp. 579–596). Hoboken, NJ: Wiley.

Yeates, K. O., Bigler, E. D., Dennis, M., Gerhardt, C. A., Rubin, K. H., Stancin, T., et al. (2007). Social outcomes in childhood brain disorder: A heuristic integration of social childhood brain disorder: A heuristic integration of social neuroscience and developmental psychology. *Psychological Bulletin, 133,* 535–556.

Yeates, K. O., Ris, M. D., & Taylor, H. G. (Eds.). (2000). *Pediatric neuropsychology: Research, theory, and practice.* New York, NY: Guilford Press.

Youngman, A. R., Riccio, C. A., & Wicker, N. (2010). Assessing and intervening with children with seizure disorders. In D. C. Miller (Ed.), *Best practices in school neuropsychology: Guidelines for effective practice, assessment, and evidence-based intervention* (pp. 767–791). Hoboken, NJ: Wiley.

Zametkin, A., Liebenauer, L. L., Fitzgerald, G. A., King, A. C., Minkunas, D. V., Herscovitch, P. et al. (1993). Brain metabolism in teenagers with attention-deficit hyperactivity disorder. *Archives of General Psychiatry, 50,* 333–340.

Zametkin, A., Nordahl, T., Gross, M., King, A. C., Semple, W. E., Rumsey, J. et al. (1990). Cerebral glucose metabolism in adults with hyperactivity of childhood onset. *New England Journal of Medicine, 323,* 1361–1366.

Zimmerman, I. L., Steiner, V. G., & Ponds, R. E. (2002). *Preschool language scale, fourth edition (PLS-4) Spanish edition.* San Antonio, TX: Harcourt.

Zonfrillo M. R., Penn J. V., & Leonard, H. L. (2005). Pediatric psychotropic polypharmacy. *Psychiatry 2005, 8,* 14–19.

About the Author

Dr. Daniel C. Miller is a professor and department chair in the Department of Psychology and Philosophy at Texas Woman's University (TWU) in Denton, Texas. Dr. Miller has been a faculty member at TWU since 1990. Dr. Miller is also the director of the KIDS, Inc.'s School Neuropsychology Post-Graduate Certification Program. Dr. Miller is Board Certified in School Psychology from the American Board of Professional Psychology and a Diplomat in School Neuropsychology from the American Board of School Neuropsychology. He is also a Fellow with the National Academy of Neuropsychologists. Dr. Miller is a Nationally Certified School Psychologist (NCSP), a Licensed Specialist in School Psychology (LSSP-TX), and a licensed psychologist (OH).

Dr. Miller has been an active leader and presenter in state and national school psychology associations since 1992. Dr. Miller served as the President of NASP in 2003 to 2004. Dr. Miller is also an active researcher in the field of school neuropsychology and early childhood assessment. Dr. Miller is the author of the *Essentials of School Neuropsychological Assessment* (2007), and the *Best Practices in School Neuropsychology: Guidelines for Effective Practice, Assessment, and Evidence-Based Intervention* (2010), and a coauthor of *Essentials of WJ III Cognitive Assessment—Second Edition* (2010).

Index

About the CD-ROM

INTRODUCTION

This appendix provides you with information on the contents of the CD that accompanies this book. For the latest information, please refer to the ReadMe file located at the root of the CD.

System Requirements

- A computer with a processor running at 120 Mhz or faster
- At least 32 MB of total RAM installed on your computer; for best performance, we recommend at least 64 MB
- A CD-ROM drive
- Adobe Flash Player 9 or later (free download from Adobe.com).

Make sure that your computer meets the minimum system requirements listed in this section. If your computer doesn't match up to most of these requirements, you may have a problem using the contents of the CD.

Note: Many popular spreadsheet programs are capable of reading Microsoft Excel files. However, users should be aware that formatting might be lost when using a program other than Microsoft Excel.

Using the CD with Windows

To access the content from the CD, follow these steps:

1. Insert the CD into your computer's CD-ROM drive. The license agreement appears (Windows 7 > Select Start.exe from the AutoPlay window or follow the same steps for Windows Vista.)

    The interface won't launch if you have autorun disabled. In that case, click Start > Run (For Windows Vista, Start > All Programs > Accessories > Run). In the dialog box that appears, type D:\Start.exe. (Replace D with the proper letter if your CD drive uses a different letter. If you don't know the letter, see how your CD drive is listed under My Computer.) Click OK.

2. Read through the license agreement, and then click the Accept button if you want to use the CD. The CD interface appears. Simply select the material you want to view.

Using the CD on a Mac

To install the items from the CD to your hard drive, follow these steps:

1. Insert the CD into your computer's CD-ROM drive.
2. The CD icon will display on your desktop; double-click to open it.
3. Double-click the Start button.
4. Read the license agreement, and then click the Accept button to use the CD.
5. The CD interface will display. The interface provides a simple point-and-click way to explore the contents of the CD.

Note for Mac users: the content menus may not function as expected in newer versions of Safari and Firefox; however, the documents are available by navigating to the Author Files folder.

WHAT'S ON THE CD

The following sections provide a summary of the software and other materials you'll find on the CD.

Content

Major Tests Classified According to the Integrated SNP/CHC Model
The CD contains a spreadsheet for use with Microsoft Office Excel. The spreadsheet contains the following fields:

- New Broad Classifications:
  - Sensorimotor Functions
  - Visuospatial Processes
  - Auditory/Phonological Processes
  - Learning and Memory Processes
  - Executive Processes
  - Allocating and Maintaining Attention Facilitators/Inhibitors
  - Working Memory Facilitators/Inhibitors
  - Speed, Fluency, and Efficiency of Processing Facilitators/Inhibitors
  - Acquired Knowledge: Acculturation Knowledge
  - Acquired Knowledge: Language Abilities
  - Acquired Knowledge: Reading Achievement
  - Acquired Knowledge: Written Language Achievement
  - Acquired Knowledge: Mathematics Achievement

- New 2nd Order Classifications—Varies based on the broad classification.
- New 3rd Order Classifications—Varies based on the broad classification and 2nd order classification.
- Test Name.
- Abbreviation—Abbreviation of the tests name (e.g., Wide Range Assessment of Memory and Learning—Second Edition = WRAML2).
- Subtest—A specific subtest name that would be classified according to the Integrated SNP/CHC Model.
- Description—A description of what the subtest is designed to measure.
- Score Type—The type of score reported (e.g., standard score).
- Age-Grade Range—The suitable age or grade range of the subtest.
- Publisher—The principle test publisher.

The purpose of this spreadsheet is to find subtests from across multiple test batteries that are all designed to measure a similar broad or narrow construct.

The filter feature within Excel has been enabled, which will allow a user to perform a variety of sorts:

1. Find subtests that are designed to measure processes/functions/skills within a particular broad or narrow classification with the Integrated SNP/CHC Model:

   a. In Row 1—Column A of the spreadsheet there is a down arrow in the right side of the field. Click on that arrow and a list of the Broad Classifications appear.

   b. Click on the box to the left of the Select All option to deselect all broad classifications.

   c. Choose one of the Broad Classifications by clicking the check box to the left of the label, then click on OK.

   d. What is displayed in the spreadsheet are all of the subtests from across the major test batteries that are classified according to the Integrated SNP/CHC Model that are designed to measure the broad classification that you have chosen.

   e. You can narrow your search further by clicking on the arrow in the cell Row 1—Column B (New 2nd Order Classifications). You can choose a narrower classification among this list following the same procedures as outlined above to find the subtests that match more specific selection criteria.

f. You can then narrow down your list of subtests even further by selecting the subtests that match the Broad Classification—2nd Order Classifications—3rd Order Classifications criteria that the user selects. Note that not all 2nd Order Classifications have 3rd Order Classifications.

Note: To start a new sort, the user must go back to each field (e.g., Broad Classification) and choose the Select All option.

2. Find a particular test and see how the individual subtests are classified according to the Integrated SNP/CHC Model.
   a. In Row 1—Column D, the field is labeled as Test Name and has a down arrow in the right-hand corner of the field.
   b. Click on the box to the left of the Select All option to deselect all broad classifications.
   c. Choose one of the test names by clicking the check box to the left of the label, then click on OK.
   d. What is displayed in the spreadsheet are all of the subtests from that chosen test classified according to the Integrated SNP/CHC Model.

An online searchable database of the major tests classified according to the Integrated SNP/CHC Model is available on the www.schoolneuropsych.com website and is kept current as new tests are published.

Neuropsychological Processing Concerns Checklist for Children and Youth—Third Edition (NPCC-3)

The CD contains both English and Spanish Versions of the *Neuropsychological Processing Concerns Checklist for Children and Youth—Third Edition* (NPCC-3). Both versions of the NPCC-3 are saved as portable document files (.pdf). The NPCC-3 (English and Spanish) are copywritten by Dr. Daniel C. Miller at KIDS, Inc.; however, users of this book are granted permission to use these forms in clinical practice free of charge.

School Neuropsychology Report Shell

The CD contains a copy of the School Neuropsychology (SNP) Report Shell (version 19.0) that operationalizes the Integrated SNP/CHC Model presented in this book. At the time of the publication of this book, this was the most recent version of the SNP Report Shell. The SNP Report Shell is updated regularly as new tests are published and as a result of ongoing validation research studies.

The SNP Report Shell is saved as a portable document file (.pdf) and is presented as an example of how a comprehensive School Neuropsychological Assessment Report could be constructed. In practice, the clinician will delete all of the extraneous tests that were not administered to the student while leaving the tests that were administered.

The SNP Report Shell is included on the CD for illustration purposes only. If a clinician wants to use the SNP Report Shell in practice, the clinician needs to obtain formal training and supervised practice in school neuropsychology (see Chapter 3 for training options).

Learning Curve Graphs

In Chapter 12 in this book, the importance of plotting the learning curves for samples of learning is discussed. Several samples of learning curves for the major tests of memory and learning are included on the CD.

These learning curve graphs were created and saved in a Microsoft Excel format (.xls). Users may enter data into the spreadsheet for a particular subtest and the respective learning curve is automatically updated. The graph may be cut and pasted into a Word document as part of an assessment report.

Sample Reports

The CD contains two sample school neuropsychological case study reports. Many referrals for school neuropsychological assessments involve complex medical histories and multiple previous diagnoses. The first case study is an example of an adolescent who had many medical challenges at birth, which have affected his growth and development. The second case study is an example of 10-year-old boy, who had his left hemisphere surgically removed when he was 5 years old due to severe seizures caused by Rasmussen's Encephalitis. These case studies illustrate how the Integrated SNP/CHC Model may be used in practice.

Summary of School Neuropsychology Assessment Results Forms

SummaryForm1.doc—A single-page document that can be used to display an overview of the student's strengths and weaknesses based on the school neuropsychological assessment findings.

SummaryForm2.pdf—A multiple-page document that can be used to show the student's normative strengths and weaknesses compared to the student's intra-individual strengths and weaknesses based on the school neuropsychological assessment findings.

Applications

Adobe Reader

Included on this CD is a link to download Adobe Acrobat Reader for viewing PDF files. For more information and system requirements, please go to www.adobe.com.

OpenOffice.org

Included on this CD is a link to download OpenOffice.org for viewing spread-sheet files. For more information and system requirements, please go to www.openoffice.org.

OpenOffice.org is a free multiplatform office productivity suite. It is similar to Microsoft Office or Lotus SmartSuite, but OpenOffice.org is absolutely free. It includes word processing, spreadsheet, presentation, and drawing applications that enable you to create professional documents, newsletters, reports, and presentations. It supports most file formats of other office software. You should be able to edit and view any files created with other office solutions.

Shareware programs are fully functional, trial versions of copyrighted programs. If you like particular programs, register with their authors for a nominal fee and receive licenses, enhanced versions, and technical support.

Freeware programs are copyrighted games, applications, and utilities that are free for personal use. Unlike shareware, these programs do not require a fee or provide technical support.

GNU software is governed by its own license, which is included inside the folder of the GNU product. See the GNU license for more details.

Trial, demo, or evaluation versions are usually limited either by time or functionality (such as being unable to save projects). Some trial versions are very sensitive to system date changes. If you alter your computer's date, the programs will "time out" and no longer be functional.

TROUBLESHOOTING

If you have difficulty installing or using any of the materials on the companion CD, try the following solutions:

- Turn off any anti-virus software that you may have running. Installers sometimes mimic virus activity and can make your computer incorrectly believe that it is being infected by a virus. (Be sure to turn the anti-virus software back on later.)
- Close all running programs. The more programs you're running, the less memory is available to other programs. Installers also typically update files and programs; if you keep other programs running, installation may not work properly.
- Reboot if necessary. If all else fails, rebooting your machine can often clear any conflicts in the system.

QuickBooks® 2012

IN DEPTH

Laura Madeira

800 East 96th Street,
Indianapolis, Indiana 46240 USA

QUICKBOOKS® 2012 IN DEPTH

Copyright © 2013 by Pearson Education, Inc.

ISBN-13: 978-0-7897-4918-5

ISBN-10: 0-7897-4918-1

The Library of Congress Cataloging-in-Publication data is on file.

Printed in the United States of America

First Printing: August 2012

Trademarks

All terms mentioned in this book that are known to be trademarks or service marks have been appropriately capitalized. Que Publishing cannot attest to the accuracy of this information. Use of a term in this book should not be regarded as affecting the validity of any trademark or service mark.

Warning and Disclaimer

Every effort has been made to make this book as complete and as accurate as possible, but no warranty or fitness is implied. The information provided is on an "as is" basis. The author and the publisher shall have neither liability nor responsibility to any person or entity with respect to any loss or damages arising from the information contained in this book or from the use of the CD or programs accompanying it.

Bulk Sales

Que Publishing offers excellent discounts on this book when ordered in quantity for bulk purchases or special sales. For more information, please contact

U.S. Corporate and Government Sales

1-800-382-3419

corpsales@pearsontechgroup.com

For sales outside of the U.S., please contact

International Sales

international@pearsoned.com

Editor-in-Chief
Greg Wiegand

Acquisitions Editor
Michelle Newcomb

Development Editor
Patrice-Anne Rutledge

Managing Editor
Sandra Schroeder

Project Editor
Mandie Frank

Copy Editor
Megan Wade

Indexer
Tim Wright

Proofreader
Paula Lowell

Technical Editors
David Ringstrom
Mary Longacre

Editorial Assistant
Cindy Teeters

Designer
Anne Jones

Compositor
Tricia Bronkella

CONTENTS AT A GLANCE

CONTENTS

ABOUT THE AUTHOR

Laura Madeira is the owner of ACS, Inc., a software sales and consulting firm located in the greater Dallas, Texas area. She is one of the original members of the elite Intuit Trainer/Writer Network. Laura is a guest speaker for Intuit, sharing "What's New for QuickBooks" each fall. She was also a founding member of the Intuit Customer Advisory Council and a recent member of the Intuit Solution Provider Council. She is an Advanced QuickBooks Certified ProAdvisor, Enterprise, and Point of Sale Certified ProAdvisor, and is also a Sage Certified Consultant representing Sage 100 Contractor.

In addition to QuickBooks 2012 In Depth, Laura's other titles from Que Publishing include *QuickBooks 2010 Solutions Guide* and *QuickBooks Essentials* DVD, which offers more than six hours of self-paced video instruction. She is also the co-author of *QuickBooks 2010 on Demand*. For more than 20 years, Laura has worked with companies of all sizes and from a variety of industries. Her focus has been to help the growing business become more successful by automating its internal accounting processes and improving its overall business financial reporting.

Additionally, Laura is a guest speaker for Intuit, providing training to thousands of consultants and accountants nationwide at numerous events. She is also a respected author for Intuit, writing technical training materials and presentations in addition to documenting and reviewing competing software.

Laura earned her accounting degree from Florida Atlantic University. She enjoys photography, art, and camping with her sisters. When Laura is not writing, she enjoys reading a good book or two!

More information can be found by visiting her website at www.quick-training.com.

ABOUT THE TECHNICAL EDITORS

I could not have completed this project without the expertise and tireless effort of two very talented individuals, my technical editors.

Being a technical editor requires patiently reading every word of the manuscript for technical accuracy. This often entails hours and hours of testing and trying the written instructions to ensure no instructional step is misstated or missing. I am so appreciative to my two technical editors who helped to form this first edition of the *QuickBooks 2012 In Depth* reference guide.

David Ringstrom has worked behind the scenes as the technical editor for 23 books. David is a CPA and owner of Accounting Advisors, Inc., an Atlanta-based software consulting firm he started in 1991. His freelance articles on Microsoft Excel have appeared internationally, and he regularly teaches classes to CPAs on Excel, QuickBooks, and other topics. More information about David can be found at www.acctadv.com/david-h-ringstrom-cpa/.

Mary Longacre has been helping companies set up, customize, and learn how to use QuickBooks since 1998. Mary is an Advanced Certified QuickBooks ProAdvisor, a QuickBooks Online Accountant Advisor, and owner of Custom Accounting Solutions LLC in Alexandria, Virginia. She is a member of the Sleeter Group, a Chapter Leader for the National Advisor Network, and a member of the "Mentor Plus" Consulting Accountants Roundtable. Mary's website is www.businessqb.com.

Dedication

To Victor, my husband, who heard the following far too many times: "I can't join you; I have a chapter to turn in." He regularly cooks, cleans, and does laundry so that I can concentrate on these writing projects.

To my family and friends who encouraged me to continue and not lose sight of the goal—to share my knowledge of QuickBooks in this one-of-a-kind reference book.

To my development editor at Que, Patrice-Anne Rutledge, who unknowingly became my cheering section with numerous emails that included the words "don't stress." It kept me going, as hard as this project really was.

To my parents, Ron and Joycelyn Demaree, who taught me from an early age that anything is possible.

Acknowledgments

Thanks to all the audiences I have had over the years who have made me test and try out how to make QuickBooks work better. To the many clients I have helped who prepared me to think "outside of the box" when finding a solution to their unique accounting need. This book is a result of all those single requests for help and information.

I am appreciative to those readers who sent in suggestions about the information provided in my previous QuickBooks training books. I have incorporated those changes in this new, comprehensive reference guide.

Thanks to the entire Intuit Product Development team who continues to keep me advised of new product features and helps me collect information during the beta testing of each new year's release of QuickBooks.

I want to thank William "Bill" Murphy for his extensive contributions and technical expertise included in Chapter 17, "Managing Your QuickBooks Database." I also want to give credit to Charlie Russell, for working with me to test and try new QuickBooks features.

I could not have done this without the technical help and guidance provided by Pearson. Michelle Newcomb, acquisitions editor, was forever patient with me as I struggled to meet the deadlines. Patrice-Anne Rutledge, development editor, worked very close with me to simplify the editing process. Megan Wade, copy editor, made sure my content was grammatically accurate.

After working with this wonderful team of experts, I am now a much more skilled technical writer thanks to their expert editing and topic guidance.

—Laura

WE WANT TO HEAR FROM YOU!

As the reader of this book, you are our most important critic and commentator. We value your opinion and want to know what we're doing right, what we could do better, what areas you'd like to see us publish in, and any other words of wisdom you're willing to pass our way.

We welcome your comments. You can email or write to let us know what you did or didn't like about this book—as well as what we can do to make our books better.

Please note that we cannot help you with technical problems related to the topic of this book.

When you write, please be sure to include this book's title and author as well as your name and email address. We will carefully review your comments and share them with the author and editors who worked on the book.

Email: feedback@quepublishing.com

Mail: Que Publishing
         ATTN: Reader Feedback
         800 East 96th Street
         Indianapolis, IN 46240 USA

Reader Services

Visit our website and register this book at quepublishing.com/register for convenient access to any updates, downloads, or errata that might be available for this book.

Introduction

Whether you are new to QuickBooks, an expert user, or somewhere "in between," you will find this book to be a comprehensive reference guide you need to successfully complete your day-to-day QuickBooks tasks.

Having worked with many different types of business the last 25 years, I know the importance of providing readers the "how and why" of common QuickBooks tasks. For both the inexperienced and expert user, this book includes easy-to-follow, step-by-step instructions accompanied by hundreds of illustrations. Additionally, you can practice what you learn using provided instructions for use with sample data installed with your QuickBooks software. In no time at all, you will be using QuickBooks like a real pro!

What truly sets this book apart from the competition are the detailed instructions for managing and troubleshooting your QuickBooks data. For the business owner, this book provides step-by-step guides, checklists, and detailed advanced discussions of what information your QuickBooks data should provide.

For the accounting professional, learn how to work efficiently with your clients' QuickBooks files using the Accountant's Copy, Client Data Review, QuickBooks Statement Writer, and other useful features included with the QuickBooks Accountant 2012 software.

How This Book Is Organized

QuickBooks 2012 In Depth offers a wealth of information gathered from the author's years of working with business and accounting professionals who use QuickBooks software. So you can find just the right information, this book is organized into specific chapters, each focused on a particular task when working with your own or a client's QuickBooks data.

- **Introduction**—Learn quickly about what's new in QuickBooks 2012.

- **Chapter 1, "Getting Started with QuickBooks"**—Learn how to create a new file, convert from other software, and set up users and permissions.

- **Chapter 2, "Getting Around QuickBooks"**—Navigation, setting preferences, using Help, and selecting a file to open are all discussed in this chapter.

- **Chapter 3, "Accounting 101"**—For the business owner, learn the basics of financial reporting. Included checklist helps you keep a close eye on the financial details.

- **Chapter 4, "Understanding QuickBooks Lists"**—Chart of accounts, items list, class list, managing lists, and fixing list errors are all detailed in this chapter.

- **Chapter 5, "Setting Up Inventory"**—Learn about the different inventory features in each version of QuickBooks, setting inventory preferences, and the proper inventory process.

- **Chapter 6, "Managing Inventory"**—How to adjust inventory, review inventory reports, and handle inventory backorders.

- **Chapter 7, "Setting Up Vendors"**—In this chapter, you will learn how to use the Home page, set vendor preferences, and use the recommended accounts payable process.

- **Chapter 8, "Managing Vendors"**—Learn about vendor reporting, correcting vendor transactions, and handling unique accounts payable transactions such as pre-paying a vendor.

- **Chapter 9, "Setting Up Customers"**—Covers tracking customer leads, customizing the Home page, setting preferences, and properly invoicing and collecting payment from your customers—a very important chapter!

- **Chapter 10, "Managing Customers"**—This chapter provides a wealth of information about properly reporting your customer balances, paying sales tax, correcting transactions errors, and handling unique customer transactions.

- **Chapter 11, "Setting Up Payroll"**—Learn about the many payroll options, setting up payroll items and employees, and the proper payroll processing steps.

- **Chapter 12, "Managing Payroll"**—Prepare your quarterly and annual payroll tax forms, troubleshoot payroll errors, and record unique payroll transactions such as a loan made to an employee.

- **Chapter 13, "Working with Bank and Credit Card Accounts"**—Learn about entering checks, credit card transactions, and bank transfers as well as reconciling tasks. Save time using the Online Banking Center to download transactions directly into QuickBooks.

- **Chapter 14, "Reporting in QuickBooks"**—Setting preferences, using the Report Center, and modifying and memorizing reports are all discussed in this chapter.

- **Chapter 15, "Reviewing Your Data"**—Step-by-step guidance on reviewing the accuracy of your data. Don't miss this chapter!

- **Chapter 16, "Sharing QuickBooks Data with Your Accountant"**—Instructions for the business owner and accountant, plus a discussion of the different types of QuickBooks files.

- **Chapter 17, "Managing Your QuickBooks Database"**—Backing up your data and upgrading your data topics are explored. For the more advanced user, learn about troubleshooting database errors and monitoring your QuickBooks database.

- **Chapter 18, "Using Other Planning and Management Tools"**—Take advantage of all the tools available with your QuickBooks software including loan management, planning, year-end guide, Microsoft Outlook contacts sync, and using the QuickBooks timer.

- **Appendix A, "Client Data Review"**—For the accounting professional, learn how to reclassify transactions in batch, track changes to lists, write-off small customer balances in batch, and fix beginning balance errors, to name just a few.

- **Appendix B, "QuickBooks Statement Writer"**—For the QuickBooks Enterprise user or accounting professional, learn how to prepare customized financials using Microsoft Excel and Word integration.

- **Appendix C, "QuickBooks Shortcuts"**—Save time and work more efficiently.

Conventions Used in This Book

The book is straightforward enough you can easily go to a specific chapter and find the needed information. It is worthwhile, however, to let you know how information is presented in this book.

Menu Commands

QuickBooks 2012 offers a variety of methods to accomplish a task. To simplify the instructions given, use the top menu bar in QuickBooks.

Menu Bar

For example, the instructions for preparing a report might look like the following:

1. From the menu bar, select Reports, Vendors & Payables.

This directive refers to clicking Reports on the menu bar and then selecting Vendors & Payables as a submenu of Reports.

Additionally, for added clarity in the topic discussion, there are many screen illustrations, which make following the instructions easy.

Web Pages and Manufacturer Information

A few web pages are listed in this book, mostly directing you to the www.intuit.com website. These web addresses were current as this book was written; however, websites can change.

Special Elements

As you read through this book, you will note several special elements, presented in what we call "margin notes." Different types of margin notes are used for different types of information, as you see here.

 tip

This is a tip that might prove useful for whatever you are in the process of doing.

 note

This offers additional related information or alternative techniques that you might want to consider.

 caution

This is a caution that something you might accidentally do might have undesirable results—so take care!

Sidebars

Learn quickly how to complete a task by following along with supplied step-by-step instructions using sample data installed with your QuickBooks software.

Learn more about this topic in another section of *QuickBooks 2012 In Depth*.

Text Conventions

Bold typeface references text you should type.

Key combinations are represented with a plus sign. If the action you need to take is to press the Ctrl key and T key simultaneously, the text tells you to press Ctrl+T.

INTRODUCING QUICKBOOKS 2012: WHAT'S NEW

Get New Insights

The latest version of QuickBooks makes it easier to stay on top of important tasks and customize QuickBooks to work the way you do.

Calendar View

The Calendar View in QuickBooks, shown in Figure 1, helps business owners see at a glance scheduled to do's and key financial tasks in one dashboard. Viewing individual transactions or tasks are just a single click away.

Excel Integration Refresh

Export QuickBooks reports to Excel to modify fonts, column headers, and cell formats; insert columns or rows; and enter formulas. Refresh your previously saved worksheet with updated data from within Excel (see Figure 2) and retain all format changes.

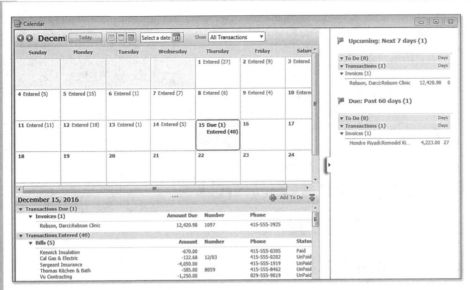

Figure 1
Customize the Calendar view to display what is important to your business.

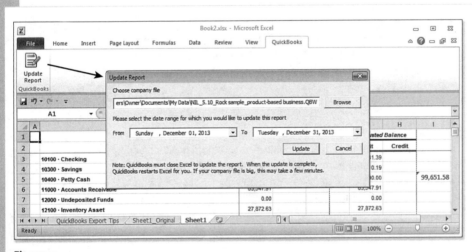

Figure 2
Refresh previously exported reports in Excel.

User-Contributed Reports

QuickBooks gives you access to industry-specific report templates created by other QuickBooks users in your industry. Search by popularity, user rating, and industry. Choose the template you like and QuickBooks will populate the report with your business data in one click. See Figure 3.

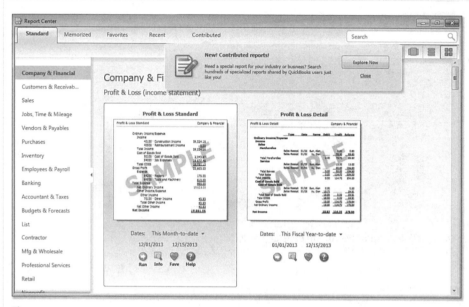

Figure 3
Find custom reports created by other QuickBooks users.

Get More Organized

Growing businesses will appreciate these new features that help business owners organize their many business building and management tasks.

Lead Center

Manage your prospects with the new Lead Center as shown in Figure 4. Track and follow up on important tasks associated with your lead activity. Convert your leads to customers with one easy click.

Document Center

Get organized by scanning and attaching receipts, estimates, and other important business documents to your QuickBooks records by simply dragging and dropping them into the Document Center. The new QuickBooks Document Center, shown in Figure 5, lets you store files locally on your hard drive on your hard drive or server.

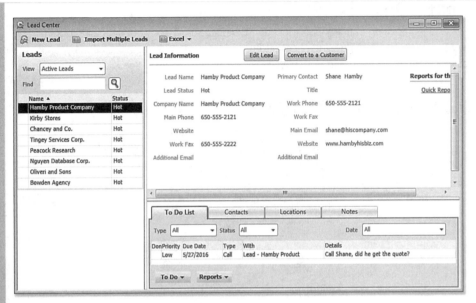

Figure 4
Keep track of critical lead activity and notes in one central place.

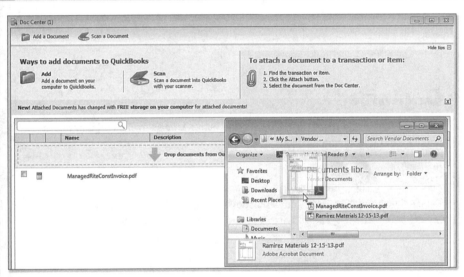

Figure 5
Easily attach documents to transactions or lists in QuickBooks.

Inventory Center

QuickBooks Premier and Enterprise centralizes inventory data in a control panel for quick access and easy management of inventory tasks, items, and reports. See Figure 6. Enterprise users can also store images of the inventory part.

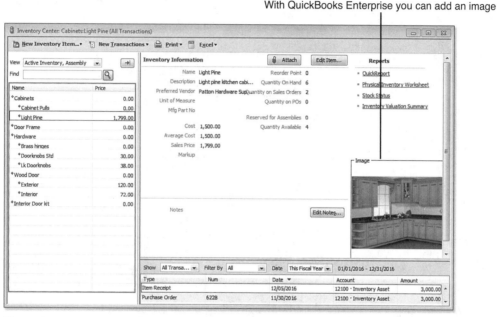

Figure 6
Manage your inventory at a glance with the Inventory Center.

Edit No Company Open

Have you struggled with multiple unused files displaying in the No Company Open dialog box? Now you can "edit" the list to hide those files you do not want displayed on the No Company Open dialog box as shown in Figure 7. The original file storage is not changed and even though you removed the file from this list you can still browse to the storage location and open the file.

QuickBooks 1099/1096 Wizard

Improved for QuickBooks 2012 is the 1099 Wizard. When your business classifies a worker as an independent contractor, you can set up QuickBooks to track and print the Form 1099-MISC at the end of the tax year. Currently, vendors paid $600 or more in a calendar year are subject to receiving a Form 1099-MISC.

Complete a few simple steps (Figure 8) in the wizard to ensure the data is properly being recorded and tracked.

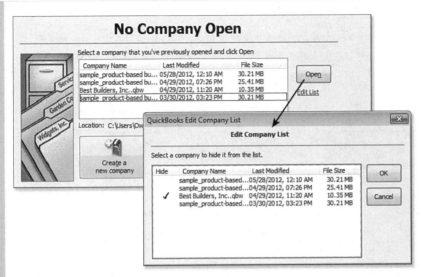

Figure 7
Edit the No Company Open list to "hide" files.

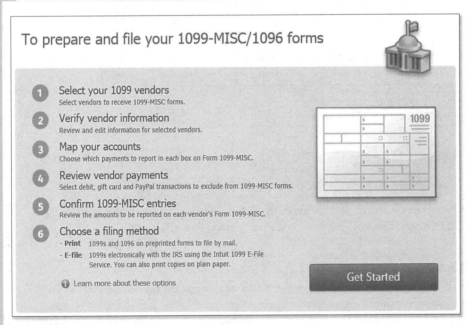

Figure 8
Track and file your vendor 1099 documents with the new wizard setup.

Get Time Back and Save Steps

Getting started with QuickBooks and completing common tasks has just gotten a whole lot easier with the release of QuickBooks 2012.

Express Start

Using Express Start, you are just three steps away from getting the basics in your file. Additionally, you can import customers, vendors, and service or product items as well as create bank accounts (see Figure 9). This information can easily be imported or added manually. That's all it takes for the new business owner to get a quick start.

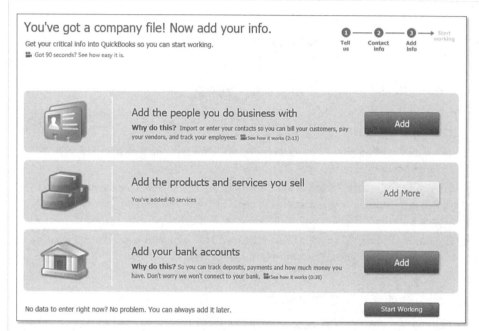

Figure 9
Add your products, services, contacts, and bank accounts easily so you can begin using QuickBooks.

Batch Timesheets

QuickBooks users who track employee's time (see Figure 10) can create a single timesheet for employees or vendors who share the same hours and, if tracked, the same service item, payroll item, and class. This single timesheet entry can then be used to prepare payroll for multiple employees or prepare checks for multiple vendors.

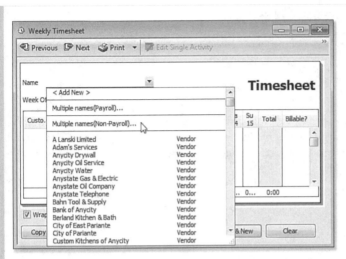

Figure 10
Do you have "crew" labor? Create multiple time sheets at once for employees or vendors.

Integrated Help/Search

Have you found yourself searching for help or separately going to the Community Forums to find answers to your QuickBooks questions?

Now, with the new Integrated Help shown in Figure 11, you can search your company file or product Help. Help content includes how-to documents, knowledge base articles, and links to related community discussions.

The icon bar also includes a new "always on" search box with the option to search your QuickBooks file or Help (this can be removed in the Customize Icon Bar dialog box).

Figure 11
Search your data file or product Help right from the icon bar.

Transaction Tab

With the Transactions tab shown in Figure 12, linked transaction data is at your fingertips. No need to click through multiple menus to get answers to questions about transactions. With a displayed QuickBooks transaction, users can view summary information, related transactions, and notes.

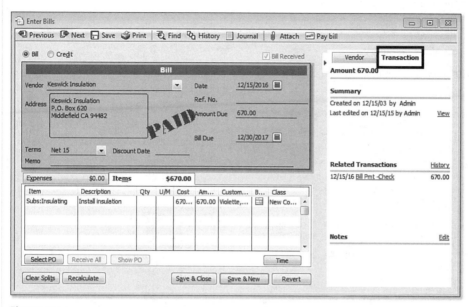

Figure 12
Find related transactions easily from the Transaction tab.

QuickBooks Enterprise Solutions

These new features are unique to using QuickBooks Enterprise Solutions 12.0. Each year, QuickBooks adds features that differentiate the products. This year, inventory management has been significantly improved.

Enhanced Inventory Receiving

For some larger companies, having the vendor item receipt also become the bill leads to confusion about what date was important—the date the items were received or the date they received the vendor's bill. Older versions of QuickBooks did not distinguish between the two different documents.

Enhanced Inventory Receiving (see Figure 13), available with QuickBooks Enterprise, improves how you receive and pay for inventory in QuickBooks. You can enable this feature on the Items & Inventory—Company Preferences tab on the Preferences dialog box (select Edit, Preferences from the menu bar). Before doing so in your file, make a backup. Some important notes about this new feature:

- The change is irreversible; once it is turned on, it cannot be turned off.

- The change will modify your existing accounting.

After you enable Enhanced Inventory Receiving:

- Item receipts do not increase accounts payable.

- Bills do not affect inventory.

- Bills issued against item receipts no longer replace the original item receipt.

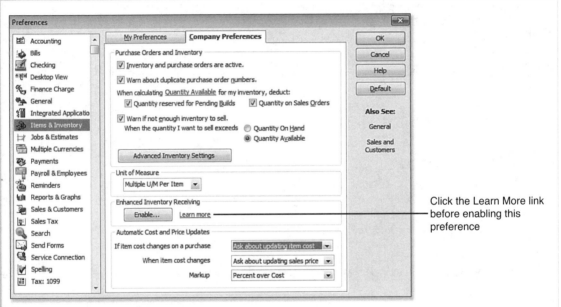

Click the Learn More link before enabling this preference

Figure 13
QuickBooks Enterprise 12.0 offers many new features around inventory management.

First In First Out (FIFO) Inventory Costing

For some companies, having a choice about how inventory costs are calculated will be a welcomed change. For all prior versions of QuickBooks, inventory has been calculated using the Average Costing method, or value of inventory = total purchased / total paid.

FIFO (first in, first out) is a method of calculating the value of inventory sold and on hand. When you enable FIFO, QuickBooks calculates inventory values based on the assumption that the first inventory items received are the first ones sold.

Turning on FIFO changes the following reports:

- Inventory Valuation reports

- Balance Sheet reports

- Profit & Loss reports (cost of goods sold)

So, with this in mind it is very important to make a backup of your data file before enabling the FIFO preferences settings.

Inventory Auto Cost, Sales Price, Markup

In previous versions of QuickBooks, when a user entered a purchase transaction with an item cost different than the item record's default cost, the QuickBooks user was prompted to update the default cost.

In QuickBooks Enterprise 12.0, you choose your preference setting on how to handle the change in the item's cost (see Figure 14).

If item cost changes on a purchase transaction you can choose to:

- Always update item cost

- Never update item cost

- Always ask about updating item cost

- Use default, but ask about updating

For calculating the sales price when and item cost changes you can choose to:

- Always update sales price

- Never update sales price

- Always ask about updating sales price

- Use default sales price, but ask about updating

Figure 14
QuickBooks can automatically manage your cost, sales price, or markup changes.

Inventory Lot/Serial Number Tracking

QuickBooks Enterprise Solutions 11.0 with an Advanced Inventory subscription included the multiple inventory site tracking. Now with QuickBooks Enterprise Solutions 12.0, additional features include Lot/Serial Numbers tracking as shown in Figures 15 and 16.

If you subscribe to Advanced Inventory (only available with QuickBooks Enterprise), you can track serial numbers or lot numbers. You cannot track both. Once the feature you choose is enabled, QuickBooks will add the field to most purchase and sales transactions.

You can also assign serial/lot numbers when you build assemblies and adjust inventory. Also, you do not need to assign serial or lot numbers to existing inventory to start tracking this information.

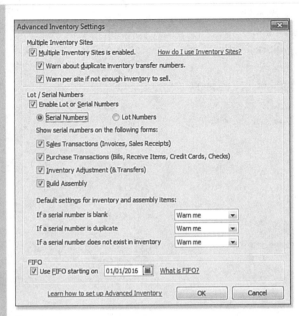

Figure 15
Only QuickBooks Enterprise offers these advanced inventory management features.

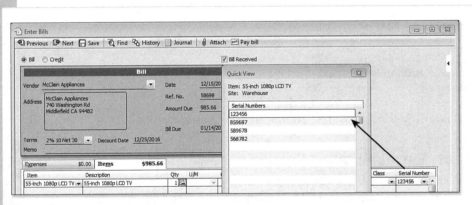

Figure 16
Track inventory serial or lot lumbers with QuickBooks Enterprise Solutions 12.0.

For the Accounting Professional

If you are an accounting professional, you will want to use the QuickBooks Accountant 2012 or QuickBooks Enterprise Solutions Accountant 12.0 software to take advantage of these new features.

Accountant Center

Over the last several years, QuickBooks has delivered some pretty amazing accountant tools and features, especially if you work with multiple clients' files.

However, for some it was hard to find and use these features. With QuickBooks Accountant 2012, there is a new Accountant Center (see Figure 17). This customizable center offers all the tools and resources needed to work efficiently with client's files.

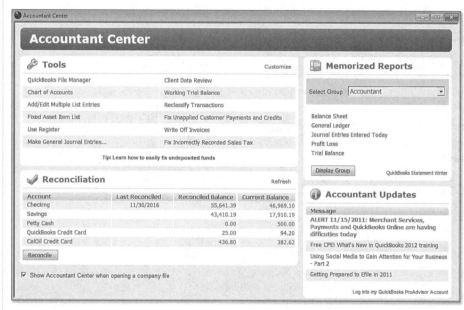

Figure 17
Accounting professionals work more efficiently with client's files when accessing important tasks from the Accountant Center.

The many great reasons to use the Accountant Center include:

- It's customizable; add just the tools and resources you need once and all of your customization is ready for the next client's file.

- Access your most common Memorized Report Groups and link to the new QuickBooks Statement Writer.

- With the Reconciliation panel, you do not need to open the bank reconciliation window or print reports to find this critical information.

Starter Copy

The accounting professional can now work more efficiently by creating a new client's company file from an existing client's file or "template." Only non-sensitive information is imported from the original file including:

- Preferences (except those related to checking or credit card accounts)

- Items List (only sales tax items)

- Memorized Reports (only if they do not filter for specific accounts, customers, vendors, jobs, items, or employees)

- Chart of Accounts (no sensitive accounts such as checking or credit cards)

- Type of Tax Form

Period/Archive Copy

The Period/Archive Copy feature is for the accounting professional who might be requested by a third party on behalf of their client to provide a data file for a specific period of time. Transactions before and after a selected date can be removed when creating a Period Copy of a client's file.

Another great use for this might be when a company needs to "archive" data for a date in the past, including balances forward, creating a smaller sized current file.

In the examples shown in Figure 18, when "Don't Create a Summary" option is selected, a Balance Sheet prepared for 12/31/14 will have a net -0- balance for all accounts.

 note

When creating a Period Copy, a copy of the original company file is made before removing any data.

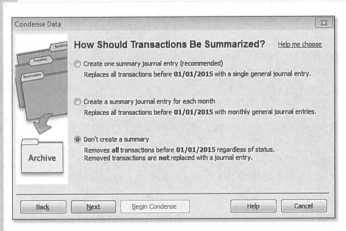

Figure 18
Accounting professionals can create a file where only specified year's data is included.

QuickBooks Statement Writer

Although Quickbooks Statement Writer is a new named feature, it was formerly known as Intuit Statement Writer. Now QuickBooks Statement Writer is included with your purchase of QuickBooks Accountant 2012 and with all editions of QuickBooks Enterprise Solutions 12.0.

QuickBooks Statement Writer (QSW) connects your QuickBooks data to Excel and Word (see Figure 19). QSW is particularly useful for accounting professionals who need to customize their clients' financials. QSW can be used to create a "template" format for financials and then use this template with multiple client files.

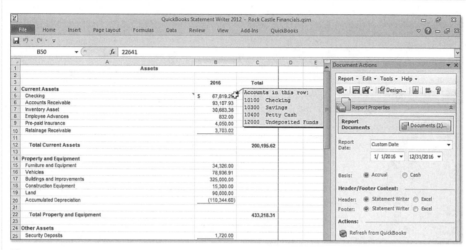

Figure 19
Customize QuickBooks financials in Excel.

GETTING STARTED WITH QUICKBOOKS

Understanding QuickBooks

This comprehensive reference book offers the reader clear and concise, step-by-step, written instructions accompanied by detailed illustrations for using QuickBooks Pro and Premier 2012. Most of the content is also applicable to Enterprise Solutions 12.0. Written for the business owner, accountant, or bookkeeper, *QuickBooks 2012 In Depth* truly offers readers a complete guide to the software they use every day.

The QuickBooks software comes in a version that is just right for your business needs. For a complete comparison visit the following website: http://quickbooks.intuit.com/product/accounting-software/quickbooks-comparison-chart.jsp or Google "QuickBooks comparison." A few of the differences are detailed in Table 1.1.

Table 1.1   QuickBooks Software Summary

Software Version	Number of Users	Invoice Customers, Pay Vendor Bills, Prepare Payroll (*)	Industry-Specific Versions	Accountant-Specific Tools and Features
QuickBooks Online Plus	Up to 5	✓		
QuickBooks for Mac	Up to 5	✓		
QuickBooks Pro	Up to 3	✓		
QuickBooks Premier	Up to 5	✓	✓	
QuickBooks Accountant	Up to 5	✓	Can toggle to all industry editions	✓
QuickBooks Enterprise	Up to 30	✓	✓	
QuickBooks Enterprise Accountant	Up to 30	✓	Can toggle to all industry editions	✓

*Payroll Subscription Required

This book does not cover the setup or use of QuickBooks Online or QuickBooks for Mac. The illustrations and content are from working with QuickBooks Premier or QuickBooks Accountant. Often the author has included content specific for an industry edition or for QuickBooks Enterprise Solutions.

Additionally, this book is be a perfect companion to the QuickBooks LiveLessons video training, combining the best of audio learning and book reference functionality.

The primary purpose of this book is to teach the businesses owner or accounting professional how to use QuickBooks software quickly and accurately. Most chapters also include troubleshooting content that sets this book apart from other how-to books. This chapter helps you get started quickly and provides you with quick steps to begin using your QuickBooks software. If you would like to practice what you are learning, open one of the sample files installed with your QuickBooks software. I teach you how to do that first!

Over the years, I have helped hundreds of businesses troubleshoot problems with getting the proper financial and management information out of their QuickBooks data. I have found that improper setup of the data file was most often the primary cause, second only to judgment errors in posting transactions to the incorrect account.

A word of caution: It is not my intention to offer any tax advice; I make comments throughout the text encouraging you to consult your accounting or tax professional before making any data corrections that might have a significant impact on a company's financials.

Using QuickBooks Sample Data

You can open one of the sample data files installed automatically with your QuickBooks software and begin trying what you are shown in this book. With this data you can test creating transactions, review how lists are set up, and process reports with ready-made data.

The number and type of sample data files installed will differ depending on the version of QuickBooks you purchased.

To open a sample file with sample data, follow these steps:

1. Launch QuickBooks from the icon on your desktop.

2. From the menu bar, select File, Close Company/Logoff. The No Company Open dialog box displays.

3. Click the Open a Sample File button and select a sample file from the drop-down list as shown in Figure 1.1.

> **🛆 caution**
>
> Do not enter your own business data into the supplied sample files; they should only be used for testing how to create transactions and reviewing reports populated with the sample data. Additionally, any customizing that you do with the sample data will not be saved to other files, including your own business file.

Figure 1.1
Practicing with sample data can help you feel more confident about using QuickBooks.

After creating your own data file, the next time you launch QuickBooks your file (not the sample file) will default as the file that QuickBooks opens.

If you want to quickly access previously opened QuickBooks files, including the sample file, select File, Open Previous Company from the menu bar. QuickBooks displays a menu of previous files to choose from.

If you do not see other files listed, you might need to change the number of files displayed on this list. To do so, first open any data file. Then, select File, Open Previous Company, Set Number of Previous Companies from the menu bar, and enter a number between 1 and 20. The No Company Open dialog box will now display the most recent files you have opened with the software.

> **🔍 note**
>
> This book uses the Sample product-based business file included automatically when you install QuickBooks on the computer. The company name associated with this fictitious data file is Sample Rock Castle Construction. The images and exercises used in the book are from this sample file, but you can read along and practice with any of the installed sample files.

    For more information, see "Selecting a Company File to Open," p. 54.

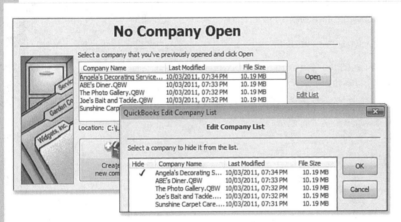

> ### 〰 tip
>
> New for QuickBooks 2012! Does the No Company Open dialog box include old, unused QuickBooks files? Would you like to only see QuickBooks files you currently are using?
>
> Click the Edit List link (see Figure 1.2) and place a checkmark next to each company name you want to hide. Click OK to save the changes. Note that the file remains on your computer or server and can later be opened by selecting File, Open or Restore Company from the menu bar.

Figure 1.2
Edit the No Company Open dialog box to remove old, unused data files.

Creating a New QuickBooks File

If you are new to QuickBooks, the first task is to create a data file. In the No Company Open dialog box, click the Create a New Company button. The QuickBooks Setup dialog box displays with the following three options:

- **Express Start**—Create a file quickly with the least amount of initial setup time.

- **Advanced Setup**—Answer a series of questions to help you set up your new file. This feature was formerly known as EasyStep Interview in previous versions of QuickBooks.

- **Other Options**—Open an existing file, convert Quicken data, or convert other accounting software data.

> *To learn more about other options your accounting professional might have with QuickBooks Accountant 2012, see "Creating a New File from an Existing Company File," p. 33.*

Choose from one of the three options that best suits your needs; each one is detailed in the following sections.

➡ *To learn more about upgrading to QuickBooks 2012 from an older version of QuickBooks, see "Upgrading Your QuickBooks Version," p. 559.*

Express Start

With Express Start you can be using your new file in just three easy steps. Express Start will guide you through the basics of entering your company information, contact information, and—optionally—contacts, products, services, and bank accounts.

From the menu bar, select File, Create a New Company, and then click the Express Start button in the QuickBooks Setup dialog box. Alternatively, click the Create a New Company button in the No Company Open dialog box and then click the Express Start button.

Step 1—Tell Us

Enter the required information about your business including Company Name, Industry, and Company Type. Click Help Me Choose to see the choices available for Industry and Company Type. (Based on your selections, QuickBooks will assign an industry-specific chart of accounts that can be modified.) Optionally, enter your company's federal tax identification number as shown in Figure 1.3. When finished, click Continue.

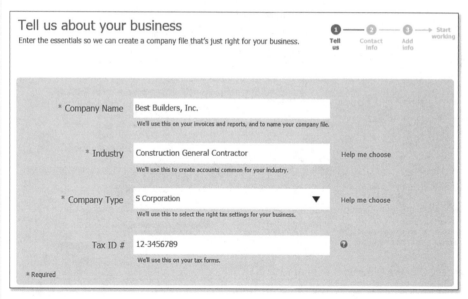

Figure 1.3
With Express Start you can be using your file in no time!

Step 2—Contact Info

Enter your business contact information. This information can be included on your customer invoices and other forms in QuickBooks.

To open the Preview Your Company Settings dialog box, click the link with the same name. Here is where you can review your current settings. Click each of the displayed tabs to see the features, chart of accounts, and company file location QuickBooks suggests for you based on your answers in Step 1. If you need to change the location where your QuickBooks data file will be stored, click Change Location on the Company File Location tab.

Don't worry too much about the other settings just yet, as they are easy to modify later in your file and will be addressed in later chapters of the book. Click OK to close the Preview Your Settings dialog box.

Click the Create Company File button to continue to the next step. QuickBooks now creates your file and saves it on your hard drive or to a specific location you selected in Step 2—Contact Info. Optionally, click the Back button to review or change previous settings.

Step 3—Add Info

In this step, you can add your contacts, products, services, and bank accounts to your new data file.

If you wish to skip this step, click the Start Working button in the lower-right corner (see Figure 1.4) to launch the QuickBooks Home page.

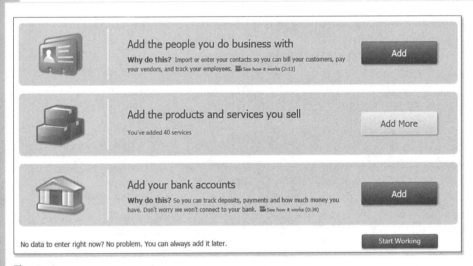

Figure 1.4
Adding your lists is easy with the QuickBooks Setup wizard.

Adding Contacts   Now would be the perfect time to add the people you do business with to your newly created file. This list includes customers, vendors, and employees. Adding contacts is a three-step process: choose how to add contacts, select who to add, and review and finish. Later, to learn more about these lists, see Chapter 7, "Setting Up Vendors" and Chapter 9, "Setting Up Customers."

To add contacts using the QuickBooks Setup wizard, follow these steps:

1. Click the Add button in the Add the People You Do Business With box (or click Add More if you've already entered some names) to import or enter the names of people you do business with.

2. If you selected the Add option, you can choose how to add from these choices:

   ■ **Import From Outlook, Yahoo, or Gmail Email**—Follow the instructions for importing from one of the listed mail carriers. You will be able to specify which contacts you want imported into QuickBooks. For Outlook, if you have more than one address book, you can choose which one to use for the import. For other mail carriers you might receive an email message that you have shared your address book with QuickBooks.

   ■ **Paste From Excel or Enter Manually**—Your imported contacts will display in the spreadsheet-like form shown in Figure 1.5. Be sure to scroll to the right to see additional data fields. You can also copy and paste from Excel or manually enter contacts directly in the form before importing.

 caution

If you are not sure how to enter information into this grid, you can skip this step and then enter your contact information later. QuickBooks also makes it easy to edit the information imported later.

Figure 1.5
Adding the people you do business with is easy when getting started with QuickBooks.

3. If you selected Add More, you are returned to the Add the People You Do Business With dialog box with the same choices as listed in step 2 previously.

4. After importing or entering manually, click Continue to review and finish. QuickBooks Setup will check your list for duplicate names or emails. If any duplicates are detected, you will need to change the Name field (not the Company Name field) so no duplicates are imported.

5. Click the Fix button and QuickBooks displays any contacts that have duplicate names. Change the Name field to make it unique.

6. Click Continue after fixing. QuickBooks will show how many contacts are ready to be added and how many need to be fixed. Follow step 5 again if needed.

7. Click Continue. QuickBooks returns you to the dialog box for you to add more contacts or to add products, services, or bank accounts.

Adding the Products and Services You Sell   You can add the products and services you sell in just a few steps. If your business tracks inventory, you will not want to enter your items here.

To learn more about setting up inventory, see Chapter 6 "Managing Inventory."

To add products and services, follow these steps:

1. In the Add the Products and Services You Sell section, click Add (or Add More if you've already entered some items).

2. Choose an item type and click the Continue button. Non-inventory item types can be changed to inventory later. Item type options in this menu feature include the following:

   ▪ **Service**—work performed by you such as an hour of labor

   ▪ **Non-inventory part**—products you sell but *do not* want to track as inventory

3. Copy and paste from a list you already have in Excel, or manually enter the item details including the optional description, price, and manufacturer's part number. Click Continue.

4. QuickBooks will check for any item duplicates or if any items to be imported are already in your QuickBooks file. Click Fix if needed. Click Continue to add the items to your file.

Adding Bank Accounts

Click Add to create accounts to track deposits, payments and how much money you have. Enter the Account Name (required) such as Checking or Savings and optional Account number. You can choose to enter your opening balance here or wait until you have reviewed the information in Chapter 3. If you choose to enter your opening balance, QuickBooks will offset the entry to the Opening Balance Equity account. Ask your accountant to help you reassign this entry to the appropriate account.

 tip

QuickBooks does not allow you to have duplicated entries in the Name field across the many lists. For example, an employee name cannot be the same as a vendor name. An easy fix for this is to add a "V" to the end of the Name field for the vendor listing who is also included on the employee list.

 tip

The bank account information you enter is necessary for you to properly reconcile your QuickBooks bank account. For example, if you are going to use 10/1/16 as your new start date, you would enter your Opening balance which would be the 9/30/16 statement ending balance *not including* any uncleared checks or deposits. You will enter these individually later. For the Opening balance date you would use 9/30/16 in this example.

To add your bank accounts into your new QuickBooks file, follow these steps:

1. Click the Add button in the Add Your Bank Accounts dialog box.

2. Type your Account Name, Account Number (optional), Opening Balance (optional), and Opening Balance Date (optional).

3. Click Continue. QuickBooks displays information about ordering checks from Intuit.

   - Select Yes, Remind Me Later (you will be prompted to create an alert); when done, proceed to step 4.

   - Select No Thanks and proceed to step 4.

   - Select Order Now, follow the prompts to complete this action, then proceed to step 4.

4. Click Continue and QuickBooks adds the bank account to your data file.

You are now ready to begin working with your QuickBooks file. Simply click the Start Working button. The Ready to Start Working dialog box displays with useful links to start entering transactions right away. Click the "X" in the red box top-right corner to close this dialog box.

Remember, everything you have entered so far is completely modifiable in your newly created QuickBooks file.

You can now skip to the section in this chapter titled, "Setting Up Users and Permissions."

Advanced Setup Using EasyStep Interview

For help in creating a new file, earlier editions of QuickBooks did not have the Express Start option but instead offered the QuickBooks EasyStep Interview, which is now accessed from Advanced Setup in QuickBooks 2012.

If you select the Advanced Setup option, QuickBooks provides a series of question-and-answer type choices to help you properly set up your data file and certain default features.

Information to Collect

Having the following information on hand before starting the Advanced Setup can help you when entering the details:

- **Company name**—This should be the company name or a name that best describes the business. By default, this is the filename given to the data file (.QBW extension) on your computer.

- **Legal name**—The legal name displays on certain reports and federal tax forms.

- **Tax ID**—Although this ID is not required to begin using QuickBooks, it is required if you want to sign up for one of the QuickBooks payroll services or use QuickBooks to print 1099s.

- **Remaining information**—This includes a phone number, email address, website, and so on (see Figure 1.6). This information can optionally be included on a customer invoice.

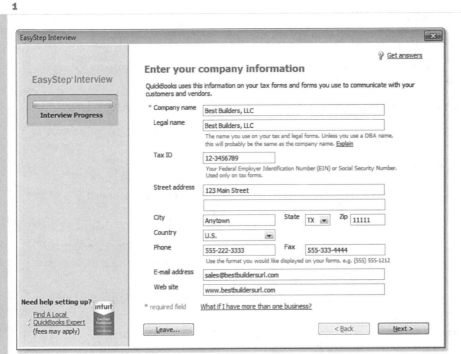

Figure 1.6
Selecting Advanced Setup provides access to the EasyStep Interview.

If you need to leave the EasyStep Interview at any time after saving the file, QuickBooks returns to the point you left off when you open the data file again.

The EasyStep Interview now prompts you for certain information based on what industry you selected. Your answers to the remaining questions will make certain features in QuickBooks the default. The purpose of this chapter is not to define each of these choices; most are self-explanatory or are included in various chapters in this book. However, discussing the effect of several important choices is useful at this time.

Using Advanced Setup (EasyStep Interview)

You may prefer to have a bit more control of the setup process up front. This is exactly what the Advanced Setup (also known as the EasyStep Interview) offers.

To create a new file using Advanced Setup, from the menu bar, select File, Create a New Company, and then click the Advanced Setup button in the QuickBooks Setup dialog box. Alternatively, click the Create a New Company button in the No Company Open dialog box and then click the Advanced Setup button.

- **Enter Your Company Information**—Enter your Company Name, Legal Name, Tax ID, and other information that can be included on customer invoices and other forms within QuickBooks. Click Next.

■ **Select Your Industry**—QuickBooks can help you get started quickly, by providing basic information for particular industries (see Figure 1.7). Pick an industry that closely matches your own. Click Next.

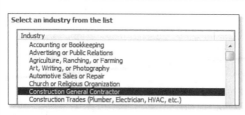

Figure 1.7
QuickBooks includes customized settings for your specific industry.

■ **How Is Your Company Organized?**—Select the legal organization your company selected when obtaining your Federal Identification Number. This choice will create unique Equity accounts to match your legal selection. Click Next.

■ **Select the First Month of Your Fiscal Year**—Select the month your fiscal year starts in. This will default certain reports to display the correct fiscal year dates. Click Next.

■ **Set Up Your Administrator Password**—It is recommended that you set up an administrator password. If you do not set one during the EasyStep Interview, you can open a QuickBooks file with the default username of Admin and leave the password blank. Using a blank password is fine during the initial setup, but you should put more security in place after you enter sensitive information. You can also set up this password later. Click Next and QuickBooks will create your company file.

■ **Create Your Company File**—QuickBooks requires that you store the company data file and provide a name for the file. Click Next. Browse to select a location to store your file or accept the default location and name suggested by QuickBooks. Click Save. QuickBooks displays a progressive message that your file is being created.

 note

Do not worry if you cannot complete the entire set of questions at one time. After QuickBooks creates the file you can click the Leave button. QuickBooks saves your choices and when you reopen the data file, QuickBooks will return you to that same section.

■ **Customizing QuickBooks for Your Business**—After reading the information, click Next.

■ **What Do You Sell?**—Choose from Services, Products, or Both Services and Products. This preference affects the type of default invoice form that is selected when you begin using QuickBooks. Click Next.

■ **Do You Charge Sales Tax?**—Specify whether or not you want to charge sales tax, choosing from the Yes or No option button. (You can change this later if necessary.) Click Next.

■ **Do You Want To Create Estimates in QuickBooks**—Select the Yes or No option button. If you provide a proposal to your clients or multiple proposals, you will want to enable this feature. Click Next.

■ **Tracking Customer Orders In QuickBooks**—Choose from Yes or No options. (This feature is only available in QuickBooks Premier, Accountant, or QuickBooks Enterprise Solutions.) For more information, see "Using QuickBooks Sales Orders," p. 292. Click Next.

 note

Not certain which choice to make when completing the Advanced Setup (EasyStep Interview)? No worries, QuickBooks will select the recommended option based on the industry you selected in Step 2.

■ **Using Statements in QuickBooks**—Choose between Yes or No. This option will enable you to print past-due statements for your customers. Click Next.

■ **Using Invoices In QuickBooks or Using Progress Invoicing in QuickBooks**—Choose from Yes or No. Selecting Yes enables the use of customer invoices. In selected industries you might be prompted to enable progress invoicing. Progress invoicing is "milestone billing" (when you invoice a customer progressively during a job).

■ **Managing Bills You Owe**—Choosing Yes enables you to enter vendor bills and pay those bills at a later date. Working with vendors is discussed in Chapter 8, "Managing Vendors." Click Next.

■ **Tracking Inventory in QuickBooks**—Select Yes or No to enable this feature. Remember, these features can later be enabled in Preferences. To learn more about inventory review Chapter 5, "Setting Up Inventory" and Chapter 6, "Managing Inventory." Click Next.

■ **Tracking Time In QuickBooks**—Tracking time enables you to bill customers for time, analyze time on projects and pay hourly employees. Select Yes or No. Click Next.

■ **Do You Have Employees?**—Choose either W-2 employees or 1099 contractors. If you selected Yes to W-2 employees, QuickBooks will create the needed Chart of Accounts items. This setting can be modified later. Click Next.

■ **Using Accounts In QuickBooks**—Click the link "Why Is the Chart of Accounts Important" to learn more about this list in QuickBooks. This list is also discussed in Chapter 4, "Understanding QuickBooks Lists." Click Next.

■ **Select A Date To Start Tracking Your Finances**—Choose from Beginning of This Fiscal Year: 01/01/2016 (for example) or Use Today's Date or The First Day of the Quarter or Month. These are examples of potential start dates. Click Next when completed with this selection.

■ You start using QuickBooks immediately upon starting your business with no prior expenses or income. This date is the easiest one to work with because you have no historical balances or transactions to consider. You begin by paying vendors and invoicing customers. Everything else will fall into place.

■ At the beginning of a calendar year, such as January 1, 20xx. This choice is common when the decision to begin using QuickBooks is at the end of a year or not very far into the new year. Again, if the company has previously had business transactions, there will be beginning balances to enter.

➡ *To learn more, see "Setting Up a QuickBooks Data File for Accrual or Cash Basis Reporting," p. 63.*

- At the beginning of your fiscal year, (for companies whose tax year does not coincide with the calendar year).

- The first day of a month during the current calendar or fiscal year.

- **Review Income and Expense Accounts**—You are provided the opportunity to include or exclude certain default chart of accounts from your new data file. Click Next.

- **Congratulations**—You are finished with the Advanced Setup. Click Go to Setup.

- **You've Got a Company File!**—You can now add contacts, products and services, and bank accounts as discussed in the "Express Start" section earlier in this chapter.

 tip

If you select the incorrect first month of your fiscal year during the EasyStep Interview, you can easily change it by selecting Company, Company Information from the menu bar. Changing this month does not affect individual transactions but does ensure that the reports that are based on a fiscal year are correct.

Creating a New File from an Existing Company File

New for QuickBooks Accountant 2012 and QuickBooks Enterprise Solutions Accountant 12.0 is the option to use an existing QuickBooks data file to create a new data file from as shown in Figure 1.8. Your original file is left unchanged in the process.

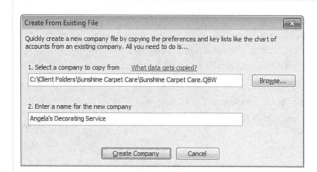

Figure 1.8
Create a new file from an existing file, available only with QuickBooks Accountant 2012 or Enterprise Solutions Accountant 12.0.

To create a new file from an existing file, follow these steps:

1. From the QuickBooks Setup dialog box, click the Other Options button and select Create from Existing Company File from the drop-down list.

   The Create from Existing Company File dialog box opens.

 note

Use by accounting professionals that want to create a new file from an existing file. Sensitive data is not copied.

2. By default, the currently opened company is selected as the file to be copied from. To select a different QuickBooks file, click the Browse button.

3. Enter a Name for the new company file.

4. Click Create Company.

5. Accept the default Filename and location for saving your new file or modify as needed.

6. Click Save.

Using the Create from Existing Company File process, QuickBooks copies only the following information from one file to another:

- **Preferences**—Not including those for bank or credit card accounts

- **Items List**—Only sales tax items, no products or services

- **Memorized Reports**—Only those that do not filter for specific accounts, customers or jobs, vendors, items, or employees

- **Type of Tax Form**—Useful if you are going to integrate with tax preparation software

- **Chart of Accounts**—No bank accounts are copied

If you find that you wanted more details copied from the original file, or wanted to remove specific year's transactions, ask your accounting professional to use QuickBooks Accountant 2012 software and provide you with a newly created "Condensed Data" file.

Hopefully you found one of these options best for your needs in starting your new QuickBooks file. The next section in this chapter covers converting other accounting software to a QuickBooks file.

 tip

Not using the Accountant version of QuickBooks software? Or would you like to be able to copy the products and services from one file to another? Consider using the IIF (Intuit Interchange Format) export. From the menu bar, select File, Utilities, Export, Lists to IIF Files.

With this option, you are able to select a specific list (not transactions) that you want to import into another QuickBooks file.

Converting from Other Accounting Software

QuickBooks has automated the process of converting files from other financial software into QuickBooks files. The other programs you can convert from include the following:

- Quicken

- Peachtree by Sage

- Microsoft Small Business Accounting

- Microsoft Office Accounting

This section provides specific details about how QuickBooks handles the conversions and what you need to consider when making the choice to convert existing data from one of the listed financial software programs to a QuickBooks data file.

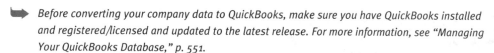 *Before converting your company data to QuickBooks, make sure you have QuickBooks installed and registered/licensed and updated to the latest release. For more information, see "Managing Your QuickBooks Database," p. 551.*

Even with the automation of the process, you should consider finding a QuickBooks Certified ProAdvisor in your area to assist with the conversion. From the Help menu in QuickBooks, select Find a Local QuickBooks Expert.

Converting from Quicken to QuickBooks

To begin the conversion from Quicken, open QuickBooks, select File, New Company from the menu bar, and then select Convert Quicken Data from the Other Options drop-down list in the QuickBooks Setup dialog box. The Conversion tool copies your Quicken data to a new QuickBooks file, leaving your original Quicken data file unchanged.

Table 1.2 shows you how the Quicken accounts are converted into QuickBooks accounts.

Table 1.2   Quicken Account Conversion

This Type of Account in Quicken:	Becomes this Type of Account in QuickBooks:
Checking	Bank
Credit Card	Credit Card
Asset	Other Current Asset
Liability	Other Current Liability
Investment	Other Current Asset

Because QuickBooks does not offer the Investment tracking feature that is in Quicken, you can choose whether to include or exclude the value of your investments in the resulting QuickBooks balance sheet. If you choose to include them, QuickBooks converts the investment accounts into the Other Current Asset chart of account type.

If you choose to exclude the investments, you are given the opportunity to delete the accounts before converting to QuickBooks. Any transfers that were recorded to or from the deleted accounts are recorded to your opening balance equity account. This is in keeping with the "debits equal credits" accounting that is going on behind the scenes in QuickBooks.

You are asked whether there is a Quicken Accounts Receivable account with customer payments. If you click Yes, the QuickBooks Conversion tool asks you to identify your Quicken Accounts Receivable account. QuickBooks then begins converting the Quicken transactions to QuickBooks Accounts Receivable transactions. This process can take several minutes.

During the conversion:

- QuickBooks creates an Opening Balance Equity account to compensate for deleted Quicken accounts.

- Memorized Invoices in Quicken might need to be reviewed, making sure the items memorized in Quicken remain on the invoice in QuickBooks.

- Duplicate check, invoice, or credit memo numbers are stored in a QBwin.log for review. You will learn more about this log in Chapter 17., "Managing Your Quickbooks Database."

- Every payee name in Quicken must be on a QuickBooks list.

Because QuickBooks cannot determine which list a name belongs to, it places all names on the Other Name list (see Figure 1.9).

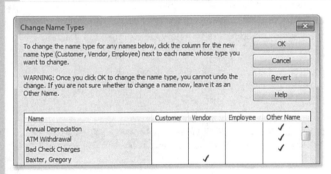

Figure 1.9
After converting from Quicken you will need to reassign most of the names on the other names list to the Customer, Vendor, or Employee Lists.

From the menu bar, select Lists, Other Names List to open the Other Name List dialog box. Right-click this dialog box and then select Change Other Name Types for a one-time option to change the payee from an Other Name list item to a vendor, employee, or customer. If you do not need to use a name on vendor form or customer form, you can leave the name on the Other Names list.

 caution
After you click OK to change the name type, you cannot undo the change. If you are not sure what list the payee belongs to, leave it as an Other Name.

Converting from Peachtree, Small Business Accounting, or Office Accounting to QuickBooks

Just as in the Quicken conversion, QuickBooks can convert your Peachtree, Small Business Accounting, or Office Accounting data to QuickBooks data directly from the EasyStep Interview dialog box. The conversion process leaves your original Peachtree, Small Business Accounting, or Office Accounting data untouched.

To download the free conversion tool, follow these steps:

1. From the menu bar, select File, New or, alternatively, click the Create a New Company button in the No Company Open dialog box. The QuickBooks Setup dialog box displays.

2. From the Other Options drop-down list, select Convert Other Accounting Software Data (Internet connection required).

3. Follow the helpful links to get the free conversion tool or to read a Conversion Tool FAQs document.

The free downloadable tool converts Peachtree (2001–2011 versions), Microsoft Small Business Accounting, or Office Accounting (2007–2009 versions). You can convert to a QuickBooks Pro, Premier 2008 or later, or Enterprise Solutions 8.0 or later. The tool can be used to convert multiple company files from any of the named software.

The download link as of the time of this writing for the free conversion tool: http://www.quickbooksdirect.com/convert (if you are not an accountant) or http://accountant.intuit.com/convert (if you are an accountant or QuickBooks ProAdvisor).

In the conversion process, you can select the specific Peachtree, Microsoft Small Business Accounting, Microsoft Office Accounting, or Office Accounting Express file and the QuickBooks product version to which you will be converting it. Additionally, you can specify the conversion of lists and transactions (including historical transactions) or lists only.

Because of the differences between the two products, you are also given a choice to identify customers and vendors in QuickBooks with the name of the Peachtree, Microsoft Small Business Accounting, Microsoft Office Accounting, or Microsoft Office Express ID value. You must choose to use the name or the ID value in QuickBooks, so making this decision before performing the conversion is best.

Key lists that are converted include the following:

- Chart of accounts

- Customer/prospects

- Jobs

- Employees/sales reps

- Vendors

- Inventory item

- Custom fields

- Balance information

Open transactions include the following:

- Open invoices
- Open vendor bills

Customer transactions include the following:

- Estimates
- Sales orders
- Invoices
- Payment receipts
- Deposits
- Credit memos

Vendor transactions include the following:

- Purchase orders
- Bills
- Bill payments
- Checks
- Bill credits

Setting Up Users and Permissions

QuickBooks always creates a default user with the username Admin. The Admin user has full rights to all settings and preferences in QuickBooks. If your company is going to have multiple users accessing the QuickBooks data file, it is recommended that you create a unique user login for each person and assign specific permissions if needed. With unique usernames for each person, QuickBooks will be able to tell you who entered, modified, or deleted a transaction on the Audit Trail report.

External Accountant

Business owners who plan to share data with their accountant at tax time or for other purposes should create a unique user for your accountant. The External Accountant user type has all the controls of the Admin, except that the accountant cannot:

- Add, delete, modify, or view sensitive customer credit card details
- Add, delete, or modify other QuickBooks user settings

To create a user login for your accountant, follow these steps:

1. From the menu bar, select Company, Set Up Users and Passwords, Set Up Users.

2. In the User List dialog box, click the Add User button.

3. Enter a User Name and Password (optional but recommended) and then enter the password again to confirm.

4. If you need to add additional licenses to your QuickBooks file, click the Explain link for more information about Intuit's licensing policy.

5. Click the Next button. If you didn't enter a password in step 3, QuickBooks opens the No Password Entered dialog box. Click Yes to create a password or No to skip this step.

6. Select the External Accountant option button, as shown in Figure 1.10, and click Next to continue.

note

Table 1.1 listed the number of users that can work in a company file at the same time, based on the version of the software that you have. If you need to buy additional licenses from the menu bar, select Help, Manage My License, Buy Additional User License.

Access for user: Laura

What do you want this user to have access to?

- All areas of QuickBooks

- Selected areas of QuickBooks
  (You will make the selections in the screens that follow)

- External Accountant
  (Access to all areas of QuickBooks except sensitive customer data, such as credit card numbers)

Figure 1.10
Creating an External Accountant user for your accounting professional limits access to sensitive customer information.

7. In the Warning dialog box, click Yes to confirm you want to give the user access to all areas of QuickBooks, except credit card information.

8. Click Finish. If a Warning dialog box opens, click OK to confirm that you understand that the Admin user is being assigned to integrated applications.

9. Click Close to close the User List dialog box.

To log in to the file as the new External Accountant user, select File, Close Company/Logoff from the menu bar. From the No Company Open dialog box, select the file from the list. Click Open and enter the username and password.

tip

If you are an accounting professional using QuickBooks Accountant 2012 you can use the QuickBooks File Manager 2012 to store your client's assigned username and password for you. When you open the client's file from within File Manager, QuickBooks will automatically log you in, bypassing the username and password dialog. This works with QuickBooks Pro, Premier, or Enterprise 2011 or newer files.

Other QuickBooks Users

Setting up users with permissions is recommended when you have multiple users working in the same QuickBooks file. Transactions are assigned to users and many changes to the file are also tracked to the user who logged into the file.

To create a user login and set permissions for additional users, follow these steps:

1. From the menu bar, select Company, Set Up Users and Passwords, Set Up Users.

2. From the User List dialog box, select Add User.

3. Enter a User Name and Password (optional but recommended) and enter the password again to confirm.

4. If you need to add additional licenses to your QuickBooks file, click the Explain link.

5. If you didn't enter a password, click Yes to create a password or No to skip this step.

6. Select the access option:

   ■ **All areas**—Provides access to all parts of QuickBooks except those which require Admin access.

   ■ **Selected areas**—Allows you to choose the options for access to each sensitive area of your QuickBooks data.

7. You will now work through nine different permission screens and on the tenth screen (see Figure 1.11) you can review the permission settings. Each dialog box offers details about the access levels and most include some or all of the following permission levels:

   ■ No Access

   ■ Full Access

   ■ Selective Access—Includes all or some of these options:

      ■ Create transactions only

      ■ Create and print transactions

      ■ Create transactions and create reports

If you are uncertain about the limitations of a permission setting, I recommend you set it for the Create Only option—the highest level of security. Then log in as that new user and attempt to access an area the employee will work in or an area they shouldn't be in and determine if the permissions assigned provide the controls you need. QuickBooks will tell you what level of permission is needed for any task you attempt.

With QuickBooks 2012, you have gotten off to a quick start in setting up your new file (or converting from other accounting software) and setting up users with specific permissions. You will also find it helpful to use the QuickBooks sample data when you want to practice or follow along with much of the content in this book.

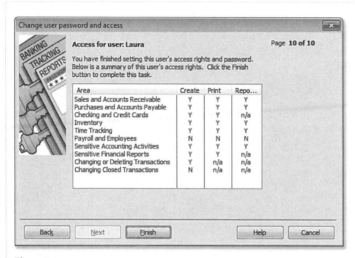

Figure 1.11
You can review a summary of the access rights assigned to a QuickBooks user.

2

GETTING AROUND QUICKBOOKS

Home Page and Navigation

You can make the most of your QuickBooks software when you learn how to navigate and customize the options available to meet your business's specific needs. This chapter will show you just how easy that task can be. For example, if your business does not need to track inventory, you can turn off that feature. However, as your business grows and the products and services you offer change, you can later reenable the same features.

QuickBooks 2012 makes it even easier to customize and navigate this easy-to-use and very popular accounting software. Let's start by making this *your* software!

Title Bar

At the top of your open QuickBooks file is the title bar as shown in Figure 2.1. The title bar indicates the following information about your file:

 caution
If you are following along this text using one of the sample data files installed with your QuickBooks file, take note of any customization you do. This customization in the sample file will not affect your own QuickBooks file.

- Name of your file as it is assigned in Company Name field in the Company Information dialog box (select Company, Company Information from the menu bar to open this dialog box).

- Your QuickBooks software year and edition; including Pro, Premier, or Enterprise. Also indicated (if applicable) is the industry specification such as accountant, retail, professional services, and so forth.

- Multi-user and the currently logged in username, if more than one user has access to the company file at a time.

Title bar   Icon bar

Menu bar

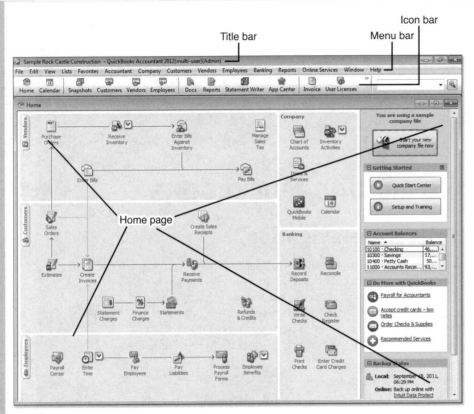

Figure 2.1
QuickBooks' many navigation points make it easy to work with.

Menu Bar

The menu bar includes nearly all of the tasks, reports, forms, and functionality available in QuickBooks. If you are a new QuickBooks user, I encourage you to review all the menus and submenus. Just look at what is included in the Company menu shown in Figure 2.2. Discovering these features can be valuable for your business as many of these additional QuickBooks tools are beyond the scope of this book.

This book uses the menu bar when providing instructions for getting around QuickBooks. You might also want to access the same tasks from the customizable icon bar or Home page.

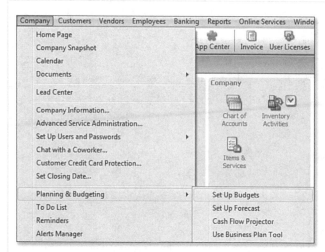

Figure 2.2
Review the menus for useful tools and features not shown on the Home page or icon bar.

Icon Bar

The icon bar (see Figure 2.1) provides quick access to the tasks and reports you frequently use. You can customize the icon bar by adding or removing shortcuts and it is uniquely customizable for each user.

To customize the icon bar for a particular user, make sure you are logged in to the file with that username before making any changes.

> *For more information about setting up users and permissions, see "Getting Started with QuickBooks," p. 21.*

You can customize the icon bar by:

- Adding icons (shortcuts)

- Editing existing icons

- Rearranging the order of the icons

- Grouping icons

- Removing icons

Customizing the Icon Bar

The icon bar provides quick access to the most common tasks. You can customize the icon bar for your specific needs.

To add the Calc icon (calculator) to your icon bar next to the Calendar icon, follow these steps:

1. On the icon bar, click the small double arrows on the far right near the search box and select Customize Icon Bar. The Customize Icon Bar dialog box, shown in Figure 2.3, will display your currently selected icons.

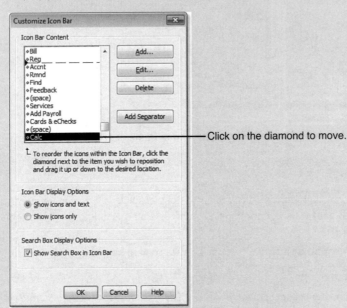

Click on the diamond to move.

Figure 2.3
Add, remove, and reposition icons on your personal icon bar.

2. Click Add and select Calculator in the Add Icon Bar Item dialog box. The Calculator icon image is selected for you, but you can choose another icon image from the available choices.

3. Accept or edit the default Label. Keep the text as short as possible here; long labels can crowd the available space on the icon bar.

4. Accept or edit the default Description. The description displays when you hover over the icon with your cursor.

5. Click OK to close the Add Icon Bar Item dialog box.

6. To reposition the Calc icon next to the Calendar icon, click the diamond in front of the Calc item. Drag the item up the list (refer to Figure 2.3), releasing the mouse when the Calc icon is next to the Calendar icon. Look at your icon bar and you will see the Calc icon is next to the Calendar icon. How easy was that!

7. In the Icon Bar Display Options section, keep the default Show Icons and Text option or select Show Icons Only.

8. Optionally, select the Search Box Display Options checkbox to display the search bar on the far right of the icon bar.

9. Click OK to close the Customize Icon Bar dialog box.

Home Page

The best place to start customizing QuickBooks specifically for your business needs is on the Home page. The Home page displays by default when you create a new QuickBooks file and includes tasks and workflows you can customize (refer to Figure 2.1). You can add or remove icons from the Home page. You cannot rearrange the order or placement of icons on the Home page. (Some Home page icons cannot be removed if related preferences are enabled.)

 tip

Now that you know how to "drag and drop" a list item, you will be able to rearrange many other QuickBooks lists this way!

When you customize the Home page to include or remove specific icons, you are often redirected to the related preference. For more detailed instructions on working with individual preferences, see the "Preferences" section in this chapter or the related preference section included with most chapters in this book.

The Home page icons require you to be logged into the file as the Admin or External Accountant user (see Chapter 1).

Customizing Icons (Tasks)

The QuickBooks Home page displays common tasks and workflow for Vendors, Customers, Employees, and other activities and information. Some tasks can be added or removed depending on the needs of your business.

If your Home page did not automatically display, you can always open it by clicking the Home page icon on the icon bar as displayed in Figure 2.1. In this section, you will learn to manage the preference to display the Home page each time you launch QuickBooks.

The Admin User in QuickBooks

Not sure if you are logged into the file as the Admin user? If you are working with a multi-user file (see Chapter 17, "Managing Your QuickBooks Database," for more details), the title bar will show the user currently logged into the opened file (see Figure 2.1). However, if you are in the file in single-user mode or if you renamed the Admin user, the username may or may not display "Admin."

To determine if you are currently logged into the file as the originally created default Admin user, select Company, Set Up Users and Passwords, Set Up Users from the menu bar to open the User List dialog box. Figure 2.4 shows how the original Admin user was renamed to "Laura." A renamed Admin user will still have all the same privileges as the original Admin user.

Many preferences and features require you to be logged into the file as the Admin user. If you are not currently logged in as the Admin user, you can log off by selecting File, Close Company/ Logoff from the menu bar.

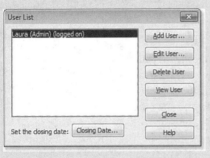

Figure 2.4
Viewing the User List will show if the Admin user was renamed (not recommended).

If you want to make changes to the Home page icons, follow these steps:

1. First, log into your file as the default Admin or External Accountant user. Enter the appropriate password if one was set.

2. From the menu bar, select Edit, Preferences to open the Preferences dialog box, which displays the preferences available in your file.

3. Select the Desktop View preference in the left column.

4. Select the Company Preferences tab at the top of the Preferences dialog box. The following options are provided:

   - **Customers**—Choose to add or remove the following Home page icons:

     - **Invoices**—Can only be removed if Estimates, Sales Orders, and Sales Tax tracking is disabled. Either Sales Receipts or Statement and Statement Charges must be enabled to remove Invoices from the Home page.

     - **Sales Receipts**

     - **Statements and Statement Charges**

   - **Vendors**—Option to remove *both* the Enter Bills and Pay Bills icons. If this option is grayed out, it is because another preference is enabled that is dependent on using vendor bills. For example if Inventory is enabled you cannot remove the vendor icons of Enter and Pay Bills.

   - **Related Preferences**—Enable or disable features globally for all users. These preference settings will be discussed in more detail in their related chapters.

     - **Estimates**—See Chapter 9.

     - **Sales Tax**—See Chapter 9.

- **Sales Orders**—See Chapter 9.

- **Inventory**—See Chapter 5.

- **Payroll**—See Chapter 11.

- **Time Tracking**—See Chapter 11.

5. Click OK to close the Preferences dialog box.

If you know you want to remove an icon (task) from the Home page by deselecting it in the Preferences dialog box, you can safely do that. These icons can later be reinstated to your Home page.

> ### ⚠ caution
> Read the referenced chapter before adding a new Home page icon. Often other unique settings will need to be defined when adding a new icon to your Home page.

Customizing Lists Displayed on Home Page

The right side of the Home page (see Figure 2.5) displays several additional panels of information. Click the plus sign (+) to expand the details; click the minus sign (–) to collapse them.

Click the (-) or (+) ——
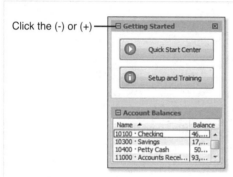

Figure 2.5
Each panel of information can be expanded or collapsed.

These panels include:

- **Getting Started**—Click Quick Start Center for useful links and videos to help you get started with common tasks. Click Setup and Training for information on getting assistance from Intuit. Optionally, click the "x" in the top-right corner to remove this panel from your Home page. You can later reinstate it in on the My Preferences tab of the Preferences dialog box (select Edit, Preferences from the menu bar to open this dialog box).

- **Account Balances**—Click the column headers to sort the accounts by the Name or Balance column.

- **Do More with QuickBooks**—Links to other products or services offered for QuickBooks users.

- **Backup Status**—Notification of when the last backup was completed and links to information on storing your data online.

- **Reminders and Alerts**—Links to view the reminders and alerts you have enabled in your QuickBooks file.

Open Windows List

Are you ready for another personal preference for navigating in QuickBooks? Try the Open Windows list. With computer monitors getting larger and larger, you will most likely have plenty of room to use it with your QuickBooks file.

From the menu bar, select View, Open Window List. The Open Windows list displays on the left side of your Home page (see Figure 2.6), which enables you to move between many different open reports or forms easily by clicking on their name in this list.

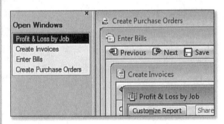

Figure 2.6
The Open Windows list is useful when you have multiple windows open at the same time.

Your open windows might cascade one over the top of another open window. If you find this distracting, select View, One Window from the menu bar to make all of the windows use the full QuickBooks desktop area. You can also resize an open dialog box by dragging its top, bottom, sides, or corners.

Tutorials

In your QuickBooks software are several tutorials to help you get started quickly. You can watch these to supplement this *In Depth* guide to working with QuickBooks 2012.

To do so, select Help, Learning Center Tutorials from the menu bar. Click a category on the left or select quick links to What's New to jumpstart your use of QuickBooks. When you are finished viewing the tutorials, click Go to QuickBooks to close the Learning Center.

 tip

Click any icon on the Home page (other than the Home icon) and see the Open Windows list on the left grow with each transaction or task that is opened. Would you like to close all open windows quickly? Select Window, Close All from the menu bar.

After closing all open windows, if you wish to return to the Home page, click the Home icon on the icon bar.

Preferences

You can customize QuickBooks to suit your specific business needs while maintaining individual preferences.

You are required to save your changes as you work with each preference. Some preferences might have you close all open windows to effect the change. Simply return to the Preferences dialog box until you are finished specifying all your preferences by selecting Edit, Preferences from the menu bar.

To return to the original preference setting, select a preference on the left side of the Preferences dialog box and click the Default button. Be aware the Default button is not available for all preferences. Click OK to close the Preferences dialog box.

Preferences come in two important types:

- **Company Preferences**—Affect all users of the currently opened QuickBooks file. Only the QuickBooks Admin and External Accountant user have full rights to set these preferences. Learn more about different types of users and user permissions in Chapter 1.

- **My Preferences**—Specific to the currently logged in user and do not affect the settings for other users of the same file or other QuickBooks files.

This section will provide a review of the most common, general use preferences. Most of the preference settings are self-explanatory and do not need to be discussed here. However, specific details on important preferences are provided in each chapter of this comprehensive guide.

Accounting—Company Preferences

These are global preferences and when modified will affect all users of the opened QuickBooks file:

- **Date Warnings**—A new file defaults to Warn if Transactions Are 90 day(s) in the Past and Warn if Transactions Are 30 day(s) in the Future (see Figure 2.7). At times, you might want to edit these date ranges, such as when you are just starting to use QuickBooks and need to enter data for a period in the past.

Figure 2.7
QuickBooks can warn when transaction dates do not fall within a specific date range.

Desktop View—My Preferences

These are personal preferences and, when modified, will only affect the currently logged in user:

tip

To simplify your daily QuickBooks use, select the One Window option and select View, Open Window List from the menu bar.

- **View**—One Window or Multiple Windows per user preference. This preference also can be selected from the View menu on the menu bar.

- **Desktop**—Includes the following options:

  - **Save When Closing Company**—Default setting that saves every open window when a QuickBooks session is closed. When QuickBooks is reopened, each report and form left open in the last session will be restored. This preference is not recommended for a file that has multiple users logging into the file simultaneously. Restoring multiple windows, forms, or reports at startup can slow down the time it takes for the QuickBooks file to open.

  - **Don't Save the Desktop**—Closes each open window automatically when the QuickBooks program is closed. This is the most efficient choice and will notify you if a transaction has not been completed before closing the form as well as give you the option to save any unmemorized custom report settings.

  - **Save Current Desktop**—When you reopen QuickBooks, any previously opened non-transaction window will be displayed. Additionally, the preference to Keep Previously Saved Desktop will be automatically selected.

  - **Keep Previously Saved Desktop**—Selected for you automatically. QuickBooks will open with all previously opened non-transaction forms and reports.

Certain preferences will override these defaults, particularly if you have selected the following preferences:

  - **Show Home Page When Opening a Company File**—When selected, the Home page will always open when you launch QuickBooks.

  - **Show Getting Started Window**—Useful if you are still setting up your file.

General—My Preferences

These are personal preferences and, when modified, will only affect the currently logged in user:

tip

If you selected the preference "Pressing Enter moves between fields" and you wish to save a transaction or activate a highlighted command, use the combination of Ctrl + Enter from your keyboard.

- **Pressing Enter Moves Between Fields**—When this is *not* selected you will use the Tab key to move between fields and the Enter key to save a transaction or activate a highlighted command.

  If you wish to use the Enter key to move between fields (perhaps you have grown accustomed to using the Enter key in this way with other software) then place a checkmark in this preference.

- **Automatically Place a Decimal Point**—When selected, displays .01 rather than 1.00 when you type the number "1" in QuickBooks.

- **Bring Back All One Time Messages**—If data entry mistakes have been ignored in the past, turning on this warning can call attention to possible mistakes in the future.

- **Keep QuickBooks Running for Quick Startups**—When selected, the QuickBooks software might open faster. This is the only preference that will also affect other data files.

Spelling—My Preferences

These are personal preferences and, when modified, will only affect the currently logged in user.

Options include being able to always check spelling or ignore specific words or word with numbers, Internet addresses, and so forth.

When enabled, the Description, Memo, Notes, and Message fields of the following forms are spell checked: invoices, estimates, sales receipts, credit memos, and purchase orders.

If you do not select the option to always check spelling, on certain forms you will be able to manually spell check.

Help Options

As a business owner or accounting professional new to QuickBooks, you will find there are many resources for getting the help you need. To access Help in QuickBooks you can press the F1 key on your keyboard, or choose Help, QuickBooks Help from the menu bar.

New for QuickBooks 2012 is the search tool on the right side of the icon bar. From the drop-down list on the icon bar search field, select Search Company File if you want to search through your lists or transactions, or Help if you want to search technical resources.

QuickBooks provides help in several distinct ways and allows you to search each with a single dialog box, as shown in Figure 2.8.

Options include

- **How To**—Links to more detailed information; content is sensitive to the area of QuickBooks you currently have opened.

- **Troubleshooting**—Links to knowledge-base resources including tools, features, or articles addressing your specific search term.

- **Community**—Connect with other users and see if your question has already been answered.

Would you prefer to have a local QuickBooks experienced professional come to your place of business to help you get started quickly? If so, choose Help, Find a Local QuickBooks Expert from the menu bar. You will be asked for your ZIP code to help locate a list of QuickBooks Certified ProAdvisors in your area and fees may apply.

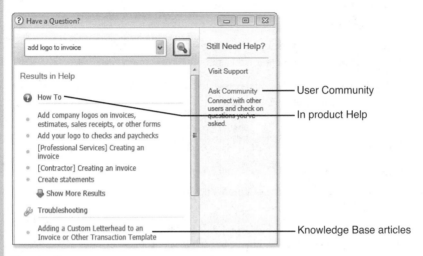

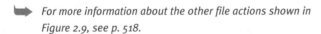

Figure 2.8
Search multiple help resources all at once.

Selecting a Company File to Open

In general, you will not have any trouble opening your QuickBooks file because the software will automatically select your file each time you open QuickBooks. There are, however, several ways to open your QuickBooks data. Listed here are the most common.

Opening Your Data for the First Time

After creating your new file, it launches automatically when you open QuickBooks. However, if you are opening your data for the first time on a new computer you will need to follow these steps:

1. Launch your QuickBooks software by clicking the QuickBooks icon on your desktop.

2. From the menu bar, select File, Open or Restore Company.

3. In the Open or Restore Company dialog box, select the Open a Company File option button, as shown in Figure 2.9.

> ➡ *For more information about the other file actions shown in* *Figure 2.9, see p. 518.*

4. Click Next.

5. QuickBooks will default to the last known folder that a QuickBooks file was opened from or you can browse to locate where you stored the file. Select the file and click Open. If required, enter your username and password to open the file.

> **⊙ tip**
>
> Chapter 16, "Sharing QuickBooks Data with Your Accountant," discusses in more detail different file types and their purposes. The QuickBooks instruction of selecting File, Open will only open a file with the extension of .QBW.

Figure 2.9
If you have moved your file to a new computer, select the Open a Company file option and browse to the location of the stored file.

Choosing from a List of Multiple Data Files

Chapter 1 introduced you to working with the QuickBooks sample data that installs automatically with your QuickBooks software. Using sample data can give you the freedom to practice what you learn and gain confidence in working with your software.

You also learned in Chapter 1 how to create your company's QuickBooks file using a variety of different methods.

In this section, you will learn how to open a QuickBooks file from a list, which is especially useful if you have multiple data files or want to open the sample data again after working in your own file.

To choose from a list of multiple data files, follow these steps:

1. From the menu bar, select File, Open Previous Company. A list of previously opened files (up to a maximum of 20) displays, as shown in Figure 2.10.

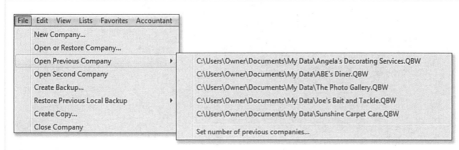

Figure 2.10
Access previously opened QuickBooks files easily.

2. Select a file in the list to open it.

3. Enter your username and password, if required.

If you need to increase the number of files shown, from an *opened* QuickBooks file, select File, Open Previous Company, Set Number of Previous Companies from the menu bar. QuickBooks can display up to 20 different data files in this list. Enter the number you want to include in your list and click OK when finished.

In Chapter 1, you learned how to open and test with sample data and create your own file. In this chapter, you learned how to navigate the many features and tools found in QuickBooks. Let's take a quick break from QuickBooks and discuss some basic accounting in the next chapter, Chapter 3, "Accounting 101." I promise it will be worth your time and help you make better use of your QuickBooks file.

3

ACCOUNTING 101

Basic Principles of Accounting

This chapter provides a quick review of some of the more important accounting concepts, written especially for the non-accountant business owner. While there is much more to learn about accounting principles than this chapter covers, you will learn at least enough to help you manage the financials of your business.

You made an important choice when you selected the QuickBooks software to help you track the day-to-day financial transactions of your business. QuickBooks completes most of the accounting behind-the-scenes, so you can focus on what you do best.

 note

This book does not offer tax or accounting advice. Be sure to consult your accounting professional when necessary.

The Matching Principle

The matching principle of accounting refers to recognizing revenue and associated expenses in the same period. Matching income and costs in this manner gives you a much more accurate representation of your financial situation and performance.

Most businesses offer products or services that have related costs, such as:

- **Asset Purchases**—Balance Sheet accounts. Inventory for sale, or fixed assets (equipment) used in the production of your product or service.

- **Cost of Goods Sold Expenses**—Direct expenses incurred when making your product or providing a service. Cost of material or labor expenses are examples.

- **Expenses**—Overhead fixed and variable expenses such as rent, office supplies, advertising, and so forth.

- **Other Expenses**—Expenses of the business not related to the product or service you provide. For example, interest expense or depreciation expense.

note

Inventory you purchase is an asset purchase and later becomes a cost of goods sold expense when you sell it.

It is important to understand the different account types when recording costs, so that you will categorize your bills or expenses correctly.

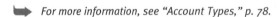 *For more information, see "Account Types," p. 78.*

Any discussion of the matching principle isn't complete without defining revenue. Revenue (income) is usually the funds received from customers. Income is typically one of the following:

- **Operating Income**—Income derived from selling your business's product or service.

- **Other Income**—Income derived from sources other than selling your product or service. For example, interest income.

I expect that you already understand the general concept of revenue versus expense. So what does the matching principle have to do with accounting?

A retail bike store might keep parts, such as wheels, pedals, and chains on hand in its inventory so it can assemble bicycles for its customers. The matching principle requires this store to record the costs of the bike at the time of sale. The initial purchase of inventory is not an expense, it is simply trading one asset, cash, for another asset, inventory. When the asset is sold, the initial purchase cost becomes an expense, which reduces the resulting revenue.

Inventory management, as discussed in this example, is pretty straightforward. QuickBooks will track your initial purchase as an asset, and then record the average cost of each part as an expense when you create an invoice to record the sale to a customer.

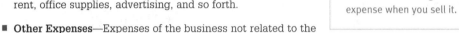 *For more information, see "Setting Up Inventory," p. 111 and "Managing Inventory," p. 159.*

However, let's tackle something a bit more difficult. In this same business, you are required to prepay six months of general liability insurance. Recording this entire balance as an expense in a single month would make that month's net income appear artificially lower, along with making net income for the next five months artificially higher. To match the expense, you would assign the initial payment to a prepaid expenses account on your balance sheet. You would then use a journal entry each month to record an increase in insurance expense and a decrease in the prepaid expenses account. Each month would then have the cost for insurance that belonged in a single month.

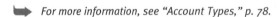 *For more information, see "Recording Vendor Prepayments," p. 245.*

QuickBooks accrual basis reporting can help view your financials in a format that matches revenue with expense. More information is provided in the next section.

Accrual Versus Cash Basis Reporting

Although the purpose of this book is not to give specific accounting or tax advice on any of the topics covered, it is worth discussing the nature of accrual versus cash basis reporting as it pertains to creating a new data file.

Cash basis accounting follows these rules:

- **Revenue**—Recognized when the customer payment is received, not necessarily the same day or month the service or product was provided.

- **Expenses**—Recognized when the payment is made to the vendor or employee, not necessarily the same day or month the expense relates to.

Accrual basis accounting follows these rules:

- **Revenue**—Recognized as income on the date of the customer invoice transaction regardless of when the customer pays the invoice.

- **Expenses**—Recognized as a cost on the date of the vendor bill, check, or credit card charge, regardless of when you make the payment.

Understanding the basics of these two types of reporting is important. When filing a tax return, businesses must specify cash or accrual as their accounting method. However, for management purposes, business owners can view one or both types of reports when making internal decisions. The capability to view reports in either accrual or cash basis is one of the features that sets the QuickBooks software apart from other accounting solutions.

Cash basis reporting can give you a sense of how cash flows through your business, while accrual basis reporting uses the matching principle to give you a much more accurate representation of how revenue and expenses are related.

The difference between the two methods is in the timing of when income and expenses are recognized in your financials. Table 3.1 shows how QuickBooks treats the different types of transactions in both reporting methods on the Profit & Loss statement.

Table 3.1   Accrual Versus Cash Basis Accounting

Transaction Type	Profit & Loss Accrual Basis	Profit & Loss Cash Basis
Customer Invoice	Revenue is recognized on the date of the invoice.	Revenue is recognized on the date of the customer payment transaction.
Customer Credit Memo	Revenue is decreased on the date of the credit memo.	No impact.
Vendor Bill	Cost is recognized on the date entered on the vendor bill transaction.	Cost is recognized on the date of the bill payment check.
Vendor Credit Memo	Cost is decreased on the date of the vendor credit memo.	No impact.

Table 3.1   Continued

Transaction Type	Profit & Loss Accrual Basis	Profit & Loss Cash Basis
Check	Cost is recognized on the date entered on the check transaction.	Cost is recognized on the date entered on the check transaction.
Credit Card	Cost is recognized on the date entered on the credit card transaction.	Cost is recognized on the date entered on the credit card transaction.
General Journal	Cost or revenue is recognized on the date entered on the general journal transaction.	Cost or revenue is recognized on the date entered on the general journal transaction.
Inventory Adjustment	Date of inventory adjustment is the date the financials are affected.	Date of inventory adjustment is the date the financials are affected.

In QuickBooks preferences you can set a global default basis for all reports. Log into the file as the Admin or External Accountant user type, and from the menu bar, choose Edit, Preferences, Reports & Graphs. Select the Company Preferences tab and choose Accrual or Cash from the Summary Reports Basis section. You can also modify the basis of many reports individually. From a displayed report, select Customize Report and select Accrual or Cash in the Report Basis section.

For management analysis, I encourage every business owner to view their financials often using accrual basis reporting. When you review accrual basis reports, you can see trends from one period to the next. Management decisions based on accrual basis reports might be very different when making the same decisions based on cash basis reports.

Basic Financial Reports

This section describes financial reports that are key to your business.

 *For more details on working with reports, see "Reviewing Your Data," p. 495.*

Balance Sheet

The balance sheet represents the overall financial health of the business. Of the financial statements detailed here, the balance sheet is the only statement that applies to a single date in the business' calendar year.

A standard company balance sheet has three sections and is represented by this equation: Assets = Liabilities + Equity. The categories include:

- **Assets**—Cash, along with economic resources that can be converted to cash.

  - **Current Assets**—Cash, accounts receivable, inventory, and pre-paid expenses to name a few.

  - **Fixed Assets and Depreciation**—Buildings and equipment and their depreciation.

  - **Other Assets**—Goodwill, trademarks, and copyrights.

- **Liabilities**—A debt the business is obligated to pay.

  - **Current Liabilities**—Debt that typically will be paid back within one year.

  - **Long-term Liabilities**—Debt that is expected to take longer than one year to pay back.

- **Equity**—Owner's investments and draws and residual net income or loss in the business over time.

Business owners should review the balance sheet as often as they review the income statement. Most business owners that review the balance sheet will have a pretty good idea if the information is accurate just by looking at the balances.

Income Statement

The income statement also is referred to as a profit and loss statement in QuickBooks. My experience over the years is that business owners review this report often. In QuickBooks, a simple income statement includes these basic sections:

- **Income**—Monies received from the sale of products and services.

- **Cost of Goods Sold**—Direct costs of producing your product or service.

- **Gross Profit**—Income less cost of goods sold.

- **Expense**—Costs associated with your business that aren't directly related to producing goods or services, often referred to as overhead.

- **Net Ordinary Income (Loss)**—Income or loss from operations.

- **Other Income/Expense**—Income or expense not related to operations, such as interest income or interest expense.

- **Net Income (Loss)**—Income or loss from operations less other income/loss.

QuickBooks offers you the flexibility to review your Profit & Loss Standard report in either accrual or cash basis. Creating an income statement that shows 12-month periods on the accrual basis makes it easy to spot changes and trends from period to period.

Statement of Cash Flows

The primary purpose of this report is to show the sources and uses of cash in the business. The statement of cash flows includes the following groups:

- Operating activities

- Investing activities

- Financing activities

Additionally, the following information is included in the statement of cash flows report:

- Net cash increase for the period

- Cash at the beginning of the period

- Cash at the end of the period

QuickBooks automatically assigns a specific chart of accounts to cash flow report categories based on the account type selected.

You also can manually assign a chart of accounts to a specific section of the statement. You must log into the file as the Admin or External Accountant user to set this preference. From the menu bar, select Edit, Preferences, Reports & Graphs, and select the Company Preferences tab. Click the Classify Cash button and follow the instructions on the screen.

Other Accounting Reports

The reports references are simply the basic reports used to analyze the financial health of a business. There are many other reports worth reviewing. Many chapters in this book include sections that detail specific reports relevant to the topic.

Accounting Checklist to Help You Manage Your Financials

This checklist is provided to help the business owner or accounting professional take an organized approach to periodically reviewing a QuickBooks file. This book includes several chapters that will help you learn how to accurately and efficiently manage your data.

Client Name: _____

Date Due: _____

Data for Year Ended: _____ 201___

QuickBooks Version: _____ QuickBooks Release: _____

Method of Accessing Client Data (circle one):

On-site   .QBB Backup Data

.QBM Portable Co. File   .QBX Accountant's Copy

Remote Access

External Accountant Username and Password: _____

Or Client Admin Password: _____

___ Backup of Data Made Before Correcting Transactions

___ Review of Working Trial Balance Ending Balances from Prior Year

___ Prior-Year Balances Changed? Print Audit Trail, Voided/Deleted, Retained Earnings QuickReport

___ Review Chart of Accounts for Any Newly Created Accounts

    ____ Proper account type selected?   ____ Duplicated accounts?

    ____ Assign as sub-account?

___ Item List Review—Print Reports—For The Item List Include Account and COGS Account

    ____ Proper accounts assigned?   ____ Duplicated items?

    ____ Assign as sub-item?

___ Review Accounts Receivable

    ____ Small open balances   ____ Unapplied credits

    ____ Undeposited Funds

___ Review Accounts Payable

    ____ Paid open vendor bills   ____ 1099 Misc. Income form setup

    ____ Unapplied vendor credits

___ Review Payroll

    ____ Non-payroll transactions   ____ Employee defaults

    ____ Payroll item mapping

    ____ Completed run payroll checkup

___ Review Completed Bank Reconciliations

    ____ Account(s) reconciled   ____ Agrees with balance sheet?

    ____ Review uncleared bank transactions

___ Review Inventory Setup

    ____ Inv. valuation summary asset total agrees with balance sheet

    ____ Old outdated item receipts   ____ Journal entries posted to inventory asset account

Setting Up a QuickBooks Data File for Accrual or Cash Basis Reporting

If you have just recently started a new business and QuickBooks is the first financial tracking software you have used, rest easy. You can skip this section because QuickBooks makes it possible for you to do the daily tasks of paying vendors or employees and invoicing customers without any complicated startup procedures. Later, you can view reports in either cash or accrual basis.

However, you may have to manually enter open customer, vendor, and bank balances, in addition to additional balance sheet balances if you are converting to QuickBooks from a software application other than those currently supported with the QuickBooks conversion tool.

For more information, see "Converting from Other Accounting Software," p. 34.

When you begin using QuickBooks you will need to define a start date—the date you first want QuickBooks to track your financial accounting. If the business had expenses or sold products and services before this start date, you most likely have open transactions. For example, if your start date is January 1, 2017, then your beginning balances would be dated as of December 31, 2016.

The following is a brief list of what you need to collect when creating a new QuickBooks data file. These lists should represent their respective value as of the day before your QuickBooks start date:

- **Accounts Receivable**—List by customer of what customers owed you on the day before your start date, including any invoices where the payment was received, but not deposited by the start date.

- **Accounts Payable**—List by vendor of those bills you had not paid as of your start date.

- **Bank Ending Balance**—Ending balance from your bank statement on the day before your start date.

- **Uncleared Checks and Deposits**—List of all checks and deposits that have not yet cleared your bank account as of your start date.

- **Other Balances**—List of all other assets, liabilities, and equity you have in the business.

- **Payroll**—Year-to-date totals for each employee (if using payroll in QuickBooks).

To get your QuickBooks data ready for entering current transactions, you need to record these open balances. However, before doing so, you need to have a few things already set up in QuickBooks. You might refer to the following items as "Master Lists."

Before You Begin Entering Opening Balances

Before you begin entering these startup balances, make sure to have the following created in your QuickBooks data file. Each list item below has its own chapter in this book to help you with this task:

- Chart of Accounts
- Items List
- Customer and Job Names
- Vendor Names
- Employee Names
- Payroll Items

The following options are available when you are creating startup or opening transactions for a business for which you are beginning to use QuickBooks after previously using some other software or manual accounting method.

Cash or Accrual Basis Startup Transactions: Accounts Receivable

After you have completed creating your new data file, you need to take some additional steps that are important to the successful setup of your new QuickBooks file.

To create a customer or job from the Customer Center, select New Customer & Jobs or select the menu to Add Multiple Customer:Jobs. You can enter an opening balance in the New Customer or New Job dialog box (see Figure 3.1). However, as I explain in this section, I don't recommend entering the beginning balance here.

When you enter an amount in the Opening Balance field on a new Customer or Job record, QuickBooks will create a single invoice for the entire amount owed, whereas your own records may include multiple invoices for the amount owed. Additionally, when preparing cash or accrual basis reports take this into account:

- **Accrual Basis Reporting**—For this type of reporting, the Opening Balance field increases Accounts Receivable (debit) and increases Uncategorized Income (credit) assigned the date in the "as of" field on the New Customer or New Job dialog box.

- **Cash Basis Reporting**—For this type of reporting, the field has no effect until the date of customer payment. When the customer payment is received, it increases (debit) the account you assign to customer payments (either the QuickBooks Undeposited Funds or the bank account) and increases Uncategorized Income (credit).

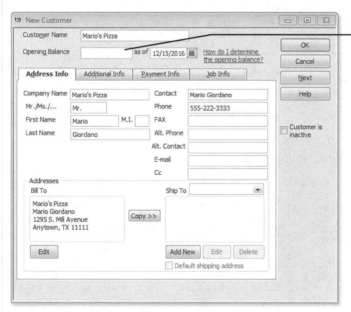

Better option is to create an invoice for the opening balance. When you enter individual invoices for the ope balance you can track more accura which invoices your customers has not yet paid.

Figure 3.1
The Opening Balance field in a New Customer dialog box.

You might well imagine that recording open customer invoices in the New Customer or New Job dialog box is generally not recommended. Instead, follow these steps to create open customer invoices as of your start date:

1. From the menu bar, select Customers, Create Invoices (see Figure 3.2).

2. Select the customer or job from the Customer:Job drop-down list.

 tip

To access this dialog box, you also can use the shortcut key Ctrl+I or access it directly from the opening screen in QuickBooks, known as the Home page.

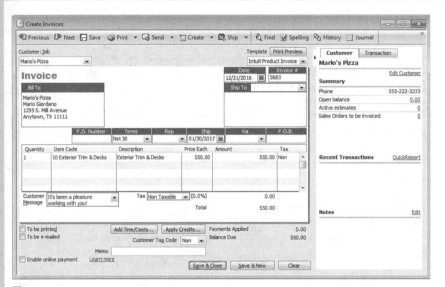

Figure 3.2
Create an open customer invoice.

3. Enter the original invoice date in the Date field (it should be before your start date).

4. Enter the originally assigned invoice number.

5. In the Item column, enter the item(s)—the products or services that were sold—if you want to accurately track your revenue from this item. It should be the same item(s) that appeared on the original invoice to the customer.

6. If applicable, enter a value in the Quantity column.

7. If the rate did not prefill (because it was not included when the list item was created), enter a value in the Rate column.

8. The correct tax status on the line should prefill if the list item was set to the proper sales tax status. If some customers pay sales tax and others do not, you must first indicate the taxable status of an item by clicking Lists, Item List. Highlight the item in question, select the Item button, and select Edit Item. The Edit Item dialog box opens, and you can mark the item with the appropriate sales tax code.

   QuickBooks first determines whether an item is taxable, and then it checks whether the customer is a sales tax–paying customer before assessing sales tax on a customer balance.

9. Make sure the To Be Printed and To Be E-mailed check boxes in the lower left are not selected. However, you will want to select the appropriate box here when you create your first new invoice in QuickBooks. Going forward, QuickBooks will remember the setting from the last saved or edited invoice.

10. Check your Balance Due to make sure it agrees with the list item total from which you are working.

11. Click Save & Close if you are finished, or click Save & New if you have more invoice transactions to record.

Partially Paid Open Customer Invoices on Cash Basis Reporting

To properly prepare reports on a cash basis and to properly report on sales by item, you should perform additional steps for those open invoices that had partially paid balances paid as of your startup date. These steps are required if you want to accurately track sales by item:

1. From the menu bar, select Lists, Chart of Accounts.

2. In the Chart of Accounts dialog box, select New from the Account drop-down list. The Add New Account dialog box opens.

3. Select the Bank account type and click Continue.

4. In the Account Name field, name the new bank account Prior Year Payments Account. This is a temporary account that will later have the balances moved to the Opening Balance Equity account in Step number. 15. Click Save & Close.

5. From the menu bar, select Lists, Item List.

6. Select New from the Item drop-down list. The New Item dialog box opens.

7. Select Payment from the Type drop-down list and name it Prior Year Payments in the Item Name/Number field.

8. Assign the Prior Year Payments account created in step 1 as the account to Deposit To (see Figure 3.3). Click OK.

9. To create the open invoice, select Customers, Create Invoices from the menu bar.

10. Select the Customer:Job from the drop-down list.

11. Enter the original invoice date (it should be before your QuickBooks start date), and enter the invoice number originally presented to the customer for payment.

Figure 3.3
Create a payment item type to use on partially paid startup invoices.

12. On line 1 (or more if needed) of the customer invoice, enter your normal service or product item you sold to the customer. On the next available line, use the new Prior Year Payments item you created and enter the total of the customer's prior payments as a negative amount (see Figure 3.4). Click Save & Close if you are finished, or Save & New to create additional open customer invoices.

13. Verify that the Balance Due amount on the invoice accurately matches the open invoice total from your prior accounting list or report.

14. Compare your QuickBooks A/R Aging Summary report to your open invoices startup list total. If the balances agree, go to Step 15. If they do not agree, review either the Summary or Detail A/R Aging report and identify which customer(s) balances are incorrect.

15. When your totals agree, click Banking, Use Register, and select the Prior Year Payments bank account.

16. To close the fictitious bank account balance to the Open Balance Equity account, enter the following on the next available line of the register.

    For the date, enter the day before your startup date. Optionally for the number, use the term Closing. In the payment column, enter the same dollar amount as the register total displayed prior to this transaction. In the Account field, select the QuickBooks-created equity account named Opening Balance Equity.

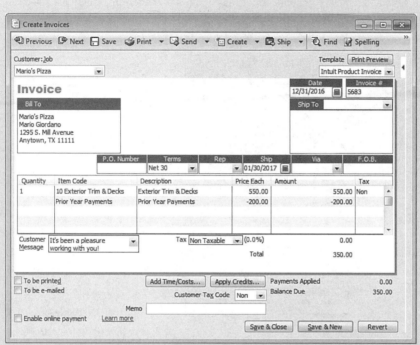

Figure 3.4
Creating an invoice that was partially paid before the start date.

17. Click Record to save the transaction.

Your Prior Year Payments bank register should now have a zero balance.

 For more information, see "Closing Opening Balance Equity into Retained Earnings," p. 513.

Cash or Accrual Basis Startup Transactions: Accounts Payable

Accounts Payable startup refers to those vendor bills that were not paid as of your start date. Presumably, these are the vendor bills you will be paying out in your first month of using QuickBooks.

Correctly setting up the starting Accounts Payable balance is just as important to your financials as setting up Accounts Receivable.

note

Entering invoices using the method described in the side bar provides you with sales reports by item. If this level of detail is not needed on past transactions, you could simply enter a net amount due on the invoice.

1. From the menu bar, select Vendors, Enter Bills. From the Vendor drop-down list select the appropriate vendor (see Figure 3.5).

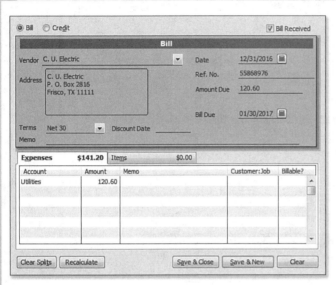

Figure 3.5
Enter a vendor bill that was unpaid at your start date.

2. Enter the bill Date. This date should be on or before your QuickBooks start date, and it is often the date on the vendor's bill you received.

3. Enter the vendor's bill number in the Ref. No. field. This serves two important purposes: One is to optionally print the reference number on the bill payment stub that is sent to the vendor, and the other is to allow QuickBooks to warn you if a duplicate bill is later entered with the same Ref. No.

4. Enter a number in the Amount Due field, if you previously paid part of the bill; the amount should equal the balance remaining to be paid. (See the sidebar "Partially Paid Open Vendor Bills on Cash Basis Reporting.")

5. QuickBooks defaults the Bill Due date to the terms specified on the Additional Info tab in the New Vendor or Edit Vendor dialog box; however, you also can override the Bill Due date on this screen, if necessary.

6. Click the Expenses tab and assign the appropriate expense account. If you are tracking costs by items, use the appropriate item on the Items tab. In accrual basis, the account or item selected is not as important because the expense was recorded on the vendor's bill date in your previous software or accounting method. For cash basis, it is most important because the cost is recorded to the expense account or item not when the bill is dated, but on the date of the bill payment check transaction, which should occur after the start date.

7. Click Save & Close.

8. From the menu bar, select Report, Vendors & Payables, A/P Aging Summary (or A/P Aging Detail), and compare the totals with your previous accounting software or manual records.

9. If the open bills you are entering are for inventory, make sure you read the details in Chapter 5, "Setting Up Inventory."

Partially Paid Open Vendor Bills on Cash Basis Reporting

To properly prepare reports on cash basis, you should perform additional steps for those open vendor bills that have partial payments as of your startup date. These steps are required if you want to accurately track your costs by item.

Use the Prior Year Payments bank account that you created in the previous set of steps. This is a temporary account that will later have the balances moved to the Opening Balance Equity account in Step number 9.

1. From the menu bar, select Lists, Item List. The Item List dialog box opens.

2. Select New from the Item drop-down list.

3. In the New Item dialog box, select the Other Charge item type. In the Item Name/Number field, type Prior Year Vendor Payments (see Figure 3.6). Assign it to the Prior Year Payments bank account by selecting it from the Account drop-down list. (This account was created in the previous set of steps. See the sidebar "Partially Paid Open Customer Invoices on Cash Basis Reporting.") Click OK to save.

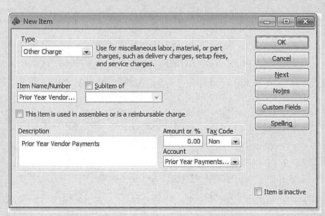

Figure 3.6
Create an Other Charge type item to record prior year vendor payments.

4. Follow steps 1–6 in the preceding section titled "Cash or Accrual Basis Startup Transactions: Accounts Payable" with the exception that you want to record the full amount of the original bill. You can use the Expenses tab and assign the appropriate expense account, or if you are tracking costs by item, use the Items tab and assign the correct item.

5. On the Items tab of the Enter Bills dialog box, add the Other Charge type item called Prior Year Vendor Payments. Enter a negative amount equal to the total of all previous bill payments (see Figure 3.7).

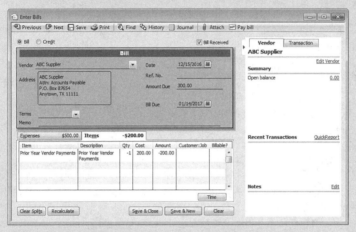

Figure 3.7
Create an open vendor bill including any prior year vendor payment line detail.

6. Verify that the Amount Due amount on the Enter Bills dialog box accurately matches the open vendor invoice total from your previous software (or accounting method) report.

7. Compare your QuickBooks A/P Aging Summary report to the open vendor bill startup list total from your previous software. If the balances agree with each other, go to the next step. If they do not agree, review either the Summary or Detail A/P Aging report and identify which vendor(s) balances are incorrect and make the needed changes.

8. When the totals of your prior accounting Payables agree with the new QuickBooks A/P Summary report, select Banking, Use Register from the menu bar, and select the Prior Year Payments fictitious bank account in the Use Register dialog box. Click OK.

9. On the next available register line, enter the day before your startup date and the word *Closing* for the number. In the Deposit column, enter the total amount you see in the balance column of this register. In the Account field, select the QuickBooks-created equity account named Opening Balance Equity.

10. Click Record to save your transaction.

When completed, your Prior Year Payments account will have a zero balance.

 For more information, see "Closing Opening Balance Equity into Retained Earnings," p. 513.

Cash or Accrual Basis Startup Transactions: Bank Account Statement Balance

In addition to setting up the Accounts Payable and Receivable startup transactions, you also must record the balance the bank had on record as of the start date. Having accurate information is necessary when you are ready to reconcile the bank account in QuickBooks to the bank's records.

 tip

To track these expenses using one of the many Job Profitability reports, you need to enter your cost detail on the Items tab of the related dialog box.

To create your beginning bank balance, follow these steps:

1. From the menu bar, select Banking, Make Deposits to record your bank statement balance (if a positive balance). However, if you have been using QuickBooks for recording payments before you entered your beginning bank balance, you may need to close the displayed Payments to Deposit dialog.

2. In the Deposit To field, enter your bank account from your chart of accounts list. The Date should be the same as your bank statement ending date, usually the day before your QuickBooks start date.

3. Select Opening Balance Equity from the From Account drop-down list (see Figure 3.8). The balance really belongs in Retained Earnings, but posting it here first gives you a chance to make sure the opening entries for your cash account are correct. (See Chapter 13, "Working with Bank and Credit Card Accounts," for a complete discussion on moving the Opening Balance Equity balance to Retained Earnings.)

4. Enter an optional Memo.

5. Enter the Amount. The amount recorded here is the ending balance from the bank statement the day before your QuickBooks start date. This amount *should not* include any uncleared checks or deposits that have not cleared the bank funds.

6. Click Save & Close to record the transaction.

 tip

To check if your bank account has the correct balance, from the menu bar, select Banking, Use Register, and select your bank account to open the register.

If the amount is correct and agrees with your bank's statement ending balance, no further action is required. Otherwise, double-click the transaction and edit the amount. If you don't yet have a beginning balance, follow the steps listed in this section.

 tip

If your bank account had a negative balance as of your start date, you can use a check to record that amount.

If you have outstanding deposits that did not clear your bank funds, the way you enter them depends on the basis of accounting used:

- Accrual basis users create the deposit(s) using the same steps as outlined for entering the beginning bank balance and date the transactions before the start date.

- Cash basis users select Customers, Receive Payment from the menu bar, and apply the deposit to an open invoice, which you created earlier in this chapter. Date this transaction *on* or *after* your start date.

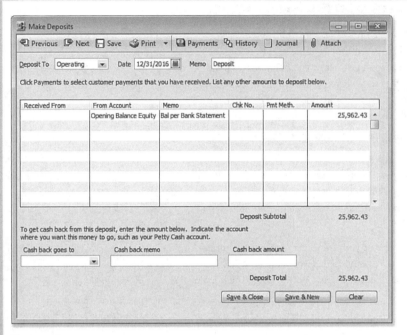

Figure 3.8
Entering the statement ending balance from the bank.

Cash or Accrual Basis Startup Transactions: Recording Uncleared Bank Checks

You are almost finished with the startup entries. The last thing to do is to record the checking account's uncleared checks and debits, as shown in Figure 3.9. To complete the startup process for your banking transactions, follow these instructions to create your uncleared checks:

1. From the menu bar, select Banking, Write Checks.

2. In the Write Checks dialog box, enter the actual check number that was issued in the No. field.

3. Enter the date of the original check in the Date field, which should be before the start date.

4. Select the payee from the Pay to the Order Of drop-down list.

5. Enter the amount of the check.

6. Enter the Opening Balance Equity account on the Expenses tab (see Figure 3.9). (This account is used because in both accrual and cash basis reporting, the check expense amount was included in our prior software or accounting method Profit & Loss totals.)

7. Click Save & Close (or Save & New) until you are completed with this task.

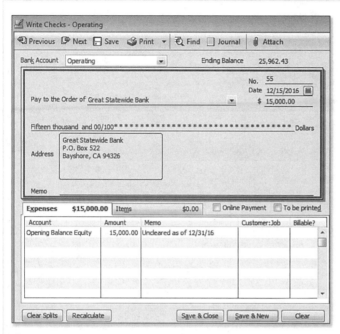

Figure 3.9
Entering a check that was not cashed by the bank as of the start date.

To verify the accuracy of the information, select Reports, Company & Financial, Balance Sheet Standard from the menu bar, and set the date to be one day before your start date. Your bank account balance(s) should be equal to Bank Statement Ending Balance plus Outstanding (uncleared) Deposits less Outstanding (uncleared) Checks.

UNDERSTANDING QUICKBOOKS LISTS

QuickBooks offers several methods for tracking and reporting on your accounting data so you can review how your business is doing financially.

With QuickBooks you can use the following lists to help with analyzing your business:

- **Chart of Accounts**—For organizing your daily transactions.

- **Items List**—For tracking the profitability of individual services and products sold.

- **Class List**—For tracking different corporate profit centers (divisions).

- **Customer Type List**—For viewing your gross profit by user defined-customer types.

 tip

A well-defined QuickBooks data file most likely includes the use of items, classes, and customer types, in addition to the chart of accounts.

The QuickBooks chart of accounts is easy to set up. It might already exist if you created your file with the Express Start discussed in Chapter 1 "Getting Started with QuickBooks." What becomes problematic for some is how to efficiently use each of the available list types when you want to segment the business reporting activity in QuickBooks. We will start first with the chart of accounts.

Chart of Accounts

The chart of accounts is a list of asset, liability, equity, income, and expense accounts to which you assign your daily transactions.

This list is one of the most important lists you will use in QuickBooks; it helps you keep your financial information organized. When this list is created with summary accounts and you use the other list types for detail, you can capture information in a timely manner, which will help you make good financial and management decisions for the business.

Account Types

Understanding the chart of accounts isn't complicated. There are six standard account categories used for tracking the financial activity of your business: assets, liabilities, equity, income, cost of goods sold, and expense.

Assets

Assets include something you have purchased in the past that will be used in the future to generate economic benefit. QuickBooks offers these categories in the order of how liquid the asset is, or in simple terms how quickly you can turn the asset into cash:

- **Bank**—You use this account type to track your cash in and out of the business. This account type and the credit card account type are the only account types you can select as the payment account in the Pay Bills or Write Checks dialog box.

- **Accounts Receivable**—This account type requires a Customer or Customer and Job name with each entry. You use this account type when generating an invoice or credit memo transaction or when receiving a customer payment. You can create more than one Accounts Receivable account if needed, however I do not recommend it as it adds extra work when recording customer payments.

- **Other Current Asset**—This account type is general in nature and includes the QuickBooks Inventory Asset and the Undeposited Funds account. The Undeposited Funds account is used like a "desk drawer" in that it holds customer payments to be totaled together on one deposit ticket.

- **Fixed Asset**—This account type shows purchases of tangible property that will have a useful life of longer than one year. Accumulated Depreciation totals are also held in this account type as a negative fixed asset.

- **Other Assets**—Intangible assets that have a life of more than one year; also any asset that is not a Fixed Asset or Current Asset.

Liabilities

Liabilities are the debts the company has yet to pay. QuickBooks includes these subgroups:

- **Accounts Payable**—This account type is reserved for the QuickBooks Accounts Payable account where vendor bills and bill payments reside.

- **Credit Cards**—Optionally users can use this grouping to track the charges and payments made against a company credit card. One benefit is that you can reconcile this account as you do your bank account and download your credit card transactions directly into QuickBooks.

- **Other Current Liability**—This is debt that is expected to be paid within one year. This grouping includes the QuickBooks-created Payroll Liabilities account and Sales Tax Payable account, in addition to other user-defined liability accounts.

- **Long-Term Liability**—This is debt that will not be paid within one year.

Equity

The Equity account category holds the owner's (or owners') residual interest in the business after the liabilities are paid. Accounts in this category include common stock; owner's investments and draws; retained earnings; and opening balance equity (an account created by QuickBooks that is discussed in more detail in "Closing Opening Balance Equity into Retained Earnings" in Chapter 15, "Reviewing Your Data").

Income

Money earned from the sale of your products or services is recorded as income. Your company might have one income account or several depending on the detail needed for your financial analysis. Another category of income is Other Income, or income generated from the sale of a product or service not normal to your operations. Interest Income is an example of an Other Income account type.

Cost of Goods Sold

The Cost of Goods Sold account is for costs directly related to producing a service or good for sale. There is a direct relationship between these costs and your revenue. If your company sells a product, your cost of goods sold (COGS) expenses would be the material, labor, and other costs incurred to make and sell the product. By contrast, your office expenses for rent or advertising are considered indirect and should not be posted to the Cost of Goods Sold account type.

Expense

An expense is recorded when an asset is used or there is an outflow of cash. The expense accounts were created during the Express Start or Advanced Setup and provide you with the basic classifications needed for properly tracking your expenses.

Although QuickBooks does not automatically create other groupings within the expenses category, a recommendation would be to group your expenses by fixed (or uncontrollable) and variable (or controllable) costs. When you review your costs, these additional groupings make easy work of determining which costs you have more control over.

 tip

When you are creating your Cost of Goods Sold accounts, consider using summary accounts, such as material, labor, and subcontract, and letting your Item List track more detail. For example, if you are a construction company and you have expenses for site work, concrete, framing, painting, and so on, rather than have a Cost of Goods Sold account for each cost type, use the Item List for these. See the section in this chapter titled "Adding an Item" for more details. Reports by item are available to break down the total of Cost of Goods Sold account into more detail.

You can also categorize an expense as an Other Expense, which is an expense that is not normal to your operations. You should contact your accountant for advice on what expenses are appropriate to record to an Other Expense category type.

Adding a New Account

If you created your own new data file using one of the methods taught in Chapter 1, you might already have the basics of your chart of accounts created for you. Let's think positively and use the example that your business is doing so well you have opened a new money market account with your bank. You know you need to create a new bank account in QuickBooks so that you can reconcile your banking activity with your financial institution's records.

Creating a New Account

To practice adding a new account record open the sample data file as instructed in Chapter 1. If you are working in your own file use these instructions to create a new bank (or other type of account) in your chart of accounts:

1. From the menu bar, select Lists, Chart of Accounts.

2. In the Chart of Accounts dialog box, select New from the Account drop-down list. Optionally, use the keyboard shortcut Ctrl+N.

3. In the Add New Account dialog box (see Figure 4.1), select the Bank option button and click the Continue button.

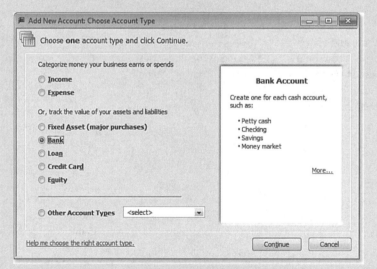

Figure 4.1
When creating a new account, useful information about the account type is displayed on the right.

4. Enter **Money Market** in the Account Name field and **10500** in the Number field (if account numbering is enabled), as shown in Figure 4.2.

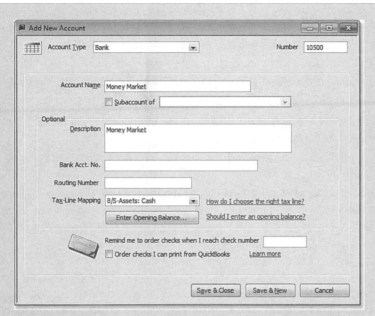

Figure 4.2
Adding a new account when account numbering is enabled.

5. Optionally, select the Subaccount Of check box and select the account you wish to associate this account with. (It is not common to make a bank account a subaccount of another account.)

6. Enter an optional description; this description can be printed on certain reports.

7. Accept the default Tax-Line Mapping, which comes from your sample data file or the choices you made when creating your own new file using the Express or Advanced Setup option discussed in Chapter 1. You can also select the drop-down list and choose a different tax line assignment or click the "How do I choose the right tax line?" link for more information. If opened, close the help dialog box to continue.

   The tax line is only necessary if you or your accountant prepares the business' tax return using software that integrates with QuickBooks such as Intuit's Turbo Tax.

8. Click Save & Close.

The Add New Account dialog box also includes several other important fields:

- **Bank Accnt No.**—This information will be used if you set up your QuickBooks bank account for online banking downloads. For more information, see Chapter 13, "Working with Bank and Credit Card Accounts."

- **Routing Number**—This information will be used if you set up your QuickBooks bank account for online banking downloads (see Chapter 13).

■ **Enter Opening Balance**—This button opens the Enter Opening Balance dialog box where you can enter your Statement Ending Balance and Statement Ending Date. Select the "Should I enter an opening balance?" link for help in entering these important starting numbers.

➡ *For more information about beginning balances, see, "Setting Up a QuickBooks File for Accrual or Cash Basis Reporting," pg. 63.*

This dialog box also enables you to request a reminder to order checks when you reach a specific check number or order checks directly from Intuit.

The specific details required when creating a new account will vary depending on the type of account you are adding to the chart of accounts.

Creating a new account in the chart of accounts is simple. However, if after reviewing the content in this chapter you find the need to make corrections, read the section in this chapter titled "Modifying an Account in the Chart of Accounts."

Items

Items are what you sell or buy and are used on all customer transactions and optionally on purchase transactions. Items provide a quick means for data entry. However, a more important role for items is to handle the behind-the-scenes accounting while tracking product- or service-specific costs and revenue detail.

Adding an Item

Adding items to your QuickBooks file takes some planning, but the effort will pay off with improved reporting on the different services or products your company provides.

In this example, you will be adding a new service item type to the sample data file.

Adding a New Service Item

To practice adding a new service item, open the sample data file as instructed in Chapter 1. If you are working in your own file use these instructions to begin creating your own service items.

1. From the menu bar, select Lists, Item List to open the Item List dialog box.

2. Select New from the Item drop-down list. Optionally, use the keyboard shortcut Ctrl+N.

3. In the Add/Edit Multiple List Entries dialog box, click OK. Optionally, select the Do Not Display This Message in the Future check box. For more information on this feature, review the "Add/Edit Multiple List Entries" section later in this chapter.

4. From the Type drop-down list select Service.

5. Type Inspection in the Item Name/Number field.

6. Select the This Service Is Used in Assemblies or Is Performed by a Subcontractor or Partner check box, as shown in Figure 4.3. This makes the item "two-sided," assigning both an expense account when used with a purchase transaction and an income account when used with a sales transaction.

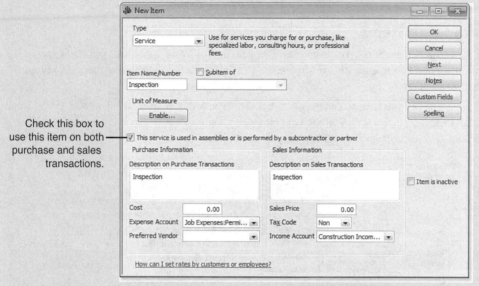

Check this box to use this item on both purchase and sales transactions.

Figure 4.3
Items are used on customer sales transactions and purchase transactions.

7. Type **Inspection** in the Purchase Information text box.

8. Optionally, enter a default Cost. This amount will default on a purchase transaction, but can also be changed at the time of entry.

9. In the Expense Account field, select the appropriate account. For this example, we will use the Cost of Goods Sold account because the item is directly related to our Customers or Jobs.

10. Optionally, select a default Preferred Vendor.

11. Accept the default description in the Sales Information text box or type a unique description. This description will default on your sales transactions for this item.

12. Optionally, enter a default Sales Price. This amount will default on sales transactions, but can be changed at the time of entry.

13. Select the tax code, choosing Tax if the item is subject to sales tax or Non for Non-taxable services. Check with your state's taxing authority if you have any questions about an item you sell being taxable or not.

14. From the Income Account drop-down list, select the Subcontracted Labor Income account.

15. If you are finished adding items, click OK to save and exit the New Item dialog box.

16. If you want to continue adding items, click Next to continue to the next item.

For more information about tracking product inventory, see "Inventory Item Type Descriptions," p. 118.

For more information about other uses of the items list, see "Unique Customer Transactions," p. 366.

Understanding Items

Using the contractor example, you could create an item for Site Work, Electrical, and Plumbing Subcontractor and assign each item to your single Cost of Goods Sold—Subcontractors account in the chart of accounts.

Using items enables you to capture cost detail by labor type rather than creating an account for each type. Then when you view your Profit & Loss statement, you can easily see what your total Cost of Goods Sold—Subcontractors is for all labor types. See Figure 4.4.

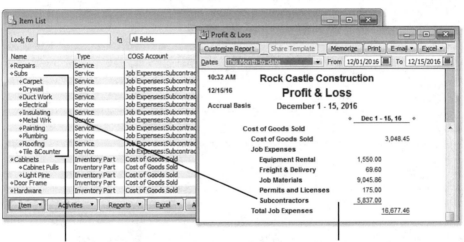

Use the Items List for detailed reporting.   Use the Profit & Loss for summary reporting.

Figure 4.4
Detailed items can report to a single account making the Profit & Loss easier to read.

From the menu bar, select Reports, Jobs, Time and Mileage for reports that provide detailed information about transactions assigned to items including:

- Job Profitability Summary or Detail

- Job Estimates vs. Actuals Summary or Detail

- Item Profitability

- Time by Item

These reports are useful for a business owner who would like to know the profitability of individual customers or jobs.

tip
Using the Items tab on expense transactions such as Write Checks or Enter Bills to ensure that you have the detailed reporting you need to review customer or job profitability.

Item Types

QuickBooks has 11 item types to choose from (not including the Fixed Asset Item), although some of the items might not be listed in your data file if the related feature is not enabled. You can choose the type to assign to a list item; however, each type has certain unique characteristics. Here are some general guidelines about the proper use for item types:

- **Service**—Create this type for services you offer and, optionally, have supplied by subcontractors.

- **Inventory Part**—This type displays only if you select the Inventory and Purchase Orders are Active check box on the Items & Inventory—Company Preferences tab of the Preferences dialog box. (Access from the menu bar by selecting Edit, Preferences.) Inventory is used to track products you make or buy, place in a warehouse location, and later sell to a customer. Inventory is increased with a received purchase order or bill and is decreased on a customer invoice.

  ➡ *For more information, see Chapter 5, "Setting Up Inventory," and Chapter 6 "Managing Inventory."*

- **Inventory Assembly**—This type is an assembling of multiple inventory components, as in a Bill of Materials. When an inventory assembly is built, the individual items (components of the assembly) are deducted from inventory and the quantity of the finished product is increased. The assembly functionality is only available in QuickBooks Premier, Accountant, or Enterprise.

- **Non-inventory Part**—This type is used for products you purchase, but do not track as inventory. Correct use of this type would include products you purchase that are ordered for a specific customer and directly shipped to the customer, or for materials and supplies you purchase, but do not sell to the customer.

- **Other Charge**—This is a multipurpose item type. Freight, handling, and other miscellaneous types of charges are examples of the proper use of the Other Charge item type. Using this type makes it possible to see your services separate from the other charge types of revenue and expense.

- **Subtotal**—This type is used to add subtotal line items on sales and purchase transactions. This item is especially useful if you want to calculate a specific discount on a group of items on a customer invoice.

- **Group**—This type is used to quickly assign a grouping of individual items on sales and purchase transactions. Unlike assemblies, groups are not tracked as a separate finished unit. Groups can save you data entry time and enable you to print or not print the details on a customer's invoice.

- **Discount**—This type facilitates dollar or percent deductions off what your customers owes. This item type cannot be used on purchase transactions.

- **Payment**—This item type is not always necessary to set up. You create this item type if you record the payment directly on an invoice as a line item, such as is done with a Daily Sales Summary (see the QuickBooks Help menu). On typical customer invoices, you should not record payments in this manner because there is no tracking of the customer's check or credit card number.

- **Sales Tax Item**—This type is available only if you enabled sales tax on the Sales Tax—Company Preferences tab of the Preferences dialog box. (Access from the menu bar by selecting Edit, Preferences.) In most cases, QuickBooks automatically assigns this item to an invoice. In some states or industries where there are multiple sales tax rates for a given sale, you can also add this item to an invoice as a separate line item.

- **Sales Tax Group**—This type is used to group multiple tax district flat-rate sales tax items that are combined and charged as one sales tax rate.

> ### 🔔 caution
>
> Carefully determine the correct item type to use when creating items. After they are created, the following item types cannot be changed to any other item type: service, inventory assembly, subtotal, discount, payment, sales tax item, and sales tax group.
>
> If you find you have set up the wrong item type, correcting it might require making an accounting adjustment. To avoid using the incorrect item on future transactions, mark the item as inactive by selecting Lists, Item List from the menu bar to open the Item List dialog box. Select Edit Item from the Item drop-down list and then select the Item is Inactive check box. When this box is selected, as Figure 4.5 shows, the item is not included in any drop-down lists on transactions, but is included in reports if used during the period being reported.
>
> However, do not make an inventory type inactive if QuickBooks still shows available inventory quantity.

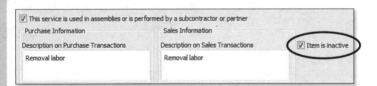

Figure 4.5
Marking a list item inactive only removes it from drop-down lists, not reports.

Class

Another method for segmenting your QuickBooks financial information is by using classes. The use of classes is a preference setting and must first be enabled by logging in to the data file as the Admin or External Accountant user.

To enable classes, follow these steps:

1. From the menu bar, select Edit, Preferences.

2. In the Preferences dialog box, select the Accounting preference on the left.

3. Select the Company Preferences tab.

4. Select the Use Class Tracking check box, as shown in Figure 4.6.

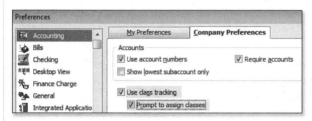

Figure 4.6
Class tracking provides another method for financial reporting for management purposes.

5. Click OK to save your changes and close the dialog box.

Classes are typically used when a company has multiple revenue-generating business types or multiple profit centers. These class list items are then assigned to each transaction, as in Figure 4.7. Examples of classes might be a construction company that offers either new construction or remodel services, or a restaurant with multiple locations. In both examples, using classes that are assigned to each transaction line for both revenue and costs enables you to report profit and loss by class.

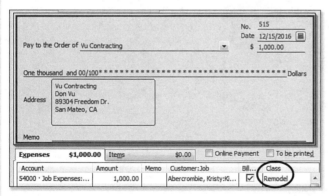

Figure 4.7
Assigning a class list item to a check transaction line provides additional management reporting.

tip

When deciding to use classes, it is important you have only one primary purpose for the class structure. If you try to track more than one "type" of class, the value in the reporting is diminished. For example, your company has both an east coast and west coast division. These represent a single use of the QuickBooks class feature. However, using classes to also track the source of the business—for example, *Yellow Pages*, email marketing, and so on—would diminish the success of class reporting because you would be tracking two unrelated groupings. Instead, you can use classes for one purpose and customer types for another.

Customer Type

You can use customer types to categorize your customers in ways that are meaningful to your business. A retailer might use customer types to track retail versus wholesale; a medical office might track types of services; a service company might track what marketing event brought in the customer. You can filter certain reports by these customer types, giving you critical information for making business management decisions. These customer types can also be useful for marketing purposes when you want to direct a letter to a specific customer type.

To create or edit a customer record and assign a customer type, follow these steps:

1. On the Home page, click the Customer button.

2. Select a customer in the list that displays by double-clicking the name.

3. In the Edit Customer dialog box, click the Additional Info tab and select a type from the Type drop-down list. Optionally, select Add New from the drop-down list to add a new type, as shown in Figure 4.8.

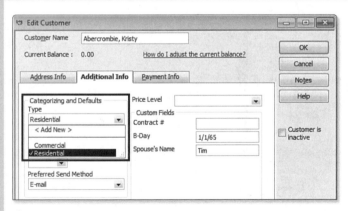

Figure 4.8
Assign a customer type for additional segmented reporting.

4. Click OK to save your changes.

Many of the customer reports can be filtered for customer type, making it another useful list for management reporting.

Managing Lists

You have learned about some of the more important lists to set up in your QuickBooks file. This section will share details on managing these lists, including preference settings that can help you be more efficient and accurate with your daily data entry.

This section also provides you with multiple options for importing your lists (not transactions) into your new QuickBooks file and managing these lists once they are already in QuickBooks. When importing your lists you can select from multiple methods including:

- Adding or modifying the list directly in QuickBooks, one item at a time.

- Adding or modifying your lists using Add/Edit Multiple List Entries, adding or modifying multiple records at a time in a single list.

- Importing a list from another QuickBooks file using the IIF (Intuit Interchange File) format.

If you are starting with a new QuickBooks file, you might first want to review the preference settings that affect the chart of accounts.

Chart of Account Preferences

Setting preferences in QuickBooks can help you be more accurate and efficient with your data entry. In Chapter 2, "Getting Around QuickBooks," you learned about Company Preferences that are global for all users and My Preferences that only affect settings for the currently logged-in user.

Using specific preferences, you can modify how many of the QuickBooks features work. To do so, from the menu bar, select Edit, Preferences and select the Accounting—Company Preferences tab as previously displayed in Figure 4.6.

Here is a list of the preferences found in the Accounting—Company Preferences tab that affect the chart of accounts.

- **Use Account Numbers**—Selecting this option turns on the data field that holds a numeric assignment for each chart of accounts. By default, this feature is not selected in a newly created QuickBooks file.

- **Show Lowest Subaccount Only**—You can select this preference only if you selected the Use Account Numbers check box and if every account has been assigned an account number. If you have created a subaccount listing under a main (parent) listing, when you type the subaccount name only the subaccount name

 tip

For accounts that have an account number assigned, not selecting the Use Account Numbers option does not remove the account number—it simply makes the field not visible. For accountants, turn on the feature and assign your desired account numbers, and then turn the feature off when the file is returned to your client. When you review the file again, any accounts created since your last review will not have an account number, which makes locating them easy.

This is only one method you can use. Accountants who use the QuickBooks Accountant 2012 software can track changes made to the chart of accounts including additions, renames, deletions, or merges made using the Client Data Review tools.

and account number will display in transactions. Without the feature selected, when you type a subaccount name on an expense transaction you will see both the main account name and subaccount name.

- **Require Accounts**—By default, this feature is selected in a newly created QuickBooks file. If this feature is not selected, any transactions saved without an appropriate income or expense account will be posted to an automatically created uncategorized income or uncategorized expense account. This process follows the rule that there must always be a debit and credit side to each transaction. Fortunately, you do not have to know how to post a debit or credit because QuickBooks does this thinking for you with each transaction.

 note

On a report, if you see an amount reporting to an "Other" subaccount row title under a main account, it might be due to someone posting to the main (or parent) account rather than to the appropriate subaccount.

Add/Edit Multiple List Entries

Adding or modifying several entries in a single QuickBooks list can be a daunting task when you have to work with one list entry at a time. In Chapter 1, you might have created your lists using the QuickBooks Setup to add the people you do business with, the products or services you sell and your bank accounts.

With the Add/Edit Multiple List Entries feature (see Figure 4.9), you can add to or modify customer or vendor records. You can also add or modify your service, inventory, and non-inventory items. Using this feature can save you precious time, particularly when you want to add or make changes to multiple entries on a list all at once.

Practice Using the Add/Edit Multiple List Entries Feature

Learn how to use the Add/Edit Multiple List Entries feature by adding a customer record and customizing the columns of data displayed. To complete this task, open the sample data as instructed in Chapter 1.

Figure 4.9
Use the Add/Edit Multiple Lists Entries to add or modify your lists efficiently.

1. From the menu bar, select File, Open Previous Company and select the sample data file you previewed in Chapter 1.

2. From the menu bar, select Lists, Add/Edit Multiple List Entries.

3. In the Add/Edit Multiple List Entries dialog box, the Customer list should default in the List drop-down list. (If you are adding or modifying one of the other supported lists your data fields will vary from the figures shown here.)

4. Click the Customize Columns button on the right side. The Customize Columns dialog box displays.

5. From the Available Columns panel on the left, select the Terms field and click Add>. The Terms data field is now added to the Chosen Columns panel.

6. Click the Move Up or Move Down button with Terms selected to reposition the location of that data column. Adding, removing, or repositioning columns can be very useful if you are copying data from an existing Excel worksheet.

7. With your cursor, select the M.I. (middle initial) field in the Chosen Columns panel. Click the Remove button.

8. Click OK to close the Customize Columns dialog box.

9. Optionally, select the View drop-down list to filter the list results or type in the Find box a specific search term to add as an additional filter to the resulting list.

10. For practice in this sample data, enter your name as a customer. Or, if your own business' customer list is already in an Excel spreadsheet, use Excel's cut and paste functionality to add the customer details to the Add/Edit Multiple List Entries grid.

11. Click Save Changes. QuickBooks indicates the number of customer record(s) that have been saved. Click OK. You might want to save your work as you go often.

12. Click Close to close the Add/Edit Multiple List Entries dialog box when you have completed your additions or modifications.

 tip

If a sample file is not listed, select File, Close Company or File, Close Company/Logoff. In the No Company Open dialog box, select a file to practice with from the Open a Sample File drop-down list.

 caution

On the Customers list, the Name field is the "look-up" or internal name you give a customer. It can be the same as the Company Name field or different. The customer invoice will display the name you type in the Company Name field so be sure not leave it blank.

If you type a name in the Name column that already exists, QuickBooks will highlight the duplicate name and require you to append the name. You cannot have the same Name field duplicated on a single list or other lists. For example, a customer ABC Services cannot exist more than once on the customer list and cannot also be a vendor with the same spelling. If you have a customer that is also a vendor, modify the vendor listing to ABC Services-V and put the actual name of the vendor in the Company Name field and Print on Check As field in the vendor record.

caution

When working in your own data file, make sure your columns of data in Excel match the Add/Edit Multiple List Entries columns when cutting and pasting from Excel.

From the grid, you can right-click with your cursor for other functionality. From this menu, you can use Copy Down, Duplicate Row, Clear Column, and other useful features.

Using the Add/Edit Multiple List Entries dialog box for importing via Excel's cut and paste can be an efficient way to get started and to update existing lists.

Importing an Intuit Interchange Format File (IIF)

The term *Intuit Interchange Format (IIF)* refers to data exchange functionality that has been around for some time. It is a method for exporting lists from one QuickBooks file and importing these lists into a new QuickBooks file. The process creates a comma-separated value format file with the extension of .iif. You can view and edit this file using Excel.

The most common use for this tool is to export lists from one QuickBooks data file to a new QuickBooks data file. The process is easy and relatively error free. Other uses for the tool include transaction imports. This book does not cover the topic of transaction imports using IIF-formatted files; however, you can find more information about this utility by typing **IIF** in the search field at www.quickbooks.com\support.

The IIF format is a preferred and easy method to use if you already have a QuickBooks file with a chart of accounts (or other lists) that you want to replicate in another file.

The only disadvantage to working with an IIF format file is all the extra information that is in the worksheet, making it awkward to edit or add to the existing information.

To export an IIF-formatted chart of accounts file from an existing QuickBooks file, follow these steps:

1. From the menu bar, select File, Open or Restore Company to open the QuickBooks file that has the chart of accounts (or other lists) you want to export and duplicate in another file.

2. From the open QuickBooks file, on the menu bar, select File, Utilities, Export, Lists to IIF Files.

3. In the Export dialog box, select the Chart of Accounts check box (or other type of list you want to export), as shown in Figure 4.10.

 tip

Creating individual IIF files for each of the master lists you want to export is preferred to creating one combined file. In other words, create one file for your chart of accounts separate from a file for vendors or customers. This way, if one list has trouble importing, it won't prevent the other lists from importing.

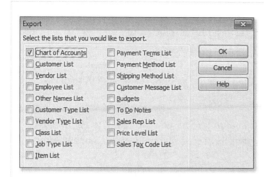

Figure 4.10
The Export dialog box shows choices of lists available for export.

4. Click OK. You will be prompted to provide a filename and to save the file. Remember the location you stored the file in; you will need to browse to the file to import into another QuickBooks file.

Figure 4.11 shows the exported QuickBooks chart of accounts in the IIF format in an Excel workbook. You can see it is not as user friendly as the Add/Edit Multiple List Entries dialog box discussed previously.

	A	B	C	D	E	F	G	H	I	J	K	L
1	!HDR	PROD	VER	REL	IIFVER	DATE	TIME	ACCNTNT	ACCNTNTSPLITTIME			
2	HDR	QuickBool	Version 22.0D	Release R1P	1	12/15/2016	1.48E+09	N	0			
3	!ACCNT	NAME	REFNUM	TIMESTAMP	ACCNTTYF	OBAMOUNT	DESC	ACCNUM	SCD	BANKNUN	EXTRA	HIDDEN
4	ACCNT	Checking	2	933270541	BANK	46,969.10	Cash	10100	1535			N
5	ACCNT	Savings	3	933270541	BANK	17,910.19	Savings	10300	1535			N
6	ACCNT	Petty Cash	85	1071509830	BANK	500	Petty Cash	10400	1535			N
7	ACCNT	Accounts I	4	933270541	AR	93,007.93	Accounts I	11000	1537			N
8	ACCNT	Undeposi	8	933270541	OCASSET	2,440.00	Undeposi	12000	1547		UNDEPOS	N
9	ACCNT	Inventory	6	933270541	OCASSET	30,683.38	Inventory	12100	1547		INVENTOI	N
10	ACCNT	Employee	5	933270541	OCASSET	832	Employee	12800	1547			N
11	ACCNT	Pre-paid I	55	1071514466	OCASSET	4,050.00	Pre-paid I	13100	1547			N
12	ACCNT	Retainage	7	933270541	OCASSET	3,703.02	Retainage	13400	1547			N

Figure 4.11
A chart of accounts IIF format file that can be imported into another QuickBooks file.

To import the saved IIF file into a new QuickBooks file, follow the steps:

1. From the menu bar, select File, Open or Restore Company, and select the QuickBooks file you want to import the previously exported list into.

   If you have not already created your new file, select File, New, and follow the prompts. (See Chapter 1 for more information.)

 caution

The IIF file format is a CSV (Comma Separated Values) format with an extension of .iif. Be sure to keep this format when saving your changes and not save as an .xls or .xlsx Excel file type.

2. From the menu bar, select File, Utilities, Import, IIF Files.

3. In the Import dialog box, browse to the location of the stored IIF formatted file.

4. With your cursor, select the file and click Open.

5. QuickBooks then imports the IIF-formatted file into the QuickBooks data file. Click OK to close the "Your data has been imported" message box.

Now that you have your new data file with new lists from another file, you are ready to begin entering transactions. Just think of all the time you saved by not having to manually create each list item in the new file.

Reporting on Lists

With a QuickBooks file created and lists entered, you can now review the efforts of your work.

Let's start with a simple listing of your vendors.

1. From the menu bar, select Reports, List. Take a moment of your time to review the many lists available for reporting on in this menu. Some lists will only display if the associated preference in QuickBooks is enabled.

2. Select the Vendor Contact List. Optionally click the Customize Report tab.

3. The Modify Report dialog opens with the Display tab selected. From the Columns listing, add or remove checkmarks to include or exclude information from the list report.

4. Click OK when completed.

You will learn more about modifying these and other reports in Chapter 14, "Reporting in QuickBooks."

Reviewing your lists before you begin entering transactions can ensure that the information provided in reports is correct.

Finding and Fixing Chart of Account Errors

When searching for reasons why your financial statements do not appear correct, the first place to look is often the chart of accounts. It is also important to carefully consider the impact of the change on your financials and make sure you choose the right method for correction.

There are many ways to resolve errors found on the chart of accounts. However, before attempting any of the suggested methods here, you should consider the following:

- The effect the change could have on prior-period financials

- The effect the change could have on previously recorded transactions

- The impact the changes would have on the records your accountant has kept for the company

A quick review of the chart of accounts should include the following:

- Duplicated accounts
- Unnecessary accounts (too much detail)
- Accounts placed in the wrong account type category
- Misplaced subaccounts

QuickBooks Required Accounts

The chart of accounts listed here is required for specific functionality of a transaction. If you have previously removed the account, QuickBooks will recreate it when you use a transaction that is dependent on that specific account. Additionally, these accounts are automatically created when a related transaction is opened for the first time:

- Accounts Receivable
- Inventory Asset
- Undeposited Funds
- Accounts Payable
- Payroll Liabilities
- Sales Tax Payable
- Opening Balance Equity
- Retained Earnings
- Cost of Goods Sold
- Payroll Expenses
- Estimates (non-posting)
- Purchase Orders (non-posting)

Making an Account Inactive

Marking an account inactive is usually the best choice when you have duplicate or extra list entries on your chart of accounts. Making an account inactive removes it from any drop-down list where the item can be selected. However, for reporting periods where the account has a value, any reports generated for this time period includes the inactive account balance.

Need to mark several accounts as inactive? Simply select the Include Inactive check box at the bottom of the Chart of Accounts list as shown in Figure 4.12. You can mark any list items you want

 note

In earlier versions of QuickBooks, you might have accounts that have an asterisk (*) in front of the name to indicate a duplicate account name. This situation usually only happens when you did not select to use one of the sample charts of accounts. QuickBooks has certain accounts that it creates automatically. For example, if you did not select a sample default chart of accounts and created your own Accounts Receivable account, later when you opened a customer invoice, QuickBooks created the Accounts Receivable account but recognized that one existed with the same name. You should merge your created account (the one without the *) into the QuickBooks-created account. See the later section titled "Merging Duplicated Accounts" for instructions on how to merge two like accounts.

to become inactive by clicking in front of the list item name. If the Include inactive is grayed out, right-click an account and choose Make Account Inactive. You will now have the option to place a checkmark in the Include inactive box.

In the future if you try to use an inactive account QuickBooks will prompt you to "Use it once" or "Make it active."

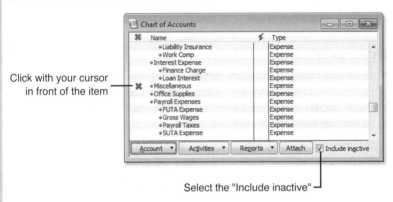

Click with your cursor
in front of the item

Select the "Include inactive"

Figure 4.12
Easily mark accounts inactive from the Chart of Accounts dialog box.

Merging Duplicated Accounts

Another method to remove duplicated accounts is to merge the similar accounts. To perform a chart of accounts merge, both accounts must be in the same chart of accounts category; in other words, you cannot merge an Asset with a Liability type account.

Before merging accounts, perform a backup of your data, just in case the result is not what you expected. When the accounts are merged, all transactions previously assigned to the removed account now appear as if they were always assigned to the remaining account.

 caution

This method potentially changes your financials and should be cautiously performed only after you have discussed the effect with the company's accountant and have made a backup of the data file.

To merge two accounts, follow these steps:

1. From the menu bar, select Lists, Chart of Accounts, and highlight the account you want to remove with the merge. With the account highlighted, press Ctrl+E on your keyboard to open the Edit Account dialog box.

2. If you are using account numbering, replace the account number with the account number for the account you want to retain. Or optionally, you can type the exact spelling of the name of the other account you are merging this one into the Account Name field.

   QuickBooks cautions you that the name is already being used and asks whether you want to continue (see Figure 4.13). If you do not get this message, you didn't type the name or account number exactly the same. You will want to try again.

Figure 4.13
QuickBooks offers a word of caution when you are merging two Charts of Accounts lists.

    3. Click Yes to merge the accounts together.

Modifying an Account in the Chart of Accounts

The mistake most often made when creating your own chart of accounts is assigning the wrong account type. QuickBooks provides additional subcategories under the six standard accounting categories, as identified in the "Account Types" section at the beginning of this chapter.

The Add New Account dialog box, previously shown in Figure 4.1, can help you reduce errors that occur when creating a new account. When you select an account type QuickBooks provides a general description of the proper use of the selected account.

Changing an account type can also be advantageous when you want to fix future transactions and prior-period transactions. For example, suppose you created a Current Asset account type instead of the correct Expense account type. Simply changing the account type via the Edit Account dialog box (see following steps) corrects all prior-period and future transactions to be assigned to the new account type.

However, you will not be able to change an account type or merge a chart of an account if there are subaccounts associated with that chart of account list item. For more information, refer to the note on page 99.

To change an account type, follow these steps:

    1. From the menu bar, select Lists, Chart of Accounts (or press Ctrl+A). The Chart of Accounts dialog box displays.

    2. Select the account for which you want to change the type.

    3. From the Account drop-down list, select Edit Account (or press Ctrl+E to open the account for editing). The Edit Account dialog box displays.

 caution

Chart of accounts, customers, jobs, vendors, and other names lists can all be merged within their own type or category. Be careful—there is no undo function, making the action irreversible.

 caution

Exercise caution before changing an account type. The change affects any prior-period financials. If this consequence is a limitation for your company, a simple solution would be to create a general journal entry to remove the amount from one account and assign it to another dating the transaction in the current period. This method preserves the integrity of prior-period financials.

The Audit Trail report in QuickBooks does not track that a change was made to an account type. However, if your accountant views your data with her QuickBooks Accountant 2012 software, she can view the changes you or your employees made to an account type.

4. Click the drop-down arrow next to Account Type (see Figure 4.14) and choose a new account type from the list.

5. Click Save & Close.

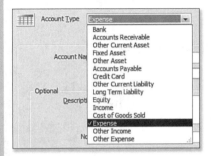

Figure 4.14
When needed, you can change the account type of most accounts (not all).

note

Not all account types can be changed. Accounts Receivable, Accounts Payable, Credit Cards (with online access configured), and any of the default accounts created by QuickBooks cannot be changed to a different type. In addition, for any Balance Sheet account that the account type is changed to a non-Balance Sheet account type, QuickBooks warns that you can no longer use a register for this account or enter transactions directly into this account.

Assigning or Removing a Subaccount Relationship

Often in accounting reports, you have specific accounts for which you want to see a more detailed breakdown of the costs. You can get this breakdown easily by creating the main account and associating subaccounts with the main account.

Figure 4.15 shows Utilities as a main account with an indented subaccount for each type of utility expense.

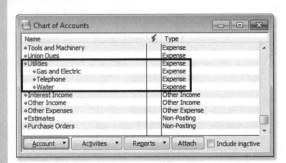

Figure 4.15
Chart of Accounts showing a subaccount relationship to main account.

To edit an existing account to be a subaccount of another main account, follow these steps:

1. From the menu bar, select Lists, Chart of Accounts (or press Ctrl+A). The Chart of Accounts dialog box displays.

2. Select the account that you want to be a subaccount of another account.

3. From the Account drop-down list, select Edit Account (or press Ctrl+E to open the account for editing). The Edit Account dialog box displays.

4. Select the Subaccount Of check box and choose the account you want it to be associated with from the drop-down box. (It must be of the same account type.)

5. Click Save & Close.

Users can assign a subaccount that is only in the same general account type. For example, an Expense type cannot be a subaccount of a Current Asset type account (see Figure 4.16).

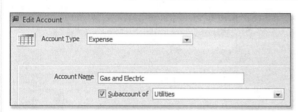

Figure 4.16
Assigning a subaccount to main account.

Another method for changing the assignment of a subaccount to a main account is easily done directly from the list view.

To remove or add a subaccount directly from the list, follow these steps:

1. In the Chart of Accounts dialog box, click with your cursor over the diamond in front of the list item (see Figure 4.17).

2. Drag the diamond so the selected account is immediately below the main account grouping (see Figure 4.17).

3. Drag the diamond to the right to create a subaccount account relationship to the main account. Or optionally, drag the diamond to the left to remove the subaccount relationship.

   The Chart of Account list shows the corrected relationship (see Figure 4.18).

 note

If you need to change the subaccount to another General Ledger account type, first deselect the Subaccount Of check box. Click Save & Close to save the change. Then edit the account and change the type. You cannot change subaccount types when they are associated with a main account. You also cannot change the account type when that account has subaccounts associated with it.

Financial reporting is more accurate when you take the time to review and correct your chart of accounts setup. Often, you can manage the information better when you group similar income or expense accounts using the subaccount feature.

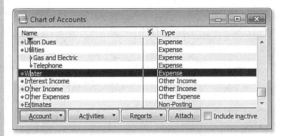

Figure 4.17
Dragging the diamond in front of an account is an easy way to change the subaccount relationship within the same category type.

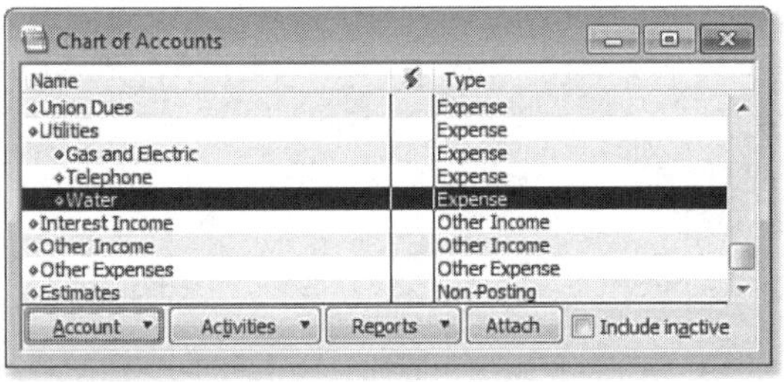

Figure 4.18
The Chart of Accounts viewed after changing the subaccount relationship.

Finding and Fixing Item List Errors

Want to quickly fix some of the most common errors in QuickBooks? Reviewing and correcting items in QuickBooks can be an efficient way to repair a company's data file accounting errors. Often the reason or misstatement on a company's financials can be traced to incorrectly set up items. Some indicators of this might be understated revenue, negative costs, or just an overall lack of confidence in the financials. This is because QuickBooks items are "mapped" to the chart of accounts, if an item is improperly assigned to the wrong type of an account, this could create errors in accurate financial reporting.

To help you in those instances where incorrectly set up items might not be so apparent, the following sections offer a few methods for reviewing the item list.

Reviewing the Item List on the Computer Screen

Adding and removing columns you view in the Item List can help you notice any setup errors that exist. To customize the Item List that displays for items, do the following:

Customizing the View of the Item List

To modify the columns that display on the items list follow these instructions:

1. In the Item List dialog box (select Lists, Item List from the menu bar), right-click and select Customize Columns.

2. In the Customize Columns dialog box, as shown in Figure 4.19, add the COGS Account by highlighting it in the Available Columns pane and clicking Add to include the account in the Chosen Columns pane on the right. Add (or remove) from the Chosen Columns pane those fields that you want (or don't want) to see when viewing the Item List dialog box.

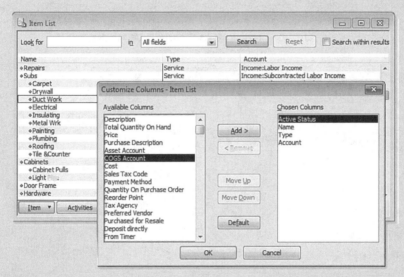

Figure 4.19
Customizing columns on the item list can help you see item errors easily.

3. Click the Move Up or Move Down buttons in the center of the dialog box to customize the order in which you want to view the columns and then click OK.

4. Optionally, to widen columns of displayed data on your computer screen, place your mouse on the right edge of a column header and drag to make the column wider or smaller.

5. Optionally, click a header column to sort the displayed data by the selected column.

6. Click the X in the top-right corner to close the Item List.

Now, you can conveniently review the list on the computer screen for those items that do not have a Cost of Goods Sold or Expense account assigned, or might have the wrong account assigned. Not having an expense account assigned becomes problematic when the item is both purchased and sold; both types of transactions will report only to the single account selected as the Income Account.

See the "Correcting One-Sided Items" section of this chapter for a more detailed discussion of how to properly fix this issue. Refer back to Figure 4.3 for details on creating a two-sided item in QuickBooks.

Item Listing Report

Another method to review the item list setup is the Item Listing report (by choosing Reports, Lists, Item Listing from the menu bar). Click Customize Report from the top left of the displayed report. In the dialog box that displays, click the Display tab to select the columns to view. Useful columns include Item, Description, Type, Account, Asset Account (for inventory items only), COGS Account, and Sales Tax Code, as shown in Figure 4.20. Whenever the item is used on a purchase or sales transaction (such as an invoice, a sales receipt, a bill, a check, and so on), these columns show to which accounts QuickBooks records the transaction on the chart of accounts.

Figure 4.20
Modify the item listing report to provide just the details you need.

What exactly are you looking for on the list item report shown in Figure 4.21? One thing you are looking for are items you use on both purchase and sales forms, but that have only the Account column details. Alternatively, you might also be looking for items with the incorrect account assigned. If you collect sales tax, be sure the correct sales tax code is selected.

➡ *For a more detailed discussion of sales tax in QuickBooks, see "Setting Up Sales Tax," p. 274*

Profit & Loss Standard Report

If you suspect errors with your financials, drilling down (double-clicking with your cursor) on the Total Income, Cost of Goods Sold, or Expense totals from a Profit & Loss Standard report might provide clues to the mistakes. To generate this report for your data, follow these steps:

1. From the menu bar, select Reports, Company & Financial, Profit & Loss Standard.

2. On the Profit & Loss Standard report, double-click the Total Income subtotal, as shown in Figure 4.22. A Transaction Detail by Account report displays, showing each line of detail that makes up the amount you viewed on the original Profit & Loss Standard report.

These items do not have an expense account assigned.

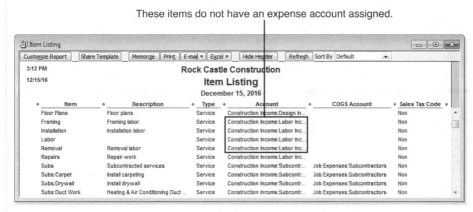

Figure 4.21
Review the Item Listing report for item setup errors or missing information.

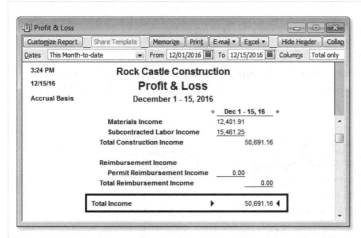

Figure 4.22
Drill down to review the details of your business Total Income dollars.

3. On the Transaction Detail by Account report, click Customize Report. In the dialog box that displays, click the Filters tab. In the Choose Filter pane, scroll down to select Transaction Type.

4. In the Transaction Type drop-down list, select Multiple Transaction Types, as shown in Figure 4.23. The Select Transaction Type dialog box displays. Click to place a checkmark next to each transaction type that normally would *not* be reported to an income account, such as a check, bill, credit card, and so on, and then click OK.

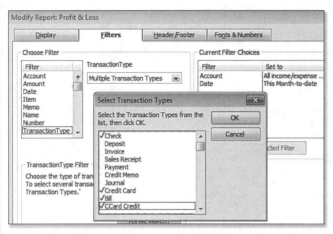

Figure 4.23
Filter the report to include transaction types that should not be reporting to income accounts.

The resulting report now shows all purchase type transactions (or whatever transaction types you selected) that were recorded to income accounts. In the example shown in Figure 4.24, a vendor bill transaction type displays in the totals for income. This is because on the vendor bill an item was used that had only an income account assigned. After you determine you have these types of errors in posting, you should review your item list for any one-sided items. This topic is discussed in the next section.

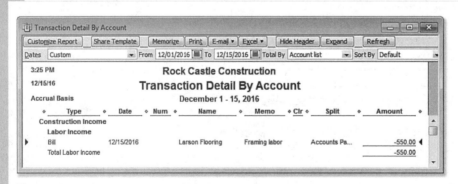

Figure 4.24
The Transaction Detail by Account report shows a purchase type transaction reporting to an income account in error.

As with any data correction in QuickBooks, you should make a backup of the data before attempting these methods. The preferred backup method is a QuickBooks backup (a file with the extension of .QBB). You can create a data backup by selecting File, Create Backup from the menu bar. If the result after fixing items is not what you expected, you can easily restore the backup file.

This section has shown some effective ways to determine whether your items were incorrectly set up. In the next section, you learn the methods of fixing these item setup errors in QuickBooks.

If you are an accounting professional, you will want to review your client's item setup and possible errors using the Client Data Review features and tools available only with QuickBooks Accountant 2012. More information can be found in Appendix A, "Client Data Review."

> **tip**
>
> These methods might affect your financials for prior accounting periods. You should take care when selecting a method that will impact financial periods that have already been used to prepare your tax documents. Discuss these choices with your accountant before making the changes.
>
> If you would like to be warned when making changes to prior periods, consider entering a Closing Date into your file. For more information, see Chapter 16 "Sharing QuickBooks Data with Your Accountant."

Correcting One-Sided Items

A one-sided item is an item that only has one account assigned. See Figure 4.25, which shows the Framing item setup. Notice the only account assigned to this item is Income:Labor. When this item is used on a customer invoice, it increases the Income:Labor amount. However, if the same item is used on a check or bill, the amount of the expense records directly to the Income:Labor income account as a negative number. This would cause both income and cost of goods sold to be understated.

You should not have one-sided items if you plan to use the same item on both purchase transactions and sales transactions.

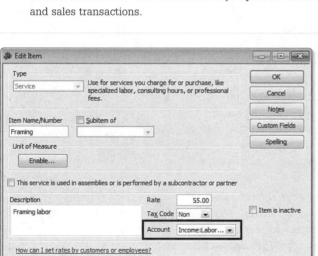

Figure 4.25
Items with only one account assigned can misstate financials if used on both purchase and sales transactions.

CHAPTER 4

You might have several items on your list that can qualify to be one sided because they are used only on sales transactions and never on purchase transactions, or always on purchase transactions and never on sales transactions. What can become problematic is that at some time, a user will mistakenly use the item on the other transaction type.

Inventory items will default as two sided. For the other item types, I recommend you create them all as two-sided items (see Figure 4.26). You do so by selecting the check box labeled This Service Is Used in Assemblies or... (the rest of the label depends on what item type is selected) in the New or Edit Item dialog box.

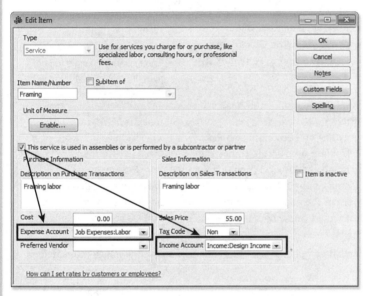

Figure 4.26
The corrected one-side item now has both an expense and income account assigned.

The results are new Purchase Information and Sales Information panes. Now, the "Account" has become an "Income Account" and you have a new Expense Account field to assign your proper expense account. This way, if you use the item on both a vendor bill or check and a customer sales transaction, your financials show the transaction in the proper account.

The decision made at this time to change the account assignment is critical to your financials. Selecting Yes to updating existing transactions causes all previous transactions to now report to the new account assigned. If you are attempting to fix historical transactions, this can be a timesaving feature because you do not have to change each individual transaction manually.

 caution

Before making these suggested changes, have you made a backup of your data? Remember some of the recommended changes are not reversible.

You might even consider printing reports before and after to compare and verify that you achieved the desired end result with your change.

Click No if you do not want to update prior period transactions. This option might be recommended if you have already prepared your tax data with QuickBooks financial information. The change then takes effect only for future transactions.

Additional Warnings for One-Sided Items

You aren't completely on your own when it comes to locating one-sided item errors in item assignments. QuickBooks helps you recognize the potential error by displaying a warning message when you are using an item on a purchase transaction that is only assigned to an income account. Figure 4.27 shows the warning message you see when a check is being written to a vendor but the item used is only assigned to an income account. Be aware that this warning only displays if you have not checked the Do Not Display This Message in the Future check box.

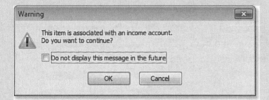

Figure 4.27
The warning message displayed when you use an item on a purchase transaction that is only mapped to an Income Account.

If you ignore the message, in this example QuickBooks posts the expense to the revenue account selected in the New or Edit Item dialog box. The effect of this is to understate revenue (an expense is a negative amount in the revenue account) and to understate your costs (because no cost was recorded to an expense account). Both of these messages distort your financial details, so be sure you don't disregard this important message.

 note

Users often ignore these one-time messages and select the Do Not Display This Message in the Future check box (refer to Figure 4.27). To enable these messages again, select Edit, Preferences from the menu bar. In the Preferences dialog box, select the Bring Back All One Time Messages check box on the General—My Preferences tab as shown in Figure 4.28. This preference setting is only for the currently logged-in user; so don't forget to have other users enable this same preference, if desired.

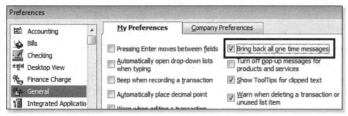

Figure 4.28
To be notified of transaction errors previously disregarded, select the Bring Back All One Time Messages check box.

Making an Item Inactive

If you have found errors in your item list, a safe method for avoiding future mistakes by using the incorrect items is to make them inactive. An inactive item still displays in reports, but is not included in any drop-down lists on sales or purchase transactions.

To mark an item as inactive:

1. From the menu bar, select Lists, Item List.

2. Select the item you want to make inactive by clicking it once.

3. Right-click the selected item.

4. Select Make Item Inactive.

5. If a warning message displays (such as the item being part of a group), click Yes to make the item inactive or No to cancel your change.

Making an item inactive does not have any impact on the company's financials. If you want to correct your financials, you need to choose one of two options:

- Edit the account assignment on each item. This gives you the option to fix all previous transactions that used this item retroactively. (Use this cautiously because it changes prior-period financials.) The effect of changing an account assignment on an item is the same as the one discussed in the section of this chapter titled "Correcting One-Sided Items."

- Create a General Journal Entry transaction to reassign the amounts from one account to another. This method is typically completed by your accountant.

Before making changes, make a backup of your data and always discuss the method you choose with your accountant.

Marking most items inactive is okay. The exception is inventory items. Only inventory items with a zero quantity on hand should be made inactive. See Chapter 6 "Managing Inventory" for more details on handling inventory errors.

 tip

Open the Item List by selecting Lists, Item List from the menu bar. Select the Include Inactive check box (in the lower center of the dialog box). Click once to the left of any list item to make the item inactive, as shown in Figure 4.29.

If the check box is grayed out, you have not yet made any item inactive. After making the first item inactive, you can select the check box.

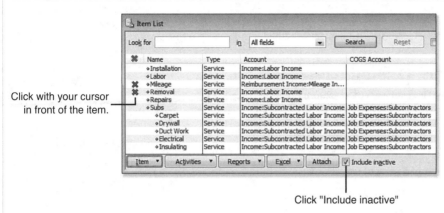

Click with your cursor in front of the item.

Click "Include inactive"

Figure 4.29
Marking Item List elements inactive causes the item not to show on drop-down lists.

Merging Items

If you have duplicated items, one easy method for fixing the problem is to merge items of the same type. When merging two items, you first need to decide which item is going to be merged into the other item. The item merged will no longer exist on your item list.

To merge two items, follow these steps:

1. From the menu bar, select Lists, Item List.

2. Review the list for duplicate items; note the name of the item you want to remain.

3. Double-click the item you want to merge into another item. The Edit Item dialog box displays.

4. Type in the Item Name/Number field the name exactly as you noted it in step 2. You can also use the copy and paste command to avoid typing lengthy names or long numbers.

5. Click OK to save your change. QuickBooks provides a warning message that you are merging items (see Figure 4.30).

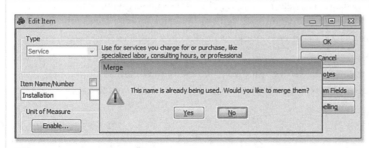

Figure 4.30
A warning displays when you merge two items.

Carefully consider the consequences of merging before you do it (and be sure you have a backup of your QuickBooks file). All the historical transactions merge into the remaining list item.

Creating Items as Subitems

Creating an item as a subitem of another item is one way to easily organize reports for a group of similar items. Your accounting data is not affected by having or not having items as subitems.

To make an item a subitem of another item, follow these steps:

1. From the menu bar, select Lists, Item List.

2. Double-click the item you want to assign as a subitem. The Edit Item dialog box opens.

3. Select Subitem Of check box, as shown in Figure 4.31.

caution

You can merge only items of the same type together. Duplicate service item types can be merged together, but a service item type cannot be merged with a non-inventory item type. It is not recommended to merge inventory items together; see Chapter 6, "Managing Inventory" for more detail.

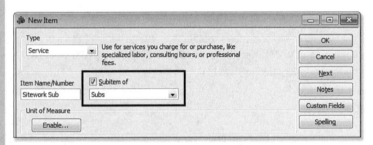

Figure 4.31
The Sitework Sub service item is being made a subitem of Subs (short for Subcontracted).

4. From the drop-down list, select the item you want to relate this subitem to.

You can create a subitem only within the same item type. For example, service items cannot be subitems of inventory items.

You can also rearrange the list by assigning a subitem to another item by using your mouse pointer on the Item List to move the item up or down and to the right or left. This functionality is the same as the example discussed in the section titled "Assigning or Removing a Subaccount Relationship" in this chapter.

You have now completed the important steps in getting your file ready to work with. In the next few chapters, you will learn about inventory, vendor and customer activities, and much more!

SETTING UP INVENTORY

Overview of Accounting for Inventory

Inventory can be described as a company's merchandise, raw materials, and finished and unfinished products that have not yet been sold.

QuickBooks can track the products you purchase, stock, and then later sell to customers. QuickBooks can also track the products you assemble (a component) and use to create a product for sale (finished good). QuickBooks has a perpetual inventory system, meaning each time you record a purchase transaction, inventory is increased, and when you record a sales transaction, inventory is decreased. (See the "Proper Inventory Processes" section later in this chapter.)

QuickBooks Pro, Premier, and Enterprise Solutions record the cost of inventory using the Average Cost method as opposed to LIFO (Last In First Out) or FIFO (First In First Out). This means that the cost recorded at the time a product is sold is equal to the number of inventory units purchased divided by the total cost of the units. QuickBooks automates this process for you. As long as you record your documents correctly and date them appropriately, QuickBooks will assign the correct average cost.

If you are using QuickBooks Enterprise Solutions 12.0, you also have the *option* to use FIFO costing, or First In First Out method. The feature differences between the editions of QuickBooks can be found in the section titled "Inventory Features by QuickBooks Edition." This book does not detail the specific use of QuickBooks Enterprise (QBES) 12.0; however a QBES user will find this book to be a useful resource as most of the menus and processes are the same as when working with Pro or Premier.

Ask yourself these important questions to differentiate between using inventory or non-inventory items in QuickBooks:

- **Will you be selling what you buy, and you do not know the customer at the time of purchase?**—An example might be a furniture store that purchases furniture for resale to customers, or a retail store that purchases medical supplies that are sold to customers. These qualify as the proper use of inventory items.

- **Are you manufacturing what you sell?**—In other words, you buy components (raw materials) and later assemble the components into a finished product that is sold to a customer. An example might be a bike store that purchases wheels, steering columns, chains, and so on and then assembles the components into a completed bike for sale to the customer. This qualifies as the proper use of inventory items.

- **Are you purchasing materials that you use, but do not sell?**—For example, a car repair business might purchase buffing pads and paint supplies. These items are stored in inventory, but are not sold directly to a customer. This example is a more appropriate use of non-inventory items.

- **Is the dollar value of your inventory not significant?**—Often, companies carry a small amount of inventory, but the majority of their sales are drop-shipped directly to the customer from the vendor that the product is purchased from. For example, a construction company can order appliances for a new home, but does not generally stock them. Instead, they have the appliances shipped directly to the new home from the vendor. This example is a more appropriate use of a non-inventory item.

Making the decision to track inventory takes commitment on your part. QuickBooks can help you efficiently and accurately track your inventory with features unique to each edition of QuickBooks.

Inventory Features by QuickBooks Edition

The release of QuickBooks 2012 has dramatically changed the features available when your business tracks inventory. Now, more than ever before, you need to review those features you need the most and make sure you are working in the right QuickBooks edition for your business inventory tracking needs.

There are many other features differences between the versions that are not discussed in this chapter or book. You can view the differences by visiting www.quickbooks.com.

If you are using the QuickBooks Pro or Premier editions and later decide your business would benefit from the features available only with QuickBooks Enterprise Solutions, you can expect the transition to be seamless. When you are ready to upgrade, you will open your company file in Enterprise Solutions and your lists, data, report templates, and user permissions automatically transfer.

QuickBooks Pro 2012

QuickBooks Pro 2012 is easy to set up and learn to use. With QuickBooks Pro you can have up to three simultaneous users working in the same data file. QuickBooks Pro *does not* come in industry-specific editions.

QuickBooks Pro has the most basic of inventory features including:

- Inventory Items, which includes Inventory Part and Non-inventory Part

- Purchase Orders

- Change Item Prices in Batch

- Warn If Not Enough Inventory to Sell, which is found in Preference Settings

- Integrate Your FedEx, UPS, and USPS Software with QuickBooks

Inventory features such as Multiple Unit of Measure can be viewed in a Pro file (once the feature has been enabled in a Premier edition of QuickBooks), but you cannot add, edit, or modify the Unit of Measure settings in a QuickBooks Pro file.

You can easily convert a QuickBooks Pro file to QuickBooks Premier or Enterprise.

More information about upgrading your file can be found in Chapter 17, "Managing Your QuickBooks Database."

QuickBooks Premier 2012

QuickBooks Premier 2012 offers several different industry-specific editions. The inventory features include everything offered with QuickBooks Pro 2012 and:

- **Inventory Center**—Central location for inventory activities and reporting.

- **Inventory Assembly**—Creating a finished good from a bill or materials.

- **Sales Orders**—Handling customer preorders.

- **Quantity Available**—Preference settings for handling how quantity available is calculated.

- **Multiple Unit of Measure**—When you purchase one unit and sell in another. (Available only in selected Premier or Enterprise editions.)

If you have purchased the QuickBooks Premier Manufacturing & Wholesale 2012 edition, you will have all of the above features plus the following:

- **Sales Order Fulfillment Worksheet**—Ease in filling orders.

- **Create Customer Return Materials Authorization Form**—Creates a Word template for you to enter information in.

- **Report on Non-conforming Material Report**—Creates a Word template for you to enter information in.

- **Damaged Goods Log**—Creates a Word template for you to enter information in.

- **Several Industry-Specific Reports**—Includes Inventory Reorder Report by Vendor.

QuickBooks Enterprise Solutions 12.0

The release of QuickBooks Enterprise Solutions 2012 has created the most excitement in years, specifically for companies that track inventory. This book lists the features, but does not cover in detail the setup or use of these new features. Options include:

- QuickBooks Enterprise Solutions 12.0

- QuickBooks Enterprise Solutions Manufacturing & Wholesale 12.0

- Either of the two above with an Advanced Inventory subscription

QuickBooks Enterprise Solutions 12.0

QuickBooks Enterprise Solutions 12.0 includes all of the features mentioned previously as well as:

- **Enhanced Inventory Receiving**—New workflow records and tracks the item receipt separate from the vendor bill.

- **Automatic Cost and Price Updates**—When an item's cost changes, set a preference for automatically handling charges to the default cost, sales price, and markup.

- **Edit Markup**—Defines how markup is calculated from cost.

- **Inventory Center Add Image**—Ability to attach an image to an item record. (Currently, you cannot attach an image to a transaction.)

- **Custom Fields**—Used to track additional specific detail for your inventory items. Custom fields can be required upon entry and can be defined by type of data, numbers, date, phone, and so on.

QuickBooks Enterprise Solutions Manufacturing & Wholesale 12.0

If you purchased the QuickBooks Enterprise Solutions Manufacturing & Wholesale 12.0 edition, you will have the same industry-specific tools available with QuickBooks Premier Manufacturing & Wholesale 2012 including:

- **Sales Order Fulfillment Worksheet**—Offers ease in filling orders.

- **Create Customer Return Materials Authorization Form**—Creates a Word template for you to enter information in.

- **Report on Non-conforming Material Report**—Creates a Word template for you to enter information in.

- **Damaged Goods Log**—Creates a Word template for you to enter information in.

- **Inventory Reorder Report by Vendor**—One of a few industry-specific reports.

Advanced Inventory Subscription

QuickBooks Enterprise Solutions 12.0 or QuickBooks Enterprise Solutions Manufacturing & Wholesale 12.0 with an Advanced Inventory subscription includes the additional following features:

- **Multiple Inventory Sites**—Reporting and tracking of inventory in multiple locations.

- **Lot or Serial Numbers**—Tracking one or the other and a variety of related preference settings.

- **FIFO**—(First In First Out) Inventory Costing.

The optional Advanced Inventory functionality is built into QuickBooks Enterprise Solutions, has an annual fee, and requires a current Full Support Plan (annual fee).

QuickBooks has a version right for your business inventory tracking needs. You can also visit www.quickbooks.com to compare the different editions feature by feature.

Enabling Inventory Preferences

To begin using QuickBooks to track inventory, you must first turn on the feature found in the Items & Inventory preference in QuickBooks. By default, when creating a new company data file, inventory management is not enabled.

To turn on the inventory feature, follow these steps:

1. Log into the data file as the Admin or External Accountant user.

2. From the menu bar, select Edit, Preferences to open the Preferences dialog box.

3. On the Items & Inventory—Company Preferences tab, select the Inventory and Purchase Orders Are Active checkbox.

4. Click OK to save the preference.

The preferences displayed in Figure 5.1 do not affect the accounting for inventory, but rather enable specific features and preferences within inventory management. The preferences available in your QuickBooks data might differ depending on the year and edition of QuickBooks you are using.

Your QuickBooks Home page now shows the inventory workflow (see Figure 5.2). To view the Home page, if it does not automatically open, select Edit, Preferences from the menu bar. On Desktop View—My Preferences tab of the Preferences dialog box, select the Show Home Page When Opening a Company File checkbox.

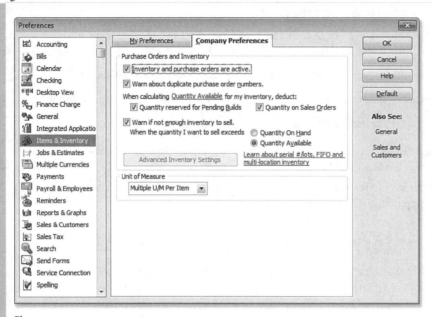

Figure 5.1
Preferences that enable QuickBooks inventory tracking.

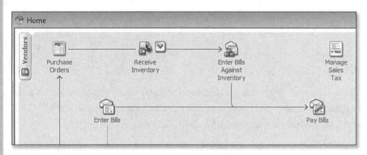

Figure 5.2
Home page workflow with inventory and purchase orders enabled.

One additional preference that can affect your setup of inventory is found in the Time & Expenses—Company Preferences tab (accessed as you did previously for the Items & Inventory preference). When you enter a percentage in the Default Markup Percentage field, QuickBooks automatically makes the default Sales Price to be the cost multiplied by the markup on a new item when the cost is first recorded (see Figure 5.3). As part of the setup you will be required to select an account for the Markup amount; usually this is an income account type.

For example, when you create a new inventory list item and enter a cost of $3.00, QuickBooks will default the sales price of $3.30, or $3.00 + 10% markup, as shown in Figure 5.4.

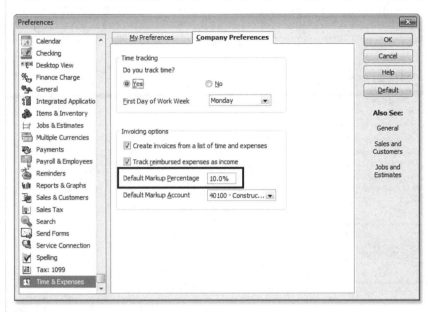

Figure 5.3
Including a Default Markup Percentage will make the sales price of a newly created inventory item to be cost multiplied by the markup.

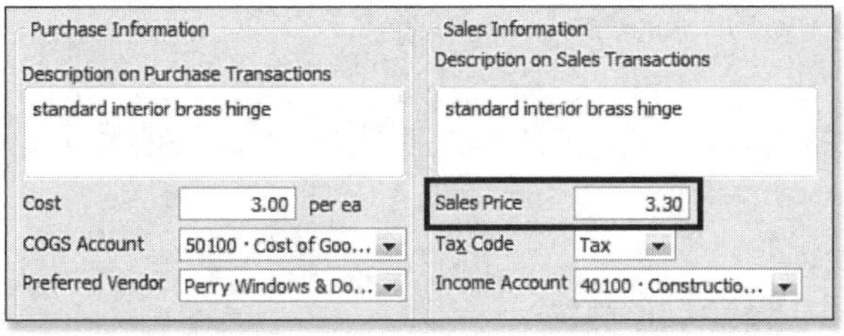

Figure 5.4
QuickBooks automatically calculates the sales price when you set the preference for default markup in the Time & Expenses preference.

Another feature for inventory management is the Unit of Measure (on the Items & Inventory—Company Preferences tab). When selecting this preference (see Figure 5.5), you can define the following for inventory items or non-inventory items in QuickBooks:

- **Single Unit of Measure**—Choose this if you buy, stock, and sell each item by the same unit of measure. For example, if you buy by the pound, sell by the pound, and track your inventory by the pound, this option is the best choice.

- **Multiple Unit of Measure**—If you buy in one measurement, for example, you purchase by the skid (multiple cases of soda) and sell to the customer in single units (a can of soda), but ship by the case (multiple cans of soda), the Multiple Unit of Measure option is the best choice.

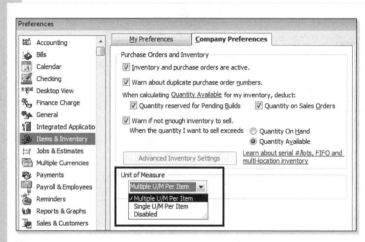

Figure 5.5
QuickBooks Premier or Enterprise includes Multiple Unit of Measure preference.

When you select Multiple Unit of Measure and assign it to an inventory or non-inventory item, you can also define your default units of measure for purchase, sales, and shipping transactions.

For more information, see "Setting Up Multiple Unit of Measure," p. 134.

Unit of Measure settings indirectly affect your accounting by defaulting the unit and the associated cost and sales price. Using this feature can improve your buying and selling accuracy on your documents and can help ensure that proper inventory quantities are recorded.

Inventory Item Type Descriptions

QuickBooks provides several different item types for use in the management of inventory and non-inventory. These items can be used on purchase and sales transactions. This section details the purpose of these QuickBooks item types used primarily with inventory management.

For details on additional types of QuickBooks items, see Chapter 4, "Understanding QuickBooks Lists" and Chapter 9, "Setting Up Customers."

Inventory Part

Create an Inventory part if any of the following apply in your business:

- Items that are purchased and sold

- Items that are stored in stock and later sold

- Items purchased and used as components of a finished product (assembled)

The ability to create an assembled good and track the quantity on hand of the finished product is only available in QuickBooks Premier (all editions) and QuickBooks Enterprise (all editions).

Non-inventory Part

Create a non-inventory part if any of the following applies to the specific part:

- Purchased but not sold

- Sold but not purchased

- Purchased and resold, but not tracked as stock (drop-shipped directly to the customer)

> ➡ *For more information, see "Adding or Editing Inventory Items," p. 121.*

Group Items and Inventory Assemblies

Using the group item types and inventory assembly types are similar in that they both let you record multiple items with a single entry on purchase or sales transactions. The group item type is included with QuickBooks Pro, Premier (all editions) or Enterprise (all editions). Inventory assemblies are only included with QuickBooks Premier (all editions), Accountant or QuickBooks Enterprise (all editions), and Enterprise Accountant.

Here are a few reasons you might want to use assemblies in QuickBooks:

- Track finished goods separately from individual inventory items.

- Customize the price of assembled items. You can specify a price for an assembly, which is different from the sum of the costs of its component items.

- Detailed information about your finished goods including date they were assembled, quantity and cost, and list of component items.

- Ability to set reminders for future builds.

If you are using QuickBooks Premier (all editions) or QuickBooks Enterprise Solutions (all editions) you may benefit from creating Group Items.

What are some reasons you would work with a Group Item? They might include:

- Detailed sales, cost, and budget reporting for multiple items.

- Option to show a single line of detail when invoicing the customer.

Inventory assemblies can be added to both purchase and sales transactions. Group Items are only available to be added to sales transactions. Both help to automate the process of entering multiple items on transactions.

Table 5.1 compares the details of using the Group Item or Inventory Assembly Item. This detail should help you determine the proper type to use for your business:

Table 5.1   Comparing Group and Assembly Items

Group Item	Inventory Assembly Item
Can include any item type except other groups.	Can include any of the following item types: service, inventory part, inventory assembly (sub-assemblies), non-inventory part, and other charge.
Ability to print on sales transactions the individual items in the group item.	Prints only the assembly name, not the component part names on sales transactions.
No reports specific for group items.	On standard inventory reports including pending builds report.
Quantity on hand of each individual item is adjusted at the time of sale.	Quantity on hand of each individual item is adjusted at the time of build.
Sales tax is calculated by individual items.	One sales tax code (rate) applies to the entire assembled (finished) good.
Cannot be included in another group item.	Can be included (nested) in other assemblies and in group items.
Does not track the finished item; only the individual parts are tracked.	Tracks the quantity of the finished product, and depletes the quantity of components.
Price of the group item is the sum of the parts (you can include another item to adjust the sales price).	Sales price of an assembly item defaults to the sales price of the sum of the parts, but can be manually adjusted.
Can include both taxable and non-taxable items.	Must be entirely designated as either taxable or non-taxable.

Included in the next section are details on creating both the group item and inventory assembly. Both are used to save data entry time and improve accuracy when recording purchase and sales transactions with the same multiple items.

Adding or Editing Inventory Items

With inventory and purchase order tracking enabled in your QuickBooks file, you can add your inventory or non-inventory products to the Item list. You will have several options for adding or modifying your list of products. Choose the method that best meets your needs.

Before you begin tracking inventory, you should know the commitment you are making to additional accounting responsibilities. When choosing to track inventory in the normal course of your business, you need to use purchase transactions to increase inventory, and sales transactions to decrease inventory. You also need to commit to periodic inventory counts because your inventory can often get out of sync with your accounting information.

Adding or Editing Individual Items

You can choose to add or modify an individual inventory or non-inventory item in QuickBooks.

Inventory Part

When you purchase or build your product, then stock it in your warehouse for future sale to your customer, you will want to create an inventory part (see Figure 5.6).

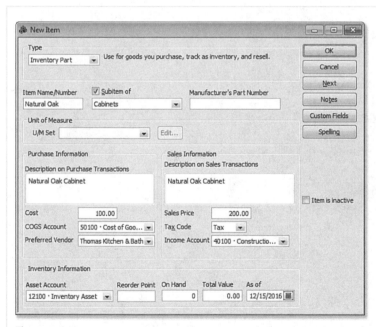

Figure 5.6
Adding a new inventory part item.

When inventory is used, an Inventory Asset account is increased when you purchase and stock the product. The income and related cost is not recorded until you include the inventory item on your customer's invoice.

Adding an Inventory Part

To practice adding a new inventory part item, open the sample data file as instructed in Chapter 1, "Getting Started with QuickBooks":

1. On the Home page, click the Items & Services icon. The Item List displays.
2. From the Item drop-down list, select New or use the keyboard shortcut of Ctrl+N.
3. If the New Feature dialog box for Add/Edit Multiple List Entries displays, click OK to close (this will be taught in the next section). The New Item dialog box displays.
4. From the Type drop-down list, select Inventory Part.
5. In the Item Name/Number field, type **Natural Oak Cabinet**.
6. Select the Subitem Of checkbox and then select Cabinets from the drop-down list.
7. Leave the boxes for Manufacturer's Part Number and U/M Set (for Unit of Measurement) blank.
8. In the Description on Purchase Transactions box, select the newly created item, Natural Oak Cabinet.
9. In the Cost field, enter **100.00**.
10. From the COGS Account drop-down list, select the Cost of Goods Sold account if it isn't automatically selected by QuickBooks.
11. In the Preferred Vendor field, select or type **Thomas Kitchen & Bath**.
12. In the Sales Price field, type **200.00**.
13. Leave the default of Tax assigned in the Tax Code field.
14. From the Income Account drop-down list, select the Construction Income:Materials Income account. You can also select the account by typing the account number 40140 (the subaccount number) in this example.
15. In the Asset Account drop-down list, leave the Inventory Asset account that displays by default.
16. Optionally, enter a quantity for Reorder Point reporting.
17. Leave the On Hand field blank. See the caution that follows these steps about entering your quantity on hand in this manner. If you choose to enter an On Hand quantity, QuickBooks will enter a financial transaction that will increase the inventory asset account and increase the Opening Balance Equity account.
18. If you entered an On Hand quantity, QuickBooks will automatically calculate the Total Value field by taking the On Hand quantity times the amount recorded in the Cost field. You can override this calculated Total Amount field, but only if the resulting value is the proper amount to record for this asset.
19. If you entered an On Hand quantity (not recommended), select the As Of date you want to record the increase in your inventory asset value.
20. Click OK to save your changes and close the New Item dialog box.

tip

The Cost field in a new (or edit) inventory part record is optional. Entering a default cost can be useful for automating entry on purchase transactions, and in some instances can help with properly reporting a change in value when an inventory adjustment record is recorded.

 caution

Converting to QuickBooks after having used other software to track inventory? It is recommended you use an Inventory Adjustment transaction to enter your opening quantity on hand instead of entering a quantity in the On Hand field of a new inventory item record. For more information, see "Adjusting Inventory," p. 159.

Offering a new product for sale to your customers? You should not enter an amount in the On Hand field; instead use a Create Purchase Orders, Enter Bills, or Write Checks transaction to record the purchase of this new inventory item.

Once you save a new item record, many fields cannot be edited, including the On Hand and Total Value fields.

There are optional fields or actions in an item record (depending on the version of QuickBooks you are using) that are useful:

- **U/M Set**—Used to assign defined units of measure for the selected item.

- **Notes**—Internal notes for the currently selected item.

- **Custom Fields**—Flexibility to add information that is not already tracked by QuickBooks. Review the section in this chapter titled "Inventory Features by QuickBooks Edition" to see if the custom field you need is already tracked in a different edition of QuickBooks than you are currently using.

- **Spelling**—Click Spelling and QuickBooks will spell check the description fields of the individual item being added or edited.

- **Item is Inactive**—Should only be used when the item inventory count for the selected item is zero and when you no longer want the item to be included in drop-down lists. More information on efficiently managing your items is included in Chapter 4, in the section titled "Making an Item Inactive."

Non-Inventory Part

Your company might want to create non-inventory items. For example, a construction company that orders appliances for the new homeowner but does not stock the appliance would want to create non-inventory items.

When non-inventory is used, the expense account on the non-inventory item record is used to record the cost at the time of purchase. These items never increase your inventory asset balances.

Adding a Non-Inventory Part

To practice adding a new non-inventory item, open the sample data file as instructed in Chapter 1, "Getting Started with QuickBooks":

1. On the Home page, click the Items & Services icon. The Item List displays.

2. From the Item drop-down list, select New or use the keyboard shortcut of Ctrl+N.

3. If the New Feature dialog box for Add/Edit Multiple List Entries displays, click OK to close. (this will be taught in the next section). The New Item dialog box displays.

4. From the Type drop-down list, select Non-inventory Part.

5. In the Item Name/Number field, type **Stain**.

6. Select the Subitem Of checkbox and then select Lumber from the drop-down list.

7. Leave the boxes for Manufacturer's Part Number and U/M Set (for Unit of Measurement) blank.

8. Select the This Item Is Used in Assemblies or Is Purchased for a Specific Customer checkbox (refer to the caution that follows these steps).

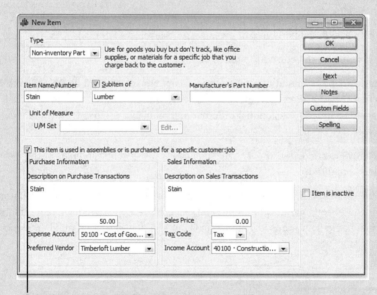

Selecting this box will add both an expense and income account.

Figure 5.7
Use Non-inventory Part type for items you stock but do not sell.

9. In the Description on Purchase Transactions box, type **Stain**.

10. In the Cost field, enter **25**.

11. From the Expense Account drop-down list, select the Cost of Goods Sold or if you prefer, the expense account of your choice.

12. In the Preferred Vendor field, select or type Timberloft Lumber.

13. In the Sales Price field, type **100.00**.

14. Leave the default of Tax assigned in the Tax Code field.

15. From the Income Account drop-down list, select the Construction Income:Materials Income account. You can also select the account by typing the account number **40140** (the subaccount number) in this example.

16. Click OK to close the New Item dialog box.

 caution

Non-inventory parts only require one account by default. This is okay if you do not purchase and sell the item. To ensure proper accounting, I recommend when creating a non-inventory item type, you place a check mark in the "This Item Is Used in Assemblies or Is Purchased for a Specific Customer:Job" box, as shown in Figure 5.7. This enables you to assign both an expense and income account in the event you purchase and sell the item.

If you are tracking inventory in your business, non-inventory parts are best used when you consume the product in your business and do not sell it on the customer's invoice.

Entering or editing each individual inventory item can be time consuming and take you away from more important tasks. The next few sections provide alternatives for adding or editing multiple inventory items at one time.

Using Add/Edit Multiple List Entries

Adding or modifying several list items in a single QuickBooks list can be a daunting task when you have to work with one list item at a time. In Chapter 1, you might have created your lists using the QuickBooks Setup to add the people you do business with, the products or services you sell, and your bank accounts.

With the Add/Edit Multiple List Entries feature (see Figure 5.8), you can add to or modify service items or inventory and non-inventory parts. Using this feature can save you precious time, particularly when you want to add or make changes to multiple items on a list all at once.

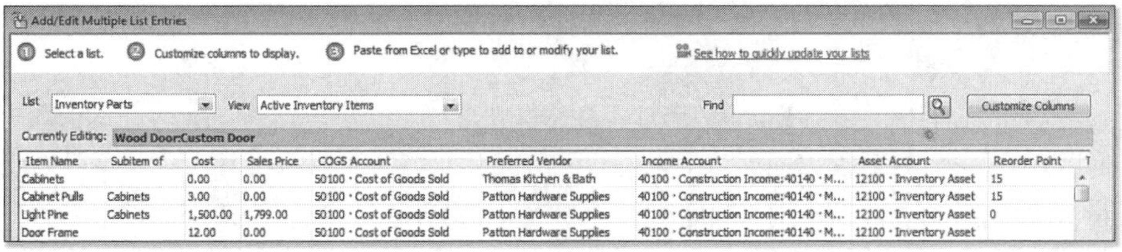

Figure 5.8
Use the Add/Edit Multiple Lists Entries feature to add or modify multiple inventory parts efficiently.

Add/Edit Multiple Items at Once

Practice using the Add/Edit Multiple List Entries feature by adding a Custom Door inventory item and customizing the columns of data displayed for editing.

Open the sample data as instructed in Chapter 1:

1. From the menu bar, select Lists, Add/Edit Multiple List Entries.

2. From the List drop-down list, select Inventory Parts.

3. From the View drop-down list, select Active Inventory Items.

4. Click the Customize Columns button on the right side to open the Customize Columns dialog box.

5. View the fields in the Chosen Columns pane. These fields are currently displayed in the Add/Edit Multiple List Entries grid.

6. To add a column to the grid, select Purchase Description and click the Add⸱⸱⸱⟩ button in the center.

7. To rearrange the order of the columns, select the newly added Purchase Description in the Chosen Columns pane and click the Move Up button several times until the Purchase Description field is immediately below the Subitem Of field.

8. Click OK to close the Customize Columns dialog box.

9. Use the scroll bar at the bottom of the Add/Edit Multiple List Entries dialog box to view the fields available.

10. Click in the next available blank row in the Item Name field. A Time Saving Tip might display. Read about how to update several list entries at a time. Click OK to close.

11. In the Item Name field, type **Custom Door**.

12. From the Subitem Of drop-down list, select Wood Door.

13. In the Purchase Description field, type **Custom Wood Door**.

14. In the Cost field, type **1,850.00**.

15. In the Sales Price field, type **2,200.00**.

16. Accept the default COGS Account: Cost of Goods Sold.

17. Optionally, select Perry Windows & Doors in the Preferred Vendor field.

18. From the Income drop-down list, select Construction Income:Materials Income account.

19. Accept the default Asset Account: Inventory Asset.

20. Type **10** in the Reorder Point field.

21. Leave the default Total Value column blank.

22. Accept the default Tax in the Sales Tax Code column.

23. Skip the Manufacturer's Part number field.

24. Skip the Qty on Hand field.

25. Click Save Changes.

26. QuickBooks displays the number of record(s) saved. Click OK to close. Click Close.

tip

Use the Tab key on your keyboard to move efficiently from one field to the next.

From the grid, you can right-click for other functionality. From the right-click menu, you can choose from Copy Down, Duplicate Row, Clear Column, and other useful features.

To view your newly added inventory item select Lists, Item List, select Wood Door in the Look For field at the top of the Item List, and press the Enter key on your keyboard. Do you see the newly created Custom Door listed? Click the Reset button to return to the original list.

Using the Add/Edit Multiple List Entries dialog box for adding data to your QuickBooks date from a formatted Excel file is easy using the Copy and Paste commands found in Excel.

 caution

Make sure your columns of data in Excel match the Add/Edit Multiple List Entries columns when cutting and pasting into QuickBooks from Excel.

Importing an Intuit Interchange Format File (IIF)

The term *Intuit Interchange Format (IIF)* refers to data exchange functionality that has been around for some time. It is a method for exporting lists from one QuickBooks file and importing these lists into a new QuickBooks file. The process creates a comma-separated value format file with the extension of .iif. You can view and edit this file using Excel.

The IIF format is a preferred and easy method to use if you already have a QuickBooks file with an items list you want to replicate in another QuickBooks file.

To export an IIF-formatted items file from an existing QuickBooks file, follow these steps:

1. Open the QuickBooks file that has the items list you want to export and duplicate for another file.

2. From the menu bar, select File, Utilities, Export, Lists to IIF Files.

3. Select the Item List checkbox.

4. Click OK. You are prompted to provide a file name and to save the exported file. Remember the location you stored the file in, you will need to browse to the .iif file to import it into another QuickBooks file.

5. Click OK to the message that your data was exported successfully.

Figure 5.9 shows the exported items list in the IIF format in an Excel workbook. You can see that it is not as user friendly as the Add/Edit Multiple List Entries previously discussed.

 caution

The IIF file format is a CSV (Comma Separated Values) format with an extension of .iif. If you edit the details of the file, be sure to keep this format when saving your changes and not save as an .xls or .xlsx Excel file type.

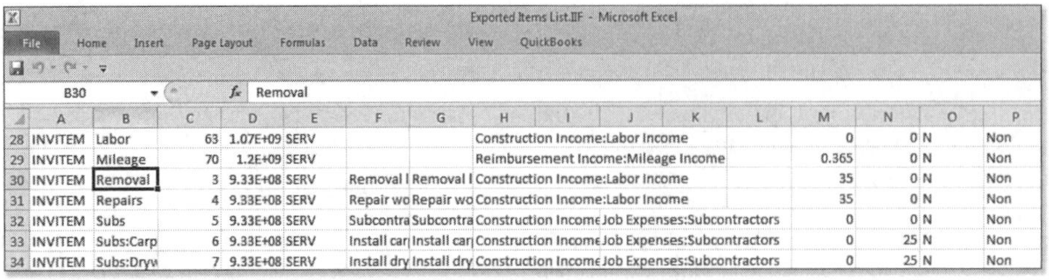

Figure 5.9
An exported items list in IIF format can be imported into another QuickBooks file.

To import the saved IIF file into a new QuickBooks file, follow these steps:

1. Open the QuickBooks file you want to import the previously exported list into. If you have not already created your new file, select File, New from the menu bar and follow the prompts. (For more information, see Chapter 1.)

2. From the menu bar, select File, Utilities, Import, IIF Files.

3. When the Import dialog box opens, browse to the location of the stored IIF formatted file.

4. Select the file and click Open.

5. QuickBooks then imports the IIF-formatted file into the QuickBooks data file. Click OK to the Your Data Has Been Imported message.

Now that you have your new data file with new lists from another file, you are ready to begin entering transactions. Just think of all the time you saved by not having to manually create each list item in the new file.

Changing Item Prices

Your business might have a variety of items including Service, Inventory, Non-inventory Parts, and even Other Charge items. During the course of doing business your costs of supplying these products or services will change and you might want to update your item sales prices.

Included with QuickBooks Pro, Premier, or Enterprise is the Change Item Prices (see Figure 5.10).

With this feature you can change the price of:

- One item at a time

- More than one item at a time

- Several items by a fixed amount based on Current Price or Unit Cost

- Several items by a percentage based on Current Price or Unit Cost

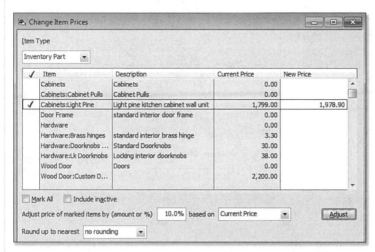

Figure 5.10
You can efficiently manage multiple inventory part sales price changes with Change Item Prices.

Practice Using the Change Item Prices

To practice using the Change Item Prices feature, open the sample data as previously instructed in Chapter 1:

1. From the menu bar, select Customers, Change Item Prices.

2. In this example, select Inventory Part from the Item Type drop-down list.

3. Place a checkmark next to the Cabinets:Light Pine item.

4. Type **10%** in the Adjust Price of Marked Items by (Amount or %) field (refer to the caution that follows these steps).

5. Leave the default of Based on Current Price selected.

6. Click Adjust. Notice the New Price is calculated based on your specifications in step 4.

7. In the Round Up to Nearest drop-down list, leave the No Rounding option selected.

8. Click OK to close the Change Item Prices dialog box.

 caution

If you desire to increase the Current Price by a percentage, be sure to type the amount with the percentage symbol. For example, if you want to increase the New Price by 15 percent, you would type 15% because without the % sign QuickBooks will consider the new price to be a fixed dollar amount.

Using the Change Item Prices dialog box can be an efficient way of updating your pricing for multiple items at one time. QuickBooks Enterprise Solutions 12.0 provides more control over changes to the default part cost, sales price, and markup when an item's cost changes. See Figures 5.11 and 5.12.

> ## caution
>
> In Chapter 9, "Setting Up Customers," you will learn about working with memorized transactions. It is important to note that changes made to item prices *do not* automatically change the prices you have previously recorded on a memorized customer invoice.

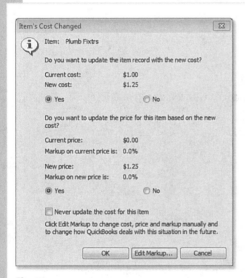

Figure 5.11
Available only in QuickBooks Enterprise is the option to update the default cost and sales price when recording a purchase transaction.

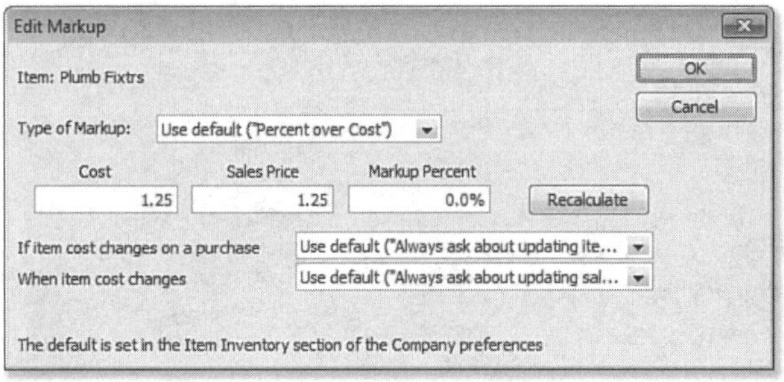

Figure 5.12
Define specific settings for handling markup % or amount, available with QuickBooks Enterprise.

Creating Inventory Assemblies

The Inventory Assembly (see Figure 5.13) can include the following item types:

- Other Assemblies (Subassemblies)

- Inventory Parts

- Non-inventory Parts

- Service Items

- Other Charge Items

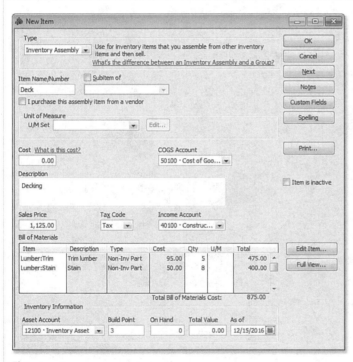

Figure 5.13
Inventory Assembly items are available in QuickBooks Premier, Accountant, or Enterprise.

Practice Using Inventory Assemblies

To practice adding a new Inventory Assembly (only if you have QuickBooks Premier or Enterprise), open the sample data file as instructed in Chapter 1:

1. On the Home page, click the Items & Services icon. The Item List displays.

2. From the Item drop-down list, select New or use the keyboard shortcut of Ctrl+N.

3. If the New Feature dialog box for Add/Edit Multiple List Entries displays, click OK to close. The New Item dialog box displays.

➡ *For more information, see "Using Add/Edit Multiple List Entries," p. 125.*

4. From the Type drop-down list, select Inventory Assembly.

5. In the Item Name/Number field, type **Deck**.

6. Leave the I Purchase This Assembly Item from a Vendor checkbox and Unit of Measure (U/M) Set field blank.

7. Leave the Cost field blank.

8. Accept the defaulted COGS Account of Cost of Goods Sold.

9. In the Description field, type **Decking**.

10. Leave the Sales Price blank.

11. Leave the Tax Code of Tax as defaulted.

12. From the Income Account drop-down list, select Account number 40140 or Construction Income:Materials Income.

13. Enter the Bill of Materials by selecting the following items from the Item drop-down list:

    • Select Trim from the Lumber item group. Enter **5** in the Qty column.

    • On the next row, select the new item you created in an earlier exercise in this chapter, Stain. Enter a Qty of **8**.

    Notice how QuickBooks calculates the Total Bill of Materials Cost, which is the sum total of the individual default costs recorded with each item record. Knowing the cost of the items can help you assign a proper Sales Price.

14. Enter $1,125.00 in the Sales Price field.

15. Leave the Asset Account as defaulted.

16. Enter 3 in the Build Point.

17. Leave the On Hand and Total Value fields blank. Leave the defaulted date value in the As of field.

18. Click OK to close the New Item dialog box.

Creating the assembly is only part of the process. You also need to "build" the assembly.

Using Inventory Assemblies can help your business track whether you have enough components in inventory to build the finished product for your customers. You can edit Inventory Assemblies, but QuickBooks does not track the revision history for an item. If you are no longer selling a particular assembled item, you can make the item inactive so it cannot be used on future purchase or sales transactions.

Creating Group Items

Previously, Table 5.1 listed in detail the differences when working with Group Items (see Figure 5.14) versus an Inventory Assembly. In this section, you will learn how to work with Group Items.

Unlike working with assemblies, when creating or editing Group Item you do not assign a cost for each item or a sales price for the Group Item. The cost and sales price is calculated for you from the respective totals for each of the included items. The sales price recorded on the invoice can be modified at the time you create the invoice if necessary.

> ⚠ **caution**
>
> Working with assemblies requires some care and attention on your part. A couple of items worth noting here:
>
> - Future changes to the Item default cost will update the costs of all assemblies that use that item.
>
> - When adding the item to the Bill of Materials of an assembly, if you leave the Qty field blank the default unit depleted when the inventory is built is 1 not 0.
>
> Carefully review the details of your assemblies by selecting the Full View on the Add or Edit Assembly dialog box.

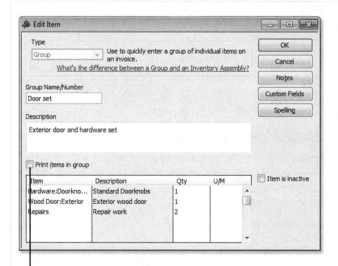

When not selected, the customer invoice will only display the detail in the Description box.

Figure 5.14
Creating Group Items can save you time when you need to enter multiple items.

Practice Using Group Items

In this exercise you will edit an existing Group Item. Open the sample data as previously instructed in Chapter 1:

1. On the Home page, click the Items & Services icon. The Item List displays.

2. Scroll down the list and select the Door Set group (near the bottom of the list in the Group section). Optionally, you can also begin typing **Door Set** in the Look for box at the top of the Item List and click the Search button.

3. Double-click to select the Door Set group. The Edit Item dialog box displays.

4. Type a Group Name/Number that will serve as reminder what items are included in this Group.

5. In the Description box is the desired detail that will display on a customer's invoice. Modify the description on the invoice if needed.

6. Don't select the Print Items in Group checkbox. This is one unique feature of working with the Group Item type. When the Print Items in Group checkbox is *not selected,* the customer's invoice will only show the Description from step 5.

7. Currently, there are two items included in the Group: Doorknobs and Exterior Wood Door. In the Item column, click the next available row and select the Service item named Repairs from the drop-down list.

8. In the Qty. column type **2**, assigning two hours of repair labor when installing this door.

9. Click OK to close the Edit Item dialog box. You are returned to the Item List and your new group is highlighted (selected).

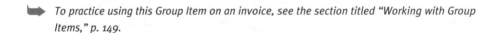 *To practice using this Group Item on an invoice, see the section titled "Working with Group Items," p. 149.*

Setting Up Multiple Unit of Measurement

If you are using QuickBooks Premier or Enterprise, you have the option to set up Multiple Unit of Measure. A benefit of using this feature is the ability to assign a specific unit default for purchases, shipping, and sales transactions.

To begin using Multiple Unit of Measure in your Premier or Enterprise file, you need to enable the preference setting. To do so, follow these steps:

1. Log into the file as the Admin or External Accountant user.

2. From the menu bar, select Edit, Preferences.

3. Select the Items & Inventory—Company Preferences tab.

4. In the Unit of Measure box, click the Enable button.

5. Select either Single U/M per Item or Multiple U/M Per Item (as shown in Figure 5.15). For more information, see "Enabling Inventory Preferences," p. 115.

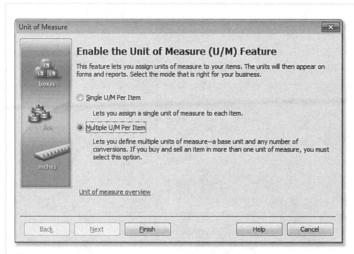

Figure 5.15
To begin using Multiple Unit of Measure, first enable the preference.

6. Click Finish. Click OK to close the Preferences dialog box.

Now that the preference is enabled, first create the different unit measurements you will be tracking.

Using Multiple Unit of Measure

After enabling the Unit of Measure preference, create multiple unit of measure for the Stain non-inventory part. This part was created in the section of this chapter titled "Non-Inventory Part":

1. From the menu bar, select Lists, Item List.

2. Select the Stain non-inventory part created earlier. Double-click the Stain item to open the Edit Item dialog box.

3. From the Unit of Measure drop-down list on an existing item, select Add New to open the Unit of Measure dialog box.

4. The Unit of Measure dialog box displays. If you do not see the desired unit displayed, select the Other option as shown in Figure 5.16 and follow the instructions to create a new base unit.

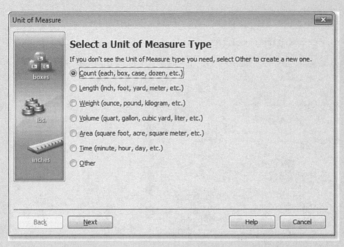

Figure 5.16
QuickBooks provides multiple units of measure types or select Other to create your own.

5. For this example, the base unit type selected is Count (each, box, case, dozen, and so on). Click Next to display the Add Related Units screen (see Figure 5.17).

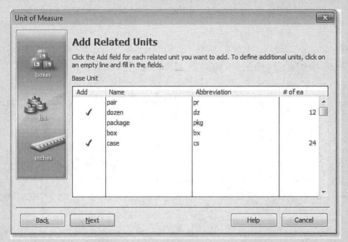

Figure 5.17
For the unit of measure created, you define the number of base units (in this example, # of ea).

6. Place a checkmark next to the individual units of measurement you want to add to the selected item (see Figure 5.17). In the # of ea column, enter the related quantity. Click Next when completed.

7. The Select Default Units of Measure screen displays. From the drop-down list, select the default units for Purchase, Sales, and Shipping transactions as shown in Figure 5.18.

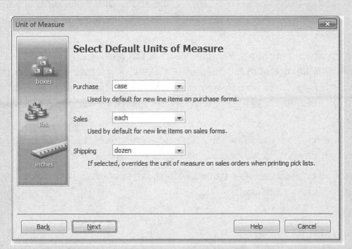

Figure 5.18
The benefit of working with Multiple Unit of Measurement is the ability to define the default units for specific transaction types.

8. Click Next.

9. The Name the Unit of Measure Set screen displays. Enter a Set Name or accept the default selected.

10. Click Finish and the U/M Set now shows the configured Multiple Unit of Measurement assigned to the selected item.

11. Click OK to close the New Item dialog box or Edit Item dialog box.

 caution

If you edit an existing unit of measure assigned to an item, you will be warned, "Any changes you make to this unit of measure set will affect all items that use this set."

With Multiple Unit of Measure defined for this item, entering inventory on transactions will be easier and more accurate.

Proper Inventory Processes

Understanding the recommended inventory process and the associated transactions can help you properly use the inventory feature. If you are new to inventory management, QuickBooks makes getting started with it easy, via the workflow outlined on the Home page, as shown previously in Figure 5.2.

Use a purchase order if you want to compare the bill the vendor sends with the original agreed quantity and cost. With purchase orders, you can also keep track of what items have been ordered and have not yet been received.

You can receive inventory in one of two ways. With one method, you receive inventory with the vendor's final bill. If you record full receipt of the quantity, QuickBooks will then mark the purchase order as closed. You can also choose to receive inventory without a bill. QuickBooks will create an Item Receipt document that is included in the accounts payable reports, but cannot yet be paid in the Pay Bills dialog box.

Rest assured that as you create the vendor's final bill, QuickBooks will recognize if you have outstanding purchase orders or item receipts you want to associate with the vendor's bill.

Table 5.2 shows a listing of all transaction types you should use when working with Inventory and their related effects on the company's accounting.

Table 5.2 Inventory Transaction Types

Transaction Type	Purpose of Transaction	Effect With Accounting
Purchase Order	Record order placed with vendor	No effect
Item Receipt without Bill	Record receipt of inventory items	Increase inventory, increase accounts payable (bill *cannot* be selected in the Pay Bills dialog box)
Item Receipt with Bill	Record receipt of inventory items	Increase inventory, increase accounts payable (bill *can* be selected in the Pay Bills dialog box)
Bill	Record bill (optionally, assign purchase order or item receipt)	Increase inventory, increase accounts payable
Check	Items tab used (optionally, assign purchase order or item receipt)	Increase inventory, decrease cash
Estimates	Record quote for sales of items to a customer	No effect
Sales Order	Manage sales of inventory by committing it for sale (used to manage back orders of inventory)	No effect, except to show the items in inventory as committed
Invoice	Record sale of inventory to customer	Decrease inventory, increase accounts receivable, increase cost of goods sold, and increase income
Sales Receipt	Record sale of inventory to customer	Decrease inventory, increase cash, increase cost of goods sold, and increase income
Inventory Adjustment— Quantity	Record a change to the quantity of stock on hand	Decrease or increase inventory and decrease or increase Inventory Adjustment account (Cost of Goods Sold type or Expense type)

Transaction Type	Purpose of Transaction	Effect With Accounting
Inventory Adjustment— Value	Record a change to the value of the stock on hand	Decrease or increase inventory value and decrease or increase Inventory Adjustment account (Cost of Goods Sold type or Expense type)

 tip

QuickBooks Enterprise Solutions 12.0 (all industry versions) includes the option to use Enhanced Inventory Receiving. When enabled, this feature will record an item receipt as an increase to Inventory and an increase to an Inventory Offset account (other current liability account). Later when the vendor bill is entered, Accounts Payable will be increased and the Inventory Offset account will be decreased.

As a business owner, you do not need to worry about the details; QuickBooks Enterprise does all the behind-the-scenes accounting for you.

Purchasing, Receiving, and Entering the Vendor Bill

An important reason to purchase accounting software is the ability to track the expenses incurred in providing products or services to your customers. In fact, the business' profitability can be improved by effectively managing your purchasing costs. In this section, you will learn a recommended purchasing process specifically for inventory items and non-inventory items. This process is similar to the steps outlined in Chapter 7, "Setting Up Vendors."

Review Table 5.2 in the previous section for how QuickBooks handles the accounting for inventory. To manage your inventory purchasing with the greatest level of control, follow these three steps:

1. Create a purchase order recording a commitment to purchase.

2. Receive inventory without a vendor bill to create an item receipt.

3. Enter a vendor bill upon receipt and associate it with the open item receipt.

 caution

There is one other transaction type that can be used to pay for your inventory purchase: Write Checks. If you use the Write Checks transaction type to enter your inventory purchases, you must use the Items tab to enter the items being purchased. However, the Write Checks transaction does not track the vendor's bill reference number.

Practice Creating a Purchase Order

Using the sample company referred to in Chapter 1, let's practice creating a purchase order and receiving the inventory:

1. On the Home page, shown in Figure 5.2, click the Purchase Orders icon to open the Create Purchase Order dialog box.

2. In the Vendor drop-down list, begin typing the letters Th and QuickBooks automatically prefills with the vendor Thomas Kitchen & Bath. Alternately, you can scroll through the drop-down list and click to select a vendor for the purchase order.

3. Use the Tab key to move to the Class field and select New Construction.

4. In this example, leave the Drop Ship To field blank. Accept the defaulted Template, Date, P.O. No., Vendor, and Ship To details.

5. From the Item drop-down list, select the Light Pine item, a subitem of Cabinets.

6. Accept the default description.

7. In the Qty field, click the icon (see Figures 5.19 and 5.20) to view the Current Availability of the item. This useful feature is available only with QuickBooks Premier or Enterprise. Click Show Details. From the Show Details for drop-down list, select Sales Orders.

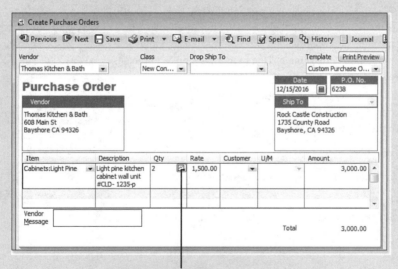

Click the icon to view Current Availability details for this part.

Figure 5.19
Creating a purchase order helps you manage your expected costs.

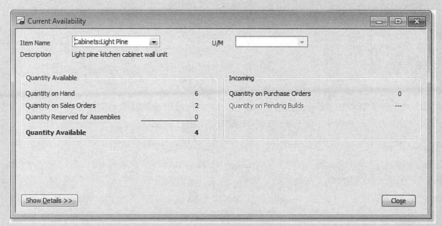

Figure 5.20
Current Availability information for inventory items is conveniently included on purchasing and sales transactions.

8. Click Close to close the Current Availability dialog box.

9. In the Qty field, type 2.

10. Accept the defaulted Rate.

11. Leave the Customer field blank. For inventory items, the cost will be assigned to the customer when the inventory item is included on a customer's invoice. Select the customer only if you are using an item type *other than* inventory and *only* if you know the customer at the time of purchase.

12. For this exercise, if U/M (Unit of Measure) is enabled, leave the field blank.

13. Accept the default Amount.

14. Optionally, type a message to the vendor in the lower-left Vendor Message field.

15. Optionally, select the To Be Printed checkbox or the To Be Emailed checkbox. Emailing forms and reports requires the Send preference be enabled. You can access this preference from the Send Forms—My Preferences tab of the Preferences dialog box (select Edit, Preferences from the menu bar).

16. Optionally, enter a Memo. This field displays on reports and can be useful when you have multiple open purchase orders for one vendor at a time.

17. For this practice, click Save & New. If the Check Spelling on Form warning displays, select the Ignore All option.

18. Preview the purchase order just created. From the Create Purchase Orders dialog box, click Previous (top left). The purchase order you created appears.

19. From the Print drop-down list (at the top), select Preview. If the Shipping Labels message displays, click OK.

20. Your newly created purchase order displays using the default purchase order template.

 For more information, see "Customizing QuickBooks Forms," p. 282.

21. Click Close to close the preview and click Save & Close to close the Create Purchase Orders dialog box.

---

 tip

Did you know by default QuickBooks would have you use the Tab key on your keyboard to advance from one field to another with certain transactions?

If you inadvertently used the Enter key on your keyboard, QuickBooks might store the incomplete transaction. If this happens to you, simply use the Previous or Next menu at the top of the open transaction to find the one you had not fully completed.

If you prefer to use the Enter key on your keyboard to advance between fields, you can set that preference on the General—My Preferences tab of the Preferences dialog box (select Edit, Preferences from the menu bar). Select the Pressing Enter Moves Between Fields checkbox and click OK to save your preference setting.

Creating the Purchase Order

If you are practicing in your own data file, make sure you have read the section in this chapter titled "Enabling Inventory Preferences."

The menu at the top of the Create Purchase Orders dialog box consists of other useful related actions and reports including:

- **Previous**—Opens the previous purchase order.

- **Next**—Advances to the next purchase order.

- **Save**—Saves your current purchase order and keeps the purchase order open in the current active window.

- **Print**—Multiple options for printing purchase order(s) or shipping label(s).

- **Email**—Multiple options for emailing the purchase order document(s).

- **Find**—Finding purchase orders with specific filter criteria.

- **Spelling**—Performs a spell check of the currently opened purchase order.

- **History**—Displays related transactions to the currently open purchase order. See the Transaction tab information later in this list.

> **tip**
>
> Did you know that you can get a detailed report of the accounting for any currently opened transaction by pressing the Ctrl + Y on your keyboard? For more information, see Appendix C, "QuickBooks Shortcuts."

- **Journal**—Creates a Transaction Journal report. Available in QuickBooks Accountant 2012 or QuickBooks Enterprise Solutions Accountant 12.0.

- **Customize**—Menu for managing templates, design, and layout of your forms. More information can be found in Chapter 9.

- **Attach**—Option to browse to a file, scan a document, or see a list of documents in the document center and attach to the currently opened form. For QuickBooks 2012 this is a free option and includes local storage on your computer or server.

- **Vendor tab**—Provides summary and recent transaction information for the vendor selected on the Purchase Order. Also includes links to edit the vendor record, create a QuickReport, and enter notes for the current transaction.

- **Transaction tab**—View summary information, related transactions, and notes for the currently displayed purchase order.

Creating a purchase order is the first step in successfully managing your inventory.

Receiving Item(s) into Inventory

Next, you will work with receiving your items into inventory and you will find many of the same additional related actions and reports as listed earlier also available on the Item Receipt transaction.

Practice Receiving Items

Continuing with our practice using QuickBooks sample data, building on the previous exercise "Practice Creating a Purchase Order" let's record the receipt of the inventory:

1. From the Home page, select Receive Inventory Without Bill from the drop-down list next to the Receive Inventory icon. The Create Item Receipts dialog box opens.

2. In the Vendor field, begin typing the letters Th and press the Tab key on your computer keyboard.

3. The Open PO's Exist dialog box displays. Click the default, Yes.

4. Click in the first column to assign the purchase order to this Item Receipt as shown in Figure 5.21.

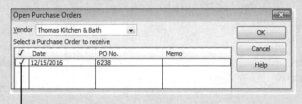

Click to select the open purchase order.

Figure 5.21
When creating an item receipt, QuickBooks will list open purchase orders.

5. Click OK and the Create Item Receipts dialog box prefills with the information from the original purchase order.

6. In this exercise, accept the default date. In the Ref. No. field, enter **1234**.

7. To continue with the practice example here, record only a partial receipt of the inventory items and replace the 2 in the Qty field with **1** as displayed in Figure 5.22.

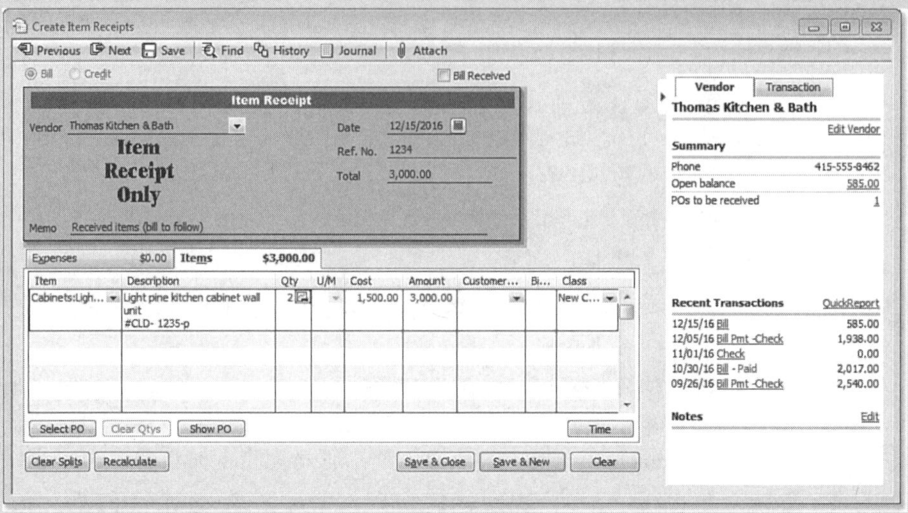

Figure 5.22
When receiving inventory without the final vendor bill, QuickBooks creates an Item Receipt.

8. Leave the Customer:Job and Billable? fields blank. Accept the default Class and PO No. assigned.

9. Notice other useful fields on the Create Item Receipts dialog box including:

    - **Select PO**—Use if you want to assign another open purchase order to this item receipt.

    - **Clear Qtys**—If you want to clear all quantity fields and enter them manually.

    - **Show PO**—To open the selected purchase order. Useful if you need to make changes to the purchase order details.

    - **Time**—Used when adding time sheet details to a vendor bill.

    - **Clear Splits and Recalculate**—These are not typically used on the Item Receipt transactions created from purchase orders.

10. To continue with the practice, click Save on the top of the Create Item Receipts dialog box. This will save the details, but leave the current transaction, displayed for this exercise.

11. Click the Transaction tab to the right to view Related Transactions including a link to the Purchase Order used to create this item receipt.

12. Click the Purchase Order link in the Related Transactions section of the Transaction tab to view the Purchase Order that the Item Receipt is linked to.

    The Create Purchase Orders dialog box now includes a column with the Backordered quantity.

13. Click Save & Close to close the Create Purchase Orders dialog box.

14. Click Save & Close to close the Create Item Receipts dialog box.

tip

Did your vendor not supply you with a vendor bill number (same as Ref. No.)? You might want to use the same date as the vendor bill in the Ref. No. field. The primary purpose of the Ref. No. field is to warn you if you enter a bill with the same reference number more than once.

Now might be a good time to advance ahead to the section titled "Inventory Reporting," p. 165. Specifically look for reports in the Report Center, Vendors and Payable section. There are several excellent purchasing reports you can review.

Entering the Vendor Bill

When it comes to inventory, the more controls you have in place surrounding your purchasing process the more accurate your accounting data will be. In the next exercise, you learn how to enter a vendor bill and assign it to the previously recorded item receipt.

 tip

Do you have freight, shipping, or handling charges to add to the vendor's item receipt? To track them as an added expense but not as part of the average cost of this inventory item, click the Expenses tab and add the additional charges.

Practice Entering a Vendor Bill and Assigning the Item Receipt

Continuing with our practice using QuickBooks sample data, record the vendor bill and assign it to the open item receipt from the previous exercise:

1. On the Home page, click the Enter Bills Against Inventory icon. The Select Item Receipt dialog box opens.

2. In the Vendor field, select Thomas Kitchen & Bath as the vendor from the drop-down list.

3. Optionally, select the Use Item Receipt Date for the Bill Date checkbox. Because QuickBooks removes the item receipt and replaces it with a bill, you want to be sure to use the date you want your financials affected. You can also set date preferences on the General—My Preferences tab of the Preferences dialog box.

4. Select the appropriate Item Receipt to associate with this bill, as shown in Figure 5.23

Figure 5.23
Be certain your item receipt is highlighted before clicking OK.

5. Click OK to close the Select Item Receipt dialog box. The Enter Bills dialog box displays and the item receipt no longer exists as an item receipt transaction.

6. In this exercise, accept the vendor's Ref. No., Qty, and Cost. When you are creating your own vendor bill transactions, you will carefully inspect that the vendor's bill details for Ref. No., Qty, and Cost agree with your records generated by the original purchase order.

7. Click Save & Close. If the message, "You have changed the transaction" displays, click Yes.

Your business will benefit from the added cost controls put in place when you use a purchase order and receive item transactions. This process is particularly useful when the vendor sends the final bill separately from the original shipment. When you do get the vendor bill in the mail, you can review the details to make sure they agree with your records.

Paying for Inventory

You have now learned how to efficiently manage your inventory beginning with the purchase order that tracks the quantity ordered and the agreed-to cost. Next, when the product is delivered to your warehouse you enter an item receipt with or without the vendor bill.

After creating a vendor bill in the previous section, you are now ready to process a payment by check, credit card, or electronic funds transfer (ACH) to your vendor.

Practice Paying for Inventory

Using the sample company referred to in Chapter 1, you will now create a payment to the vendor for the bill created in the earlier exercise:

1. On the Home page, click the Pay Bills icon. The Pay Bills dialog box displays.

2. Leave the Show All Bills option button selected.

3. From the Filter By drop-down list, select Thomas Kitchen & Bath. When you are ready to pay your bills in your own QuickBooks file, you will probably not need to filter for a specific vendor because you will want to process multiple checks for many vendors at once.

4. From the Sort By drop-down list, view the other options for sorting the bills in the Pay Bills dialog box.

5. Place a checkmark next to both of the bills in the first column on the left. Notice that after you place a checkmark, the Amt. to Pay column for each bill is now equal to the Amt. Due column (see Figure 5.24).

6. With a bill selected, click the Go to Bill button. Notice how easy it is to get to the original transaction. Press the Esc key on your keyboard to close the Enter Bills dialog box and return to the Pay Bills dialog box.

7. Click Save & Close to return to the Pay Bills dialog box. The Set Discount and Set Credits options will be discussed in the section titled "Handling Vendor Discounts and Returns."

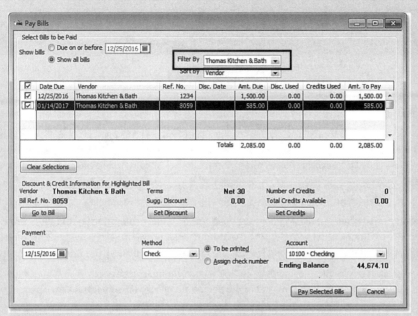

Figure 5.24
You can filter the Pay Bills dialog box for a single vendor.

8. For this exercise, leave the defaulted Payment Date. When working in your own data, enter the date you want to print on the vendor checks.

9. For Payment Method, leave selected the default of Check.

10. In the Account field, leave the default Checking named account selected. (When working with your own data you will select the account you are recording the payment from.) Notice that QuickBooks displays your Ending Balance for your bank account.

11. Click Pay Selected Bills. QuickBooks opens the Payment Summary dialog box.

12. Review the details displayed including payment date, account, and method.

13. Select the Print Checks button or click Done if you do not want to practice printing (using plain paper).

14. If you selected the option to Print Checks, the Select Check to Print dialog box displays. Leave selected the default Bank Account and the defaulted First Check Number.

15. Review the list of checks to be printed. Each will have a checkmark in the column to the left. Remove the checkmarks from any checks you do not want to print at this time.

16. Click OK to open the Print Checks dialog box. Select your printer from the Printer Name drop-down list, and then choose the proper Check Style from Voucher, Standard, or Wallet. More detailed instructions on setting check printing preferences are included in Chapter 13.

17. Click Print. For this exercise, make sure you have plain paper in your printer. A check printed to plain paper is not a negotiable document.

18. The Print Checks—Confirmation dialog box displays. In this exercise, click OK to close the confirmation.

tip

When selecting vendor bills to be paid, you can override the Amt. to Pay and type an amount of your choosing. QuickBooks will keep track of the remaining balance due to the vendor.

 tip

Did you know that you can pay your vendors by any one of a number of methods? The methods include printing a check, recording a manually written check, by credit card, and even as an online bank payment. To learn more about preferences for printing checks or making online payments directly from your QuickBooks file see Chapter 13, "Working with Bank and Credit Card Accounts."

See how easy it is to print checks paying your vendors? You can order checks from most reputable check suppliers or order directly from Intuit. To order checks from Intuit, select the Print Checks icon on the lower right of the Home page. Click the Order Checks button. An Internet connection is required.

In the next section, you will learn how to handle selling inventory on a customer invoice.

Selling Inventory

For your business to survive, you will need to sell your products (or services) to customers. The next important task discussed in this chapter shows just how easy it is to prepare invoices for your customers in QuickBooks.

First, it might be helpful for a little review on the proper accounting for inventory at the time of sale. You will recall that Table 5.2 detailed the impact an invoice or sales receipt has on accounting— namely to decrease inventory, increase accounts receivable (or cash) depending on the transaction type used, increase cost of goods sold, and increase income.

Your inventory item setup does all this complicated work for you behind the scenes. First, each inventory item in QuickBooks is assigned an inventory asset account, COGS (cost of goods sold account) and income account. Secondly, QuickBooks uses the average cost method for calculating the cost of your product at the time of the invoice.

 For more information, see "Reviewing the Recorded Average Cost Valuation," p. 170.

Practice Selling Inventory

Follow these steps to practice creating an invoice for a customer using the sample data installed with QuickBooks and discussed in Chapter 1:

1. On the Home page, click the Create Invoices or Invoices icon. The icon name will differ depending on whether you have enabled the Time and Expenses preference. If required, select Create Invoices.

2. From the Customer:Job drop-down list, select Garage Repair for the customer Baker, Chris.

3. In the Class drop-down list, select New Construction.

4. Accept the defaulted Template, Date, Invoice #, Bill To, Ship To, Terms, and Due Date fields.

5. From the Item column drop-down list, select the Doorknobs Std inventory part from the Hardware parent inventory part.

6. In the Quantity field, type 1. If you are using the QuickBooks-supplied sample data for this practice, you will have an invoice for 1 doorknob inventory part with tax.

7. For this practice, click Save on the top of the form. This saves the invoice and assigns the invoice number, but keeps the invoice open for viewing. See the Tip that follows this exercise.

8. From the top of the open invoice, select Preview from the Print drop-down list. Click OK to close the prompt about printing shipping labels. Click Close when done with the Print Preview dialog box.

9. Click Save & Close (or Save & New) to practice creating another invoice.

 tip

When you work with your own data, you have the option to select the Save button at the top. Typically, you will not need to do this each time. Instead you can choose between the Save & Close button and the Save & New button on the lower right.

QuickBooks truly does make it easy to create invoices for your customers. Now, getting your customers to pay that is another task! Join me later in Chapter 10, the section titled "Using the Collections Center," p. 326.

Working with Group Items

Using Group Items can save you time when needing to enter several items on a purchase or sales transaction.

Practice Using Group Items

Using the sample company referred to in Chapter 1, practice creating an invoice with the Group Item modified in an earlier exercise:

1. On the icon bar, click the Invoice icon. The Create Invoices dialog box displays. If you do not see this icon, you might want to review the information in Chapter 2, "Getting Around QuickBooks" in the "Home Page and Navigation" section.

2. From the Customer:Job drop-down list, select the Barley, Renee:Repairs job. Select Remodel for the Class field. Leave all other fields as defaulted.

3. In the Item column, type **Door Set**.

4. QuickBooks adds multiple rows to the invoice. Click the Save button at the top of the invoice.

5. From the Print drop-down list at the top of the invoice, select Preview. Click OK to close the message about printing shipping labels. Optionally, you can also select the Print Preview button next to the Template on the top right of the open Create Invoices dialog box.

6. Click Zoom In at the top to enlarge the detail displayed.

7. Notice that the QuickBooks customer invoice includes one line of detail for the customer, but your internal reports will show multiple lines of detail.

8. Click Close to close the preview. Click Save & Close to close the Create Invoices dialog box.

Using Group Items make data entry more efficient when you need to enter multiple items at one time. An added benefit is that using Group Items also provides the option to hide individual line details on the invoice provided to the customer.

Next, continue your practice by working with Assembly Items.

Working with Assemblies

Assemblies are used when you want to enter multiple items at one time and track the on-hand quantity for the finished good. Inventory Assemblies are only available with QuickBooks Premier (all editions), Accountant, and Enterprise (all editions).

Working with assemblies is a two-step process:

1. Create the assembly

2. Build the assembly

Practice Using Assemblies

Using the sample company referred to in Chapter 1, practice building an assembly and creating an invoice with an Assembly Item in your sample data:

1. From your Home page, select Build Assemblies from the drop-down list next to the Inventory Activities icon. The Build Assemblies dialog box opens (see Figure 5.25).

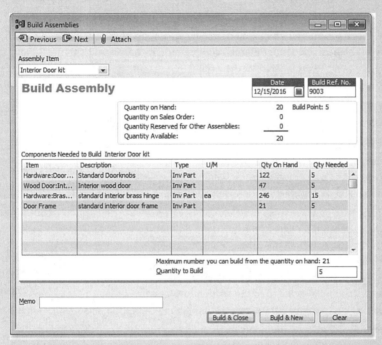

Figure 5.25
You must first build the assembly to track the quantity of finished product.

2. From the Assembly Item drop-down list, select Interior Door Kit.

3. Accept the default Date and Build Ref. No.

4. Review the individual items and note the reported maximum number of items that can be built with the stock on hand (lower right).

5. In the Quantity to Build box, type 5. Enter an optional memo for your own reporting.

6. Click Build & Close.

With the assembly now built, you are ready to add the assembly to a customer's invoice. To do so, follow these steps:

1. On the icon bar, click the Invoice icon. The Create Invoices dialog box displays.

2. From the Customer:Job drop-down list, select the Baker, Chris:Family Room job. Select Remodel for the Class field. Leave all other fields as defaulted.

3. In the Item column, select Interior Door Kit.

4. Enter a **1** in the Quantity field.

5. Enter **$125.00** in the Rate field. This rate would have defaulted if there was a sales price associated with the Inventory Assembly.

6. Click Save & Close to close the Create Invoices dialog box.

How do you handle your accounting when you do not have enough inventory on-hand to ship to a customer? Join me in the next section for details on working with sales orders to track these back-orders.

Handling Inventory Backorders

Do you want to "commit" inventory to a customer ahead of purchasing the inventory? Handling backorders for your customers is best tracked using the QuickBooks sales order transaction available with QuickBooks Premier (all editions), QuickBooks Accountant, or QuickBooks Enterprise Solutions (all editions).

With a sales order transaction you can record that you have committed inventory (backordered) for sale to the customer and provided the customer details of the sale for prepayment, and then later create the customer invoice directly from the sales order details. If you do take a prepayment from a customer you will want to review the instructions included in the section in Chapter 9 titled "Recording the Customer Payment," p. 308.

Sales orders are considered a nonposting document, meaning that when they are created they do not affect inventory, revenue, or costs until the sales order is converted to an invoice, whereas, if you use a sales receipt, you are affecting your inventory, revenue, and costs when the sales receipt is recorded.

Using this sales order transaction type is the best solution if you must provide a sales document to a customer before he or she receives the merchandise.

 tip

The sales order transaction type is only available in QuickBooks Premier (all editions) or QuickBooks Enterprise Solutions (all editions). If you need this functionality, consider upgrading your file to Premier or Enterprise. For more information, see "Upgrading Your QuickBooks Version," p. 559.

Additionally, working with sales orders is a preference that is enabled by logging into the file as the Admin or External Accountant user then selecting the Sales & Customers— Company Preferences tab on the Preferences dialog box.

Practice Working with Sales Orders

Using the same sample data discussed in Chapter 1, create a sales order:

1. From the menu bar, select Customers, Sales Orders. Sales Orders are only available only with QuickBooks Premier, Accountant, or QuickBooks Enterprise software.

2. From the Customer:Job drop-down list, select the Home Remodel Job for the customer Bauman, Mark as displayed in Figure 5.26.

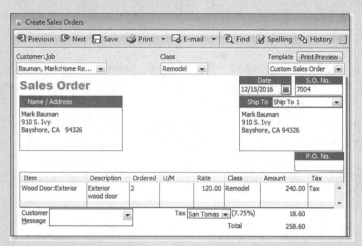

Figure 5.26
Use a Sales Order to commit inventory for a future sale.

3. For the Class field, select Remodel.

4. Leave the defaulted template, date, S.O. No., Ship To, and P.O. details.

5. In the Item column drop-down list, select the Exterior inventory part sub-item of Wood Door.

6. Enter 2 in the Ordered column. Leave the other fields on the row as defaulted. If you are using the QuickBooks-supplied sample data for this practice, you will have a Sales Order for 2 Exterior Wood Doors with tax.

7. For this exercise, click Save on the top of the transaction. This saves the sales order and assigns the sales order number, but keeps the sales order open for viewing.

8. Select Preview from the Print drop-down list at the top of the open sales order. Click OK if you receive a message about printing shipping labels. Click Close when done with the Print Preview dialog box.

9. Click Save & Close (or Save & New) to practice creating another sales order.

10. Next, create an invoice for the open sales order. From the icon bar, click the Invoice icon to open the Create Invoices dialog box again. Optionally, from an open sales order you can also click the Create Invoice icon at the top of the transaction to create the invoice.

11. From the Customer:Job drop-down list on the Create Invoices dialog box, select the Home Remodel job for the customer Bauman, Mark. The Available Sales Orders dialog box shown in Figure 5.27 displays.

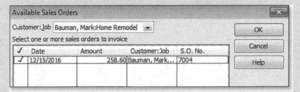

Figure 5.27
Don't forget to place a checkmark next to each open sales order you want to invoice.

12. Click in the first column to place a checkmark next to the listed open sales order(s) you want to include on the invoice to the customer.

13. Click OK. The Create Invoice Based on Sales Order(s) dialog box displays. For this exercise, select the Create Invoice for Selected Items option button as shown in Figure 5.28.

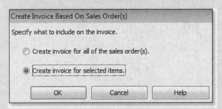

Figure 5.28
Invoicing a partial sales order.

14. Click OK. QuickBooks displays the Specify Invoice Quantities for Items on Sales Order(s) dialog box as displayed in Figure 5.29.

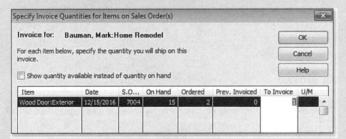

Figure 5.29
Use this dialog box to specify the quantity of the sales order items you want to invoice.

15. Optionally, select the Show Quantity Available Instead of Quantity on Hand checkbox. How quantity available and quantity on hand differ is determined by your settings in Inventory preferences (refer to Figure 5.1).

16. In the To Invoice column, type **1** (to record a partial invoice).

17. Click OK to return to the Create Invoices dialog box.

18. Review the details on the invoice (see Figure 5.30) for the Wood Door:Exterior with details for Ordered, Prev. Invoiced, and Invoiced. If you selected multiple sales orders to invoice, you will also have a column for backordered on the invoice template. Click Save on the top of the transaction.

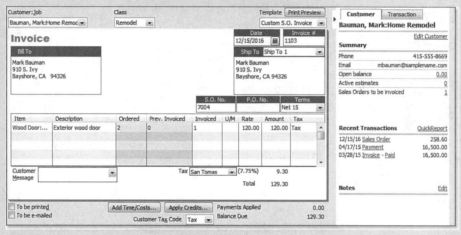

Figure 5.30
The invoice now shows separate columns for Ordered, Prev. Invoiced, and Invoiced.

19. In the Recent Transactions section on the Customer tab (on the right side of the dialog box), click the link to the Sales Order you created in this exercise.

20. The Create Sales Order dialog box displays with the details of the original sales order. Notice the new columns of detail for Backordered and Invoiced on the sales order.

If your customer orders inventory before you have made or ordered the part, using the sales order transaction can keep track of these committed sales. Reviewing your open sales orders is important for effective inventory management.

Handling Customer Inventory Returns

When your company offers an inventory product for sale, you will probably also have the occasion when a customer returns the product. In QuickBooks you will use a credit memo transaction to record the return.

Processing your customer returns correctly can be very important to your company's financials. A returned inventory product from your customer will affect the following:

- Inventory physical count and inventory valuation on the balance sheet

- Accounts receivable balance on the balance sheet

- Income and cost of goods sold

- Sales tax payable (if applicable to your business and product)

New for QuickBooks 2012, users can create a credit memo directly from the original customer invoice. This new functionality can help QuickBooks users be more accurate when recording customer returns.

Practice Recording Customer Returns

Using the same sample data discussed in Chapter 1, you can continue with the practice exercise you completed earlier when creating an invoice:

1. On the icon bar, click the Customers icon to open the Customer Center (see Figure 5.31).

Figure 5.31
The Customer Center can be the easiest place to find specific transactions.

2. From the Customers & Jobs tab, select the Garage Repair job for the customer Baker, Chris.

3. On the right side of the Customer Center you should see the invoice you created in the earlier practice. Double-click it to open the selected invoice.

4. With the customer invoice open, from the Create drop-down list (on the top of the Create Invoices dialog box) select Credit Memo for this invoice.

   The Create Credit Memos/Refunds dialog box displays with the same item(s) that were included on the original invoice.

5. Review and leave the defaulted information. In your own data you might need to add or remove items from the Create Credit Memos/Refunds dialog box.

6. Click Save & Close. The Available Credit dialog box displays, as shown in Figure 5.32, with these options:

   - Retain as an available credit

   - Give a refund

   - Apply to an invoice

Figure 5.32
Multiple options are available for handling customer credits.

7. For this practice, select the Apply to an Invoice option button. Click OK.

    The Apply Credit to Invoices dialog box displays. In this practice example, QuickBooks has automatically selected the invoice you created in the previous practice.

8. Click Done. You are returned to the Create Credit Memos/Refunds dialog box that, for this exercise, shows a Remaining Credit of 0.00 in the lower-right corner.

9. Click Save & Close. You are returned to your original invoice that now displays the Paid stamp.

10. Click Save & Close.

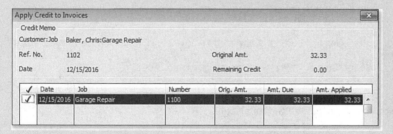

Figure 5.33
You can manually override the amount or invoice selection in how a customer credit is applied.

 tip

When applying a credit memo to an invoice in the Apply Credit to Invoices dialog box, shown in Figure 5.33, QuickBooks will match the credit to an invoice of the same amount if there are multiple invoices with open balances by default. If no match is found, QuickBooks will apply the credit to the oldest invoice(s) first.

Creating credit memos for product returns is much easier with improvements made to QuickBooks 2012. If you are using an earlier edition of QuickBooks, you can also click the Apply Credits button at the bottom of an invoice to complete the same step.

Handling Vendor Inventory Returns

Perhaps after receiving the returned inventory from your customer, you find the product was not manufactured to your specifications and needs to be returned to the vendor.

Handling these types of returns properly is important and can affect these financial balances:

- Inventory physical count and inventory valuation on the balance sheet
- Accounts payable balance on the balance sheet

To create a vendor return in your QuickBooks data file, follow these steps:

1. On the Home page, click the Enter Bills icon.

2. Select the Credit option button at the top of the Enter Bills dialog box to create a vendor credit.

3. From the Vendor drop-down list, select the vendor you are returning the product(s) to.

4. For the Date field, enter the date you want to record return of the inventory.

5. In the Ref. No. field, enter your vendor's credit authorization number if supplied.

6. Click the Items tab and select the inventory item(s) being returned.

7. In the Qty field, type the number of units being returned.

8. Review the defaulted Cost and adjust as needed to agree with your vendor's credit authorization.

9. Click Save & Close (or Save & New) to enter another vendor credit.

Entering a credit memo is just the first step in the process. When you know how your vendor applied the credit, you can complete the transaction.

MANAGING INVENTORY

Adjusting Inventory

For companies that track inventory, I find inventory balances are one of the last numbers in QuickBooks that truly gets a good look. You review your accounts receivable because you have customers that need to pay you. You keep up with your accounts payable because you have vendors that won't supply you without first getting paid. Why exactly is it then, that inventory "reconciling" is often at the bottom of the list, yet it can have the greatest impact on your company's financials?

Experience has taught me that most companies simply do not know how in QuickBooks to properly review and audit their inventory balances. This section outlines specific reports and methods you can use in QuickBooks to make sure inventory balances are correct.

If you are using inventory in your QuickBooks data, it is recommended that you view your financial reports in accrual basis. Most companies that have inventory report their tax financials in accrual basis. However, a more important reason is that on accrual basis reporting, QuickBooks will match the cost with the related sale. The exception is when using non-inventory items. These items, when purchased, do not increase an Inventory Asset account. Instead, they are recorded directly to the Cost of Goods Sold account, or the Expense account that was assigned when the item was created.

Any company that manages inventory needs to manage inventory errors. Business owners will list any of the following reasons for having to correct their accounting inventory errors:

- Errors in the physical counted results

- Damaged goods

- Theft of inventory

- Open vendor item receipts or bills that are not due to the vendor

- Incorrect valuation given to the inventory at the startup of a data file

This section discusses the methods for correcting inventory errors you might find in your QuickBooks data. If you have a good inventory count commitment and manage the resulting information from the QuickBooks Inventory Valuation Summary report, you should see little to no data entry errors and instead probably will be adjusting inventory only for damage or theft.

Performing a Physical Inventory Count

All too often, here is where I find a complacent attitude about inventory management. I agree that performing a physical inventory count is a time-consuming task. However, if effort is put to this task, your overall financials will be more accurate.

To make recording the count easier, select Reports, Inventory, Physical Inventory Worksheet from the menu bar. The report cannot be modified or filtered for specific dates, so you should run the report at the same time you plan to do your physical count (see Figure 6.1) and be certain that all your inventory-related transactions have been entered. If you want to keep a record of the original worksheet, you can export it to Excel or email it as a PDF attachment.

Item	Description	Preferred Vendor	Quantity On Hand	Physical Count
Cabinets	Cabinets	Thomas Kitchen & Bath	0	
Cabinets:Cab...	Cabinet Pulls	Patton Hardware Supplies	423	
Cabinets:Ligh...	Light pine kitchen cabinet wall unit	Patton Hardware Supplies	7	
Door Frame	standard interior door frame	Patton Hardware Supplies	21	
Hardware		Patton Hardware Supplies	0	
Hardware:Br...	standard interior brass hinge	Perry Windows & Doors	246	
Hardware:Do...	Standard Doorknobs	Perry Windows & Doors	124	
Hardware:Lk...	Locking interior doorknobs	Perry Windows & Doors	122	
Wood Door	Doors	Patton Hardware Supplies	1	
Wood Door:E...	Exterior wood door	Perry Windows & Doors	14	
Wood Door:In...	Interior wood door	Perry Windows & Doors	47	
Interior Door kit	complete interior door		20	

Rock Castle Construction — **Physical Inventory Worksheet** — December 15, 2016 (8:44 AM, 12/15/16)

Customize Report | Share Template | Memorize | Print | E-mail ▾ | Excel ▾ | Hide Header | Refresh | Sort By Default

Figure 6.1
Create a physical inventory worksheet to record the actual inventory counts.

After completing a physical inventory count, you can then confidently create an inventory adjustment so the accounting records will match your actual physical inventory.

Quantity Adjustments

If you discovered quantity differences between your accounting records and your physical inventory account, you should record an inventory quantity adjustment to correct your accounting records.

To create an inventory quantity adjustment in your date, follow these steps:

1. On the Home page, click the Inventory Activities icon and select Adjust Quantity/Value on Hand from the menu. The Adjust Quantity/Value on Hand dialog box opens, as shown in Figure 6.2.

 caution

Before creating the accounting adjustment, make sure you have created an account in the chart of accounts to hold the value of the inventory adjustment. The account type can be either a Cost of Goods Sold type or an Expense type. For the business owner, consult your accountant when making this decision.

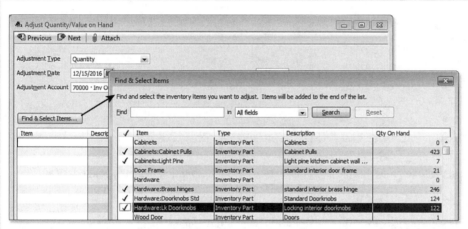

Figure 6.2
Use the Find & Select Items button to efficiently select multiple inventory items to adjust quantity.

2. From the Adjustment Type drop-down list, select Quantity.

3. Enter an Adjustment Date and optional Ref. No.

4. Select the appropriate Adjustment Account. This account is usually a Cost of Goods Sold account or an Expense account named Inventory Overage/Shortage.

5. Optionally assign a Customer:Job and select your Class if being tracked. However, Job Profitability reports will not include inventory adjustment transactions.

6. To efficiently select multiple items at once, click the Find & Select Items button. Click with your cursor to place a check mark (see Figure 6.2) next to those items you want to create a quantity adjustment for.

 caution

Inventory (and Value) adjustments assigned to a customer or job will be included in the Profit & Loss by Job reports, but will not be included in any of the other reports offered, when selecting Reports, Jobs, Time, and Mileage from the menu bar.

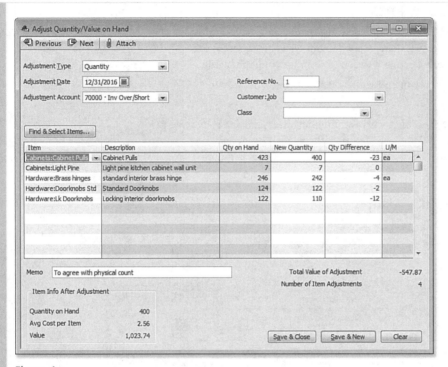

Figure 6.3
Use Inventory Adjustments to properly adjust your inventory in your accounting to match your physical counts.

7. Click Add Selected Items to return to the Adjust Quantity/Value on Hand dialog box.

8. In the New Quantity column, enter your count from the completed physical inventory or optionally enter the change in the Qty Difference column.

9. Click Save & Close when completed.

QuickBooks provides details on the Item Info After Adjustment as well as summarizes the Total Value of the Adjustment and the Number of item Adjustments.

The accounting effect of the transaction in Figure 6.3 is to reduce the quantity on hand for each of the items shown, reduce (credits) the Inventory asset balance by $547.87, and increase (debits) the Inventory Adjustments account (either a Cost of Goods Sold type or Expense type).

Value Adjustments

Timing is important when doing a valuation adjustment. Value adjustments, if appropriate, should be carefully considered for their impact on the company's resulting financials.

Value adjustments differ from quantity adjustments as they do not adjust the quantity but instead adjust the recorded value of the specific items in inventory.

To create a value-only inventory adjustment in your data, follow these steps:

1. From the menu bar, select Vendors, Inventory Activities, Adjust Quantity/Value on Hand. A dialog box with the same name opens, as shown in Figure 6.4.

2. Select Total Value from the Adjustment Type drop-down list.

3. Enter an Adjustment Date and optional Ref. No.

> **caution**
>
> Generally, this type of adjustment is not done as often as quantity adjustments. The purpose of this book is not to explore or offer tax advice, but certain guidelines exist for when an inventory valuation adjustment is appropriate. Ask your tax accountant to provide them for you.

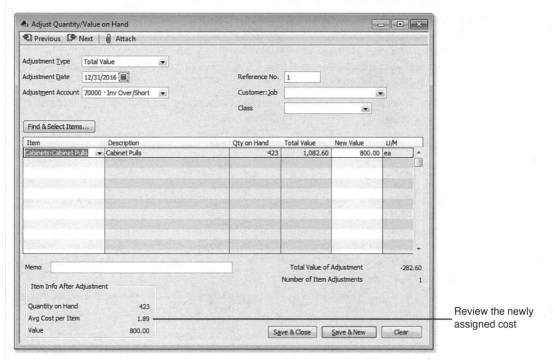

Review the newly assigned cost

Figure 6.4
Value adjustments are not used often, be sure to ask your accountant first if it is appropriate for your needs.

4. Select the appropriate Adjustment Account. This account is usually an Expense account named Inventory Overage/Shortage.

5. Optionally, assign a Customer:Job and select your Class if being tracked.

6. To efficiently select multiple items at once, click the Find & Select Items button. Click with your cursor to place a check mark next to those items you want to create a quantity adjustment for.

7. Click Add Selected Items. You are returned to the Adjust Quantity/Value on Hand dialog box.

8. In the New Value column, enter your new calculated total value you want assigned to the item.

9. Click Save & Close when completed.

 caution

Do you know how important the date is when assigning the inventory adjustment? If you backdate your inventory adjustment, QuickBooks will recalculate your Cost of Goods Sold from that date forward using the new average cost as of the date of the sales transaction. Care should be taken not to date an inventory adjustment in a prior year where tax returns have already been filed.

The accounting result of this inventory value adjustment, as shown in Figure 6.4, is no net change to inventory quantities, a decrease (credit) to your Inventory Asset account, and an increase (debit) to your Inventory Adjustments account (either a Cost of Goods Sold type or Expense type). A new average cost will be computed based on the (Original Asset Value + or − the Value Difference) / Quantity on Hand as recorded on the inventory value adjustment. You can view the newly assigned average cost in the lower left of the inventory adjustment.

The new average cost will be recorded when a sales transaction uses this item, *on or after* the date of the inventory adjustment.

 tip

There are two preferences to control dating transactions. To access them, log in as the Admin or External Accountant user in single-user mode. From the menu bar, select Company, Set Closing Date to open the Preferences dialog box with the Accounting—Company Preferences tab selected (see Figure 6.5).

Setting Date Warnings enables a user to be warned when a transaction is either dated so many days in the past or in the future. Set Date/Password is another option to "close" QuickBooks to prevent adding, modifying, voiding, or deleting transactions prior to a selected closing date. Setting a closing date and related features is discussed more fully in Chapter 16, "Sharing QuickBooks Data with Your Accountant."

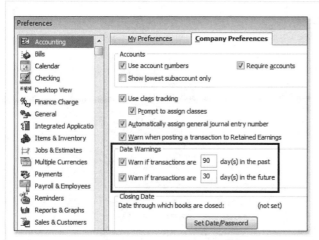

Figure 6.5
Choices for controlling past- or future-dated transactions.

Inventory Reporting

You have learned just how easy it is to buy, sell, and adjust your inventory. Good inventory management will also include frequent reviews of inventory specific reports available in QuickBooks.

In this section, you will be introduced to some of the more common reports. However, take the time to review all available reports, as you may have a specific reporting need in addition to those mentioned here.

Inventory Center

New for QuickBooks Premier 2012 (all editions) and Enterprise Solutions 12.0 (all editions) is the Inventory Center. From the Home page click the Inventory Activities icon and select the Inventory Center from the menu bar as displayed in Figure 6.6. Similar to the other "centers" in QuickBooks, the Inventory Center offers one convenient location to manage your inventory reporting and activities including:

- **New Inventory Items**—Quick access to creating an individual new inventory item or to the Add/Edit Multiple List Entries functionality.

- **New Transactions**—Quick access to all inventory-related transactions.

- **Print**—Quick access to printing the item list, information, or transaction list.

- **Excel**—Exporting to Excel the item or transaction list. Importing item list from Excel.

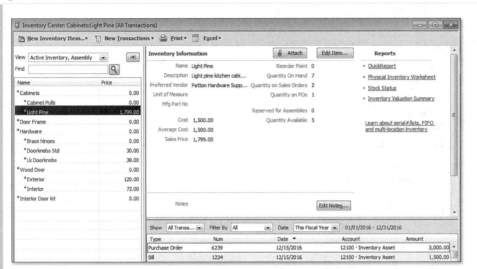

Figure 6.6
Access the most common transactions and reports for your inventory from the Inventory Center.

Click with your cursor on a specific inventory item and to the right you will see displayed detailed information, transactions, and links to some of the more common reports for managing your inventory.

Access is also provided to attach a document to the inventory item using the new free QuickBooks Attached Documents. Click the Docs icon on your icon bar to open the Doc Center.

With an item selected in the Inventory Center, you can click the Edit Item button to make changes as discussed previously in Chapter 5 in the section titled "Adding or Editing Inventory Items," p. 121.

Report Center

Use the Report Center to find the right report for your inventory management needs. See Figure 6.7.

 tip

With this new Inventory Center you can filter your inventory list by ready-made filters or custom filters of your choosing. One important selection is the ability to filter for inventory with a negative inventory quantity on hand (QOH < = zero). You will learn later in this chapter how important it is to accurate financials not to let your inventory get negative (where you have sold more than you have on hand).

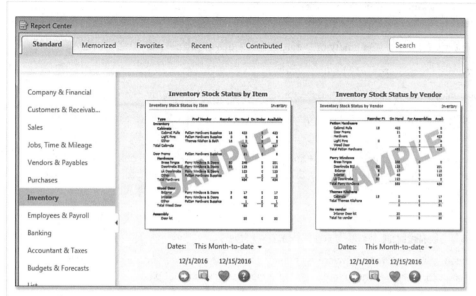

Figure 6.7
The Report Center makes finding the right inventory management report simple.

To open the Report Center, follow these steps:

1. From the menu bar, select Reports, Report Center.

2. Click the Close link to close the New! Contributed Reports! message. This feature will be detailed in Chapter 14, "Reporting in QuickBooks."

3. On the Report Center's Standard tab, select Sales.

4. Scroll down to the bottom of the page to find the Open Sales Orders—by Customer or by Item report, which is useful when managing inventory. This report is available only if you are using QuickBooks Premier or Enterprise Solutions.

5. Next, select Purchases on the Standard tab of the Report Center to view these inventory management reports:

   - **Purchases by Vendor**—Summary or Detail

   - **Purchases by Item**—Summary or Detail

   - **Open Purchase Orders**—Summary or Detail

   The Report Center provides a thumbnail image of how the data would look in the report.

6. Below each report you can change the dates, click Run to prepare the report with your data, click Info to preview a larger thumbnail image, click Fave to include the report in the Favorites section of the Reports Center, or click Help for more details.

7. Next, select Inventory on the Standard tab of the Report Center to view these inventory management reports:

- **Inventory Valuation**—Summary or Detail. More details in the next section.

- **Inventory Stock Status**—By Item or Vendor.

- **Physical Inventory Worksheet**—Used for recording your physical inventory count totals.

- **Pending Builds**—For QuickBooks Premier or Enterprise users who have assembly inventory items.

8. If you are using the Manufacturing & Wholesale edition of QuickBooks Premier or Enterprise Solutions, click Mfg & Wholesale on the Standard tab of the Report Center for additional useful inventory management reports.

Inventory Valuation and Your Financials

Another equally important task in inventory management is to compare your Inventory Valuation Summary report to your Balance Sheet Inventory Asset balance (accrual basis).

Comparing Inventory Reports to Financials

Using the sample company referred to in Chapter 1, use this exercise to practice how to compare the Inventory Valuation Summary report to the Balance Sheet Inventory Asset balance.

1. From the Report Center, select Inventory on the Standard tab. Find the Inventory Valuation Summary report and click the Run icon to display the report. Accept the defaulted report date; in Figure 6.8 the As of December 15, 2016 data is displayed.

2. Take note of the Asset Value column Total. In Figure 6.8 the total Asset Value is $31,566.37. Your sample data total might differ.

3. From the Report Center, select Company & Financial on the Standard tab, and then click Run below the Balance Sheet Standard report (scroll down to find this report). Accept the defaulted report date. In Figure 6.8 the As of December 15, 2016 data is displayed.

4. Compare the balance in the Inventory Asset account (in the Other Current Assets group) to the total from step 2.

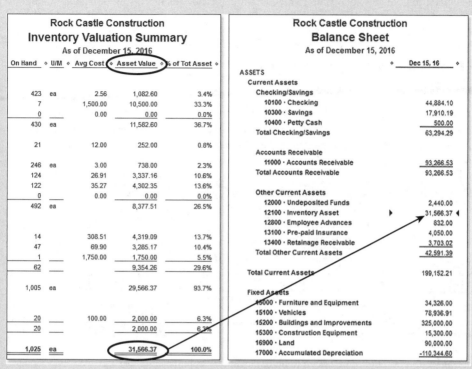

Figure 6.8
Compare your total Asset Value with your Balance Sheet Inventory Asset balance.

What if the two balances do not match? The most common cause for the two reports not to match is entering a transaction that affects the Inventory Asset account, but does not affect inventory items. The Inventory Summary report only shows the results of transactions that use inventory items. For example, if a General Journal has been used to adjust the Balance Sheet balance, those transactions will not affect the Inventory Valuation Summary report.

 caution

When working with inventory adjustments, never use a General Journal transaction. The specific reason is because a General Journal transaction does not use Items, and any adjustments using this transaction affects only the Balance Sheet balance, not the Inventory Valuation Summary report.

It is also not appropriate to use the Inventory Asset account on the Expense tab of a Vendor Bill, Credit, or Write Checks transaction. To properly use these transactions, you would use the Items tab with the appropriate inventory item.

If you need to adjust inventory, select Vendors, Inventory Activities, Adjust Quantity/Value on Hand from the menu bar, as discussed earlier in this chapter.

To find General Journal entries in your own data that might be causing the out-of-balance amount, follow these steps:

1. Double-click the Inventory Asset balance on your Balance Sheet report.

   QuickBooks creates the Transactions by Account report.

2. From the Dates drop-down list, scroll to the top and select All.

3. To locate the General Journal entries, select Type from the Sort By drop-down list (in the upper-right corner of the report), as shown in Figure 6.9. QuickBooks now organizes the data by transaction type. Look for General Journal type transactions.

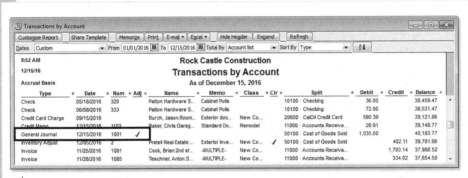

Figure 6.9
General Journal transactions should not be used to adjust inventory balances.

You should not modify, delete, or void these transactions, especially if they were used in accounting periods that have already had tax returns prepared using the current financial information. Continue with the remaining methods in the sections that follow, before making any corrections.

Reviewing the Recorded Average Cost Valuation

As mentioned earlier in this chapter, QuickBooks uses the Average Cost method for valuing inventory. From the menu bar, select Reports, Inventory, Inventory Valuation Summary. Figure 6.10 shows the value assigned to your costs when you sell an inventory item.

If you are using QuickBooks Enterprise Solutions 12.0 with FIFO (First In First Out) costing enabled, it might not be necessary to review this section because FIFO costing replaces Average Costing.

As an example, you are selling an inventory product with the following transactions as shown in Table 6.1.

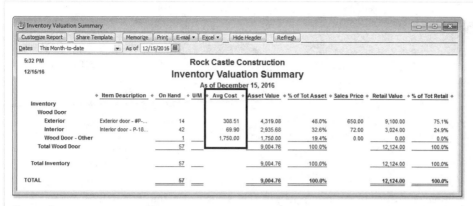

Figure 6.10
Use the Inventory Valuation Summary report to verify the cost being recorded when an inventory item is sold.

Table 6.1 Calculating Average Cost

Date	Quantity Purchased	Actual Cost per Unit	Total Cost	QuickBooks Calculated Average Cost per Unit
12/15/16	100	$10.00	$1,000.00	$10.00
12/25/16	50	$8.50	$425.00	$9.50
TOTAL	150		$1,425.00	(1425/150)

Sales transactions that are dated on or between 12/15/16 and 12/24/16 selling this item will record cost of goods sold at $10.00 per unit. (Assuming there are no other replenishing purchases made during that time.)

The average cost of the 150 units will be $9.50 each if none are sold prior to 12/26. However, any quantity sold from the first order will change the weighting of the unit cost so a different average cost will result when the second order is received.

To further explain how important it is to enter your inventory transactions daily (and not retroactively), Table 6.2 shows the resulting Average Cost calculations used when selling more inventory than is available.

In Table 6.2, the cost recorded on 12/20/16 is $10.00 per unit. However, after the replenishing transaction the actual average cost is $7.00 per unit. The costs in 2016 will be overstated by $3.00 per unit with the correcting entry to Cost of Goods Sold reported in the 2017 financials.

These details assume that no other transactions were recorded for this item except as noted in the following transactions:

Table 6.2 Calculating Average Cost When Selling Negative Inventory

Date	Quantity Purchased	Quantity Sold	Actual Cost Per Unit	Inventory Value	Calculated Average Cost
12/15/16	100		$10.00	$1,000.00	$10.00
12/20/16		–125	$10.00	($1,250.00)	$10.00
01/05/17	50		$8.50	$425.00	$9.50
Remaining Quantity	25		Remaining Value	$175.00	$7.00

Average costing is a perfect fit for a business that sells a product that does not fluctuate significantly in cost from one period to the next. However, this is not always the case, so it becomes important that you verify the relative accuracy of the average cost QuickBooks has recorded on the Inventory Valuation Summary report.

In Figure 6.10 shown previously, the average cost for the Interior Wood Door is listed as $69.90. Compare this amount to a recent vendor bill. If the amount is significantly different, you should review the purchase details for the item.

From the menu bar, select Reports, Inventory, Inventory Valuation Detail. You might want to customize and filter the report for specific dates or items. More about working with reports is available in Chapter 14.

In Figure 6.11, the Inventory Valuation Detail is shown for the Interior Wood Door. Reviewing the individual lines in the Average Cost column can help you determine whether an issue exists with the average cost. If the average cost changes dramatically, you might want to review the specific bill or check details recorded when the product was purchased.

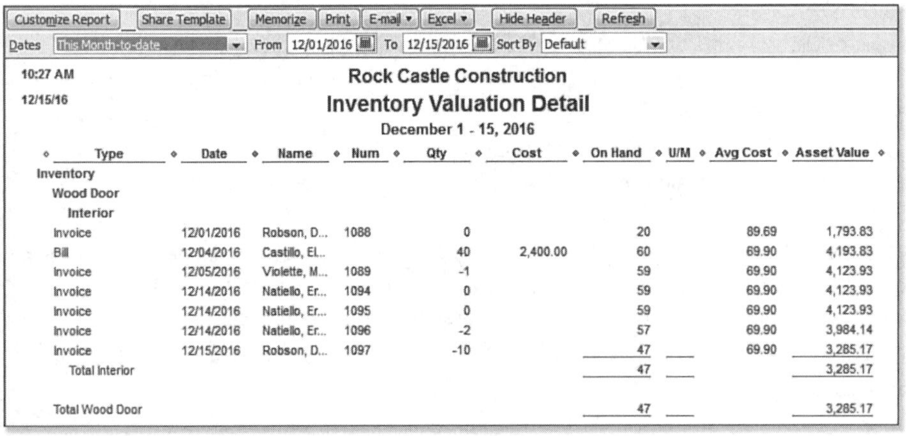

Customize Report | Share Template | Memorize | Print | E-mail | Excel | Hide Header | Refresh

Dates This Month-to-date From 12/01/2016 To 12/15/2016 Sort By Default

10:27 AM
12/15/16

Rock Castle Construction

Inventory Valuation Detail

December 1 - 15, 2016

Type	Date	Name	Num	Qty	Cost	On Hand	U/M	Avg Cost	Asset Value
Inventory									
Wood Door									
Interior									
Invoice	12/01/2016	Robson, D...	1086	0		20		89.69	1,793.83
Bill	12/04/2016	Castillo, El...		40	2,400.00	60		69.90	4,193.83
Invoice	12/05/2016	Violette, M...	1089	-1		59		69.90	4,123.93
Invoice	12/14/2016	Natiello, Er...	1094	0		59		69.90	4,123.93
Invoice	12/14/2016	Natiello, Er...	1095	0		59		69.90	4,123.93
Invoice	12/14/2016	Natiello, Er...	1096	-2		57		69.90	3,984.14
Invoice	12/15/2016	Robson, D...	1097	-10		47		69.90	3,285.17
Total Interior						47			3,285.17
Total Wood Door						47			3,285.17

Figure 6.11
Create an Inventory Valuation Detail report to research changes in average cost.

Reviewing and correcting the average cost of items is as equally important as adjusting the quantity on hand.

Reviewing Aged Item Receipts

The "Purchasing, Receiving, and Entering the Vendor Bill" section of Chapter 5 provided details about the inventory process; one of the methods of receiving inventory is without the vendor's bill.

The effect of receiving inventory without a bill is to increase your inventory asset (debit) and increase your accounts payable (credit). The unique feature of this method is that QuickBooks creates an item receipt transaction that *will not* show in the Pay Bills window. QuickBooks recognizes that because you did not receive the bill, it is not likely you should be paying it without the final bill details.

Often, goods will arrive at your business without a bill. A couple of reasons exist for a vendor to ship the goods to your place of business without a final bill:

- Shipping charges need to be added to the bill. Often, the vendor will not know the shipping charges when the goods are initially shipped.

- Vendors do not want to disclose the value of the inventory, so that those who handle the inventory during shipping will not know the value of the goods being shipped.

What you might not know is that item receipts age just like an outstanding accounts payable bill. To see whether you have open, outdated item receipts, go to the Vendor Center and click the Transactions tab (see Figure 6.12). Select the Item Receipts transaction type. Filter by All Dates and click the Date column to sort the transactions by date.

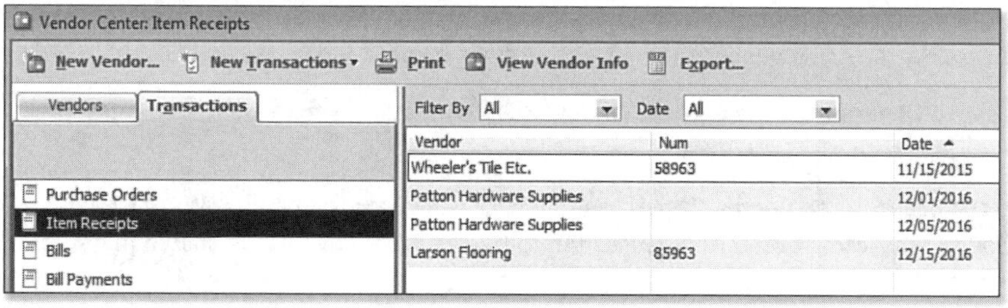

Figure 6.12
Use the Transactions tab of the Vendor Center to see all open item receipts.

If you find you have aged item receipts and you know you have paid the vendor, use the following steps to assign the check to the open item receipt. If you have also paid your vendors with a credit card, you might also want to use these same instructions substituting the credit card transaction for the check transaction:

1. From the Vendor Center, select the Item Receipts transaction type on the Transactions tab.

2. Unapplied item receipts display on the right. Click the header for the Date column to sort by date. You are looking for any old outdated item receipts.

3. If you find an aged item receipt that you know was paid to the vendor, double-click the item receipt to open the Create Item Receipts dialog box.

4. Select the Bill Received check box (top right) as shown in Figure 6.13.

Open the Item receipt document and click the Bill Received box.

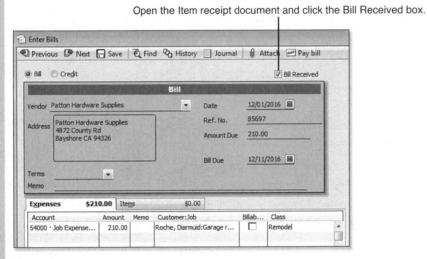

Figure 6.13
The item receipt now becomes a vendor bill.

5. Click Save & Close.

6. Next, you need to locate the check that was written to the vendor. From the Vendors tab on the Vendor Center, select the same vendor the item receipt was created for.

7. On the right, select Checks from the Show drop-down list. Optionally, select a Filter By and Date range.

8. After locating the check in the Vendor Center, double-click the check to open the Write Checks dialog box. Modify the Account on the Expenses tab to be Accounts Payable, as shown in Figure 6.14.

9. Next, assign the Vendor name in the Customer:Job column. The effect of this updated transaction is to decrease (debit) Accounts Payable and decrease (credit) Cash.

10. Click Save & Close.

11. From the Home page, click the Pay Bills icon. The Pay Bills dialog box opens.

12. In the Filter By drop-down list, select the vendor you are correcting the records for.

13. Place a checkmark next to the bill (see Figure 6.15).

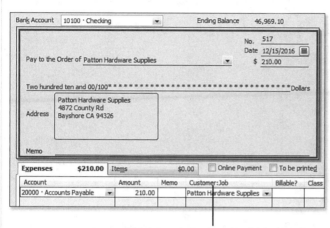

Vendor name assigned to this column

Figure 6.14
Changing the Expenses account to Accounts Payable and adding the vendor name on the same line creates a vendor credit from the check.

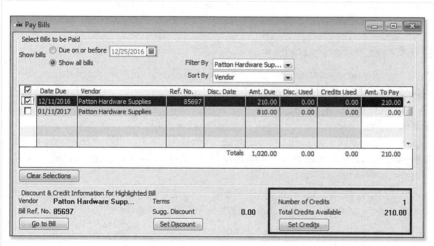

Figure 6.15
Once the bill is selected, the Set Credits option is available.

14. Click the Set Credits button to assign the modified check transaction from step 7 to the open vendor bill (see Figure 6.16).

Figure 6.16
QuickBooks automatically matches a credit with a bill of the same amount, or you can select the credit and modify the amount assigned.

15. Click Done to return to the Pay Bills dialog box. If your credit is the same amount as the open vendor bill, the Amt. To Pay column will be zero.

16. Click Pay Selected Bills. Click Done to close the Payment Summary dialog box.

Reviewing Aged Accounts Payable

At the same time you review your open item receipts, you should also review your accounts payable open invoices that have aged more than 60 days.

To review your accounts payable, select Reports, Vendors & Payables, Unpaid Bills Detail from the menu bar. If you see open vendor bills you are sure you have paid, it might be because you used the Write Checks dialog box to pay your vendor bills instead of using the Pay Bills dialog box (accessed from the Vendors, Pay Bills menu). Having both an open vendor bill and check paying for the same purchase overstates your costs or inventory.

QuickBooks tries to prevent you from doing this by providing a warning message when you try to write a check to a vendor for whom you have an unpaid bill, as shown in Figure 6.17.

If you did use the Write Checks dialog box to issue a vendor payment for a currently open vendor bill, you can resolve this problem by reassigning it. To do so, follow the steps outlined in the "Reviewing Aged Item Receipts," page 173, starting with step 7.

After completing the steps, you will have successfully assigned the check you wrote using the Write Checks dialog box to the open vendor bill that should have been paid by a check in the Pay Bills dialog box. This correction has now removed the expected overstatement in your costs and removed the bill from being included in your open Accounts Payable balances.

 tip

If you are an accounting professional and using the QuickBooks Accountant 2012 software, you will find a tool in Client Data Review that will simplify the steps outlined in this section. For more information, refer to Appendix A, "Client Data Review."

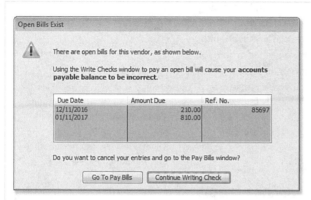

Figure 6.17
A warning displays if you try to use the Write Checks dialog box to pay a vendor instead of creating a bill payment from the Pay Bills dialog box.

How QuickBooks Handles Negative Inventory

QuickBooks enables selling of inventory, even if you do not have enough quantity available for sale. This situation is referred to as selling negative inventory. What it means is that you can include an inventory item on a customer invoice or sales receipt before you have recorded the item receipt or bill for the purchase of the item into your inventory.

When a transaction will cause you to have a negative inventory balance the user is provided with the warning message shown in Figure 6.18. The warning does not prevent the user from completing the intended transaction, but should be viewed as a need to research why QuickBooks does not have enough stock of that item in inventory to record the sale.

 caution

On the Items & Inventory—Company Preferences tab of the Preferences dialog box (select Edit, Preferences from the menu bar), you can enable a warning if there is not enough inventory quantity on hand (QOH) to sell (see Figure 6.18). Your preferences might differ depending on the version of QuickBooks you are using.

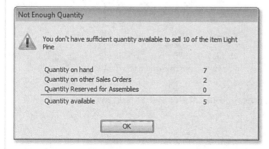

Figure 6.18
Not enough quantity warning indicates an issue with not following the recommended processes for proper inventory management.

Although ignoring the warning message can be useful for getting the invoice to the customer, it can create issues with your company's financials. The following sections detail how QuickBooks handles the costing of the inventory behind the scenes when you sell negative inventory and provides information on how to avoid or minimize the negative effect it can have on your company's financials.

 For more information, see Appendix A, "Client Data Review," p. 601.

When Inventory Has an Average Cost from Prior Purchase Transactions

If you review the Inventory Valuation Detail report (select Reports, Inventory, Inventory Valuation Detail from the menu bar) for the item(s) that have negative values, and there are previously recorded average cost amounts, QuickBooks will assign the most recent average cost dated on or before the invoice date that created negative inventory. When the purchase transaction is later recorded, QuickBooks will adjust Cost of Goods Sold or Expense type for any difference.

Figure 6.19 shows the average cost on the date of the invoice was $150.00 per unit. QuickBooks records a decrease (credit) to inventory for the two units of $300.00 total and an increase (debit) to Cost of Goods Sold of $300.00 for the two units sold.

> **tip**
>
> Included with QuickBooks Accountant 2012 Client Data Review feature you can troubleshoot inventory discrepancies between the Inventory Valuation Summary report and the inventory balance on the Balance Sheet. This new troubleshooting tool will automatically compare the balances from the two reports and detail which transactions are potentially causing the discrepancy.
>
> Additionally, this new tool will identify which items are negative (you have sold more than you have purchased) for the specific accounting period being reviewed as well as for a current date. You will find in this chapter just how important it is to not let your inventory go negative.

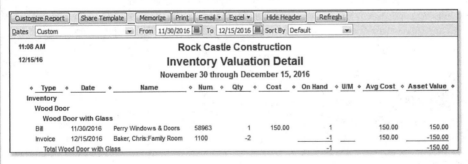

Figure 6.19
QuickBooks records the Cost of Goods Sold for negative inventory items at the last known average cost.

To show how important the date of the replenishing purchase transaction is, review the details provided below. Note, this example assumes that no additional transactions were recorded except as noted.

The new inventory asset value is calculated as

($150.00)	Inventory asset value as of 12/15/16 due to selling "negative inventory"
$600.00	12/25/16 replenishing purchase of 3 units @ $200.00 / unit
$450.00	Asset value before QuickBooks' automatic adjustment to COGS

Actual inventory value is 2 remaining units at $200 each or $400.00 total

$(50.00)	On the date of the replenishing vendor bill, QuickBooks automatically creates a transaction that decreases (credits) Inventory asset and increases (debits) COGS. See Figure 6.20. This increase in cost adjustment is not associated with the recorded per unit cost to the customer.
$400.00	Resulting Inventory Asset value on 12/25/16 as shown in Figure 6.21.

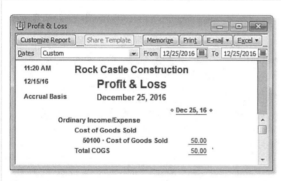

Figure 6.20
When you replenish inventory shortages, QuickBooks automatically makes an adjustment to agree with what the average cost would have been.

Type	Date	Name	Num	Qty	Cost	On Hand	U/M	Avg Cost	Asset Value
Inventory									
Wood Door									
Wood Door with Glass									
Bill	11/30/2016	Perry Windows & Doors	58963	1	150.00	1		150.00	150.00
Invoice	12/15/2016	Baker, Chris:Family Room	1100	-2		-1		150.00	-150.00
Bill	12/25/2016	Perry Windows & Doors	58975	3	600.00	2		200.00	400.00
	Total Wood Door with Glass					2			400.00

Figure 6.21
The Inventory Valuation Detail report shows the actual inventory value after recording the replenishment transaction.

When QuickBooks creates an adjustment to reflect what the average cost should have been, the adjustment is *not* assigned to customers or jobs—making it even more important to not sell negative inventory.

When Inventory Does Not Have a Prior Average Cost

There might be times when you stock a new item and you add it to a customer invoice before recording any purchase activity for the item. If this happens, you should at least record a default cost on the New Item (or Edit Item) dialog box.

When an Inventory Item Has a Default Cost

If you have assigned an inventory item that you have not yet purchased (that is, the quantity on hand is zero) to a customer invoice and if you *did* define a default cost when you first created the inventory item, QuickBooks will use this default cost as the suggested per-unit cost when the invoice is recorded.

Let's suppose you stock a new inventory item for a Wood Door with Glass. When creating the item, you record a default cost of $150.00, as shown in Figure 6.22.

 tip

What is important to note here is that QuickBooks does not retroactively record the additional cost back to the customer's negative inventory invoice date. In fact, QuickBooks records the adjustment as of the date of the purchase transaction and will not associate the adjustment with the original customer at all, overstating gross profit on a Profit & Loss by Job report.

The date of the replenishing purchase transaction becomes increasingly important to manage when you let inventory go negative at the end of a fiscal or tax year in your data.

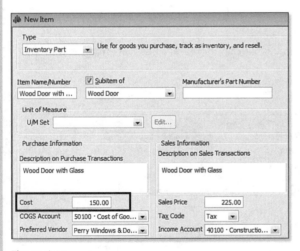

Figure 6.22
New stock item created in QuickBooks with a default cost of $150.00.

Before any purchase is recorded for this item, it is sold on a customer invoice. When you create an invoice where there are not enough inventories, QuickBooks provides a warning, as previously shown in Figure 6.18.

QuickBooks has to estimate the cost of the item and, in this example, uses the cost assigned to the item in the New or Edit Item dialog box. When you save this invoice, QuickBooks will increase (debit) Accounts Receivable, increase (credit) Income, decrease (credit) Inventory Asset, and increase (debit) Cost of Goods Sold, and in this example, will also increase (credit) Sales Tax Payable. The Transaction Journal report details the accounting automatically recorded by QuickBooks (see Figure 6.23). You can access this report by clicking Journal found at the top of a displayed transaction in QuickBooks.

Customize Report | Share Template | Memorize | Print | E-mail | Excel | Hide Header | Refresh

Dates All | From | To | Sort By Default

11:53 AM
12/15/16

Rock Castle Construction
Transaction Journal
All Transactions

Trans #	Type	Date	Num	Account	Sales Price	Debit	Credit
1781	Invoice	12/15/2016	1100	11000 · Accounts Receivable		242.44	
				40140 · Materials Income	225.00		225.00
				12100 · Inventory Asset			150.00
				50100 · Cost of Goods Sold		150.00	
				25500 · Sales Tax Payable	7.75%		17.44
						392.44	392.44

Figure 6.23
QuickBooks uses the cost assigned in the New or Edit Item dialog box when you sell inventory that you have not recorded any purchase transactions for.

This impact to your financials (positive or negative) can be significant if the actual purchase price is different from the recorded default cost on the New or Edit Item dialog box.

When an Inventory Item Does Not Have a Default Cost

If you have assigned an inventory item you have not yet purchased (that is, the quantity on hand is zero) to a customer invoice and if you *did not* define a default cost when you first created the inventory item, QuickBooks will use -0- as the default cost per unit when the invoice is recorded, showing a 100% profit margin for your financials and for that customer!

Now, using the same previous example, only *not* recording a default cost when setting up the item, as shown in Figure 6.24, QuickBooks will not calculate any cost or inventory reduction with the sale of the inventory (see Figure 6.25).

Imagine the impact this can have on your financials and the profitability reports you might review for your business or clients. Simply heeding the many warnings QuickBooks provides about the errors of selling negative inventory can prevent this from happening in your data file.

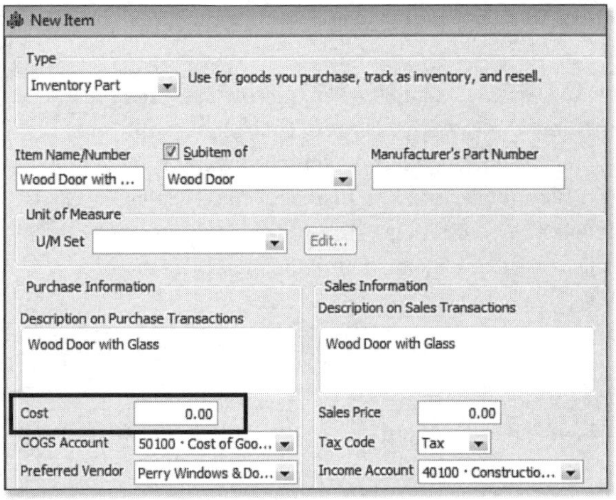

Figure 6.24
Setting up an item without including a default cost is not recommended.

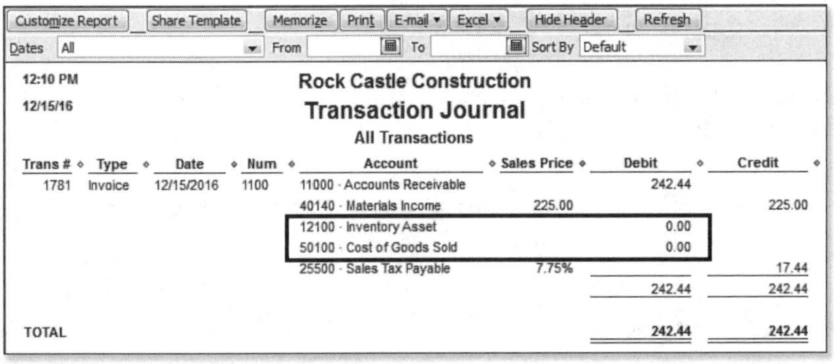

Figure 6.25
No inventory decrease or cost is recorded when selling an item you do not have in inventory, have not purchased, and did not record a default cost for.

When a Replenishing Purchase Transaction Is Created

What exactly happens when you do record purchase transactions? The date recorded on the purchase transaction is important in how QuickBooks will handle this transaction.

For example, if a sale resulting in negative inventory was dated in October and the replenishing transaction (vendor bill) was dated in November, QuickBooks records the revenue in the month of October and the cost in the month of November. From month to month, it might not be noticeable, but if the transactions cross years, revenue would be overstated in one year and costs in another.

Additionally, the revenue is tracked by the customer assigned to the invoice, but the cost *is not* tracked by the customer because the cost is recorded on the date of the purchase transactions.

To limit the negative impact, simply date your replenishing purchase transactions *before* the date of the customer invoice that caused the negative inventory. QuickBooks will recalculate the average cost of all sales transactions dated after this "replenishing" purchase transaction. And of course, it is simply best not to sell negative inventory altogether.

How to Avoid Incorrect Inventory Valuation

Troubleshooting negative inventory can be an eye opener as to how important proper inventory management is. To help with this task, rely on the Inventory Valuation Detail report, shown previously in Figure 6.21.

You can avoid these issues if the purchase transactions or inventory adjustments are dated on or prior to the date of the sales transactions creating the negative inventory. Backdating inventory adjustment transactions can be a powerful solution for correcting months of misstated financials, so use it where appropriate after discussing it with your accountant.

Solid inventory management processes and being current with your data entry will avoid recording negative inventory. If you do have negative inventory, be sure to correct it at the end of your tax year or your tax return information will potentially be incorrect.

7

SETTING UP VENDORS

Customizing Your Home Page for Vendor Activities

QuickBooks makes performing vendor activities easy with a customizable list of tasks on the Home page, as shown in Figure 7.1.

When working with Accounts Payable, you can customize the Home page to include or exclude:

- The option to enter bills and pay bills

- Inventory-related activities

- Time tracking, which is useful if you pay vendors for time worked on jobs

➡ *For more information on customizing the Home page, refer to Chapter 2, "Getting Around QuickBooks."*

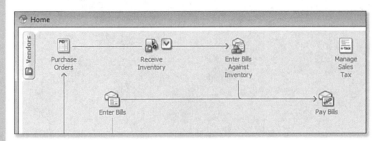

Figure 7.1
Access common vendor activities from the Home page.

Preferences That Affect Accounts Payable

Did you know that you can streamline accounts payable processes by setting certain QuickBooks preferences? Setting preferences saves keystrokes, which in turn can save data entry time.

Not every preference that affects accounts payable impacts your financials; some preferences enable specific features. Set preferences in QuickBooks by selecting Edit, Preferences from the menu bar to open the Preferences dialog box.

Preferences in QuickBooks come in two forms:

- **My Preferences**—Settings that are unique to the current user logged in the data file and are not shared by other users. Click the My Preferences tab to modify the user-specific settings for the logged-in user.

- **Company Preferences**—Settings that are common for all users. Click the Company Preferences tab to modify settings globally for all users.

The following sections detail the preferences that can affect your use of the accounts payable functionality.

Accounting

The Accounting preferences are important to review when you first create your data file. These choices affect much of how your accounting information is recorded in accounts payable.

 note

To set company preferences, you need to open the file as the Admin or External Accountant user and switch to single-user mode (if you are using the data file in a multi-user environment). The Admin user is the default user created when you begin using QuickBooks for the first time.

Proper data entry security includes limiting which employees have access to logging in as the Admin and setting company preferences that are global for all users.

Company Preferences

Company preferences are shared globally by all users. The Accounting preferences include:

- **Accounts**—These settings are important for proper management of recording revenue and expenses. The following are the preference settings for Accounts:

  - **Use Account Numbers**—Requires the use of an account number in addition to account name when creating a new chart of account list item. Users can type either the number or the name when referencing an account on a transaction line.

  - **Show Lowest Subaccount Only**—You can choose this option if account numbering is enabled and all the chart of account items have a number assigned. This setting changes how the account name is displayed. If you see an "other" named account on your financials, users recorded a transaction to the parent account and not to one of the available subaccounts.

  - **Require Accounts**—Use this option to determine whether or not QuickBooks displays a prompt when you forget to choose an account on a transaction line. If you leave the option turned off, QuickBooks will assign the transaction to Uncategorized Income or Uncategorized Expense. When creating a new data file, this default is automatically selected.

- **Use Class Tracking**—Classes in QuickBooks provide a secondary means of grouping transactions, such as into profit centers. The optional Prompt to Assign Classes allows you to enforce class tracking in a similar fashion to the aforementioned Require Accounts option. See the QuickBooks Help menu for more information on how you can use class tracking to track multiple profit centers on your income statement and for some balance sheet accounts.

- **Automatically Assign General Journal Entry Number**—This preference sequentially numbers any general journal entries automatically. Each entry number can be modified at the time of input.

- **Warn When Posting a Transaction to Retained Earnings**—You can post to the Retained Earnings account but you should not because QuickBooks uses this account at year end to close out the year's Profit or Loss totals. Note: When creating a new data file, this option is enabled by default.

- **Date Warnings**—When you create a new data file, the default date range set is from 90 days in the past to 30 days in the future, calculated from your current computer system date. Users can modify these date ranges, and QuickBooks will warn users when they enter or modify a transaction outside these dates.

- **Closing Date**—The Admin or External Accountant user login can set a date in the past for which transactions cannot be modified, added, or deleted prior to that date without entering the closing date password (if one was created).

My Preferences

My Preferences are unique to the username currently logged in to the data file. These settings are not shared globally.

Autofill memo in general journal entry—when creating a journal entry, each row memo column will autofill with the memo from the row above.

Bills

Review your Bills preferences to determine whether the defaults set by QuickBooks are appropriate for your company's needs.

Company Preferences

Company preferences are shared globally by all users. The following are the Bills preferences:

- **Entering Bills, Bills Are Due**—Specifies the default number of days vendor bills should be paid within. You can change this global default on each vendor's record information or on a specific transaction. By default, QuickBooks sets the default due date for bills (where a vendor record does not have payment terms set) to 10 days. Users can modify this for their company's specific bill-paying terms.

- **Warn About Duplicate Bill Numbers from Same Vendor**—Ensures you don't pay the same bill twice. This safeguard is an important reason for entering bills first, rather than skipping a step and instead using the write checks transaction type when you pay vendors.

- **Paying Bills, Automatically Use Discounts and Credits**—Enables QuickBooks to apply the discount to your vendor bill payments automatically if your vendor is set up with discount terms and the bill is being paid within the discount date defined. Be sure to select your preferred chart of account for recording these credits.

My Preferences

There are no My Preferences that would affect your workflow for accounts payable.

Checking

The Checking preferences improve the accuracy of your day-to-day data entry. Be sure to review them when setting up a new data file.

Company Preferences

Company preferences are shared globally by all users. The following are the Checking preferences:

- **Print Account Names on Voucher**—The default is to print the General Ledger account when using the Write Checks transaction. General Ledger accounts do not appear on checks printed via the Pay Bills transaction.

- **Change Check Date When a Non-Cleared Check Is Printed**—If you use the Pay Bills feature to queue bill payment checks ahead of printing them, this setting will change the check date to the current system date when you print the checks.

- **Start with Payee Field on Check**—This time-saving option places your curser in the Payee field when you use the write checks transaction type.

- **Warn About Duplicate Check Numbers**—QuickBooks will warn the user if she is using a check number that the system has already recorded.

- **Autofill Payee Account Number in Check Memo**—You can assign the account number your vendor has assigned to you and have this number print on the Memo field of the bill payment check. For more information, see "Assigning the Vendor Account Number to the Vendor Record" later in this section.

- **Select Default Accounts to Use**—You can assign the default bank accounts QuickBooks uses when creating paychecks or payroll liability checks.

- **Online Banking**—Users can select from two data viewing options when downloading transactions.

My Preferences

My Preferences are unique to the username logged in to the data file. These settings are not shared globally:

- Select Default Accounts to Use—Assign what account you want to use for:
  - Opening the Write Checks
  - Opening the Pay Bills
  - Opening the Pay Sales Tax
  - Opening the Make Deposits

Assigning the Vendor Account Number to the Vendor Record

To assign the vendor account number to the vendor record, follow these steps:

1. On the Home page, click the Vendors button.

2. On the left side of the page, select the vendor to which you want to assign the account number.

3. Click the Edit Vendor button.

4. If necessary, close the New Feature message by clicking OK. The Edit Vendor dialog box opens.

5. Click the Additional Info tab.

6. Type the account number the vendor has assigned to your account (see Figure 7.2). Click OK.

7. Press the Esc key on your keyboard to close the Vendor Center.

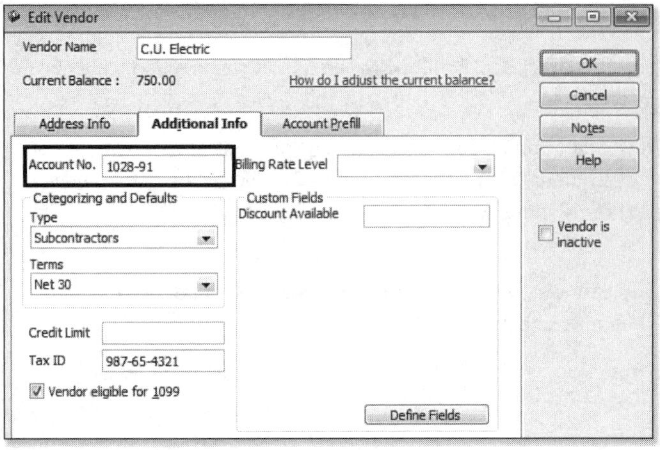

Figure 7.2
QuickBooks can optionally print the account number vendors assign to your business on the memo line of
checks created via write checks or pay bills.

General

Everyone using QuickBooks should review the settings in General Preferences. Although I have
named a couple here, many are worth selecting and customizing for your company's specific needs.

Company Preferences

Company preferences are shared globally by all users. The following are the General preferences
that might affect your use of Accounts Payable functions:

- **Time Format**—If you track your vendors' time with QuickBooks time sheets, you can default how
  portions of an hour display.

- **Never Update Name Information When Saving Transactions**—When not selected and you
  change the payee name or address, QuickBooks will prompt you if you want to update the payee's information. By default this preference is not selected in a newly created QuickBooks file.

- **Save Transactions Before Printing**—By default this preference is selected in a newly created
  QuickBooks file.

My Preferences

My Preferences are unique to the username currently logged in to the data file. These settings are
not shared globally:

- **Pressing Enter Moves Between Fields**—When this option is not selected, using the Tab key will
  advance through fields in a transaction; using the Enter key will save a completed transaction.

If the option is selected, both the Tab and Enter key can be used to advance through fields on a transaction. The keyboard combination of Ctrl+Enter will save a completed transaction.

- **Automatically Open Drop-Down Lists When Typing**—Time-saving feature that is selected by default. Useful if the chart of accounts has subaccounts.

- **Warn When Editing a Transaction**—By default this option is selected. Helps to avoid unintentional changes to a transaction being reviewed.

- **Warn When Deleting A Transaction Or Unused List Item**—By default this option is selected. Helps to avoid unintentional deletion of a transaction being reviewed.

- **Automatically Recall Information**—Select this option to recall both the previously assigned account and the amount or just the account when creating a new vendor transaction.

- **Default Date to Use for New Transactions**—Exercise caution to ensure that the appropriate choice is selected. If you are entering transactions from the past, you might want to choose the last entered date. Otherwise, I recommend setting the default to use today's date.

Reminders

When setting the Company Preferences for reminders, do not forget to also set the My Preferences for this section.

The Company Snapshot is a digital dashboard that includes a view of your reminders. Defining these preferences specific for your company affects the information users see on the Company Snapshot, reminding them of important tasks.

Company Preferences

On the Reminders preference page, you default QuickBooks reminders to show a summary, or list, or to not remind users of all checks to print, bills to pay, or purchase orders to print.

My Preferences

If you would like reminders to display when you open the QuickBooks data file, select the My Preferences tab of the Reminders preference and choose to Show Reminders List when opening a Company file.

Reports and Graphs

The person responsible for how QuickBooks reports your Accounts Payable aging will want to review these preferences choices.

Company Preferences

Company preferences are shared globally by all users. The Reports and Graphs preferences include:

- **Summary Reports Basis**—This feature is important because it tells QuickBooks what basis you want to view your Balance Sheet and Profit & Loss report in by default. You can always override the default when you prepare the report. More details about the differences between Accrual and Cash report basis is included in Chapter 3, "Accounting 101."

- **Aging Reports**—You can choose to age your reports from the due date or from the transaction date.

The remaining preferences affect the appearance of your reports.

My Preferences

My Preferences are unique to the username logged in to the data file. These settings are not shared globally:

- **Prompt Me to Modify Report Options Before Opening a Report**—By default this preference is not selected. If it is selected, each time you open a report the Modify Report dialog will display.

- **Report and Graphs**—These settings determine how a report is refreshed when the data used in the report changes. The default in a newly created QuickBooks file is the Prompt Me to Refresh. I recommend selecting the Refresh Automatically option. You can make this decision for yourself depending on the size of your QuickBooks data file and the speed of your computer's processor.

Tax:1099

Setting up your vendors for proper 1099 status is important. However, be assured that if after reviewing this information you determine the original setup was incorrect, any changes made to this preference will correct prior- and future-dated reports and forms.

The Internal Revenue Service requires that a business provide a Form 1099-MISC at the end of the tax year to any person or unincorporated business paid $600 or more for services in a given calendar year. Most incorporated businesses are not required to get a Form 1099-MISC. You should contact your accountant for more information.

Company Preferences

You can select the Do You File 1099-MISC Forms? option to let QuickBooks know that you will be providing 1099 forms to your vendors at the end of the year.

The dialog box shown in Figure 7.3 is the first step in getting ready to track your Form 1099-MISC payments.

 For more information, see "Tracking and Reporting Vendor 1099-MISC Payments," p. 226.

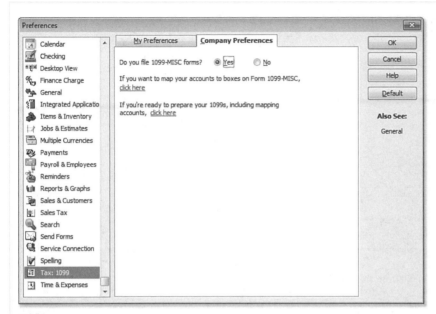

Figure 7.3
Choose Yes if you are required to submit 1099-MISC forms to the Internal Revenue Service.

My Preferences

There are no My Preferences in the Tax:1099 that you can set.

Working with the Vendor Center

QuickBooks makes adding, modifying, and researching vendor activity easy using the Vendor Center. Vendors are individuals or companies that you purchase services or products from and they are managed in the Vendor Center as displayed in Figure 7.4.

From the Vendor Center, you view contact details for your vendors and can access many tasks including:

- Create a new or edit an existing vendor.

- Access the Add Multiple Vendors dialog box (using the Add/Edit Multiple List Entries feature discussed in Chapter 4).

- Record commonly used vendor transactions.

- Print the vendor list, information, or transactions.

- Export the vendor list or transactions; import or paste vendors from Excel.

- Prepare a vendor letter and customize the vendor templates.

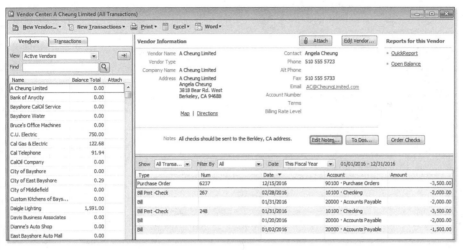

Figure 7.4
Complete common vendor tasks from the Vendor Center.

- Filter your list of vendors to include All Vendors, Active Vendors, Vendors with Open Balances, or a custom filter of your choice.

- Attach documents to the vendor record, such as attaching a copy of the signed subcontractor agreement.

- Access a map and driving directions to the vendor's location.

- Add and edit vendor notes and to do reminders.

- View and filter the list of transactions by vendor or by transaction type.

- Prepare a QuickReport or Open Balance Report for the given vendor.

Use the Vendor Center to access many of the common vendor transactions and reports you will learn about in this chapter and in Chapter 8, "Managing Vendors."

The following sections provide more details about creating a vendor and using the Vendor Center for researching transactions.

Adding or Modifying Vendors

When you are ready to purchase materials or services for your business you will need to create a vendor. You might already have a head start on adding vendors to your file if you used the Adding Contacts feature available with the Express Start QuickBooks setup discussed in Chapter 1, "Getting Started with QuickBooks."

However, there is also another less used list in QuickBooks worth mentioning here titled the Other Names list. One reason you might choose to add a payee to the Other Names list might be when you are recording a one time purchase. Later if you begin using the vendor regularly, you have the option one-time to remove the payee from the Other Names list and add it to your Vendor list.

This section offers instruction specific to setting up vendors. If your company will be using the Enter Bills process, you will have to use a payee from the vendor list; the bill will not allow you to use an Other Names list item in the Payee field.

Adding a New Vendor

To practice adding a new vendor record, open the sample data file as instructed in Chapter 1, "Getting Started with QuickBooks." If you are working in your own file use these instructions to begin entering the vendors you purchase goods and services from:

1. Click the Vendors button on the Home page. Alternatively, select Vendors, Vendor Center from the menu bar.

2. If the New Feature message displays, read the information provided. Optionally, select the Do Not Display This Message in the Future box. Click OK to close the message.

3. Select New Vendor from the New Vendor drop-down list in the upper-left corner of the Vendor Center.

4. The New Vendor dialog box displays (see Figure 7.5). Enter ABC Cleaners in the Vendor Name field. It is important to mention that no two names from any of the lists in QuickBooks can be the same.

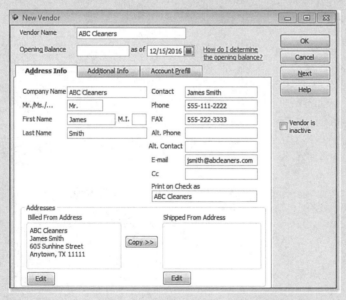

Figure 7.5
Completing the contact information for your vendor is good practice for your record keeping.

5. Leave the Opening Balance field blank. Chapter 3, "Accounting 101," discusses entering beginning balances in a new QuickBooks file (when there have already been previous accounting transactions recorded in some other accounting software or method). If you are a new business, you will later enter a vendor bill to increase the balance owed to the vendor instead of entering an Opening Balance amount in the New Vendor record.

   The As Of (date) field will not have any effect in your QuickBooks file if no dollar value was entered in the Opening Balance field.

6. On the Address Info tab, consider completing the salutation, first name, and last name fields so you have the option to send letters to your vendors in the future.

7. Complete any remaining fields you deem applicable, such as contact information and address.

8. Click the Additional Info tab. In the Account No. field enter the account number your vendor has assigned to you, if applicable. This account number can optionally be printed on the memo line of a vendor bill payment check.

9. Use the Type field in Categorizing and Defaults to create or assign a vendor type, which you can then use to filter your vendor and transaction reports.

10. Select the appropriate payment terms, such as Net 30 days, your vendor has assigned to your account. If the specific term needed is not displayed, click Add New to create a new term.

11. When applicable enter the Credit Limit established by your vendor.

12. If your vendor qualifies for receiving a Form 1099-MISC at the end of the year, enter the vendor's Tax ID and place a check mark in the box for Vendor Eligible for 1099. Note that if you do not have this information handy when you are first creating the vendor, you can add this information at later date without any loss of tracking the details.

13. If you are using QuickBooks Accountant, Premier, or Enterprise you have the option of selecting a Billing Rate Level for your vendor. Billing rates allow you to mark up billable time you will later add to a customer invoice.

14. If you have created a Custom Field, complete the value for that field. In Figure 7.6 a custom field is displayed titled Discount Available. Custom fields allow you to track supplemental information about your vendors, such as if an additional discount is available beyond what you entered in the Payment Terms. Click the Define Fields button to add or remove custom fields.

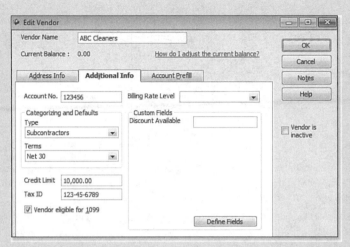

Figure 7.6
More useful information can be recorded on the Additional Info tab.

15. Click the Account Prefill tab as shown in Figure 7.7. Assign the Repairs, Building Repairs expense account. You can assign up to three different accounts that will display automatically when you create a new transaction using this vendor as the payee. If you also download transactions from your bank or credit card, click the link (not shown) to review the information provided about how Account Prefill works with Online Banking.

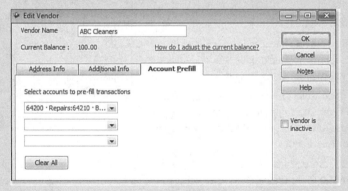

Figure 7.7
Streamline your data entry by storing the default accounts to assign to transactions for this vendor.

16. At any time you can select or deselect the Vendor Is Inactive checkbox. In such cases the vendor still appears on reports, but will not appear in drop-down lists you use for creating new transactions.

17. Click OK to save your changes and close the New Vendor dialog box, or click Cancel to discard your work. You can also click Next to add another new vendor.

 tip

Want a quick way to complete multiple name fields at once when creating a new vendor? Start with entering data in the Company Name field. When you move out of the Company Name field, QuickBooks will automatically populate the Vendor Name, Company Name, Billed From, and Print on Check as fields.

The Vendor Name field in QuickBooks is a "look-up" name; this field also controls how your vendors are automatically sorted in the Vendor Center.

If you prefer to use a different vendor "look-up" name, be sure to enter the proper vendor name in the Print On Check As field.

Now that you have created a new vendor in the sample file, you are prepared to create a list of your own vendors. Return to the Vendor Center any time you need to update a vendor's information.

Finding Vendor Transactions

The Vendor Center not only provides access for adding to or modifying your vendor's records in QuickBooks, but also includes convenient access to finding vendor transactions.

With the Vendor Center open, select a vendor to display a list of their transactions on the right. In the previously displayed Figure 7.4, vendor A Cheung Limited is selected and to the right are individual transactions for that vendor.

 caution

QuickBooks does not keep a time stamp on revisions made to your vendor's contact information. Once you make a change, all previous records will reflect the change to the address or contact information.

However, changes to the Account Prefill selection will affect newly created transactions.

You can filter the resulting transactions by selecting options in the Show, Filter By, and Date drop-down lists. The options in the Filter By list change as you make a selection from the Show list.

Figure 7.8 shows representative vendor transaction types. Your transaction types might differ from the displayed types if you do not have the related feature enabled in Preferences. The only transaction type that can have a vendor record assigned that is not included in these options is Make Journal Entry.

 For more information, see "Correcting Accounts Payable Errors," p. 235.

This chapter will discuss how to handle various situations, including incorrect journal entries that affect a vendor record.

The Transactions tab in the Vendor Center allows you to group transactions by type, rather than by vendor.

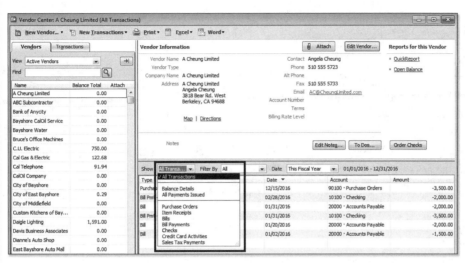

Figure 7.8
You can filter vendor transactions based on multiple criteria.

Researching Vendor Transactions

To practice finding vendor transactions by type, open the sample data file as instructed in Chapter 1. If you are working in your own file use these instructions to easily locate vendor transactions:

1. On the Home page, click the Vendors button to open the Vendor Center. Click the Transactions tab.

2. Select the Purchase Orders type as shown in Figure 7.9.

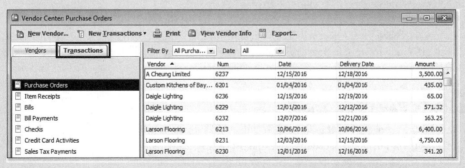

Figure 7.9
Use the Transactions tab of the Vendor Center to find like transaction types.

3. Optionally, from the Filter By drop-down list, select Open Purchase Orders.

4. Optionally, filter for a specific date range. This might be useful if you are looking specifically for older dated open purchase orders.

5. Optionally, click any column header to sort that column.

6. To view a transaction, double-click it, or right-click, and select Edit Transaction.

7. Click the Print icon to print the listed transactions.

8. Optionally, click the View Vendor Info button and click OK if the New Feature message displays. QuickBooks opens the Edit Vendor dialog box for the currently selected vendor. Click OK to close and return to the Vendor Center:Purchase Orders listing.

9. Click the Export icon to export the list of transactions to an Excel worksheet or to a comma-separated value file.

The Vendor Center provides one location to create or modify your vendor records and even research vendor transactions.

Next, you will learn about the proper Accounts Payable process so you can successfully track your vendor business expenses.

The Accounts Payable Process

QuickBooks includes a flexible payable process. Your company can choose to use the purchase order and receive item transactions for controlling and monitoring costs and delivery, or you can skip these steps and simply create a bill to be paid later.

An important reason for using a vendor bill to record your business expenses is the ability to track the vendor's bill reference number. In the event your vendor invoices you more than once for the same services or items, QuickBooks will optionally warn you when you enter a reference number that was previously recorded.

If you created your data file using the Express Start option you might need to enable the features as discussed in the earlier section "Preferences That Affect Accounts Payable" of this chapter. If you are ready to work in your own data file, make sure you have created your new file as discussed in Chapter 1.

Accounts Payable Forms

Many of the accounts payable forms use QuickBooks items. If you are considering using the accounts payable process for the first time, be sure to review Chapter 4, "Understanding QuickBooks Lists," which discusses the use of items and how to set them up properly.

If you choose to use the purchase order transaction, you will need to create items. Items are a list of the products or services you sell to customers or purchase from vendors. The primary purpose

 tip

Many users inadvertently post revenue and expenses to the same account for Services, Non-Inventory Parts, Other Charges, and Discounts. The New Item dialog box includes a checkbox (see Figure 7.10) that enables you to avoid this problem and provide separate revenue and expense account fields. Choosing to set up items correctly can be one of the most important decisions you will make in using accounts payable.

of items is to perform the accounting behind the scenes and to automate the data entry process by prefilling descriptions, costs, and sales price on purchase and sales transactions.

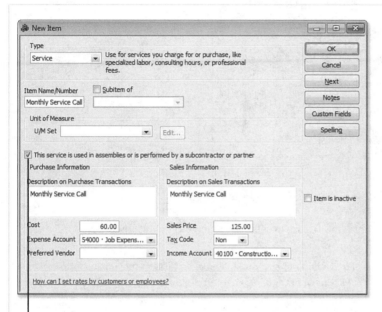

Click here to enable assigning both an Expense and Income Account for the item

Figure 7.10
You can use the same item with both customers and vendor transactions.

Should you use items even if you do not plan on using the QuickBooks purchase order or item receipt transactions? I recommend that you do, especially if you follow the instructions in the preceding tip. A powerful feature of items is that each time the item is purchased or sold, QuickBooks records the amount to the specific account(s) defined in the Add New or Edit Item dialog box, reducing or eliminating potential errors created from recording the transaction to the wrong account when using the Expense tab of a purchase transaction.

How can items help you track your customer's profitability? Many of the QuickBooks reports that provide profitability information are based on transactions recorded using items on the Items tab and will not provide the same information if the transaction is recorded using the Expenses tab.

For example, a home builder creates a budget for the project (using an estimate transaction) and wants to track actual versus budgeted expense. To take advantage of the many customer and job profitability reports, you must enter your expenses using the Items tab on an accounts payable bill (and use the same process for the check transaction), as shown in Figure 7.11.

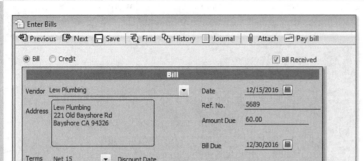

Figure 7.11
Use the Items tab to record expenses you want to track in customer or job profitability reports.

Table 7.1 lists the transaction types available in accounts payable and the purpose each type serves. You will also want to review Table 8.1 in Chapter 8, "Managing Vendors," which outlines the accounting that goes on behind the scenes with these same transactions.

Table 7.1 Accounts Payable Transactions

Accounts Payable Transaction Name	Primary Purpose of Transaction
Purchase Order	Document issued by a buyer to a seller indicating the products or services, quantity, and amounts the buyer has agreed to pay.
Item Receipt (Receiving inventory, non-inventory, or other item recorded on a purchase order)	Records receipt of inventory, non-inventory items, or other item types when the goods arrive before the vendor's final bill.
Enter Bills	Records an increase to accounts payable and the associated expense.
Vendor Credit Memo	Records a decrease of what is owed to a vendor.
Bill Payment Check	Pays the vendor bill and decreases accounts payable and cash account balances.

Accounts Payable Workflow

In this section you will learn about the importance of using the accounts payable process instead of writing a check for your business expenses. The QuickBooks Home page and Vendor Center, as shown in Figures 7.1 and 7.4, respectively, make managing all your purchasing activities easy.

Your Home page workflow might vary, depending on the version of QuickBooks you are using and the preferences you have enabled.

To perform typical vendor-related activities from the QuickBooks Home page, as shown in Figure 7.1, follow these steps:

1. Access the Vendor Center.

2. Create a purchase order to the vendor (optional).

3. Receive inventory (optional).

4. Optionally, enter bills against inventory.

5. Enter a bill to the vendor.

6. Pay the bill (typically within the agreed-upon payment terms for that vendor; for example, 30 days from the bill date).

Some companies choose not to use accounts payable transactions, but instead pay their vendors with a check (select Banking, Write Checks from the menu bar). Often, this choice is made because the process of paying a vendor with a check is quick and easy and takes fewer steps than creating and paying a vendor bill.

However, by choosing *not* to use accounts payable transactions, you ignore several important controls for managing the purchases your company makes. These purchasing controls include:

- **Associating the bill with the purchase order (or item receipt) to automatically calculate quantity and cost**—As soon as you enter the vendor's name on a bill, QuickBooks prompts you with an open purchase order (or item receipt) dialog box, as shown in Figure 7.12, and prefills the bill for you.

Figure 7.12
Warning provided when you enter a bill for a vendor that has an open purchase order.

- **Receiving a warning when entering a vendor invoice number twice**—It can happen: A vendor sends you a bill more than once and you pay it more than once. However, when you use a vendor bill (versus the Write Checks transaction) and you enter the vendor's invoice number in the Ref No. field, QuickBooks warns you if the vendors reference number was used on a previous bill, as shown in Figure 7.13.

- **Not recognizing costs in the month they were incurred**—When you opt to use the Write Checks transaction instead of a vendor bill, QuickBooks uses the date of the check as the date the expense is recorded (recognized). How often do you pay the vendor's bill the same day or month you receive it? You might be overstating or understating the expenses incurred in a specific month if you use the check instead of the bill form.

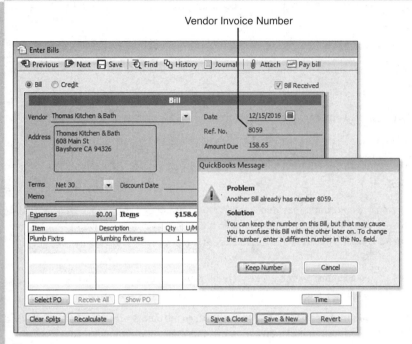

Figure 7.13
QuickBooks provides a warning message when you enter a bill with the same reference (vendor invoice) number.

- **Taking advantage of discounts offered by your vendor**—Only if you use vendor bills can you set a preference to have QuickBooks automatically calculate and record the discount if you're paying the bill within the vendors discount terms.

The purchasing controls and warnings provided in QuickBooks make using the accounts payable process a smart choice for your company. Additionally, your company will benefit from having financial statements that can be viewed in cash and accrual basis.

Entering a Purchase Order

Your business might choose to record purchase orders to track the expected product or service cost. Purchase orders are non-posting, which in accounting vernacular means when you record a purchase order you are not recording an expense or liability. Instead, a purchase order serves as a reminder that you expect to receive a bill from the vendor at a later date.

To learn more about working with purchase orders, see "Creating the Purchase Order," p. 142.

Recording Vendor Bills

You are on your way to properly using accounts payable forms to help track and report on your business expenses. Learn how to enter your vendor bills in this section.

---

 tip

Did you know by default QuickBooks requires you to use the Tab key on your keyboard to advance from one field to another on certain transactions?

If you inadvertently used the Enter key on your keyboard, QuickBooks might save and close the transaction. If this happens to you, use the Previous or Next menu at the top of the open dialog box to find the transaction you had not yet completed.

If you prefer to use the Enter key on your keyboard to advance between fields, you can set that preference in Edit, Preferences, General Preferences. On the My Preferences tab, select the Pressing Enter Moves Between Fields checkbox. Click OK to save and close your preference setting.

Practice Entering a Vendor Bill

To practice adding a new vendor bill, open the sample data file as instructed in Chapter 1. If you are working in your own file, use these instructions to begin entering bills for the products and services you have purchased:

1. On the Home page, click the Enter Bills icon to open the Enter Bills dialog box, as shown in Figure 7.14.

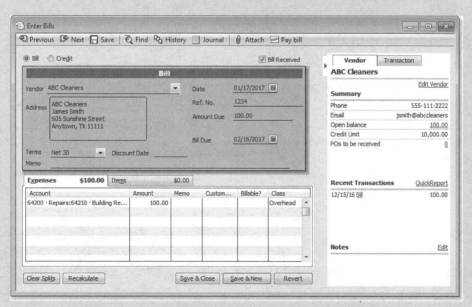

Figure 7.14
Using the bill allows you to record the expense when incurred, but pay the vendor at a later date.

2. From the Vendor drop-down list, type the first few letters of the vendor name **ABC Cleaners** (created earlier in this chapter). You might also select the vendor from the drop-down list by scrolling through the list and selecting a specific vendor.

3. Using the Tab key on your keyboard, advance to the Date field. If you are practicing, accept the default date, otherwise enter the actual date for your transaction. In your file you can use the (+) or (-) key on your keyboard to change the date by a single day forward or backward. Other shortcuts are detailed in the Appendix C, "QuickBooks Shortcuts." This date will be used to record the expense when viewing your financial reports in accrual basis.

> *More information on the accounting for transactions can be found in Table 8.1 in Chapter 8, "Managing Vendors."*

4. Type **1234** in the Ref. No. field. This represents the invoice number supplied by your vendor on his bill. If your vendor did not provide an invoice number, I often recommend using the digits of the bill date. For example, I might use 011717 as the Ref. No. if I were also dating the bill 01/17/2017.

5. Using the Tab key again, advance to the Amount Due field and type **100**. QuickBooks automatically formats the amount to be 100.00. In your own file, you can manage this preference by selecting Edit, Preferences, General, and selecting the My Preferences tab. If you enabled the Automatically Place Decimal Point option, QuickBooks would have formatted your input of 100 as 1.00 instead.

6. The Bill Due, Terms, and Discount Date will prefill from the vendor's record. You can override these inputs on the specific vendor bill you are entering. If no defaults are included in the vendor record, QuickBooks will then use the default due date calculation found on the Bills—Company Preferences tab of the Preferences dialog box (see Figure 7.15). You must be logged into the file as the Admin user or External Accountant to change the Company Preferences settings for bills.

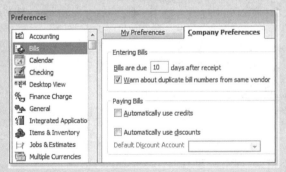

Figure 7.15
QuickBooks uses the Company Preference terms when a vendor record doesn't specify terms.

7. Optionally, enter a Memo. This memo will print on the bill payment check. If your vendor record has a stored Account No. as detailed in the section on Adding or Modifying Vendors, leave the memo field blank and QuickBooks will include the Account No. on the printed bill payment check automatically.

8. In this exercise, QuickBooks automatically prefilled the Account column on the Expenses tab with Repairs:Building Repairs. In this exercise, the account was set as a default for this vendor.

9. Optionally, enter a memo for your reporting needs. This memo will not print on the final check. Although named similarly to the Memo field on the check, this field allows you to describe the transaction line for your reporting.

10. Select a customer or job name from the list when applicable.

11. Use the Billable? field when you specify a customer or job and you want to include this expense on a future customer invoice.

12. If you are using Class tracking, enter the appropriate class.

13. Click Save & Close.

Other buttons on the Enter Bills dialog box include:

- **Clear Splits**—Useful when you want to condense multiple account rows into a single account row.

- **Recalculate**—The Recalculate button updates the Amount Due field, which is helpful when you have added additional line items.

- **Save & Close or Save & New**—Choose Save & Close if you don't need to add another bill, or Save & New to display a blank Enter Bills transaction.

- **Revert**—Click this button when you want to undo changes to a previously saved vendor bill.

Creating a Vendor Credit

Now that you are recording your business expenses with vendor bills, what about returning a product to the vendor or receiving a credit for a service not preformed to your specifications? The next section will show you how easy it is to create a vendor credit.

Practice Creating a Vendor Credit

To practice creating a vendor credit, open the sample data file as instructed in Chapter 1. If you are working in your own file, use these instructions to begin entering credits you receive from your vendors:

1. On the Home page, click the Enter Bills icon.

2. Select the Credit option at the top of the Enter Bills dialog box (see Figure 7.16). The dialog box now displays a credit, decreasing accounts payable and decreasing the account(s) assigned on the Expenses tab, or if you are using the Items tab, the account assigned to the item(s) being used.

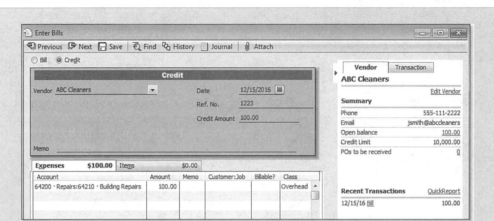

Figure 7.16
Credits reduce what you owe your vendor and the account assigned on the credit or associated with the item.

3. To continue with the practice example we used earlier, begin typing the vendor name **ABC Cleaners**. Press the Tab key on your keyboard to advance to the Date field.

4. If you are practicing, accept the prefilled date. In your own file, you can select the date from the calendar.

5. Enter **1223** in the Ref. No. field. This is the credit memo number your vendor has assigned this record.

6. In the Credit Amount field enter **100.00**.

7. Enter an optional memo. If you want the memo to display in reports based on your expense lines, be sure to use the memo field in the Expenses tab or the Description field on the Items tab.

8. In this exercise, QuickBooks used the Repairs:Building Repairs expense account assigned to the vendor record and the amount entered in the Credit Amount field. If needed, you can change the account or add additional lines.

9. Click Save & Close.

 note

For ease in typing, QuickBooks will format the date for you. For example, if your current computer system year is 2016, you would only need to type 1220 in a date field and QuickBooks will format the date as 12/20/16.

This vendor credit is currently unapplied and available to be applied when you record a bill payment. If you know that a vendor has an unpaid bill pending, you can apply the credit against that bill now, or wait until the next time you need to pay the vendor.

Paying Vendor Bills

One of the benefits of entering vendor bills is that you can record the expense during the month you incur it, but pay the balance owed at a later date.

If you are ready to pay your bills, make sure you have a vendor bill or some record of the expense being incurred. Develop a process at your business for accurately reviewing your unpaid bills.

Practice Paying Vendor Bills

To practice paying a vendor bill, open the sample data file as instructed in Chapter 1. If you are working in your own file, use these instructions to begin paying the bills you owe your vendors:

1. On the Home page, click the Pay Bills icon.

2. For this exercise, leave the Show All Bills option button selected. When working with your own data, you can filter the bills that display in the Pay Bills dialog box by selecting the Due On or Before option button and entering a date (see Figure 7.17).

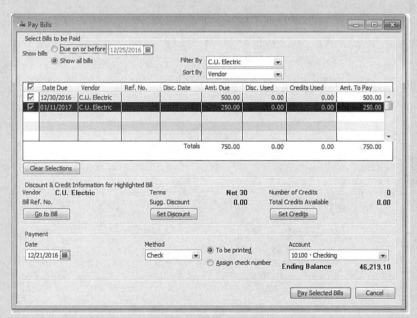

Figure 7.17
Use the Pay Bills dialog box to record payment by check, credit card, or online payment to your vendor.

3. In the Filter By drop-down list, select C.U. Electric or begin typing the name as you learned in an earlier exercise.

4. Review the choices available in the Sort By drop-down list, but leave Vendor selected.

5. Place a checkmark next to each of the bills for C.U. Electric, or optionally click the Select All Bills button. If you are printing checks, QuickBooks will create one check for the two selected bills displayed in Figure 7.17.

---

6. When working with your own data, if you did not want to pay the full balance you can manually type an amount in the Amt. To Pay column on a specific bill's row. Later when you are prepared to pay the balance, QuickBooks will include the remaining balance due in the Amt. To Pay column.

7. With a bill selected, click the Go to Bill button. QuickBooks opens the Enter Bills dialog box where, if necessary, you could make changes. Click Save & Close to return to the Pay Bills dialog box.

8. Optionally view the discount terms or credits available, QuickBooks will display a special dialog box. More details are provided about working with discounts and credits in the next section.

9. When working with your own data, you can specify payment options in the Payment section of the Pay Bills dialog box, including the following fields (for this exercise, leave the choices as displayed in Figure 7.17):

   ■ **Date**—This is the date that will print on your checks or will be assigned to the transactions in your accounting.

   ■ **Method**—Select Check if you will be printing a check or recording a manually written check. Select Credit Card if you are paying the bill with the company's corporate credit card. Select Online Bank Pmt if you are using online banking.

   ■ **To Be Printed or Assign Check Number**—If you selected Check as your method of payment, you can select the To Be Printed option button. If you manually wrote the check, you can select Assign Check Number.

   ■ **Account**—Depending on your Method selection, you will assign either the bank account or credit card account used to make the payment.

   ■ **Ending Balance**—QuickBooks displays the ending balance for your bank or credit card account selected.

10. Click Pay Selected Bills. QuickBooks opens the Payment Summary dialog box.

11. Review the details displayed in the Payment Summary dialog box including payment date, account, and method.

12. Click the Print Checks button on the Payment Summary dialog box. Optionally, you can click the Pay More Bills button to return to the Pay Bills dialog box or click Done if you do not want to practice printing (using plain paper).

13. If you selected the Print Checks button, the Select Checks to Print dialog box displays. Leave selected the default Bank Account and the prefilled First Check Number.

14. Review the list of checks to be printed. Each will have a checkmark in the column to the left. Remove the checkmarks from any checks you do not want to print at this time.

15. Click OK to open the Print Checks dialog box. Select your printer from the Printer Name drop-down list, and then choose the proper Check Style from Voucher, Standard, or Wallet.

16. Click Print. For this exercise, make sure you have plain paper in your printer. A check printed to plain paper is not a negotiable document.

17. The Print Checks – Confirmation dialog box displays. In this exercise, click OK to close the confirmation.

tip

New for QuickBooks 2012 is a feature to prepare a bill payment check for a single vendor directly from the Enter Bills dialog box.

To do so, open a previously saved vendor bill, select the Pay Bill option at the top of the Enter Bills dialog box. The Pay Bills dialog box opens with the Filter By field already selected for the same vendor as the open vendor bill.

You have now learned how to complete basic accounts payable tasks including using bills to record your expenses and preparing the payment for the vendor. In the next sections, you will learn how to work with vendor discounts and credits.

Applying Vendor Credits

Your vendor might offer discounts for timely payment or issue a credit for products or services that did not meet your expectations.

Continue your QuickBooks practice by applying the vendor credit created in an earlier practice section of this chapter.

Practice Applying Vendor Credits

To practice applying a credit, open the sample data file as instructed in Chapter 1. If you are working in your own file, use these instructions to apply vendor discounts or credits to your vendor's open balances:

1. Review your preference for applying credits. From the menu bar, select Edit, Preferences, and go to the Bills—Company Preferences tab on the Preferences dialog box. (You must log into the file as the Admin or External Accountant user type.) Refer to Figure 7.15. These settings determine if QuickBooks automatically applies any open credits for you. If you don't select the Automatically Use Credits checkbox, you will manually apply the credits. Pick the selection that best meets your business needs.

2. Click OK to close the Preferences dialog box.

3. On the Home page, click the Pay Bills icon. The Pay Bills dialog box opens.

4. For this practice, select the ABC Cleaners vendor in the Filter By drop-down list. Filtering can be useful if you have many open invoices for multiple vendors, but it is not required.

5. Place a checkmark next to the open bill you want to apply the vendor credit to. If you didn't select to apply credits automatically in step 1, QuickBooks will show the total number of credits and their total value in the Discount & Credit Information for Highlighted Bill section (see Figure 7.18).

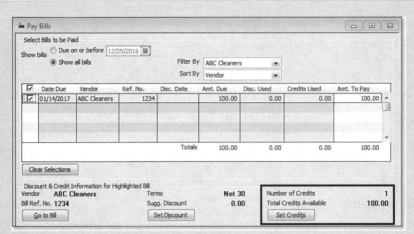

Figure 7.18
With a vendor bill selected, QuickBooks will show the number of available credits for that vendor.

6. If you want to modify the amount or which credits are selected, click the Set Credits button. The Discount and Credits dialog box displays as shown in Figure 7.19. You can modify which credit is selected by changing the checkmark from one credit to another or by manually overriding the amount in the Amt. To Use column.

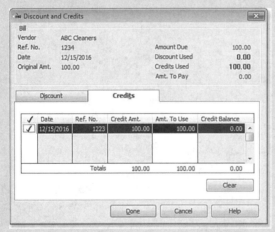

Figure 7.19
The Discount and Credits dialog box allows you to manage how the credits are applied to open vendor bills.

7. Click Done to close the Discount and Credits dialog box. Click Pay Selected Bills to exit the Pay Bills dialog box. If you are only associating a credit memo with a vendor bill, no additional check transaction will be created.

8. Click Done in the Payment Summary dialog box or click Pay More Bills if you want to return to the Pay Bills dialog box.

If you are an accounting professional and using QuickBooks Accountant or QuickBooks Enterprise Accountant you might want to use the Client Data Review feature. From one convenient window, you can assign the vendor unapplied credit memo to the open accounts payable bill, replacing the previous steps numbered 3–8.

 To learn more about time savings features for accounting professionals, see "Client Data Review," p. 601.

 note

When you need to change a prior year's open balance for a vendor, credit memos can be the safest way to not inadvertently affect prior year financials. With a credit memo you can date the correcting transaction in the current year, important if you have already used your prior year's data to prepare and file a tax return.

Taking Discounts on Vendor Bills

Your company might be able to save money by paying your vendors within their allowed discount terms. Discounts are offered by some vendors to encourage quick payment of their invoices.

Practice Taking Discounts on Vendor Bills

To practice applying a vendor discount, open the sample data file as instructed in Chapter 1. For this practice we will complete all of the steps necessary for QuickBooks to automatically calculate the discount when paying a vendor bill. If you are working in your own file, you will need to log in as the Admin or External Accountant user type to set the preference mentioned. You can then use these instructions to apply discounts to your vendors open balances:

1. From the menu bar, select Edit, Preferences and select the Bills—Company Preferences tab in the Preferences dialog box. Select the Automatically Use Discounts checkbox, as displayed previously in Figure 7.15.

2. Select Job Expenses:Less Discounts Taken as the Default Discount Account.

3. Click OK to save your selection and close the Preferences dialog box.

4. Next, you will need to assign discount terms to a vendor. From the menu bar, select Vendors, Vendor Center.

5. In the QuickBooks sample data, select Bayshore CalOil Service. To the right, click the Edit Vendor button. Click OK to the New Feature message if it displays.

6. In the Edit Vendor dialog box for Bayshore CalOil Service, click the Additional Info tab.

7. If it's not already assigned, select the 2% 10 Net 30 terms in the Terms drop-down list. When selected, QuickBooks will calculate a 2% discount if the payment is dated within 10 days of the invoice date. Otherwise, the full amount is payable within 30 days.

8. Click OK to save your changes and close the Edit Vendor dialog box.

9. From the Vendor Center, with Bayshore CalOil Service, select Enter Bills from the New Transactions drop-down list.

10. Using the Tab key, advance to the Ref. No. field. Type **567**.

11. In the Amount Due field, type **1,000.00**. QuickBooks assigns the Terms and Discount Date and adds the amount to the Expenses tab.

12. Assign Overhead to the Class column on the Expenses tab.

13. At the top of the Enter Bill dialog box, select Pay Bill.

14. Select Yes to record your changes. The Pay Bills dialog box displays with the vendor bill you just created already selected.

15. Notice that as a result of selecting Automatically Use Discounts in step 1, QuickBooks displays the terms and the Sugg. Discount (see Figure 7.20).

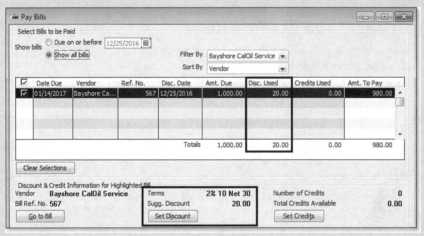

Figure 7.20
QuickBooks automatically calculates early payment discounts.

16. Optionally, you can click the Set Discount button to change the amount of the discount, assign a different discount account, and assign a discount class. Click Done to close the Discounts and Credits dialog box.

17. For this practice, click Cancel to close the Pay Bills dialog box. If you are assigning discounts to your own vendor bills, continue with the check printing process.

If you are going to assign discounts to your vendor bills, record your bills at the "gross" amount, or total amount before any discount. Then, over time you can watch the amount you have saved grow!

MANAGING VENDORS

Accounts Payable Reporting

Accounts payable mistakes often can be one of the primary reasons for misstated company financials. Knowing which reports are best to review will make you much more efficient at keeping your accounts payable "clean," meaning the data is correct and up to date. Often, the thing that makes troubleshooting data errors most difficult is not knowing exactly what you should be looking for. This problem is addressed in the next section, which explains some of the more common reports used to identify whether your accounts payable information is correct.

Reconciling Balance Sheet Accounts Payable Balance to A/P Aging Summary Report Total

An important check to do with your file is to compare your Balance Sheet report balance for accounts payable with the A/P Aging Summary report total.

With QuickBooks, you don't have to worry that the Balance Sheet accounts payable balance will not match the A/P Aging Summary report total because any transaction posting to the accounts payable account must have a vendor assigned. When providing year-end documentation to your accountant, be sure to include the A/P Aging Summary or Detail report and compare the total amount from these reports to the Balance Sheet balance for accounts payable.

To compare the Balance Sheet Standard report balance for accounts payable with the A/P Aging Summary report total, follow these steps:

1. From the menu bar, select Reports, Company & Financial, Balance Sheet Standard. On the Balance Sheet report that opens, select the As of Date you want to compare to. To accurately compare the Balance Sheet report Accounts Payable balance and the A/P Aging Summary report total, you *must* create your Balance Sheet in accrual basis. If your reporting preference default was for cash basis, you can change the reporting basis temporarily by clicking the Customize Report button on the active report window and selecting Accrual as the report basis. Click OK to return to the report.

2. Note the balance of your Accounts Payable account(s) on the Balance Sheet (see Figure 8.1).

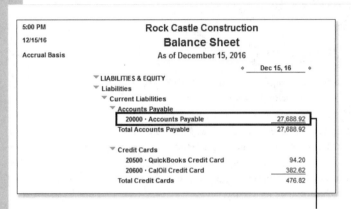

Should match total from A/P Aging Summary report

Figure 8.1
Use an accrual basis Balance Sheet report when reconciling your Accounts Payable Aging report.

3. From the menu bar, select Reports, Vendors & Payables, A/P Aging Summary. See Figure 8.2. Make sure the date is the same as the date you selected in step 1.

Your Accounts Payable balance on the Balance Sheet Standard report should match the total on the A/P Aging Summary report. If it does not, the reason might be a data integrity issue. This is discussed in more detail in Chapter 17, "Managing Your QuickBooks Database." If you find the two balances do not match first, make sure your Balance Sheet Standard report is created in the accrual basis. Then verify your data by selecting File, Utilities, Verify Data from the menu bar.

Reviewing the Unpaid Bills Detail Report

If you need more detail than the A/P Aging Summary report offers, consider the Unpaid Bills Details report instead. This report is helpful because it displays individual vendor bill lines for each open vendor transaction instead of grouping them together by aged date summarizing the information.

	Current	1 - 30	31 - 60	61 - 90	> 90	TOTAL
ABC Cleaners	0.00	0.00	0.00	0.00	0.00	0.00
Bayshore CalOil Service	1,000.00	0.00	0.00	0.00	0.00	1,000.00
C.U. Electric	750.00	0.00	0.00	0.00	0.00	750.00
Cal Gas & Electric	122.68	0.00	0.00	0.00	0.00	122.68
Cal Telephone	91.94	0.00	0.00	0.00	0.00	91.94
Daigle Lighting	52.00	1,539.00	0.00	0.00	0.00	1,591.00
Hamlin Metal	670.00	0.00	0.00	0.00	0.00	670.00
Hopkins Construction Rentals	700.00	0.00	0.00	0.00	0.00	700.00
Lew Plumbing	1,330.00	0.00	0.00	0.00	0.00	1,330.00
Middlefield Drywall	1,200.00	0.00	0.00	0.00	0.00	1,200.00
Patton Hardware Supplies	1,020.00	3,459.20	0.00	0.00	0.00	4,479.20
Perry Windows & Doors	4,957.00	1,800.00	0.00	0.00	0.00	6,757.00
Sergeant Insurance	4,050.00	0.00	0.00	0.00	0.00	4,050.00
Sloan Roofing	1,047.00	0.00	0.00	0.00	0.00	1,047.00
Thomas Kitchen & Bath	585.00	0.00	0.00	0.00	0.00	585.00
Timberloft Lumber	215.10	0.00	0.00	0.00	0.00	215.10
Vu Contracting	1,250.00	0.00	0.00	0.00	0.00	1,250.00
Washuta & Son Painting	600.00	0.00	0.00	0.00	0.00	600.00
Wheeler's Tile Etc.	1,250.00	0.00	0.00	0.00	0.00	1,250.00
TOTAL	20,890.72	6,798.20	0.00	0.00	0.00	27,688.92

Rock Castle Construction
A/P Aging Summary
As of December 15, 2016

5:03 PM
12/15/16

Should match total Accounts Payable
from the Balance Sheet report

Figure 8.2
Your A/P Aging Summary report should always reconcile with the Accounts Payable total on an accrual basis
Balance Sheet report.

By default this report is perpetual, which means that even if you create it using a date in the past,
QuickBooks will show those open vendor bills, or unapplied credit memos, as of *today's* computer
system date, including all payments recorded before and after the report date. You can override this
default, and then properly reconcile the Unpaid Bills Detail report to your Balance Sheet and your
A/P Aging Summary report for a date prior to today's date. To do so, follow these steps:

1. From the menu bar, select Reports, Vendors & Payables, Unpaid Bills Detail. As mentioned previously, this report includes all payments made before and after the report date you have chosen.

2. If you are creating this report for a date other than today, you will likely want to have the report match your Balance Sheet totals as of that same date. To do so, click the Customize Report. The Modify Report dialog box opens, with the Display tab selected.

3. Click the Advanced button to open the Advanced Options dialog box.

4. Under Open Balance/Aging, select the Report Date option, as shown in Figure 8.3, and click OK to close the Advanced Options dialog box.

5. Click OK to return to the report.

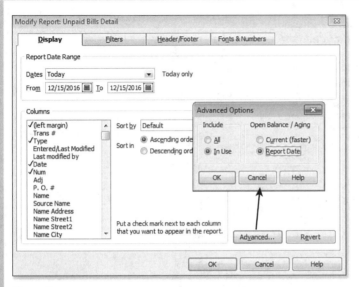

Figure 8.3
Modify the Unpaid Bills Detail report so it will agree with the Balance Sheet for a date in the past.

Modifying this report enables you to see each open vendor bill or unapplied credit detail as of some date in the past. This report becomes very useful for reconciling your accounts payable unpaid bills or open credit detail to your Balance Sheet accounts payable total. You might want to send a copy of this modified report to your accountant after verifying that it agrees with the Balance Sheet.

If an amount is listed on this report, it is presumed you owe the money, or in the event of a credit, your vendor owes you.

Reviewing Aged Open Item Receipts

Often, when goods are purchased for inventory, non-inventory, or other item types, your vendor will ship the product with a packing slip and then send the final vendor bill later. One reason for doing this is that receiving departments in a warehouse should not necessarily know the value of the goods being delivered. Another reason might be that the vendor needs to add freight and handling to the final bill before sending it to your company.

The QuickBooks Create Item Receipts transaction is used to record the receipt of the stock into your place of business, increase the quantity on hand for this item (if an inventory item), and increase your accounts payable due to that vendor.

However, because you have not yet received the final bill from the vendor, QuickBooks does not include these item receipts in the Pay Bills dialog box. This is because QuickBooks recognizes an item receipt transaction as not yet having received the final bill to be paid.

note

New for QuickBooks Enterprise Solutions 12.0 is Enhanced Inventory Receiving. If you are using this version of QuickBooks and you are tracking inventory, you have the option to enable a different method of accounting for the items received.

With Enhanced Inventory Receiving enabled, when an item receipt is recorded without the final bill, QuickBooks will increase (debit) Inventory Asset and increase (credit) Inventory Offset account, a current liability account created automatically by QuickBooks.

Later when you enter the final vendor's bill, QuickBooks will decrease (debit) the Inventory Offset account and increase (credit) Accounts Payable.

An error in your accounting can result if you entered a bill and ignored the warning message that outstanding item receipts existed for that vendor and created another bill, or perhaps you used the Write Checks transaction to pay for the same charge as recorded on the original item receipt. Both of these types of mistakes will overstate your expenses or inventory value.

First, to see if this issue is a problem for your data file, select Reports, Vendors & Payables, Unpaid Bills Detail. On the report, do you have line items with a transaction type of Item Receipt (see Figure 8.4)? If you do, these are from receiving inventory, non-inventory, or other types of items *without* receiving (or recording) the final vendor bill.

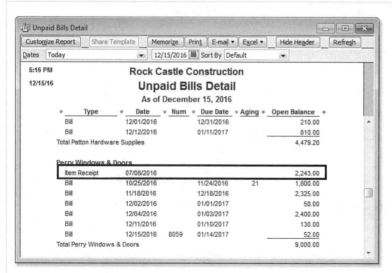

Figure 8.4
Aged item receipts are acceptable only when you have not yet received the vendor's final bill.

If after reviewing your Unpaid Bills Detail report, you find out-dated item receipts that you do not owe the vendor, determine whether they have been paid by requesting an open payables statement from your vendor. To see if the bill was paid with a Write Checks transaction instead of the proper Pay Bills transaction, follow these steps:

1. On the Home page, click the Vendors button.

2. Select the Vendor name on the left. You can also type the first letter of the name and QuickBooks will advance to the first list entry with that letter.

3. To the right, click the Show drop-down list to select the Checks transaction type, as shown in Figure 8.5.

If it would be helpful, you can print the vendor transaction list via the Print drop-down list at the top of the Vendor Center dialog box.

caution

How exactly does QuickBooks manage the use of Item Receipt transactions?

• They age like other open payables on the A/P Aging Summary report.

• The Unpaid Bills Detail report does not show any days in the aged column, yet they are aging.

• QuickBooks does not let you pay an item receipt in the Pay Bills dialog box.

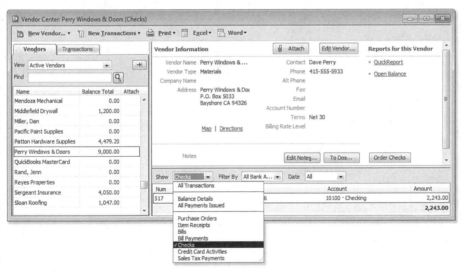

Figure 8.5
Use the Vendor Center to easily review checks written to a vendor as opposed to bill payment checks.

In Figure 8.4, shown previously, Perry Windows has an open item receipt dated 07/08/16. To see whether a check was used to pay this vendor, follow the steps listed previously to see any Write Checks transaction (not Pay Bills) transaction type that was written to the vendor.

➡ *For more information, see "Correcting Accounts Payable Errors," p. 235.*

Reviewing Item Setup

Items play an important part in the accounts payable process if you use purchase orders, item receipts, or the Items tab on a vendor bill or check.

Figure 7.10 (shown in the previous chapter) pictured a service type item with a checkmark placed in the box titled, "This Service Is Used...." Having this checkmark is important if you buy and sell the same item. If this option is not selected and you use the same item on a purchase and a sales transaction, QuickBooks will record both the revenue and the expense to the single account selected on the New Item dialog box or Edit item dialog box.

It is acceptable to create an item with only one account if you know you will never buy and sell the same item. However, I usually recommend each item be set up as two-sided, or needing an expense and an income account.

Properly setting up items is discussed in more detail in Chapter 4, "Understanding QuickBooks Lists." This section focuses on how you can determine whether your items are the cause of errors on your financials for a company data file with transactions. If your data file does not have transactions in it yet, you will not be using this report to check your item setup.

Presume an item was created with only an income account assigned. The item was used on a vendor bill and the user has to decide whether to ignore the warning shown in Figure 8.6.

Figure 8.6
The warning you receive on an expense transaction when using an item that only has an income account assigned.

To see whether this type of error affects your or your data, create the following report:

1. From the menu bar, select Reports, Company & Financial, Profit & Loss Standard.

2. Double-click the Total Income account (see Figure 8.7). QuickBooks creates a Transaction Detail by Account report, displayed in Figure 8.8.

3. On the top right of the resulting Transaction Detail by Account report, select Type from the Sort By drop-down list. QuickBooks groups all transactions by type within each income account or subaccount. Notice in Figure 8.8 that the Labor Income account has a vendor bill transaction posting to an income account.

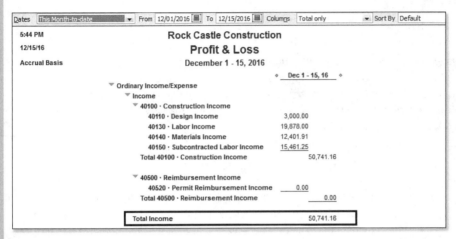

Figure 8.7
Double-click the Total Income amount to create a Transaction Detail by Account report.

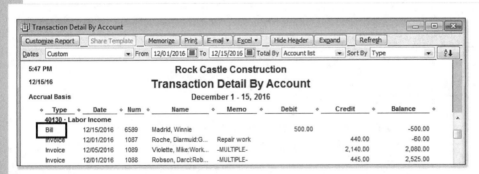

Figure 8.8
A Bill transaction type should not post to an income account, unless the item is set up incorrectly.

Accounts Payable Balance on Cash Basis Balance Sheet

The nature of accounts payable suggests that when you are reviewing your financials in cash basis, you would not see an accounts payable balance. See Table 8.1 for a listing of the transactions you can use in accounts payable and the effect the transaction has on both accrual and cash basis reporting.

Table 8.1 Accounts Payable on Accrual or Cash Basis Balance Sheet

Transaction Name	Accrual Basis	Cash Basis
Create Purchase Orders	No effect	No effect
Create Item Receipt (Receiving inventory *without* the vendor's bill)	Date of Item Receipt—increase (debit) account assigned to the item usually cost of goods sold (or expense account); increase (credit) accounts payable. Note: Item Receipts *cannot* be paid in the Pay Bills dialog box.	No effect
Create Item Receipt (Receiving inventory *with* the vendor's bill)	Date of Item Receipt—increase (debit) account assigned to the item usually cost of goods sold (or expense account); increase (credit) accounts payable. Note: Item Receipt has now become a Bill and *can* be paid in Pay Bills dialog box.	No effect
Enter Vendor Bill For Non-inventory, Other Item Types or General Expenses	Date of Bill—increase (debit), account assigned to item, or account used on the Expenses tab of the bill; increase (credit) accounts payable.	No effect until date of bill payment check
Enter Bills (Credit)	Date of Credit—decrease (debit) accounts payable; decrease (credit) inventory, account assigned to item, or account used on the Expenses tab of the credit memo.	No effect until date of bill payment check

Why exactly do you have an accounts payable balance on a cash basis Balance Sheet report? Any of the following can be the cause:

- A/P transactions have expenses or items posting to other balance sheet accounts.

- Inventory items on an invoice or credit memo (typically, inventory management should be done in accrual basis reporting).

- Transfers between balance sheet accounts.

- Unapplied accounts payable vendor payments.

- Payments applied to future-dated vendor bills.

- Preferences that contradict each other. (This can happen if you select cash basis on your summary reports and accrual basis as your sales tax preference.)

- Data corruption. To confirm, (and hopefully resolve) this problem, select File, Utilities, Verify Data. More details are included in Chapter 17, "Managing Your QuickBooks Database."

Some of the reasons why you might have an accounts payable balance on your cash basis Balance Sheet report, as shown in Figure 8.9, were listed previously.

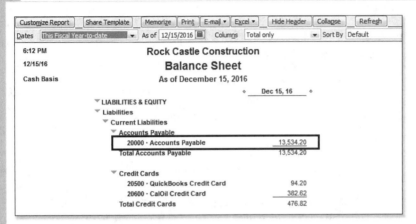

Figure 8.9
Cash basis Balance Sheet report with an Accounts Payable balance.

What can you do if you do have an accounts payable balance on your cash basis Balance Sheet? First, modify the following report to help you locate the transactions making up this balance:

1. From the menu bar, select Reports, Company & Financial, Balance Sheet Standard.

2. Click the Customize Report button to open the Modify Report dialog box with the Display tab selected.

3. Select Cash for the report basis.

4. Click OK.

5. Double-click the Accounts Payable amount in question. The Transactions by Account report is created.

6. Click the Customize Report button to open the Modify Report dialog box with the Display tab selected.

7. For the Report Date Range, remove the "From" date and leave the "To" date.

8. Click the Advanced button and from the Open Balance/Aging box, select Report Date as shown in Figure 8.10. Click OK to close the Advanced Options dialog box.

9. Click the Filters tab.

10. In the Choose Filter box, scroll down to select Paid Status.

11. Select Open for Paid Status.

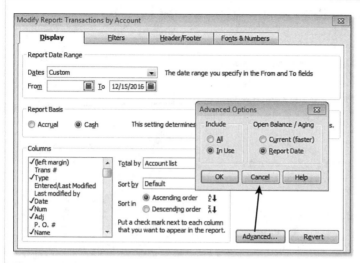

Figure 8.10
Use the Advanced button on the Modify Report dialog box to filter a report for transaction status as of a specific date in the past.

12. Click OK to return to the report and look for transactions that fall into any of the categories described earlier. The Transaction Detail report in Figure 8.11 shows several inventory transactions and a prepaid insurance transaction. All of these transactions are posting to other balance sheet accounts, one of the common causes of having an Accounts Payable balance on a cash basis Balance Sheet report.

| Dates | Custom | ▼ | From | | To | 12/15/2016 | Total By | Account list | ▼ | Sort By | Default | ▼ |

Rock Castle Construction

6:16 PM
12/15/16

Transactions by Account

Cash Basis   As of December 15, 2016

Type	Date	Name	Split	Debit	Credit	Balance
20000 · Accounts Payable						
Bill	10/25/2016	Abercrombie, Kris...	12100 · Inventory Asset		1,800.00	1,800.00
Bill	11/18/2016	Teichman, Tim:Kitc...	12100 · Inventory Asset		1,825.00	3,625.00
Bill	12/04/2016	Castillo, Eloisa:Utili...	12100 · Inventory Asset		2,400.00	6,025.00
Item Receipt	12/05/2016	Keenan, Bridget:S...	12100 · Inventory Asset		3,459.20	9,484.20
Bill	12/15/2016	Overhead	13100 · Pre-paid Insurance		4,050.00	13,534.20
Total 20000 · Accounts Payable				0.00	13,534.20	13,534.20
TOTAL				0.00	13,534.20	13,534.20

Figure 8.11
Filter for transactions that make up the Accounts Payable amount on a cash basis prepared Balance Sheet report.

Tracking and Reporting Vendor 1099-MISC Payments

If your company pays individuals and certain types of businesses, you might need to file a Form 1099-MISC at the end of the year. Currently, only vendors paid $600 or more in a calendar year are required to be reported to the IRS.

Accompanying Form 1096 is also required and summarizes the individual filed 1099 forms. QuickBooks will print both the 1096 summary and individual 1099 forms, using preprinted tax forms available through Intuit or most office supply stores. Or, new for calendar year ending 12/31/2011, Intuit is also offering the option to use Intuit's E-File Service for filing your 1099 and 1096 tax forms.

Before you begin using the QuickBooks 1099 Wizard, review your vendor settings using the following reports. To access these, select Vendors, Print/E-file 1099s from the menu bar.

 caution

The newly designed QuickBooks 1099 Wizard was updated to assist with 2011 tax year reporting changes made by the IRS. Make sure you are on the latest release of the QuickBooks software. Instructions on updating your data file are included in Chapter 17.

Press Ctrl + 1 on your keyboard to view the Product Information dialog box. The Product field lists the QuickBooks version, year, and release you are currently using.

- **Review 1099 Vendors**—Lists vendor's Tax ID, Address, and other useful information. Sort by Eligible for 1099 at the top of the report to help verify you have all the vendors selected you want to supply a Form 1099-MISC for.

- **1099 Summary Report**—Lists Box 7:Nonemployee Compensation details by vendor.

- **1099 Detail Report**—Lists individual transactions that are used to calculate the amount reported for the vendor's Form 1099-MISC earnings.

Properly setting up your 1099 tax form preferences in QuickBooks will ensure compliance with federal tax reporting guidelines. If you have specific questions about what type of vendor should receive this document, refer to the www.irs.gov website or contact your company's accountant or tax advisor. Let's get your file ready to track and report your Form 1099-MISC payments to vendors using the six steps in the new QuickBooks 1099 Wizard.

Step 1—Select Your 1099 Vendors

Not all vendors are required to receive a Form 1099-MISC at the end of the year. Make sure you have reviewed the reporting requirements on the IRS website or have asked for advice from your company's accountant or tax advisor.

To select your 1099 vendors, follow these steps:

1. Log into your file as the Admin or External Accountant user.

2. From the menu bar, select Edit, Preferences to open the Preferences dialog box, as previously shown in Figure 7.3 in Chapter 7.

3. Select the Tax:1099—Company Preferences tab. Select the Yes option for Do You file 1099-MISC Forms?

4. Select the Click Here link for If You're Ready To Prepare Your 1099's, Including Mapping Accounts. If the link does not display, close and reopen the preferences dialog.

5. Click Yes to the Save Changes message if displayed. QuickBooks opens the 1099 Wizard, displayed in Figure 8.12.

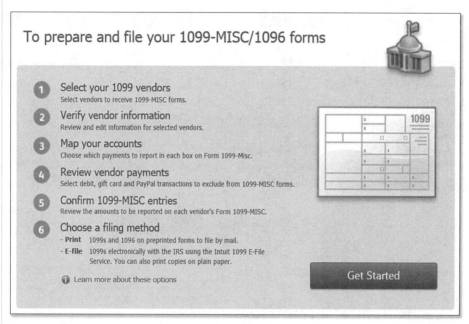

To prepare and file your 1099-MISC/1096 forms

1. **Select your 1099 vendors**
Select vendors to receive 1099-MISC forms.

2. **Verify vendor information**
Review and edit information for selected vendors.

3. **Map your accounts**
Choose which payments to report in each box on Form 1099-Misc.

4. **Review vendor payments**
Select debit, gift card and PayPal transactions to exclude from 1099-MISC forms.

5. **Confirm 1099-MISC entries**
Review the amounts to be reported on each vendor's Form 1099-MISC.

6. **Choose a filing method**
- **Print**   1099s and 1096 on preprinted forms to file by mail.
- **E-file**   1099s electronically with the IRS using the Intuit 1099 E-File Service. You can also print copies on plain paper.

Learn more about these options

Get Started

Figure 8.12
In just a few simple steps, you can use the 1099 Wizard to track vendor 1099 payments.

6. Review the steps and select Get Started.

7. Place a checkmark in front of those vendors you want to track Form 1099-MISC earnings for. Optionally click the Select All button. See Figure 8.13.

8. Click Save & Close if you are not ready to complete the remaining steps in the 1099 Wizard or click Continue to advance to the next step.

Select all the vendors who should get the required tax form. If they are not paid the IRS established threshold during the year (currently $600), QuickBooks will not include them in the forms that are to be printed. Do not worry here if you are uncertain which vendors to select. You can always come back and make changes.

Figure 8.13
Select the vendors who will receive a Form 1099-MISC.

Step 2—Verify Vendor Information

One of the important steps to take to properly tracking your vendors payments subject to 1099 filings is to record the vendors Tax ID and select the Vendor is eligible for 1099 as previously displayed in Figure 7.6 from Chapter 7. You can request this information from your vendor using the IRS form W-9, Request for Taxpayer Identification Number and Certification. This form can be downloaded from the www.irs.gov website.

If you didn't have this information available when you initially created your vendor record, you can add this information at any time during the year and QuickBooks will include the vendor payments in your 1099 reporting.

To verify vendor information, follow these steps:

1. If you selected Continue after step 7 (select your 1099 vendors), you will now verify your 1099 vendor's information.

2. For the vendors you selected, make sure you have the Tax ID, Company Name, Address, and other information for each of your selected vendors. See Figure 8.14.

3. If information is missing, click in the field and enter the missing information.

 tip

The end of any calendar year is a busy time. Consider reviewing your vendor's 1099 information throughout the year so you have time to collect the missing information before the tax forms are due.

Businesses must provide eligible vendors with their Form 1099-MISC by the end of January following a calendar year. Some will want their forms as early as possible in January, so be prepared early.

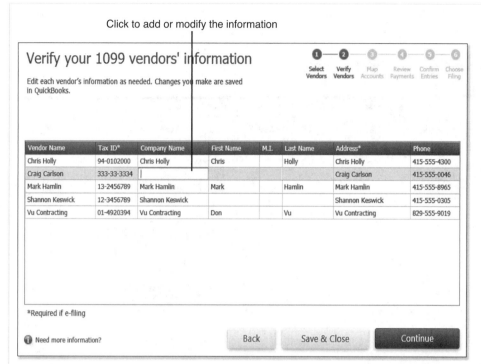

Figure 8.14
Changes made in the 1099 Wizard will automatically update the vendor's record in QuickBooks.

4. Click Save & Close if you are not ready to complete the remaining steps in the 1099 wizard or click Continue to advance to the next step.

Step 3 — Map Your Accounts

QuickBooks provides you the option of including or excluding specific chart of accounts from being used when reporting your vendor's payments. For example, you might pay your vendor for services and record it to a specific Subcontractors expense account. You might also reimburse that same vendor for materials purchases and record that portion of the expense to a different expense account.

It is not the intent of this book to provide tax filing advice, so please check with the IRS website for more details or ask your company's accountant or tax advisor.

To map your accounts, follow these steps:

1. After verifying your 1099 vendor's information (previous instructions), click Continue.

2. For the vendors you have selected, the 1099 Wizard will display the accounts that were assigned on the vendor payments. For each account displayed, you can choose to Omit these payments from Form 1099-MISC income reporting or select from several 1099 box reporting options; see Figure 8.15.

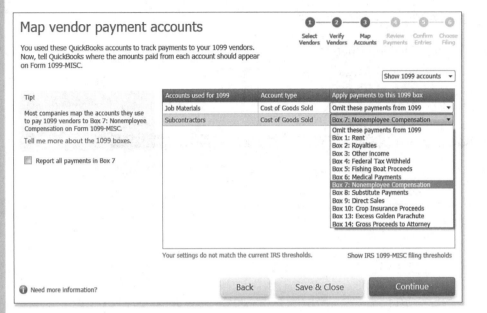

Figure 8.15
Selectively choose which accounts are reported or omitted from your 1099 reporting.

 caution

The only 1099 form that QuickBooks will print or that can be processed by Intuit 1099 E-File Service is the Form 1099-MISC. Accounts in QuickBooks can be assigned to any of the 14 boxes on the Form 1099-MISC.

Multiple cost of sales, ordinary expense, and other expense accounts can be assigned (mapped) to a single box on the Form 1099-MISC. However, a single account cannot be assigned to more than one reporting box on the form.

If a Balance Sheet account (such as a vendor prepayment) is used when recording a payment to a 1099 eligible vendor; that account will not display by default in the Map vendor payment accounts. However, if you select Show All Accounts, you are provided the option to omit the payments recorded to Balance Sheet accounts from 1099 or assign to the appropriate Form 1099-MISC box.

3. Optionally, click the Show 1099 Accounts drop-down list and select the Show All Accounts if you want to omit or map your 1099 reporting for all of your accounts on your chart of accounts.

4. Optionally, select the Report All Payments in Box 7 checkbox. By doing so, all the displayed accounts will now be assigned to Box 7:Nonemployee Compensation.

5. If you see the warning message "Your Settings Do Not Match the Current IRS Thresholds," click the Show IRS 1099-MISC Filing Thresholds link.

6. Read the information displayed in the 1099-MISC IRS Thresholds dialog box. Click the Reset to IRS Thresholds button. QuickBooks updates the thresholds with current tax information.

7. Click Save & Close to return to the 1099 Wizard.

8. Click Save & Close if you are not going to complete the remaining steps in the 1099 Wizard or click Continue to advance to the next step.

Step 4 — Review Vendor Payments

Do you pay your vendor bills by credit card? Beginning with the 2011 tax year, the IRS established new rules to exclude from Form 1099-MISC any payments you made by credit card, debit card, gift card, or third-party payment network such as PayPal. (The IRS reports that these payments are too be reported by the card issuers and third-party payment networks on Form 1099-K.) You will want to review both included and excluded payments on the Review Payments for Exclusions screen in the 1099 Wizard, displayed in Figure 8.16.

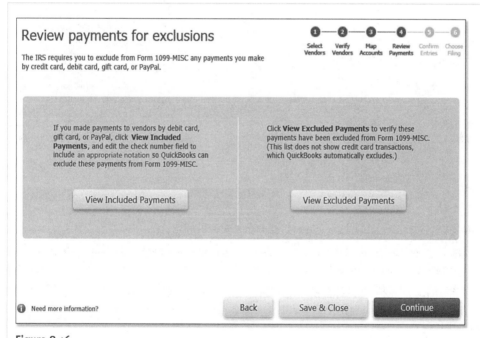

Figure 8.16
With the new 1099 rules beginning in 2011, verifying that the proper payments are included or excluded is provided as part of the 1099 Wizard.

For payments to vendors made by credit card but not recorded using the preferred Enter Credit Card Charges transaction type (such as the Pay Bills transaction using a check or the Write Checks transaction), special guidelines need to be followed. To record a vendor payment made with a credit card, debit card, or gift card, or using a third-party payment network such as PayPal, you should note the payment method in the No. field of a Write Checks dialog box. QuickBooks recognizes, and automatically excludes from Form 1099-MISC, these payments if the following notations in the check number field (limited to eight characters) are used:

- Debit

- DBT card

- Visa

- MCard

- Diners

- Debitcar

- DCard

- Masterc

- Chase

- Paypal

- DBT

- Debit cd

- MC

- Discover

tip

Save yourself time from having to modify the check number assigned to bill payment checks or other checks when recording vendor 1099 payments made by credit card using these forms. Instead, when paying a vendor bill assign the payment to a credit card account or use the Enter Credit Card Charges dialog box to record the expense (select Banking, Enter Credit Card Charges from the menu bar).

QuickBooks automatically excludes from Form 1099-MISC any bill payment made using the credit card payment method.

To view the transactions included in your 1099 reporting, follow these steps:

1. Click the View Included Payments. QuickBooks creates a report titled "Check Payments Included on Forms 1099-MISC" (see Figure 8.17).

2. If any of these payments were made by credit card, debit card, gift card, or third-party payment network such as PayPal, you will need to edit the check number, displayed in the Num column on this report.

3. Double-click to open a single transaction that was paid by credit card. The associated check displays. Modify the information in the No. field using one of the accepted notations listed previously.

4. Click Save & Close to save your changes. QuickBooks no longer includes this payment in your 1099-MISC Income reporting.

5. Click the View Excluded Payments button. QuickBooks creates a report titled Check Payments Excluded from Forms 1099-MISC. Verify that the transactions listed on this report qualify to be excluded from 1099-MISC Income reporting.

If these payments were by credit card, modify the number to agree with the acceptable notations.

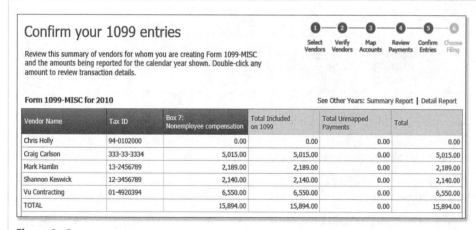

8:26 PM
12/20/11

Rock Castle Construction
Check Payments Included on Forms 1099-MISC
January through December 2010

Type	Num	Date	Name	Memo	Item	Account	Paid Amount	Original Amount
▶ Bill Pmt -Check	299	04/10/2010	Craig Carlson	ROCK-0921		Checking		-415.00 ◀
Bill		03/18/2010	Violette, Mike:Utility...	Install drywa...	Subs:Dr...	Subcontractors	-415.00	415.00
TOTAL							-415.00	415.00
Bill Pmt -Check	321	05/23/2010	Chris Holly			Checking		-289.95
Bill		03/28/2010	Violette, Mike:Utility...	Install Wash...		Subcontractors	-145.00	145.00
			Violette, Mike:Utility...	Install double...		Subcontractors	-55.00	55.00
			Violette, Mike:Utility...	Electrical wo...	Subs:Ele...	Subcontractors	-89.95	89.95
TOTAL							-289.95	289.95

Figure 8.17
Review checks recorded as payments to vendors who might have been paid by credit card.

6. Click the X in the top-right corner to close the report(s).

7. Click Save & Close if you are not going to complete the remaining steps in the 1099 Wizard or click Continue to advance to the next step.

Step 5—Confirm 1099-MISC Entries

The 1099 Wizard displays a list of the Vendors that will be receiving a Form 1099-MISC (see Figure 8.18).

Confirm your 1099 entries

①——②——③——④——⑤——⑥
Select   Verify   Map   Review   Confirm   Choose
Vendors Vendors Accounts Payments Entries   Filing

Review this summary of vendors for whom you are creating Form 1099-MISC and the amounts being reported for the calendar year shown. Double-click any amount to review transaction details.

Form 1099-MISC for 2010   See Other Years: Summary Report | Detail Report

Vendor Name	Tax ID	Box 7: Nonemployee compensation	Total Included on 1099	Total Unmapped Payments	Total
Chris Holly	94-0102000	0.00	0.00	0.00	0.00
Craig Carlson	333-33-3334	5,015.00	5,015.00	0.00	5,015.00
Mark Hamlin	13-2456789	2,189.00	2,189.00	0.00	2,189.00
Shannon Keswick	12-3456789	2,140.00	2,140.00	0.00	2,140.00
Vu Contracting	01-4920394	6,550.00	6,550.00	0.00	6,550.00
TOTAL		15,894.00	15,894.00	0.00	15,894.00

Figure 8.18
Preview vendor payments that will be included or not included in your Form 1099-MISC income reporting.

To confirm 1099-MISC entries, follow these steps:

1. Click the Summary Report link to see a summary for all vendors included in your Form 1099-MISC income reporting. Modify the dates and filters as needed.

2. Click the X in the top right to close the 1099 Summary report.

3. Click the Detail report to see a list of all transactions grouped by vendor. Modify the dates and filters as needed.

4. Click the X in the top right to close the 1099 Detail report.

5. Click Save & Close if you are not going to complete the remaining steps in the 1099 Wizard or click Continue to advance to the next step.

Step 6 — Choose a Filing Method

The QuickBooks 1099 Wizard provides information to help you choose a filing method, either printing or electronically filing the forms (see Figure 8.19).

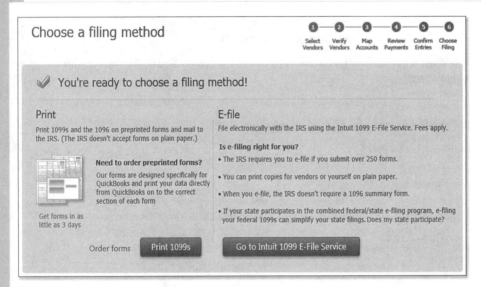

Figure 8.19
The 1099 Wizard makes it easy to print 1099 forms or file electronically.

To print the 1099-MISC Income forms, follow these steps:

1. Click the Order Forms link to order your tax forms from Intuit. You might also purchase tax forms from your local office supply store.

2. Click the Print 1099s button to print the documents on the preprinted forms you have purchased.

3. QuickBooks, 1099-MISC and 1096 Forms dialog box displays. Select the appropriate year you are printing your forms for. Typically, you would be selecting Last Calendar Year.

4. The Select 1099s to Print dialog box displays with each vendor selected. Optionally, click Select All or Select None if needed.

   QuickBooks displays the number of vendors selected and the total dollar amount for the selected vendors.

5. Click Print 1099. The Print 1099s settings display. Place the tax forms in your printer and select Print. You will need to print on preprinted forms; unlike W-2s, the IRS does not accept 1099 forms on plain paper.

6. View the documents that printed. When you have completed printing 1099, click Print 1096 and insert in your printer the preprinted form.

7. Enter the Contact Name in the 1096 Information dialog box. If circumstances warrant select This is My Final Return.

8. Select your printer and click Print. QuickBooks returns to the Select 1099s to Print dialog box.

9. When complete, click the X in the top-right corner to close the Select 1099s to Print dialog box.

If you will be E-Filing, click the Go to Intuit 1099 E-File Service. Follow the instructions for filing. You will complete three steps:

1. **Sign up for the Service**—Using your Intuit Account username and password.

2. **Set up Intuit Sync Manager**—Enables QuickBooks to send your information to the Intuit E-File 1099 Service.

3. **Purchase, Print and E-File**—Print and E-File your returns with a click of a button.

The information window provides a toll-free number to call if you have any questions. 1099 forms for a given tax year cannot be filed until January of the following year.

You have successfully completed the steps to properly track and report your vendors' Form 1099-MISC income payments.

Correcting Accounts Payable Errors

Chapter 7, "Setting Up Vendors," provides a recommended work-flow and preference settings that will help you avoid making mistakes with your accounts payable transactions. This chapter provides specific details about methods you can use to correct existing accounts payable errors.

The purpose of this book is not to give your business specific accounting or tax advice, but rather to introduce you to ways you might consider fixing specific mistakes you have found.

 caution

Before making any of the suggested changes, be sure you have made a backup of your data in case the change does not give you the desired result. Additionally, contacting your accountant and obtaining his advice on the changes you are going to make would be prudent.

Open Vendor Bills Paid with a Write Checks Transaction

Earlier in this chapter, in the "Reviewing the Unpaid Bills Detail Report," section, you were provided a way to reconcile your A/P Aging Summary report total to your Balance Sheet accounts payable total (refer to Figure 8.2). As important as this task is, it is also necessary for you to review those items listed as unpaid to your vendor. If you notice an open vendor bill that you know you do not owe the vendor, it might be because you paid the vendor with a Write Checks transaction instead of the proper Pay Bills transaction type.

You should experience fewer of these types of mistakes in recent years because QuickBooks directs you to the Pay Bills dialog box, as shown in Figure 8.20, when you attempt to write a check to a vendor with open bills.

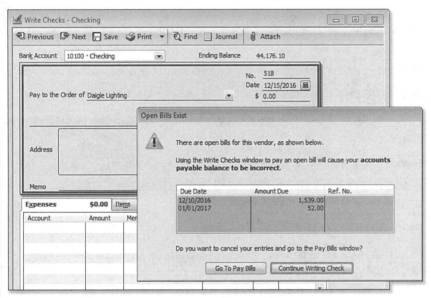

Figure 8.20
The warning provided if you attempt to create a check to pay a vendor with open bills.

If you choose to modify the original vendor check, carefully consider the accounting effect this type of correction will have on your financials:

- Is the change a significant dollar amount? Both cash and accrual basis reports will be affected.

- Consider the date of the check and the date of the bill—are they in different tax years?

- Is the correction going to affect a year where the data has already been used to prepare a tax return?

If you answered yes to any of these questions, be sure to discuss with your accountant the impact this change could have on your financials.

You can modify this check, making it become a vendor credit. In other words, it will decrease (debit) accounts payable and maintain the original decrease (credit) to your cash account. To do so, follow these steps:

1. Locate the Write Checks transaction used to pay the vendor. One easy way is to click the Vendors button on the Home page to open the Vendor Center. Select the vendor from the list on the left and select Checks from the Show drop-down list as displayed previously in Figure 8.5.

2. Double-click the check to open the Write Checks dialog box for the selected transaction.

3. On the Expenses tab, in the account column, replace the currently listed account with the accounts payable account as shown in Figure 8.21. This creates a decrease (debit) to the accounts payable account.

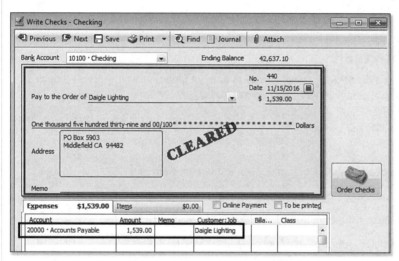

Figure 8.21
Using a check to record a vendor pre-payment (debit to Accounts Payable).

4. Select the vendor name from the drop-down list in the Customer:Job column. If you had previously listed a Customer:Job in this field you will be warned to choose a Vendor name instead. This assigns the accounts payable decrease to a specific vendor. You cannot save the transaction without assigning a vendor name.

5. Click Save & Close, and then click Yes to record your changes.

6. From the menu bar, select Vendors, Pay Bills, and use the arrow key on your keyboard to move up and down through the list of vendors in the Pay Bills dialog box. Or, optionally, select the vendor name from the Filter By drop-down list. Before placing a checkmark in the box next to the vendor's specific invoice, QuickBooks will show the total number of credits and their total value in the Discount & Credit Information for Highlighted Bill section. (See Figure 7.18 in Chapter 7.)

7. When you have located the correct bill, place a checkmark in the box to the left of the Date Due column. When an invoice is selected, QuickBooks will automatically apply the available credits to the selected vendor invoice (if the preference was set). If not and you want to modify the amount or which credits are selected, click the Set Credits button. The Discount and Credits dialog box displays (previously shown in Figure 7.19 in Chapter 7). Users can modify which credit is selected by changing the checkmark from one credit to another or by manually overriding the amount of the credit.

8. Click the Done button when the credit is assigned.

9. QuickBooks shows in the Pay Bills dialog box that the bill is being paid by a credit (if the entire bill is being paid by the credit, QuickBooks will not create a check). Click Pay Selected Bills when you are finished.

10. QuickBooks offers you Pay More Bills or Done choices. Click Done, if you do not have any other transactions to correct using this method.

Misapplied Vendor Credit

Have you ever been given a credit from a vendor, only to find out later that your vendor applied the credit to a different open bill than you did in your data?

QuickBooks makes it easy to reassign a vendor credit from one accounts payable bill to another bill. You will temporarily assign the credit to another vendor, and then reapply it to the correct vendor. To do so, follow these steps:

1. On the Home page, click the Vendors button to open the Vendor Center.

2. Select the vendor with the misapplied credit.

3. From the Show drop-down list, select Bills (this will also list vendor credits).

4. From the transactions listed, select the misapplied credit memo by double-clicking it. The Enter Bills dialog box with the word *Credit* displayed, opens for the selected transaction.

5. On the vendor line of the credit, select a different vendor. (Remember to whom you assign it.)

6. Click Save & Close. QuickBooks removes the credit transaction from the vendor bill it was previously associated with.

7. QuickBooks also warns that the transaction you are editing will no longer be connected. Click Yes to continue (see Figure 8.22).

Figure 8.22
Warning when you unapply a previously applied vendor credit.

8. From the same Vendor Center, select the other vendor to which you assigned the credit. From the Show drop-down list, select Bills and double-click the credit you just assigned in step 5. The Enter Bills dialog box, with the word *Credit* displayed, opens for the selected transaction.

9. On the vendor line, select the original vendor.

10. Click Save & Close and Yes to making the change.

QuickBooks now shows the credit as unapplied to your original vendor, and you can follow the steps outlined previously for applying the credit to the correct open vendor bill.

Removing Aged Open Item Receipts or Vendor Bills

One of the more important tasks you can do to maintain a correct data file is to remove old, aged item receipts or payables you do not owe.

You have three options when you want to remove these aged (old) transactions:

- Create a credit memo and apply it.

- Void the item receipt or bill.

- Delete the item receipt or bill.

To create and apply a credit memo to a vendor bill, follow the same steps as listed in Chapter 7 in the section, "Applying Vendor Discounts or Credits."

You must give special consideration to applying a credit memo to an open item receipt. First, convert the item receipt to a bill. To do so, follow these steps:

1. Locate the open item receipt using any of the methods suggested in Chapter 7.

2. When you select the open item receipt, QuickBooks opens the Create Item Receipts dialog box. Place a checkmark in the Bill Received box at the top right, as shown in Figure 8.23.

You can now apply your credit memo to the item receipt, which has been converted to a bill.

When considering whether to void or delete, I always prefer the void option because it leaves a record of the original transaction.

Before voiding or deleting, you need to verify that the aged open item receipts or bills do not have any other transactions associated with them. To verify this, follow these steps:

1. Open the item receipt or bill using any one of the many methods discussed in Chapter 7.

2. Open a previously recorded bill or create item receipts, click the transaction tab to the right. QuickBooks displays in the Summary box information about when the transaction was created and edited (if applicable). In the Related Transactions box, links are provided to the original transactions (if any).

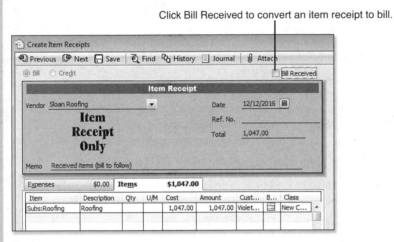

Click Bill Received to convert an item receipt to bill.

Figure 8.23
Converting an open item receipt to a bill is necessary before applying a vendor credit memo.

If you had voided or deleted the vendor bill shown in Figure 8.24, you would have created an unapplied vendor payment (the Bill Pmt-Check listed in the Related Transactions section). In effect, you would have traded one correction for another problem. So be careful when making corrections to your accounts payable transactions.

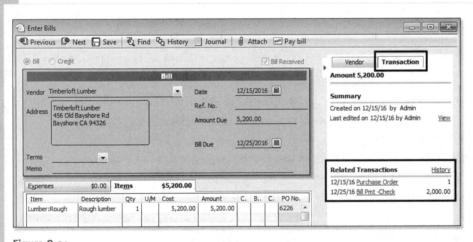

Figure 8.24
Before voiding, deleting, or modifying a bill, click the Transaction tab to the right to see whether any transactions are associated with this bill.

Making General Journal Adjustments to Accounts Payable

All too often, I find that accounting professionals are quick to make adjustments to accounts payable using the Make General Journal Entries dialog box, also referred to as a journal entry. The following are some of the issues surrounding the use of the journal entry transaction type:

- Only a single vendor or a customer name can be in the Make General Journal Entries dialog box, not both a vendor and customer in the same transaction, minimizing the usefulness of the transaction for large-volume corrections.

- General journal entries do not include the option to assign an item, including service, non-inventory, inventory, and so on. The adjustment would affect the Profit & Loss reports, but not specific QuickBooks reports that use item information, such as the Job Profitability reports or Inventory Valuation reports.

- You will still need to go to the Pay Bills dialog box to assign the balance generated by the general journal to the other related vendor transactions.

caution

Often, the use of the general journal entries does not provide the desired results in your reporting. Did you know that the first line of any general journal entry is considered a "source" line? Specifically, this means that if the first line of a multiple-line general journal entry includes a vendor, customer, or any list item name in the Name column, as shown in Figure 8.25, that name element will display in reports on the lines below the first line, even if there is no relationship (see Figure 8.26).

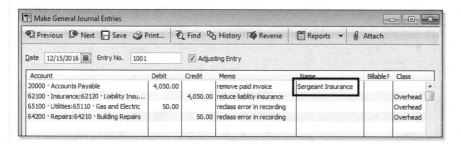

Figure 8.25
When the first line of a multiple-line general journal includes a list name in the Name column, QuickBooks associates the name entry with all lines of the form.

This type of error is more apparent when a Customer:Job Name is included on the first line of a multiple-line general journal entry form. When preparing a Profit & Loss by Job report, QuickBooks would include all lines of the general journal entry as belonging to that job!

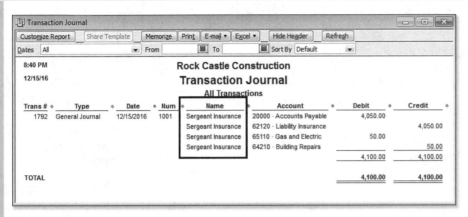

Figure 8.26
QuickBooks associated the vendor's name with all lines of the journal entry because the vendor list name was on the first line of the general journal.

A quick fix is to add a blank line at the beginning of each general journal entry. Another recommendation is to create a fictitious bank account and call it Adjusting Entries, but then leave the debit and credit fields blank. If you assign the first line of the entry to this account, QuickBooks provides a "register" for you to locate these types of transactions and at the same time avoid the issue addressed in this section. See Figures 8.27 and 8.28 to see how adding the line at the beginning of the transaction solves the problem in reporting.

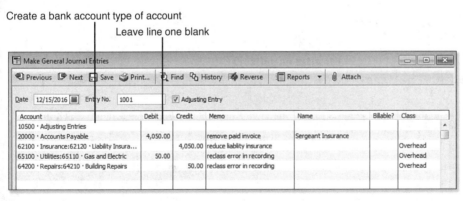

Figure 8.27
Including the fictitious bank account on the first line of a general journal entry prevents the source line (line 1) from being associated with additional unrelated lines.

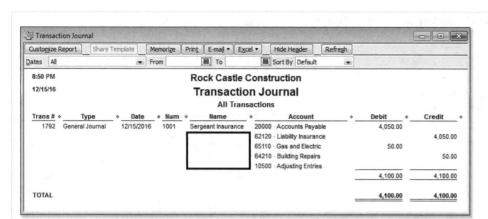

Figure 8.28
QuickBooks no longer associates the vendor's name with the unrelated general journal lines.

Often, just these simple tips can help make your QuickBooks reporting much more accurate!

If you have journal entries recorded to your accounts payable, your unpaid bills report might look something like Figure 8.29.

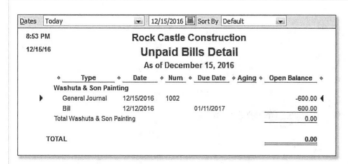

Figure 8.29
Your Unpaid Bills Detail report might show the general journal entry as unapplied.

If your Unpaid Bills Detail report includes journal entries, see "Applying Vendor Credits," p. 211.

Handling Unique Accounts Payable Transactions

So far you have learned about the accounts payable forms and workflow, preferences you can set to improve your data entry, reports to review when troubleshooting errors, and methods of correcting accounts payable errors. This section offers specific solutions to some of those unique transactions you might need to record.

Bartering Services with Your Vendors

Having a vendor who is also a customer is commonly referred to as *bartering*. This is when your vendor also purchases your goods or services and you are going to "swap" and not pay each other for the items purchased from each other.

To track the exchange of goods, follow these steps:

1. From the menu bar, select Lists, Chart of Accounts.

2. From the Account drop-down list, select New to create a new bank account type named Bartering. If you have account numbering turned on, you will also need to assign an account number. This bank account will always have a net zero balance if the transactions are recorded properly.

3. Click Save & Close.

4. From the menu bar, select Vendor, Enter Bills to record your vendor bill as if you were going to make the purchase from the vendor.

5. From the menu bar, select Vendor, Pay Bills. The Pay Bills dialog box opens. Select the bill for the vendor you will barter with.

6. In the Pay Bills dialog box, select the Bartering Account as the payment account (as displayed in Figure 8.30). You can then choose to assign a fictitious check number.

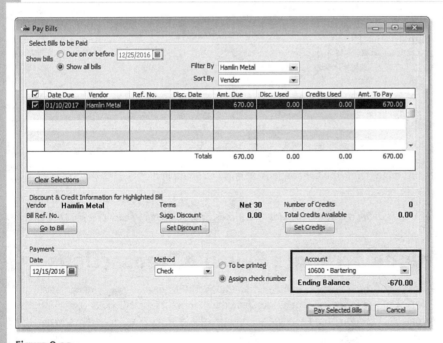

Figure 8.30
When you are bartering goods with your vendor, choose the fictitious bank account when recording the "payment" of the vendor bill.

7. On the Home page, click the Customers button to open the Customers Center.

8. From the New Customer & Job drop-down list, select New Customer and complete the contact information for the new customer; otherwise, double-click the customer or job you will be bartering with to select it.

9. From the Customers Center, select Invoices from the New Transactions drop-down list. Prepare the invoice to the new customer (also your vendor) using the same items on the invoice as if you were selling them to a customer. Click Save & Close.

10. From the Customers Center, select Receive Payments from the New Transactions drop-down list. Record the fictitious payment from the customer (your vendor). Click Save & Close.

 note

QuickBooks will not allow the same name to reside on multiple lists. To get around this limitation, when creating the customer name for your vendor, follow this convention: Johns Plumbing – C. I have added a – C after the "vendor name" on my customer list. This is helpful when picking the name from a list and you need to be certain to select the customer list item.

11. Depending on how your preferences are set up for customer payments, deposit the fictitious customer payment into the same Bartering bank account created earlier.

12. If the value of what you purchased is equal to the value of what you sold, your Bartering bank account will have a net zero ending balance. If not, you will need to enter an adjusting entry to remove the balance or adjust your purchase or sales transaction total. If needed, you can create this entry by selecting Banking, Use Register from the menu bar and selecting your Bartering bank account from the Use Register drop-down list. On the next available line in the account register, record a payment or deposit as needed to clear the account. You will want to ask your accountant what account is appropriate for the adjustment.

Recording Vendor Prepayments

If your business is required to prepay your vendor for purchases, you can choose from a couple of methods:

- Assign expenses to the other current asset type account typically named Prepaid Expenses.

- Record a decrease (debit) transaction to the accounts payable account.

Often you will have expenses that must be paid in advance of the benefit of the service or product being purchased. An example is a business's general liability insurance. Typically, you pay several months in advance for this type of insurance. To record this annual or semi-annual expense all in one month would make that month unfairly take on the total expense.

A preferred method is to record the expense in equal monthly increments. The following steps show you how to record the original prepaid expense and record the expense to the individual months.

To accomplish this task, you will pay the insurance vendor, assign the expense to the other current asset account, and then create a recurring entry that QuickBooks uses to remind you to enter the expense; or QuickBooks will automatically enter the expense each month, depending on how you set up the reminder. This example shows how you would prepay a general liability insurance bill of $12,000 for 12 months of coverage.

To record vendor prepayments, follow these steps:

1. Complete an Enter Bills or Write Checks transaction payable to your insurance provider (or whatever type of prepaid expense you are recording). Instead of assigning the usual expense account on the transaction, assign the prepaid other current asset type account. In this example, the account is Pre-paid Insurance.

2. Pay the bill to the vendor as normal.

3. Set up a recurring transaction to charge 1/12 of the total to each month. If the amount remains the same from month to month, set up the recurring entry to automatically post to QuickBooks. To do so, select Company, Make General Journal Entries from the menu bar. Create a journal entry with a debit to your expense account and a credit to the prepaid other current asset type account.

Did you know that you can memorize repeating transactions and let QuickBooks remind you or even automatically record them? To do so, follow these steps:

1. Create the transaction you want to memorize. You can also use this process to memorize any of the QuickBooks transaction types, checks, bills, invoices, and so on.

2. With the transaction displayed, press Ctrl+M on your keyboard or select Edit, Memorize from the menu bar to open the Memorize Transaction dialog box.

3. Choose to have QuickBooks remind you on a specific frequency, or choose to have QuickBooks automatically enter the transaction (see Figure 8.31).

Figure 8.31
To automate data entry, memorize the transaction.

 tip

QuickBooks will list memorized transactions on the Memorized Transaction List, which is available by pressing Ctrl+T on your keyboard. You can also access by selecting Lists, Memorized Transaction List from the menu bar.

You might want to check your company reminders to be sure you enable a reminder for showing your memorized transactions. To do so, select Edit, Preferences from the menu bar, and then select the Reminders tab on the Preferences dialog box.

The other method discussed here is to record a debit balance to the vendor's accounts payable account. This would be appropriate if you are going to be using the prepayment soon as payment towards the final vendor bill. To do so, follow these steps:

1. From the menu bar, select Banking, Write Checks.

2. In the Pay to the Order Of field, select the vendor's name.

3. Enter the amount of the prepayment.

4. On the Expenses tab, in the account detail area, select the accounts payable account (see Figure 8.32).

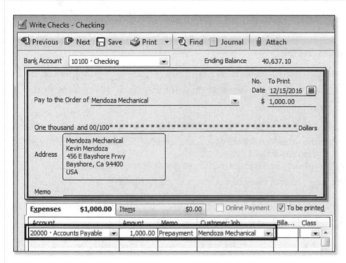

Figure 8.32
Assign the Accounts Payable account and the vendor name to a check when recording a vendor prepayment.

5. In the Customer:Job column, enter the vendor's name (must be a vendor type for this method to work).

6. Click Save & Close.

QuickBooks now records a vendor credit (debit to accounts payable) as shown in Figure 8.33.

At a later date, you would record a bill for the full purchase price and assign this credit.

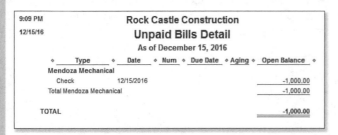

Figure 8.33
QuickBooks records the vendor prepayment as a negative entry to accounts payable (or a debit to accounts payable).

Entering Mid-Year 1099 Balances

If you start your QuickBooks data file mid-year (or at some other time than the first of a new calendar year), you might have amounts paid previously to vendors who are eligible to receive the Form 1099-MISC.

To properly record the amounts paid to vendors in your prior accounting software and to make sure that QuickBooks reports all amounts paid to the vendor on the Form 1099-MISC, follow these steps:

1. From the menu bar, select Company, Make General Journal Entries. If you use any of the job profitability reports, leave the first line (source line) of the journal entry blank.

2. On the following lines (one line per vendor), in the Account column, enter the cost of goods sold account or expense account assigned in the preferences for Tax:1099.

3. For each Debit line amount, be sure to select the vendor's list name (this must be a vendor type) in the Name column.

4. On the last line, enter one line total assigning the same account as the other lines so that the Debit column is equal to the Credit column (see Figure 8.34).

Figure 8.34
When starting a QuickBooks file mid-year, create a general journal entry to record year-to-date vendor Form 1099-MISC Income tax payments.

Your overall financials will not change because the same account was used for both the debit and credit side of the transaction. Including the vendor name on the debit side of the transaction lines causes QuickBooks to include the amount in the reported Form 1099-MISC income amount.

Memorizing Recurring Transactions

QuickBooks can also make help you not forget a recurring accounts payable bill. Memorized bills work best if the amount being paid is the same from month to month (or whatever frequency you set). An example might be your rent payment.

To memorize a recurring accounts payable transaction, follow these steps:

1. Create a vendor bill as normal, assigning the amount and expense account with which you want it to be associated.

2. With the Enter Bills dialog box open, press Ctrl+M to open the Memorize Transaction dialog box (see previous Figure 8.31).

3. Enter a name that identifies this transaction in the memorized transaction list.

4. Choose one of the available options:

   ■ **Add to My Reminders List**—If you select this option, you need to choose how often and the next date you want to be reminded.

   ■ **Do Not Remind Me**—Use this option if you want to stop permanently, or even temporarily, your reminders for this transaction.

   ■ **Automate Transaction Entry**—Use this option if you want QuickBooks to create the entry automatically.

 note

New for QuickBooks 2012: If you assign the Automate Transaction Entry option for memorizing a transaction, QuickBooks will provide a new reminder dialog box that will display when you log into the QuickBooks file.

From the Enter Memorized Transactions dialog box, you can enter all of the selected transactions, select those you want to enter, or enter them all later (see Figure 8.35).

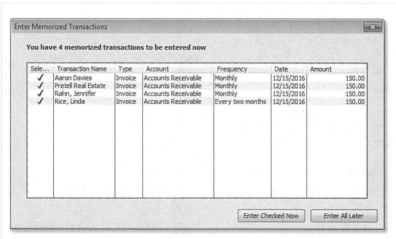

Figure 8.35
QuickBooks reminds you to process Memorized repeating transactions.

- **Add to Group**—You can assign multiple transactions to a group and then process them with one keystroke. First, create a group by choosing Lists, Memorized Transaction List from the menu bar. From the Memorized Transaction drop-down list, select New Group. Give the group a name and choose options for the group from the following options: Remind Me, Do Not Remind Me, or Automatically Enter.

5. Click OK to close the Schedule Memorized Transaction dialog box.

6. Click Save & Close on your bill only if you want to create the vendor bill now and also add it to your memorized transaction list. If not, select Clear to remove the bill details, knowing that QuickBooks will prompt you to enter it on the frequency and date you selected.

To manually enter the transactions (if they're not set to Automate Transaction Entry), choose Lists, Memorized Transaction List from the menu bar, or press Ctrl+T on your keyboard to quickly call up the list. Select the group or individual transactions you want to post by double-clicking the group or individual item from the memorized transaction list.

If you clicked on a memorized group, QuickBooks will create each of the transactions in the group, asking you to assign a transaction date globally to all the transactions in the group. Use the memorized transaction tool to save time and to remind you to pay those important recurring bills.

Depositing a Vendor Refund

On occasion, you might receive a refund from your vendor whom you previously paid. To add a vendor refund check to your bank deposit, follow these steps:

1. Create your deposit (normally done with customer invoice payments) as usual.

2. On the next available deposit line, choose one of two options:

   - If you do not have an open vendor credit in your Accounts Payable, enter the vendor name in the Received From column, and select the expense account you want to reduce in the From Account column.

   - If you do have an open vendor credit that you want to associate this refund with, enter the vendor name in the Received From column, and select the Accounts Payable account in the From Account column. Then apply the deposit to the open credit.

3. Enter an optional memo.

4. Enter the amount.

5. Click Save & Close when the total of the deposit agrees with the bank deposit total.

Although this method is quite easy to use, it does not allow you assign an item so any refund recorded this way will not be included in certain job cost reports that are prepared from the use of items.

Instead, you would create a vendor credit memo to record the reduction in a job cost, then follow the preceding instructions for applying the deposit to the open vendor credit.

Paying and Recording a Credit Card Bill

You have flexibility in how you choose to record and pay your credit card bills. The decision is based on your own circumstances because no one way is the right way.

Options for recording credit card expenses include the following:

- Enter a bill to the credit card vendor, summarizing the total charges on one bill and entering a separate line for each expense account amount.

- Enter individual credit card charges. From the menu bar, select Banking, Enter Credit Card Charges. You might be prompted to add a credit card account to QuickBooks.

- Use the QuickBooks Online Banking feature and automatically download your credit card charges and payments directly into your QuickBooks data file. Not all credit card providers offer this functionality. To see whether your card offers this option, select Banking, Online Banking, Participating Financial Institutions from the menu bar.

➡ *For more information, see "Online Banking Center," p. 449.*

Options for paying your credit card bill include the following:

- If you selected to enter a bill to your credit card vendor, simply pay the bill as you do other bills, paying it partially or in full.

- If you selected one of the other two options, you need to create a vendor bill or check and in the Account column of the transaction assign the Credit Card type account you previously recorded the transactions to. The vendor bill simply decreases the balance owed on the credit card liability account.

The cash basis Balance Sheet often shows this amount if it is not paid by the date you prepare your financials.

➡ *For more information about how QuickBooks handles certain accounts on a cash basis, see "Accounts Payable Balance on Cash Basis Balance Sheet," p. 222.*

Have you ever found that QuickBooks users will assign a different expense account each time they create a check or bill to pay for costs of the business? This can make reviewing your specific expenses for the business less accurate.

QuickBooks offers two choices with the Automatically Recall Information preference (select Edit, Preferences from the menu bar and select the General—My Preferences tab):

- **Automatically recall last transaction for this name**—will recall both the account and the previous amount.

- **Prefill accounts for vendor based on past entries**—will only recall the account(s) used and will not recall the amount.

A more efficient process is to assign up to three different default chart of accounts to each vendor record. To add these accounts, follow these steps:

1. From the Home page, click Vendors to open the Vendor Center.

2. Select the vendor to which you want to assign accounts, and click Edit Vendor to open the Edit Vendor dialog box.

3. Click OK to close the New Feature message if it displays.

4. Click the Account Prefill tab. In the fields provided, select the desired accounts from the drop-down list, as shown on Figure 7.7 in Chapter 7.

If you rarely use the additional accounts, you might want to consider adding them only when needed. All newly created transactions will include up to the three lines assigned. If these lines are not removed, they will lead to blank lines of data in many reports.

The selected accounts will override any preference setting for Recall or Prefill and will instead insert these accounts automatically on a Write Checks or Enter Bills transaction. This is just another method you will find to help you keep your accounting accurate.

SETTING UP CUSTOMERS

Introduction

It is not surprising to me and perhaps not to you either that the Accounts Receivable process is the most organized and "cared for" task in QuickBooks. The process of producing a customer invoice is completed quickly because you have to provide a document to a customer to get paid.

In this chapter, you will find useful information to help you:

- Customize and set important preferences

- Work with prospecting activities

- Set up customers, jobs, and supporting lists

In Chapter 10, you will find information useful for managing your customers by:

- Creating accounts receivable reports

- Troubleshooting accounts receivable issues

- Handling unique customer transactions

Whether you are a first-time QuickBooks user or you have been using the software for years, the details in this chapter will help you set up your customers correctly.

Customizing Home Page Customer Activities

QuickBooks makes performing customer activities easy with a customizable list of tasks on the Home page (see Figure 9.1).

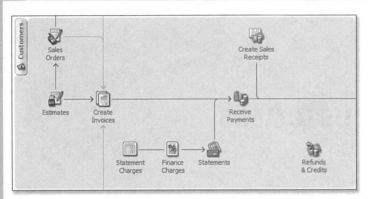

Figure 9.1
The Home page provides easy access to common customer activities.

Depending upon your version of QuickBooks, you can add or remove tasks from your Home page:

- **Sales Orders**—Commitment of a sale to a customer (QuickBooks Premier, Accountant, or Enterprise).

- **Estimates**—Providing customers with quotes for your product or service, and most importantly, provides the basis for Customer or Job budgets.

- **Sales Tax Tracking**—Collecting sales tax from your customers and remitting to the taxing authority.

> *For more information on customizing the Home page, refer to Chapter 2, "Getting Around QuickBooks."*

Details about the selected features that can be enabled or disabled on the Home page are discussed in the next section.

Preferences That Affect Accounts Receivable

You can simplify your Accounts Receivable tasks by setting certain QuickBooks preferences. Some of these preferences save you keystrokes, which can save data entry time.

Not every preference that affects Accounts Receivable impacts your financials. Some preferences enable specific features such as shown in Figure 9.2. To set preferences in QuickBooks, select Edit, Preferences from the menu bar, and choose the type of preference on the left side of the Preferences dialog box.

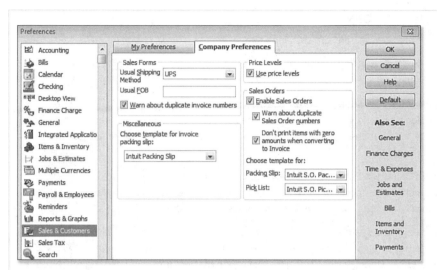

Figure 9.2
Preferences enable features and specific types of customer transactions.

Preferences in QuickBooks come in two forms:

- My Preferences are settings that are unique to the user logging into the data file and are not shared by other users.

- Company Preferences are settings that are common for all users. When a preference is modified on the Company Preferences tab of the Preferences dialog box, the change affects all users.

To set company preferences, open the file as the Admin or External Accountant user and switch to single-user mode (if you are using the data file in a multi-user environment).

The sections that follow outline the preference settings that will improve your QuickBooks Accounts Receivable workflow. There are many preferences that can help you work more efficiently in QuickBooks. Be sure to have each user log into QuickBooks with their user name and review all of the available preferences.

 caution

The Admin user is the default user that is created when your first start using QuickBooks. Proper controls should be in place to allow only certain individuals to log into the data file as the Admin user. For more information, see "Setting Up Users and Permissions," p. 38.

Payments

These preferences will help you with customer payment processing and improve your overall process for receiving money from customers. Select Edit, Preferences from the menu bar, and the Payments preference on the left side of the Preferences dialog box.

Company Preferences

Here are the specific preferences that are set for all users:

- **Receive Payments**—These settings make it easier for you to assign customer payments to the customers' invoices:

  - **Automatically Apply Payments**—When you select this option and record the receive payment transaction, QuickBooks applies the payment to an invoice of the same amount, or if no invoice amount matches the exact dollar amount the payment is applied to the oldest invoice first. See Figure 9.48.

  - **Automatically Calculate Payments**—When this option is selected, you do not need to put a total in the Amount box on the Receive Payments dialog box. QuickBooks calculates and pre-fills the amount as the sum total of each of the invoices marked as received.

  - **Use Undeposited Funds as a Default Deposit to Account**—When selected, this preference causes QuickBooks to place all customer payments into a current asset account that is created by QuickBooks. Undeposited Funds are like a safe that holds your customer payments before they are taken to the bank for deposit. When you record a make deposit transaction, QuickBooks will remove the funds from the Undeposited Funds account and place them in your bank account.

- **Invoice Payments**—After signing up for Intuit PaymentNetwork, your customers can pay your invoices online by ACH, or a debit to their bank account (similar to paying with a company check):

  - **Sign Up for Intuit PaymentNetwork**—Click Learn More to sign up for the Intuit PaymentNetwork service.

  - **Include Online Payment Link on Invoices**—Adds a payment web address to all invoices you email from QuickBooks. Select the Explain link to learn more.

  - **Include On Printed Invoices**—Adds a payment web address to invoices you print.

  - **Intuit PaymentNetwork Email**—Enter the email address you use (or plan to use) to sign into Intuit PaymentNetwork.

  - **Turn Off Online Payments**—This action turns links off for all invoices and all customers. If you resend a past invoice that included the link, the newly sent invoice will not include the online payment link.

My Preferences

There are no My Preferences for Payments settings.

Sales & Customers

These preference settings enable you to customize QuickBooks around the tasks you use to manage customer activities. You can also make it easier for your employees to do their daily tasks by customizing the Home page so the needed forms are available. Select Edit, Preferences from the menu bar, and Sales & Customers preference on the left side of the Preferences dialog box.

Company Preferences

Here are the specific preferences that are available for all users:

- **Sales Forms**—These settings enable you to set a default shipping method that will display on customer forms. You can also choose to be warned when duplicate invoice numbers are detected.

- **Miscellaneous**—A drop-down list allows you to select the default packing slip form.

- **Price Levels**—Click the Use Price Levels check box to enable the use of price levels. Price levels are assigned to your customers and automate unique customer pricing. An example might be using price levels to offer wholesale pricing to certain customers, while charging retail to others.

- **Sales Orders**—Available with QuickBooks Premier, Accountant, or QuickBooks Enterprise Solutions. Use sales orders to commit sales to customers and track backorders. Preferences include warning about duplicate sales order numbers, printing options for items with zero amounts. Choosing templates for Packing Slips and Pick List.

My Preferences

These settings affect the current logged-in user:

- **Add Available Time/Costs to Invoices for the Selected Job**—Determines how QuickBooks will prompt the logged-in user when unbilled costs exist for a Customer or Job, options include:

  - Prompt for time/costs to add

  - Don't add any

  - Ask what to do

- **Show Payment Toolbar on Receive Payment and Sales Receipt Forms**—This setting turns on or off the payments toolbar (see Figure 9.49). The payments toolbar provides links for signing up for credit card and eCheck processing.

Checking

The Checking Preferences are for defining specific bank accounts for sales-related activities, such as depositing a customer's payment into a predefined bank account. Select Edit, Preferences from the menu bar and then select the Checking preference on the left side of the Preferences dialog box.

Company Preferences

There are not any Checking Company Preferences that would affect your workflow for Accounts Receivable.

My Preferences

The Open the Make Deposits form preference is optional. Use this preference to specify the default bank account selected for making deposits. If you have multiple bank accounts you make deposits to, you might not want to set a default on this tab. When no preference is set, the first bank account on the list will default.

Finance Charge

Does your company charge late-paying customers finance charges on open balances? If so, you will want to set these preferences. Select Edit, Preferences from the menu bar and then select the Finance Charge preference on the left side of the Preferences dialog box.

Company Preferences

These preferences set your company's annual interest rate, minimum finance charge, grace period, and income account you want to credit.

The additional sub-settings for each preference will affect your financial reports and how much you want calculated for finance charges:

- **Annual Interest Rate (%)**—Enter the interest rate you want to use when calculating finance charges on late payments.

- **Minimum Finance Charge**—Enter a dollar amount that will be used as the minimum finance charge.

- **Grace Period (days)**—Used to calculate a grace period before finance charges apply.

- **Finance Charge Account**—Enter the account you will use to track the finance charges you collect from your customers. Typically you would select an income account type.

- **Assess Finance Charges on Overdue Finance Charges**—When selected, this option includes unpaid finance charge amounts previously invoiced in the new amount used to calculate additional late fees. It has been my experience that when you use this option, you become the "squeaky wheel" that gets paid.

- **Calculate Charges From**—The choices are Due Date or Invoice/Billed Date. For example, if you create an invoice for a customer for $1,000 that is due in 30 days, and you select the Calculate Charges From Due Date option, the amount is not considered overdue until 30 days from the invoice due date.

- **Mark Finance Charge Invoices "To Be Printed"**—If this option is not selected, you can send a statement to the customer at the end of your billing cycle to communicate the amounts that are owed instead of sending an invoice for the finance charges assessed.

My Preferences

There are no My Preferences for Finance Charge settings.

Jobs & Estimates

The preference settings found in this section enable certain accounts receivable transaction types in QuickBooks. Select Edit, Preferences from the menu bar and then select the Jobs & Estimates preference on the left side of the Preferences dialog box.

Company Preferences

These choices have to do with enabling specific estimating and invoicing features in QuickBooks as well as defining custom job status descriptions:

- **Job Status Descriptions**—You can choose to modify the job status descriptions, such as changing Not Awarded to Lost.

- **Do You Create Estimates?**—Selecting Yes will add an icon to the Home page for Estimates.

- **Do You Do Progress Invoicing?**—Selecting Yes will enable a dialog box when creating an invoice from an estimate. The dialog box includes the options to create an invoice for all, a percentage, or selected items from a multi-line estimate.

- **Warn About Duplicate Estimate Numbers**—Selecting this option provides good internal controls over your documents.

- **Don't Print Items That Have Zero Amount**—Useful when creating a progress invoice with many lines. This selection is available if you selected Yes to the Progress Invoicing option.

My Preferences

There are no My Preferences for Jobs & Estimates.

Reminders

The Reminders preferences can be useful if you want QuickBooks to prompt you when certain accounts receivable tasks are due. Select Edit, Preferences from the menu bar and then select the Reminders preference on the left side of the Preferences dialog box.

Company Preferences

The Company Preferences for Reminders, as shown in Figure 9.3, determines how QuickBooks shows reminders. Options include Summary, List, or Don't Remind Me. Accounts Receivable reminders include Invoices/Credit Memos to Print, Overdue Invoices, Almost Due Invoices, and other customer activity–related reminders.

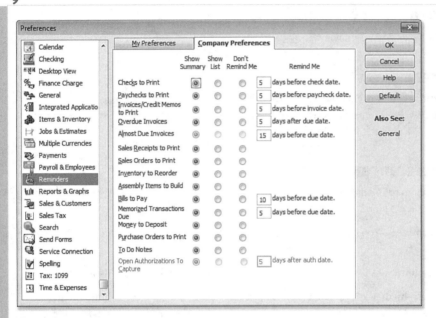

Figure 9.3
The selections on the Company Preferences tab determine how QuickBooks reminds all users.

My Preferences

Users can specify whether they want to see the reminders when they open the QuickBooks data file. Regardless of this setting, users can select Company, Reminders from the menu bar at any time to review the reminder list contents.

Reports & Graphs

Review the Personal preferences and Company preferences for working with reports and graphs. The defaults set here can be overridden at the time a particular report is prepared. Select Edit, Preferences from the menu bar and then select the Reports & Graphs preference on the left side of the Preferences dialog box.

Company Preferences

Review each of the listed preferences; they will often affect how certain accounts receivable reports will calculate:

- **Summary Report Basis**—Although this setting affects many reports in QuickBooks, Accounts Receivable reports can only be prepared on the accrual basis.

- **Aging Reports**—This option sets the default for calculating overdue invoices. You can choose to age from due date or from transaction date. Typically, aging from transaction date causes invoices to show as overdue earlier than if you aged from due date.

■ **Format**—This option enables you to override the default header, footer, and font for all QuickBooks reports. You should not override the Report Title, Subtitle, or Date Prepared because QuickBooks will accurately fill in this information for you each time you prepare a report.

■ **Reports - Show Accounts By**—This setting offers you the following options for displaying reports:

   ■ **Name Only**—Reports display the name and account number (if the preference to enable account numbers is selected).

   ■ **Description Only**—Reports display the description typed in the New or Edit Account dialog box (see Figure 9.4). No account numbers are displayed on the reports.

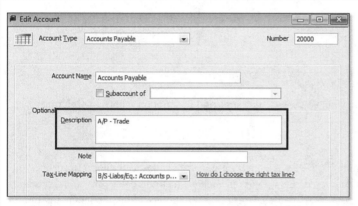

Figure 9.4
Enter an optional description on the New or Edit Account dialog box; reports can display this description.

   ■ **Name and Description**—Reports display the account number (if enabled in preferences), the name, and the description as typed in the New Account or Edit Account dialog box in parentheses (see Figure 9.5).

■ **Classify Cash**—If you will be preparing a cash flow statement, QuickBooks uses these settings to determine which accounts are considered Operating, Investing, or Financing. This preference does not specifically relate to accounts receivable.

My Preferences

The My Preferences selections include:

■ **Prompt Me to Modify Report**—Selecting this opens the Modify Report dialog box with each created report. (This action is the same as selecting Customize Report from a displayed report.)

■ **Reports & Graphs**—Refresh options for reports and graphs when data changes. These prompt the user to refresh or not to refresh.

■ **Graphs Only**—Specific display settings when preparing graphs.

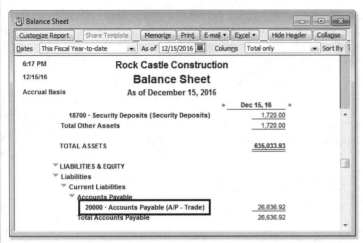

Figure 9.5
Reports show the additional description when you select the Name and Description reporting preference.

Sales Tax

The Sales Tax preference shown in Figure 9.6 is important if your business is required to collect sales tax on sales made to your customers. Be sure to research each state's sales tax regulations so you can comply with the laws and avoid penalties. Select Edit, Preferences from the menu bar and then select the Sales Tax preference on the left side of the Preferences dialog box.

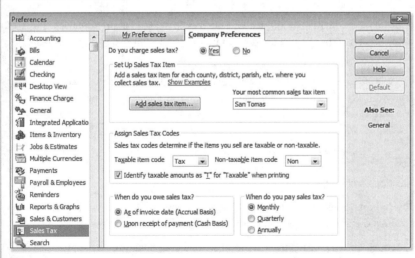

Figure 9.6
Use these Company Preferences to configure Sales Tax defaults in QuickBooks.

Company Preferences

To enable sales tax tracking, select Yes next to the Do You Charge Sales Tax? field. Additionally, complete the following selections:

- **Set Up Sales Tax Item**—When you click the Add Sales Tax Item button, QuickBooks opens the New Item dialog box with the Sales Tax item type selected. Here, you will define a name for the sales tax item, type a description, rate, and assign the tax agency you will be remitting the collected tax to. A separate drop-down list allows you to select your most common sales tax item.

- **Assign Sales Tax Codes**—This is the name of the code that will be assigned to your product or service items. Usually the default of Tax and Non are considered appropriate. You can select to have a "T" print on your customer invoices for items that are taxable. This option is useful if on one invoice you sell both taxable and nontaxable items.

- **When Do You Owe Sales Tax?**—If you are not sure what each state department of revenue requires, review their websites or call to get the correct information.

- **When Do You Pay Sales Tax?**—This setting tells QuickBooks what date range to select automatically when paying your sales tax. For example, if you select Monthly, QuickBooks will compute the amount owed for the previous month in the Pay Sales Tax Liability dialog box.

My Preferences

There are no My Preferences for Sales Tax.

Send Forms

For sending forms, users have the option to use Web Mail, Outlook, or QuickBooks E-mail. Select Edit, Preferences from the menu bar and then select the Send Forms preference on the left side of the Preferences dialog box.

Company Preferences

This preference, as shown in Figure 9.7, enables you to set email defaults including a default message when sending supported forms or reports. Select the different forms from the Change Default For drop-down list. Click the Spelling button to check your template content for spelling errors.

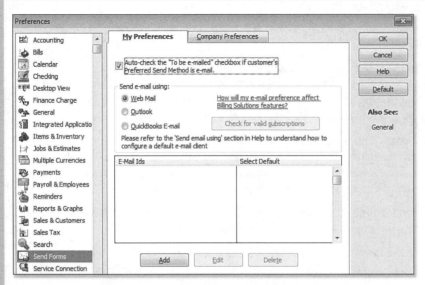

Figure 9.7
QuickBooks provides multiple choices for using email to send reports or forms.

My Preferences

These settings affect the current logged-in user:

- **Auto-Check The "To Be E-Mailed"…**—If enabled QuickBooks will automatically select the "To Be E-Mailed" checkbox on newly created invoices.

- **Send E-mail Using**—You can select your preferred method for sending transactions and reports:

  - Web Mail

  - Outlook

  - QuickBooks Email (Using Billing Solutions)

QuickBooks users can use Outlook, Outlook Express, other web-based email (such as Gmail or Hotmail), or the QuickBooks email server as the preferred method for sending reports and transactions from within QuickBooks. If you select Outlook, however, your preference can affect certain Billing Solutions features. Click the link to learn more or from the Help menu type "billing solutions" in the search box.

Spelling

This preference determines how QuickBooks assists you with spelling on accounts receivable transactions. Select Edit, Preferences from the menu bar and then select the Spelling preference on the left side of the Preferences dialog box.

Company Preferences

There are no Company Preferences for the Spelling Preference.

My Preferences

Users can set QuickBooks spelling preferences for sales and purchase transactions and include custom-added spelling words.

Time & Expenses

Time & Expenses is a specific method of invoicing common to the professional services industry, where customers' sales are invoiced based on hours or costs of the project plus an agreed-to markup and/or overhead fee. Select Edit, Preferences from the menu bar and then select the Time & Expenses preference on the left side of the Preferences dialog box.

Company Preferences

If your company needs to provide customers with an invoice showing your individual costs plus an added markup, enable this preference (see Figure 9.8) by selecting from the following:

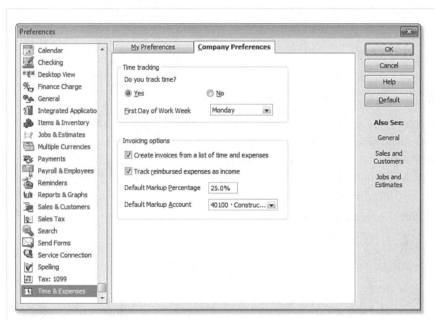

Figure 9.8
Enable these preferences if your company tracks time or bills customers for reimbursement of costs.

■ **Time Tracking**—Select Yes for Do You Track Time? to enable time recording on timesheets, which can be transferred to payment transactions and customer invoices. You can also define the first day of the work week here.

■ **Invoicing Options**—Includes the following:

   ■ **Create Invoices from a List of Time and Expenses**—Select Yes for Do You Track Time? to enable time recording on timesheets, which can be transferred from payment transactions to customer invoices. This is useful when your company will be including on a customer's invoice amounts paid to vendors, employees, or payees on the Other Names list.

   ■ **Track Reimbursed Expenses as Income**—Select this checkbox if you want to track costs invoiced to customers as income. An example might be a law firm that charges the customer for costs incurred for shipping charges and wishes to show the amount as income. The income would be offset by the expense, usually in an overhead expense account.

   ■ **Default Markup Percentage**—Option to define a percentage to add to the customer's invoice when billing for time and costs. An example would be including a 10% markup adding $10.00 to a $100.00 cost reimbursement invoice.

   ■ **Default Markup Account**—Option to select a default account (typically an Income category) for tracking all amounts charged to the customer as markup.

My Preferences

There is no My Preferences for the Time & Expenses settings.

Working with the Customer Center

Are you new to using QuickBooks? I expect one of the first lists you have already added to in QuickBooks is the customer list. You might have imported your customers while creating your new file using the Express Start.

The Customer Center (see Figure 9.9) provides one location for viewing contact details and accessing many customer tasks and reports including:

■ Create a new or edit an existing Customer or Job.

■ Access the Add Multiple Customers:Jobs feature.

■ Record commonly used customer transactions.

■ Print the Customer & Job list, information, or transactions.

■ Export the Customer list or transactions as an Excel or CSV file; import or paste customers from Excel.

■ Prepare customer letters and customize the built-in letter templates.

■ Access the Collections Center.

- Filter your list of customers to include All Customers, Active Customers, Customer's with Open, Overdue, or Almost Due Balances, or a custom filter of your choice.

- Attach documents to the customer record, such as a copy of a signed agreement.

- Access a map and driving directions to the Customer or Job location.

- Add or edit customer notes and to do reminders.

- View and filter transactions by customer or by transaction type.

- Prepare a QuickReport, Open Balance Report for the currently selected customer.

- Show Estimates and Customer Snapshot for the currently selected customer.

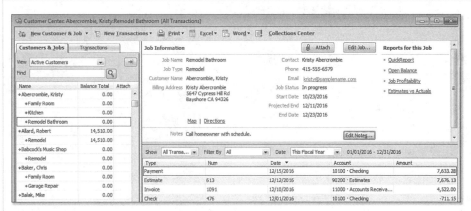

Figure 9.9
From the Customer Center, you can access most customer activities and useful reports.

The following sections will provide more details about creating a Customer or Job and using the Customer Center for researching transactions. The Customer Center provides quick access to common customer tasks and reporting.

Adding or Modifying Customers and Jobs

Customers are the individuals or businesses that you sell your product or service to. QuickBooks can also track a job for customer, in the event you want to track the profitability for different projects for the same customer. For example, if you're renovating a house, you might create a job for each room. Or an attorney might track the revenue and costs for individual legal matters for the same customer.

Creating jobs is not required in QuickBooks, but is helpful when you have multiple projects for a single customer. This section offers instructions specific for setting up customers and jobs of customers.

Creating a Customer and Job Record

To practice adding a new customer record and assigning a job to that customer, open the sample data file as instructed in Chapter 1. If you are working in your own file, use these instructions to begin entering your customers you sell your product or service to:

1. Click the Customers button on the Home page, or select Customers, Customer Center from the menu bar.

2. From the New Customer & Job drop-down list, select New Customer.

3. If necessary, click OK to close the New Feature message. To learn more about adding multiple customer records, see "Add/Edit Multiple Lists," p. 90.

4. The New Customer dialog box displays (see Figure 9.10). Type **ABE's Diner** in the Customer Name field. It is important to mention that no two names from any of the lists in QuickBooks can be the same.

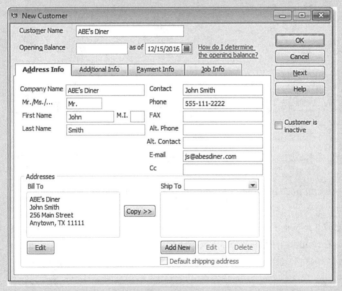

Figure 9.10
Completing the contact information for your customer is good practice for your record keeping.

5. Leave the Opening Balance field blank. To learn more about entering opening balances in QuickBooks, see Chapter 3, "Accounting 101." If you are a new business, the amounts your customer will owe you will be recorded using the accounts receivable transactions detailed in this chapter.

6. The As Of (date) field supports the Opening Balance field and has no effect when no dollar value is entered in the Opening Balance field.

7. Complete the remaining fields for this practice by adding the contact information and address. Consider completing the salutation, first name, and last name fields. Doing so enables you to send professional-looking letters to your customers in the future.

8. Click the Additional Info tab. If working in the practice file, select Commercial from the Type field, or select Add New to create your own customer type. Many sales reports can be filtered by customer type.

9. From the Terms drop-down list, select Net 30 for this new customer. This instructs QuickBooks to calculate due dates that are 30 days from your invoice dates. Use the Add New choice to create terms that suit your specific needs.

10. Leave the Rep field blank for this exercise. In your own data, you can select the Rep field if you will be tracking sales by Rep.

11. Although optional, the Preferred Send Method allows you to determine whether QuickBooks automatically selects the To Be Emailed or To Be Printed checkboxes when you create new accounts receivable transactions.

12. Accept the defaulted Sales Tax Information. Or, if you are working in your own file, modify the information as needed.

13. For this exercise, leave the Price Level field blank.

14. For this exercise, leave the custom fields blank. When working with your data you can select the Define Fields button and add custom fields you can assign to your Customer, Vendor, or Employee records. These custom fields can also be added to your sales transactions and included in many reports.

15. From the Payment Info tab, complete the following:

    • **Account No.**—This field can be added to the customer transactions.

    • **Credit Limit**—Enter a value here to be informed when a transaction will exceed the stated credit limit.

    • **Preferred Payment Method**—Select Check for this sample exercise. This option allows you to store credit card information in your own data, or indicate that a customer typically pays by cash or check.

    • **Online Payments**—Use this option to determine whether a link for making an online payment displays on the customer's invoices. Using this feature requires an Intuit Merchant account for accepting online payments by credit card, or an Intuit PaymentNetwork account for accepting online payments by business check.

16. Select the Job Info tab. For this exercise, leave the Job Status information blank. In your own file, if you are tracking project activity at the customer level, complete the fields as needed. Some of the job profitability reports can be filtered by these fields.

17. Click OK to close the New Customer dialog box. You will be returned to the Customer Center and ABE's Diner will be selected.

18. From the New Customer & Job drop-down list, select Add Job.

19. If necessary, click OK to dismiss the New Feature message referenced in step 3.

20. Type **Kitchen Remodel** for the Job Name. Complete any other fields as desired on each of the New Job tabs.

21. Click OK to add this job record to the ABE's Diner customer record. You will be returned to the Customer Center and Kitchen Remodel will appear beneath ABE's Diner, as shown in Figure 9.11.

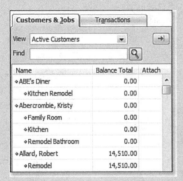

Figure 9.11
Create jobs to track costs and revenue for multiple projects for the same customer.

---

 tip

If you begin typing the name of your customer or job in the Company Name field, QuickBooks will populate the Customer Name and Bill To name field.

---

caution

Specifying terms is part of the process for managing your accounts receivable balances. You will also want to review the Reporting—Company Preferences tab on the Preferences dialog box for settings that affect A/R Aging reports. You can select to have the A/R Aging or Detail reports age from the invoice due date or age from invoice transaction date.

Now that you have created a new customer in the sample file, you are prepared to create a list of your own customers. When your customers address or contact information changes, you can return to the Customer Center to edit the same information.

Finding Customer Transactions

The Customer Center provides access for adding to or modifying your customer or job records in QuickBooks, but also includes convenient access to finding customer transactions.

With the Customer Center open, select a customer or job with your cursor. With a customer or job selected, individual transactions assigned to that customer or job display on the right. Earlier in Figure 9.9, the job Remodel Bathroom for customer Abercrombie, Kristy is selected and to the right are individual transactions for that job.

You can filter the resulting transactions by selecting options in the Show, Filter By, and Date drop-down lists. The options available will differ depending on the type of transaction being filter for.

In Figure 9.12, the options available for filtering include customer transactions. Your transaction types might differ from the displayed types if you do not have the related feature enabled in preferences. The only transaction type that can have a customer or job record assigned that is not included in these options is the Make Journal Entry.

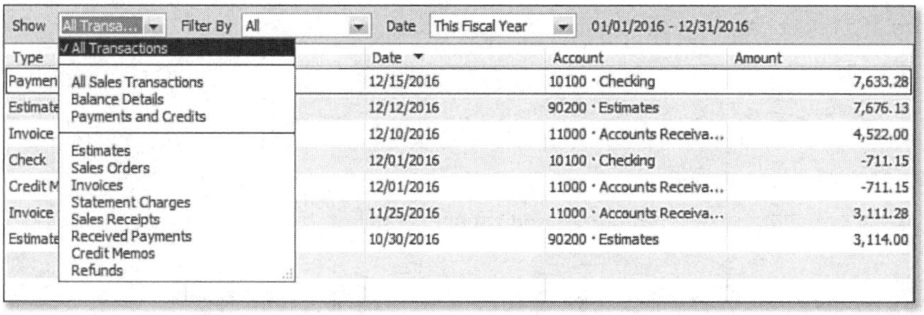

Figure 9.12
Conveniently filter for specific transactions types and dates for the selected customer.

Another useful feature of working with the Customer Center is available on the Transactions tab. On the Transactions tab, you can locate similar transaction types for all customers.

To do so, follow these steps:

1. From the Customer Center, click the Transactions tab.

2. Select the Estimates type as shown in Figure 9.13.

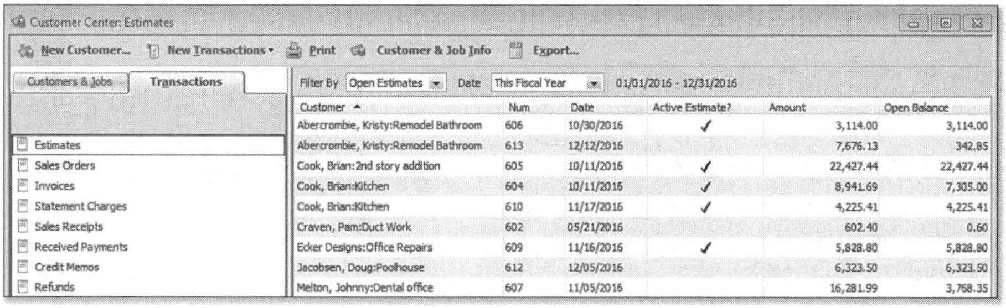

Figure 9.13
Use the Transactions tab of the Customer Center to find like transaction types.

3. From the Filter By drop-down list, select Open Estimates.

4. Optionally, filter for a specific date range.

5. Click any column header to sort the data by that column.

6. Double-click any transaction to open the selected transaction. Click Save & Close to return to the Transactions tab details.

7. Click the Print button to print the listed transactions. Click OK to close the Transaction Report message. Click Print to print the list of transactions or click Cancel to return to the Customer Center's Transactions tab.

8. Optionally, click the Customer & Job Info. If necessary, click OK to close the New Feature message. QuickBooks displays the Edit Customer or Job dialog box for the selected customer or job. Click OK to close and be returned to the Customer Center:Estimates listing.

9. Click the Excel button to export the list of transactions to an Excel worksheet or CSV file format.

The Customer Center provides a single location from which you can create or modify your customer records or research customer transactions.

In the next section, you will learn about managing your prospects using the Lead Center.

Working with Prospects in the Lead Center

New for QuickBooks 2012 is the Lead Center to help you keep track of your business prospecting activities. From the menu bar, select Customers, Lead Center to open the Lead Center (see Figure 9.14).

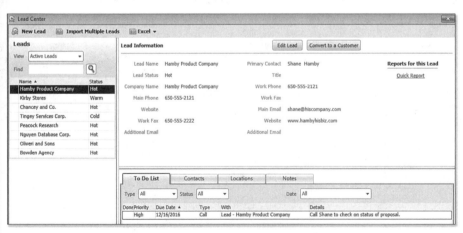

Figure 9.14
Keep track of prospect contacts and activities in the Lead Center.

From the Lead Center, you can click the following buttons:

- **New Lead**—Enter a single new lead.

- **Import Multiple Leads**—Using a preformatted grid you can enter multiple leads row by row, or copy and paste from an existing Excel worksheet.

- **Excel**—Export a Lead Contact List, Lead Status List, or a list of Converted Leads (those leads that become customers).

Creating a New Lead

To practice creating a new lead record, open the sample data file as instructed in Chapter 1, "Getting Started with QuickBooks." You might also use these instructions if you are getting started with lead management in your own data file:

1. In the Lead Center, click New Lead.
2. In the Name field enter your own name.
3. Complete the remaining fields on the Company and Contacts tab.
4. Optionally, add additional locations or contacts for this new lead.
5. Click OK to complete adding the lead.
6. With the lead selected on the left, click the To Do button on the To Do List to add a new reminder activity. See Figure 9.15. These To Do activities will be included in your calendar reminders. See Chapter 18, "Using Other Planning and Management Tools."

Figure 9.15
Stay organized with your prospecting activities by adding To Do's to the lead record.

7. Click any header column to sort the data by that column.

8. Click the Contacts, Locations, or Notes tab to view additional information about your lead.

9. Continue adding a few more leads using any of the mentioned methods.

10. In this exercise, select a lead from the list and click Convert to Customer. QuickBooks creates a new customer record from the details in the Lead Center.

11. The lead is no longer listed in the Lead Center. Open the Customer Center to view the new customer record.

Use the new Lead Center to track important business prospecting activities and save time when creating customer records from your lead base.

Setting Up Sales Tax

In QuickBooks you can collect and remit sales tax on behalf of governmental authorities. To do so, you need to establish sales tax items and codes. You might also need to create sales tax groups.

Creating Sales Tax Items

Sales tax items are used to identify specific rates charged to your customers and the tax authority vendor to which you remit the sales tax. You might have one sales tax item, or several, on your item list.

tip

Each state has different requirements and rates for reporting sales tax. It is critical you research the applicable regulations and set up QuickBooks correctly. Otherwise your business could be subjected to expensive—and avoidable—penalties.

To create a sales tax item in your data file, follow these steps:

1. From the menu bar, select Lists, Item List.

2. From the Item drop-down list, select New to open the New Item dialog box.

3. If necessary, click OK to close the New Feature message. The Add/Edit Multiple List Entries feature does not include the ability to add or edit sales tax items.

4. Choose Sales Tax Item in the Type drop-down list, as shown in Figure 9.16.

5. Enter a sales tax name for the sales tax item; the name should identify the applicable jurisdiction (see Figure 9.17).

6. Enter a Description you want printed on the customer's invoice.

7. In the Tax Rate (%) box, enter the rate the taxing authority charges.

8. From the Tax Agency (vendor you collect for) drop-down list, select the vendor to which you remit your sales tax payments. If your vendor is not set up in QuickBooks, select Add New at the top of the list to create a sales tax vendor record.

9. Click OK to save the sales tax item.

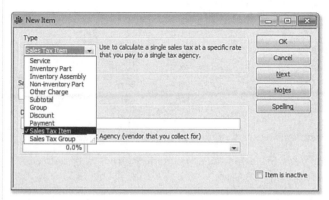

Figure 9.16
Sales tax is properly calculated and tracked in QuickBooks when you use the Sales Tax Item type.

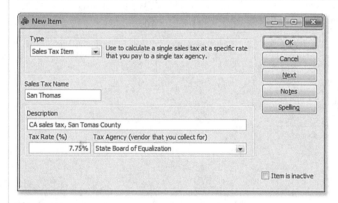

Figure 9.17
Setting up your sales tax item with the proper rate and vendor ensures you collect and remit sales taxes correctly.

With sales tax items created, you can group them into sales tax groups if the state requires collection and reporting on multiple tax entities.

Creating Sales Tax Group Items

Sales tax groups are optional in QuickBooks. In many states, you are required to report the collection of sales tax for a combination of city, county, and state, but you want to show the customer a single tax rate. In QuickBooks, you can accomplish this by first creating your individual city, county, and state sales tax items, and then assigning them to a Sales Tax Group item type. The Sales Tax Group item is then assigned to the customer.

CHAPTER 9

To create a Sales Tax Group item in your data file, follow these steps:

1. From the menu bar, select Lists, Item List.

2. From the Item drop-down list, select New to open the New Item dialog box. If necessary, click OK to close the New Feature message.

3. Select Sales Tax Group item from the Type drop-down list.

4. Enter a Group Name or Number that identifies the group.

5. In the Description box, enter the description you want printed on the customer's invoice.

6. In the Tax Item column, from the drop-down list, select the appropriate city, county, or state sales tax items previously created (refer to Figure 9.17).

7. Click OK to save the new Sales Tax Group item.

In the example shown in Figure 9.18, you are going to collect and remit the sales tax at a rate of 8.05%. In this example, part of the payment will be made to the State Board of Equalization and the other portion will be paid to the City of East Bayshore. However, when this tax group is assigned to a customer, the invoice will show a single rate of 8.05%.

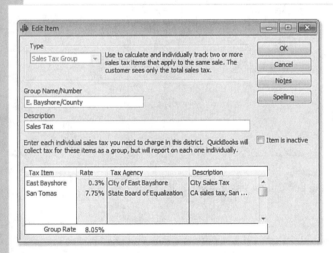

Figure 9.18
Use sales tax groups to track multiple taxes, but show one tax rate on a customer's invoice.

Creating Sales Tax Codes

The primary purpose of sales tax codes in QuickBooks is to identify a product or service as taxable or non-taxable and identify a customer as taxable or non-taxable. If you track sales tax, you must have at least one taxable code but might have multiple non-taxable tax codes.

Another use of sales tax codes is for when the state has reporting requirements on the types of non-taxable sales you make. Creating a unique non-taxable sales code for each of these non-taxable sales types enables you to report the total sales by non-taxable sales tax type.

Examples of non-taxable tax codes might include some or all of the following:

- Non-taxable reseller

- Out-of-state sales

- Sale to a nonprofit organization

- Government entity

To see a list of suggested non-taxable tax codes, select Help from the drop-down list to the right of the search box on the icon bar. Type "sales tax code" and select the Non-taxable sales tax codes examples topic. QuickBooks will provide a list of commonly used sales tax codes. See Figure 9.19 for a sample sales tax code list.

Figure 9.19
Sales Tax Codes are assigned to your customers and help with reporting requirements by your taxing authority.

When creating a customer invoice and before charging sales tax to the customer, QuickBooks determines whether the item being sold is taxable and whether the customer is assigned a taxable or non-taxable sales tax code before computing any sales tax charge on an invoice.

To create a sales tax code list or edit the existing sales tax codes in your data file, follow these steps:

1. Make sure you have enabled the sales tax preference as discussed earlier in this chapter.

2. From the menu bar, select Lists, Sales Tax Code List.

3. From the Sales Tax Code drop-down list, select New to create a new code. Alternatively, select a sales tax code from the list and then select Edit Sales Tax Code from the Sales Tax Code drop-down list. (Note that a new QuickBooks data file defaults with one taxable tax code and one non-taxable tax code.)

4. In the New Sales Tax dialog box (or Edit Sales Tax dialog box), enter a three-character code in the Sales Tax Code field. Make the three-character code something meaningful. You will see this code on the following dialog boxes: a New Item, Edit Item, New Customer, or Edit Customer; and optionally, on the lines of the customer's invoice.

In the next section, you will complete the process, and assign the appropriate code to your customer record.

Assigning Sales Tax Codes to Products or Services

Items are created in QuickBooks for use on sales and purchase transactions. The primary purpose of creating items is to handle the behind-the-scenes accounting and to assign the taxable status for an item on a customer invoice.

The following items in QuickBooks enable you to assign a taxable code, as shown in Figure 9.20:

- Service Item

- Inventory Part

- Inventory Assembly

- Non-inventory Part

- Other Charge

- Discount

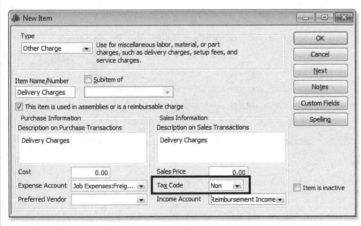

Figure 9.20
When an item is set up with a Tax Code, no tax will be calculated even if the customer is taxable.

If you expect to charge sales tax on an item, it should be marked as taxable even if it is sold to a non-taxable customer. QuickBooks will validate whether an item is taxable and then verifies the customer is taxable before it charges sales tax.

If the item is always non-taxable, even if it is sold to a taxable customer (for example, labor), it should be assigned a non-taxable sales tax code so it will never have sales tax calculated on the sale of that item.

 note

Items are typically assigned a generic taxable or non-taxable sales tax code. You might create other sales tax codes for resellers or out-of-state sales, which you will assign to customers, but not items.

Some states require the sale of labor services to be taxed if they are invoiced with products and not taxed if they are invoiced separately. Although this might not be the requirement for the state jurisdictions you sell in, to handle this situation, create two Labor Service type items—one named Taxable Labor and assigned a taxable tax code, and another named Non-Taxable Labor and assigned a non-taxable tax code. You can then select the appropriate item when you invoice your customers.

Assigning Sales Tax Codes and Sales Tax Items to Customers

Enabling the sales tax preference and creating sales tax items, groups, and codes are part of the sales tax setup. You also need to assign a tax code and a tax item to each customer.

To assign or edit an existing customer's tax code (as well as tax item), as shown in Figure 9.21, follow these steps:

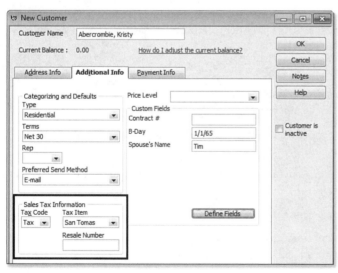

Figure 9.21
Assign the proper sales tax code and sales tax item to each of your customers.

1. On the Home page, click the Customers button to open the Customer Center.

2. Select the customer for whom you want to assign or edit a tax code.

3. If necessary, click OK to close the New Feature message.

4. Click the Edit Customer button.

5. In the Edit Customer dialog box, click the Additional Info tab.

6. Select the appropriate Tax Code and Tax Item from the drop-down lists in the Sales Tax Information box.

Creating Price Level Lists

Each time you sell a product or service to a customer with an assigned price level, QuickBooks defaults the sales price to match the price level. (This feature is available in the QuickBooks Premier, Accountant, or Enterprise Solutions editions.) The price level assigned to a customer affects all sales to the customer for the selected item(s). Price levels cannot be based on discounts earned from buying a product in bulk.

To create a price level, follow these steps:

1. From the menu bar, select Lists, Price Level List. After creating the price level, assign the price level to the appropriate customers.

2. Calculate the price level using one of two methods:

   - **Fixed Percentage Price Levels**—An example would be to create a Price Level that will award that customer a 10% discount on all purchases.

   - **Per Item Price Levels**—You might have preferred customers who get a specific rate for a particular item.

3. To assign a price level to a customer, from the Customer Center select a customer list item on the left.

4. Click the Edit Customer button and choose the Additional Info tab.

5. From the Price Level drop-down list, select the proper price level to assign to this customer. You can assign one price level per customer. Refer to Figure 9.21.

Price levels automate the pricing adjustments you have negotiated with your customers. You might instead consider using a discount item. With a discount item your customer can see the original price for the product or service and the discount that you provided.

 caution

You can assign one tax code and one tax item to each customer. You cannot assign a tax code or tax item to a job. If you have a customer with multiple locations and you are required to charge different sales tax rates for each location, you need to create a unique customer for each location.

The sales tax code defines the customer as taxable or not. The sales tax item defines the rate to be charged to the customer.

Because QuickBooks enables you to save a customer record without one or both of these settings, be sure to review your customer sales tax list often to ensure your sales tax is assigned to each of your customers.

Creating Payment Terms

QuickBooks terms offer a shortened description and calculate on an invoice when you expect to receive payment from a customer or when a vendor expects to receive payment from you. For example, 1% 10 Net 30 is an expression for payment due in 30 days, 1% discount if paid within 10 days.

Creating a Payment Term

To practice creating a payment term, open the sample data file as instructed in Chapter 1, "Getting Started with QuickBooks." You might also use these instructions if you are creating a new payment term in your own data file:

1. From the menu bar, select Lists, Customer & Vendor Profile Lists, Terms List. A list of terms displays, as shown in Figure 9.22.

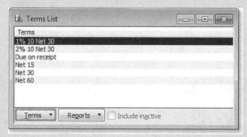

Figure 9.22
Terms lists can be used on customer and vendor transactions.

2. From the Terms drop-down list, select New. The New Terms dialog box displays (see Figure 9.23).

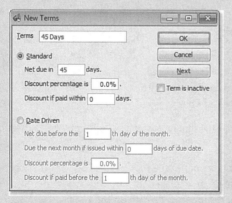

Figure 9.23
Complete all of the fields when creating a new payment term.

3. In the Terms field, type **45 Days**.

4. Select the Standard option and type **45** in the Net due in field.

5. Click OK. You are returned to the Terms List.

6. Optionally, click the Reports button and then select QuickReport to prepare a report of transactions using the selected term.

7. You can now assign this term to customer and vendor transactions.

Customizing QuickBooks Forms

You can customize most forms in QuickBooks, such as sales orders and customer invoices. Customization options include:

- **Overall Design**—Includes how the form looks, if the form has a design imprint or if field titles are shaded as well as other format options.

- **Data Fields**—Customizing the data layout on a form.

Using the Customize My Forms Wizard

To create a consistent look and feel for your printed forms, consider using the Intuit—Customize My Forms wizard. This feature is free for the first 30 days for each QuickBooks data file. After 30 days, if you need to make changes to a design the fee is $4.99 per design. Any changes you pay for come with a 60-day satisfaction guarantee.

In just a few simple steps, you can add a professional look to all of the QuickBooks forms.

To customize QuickBooks forms, follow these steps:

1. From the menu bar, select Lists, Templates. A list of current templates displays. You can also access this tool from an open dialog box, by selecting the Customize button at the top of the dialog box (such as from the Create Invoices dialog box).

2. In the lower-left corner of the displayed Templates dialog box, click the Templates button. Choose the Create Form Design menu option.

3. The QuickBooks Forms Customization dialog box opens (see Figure 9.24). An Internet connection is required. Choose a background that is specific to your business from the Industry drop-down list. As you select a background the resulting design is displayed on the right.

4. Click the Add button under Company Logo to browse for your logo file. If you do not have a company logo, click the Need a Logo? Get Started button. Intuit has partnered with 99designs to offer very affordable custom made design services.

 note

If you would like to "practice" using this tool before committing the changes to your own forms, use the Rock Castle Construction file as instructed in Chapter 1.

Using the sample data you will not be able to save the design or apply it to your own data's QuickBooks forms.

Figure 9.24
Add a professional look to your business forms.

5. Click Next to display Step 2—Colors and Fonts as shown in Figure 9.25. Select your font and grid colors overall, or for specific fields by clicking the appropriate drop-down list. A gray-out field indicates the data for that field does not exist in your QuickBooks data file. Optionally, place a checkmark in the box to indicate you mail your invoices in window envelopes. Click Next.

6. Step 3—Select a Grid Style displays. Click to select a shaded style grid of your choice. Click Next.

7. Step 4—Review Design displays. Click the Back button to make changes. Click Continue to select the forms to assign the design to. Click No Thanks to cancel your changes. You are redirected to a website that displays matching business forms.

8. The Apply Design dialog box displays (see Figure 9.26). Place a checkmark next to each of the forms to which you want to apply the customized design. You can select from the many QuickBooks forms (Invoice, Sales Receipt, Purchase Order, and so on), making it easy to customize several forms all at once!

 note

I used this Intuit design service to create the logo displayed on my website, www.quick-training.com.

 note

If you are prompted for payment to apply the designs to your forms, this indicates that you have previously used the initial free service. After a period of time, the service is available but requires a minimal fee.

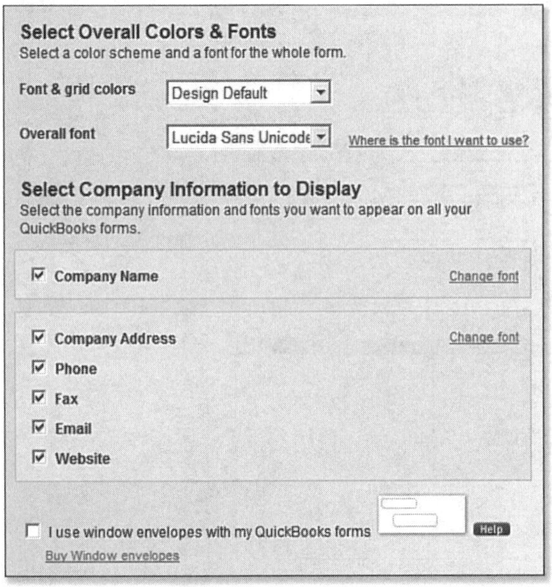

Select Overall Colors & Fonts
Select a color scheme and a font for the whole form.
Font & grid colors
Design Default
Overall font
Lucida Sans Unicode
Where is the font I want to use?
Select Company Information to Display
Select the company information and fonts you want to appear on all your QuickBooks forms.
Company Name
Change font
Company Address
Change font
Phone
Fax
Email
Website
I use window envelopes with my QuickBooks forms
Help
Buy Window envelopes

Figure 9.25
Select font and grid colors and other design options for your customized forms.

Apply Design
When you click Apply, QuickBooks will:
• Make copies of the template you select, then
• Apply your design to the copies
(Don't worry, your original templates won't change.)
Form
Template
Invoice
Intuit Product Invoice (default)
Credit Memo
Custom Credit Memo (default)
Sales Receipt
Custom Sales Receipt (default)
Purchase Order
Custom Purchase Order (default)
Stmt Charge
Intuit Standard Statement (default)
Estimate
Retail Estimate (default)
Sales Order
Custom Sales Order (default)
Select All
Clear All
Show All Templates
Design Preview
Apply
Cancel

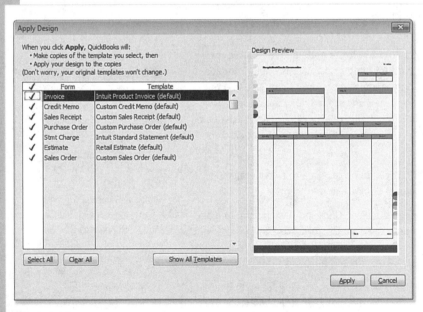

Figure 9.26
Apply the design customization to multiple forms all at once.

9. Click Apply and the Design Applied dialog box displays with instructions for identifying your customized templates on the Templates list. After reading the details, click OK to close the message.

10. The Save Design Online dialog box displays with these options:

   - Click Save the Design for Future Editing; you will be prompted to define a name for the design and to create a secure login for future editing. A message displays showing the date the form was customized and the last day to make changes without an additional fee. Click OK to close.

   - Click No Thanks if you do not want to save the design. A warning message displays; click OK to close and you are redirected to a website showing other business items that match your customized style. Close the open web pages when completed reviewing the information.

11. The Intuit Business Forms web page displays. Click the X in the top-right corner to close the web page when you complete your review of the information.

Using the Customize Data Layout Tool

Use the Customize Data Layout tool to create a new template or edit the layout and design of an existing invoice, purchase order, or other template. One distinct difference from the method taught previously is the changes you make now are only for the currently selected form. If you want to make changes to the format for multiple forms at one time, use the method discussed in the previous section.

Creating an Invoice Template

In this exercise you are going to create a new invoice template using the sample data as instructed in Chapter 1. Your selection options might differ depending on the version of QuickBooks you are using and if you are using using a different sample data file:

1. From menu bar, select Lists, Templates.

2. From the Templates drop-down list, select New.

3. In the Select Template Type dialog box, choose the Invoice type. Click OK.

   The Basic Customization dialog box displays.

4. Click Manage Templates. QuickBooks shows a preview of the form and allows you to provide a Template Name. If you are practicing, you might want to name the template Test Invoice Template. If you are creating a new template for your own file, enter a name of your choosing. For your own data, if you have multiple invoice templates, type a descriptive name.

5. Click OK to return to the Basic Customization dialog box.

6. Optionally, select any of the following:

   • **Use Logo**—Browse for your logo image file to attach to the form. QuickBooks will copy the logo to a folder that resides in the same location as your QuickBooks data file.

   • **Select Color Scheme and Apply Color Scheme**—Alter the color of borders and header fonts.

   • **Change Font For and Change Font**—Select a data field and choose the Change Font to change the font for that specific field.

   • **Company & Transaction Information and Update Information**—Click to select the fields you wish to display on your form and then select the Update Information button.

7. If you added any fields to your form, you might be prompted with a Layout Designer message. For this exercise, click OK to dismiss the message.

8. Click Print Preview to take a closer look at the changes.

9. If you'd like even more control over your form, click Additional Customization. See Figure 9.27. Modify the following for your newly designed invoice form. View the changes as they are made in the image to the right.

Figure 9.27
Customize your forms for which fields to display and print.

   • **Header**—Each field selection offers the option to view on the screen, print on the invoice, and add a title.

   • **Columns**—Each field offers the option to select which columns appear onscreen and in print, and in what order. Accept the default title or assign a new title to each field. See Figure 9.28.

- **Prog Cols**—If you have enabled Estimates or Sales Orders, these fields allow you to select which columns appear onscreen or in print, and in what order. Accept the default title or type a new title in the field.

- **Footer**—These fields allow you to manage the data that appears at the bottom of forms onscreen and in print. Accept the default title or assign a new title to the field. Optionally, select to include a long text disclaimer on your invoice and to include the Intuit PaymentNetwork link on printed invoices.

- **Print**—Settings for managing the printing of the invoice, adding page numbers, and an option to print trailing zeros.

Figure 9.28
For your customized forms, define the order of the displayed and printed fields.

10. Click Layout Designer, shown in Figure 9.29. Use the layout designer to

   - Modify the properties for the selected field's font, text, border, and background.

   - Add a text box, data field, or image.

   - Copy or remove a field.

   - Use the Copy Format button to apply formatting from one field to others. Click End Format to turn off this feature.

   - Make multiple fields the same height, width, or size by holding down the Ctrl key on your keyboard while selecting the desired fields.

   - Click Center to place a selected field in the center of the form.

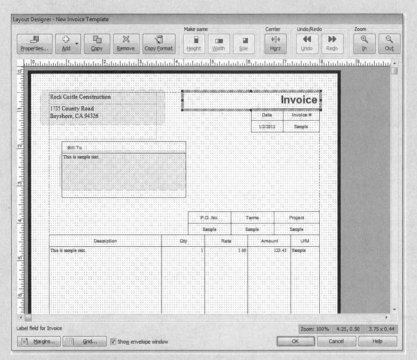

Figure 9.29
Use the Layout Designer to rearrange the fields or modify the attributes of the field.

11. Click Undo or Redo as needed.

12. Use the Zoom In or Out buttons to see the detail more closely.

13. Click the Margins button to set the margins for the form. Click OK to close.

14. Click the Grid button for various options related to the grid. Click OK to close.

15. If you use window envelopes, click Show Envelope to determine if your address is positioned correctly.

16. Click OK to save your changes, or select Cancel or Help. Select Yes to the Layout Designer message and to be returned to the Additional Customization dialog box.

17. Click OK to close the Additional Customization window. Click OK to close the Basic Customization dialog box.

The newly created or modified invoice form can be used when preparing an invoice for your customers.

tip

To download ready-made forms, select Lists, Templates from the menu bar. In the Templates dialog box, select the Templates button and select Download Templates. Click OK to the optional message that you will need an Internet connection for the download.

QuickBooks directs you to the QuickBooks Community Forms library, where you can download pre-made custom invoice forms as well as other types of forms.

Accounts Receivable Process

Within QuickBooks, you have some flexibility in how you handle your company's receivables workflow. Your company might use some or all of the forms listed in this chapter, depending on the product or service that you sell.

In the section titled "Preferences That Affect Accounts Receivable" in this chapter, I discussed the preferences you can define after you determine what sales transaction type or feature you need.

Table 9.1 details the transactions that are used in the Accounts Receivable module and their primary purpose.

Table 9.1   Accounts Receivable Transactions

Transaction Types	Primary Purpose
Estimates	Create a job budget and proposal
Sales Orders	Record a committed sale
Invoices	Record the sale of services or products on account
Sales Receipt	Record the sale of services or products COD (Cash at the time of sale)
Receive Payment	Record customer payment of invoices
Online Payments	Download online customer payments (requires a monthly subscription)
Record Deposits	Recording the bank account deposit
Statement Charges	Assessing customers' recurring charges
Finance Charges	Assessed to customers with a past-due balance
Statements	Periodic statement provided to the customer of account activity
Refunds & Credits	Returns or credits given to customers

So whether you start with an estimate, sales order, or prepare an invoice for a customer, the proper workflow for recording a sale has some or all of these steps:

1. Optionally, create a quote using an estimate. Estimates are useful if you will be providing a quote or multiple quotes for a prospect. Estimates not won can be marked as inactive.

2. Optionally, create a sales order. Sales orders are best when you have a commitment for sale to a customer, but you cannot fulfill it at the time the order comes in. Sales orders can be created directly from an estimate.

3. Prepare an invoice, sales receipt, or statement charge. The invoice transaction can be created directly from the estimate or sales order.

4. Receive the customer payment into an Undeposited Funds account.

5. Record the deposit into your bank account.

Performing these related tasks in QuickBooks is easy from the Home page, as shown in Figure 9.1. Whether you are new to QuickBooks or are an experienced user, you will find the Home page useful in getting around QuickBooks and in determining what the next transaction process should be.

What I have noticed over the years of consulting with clients is that many do not know the proper Accounts Receivable process. By following a recommended workflow, some of the more common errors can be avoided rather than having to be fixed at a later date.

Using QuickBooks Estimates

Use a QuickBooks estimate to provide prospects a quote for your product or services. The estimate will help you keep track of the sales price you have quoted. In accounting terms, the estimate is considered "non-posting," which means when you record an estimate you are not yet recording revenue.

Estimates also provide the means for QuickBooks to prepare a budget (expected costs and revenue) for a customer or job. There are many job costing reports that use the estimate details. You can view these reports using the sample data referred to in Chapter 1. From the Reports menu, select Jobs, Time & Mileage, and view the Job Estimates vs. Actuals Summary or Detail (to name just a couple).

Creating an Estimate

To practice creating a new estimate, open the sample data file as instructed in Chapter 1. If you are using your own data file, make sure you have enabled estimates as discussed in the preferences sections of this chapter:

1. On the Home page, click the Estimates icon. The Create Estimates dialog box displays (see Figure 9.30).

2. From the Customer:Job drop-down list, select the Remodel job for the customer Allard, Robert.

3. Leave Estimate Active selected. Select Remodel for the Class field.

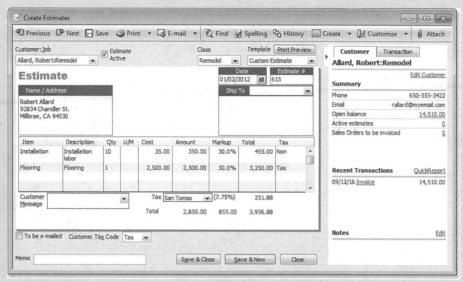

Figure 9.30
Use estimates to track your projected job costs and to save time creating invoices to the customer.

4. For this exercise, leave the prefilled values in the Template, Date, Estimate #, and Name/Address fields.

5. Click the first field in the Item column and use Installation. Accept the prefilled description.

6. In the Qty field, type **10**.

7. Leave the U/M (Unit of Measure) field blank.

8. Accept the Cost field default of $35.00.

9. In the Markup field, type **30%**.

10. In the Item column on the next available row, select the non-inventory part, Flooring.

11. In the Qty field, type **1**.

12. Leave the U/M (Unit of Measure) field blank.

13. In the Cost field, type **2,500.00**.

14. In the Markup field, type **30%**.

15. Click Save & Close to complete the estimate, or Save & New to practice creating another estimate.

note

When the Estimate Active checkbox is selected, QuickBooks will display this estimate in drop-down lists, such as creating an invoice from an estimate. You can also filter reports on the Estimate Active field.

 caution

If you want the markup to be % over cost, you must also type the percentage (%) character. To charge a fixed dollar amount over cost, type the dollar amount.

If you do not include anything in the Markup column, QuickBooks job budget vs. cost reports will consider the amount in the Cost column the same as the Total which is, in effect, the Sales Price. Best practice is to include a markup % or amount.

You now have an estimate and can track the quote you have provided to your prospect. When your prospect becomes a customer, create the invoice from the estimate.

Estimates can also be used to create Sales Orders referred to in the next section.

Using QuickBooks Sales Orders

Sales orders are used to record the sale of products you do not have in stock or services you have scheduled to provide at some future date. Sales orders are perfect for tracking "back orders." Sales Orders are not available with QuickBooks Pro, but are included with all other editions of the QuickBooks for Windows desktop products.

You can start with a blank sales order, of if you created an estimate, you can create the sales order from the estimate.

The Sales & Customers—Company Preferences tab on the Edit Preferences dialog box offers settings you can adjust, which will make working with Sales Orders more efficient for your business.

 For instructions on creating Sales Orders, see "Handling Inventory Backorders," p. 152.

Creating Customer Invoices

If my guess is correct, this is one of the first sections of the book you have turned to. My clients typically are quick to get an invoice to a customer for payment for the product or service being sold.

This section provides some basic instruction in using multiple forms of invoicing in QuickBooks. You might even learn some new techniques.

Basic Invoice

QuickBooks makes it easy to prepare and send invoices to your customers. A basic invoice might contain a single line, or many lines, depending upon the nature of the products and services you provide.

Creating an Invoice

To practice creating an invoice, open the sample data file as instructed in Chapter 1. You might also use these instructions if you are creating an invoice for your own customers:

1. On the Home page, click the Create Invoices icon. Depending on the sales and customer preferences you have enabled, you might have to select Create Invoices from the drop-down list next to the Invoices icon. See Figure 9.31.

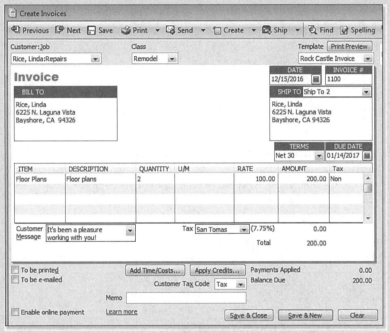

Figure 9.31
Creating a basic invoice is simple using QuickBooks.

2. Select the Repairs job for Rice, Linda.

3. Select Remodel in the Class field.

4. Leave the prefilled Template, Date, Invoice #, Bill To, and Ship To details. If you are working in your own data, optionally choose a different template.

5. Select the Floor Plans item in the Item column.

6. Accept the prefilled description.

7. In the Quantity field, type **2**.

8. In the Rate field, type **100.00**. QuickBooks did not include a rate because the item record did not have a value recorded in the Sales Price field. QuickBooks automatically calculates the row total.

   The item used, Floor Plans, is a non-taxable item (per the original setup of this item) even though the customer is taxable.

9. To preview this invoice, click Save at the top of the Create Invoices dialog box.

10. From the Print drop-down list, select Preview. Optionally, click the Zoom In button to see more details.

11. Click Close to return to the Create Invoices dialog box.

12. Click Save & Close if you are completed with this task or click Save & New to practice creating another invoice.

 tip

When entering data you can use common keyboard shortcuts to complete transactions. For this exercise, start typing Rice in the Customer:Job field and the customer Rice, Linda displays.

Without leaving the field, press the Ctrl key while you tap the down arrow key to navigate through the list from that point forward.

When you have the proper job selected, use the Tab key to advance to the next field.

Do you routinely add multiple items to your invoices? QuickBooks Enterprise Solutions 12.0 (all editions) includes the ability to select multiple items (see Figure 9.32) in one easy, searchable window. For learning more about the differences between QuickBooks Pro, Premier, or Enterprise Solutions, see the author's website: www.quick-training.com.

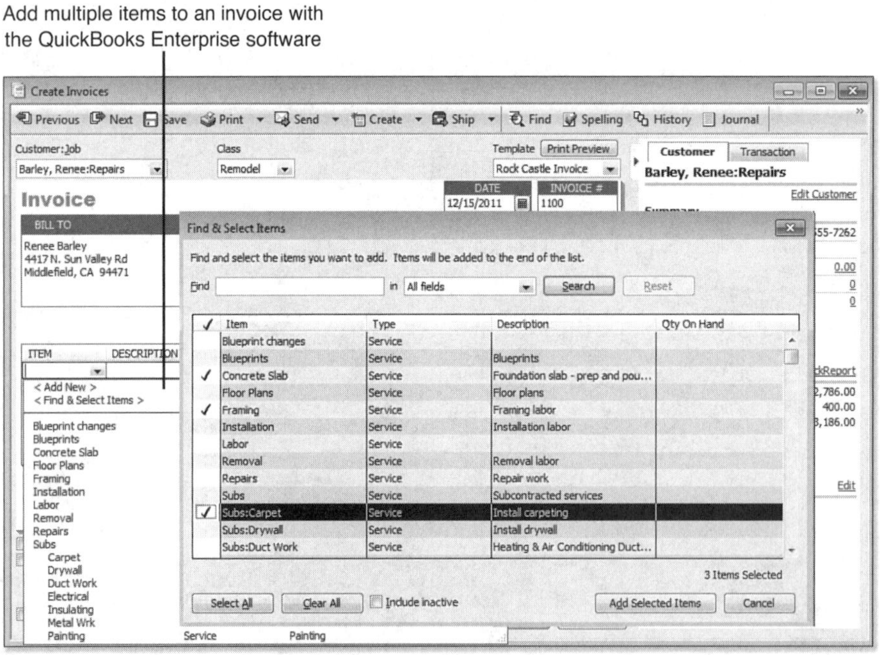

Add multiple items to an invoice with
the QuickBooks Enterprise software

Figure 9.32
QuickBooks Enterprise includes the ability to quickly add multiple items to an invoice.

Batch Invoicing

Do you issue recurring invoices to a group of customers for:

- Same service or product item?
- Same price?
- Same billing frequency?
- Same invoice template?

If you answered yes to each of these questions, you will save time invoicing using the QuickBooks Batch Invoicing feature.

There are three basic steps when working with Batch Invoicing:

1. Creating your billing group involves naming the group, and then assigning customers and/or jobs.

2. Selecting the line items and rates for the batch invoices.

3. Reviewing the list of invoices to be prepared.

Using Batch Invoicing

To practice using Batch Invoicing, open the sample data file as instructed in Chapter 1. You might also use these instructions if you are creating Batch Invoicing with your own data:

1. From the menu bar, select Customers, Create Batch Invoices.

2. If the warning message "Is Your Customer Info Set Up Correctly" displays, read the information provided. Your success with using Batch Invoicing is dependent on how well your customer records are set up. The message refers to the following fields that should be defined for each customer before creating invoices using the Batch Invoicing feature:

    - Customer payment terms
    - Customer sales tax rates
    - Customer and Job preferred send method

3. Click OK to dismiss the message for this practice.

4. The Batch Invoice dialog box displays. Click the Billing Group drop-down list, and select Add New.

5. Type **Monthly** in the Group Name field, and then click Save. Or, if you are creating a Billing Group in your own data, provide a name that is meaningful to your business. Click Save.

6. In the Search Results box, which displays all active jobs, select a few jobs of your choice. In this example, three jobs were selected as displayed in Figure 9.33. Notice you can Search for a specific list of customers or choose Select All or Clear All for ease in setting up your Billing Group.

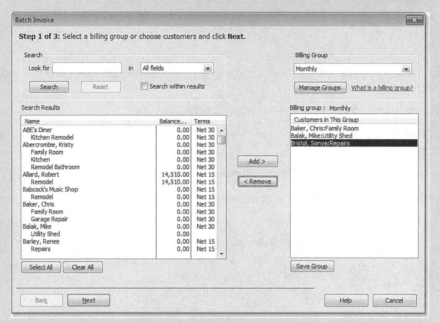

Figure 9.33
When creating a Billing Group select the Customers or Customer:Jobs you want to issue a recurring invoice to.

7. Click Save Group. You can return to this dialog box at any time to modify the list of customers or jobs included.

8. Click Next. Step 2 of 3 displays as shown in Figure 9.34. Leave the Rock Castle invoice template selected. If you are working in your own data, select the invoice template you want to use.

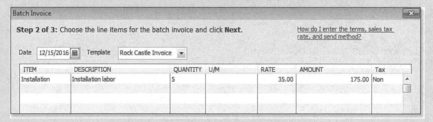

Figure 9.34
Batch invoices share the same item, description, quantity, rate, and tax status.

9. In the Item column, select Installation.

10. In the Quantity column, type 5.

11. Leave the U/M (Unit of Measure) blank.

12. Leave the prefilled rate of $35.00 as was originally stored with the item record. QuickBooks calculates the Amount field and assigns the Tax status recorded with the item record.

13. Optionally, select or add a new Customer Message.

14. Click Next. Step 3 of 3 displays as shown in Figure 9.35. Deselect any customers or jobs you don't want to invoice.

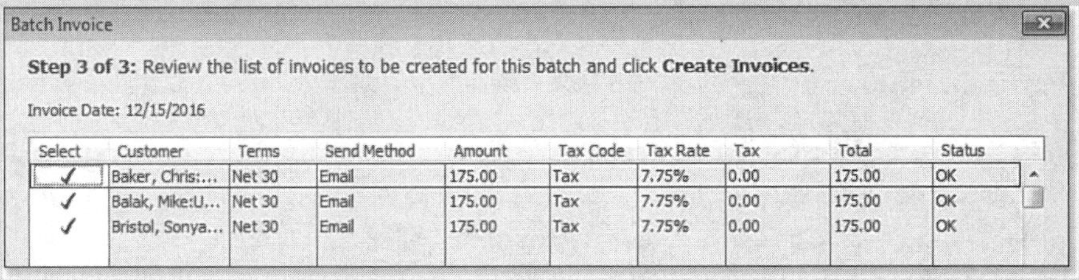

Select	Customer	Terms	Send Method	Amount	Tax Code	Tax Rate	Tax	Total	Status
✓	Baker, Chris:...	Net 30	Email	175.00	Tax	7.75%	0.00	175.00	OK
✓	Balak, Mike:U...	Net 30	Email	175.00	Tax	7.75%	0.00	175.00	OK
✓	Bristol, Sonya...	Net 30	Email	175.00	Tax	7.75%	0.00	175.00	OK

Batch Invoice

Step 3 of 3: Review the list of invoices to be created for this batch and click **Create Invoices**.

Invoice Date: 12/15/2016

Figure 9.35
Review the listed terms, send method, and tax settings before creating the invoices.

15. Click Create Invoices when you are ready. If any of the fields displayed are blank or show incorrect information, click Cancel. Update the corresponding customer records and then return to the Batch Invoicing menu to complete the steps listed here.

16. Once you click Create Invoices, the Batch Summary dialog box displays. Here, you can print or email the newly created invoices. If a Preferred Send method was not indicated in the Customer or Job record, the invoice will be included in the unmarked total.

You might be asking, what if my customers have different items or rates, but on a recurring basis? The next section details using Memorized Invoice transactions when Batch Invoicing won't meet your specific needs.

Memorized Transaction Group

Memorized transactions offer a recurring invoice alternative to Batch Invoicing. With Memorized Transactions you can assign different items or prices to each customer, yet still create a group of invoices all at once.

When working with a memorized group you need to

1. Create a memorized group.

2. Define the frequency of the recurring transactions.

3. Assign memorized transactions to the group.

Creating Memorized Transactions

To practice using a Memorized Transaction Group of customer invoices, open the sample data file as instructed in Chapter 1. This practice will build on the exercise completed in the section titled "Basic Invoicing":

1. From the menu bar, select Lists, Memorized Transaction List.

2. From the Memorized Transaction drop-down list, select New Group.

3. Type a group name. In this practice, type **Monthly**. See Figure 9.36.

Figure 9.36
Create the Memorized Transaction Group first.

4. Choose Monthly from the How Often drop-down list.

5. For this exercise, you can accept the date that QuickBooks prefills in the Next Date field, or assign a different date if you are using your own data.

6. Click OK to close the New Memorized Transaction Group message. You are returned to the Memorized Transaction List and your newly created Group name is in bold text.

   Next you will add a previously recorded invoice to your memorized group.

7. On the icon bar, click the Invoice icon.

8. From the top left of the Create Invoices dialog box, select Previous. A recorded invoice is displayed. Alternatively, create a new invoice from scratch.

9. From the Create drop-down list at the top of the invoice, select Memorize Transaction.

10. In the Name field, type a descriptive name such as the customer or job name on the invoice. When creating a memorized transaction (see Figure 9.37) in your own data file, type a name that will be helpful for you to identify the transaction in a group.

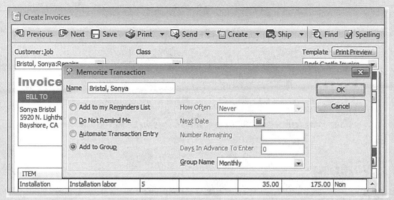

Figure 9.37
Click the Create drop-down list on the invoice and choose to Memorize Transaction.

11. Click to select Add To Group and then select your newly created group from the Group Name drop-down list.

12. Click OK.

13. Return to the Memorized Transaction List (see Figure 9.38) to see your memorized transaction.

Figure 9.38
The Memorized Transaction Group name will be in bold text, with the invoices assigned indented to the right.

14. To process this recurring memorized transaction list, double-click the group name, Monthly.

15. QuickBooks prefills the Date. Alternatively, choose an invoice date.

16. Click OK and QuickBooks creates the invoices. Click OK to close the message indicating that the transactions in the group were entered (see the tip that follows these steps).

note

Use your mouse cursor on the sides or corners of the Memorized Transaction list to expand the information, or click the top right box (next to the X) to expand the list contents.

tip

Do you need to print or email your newly created forms? Select File, Print Forms, or Send Forms and follow the instructions.

Progress Invoicing

The Progress Invoicing feature allows you to generate multiple invoices from a single estimate. To use progress invoicing you must first enable the preference on the Jobs & Estimates—Company Preferences tab of the Preferences dialog box. (You must log into the file as the Admin or External Accountant User type.)

Certain industries you do business with might require the work performed or products being made are invoiced in stages of completion. This method of invoicing is often referred to as percentage of completion. Conversely, you would not need to use Progress Invoicing in cases where you present a single invoice at point of delivery or project completion.

Creating a Progress Invoice

To practice creating a progress invoice for a customer, open the sample data file as instructed in Chapter 1. If you are working in your own data, the company preferences for progress invoicing must be enabled on the Jobs & Estimates—Company Preferences tab of the Preferences dialog box.

This practice exercise will continue with the estimate created earlier:

1. On the icon bar, click the Invoice icon to open the Create Invoices dialog box.

2. From the Customer:Job drop-down list, select the Allard, Robert:Remodel customer.

3. Select the estimate in the Available Estimates dialog box. The selected row will be shaded black as shown in Figure 9.39.

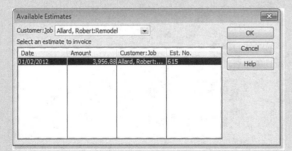

Figure 9.39
Select the Estimate you want to use for creating the progress invoice.

4. Click OK and QuickBooks displays a Create Progress Invoice Based on Estimate message.

5. For this exercise, select Create Invoice for selected items or for different percentages of each item and then click OK. You might also want to familiarize yourself with the other options. See Figure 9.40. Click OK.

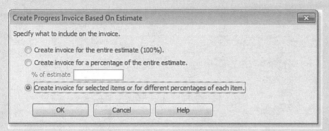

Figure 9.40
When progress invoicing is enabled, you can choose from these options when creating an invoice.

QuickBooks opens the Specify Invoice Amounts for Items on Estimate dialog box.

6. Toggle the Show Quantity and Rate and Show Percentage options to see how the transaction changes. For this exercise, remove the checkmark next to Show Percentage.

7. In the Qty column for Installation, type **9**. In the same column for Flooring, enter **.50** (invoicing for 50% of the materials). Figure 9.41 displays the result of entering these values.

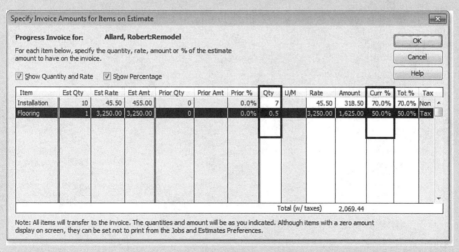

Figure 9.41
Enter either a Qty or a percent in the Curr % column to add line items to the customer's progress invoice.

8. Review the dollar total by row displayed in the Amount column.

9. When you click OK, QuickBooks adds the items to your invoice.

10. From the top-right corner of the invoice, select the Progress Invoice template from the Template drop-down list (see Figure 9.42).

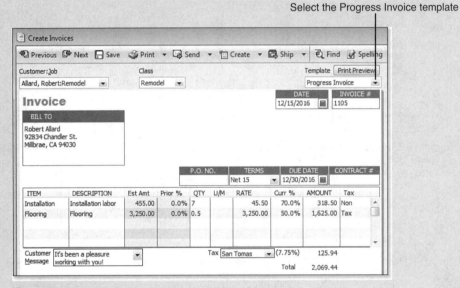

Select the Progress Invoice template

Figure 9.42
The Progress Invoice template includes columns for Estimate Amount and Prior Percentage invoiced.

11. For this exercise, click Save & New to practice creating a second invoice. A blank Create Invoice dialog box displays.

12. Repeat steps 2–4.

13. On the Create Progress Invoice Based on Estimate dialog box, select Create an Invoice for the Remaining Amounts of the Estimate. Click OK.

14. QuickBooks prepares the transaction. Click the arrow next to the Print button, and then select Preview to see the completed invoice.

15. Click Close to return to the Create Invoices dialog box. Click Save & Close.

 caution

Are you tracking inventory in your QuickBooks data file? Be careful to only progressively bill whole increments of inventory part items, such as 3 wheels, rather than 2.5 wheels.

If instead, you are trying to create a printable document to record a customer's deposit or pre-payment, use the instructions in Chapter 10 in the section titled "Unique Customer Transactions."

caution

If the Est Amt and Prior % columns do not appear on your invoice, confirm that you have selected the Progress Invoice template.

Time and Expense Invoicing

Time and Expense invoicing allows you to charge your customers the costs you incur on their behalf plus an agreed-upon markup (to cover for overhead costs and profit).

The Time and Expenses feature is available in QuickBooks Pro, Premier (all editions), Accountant, and QuickBooks Enterprise Solutions (all editions). You can enable this feature on the Time & Expenses—Company Preferences tab of the Preferences dialog box.

Before you begin creating a Time and Expense invoice you must first have billable charges for your customer. The Write Checks, Enter Bills, and Make General Journal Entries transactions can all have costs selected as billable as shown in Figure 9.43.

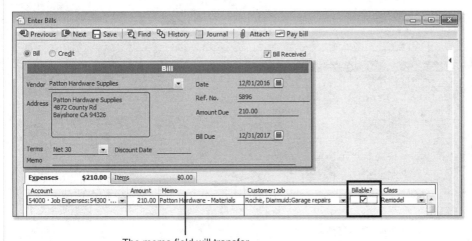

The memo field will transfer
to the customer's invoice

Figure 9.43
When creating a customer or job related expense place a checkmark in the Billable column if you need to add the charge to a future customer invoice.

You can review the costs marked as billable by selecting Reports, Jobs, Time & Mileage, Unbilled Costs by Job from the menu bar.

 note

It is not necessary to add or remove the checkmark in the billable column if you are not providing your customers a Time and Expense invoice.

Creating a Time and Expense Invoice

To practice creating a Time and Expense invoice, open the sample data file as instructed in Chapter 1. You might also use these instructions if you are creating a Time and Expense invoice for your own customers:

1. On the Home page, select Invoice for Time & Expenses from the drop-down list next to the Invoices icon. This menu option is only available if you have enabled the Create Invoices from a List of Time and Expense option on the Time & Expenses—Company Preferences tab of the Preferences dialog box.

2. If necessary, close Choose Multiple Customers to Invoice for Time and Expenses by clicking OK.

3. The Invoice for Time & Expenses dialog box displays. Select a Date Range. For this practice exercise, accept the prefilled To Date of 12/15/2016 as shown in Figure 9.44.

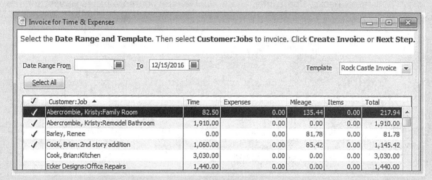

Figure 9.44
Invoice multiple customers in a batch after enabling the preference to create invoices from a list of time and expenses.

4. In the sample company, select the Rock Castle Invoice template, or select a template from your data that suits your needs.

5. Optionally, click any header column to sort the list.

6. For this exercise, place a checkmark next to the Abercrombie, Kristy:Family Room.

7. Select the Let Me Select Specific Billables for This Customer:Job checkbox at the bottom of the dialog box.

8. Click Create Invoice. QuickBooks displays the Choose Billable Time and Costs dialog box. From here, you can view expenses marked billable from the following tabs:

   - **Time**—Employees time from paychecks, click the Options button to see choices for transferring employee time to the customer's invoice. Click OK to return to the Choose Billable Time and Costs dialog box.

   - **Expenses**—Costs from the Expense tab of a write check, vendor bill, or journal entry.

   - **Mileage**—Costs recorded using the menu Company, Enter Vehicle Mileage.

   - **Items**—Costs from the Items tab of a write check or vendor bill.

9. From the Time tab, place a checkmark in the first column next to the time entry for Gregg O. Schneider. Or, optionally, click Select All for this practice. In your own data, you can choose which costs you want to include on the customer's invoice.

10. Click OK; QuickBooks transfers the charges you selected to the invoice. The Description on the invoice will default from the item record, or the memo field included in most expense transactions (see Figure 9.43).

11. Click Save & Close. QuickBooks replaces the Billable checkmark on the originating expenses transactions with an invoice icon. This indicates the cost has been included on a customer invoice.

 note

The Choose Billable Time and Costs dialog box enables you to review the expenses invoiced to your customer. You can then click the Hide column at the right to indicate you won't be invoicing the customer for certain charges.

Choosing to Hide an expense does not remove the expense from your own records; instead it will be excluded from this or future Time and Expense invoices.

Do you invoice your customers for the services of vendors or employees? If necessary, you can create billing rate levels you associate with your vendors and/or employees. In turn QuickBooks applies the proper billing rate when you add charges to an invoice. See Figure 9.45.

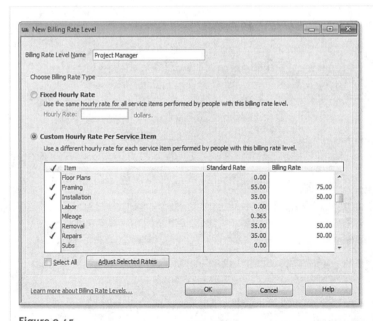

Figure 9.45
Billing Rate Levels are assigned to vendors, customers, and the other names list, and defaults the sales price for a person when time is tracked to specific service items.

To use billing rates, follow these steps:

1. Create your service items.

2. Create your billing rate levels.

3. Assign each billing rate level to vendors, employees, or other names as needed.

4. Invoice your customers using Add Time/Costs. QuickBooks will use the corresponding billing rate you have assigned.

Use Time and Expense invoicing when you are permitted to add a markup to job expenses.

Recording a Sales Receipt

Use a QuickBooks Sales Receipt when you are recording a sale and taking payment at the time of sale, commonly referred to as "Cash on Delivery" or COD. Recording a sales receipt does not increase Accounts Receivable because you are receiving payment at the time of sale.

QuickBooks Sales Receipts can be added or removed from the Home page on the Desktop View—Company Preferences tab of the Preferences dialog box. To change this preference you need to log into the file as the Admin or External Accountant User.

Sales receipts are a perfect choice for a company that does not offer terms to their customers. Some retail establishments might summarize the day's cash register tally into a Sales Receipt for a generic customer named "Daily Sales."

Creating a Sales Receipt

To practice creating a sales receipt, open the sample data file as instructed in Chapter 1. You might also use these instructions if you are creating a sales receipt in your own data:

1. On the Home page, click the Create Sales Receipts icon. The Enter Sales Receipts dialog displays as shown in Figure 9.46.

2. From the Customer:Job drop-down list, select Sage, Robert:Remodel job.

3. In the Class field, select Remodel.

4. For this exercise, leave the Template, Date, and Sale No. as prefilled by QuickBooks.

5. In the Check No. field, type **1234**. From the Payment Method drop-down list, select Check.

6. In the Item column, select Repairs.

7. Using the Tab key on your keyboard, advance to the Qty field and type **5**.

8. Optionally, select a Customer Message.

9. For this exercise, click Save. From the Print drop-down list, you can preview, print, or choose from other useful commands.

10. Click Save & Close to complete the Sales Receipt or Save & New to practice creating another one.

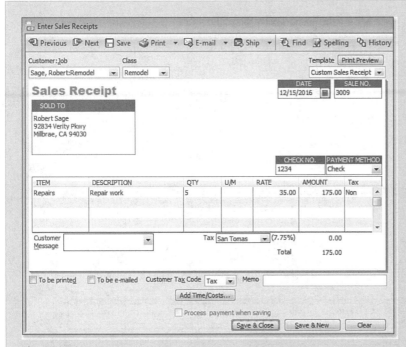

Figure 9.46
Enter sales receipts when payment is collected at the time of sale.

You might be asking where did the money go that I just recorded go in my accounting records? First, you will want to review your Payments preference as discussed earlier in this chapter and then learn how to add these payments to a bank deposit in the section "Making the Bank Deposit."

Recording a Statement Charge

Statement charges are useful if you want to accumulate charges before requesting payment, or if you assess a regular monthly charge to your customer. Use statement charges when you are not going to be providing the customer with an invoice, but instead will provide the customer with a periodic statement.

Recording a Statement Charge

To practice recording a statement charge, open the sample data file as instructed in Chapter 1:

1. On the Home page, click the Statement Charges icon.
2. From the Customer:Job drop-down list, select the Babcock's Music Shop:Remodel job.
3. For this exercise, place your cursor in the next available row and accept the prefilled date.
4. In the Item field, select Repairs.
5. In the Qty field, type **8**. See Figure 9.47.
6. In the Class field, select Remodel.

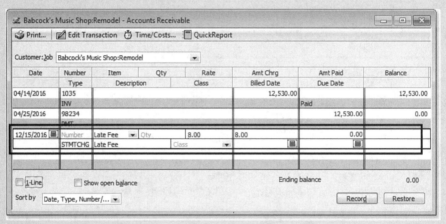

Figure 9.47
Use statement charges for a customer or job when you are not providing an invoice for the charges.

7. Click Record to enter the charge on the customer's register. Repeat steps 2–7 as needed to add additional statement charges.

Recording statement charges one customer at a time can be very time consuming. If this charge is recurring, consider adding them to a Memorized Transaction Group discussed previously.

Recording the Customer Payment

Sales Receipts record your customer's payment at the time of the sale. However, businesses issue invoices or statement charges and expect the customer to remit payment within an agreed-upon number of days.

When your customer pays in full or in part an amount that is due, you will record a receive payment transaction.

When a customer payment is posted to your bank account will depend on your payment preference settings.

To review your current settings, log into the file as the Admin or External Accountant user type and view the Payments—Company Preferences tab on the Preferences dialog box as shown in Figure 9.48.

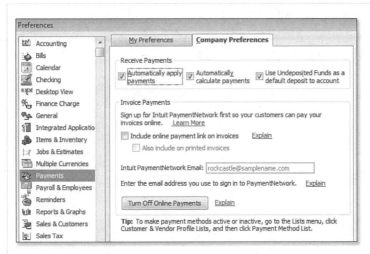

Figure 9.48
The Company Preferences for Receive Payments will determine how QuickBooks records money received from customers.

Recording a Customer Payment

To practice recording a customer payment, open the sample data file as instructed in Chapter 1:

1. On the Home page (as shown in Figure 9.1), click the Receive Payments icon.
2. The Receive Payments dialog box displays. To the left is a panel that provides links to accepting credit cards or eCheck processing from your customers. Follow the links for more information. Send a request to the author at info@quick-training.com to receive a quote for discounted merchant service rates.
3. From the Received From drop-down list, select Melton Johnny:Dental office.
4. In the Amount field, type **5,000.00**.
5. Select Master Card in the Pmt. Method field. See Figure 9.49.

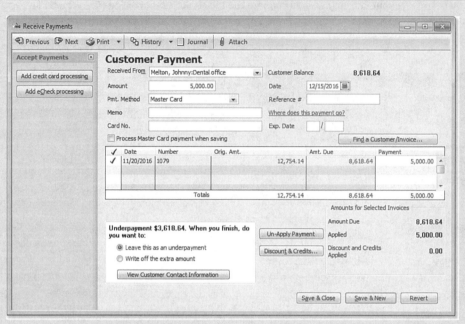

Figure 9.49
Record a Receive Payments transaction when a customer remits funds to you.

6. If you selected the preference to Automatically Apply Payments, QuickBooks will first try to match the payment with an invoice for the same amount. If a match is not found, it will apply the payment to the oldest invoice.

7. For this practice, QuickBooks displays an underpayment message as well as a link to View Customer Contact Information. Accept the default choice of Leave This as an Underpayment.

8. Click Save & Close to complete this exercise or Save & New to practice adding more customer payments.

 note

If the Accept Payments panel does not display, you can enable it on the Sales & Customers—My Preferences tab on the Edit Preferences dialog box. Select the Show Payment Toolbar on Receive Payment and Sales Receipt Forms checkbox to display this panel.

 tip

Often your customer will send in a payment but will not indicate on the payment what invoice they are paying for.

Click the Find a Customer/Invoice button to search by selected fields.

From the displayed results, select any of the matches and click the Use Selected Customer or Transaction.

This Receive Payments transaction has reduced the balance your customer owes you and increased the balance in your Undeposited Funds account. In the next section, you will learn how to add this and other monies received to make a deposit.

Making the Bank Deposit

When receiving payments from your customers, you will record the payments and then physically store the checks or cash received in a safe place until you can go to the bank.

Depending upon the preferences you set, QuickBooks uses an account titled Undeposited Funds account to hold payments received, but not yet included on a bank deposit ticket.

The Undeposited Funds account also plays an important role in making the bank reconciliation process easier and more accurate. If you list multiple customer payments on one deposit ticket taken to the bank, you need to match this deposit ticket total to the make deposit transaction recorded in QuickBooks. By setting the preference to have QuickBooks forward all your customer payments into a temporary Undeposited Funds account (see Figure 9.48), you can then "group" these individual payments in QuickBooks using the Make Deposits transaction. The deposits in your bank account register will now match the deposit amounts on your bank statement.

Check and Cash Payment Deposits

Creating a bank deposit for your cash and check payments correctly is one of the important tasks to properly tracking the balance of funds you have in your bank account.

Recording a Bank Deposit

To practice making a deposit, open the sample data file as instructed in Chapter 1.

1. On the Home page, click the Record Deposits icon.

2. Using the sample data for practice, the Payments to Deposit dialog box displays a listing of payments received that have not yet been recorded as a deposit into the bank account. When you are working in your data if this message does not display, you do not have any payments that were recorded to the Undeposited Funds account.

3. From the View Payment Method Type drop-down list, select Cash and Check. This step is optional, but helps to group the payments by the type of deposit.

4. Click the Select All button to place a checkmark next to each of the amounts listed. See Figure 9.50. Your total might differ if you did not complete the exercise in the previous section.

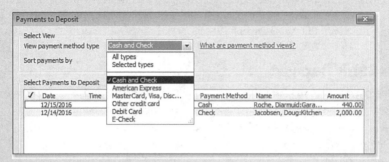

Figure 9.50
The Payments to Deposit can be filtered for specific payment types, helping you group the payments to agree with your bank's deposit records.

5. Compare your deposit ticket total to the payments subtotal on the Payments to Deposit dialog box. See Figure 9.51.

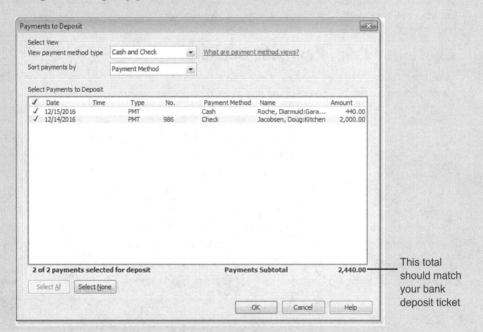

This total should match your bank deposit ticket

Figure 9.51
Place a checkmark next to each payment item that is included on your deposit ticket.

6. When you click OK, QuickBooks adds the selected payments to the Make Deposits dialog box.

7. Confirm the Deposit To account is correct and select the Date your bank will credit your account with the funds. Entering details in the Memo field will display in reports.

8. From the Print drop-down list, select to print a deposit slip (pre-printed forms necessary) or print a deposit summary for your file. See Figure 9.52.

9. Click Save & Close to complete the task or Save & New to record another bank deposit.

Print a deposit slip ticket to take to the bank.

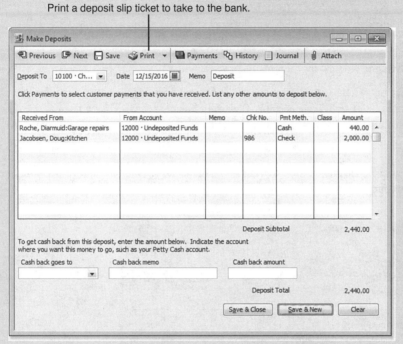

Figure 9.52
Using the Make Deposits dialog box is the final step in recording customer payments.

Recording Credit Card Deposits Less a Discount Fee

If you collect credit card payments from your customers, having a defined Receive Payments and Make Deposits process you can consistently follow is important. Because you don't physically hold the payment from your customer as you do with cash or check payments, tracking these credit card payments accurately and reconciling with the bank's monthly statement helps you avoid some common mistakes.

When your business accepts credit card payments from your customers, your merchant account vendor charges you, the seller a discount fee. Your credit card processor might charge the fee at the time of the deposit, at the end of the billing cycle, or a combination of both.

If you are charged a fee at the end of the month, you can enter the fee into your checkbook register in QuickBooks or create a journal entry with a debit to your credit card expense account and a credit to your bank account.

What if your merchant vendor reduces the amount of your customer's payment credited to your bank account? To help you keep accurate records, follow these steps:

1. Follow the instructions in the section titled "Recording the Customer Payment," p. 308.

2. Next, confirm the amount of the deposit made to your bank from your credit card merchant. If you have online access to your bank institution, you can find this information timely without having to wait for the monthly bank statement.

3. On the Payments to Deposit dialog box, select the credit card payments that were included in the batch transmitted to your bank account. Does your business receive many payments by credit card? It can be helpful to have a printout of the batch details from your merchant vendor.

4. Click OK and QuickBooks includes these credit card payments on a make deposits transaction.

5. On the next available line, in the From Account column, enter your credit card discount fees expense account. See Figure 9.53.

 tip

I teach my clients to leave credit card deposits in the QuickBooks Undeposited Funds account until they know the exact amount and date that money was deposited to their bank.

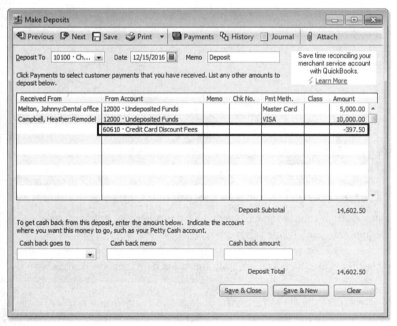

Figure 9.53
Record discount fees as part of your credit card deposit.

6. In the Amount column, enter a negative amount equal to the fee charged.

7. Confirm that the deposit total on the make deposits transaction agrees with the exact amount credited to your bank account by the merchant. Click Save & Close if you are done. Click Save & New to record another deposit.

Recording and Applying a Customer Credit Memo

Use the Create Credit Memos/Refund transaction when a customer returns a product or you want to record a credit toward a future purchase.

Creating a Customer Refund Check

To practice refunding an overpayment with a check, open the sample data file as instructed in Chapter 1:

1. On the icon bar, click the Customers icon to open the Customer Center.

2. For this exercise, scroll through the Customers & Jobs list and select the Hendro Riyadi:Remodel Kitchen job.

3. Double-click the invoice listed on the right.

4. From the Create drop-down list (see Figure 9.54) at the top of the Create Invoices dialog box, select Credit Memo for This Invoice.

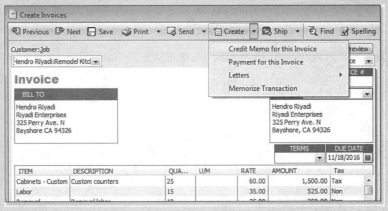

Figure 9.54
You can create credit memos efficiently from the original customer invoice.

5. QuickBooks duplicates the details from the original invoice to a new Create Credit Memos/ Refunds transaction.

6. Review the lines included on the newly created credit memo. When working in your own data, remove individual lines as needed to agree with the products returned or services to be credited.

7. Click Save & Close. QuickBooks displays the Available Credit message.

8. Select the option to Apply to an Invoice as shown in Figure 9.55.

Figure 9.55
Choose how you will record the available credit in QuickBooks.

9. QuickBooks displays the Apply Credit to Invoices dialog box. From here, you can change which invoice or how much of the credit is applied. For this exercise, leave the transaction as shown in Figure 9.56.

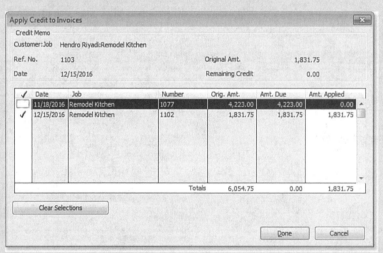

Figure 9.56
Make sure your records for applying the credit agree with your customer's.

10. Click Done.

11. QuickBooks returns to the Create Invoices dialog box. In this practice exercise, a paid stamp is displayed on the resulting credit memo offsetting the open balance. Click Save & Close to complete the activity or Save & New to create another credit memo.

tip

To efficiently remove lines on a newly created transaction, with your cursor select a row and press the Ctrl+Delete key on your keyboard to remove an entire line one at a time.

Refunding a Customer's Overpayment

Has your company received an overpayment from a customer? Although it is rare during difficult economic times, knowing how to handle the transaction can help keep your financial records correct and your customer happy.

When you receive an overpayment you can leave the overpayment in your books and apply it to future invoices, similar to the process for applying credit memos to open invoices.

However, your customer might request you refund the overpayment.

Refunding a Customer's Overpayment

To practice refunding an overpayment with a check, open the sample data file as instructed in Chapter 1:

1. First, you need to record an overpayment in this sample file you are using. On the Home page, click the Receive Payments icon.

2. From the Received From drop-down list, select the Robson, Darci:Robson Clinic job.

3. The customer balance displays on the Receive Payments dialog box. In the Amount field, type **12,500.00**.

4. QuickBooks displays a message about the overpayment. Select Refund the Amount to the Customer as shown in Figure 9.57.

5. Click Save & Close.

6. QuickBooks opens the Issue a Refund dialog box. Select Check from the Issue This Refund Via drop-down list.

7. Leave selected the prefilled bank account as is.

8. Optionally, enter a Class and Memo.

9. Check or remove the checkmark from the To Be Printed checkbox.

10. Click OK.

11. To print the check, select File, Print Forms, Print Checks from the menu bar, and enter the check number you are placing in your printer.

12. You can also modify the To Be Printed status of a transaction in the Number/Type field in the bank register by selecting Banking, Use Register from the menu bar.

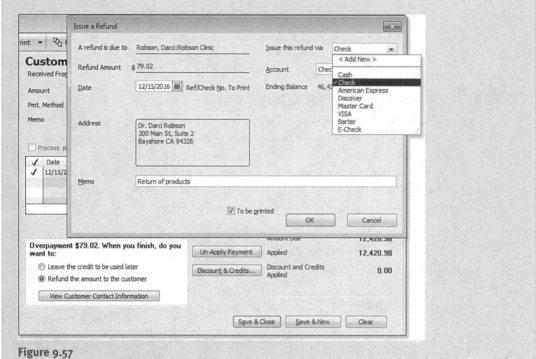

Figure 9.57
Be sure to specify a method when you issue a customer refund.

If you did not apply the credit when you first created it, you can later process the credit as a refund or apply to an open invoice by selecting the Credit To drop-down list from the Create Credit Memos/Refunds dialog box.

MANAGING CUSTOMERS

Accounts Receivable Reporting

You have learned how to use some of the most common customer-related transactions and carry out important customer-related activities in your QuickBooks data file.

There are a wide variety of reports available for documenting sales, customer balances, and other useful management reporting. Details on working with QuickBooks reports are included in Chapter 14, "Reporting in QuickBooks," including accessing a wide variety of customer-related reports from the following menus:

- Reports, Report Center; select the Customers & Receivables or Sales reports from the Standard tab.

- Company, Company Snapshot; select the Payments or Customer tab.

The next several sections in this chapter will help you review and trouble-shoot your own data for accuracy. Following are some of the more common reports used to identify whether or not your Accounts Receivable information is correct.

Reviewing A/R Aging Summary and Detail Reports

Preparing your customer invoices and recording the customer's payments are important to the accuracy of your financials. There are several reports that summarize the status of unpaid or unapplied customer transactions included in your Accounts Receivable balance on the Balance Sheet report.

You can prepare these reports with your own data, or review the report details using the sample data discussed in Chapter 1, "Getting Started with Quickbooks."

From the menu bar, select Reports, Customers & Receivables, and then select one of the following from the submenu:

- **A/R Aging Summary**—Report groups open customer transactions by job into a series of aged date ranges (see Figure 10.1). Use this report for a quick view of those customers who have older unpaid balances.

	Current	1 - 30	31 - 60	61 - 90	> 90	TOTAL
Allard, Robert						
Remodel	0.00	0.00	0.00	14,510.00	0.00	14,510.00
Total Allard, Robert	0.00	0.00	0.00	14,510.00	0.00	14,510.00
Burch, Jason						
Room Addition	1,005.00	0.00	0.00	0.00	0.00	1,005.00
Total Burch, Jason	1,005.00	0.00	0.00	0.00	0.00	1,005.00
Campbell, Heather						
Remodel	13,900.00	0.00	0.00	0.00	0.00	13,900.00
Total Campbell, Heather	13,900.00	0.00	0.00	0.00	0.00	13,900.00
Cook, Brian						
2nd story addition	5,418.00	0.00	0.00	0.00	0.00	5,418.00
Kitchen	3,279.33	0.00	700.00	0.00	0.00	3,979.33
Total Cook, Brian	8,697.33	0.00	700.00	0.00	0.00	9,397.33

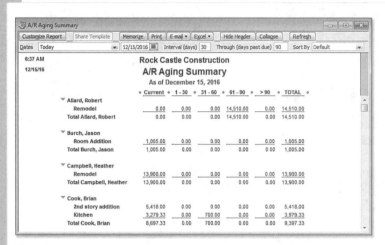

Figure 10.1
Use the A/R Aging Summary report to identify which customers have overdue balances.

- **A/R Aging Detail**—The report shown in Figure 10.2 provides a single line of detail for all open customer transactions, grouped by aging period.

Type	Date	Num	P. O. #	Name	Terms	Due Date	Class	Aging	Open Balance
1 - 30									
Invoice	11/18/2016	1077		Hendro Riyadi:Remodel Kitchen		11/18/2016	Remodel	27	4,223.00
Invoice	11/15/2016	1076		Vitton, David:Remodel Kitchen	Net 15	11/30/2016	Remodel	15	700.00
Invoice	11/28/2016	1085		Teschner, Anton:Sun Room	Net 15	12/13/2016	New Co...	2	565.95
Total 1 - 30									5,488.95
31 - 60									
Invoice	10/20/2016	1068		Mackey's Nursery and Garden Supply:G...	Net 15	11/04/2016	New Co...	41	13,900.00
Invoice	10/10/2016	1065		Pretell Real Estate:155 Wilks Blvd.	Net 30	11/09/2016	New Co...	36	2,239.00
Invoice	10/15/2016	1066		Cook, Brian:Kitchen	Net 30	11/14/2016	Remodel	31	700.00
Total 31 - 60									16,839.00
61 - 90									
Invoice	09/12/2016	1058		Allard, Robert:Remodel	Net 15	09/27/2016	Remodel	79	14,510.00
Total 61 - 90									14,510.00

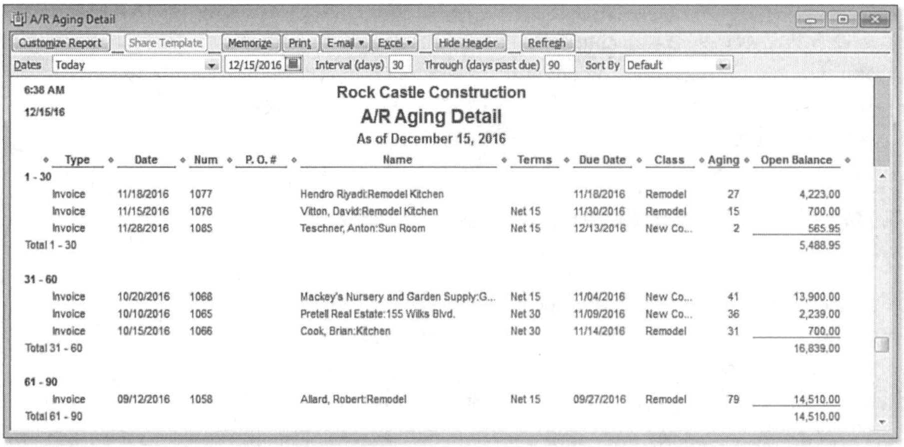

Figure 10.2
The A/R Aging Detail report groups aged customer transactions by overdue date status.

Use these reports to identify those customers who are in need of collection efforts and use the tools discussed in the section of this chapter titled "Using the Collections Center."

Reviewing the Open Invoices Report

Unlike the A/R Aging Summary report, the Open Invoices report is useful because it shows individual lines for each open transaction grouped by customer and job. This report is a "perpetual" report, meaning it will show open invoices as of today's date and not some fixed time in the past unless you modify the reports as detailed here.

To modify an Open Invoices report so you can compare it to your Balance Sheet report for some specific date in the past, follow these steps:

1. From the menu bar, select Reports, Customers & Receivables, Open Invoices. This report includes all payments made by your customer as of today's computer system date.

2. If you are creating this report for some date in the past, click the Customize Report button and then click the Advanced button on the Display tab of the Modify Report dialog box.

3. In the Open Balance/Aging box of the Advanced Options dialog box, select the Report Date option (see Figure 10.3). This modification to the report enables you to see each invoice balance detail as of the prior report date. If you do not modify this report, QuickBooks displays the prior date on the report, but also reduces the balances owed for payments made after the report date.

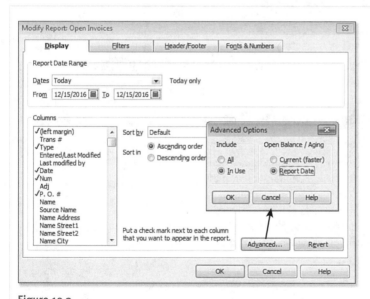

Figure 10.3
The Open Invoices report, when modified, can be compared to the totals on your Balance Sheet report for a previous date.

4. On the Open Invoices report (see Figure 10.4), view details of all open balances and any unapplied credits grouped by customer and job.

Open Invoices								
Customize Report	Share Template	Memorize	Print	E-mail ▼	Excel ▼	Hide Header	Refresh	
Dates Today		12/15/2016	Sort By Default					

6:46 AM
12/15/16

Rock Castle Construction
Open Invoices
As of December 15, 2016

Type	Date	Num	P.O. #	Terms	Due Date	Class	Aging	Open Balance
Allard, Robert								
Remodel								
Invoice	09/12/2016	1058		Net 15	09/27/2016	Remodel	79	14,510.00
Credit Memo	12/15/2016	1100			12/15/2016	Remodel		-500.00
Total Remodel								14,010.00
Total Allard, Robert								14,010.00
Burch, Jason								
Room Addition								
Invoice	11/25/2016	1083		Net 30	12/25/2016	New Co...		1,005.00
Total Room Addition								1,005.00
Total Burch, Jason								1,005.00
Campbell, Heather								
Remodel								
Invoice	12/10/2016	1092		Net 15	12/25/2016	Remodel		13,900.00
Total Remodel								13,900.00

Figure 10.4
Unlike the Aging Summary report, the Open Invoices report groups open or unapplied transactions by customer or job rather than by aging date.

Reconciling Balance Sheet Accounts Receivable Amount to A/R Aging Summary Total

With QuickBooks, you don't have to worry that the Balance Sheet report and the Accounts Receivable Aging Summary report match because any transaction posting to the Accounts Receivable account must have a customer assigned. You want to make sure you always create your Balance Sheet with the Accrual Basis because the A/R Aging Summary report provides details only on an Accrual Basis:

To prepare the reports needed for this comparison, follow these steps:

1. From the menu bar, select Reports, Company & Financial, Balance Sheet Standard. The selected report is displayed. For the date, select the As of Date you want to compare to.

 tip

To compare your Balance Sheet report with the A/R Aging Summary report, you must create your Balance Sheet in accrual basis. If your reporting preference default is for cash basis, you can change it temporarily to accrual basis in the active report. Just click the Customize Report button at the top of the report and select Accrual as the reporting basis.

2. In the Balance Sheet report that displays, note the balance in your Accounts Receivable account (see Figure 10.5).

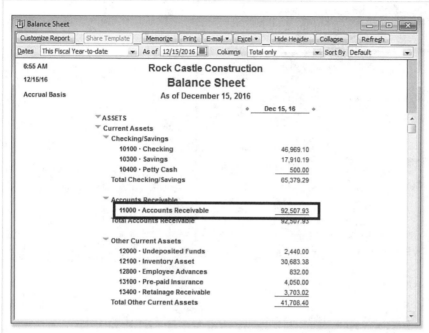

Figure 10.5
Use your Balance Sheet report (accrual basis) to reconcile your Accounts Receivable report.

3. From the menu bar, select Reports, Customers & Receivables, A/R Aging Summary, making sure the field shows the same date as the date selected in step 1. The image shown in Figure 10.6 has been "collapsed" to make viewing the information easier. To expand to see more detail, click the Expand button at the top of the report.

The balance from the Balance Sheet report should match the total on the A/R Aging Summary. If it does not, the cause might be a "broken" transaction link. You can detect these types of issues by selecting File, Utilities, Verify Data from the menu bar; additional details are provided in Chapter 17, "Managing Your Quickbooks Database."

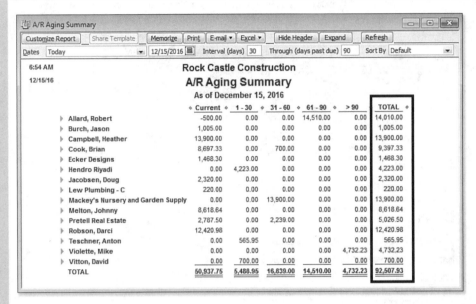

Figure 10.6
A/R Aging Summary report collapsed for reviewing report totals.

Viewing the Accounts Receivable Balance on a Cash Basis Balance Sheet

The nature of Cash Basis reporting implies you would not see an Accounts Receivable balance on your Balance Sheet. In short, cash basis accounting doesn't recognize revenue until you deposit the funds.

What should you do if you see an Accounts Receivable balance on a Cash Basis Balance Sheet? Any of the following can be the cause:

- A/R transactions have items posting to other Balance Sheet accounts.

- Inventory items on an invoice or credit memo (inventory management should be reported in Accrual Basis reporting).

- Transfers between Balance Sheet accounts.

- Unapplied Accounts Receivable customer payments.

- Customer payments applied to future-dated Accounts Receivable invoices.

- Preferences that contradict each other. (This situation can happen if you select Cash Basis on your Summary Reports, but Accrual Basis as your Sales Tax preference.)

- Data corruption (select File, Utilities, Verify Data from the menu bar to check for data corruption).

Accounts Receivable Balances on Cash Basis Balance Sheet

To determine why an Accounts Receivable balance displays on a Cash Basis Balance Sheet, follow these steps:

1. From the menu bar, select Reports, Company & Financial, Balance Sheet Standard report as displayed in Figure 10.7.

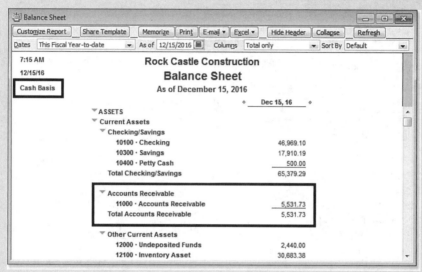

Figure 10.7
The Cash Basis Balance Sheet shows an Accounts Receivable balance.

2. Click the Customize Report button.

3. The Modify Report dialog box opens, with the Display tab selected. Select Cash for the report basis.

4. Click OK.

5. Double-click the Accounts Receivable amount in question. The Transaction by Account report is created.

6. Click the Customize Report button. The Modify Report dialog box opens, with the Display tab selected.

7. For the Report Date Range, remove the From date and leave the To date.

8. Click the Advanced button, and from the Open Balance / Aging box, select Report Date.

9. Click the Filters tab.

10. In the Choose Filters box, scroll down to select Paid Status and select the Open option.

11. Click OK.

Look for transactions that fall into any of the categories described previously. Figure 10.8 shows an item was used on Invoice No. 1090 that debited another Balance Sheet account named Retainage. Any item used on a customer invoice that is mapped to another Balance Sheet account (including inventory) will display on a Cash Basis Balance Sheet report.

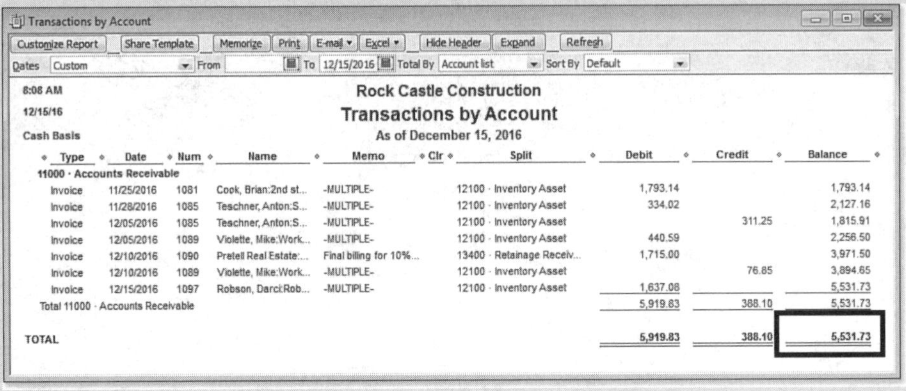

8:08 AM
12/15/16
Cash Basis

Rock Castle Construction
Transactions by Account
As of December 15, 2016

Type	Date	Num	Name	Memo	Clr	Split	Debit	Credit	Balance
11000 · Accounts Receivable									
Invoice	11/25/2016	1081	Cook, Brian:2nd st...	-MULTIPLE-		12100 · Inventory Asset	1,793.14		1,793.14
Invoice	11/28/2016	1085	Teschner, Anton:S...	-MULTIPLE-		12100 · Inventory Asset	334.02		2,127.16
Invoice	12/05/2016	1085	Teschner, Anton:S...	-MULTIPLE-		12100 · Inventory Asset		311.25	1,815.91
Invoice	12/05/2016	1089	Violette, Mike:Work...	-MULTIPLE-		12100 · Inventory Asset	440.59		2,256.50
Invoice	12/10/2016	1090	Pretell Real Estate:...	Final billing for 10%...		13400 · Retainage Receiv...	1,715.00		3,971.50
Invoice	12/10/2016	1089	Violette, Mike:Work...	-MULTIPLE-		12100 · Inventory Asset		76.85	3,894.65
Invoice	12/15/2016	1097	Robson, Darci:Rob...	-MULTIPLE-		12100 · Inventory Asset	1,637.08		5,531.73
Total 11000 · Accounts Receivable							5,919.83	388.10	5,531.73
TOTAL							5,919.83	388.10	5,531.73

Figure 10.8
This modified report identifies the individual transactions that are included in the Accounts Receivable amount showing on a Cash Basis Balance Sheet.

Now that you have been reviewing your customers open and aged balances, you will appreciate the tools available in your QuickBooks software to help you with critical collection tasks.

Using the Collections Center

If your business sends invoices to customers for payment, you have offered the customer terms of payment. Those terms might be Net 30 or Net 60 and might include discounts if early payment is received.

Using the A/R Aging Summary, Detail or Open Invoices reports will help you to identify customers who are late in paying. Other useful reports included in the Reports, Customers & Receivables menu that assist with collections analysis include:

- Customer Balance Summary
- Customer Balance Detail
- Collections Report
- Average Days to Pay Summary
- Average Days to Pay

The QuickBooks Collections Center as shown in Figure 10.9 provides a place for you to record notes about your collection efforts and prepare reminder notices for clients with overdue and almost due balances.

Figure 10.9
Click the Note icon to document your collection activities.

1. On the Home page, click the Customers button.

2. The Customer Center opens, with the Customers & Jobs tab selected. From the top of the Customer Center, click the Collections Center button.

3. The Collections Center opens, with the Overdue tab selected. Click any column header to sort by that column.

4. Click the Notes/Warnings icon next to any open item and QuickBooks will populate the date and time and you can add your collection notes. Click Save. These notes become part of the customer or job notes record and can be viewed from the Customer Center. After the note is saved, hover your mouse over the Notes/Warnings icon and QuickBooks displays the contents without opening the note.

5. Click the Select and Send Email link.

6. Place a checkmark next to each overdue invoice you want to send a collection notice to. Select all or deselect all using the checkmark in front of the Customer Name column header.

7. To the right, modify the template text that will be included in the email communication. Add the From, Cc:, and Bcc: email addresses. You can set your default text for these communications on the Send Forms—Company Preferences tab of the Preferences dialog box.

   QuickBooks will use the email provider you designated on the Send Forms—My Preferences tab of the Preferences dialog box.

8. Repeat steps 4–7 for customers with open invoices listed on the Almost Due tab.

9. Click the X in the top right to close the Collections Center.

The notes assigned to the overdue invoice will also track the day and time an email was sent.

Even with your best efforts, sometimes you are just not able to collect the money that is owed to you. For these instances, you will want to accurately write off the balance to your Bad Debt expense account. Review the "Removing an Open Balance from a Customer Invoice" section for details.

Generating the Missing Customer Invoices Report

Most companies establish some control over the process of creating customer invoices. One control, if invoices are created manually in the field and later entered into QuickBooks, is to maintain a numeric invoicing pattern. Usually each invoice is one number larger than the prior invoice. This method of invoice record keeping can be an important process to have if your company is ever audited and you are required to provide a list of all invoices.

To see whether your data has any missing numbers in the invoicing sequence, follow these steps:

1. From the menu bar, select Reports, Banking, Missing Checks.

2. In the Missing Checks dialog box, select Accounts Receivable from the Specify Account drop-down list, and click OK to generate the report (see Figure 10.10).

Figure 10.10
Create a report that lists all your customer invoices by invoice number.

3. Rename the report by choosing Customize Report, clicking the Header/Footer tab, and typing a new title for the Report Title field, such as Invoice List.

4. Click OK to display the newly renamed report.

This customized report makes the process of identifying missing or duplicated invoice numbers easy (see Figure 10.11). Use this information to determine whether you need better company practices to avoid this situation.

 caution

The customized Missing Invoices report filter omits credit memos. With the customized report displayed, you can add credit memos to the transactions reported. Click the Customize Report button and select the Filters tab. In the Choose Filter box, select Transaction Type. From the Transaction Type drop-down list, select Multiple Transaction types including invoice, credit memo, and others you want included.

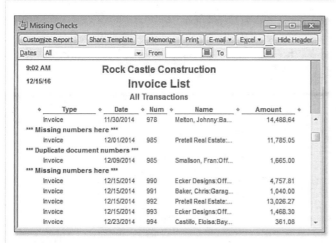

Figure 10.11
This modified report shows a list of all missing or duplicated invoice numbers.

Sales Tax Payable Reports

I recommend you review these reports each time you prepare to pay your sales and use tax to the taxing authority. Properly "reconciling" these reports to each other helps minimize any chance that your QuickBooks data will not support what you filed on your sales tax return.

Reviewing Customer Lists for Tax Code and Tax Item Assigned

Check your customers' taxable status often. This task is quite easy to do and helps prevent the costly mistakes caused by not charging sales tax or charging the incorrect rate.

1. From the menu bar, select Reports, List, Customer Phone List.

2. Click the Customize Report button on the top left of the report.

3. In the Modify Report dialog box that opens, place a checkmark in the Columns box next to items you want to review for the list, including Sales Tax Code and Tax Item, and include the Resale Num if you track this number for your wholesale customers.

4. Optionally, select Sales Tax Code from the Sort By drop-down list.

5. Optionally, click the Header/Footer tab to change the report title. Click OK.

> **caution**
>
> When you make a change to a customer's assigned tax code or tax item or to the tax code assigned to a product or service you sell on your item list, QuickBooks will *not* correct or modify prior saved transactions. New transactions will show the change in the sales tax status or rate.

From this list, shown in Figure 10.12, double-click any line item detail to open the Edit Customer dialog box and make needed changes.

Figure 10.12
Prepare this report often to review the accuracy of the sales tax codes and items assigned to your customers.

Reviewing the Item List for Tax Code Assigned

Another review that I recommend you do periodically is to look at the list of services and products you sell and determine whether the proper tax code has been assigned (see Figure 10.13).

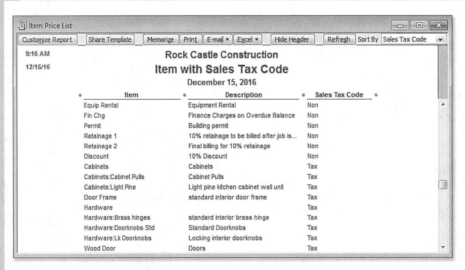

Figure 10.13
Prepare a report of the sales tax codes assigned to your items.

To review the Item Price List report, follow these steps:

1. From the menu bar, select Reports, List, Item Price List.

2. Click the Customize Report button at the top left of the report.

3. In the Columns box of the Modify Report dialog box, remove checkmarks from those data fields you do not want displayed on this report. Place a checkmark next to date fields you want to review for the list, including Sales Tax Code.

4. Optionally, select Sales Tax Code from the Sort By drop-down list.

5. Optionally, click the Header/Footer tab to change the report title. Click OK.

Reconciling Total Sales to Total Income

The term *reconciling* (also known as proofing) refers to the need to compare two related numbers from two different reports. The importance of this task cannot be overstated. If your company is selected to have a sales tax audit, one of the first numbers the auditor will want to determine is the total sales you reported on your tax returns for the time period being audited.

When comparing these two reports, it is imperative you know the basis you have selected for your sales tax.

For more information, see "Setting Up Sales Tax," p. 274.

To compare your total sales on the Sales Tax Liability report to your total income on the Profit & Loss report using the same basis as your sales tax preference, follow these steps:

1. From the menu bar, select Reports, Vendors & Payables, Sales Tax Liability.

2. Make a note of the date range and total sales on this report, as shown in Figure 10.14.

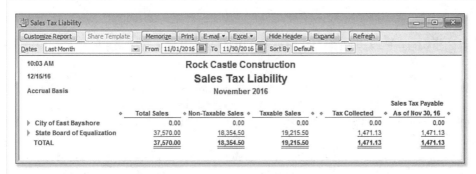

Figure 10.14
Compare total sales on the Sales Tax Liability report to total income on the Profit & Loss report.

3. From the menu bar, select Reports, Company & Financial, Profit & Loss Standard.

4. Select the same date range used for your Sales Tax Liability report in step 1.

5. Verify the same basis is used on this report that was used on the Sales Tax Liability report. If necessary, click Customize Report to change.

6. Compare total income (see Figure 10.15) to the total sales from the Sales Tax Liability report. Note: You might have to deduct any non-sales income on your Profit & Loss Total Income amounts.

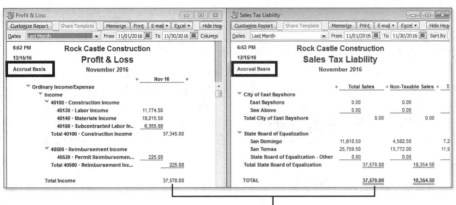

Both of these totals should match each other

Figure 10.15
Compare the total income on the Profit & Loss report to the total sales on the Sales Tax Liability report.

If your totals on these two reports do not match, review the instructions included in the "Correcting Sales Tax Errors" section of this chapter.

Reconciling Sales Tax Liability to Balance Sheet Sales Tax Payable

Another important comparison to make is between the amount reported for Sales Tax Payable on the Balance Sheet report and the Sales Tax Payable total on the Sales Tax Liability report. Carefully check that you are using the same Cash or Accrual Basis for each report when completing this review.

If you created your own Sales Tax Payable account, you might not be able to correctly compare the two reports. QuickBooks creates a Sales Tax Payable account automatically.

To compare the Balance Sheet Sales Tax Payable account balance with the Sales Tax Payable total on the Sales Tax Liability report, follow these steps:

1. From the menu bar, select Reports, Company & Financial, Balance Sheet Standard (see Figure 10.16).

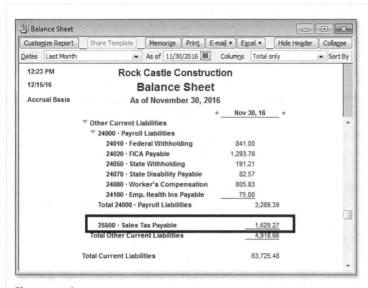

Figure 10.16
Balance Sheet Sales Tax Payable amount should agree with your Sales Tax Liability report.

2. On the report, select the As of Date you are comparing to (this date must be the same ending date you will use when you prepare your Sales Tax Liability report in the next step).

3. From the menu bar, select Reports, Vendors & Payables, Sales Tax Liability. See Figure 10.17. QuickBooks defaults the date range depending on your sales tax preference setting.

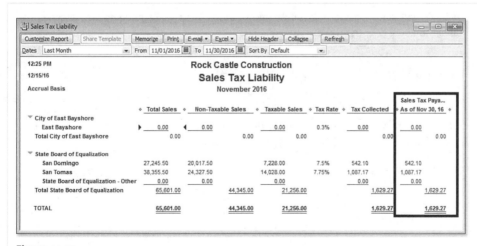

Figure 10.17
The total sales tax liability payable should agree with your Balance Sheet Sales Tax payable.

Each month before preparing your sales tax return, compare the total of these two reports. Later in this chapter, you will learn about methods you can use to troubleshoot these totals when they do not match.

When a Check or Bill Was Used to Pay Sales Tax

A common mistake when recording payment of the sales tax payable is to use a Write Checks or Enter Bills transaction. If these types of transactions are used and the Sales Tax Payable account is assigned on the form, QuickBooks reduces the Sales Tax Payable amount on the Balance Sheet, but does not make the same adjustment in the Pay Sales Tax dialog box. Instead this type of transaction will be included in the Pay Sales Tax dialog box as a negative Amt. Due.

To find the transaction(s) that might be the cause of not being able to compare your Balance Sheet Sales Tax Payable amount to your Sales Tax Liability report amount to be paid, follow these steps:

1. On the Home page, click the Vendors button to open the Vendor Center.

2. Select your sales tax vendor from the Vendors list.

3. From the Show drop-down list, select Checks (or Bills), making sure you are looking in the appropriate date range.

If you have found checks or bills, this could be one of the reasons your two reports do not agree with each other. The correct sales tax payment transaction is named TAXPMT when viewing transactions in your bank register. The following section details how to properly record the payment of the collected sales tax in your QuickBooks data.

Paying Sales Tax

Now that you have your sales tax correctly set up and you have reviewed your sales tax payable reports, you need to know how to properly pay your sales tax.

Paying Sales Tax Without an Adjustment

As mentioned earlier, when you collect sales tax, you are acting as an agent for the state. Most often, you will pay the state or city taxing authority the same amount that you collected from your customers. Sometimes the state might allow you to discount the sales tax due for prompt payment or charge a penalty for paying late. Each of these situations is discussed in detail in this section.

Paying Sales Tax Without an Adjustment

To practice paying sales tax without an adjustment, open the sample data file as instructed in Chapter 1. Use these instructions when creating your own sales tax payments—selecting accounts and dates that are correct for your needs:

1. From the menu bar, select Vendors, Sales Tax, Pay Sales Tax. The Pay Sales Tax dialog box displays (see Figure 10.18).

Figure 10.18
Use this transaction type to properly remit your sales tax payable amount.

2. For this exercise, in the Pay From Account field leave selected the Checking account.

3. In the date field, select December 31, 2016.

4. In the Show Sales Tax Due field, select December 31, 2016. This date should default to your preference setting. If the date is not the date you want to pay through, you can override it here.

5. Leave the Starting Check No. unchanged.

6. Place a checkmark in the Pay column on the left for the individual items you want to pay. QuickBooks creates or prints a separate check transaction for each line item with a different vendor.

7. Verify that the Amt. Paid column is in agreement with your Sales Tax Liability report for the same period.

8. Click OK; QuickBooks creates a transaction with the TAXPMT type viewable from your checkbook register, as shown in Figure 10.19.

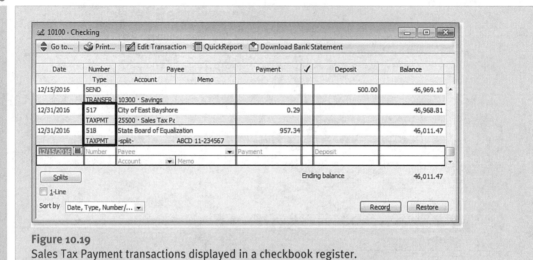

Figure 10.19
Sales Tax Payment transactions displayed in a checkbook register.

 tip
You can set a user-specific default account for paying the sales tax liability from. From the menu bar select Edit, Preferences and choose the Checking, My Preferences tab.

Paying Sales Tax with an Adjustment

There are many reasons why your Sales Tax Payable doesn't agree with the amount the agency is expecting you to pay, including the following:

- Discount offered for early payment

- Penalty or fee assessed for late payment

- Credit received for overpayment on a prior period's sales tax return

- State sales tax holiday or rate reduction

- Rounding errors

If any of these apply to your business, follow these steps:

1. Perform steps 1–5 listed in the preceding section ("Paying Sales Tax Without an Adjustment") making sure to select the proper accounts and dates for your specific needs.

2. In the Pay Sales Tax dialog box, click Adjust to open the Sales Tax Adjustment dialog box, as shown in Figure 10.20.

 note
If you select the items to be paid *first*, and then select the Adjust button recording the discount or increase, QuickBooks will provide a warning that your previously selected checkmarks will be removed and you will need to select the line items again, including the new adjustment to be included with the payment.

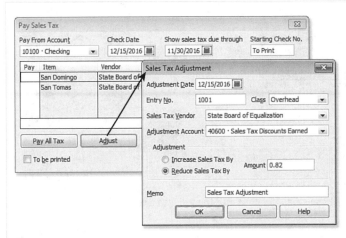

Figure 10.20
Use the Sales Tax Adjustment dialog box to increase or decrease your sales tax payment.

3. Select the appropriate Adjustment Date. This date should be on or before the Show Sales Tax Through date.

4. Enter an Entry No. or QuickBooks will default a number if that preference is set.

5. Select the Sales Tax Vendor for which you are decreasing or increasing your payment.

6. Select from your chart of accounts the Adjustment Account. Ask your accountant what he prefers; the account might be either of the following:

   - Other Income, if you are recording a discount for early payment.

   - Expense, if you are recording a penalty or fine.

7. Select the option to Increase Sales Tax By or Reduce Sales Tax By and enter the appropriate dollar amount.

8. In the Memo section, enter a description for your reports or accept the default description.

9. Click OK to record the sales tax adjustment.

10. Click OK to close the warning message when recording a sales tax adjustment.

11. QuickBooks now shows the Pay Sales Tax dialog box with an additional line showing the adjustment. This example shows a reduction in sales tax due (see Figure 10.21).

QuickBooks creates a general journal entry when the sales tax adjustment is recorded.

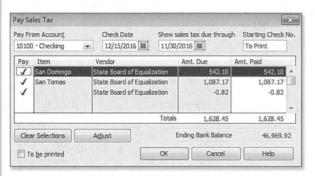

Figure 10.21
When preparing your sales tax payment select the sales tax lines and the adjustment line.

Correcting Accounts Receivable Errors

After reviewing your accounts receivable reports, you might have identified some data entry errors. Before you can fix these, you need to determine the best method to correct the errors. When deciding which method is best, you should ask yourself the following:

- **Are the errors in an accounting year that I have already filed a tax return for?**—If yes, then adjusting these transactions by dating the modifying entry in the current tax year and not modifying the original transaction is best. Some methods listed in this section will not enable you to select a date different from the original transaction date.

- **Are the errors significant in the dollar amount, collectively or individually?**—If yes, you should obtain the advice of your accountant before making any adjustments so changes that will affect your tax status are carefully considered.

- **Am I going to fix detail or summary information?**—In other words, are you going to fix individual invoices or correct a group of customer invoices with one adjusting transaction?

- **Am I modifying an invoice with sales tax recorded on the invoice?**—If yes, refer to the "Correcting Sales Tax Errors" section in this chapter for a detailed discussion on adjusting invoices with sales tax. These corrections should only be made with transactions dated in the current accounting month.

Removing an Open Balance from a Customer Invoice

There are several reasons you might have open balances on your Accounts Receivable invoices. There are also several methods to correct overstated or understated balances, each with its own effect on your company's financials.

If you are an accounting professional and you are using QuickBooks Accountant 2012 or QuickBooks Enterprise Solutions Accountant 12.0 software, you will want to review Appendix A, "Client Data Review."

Included in the Client Data Review (CDR) used by accountants, are useful tools that streamline applying open customer payments and credits to open customer invoices and simplify writing off small open balances in batch.

The following sections are methods you can use to remove open customer balances with your QuickBooks Pro, Premier, or Enterprise software.

Writing Off a Customer Balance by Modifying the Original Customer Receive Payments Transaction

This method of modifying the original customer payment to write off a customer balance records the change as of the date of the Receive Payments transaction and permits a write-off amount equal to the underpayment amount. You can write off the amount at the time you first record the payment or at a later date.

On the Home page, click the Customers button and select the appropriate customer. From the Show drop-down list, select Payments and Credits or just Received Payments and any other date criteria you want to use, as shown in Chapter 9, Figure 9.9.

Double-click the selected customer payment to open it. In the example shown in Figure 10.22, the customer paid $510.00 less than the amount due. Write off this amount by selecting Write Off The Extra Amount option on the lower left of the Receive Payments dialog box. When you select Save & Close, QuickBooks then prompts you for an account to assign for the write-off amount.

Figure 10.22
When you select to write off an amount due, QuickBooks requires you assign the amount to an account and optionally to a class.

Recording a Discount to Remove a Customer Balance

Another way to remove an open customer balance is to record a discount. This method records the change as of the date of the Receive Payments transaction. A discount can be recorded initially when the customer's short payment is recorded, or on a later date by creating a new payment without placing any dollars in the Amount field and choosing the Discounts & Credits option. However, the discount amount cannot be in excess of the amount due.

If the amount due is an insignificant amount, you might not want to take the time to collect it. The easiest method of dealing with it would be to write off the remaining amount on the date the payment is recorded. If you do not write off the remaining amount, QuickBooks will warn you of the underpayment.

The difference between a write-off and discount is the placement on the Profit & Loss statement. A write-off is used when the debt has gone bad and cannot be collected and is often an expense type. In contrast, the discount is used when you decide to reduce the sale price and this account is typically an income type.

To record a discount, click the Discount & Credits button on the Receive Payments dialog box. Similar to the Write Off Amount dialog box, you will be asked to identify an account to post the amount to (see Figure 10.23).

Figure 10.23
Assign the account and other details when recording a customer discount.

Recording a Credit Memo to Remove a Balance Due

The most accurate method for removing a balance due is to record a credit memo, because it creates a good audit trail. You can date the credit in a period you want to reduce the appropriate income account and, if applicable, sales tax due.

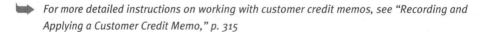

For more detailed instructions on working with customer credit memos, see "Recording and Applying a Customer Credit Memo," p. 315

Recording a Journal Entry to Remove (or Increase) a Customer Balance

Another way to remove or increase a customer balance is to record a journal entry. This type of transaction is often created by the company's accountant when adjusting Accounts Receivable.

If you are going to record a journal entry adjustment, you need to keep in mind the following:

- Only one customer is allowed per journal entry.

- If the general journal entry has other noncustomer-related adjustments, the first line of the journal entry should remain blank.

- The date of the general journal entry is the date the transaction will impact your financials for Accrual or Cash Basis.

- If you print cash basis reports, make sure the income account is *not* recorded on the first line of the journal entry.

- You can enter and apply one lump sum to multiple open customer invoices.

 caution

Did you know that if you use a customer on the first line of a journal entry, every other adjustment made—even noncustomer adjustments—will display on the Profit & Loss by Job report for that customer? This situation is due to the first line of any journal entry being a source line and causing a relationship with transactions below the first line.

To avoid this problem, always leave the first account line of a journal entry blank, as shown in Figure 10.24. Including a memo on the first line is acceptable.

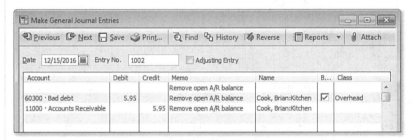

Figure 10.24
Journal entries that adjust accounts receivable balances should then be applied against a customer's open invoice(s).

To record a journal entry adjustment to a customer balance, follow these steps:

1. From the menu bar, select Company, Make General Journal Entries.

2. In the Make General Journal Entries dialog box, record a debit to increase Accounts Receivable or credit to reduce Accounts Receivable (refer to Figure 10.24). Be sure to assign the customer name to each line (except the first line, see the previous Caution) so a Profit & Loss by Job report will show the adjustment.

3. Assign the General Journal Entry to the appropriate customer invoice. From the menu bar, select Customers, Customer Center.

4. Select the correct customer from the list on the left, and in the Show drop-down list, select Invoices. Double-click the appropriate invoice list item.

5. The Create Invoices dialog box opens. Select Apply Credits. QuickBooks then provides a list of available credits to choose from (see Figure 10.25).

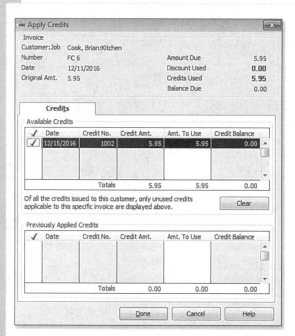

Figure 10.25
Applying an open credit to an open customer invoice balance.

6. On the Apply Credits dialog box that opens, select the appropriate credits by placing a checkmark next to the credit. Click Done to assign the credit(s) to the customer invoice.

7. Click Save & Close.

Correcting Customer Payments

Applying the customer's payments exactly as the customer intended is important. If you apply the customer's payment to an invoice of your own choosing, communicating any discrepancies with open invoice balances can be more confusing than necessary.

However, many times your customer does not provide you with the correct invoice number and you might apply his payment to an incorrect invoice. QuickBooks makes changing how you applied the payment to an invoice easy.

Fixing Unapplied Customer Payments and Credits

When reviewing your Open Invoices report, you might also notice there are unapplied payments included in the report (see Figure 10.26). This would happen when the payment was recorded and the QuickBooks user did not assign the payment to any open invoice.

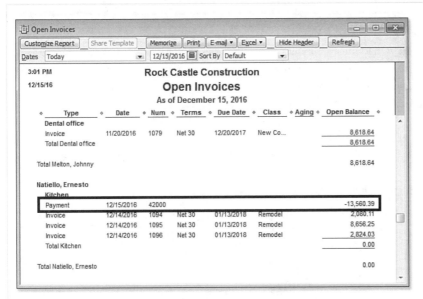

Figure 10.26
Unapplied Receive Payments transactions will show on the Open Invoices report as a credit for that customer.

To correct this, click the Payment transaction listed on the report, and add the checkmarks to the invoice(s) being paid. This transaction change will affect prior year financials in Cash Basis reporting, so be sure to notify your accounting professional of the change.

Fixing a Payment Applied to the Wrong Invoice Number

If, after you compare your customer's records with yours, you find you have applied the payment to the wrong invoice, follow these steps to unapply the payment and then reapply to the correct invoice:

1. From the menu bar, select Customers, Customer Center.

2. On the list on the left, select the appropriate customer.

3. In the pane to the right of the customer list, select Payments and Credits from the Show drop-down list.

4. Optionally, select specific payment methods or select a specific date range from the appropriate drop-down list. QuickBooks will list all received payment transactions for this customer.

5. Double-click the payment that was misapplied.

6. The Receive Payments dialog box opens. Remove the checkmark from one invoice and place it next to the correct invoice. Be careful that the amount of the payment total does not change. Click Save & Close.

Fixing Payment Applied to the Wrong Customer or Job

From the Customer Center, find the appropriate customer, filter for Received Payments, and locate the payment in question as instructed in previous sections.

Determine whether the payment has already been included on a deposit by clicking History in the receive payments screen. If you attempt to change the customer name on the payment screen, QuickBooks warns you that the payment first needs to be deleted from the deposit.

If the payment has been included on a deposit, follow these steps to correct the customer or job assigned. You will temporarily remove the amount from a deposit and then add back in the corrected payment.

To reassign a payment received to another customer or job, follow these steps:

1. From the Receive Payments dialog box for the payment assigned to the incorrect customer or job, click History as shown in Figure 10.27.

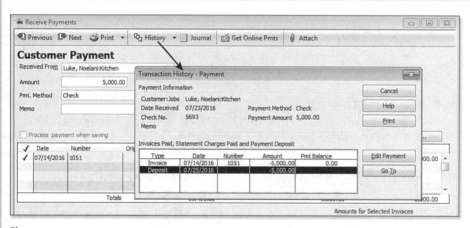

Figure 10.27
To reassign a recorded payment to a different customer or job you first have to remove the payment from the deposit.

2. From the Transaction History—Payment dialog box, select the deposit and click Go To. The deposit opens.

3. Record on paper the total deposit amount and date. You will need this information later in step 8.

4. If multiple payments are on the deposit, go to step 5. If the payment amount being corrected is the only deposit line item, then go to step 9.

5. Highlight the line item to be removed, as shown in Figure 10.28, and press Ctrl+Delete on your keyboard. Click OK to the Delete warning message. Then click Save & Close. This step removes the line item from the deposit. QuickBooks will also warn you if the item has previously been cleared.

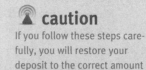

caution

If you follow these steps carefully, you will restore your deposit to the correct amount and you will not have any reconciliation differences.

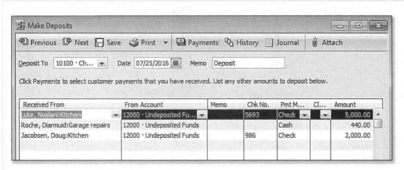

Figure 10.28
To remove an entire line, use Ctrl+Delete on your keyboard.

6. Locate the customer payment that was in error and change the Customer or Job assigned.

7. Return to the bank register and locate the deposit. Double-click the deposit. With the deposit open, select Payments at the top and place a checkmark next to the payment with the corrected Customer or Job (see Figure 10.29). Click OK to add the payment to the deposit.

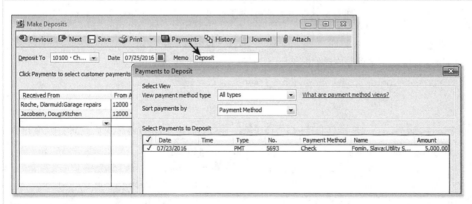

Figure 10.29
With the original deposit open, click the Payments icon to add back the corrected payment.

8. Verify that the total of the deposit agrees with the original amount you recorded on paper. When this transaction is saved with the same original amount, your bank reconciliation will not show a discrepancy. The process is now complete (see Figure 10.30).

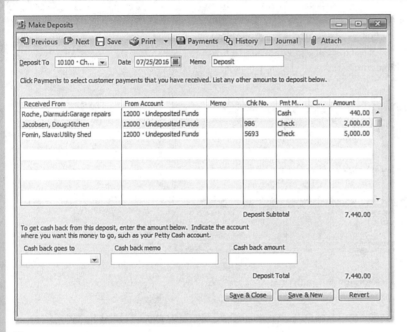

Figure 10.30
The corrected payment has been added to the original deposit, preserving the cleared bank status of the original deposit.

9. If the payment you are correcting is the only deposit line item, select Customers, Receive Payments from the menu bar and record the information for the correct customer or job. Then, follow steps 7 and 8 to assign your newly created payment to the existing deposit. Next, delete the incorrect line item and save the deposit.

10. From the Customer Center, locate the incorrect payment and void or delete it.

When a Credit Memo Is Applied to the Wrong Customer Invoice

It often happens that you create a credit memo and apply it to a specific invoice. Then, when you communicate with the customer, you find out he or she applied it to a different invoice. When you are making those credit and collections calls, the discrepancy can end up costing you critical time in getting paid on invoices that you show as open. If in the end the total due from the customer remains the same, I find it easier to agree with the customer's records when applying credit memos.

Without agreeing with the customer, your collections process would be delayed as both parties sort out what remains unpaid. This process will temporarily have you reassign the credit memo to another customer.

The steps that follow will help you reassign the credit memo to the correct invoice, or at least the same invoice your customer assigned it to:

1. From the Customer Center, locate the customer who had the credit memo applied to the wrong invoice. If you are not sure, click the Customer Center's Transactions tab and select Credit Memos from the list of available transaction types. You can filter for Open or All Credit Memos as well as transaction dates to narrow your search.

2. To reassign the incorrectly assigned credit memo to another invoice, open the credit memo and temporarily change the Customer or Job name to any other customer or job name.

3. Make a note of the new customer assigned to the changed credit memo. Click Save at the top of the Create Credit Memos/Refunds dialog box.

4. QuickBooks warns that the transaction is connected to other transactions and changing it will remove them. Click Yes to close the message.

5. With the open credit displayed showing a Remaining Credit balance assigned to the temporary customer, click the Customer:Job drop-down list and select the correct Customer or Customer:Job.

6. QuickBooks might display a warning about switching between customers with sales tax or prices levels. Click OK to close the message.

7. Click Save at the top of the Create Credit Memos/Refunds dialog box. Click Yes to changing the transaction. The remaining credit amount displays in the dialog box.

8. Click the Use Credit To icon at the top right of the Create Credit Memos/Refunds dialog box and select Apply to invoice.

9. The Apply Credit dialog box opens. Place a checkmark next to the appropriate credit amounts. QuickBooks will, by default, select the invoice with an exact match. You can override this selection by unchecking the default and apply the credit as needed.

10. Select Done. Click Save & Close.

When Deposits Were Made Incorrectly

Four steps are basic to Accounts Receivable management:

1. Create a quote using an estimate or sales order (optional).

2. Prepare an invoice, sales receipt, or statement charge.

3. Receive the customer payment into an Undeposited Funds account.

4. Record the deposit into your bank account.

This section details how to correct your QuickBooks data when the receive payments step was skipped in recording deposits to the bank account.

How can you know when this situation happens? You need to do a little troubleshooting first to identify the problem:

- Do you have open invoices for customers who you know have paid you?

- Is your bank account balance reconciled and correct?

- Does Income on your Profit & Loss Report appear to be too high?

If you answered yes to these questions, you need to determine just how the deposits in the bank account register were recorded.

Viewing Deposits in the Bank Register

To determine how deposits were made to the bank account, view the deposits in your bank register. To open a bank register, select Banking, Use Register from the menu bar and select the appropriate bank account.

The two deposits dated 12/15/16 (see Figure 10.31) were each individually recorded to the account by assigning checking on the receive payment form. This would be acceptable if the individual checks were on different deposit tickets taken to your bank and if the date of the receive payment was also the same date as the deposit. Often these are not the normal conditions and having the payment recorded to the Undeposited Funds would be the best process.

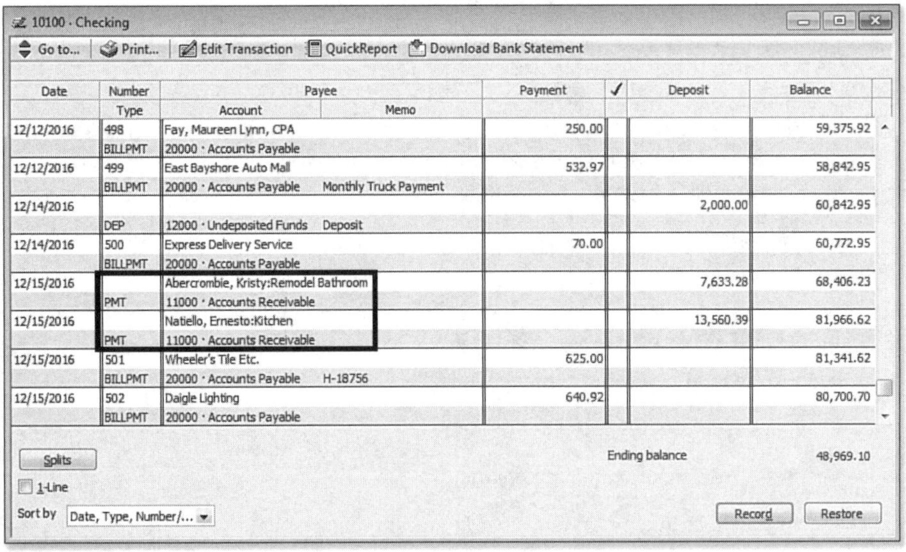

Figure 10.31
The checkbook register indicates the record type for each deposit.

In the checkbook register view, the account shown represents the account from which the transaction originated. You might see Accounts Receivable, an income account or you will see "-Split-," which indicates that there are several lines of detail for this single transaction. To view the "-Split-" detail, just double-click the transaction itself to open the originating QuickBooks transaction.

By contrast, look at the deposit dated 12/14/2016 for $2,000.00 in Figure 10.31. The account shown is Undeposited Funds, which is the account where the transaction originated.

To summarize, look for a "pattern" of how deposits were made to your QuickBooks data. The examples here show two types of deposits: those that were recorded to the checking account and others that first went through the Undeposited Funds account. You might have others in your data where the account shown is your income account. This type of transaction is discussed in the next section, "Viewing the Deposit Detail Report."

You will also be looking to see which transactions have been cleared in the bank reconciliation and which deposits remain uncleared. Chapter 13, "Working with Bank and Credit Card Accounts," discusses the bank reconciliation topic. In fact, it would be best if the reconciliation task were completed before you begin fixing your deposit details. Why? If you see an uncleared deposit, it would help you identify your potential errors in the Undeposited Funds account.

Viewing the Deposit Detail Report

Use this report to review how deposits were recorded to the bank account in QuickBooks and identify deposits that did follow the recommended process of being recorded first to the Undeposited Funds account.

To open the Deposit Detail report, follow these steps:

1. From the menu bar, select Reports, Banking, Deposit Detail.

2. Click the Customize Report button at the top of the report.

3. Click the Filters tab. In the Choose Filter box, the Account filter is already selected. From the drop-down list, select your bank account or use the default of all bank accounts. Click OK to prepare the report.

In Figure 10.32, the deposit for $2,000.00 was recorded using the recommended process of automatically assigning the payment to the Undeposited Funds account. The other payments did not follow this same process and details for correcting these are provided in the next sections.

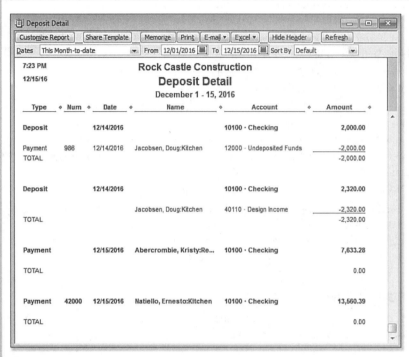

Figure 10.32
The Deposit Detail report also indicates the record type of each deposit.

Creating a Payment Transaction List Detail Report

Do you find the Deposit Detail report too lengthy and difficult to read? You can create a report that shows the detail in a list form and provides a total of the column detail using these steps:

1. From the menu bar, select Reports, Custom Reports, Transaction Detail. The report opens with the Display tab selected.

2. Select the Report Date Range you want to view, as well as the columns you want to see on the report.

3. From the Filters tab, in the Choose Filter box, select Account and choose a specific bank account.

4. Set an additional filter for Multiple Transaction Types, including the deposit, payment, and journal (although less likely a journal was used).

5. Click OK to close the Transaction Type filter and OK to display the report with the selected transactions.

Now you can view in a list format all payments that were recorded to the Checking account (see Figure 10.33).

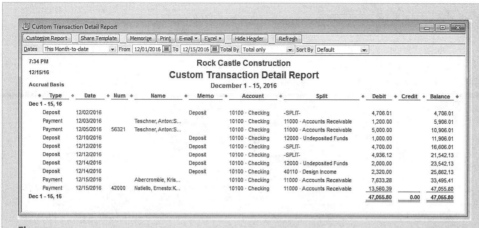

Figure 10.33
Use a filtered custom transaction detail report for a simple view of all deposits into the bank account.

Assigning the Make Deposits Transaction to the Open Customer Invoice

Did your research reveal Make Deposits transactions recorded directly to an income account instead of using the Receive Payments transaction? For the business owner, assigning the deposits to the customer invoice is a two-step process. If you have the time to correct individual transactions, this method retains your bank reconciliation and identifies the payment with the customer's open invoice. Be prepared for a bit of tedious work. You need to have a good record of which deposit was paying for which customer invoice. Remember, these steps are to correct transactions that have been recorded incorrectly.

To manually correct recorded Make Deposits follow these steps:

1. From the menu bar, select Banking, Use Register.

2. The Use Register dialog box opens. Select the bank account to which the deposit was made.

3. Locate the deposit in the checkbook register and double-click it to open the Make Deposits transaction. Change the account assigned in the From Account column from Income to Accounts Receivable. The effect of this step is to "credit" Accounts Receivable (see Figure 10.34). Click Save & Close.

4. From the menu bar, select Reports, Customers & Receivables, Open Invoices, and double-click the invoice.

5. Click the Apply Credits button and select the credit that pertains to this invoice.

6. Click Done to close the Apply Credits dialog box. Click Save & Close.

 tip

I like using the Open Invoices report because I can see both the credit and open invoices grouped by customer or job.

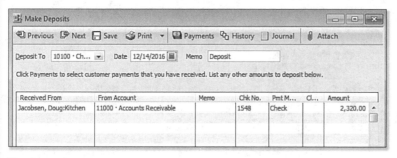

Figure 10.34
Changing the From Account on a deposit to Accounts Receivable will create a credit for the customer listed in the Received From column.

You have now corrected the deposit and assigned the amount to the open customer invoice, all without changing your bank reconciliation status of the item. This process works well, but can be tedious if you have many transactions with this type of error.

Grouping Deposited Items to Agree with Bank Deposit

Unless you take each and every check or cash payment from your customers to the bank on a separate bank deposit ticket, your customer payments should be grouped together with the total matching your bank deposit slip.

If you group your customer payments together on the same deposit transaction and match the total deposited to your bank deposit ticket, your bank reconciliation will be much easier to complete each month.

You should not attempt this method if you have reconciled your bank account in QuickBooks. Also, if you are correcting years of unreconciled transactions, this method might just be too tedious.

The easiest place to see the problem is in your bank account register. From the menu bar, select Banking, Use Register, and select the appropriate bank account.

As shown in Figure 10.31, assume the deposit total per the bank statement was $21,193.67, but in the checkbook register, you recorded two individual deposits.

This situation was caused by choosing Checking as the Deposit To account when receiving the customer's payment (see Figure 10.35). The preferred method would have been to select Undeposited Funds and group them together on one deposit transaction.

To correct these errors (be aware, it is a time-intensive process) if you have many months or years of transactions follow these steps:

1. From the displayed Receive Payments transaction that was originally deposited directly to the bank account, select the Deposit To drop-down list and choose Undeposited Funds.

2. From the menu bar, select Banking, Make Deposits. QuickBooks displays a list of all the payments received, but not yet included in a deposit (included in the Undeposited Funds balance sheet account balance).

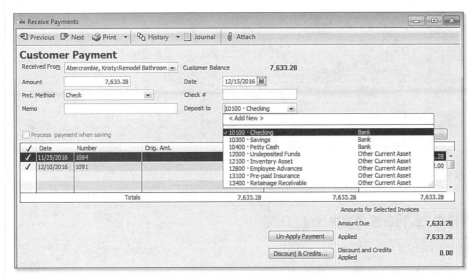

Figure 10.35
This customer payment won't be grouped with other customer finds on the same bank deposit ticket.

3. Click to place a checkmark next to the grouped payments, and verify the total deposit agrees with your bank deposit.

4. Click OK. The make deposit now agrees with the actual bank deposit recorded by the bank.

Eliminating the Print Queue for Customer Invoices Marked to Print

At the bottom left of each customer invoice is the option to select the invoice to be printed. QuickBooks remembers the setting from the last stored invoice, which can sometimes hinder your own company process.

If you find that you have many invoices selected to print and you don't intend to print them, try this easy solution:

1. Place one or two sheets of paper in your printer. From the menu bar, select File, Print Forms, Invoices. The Select Invoices to Print dialog box displays the invoices that are marked to be printed (see Figure 10.36).

2. The checkmark next to the invoice tells QuickBooks you want to print the invoice on paper. Click OK to send the forms to the printer.

3. After a couple of invoices print, a message displays showing a list of the forms that did not print. Because you don't want to print them, click OK and each transaction will be marked in QuickBooks as if it were printed. You might also need to cancel the print job at your printer. Another option is to print the invoices to a PDF printer (file).

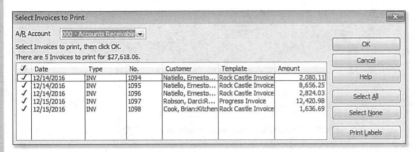

Figure 10.36
View the invoices selected to print.

Correcting Sales Tax Errors

Sales tax errors can be a bit tricky to fix, so make sure you answer the following questions:

- Have you made a backup of your data?

- Have taxes or financials been prepared using the current data in its current state? If yes, then you need to be concerned about the dates and types of the corrections you make.

- If the QuickBooks sales tax due is incorrect, have you determined outside QuickBooks how much was or is due?

Print your sales tax reports before you begin to make corrections to your data file. Then, when your corrections are complete, print the same reports to be sure you achieved the desired end result. Of course, keep good paper documentation of why you did what you did in case you are subject to a sales tax audit.

When a Check or Bill Was Used to Pay the Sales Tax

In newer versions of QuickBooks, the error of using a check or bill to pay sales tax should happen less often. QuickBooks provides messages to users attempting to pay their sales tax vendors incorrectly.

When you pay a vendor and assign the Sales Tax Payable account (created by QuickBooks) on a check or bill, QuickBooks provides the warning shown in Figure 10.37.

When you locate a sales tax payment made by check (or bill), first determine whether the check has been included in the bank reconciliation. If it has not, void the check and re-create the check per the instructions in the section titled "Paying Sales Tax."

Figure 10.37
You are warned when using a check to record a sales tax payment.

If the check has already been included in the bank reconciliation, use the following method to assign the check or bill to the line items in the Pay Sales Tax dialog box:

1. From the menu bar, select Vendors, Vendor Center. Select the vendor whom sales tax payments are made to.

2. From the Show drop-down list to the right, double-click the check or bill to open the Write Checks dialog box or Enter Bills dialog box.

3. Assign the Sales Tax Payable liability account in the Account column of the Expenses tab.

4. In the Customer:Job column, select the Sales Tax Vendor from the list of vendors (make sure it is a vendor and not an "other name" list item).

5. Click Save & Close to close the check (or bill).

6. From the menu bar, select Vendors, Sales Tax, Pay Sales Tax. The corrected transaction will display if it is dated on or prior to the Show Sales Tax Due Through date.

7. When you are ready to pay your next period's sales tax, place a checkmark next to each sales tax line item, including the line item with the correction to associate the check or bill payment with the sales tax due (see Figure 10.38). If the net total amount is zero, select each of the items the next period you pay your sales tax.

If the net Amt. Due is zero, place a checkmark next to each item and QuickBooks will associate your check or bill payment with the related sales tax due. When you return to the Pay Sales Tax dialog box the amount previously showing as unpaid will no longer be there. If the Amt. Due does not agree with your records, you might need to create a sales tax adjustment before making your next sales tax payment.

 note

If you are an accounting professional working with QuickBooks Accountant 2012 software, review Appendix A "Client Data Review." CDR includes a tool that will help you efficiently correct sales tax payments that were recording using the incorrect payment transaction type.

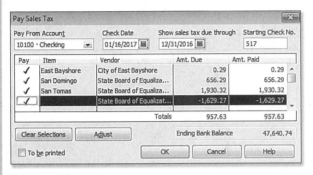

Figure 10.38
Include the corrected check (or bill) with your next period sales tax payment.

When the Sales Tax Liability Report Shows Past Sales Tax Due

If your collected sales tax amount and the amount showing payable on the Sales Tax Liability report do not match, as shown in Figure 10.39, it is because there are sales taxes collected prior to the current report's Show Sales Tax Through date that remain unpaid. Perhaps the payments were incorrectly paid using a check or bill, in which case you should correct these errors following the instructions provided in the previous section.

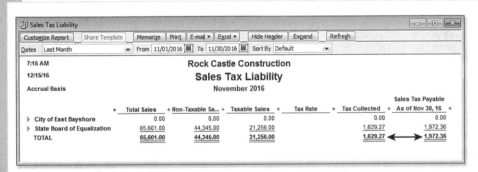

Figure 10.39
When the tax collected and the sales tax payable do not match, prior sales taxes have not been properly remitted.

To verify the totals and to make the needed corrections, follow these steps:

1. From the menu bar, select Vendors, Sales Tax, Sales Tax Liability.

2. From the Dates drop-down list, select This Month-to-Date.

3. If the Tax Collected and Sales Tax Payable totals agree with each other for today's date, your sales tax payment made previously was given the wrong Show Sales Tax Through date. To fix this error, you can void and reissue the payment or know that the QuickBooks report prepared for a future date should reflect the payment accurately.

4. If the two totals do not match, verify that the tax collected for the current period is correct. You can verify this amount by reviewing the invoices you have issued for the month.

5. Verify that the tax collected for the prior period was correct.

6. Determine to what account(s) your sales tax payments were incorrectly recorded. The previously made payments would cause these accounts to be overstated.

   In the correcting entry in example in Figure 10.40, your research found that a Sales Tax Expense type account was used when recording a sales tax payment in error.

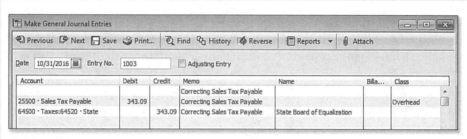

Figure 10.40
Journal entries can correct sales tax payable errors.

7. From the menu bar, select Company, Make General Journal Entries to create a correcting entry.

8. Date the entry in the period you are correcting.

9. Give the entry a number, or let QuickBooks automatically number it if that is a preference you have set.

10. Leave the first line of the general journal blank.

11. On the second line in the Account column, select the Sales Tax Payable liability account.

12. Enter a debit amount if you are decreasing your sales tax payable amount. Enter a credit amount if you are increasing your sales tax payable amount.

13. On the third line, select the account that was discovered to be overstated or understated in your review (see step 6).

14. Enter the same amount from line 2 in the opposite column (debit or credit) from the previous line. Verify that your debits are equal to your credits.

15. Click Save & Close to close the general journal.

You will now be able to select this line item with other sales tax lines for future tax payments, similarly to what was shown in Figure 10.38.

You might opt for this method to fix many months' errors with one journal entry and then have in place better controls for future sales tax management.

When Total Sales Does Not Equal Total Income

One of the important comparisons to make is the Sales Tax Liability total sales with the Profit & Loss Standard total income. Both of these reports were discussed in the section "Reconciling Total Sales to Total Income." Before comparing the reports, be sure to create both using the same accounting basis: accrual or cash. The default basis for the sales tax report comes from the Sales Tax Preference discussed earlier in this chapter. With the report displayed, you can click the Customize Report button to change the basis being used for that report.

What can cause your total sales on your Sales Tax Liability report not to match your total income on your Profit & Loss report? Some of the reasons might be the following:

- **Different accounting basis between reports**—Your Sales Tax Liability report basis is in conflict with your Profit & Loss reporting basis. The basis of the report is by default printed on the top left of the report. Both reports must be either Accrual Basis or both must be Cash Basis before comparing.

- **Non-sales type transactions recorded to income accounts**—A method to locate these transactions is to double-click the total income amount on your Profit & Loss report. Doing so opens the Transaction Detail by Account report. At the top right of the report, select Sort By and choose Type. Within each income account group, QuickBooks will sort the transactions by transaction type. Review the report for non-sales transaction types such as General Journal or Bill (to name a couple). If you find an expense transaction in this report, often the cause is from using items on expense transactions, when the item record only has an assigned income account. More details on properly setting up items can be found in Chapter 4, "Understanding QuickBooks Lists."

- **Using items on sales forms that are assigned to a non-income account**—As an example, a company that collects customer deposits might be using an item that is assigned to a current liability account. Total sales on the Sales Tax Liability report would include this amount, but the Profit & Loss would not.

- **Income recorded as a result of vendor discounts**—If you have set up an income account for your vendor discounts in your bills preferences setting, you will need to deduct this amount from your total revenue when you compare the two totals. If you are using an income account, create a separate income account for these discounts so that you can easily identify them.

The first two previous bullet points can be corrected by changing the reporting basis or correcting the original item record (select Lists, Item List from the menu bar) to include both an income and an expense account.

The last two bullet points are less likely to be changed in your process. You might instead need to prepare specific reports to proof your totals, making sure that when you file your sales tax return you are using the correct information.

In the following exercise, we will use the sample data to see how these reports can help you reconcile these differences.

Reconciling Financials and Sales Tax Reports

To practice reconciling (proofing) the Profit & Loss total income to the sales tax payable on the Sales Tax Liability report, open the sample data file as instructed in Chapter 1. Your totals might differ from those shown in the figures here, but the process remains the same:

1. From the Reports menu, open these two reports:

    - **Company & Financial, Profit & Loss Standard**—from the Dates drop-down list, select Last Month.

    - **Vendors & Payables, Sales Tax Liability**—by default, the Last Month is selected in the Dates field.

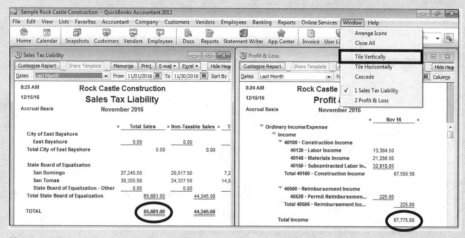

Figure 10.41
When comparing two reports, select Window, Tile Vertically.

2. Notice in this exercise that the Total Sales from the Sales Tax Liability report and Total Income from the Profit & Loss report (on the right in Figure 10.41) do not match. The difference between the two amounts in this example is $2,174.50.

3. Next, select Reports, Sales, Sales by Item Summary from the menu bar. From the Dates drop-down list, select Last Month.

4. Click Customize Report and remove the checkmarks for COGS, Ave. COGS, Gross Margin, and Gross Margin % because we do not need this information for our analysis. Click OK.

5. To make this report easier to read, you might consider selecting the Collapse button at the top right of the open report.

6. What exactly are you looking for? Because this report shows all items sold on customer sales forms during the same month being "reconciled" you are looking for items that do not map to ordinary income accounts. In Figure 10.42, our difference is easy to spot: The Retainage 1 item was used on sales transactions during the month. A review of the item record shows the account assigned is a Balance Sheet account (see Figure 10.43).

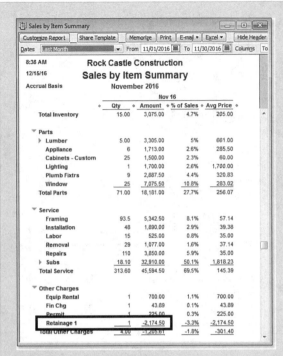

Figure 10.42
Report differences might arise when items with non-income accounts assigned are included on sales transactions.

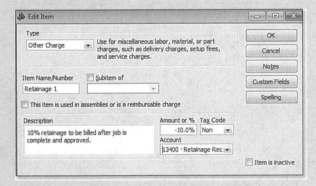

Figure 10.43
When reviewing differences, review the account assigned to items sold during the period.

 tip

Because you want to compare the totals, try this: From the menu bar, select Window, Tile Vertically. Both reports will be displayed side-by-side as shown in Figure 10.41 if these are the only currently open windows.

Now that you have identified the difference, what exactly does it mean? If your state requires you report total sales as income earned on your sales tax reports, in this example the proper amount to report would come from your Profit & Loss report. Your company's results might differ and might be more difficult to identify.

Instead, you might want to try customizing the Sales Tax Liability report. Click the Customize Report button, select the Filters tab on the Modify Report dialog box, and select All Ordinary Income Accounts from the Accounts drop-down list. From here, review the amount displayed in the Total Sales Column. If this amount now agrees with your Profit & Loss report, you can be sure there are items on invoices that are mapped to non-ordinary income accounts.

Correcting Undeposited Funds Account Errors

Did you make it through the review of each of the referenced reports in the earlier sections of this chapter? You don't want to jump into fixing transactions that affect accounts receivable without due diligence in researching what the correct balance should be. Without the review and troubleshooting time, you might hastily delete, void, or modify a transaction only to compound the problem.

This section details specific steps for correcting the errors you might find. It was important to first discover why the error was made and then fix it so you can avoid the same error on future transactions.

Reviewing the Balance in the Undeposited Funds Account

Before you can begin to agree or disagree with your Undeposited Funds account balance, it is best to review your QuickBooks data, concentrating on certain reports that will help you simplify the review process.

This section provides instructions on creating specific reports you can use for this task.

Creating an Undeposited Funds Detail Report

The first report I create for a client is a custom report titled "Undeposited Funds Detail." This is not a ready-made report in QuickBooks, but it is easy to create, as you will see.

This report is fundamental because you cannot troubleshoot a total balance for the undeposited funds you see on a balance sheet report without knowing the detail behind the numbers. If you print the register for the account, too much data will display, making it difficult to identify what is not deposited.

How do transactions get to this account? When you select the Undeposited Funds account as the deposit-to account (or you set the preference to have QuickBooks automatically do this), QuickBooks increases the balance in the Undeposited Funds account. Then, when you complete a make deposit,

 caution

Before you troubleshoot your Undeposited Funds Detail, reconcile your bank account. Identify what transactions have cleared your bank and which transactions have been recorded in QuickBooks but did not clear your bank in a timely manner.

For more information, see "Reconciling the Bank or Credit Card Account," p. 458.

QuickBooks reduces the Undeposited Funds account balance, and behind the scenes, it marks the original increase and the new decrease as cleared. Table 10.1 shows the relationship of these transactions to your accounting.

Table 10.1 Transaction Effect on Undeposited Funds Account

Transaction Type	Accounts Receivable	Undeposited Funds	Bank Account
Customer Receive Payments with Undeposited Funds Account Selected as the "Deposit to" Account	Decreases (credit)	Increases (debit)	No effect
Make Deposits	No effect	Decreases (credit)	Increases (debit)

Before we dig too deep, let's see if you agree with the detail of the Undeposited Funds balance in your QuickBooks data. You also might want to memorize this report for the convenience of reviewing the detail often, avoiding any data entry errors this section might help you uncover.

To create this Undeposited Funds Detail report, follow these easy steps:

1. From the menu bar, select Reports, Custom Reports, Transaction Detail. The Modify Report dialog box opens.

2. Display the date range as All.

3. For Total by, select Payment Method from the bottom of the list.

4. For Columns, select those you want to view on the report.

5. Click the Filters tab. In the Choose Filter box, select Account, and choose the account named Undeposited Funds from the drop-down list.

6. Also from the Filters tab, select Cleared and click the No button.

7. Click the Header/Footer tab. Change the report title to Undeposited Funds Detail. Click OK.

tip

For the date range field, type an "a" without the quote marks to make the date range default to All.

caution

The modified custom report you named Undeposited Funds Detail will always show the present state of the transaction, which means when a payment is received and is included on a Make Deposits transaction the report for a prior date will no longer show that item as undeposited. Behind the scenes, QuickBooks is marking the transaction as "cleared" as of the transaction date; therefore, you cannot get a historical snapshot with this report.

This report provides the details of the amounts that are included in the Undeposited Funds account balance. You might want to include preparing this report at the end of each month for your records. Following are other reports you might also find useful when reviewing the balance in your Undeposited Funds account.

Creating a General Ledger Report of the Undeposited Funds Account

You can review a General Ledger report of the Undeposited Funds account balance that will agree with the ending balance on your Balance Sheet report, but without quite a bit of manual work, you cannot identify each individual transaction that makes up the Undeposited Funds account for a specific prior period. Why? Because each time you deposit a receive payment, QuickBooks marks the original dated line item as cleared. This is why we first create a custom report to see if the current (today's date) detail is correct.

If you review your balances monthly, you need to print out the Undeposited Funds Detail report you created earlier in this chapter, on the last day of your accounting month. Save this report in your paper file for future reference because you cannot go back to a historical date and get the same information.

If you take credit cards as payments from your customers, I recommend you not complete the "Make Deposits" task until you view a bank statement showing the funds deposited into your bank account. This does not mean waiting a month for the statement to arrive, because most financial institutions now offer online account access to your account statements.

For those clients, particularly retail businesses, where there is often a large volume of customer receipts in any day, I recommend reviewing the modified report as part of the month, quarter, or year-end process. Notice whether any old dated transactions are on the list. If you find none, you can assume the Balance Sheet balance in Undeposited Funds as of the prior period date is probably correct.

To generate a General Ledger report, follow these steps:

1. From the menu bar, select Reports, Accountant & Taxes, General Ledger.

2. Select Customize Report from the report screen.

3. In the Modify dialog box that opens, enter an appropriate Report Date Range.

4. From the Columns box, select the columns you want to see. (You might want to include Clr for seeing the cleared status of transactions.)

5. Click the Advanced button and select to Include In Use. This will streamline the data that results on the report.

6. Click the Filters tab, choose to filter for Account, and select the Undeposited Funds account from the drop-down list.

7. Click OK.

You can use this General Ledger report to see details for the Undeposited Funds account and to verify if the running balance in this report agrees with your Balance Sheet report. However, you still cannot use this report to identify which Receive Payments transaction was not deposited as of the report date because QuickBooks does not capture the information with an "as of" date.

Removing Old Dated Payments in the Undeposited Funds Account

Did your review of the data uncover old dated payment transactions still in the Undeposited Funds account? If yes, use the following method to remove these payments without editing or modifying each transaction.

This method of correcting makes the following assumptions:

- Your bank account is reconciled before making these changes.

- You have reviewed and corrected your Accounts Receivable Aging reports.

- You have identified which payment amounts are still showing in the Undeposited Funds account, and these are the same amounts that have already been deposited to your bank register by some other method.

- You have identified the specific chart of accounts (typically income accounts) to which the deposits were originally incorrectly recorded.

This method enables you to remove the unwanted balance in your Undeposited Funds account with just a few keystrokes. To remove old payments in the Undeposited Funds account, follow these steps:

1. If the funds that remain in your Undeposited Funds account are from more than one year ago, you first should identify the total amount that was incorrectly deposited for each year. See the sidebar titled "Creating a Payment Transaction List Detail Report," in this chapter. Filter the report for the specific date range.

2. Now start the process of "removing" these identified Undeposited Funds items by selecting Banking, Make Deposits from the menu bar.

3. In the Payments to Deposit dialog box, select all the payments for deposit with dates in the date range you are correcting by placing a checkmark next to the payment items (see Figure 10.44). Click OK.

   The Make Deposits dialog box opens with each of the previously selected payments included on a new make deposit.

4. On the next available line, enter the account to which the incorrect deposits were originally recorded. In this example, you discovered that the Construction Income account was overstated by the incorrectly recorded deposits. The effect of this new transaction is to decrease (debit) the Construction Income account and decrease (credit) the Undeposited Funds account without any effect on the checking account, as shown in Figure 10.45.

5. Make sure to reconcile this net -0- deposit in your next bank reconciliation.

 caution

The date you give the Make Deposits transaction is the date the impact will be recorded in your financials. You have several important considerations to take into account when selecting the appropriate date:

- Are the corrections for a prior year?

- Has the tax return been prepared using current financial information from QuickBooks for that prior period?

- Has another adjustment to the books been done to correct the issue?

If you answered yes to any of these, you should contact your accountant and ask her advice on the date this transaction should have.

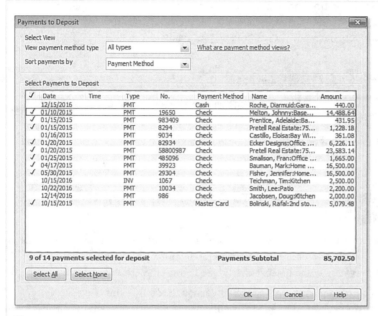

Figure 10.44
The older payments in Undeposited Funds were posted to the cash account by some other method.

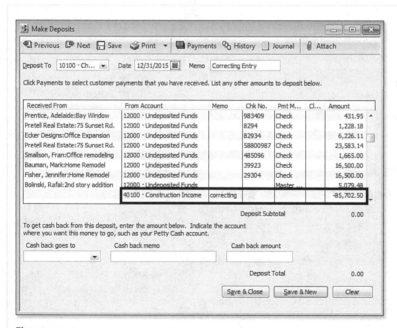

Figure 10.45
Enter a line with a negative amount recorded to the account that was previously overstated.

You should now be able to review the Undeposited Funds Detail report and agree that the items listed on this report as of today's date are those you have not yet physically taken to your bank to be deposited or the credit card vendors have not yet credited to your bank.

Unique Customer Transactions

This chapter has provided ways you can review and troubleshoot your data, and provided instructions on how to fix many of the common Accounts Receivable errors.

This section of the chapter shares some ways to handle unique transactions—the type of transaction you might come across but just are not sure how to enter.

Recording Your Accountant's Year-End Adjusting Journal Entry to Accounts Receivable

Often, adjustments at tax time might include adjustments to your Accounts Receivable account. This transaction is typically created by your accountant using a general journal transaction. What can make the entry more difficult for you is when no customer(s) are identified with the adjustment.

You can request a breakdown by customer of the adjustments made to the Accounts Receivable account. If that is not available, and you need to enter the adjustment, you might want to consider using the following method:

1. From the Customer Center, create a fictitious customer name—something such as Accountant YE Adj.

2. Use this customer to apply the line item to the make journal entry. Remember that this is a temporary fix and the balance for the fictitious customer will display on your Open Invoices report.

Later, when you are able to collect from the actual customer(s) who make up the adjustment, you can enter a reversing entry to the fictitious customer and new entries to the correct customers.

When a Customer Is Also a Vendor

Often, I am asked how to handle a transaction when you are selling your company's product or service, but instead of getting paid, you are trading it for the products or services of your customer.

To keep track of the revenue and costs in this bartering arrangement, follow these steps:

1. From the menu bar, select Lists, Chart of Accounts to open the Chart of Accounts dialog box.

caution

You can add new customers by selecting the Customer Center from the QuickBooks Home page.

However, QuickBooks does not let you use the same name on the customer list as the vendor list. A little trick can help with this; when naming the new "fictitious" customer, enter a "- C" after the name. This naming convention will not display on invoices, but when selecting this name from lists, it will bring to your attention that you are using the "customer" list item.

2. Click the Account button. Select New and create an account named Barter Account as a bank account type following the instructions on the screen. Click Save & Close.

3. From the menu bar, select Customers, Create Invoices. Select the new customer you created (your vendor is now added to the customer list). Enter the information as if you were selling your products or services to this customer. Click Save & Close.

4. From the menu bar, select Customers, Receive Payments. Select the new customer you created and record the amount of the payment, placing a checkmark next to the appropriate "fictitious" invoice.

5. Select the new Barter Account as the Deposit To account and click Save & Close to finish the revenue part of the transaction.

6. From the menu bar, select Banking, Make Deposits to open the Payments to Deposit dialog box. Place a checkmark next to the fictitious transaction, and click OK to advance to the Make Deposits dialog box.

7. In the Make Deposits dialog box, select the Barter Account as the Deposit To account and select the date you want this transaction recorded. Click Save & Close when done.

 caution

If your default preference is set to have all customer payments go to Undeposited Funds account, you will need to change that preference temporarily.

From the menu bar, select Edit, Preferences and choose the Payments preference. Remove the checkmark in the Use Undeposited Funds as a Default Deposit to Account.

You have recorded the "potential" revenue side as well as the "fictitious" payment of the invoice of the barter agreement. Now you need to record the expense side of the transaction.

I recommend that the transactions going in and out of the barter account are equal in value; if not, you will need to make an adjustment in the register. (Select Banking, User Register from the menu bar.) Select the Barter Account and increase or decrease the amount to an income or expense account as determined by the amount left in the account.

To record the expense with a check, follow these steps:

1. Create a vendor list item for your customer who is also a vendor. I append the name with a – V so when I select the name, I will know I am using the Vendor list item and not the Customer list item.

2. To create an expense transaction, select Banking, Write Checks from the menu bar.

3. Select the Barter Account as the checking account.

4. For the check or reference number, use any number or alphanumeric characters you want.

5. For the payee, use the newly created vendor list item (a vendor record for your customer).

6. Record to the normal expense account an amount as if you were purchasing the goods or services with a check.

7. Click Save & Close. If paying by check, the process is complete. If you recorded a vendor bill, continue with the following steps.

8. To pay the bill, select Vendors, Pay Bills from the menu bar.

9. Place a checkmark next to the appropriate bill that has been paid by providing the vendor with your product or services.

10. In the Payment Method box, select the choice to assign check number because we don't expect to print a check to give to the vendor.

11. In the Payment Account box, select the newly created Barter Account as the payment account.

12. Click Pay Selected Bills to open the Assign Check Numbers dialog box. Assign a fictitious check number of your choosing. You can even put the term "Barter" in for the check number. Click OK and QuickBooks displays a payment summary. Select Done.

When this process is finished, your Barter Account should have a zero balance as indicated earlier in this section. You might even want to perform a bank reconciliation of the Barter Account to clear both equal sides of the transaction.

Recording a Customer's Bounced Check

If you have ever had a customer's payment check bounce, you know how important correct accounting is. When a check is bounced, often your banking institution automatically debits your bank balance and might also charge an extra service fee.

So just how do you record these transactions and also increase the balance your customer now owes you? Follow these steps:

1. To create a bounced check item, select Lists, Item List from the menu bar. Click the Item button and select New. If necessary, select OK to dismiss the New Feature message.

2. The New Item dialog box displays. Select an Other Charge item type. In both the Number/Name field and Description field, type **Bounced Check**.

3. Leave the Amount field blank; assign Non as the Tax Code. For the Account, select the bank account that was deducted for the returned check (see Figure 10.46).

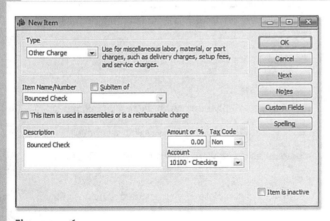

Figure 10.46
This item will be used to record the deduction to your bank account for the bounced check amount.

4. Using the preceding steps, create an additional Other Charge item type to be used to invoice the customer for the bank fee you incurred. Name the item Bad Chk Chg.

5. Leave the Amount blank, set the Tax Code as Non, and for the Account, select an income account, such as Returned Check Charges.

6. From the menu bar, select Customers, Create Invoices, and in the dialog box that displays, select the customer with the bounced check. On the first line of the invoice, use the Bounced Check item and assign the amount of the bounced check. On the second line of the invoice, use the Bad Chk Chg item and assign the amount of the fee your bank charged you (see Figure 10.47). Click Save & Close.

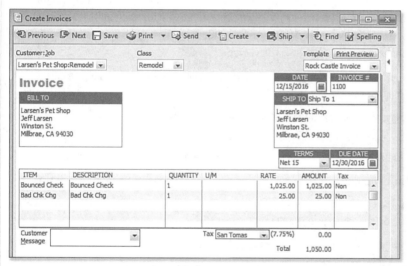

Figure 10.47
Create an invoice to collect the NSF funds and recover the bank fee from the customer.

The impact is to increase Accounts Receivable (debit), increase Income for the bank fee (credit), and decrease your bank account (credit). The reduction in the bank account is to record the fact that the bank deducted the amount from your account.

When you reconcile your bank account, be sure to enter the service fee charged.

Although this method provides a process to charge your customer again for the returned check as well as the bank fee, it does have one side effect you might want to consider. When you create a Balance Sheet on a cash basis, you might see this amount in Accounts Receivable.

Tracking Customer Deposits in QuickBooks

Do you require your customers to pay a deposit in advance of the product shipping or the service being provided? You might want to track these in one of two ways:

- As a credit to Accounts Receivable for the specific customer

- As a credit to an Other Current Liability account

You might want to ask your company accountant which method is preferred. Using the first method is often easier and takes fewer steps. The second method of using a current liability account reports the pre-payment in the proper category on the business' balance sheet.

If you are choosing the first method listed you would create a receive payment when your customer pays and not assign the payment to an invoice. In effect, this debits (increases) your Undeposited Funds account or bank account and credits (reduces) accounts receivable.

If you choose to use the second method, follow these steps:

1. If needed, start the process to create a Customer Deposits account by selecting Lists, Chart of Accounts from the menu bar.

2. Click the Account button at the bottom of the screen and select New.

3. In the Add New Account dialog box that opens, from the Other Account Types drop-down list, select the Other Current Liability type account and follow the remaining steps on the screen.

4. Next, you will create an item to be used on invoices for this pre-payment. From the menu bar, select Lists, Item Lists.

5. Click the Item button on the bottom of the list and select New.

6. From the New Item type drop-down list, select Other Charge.

7. In the Item Name/Number field, type a name such as **Customer Deposits**. Enter an optional description and select the Customer Deposits other current liability account from the Account drop-down list.

8. Prepare your invoice to the customer for the amount of the pre-payment you are requiring. When the customer pays, record the Receive Payments transaction.

9. When the project is completed and you are ready to recognize the revenue associated with the sale, create your invoice using the item(s) that were sold to the customer. On the next available line of your invoice use the Customer Deposit item, only this time enter a negative amount.

QuickBooks will then record the revenue in the period the sale was complete, and the final invoice will be reduced by the amount of the deposit previously paid.

Using the method described here does have a tradeoff. If you are a cash basis taxpayer, you would not expect to see a balance in your Accounts Receivable account when the Balance Sheet report is prepared on a cash basis. However, when you use this method, you will see an Accounts Receivable balance on a cash basis Balance Sheet report. One of the causes of this is that QuickBooks reports an Accounts Receivable balance on a cash basis Balance Sheet report when items are used that map to other Balance Sheet accounts.

Unique Sales Tax Transactions

Over the years, I have come across some unique sales tax transaction tracking needs. This section addresses several that you might find useful if your state has similar guidelines.

As always, because you are acting as the "agent" for the state in collecting sales tax from your customers, you should take the time to research the sales tax regulations for each state where you do business.

The state you sell in might require you to collect and track multiple sales tax rates depending on where the customer is located. If you have a customer with different tax rate locations, you need to create a customer for each tax location if you want QuickBooks to automatically collect the correct tax amount because QuickBooks tracks the sales tax rate to the customer and not to the job.

When Your State Imposes a Maximum Sales Tax

I have encountered having to track a state-imposed maximum sales tax a few times. If your state imposes a maximum sales tax for a certain type of sale, I recommend the following method:

1. From the menu bar, select Lists, Item List. (If the New Feature dialog box displays, click OK.) From the Item drop-down list, select New to create a new list item. The New Item dialog box displays.

2. If you do not have a subtotal item on your list, select Subtotal from the Type drop-down list.

3. To create the invoice to your customer, select Customers, Create Invoices from the menu bar.

4. Enter the taxable items on the invoice, making sure the Tax column has "Tax" listed.

5. Enter a subtotal item—you might even want to type in the description that this amount is subject to sales tax.

6. Enter the next sale item that is normally taxed. If you have met a threshold defined by your state, select Non in the Tax column. See Figure 10.48.

QuickBooks will now record the total sales (in this example) of $6,000.00, but it shows only $5,000 in the Taxable Sales column of the Sales Tax Liability report, as shown in Figure 10.49.

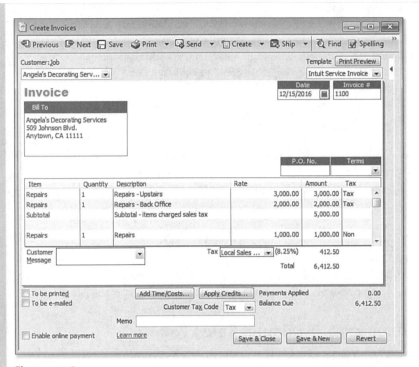

Figure 10.48
Adding a subtotal and adjusting the Tax column helps when your state has a threshold for sales tax charges on a single invoice.

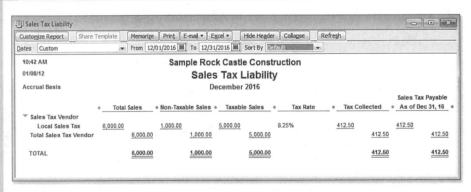

Figure 10.49
QuickBooks records the taxable revenue amount from the non-taxable sale amount.

Multiple Sales Tax Rates on One Invoice

In particular, if your business sells retail items, liquor, and food all on one sales form, chances are each item type is subject to a unique sales tax rate. Follow these steps for creating the subtotal item and 0% sales tax item. Assign this 0% named "See Above" sales tax item to your customer.

Next, create your customer's invoice as detailed in the previous section, following these additional steps:

1. Create these items:

   - **Subtotal Item**—Using the steps outlined in the previous section.

   - **Sales Tax Item**—Use the name See Above and the same, See Above, for the description. Tax Rate will be 0.0%. Tax Agency should be your most common Tax Agency vendor.

   - **Sales Tax Items**—Representing the tax jurisdictions you are required to collect and report on. Name them clearly so your customer can identify them.

2. Enter the line item(s) subject to one tax rate.

3. Enter a subtotal line.

4. Enter the appropriate sales tax item.

5. Enter additional invoice lines, each with a subtotal and appropriate sales tax items.

QuickBooks will collect and report on the correct amount of sales tax charged for the different item types being sold.

To further clarify this point, the example shown in Figure 10.50 does not track sales by customer, but just a retail summary for the day's sales. The example also shows how to charge multiple sales tax rates on a single invoice by placing a subtotal after each group of sales and then placing the correct sales tax rate after the subtotal.

If you would like more information on this, you can press the F1 key on your keyboard to open QuickBooks Help. Click the Search tab and on the top search bar, type "sales summaries," and follow the link for more information on this topic.

Figure 10.50
Creating an invoice with multiple sales tax rates charged.

Issuing Credit Memos When Sales Tax Should Not Have Been Charged

Issuing customer credit memos is necessary for correct reporting when you file your sales tax on accrual basis (sales tax payment liability accrued as of the date of the customer invoice) and not required when you report sales tax liability on cash basis (sales tax payment liability not accrued until the date of customer's payment). However, I still recommend having controls in place, which limit the ability to modify an invoice from a prior month.

After you have filed your sales tax return with your state, you should not adjust any invoices or sales tax payments recorded on or before your file-through date. If you do, QuickBooks recalculates the taxable sales, non-taxable sales, and amount owed, and your return as filed with the state will no longer agree with your QuickBooks data.

Instead of adjusting a customer's invoice, consider using the QuickBooks customer credit memos/refund. For example, suppose you charged sales tax to a non-taxable customer by mistake. Let's also assume you have filed your accrual basis sales tax return for the month of that invoice, overstating taxable sales.

Creating a credit memo reduces taxable sales, increases non-taxable sales, and credits the customer's invoice for the sales tax amount, all within the current sales tax month.

Follow the same steps outlined in the section in Chapter 9 titled, "Recording and Applying a Customer Credit Memo" earlier in this chapter for creating a credit memo from the original customer invoice. You will want to be sure you date the credit memo in the current month you have not yet filed your state sales tax reports for. The credit memo will then reduce your sales tax you owe for the current period.

 note

In Chapter 16, "Sharing QuickBooks Data with Your Accountant," I discuss setting a closing date for your data. I recommend this same control be placed in your file after preparing your monthly or quarterly sales tax returns for your state.

SETTING UP PAYROLL

Getting Started

When your business hires employees, one of the more important tasks you will have is making sure your QuickBooks data is set up correctly to handle this responsibility. This chapter details for you the proper setup of your payroll. In Chapter 12, "Managing Payroll," you will learn how to efficiently review your payroll data, and handle some of those unique payroll transactions.

A common definition of an employee is "a person in the service of another under any contract of hire, express or implied, oral or written. The employer also has the power or right to control and direct the employee in the material details of how the work is to be performed." If your company hires individuals who meet this criteria, your company is responsible for paying wages, collecting and paying certain federal and state payroll taxes, and filing quarterly and annual forms.

Your company becomes an agent of the federal and state governments because the company must collect certain payroll-related taxes and pay these on predetermined payment schedules.

 note

Are you already using QuickBooks for your payroll processing? Why not start with the QuickBooks Run Payroll Checkup, discussed on pg. 397.

Payroll Process Overview

QuickBooks is designed to help you set up and manage your company's payroll. Payroll tasks are easily completed using the Employee Center and Payroll Center. Scheduling your payroll and related liability payments practically eliminates the chance of making errors.

The recommended payroll workflow detailed here, when combined with the frequent review of reports, can help you manage your company's payroll efficiently and accurately:

1. Sign up for an Intuit QuickBooks payroll subscription.

2. Set Payroll and Employee preferences for your company.

3. Complete (if your data is new) the Payroll Setup process or use the Run Payroll Checkup diagnostic tool included with your QuickBooks software.

4. Set up scheduled payrolls to pay your employees.

5. Pay your scheduled payroll liabilities.

6. Reconcile your bank account each month verifying that the paychecks distributed were cleared for the proper amounts.

7. Review and compare your business financials and payroll reports.

8. Prepare your quarterly and annual state and federal payroll forms directly in QuickBooks (depending on which payroll subscription you have purchased).

When managing payroll in QuickBooks, you will use these transactions:

- **Paycheck**—Record payment to an employee and automatically calculate all additions and deductions. You can identify these in your bank register as the transactions with a PAY CHK transaction type, as shown in Figure 11.1.

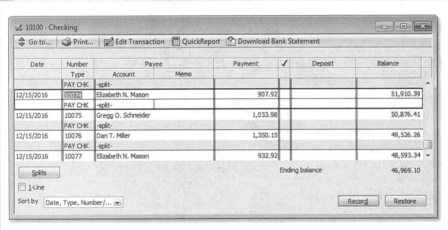

Figure 11.1
Properly created employee paychecks have PAY CHK as the transaction type.

- **Liability Adjustment**—Modify the payroll liability amounts computed from actual paychecks. You can identify these transactions in your bank register as transactions with a LIAB CHK transaction type.

■ **Refund Deposit for Taxes and Liabilities**—Record any refund received from overpaying your payroll liabilities. You will learn more about this transaction type in Chapter 12, "Managing Payroll."

Each of these transactions are accessible from the Payroll Center or by selecting Employees, Payroll Center from the menu bar.

When you use the proper payroll transactions, QuickBooks will include the amounts in preparing payments of payroll liabilities due or when preparing state and federal payroll reports in QuickBooks.

Selecting and Activating a Payroll Service Subscription

For QuickBooks to automatically calculate your payroll, you need to purchase a payroll service subscription from Intuit in addition to the purchase of your QuickBooks financial software.

QuickBooks financial software partnered with an Intuit-provided payroll service makes setting up payroll, collecting taxes, remitting timely payments of the collected taxes, and filing the required payroll reports trouble free.

Purchase your payroll service subscription at www.payroll.com, or click the Learn About Payroll Options on the Home page and select a plan that works for your company.

As of the writing of this book, Intuit offers four payroll service options, one of which is sure to meet the needs of your company.

 note

You can enable manual payroll in QuickBooks without purchasing a subscription. With manual payroll, QuickBooks will not calculate the payroll taxes or prepare the payroll forms. I do not recommend this method unless you have only a few payroll checks that are always the same amounts each pay period.

From the menu bar, select Help, QuickBooks Help. In the search box, type "process payroll manually" and select the link with the same name. Read the information and follow the provided instructions.

Preparing and Printing Paychecks Only

On the Home page, select Learn About Payroll Options. Choose the "I Want My Accountant..." option. This option is the Intuit Payroll Basic subscription and includes:

■ The capability to enter employee hours and let QuickBooks automatically calculate payroll taxes, additions, and other deductions.

■ The option to print checks; or, for a small per check fee, you can direct deposit the earnings into your employees' bank accounts.

■ A variety of reports your accountant can use to complete payroll tax forms.

Preparing and Printing Paychecks and File Tax Forms

On the Home page, select Learn About Payroll Options. Choose the "I Want To Pay & File..." option. This option is the Intuit QuickBooks Payroll Enhanced subscription and includes:

■ Ability to enter employee hours and let QuickBooks automatically calculate payroll taxes, additions, and other deductions.

- Option to print checks, or for a small per check fee, direct deposit the earnings into your employee's bank accounts.

- Automatic preparation of federal and most state tax forms for you to print or E-File.

If you are an accounting professional, you can select the Intuit QuickBooks Payroll Enhanced for Accountant's subscription. With this subscription you can do all of the tasks named previousy plus:

- Create after-the-fact payroll

- Calculate net-to-gross paychecks

- Support up to 50 FEINs with your paid payroll subscription

- Prepare Client Ready Payroll Reports (using Excel)

More details can be found by visiting the www.proadvisor.intuit.com website.

Allowing Intuit Payroll Experts Prepare Your Payroll

On the Home page, select Learn About Payroll Options. Choose the "I Want Intuit Payroll Experts..." option. You can choose from two subscriptions, both detailed here:

- Assisted Payroll Subscription

  - Work with a payroll specialist to set up your first payroll.

  - Enter hours into QuickBooks to create paychecks. All of your taxes, additions, and deductions are calculated automatically.

  - Print checks or offer direct deposit into your employees' bank accounts.

  - Allow Intuit to process tax payments and forms for you, guaranteed accurate and on time.

- Intuit Full-Service Payroll Subscription

  - Work with Intuit payroll experts to set up or transfer all your employee data.

  - Enter hours into QuickBooks to create paychecks. All of your taxes, additions, and deductions are calculated automatically.

  - Print checks or offer direct deposit into your employees' bank accounts.

  - Allow Intuit to process tax payments and forms for you, guaranteed accurate and on time.

 note

If you currently use an outsourced payroll solution that does not integrate with QuickBooks, consider one of the I Want Intuit Payroll Experts... subscriptions. Entering payroll into QuickBooks can save time and improve accuracy.

Using Intuit Online Payroll

With an Intuit Online Payroll subscription you can prepare payroll anytime, anywhere with an Internet connection. With Intuit Online Payroll you can:

- Enter employee hours online and paycheck additions, and deductions automatically calculate.

- Receive email reminders when it's payday or tax filing deadlines.

- Print paychecks or direct deposit employees' paychecks into their bank accounts.

- Process electronic payments and tax filings.

- Allow employees to view their pay stub information online.

- Process payroll using your mobile device.

- Prepare many detailed payroll reports.

- Process an unlimited number of payrolls each month.

- Import the transactions into QuickBooks (as a Write Checks transaction).

 note

Are you an accounting professional? Would you like to share responsibility with your client for payroll processing?

With Intuit Online Payroll for Accounting Professionals subscription, your client can enter the payroll hours and leave the responsibility for tax filings to you. Visit www.accountant.intuit.com and select the Payroll tab to learn about each of the payroll offerings.

Updating Payroll Tax Tables

Your purchase of an Intuit payroll subscription includes periodic tax table updates. When the federal or state government makes changes to payroll taxes or forms, you will be notified that a new tax table is available.

To update your tax tables make sure you are connected to the Internet and you have a current payroll subscription.

To update payroll tax tables, follow these steps:

1. From the menu bar, select Employees, Payroll Center. Your payroll subscription status is detailed to the left. See Figure 11.2.

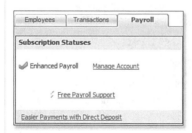

Figure 11.2
Check the status and manage your payroll subscription from the Payroll Center.

2. From the menu bar, select Employees, Get Payroll Updates.

3. Click the Payroll Update Info button for details about the currently installed tax table version.

4. Select the option to download only changes and additions to the installed payroll files or download the entire payroll update. Click the Update button.

5. Click OK to close the Payroll Update message that tells you a new tax table or updates were installed. Click Troubleshooting Payroll Updates if the update does not install successfully.

6. QuickBooks opens the Payroll Update News dialog box. Click through the tabs of information to learn more about changes made with the installed update. Press the Escape key on your keyboard to close.

7. From the menu bar, select Employees, Payroll Center.

8. On the left side of the Payroll Center, view information about your payroll subscription statuses.

Employer Resources

Getting started with payroll can seem like a daunting task. In this section I share many resources that will help you successfully get started with payroll.

Classifying Workers as Employees

Your business might hire employees and independent contractors (discussed in Chapter 7, "Setting Up Vendors"). Use these IRS guidelines when classifying a worker as an employee:

- **Behavioral**—Does the company control or have the right to control what the worker does and how the worker does his or her job?

- **Financial**—Are the business aspects of the worker's job controlled by the payer? (These include things like how the worker is paid, whether expenses are reimbursed, if the business owner provides tools and supplies.)

- **Type of Relationship**—Are there written contracts or employee type benefits (that is, pension plan, insurance, vacation pay, and so on)? Will the relationship continue and is the work performed a key aspect of the business?

The IRS provides additional comments on this topic on its website, www.irs.gov. Type "contractor or employee" in the help search box and click the links provided for more details.

Federal and State Required Identification

Your business will likely have identification numbers assigned by federal, state, and local governments. The identification numbers detailed here represent the basic identification numbers you will need to properly report and pay payroll liabilities.

As mentioned earlier, your company becomes an agent of the state and federal government when it collects from employees certain taxes that are required to be reported and paid to the respective legal entity. Your company will need the following identification numbers for properly reporting and remitting your payroll taxes:

 tip

The reporting regulations for federal and state governments can be time consuming to learn about. Hiring legal and accounting professionals to guide you through the process can save you time and allow you to concentrate on building your business.

- **Federal Employer Identification Number**—Commonly referred to as FEIN. This number is obtained from the Internal Revenue Service. Visit www.irs.gov for instructions.

- **State Withholding Tax ID**—Issued by the states you do business in and used to file and pay state income tax withheld from your employees' paychecks. Some states might also require IDs by city, county, or both. Call your state tax department or search your state's website for more details.

- **State Unemployment ID**—Issued by the states you do business in and used to pay and file state unemployment reports. Call your state tax department or search your state's website for more details.

- Other identification numbers as required by the state, county, or city jurisdictions you do business in.

You might be processing payroll before you have your assigned identification numbers. Check with your state taxing authority for instructions on paying these liabilities while you wait for your proper identification number to be assigned.

IRS and Other Forms

Your business is required to have on file for each employee a Form W-4: Employee's Withholding Allowance Certificate. You can access this form and other useful forms for your business in the Your Taxes section of the following website: http://payroll.intuit.com/support/forms/index.jsp. If the forms provided at this site are not the most current, you can also go to www.irs.gov.

State Reporting

Each state that you have employees working in will have specific filing requirements. You are even required to report new hires and in some states report independent contractors. Your state might also require city and county reporting. You can access information from each state's website, or Intuit provides useful information on the following websites:

- http://payroll.intuit.com/support/PTS/

- http://payroll.intuit.com/support/PTS/statelocaltax.jsp

Properly tracking and reporting to the state your payroll activity will help you avoid costly penalties for not filing timely.

Other General Requirements

There are many other requirements of the business owner when paying employees, including displaying the most current federal and state labor law posters at your place of business. More information can be found at www.freeposteraudit.com.

Because payroll requirements are changing all the time, make sure you have an accounting professional who can review your payroll setup or who can file the returns for you.

Creating Payroll Accounts in the Chart of Accounts

Proper payroll tracking includes having the necessary payroll liability and expense accounts in the chart of accounts.

Review your data to make sure you have these accounts or create them as needed. Adding subaccounts (see Figure 11.3) to the default accounts created by QuickBooks can help you track the financial details of payroll more efficiently.

Figure 11.3
Create subaccounts for payroll liability and expenses for more detailed reporting.

> See "Chart of Accounts," p. 77 for more information on creating these subaccounts.

Typical accounts to create for working recording payroll transactions include:

- **Bank Account**—QuickBooks does not require that you have a separate bank account for payroll transactions. Companies with large amounts of funds from operations might choose to have another bank account for payroll transactions. Having a separate bank account for payroll can limit the business' financial exposure from fraud.

- **Payroll Liabilities—Other Current Liability**—QuickBooks uses this account type to track the amount owed to federal or state governments, health insurance providers, and so on. QuickBooks creates this account for you automatically. Include the following as subaccounts to this account and add additional subaccounts as needed:

  - FICA/Medicare Payable (also referred to a 941 taxes). For simplicity, I recommend a single account combining the employee deductions and employer contributions.

- State Unemployment Payable (also referred to as SUTA).

- Federal Unemployment Payable (also referred to as FUTA).

- Health Insurance Payable.

- Wage Garnishments.

- **Job Costs**—Cost of Goods Sold. Many industries track the costs associated with providing a service or product to their customers or jobs. To track these properly on your Income Statement, use the Cost of Goods Sold account category. Do not overuse this category by adding too many to the chart of accounts; instead use QuickBooks items for greater detail.

- **Overhead Costs**—**Expense**—When you create a company-paid payroll item you will assign an account for the expense. Payroll items are used on paycheck transactions and have account(s) assigned to them. QuickBooks automatically creates a Payroll Expenses account. Typically, you would add the following as subaccounts:

  - **Salaries & Wages**—Assign to payroll compensation items.

  - **Payroll Taxes**—Assign to the employer Social Security and Medicare payroll items.

  - **State Unemployment**—Assign to your state(s) unemployment payroll item.

  - **Federal Unemployment**—Assign to the Federal Unemployment payroll item.

  - **Employee Benefits**—Assign to company-paid benefits including health, dental, life insurance, and other types of benefits.

A comprehensive chart of accounts that includes subaccounts for liabilities and expenses will make it easy for you to review your payroll and fix any errors.

Setting Up Payroll Tax Vendors

Tracking, paying, and reporting payroll liabilities balances can be improved if you identify the vendors by the tax or benefit being paid. This is important for states or other agencies that have the same payee name for multiple payroll liabilities.

 tip

Have you been recording QuickBooks payroll transactions without using these recommended subaccounts? Create the desired subaccounts, then edit the payroll items assigning the newly created subaccount.

QuickBooks will reassign all previous transactions to the newly created subaccounts. Always make a backup of your data before attempting a procedure such as this.

 caution

Do you have employees who work in the office doing administrative tasks and other employees who perform work related to customers and jobs? If you do, proper recording of payroll costs would assign the costs of administrative payroll to an overhead expense account, and customer or job payroll expenses to cost of goods sold account.

However, QuickBooks has a limitation with this process. Company-paid payroll tax items only allow a single-expense account. The result is each specific company-paid payroll tax expense is reported to a single account. Keep this in mind when you are reviewing your financials.

Creating separate vendor records is recommended, but not required. When processing the payroll liability payments from the Payroll Center, QuickBooks will prepare a separate liability check for each:

- Unique liability payroll item assigned to a specific payee.

- Liability payment with a different due date.

When preparing the Federal 941/944 and Federal 940 payments, QuickBooks will create a separate check for each type of liability or for same payroll item types but with different due dates. See the Pay Scheduled Liabilities section in Figure 11.4. This is necessary so that the reporting and payment for these liabilities follow strict due date guidelines dictated by the state, federal government, or other entity being paid.

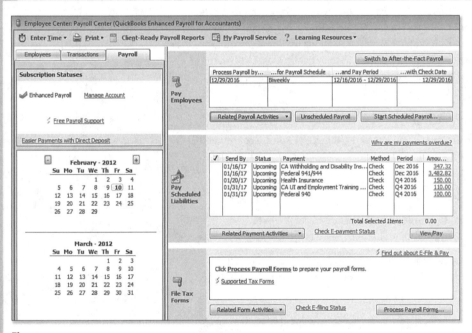

Figure 11.4
QuickBooks will prepare individual checks for the different payroll items and for the same payroll items but with different due dates.

➡ *To learn more about creating your vendor records, see "Adding or Modifying Vendors," p. 194.*

The following is a list of some of the more common payroll vendors you should create when you are managing payroll:

- United States Treasury—941

- United States Treasury—940

- State income tax vendor

- State unemployment tax vendor

- Health insurance vendor

Payroll Preferences

After you sign up for one of the Intuit Payroll Service subscriptions, you need to enable payroll and set some payroll-specific and employee-specific preferences. There are two types of preferences in QuickBooks:

- **My Preferences**—Settings that are unique to the user logged into the data file and are not shared by other users.

- **Company Preferences**—Settings that are common for all users. When a preference is modified on the Company Preferences tab, the change affects all users.

For this section, reference is only made to Company Preferences, as there are not any My Preferences that directly affect the payroll process. Log into the file as the Admin or External Accountant user in single-user mode to set the following preferences.

Payroll and Employee Preferences

These specific preferences are set for all users. To set up payroll and employee preferences, follow these steps:

1. From the menu bar, select Edit, Preferences to open the Preferences dialog box. Select the Payroll & Employees—Company Preferences tab as shown in Figure 11.5.

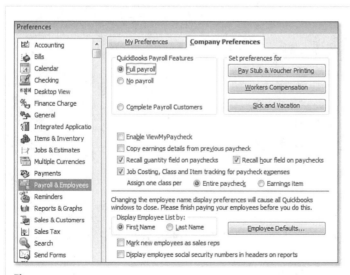

Figure 11.5
Setting defaults improves accuracy and efficiency when working with payroll activities.

2. Select the Full Payroll option button in the QuickBooks Payroll Features box. This button enables the remaining features in the Preferences dialog box.

3. Select the checkbox next to the features that are appropriate to your business:

   - **Copy Earnings Details from Previous Check**—Copies hours, rates, and Customer:Job from prior paycheck.

   - **Recall Quantity Field on Paychecks**—Recalls line 1 of a previous paycheck, payroll item, and rate only; no Customer:Job recalled.

   - **Recall Hour Field on Paychecks**—Recalls total hours only and places total number of hours on a single line even if prior paycheck had several lines.

   - **Job Costing, Class, and Item Tracking for Paycheck Expenses**—Enables QuickBooks to add the cost of company-paid taxes to the burdened costs for time that is assigned to a Customer:Job. QuickBooks also offers the Class Tracking by Paycheck or Earnings Item option if you have the class tracking preference enabled.

4. Choose the default for displaying employee names on reports. Choose to display by First Name or Last Name.

5. Select the Mark New Employees as Sales Reps checkbox if you want new employees automatically added to the sales rep list. An employee who is also a sales rep can be listed on a customer invoice transaction so you can report on sales by rep.

6. Select the Display Employee Social Security Numbers in Headers on Reports checkbox if you want to display this sensitive information on reports.

7. Click the Employee Defaults button to set the following defaults for new employees:

   - Earnings items and rate

   - Time data to create paychecks

   - Additions, deductions, or company contributions payroll items

   - Employee coverage by qualified pension plan

   - Payroll schedule or pay frequency

   - Class (if the QuickBooks Class preference is enabled)

   - Taxes for federal and state tax settings

   - Sick and vacation settings

8. Click OK to close the Employee Defaults dialog box.

9. Click the Set Preferences for Pay Stub and Voucher Printing button to open the Payroll Printing Preferences dialog box shown in Figure 11.6. In this dialog box, you can customize what detail will print on employees' paycheck stubs.

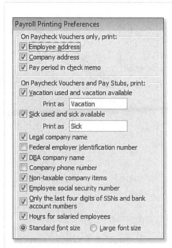

Figure 11.6
Customize the information that will print on the employee's paychecks or paystubs.

10. Click the Workers Compensation button to set the preference to track worker's comp, to be warned when worker's comp code is not assigned, and to exclude overtime hours from worker's compensation calculations.

11. Click the Sick and Vacation button to set default accrual period, hours accrued, maximum number of hours, and if the hours should be reset each new year.

Checking

These specific preferences are set for all users. From the menu bar, select Edit, Preferences to open the Preferences dialog box. Select the Checking preference from the left side and click the Company Preferences tab.

In the Select Default Accounts to Use box, select the Open the Create Paychecks checkbox or the Open Pay Payroll Liabilities checkbox and specify a bank account from the drop-down list.

Time and Expense

These specific preferences are set for all users. To set up time and expense preferences, follow these steps:

1. From the menu bar, select Edit, Preferences to open the Preferences dialog box and select the Time & Expenses—Company Preferences tab.

2. Select Yes in the Time Tracking box if you plan to use timesheets to record employee work hours.

3. If necessary, change the First Day of Work Week from the drop-down list.

 note

Do you invoice customers for time, expense, and a markup percentage? If yes, the Invoicing Options will help you with this task. For more information, see "Time and Expense Invoicing," p. 303.

Using the Payroll Setup Interview

The Payroll Setup Interview is helpful for new and existing QuickBooks payroll users. New users will appreciate how it walks you through setting up your first payroll.

For existing QuickBooks Payroll users, the Payroll Setup will help you by identifying missing information necessary for properly preparing, reporting, and paying payroll. If you do not have all of the information needed at the time of setup, select Finish Later to exit the Payroll Setup. You can return later to update the information.

Information Needed to Set Up Payroll

The following information should be collected, where possible, before beginning to set up your payroll:

- **Compensation types**—Compile a list of the types of pay you offer, such as hourly, salary, overtime, vacation, and so on. You will be establishing a QuickBooks payroll item for each of these.

- **Other additions or deductions to payroll**—Some examples: dental insurance, uniforms, and union dues to name just a few.

- **Employee names, addresses, and Social Security numbers**—Form W-4: Employees Withholding Allowance Certificate.

- **Payroll tax payment schedules and rates**—That is, what frequency your business is required to pay payroll taxes, including the rate you pay for your state unemployment tax and other taxes.

- **A year-to-date payroll register from your previous payroll system**—If you're transferring your payroll process to QuickBooks at any other time than the first of a calendar year, request a year-to-date payroll register from your previous payroll system.

     For more information, see "Mid-Year Payroll Setup," p. 394.

- **Any year-to-date payroll tax and other liability payments made prior to using QuickBooks**—These will help you to prepare your startup payroll records in QuickBooks.

With this information collected, you are ready to begin using the Payroll Setup Interview. This handy tool uses a question-and-answer format to walk you through customizing your payroll settings. When completed, you can begin preparing payroll checks for your employees.

Introduction

The Payroll Setup Interview will guide you through adding the necessary payroll items needed to begin processing payroll.

> **note**
>
> If you have been using QuickBooks for preparing payroll, consider using the Run Payroll Checkup diagnostics. From the menu bar, select Employees, My Payroll Services, Run Payroll Checkup. To learn more about working with this feature, see "Using the Run Payroll Checkup Diagnostic Tool," p. 397.

After purchasing a payroll service subscription, launch Payroll Setup (see Figure 11.7) by selecting Employees, Payroll Setup from the menu bar. Optionally, click the link Payroll Item Checklist (not shown in Figure 11.7). Click Continue.

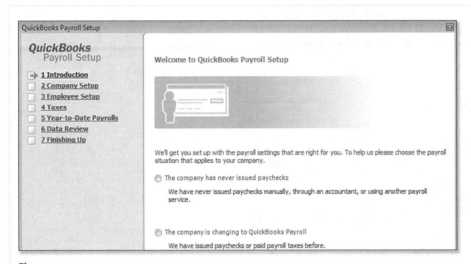

Figure 11.7
Selecting the right option for setting up payroll will affect the menus provided in the QuickBooks Payroll Setup dialog box.

Choose one of the following that best describes your business payroll setup needs:

- **The Company Has Never Issued Paychecks**—Manually through an accountant or using another payroll service.

- **The Company Is Changing to QuickBooks Payroll**—Paychecks have been issued in the same year you are starting to use QuickBooks payroll.

The instructions that follow assume no prior paychecks have been issued. Your menu options will differ if you selected the Company Is Changing to QuickBooks Payroll.

Company Setup

The Company Setup introduction provides two methods for creating pay types and benefits:

- **Typical New Employer Setup**—QuickBooks automatically creates common payroll items.

- **Custom Setup**—Select this option if you need to set up sick time, vacation time, or insurance benefits.

    To learn more about adding custom payroll items, see "Adding or Editing Payroll Items," p. 406.

The instructions that follow will assume you selected Typical New Employer Setup. Click Continue to begin setting up your employees (see Figure 11.8).

Employee John Smith

Enter employee's name and address

Legal name

First name | John | M.I. |

* Last name | Smith |

Print on check as | John Smith |

Employee status | Active ▾ | Explain

Contact information

* Home Address | 400 Oak Shores Road |
| |

* City | Anytown |

* State | CA - California ▾ |

* Zip Code | | Enter employee home zip code for printing on W-2.

Figure 11.8
Be sure to have your employees' information ready when you run the Payroll Setup Interview so you can complete each of the required fields.

Employee Setup

You can work most efficiently with entering your employees if you have all of the required information listed here. Complete the following information:

- Legal Name.

- Contact Information.

- Employee type and other hiring information.

- Payroll schedule, pay type, and rate (see Figure 11.9).

- Additions or deductions to employee's payroll.

- Determine what method of payment will be made for the payroll—check, direct deposit to an Intuit Pay Card, bank account, or splitting the amount into multiple direct deposit bank accounts.

- The state worked in and state subject to withholding taxes.

- Federal tax information from the employee's Form W-4, and select the proper withholdings and credits. Most employees' wages are subject to Medicare, Social Security, and Federal Unemployment.

- Whether the employee is subject to any special local taxes.

 tip

If you do not have all of the needed information for the employee, enter as much detail as possible. Then click the Finish Later button (lower left). You can return later to the Payroll Setup Interview and complete the missing information.

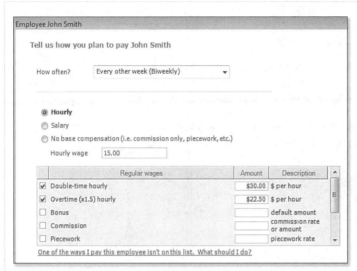

Figure 11.9
Assign the pay frequency and rate to improve the accuracy of the prepared paycheck.

Information required will differ from state to state.

Click Finish (not shown in Figure 11.9) to complete the setup for this employee. If you have not completed all of the information you might get a Missing Information error message. Read the information and click OK to close the message or Cancel to return to the setup. Choose Add New to continue with the next employee setup or select an employee from the list and click Edit, Delete, or Summary.

First Paychecks

With the few steps you have completed you can immediately create paychecks. If you are in a hurry to prepare paychecks, click the Create Paychecks button. However, I recommend completing the setup by selecting the second option listed:

- Click the Create Paychecks button to be returned to the Payroll Center where you can immediately pay your employees.

- Click the Continue button to Complete the Tax Setup, providing agency information (recommended).

Tax Setup

Continuing with the payroll setup, review the tax items created automatically for you and enter the rates your business pays for federal and state taxes:

- **941/944 Form**—Identify which tax form you file.

- **Federal Taxes**—Review the federal payroll tax items created for you (you will add to or edit them later).

- **State Tax**—Click Add New to create a specific local/custom tax and define the state you are creating a payroll tax item for. Click Finish. Click Add New, Edit, or Delete. Click Continue when you have finished setting up state tax payroll items.

- **Schedule Payments**—Assign the tax item deposit method of check or E-pay, payee, and payment frequency. If you are uncertain what payment schedule your business should follow, contact your tax accountant or click the link "How Often Should I Pay These Taxes" for additional resources.

When a "Fix This Error Now" icon displays during Payroll Setup, heed the warning. If you don't, your payroll transactions or reporting might be incorrect. See Figure 11.10.

Figure 11.10
The QuickBooks Payroll Setup detects any setup errors or missing information.

Mid-Year Payroll Setup

In the accounting community, the term "mid-year" refers to setting up payroll at any other time other than at the beginning of the current calendar year.

This method is needed only for companies converting to QuickBooks payroll in a calendar year that had prior payroll produced using software or through a payroll service provider.

When you make the decision to begin using QuickBooks payroll in a year that you have already had payroll transactions, you can:

- Manually re-create in detail all your previous payroll transactions, you will not need to follow the steps in this section.

- Record year-to-date totals for previously issued payroll checks and liability payments, following the steps given in this section.

> **caution**
>
> If creating mid-year payroll records, you will need to complete each of the following: paychecks, tax payments, and non-tax payments. Failure to complete each of these will result in misleading information in the QuickBooks payroll module.

🔍 note

The Enter Paychecks by Employee option *will not* create any accounting entries (it has no effect on Balance Sheet or Profit & Loss). However, the entries *will* affect payroll reports and forms you file for your state and the federal government. The transactions entered here are used to properly calculate certain taxes on future paychecks and for completing quarterly and annual payroll forms using QuickBooks.

You will separately record the payroll liability balances for the Balance Sheet and payroll expenses for the Profit & Loss reports with a beginning trial balance entry provided by the company accountant.

Before beginning this process, make sure you have accurate records of the prior period payrolls, preferably subtotaled by calendar quarter. To set up mid-year payroll totals using the Payroll Setup, follow these steps:

1. On step 1 of the Payroll Setup (select Employees, Payroll Setup from the menu bar), select The Company Is Changing to QuickBooks Payroll. QuickBooks will add additional menus to the Payroll Setup necessary for completing YTD entries.

2. Complete steps 2–4 entering the required information for Company, Employee, and Taxes setup as detailed previously.

3. On step 5 (Year-to-Date Payrolls), select Determine If Needed.

4. Click Yes to Has Your Company Issued Paychecks This Year?

5. Click Continue. QuickBooks opens the Enter Paychecks by Employee dialog box as shown in Figure 11.11. This dialog box, with functionality similar to Microsoft Excel's, streamlines the task of entering year-to-date payroll totals for your employees.

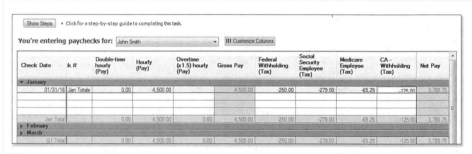

Figure 11.11
Use this worksheet in QuickBooks Payroll Setup to record prior year paychecks.

6. Click the Show Steps button to have QuickBooks provide a pop-up dialog box of the steps for entering the information to be typed in each cell.

7. Click the Customize Columns button to arrange the columns of data to match the reports from your prior software or payroll provider, which simplifies the data entry process.

8. To begin entering data for your employees, click the drop-down list for You're Entering Paychecks For and select the employee name.

9. Right-click to conveniently copy, paste, delete, or insert rows. This functionality is especially useful when entering repeating information such as for salaried employees.

10. Conveniently check your monthly and annual totals as you type directly from the Enter Paychecks by Employee dialog box to make sure your data entered agrees with your prior payroll records.

11. Click View Reports, and QuickBooks includes two reports to help report on the accuracy of the setup details. Once the reports are displayed you can print the report, export the report to Excel, or compress the report to fit on the printed page. See Figure 11.12.

 note

If you previously started using the Payroll Setup, step 5 will instead display the Payroll Summary. Click Edit next to the desired information you need to complete including paychecks, tax payments, or non-tax payments.

 caution

The Enter Paychecks by Employee dialog box will only allow you to enter payroll check dates in the current calendar year (determined by the year on your computer).

Check Date		Gross Pay	Federal Withholding (Tax)	Social Security Company (Tax)	Social Security Employee (Tax)	Medicare Company (Tax)	Medicare Employee (Tax)	Federal Unemployment (Tax)	CA - Withholding (Tax)	CA - Unemployment (Tax)	CA - Employment Training Tax (Tax)	Net Pay
2016 Paychecks		4,500.00	-250.00	279.00	-279.00	65.25	-65.25	27.00	-125.00	153.00	4.50	3,780.75
Q1 Jan-Mar		4,500.00	-250.00	279.00	-279.00	65.25	-65.25	27.00	-125.00	153.00	4.50	3,780.75
January		4,500.00	-250.00	279.00	-279.00	65.25	-65.25	27.00	-125.00	153.00	4.50	3,780.75
1/31/16												
	John Smith	4,500.00	-250.00	279.00	-279.00	65.25	-65.25	27.00	-125.00	153.00	4.50	3,780.75
	1/31 Total	4,500.00	-250.00	279.00	-279.00	65.25	-65.25	27.00	-125.00	153.00	4.50	3,780.75
February												
March												

Figure 11.12
The Historical Paycheck—Basic report is useful to review and compare to the payroll records you have before using QuickBooks.

- **Historical Paycheck Report—Basic**—The report details the gross pay and any deductions or company expenses. This report should be reviewed carefully to make sure the totals match your prior payroll records.

- **Historical Paycheck Report—Advanced**—Click the Switch to Advanced Report. The Advanced report compares the combination of historical paycheck detail with any employee or company payroll liability adjustments. If your historical payroll and adjustments (if needed) were correctly entered, the QuickBooks-Calculated amount column should equal your totals for those payroll tax items as reported to your federal and state governments.

12. Click the X in the top-right corner to return to the Enter Paychecks by Employee dialog box.

13. Click the Done Entering Paychecks button to return to the QuickBooks Payroll Setup dialog box. As each paycheck, tax payment, and non-tax payment are entered, the boxes will be shaded green progressively until each task is complete, making it easy to return where you left off.

> **note**
>
> After clicking View Reports, if your computer has Internet security settings enabled, you might see a yellow bar near the top of your Internet browser. Click the yellow bar, select Allow Blocked Content, and click Yes if prompted.

Congratulations, you have completed the tasks necessary to set up your year-to-date payroll and you can now process new payroll transactions. Now would be a good time to complete the Run Payroll Checkup diagnostics discussed in the next section.

Using the Run Payroll Checkup Diagnostic Tool

After you complete the payroll setup and you have created payroll checks or year-to-date entries in QuickBooks, you are ready to review your data using the Run Payroll Checkup diagnostic tool.

This feature is similar to the previously listed Payroll Setup feature. In fact, when you open the Run Payroll Checkup diagnostic tool, it also opens the Payroll Setup feature, but some of the menu choices are different.

What makes the Run Payroll Checkup tool different from the Payroll Setup tool? After you have set up your payroll, you will most likely use the Run Payroll Checkup tool to diagnose errors with setup and transactions.

The QuickBooks Run Payroll Checkup enables you to "Finish Later" and return where you left off. Before you begin the Run Payroll Checkup dialog box, make sure you have the following information available in case any of it is missing or incorrect:

- Employees' names, addresses, and Social Security number.

- Compensation, benefits, other additions, or deductions your company offers.

- Missing or incomplete information when you originally set up the employees; an example was shown previously in Figure 11.10.

- Compensation items, other additions, and deductions for missing or incomplete information.

- For existing data, review of actual wage and tax amounts provides an alert if any discrepancy is found, as shown in Figure 11.13.

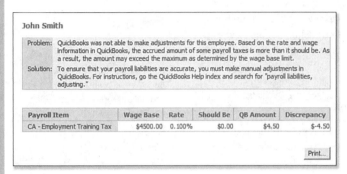

John Smith

Problem: QuickBooks was not able to make adjustments for this employee. Based on the rate and wage information in QuickBooks, the accrued amount of some payroll taxes is more than it should be. As a result, the amount may exceed the maximum as determined by the wage base limit.

Solution: To ensure that your payroll liabilities are accurate, you must make manual adjustments in QuickBooks. For instructions, go the QuickBooks Help index and search for "payroll liabilities, adjusting."

Payroll Item	Wage Base	Rate	Should Be	QB Amount	Discrepancy
CA - Employment Training Tax	$4500.00	0.100%	$0.00	$4.50	$-4.50

Print...

Figure 11.13
QuickBooks Payroll Setup detects certain payroll tax computation errors.

To have the payroll diagnostic tool within QuickBooks review your payroll setup for missing information and paycheck data for discrepancies, do the following:

1. From the menu bar, select Employees, My Payroll Service, Run Payroll Checkup. Follow each of the dialog boxes, clicking Continue through each step.

2. In the Data Review dialog box, click Yes. QuickBooks will review the wages and taxes in the payroll records.

3. If errors are detected, click the View Errors button. QuickBooks opens the error detail, as shown in Figure 11.13.

4. Click the Print button in the Payroll Item Discrepancies dialog box.

5. If you click the Continue button, some errors will require you to fix them before proceeding.

6. Click the Finish Later button to close the Run Payroll Checkup diagnostic tool so you can create correcting entries.

 tip

The Run Payroll Checkup diagnostic tool is optional for Intuit's Basic or Enhanced Payroll subscribers. However, I recommend you process the Run Payroll Checkup regardless of what payroll option you select. Using the tool as often as once a quarter before preparing quarterly payroll tax returns can help ensure your data is correct.

Be prepared to take the time to fix the errors that are detected. The QuickBooks Run Payroll Checkup diagnostic tool allows you to ignore warnings, but doing so might create additional payroll calculation errors.

 caution

Carefully consider the adjustments that need to be made if they affect a prior calendar quarter you have already filed with the state or federal government.

Be prepared to promptly file a correcting return with the appropriate agency when you adjust your QuickBooks payroll data from what was previously reported.

Correcting prior quarters can often be the best choice, especially if your data is ever audited.

Using the errors displayed earlier in Figure 11.13 as an example, the following are the typical steps for correcting them. (Your errors will be different and might require adjustments to other types of payroll items than are detailed here.)

1. From the menu bar, select Reports, Employees & Payroll, Payroll Summary. Review this report for either prior or current payroll quarters (depending on where the error was detected). In Figure 11.14, compare the Payroll Summary report to the Payroll Item Discrepancies report in shown earlier in Figure 11.13. The Should Be amount should equal what your Payroll Summary report shows when prepared today.

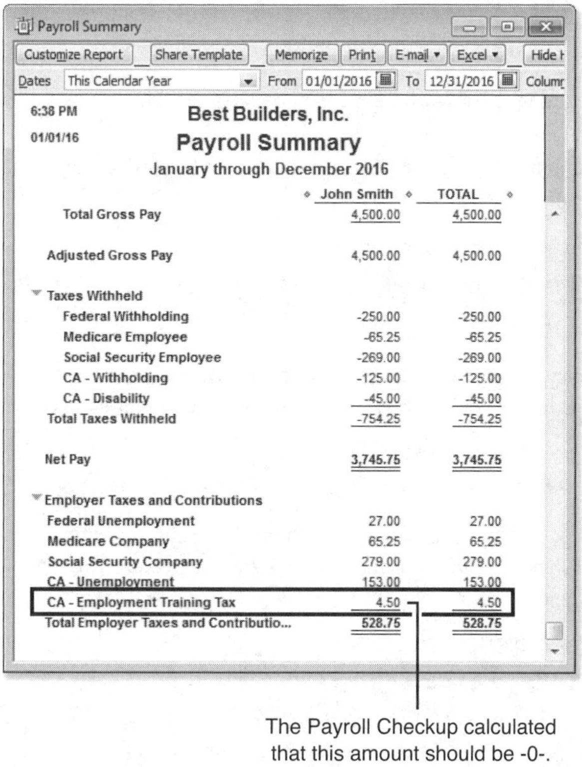

The Payroll Checkup calculated
that this amount should be -0-.

Figure 11.14
The amounts included in the Payroll Summary report should match the Should Be amounts in the Payroll Item Discrepancies report.

2. From the menu bar, select Employees, Payroll Taxes and Liabilities, Adjust Payroll Liabilities; see Figure 11.15.

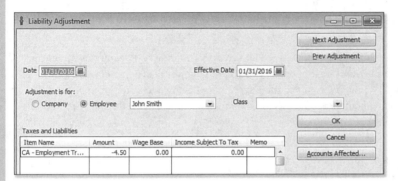

Figure 11.15
Create a liability adjustment to correct any errors found in the Payroll Item Discrepancies report.

3. Enter the Date and Effective Date. Both should be dated in the quarter you want to effect the change.

4. Select either Company or Employee for the adjustment. Company indicates it is a company-paid adjustment. Employee indicates an employee-paid adjustment and will affect W-2 reported amounts.

5. Optionally, assign a class if your business tracks different profit centers.

6. Click Accounts Affected only if you do not want to affect liability and expense account balances. This would be necessary if your Balance Sheet is correct, but the Pay Scheduled Liabilities balances in the Payroll Center are incorrect.

7. If opened, click OK to close the Accounts Affected dialog box. Click OK to save the transaction.

8. Return to the Run Payroll Checkup menu to review your payroll data again after the correction. If your adjustments were successful, QuickBooks displays a Congratulations message showing all adjustments have corrected the discrepancies.

Need to Run Payroll Checkup for a Prior Year?

If you need to complete a Run Payroll Checkup diagnostic for a prior year follow these instructions. If you are working in a multi-user environment, ask everyone to log out of the QuickBooks file and close the data file.

Next, change your computer system date to a date in the prior year. When selecting the date, keep in mind how QuickBooks will review and report on "prior quarters" dependent on this new system date.

Run the Payroll Checkup diagnostic; QuickBooks now checks the payroll data that corresponds to the year of your computer's system date.

Don't forget to close the file and then reset your computer date to the current date before opening the file again and allowing other users into the system.

You might want to contact your computer hardware professional before changing the system date in a networked environment, because it might impact other running programs.

Managing Employees

If you are a new QuickBooks payroll user, I recommended using the Payroll Setup for adding payroll items and employees. You can return to the Payroll Setup to add additional employees or use the following instructions to add or edit employee information. Refer to the instructions in the "Employee Setup" section of "Using the Payroll Setup Interview" in this chapter.

Using the Employee Center

QuickBooks makes adding, modifying, and researching employee activity easy from the Employee Center as displayed in Figure 11.16.

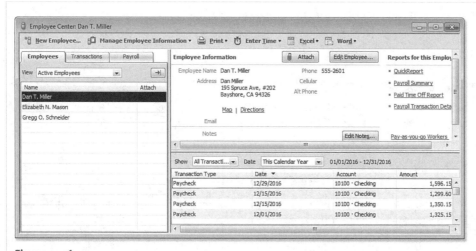

Figure 11.16
The Employee Center provides one place to access common employee tasks and reports.

On the Home page, click the Employees button to open the Employee Center. Alternatively, you can also click the Employees icon on the icon bar.

From the Employee Center, you can view contact details for your employees and access many payroll-related tasks to

- Add a new employee or edit an existing employee's information.

- Manage employee sales rep information and new employee defaults.

- Print paychecks, paystubs, and other useful list information.

- Enter time for employees.

- Export to Excel employee lists and transactions.

- Export to Excel Client Payroll Reports (requires a payroll service subscription for accounting professionals).

- Prepare employee letters and customize vendor letter templates using Word.

- Filter the list of employees to include All Employees, Active Vendors, or Released Employees.

- Attach documents to the employee record.

- Access a map and driving directions to the employee's address.

- Add and edit employee notes and to do reminders.

- View and filter the list of transactions by employee or by transaction type.

- Prepare a QuickReport, Payroll Summary, Paid Time Off Report, or Payroll Transaction Detail report for the selected employee.

Use the Employee Center to access many of the common employee transactions and reports you will learn about in this chapter.

Adding or Editing Employee Information

Have you completed the steps outlined in the Payroll Setup? You can now easily add a new employee or modify the information for an existing employee in the Employee Center.

 caution

Is this your first time setting up employees in QuickBooks? You might want to start by using the Payroll Setup. For more information, see "Using the Payroll Setup Interview," p. 390.

Adding an Employee

To practice adding a new employee record, open the sample data file as instructed in Chapter 1. If you are working in your own file, follow these instructions to add a new employee:

1. From the menu bar, select Employees, Employees Center. Click New Employee.

2. Complete the fields in the Personal, Address and Contact, and Additional Info tabs. For this exercise, enter fictitious information into each of the fields. On the Additional Info tab your QuickBooks version might offer a Billing Rate Level selection. For more information, see "Billing Rate Levels," p. 305.

3. Enter pay rate information by selecting Payroll and Compensation Info from the Change Tabs drop-down list. See Figure 11.17.

Use this to change the information tabs.

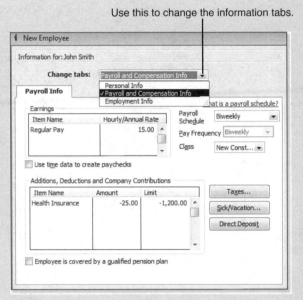

Figure 11.17
Use the Change Tabs field to edit employee information.

4. The Regular Pay wage item defaults in the Item Name column of the Earnings box. Type **15.00** in the Hourly/Annual column. To view other compensation items, click the down arrow next to Regular Pay.

5. For this exercise, do not select either of these options: Use Time and Expense Data to Create Paychecks, or Employee is Covered by a Qualified Pension Plan.

6. Record other Additions, Deductions, and Company Contributions for this employee. Select Health Insurance from the Item Name drop-down list for this exercise. Type **25.00** in the amount column and accept the defaulted Limit—QuickBooks will deduct this amount from each paycheck. The Limit refers to any upper limit and if the limit is reset annually. The Limit amount can be defined globally for all employees when setting up the deduction, or the Limit can be a unique amount for each employee.

7. Select Biweekly payroll schedule. QuickBooks displays payroll schedules in the Payroll Center. Payroll schedules allow you to group employees who share the same pay frequency.

8. In the Class field, select New Construction. The option to assign a single class (department) to the entire paycheck or assign multiple classes to a single paycheck is defined in the Payroll & Employee preferences section. From the menu bar, select Edit, Preferences, Payroll & Employees, Company Preferences.

9. Click the Taxes button to see the information displayed in Figure 11.18. The information selected in the fields on the Federal, State, and Other tabs determines how the respective taxes are calculated. Use the information on the employee's completed Form W-4 when selecting Filing Status, Allowances, and Extra Withholding settings. Click OK to close. If you did not select a State Worked, you might be prompted to complete the setup.

Figure 11.18
Assign the employee's federal, state, and other tax status.

10. Click the Sick/Vacation button. Use these settings to accrue and track employees sick and vacation time. Click OK to close.

11. The Direct Deposit button is inactive in the sample data being used for this exercise. In your own file, you might be directed to a QuickBooks dialog box to verify your company information, enter bank information, and select check security limits.

12. Optionally, select the Employee Info and Workers Compensation from the Change Tabs drop-down list to view additional information that can be tracked.

13. Select any of the menus from the Change Tabs drop-down list to review the information.

14. Click OK to close the New Employee dialog box.

Managing your employees' information from the Employee Center is easy. To edit an employee's information, select an employee on the left side of the dialog box and click the Edit Employee button (top right).

Finding Payroll Transactions

The Employee Center provides a single location for maintaining employee records and reviewing payroll transactions in QuickBooks.

On the Home page, click the Employees button to open the Employee Center. Select an employee on the left side of the dialog box to display individual transactions assigned to that employee on the right. With the employee Dan T. Miller selected

 tip

If working in your own file, you select Use Time and Expense Data to Create Paychecks, QuickBooks will use that time data from time cards to pre-fill the hours on a paycheck. This can save you time making your payroll processing more efficient.

Learn more about using the QuickBooks Timer, p. 596.

in the Employee Center, QuickBooks displays individual transactions for that employee. See Figure 11.19.

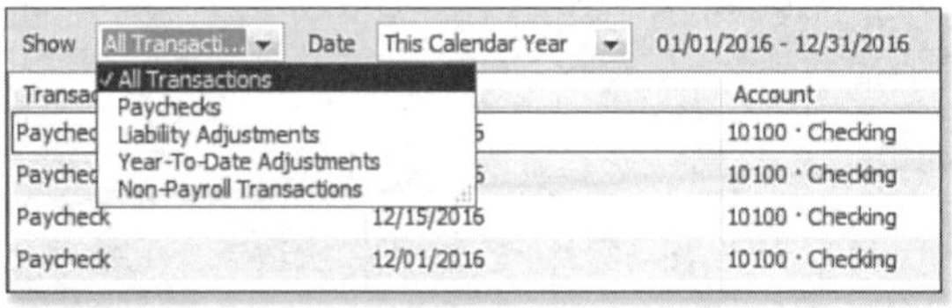

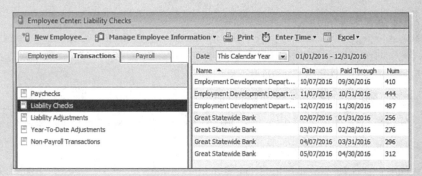

Figure 11.19
Filter for specific transactions types and dates for the selected employee.

Another useful feature of working with the Payroll Center is found on the Transactions tab. From the Transactions tab in the Employee Center, you can easily locate payroll and non-payroll transactions for all employees.

Researching Payroll and Non-Payroll Transactions

To practice finding employee transactions by type, open the sample data file as instructed in Chapter 1. If you are working in your own file use these instructions to locate your own employee's transactions.

1. From the Employee Center, click the Transactions tab.

2. Select the Liability Checks type as shown in Figure 11.20.

Figure 11.20
Use the Transactions tab of the Employee Center to research by transaction type.

3. From the Date drop-down list, select This Calendar Quarter (if you are using the QuickBooks-supplied sample data, the date selected might be some time in the future).

4. Click any column header to sort the data by that column.

5. Double-click any transaction to open it. Click Save & Close to return to the Transactions tab details.

6. Click the Print icon to print the listed transactions.

7. Click the Enter Time drop-down list to enter a Weekly Timesheet or Time/Enter Single Activity.

8. Click the Excel icon to Export Transactions or Summarize Data in Excel. If you are an accounting professional using Enhanced Payroll for Accountants, you will also have the option to export to Excel, Client-Ready Payroll Reports.

In the next section you will learn about managing your payroll items.

Managing Payroll Items

QuickBooks uses payroll items to calculate and track compensation, additions, deductions, and company expenses that result from paying employees. You need to set up your payroll items only once, which in turn makes processing payroll as easy as reporting the time an employee works.

Adding or Editing Payroll Items

If you are new to QuickBooks payroll, I recommend that you begin by using the Payroll Setup. During the Payroll Setup you were provided with two options for creating your list of payroll items:

- **Typical New Employer Setup**—QuickBooks adds the most common payroll items for you.

- **Custom Setup**—Select this option if you need to set up sick time, vacation time, or insurance benefits.

If you have been using QuickBooks for payroll you will no longer see these two options. The fields required to be completed will differ depending on the type of payroll item.

To add a deduction payroll item, follow these steps:

1. From the menu bar, select Lists, Payroll Item List.

2. Select New from the Payroll Item drop-down list (or use the Ctrl+N keyboard shortcut).

3. Select one of the following methods:

    - **EZ Setup**—Opens the Payroll Setup using standard settings, recommended for most users. To learn more about using this option, see "Using the Payroll Setup Interview," p. 390.

    - **Custom Setup**—Offers a more traditional approach to setting up payroll items, recommended for expert users.

4. If you selected Custom Setup in step 3, the Add New Payroll Item dialog box displays.

5. Select a payroll item type, such as Deduction (shown in Figure 11.21), and then click Next.

6. Type a name for the payroll item. This name will display on paychecks and in reports. Selecting the Track Expenses by Job might be suitable for most company contribution and addition items and would include this payroll item in Job Profitability reports. Click Next.

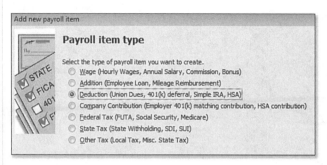

Figure 11.21
Select the appropriate payroll item type to be created.

7. On the Agency for Employee-Paid Liability screen, enter the following:

   ■ From your vendor list, select the agency to which you pay the liability. If necessary, click Add New to create a new vendor record. Skip this field if the deduction is not being paid to anyone as Figure 11.22 shows creating a cell phone deduction to employees checks.

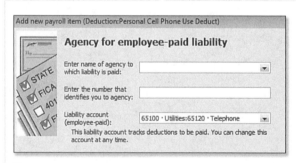

Figure 11.22
Payroll deductions can recover from the employee a portion of a business paid expense.

   ■ Optionally, enter the account number that identifies you to the agency you pay the liability to.

   ■ Make a selection from your chart of accounts. In this example, Payroll Liabilities is selected. If you followed the previously recommended process for creating detailed payroll accounts on your chart of accounts, select the appropriate subaccount. If the deduction payroll item is used to recover a business-paid expense from employees, select the corresponding expense account. Click Next.

8. Select the appropriate Tax Tracking Type or None if none of the types apply, as shown in Figure 11.23. This choice is very important to proper set up your payroll items. If you are unsure, ask your accountant for advice. Click Next.

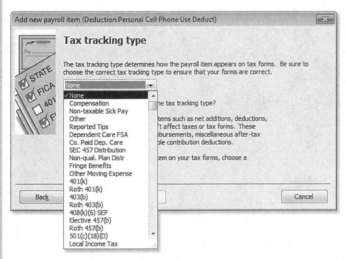

Figure 11.23
Carefully reviewing the Tax Tracking Types can help with accurately setting up payroll.

9. The Taxes screen displays. In most cases, you will not need to modify the settings in this screen. Click Default to return to the original settings. Click Next.

10. The Calculate Based on Quantity screen offers the following choices:

- Calculate This Item Based on Quantity

- Calculate This Item Based on Hours

- Neither

11. After making a selection, click Next.

12. Select to calculate the deduction from Gross Pay or Net Pay. If you are unsure, ask your accountant as the correct selection will depend on the item being set up. Click Next.

13. Enter a Default Rate, optional Default Upper Limit, and specify if the limit is annually reset. If the rate or upper limit differs for each employee, do not enter amounts here. The rate and limit can be added individually to each employee's record. Click Finish.

14. Click OK after reading the Schedule Payments message. For more information, see "Creating or Editing a Payroll Schedule," p. 413.

 note

You can always edit the settings for a specific payroll item. However, some changes will only affect future payroll checks and not those recorded prior to making the change.

Reporting About Payroll Items

Review your payroll items list after adding to or modifying it. From the menu bar, choose Lists, Payroll Item List. QuickBooks displays the Payroll Item List dialog box (see Figure 11.24). To expand the report for better viewing, double-click the words "Payroll Item List" at the top of the dialog box. To add or remove columns, right-click and select Customize Columns.

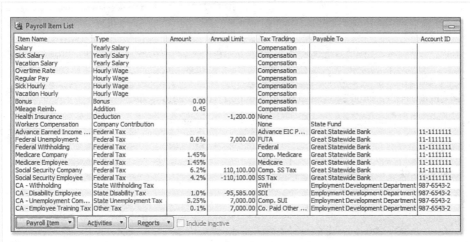

Figure 11.24
View the Payroll Item List for information about the setup and accounts assigned to the payroll items.

The following information is displayed when viewing the Payroll Item List:

- **Item Name**—Displayed on paychecks and reports.

- **Type**—This is from a predefined list in QuickBooks. The type determines whether it is added to gross wages or deducted

- **Amount**—This figure is determined by the QuickBooks-provided payroll tax tables, with the exception of State Unemployment, city, and local taxes, which are user defined.

- **Annual Limit**—This figure is determined by the QuickBooks-provided tax tables and is not modifiable by the user. Incorrect limits could be due to a payroll tax table that is not current.

- **Tax Tracking**—When you create a new payroll item and select a payroll item type, QuickBooks provides a predetermined list of tax tracking types associated with that item type. Tax tracking determines how QuickBooks treats the item on the W-2 year-end employee tax form.

- **Payable To**—Checks are payable to the named entity.

- **Account ID**—The identification number your tax payment agency has assigned to your company.

- **Expense Account**—If the payroll item type is considered an expense, users can define the default expense account from the chart of accounts list in the payroll setup. QuickBooks defaults this account to a generic Payroll Expense account, which is created automatically by QuickBooks when payroll is enabled.

■ **Liability Account**—This account is used for payroll items that are accrued with payroll and paid to the state or federal government. QuickBooks defaults these items to a generic liability account created when payroll is enabled. You can define what liability account is assigned. If you are creating a new account, it should be a subaccount of the one QuickBooks provides if you want to see certain warnings that are provided when you try to create a transaction incorrectly.

 tip

To add or remove specific columns of data, right-click and select Customize Columns.

Additionally, from this screen view of the payroll items list you can access the following:

■ **Payroll Item**—Add, edit, delete, make item inactive, find in transactions, and print list.

■ **Activities**—Access the Payroll Setup and other common payroll item tasks.

■ **Reports**—Access summary or detail reports of payroll item transactions.

Paying Employees

Having completed your Payroll Setup and Run Payroll Checkup, you are ready to begin paying your employees. If you previously paid your employees' payroll with other software or by a payroll agency, record the year-to-date payroll totals for each employee.

➡ *For more information, see "Mid-Year Payroll Setup," p. 394.*

The next sections provide details on preparing payroll for your employees.

Payroll Home Page Workflow

With a paid payroll subscription you might have all or some of the following icons on your Home page providing easy access to the typical payroll workflow. Your icons might differ from those shown in Figure 11.25 depending on the payroll subscription purchased and the preferences you have set in QuickBooks.

Figure 11.25
The Home page provides access to the proper payroll workflow.

Entering Employee Time

QuickBooks includes a weekly or activity timesheet you can use to record employee work time and create paychecks. You can access timesheets by clicking the Enter Time icon on the Home page.

Using timesheets will simplify the process of creating payroll records if you track employees' time by customers, jobs, or service items. Timesheets are not necessary if your employees are paid a fixed amount (salary) or work the same hours each pay period. Features of using timesheets in QuickBooks include:

- Using a stopwatch to time an activity as it is performed.

- Entering the time manually using a weekly timesheet or individually by the activity as shown in Figures 11.26 and 11.27.

- Adding the time to a customer's invoice. For more information, see "Time and Expense Invoicing," pg. 303.

> ### 🔍 note
>
> Time tracking is enabled in the Preferences dialog box. From the menu bar, select Edit, Preferences to open this dialog box and select the Time & Expenses—Company Preferences Tab.
>
> Time sheet entries can help you efficiently create payroll records each pay period. On the Payroll Info tab for each employee (see Figure 11.17), select the Use Time Data to Create Paychecks check box.

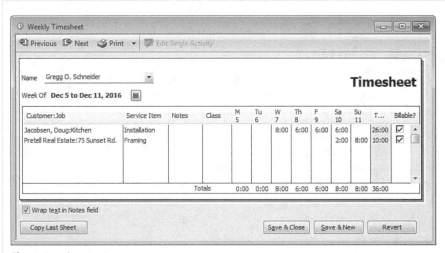

Figure 11.26
Weekly timesheets can be used to create payroll transactions.

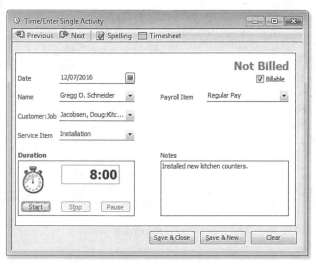

Figure 11.27
The Time/Enter Single Activity includes a stopwatch.

To record payroll timesheet activity, follow these steps:

1. On the Home page, click the drop-down list next to the Enter Time icon and select Use Weekly Timesheet or Time/Enter Single Activity. The following instructions presume you selected the Weekly Timesheet.

2. From the Name drop-down list, select the employee whose time you want to enter. If you want to enter multiple names, select Multiple Names (Payroll) from the list. Adding multiple names to a timesheet can be useful if you have crew labor that performs the same service items for the same customers or jobs.

3. Click Copy Last Sheet if you need to repeat the detail from a previously recorded timesheet.

4. Enter data in each of the columns. Your columns might differ depending on your purchased payroll subscription and payroll preferences you enabled.

5. Optionally, click the Print button to print the current timesheet with a signature line. If you want to print a blank timesheet, click the down arrow to the right of the Print button and select Print Blank Timesheet.

6. Click Save & Close when completed with the timesheet entry.

 tip

Want to have employees track their own time on jobs at their computer even if they do not have access to the QuickBooks file? Enter "QuickBooks Timer" in the search box in the upper-right corner of the menu bar, select Help from the drop-down list, and click the Search button. Follow the links for installing and working with the QuickBooks Timer.

For more detailed information and instructions, see "Using the QuickBooks Timer," p. 596.

Preparing Employee Paychecks

You are now ready to create paychecks for your employees. Following the instructions provided in this chapter can help to make this process efficient and accurate.

Creating or Editing a Payroll Schedule

A payroll schedule defines the payroll frequency, the pay period end date, and the date that should print on the employee's paycheck. If you create at least one payroll schedule, the Payroll Center will display the next scheduled payroll. Another use for payroll schedules is to separate your employees into different groups. If your business pays the administrative staff biweekly but your operations employees weekly, you would set up two payroll schedules.

To create or edit a payroll schedule, select Employees, Add or Edit Payroll Schedules from the menu bar. Complete the information required and click OK to save the schedule. Press the Esc key on your keyboard to close the Payroll Schedule List.

Next, assign your employees to the newly created scheduled payroll.

➡️ *For more information see, "Adding an Employee," pg. 402.*

Paying Employees

To prepare your QuickBooks payroll paychecks, follow these steps:

1. On the Home page, click the Pay Employees icon. The Payroll Center opens (refer to Figure 11.4).

2. Select a Payroll Schedule and click Start Scheduled Payroll.

3. From the Enter Payroll Information dialog box:

   ▪ Accept the default Pay Period Ends and Check Date or change as necessary.

   ▪ Place a checkmark next to each employee you want to pay. Optionally, click the Check All or Uncheck All button as shown in Figure 11.28.

   ▪ Optionally, use the Sort By and Show/Hide Columns to customize how the information is displayed.

   ▪ Verify that the affected employee records have the Use Time Data to Create Paychecks option selected (refer to Figure 11.17) if the time did not import. This is valid only if you created timesheets or individual time activities and allowed QuickBooks import the time detail.

   ▪ Optionally, enter your employee's hours in the Enter Payroll Information dialog box.

   ▪ Optionally, click the Open Paycheck Detail to review and or edit information not displayed on the Enter Payroll Information dialog box. Click Save & Next or Save & Close to return to the Enter Payroll Information dialog box.

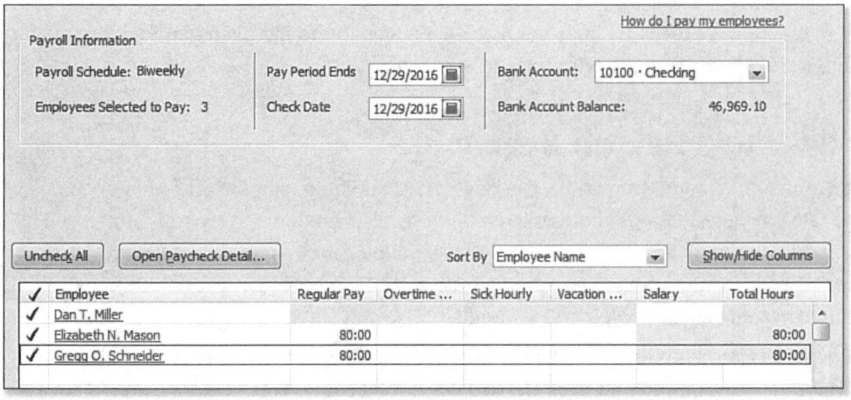

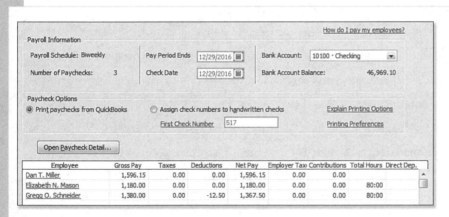

Figure 11.28
The payroll information defaults from the scheduled payroll setup and employee's salary or time sheet details.

4. Click Continue. The Review and Create Paychecks dialog box displays as shown in Figure 11.29.

Figure 11.29
Select paycheck printing options and review paycheck details.

5. Change the Bank Account if necessary.

6. Choose to Print Paychecks from QuickBooks or Assign Check Numbers to Handwritten Checks.

7. Click Create Paychecks.

The following section details printing of paychecks or paystubs.

Printing Paychecks or Paystubs

The last step in preparing payroll for your employees is printing the checks. There are two options available:

- **Print Paychecks**—Prints on check stock for employees to deposit or cash.

- **Print Paystubs**—Creates a non-negotiable document detailing the employee's earnings. Use this dialog box when an employee is paid by direct deposit.

When you click Create Paychecks, the Confirmation and Next Steps dialog box displays as shown in Figure 11.30.

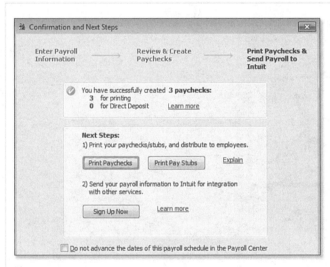

Figure 11.30
You can print paychecks now, or later by selecting File, Print Forms, Print Paychecks, or Print Paystubs from the menu bar.

After successfully printing your employees' paychecks, you will want to promptly pay the payroll liabilities to avoid costly penalty and late fees.

➡ *To learn more about printer settings in QuickBooks, see "Setting Form Defaults and Making Printer Adjustments," p. 443.*

Preparing Payroll Liability Payments

When your business pays employees, you also become responsible for paying the liabilities associated with the payroll to governmental and other entities.

Paying Scheduled Liabilities

To pay scheduled payroll liabilities, follow these steps:

1. On the Home page, click the Pay Liabilities icon. QuickBooks opens the Payroll Center. The Pay Scheduled Liabilities lists each payroll liability (amount you owe), with the Due Date, Status, Payment Description, Method, Period, and Amount (refer to Figure 11.4).

2. To process a payment, place a checkmark next to the payroll item you want to pay. Optionally, double-click the Amount to view a listing of the transactions that are included in the amount due.

3. Click View/Pay. QuickBooks prepares a Liability Payment for your review, as shown in Figure 11.31.

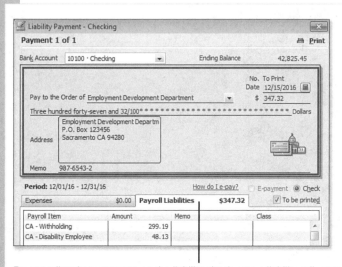

Do not adjust item amounts on the liability check; use a liability adjustment transaction instead.

Figure 11.31
QuickBooks payroll calculates the tax payments automatically.

4. Change the Bank Account if needed. The payroll items and amount included on the liability payment are calculated from payroll transactions. Check E-Payment to process your payment electronically, or for more information click the How Do I E-Pay link.

5. Print the checks from the top-right Print icon, or later by selecting File, Print Forms, Print Checks from the menu bar.

6. Click Save & Close when completed to return to the Payroll Center, Pay Scheduled Liabilities.

caution

If you do not see all of the payroll liabilities you accrue each pay period, you might not have the correct payroll liability due date assigned. From the Payroll Center, in the Pay Scheduled Liabilities box, select the Related Payment Activities drop-down list.

When you select Edit Payment Due Dates/Methods, QuickBooks opens the Payroll Setup. Review and edit the Scheduled Tax Payments List.

Adjusting Payroll Liabilities

QuickBooks automatically calculates payroll liabilities as you process paychecks. If you determine that an amount is not calculating correctly, review the settings for that payroll item.

Your accounting professional might choose to create a journal entry to correct the business financials. However, this type of transaction will not affect the amounts included in the Pay Scheduled Liabilities in the Payroll Center or the payroll reporting forms. Instead, use the Liability Adjustment dialog box for changes to the amounts that are reported as liabilities and to affect federal and state reporting forms.

After reviewing your payroll reports (see the next section), you can adjust payroll liabilities. To do so, follow these steps:

1. From the menu bar, select Employees, Payroll Taxes and Liabilities, Adjust Payroll Liabilities (refer to Figure 11.15).

2. Select the Date and Effective Date. These dates might affect your payroll reporting forms, so specify the date carefully.

3. Select Company if the adjustment is for a company-only payroll item, such as a company-paid health insurance benefit.

4. Select Employee if the adjustment is for an employee-reported liability or if you need to effect a change to the employee's W2 amounts. Select Class if using this feature in QuickBooks.

5. From the Item Name drop-down list, select the payroll item or items to be adjusted.

6. Enter an Amount (positive or negative).

7. Enter the Wage Base (positive or negative) if the payroll item being adjusted is subject to a wage threshold similar to federal or state unemployment.

8. Enter the Income Subject to Tax (positive or negative) to adjust the amount reported on tax forms.

9. Optionally, enter a Memo.

10. Optionally, click Accounts Affected. The default is to affect liability and expense accounts. If your financials are correct, but the payroll reporting and liabilities are incorrect, select Do Not Affect Accounts. Click OK to close the message.

11. Click Next Adjustment to add an additional record, or click OK to close the Adjust Payroll Liabilities dialog box.

A good practice is to review your payroll reports again after making the adjustments to be certain they provide the result expected.

MANAGING PAYROLL

Payroll Reporting

You will find that reporting on payroll activity is necessary to properly managing your business payroll activity.

QuickBooks offers several payroll reports that can be customized to suit your needs. For more details on customizing reports, see Chapter 14, "Reporting in QuickBooks."

Report Center Payroll Reports

Whether you are new to QuickBooks, or an expert, you will benefit from the payroll reports in the Report Center. To open the Report Center, select Reports, Report Center from the menu bar. Select any of the icons on the top right to change the viewing method for the Report Center:

- Carousel View

- List View

- Grid View

By default, the Report Center opens with the Standard tab selected and displays several report categories. Click Employees & Payroll. To the right displays sample payroll reports, as shown in Figure 12.1, using the Grid View.

Underneath each sample report, you can click to prepare the report using your data and a date you select, get more information about the report, mark the report as a favorite, or access help information for the report.

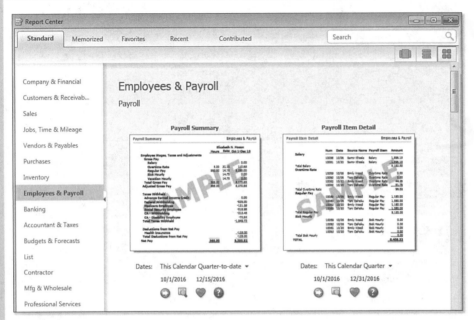

Figure 12.1
Preview and prepare payroll reports in the Report Center.

The Report Center also offers these additional tabs:

- **Memorized**—From any displayed report, click Memorize to add the report to this tab in the Report Center.

- **Favorites**—Mark a report as a Favorite to include the report in this tab group.

- **Recent**—QuickBooks lists reports you have recently prepared here.

- **Contributed**—Custom reports created by Intuit or other QuickBooks users can be downloaded and used with your data. You can also share reports you create with the community at large. When sharing a report you are not sharing sensitive information, just the format of the report.

You can also type a descriptive search term into the search box in the Report Center and a list of relevant reports will display. Additional payroll reports are available in QuickBooks using pivot tables in Microsoft Excel. The next section details these reports.

Excel Reports

If you did not find the report you needed in the Report Center, check out the many reports that use pivot tables in Microsoft Excel. These reports are included with your QuickBooks software.

To access these reports, select Reports, Employees & Payroll, Summarize Payroll Data in Excel (or More Payroll Reports in Excel) from the menu bar. A few of the reports prepared in Excel with your data include:

- Summarize Payroll Data in Excel (see Figure 12.2)

- Payroll Summary by Tax Tracking Type

- Employee Time & Costs

- Employee Sick & Vacation History

- Employee Direct Deposit Listing

- Tax Form Worksheets

- Payroll Liability Accruals & Payments

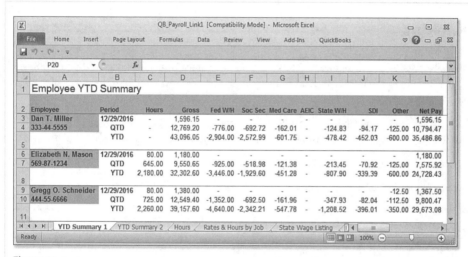

Figure 12.2
This and many other payroll reports prepared with your data use Excel pivot tables.

With the Report Center, Excel Reports, and the Employees & Payroll reports accessible from the Reports menu on the menu bar, you have plenty of options for finding the right payroll report for your needs.

Tax Forms and Filings

Up to this point, you have set up payroll, managed employees and payroll items, paid your employee and the liabilities, and prepared payroll reports. You will now see how QuickBooks helps you be compliant with the required payroll reporting.

In Chapter 11, "Setting Up Payroll," you learned about the many payroll subscription offerings you can choose from. If you want your QuickBooks software to automatically calculate your payroll trans-actions and prepare federal and state forms, you will need to have the Intuit QuickBooks Payroll Enhanced subscription. For accounting professionals who prepare payroll for multiple clients, Intuit QuickBooks Payroll Enhanced for Accountants is the subscription most suitable for working with multiple client files.

QuickBooks can print required federal and state payroll forms or E-File them for you; it just couldn't be easier to complete your payroll reporting tasks.

Preparing and Printing Tax Forms

Before preparing your first payroll tax form, complete the Payroll Tax Information box on the Company Information dialog box. To do so, select Company, Company Information from the menu bar. In the lower-right corner include the Contact Name, Title, and Phone # that will be included on the prepared payroll tax forms.

To prepare your federal or state forms, follow these steps:

1. On the Home page, click the Process Payroll Forms icon.

2. Select Federal Form or State Form. Click OK. If a message displays informing you to update your tax tables go to step 3, if not go to step 7.

3. Click Check Now or Skip. I recommend that you select the Check Now for updating the tax tables and forms. Click OK to the message that the payroll tax updated, installed, or did not install successfully.

4. Click OK to close the Payroll Update message. QuickBooks provides a window displaying the details of the Payroll Updates. Press the Esc key on your keyboard to close.

5. On the Home page, click the Process Payroll Forms icon.

6. Select a federal form or state form. Click OK. See Figure 12.3.

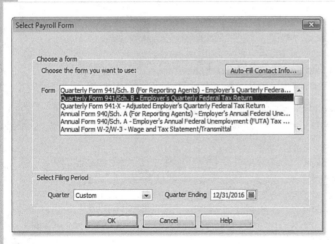

Figure 12.3
With the Enhanced Payroll Subscription, QuickBooks can prepare all of your federal forms and many state forms.

7. Choose a form to prepare. For accounting professionals, choose the option for Reporting Agents.

8. Optionally, click the Auto-Fill Contact Info button. This is the default information that will be included with your payroll forms.

9. Select Filing Quarter and Quarter Ending date. Click OK. If a warning displays about download-ing the latest payroll update, read the warning and click OK to close the warning.

10. Complete any required fields on the displayed form. If you have questions about the form details, click the provided links. When you have completed the form, click Check for Errors. If any errors display, click the error and QuickBooks will advance to that section of the form for you to com-plete or correct.

11. Click Next to advance to the next form page.

12. Click Save & Close allowing you to return later to your saved work.

13. Click Save as PDF to save a PDF for your records, Print to prepare a paper copy, or Submit Form if you have signed up for E-Filing (discussed in the next section).

E-Filing Tax Payments and Forms

If you selected the Intuit QuickBooks Payroll Enhanced subscription or the Intuit QuickBooks Payroll Enhanced for Accountant's subscription for your business, you can sign up for the E-File and E-Pay service.

With E-File and E-Pay, you prepare your payroll liability payments in QuickBooks and select E-Pay. Intuit will debit your bank account for the funds and remit them directly to the IRS on your behalf.

With E-File of your payroll forms, you can select Submit Form and QuickBooks will process your payroll form and send it to the IRS. You will receive email notification that the form was accepted (or rejected) by the IRS. To take advantage of the E-File and E-Pay Service, you need:

- An active Enhanced Payroll subscription.

- A supported version of QuickBooks (typically not older than three years back from the current calendar year).

- An Internet connection.

- The most recent payroll tax update.

- Enrollment with the Electronic Federal Tax Payment System (EFTPS); used by the IRS for employer payments. For more information, visit www.eftps.gov.

More detailed information is provided by clicking the Find Out About E-File & Pay link on the Payroll Center. As your business E-Pays and E-Files, you can click the link to Check E-Filing Status, which displays documentation that the payments and forms were successfully transmitted to the IRS.

Troubleshooting Payroll

Using the QuickBooks Run Payroll Checkup diagnostic tool is a recommended way to review and validate the accuracy of your payroll data. You can also review your data setup and accuracy manually by reviewing the reports detailed in this section.

Reviewing the Payroll Item Listing can also be helpful when needing to troubleshoot payroll issues.

➡ *For more information, see "Reporting About Payroll Items," p. 409.*

Comparing Payroll Liability Balances to the Balance Sheet

It's important to periodically compare your Balance Sheet payroll liabilities account balance to the amount on the Payroll Liabilities Balances report. To do so, follow these steps:

1. From the menu bar, select Reports, Company & Financial, Balance Sheet Standard.

2. Select the As Of date for the period you are reviewing.

3. From the menu bar, select Reports, Employees & Payroll, Payroll Liability Balances.

4. Click the Dates drop-down list and select All from the top of the list. Leave the From date box empty. In the To date box, enter the same date that was used on the Balance Sheet Standard report. Doing so ensures you are picking up all transactions for this account, including any unpaid balances from prior years. Click Print if you want to have a copy of this report to compare to your Balance Sheet payroll liabilities balance.

These two reports should have matching totals. In the examples shown in Figures 12.4 and 12.5, the Balance Sheet and Payroll Liabilities reports do not match.

The totals might not match because of non-payroll transactions being used to record adjustments or payments to payroll liabilities using non-payroll transactions, including make journal entry, enter bill, or write check transaction types.

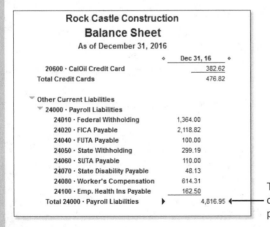

Rock Castle Construction
Balance Sheet
As of December 31, 2016

	Dec 31, 16
20600 · CalOil Credit Card	382.62
Total Credit Cards	476.82
▼ Other Current Liabilities	
▼ 24000 · Payroll Liabilities	
24010 · Federal Withholding	1,364.00
24020 · FICA Payable	2,118.82
24040 · FUTA Payable	100.00
24050 · State Withholding	299.19
24060 · SUTA Payable	110.00
24070 · State Disability Payable	48.13
24080 · Worker's Compensation	614.31
24100 · Emp. Health Ins Payable	162.50
Total 24000 · Payroll Liabilities	4,816.95

This amount will not match if any liability calculations do not have an assigned payment due date or method.

Figure 12.4
Compare the Balance Sheet payroll liabilities amount to the payroll liability reports.

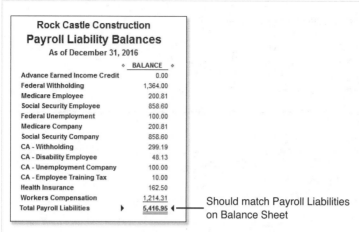

Rock Castle Construction
Payroll Liability Balances
As of December 31, 2016

	BALANCE
Advance Earned Income Credit	0.00
Federal Withholding	1,364.00
Medicare Employee	200.81
Social Security Employee	858.60
Federal Unemployment	100.00
Medicare Company	200.81
Social Security Company	858.60
CA - Withholding	299.19
CA - Disability Employee	48.13
CA - Unemployment Company	100.00
CA - Employee Training Tax	10.00
Health Insurance	162.50
Workers Compensation	1,214.31
Total Payroll Liabilities ▶	**5,416.95** ◀

Should match Payroll Liabilities on Balance Sheet

Figure 12.5
Payroll Liability Balances report should match the Balance Sheet amount for the same account.

To troubleshoot payroll liabilities differences, I prefer to work with the Custom Transaction Detail report. To access the report, follow these steps:

1. From the menu bar, select Reports, Custom Reports, Transaction Detail. The Modify Report dialog box opens.

2. Click the Dates drop-down list and select All. Leave the From date box empty; in the To date box, enter the date you used on the Balance Sheet Standard report.

3. In the Columns box, remove or add a check mark for the information you want to display on the report. Be sure to include Type.

4. On the Sort By drop-down list, select Type.

5. Click the Filters tab; in the Choose Filters box, the Accounts filter is already selected. From the Accounts drop-down list to the right, select the Payroll Liabilities account.

6. Click OK to create the report.

QuickBooks creates a useful and telling report, as shown in Figure 12.6. When this report is sorted by type of transaction, you can easily see what non-payroll-related transactions are affecting your Balance Sheet Standard report Payroll Liability balance and are not affecting your Payroll Liability Balances report.

If you are an accounting professional working with the Client Data Review feature, you can also select the Find Incorrectly Paid Payroll Liabilities custom report from the Accountant menu.

➡ *For more information, see "Find Incorrectly Paid Payroll Liabilities," p. 643.*

You can double-click any of the listed transactions to see more detail about the transaction that was used to create the adjustment to the Balance Sheet.

General Journal will not adjust your scheduled payroll liabilities.

6:02 PM		\multicolumn{5}{c}{**Rock Castle Construction**}
12/15/16		\multicolumn{5}{c}{**Custom Transaction Detail Report**}
Accrual Basis		\multicolumn{5}{c}{December 2016}
Type	Date	Num	Name	Memo	Amount	
Dec 16						
General Journal	12/31/2016	1002		To Agree wtih Ins Bill	-600.00	◄
Liability Check	12/07/2016	487	Employment Devel...	987-6543-2	-99.77	
Liability Check	12/07/2016	487	Employment Devel...	987-6543-2	-195.21	
Liability Check	12/07/2016	488	Great Statewide B...	00-7904153	0.00	
Liability Check	12/07/2016	488	Great Statewide B...	00-7904153	-849.00	
Liability Check	12/07/2016	488	Great Statewide B...	00-7904153	-122.61	

Figure 12.6
Use the Custom Transaction Detail report to easily identify non-payroll transactions that are recorded to the Payroll Liabilities account.

Comparing Payroll Summary to Filed Payroll Returns

Has your company ever received a notice from the IRS indicating your year-end payroll documents do not agree with your quarterly payroll return totals, or have you received a similar notice from your state payroll tax agency?

Listed in this section are some basic comparisons you should do both before filing a payroll return and after, in the event you allow users to make changes to transactions from previous payroll quarters.

➡ *For more information preventing these changes, see "Set a Closing Date," pg. 533.*

Compare the following items routinely while doing payroll in QuickBooks and ensure that:

- Each calendar quarter QuickBooks payroll totals agree with your filed payroll return totals. Look at these specific totals when reviewing the Payroll Summary:

  - Total Adjusted Gross Pay in QuickBooks agrees with the Federal 941 Form, Wages, Tips, and Other Compensation.

  - Federal Withholding in QuickBooks agrees with the Federal 941 Form, Total Income Tax Withheld from Wages, and so on.

  - Employee and Company Social Security and Medicare in QuickBooks agree with the computed Total Taxable Social Security and Medicare on the Federal 941 Form.

- Total payroll tax deposits for the quarter in QuickBooks agrees with your paper trail. Whether you pay online or use a coupon that you take to the bank, make sure you recorded the correct calendar quarter with the IRS for your payments.

- Total Adjusted Gross Pay for the calendar year in QuickBooks agrees with the reported Gross Wage total on the annual Federal Form W-3, Transmittal of Wage, and Tax Statements.

- Total Adjusted Gross Pay for the calendar quarter in QuickBooks agrees with the Total Gross Wage reported to your state payroll agency.

- Total Payroll expense from the Profit & Loss report agrees with total Adjusted Gross Pay on the Payroll Summary report.

Comparing these critical reports with your federal and state tax filings will ensure your data agrees with the payroll tax agency records.

Reconciling Payroll Reports to Business Financials

When applying for a business loan from your bank, your company might be required to produce reviewed or audited financials. One of the many items that will be reviewed is the comparison of payroll costs included in the business financials to those in the payroll returns filed with federal or state governments.

If you are uncertain about which accounts within your chart of accounts to review, refer to the account you assigned to the payroll item. Here are a few selected comparisons you can do yourself as a business owner:

- Compare Federal Form 941 Wages, Tips, And Other Compensation (Box 2) to the expense accounts used to report salaries and wages. You might need to add multiple accounts together to match the total in Box 2.

- Compare the company portion of the payroll taxes reported to federal or state governments. If you are uncertain about the amount, ask your accountant or view information about payroll taxes on the www.irs.gov website.

Recording Unique Payroll Transactions

The following sections detail several common payroll transactions you might need in your business.

Employee Loan Payment and Repayment

Your business might offer a loan to an employee in advance of payroll earnings. This amount should not be taxed at the time of payment if you expect the loan to be paid back to the company.

Paying an Employee Paycheck Advance

When you offer to pay employees an advance on their earnings, you are creating a loan payment check. If this is a loan to be paid back to the company, follow these steps:

1. From the menu bar, select Employees, Pay Employees, Unscheduled Payroll. The Enter Payroll Information dialog box opens.

2. Place a checkmark next to the employee you are creating the loan check for.

3. QuickBooks might warn that a paycheck for that period already exists. Click Continue if you want to create the loan payment check. You are returned to the Enter Payroll Information dialog box.

4. To modify the check to be an employee loan check, click the Open Paycheck Detail button.

5. In the Preview Paycheck dialog box, remove any amounts from the Earnings box (if you expect to be repaid this amount, the amount is not considered taxable earnings).

6. From the Other Payroll Items drop-down list, select the Employee Advances addition type payroll item, as shown in Figure 12.7, and skip to step 15.

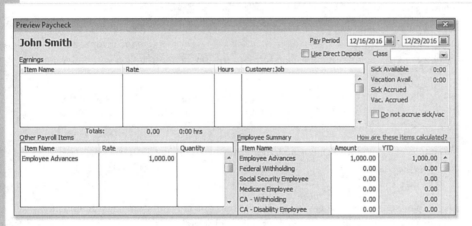

Figure 12.7
Use an Addition type payroll item in the Other Items box to record a nontaxable loan (advance).

If you do not have an employee advance payroll item, you can easily create one right from the Preview Paycheck dialog box. Click Add New from the Other Payroll Items box drop-down list.

7. From the Add New Payroll Item dialog box, select the button for the Addition type and click Next.

8. The Add New Payroll Item (Addition) dialog box opens. Name the item Employee Advance (if displayed, do not select the Track Expenses by Job box). Click Next.

9. From the Expense Account drop-down list, select the Employee Loans, Other Current Asset account. You can also scroll to the top of this list and click Add New in this dialog box to create the Other Current Asset account if needed. Click Next.

10. On the Tax Tracking Type screen, select None (at the top of the list) and click Next.

11. Do not place a checkmark next to any of the Taxes options. Click Next.

 caution

Carefully consider what option you choose when selecting the Tax Tracking type for a new payroll item or editing an existing payroll item. The selection you choose here affects how QuickBooks taxes or doesn't tax the payroll item on paychecks and how QuickBooks handles reporting the payroll item on forms, such as the W-2 form given to employees at the end of a calendar year.

When you select each Tax Tracking type, QuickBooks provides detailed information about how it will be treated for tax calculations and form preparation. Be sure to take the time to read these. If you are unsure of the proper tax tracking type, consult your accounting professional.

12. The Calculate Based on Quantity screen opens. Leave the default of Neither selected and click Next.

13. On the Gross vs. Net screen, leave the default of Gross. This setting has no impact because you are setting it up with a tax tracking type of None. Click Next.

14. The Default Rate and Limit screen opens. Leave it blank because you define the limit amounts individually for each employee. Click Finish to close the Add New Payroll Item (Addition) dialog box.

15. You are returned to the Preview Paycheck dialog box. From the Other Payroll Items box, in the Item Name column, select the Employee Advance payroll addition item from the drop-down list. Enter the dollar amount of the loan you are providing the employee in the Rate column. QuickBooks creates a payroll advance check without deducting any payroll taxes (see Figure 12.7 shown previously). (Note: You do not need to enter anything in the Quantity column.)

QuickBooks now has on record a loan paid to the employee. If you have defined payment terms with the employee, you need to edit the employee's record so that on future payroll checks the agreed-to amount will be deducted.

Automatically Deducting the Employee Loan Repayments

When a company provides an advance to an employee that is to be paid back in installments, you can have QuickBooks automatically calculate this amount and even stop the deductions when the total of the loan has been completely paid back to the company.

QuickBooks will automatically deduct the loan repayments from future payroll checks. Follow these steps to record a payroll deduction on the employee's setup:

1. From the menu bar, select Employees, Employee Center.

2. Select the employee who was given a payroll advance or loan.

3. Click the Edit Employee button in the Employee Center. The Edit Employee dialog box opens.

4. From the Change Tabs drop-down list, select Payroll and Compensation Info. The Payroll Info tab displays.

5. In the Item Name column of the Additions, Deductions, and Company Contributions box, select your Employee Loan Repay deduction item (and skip to step 14) or click Add New to open the Add New Payroll Item dialog box.

6. If creating a new item, select type Deduction and click Next.

7. Name the item Employee Loan Repay and click Next.

8. The Add New Payroll Item (Deduction) dialog box opens. Leave the agency name and number fields blank. For the Liability Account, select the drop-down list and select your Employee Loans, Other Current Asset account created when you made the employee advance check. See Figure 12.8. Click Next.

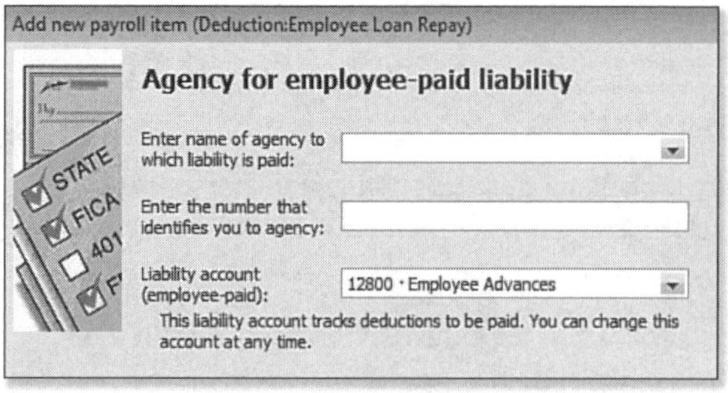

Figure 12.8
Assign the Other Current Asset Employee Loan Advances account for the paycheck deduction.

9. The Tax Tracking type screen displays. Leave the default for Tax Tracking type of None and click Next.

10. The Taxes screen displays. Accept the default of no taxes selected and click Next.

11. The Calculate Based on Quantity screen displays. Leave the default of Neither selected and click Next.

12. The Gross vs. Net screen displays. Leave the default of Gross Pay. This setting has no impact because you are setting it up with a tax tracking type of None. Click Next.

13. The Default Rate and Limit screen displays. Leave it blank because you define the limit amounts individually for each employee. Click Finish to return to the New Employee dialog box or Edit Employee dialog box.

14. In the Item Name column of the Additions, Deductions, and Company Contributions box, select your Employee Loan Repay deduction item you just created.

15. In the Amount column, enter the per pay period amount you want to deduct.

16. In the Limit column, enter the amount of the total loan. QuickBooks stops deducting the loan when the limit is reached. Click OK to record your changes to the employee setup.

QuickBooks is now properly set up to deduct the stated amount on each paycheck until the employee loan has been fully paid back. If you provide additional employee loans, do not forget to go back to step 15 and add the new amount to the previous loan total.

Reporting Employee Loan Details

It is equally important to track the actual details of the employee loan. To open a modified version of my favorite report, the Transaction Detail report (as shown in Figure 12.9), follow these steps:

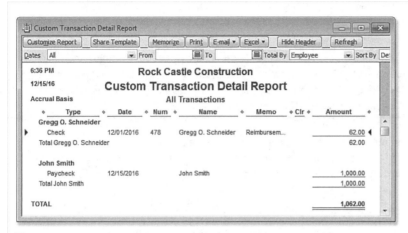

Figure 12.9
Create a report to track your employee loan details.

1. From the menu bar, select Reports, Custom Reports, Transaction Detail. The Modify Report dialog box displays.

2. From the Report Date Range drop-down list, select the date range you are reviewing.

3. In the Columns box, select or deselect the detail you want to see displayed on the report.

4. From the Total By drop-down list, select Employee.

5. Click the Filters tab; Account is already selected in the Choose Filters box. From the Account drop-down list to the right, select the Employee Loans, Other Current Asset account.

6. In the Choose Filters box, select the Amount filter and optionally select an amount greater than or equal to .01. Doing so provides a report of only those employees with non-zero balances.

7. Optionally, click the Header/Footer tab and customize the report title.

8. Click OK to view the modified report.

9. Optionally, click Memorize to save the report for later use.

You are now prepared to advance money to an employee and track the employee's payments against the loan accurately. Don't forget to review the balances and to increase the limit when new loans are paid out.

Reprinting a Lost Paycheck

When any other check in QuickBooks is lost, you typically void the check in QuickBooks and report it to your bank so it cannot be cashed.

With payroll, you need to be a bit more cautious about voiding the transaction because when you void a payroll transaction and then reissue it, payroll taxes could be recalculated on the replacement check differently from the originally issued payroll check.

Certain payroll taxes are based on limits; for example, Social Security, federal unemployment, and state unemployment taxes are examples of taxes that are charged to employees or to the company up to a certain wage limit. When you void a previously issued check, QuickBooks recalculates these taxes for the current replacement check, and these amounts might differ from the original check, potentially affecting the net amount of the check.

Proper control would be to report the missing check to your bank so it cannot be cashed. In QuickBooks, instead of voiding the payroll check and then re-creating it, print a new payroll check (from the same original payroll check details), record the new check number, and then separately create a voided check for the lost check.

To record these transactions, follow these steps:

1. Locate the lost check in your checking register by choosing Banking, Use Register.

2. From the Select Account drop-down list, select the bank account that has the missing check and click OK to open the bank register.

3. Find the check in the register that was reported missing. Double-click the specific check to open the Paycheck dialog box (see Figure 12.10). Make a note of the check number, date, and payee.

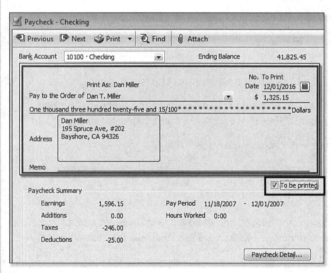

Figure 12.10
Do not recreate a lost paycheck; instead select the To Be Printed check box on the original paycheck.

4. In the open Paycheck dialog box, select the To Be Printed check box.

5. Print the paycheck singly or with others by clicking the Print button at the top of the check.

6. Enter the Printed Check Number. After printing the check, QuickBooks assigns the new check number and uses the check date and totals assigned to the original check.

7. To keep track of the lost check in your accounting, select Banking, Write Checks from the menu bar. Using the original check number, date, and payee record the check with a zero amount to an account of your choosing. You might get a message warning not to pay employees with a check, but because you are recording a zero transaction, you can ignore this warning.

8. With the lost check created in step 7 still open, click Edit, Void Check. QuickBooks prefills with a "0" amount and the Memo line of the check with "Void." This now shows this check as voided in your register just in case the employee was able to cash the check. You would notice when reconciling that you have marked it as voided.

Using this method for printing a lost payroll check ensures you do not inadvertently change any prior period payroll amounts and reported payroll totals; at the same time, recording the lost check helps keep a record of each check issued from your bank account.

Paying a Taxable Bonus

Use an unscheduled payroll to issue bonuses to your employees. This payroll is included in their total taxable wages. To do so, follow these steps:

 note

When issuing a bonus paycheck, QuickBooks might display a warning that a paycheck already exists for the date you have selected. Click Continue to close the warning. You are returned to the Enter Payroll Information dialog box.

1. From the menu bar, select Employees, Pay Employees, Unscheduled Payroll. The Enter Payroll Information dialog box displays.

2. Place a checkmark next to the employee(s) receiving a bonus check.

3. If the employee is paid hourly, you can adjust the hours from the regular pay column.

4. Often, you want to edit or remove the default Gross Earnings or Federal Taxes Withheld on a bonus check. To adjust this detail, click the Open Paycheck Detail button to modify the default amounts.

5. If you are using Intuit QuickBooks Payroll Enhanced subscription, you can also select the check box to Enter Net/Calculate Gross on the paycheck detail. Selecting this option enables you to specify the net amount and QuickBooks then calculates what the gross amount should be to cover taxes and withholdings.

6. QuickBooks might display a warning dialog box titled "Special Calculation Situation" to inform you certain payroll items have reached their limits.

7. In the example shown in Figure 12.11, the Federal Withholding amount that was automatically calculated was removed. QuickBooks now shows that this paycheck was adjusted.

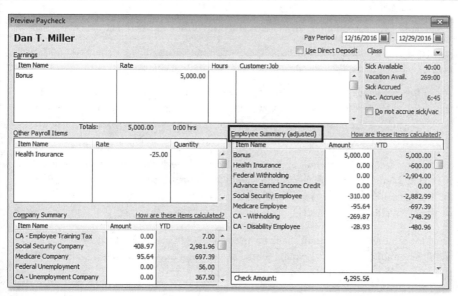

Figure 12.11
QuickBooks identifies when automatic payroll calculations have been manualy adjusted.

Adjust paychecks cautiously, making sure you do not adjust those items that have a predefined tax table amount, such as Social Security and Medicare. If you do, and the adjustment causes the calculated totals to be incorrect for the year, QuickBooks "self-adjusts" the taxes on the next payroll check you create for this employee. You should also obtain the advice of your tax accountant before adjusting taxes withheld on bonus payroll checks.

Adjusting an Employee Paycheck

You should rarely need to adjust a paycheck record in QuickBooks. One example is where you hand-prepare a check, and then later discover QuickBooks calculated a different net pay amount.

In this example, the check amount cashed by the employee differs from what QuickBooks computed, so adjusting the QuickBooks paycheck is acceptable.

To adjust a prepared employee check before it is printed, or to adjust a paycheck that had the wrong amount in QuickBooks from what was recorded on the actual check, follow these steps:

1. Locate the paycheck in your checking register by clicking the Check Register icon on the QuickBooks Home page.

2. If you have multiple checking accounts, select the account the paycheck was recorded to and click OK to open the bank register.

3. Find the check with the incorrect amount; open the paycheck transaction by double-clicking the check.

4. Click the Paycheck Detail button to display the detail of the check to be modified.

5. Click Unlock Net Pay and review the message QuickBooks provides about cautiously changing net pay on existing checks. Click OK to close the message, as shown in Figure 12.12.

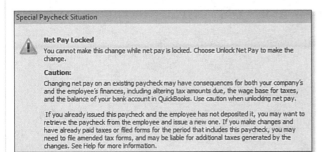

Special Paycheck Situation

⚠ **Net Pay Locked**
You cannot make this change while net pay is locked. Choose Unlock Net Pay to make the change.

Caution:
Changing net pay on an existing paycheck may have consequences for both your company's and the employee's finances, including altering tax amounts due, the wage base for taxes, and the balance of your bank account in QuickBooks. Use caution when unlocking net pay.

If you already issued this paycheck and the employee has not deposited it, you may want to retrieve the paycheck from the employee and issue a new one. If you make changes and have already paid taxes or filed forms for the period that includes this paycheck, you may need to file amended tax forms, and may be liable for additional taxes generated by the changes. See Help for more information.

Figure 12.12
QuickBooks protects inadvertent changes by requiring you to unlock net pay before modifying a paycheck record.

6. Modify the check as needed, being careful not to modify the Social Security or Medicare taxes. Modify the check to reflect the actual check amount that cleared.

7. Click OK to close the dialog box.

8. Click Save & Close to save the changes to the paycheck.

Cautiously consider the effect of changes you make to existing paychecks will have on previously filed payroll tax returns.

Depositing a Refund of Payroll Liabilities

If you received a refund from an overpayment of payroll taxes, you would not want to add it to a Make Deposits transaction (like other deposits you create). If you did, the refunded amount would not correct your overpayment amount showing in the payroll liability reports and in certain payroll forms.

This type of payroll error should rarely, if at all, occur in current versions of QuickBooks thanks to improved messaging and ease of creating payroll transactions from the Payroll Center.

However, if you were paying your payroll liabilities outside the QuickBooks payroll menus and you had an overpayment you requested and received a refund for, you can record the deposit to reflect receipt of the overpayment in your payroll reports. To do so, follow these steps:

1. From the menu bar, select Employees, Payroll Taxes and Liabilities, Deposit Refund of Liabilities. The Refund Deposit for Taxes and Liabilities dialog box displays.

2. Select the name of the payroll tax liability vendor.

3. Enter the Refund Date (the date of your deposit).

4. Enter the For Period Beginning date (this should be the payroll quarter the overpayment was in).

5. Enter the Deposit Total of the refund.

6. Select the Group with other undeposited funds button if this item is included on a bank deposit ticket with other deposit amounts; or select the Deposit To button to create a single deposit entry and select the appropriate bank account from the drop-down list.

7. Select the Payroll Item that needs to be adjusted.

8. Optionally, add a Memo, and click OK.

See Figure 12.13 for a completed Refund Deposit for Taxes and Liabilities transaction.

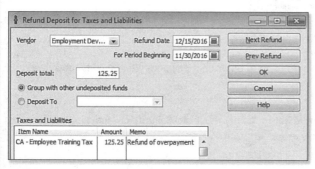

Figure 12.13
Use the proper transaction when recording a refund of overpaid payroll liabilities.

13

WORKING WITH BANK AND CREDIT CARD ACCOUNTS

Importance of Bank and Credit Card Balances

You might wonder why I would have to point out the importance of having the correct bank or credit card balances in your QuickBooks data, yet incorrect account balances are often one of the most common problems I find when troubleshooting a client's QuickBooks data. One of the first questions I ask new clients is whether they have reconciled their bank or credit card accounts in QuickBooks. Most tell me they have. I then review any transactions that are not marked as cleared and I will usually find older, dated transactions that have not cleared. For more information, see "Reviewing Uncleared Transactions," in this chapter.

One of the most important reconciliations you should do in QuickBooks is match your bank or credit card transactions recorded in QuickBooks with the same transactions reported by the financial institution in their monthly statement. Just reconciling your account balances can correct many errors on the Profit & Loss statement.

Preferences that Affect Banking and Credit Card Management

Did you know that you can streamline your banking and credit card processes by setting certain QuickBooks preferences? Setting preferences saves keystrokes, which in turn can save data entry time.

Not every preference that affects banking or credit card management impacts your financials; some preferences enable specific features. Set preferences in QuickBooks by selecting Edit, Preferences from the menu bar.

Preferences in QuickBooks come in two forms:

- **My Preferences**—Settings that are unique to the current user logged in the data file and are not shared by other users.

- **Company Preferences**—Settings that are common for all users.

 For a detailed review of the preferences that affect working with banking and credit card activities see "Preferences That Affect Accounts Payable," p. 186.

Working with Write Check Transactions

An important task for any financial management software is the ability to record the expenses that a business has in providing the product or service to its customers.

QuickBooks offers multiple transactions for recording your business expenses. The Write Checks transaction offers a quick method for entering costs. Another transaction for recording expenses is the Enter Bills transaction (to enter vendor bills).

Both the Write Checks transaction and the Enter Bills transaction can be used to record expenses. However, there are some notable differences between the two:

- Using a vendor bill allows you to track what is owed while using a write check simply records the cost as of the date of the check.

- If you use a vendor bill, QuickBooks will warn you if you enter the same reference number that has already been recorded. This warning helps to control inadvertently paying a vendor more than once for the same product or service.

You might want to use a vendor bill for selected vendor costs rather than writing a check. This chapter is specific to working with the costs you will be recording using the Write Checks or Enter Credit Card Charges transactions.

 note

To set company preferences, you must log into the file as the Admin or External Accountant user and switch to single-user mode (if you are using the data file in a multi-user environment). The Admin user is the default user created when you begin using QuickBooks for the first time.

Proper data entry security includes limiting which employees have access to logging in as the Admin and setting company preferences that are global for all users. For more information see, "Setting Up Users and Permissions," p. 38.

caution

The Write Checks transaction is *not* the proper type of transaction for recording payment of a bill entered into QuickBooks, paychecks for employees, payroll liability payments, or sales tax liability payments. More detailed information about using the proper transaction type for these can found in the respective chapters in this book.

Using the Expenses Tab and Items Tab

The QuickBooks Write Checks dialog box includes an Expenses and Items tab. The information entered on these tabs provides financial detail about the cost being recorded as well as other useful information. See Figure 13.1.

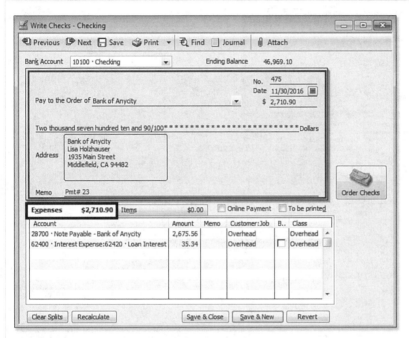

Figure 13.1
Use the Expenses tab to record administrative or overhead costs.

The Expenses and Items tabs on a check or vendor bill affect QuickBooks reports in different ways. Costs recorded on either tab will be included in all of the Profit & Loss reports. However, if your business wants to use the job profitability reports, you must consistently use the Items tab for recording job-related expenses as shown in Figure 13.2.

From the menu bar, select Reports, Jobs, Time & Mileage. Many of the listed reports are dependent on the information entered on the Items tab of the write checks transaction.

➡ *For more information, see "Items," p. 82.*

Another useful purpose of the Items tab is to automate assigning the expense to a specific chart of account. An example is recording telephone expenses. A business that has multiple vendors for telephone, fax, or cell phone services can create an item named "Telephone." This item would be mapped to the appropriate chart of account. When a bill is received, the cost can be recorded on the Items tab using the Telephone item. QuickBooks will automatically assign the cost to the expense account included in the item setup.

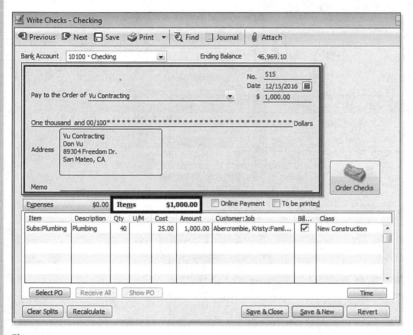

Figure 13.2
Use the Items tab to record customer- or job-related expenses.

Writing a Check

Writing a check is an easy way to record expenses. I recommend using it for one-time purchases from a supplier or service provider, or for recording debit card or ACH payments from your bank account.

Writing a Check

To practice writing a check, open the sample data file as instructed in Chapter 1, "Getting Started with QuickBooks." If you are working in your own file, use these instructions to enter checks:

1. From the menu bar, select Banking, Write Checks.

2. On the Write Checks dialog box, leave the prefilled Bank Account—Checking.

3. In the Pay to the Order Of field, begin typing **Davis Business Associates** until the appropriate vendor displays (also see the tip that follows this sidebar). QuickBooks will prefill if the name is recognized in any of the lists in QuickBooks (see Figure 13.3). To continue with the sample exercise, skip to step 9; if you're working in your own file, continue to step 4.

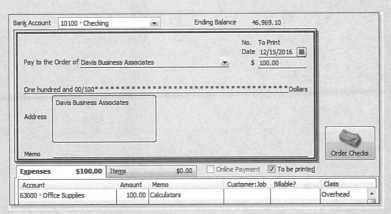

Bank Account 10100 · Checking   Ending Balance   46,969.10

No. To Print
Date 12/15/2016

Pay to the Order of Davis Business Associates $ 100.00

One hundred and 00/100************************************Dollars

Davis Business Associates

Address

Memo   Order Checks

Expenses $100.00 Items $0.00   ☐ Online Payment   ☑ To be printed

Account	Amount	Memo	Customer:Job	Billable?	Class
63000 · Office Supplies	100.00	Calculators			Overhead

Figure 13.3
Create a check to record a business expense.

4. When you are entering checks in your own file and the payee is not included in a list, select Add New at the top of the Pay to the Order Of drop-down list.

5. When adding a new payee, the Select Name Type message displays where you will assign the new payee as a Vendor, Customer, Employee, or Other. After selecting the appropriate list, click OK.

6. Complete the details for the newly created list item.

7. Optionally, instead of selecting Add New in step 4, if you begin typing the name in the Payee field, QuickBooks will offer these choices:

      • **Quick Add**—Creates a new list record with just the name field.

      • **Set Up**—Opens up the Select Name Type. Choose from Vendor, Customer, Employee, or Other names list.

      • **Cancel**—Select to not add the new payee.

8. Complete the remaining fields for adding the new name to the selected list. This process varies depending on whether you are adding a new vendor, employee, customer, or someone else. Click OK to return to the Write Checks dialog box.

9. Accept the prefilled Date. The cost will be recorded in the business financials as of this date.

10. In the amount field, type **100.00**.

11. Optionally, complete the address details. (When you save the record, QuickBooks will prompt you asking whether you want to save the changes for future transactions.)

12. Enter an optional Memo (the field below the address box). This memo will print on the check. If the Memo field is left blank, QuickBooks can insert the Account Number from the vendor record. For more information, see the section, "Adding or Modifying Vendors," in Chapter 7.

13. On the first line of the Expenses tab, begin typing the account **Office Supplies**.

14. Use the Tab key on your keyboard to advance to the following fields:

    • **Memo**—Enter an optional memo that will be included in reports (not on the printed check).

    • **Customer:Job**—Leave blank for this exercise. It is recommended to use the Items tab when assigning costs to jobs with budgets.

    • **Billable**—Leave the field blank. For more information, see "Time and Expense Invoicing," p. 303.

    • **Class**—Select Overhead.

15. Leave the following fields unselected:

    • **Online Payment**—Select if your bank offers payment of expenses through your QuickBooks file. For more information, see the section in this chapter titled "Online Banking Center."

    • **To Be Printed**—When selected, QuickBooks removes any prefilled check number. The check number will be assigned when the check is printed.

16. Optionally, click any of the following to help complete the transaction:

    • **Clear Splits**—Condenses multiple rows into one.

    • **Recalculate**—Useful if after entering an amount at the top of the record, you add additional lines of detail to the Expenses or Items tab.

    • **Revert**—Undo of any previous changes.

    • **Save & Close**—Save and close the dialog box.

    • **Save & New**—Save and continue with another record.

 tip

QuickBooks can automatically open drop-down lists when typing. From the menu bar, select Edit, Preferences, and select the General—My Preferences tab on the Preferences dialog box. Select the Automatically Open Drop-Down Lists When Typing checkbox. Click OK to close the dialog box and save your changes.

 note

You will not have the Class field in your data if Class Tracking in the Preferences dialog box is not enabled. To enable class tracking, from the menu bar select Edit, Preferences. Select the Company Preferences tab for Accounting.

Printing Checks

Printing checks from QuickBooks can save you time over manually writing checks and later recording them in your software. Printing also helps to limit any confusion about the amount the transaction is approved for.

Ordering QuickBooks Checks

Many check printing suppliers offer QuickBooks-compatible checks. When ordering, confirm with your check supply source that it guarantees the format supplied will work with the QuickBooks software. In QuickBooks, only a few minor adjustments can be made to the placement of data on the printed check.

You can also purchase checks directly from Intuit. For more information, see the "Do More with QuickBooks," panel on the QuickBooks Home page.

Setting Form Defaults and Making Printing Adjustments

Before printing checks from your QuickBooks file, review the printing defaults assigned to checks or paychecks. From the menu bar, select File, Printer Setup. From the Form Name drop-down list, select Check/PayCheck as shown in Figure 13.4.

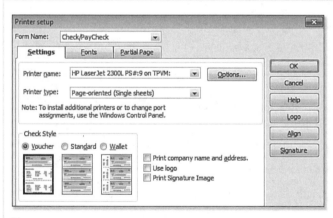

Figure 13.4
Select the check style you will be printing and other settings.

From the Settings tab, you can select

- Printer Name and Printer Type.

- Check Style. Select from Voucher, Standard, or Wallet.

- Print Company Name and Address, Use Logo, or Print Signature Image. Click the Signature button to the right to locate the electronically stored signature image.

Select the Fonts tab to modify the Font used on the check. Select the Partial Page tab if you print standard or wallet format style checks. Use this setting to define how a single check is to be positioned in the printer.

After printing a check, you might find it necessary to make minor alignment modifications to the printed check. Click the Align button. Select amounts to move the text in 1/100-inch increments (as shown in Figure 13.5). Click Print Sample to check your new settings. Click OK to close the Printer Setup when completed with this task.

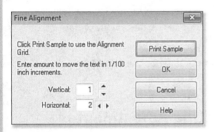

Figure 13.5
Use the fine alignment setting for check printing adjustments.

Printing Checks

With QuickBooks, you can print checks individually or in a batch of checks all at one time.

To print a check when using the Write Checks dialog box, make sure the To Be Printed box is selected (see Figure 13.3).

To print a check, follow these steps:

1. If the Write Checks dialog box isn't already open, select Banking, Write Checks from the menu bar, and prepare your check for printing.

2. From the Print drop-down list, select from the following:

   - **Print**—Enter the check number you are printing to.

   - **Print Batch**—Select the Bank Account. Enter the First Check Number and remove the checkmark for any check you will not be printing in the batch.

3. The Print Checks dialog box displays. Change the defaults as necessary.

4. If you are printing a single check using the Standard or Wallet check style, click the Partial Page tab. Review the settings specific for how your printer needs the single check positioned before printing.

5. Click the Print button to print your checks.

6. The Print Checks—Confirmation dialog box displays as shown in Figure 13.6.

Figure 13.6
Make sure each check printed correctly before selecting OK on the Print Checks—Confirmation dialog box.

7. Review the checks that just printed. If each check printed successfully, click OK on the Print Checks—Confirmation dialog box. If any check did not print successfully, place a checkmark in the Reprint column. You can return to step 2 and reprint the checks selected.

Entering a Bank Debit Charge

If your business uses a debit card for making purchases, you need to record these expenses like any other purchase transaction. A debit card transaction is debited from your bank's available cash balance, unlike a credit card where the payment for the purchase is made at some later date.

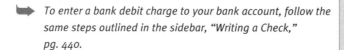   To enter a bank debit charge to your bank account, follow the same steps outlined in the sidebar, "Writing a Check," pg. 440.

Instead of printing a check, remove the To Be Printed checkmark and in the No. field enter a notation as referred to in the Caution in this section. Or, you can enter some notation of your own that will help you identify the charge as a debit when reconciling the bank account.

 tip
You can review both printed and to be printed check transactions by clicking the Check Register icon on the Home page and selecting the appropriate bank account.

 caution
If you are recording a debit card payment made to vendor for whom you issue a year-end FORM 1099-MISC, there are specific notations that should be used in the No. field. For more information, see "Tracking and Reporting Vendor 1099-MISC Payments," p. 226.

Entering Credit Card Charges

QuickBooks uses the Enter Credit Card Charges transaction to record business purchases made on credit. Has your business been using this transaction type? If not, you might have recorded credit card purchases using a vendor bill payable to the credit card merchant. Listed here are a few of the reasons to use a credit card receipt to record payments made by credit card:

- Track the vendors paid for the service or product.

- Track the date the purchase was made.

- Reconcile the credit card activity to the monthly statement from your credit card provider.

Recording a Credit Card Charge

To practice recording a credit card charge, open the sample data file as instructed in Chapter 1. If you are working in your own file use these instructions to enter a credit card charge:

1. From the menu bar, select Banking, Enter Credit Card Charges.

2. Leave the prefilled QuickBooks Credit Card account (see Figure 13.7).

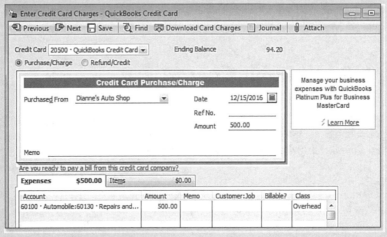

Figure 13.7
Recording expenses made with the company credit card.

3. For this exercise, leave selected Purchase/Charge. When working in your own data you can select Refund/Credit when necessary.

4. From the Purchased From drop-down list, start typing **Dianne's Auto Shop**. To add a new payee when necessary, select Add New at the top of the list. Select an appropriate type from the Select Name Type dialog box that displays (also see the tip that follows these steps).

5. For this exercise, leave the prefilled date. When working with your own data this would be the date the charge was incurred.

6. Optionally, enter a Ref. No.

7. Type the amount of **500.00**

8. Optionally, enter a Memo.

9. On the Expenses tab, the account has prefilled from the default settings with that vendor or from past credit card purchases.

10. Leave Memo and Customer:Job blank.

11. Leave the Billable column blank and select the Overhead class.

12. Optionally, click any of the following to help complete the transaction:

   - **Clear Splits**—Condenses multiple rows into one.
   - **Recalculate**—Will recalculate the Amount field from the total of the rows.
   - **Revert**—Undo previous changes.
   - **Save & Close**—Save and close the dialog box.
   - **Save & New**—Save and continue with another record.

 tip

Often credit card purchases are made from one-time suppliers. I recommend that you select the Other name type when adding this type of payee. This will keep your vendor list limited to those you do frequent business with.

Paying the Credit Card Bill

As you enter credit card charges, QuickBooks increases the amount you owe your credit card institution. Because the individual charges have already been recorded, when you pay your bill you need to reduce your bank balance and the amount you owe the credit card company.

If you are using a check to record the payment, select Banking, Write Checks from the menu bar. Follow the instructions for writing a check, with one exception. On the Expenses tab, in the Account column select the other current liability account associated with the credit card bill you are paying (see Figure 13.8).

If you choose to enter a bill, select Vendors, Enter Bills from the menu bar.

➤ *For more information on working with vendor records, see "Recording Vendor Bills," p. 205.*

On the Expenses tab, in the Account column select the other current liability credit card account. Process the payment for the vendor bill as with other bills.

Include reconciling your credit card account in your list of monthly accounting tasks; doing so will help you manage your credit card activity as discussed in this chapter.

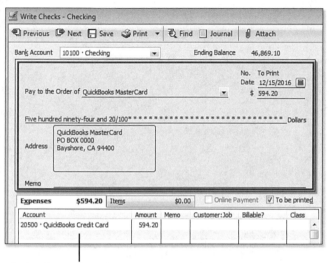

Assign the credit card account
in the Account column.

Figure 13.8
Properly record the payment of your credit card bill.

Transferring Funds Between Bank Accounts

If your business has more than one bank account, at some time you will probably need to transfer funds from one account to another account. If you need to physically take a printed check to the bank, use the instructions in the sidebar "Writing a Check" earlier in this chapter. Or, create a bill and pay the bill as instructed in Chapter 7, "Setting Up Vendors." The exception with these two types of transactions is on the Expenses tab. In the Account column, select the bank account you are depositing the funds into.

If you transfer the funds between accounts using your banks online portal, then you can record the transaction using the Transfer Funds Between Accounts dialog box using these steps:

1. From the menu bar, select Banking, Transfer Funds.

2. Enter the date the transfer was effective.

3. Select the Transfer Funds From account and the Transfer Funds To account.

4. Enter the Transfer Amount $.

5. Optionally, enter a memo, which will display in reports.

6. Select the Online Funds Transfer if you have signed up for Online Banking within QuickBooks and you are transferring funds between two accounts at the same bank. QuickBooks will automatically process the transfer using your Online Banking credentials.

Online Banking Center

QuickBooks provides a user-friendly interface with your bank or credit card accounts. The interface enables you to download your transactions for easy matching and reconciliation, examine recent bank transactions, transfer money between two online accounts, and pay bills online.

You don't have to use all the online services offered by your financial institution. Checking balances and transferring funds are typically free services, but many banks charge a monthly fee or per-transaction fee for bill payment services. You should weigh this fee against the cost of postage and paper supplies and the time you save to determine whether the service is worthwhile to you.

Choosing an Online Banking Mode Preference

QuickBooks users have the option to choose between two different methods of viewing the information that is to be downloaded. Try both methods and see which one works best for you.

From the menu bar, select Edit, Preferences, and select the Checking—Company Preferences tab. The Online Banking box offers two choices:

- Side-by-Side Mode

- Register Mode

Click the What's the Difference? link for more information or give them both a try. You can choose to work with one and then later switch back to the other method.

The remaining sections on the QuickBooks Online Banking feature will be shown using the side-by-side mode.

Activating Online Services with Your Financial Institution

The first step in using online banking services is getting access to a bank that provides the services you need. After you have opened a bank account and established online privileges, you are ready to put QuickBooks to work. With an Internet connection, you will be able to access your bank account directly from your QuickBooks program.

To initiate the QuickBooks online banking feature, follow these steps:

1. From the menu bar, select Banking, Online Banking, Set Up Account for Online Services.

2. From the Select Your QuickBooks Account drop-down list, select the QuickBooks bank account (or credit card) for which you want to set up online services or select Add New if you are creating a new bank or credit card type account. (Remember, you must have online services enabled with your financial institution before you can set up the services within QuickBooks.) Click Next.

3. From the Enter The Name Of Your Financial Institution drop-down list, select your banking or credit card institution. *Hint:* You can also begin typing the name and QuickBooks will prefill the list with possible matches. Click Next.

4. You might be prompted with a Select Option dialog box if your financial institution has multiple related financial entities. Choose where the account is held if applicable, and click OK.

5. If your financial institution provides more than one method for connecting, you will be given the option to choose which connection to use. Select Direct Connect if you want to connect to your bank or credit card directly from within QuickBooks. (This is the most efficient method.) See Figure 13.9.

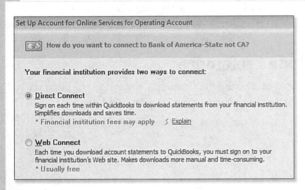

Figure 13.9
Choose between two methods for downloading transactions into QuickBooks.

6. Select Web Connect if you want to first sign into your financial institution's website before downloading transactions (this method is more manual and time consuming).

7. Click the Compare These Options link if you are unsure which to choose. Click Next.

8. If prompted, select Yes if you have already activated your online access with your financial institution. Select No if you need the contact information for your financial institution. If you selected No, a dialog box will open in which you can view your bank's contact information.

9. If you selected Yes, you are prompted to enter your Customer ID and Password. Click Sign In.

10. Click to select the account you want to log onto from the list.

11. Click Next and QuickBooks will now process the request for your online financial services connection to QuickBooks.

12. Click Activate Online Bill Payments to set up the ability to pay your bills directly from QuickBooks (fees might apply).

13. Click Finish and QuickBooks opens the Online Banking Center.

 note
You can also download credit card transactions directly into your QuickBooks data file.

Retrieving Online Transactions

After you have activated online services with your bank, you can request to review and download your bank or credit card transactions that have recently cleared your financial institution.

1. From the menu bar, select Banking, Online Banking, Online Banking Center.

2. If the Choose Your Online Banking Mode dialog box displays, select Continue to use your existing mode or switch the mode by selecting Change Mode. The selection is not permanent, so you can test each method and pick what works best for you.

3. If you have more than one online account, verify that the correct account name displays in the Financial Institution box. If you have multiple online services, use the Select drop-down list to select the proper online service you want to work with in the current online banking session. See Figure 13.10.

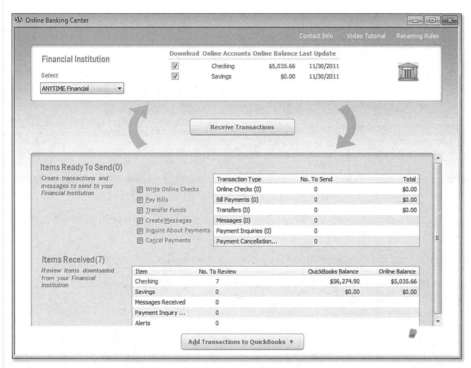

Figure 13.10
Review and add downloaded transactions to your QuickBooks file.

4. Click the Receive Transactions button to automatically connect through the Internet with your selected financial institution.

5. Enter your PIN into the Access dialog box for your financial institution that displays.

6. Click OK.

QuickBooks will provide a status message as it downloads current transactions into the QuickBooks Online Banking Center. In the Online Banking Center, you can control which transactions you download into your QuickBooks financial institution register.

Now that you have successfully retrieved your financial institution's transactions, follow the steps in the next few sections to properly download the transactions into your QuickBooks file.

Adding Downloaded Transactions to QuickBooks

You can conveniently add transactions one at a time to your QuickBooks data file (see Figure 13.11). Activating Online Banking Services can save you time and improve your data entry accuracy.

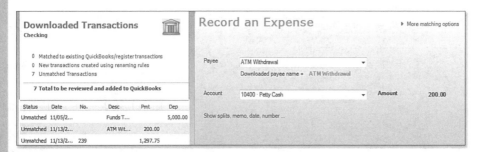

Figure 13.11
Choose to add the transactions to QuickBooks one at a time.

1. To open the Online Banking Center, select Banking, Online Banking, Online Banking Center from the menu bar.

2. To review the items downloaded, click Bank, Credit Card, Messages Received, or Alerts in the Items Received section.

   The Add Transactions to QuickBooks dialog box displays the transactions, messages, or alerts.

3. Click a single transaction on the left. (You might optionally click Add Multiple. A list of Renamed or Unmatched transactions displays as shown in Figure 13.12.)

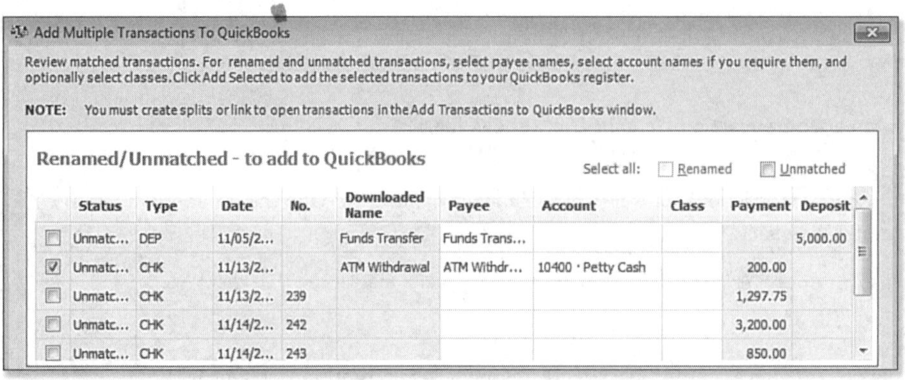

Figure 13.12
Work efficiently by downloading multiple transactions at once into QuickBooks.

4. The Payee field will automatically populate if the QuickBooks online banking services recognizes the payee. If it doesn't populate, simply click the drop-down list to select from your QuickBooks lists (vendors, employees, customers, other names) or begin typing the name and have QuickBooks add it to your lists.

5. The Account field will automatically populate if the QuickBooks online banking service recognizes the payee from a previous downloaded transaction. If it doesn't populate, simply begin typing the account name or click the drop-down list to select from a list of your accounts.

6. Click the More Matching Options link to select to record the expense, assign the payment to an open vendor bill, or match to an existing QuickBooks transaction. (Your options might differ depending on the type of transaction being added.)

7. Optionally, click Show Splits, Memo, Date, and Number and modify as needed.

8. In the Account field, if the account did not automatically populate, type the account name or select one from the drop-down list.

9. Accept the default amount that displays or click in the amount column to modify if needed.

10. Optionally, assign the expense to a customer using the Customer:Job field.

11. Select the Billable check box if you will be using QuickBooks Add Time and Costs feature to invoice the customer for the expense.

12. Assign a class with the Class field if you departmentalize your company's Income Statement (and use Classes for other reporting).

13. Click Remove Selected to clear the line detail above the currently selected line.

14. Click Hide Splits, Memo, Date, Number to return to the less-detailed entry dialog box.

15. Click Add to QuickBooks, and the transaction will now be included in the QuickBooks register for that financial institution.

16. Click Finish Later to return to QuickBooks and exit the Online Banking Center.

Renaming Rules in Online Banking

Renaming rules automate and standardize the names of downloaded banking transactions into QuickBooks. Your financial institution might include a transaction number in the downloaded payee name field. In such cases, QuickBooks might then create a new vendor for each transaction, but you can use the Aliasing feature to avoid this problem.

For example, you purchase mobile phone services from Verizon Wireless. When the transaction is downloaded, the vendor name is "Verizon Wireless - <transaction code or location>." You can create a renaming rule that will instruct QuickBooks to ignore the transaction code and assign it to the proper vendor. Renaming rules are based on several options: begins with, ends with, contains, or exactly matches.

To modify the renaming rules created automatically by QuickBooks Online Banking, follow these steps:

1. Click Renaming Rules in the top-right corner of the Online Banking Center.

2. In the Edit Renaming Rules dialog box (see Figure 13.13), click the name for which you are modifying the renaming rule from the list on the left.

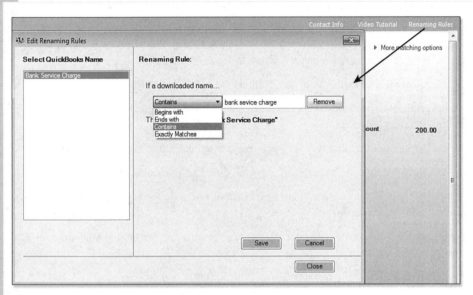

Figure 13.13
Renaming rules help QuickBooks recognizes the payee name on your list and accounts assigned for future transactions.

3. In the If a Downloaded Name drop-down list, choose from the Begins with, Ends with, Contains, or Exactly Matches options.

4. Type the criteria to be used. This can be very useful for vendors that append their name with a unique transaction number for each charge.

5. Click Remove if you want to clear your selection. Click Save to assign the renaming rule.

Other Online Banking Features

There are many other features of QuickBooks Online Banking.

note

Did you know that the QuickBooks Online Banking feature will create a renaming rule automatically when you assign the transaction to an existing QuickBooks name for the first time? You can then modify the renaming rule created.

Assigning Transactions to Open Vendor Bills

If you would like to associate a downloaded transaction to an open vendor bill in QuickBooks, effectively paying the open vendor bill with the downloaded transaction, you can use the Add Transactions dialog box.

To assign transactions to open vendor bills, follow these steps:

1. In the Online Banking Center, click the Add Transactions to QuickBooks button.

2. Select the More Matching Options link at the top right of the Add Transactions to QuickBooks dialog box.

3. Click, Select Open Bills to Pay.

4. Select the Payee from the drop-down list, or begin typing the payee name. QuickBooks will find list names that match. See Figure 13.14.

Figure 13.14
Assign downloaded payments to open vendor bills.

5. Accept the prefilled Accounts Payable account, or select the proper account if you have more than one Accounts Payable type account.

6. Accept the prefilled Date or change as needed.

7. Enter an optional Memo.

8. Enter an optional transaction number or name in the Number field if no number displays.

9. Place a checkmark next to the open bill or bills that are being paid by this downloaded transaction.

10. Click the Add to QuickBooks button to record this transaction to your financial institution register in QuickBooks.

11. Click Finish Later to leave the dialog box.

12. Select Yes or No to saving the changes made.

Assigning Deposits to Open Customer Invoices

QuickBooks Online enables you to match your downloaded banking deposits to open customer invoices or previously recorded deposits into your bank account using the Make Deposit forms.

To assign deposits to open customer invoices, follow these steps:

1. In the Online Banking Center, click the Add Transactions to QuickBooks button.

2. In the Add Transactions to QuickBooks dialog box, click a deposit transaction item from the list on the left as displayed in Figure 13.15.

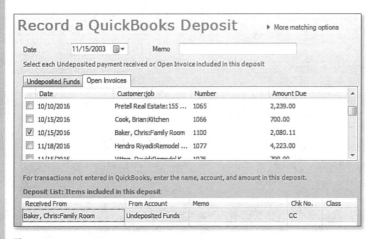

Figure 13.15
Assign bank deposits to open customer invoices.

3. Accept the default Date or modify as needed.

4. Enter an optional Memo.

5. Click to place a checkmark next to each invoice that was included in the deposit downloaded. Modify the amount in the Deposit List pane if you are not receiving full payment. Continue with the following steps not displayed in Figure 13.15.

6. Click Remove Selected to clear the contents of the Deposit List box.

7. Click Add to QuickBooks, and your transaction will be included in your financial institutions register in QuickBooks.

8. Click Finish Later to exit and return later to finish recording.

9. If you opt to finish recording information later, QuickBooks presents a prompt box. Click Yes to discard your changes.

10. Click No to save your changes and return to the dialog box.

11. When you finish assigning deposits, close the Online Banking Center dialog box by clicking the Close (x) button in the upper-right corner.

Adding or Deleting Multiple Transactions

QuickBooks Online Banking Services can save you data entry time by enabling you to add multiple transactions at once.

To add or delete multiple transactions, follow these steps:

1. In the Online Banking Center, click the Add Transactions to QuickBooks button.

2. In the Add Transactions to QuickBooks dialog box, click the Add Multiple button.

3. In the No. field, you can optionally add a transaction number.

4. Click the Payee field to select the payee from your QuickBooks lists.

5. Click the Account field to select the account from your QuickBooks chart of accounts.

6. Optionally, select the Class field and choose a class if you are tracking these in your data file.

7. To select all the transactions, place a checkmark in the Renamed or Unmatched boxes. If not selected, you can manually add or remove individual checkmarks for individual items you want to add to your financial institution register.

8. Leave the default checkmark in Select All Matched, and QuickBooks Online Banking will remove these "matched" transactions from future downloads.

9. Optionally, click the checkboxes to add or remove individual checkmarks.

10. Click Add Selected to add the selected transactions to your QuickBooks register for this financial institution.

11. If you click Cancel, you will be given the choice to keep or discard your changes to the transactions.

 note

You can also delete selected transactions. Once deleted, those transactions will no longer be included in future downloads. Click the Select Items to Delete button and place a checkmark next to those transactions you want to remove.

Making or Canceling Online Payments

Online Bill Payment from the QuickBooks Online Services lets you pay your vendors electronically through QuickBooks.

After the service is enabled (your bank might charge a fee for this), you can use QuickBooks to record the bills being paid and send instructions to your financial institution. Your financial institution's payment processor will make the payments electronically or print and mail the check for you.

To make or cancel online payments, follow these steps:

1. If you activated your online bill payment service, as discussed in the "Activating Your QuickBooks Online Services" section, you will have a link to Write Online Checks or Pay Bills in the Online Banking Center.

2. Click Write Online Checks to create a check that will be sent to your financial institution for payment directly to the vendor. Optionally, click Pay Bills to write a bill payment check in QuickBooks. Click Save and Close.

3. The Online Payment dialog box displays instructing you to click the Send/Receive Transactions to complete the process. Optionally, click Do Not Display the Message in the Future. Click OK.

4. Click Send/Receive Transactions in the Online Banking Center.

5. Enter your PIN if requested.

6. The Online Transmission Summary dialog box displays. Click Print to optionally print the summary.

7. Click Close to exit the Online Transmission Summary details and return to the Online Banking Center.

 note

Your financial institution doesn't offer bill pay service? Consider signing up for the Intuit QuickBooks Bill Pay Service. Select Banking, Online Banking, Learn About Online Bill Payment. Information and instructions are provided for signing up for the service.

Reconciling the Bank or Credit Card Account

Are you reconciling your bank or credit accounts in QuickBooks? If the answer is no, are you reconciling these accounts on the monthly paper statement provided by the financial institution? If you still answered no, then you will certainly find value in learning how easy it is to reconcile these accounts in QuickBooks.

Why exactly is it so important? A significant amount of most business' income and expenses are recorded through bank or credit card activity. When the reconciliation is not completed in the software, how certain are you that the financial reports are accurate?

There are a few exceptions to income and expenses flowing through a bank account. For example, a restaurant or bar might manage a significant amount of cash during the course of doing business. Do not limit yourself to thinking the task of reconciling is limited to bank or credit card accounts. If you have a cash safe, drawer, or box at the office, reconcile the ins and outs of the cash in your QuickBooks data.

 note

If your work is interrupted while you are reconciling a bank statement, you can click Leave in the Reconcile–Account dialog box. Clicking Leave will keep the checkmarks you have assigned to transactions and let you return to finish your work later.

To begin reconciling your bank or credit card accounts, follow these steps:

1. From the menu bar, select Banking, Reconcile to open the Begin Reconciliation dialog box as shown in Figure 13.16.

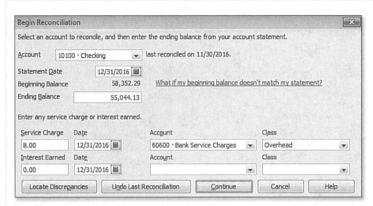

Figure 13.16
Reconcile your accounting records to your financial institution's monthly statement.

2. From the Account drop-down list, select the appropriate account. (Any Balance Sheet type account can be reconciled.)

3. Select the Statement Date that matches the ending statement date from your financial institution.

4. Review the Beginning Balance, which should equal the same number provided by your financial institution. Later sections in this chapter will detail methods of troubleshooting errors in the Beginning Balance.

5. Enter the ending balance from your financial institution's period statement.

6. Optionally, enter any Service Charge or Interest Earned, selecting the appropriate date, account, and Class if tracking the use of Classes.

7. Click Continue. The Reconcile–*Account Name* dialog box opens.

8. Select the Hide Transactions After the Statement End Date check box. This will make the task of reconciling much easier.

9. Place individual checkmarks next to cleared Checks, Payments, Deposits, and Other Credits that are included in the statement from your financial institution.

10. Click Reconcile Now only when the Difference is 0.00. See Figure 13.17. This indicates that your cleared transactions match those provided by the financial institution.

 note

Where does the beginning balance originate from on the Begin Reconciliation dialog box? It is the sum total of all previous transactions, for the selected account that are marked as cleared.

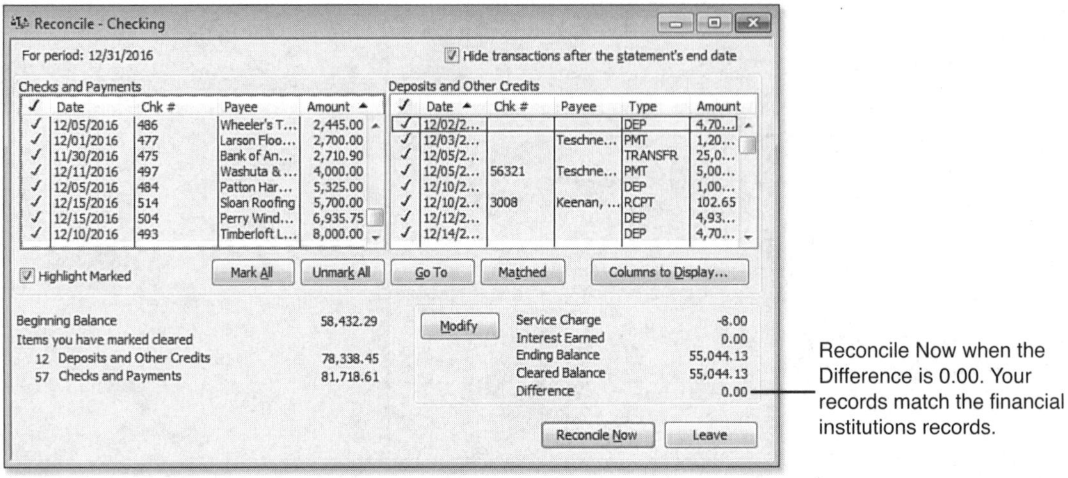

Figure 13.17
Reconcile your bank account to match transactions that cleared your bank or credit card account.

For more information, see "Reconciling with an Adjustment," p. 471.

11. Follow the prompts to print the reconciliation report to attach to your financial institution's statement for safekeeping.

Other useful features of working with the Reconcile feature in QuickBooks include:

- **Highlight Marked**—Will make it easier to differentiate the cleared from the non-cleared transactions on the computer screen.
- **Mark All or Unmark All**—Use to automatically add or remove checkmarks from transactions during the bank reconciliation process.
- **Go To**—Open the currently selected transaction. Useful if you need to modify the transaction.
- **Matched**—For matching downloaded transactions to the transactions in QuickBooks.
- **Columns to Display**—Add or remove the columns of data displayed.
- **Modify**—Click to change the reconcile For Period date or the Ending Balance amount.
- **Leave**—Click to save your work and close the Begin Reconcile window.

You can also click any column header to sort the data in that column.

Reconciliations are easiest when done each month. However, you might have been using QuickBooks for some time before learning how to complete the reconciliation task. The following section of this chapter will help you learn how to troubleshoot the first reconciliation or fix errors in previous reconciliations.

Troubleshooting Reconciliations

A simple way to determine whether your bank account is correctly reconciled is to compare your bank statement beginning balance to the QuickBooks Beginning Balance amount in the Begin Reconciliation dialog box. From the menu bar, select Banking, Reconcile, and select the appropriate Account. If you find your QuickBooks beginning balance does not agree with your bank statement, you can use one or a combination of several methods listed in this chapter to figure out why.

 note

What makes up the Beginning Balance, as shown in Figure 13.16? The beginning balance is the sum of all previously cleared checks, deposits, and other transactions. A checkmark next to a transaction item in the bank account register indicates it has previously been cleared in the bank reconciliation in QuickBooks. An asterisk indicates the item is currently being reconciled, as shown in Figure 13.18. A lightning bolt (not shown) next to a transaction indicates it has been downloaded and matched, but has not yet been marked cleared.

Transactions with a checkmark (✓) are previously cleared.
Transactions with an asterisk (*) are in the process of being cleared.

Date	Number	Payee		Payment	✓	Deposit	Balance
	Type	Account	Memo				
11/30/2016	473	Wheeler's Tile Etc.		686.00	✓		56,213.54
	BILLPMT	20000 · Accounts Pa					
11/30/2016	474	Dianne's Auto Shop		218.00	✓		55,995.54
	CHK	60100 · Automobile:: Monthly Vechiicle Rep					
11/30/2016	475	Bank of Anycity		2,710.90	*		53,284.64
	CHK	-split-	Pmt# 23				
12/01/2016	476	Abercrombie, Kristy:Remodel Bathroom		711.15	*		52,573.49
	CHK	11000 · Accounts Re					

Ending balance   53,918.15

Figure 13.18
View the cleared status of transactions in your account register.

Determining If the Account Has Been Reconciled

If your business is just starting, it is a good time to make it part of your regular routine to reconcile your bank account in QuickBooks with the statement you receive each month. However, what if you have been using QuickBooks for years or months and have never reconciled the bank account in the software?

How can you tell whether your bank account has been reconciled? An easy method is to begin the bank reconciliation. From the menu bar, select Banking, Reconcile, and select the desired account. Review the "last reconciled on (date)" in the Begin Reconciliation window. A month/day/year indicates that the account has previously been reconciled (see Figure 13.16). If you have a Beginning Balance amount but no "last reconciled on (date)," no reconciliation has been completed. This beginning balance was most likely from entering your bank balance when you first created your QuickBooks file.

➡️ *For more information, see "Express Start," p. 25.*

 tip

Are you an accounting professional? Included with QuickBooks Accountant 2012 and QuickBooks Enterprise Accountant 12.0 is the new Accountant Center as displayed in Figure 13.19.

Open a client's file and the Accountant Center will summarize important information about your client's account reconciliations.

Figure 13.19
The Accountant Center is available with the Accountant editions of QuickBooks.

Have there been no reconciliations completed? First, determine how many months have gone by. Catching up with a few months of bank statement reconciliations takes much less effort than having to do several years or months of bank statement reconciliations. If you are going to go back to the beginning of the business and reconciling each month, you need to start with the first month of your bank activity and work your way month by month to the current month. Completing your bank reconciliation for each month is the most accurate and thorough process and provides a separate reconciliation report for each month.

⚠️ **caution**

As with any major task or adjustment you plan to make in your QuickBooks data, I recommend you make a backup copy. You can easily create this backup by selecting File, Create Backup from the menu bar, and then following the instructions on the screen.

However, it is often not practical to go back to the start of your business when you simply want to get the bank account reconciled in the current month.

Complete the recommendations in the following sections before attempting to complete a multiyear or multimonth bank reconciliation.

Verifying That All Account Transactions Have Been Entered

Ensuring that all checks, bill payments, payroll checks, customer payments, and any other banking-related transactions have been entered in the QuickBooks data file is critical to the success in accurate reporting in your own or your client's QuickBooks file. You don't want to complete a multiyear or multimonth bank reconciliation if handwritten checks or other bank transactions have not been recorded in the data.

Creating a Missing Checks Report

To help you determine whether any check transactions are missing, create a Missing Checks report. To do so, follow these steps:

1. From the menu bar, select Reports, Banking, Missing Checks report.

2. In the Missing Checks dialog box, select the bank account from the drop-down list.

The resulting Missing Checks report shows all check or bill payment check type transactions sorted by number (see Figure 13.20). Look for any breaks in the detail with a ***Missing* or ***Duplicate* warning.

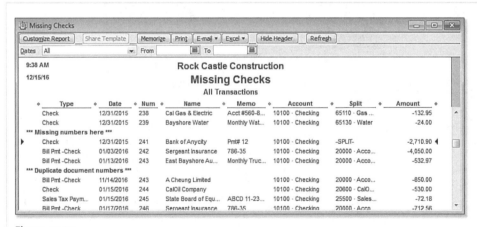

Figure 13.20
The Missing Checks report can help you determine whether you need to enter any missing transactions before you reconcile.

Creating a Custom Transaction Detail Report

Another method used to verify you have recorded all your transactions requires a bit more effort on your part. Manually add the total of all deductions and additions from the statements your bank provides you and compare it to the Custom Transaction Detail report.

To do so, follow these steps:

1. From the menu bar, select Reports, Custom Reports, Transaction Detail. The Modify Report dialog box opens.
2. Select the From and To dates to match the period you are desiring to reconcile. If from the beginning of the file, you might want to leave the From date blank and only enter the To date.
3. Click the Filters tab.
4. In the Choose Filter box, with the Account filter highlighted, choose the bank account from the drop-down list.
5. Select OK.

This report (see Figure 13.21) totals all debits (money into your bank account) and credits (money out of your bank account). To these totals, you have to add in checks and deduct deposits that have not yet cleared the bank. If the resulting totals are exact or close to your manual totals, you can feel confident reconciling multiple years or months at one time.

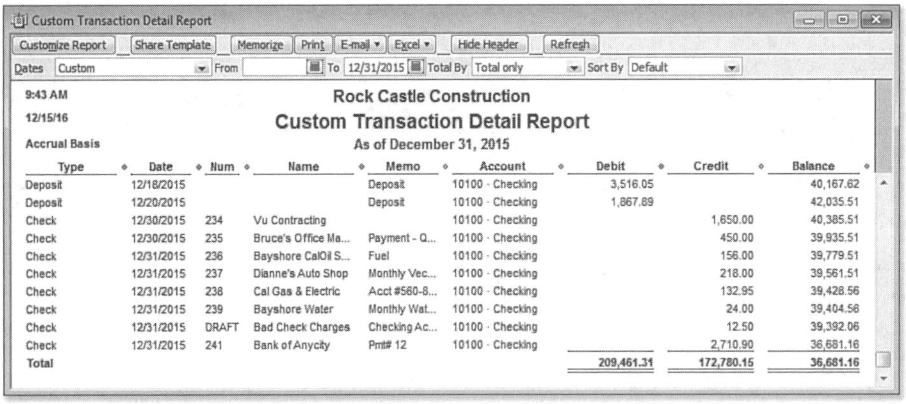

9:43 AM
12/15/16
Accrual Basis

Rock Castle Construction
Custom Transaction Detail Report
As of December 31, 2015

Type	Date	Num	Name	Memo	Account	Debit	Credit	Balance
Deposit	12/18/2015			Deposit	10100 · Checking	3,516.05		40,167.62
Deposit	12/20/2015			Deposit	10100 · Checking	1,867.89		42,035.51
Check	12/30/2015	234	Vu Contracting		10100 · Checking		1,650.00	40,385.51
Check	12/30/2015	235	Bruce's Office Ma...	Payment - Q...	10100 · Checking		450.00	39,935.51
Check	12/31/2015	236	Bayshore CalOil S...	Fuel	10100 · Checking		156.00	39,779.51
Check	12/31/2015	237	Dianne's Auto Shop	Monthly Vec...	10100 · Checking		218.00	39,561.51
Check	12/31/2015	238	Cal Gas & Electric	Acct #560-8...	10100 · Checking		132.95	39,428.56
Check	12/31/2015	239	Bayshore Water	Monthly Wat...	10100 · Checking		24.00	39,404.56
Check	12/31/2015	DRAFT	Bad Check Charges	Checking Ac...	10100 · Checking		12.50	39,392.06
Check	12/31/2015	241	Bank of Anycity	Pmt# 12	10100 · Checking		2,710.90	36,681.16
Total						209,461.31	172,780.15	36,681.16

Figure 13.21
The modified Custom Transaction Detail Report shows the total of all money in and out of a bank account for the time period selected.

Identifying All Uncleared Transactions

Make a list of all the uncleared bank transactions as of the month and year you are reconciling. If you have been manually reconciling your bank account, simply find the paper statement for the selected month and look for the list of uncleared transactions.

For example, suppose it is April 2016 and you want to reconcile multiple years or months through December 31, 2015. Collect your bank statements for January through March of 2016. Identify any cleared transactions from these 2016 bank statements where the transaction date was on or before December 31, 2015, but did not clear your bank until year 2016.

Completing the Multiyear or Multimonth Bank Reconciliation

To complete the multiyear or multimonth bank reconciliation, follow these steps:

1. From the menu bar, select Banking, Reconcile. The Begin Reconciliation dialog box displays (refer to Figure 13.16).

2. Select the desired Account from the drop-down list, and type the Statement Date you want to reconcile through. Enter the Ending Balance from the bank statement and click Continue. The Reconcile–Account dialog box displays. This example shows the bank reconciliation through December 31, 2016.

3. Select the Hide Transactions After the Statement's End Date checkbox at the top right. Checking this box makes working with the remaining transactions easier.

4. Click the Mark All button. Now each transaction is marked as if it has cleared. Remove the checkmark from any transaction you previously identified as uncleared. Your work is complete when the reconciliation shows a Difference of 0.00 at the lower right of the Reconcile–Account dialog box.

5. Click Reconcile Now. QuickBooks creates a bank reconciliation report you can print.

For added convenience when reconciling, you can sort the uncleared transactions by clicking once on any of the column headers in the Reconcile–Account dialog box.

Not all bank account reconciliations are this easy to troubleshoot and correct. Often, you need to dig deeper into the possible causes of reconciliation errors. QuickBooks makes this task much easier by providing many different tools and reports to help with this important process.

 tip

If you are choosing to complete a multiyear or multimonth bank reconciliation, consider reconciling through the last month of your previous fiscal year, which for most companies would be your statement ending December 31, 20xx. Choosing a month to reconcile through that is two to three months in the past will make identifying the transactions that have not cleared the bank as of the month you are reconciling much easier.

caution

What if the reconciled difference is not 0.00? First determine whether the amount is significant. If the answer is yes, the best method for finding errors is to review each item marked cleared in QuickBooks with the transactions listed on your bank statements.

If you choose to record the adjustment, QuickBooks records this amount into an automatically created Expense account called "Reconciliation Discrepancies." For more information, see "Reconciling with an Adjustment," p. 471.

Reviewing Uncleared Transactions

If your bank account has previously been reconciled, reviewing your uncleared bank transactions is the best place to start when troubleshooting an incorrectly reconciled bank account.

Creating an Uncleared Transactions Detail Report

This report is one of the most useful to you as you research your bank reconciliation errors. You might want to memorize this report so it can be reviewed again if needed.

To create an uncleared bank transactions report, follow these steps:

1. From the menu bar, select Reports, Custom Reports, Transaction Detail. The Display tab of the Modify Report dialog box opens. In the Report Date Range box, select All Dates. If you have more than one bank account, in the Total By drop-down list, select Account List to keep each bank account with separate totals. From the Columns box, select the data you want to appear in the report.

2. Click the Filters tab. In the Choose Filter box, with Account highlighted, select All Bank Accounts. Scroll down the Choose Filter list and select Cleared, and then click No next to the list, as shown in Figure 13.22.

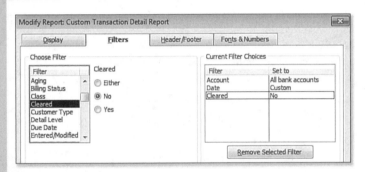

Figure 13.22
Filter the report to show only uncleared bank transactions.

3. This report will be useful to you in the future, so go ahead and give it a specific name by clicking the Header/Footer tab and changing the Report Title as desired.

4. Click OK to create the report (see Figure 13.23).

5. Optionally, click Memorize to have QuickBooks store the report for future use. QuickBooks asks you to provide a name for the report.

6. Click OK to save the memorized report.

> **tip**
>
> Another option is to add this report to your icon bar. With the report displayed, select View, Add *<name of report>* to Icon Bar.

Memorizing customized reports for later use is easy. First, make sure your Dates selection is appropriate. If your Dates selection is Custom, each time you create this report, it uses the custom dates. Selecting Dates, such as the generic This Month-to-Date or any of the other choices, makes the memorized report more valuable in future months.

With the report displayed, click Memorize. QuickBooks stores the report with the header name or you can rename it.

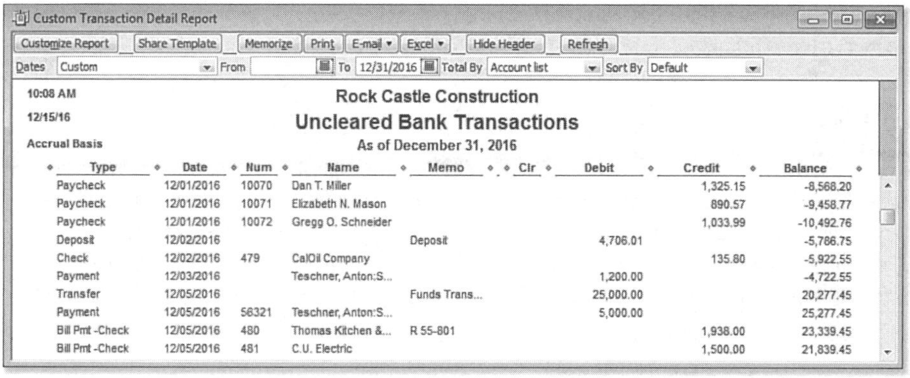

Type	Date	Num	Name	Memo	Clr	Debit	Credit	Balance
Paycheck	12/01/2016	10070	Dan T. Miller				1,325.15	-8,568.20
Paycheck	12/01/2016	10071	Elizabeth N. Mason				890.57	-9,458.77
Paycheck	12/01/2016	10072	Gregg O. Schneider				1,033.99	-10,492.76
Deposit	12/02/2016			Deposit		4,706.01		-5,786.75
Check	12/02/2016	479	CalOil Company				135.80	-5,922.55
Payment	12/03/2016		Teschner, Anton:S...			1,200.00		-4,722.55
Transfer	12/05/2016			Funds Trans...		25,000.00		20,277.45
Payment	12/05/2016	56321	Teschner, Anton:S...			5,000.00		25,277.45
Bill Pmt -Check	12/05/2016	480	Thomas Kitchen &...	R 55-801			1,938.00	23,339.45
Bill Pmt -Check	12/05/2016	481	C.U. Electric				1,500.00	21,839.45

Figure 13.23
Create a customized report to easily view uncleared bank transactions.

Sorting Transactions

Another method for reviewing uncleared bank transactions is to open your bank register and follow these steps:

1. From the menu bar, select Banking, Use Register.
2. Select the desired bank account in the Use Register dialog box.
3. On the lower left of the register is a Sort By drop-down list. Select the Cleared status from the drop-down list.
4. Scroll through the register and view those transactions that are either:
   - **Cleared**—noted by a checkmark
   - **Process of being cleared**—noted by an * (asterisk)
   - **Not cleared**—no checkmark or * (asterisk)

Often, a transaction that is cleared and should not have been cleared or a transaction that is uncleared and should have been cleared can be the cause of the opening balance not matching.

If you need to unclear a transaction or two, double-click the checkmark next to the item in the bank register. QuickBooks replaces the checkmark with an asterisk. You can also click once more to remove the asterisk if desired.

If you attempt to make a change to the cleared status of a transaction while in the bank register, QuickBooks provides a warning message.

Using additional reporting tools in QuickBooks can help you find changes made to previously reconciled transactions. You will find that using a combination of the following reports when troubleshooting reconciliation errors is useful.

Reviewing Previous Bank Reconciliation Reports

If you determine that the file has been previously reconciled but no paper copy was kept, no need to worry. From the menu bar, select Reports, Banking, Previous Reconciliation. In the Select Previous Reconciliation Report dialog box, select the Statement Ending Date to view (see Figure 13.24). QuickBooks displays the last stored reconciliation report (available only in QuickBooks Premier, Accountant, and Enterprise). Choose from the following view options: Summary, Detail, or Both.

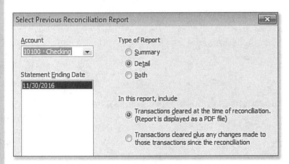

Figure 13.24
Select the previous bank reconciliation report when troubleshooting errors.

Additionally, you can view the reports in two ways:

- **Stored PDF Bank Reconciliation**—This stored report shows the bank reconciliation details as they were completed at the time the account was reconciled.

- **Transactions Cleared Plus Any Changes**—View this report to see how the bank reconciliation would look today, real time.

Compare the stored PDF with the Transactions Cleared Plus Changes report. Any differences between the two should indicate what your discrepancies are. You might be able to find these discrepancies easily with the Reconciliation Discrepancy report, as discussed next.

Locating Bank Account Reconciliation Discrepancies

From the menu bar, select Reports, Banking, Reconciliation Discrepancy to open the Reconciliation Discrepancy Report dialog box. Choose the bank account from the drop-down list and select OK to create the report. This report identifies any transaction modified after being cleared in the bank reconciliation process. For each transaction on this report, you see the modified date, reconciled amount, type of change (amount added, deleted, or voided), and the financial effect of the change (see Figure 13.25).

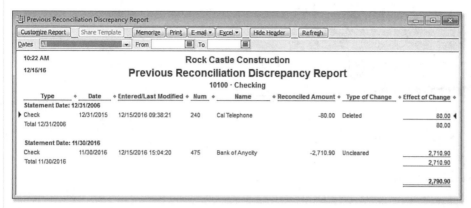

Figure 13.25
View details of previously cleared transactions that have been modified, deleted or voided.

You can click Modify Report and add the username that modified the transaction to help in identifying who made the change to the transaction.

After you have found the reconciliation discrepancy, you can view the Voided/Deleted Report (discussed in the next section) to help recreate the transaction(s).

Reviewing the Voided/Deleted Transactions Reports

Other reporting tools that help locate problem transactions are the Voided/Deleted Transactions Summary report and the Voided/Deleted Transactions Detail reports.

To create the Voided/Deleted Transactions Summary report, shown in Figure 13.26, select Reports, Accountant & Taxes, Voided/Deleted Transactions Summary from the menu bar. Alternately, you can select Voided/Deleted Transactions Detail from the submenu to view the detailed reported.

If you are having trouble finding the problem, particularly when the beginning balance has changed, this report can help you find the problem transaction(s).

 caution

Troubleshoot your bank reconciliation beginning balance differences with the previous Reconciliation Discrepancy report before completing the next month's reconciliation. Doing so is important because QuickBooks removes all detail from the discrepancy report when you complete a new reconciliation. This is due to QuickBooks determining that you have solved the issue or you would not have completed the next month's bank reconciliation.

This report does *not* track discrepancies caused by changing the bank account associated with a transaction.

Use this report for recreating the voided or deleted transactions as part of the process of fixing your bank reconciliations.

If there are more than a few transactions in error, restarting or undoing the previous bank reconciliation might be easier than researching each transaction marked as cleared.

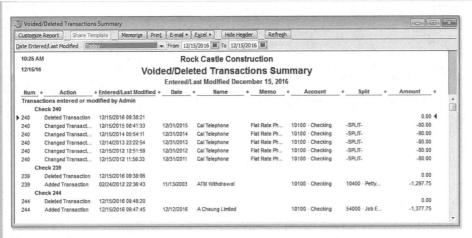

Figure 13.26
Use the Voided/Deleted Transactions Summary report to locate transactions that are possibly causing your reconciliation errors.

Restarting a Previously Completed Bank Reconciliation

If your review shows a few minor issues with bank reconciliation accuracy, restarting your reconciliation might be the best action to take. To do so, select Banking, Reconcile, Locate Discrepancies from the menu bar. The Locate Discrepancies dialog box displays. From this dialog box, click Restart Reconciliation.

Restarting your bank reconciliation retains your checkmarks on the cleared transactions, but enables you to put in a new statement date and ending balance. You can only restart the last month's banking reconciliation.

If you need to restart the reconciliation for more than one banking month, click Undo Last Reconciliation. You can repeat this undo for several months in a row all the way back to the first reconciliation if desired.

Undoing a Previous Bank Reconciliation

If you have determined the integrity of the completed bank reconciliations is in question, you can easily undo each month's reconciliation, one month at a time. From the menu bar, select Banking, Reconcile, and click Undo Last Reconciliation.

QuickBooks opens the Undo Previous Reconciliation dialog box, providing you with ample information about what to expect and recommending that you back up your company data file first. As each month is undone, QuickBooks shows you the Previous Beginning Balance. You need only to undo bank reconciliations until you reach a statement where this amount agrees with the same month's bank statement beginning balance, so watch it closely.

Click Continue after reviewing the message in Figure 13.27. You can undo the bank reconciliation one month at a time. You will know you are back to the first statement when the Undo Previous Reconciliation dialog box shows the Previous Beginning Balance as 0.00. When you return to the Begin Reconciliation dialog box, you no longer see a "last reconciled on date" or a "beginning balance" amount.

Figure 13.27
Details of what you can expect when you complete an Undo Previous Reconciliation transaction.

 tip

Use the Undo a Previous Bank Reconciliation transaction when an incorrect statement date was entered on the bank reconciliation. QuickBooks defaults the next bank statement date to 30 days from the last statement date. Before beginning the bank reconciliation in QuickBooks, verify that the statement date and beginning balance are correct.

Reconciling with an Adjustment

QuickBooks will create an adjustment to your bank account and financials if you choose to reconcile a bank account that does not have 0.00 in the Difference row of the Reconcile dialog box.

When you decide to reconcile with an adjustment for the difference amount (see Figure 13.28), you need to first consider the following:

- Have you made every attempt to find the difference using those techniques and reports you have read in this chapter?

- Is the difference as reported on the QuickBooks Reconcile dialog box not a significant dollar amount?

If you can answer *yes* to these two items, let QuickBooks make an adjustment to your financials for the difference.

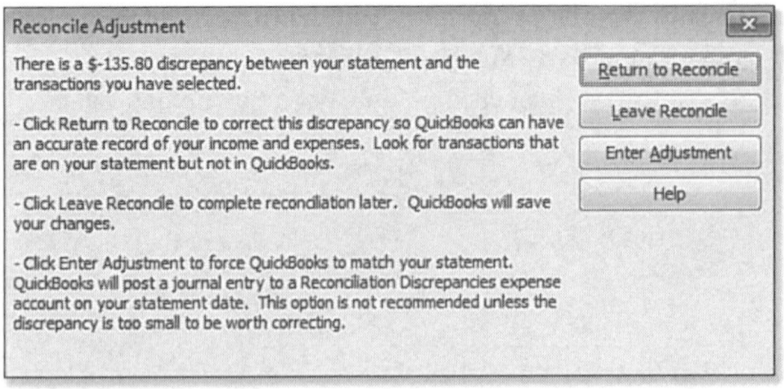

Figure 13.28
Letting QuickBooks enter an adjustment for the reconciliation difference.

To reconcile with an adjustment created by QuickBooks, click Reconcile Now in the Reconcile–Account dialog box or the Enter Adjustment in Reconcile Adjustment dialog box.

QuickBooks details the amount of the adjustment and limits your choices to do the following:

tip

One of my favorite tricks for tracking down an unreconciled balance: If the amount is evenly divisible by 9, then there's a very strong probability the digits of a transaction amount were transposed when the transaction was entered.

- **Return to Reconcile**—Click this option if you want to look for the difference.

- **Leave Reconcile**—QuickBooks saves your changes so you can return later and review your work.

- **Enter Adjustment**—This option forces QuickBooks' accounting to match your bank statement.

When you choose to use Enter Adjustment, QuickBooks creates a journal entry and posts the difference to a Reconciliation Discrepancies expense account on the profit and loss report.

I never recommend reconciling with an adjustment. Sooner or later, you will have to identify where the adjustment was from and where it should be posted. However, making an adjustment for a small balance can often save time that would be better spent on activities that grow the business. Always put in place better processes so these types of errors do not occur again.

note

Any Balance Sheet type account can be reconciled, not just bank account types. Reconciling credit card accounts provides the same control over the accuracy of your financials. Did you know that any account that transactions flow in and out of can be reconciled? Do you have a car loan? Have you reconciled your car loan account to the lending institution's statement? Do you loan money to employees and then have them pay the loan back? These are all examples of accounts that would benefit from the same reconciliation process used for bank accounts.

14

REPORTING IN QUICKBOOKS

Using the Company Snapshot

The QuickBooks Company Snapshot offers a real-time view of your company's critical information. The Company Snapshot provides insight into your business using a variety of analytic and performance indicators ready-made for your use.

The Company Snapshot (see Figure 14.1) is one convenient place to review company information and perform important tasks.

Customizing the Company Snapshot

QuickBooks offers the ability to customize the snapshot information on both a user and company file-specific basis, which can be helpful in multi-user environments. To customize your Company Snapshot, follow these steps:

1. From the menu bar, select Company, Company Snapshot to view the default graphs and reports.

2. Click Add Content to view and select from additional graphs and reports. See Figure 14.2.

3. Click the + Add button next to a graph or report to add it to your Company Snapshot.

4. Click Restore Default to remove any graphs or reports you added.

5. Click Done to view your modified Company Snapshot.

6. To rearrange the order or placement of a graph and report, click and hold your left mouse button (a move icon displays), drag the item to a new location, and release the button.

Figure 14.1
The Company Snapshot offers a wealth of useful information.

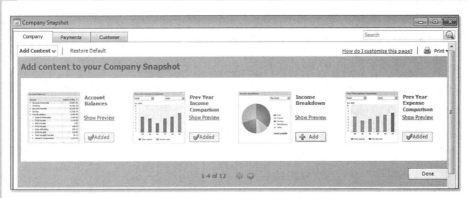

Figure 14.2
Customize the Company Snapshot by adding or removing content.

7. Optionally, select one of the following options from the Print menu in the upper-right corner to print your snapshot or prepare it for printing: Print, Print Preview, or Set Orientation.

Get an immediate view of the bottom line of your business with these reports available on the QuickBooks Company Snapshot:

- **Account Balances**—By default only Balance Sheet accounts are shown. You can add any other account type to this view by clicking the Select Accounts link.

- **Previous Year Income Comparison**—View how much money you are making this year compared to previous years for any or all accounts. You can view monthly, quarterly, weekly, or yearly comparisons.

- **Income Breakdown**—This section shows your company's largest sources of income.

- **Previous Year Expense Comparison**—Compare how much money you are spending this year to previous years for any or all accounts. You can view monthly, quarterly, weekly, or yearly comparisons.

- **Expense Breakdown**—This section shows your company's biggest expenses.

- **Income and Expense Trend Graph**—This section of the Company Snapshot shows money going in and out of your business.

- **Top Customers by Sales**—Easily report on who your top five customers are based on sales for a given period of time.

- **Best Selling Items**—This section shows you which items and services customers are buying the most during a given period of time. You can view the data by amount or by units

- **Customers Who Owe Money**—Review those customers who owe your company money. Overdue items are shown in red. To sort any of the columns, click the column header in any of the panes. The Due Date shown is the earliest due date for all invoices or statement charges for that customer.

- **Top Vendors by Expense**—This section shows who your top five vendors are based on expenses for a given period of time.

- **Vendors to Pay**—Skip running the aged payables report by adding this section to your Company Snapshot. Amounts shown in red are past due. To sort any of the columns, click the column header. The Due Date shown is the earliest due date that the vendor bills are due. The Amt Due column is the total ending balance for that vendor.

- **Reminders**—Never forget important tasks. Include these critical reminders on your Company Snapshot. Click the Set Preferences link in the Reminders box to customize what information you want displayed.

⚡ caution

If your company has created user restrictions in QuickBooks, the user will have access only to activities of the Company Snapshot that he has been provided permission to access. If you do not want the user to see the Income and Expense of the company, you will have to set restrictions for both the Sensitive Accounting Activities and Sensitive Financial Reporting. To modify a user's security rights, you must be logged into the data file as the Admin user.

After you have set up the security, log in as that user and verify whether the behavior is what you were expecting. For more comprehensive user security settings, consider using QuickBooks Enterprise Solutions 12.0.

Defaulting the Company Snapshot as Home Page

If you wish to have the Company Snapshot display when you first open a company file, follow these steps:

1. Click the Company Snapshot icon on the icon bar to open the Company Snapshot. Alternatively, select Company, Company Snapshot from the menu bar.

2. With the Company Snapshot displayed, select Edit, Preferences from the menu bar and select Desktop View on the left side of the Preferences dialog box.

3. On the My Preferences tab, select the Save Current Desktop option button. See Figure 14.3.

Figure 14.3
The desktop preference settings control what opens automatically when you launch QuickBooks.

4. Uncheck the option to Show Home Page When Opening Company File. When you open your data file, the Company Snapshot will automatically display.

Report Center

Up to this point in the book, you have learned how to get started with QuickBooks and create a variety of transactions. In this chapter you will learn from step-by-step instructions for creating specific reports to assist you with your QuickBooks setup or review.

If you are new to QuickBooks or if you have never reviewed the QuickBooks Report Center, in this section you can find out about the many features available for simplifying your reporting needs in QuickBooks.

The Report Center is available in the following editions of QuickBooks: Pro, Premier, Accountant, and Enterprise.

To open the Report Center, click Reports on the icon bar or, alternatively, select Reports, Report Center from the menu bar. The Report Center displays, as shown in Figure 14.4. Features of the Report Center include:

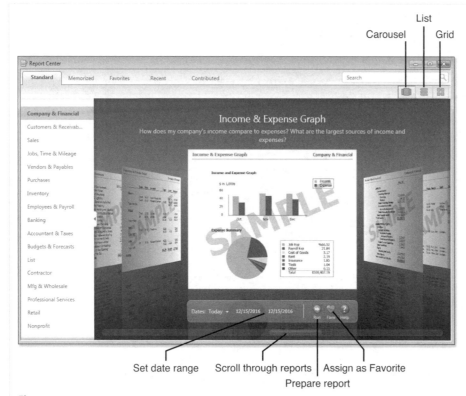

Figure 14.4
The QuickBooks Report Center in Carousel View.

- Option to view the reports or graphs in Carousel View, List View (see Figure 14.5), or Grid View (see Figure 14.6) by selecting one of the icons on the top right of the Report Center.

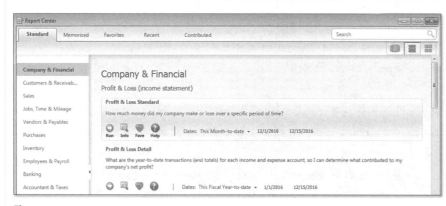

Figure 14.5
Optionally view your reports in List View.

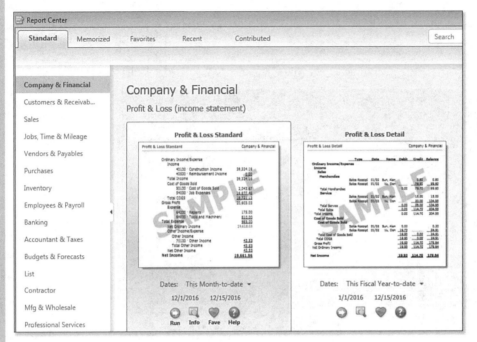

Figure 14.6
Use the Grid View to find reports for your business.

- Select a grouping of reports from the Standard tab. Your displayed report groups might differ from those shown in Figure 14.4 depending on the version of QuickBooks you are using.

- In Carousel View, use the scroll bar at the bottom of the displayed report to move through samples of the reports available in the selected report group. Data displayed is sample data.

- Click the Dates drop-down list to select a specific date, or accept the default date. (You can also click the dates to modify.)

- Click the Run icon to display the report details with your company data.

- Click the Fave icon to mark or unmark as favorite. Marking a report as a favorite places it on the Favorites Report Center tab.

- Click the Help icon to open Help information about the specific report.

- Optionally, click the arrow notch on the left of the Carousel view to close the menu report group listing.

The Report Center also includes a new tab in QuickBooks 2012 named Contributed, which displays reports shared by other QuickBooks users. QuickBooks does not share any financial data from your company file. When you share a report, you are only sharing the report structure. If the report is filtered for specific chart of accounts or other unique user-defined data, the report might not be able to be shared.

To share a report from the Memorize Report dialog box (see Figure 14.16) select the Share the Report Template With Others and follow the prompts to give the report a title and brief description.

Reports & Graphs Preferences

QuickBooks makes it easy for you to customize reports globally through the use of the Reporting Preferences. Reporting Preferences come in two types: My Preferences, which are unique to a logged-in user, and Company Preferences, which can be set only by the Admin or External Accountant user and represent global settings for all users.

My Preferences

The My Preference setting for reports is user specific. These preferences are set only for the currently logged-in user. To access user-specific preferences for reports, select Edit, Preferences from the menu bar. In the Preferences dialog box, select Reports & Graphs and click the My Preferences tab.

You can specify the following settings that will be unique for the currently logged-in user (if using QuickBooks in a multi-user mode):

- **Prompt Me to Modify Report Options Before Opening a Report**—When selected, this option causes QuickBooks to open the Modify Report dialog box each time a report is opened.

- **Reports and Graphs**—You have a choice, when report details have changed, to request QuickBooks to select one of the following options: Prompt Me to Refresh (this is the default option for a new data file), Refresh Automatically, or Don't Refresh. (I usually select the Refresh Automatically option.) However, if the report is lengthy and you have multiple users entering data, you might want to review a report, make changes, and not have QuickBooks refresh at the time the change is made.

- **Graphs Only**—This option offers settings for drawing in 2D (which is faster) or using patterns.

Company Preferences

Different from the My Preference setting for Reports and Graphs, the Company Preferences can only be set by the Admin or External Accountant user and are global settings for all users.

To access Company Preferences for reports, log in as the Admin or External Accountant user in single-user mode and select Edit, Preferences from the menu bar. In the Preferences dialog box, select Reports & Graphs, click the Company Preferences tab, and set global defaults (for all users) for the following items:

- **Summary Report Basis**—You can choose Accrual (default) or Cash Basis. For business owners, I suggest that you discuss this option with your accountant.

- **Aging Reports**—You can choose to age from the due date (default) or age from the transaction date. This setting determines the aged status of your accounts receivable or accounts payable reports.

- **Format**—Click the Format button to set the following options globally for all reports:

  - **Show Header Information**—I recommend leaving each of these choices selected and not modifying them in this window.

  - **Show Footer Information**—Here you can enter an additional footer line, such as "Confidential Information" or the like.

  - **Page Layout**—Standard (the default), left, right, or center justified.

  - **Fonts**—You can set this on the Fonts & Numbers tab. Use this to set fonts for all text or specific text lines. As you select the text line on the left, QuickBooks will display the current font choice and size for that text.

  - **Show Negative Numbers**—Format choices include normal –300.00; in parentheses (300.00) or with a trailing minus 300.00–. Optionally, you can select to have these numbers print in red.

  - **Show All Numbers**—Use this setting to divide all numbers by 1,000, to not show zeros, or to show numbers without the cents. These options are most often used by accounting professionals when providing a statement to a bank and so on.

You can display accounts by Name Only (the default), Description Only, or Name and Description. These are fields you completed in the Add New Account or Edit Account dialog boxes, as shown in Figure 14.7.

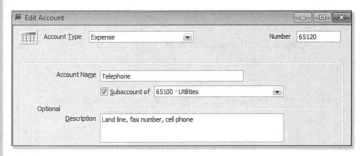

Figure 14.7
Optionally, include a description in addition to the account name.

- **Reports**—Show accounts by:

  - **Name Only**—Shows account name and account number, as shown in Figure 14.8 (if the Use Account Numbers preference is enabled).

  - **Description Only**—Shows only the information typed in the Description field (shown in Figure 14.9).

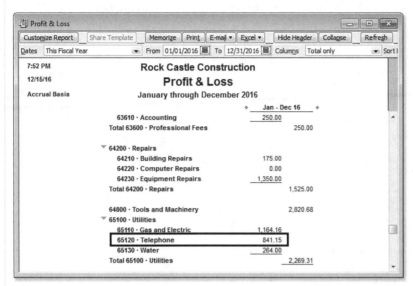

Figure 14.8
Resulting report when the Name Only report preference is selected in addition to having the account numbering preference enabled.

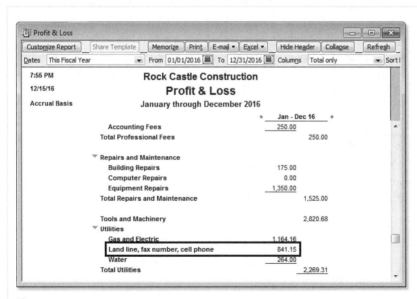

Figure 14.9
Resulting report when the Description Only report preference is selected.

- **Name and Description**—Shows account number, account name, and description, as shown in Figure 14.10.

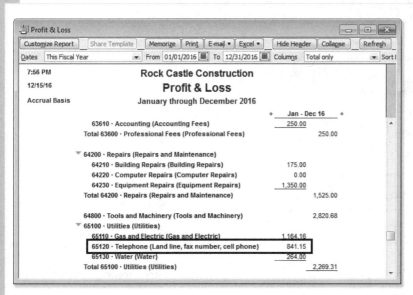

Figure 14.10
Resulting report when the Name and Description report preference is selected in addition to account numbering preference enabled.

- **Statement of Cash Flows**—Click the Classify Cash button to open the Classify Cash dialog box. From there you specify your Balance Sheet accounts as Operating, Investing, or Financing cash flow types.

Modifying Reports

QuickBooks makes gathering information from your data quick and easy. Though many reports are already created and organized for your use, you might on occasion want to modify an existing report.

This section briefly discusses the options available when you want to modify a report.

Modifying Options Available on the Report Window

A few of the options to modify a report are available directly on any active report dialog box. The options include:

- **Hide Header**—Removes the header, or report title section, from the report. Click Show Header when you want it to appear.

- **Collapse**—You can also collapse the information, as shown in Figure 14.11. When you click the Collapse button, QuickBooks removes the subaccount detail from view only. This allows you to toggle a report between summary and detail views on the fly.

Before clicking the Collapse Button

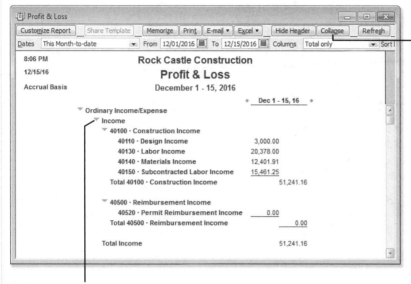

Collapse all rows in the report.

Collapse the selected account only.

After clicking collapse

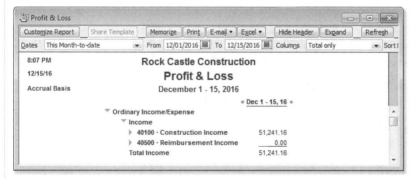

Figure 14.11
Click the Collapse button on a report to roll up the subaccounts into the main account.

- **Columns**—For certain reports, you can easily control how the data is subtotaled or grouped and add additional columns or sub-columns.

- **Sort By**—Use this to group the detail into useful ways for your review. I use this frequently, especially when looking at reports with many lines of detail. Your sort by options will vary based on the type of report you have displayed.

Other options on the active report window are also discussed in this chapter.

Customizing Reports

Click the Customize Report button at the top left of the open report dialog box. The options for modifying reports vary by report type. Some reports offer the following choices (others might not offer the same report modification choices):

- **Display tab**—This tab opens automatically when you choose to customize an existing report. The choices you have on the Display tab will vary depending on the report being modified. These choices might include:

  - **Report Date Range**—Choose from the QuickBooks predefined date ranges, or set a custom date range for your report.

  - **Report Basis**—You can choose Accrual or Cash. This option is not available on all reports. This allows you to override the default preference you might have set in Reports & Graphs preferences.

  - **Columns**—This setting is useful for selecting what information you want to see and whether you want it sorted or totaled by a specific field on the resulting report.

  - **Advanced Button**—This button is often overlooked, but its settings enable users to display active, all, or non-zero rows as well as the desired reporting calendar.

  - **Revert Button**—Undo of any changes made to the settings.

- **Filters tab**—Use these options to filter for specific accounts, names, or transaction types as well as many other fields that can be filtered on.

- **Header/Footer tab**—Use this tab to modify the report title and the appearance of the information that displays on the report. You can set this information globally for all users; see the section, "Company Preferences" earlier in this chapter.

- **Fonts & Numbers tab**—Use this tab to specify fonts for specific line text as well as how numbers appear in your reports. You can set this information globally for all users; see the section, "Company Preferences" earlier in this chapter.

 tip

New for QuickBooks 2012: Each line on a report can be collapsed or expanded manually. Click the gray arrow in front of any row report detail. This feature was included in one of the product updates. For more information about product updates, see "Installing a QuickBooks Maintenance Release," p. 560.

 tip

Filtering a report is easy and convenient to do when you want only specific information from a longer report.

If you do filter, you might want to modify your report title so it identifies what has been filtered. For example, if you are filtering a report to show employee advances detail, you might want to modify the report title on the Header/Footer tab to *Employee Advances Detail* so those who read the report will know it is pulling out specific information.

Report Groups

Users often overlook report groups, which allow you to run two or more reports in QuickBooks at once. This feature can streamline your reporting process. This section highlights how to create, use, and manage report groups.

Creating Report Groups

For accountants, this feature can save you precious time each period you work with your client's data. You can create a group of reports that you review each time you work with the client's file.

To create a report group, follow these steps:

1. From the menu bar, select Reports, Memorized Reports, Memorized Report List. The Memorized Report List dialog box displays (showing predefined groups and associated reports).

2. Click the Memorized Report drop-down list at the bottom of the list and select New Group.

3. In the New Memorized Report Group dialog box, provide a name for the group. Click OK to return to the Memorized Report List. QuickBooks places your new group alphabetically in the existing list of report groups.

4. Click the X in the upper right to close the Memorized Report List.

If you are going to create several reports that are included as part of this report group, you should move this newly created report group to the top of the list. As you memorize reports for this group, QuickBooks defaults the report group in the Memorize Report dialog box to the first Report Group on the list.

When you are done memorizing the reports to this report group (see the next section), you can move the group list item back alphabetically within the rest of the memorized reports or groups.

To move a report group up or down the list, place your cursor over the diamond shape in front of the report group name. Drag the item up or down. Figure 14.12 shows the new Monthly Reports group being moved to the top of the list.

tip

If a client were prone to making mistakes when entering data, I would teach him how the data should look, give him his own report group, and request that he review these reports before my appointment.

note

If you work in the file with Multi-user access enabled, select File, Switch to Single User Access before attempting to move a group of reports on the list.

Using Report Groups

The primary purpose of report groups is to simplify displaying or printing multiple reports at one time.

Figure 14.12
Create a report group so you can easily display or print multiple reports at one time.

To display a group of reports, follow these steps:

1. From the menu bar, select Reports, Process Multiple Reports. The Process Multiple Reports dialog box displays.

2. From the Select Memorized Reports From drop-down list, select the specific report group you want to create, as shown in Figure 14.13.

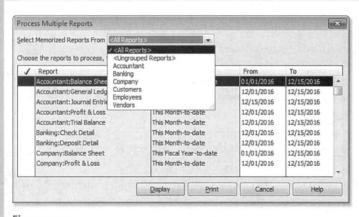

Figure 14.13
The Process Multiple Reports dialog box enables you to choose what group you want to conveniently display or print.

3. Remove the checkmark for any report you do not want to process in the group. Figure 14.14 shows a sample of selected reports.

4. In the From and To columns, change the date as needed. Be aware that these changes are not permanent. The next time you create the report group, the original date range stored with the report appears. If you want the new dates to appear next time, you need to memorize the report again and select the Replace button to replace the previously stored report with the new date range.

Figure 14.14
The Banking report group has been selected, and those reports memorized with this group are shown.

5. Click Display to view the reports on your computer screen or click Print to send the selected reports to your printer.

Your report group will now generate the multiple reports for you to view or print. I often create a report group for my clients named either Monthly or Quarterly Reports. In this group, I put certain reports I want them to review before my appointment. This method helps them help me in keeping their QuickBooks data reporting organized.

Managing Report Groups

To manage a report group, follow these steps:

1. From the menu bar, select Reports, Memorized Reports, Memorized Report List. The Memorized Report List dialog box displays (showing predefined groups and associated reports).

2. Click the Memorized Report button at the bottom of the list to choose the following memorized report list options:

> **⚠ caution**
>
> When memorizing a report you will add to a report group, be aware of the date range selected. If you want to generate a report for the current month-to-date, you would select This Month-to-Date as the default date range. When the report is generated, QuickBooks will use data from the current month-to-date.
>
> If you select a specific range of dates on a memorized report, QuickBooks considers those dates custom and will always generate the report with those specific dates.

- **Edit Memorized Report**—Edit the name of an existing report list item or which group it is associated with (you do not edit the date ranges or filters from this dialog box).

- **New Group**—Used to create an association of multiple reports, discussed in the previous section.

- **Delete a Memorized Report**—Helpful in managing the list and changes over the years.

- **Print the List**—Do this if needed to manage what reports are useful.

- **Re-sort the List**—Not often needed with this list, but if used, your list will return to its original order before any custom changes to the organization of the list items.

- **Import or Export a Template**—Create and then use reports for multiple client data files.

   For more information, see "Exporting and Importing Report Templates," p. 489.

3. To rearrange your reports, place your cursor on the diamond in front of the report name, and click and drag down and to the right, as shown in Figure 14.15. Release the mouse button when the report is in the desired position.

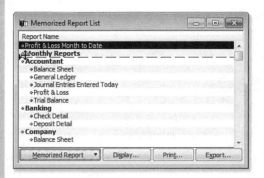 

Before rearranging the reports   After rearranging the reports

Figure 14.15
Click and drag the diamond in front of any report or group to rearrange the list manually.

From the memorized report list, you can also export your reports to Excel without first displaying them in QuickBooks. Use these report groups to streamline your data reviews. You can use the Memorize feature for many of the special reports discussed in this book and place them in a report group for easy and frequent access.

Memorized Reports

After you have created a report group, you can use the memorize feature for the reports you want in that group. Placing your memorized reports in a group is optional, but using groups helps keep your memorized reports organized.

To memorize a report, click the Memorize button at the top of an open report, as shown in Figure 14.16. QuickBooks requires you to give the report a name and optionally lets you assign it to a report group or share it with others (optional). (You must first create the report group so it displays in the drop-down list in the Memorize Report dialog box.)

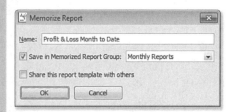

Figure 14.16
Click Memorize on any displayed report, give the report a name, and (optionally) assign it to a report group or share the template with others.

If you choose not to assign a report group, your memorized reports are listed individually at the top of the Memorized Report List, as shown previously in Figure 14.15.

Exporting and Importing Report Templates

QuickBooks offers the option to export and import report templates. This feature is useful for accountants who want to save time by having several clients use the same report template.

Only the format and filter settings are stored with report templates. If you create a report template and then have several clients use it, when the client imports it, the desired report is generated with the current client's data, not the data it was created with.

You can export and import a single report or a group of reports only from the Memorized Report List. So before you attempt to export a report, be sure to memorize it first.

Exporting a Report or Report Group Template

To export a report or report group template, follow these steps:

1. From the menu bar, select Reports, Memorized Reports, Memorized Report List.

2. From the Memorized Report drop-down list, select Export Template.

3. The Specify File Name dialog box displays, enabling you to select a location to store the template (.QBR extension).

4. Attach the stored report template or report group to an email, or copy it to a removable storage device such as a USB drive to share with other QuickBooks data files.

 caution

Certain restrictions exist when creating a template for export. For example, if you filter for a specific chart of account or customer name that might not be present in every customer's file, QuickBooks will provide the message shown in Figure 14.17 warning that this report cannot be exported.

Figure 14.17
If your report has specific filters, you might not be able to export and share it with multiple data files.

Importing a Report or Report Group Template

To import a report or report group template, follow these steps:

1. From the menu bar, select Reports, Memorized Reports. The Memorized Reports List dialog box displays.

2. Select Import Template from the Memorized Reports List drop-down list.

3. The Specify File Name dialog box displays, enabling you to select the stored location of the .QBR template.

4. Select the appropriate .QBR report or report group template.

5. Click Open. The Memorize Report dialog box displays for you to assign a name for the report and optionally assign it to a group.

6. Click OK to add the report to your memorized report list.

Exporting Reports to a .CSV File or to Excel

You might have occasions where you want to export your reports to Excel to manipulate them in some more extensive manner than is available within QuickBooks.

To export a report to either .CSV or Excel format, follow these steps:

1. From any report window, click the Excel button at the top of the report.

2. Click Create a New Worksheet. (If you are updating a previously exported report select Update Existing Worksheet and follow the prompts to browse to the file location.)

3. The Send Report to Excel dialog box displays with these options:

   - Create New Worksheet, in a new workbook or in an existing workbook

   - Update an existing worksheet

   - Create a comma separated values (.csv) file

 tip

Did you know that an abundance of reports are already created for you to import into your or your client's data file?

Both business owners and accountants will find these reports useful and unique to what you already have in QuickBooks.

Go to http://community.intuit.com/quickbooks. On the right, select Library from the More Resources section. Select the Reports For QuickBooks 2012 And Above link in Reports section. From the Search drop-down menu, select All Reports or select a specific category.

 caution

I generally try to discourage exporting to Excel and do my best with a client to find the appropriate report in QuickBooks, simply because any changes you make to your report in Excel do not "flow" back into your QuickBooks data file. However, new with the release of QuickBooks 2012, you can link exported reports, so changes made in your QuickBooks data will update your spreadsheet.

4. Optionally click the Advanced tab of the Export Report dialog box for options to preserve QuickBooks formatting, enabling certain Excel features, and printing options. Try different configurations of these settings to see what best suits your needs. See Figure 14.18. Changes made to the Advanced tab settings affect future exported reports. Click OK.

Figure 14.18
Advanced Excel includes options for formatting the exported QuickBooks report.

5. Click Export to create the exported report, as shown in Figure 14.19.

6. Select the QuickBooks Export Tips worksheet tab for additional useful hints in working with exported reports. The Advanced button includes an option to Turn Off creating the QuickBooks Export Tips worksheet.

Remember, however, that changes made in Excel to the exported report details are "static"—their information is fixed in time. Changes made to the Excel report do not transfer back into QuickBooks.

However, you can send changes in QuickBooks out to your Excel report by selecting Update an Existing Worksheet. Another method for updating a saved Excel exported report is to select the QuickBooks tab in Excel's ribbon interface and select Update Report. See Figure 14.20.

Update the saved exported report from within Excel.

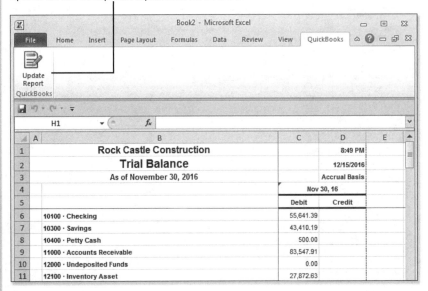

Figure 14.19
Easily convert any QuickBooks report or list to an Excel or .csv format.

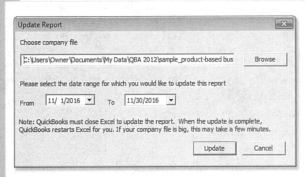

Figure 14.20
New for QuickBooks 2012, update the saved file from the QuickBooks tab in Excel.

Emailing Reports

Did you know that you can email reports from within QuickBooks? This can be a convenient way to get information to your customers, vendors, and even accountant. You can email reports as two types of attachments: individual Adobe PDF files or Excel workbooks. You must have an Internet connection on the computer that is used to send the report.

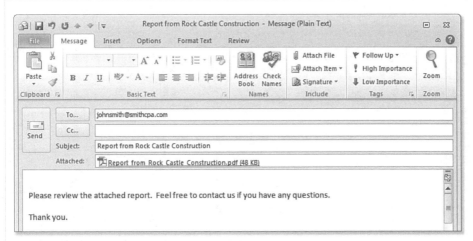

Figure 14.21
Reports sent as PDF or Excel attachments can use your own Outlook account to send.

If you want to set Outlook as your default email, select Edit, Preferences, Send Forms from the menu bar. Select the My Preferences tab where you can set the default email application to be QuickBooks or Outlook. You can also choose from other email providers.

To email a report, follow these steps:

1. From the open report, click Email and choose whether to Send Report as Excel or to Send Report as PDF (see Figure 14.21).

2. If a security message displays, indicating that sending information over Internet email is not secure, click OK to continue or click Cancel.

3. If you are sending the report through Outlook, add your email address and any additional comments to the email. Click Send when you're done. You are returned to your QuickBooks data file, and the email is stored in your Outlook sent folder.

   If you are not using Outlook for email, click Send Now and QuickBooks transmits the email for you.

note

If you do not use Outlook for your email, QuickBooks continues to send the email through QuickBooks Business Solutions, which has been available for years. Figure 14.22 shows how the email is created within QuickBooks when Outlook is not your email program.

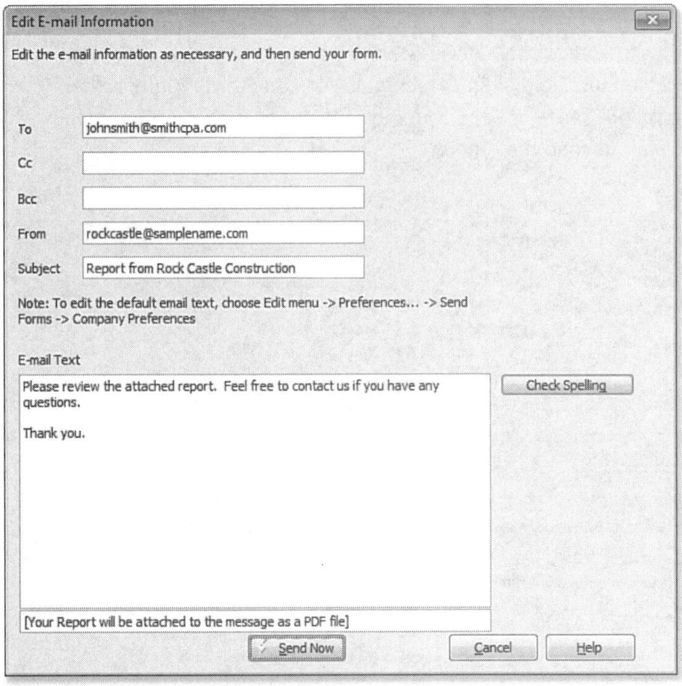

Figure 14.22
Send a report as an attachment through QuickBooks (when you don't use Outlook).

REVIEWING YOUR DATA

Importance of Reviewing Your Data

This book would not be complete without a few pages of instructions about what reports you should review for your business. These reports are not the only reports you will find useful in QuickBooks, but they are important for you to review in your file periodically.

These reports are only a subset of the many reports in QuickBooks, but are typically used by accounting professionals to verify the accuracy of your data.

Reviewing the Balance Sheet

Did you know that the report a business owner is least likely to look at is also one of the most important? To the business owner, the Balance Sheet report shows the balance of assets (what the business owns), liabilities (what the business owes others), and equity (what was put into the business or taken out of the business). Because these numbers are important, a business owner should first review this report.

This section details specific reports to use when reviewing your data. Each report is prepared in accrual basis unless otherwise mentioned. Begin by creating a Balance Sheet report of your data; this is the primary report we use for review.

From the menu bar, select Reports, Company & Financial, Balance Sheet Standard.

Leave the report with today's date. You are going to first review your data with today's date before using any other date. In the following instructions, if a different date is needed, it will be noted in the step-by-step details. Verify that the top left of the report shows Accrual Basis. If not, click the Customize Report button on the report, and select Accrual Basis from the Report Basis options.

Figure 15.1 shows a sample data Balance Sheet Standard report.

2:40 PM
12/15/16
Accrual Basis

Rock Castle Construction
Balance Sheet
As of December 31, 2016

Figure 15.1

Review your Balance Sheet first, as in this example.

	Dec 31, 16
ASSETS	
Current Assets	
Checking/Savings	
10100 · Checking	46,969.10
10300 · Savings	17,910.19
10400 · Petty Cash	500.00
Total Checking/Savings	65,379.29
Accounts Receivable	
11000 · Accounts Receivable	93,007.93
Total Accounts Receivable	93,007.93
Other Current Assets	
12000 · Undeposited Funds	2,440.00
12100 · Inventory Asset	30,683.38
12800 · Employee Advances	832.00
13100 · Pre-paid Insurance	4,050.00
13400 · Retainage Receivable	3,703.02
Total Other Current Assets	41,708.40
Total Current Assets	200,095.62
Fixed Assets	
15000 · Furniture and Equipment	34,326.00
15100 · Vehicles	78,936.91
15200 · Buildings and Improvements	325,000.00
15300 · Construction Equipment	15,300.00
16900 · Land	90,000.00
17000 · Accumulated Depreciation	-110,344.60
Total Fixed Assets	433,218.31
Other Assets	
18700 · Security Deposits	1,720.00
Total Other Assets	1,720.00
TOTAL ASSETS	**635,033.93**
LIABILITIES & EQUITY	
Liabilities	
Current Liabilities	
Accounts Payable	
20000 · Accounts Payable	26,636.92
Total Accounts Payable	26,636.92
Credit Cards	
20500 · QuickBooks Credit Card	94.20
20600 · CalOil Credit Card	382.62
Total Credit Cards	476.82
Other Current Liabilities	
24000 · Payroll Liabilities	
24010 · Federal Withholding	1,364.00
24020 · FICA Payable	2,118.82
24040 · FUTA Payable	100.00
24050 · State Withholding	299.19
24060 · SUTA Payable	110.00
24070 · State Disability Payable	48.13
24080 · Worker's Compensation	1,214.31
24100 · Emp. Health Ins Payable	150.00
Total 24000 · Payroll Liabilities	5,404.45
25500 · Sales Tax Payable	957.63
Total Other Current Liabilities	6,362.08
Total Current Liabilities	33,475.82
Long Term Liabilities	
23000 · Loan - Vehicles (Van)	10,501.47
23100 · Loan - Vehicles (Utility Truck)	19,936.91
23200 · Loan - Vehicles (Pickup Truck)	22,641.00
28100 · Loan - Construction Equipment	13,911.32
28200 · Loan - Furniture/Office Equip	21,000.00
28700 · Note Payable - Bank of Anycity	2,693.21
28900 · Mortgage - Office Building	296,283.00
Total Long Term Liabilities	386,966.91
Total Liabilities	420,442.73
Equity	
30000 · Opening Bal Equity	38,773.75
30100 · Capital Stock	500.00
32000 · Retained Earnings	61,756.76
Net Income	113,560.69
Total Equity	214,591.20
TOTAL LIABILITIES & EQUITY	**635,033.93**

Assets are typically listed in the order that they could most easily be converted to cash.

Current liabilities are expected to be paid in one year or less.

Long term liabilities represent the portion of debt that will not be paid back in a year.

Equity is the original and additional investments, owner's draws and Retained Earnings (or loss) from prior years.

Did you know that proper accounting would have the Open Bal Equity account with no balance? See "Troubleshooting Opening Balance Equity" section of this chapter.

Account Types

Reviewing the account types assigned requires some basic knowledge of accounting. If as a business owner you are unsure, this review provides the perfect opportunity for your accountant to take a quick look at how your accounts are set up.

Review the names given to accounts. Do you see account names in the wrong place on the Balance Sheet? For example, does an Auto Loan account show up in the current asset section of the Balance Sheet?

Follow these steps if you need to edit an account type. From the menu bar, select Lists, Chart of Accounts.

Select the account in question with one click. From the Account drop-down menu, select Edit. On the Edit Account dialog box (see Figure 15.2), you can select the drop-down menu for Account Type to change the currently assigned account type.

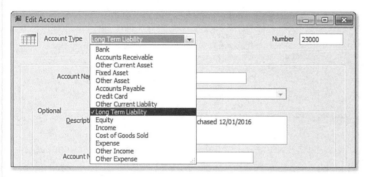

Figure 15.2
The Edit or New Account dialog box is where you assign the account type for proper placement of financial reports.

Prior Year Balances

You should provide a copy of your Balance Sheet dated as of the last day of your prior tax year (or fiscal year) to your accountant and request that she verify that the balances agree with her accounting records used to prepare your tax return. This is one of the most important steps to take in your review because Balance Sheet numbers are cumulative over the years you are in business.

 For more information, see "Accrual Versus Cash Basis Reporting," p. 59.

You can also create a two-year balance sheet to provide to your accounting professional:

From the menu bar, select Reports, Company & Financial, Balance Sheet Prev Year Comparison (see report displayed in Figure 15.3). If necessary, click the Customize Report button to change the Report Basis.

 tip
You might want to provide the Balance Sheet Prev Year Comparison report to your accountant using both Accrual and Cash Basis reporting. To change the basis of the report, click the Customize Report button and select the desired Report Basis on the Display tab.

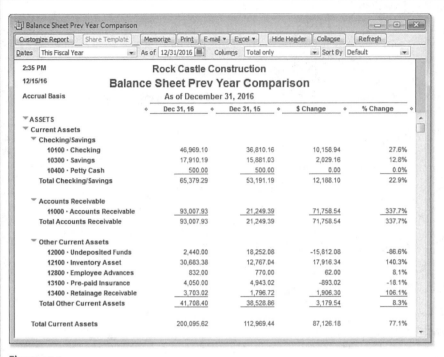

Figure 15.3
The Balance Sheet Prev Year Comparison report is a useful report to give your accounting professional at tax time.

Bank Account Balance(s)

Compare your reconciled bank account balances on the Balance Sheet report to the statement your bank sends you. Modify the date of the Balance Sheet to be the same as the ending statement date on your bank statement. Your QuickBooks Balance Sheet balance for your bank account should be equal to the bank's ending statement balance plus or minus any uncleared deposits or checks/withdrawals dated on or before the statement ending date.

At tax time, provide your last month's bank statement and QuickBooks bank reconciliation report to your accounting professional.

Accounts Receivable

The Accounts Receivable balance on your Balance Sheet report should agree with the A/R Aging Summary Report total, as shown in Figure 15.4.

To create the A/R Aging Summary report, choose Reports, Customers & Receivables, A/R Aging Summary or A/R Aging Detail from the menu bar. Click Collapse on the top of the report to minimize (remove from view) the line detail, making the report easier to view at a glance. The total should match the Accounts Receivable balance on the Balance Sheet report, as shown in Figure 15.1.

Report before
collapsing

Report after
collapsing

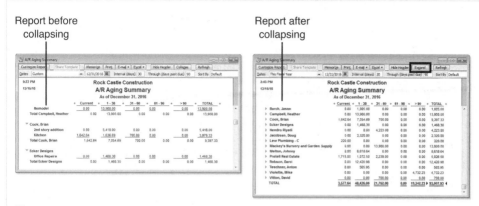

Figure 15.4
Use Expand or Collapse at the top of the report to change the level of detail displayed.

Undeposited Funds

The Undeposited Funds amount should agree with funds not yet deposited into your bank account, as shown in the custom report displayed in Figure 15.5 (use today's date on your Balance Sheet report).

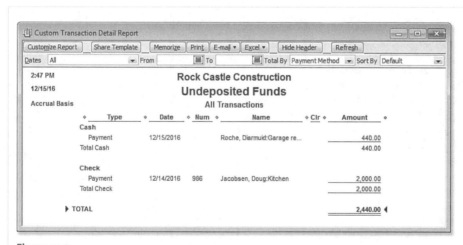

Figure 15.5
The amount of funds shown on this report should agree with the amount of funds you have not yet taken to the bank.

Create the following custom report to review the Undeposited Funds detail sorted by payment method:

1. From the menu bar, select Reports, Custom Reports, Transaction Detail. The Modify Report dialog box opens.

2. In the Report Date Range box, select All (type an "a" without the quotation marks and the date range defaults to All).

3. In the Columns box, select those data fields you want to view on the report and select Payment Method in the Total By drop-down menu.

4. Click the Filters tab; Account is already highlighted in the Choose Filter box. Choose Undeposited Funds from the Account drop-down menu to the right.

5. Also in the Choose Filter box, scroll down to select Cleared; on the right, choose Cleared No.

6. Optionally, click the Header/Footer tab and change the report title to Undeposited Funds. Click OK to view the report.

Inventory

The Inventory balance on the Balance Sheet report (refer to Figure 15.1) should agree with the Inventory Valuation Summary Asset Value report total, as shown in Figure 15.6. The ending dates of both reports need to be the same.

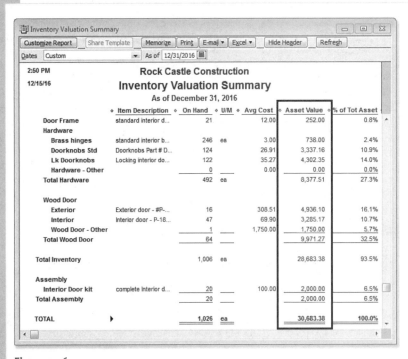

Figure 15.6
The total of the Asset Value column should agree with the Inventory balance on the Balance Sheet report.

To create the Inventory Valuation Summary report, select Reports, Inventory, Inventory Valuation Summary from the menu bar. More details about working with inventory reporting can be found in Chapter 6, "Managing Inventory."

Other Current Assets

The Other Current Asset accounts can differ widely by company. If you have employee advances, make sure your records agree with employees' records. For any other accounts in the Other Current Assets category, look to documentation outside QuickBooks to verify the reported balances.

Need an easy report to sort the detail in these Other Current Asset accounts by a list name? In this example, I created a detail report of the Employee Advances account sorted and subtotaled by payee, as shown in Figure 15.7. You can create this same report for any of your accounts, sorting in a way that improves the detail for your review.

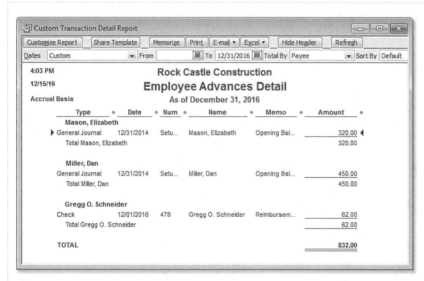

Figure 15.7
You can create a custom report to review balances in an Employee Advances account or any other asset account.

To create a detail report of your Other Current Asset accounts (in addition to other types of accounts), follow these steps:

1. From the menu bar, select Reports, Custom Reports, Transaction Detail. The Modify Report dialog box displays.

2. On the Date Range drop-down menu, select All.

3. In the Columns box, select the specific data you would like to see in the report.

4. Also in the Columns box, select Payee from the Total By drop-down menu.

5. Click the Filters tab.

6. The Choose Filter box already has selected the Account filter. On the right, from the Account drop-down menu, select the Employee Advances account (or select the specific account for which you want to see detail).

7. Optionally, click the Header/Footer tab and provide a unique report title. Click OK to create the modified report.

Verify the balances reported here with either the employees or outside source documents.

tip

Reconciling accounts like these can be useful. An example might be when an employee pays back the loan. Complete a reconciliation for this account, marking each transaction for this employee as "cleared."

You can then filter the report for "uncleared" only, limiting the amount of information that is displayed.

Fixed Assets

Fixed assets are those purchases that have a long-term life and for tax purposes cannot be expensed all at once but instead must be depreciated over the expected life of the asset.

Accountants can advise businesses on how to classify assets. If the account balances have changed from year to year, you might want to review what transactions were posted to make sure they are fixed asset purchases and not expenses that should be reported on the Profit & Loss report.

If you have properly recorded a fixed asset purchase to this account category, provide your accountant with the purchase receipt and any supporting purchase documents for their depreciation schedule records.

If you see a change in the totals from one year to the next, you can review the individual transactions in the account register by clicking Banking, Use Register, and selecting the account you want to review. Figure 15.8 shows the register for Fixed Assets—Furniture Equipment. If a transaction was incorrectly posted here, you can edit the transaction by double-clicking the line detail and correcting the assigned account category.

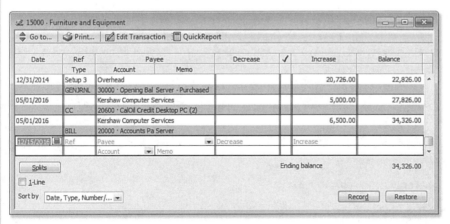

Figure 15.8
Use registers for certain accounts to see the transactions that affect the balances.

Accounts Payable

The Accounts Payable balance on the Balance Sheet report should agree with the A/P Aging Summary report total, as shown in Figure 15.9.

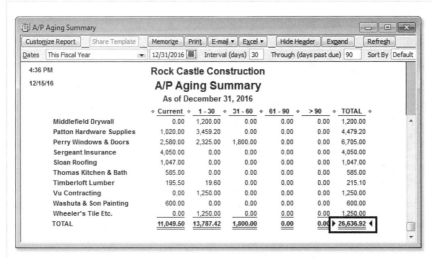

Figure 15.9
The A/P Aging Summary report total should agree with your Balance Sheet, Accounts Payable balance.

To create the A/P Aging Summary or Detail report, from the menu bar, select Reports, Vendors & Payables, A/P Aging Summary or Detail. For more information, see Chapter 8 "Managing Vendors."

Credit Cards

Your Credit Card account balance should reconcile with those balances from your credit card statement(s). You might have to adjust your Balance Sheet report date to match your credit card vendor's statement date. Or you could request that your credit card company provide you with a statement cut-off at the end of a month.

For more information on working with reconciliation tasks, see Chapter 13 "Working with Bank and Credit Card Accounts."

Payroll Liabilities

The Payroll Liabilities balance on the Balance Sheet report should agree with your Payroll Liability Balances report total. Be careful with the dates here. If you have unpaid back payroll taxes, you might want to select a date range of All for this report. See Figure 15.10.

To create the Payroll Liability Balances report, select Reports, Employees & Payroll, Payroll Liability Balances from the menu bar. Totals on this report should match your Balance Sheet report for the Payroll Liabilities account.

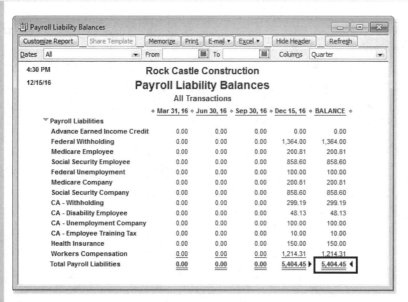

Figure 15.10
The Payroll Liability Balances report total should agree with the same total on the Balance Sheet report.

Sales Tax Payable

The Sales Tax Payable balance on the Balance Sheet report should agree with the Sales Tax Liability report balance. You might need to change the Sales Tax Payable report date to match that of your Balance Sheet.

To create the Sales Tax Liability report, select Reports, Vendors & Payables, Sales Tax Liability from the menu bar.

Make sure the To Date matches that of the Balance Sheet report date. The total, shown in Figure 15.11, should match the Sales Tax Payable total on your Balance Sheet report.

 caution

If you have set up your Sales Tax preference as Cash Basis, you cannot compare this balance to an Accrual Basis Balance Sheet report.

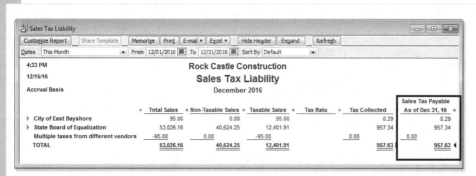

Figure 15.11
The Sales Tax Liability report total should match the Sales Tax Payable balance on your Balance Sheet report.

Other Current Liabilities and Long-Term Liabilities

Any other accounts you might have in the Other Current Liabilities and Long-Term Liabilities account types should be compared with outside documents from your lending institutions.

Reconcile these accounts like you do your bank account to verify that your balances agree with the lending institution's records.

Equity

Equity accounts differ for each company. These account balances should be reviewed by your accountant and might have tax adjustments made to them at year-end or tax time.

The reports discussed in this chapter do not make up an exhaustive, end-all list for reviewing your Balance Sheet, but they are a great start to reviewing your own data or your client's data.

> **note**
>
> If you have an account called Opening Balance Equity with a balance, this account should have a zero balance after the data file setup is completed. For more information, see "Closing Opening Balance Equity to Retained Earnings," p. 513.

Reviewing the Profit & Loss Report

My experience over the years has been that business owners do not look at the Balance Sheet report very often if at all. However, nearly every business owner I have worked with has reviewed the Profit & Loss Standard report for their business. The reason might be that the Profit & Loss report is easier to interpret than the Balance Sheet report.

Even with the simple organization (money in, money out) of the Profit & Loss report, a careful review is prudent for the business owner who wants to track how well the business is doing financially. To create a Profit & Loss Standard report, select Reports, Company & Financial, Profit & Loss Summary (or Profit & Loss Detail) from the menu bar.

There are two methods for reviewing your Profit & Loss:

- **Cash Basis**—Income is recognized when received. Expenses are recognized when paid.

- **Accrual Basis**—Income is recognized as of the date of the invoice. Expenses are recognized as of the date of the vendor bill, paycheck, and so on.

Cash basis reporting's primary focus is how much money is in the bank, and secondly are the bills paid. Additionally, many companies file their annual tax return using cash basis reports. There is nothing wrong with looking at reports prepared with cash basis accounting. However, I encourage all of my clients to consider reviewing the Profit & Loss Standard report in accrual basis.

Accrual basis, although more complex, provides so much more information about the business:

- **Matching Principle**—Revenue (customer invoice) is recorded in the same accounting period as the expenses (vendor bills, paychecks, and so on.) associated with services or products sold on the customer's invoice.

- **Seasonal Variations**—Track how your business performs financially; for example, by comparing the same month across multiple years.

- **Tracking Receivables and Payables**—This information helps with both short-term and long-term forecast planning.

With QuickBooks, you can easily change the report from cash to accrual basis by clicking the Customize Report button and manually selecting Cash or Accrual Basis on the Display tab of the Modify Report dialog box.

When reviewing the details of your Profit & Loss Detail report, you might want to look for these types of transactions:

- Monthly charges, such as rent, utility, equipment lease expenses, or other recurring expenses. Verify that the correct number of these charges is recorded, such as 12 monthly payments for rent.

- Credit card expenses reported to the proper expense accounts.

- Non-payroll payments to owners, which normally are recorded to draw or equity type accounts.

- Purchase of equipment with a significant cost, which should have been recorded to an asset account.

- Principle loan payments for vehicles or equipment; these should have been recorded to liability accounts.

A business owner who takes the time to review the Profit & Loss Detail report can feel more confident that business decisions founded on financials are as accurate as possible.

Other Reviews

You have completed the basic Balance Sheet and Profit & Loss Report reviews. These are very important and you are well on your way to being more confident about the information. There are, however, other equally important reviews that I have detailed in this section.

Tracking Changes to Closed Accounting Periods

Did you know that you can "lock" your QuickBooks data and prevent users from making changes to prior accounting periods? This process is what we accountants call a "soft close." This means that at any time if you do need to add or modify a transaction in a prior period, the Admin user (or someone with security rights) can return and "unlock" the accounting period.

To have QuickBooks track information for the Closing Date Exception report, you first had to set a closing date and optionally set specific users' access to adding or modifying transactions on or before this date.

If you have compared your own or your clients' data to prior year financials or tax returns and the ending balances prior to the closing date have changed, you should view the Closing Date Exception report to see exactly who made the change and what specific transactions were affected. For more information on working with client's files see Chapter 16, "Sharing QuickBooks Data with Your Accountant."

 caution

Exceptions, additions, and changes are not tracked unless a closing date has been set for a QuickBooks file.

To create the Closing Date Exception report (see Figure 15.12), select Reports, Accountant & Taxes, Closing Date Exception from the menu bar. If you have not set a closing date, a warning prompt will display.

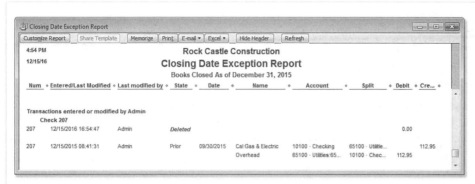

Figure 15.12
Review the Closing Date Exception report for changes made to transactions dated on or before a closing date.

This report enables you to identify changes that were made to transactions dated on or before the closing date. For modified transactions, the report details both the latest version of a transaction and the prior version (as of the closing date). If your QuickBooks access rights allow you to change closed period transactions, you can then re-create the original transaction or change the date of added transactions so you can once again agree with the ending balance from the previously closed period.

The Audit Trail report is available in all desktop versions of QuickBooks. To create the Audit Trail report shown in Figure 15.13, select Reports, Accountant & Taxes, Audit Trail from the menu bar.

Using the Audit Trail Report

The Audit Trail report provides details of additions and changes made to transactions, grouping the changes by username. The detail on this report shows the prior and latest version of the transaction, if it was edited. You can filter the report to show a specific date range to narrow the amount of detail.

For accounting professionals, see Appendix A, "Client Data Review" for details on using the Troubleshoot Beginning Balances feature in QuickBooks Accountant.

If you find undesired transaction changes, consider setting a closing date password and setting specific user security privileges.

➡ *For more information, see "Set a Closing Date," p. 533.*

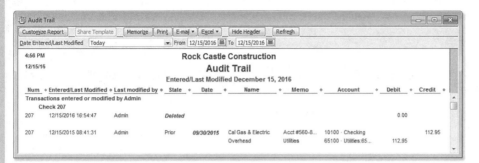

Figure 15.13
The QuickBooks Audit Trail report helps to identify what changes were made to transactions and by which user.

Using the Credit Card Audit Trail Report

QuickBooks users can stay in compliance with credit card industry security requirements by enabling security around who can view, add, or edit your customer's credit card numbers.

Individual users can be included or excluded from accessing customer's sensitive credit card information. Also, for the company accountant, there is a user type called External Accountant. When this type is assigned to your accountant, she cannot view these sensitive customer credit card numbers.

Additionally, when enabled, you can track which user viewed, edited, added, or removed a customer's credit card number with the Credit Card Audit Trail report.

To use this feature correctly, follow these three basic steps:

1. Enable the customer credit card protection feature.

2. Select which users are given security rights to view the credit card numbers and which users are not given this privilege.

3. View the new Credit Card Audit Trail report to track viewing, editing, adding, and deleting activity with your customer's credit cards.

The first step to viewing details on the Credit Card Audit Trail report is to enable Customer Credit Card Protection in QuickBooks. To do so, follow these steps:

1. Log in to the data file as the Admin user. From the menu bar, select Company, Customer Credit Card Protection.

2. Click the Enable button to open the Customer Credit Card Protection Setup dialog box. Type a complex password. The new complex password must be seven characters, including one number and one uppercase character. For example, coMp1ex is a complex password. This password is now required when the Admin user logs in.

3. You are also required to choose a Challenge Question from the drop-down menu and provide an answer to a question. This question will be used to reset your password if you forget it. Click OK.

4. A message box opens letting you know the next steps and that you will be reminded in 90 days to change the password. Click OK.

5. QuickBooks notifies you that you have enabled Customer Credit Card Protection and details how to allow access by user to the credit card numbers (see step 6). Click OK. You are now returned to QuickBooks logged in as the Admin user.

6. To select which employees have access to view the full credit card numbers, or add or change customer credit card numbers, select Company, Set Up Users and Passwords from the menu bar, and select the Set Up Users option.

7. The QuickBooks login dialog box opens and requires you to enter the Admin password to gain access to user security settings. Click OK to open the User List dialog box.

8. Select a username and click the Edit button. Optionally, edit the username or password, or click Next to accept these fields as they are.

9. The Access window for the specific user opens. Choose the Selected Areas of QuickBooks option. Click Next.

10. The Sales and Accounts Receivable access options display. Choose either Full Access or Selective Access; either of these choices combined with a checkmark in the View Complete Credit Card Numbers box (as shown in Figure 15.14) enables the user to view and add, delete, or modify the credit card number. If no checkmark is placed, the user sees only the last four digits of the customer's credit card when recording transactions that use this sensitive information.

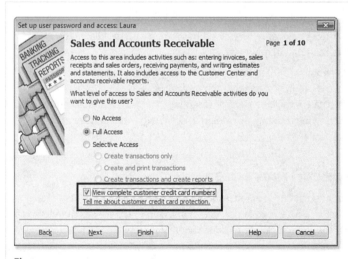

Figure 15.14
User-specific access to viewing complete customer credit card numbers.

11. Click Finish if this is the only setting you want to modify or click Next to advance through additional security settings.

You have now properly enabled the customer credit card protection and granted or removed user access to these confidential credit card numbers.

With this feature enabled, your data file is now tracking critical user activity about your customer's credit card numbers. Track when the credit card security was enabled, and track when a user entered a credit card number, modified a credit card, or even viewed the credit card audit trail report (see Figure 15.15).

tip

When creating a login user for your accountant, select the user type "External Accountant." By default, this user type cannot view your customers' stored sensitive credit card numbers.

Figure 15.15
The Customer Credit Card Audit Trail report cannot be modified, filtered, or purged.

This Customer Credit Card Audit Trail report is always tracking customer credit card activity as long as the feature remains enabled. This report can only be viewed by logging into the file as the Admin user. The report cannot be filtered or modified in any way.

If you want to disable this setting, you must first log in to the data file as the Admin user, enter the complex password that was created when you enabled the protection, and select Company, Customer Credit Card Protection, and select the Disable Protection button. Click Yes to accept that your customer's credit card number viewing, editing, and deleting activity by QuickBooks users is no longer being tracked for audit purposes.

Reporting on Voided/Deleted Transactions

QuickBooks offers flexibility for handling changes to transactions. If you grant users rights to create transactions, they also have rights to void and delete transactions. Don't worry—you can view these voided transaction changes in the Voided/Deleted Transactions Summary (see Figure 15.16) or Voided/Deleted Transactions Detail reports.

To create the Voided/Deleted Transactions Summary report, select Reports, Accountant & Taxes, Voided/Deleted Transactions Summary (or Voided/Deleted Transactions Detail) from the menu bar.

Use this report to view transactions before and after the change, and to identify which user made the change.

7:13 PM
12/15/16

Rock Castle Construction
Voided/Deleted Transactions Summary
Entered/Last Modified December 15, 2016

Num	Action	Entered/Last Modified	Date	Name	Memo	Account	Split	Amount
Transactions entered or modified by Admin								
Check 207								
207	Deleted Transaction	12/15/2016 16:54:47						0.00
207	Changed Transact...	12/15/2015 08:41:31	09/30/2015	Cal Gas & Electric	Acct #560-8...	10100 · Checking	65100 · Utilitie...	-112.95

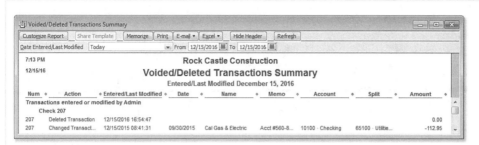

Figure 15.16
The QuickBooks Voided/Deleted Transactions Summary report quickly identifies which transactions were either voided or deleted, making troubleshooting easy!

Viewing the Transactions List by Date Report

Although the title of Transaction List by Date report doesn't indicate as much "power" as the other reports discussed in this chapter, I use this report most often when reviewing a data file.

If you are new to QuickBooks, you will soon learn that the date you enter for each transaction is important. The year you assign to the transaction is the year QuickBooks reports the transaction in your financials. For example, if you record a transaction with the year 2061 instead of 2016, this date would cause your financials not to show the effect until year 2061.

To create the Transaction List by Date report, shown in Figure 15.17, from the menu bar, select Reports, Accountant & Taxes, Transaction List by Date. From the Dates drop-down menu, select All dates.

7:21 PM
12/15/16

Rock Castle Construction
Transaction List by Date
All Transactions

Type	Date	Num	Name	Memo	Account	Clr	Debit	Credit
Paycheck	12/15/2016	10075	Gregg O. Schneider		10100 · Checking			1,033.98
Credit Card Char...	12/15/2016		Bayshore CalOil S...		20600 · CalOil Cre...			10.60
Paycheck	12/15/2016	10076	Dan T. Miller		10100 · Checking			1,350.15
Paycheck	12/15/2016	10077	Elizabeth N. Mason		10100 · Checking			932.92
Paycheck	12/15/2016	10078	Gregg O. Schneider		10100 · Checking			1,062.12
Paycheck	12/15/2016	10079	Gregg O. Schneider		10100 · Checking			1,062.12
Bill	12/15/2016		Sergeant Insurance		20000 · Accounts...			4,050.00
Bill	12/15/2016	8059	Thomas Kitchen &...		20000 · Accounts...			585.00
Bill	12/15/2016		Vu Contracting		20000 · Accounts...			1,250.00
Check	12/15/2016	515	Vu Contracting		10100 · Checking			1,000.00
Sales Tax Paym...	12/15/2016	516	State Board of Equ...	ABCD 11-23...	10100 · Checking			1,629.27
Total								

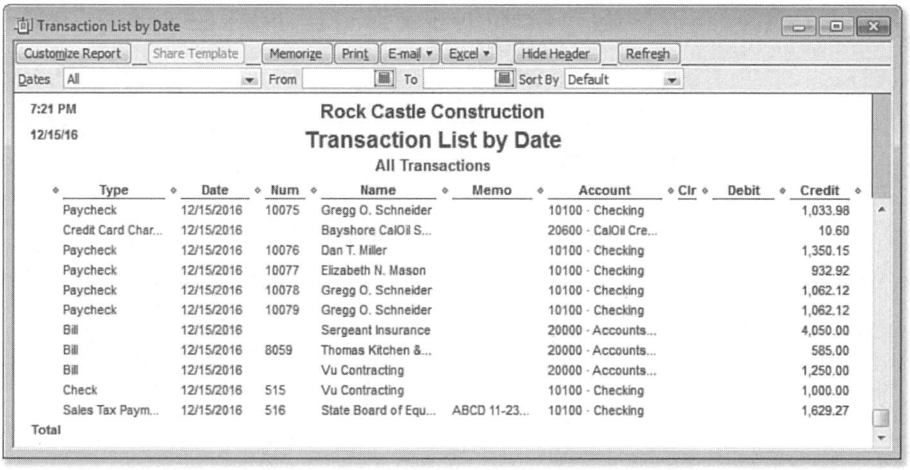

Figure 15.17
The QuickBooks Transaction List by Date report can be used to identify whether any incorrectly dated transactions exist.

You can use this report to see both the oldest dated transaction (when the file was started) and the furthest dated transaction (to identify whether date errors have been made). Then, as with all other QuickBooks reports, double-click a specific transaction to change the date if needed.

 tip

Fortunately, QuickBooks preferences help avoid transaction dating errors by enabling you to set a warning for date ranges.

To open the date warning preference, follow these steps:

1. Log into the QuickBooks data file as the Admin or External Accountant user.

2. From the menu bar, select Edit, Preferences. In the Preferences dialog box, choose the Accounting preference on the left.

3. Click the Company Preferences tab.

4. Type in the user-defined date warning range you want to work with for past-dated transactions and future-dated transactions. QuickBooks sets the default warnings at 90 days in the past and 30 days in the future. An attempt to enter transactions dated before or after this date range prompts QuickBooks to give the user a warning message, as shown in Figure 15.18.

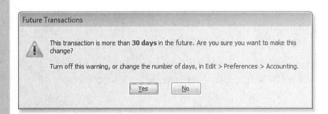

Figure 15.18
Set the Date Warning preference so users will be warned when dating a transaction outside an acceptable date range.

Be cautious when making changes to the dates, especially if the year in question has already had a tax return prepared on the existing information.

Troubleshooting Open Balance Equity Account

QuickBooks automatically records the following transactions to the Opening Balance Equity account:

- Your ending bank statement balance transaction when you created a new bank account in the Express Start setup

- Opening balances for other Balance Sheet report accounts created in the Add New Account dialog box

- Inventory total value balances entered in the New Item dialog box

- Bank reconciliation adjustments for older versions of QuickBooks

Other common transactions that a user might assign to this account include:

- Accrual basis opening accounts payable transactions as of the start date

- Accrual basis opening accounts receivable transactions as of the start date

- Uncleared bank checks or deposits (accrual or cash basis) as of the start date

Closing Opening Balance Equity into Retained Earnings

The Opening Balance Equity account should have a zero balance when a file setup is complete and done correctly. When I refer to a completely and correctly set up QuickBooks file, I assume the following:

- You *are not* converting your data from Quicken, Peachtree, Small Business Accounting, or Office Accounting. Each of these products has an automated conversion tool available free from Intuit, which eliminates the need to do startup transactions if you convert the data and not just lists.

- Your company *did not* have any transactions prior to the first use of QuickBooks. In this case, you simply enter typical QuickBooks transactions after your QuickBooks start date with no need for unusual startup type entries.

 caution

While Intuit offers certain ready-made tools to convert other software to QuickBooks, some may not convert the data as expected. It would be prudent of you to verify the information is correct after the conversion.

- Your company *did have* transactions prior to the first use of QuickBooks. You have chosen to enter these transactions one-by-one as regular transactions. You will not need to record any transactions to the Opening Balance Equity account.

- Your company *did have* transactions prior to the first use of QuickBooks, but there are so many it is not feasible to recreate them in QuickBooks. Instead you follow the directions in Chapter 3, "Setting Up a QuickBooks Data File for Accrual or Cash Basis Reporting" p. 63.

- You have entered each of your unpaid customer invoices, unpaid vendor bills, and uncleared bank transactions and dated them prior to your QuickBooks start date.

- You have entered and dated your trial balance one day before your QuickBooks start date. (You might need to request the trial balance numbers from your accountant if you are not converting from some other financial software that provides you with a trial balance.)

- When you create a Trial Balance report in QuickBooks dated one day before your QuickBooks start date, it agrees with your accountant's trial balance or with the trial balance from your prior financial software with the exception that you have a balance in the Opening Balance Equity account.

If you answered yes to each of these assumptions, I would expect that your Opening Balance Equity account is equal to the Retained Earnings balance from your accountant's financials or from your prior software. If it doesn't agree, you need to continue to review the data to determine what the errors are. If it does agree, you are prepared to make the final entry in your start-up process.

To create this closing entry using a General Journal Entries transaction, follow these steps:

1. From the menu bar, select Company, Make General Journal
   Entries.

2. Enter a Date (it should be one day before your QuickBooks
   start date).

3. Type an Entry No.

4. Leaving line 1 of the transaction blank, on line 2 of the Make
   General Journal Entries transaction (using the example as
   shown in Figure 15.19), decrease (debit) Opening Balance
   Equity by $38,773.75 and increase (credit) Retained Earnings
   by the same amount. This action "closes" Opening Balance
   Equity to Retained Earnings. Click Save & Close.

 caution

Leave the first line of any Make
General Journal Entries transaction blank because QuickBooks
uses this line as the source line.
Any list item in the name column
on the first line (source line) of a
general journal entries transaction will also be associated in
reports with the other lines of
the same general journal entries
form. For more information about
working with multiple line journal entries, see the caution on
page 341 of Chapter 10.

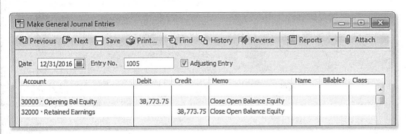

Figure 15.19
Use a Make General Journal Entries transaction to close Opening Bal Equity to Retained Earnings.

5. Click OK to the QuickBooks warning that displays; QuickBooks saves the transaction. The warning advises that you are posting to a Retained Earnings account and that QuickBooks has a
   special purpose for this account. It is appropriate to post this entry to Retained Earnings. This
   warning is a result of a preference setting you can access from the menu bar by selecting Edit,
   Preferences, Accounting. Select the Company Preferences tab and choose the option to enable
   the warning. (You must be logged in as Admin or External Accountant user and in single-user
   mode to access this preference.)

When the transaction is saved, create the Balance Sheet Standard report as explained earlier in this
chapter and verify that your ending numbers are accurate; that is, that they match your accountant's or your prior software trial balance for the same period. Figure 15.20 now shows the proper
Retained Earnings balance, and you no longer have a balance in Opening Balance Equity.

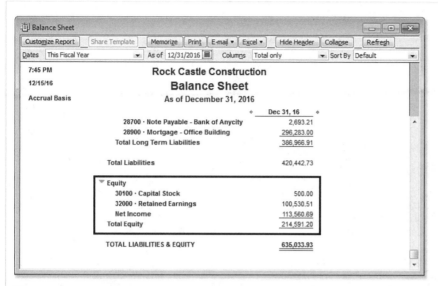

Figure 15.20
The Balance Sheet viewed after "closing" Opening Balance Equity to Retained Earnings.

16

SHARING QUICKBOOKS DATA WITH YOUR ACCOUNTANT

Overview

One feature that truly sets QuickBooks apart from other business accounting software is the ease and flexibility of sharing a copy of the data between the business owner and the accounting professional. This chapter shares useful details for both the business owner and the accountant.

Accounting professionals can work more profitably with their client's files by partnering the Accountant's Copy functionality with the expanded Client Data Review feature. The Client Data Review feature is available in Intuit QuickBooks Accountant 2012 and QuickBooks Enterprise Solutions Accountant 12.0.

➡ *For more information, refer to Appendix A "Client Data Review."*

Benefits for the Business Owner

As a business owner, you will want to have your accounting professional review your data. After all, you are using this data to make important management decisions. Additionally, you need to provide your data to your accountant for preparation of your federal and state tax returns.

So what might be some of the benefits of sharing your QuickBooks business data with your accountant? Benefits include:

- You can share an Accountant's Copy of your data, which allows your accountant to review and provide timely feedback without interrupting your daily workflow.

- You have less stress because you do not need to prepare multiple reports for your accountant to review.

- You can delegate critical tasks to your accountant, such as reconciling a bank account (Accountant's Copy File sharing method).

- Your accountant can use your data to compile the information needed for your tax returns.

- You can choose from multiple sharing methods, and select one that is just right for your business.

- Periodic review of your data by your accountant can save precious time at year-end and provide more accurate financials during the year.

Benefits for the Accountant

Periodically reviewing your client's data has become more important in recent years, as strict accounting guidelines tighten further. Often your clients are even unaware of these changes.

As an accountant, you can benefit from access to your client's data by doing the following:

- Review your client's data at your office at a time convenient for you or your staff.

- Complete key reviewing tasks, while enabling your client to continue their day-to-day transactions (Accountant's Copy File sharing method).

- Use the many accountant-specific tools to facilitate this review offered in the QuickBooks Accountant or QuickBooks Enterprise Solutions Accountant including the Client Data Review feature.

- Complete critical tasks for your client, such as reconciling a bank account, making your services more valued by the client (Accountant's Copy File sharing method).

- Provide your clients with more frequent and timely analysis of their data.

This chapter is a guide for how both the business owner and the accountant can share QuickBooks data. Of particular interest are the improvements to the Accountant's Copy File sharing method in QuickBooks 2012.

QuickBooks File Types

There is much flexibility in how a business owner or accountant can share a common QuickBooks data file. Some of the benefits of sharing data using the Accountant's Copy File were previously listed. This chapter discusses details of all the choices offered in facilitating this sharing.

Table 16.1 lists the common QuickBooks file types used for sharing data. Knowing these file types is important as you make decisions on the best method for your business or your clients' data sharing needs.

Table 16.1 QuickBooks File Types

Extension	File Type	Description	QuickBooks Editions*
.QBW	QuickBooks for Windows regular working file	This is the working data file type created when a user creates a new QuickBooks file.	Pro, Premier (all editions), Accountant Enterprise (all editions)
.QBB	QuickBooks for Windows backup file	The most secure and complete method for protecting your data with a backup.	Pro, Premier (all editions), Accountant Enterprise (all editions)
.QBM	QuickBooks for Windows portable company file	This is a compressed version of your QuickBooks .QBW data file. Used primarily to email or move the file to another location.	Pro, Premier (all editions), Accountant Enterprise (all editions)
.QBX	Accountant's Copy (export file)	This is created by the business owner to save or send data to the accountant.	Pro, Premier (all editions), Accountant Enterprise (all editions)
.QBA	Accountant's Copy (converted .QBX file)	QuickBooks creates this file when open/convert a .QBX file is performed (usually by the accountant).	QuickBooks Accountant or Enterprise Accountant
.QBY	Accountant's Copy (import file)	This is the file the accountant sends to the business owner after making changes.	QuickBooks Accountant or Enterprise Accountant

Not shown in Table 16.1 are QuickBooks Online and QuickBooks for Mac. Both of these versions have a different file structure, and neither of them supports the Accountant's Copy feature discussed at length in this chapter.

How the QuickBooks Year and Version Affect Your Data Sharing Choices

The choices of how you can share your data with your accountant depend on the version and release year of QuickBooks you and your accountant use.

The QuickBooks product line includes Pro, Premier (general and industry-specific versions), Accountant, Enterprise (general and industry-specific versions), QuickBooks for Mac, and QuickBooks Online.

Additionally, Intuit releases a new QuickBooks version each year, often represented by the year included in the name. For example, QuickBooks Premier 2012 is the Premier version usually released in the fall prior to the stated year. This version is separate from the release updates QuickBooks provides throughout a year to add functionality and fix issues discovered with a version.

To determine your current version and release, with QuickBooks open, press Ctrl+1. At the top of the Product Information dialog box that displays is the product name (and industry edition if Premier or Enterprise), year, and release number.

So you can see how the version year can affect your choices for sharing data, in this chapter I discuss the Accountant's Copy features, which are not available for QuickBooks Online, the QuickBooks for Mac edition, or for any QuickBooks product prior to the 2007 version.

Choosing a Method to Share Data

QuickBooks offers flexibility in how data is shared between a business owner and the accountant. Different methods can be used at different times during the year, depending on the nature of the changes to be made.

Options available might also be determined by the edition of QuickBooks you use and whether your data is in an older version of QuickBooks. The enhancements made in recent years for sharing your data with your accountant make it a perfect time to upgrade to the newest release.

To compare different QuickBooks products, go to www.intuit.com.

You might even choose to use multiple data sharing methods during the course of a year, after you know the advantages and limitations associated with each type.

Before choosing an option, review the details of each file type (shown earlier in Table 16.1) and in the sections that follow.

.QBW: Regular Working Copy of the Data

Each client file is originally created in this file type. Here is a list of some of the advantages and limitations of sharing this type of data file:

- The accountant *cannot* take the file to his office, work in the file, and later merge changes into the business owner's file unless the client agrees not to work in the file while the accountant has possession of it.

- The accountant has access to all transaction activities.

- The accountant can access this file at the business owner's office or with a remote Internet-assisted program. QuickBooks partners with Remote Access by WebEx, but there are several others in the market including LogMeIn or GoToMeeting.

- The file can often be too large to send as an attachment in an email.

To open a working copy of the data, select File, Open or Restore Company, Open a Company File from the menu bar.

.QBB: QuickBooks Backup File

This file type remains as it has for years—it's the best choice for securing a data backup of your work. If needed, this file can be restored to a .QBW file. Here is a list of some of the advantages and limitations of sharing this type of data file:

- The file cannot be opened first without being restored.

- When restored, the file extension becomes a .QBW (see the pros and cons listed earlier).

- Changes made to a restored version of this file type *cannot* be merged later into the original data file.

To restore a backup file, select File, Open or Restore Company, Restore a Backup Copy from the menu bar.

.QBM: QuickBooks Portable Company File

This file type has been offered for the last few years; however, it does not replace the usefulness of the QuickBooks .QBB file type. Here is a list of some of the advantages and limitations of sharing this type of data file:

- The compressed file size makes a .QBM a perfect choice for attaching to an email or moving from one computer location to another.

- The file type does not replace a .QBB backup because it lacks some of the needed transaction logs.

- The file cannot be opened until it is restored.

- When restored, the file extension becomes a .QBW (see the pros and cons listed earlier).

- Changes made to a restored version of this file type *cannot* be merged later into the original data file.

To restore a portable company file, select File, Open or Restore Company, Restore a Portable File from the menu bar.

.QBX: Accountant's Copy (Export File)

As a business owner, if you choose to share your data with your accountant using the Accountant's Copy functionality, you will send this file type to your accounting professional. Here is a list of some of the advantages and limitations of sharing this type of data file:

- This file type is created by the business owner and enables your accountant to review and make needed changes to your data while you continue recording your day-to-day transactions in the file at your office.

- Any changes or additions your accountant makes *can* be imported (merged) into your company's data file.

- The compressed file size makes it a perfect choice for attaching to an email or moving from one computer location to another.

- The file type does not replace a .QBB backup because it lacks some of the needed transaction logs.

- The file cannot be opened; it must be converted to a .QBA file type.

The accountant will convert this file to a .QBA file type from within the QuickBooks Accountant or QuickBooks Enterprise Accountant software.

.QBA: Accountant's Copy (Working File)

Only the accountant will work with this type of file. Listed here are some of the advantages and limitations of sharing this type of data file:

- This file type is a converted .QBX file and is created by the accountant from within the QuickBooks Accountant or QuickBooks Enterprise Solutions Accountant.

- The .QBA file type is the file the accountant will make changes to. It will be converted to a .QBY file for the client to import.

- The file can be saved to the accountant's computer and be opened and closed as needed while she (the accountant) does her review work.

.QBY: Accountant's Copy (Import File)

The business owner receives this file from the accountant, and it includes any accounting changes made to the original .QBX file. Here is a list of some of the advantages and limitations of sharing this type of data file:

- This file type is created by the accountant using QuickBooks Accountant or QuickBooks Enterprise Solutions Accountant software.

- The file includes the changes made by the accountant to the original .QBX file the business owner provided the accountant.

- The file cannot be opened; it must be imported into the data file that *originally created* the Accountant's Copy data file.

QuickBooks offers your business many options in how you want to share your data with your accountant. Select a solution that works for you and your accountant.

Data Sharing for the Business Owner

Few business owners with whom I have worked over the years have a college degree in accounting. That situation is exactly what makes QuickBooks so appealing to a growing business—you don't need to be an accountant to use it. However, you will need an accountant to review your financials, perhaps at tax time or when you need a statement of your business's financial condition to give to a bank when requesting a business loan.

QuickBooks provides several different methods of sharing data with your accountant. See the previous Table 16.1 for details on the QuickBooks file types the business owner can choose.

When Your Accountant Is Using QuickBooks Accountant 2012

If you are using a version of QuickBooks 2011 or newer or Enterprise Solutions version 11.0 or newer and you choose to share your data using the Accountant's Copy feature, your accountant can use the QuickBooks 2012 Accountant or Enterprise Solutions Accountant 12.0 version to open your 2011 or 2012 company file and make changes. When the file is returned with the accountant's changes, you will be able to import the changes back into your QuickBooks file, even though the accountant used a newer version of QuickBooks. The QuickBooks Accountant 2012 and Enterprise Solutions Accountant 12.0 offer a degree of backward compatibility.

If you are sharing any other file type (other than the Accountant's Copy) with your accountant, there is no backward compatibility. When your accountant restores a .QBB (backup) or .QBM (portable) company file in her 2012 version, the file will be updated to 2012; if the file is returned to you, you need to update your QuickBooks version to the same release year as your accountant.

For example, suppose you are currently using a QuickBooks 2011 version. Your accountant is using QuickBooks 2012 Accountant. When your accountant restores your QuickBooks file backup, she will have to update the file to the QuickBooks 2012 release. If your accountant returns the data to you, you will not be able to open it with your QuickBooks 2011 software.

So, as you decide which method to use, consider discussing with your accountant the QuickBooks version and release year you are using. QuickBooks accountants who have serviced companies for many years often have several versions of QuickBooks installed.

Keep in mind that QuickBooks Enterprise Solutions presents its own set of special requirements. If you open a Pro or Premier data file with the Enterprise Solutions software you will no longer be able to open the same data file in its original QuickBooks Pro or Premier edition.

Reviewing Your QuickBooks Data

No matter what method you choose to share your data file with your accountant, one of the most important things you can do is review your data for accuracy, especially in the areas of Accounts Payable and Accounts Receivable—areas that you will know better than your accountant.

To begin, pick a chapter of this book that covers the area of QuickBooks you need to review. You might want to start with Chapter 15, "Reviewing Your Data." This chapter shows you quick and easy data checks you can do before your accountant formally reviews your data. Performing this quick review can also help you identify any potential errors for which you will need your accountant's guidance when correcting.

Creating an Accountant's Copy of Your Data

The Accountant's Copy method of sharing your data is the most efficient because it enables your accountant to work in the data file from her office without interrupting your day-to-day work pattern.

 caution

Only the Admin or new External Accountant user can create an Accountant's Copy or import the .QBY Accountant's Copy import file that contains the changes the accountant made to your data.

You must consider the following before making the choice to use the Accountant's Copy file sharing type:

- If you choose to create an Accountant's Copy, you will need to determine how you will get the Accountant's Copy data file to your accountant. QuickBooks offers you these options:

  - Send an encrypted copy of your data to your accountant via Intuit's secure Accountant's Copy File Transfer service.

  - Attach the saved file to an email.

  - Copy it to a storage device such as a USB drive or CD.

  - Use an online file sharing service like YouSendIt or DropBox.

- You also will be required to set a dividing date, as shown in Figure 16.1. The dividing date is a specific date in the past that determines the restrictions you and your accountant will have when adding or editing transactions.

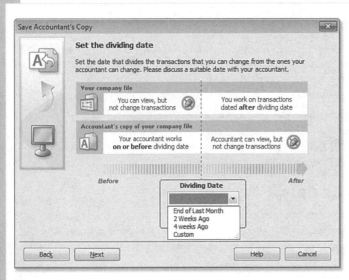

Figure 16.1
Setting a dividing date is required when creating an Accountant's Copy.

The following list briefly identifies the date restrictions with a dividing date in place when you share an Accountant's Copy of your data with your accountant. For example, if you choose a sample dividing date of 12/31/11, the following restrictions exist:

- **On or before the dividing date**—You (the business owner) cannot add, delete, or modify transactions. The accountant can add, delete, or modify transactions.

- **After the dividing date**—You (the business owner) can add, delete, or modify transactions. The accountant can add transactions, but cannot delete or modify them.

For more information, see "What the Business Owner Can and Cannot Do" later in this chapter for any restrictions that affect you, the business owner.

The business owner has these options for delivering the QuickBooks data file to the accountant:

- **Send To Accountant**—Send an encrypted copy of your data to your accountant via Intuit's Accountant's Copy File Transfer service (free for the business owner).

- **Save File**—Use this option to attach the file to an email or copy to USB or other portable medium.

caution

When a dividing date is set, you cannot add, modify, delete, or void any transaction dated prior to the dividing date, including nonposting documents such as estimates, sales orders, and purchase orders. This limitation can be terribly inconvenient for the business owner, so discuss it ahead of time with your accountant. If appropriate, you should change the date of these pending "nonposting" documents to a date after the expected dividing date.

Method 1: Using the Send File Method via the Web

Offered with QuickBooks Pro, Premier, and Enterprise is the option to use a secure, Intuit-hosted site to encrypt and transfer data to your accountant without needing to create a file and attach it to an email.

To send data to your accountant with the secure encrypted file service, follow these steps:

1. From the menu bar, select File, Accountant's Copy, Client Activities, Send to Accountant. The Confirm Sending an Accountant's Copy dialog box displays, shown in Figure 16.2. This message details the service and what types of shared work are recommended with this type of file and what types are not.

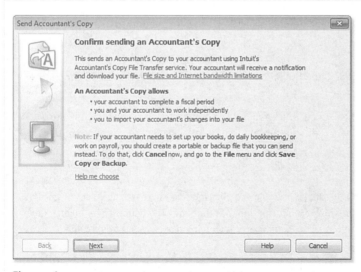

Figure 16.2
Confirming that the Accountant's Copy is the appropriate choice for the shared work you and your accountant will be doing.

2. Click Next. The Set the Dividing Date dialog box displays.

3. From the Dividing Date drop-down list, choose one of the date options shown in Figure 16.1, or choose Custom to select your own specific dividing date.

4. Click Next. The Information For Sending The File (1 of 2) dialog box displays, as shown in Figure 16.3. Type the email address to notify your accountant and include your name and return email. Your accountant will receive an email notification that your data file is ready to download. The download is only available for 14 days.

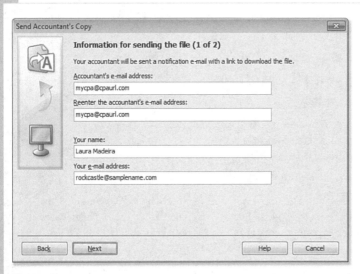

Figure 16.3
Identify the email address where your accountant should be notified, as well as your own name and email address.

5. Click Next. The Information for Sending the File (2 of 2) dialog box displays, as shown in Figure 16.4.

6. Enter a strong password that is seven characters long and contains at least one capital letter and one digit. Optionally, type a note to your accountant, but do not include the password in the communication.

7. Click Send.

8. Click OK to the message that QuickBooks has to close all windows to create the Accountant's Copy. Note: QuickBooks also provides an information message only (no action to be taken) that the transfer might take a few minutes, so don't worry if QuickBooks seems unresponsive.

9. Click OK on the QuickBooks Information dialog box that displays, which indicates the file was uploaded to the Intuit Accountant's Copy File Transfer server successfully.

Figure 16.4
Set a strong password and add an optional note for your accountant.

The QuickBooks title bar identifies your file as having Accountant's Changes Pending, as shown in Figure 16.5. This title bar change indicates you have successfully created a file for your accountant to review, edit, modify, and later return the changes to you without interrupting your work.

Figure 16.5
Your QuickBooks title bar will indicate whether you have accountant's changes pending.

Method 2: Using the Save File Method

Another method is to create the file, save it to your computer, and then email it or provide the file to your accountant on a USB device. To create an Accountant's Copy file of your data that your accountant can review and modify while you continue to do your daily transactions, follow these steps:

1. Close all your active QuickBooks windows. From the menu bar, select File, Accountant's Copy, Client Activities, Save File.

2. Choose the Accountant's Copy option, as shown in Figure 16.6. (The other option includes the Portable Company. This method will not allow the accountant to export any changes made or you to import the changes.)

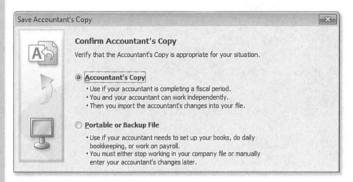

Figure 16.6
Saving a file as an Accountant's Copy creates a file that your accountant can work in and later merge the changes with your file.

3. Click Next. The Set the Dividing Date dialog box opens.

4. From the Dividing Date drop-down list, select one of the date options as previously shown in Figure 16.1, or choose Custom to select your own specific dividing date. For more information on the importance of this date, see "What the Business Owner Can and Cannot Do," p. 529.

5. Click Next. QuickBooks opens the Save Accountant's Copy dialog box, where you can browse your computer for the location where you want to save the Accountant's Copy export file (.QBX file).

6. Click the Save button. QuickBooks provides the message shown in Figure 16.7, indicating that you successfully created an Accountant's Copy and telling you where the file was saved, as well as other useful information.

Figure 16.7
QuickBooks provides information about where the file was saved.

7. Click OK. As previously shown in Figure 16.5, the QuickBooks title bar now identifies your file as having Accountant's Changes Pending.

8. Now send this .QBX file to your accountant as an email attachment, or copy it to a removable data storage device.

What the Business Owner Can and Cannot Do

With the useful features of Accountant's Copy, your accountant can be assured the information in the file she is working in will not change for dates prior to the dividing date.

The following list details what you can and cannot do with your data file while an Accountant's Changes are pending:

- **Transactions**—You can add, edit, and modify transactions with a date after the dividing date.

- **Accounts**—You can add a new chart of accounts list item.

- **Subaccounts**—You cannot add a subaccount to an existing account.

- **Editing, merging, or inactivating accounts**—You cannot edit, merge, or inactivate a chart of accounts item (your accountant can).

- **Editing lists (other than the chart of accounts)**—You can add, edit, and inactivate your list items. If you and your accountant make changes to the same item, the accountant's changes will override your changes.

- **Deleting lists**—You cannot delete or merge list items (your accountant can).

- **Reconciling the bank account**—In the .QBW file with pending Accountant's Copy, if the statement date and all transactions involved into the reconciliation are *after* the dividing date and the accountant didn't reconcile this account in the Accountant's Copy, reconciliation work remains in the .QBW file after the import. Bank reconciliations for dates *on or before* the dividing date are removed when you incorporate your accountant's changes file.

Reconciling While an Accountant's Copy Is Pending

When choosing to use the Accountant's Copy to share your data, you can only complete the bank reconciliation for reconciliations where the bank statement date and all transactions to be cleared are dated after the selected dividing date.

From the menu bar, select Banking, Reconcile, and select your bank account. The bank reconciliation dialog box opens. In this dialog box, dates entered must follow these guidelines:

- **Statement Date**—Must be a date after the specified dividing date.
- **Service Charge Date**—Must be a date after the specified dividing date.
- **Interest Earned Date**—Must be a date after the specified dividing date.

Your bank reconciliation work will remain after the import of your accountant's changes if:

- None of the transactions you mark as cleared are dated on or before the Accountant's Copy dividing date.
- Your accountant did not also complete the bank reconciliation for the same bank account.
- Your accountant doesn't undo any bank reconciliations for this account in the Accountant's Copy.

There can be value in reconciling, even if the accountant's copy import will undo it, simply to verify that your bank balances are correct.

Importing Your Accountant's Changes

When you make an Accountant's Copy from your data file, QuickBooks creates a file for you to give to your accountant. Your accountant then works in this file, adding and editing transactions, and even reconciling your bank account. When the accountant finishes with the review, she exports the changes for you, which generates a .QBY file, also referred to as an Accountant's Copy Import File.

Your accountant has two options for sending you the file with her changes:

- **Send Changes to Client**—This method allows the business owner to incorporate the changes from a menu in QuickBooks. There is no charge to the business owner for this service and only a nominal fee for the accounting professional (included free with the QuickBooks ProAdvisor Program).

- **Create Change File**—This method can be attached to an email or stored on a removable device. There is no fee for the business owner or the accountant using this method.

Encourage your accountant to use the Send Changes to Client method—of the two methods, it is the easiest for the business owner.

Method 1: Importing Changes from the Web

You can tell if your accountant used this method if you receive an email from Intuit, providing instructions for incorporating the changes your accountant made to your file. This method does not require attachments to emails or files on flash drives—making it the simplest method to use.

To import changes from the Web, follow these steps:

1. With your QuickBooks data file open, verify that the title bar indicates that the accountant's changes are pending (refer to Figure 16.5). You might also see the message shown in Figure 16.8 when you open your data file.

2. From the menu bar, select File, Accountant's Copy, Import Accountant's Changes From Web.

   The Incorporate Accountant's Changes dialog box opens, enabling you to view the details of the changes to be imported (see Figure 16.9).

Figure 16.8
QuickBooks' message when you open the data file indicating that your accountant's changes are pending.

Click the (+) to expand the detail

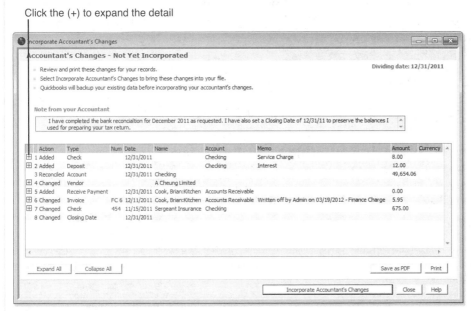

Figure 16.9
View the accountant's changes and notes before they are incorporated into your data.

3. Click the + (plus sign) in front of a transaction to see more details about that specific transaction, or click Expand All to see the details of all the transactions.

4. Click Save as PDF or Print to save the details for your future reference.

5. Click the Incorporate Accountant's Changes button when you have finished reviewing the changes.

6. The Accountant Import dialog box opens, instructing you to close any open QuickBooks windows. Click OK.

7. The Save Backup Copy dialog box opens, indicating that you must first make a backup of your data before the import. In the Save In drop-down menu select a location to save the backup file and in the File Name field, type a name if you don't want to accept the default name provided.

8. If a message displays about backing up your data to the same location as your data, read the message and select Change Location or Use This Location.

9. Click OK to close the message that informs you where the backup was stored. QuickBooks displays a progress indicator while it is incorporating the changes. When it's finished, the Accountant's Changes Incorporated dialog box displays.

10. Click OK in the QuickBooks Information dialog box, which informs you about the PDF file of the changes that QuickBooks created and stored in the same location as your company file.

11. Click OK to close the message that your accountant has been notified that you have imported the changes.

12. Click Print or Save As PDF to store a copy of the changes in addition to the PDF created in step 11.

13. Click Close to close the Incorporate Accountant's Changes dialog box.

The changes made by your accountant are now incorporated into your file.

Method 2: Importing Changes From the Transfer File

Use this method if the accountant provided you with a file with an extension of .QBY. She might have provided it to you via an email attachment or brought it by your office on a flash drive or other removable device.

To import changes from the transfer file, follow these steps:

1. With your QuickBooks data file open, verify that the title bar indicates that the accountant's changes are pending (refer to Figure 16.5). If the Accountant's Copy message displays, click OK to close.

2. Click File, Accountant's Copy, Import Accountant's Changes From File menu option.

3. Browse to the location where you stored the .QBY Accountant's Copy (import file) your accountant sent you.

4. Select the file and click Open. The Incorporate Accountant's Changes dialog box opens, enabling you to view the details of the changes to be imported (refer to Figure 16.9).

5. Click the + (plus sign) in front of a transaction to see more details about that specific transaction, or click Expand All to see the details of all the transactions.

6. Click Print or Save As PDF to save the details for your future reference.

7. Click the Incorporate Accountant's Changes button when you have finished reviewing the changes.

8. The Accountant Import dialog box opens, instructing you to close any open QuickBooks windows. Click OK.

9. The Save Backup Copy dialog box opens, indicating that you must first make a backup of your data before the import. In the Save In drop-down menu select a location to save the backup file and in the File Name field, type a name if you don't want to accept the default name provided. Click Save.

10. Click OK to close the message that informs you where the backup was stored. QuickBooks displays a progressive message that it is incorporating the changes. When it's finished, the Accountant's Changes Incorporated dialog box displays.

11. Click OK to the QuickBooks Information dialog box about the PDF file of the changes that was created and stored in the same location as your company file.

12. Click Close after viewing the Accountant's Changes Incorporated dialog box. Optionally, click Print or Save As PDF to store a copy of the changes in addition to the PDF created in step 11.

13. Click Close to close the Incorporate Accountant's Changes dialog box.

Set a Closing Date

When the accountant's changes are imported, the dividing date and all the restrictions associated with it are removed. The accountant can include with his changes a closing date that transfers to your file so you do not inadvertently add, delete, or modify transactions prior to the closing date. If a closing date was set, you will see the details in the Incorporate Accountant's Changes report you view prior to importing the changes.

If your accountant did not send back a closing date and password, I recommend that you set a closing date the same as the dividing date to protect the accountant's work.

To set a closing date for your file, follow these steps:

1. Log in as the Admin user and from the menu bar, select Company, Set Closing Date.

2. The Preferences dialog box displays. Click the Set Date/Password button. The Set Closing Date and Password dialog box displays.

3. Select a closing date, typically the same date used for the dividing date.

4. Optionally select the Exclude Estimates, Sales Orders, and Purchase Orders from Closing Data Restrictions checkbox as shown in Figure 16.10.

5. Enter an optional password (recommended).

6. Click OK to accept the closing date and optional closing date password.

Figure 16.10
Setting a closing date will help protect the work done by the accountant.

Setting Employee Security

To be certain the Closing Date control is managed properly, review all users for their specific rights for changing transactions prior to a closing date.

1. From the menu bar, select Company, Set Up Users and Passwords, Set Up Users. (This is the menu path for QuickBooks Pro, Premier, or Accountant; QuickBooks Enterprise Solutions has more robust security setting options not discussed in detail in this book.)

2. To view existing security by user, from the User List dialog box opened in the previous step, select the user with your cursor and click the View User button.

   The View User Access dialog box opens, as shown in Figure 16.11. Any user who should not have rights to change closed period transactions should have an "N" appearing in the last menu option in the Create column.

3. If after reviewing the access for each employee, you need to edit this setting for an employee, click Leave to close the View User Access dialog box.

4. You are returned to the User List dialog box. With your cursor, select the employee and click Edit User.

5. The Access for User dialog box opens. Choose the Selected Areas option and click Continue through the screens until you reach page 9 of 10, as shown in Figure 16.12. Click Next (page 10 of 10) to see a summary of the employee's security settings or Finish to return to the User List dialog box.

6. Click Close.

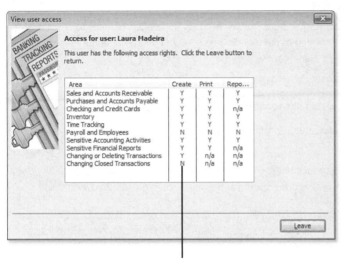

Should be "N" if you do not want the user
to change closed period transactions.

Figure 16.11
You can easily view the user's access rights from one summary window.

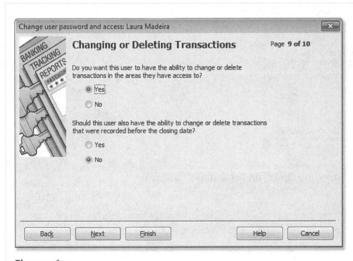

Figure 16.12
On the second option, select to prevent the user from changing transactions in closed periods.

Canceling an Accountant's Copy

It is possible for you to cancel an accountant's copy of your data if necessary. Be sure to discuss this action with your accountant before you make this change. The following are some reasons you might need to cancel the accountant's changes:

- Your accountant has delayed the review of your file.

- You have found corrections you would like to make prior to the dividing date.

- You cannot modify nonposting documents (purchase orders, sales orders, and estimates) dated prior to the dividing date.

- Your accountant needs to work in your file without any transaction restrictions, making an appointment to come to your office to work or perform the work remotely via the Internet.

Before canceling or removing restrictions on your data file, discuss this option with your accountant. After the Accountant's Copy is canceled, your accountant's changes file cannot be imported into your data file.

To remove the restrictions placed on your file by an Accountant's Copy, select File, Accountant's Copy, Remove Restrictions from the menu bar. The Remove Restrictions dialog box displays, warning you that your accountant will no longer be able to import her changes back into your file, as shown in Figure 16.13.

Figure 16.13
The Remove Restrictions warning displays when you cancel an Accountant's Copy file.

After you remove the restriction from the file, no more data restrictions are imposed by the dividing date, and the top bar of your data file no longer displays the Accountant's Changes Pending message.

Data Sharing for the Accountant

Earlier, Table 16.1 listed the types of QuickBooks files with which business owners and accountants have the options of working. This section discusses the options from the perspective of the accountant.

As the accountant, you will want to review the variety of file types and the pros and cons of using each file type for sharing data with your client.

 For more information, see "QuickBooks File Types," p. 518.

 tip

QuickBooks Accountant 2012 and Enterprise Accountant 12.0 include the QuickBooks File Manager 2012, as shown in Figure 16.14.

You can use this tool to open and manage your clients' QuickBooks files quickly and easily from one location. File Manager also makes it easy to identify what year's version and file type your client supplied you with.

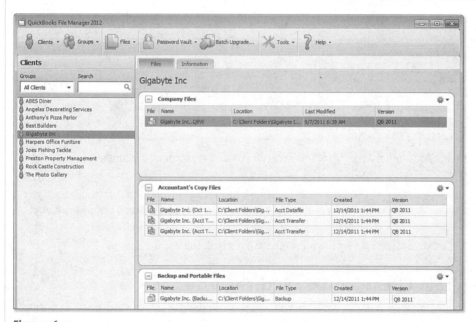

Figure 16.14
QuickBooks Accountant software includes the File Manager, which helps accountants manage multiple client files.

Creating an External Accountant User Type

When you work in a client's file, request that the client create a username specific for you and assign that username the External Accountant type as shown in Figure 16.15. Benefits and controls available when working in a client's file as the External Accountant user type include:

- Ability to separate the changes you make in the data file from the changes your client makes.

- Option to use the Client Data Review feature efficiently. For more information, see "Client Data Review," p. 601.

- Access all areas of QuickBooks except creating new users or viewing sensitive customer credit card numbers.

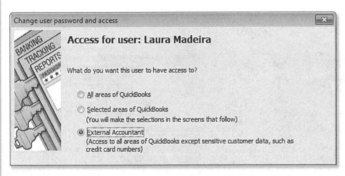

Figure 16.15
Ask your client to create an External Accountant user type for you as the company accountant.

To create this unique type of user, you must be logged into the data file as the Admin user and you or the client must create the new user *before* the client creates the Accountant's Copy file for your use.

You will then use this new login when you begin working with the client's data file.

Preparing Your Client for Data Exchange

As an accounting professional, you probably will be able to choose the method you and your client use to share the data. However, you might not be able to control the condition in which you receive the file. I am speaking specifically of accounting accuracy. Some accounting professionals don't worry much about this until they receive the data file; others might want their client to take certain steps to ensure the accuracy of the data before beginning the review. Encourage your clients to review specific chapters in this book to help better prepare their file for your review, making your review time more profitable!

Ask your client to review the following in her file before sharing the data with you:

- Accuracy of her bank balances

- The open customer invoices in Accounts Receivable

- The unpaid vendor bills in Accounts Payable

Other critical numbers to review are usually easier to reconcile by asking for documents from banks, such as a bank loan payoff statement, or comparing the business financials with filed payroll returns.

After your client has reviewed the information and provided the documents you requested, you are ready to choose a method for sharing the data with your client.

Receiving an Accountant's Copy File

After reviewing the advantages or limitations of each file type in the section titled "QuickBooks File Types," you can see that the most effective method is the QuickBooks Accountant's Copy file feature. Using this file type, your clients can continue their day-to-day accounting tasks, and from the convenience of your office you can review and make needed changes to their data, later importing these changes into the file they have been using.

Discuss the following with your clients before they prepare an Accountant's Copy of their QuickBooks data:

- The Dividing Date selected. As their accounting professional, communicate what date this should be.

- How current are the bank reconciliations in the data file? In the Accountant's Copy, your bank reconciliation work is returned to the client only for statement dates on or before the dividing date. Additionally, the client can only mark as cleared items dated after the Dividing Date.

- Verify that the user settings in the data file include restrictions for editing or modifying transactions prior to the closing date. This step is optional, but when you are working in the Accountant's Copy file, you can send back the closing date with your changes.

- Instruct them *not* to cancel or remove restrictions on the Accountant's Changes Pending file without first consulting you.

- Discuss the options for sending this file to you. Owners have these options:

  - Send you an encrypted copy of their data via Intuit's secure Accountant's Copy File Transfer service, a free service to your client. Accounting professionals pay a nominal fee (free if you are a QuickBooks ProAdvisor). Be sure your client knows the email address where you would like to be notified.

  - Attach the saved file to an email.

  - Copy it to a storage device, such as a USB drive or CD.

 tip

If you are using QuickBooks Premier Accountant 2012 or QuickBooks Enterprise Solutions Accountant 12.0, you can convert your client's QuickBooks 2011 or newer Accountant's Copy file (.QBX file extension); work with it in your Premier Accountant 2012 or Enterprise Solutions Accountant 12.0; and return it to your client to import back into their QuickBooks 2011 or 2012 version! This feature is available only with the Accountant's Copy file-sharing feature and does not apply to other file types.

QuickBooks Premier can open a Pro or Premier industry-specific edition, and when the file is returned to the client, she will be able to work again with the file in their product edition.

When you open Pro or any of the Premier industry-specific editions with QuickBooks Enterprise Solutions the file is converted to an Enterprise edition and cannot be opened again in a Pro or Premier product.

Method 1: Receiving Accountant's Copy from Client via Web

If your client chooses the Intuit's Accountant's Copy File Transfer secure server to get the data to you, you are notified at the email address the client provides in the transfer process, and you are directed to a secure site to download your client's file. This service offers your client simplicity in getting the data to you while aiding in the encrypted security of the transfer of sensitive data over the Internet. Downloads are only available for 30 days, so don't delay!

After downloading the file, follow the instructions in the next section for opening and converting the Transfer File (.QBX file extension) to an Accountant's Copy file (.QBA file extension).

Method 2: Receiving Accountant's Copy from Client via File

Have your client follow the steps to create and send you the Accountant's Copy file of the data as outlined in the section, "Create an Accountant's Copy of Your Data."

To work with your client's Accountant's Copy (.QBX) file type your client sent you or that you downloaded, follow these steps:

1. From the menu bar, select File, Accountant's Copy, Open & Convert Transfer File. The Open and Convert Accountant's Copy Transfer File dialog box displays, as shown in Figure 16.16. This summary provides you with an overview of the workflow when using an Accountant's Copy of your client's data.

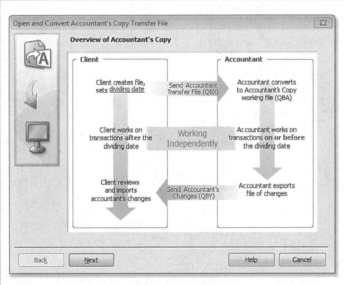

Figure 16.16
Overview of the Accountant's Copy workflow when working with your client's data.

2. Click Next. The Open Accountant's Copy Transfer File dialog box displays. This provides details on what tasks you can and cannot do when working with an Accountant's Copy. See Figure 16.17. Click Next.

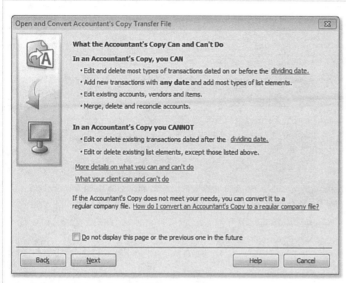

Figure 16.17
Review a summary of the tasks you can and cannot do when working with an Accountant's Copy file.

3. Browse to the location that you stored your client's QuickBooks transfer file. Select the fle and click Open. If it's displayed, click OK to the message that you have chosen an Accountant's Copy transfer file.

4. In the Save Accountant's Copy dialog box, select a location and name for the new file. I usually put the accounting period being reviewed in the name, such as <Company Name_YE_12_31_11.QBA>. Click Save and QuickBooks prompts you with a message that the conversion is taking place.

5. If you have not previously disabled this warning, the message that indicates you are opening an Accountant's Copy appears and shows you the dividing date that was chosen by your client, as shown in Figure 16.18. Click OK to close.

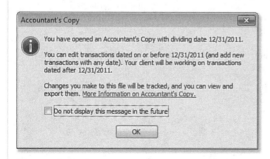

Figure 16.18
QuickBooks notification that you are opening an Accountant's Copy file and provides details of the selected dividing date.

Your QuickBooks Accountant title bar will show that you are working with an Accountant's Copy and what the dividing date for that file is (see Figure 16.19).

Figure 16.19
You can be certain you are working in the correct file by looking at the title bar of your Accountant's Copy .QBA file.

As the company's accounting professional, you can now review, add, and edit the data file and be secure that your client cannot modify the balances prior to the dividing date that was set, all while the client continues her day-to-day accounting tasks.

Reinstate Warnings

If you do not see some of the dialog boxes mentioned in this chapter, a user might have selected the Do Not Display This Message (or Page, and so on, depending on which dialog box is open), causing future users not to see these messages.

To turn these one-time messages back on, log into the file as the user and follow these steps:

1. From the menu bar, select Edit, Preferences. In the dialog box that displays, select General on the left side.

2. Click the My Preferences tab.

3. Place a checkmark in the Bring Back All One-Time Messages box and click OK.

I often do this task in my client's file (prior to making an Accountant's Copy), especially if I have found errors that might have been prevented if the user had heeded the warning of a previously dismissed message.

What the Accountant Can Do

Recent releases of the QuickBooks software have greatly improved the capabilities you have with an Accountant's Copy of your client's data.

The restrictions invoked by the dividing date set by your client affect your ability to add or edit transactions. If these restrictions prevent you from completing your tasks, you can convert the Accountant's Copy to a working QuickBooks data file (.QBW file extension). However, your changes cannot be imported into your client's file.

For more information, see "Converting the Accountant's Copy to a Regular Company File,"
p. 549.

The Accountant's Copy provides a unique feature that will help you to determine whether your changes will be sent back to the client's file. Any field that is colored beige will transfer back to your client. If the field is white, you might be able to modify it for your own purposes, but the change will not be sent back to your client.

For example, if part of your correction to your client's file was to modify an existing list item, only the fields identified in Figure 16.20 would be sent back to your client's data file. All other fields can be modified for your purposes, but would not transfer back to your client's file. If you and your client make changes to details on the same item, your changes will override the client's when the changes are imported.

Figure 16.20
When adding or modifying details in the Accountant's Copy, any fields shaded beige (non-white) will be sent back to your client's file.

The following sections describe more specifically what you, the accountant, can do (with noted limitations) while working in the Accountant's Copy of your client's file.

Accounting Activities

Recent versions of QuickBooks enhance the accounting activities you can do with the client's data when sharing an Accountant's Copy file type:

- **Reconcile the bank statements for dates prior to the Dividing Date**—You can create and edit transactions necessary to perform the bank reconciliation. Additionally, your changes to a reconciled item will also be sent back to the client.

Your client can reconcile the bank account when the statement date and all cleared transactions are dated after the selected dividing date. However, if you *also* reconcile this account, her bank reconciliation work will be rolled back to the transactions cleared status as of the time the Accountant's Copy was created.

- **Set 1099 account mappings**—You can assign the proper chart of account to the Federal Form 1099 box-Misc Income.

- **Reconcile the bank statements for dates after the Dividing Date**—You can do this if it helps your review. However, these reconciliations will not be sent back to the client's data. Any transactions added will be sent back to the client.

- **Set tax-line mappings**—Used to assign the tax form line to a chart of accounts. Use this feature if you are integrating the QuickBooks data with Intuit's tax preparation software ProSeries or Lacerte.

QuickBooks Lists

Also enhanced with recent QuickBooks releases is your ability to manage your client's list items when performing data corrections:

- **Chart of Accounts**—No restrictions, including the ability to merge charts of account list items. For more information, see "Merging Duplicated Accounts," p. 96.

- **List Items**—In general you can add, edit, delete, and inactivate list items you create in the Accountant's Copy.

- **Items List**—For lists with items dated before the dividing date, you can edit the Item Name/Number, Subitem, Expense Account, Tax Code, and Income Account and also make the item inactive. Note: If you and your client both make changes to the same item, the accountant's changes will override that of the client when the changes are imported.

- **Customer, Other Names List**—Add a new Name or edit the Name field or make the name inactive.

- **Vendor**—Add a new vendor or edit the Name, Tax ID, and identify vendor as an eligible to receive a 1099-Misc. Income form at year-end. Additionally you can assign up to three general ledger accounts on the Account Prefill tab. Your changes will override the same information in the client's file when imported.

- **Employee List**—Add a new employee or edit the Name and Social Security fields only.

- **Class List, Fixed Asset Item**—The ability to merge class list items. Additionally, you can add a new list item or edit the Name, assign Subclass of field, or make the class inactive.

- **Sales Tax Code**—Add a new sales tax code or edit the Name, Tax Agency, and make the item inactive. New sales tax items can be created, but the tax rate assigned will not transfer to the client's file.

Transactions

Generally, you can add any transaction type before or after the dividing date with the following limitations on editing, voiding, or deleting:

- **Bills and checks**—Add these types of transactions with dates before or after the dividing date. Edit, void, or delete limited to those dated before the dividing date.

- **Vendor credits**—Add these types of transactions with dates before or after the dividing date. Edit, void, or delete limited to those dated before the dividing date.

- **Item receipts**—Add or delete, but you will be unable to edit or void before and after the dividing date.

- **Bill payments by credit card**—Add or delete, but you will not be able to edit or void before and after the dividing date.

- **Inventory quantity/value adjustments**—Add or delete, but you will not be able to edit or void before and after the dividing date.

- **Customer payments**—Add or delete, but you will not be able to edit or void before and after the dividing date.

What the Accountant Cannot Do

Here is what you, the accountant, *cannot do* while working in the Accountant's Copy of your client's file:

- Add or modify payroll transactions.

- Add or modify nonposting transactions, such as estimates, sales orders, or purchase orders.

- Add or modify transfers of funds between accounts. Although you cannot use the transfer transaction, you can create the same effect on the accounts with a journal entry or deposit form.

- Add or modify the build assembly transaction.

- Add or modify the sales tax payment transaction.

Although you cannot make changes to these types of transactions in your client's file with an Accountant's Copy file type, you can conveniently make these changes in the client's file using Remote Access like Webex, LogMeIn, GoToMyPC, or others.

Returning the Accountant's Copy Change File to the Client

One of the most important features of using the Accountant's Copy to share your client's data is that when your changes are complete, you can send back an updated file for your client to import into her file.

 note

If you are working with a client's Accountant's Copy file created from a QuickBooks 2011 version, you can open the file with your QuickBooks Accountant 2012 and return the data to the client in their original QuickBooks 2011 version.

Set a Closing Date

When your client imports the changes you have made to the Accountant's Copy of her file, the dividing date restrictions are removed. If you do not want the client to add or edit transactions prior to the dividing date, make sure you also set a closing date prior to exporting the data for the client.

To set a closing date while working in the Accountant's Copy of your client's data, follow these steps:

1. Log into the client's Accountant's Copy file. From the menu bar, select Company, Set Closing Date.

2. The Company Preference dialog box displays. Click the Set Date/Password button. The Set Closing Date and Password dialog box displays.

3. Enter an optional password and a closing date—typically the same date that was used for the dividing date.

4. Click OK to accept the closing date and optional closing date password.

The closing date will transfer back to the client's file and the client will not be asked to set the closing date. The fact that a closing date was set is included in the information the client previews before incorporating the accountant's changes.

 note

If you do not set a closing date as part of your changes, when the client incorporates the changes file, a message will display asking if she wants to set a closing date.

If you want your client to have the ability to modify your changes, you might not need to set a closing date for the file.

Review the details of setting a closing date and reviewing each employee's access rights to changing transactions prior to the closing date.

 For more information, see "Setting Employee Security," p. 534.

Method 1: Send Changes to Client via Web

Using the Send Changes method is the simplest for your client to import. This service is included with a QuickBooks ProAdvisor membership or is available for a nominal annual fee. No fee is charged to the client to accept this file from you.

To return the corrected file to your client after you make all your changes, follow these steps:

1. From the menu bar, select File, Accountant's Copy, View/Export Changes for Client. The View/Export Changes for Client dialog box displays, as shown in Figure 16.21.

2. Review your changes and add an optional note for your client.

3. If you need to make additional changes or edit the changes you have made to the file, click the X in the top-right corner.

4. If your changes are complete, click Send Changes to Client. The Send Accountant's Changes dialog box displays as shown in Figure 16.22.

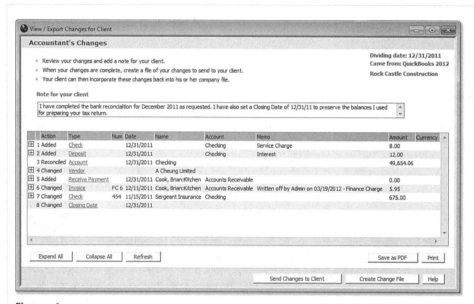

Figure 16.21
The View/Export Changes for Client dialog box, where you can review your changes and include a note for your client.

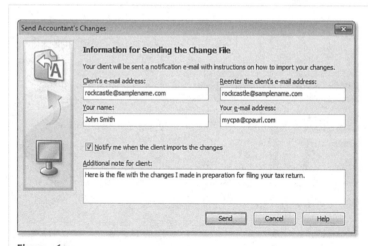

Figure 16.22
Your client will receive an email with instructions of how to incorporate your changes.

5. Enter your client's email address, your name, and your email address.

6. Click Send.

Intuit will send you an email notifying you that the file was uploaded to the Intuit Accountant's Copy File Transfer secure server. Your client will also receive an email notifying her that the file is available for downloading for 30 days. Encourage your client to follow the instructions in the email to easily incorporate your changes into her data file.

 note

If you have already exported these changes for the client, a message will display informing you that if your client has already imported the previously exported changes file, she will not be able to import these changes. Click OK if you still want to export the changes.

Method 2: Send Changes to Client via File

You might also choose to send the Changes File to the client via a file you can attach to an email or store on a flash drive or other storage device. This method requires more effort on the part of your customers. They must access the file, save it to their computer, and then import the changes into QuickBooks. Consider using the first method of sending the file via the Web, which does not require as many steps.

To create the Changes File (.QBY extension) to give to your client, follow these steps:

1. From the menu bar, select File, Accountant's Copy, View/Export Changes for Client. The View/ Export Changes for Client dialog box displays (see Figure 16.21).

2. Review your changes and optionally add a note for your client.

3. If you need to make additional changes or edit the changes you have made to the file, click the X in the top-right corner.

4. If your changes are complete, click Create Change File. The Save Accountant Changes File to dialog box displays.

5. Browse to the location where you want to save the file and optionally edit the filename to be saved. QuickBooks creates a file with .QBY extension.

6. If you have already exported these changes for the client, you will see the message informing you that if your client has already imported the previously exported changes file, she will not be able to import these changes. Click OK if you still want to export the changes.

7. Click Save. A message displays, letting you know the file was successfully created.

8. Click OK to close the message. QuickBooks returns you to the .QBA file.

To complete the process, simply give this newly created .QBY (Accountant's Copy import file) back to the client. You can copy it to a removable storage device or attach it to an email.

Instruct your client to follow the steps listed in the section, "Method 2: Importing Changes from the Transfer File," p. 532. Your client will be able to review your changes in detail before accepting or incorporating the changes into her file.

QuickBooks Remote Access for Accountants

If, as the accountant, you would like to take more control over the import of your changes into your client's file as well as setting the closing date, you might want to consider using a remote access program to log in to your client's file through the Internet.

QuickBooks partners with WebEx to bring you a solution that makes it easy to work remotely in your file or your clients' files. You can use this option if you need to make data changes that are not allowed in an Accountant's Copy. For example, making changes to payroll transactions. You can also use this tool to perform the import of your changes into your client's data file.

I find working in the remote environment a perfect choice for simplifying the entire process for clients. For more information, select Accountant, Remote Access from the menu bar in QuickBooks Accountant or QuickBooks Enterprise Accountant.

What to Request from the Client When the Import Is Complete

Clients can import your changes with simple, easy-to-follow instructions if you used the Send Changes to Client method. However, you might want to request a few items from the client after the import to be sure the process was completed successfully:

- **Trial Balance**—You should review the Trial Balance report as of the dividing date to compare with the same information from your copy of the client's file. From the menu bar, select Reports, Accountant, Trial Balance. Be sure to mention to the client the prepare the report in accrual or cash basis. They may have one or the other as the default setup in their file.

- **Closing Date**—If you want to verify that the closing date was incorporated with your changes, instruct your client to select Company, Set Closing Date from the menu bar. Doing so opens the Company Preference tab for Accounting Preferences. Have your client verify the closing date (or any date at all). Refer to Figure 16.10.

- **User Security Rights**—Verify with your client the access rights each employee has for changing transactions dated prior to the closing date. Instruct your client to select Company, Set Up Users and Passwords, Set Up Users from the menu bar. In the User List dialog box that opens, select the employee and the View User tab on the right. A "Y" in the Changing Closed Transactions permission allows that user to add or edit transactions dated prior to the closing date. If a closing date password was set, the user will have to type that password first. A creative password that I have used is "call laura," prompting the client to call me first before making the change!

Converting the Accountant's Copy to a Regular Company File

What can you do if, after beginning to work in the Accountant's Copy, you determine some of the changes that need to be made cannot be accommodated with this file type? You can convert the client's Accountant's Copy (.QBX) file type to a regular QuickBooks (.QBW) file type following these steps.

From the menu bar, choose File, Accountant's Copy, Convert Accountant's Copy to Company File/ QBW. A message displays, recommending that you contact your client to discuss this change.

You have to make the following decisions:

- Have the client manually repeat your changes in her file.

- If the client is going to use your file, the client must stop working in the file she has.

QuickBooks 2012 offers accountants more flexibility than in prior versions in how you choose to share and work in your client's data. These improvements help make the workflow for you and your client more efficient, making your accounting business more profitable.

MANAGING YOUR QUICKBOOKS DATABASE

The QuickBooks Database

If you are the typical QuickBooks user, you purchased the software to track the income and expenses of your business. By selecting software for this task, you have advanced from a manual recordkeeping system into the world of database technology.

A database is an automated version of a big file room, with information of different types stored in different cabinets, drawers, and files. Years ago, companies employed file clerks to keep track of the company's paperwork. QuickBooks uses a Database Server to perform similar tasks to a file clerk, organizing and storing the data you create.

Depending on the number of licenses you purchased, you can choose to install the software as a single user application or install it in a network environment for use by multiple users (see Figure 17.1).

Based upon your installation selection, QuickBooks either installs the personal Database Server or the network Database Server to control the flow of data from the QuickBooks application to your QuickBooks Company file. During the install, the computer operating system creates a Windows user account for this server in order to assign administrative-level access rights to the computer's resources and the QuickBooks files. When you view your list of users for your computer, included will be QBDataServiceUser22 (the default Database Server for all QuickBooks 2012 versions). During installation, the QuickBooks Database Server Manager is also installed. This utility is discussed later in this chapter.

Select for single-user install.

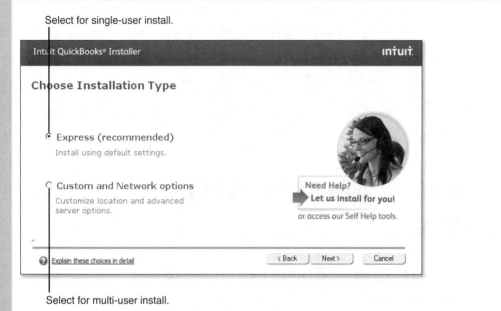

Select for multi-user install.

Figure 17.1
QuickBooks guides you through the install of the software.

System Requirements

Verify that your computer and network hardware meets the minimum requirements for QuickBooks. This list is applicable to QuickBooks 2012 versions, but you might want to check the requirements for your specific version.

Supported operating systems for QuickBooks for Windows products:

- Windows 7, either 32-bit or 64-bit versions

- Windows Vista, Service Pack 1 including either 32-bit or updated LM64-bit version

- Windows XP, Service Pack 3 and later

Computer processor, memory, and disk space requirements:

- Minimum of a 2.0 GHz processor, 2.4 GHz is recommended.

- Minimum of 1 GB of RAM for single-user configurations, 2 GB recommended.

- Minimum of 2 GB of RAM for multi-user configurations, 4 GB (or more) recommended.

⚠ caution

Do not delete the QBDataServiceUser22 (or whatever version you are running) from the user's applet within the Control Panel.

- Minimum of 2.75 GB of disk space for the application, including space required for Microsoft .NET 4.0 Runtime installed with QuickBooks (if not preinstalled on your computer). Additional space is required for your QuickBooks data files.

Additional hardware, software, and Internet connectivity:

- Hardware

  - 4x CD-ROM drive required for CD installations

  - 1024x768 or higher screen resolution

  - 100 Mbps network card, switch or router, 1000 Mbps recommended

- Software for integration capabilities

  - Microsoft Word 2003, 2007, or 2010 (including either 32-bit or 64-bit version) for preparation of QuickBooks letters.

  - Microsoft Excel 2003, 2007, or 2010 (including either 32-bit or 64-bit version) for spreadsheet integration including QuickBooks Statement Writer (optional).

  - Microsoft Outlook 2003, 2007, or 2010 (including either 32-bit or 64-bit version). When installing contact synchronization via QuickBooks Contact Sync for Outlook. For more information on this synchronization, see Chapter 18, "Using Other Planning and Management Tools."

  - Adobe Acrobat Reader, version 5.0 or later.

- Internet Connectivity

  - Internet access with at least 56 Kbps connection speed

  - Cable or DSL modem is highly recommended over dial-up service

Antivirus and firewall compatibility considerations include:

- Antivirus

  - Antivirus products (with/without firewalls) software compatibility

  - Symantec/Norton AntiVirus, Internet Security, Norton 360

  - McAfee Internet Security, Total Protection, AntiVirus Plus

  - Trend Micro Titanium or Trend Micro Worry-Free Business Security

  - ZoneAlarm

- Windows firewall compatibility

  - Windows 7 firewall (all versions)

  - Windows Vista firewall (all versions)

  - XP firewall (all versions)

Installing QuickBooks for Single-User Mode

Select the Express option (as shown in Figure 17.1) when you need to use QuickBooks from a single computer. QuickBooks installs the application and database manager in the C:\Program Files\ Intuit\QuickBooks 2012 folder; if you are using a 64-bit version of Windows the installation folder is C:\Program Files(x86)\Intuit\QuickBooks 2012.

By default, QuickBooks uses the following locations for storing your data file, although you can select a different directory if desired:

- **Windows 7:** C:\Users\Public\Public Documents\Intuit\QuickBooks\Company Files

- **Windows XP:** C:\Documents and Settings\All Users\Documents\Intuit\QuickBooks\Company Files

- **Windows Vista:** C:\Users\Public\Public Documents\Intuit\QuickBooks\Company Files

QuickBooks prompts you to enter the license and product numbers; these numbers are provided on a bright yellow sticker on the QuickBooks CD sleeve or if you have downloaded the software, you will receive an email with the registration details. Follow the remaining instructions for installing the QuickBooks software.

Installing QuickBooks for Multi-User Mode

QuickBooks 2012 streamlines the process of installing QuickBooks for multi-user simultaneous access to your company data. As discussed in the introduction, when QuickBooks is going to be used in a multi-user configuration there must be one computer on your network that will act as the QuickBooks Server to host your data files and the QuickBooks Database Server.

It is not necessary to use an actual Windows Server as your QuickBooks host because QuickBooks runs equally well on peer-to-peer and client-server domain networks. When you install QuickBooks on a network, you should always perform the installation on the server before installing QuickBooks on any workstations.

During installation, QuickBooks will prompt you to select the installation type as shown in Figure 17.1. Select Custom and Network Option for all network installations, including server (host) and workstations (clients). Follow the remaining prompts to select the installation options that best fit your network requirements for the specific computer you are installing. The choices include

- **I'll Be Using QuickBooks on This Computer**—If you are installing QuickBooks on a computer that will only access the Company files across the network.

- **I'll Be Using QuickBooks on This Computer, AND I'll Be Storing Our Company File Here So It Can Be Shared Over Our Network**—You will possibly run QuickBooks from this machine and have it act as your QuickBooks Server, which hosts your company files.

 tip

Using the "I'll Be Using QuickBooks on This Computer, AND I'll Be Storing Our Company File Here...." option is the preferred server option even if QuickBooks will not routinely be used on this machine. Selecting this option allows the QuickBooks application to be opened on the server to perform certain file-related functions, including back-up activities.

■ **I Will NOT be Using QuickBooks on This Computer...**—You can elect to install only the QuickBooks Database Server and QuickBooks Database Server Manager Utility on the hosting computer. This install does not require a license.

 caution

If you selected I Will NOT be Using QuickBooks... option, you should also review the section in this chapter titled, "The QuickBooks Database Server Manager."

You will then be prompted to enter your license and product numbers. Follow all additional prompts to complete the install process.

If you do not have a version of QuickBooks already installed, the Installation Location Options screen appears. Browse to select the desired location you want to install the new version to.

Once all your settings are correct for your network, click Install from the Ready to Install dialog box. As with the Express install, QuickBooks will display a progress bar indicating the status of the install process.. The Congratulations dialog box will display when the installation is finalized. You can either launch QuickBooks to begin creating a new file or open an existing file or practice file.

For more information, see "Getting Started with QuickBooks," p. 21.

The QuickBooks Database Server Manager

Automatically installed is the QuickBooks Database Server Manager Utility, if you selected the option I Will NOT Be Using QuickBooks on This Computer. I Will Be Storing Our Company File Here So It Can Be Shared Over Our Network (A License Is Not Required For This Option). This utility will launch automatically once the installation is complete.

 note

The QuickBooks Database Server Manager is only needed if you are using QuickBooks in multi-user mode.

Changing to Multi-User Access

If you initially installed QuickBooks for single-user access and want to change it to multi-user access, follow these steps to enable the Database Server Manager utility:

1. From the menu bar, select File, Utilities, Host Multi-User Access.

2. Click Yes to the Start Hosting Multi-User Access message that displays.

3. Click Yes to the Company file must be closed. If prompted, click Continue to allow Windows administrator permissions and Yes to allowing the changes to be made to your computer.

QuickBooks installs the network database server as a windows service/process and it is configured to run under the QBDataServiceUser22 user account. (This is the user account assigned to QuickBooks 2012.)

The QuickBooks Database Server Manager utility provides users access to configure the database server. It is critical that this utility be running and properly configured to permit multi-user simultaneous access to your QuickBooks Company data files.

Opening the QuickBooks Data Server Manager

Your computer might display the utility in your system tray in the lower right of your computer task bar. If not, you can open the QuickBooks Data Server Manager by following these steps:

1. From the Windows Orb or Windows Start button (lower-left corner of windows taskbar), click All Programs.

2. Scroll to find and select the QuickBooks folder.

3. Click the QuickBooks Database Server Manager to launch it, as shown in Figure 17.2. The data path displayed in this figure might differ from your own data path.

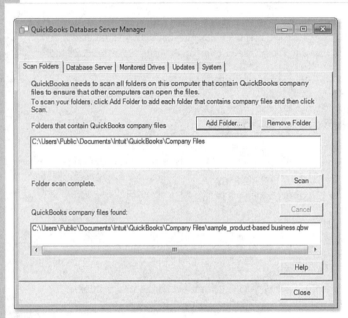

Figure 17.2
The Database Server Manager is used to configure proper multi-user hosting.

The Scan Folders tab consists of two main panels, each performing critical functions. The first is to identify the various windows folders on the QuickBooks server computer that contain QuickBooks data files. To add folders click the Add Folder button and use the Windows directory service display to locate all folders appropriate for your network configuration.

Once all folders containing QuickBooks data files are displayed in the top panel, perform a scan of those folders to locate your QuickBooks files; these files will then appear in the lower panel. A result of this scanning process is that the Database Server creates a *.QBW.ND file for every QuickBooks Company file. This Network Description file contains critical information about the Database Server's location on your network including the server name and IP address. When a QuickBooks workstation accesses the Company file the companion *QBW.ND file advises QuickBooks where and how to find the Database Server.

The QuickBooks Administrator should also configure the Monitored Drives tab, selecting the computer disk drive(s) containing the folders where QuickBooks Company files are located. The utility will then monitor these drives to identify new *.QBW or *.QBA files that might be added to those drives and directories.

➥ *For more information about these named QuickBooks file types, see "Choosing a Method to Share Data," p. 520.*

The Database Server tab displays information about the Database Server, the current QuickBooks Company file(s) in use, and the name of the user logged in. The Updates tab provides information about the current version of the QuickBooks Database Server; it is essential the Database Server version always match the QuickBooks version in use.

For QuickBooks to operate properly, you should never close the QuickBooks Database Server Manager unless you must also shut down the Server for other reasons. A best practice is to minimize the utility.

 tip

If your QuickBooks network suddenly starts suffering from inability to connect one or more workstations in multi-user mode to your Company file, you should promptly check to ensure that the QuickBooks Database Server Manager is running and still configured on the hosting computer.

Some Windows updates require a reboot of the computer. The QuickBooks Database Server Manager Service might have been stopped in the process. Contact your IT professional to restart the process. You might also need to perform the Scan function again to locate the data files on your computer.

Windows Permissions Required for QuickBooks

Simply installing QuickBooks for single-user or multi-user configuration will not guarantee that it will work properly. Certain Windows user permissions must be established to ensure proper access. All QuickBooks users must have full control including read/write privileges for any directory from which Company data files will be accessed.

Setting Permissions in Windows 7 or Windows Vista

To properly configure Windows 7 or Windows Vista user permissions, follow these steps:

1. Using Windows Explorer, locate the folder containing your QuickBooks Company files.

2. Right-click the folder and select Properties.

3. Click the Sharing tab and then click the Share button.

4. In the File Sharing window, use the drop-down list to select each User needing access to QuickBooks and click Add.

5. In the Permission Level column, click the Read drop-down list and select Read/Write.

6. Click the Share button to close the File Sharing window, and then click the Security tab in the Properties window.

7. Click the Edit button for the Group or usernames section.

8. Click the QBDataServiceUser22 User.

9. In the Permissions for QBDataServiceUser22, check the Full Control checkbox in the Allow column, and click OK.

10. Click Close.

Setting Permissions in Windows XP Professional

To properly configure Windows XP Professional user permissions, follow these steps:

1. Using Windows Explorer, locate the folder containing your QuickBooks Company files.

2. Right-click the folder and select Properties.

3. Click the Sharing, Share this folder option.

4. Click the Permissions button.

5. In the Group or usernames section, select Everyone.

6. In the Permissions for Everyone section, check the Full Control checkbox in the Allow column.

Using the QuickBooks Connection Diagnostic Tool

The QuickBooks Connection Diagnostic Tool assists users in diagnosing and correcting various problems preventing proper connections between the QuickBooks application, the Database Manager, and QuickBooks Company files. This tool can troubleshoot the most common networking and multi-user errors (including H-series or 6000-series errors) that occur when trying to open a Company file.

To download this free tool, visit the QuickBooks support website (http://support.quickbooks.intuit.com) and search for Connection Diagnostic Tool. Click the supplied link for the tool.

Once it has downloaded, click the .exe file and follow the install prompts. To launch the tool (see Figure 17.3), follow these steps:

1. Click the QuickBooks Connection icon from your desktop.

2. Click OK, if an information message displays.

3. If necessary, click Yes to the User Account Control message, allowing the program to make changes to your computer.

Browse to the location of your QuickBooks file and click the Test Connectivity button. QuickBooks will perform certain diagnostics. If any error messages display, click the appropriate links for more information or for help in resolving problems.

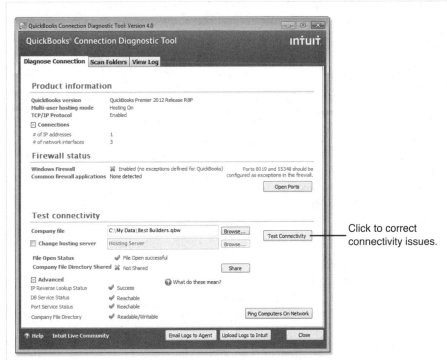

Click to correct
connectivity issues.

Figure 17.3
Used to diagnose and assist in repair of network connection issues.

Keeping Your Software Current

Intuit has a service discontinuation policy on its software. Live technical support and add-on business services such as payroll, credit card processing, QuickBooks Email, and online banking will be discontinued for versions three years or older.

Typically, you will need to upgrade your software by May 31st of each year for versions of QuickBooks 3 years or older to retain these active services if you are using a version of QuickBooks that is three years or older.

Upgrading Your QuickBooks Version

To keep your QuickBooks software supported, you will need to upgrade at least every three years, and if you are like me, you will want to upgrade each year to take advantage of the newest features. I offer a document on my website each fall detailing the newest features with each release. You can access this by visiting my blog and searching for "What's New" i the blog title: www.quick-training.com/blog.

If you are using QuickBooks Enterprise and you subscribe to the annual Full Service Plan, you will receive the newest software version each year at no additional cost, in addition to having access to elite technical support.

If you have used QuickBooks before, then when you purchase the newest year edition, you will be upgrading your QuickBooks file. QuickBooks Pro and Premier both can be upgraded to a QuickBooks Enterprise Solutions file. QuickBooks Enterprise Solutions cannot be downgraded to a QuickBooks Pro or Premier file.

The upgrade process is quite simple. If a prior installation of QuickBooks is detected, you will have the option to Upgrade or Change Installation location. If you want to upgrade the prior version, select Replace the Version Selected Below with the Version I'm Installing Now. From the drop-down list, select the version you want to upgrade. The windows path for your current version of QuickBooks displays.

However, if you want to install QuickBooks 2012 without upgrading any existing version, select the Change the Install Location option. Select a different location by clicking the Browse button and locating a new installation folder. If the folder you want to use does not exist, click the Create New Folder icon for your installation. Follow the instructions for completing the install process.

Installing a QuickBooks Maintenance Release

After a version is released, changes, improvements, and fixes are provided in the form of a maintenance release. Often, Intuit will offer the release as a manual download only. This is usually during the testing phase and you may not want to install the update in this phase.

 note

An Internet connection is required to download and install the release patches.

To choose how QuickBooks detects if there is a maintenance release, follow these steps:

1. From the menu bar, select Help, Update QuickBooks.

2. The Overview tab displays on the Update QuickBooks dialog box. Read the provided information. Optionally, click Update Now if you want to complete the task.

3. Click the Options tab and select from the following:

   - **Automatic Update**—If you select Yes, QuickBooks will automatically download the update and provide a dialog box for you to install the update the next time you launch QuickBooks.

   - **Shared Download**—If you work with multi-users accessing QuickBooks, you should select Yes to share the download with the others. This will save time and ensure that other users can access the newly updated file.

   - **Download Location**—QuickBooks displays the location and name of the downloaded file.

4. You can then choose which updates to install, choosing from:

   - Payroll

   - Federal Forms

   - Forms Engine

5. Click Save if you have made your changes, click Revert to return to the original settings or Close if you have not made any changes. Optionally, click Help for more guidance.

6. Click the Update Now tab. From this tab, you can choose which updates to install, when they were last checked, and the status.

7. Optionally, select the Reset Update to reinstall the entire update or select Get Updates.

8. A progress message displays. Click Close when finished.

To confirm that the newest maintenance release installed, you may need to close QuickBooks and relaunch the software. You can also check the product information window from an open QuickBooks file by selecting the F2 key on your keyboard and reading the Product line at the top. Refer to Figure 17.7.

Protecting Your QuickBooks Database

It is a good practice to protect your QuickBooks data and safeguard it against some unforeseen catastrophic event. In addition to making a backup of your data regularly, you might also consider including power protection, virus protection, and computer disk defragmentation.

Creating a QuickBooks Backup

Even with the best planning and safeguards, unforeseen catastrophic events can happen. Safeguard your company data by creating a regular backup.

Ideally, you should back up your company at the end of each session. However, if you are working in a multi-user environment, you should routinely wait until the end of each workday to back up. If your computer has more than one drive, you can back up onto a different disk drive from the one where your QuickBooks data is normally stored. If you only have one hard drive then you should back up onto some type of removable media such as a USB flash memory drive.

 note

You can perform a backup with multiple users logged in to the file. However, the backup process will not perform the recommended verification of the data as part of the backup.

To make a backup of your QuickBooks data, follow these steps:

1. From the menu bar, select File, Create Backup.

2. Select Local Backup.

3. Click Options. The Backup Options dialog box displays as shown in Figure 17.4. You can skip this step if you do not need to adjust your backup options.

4. Choose the Browse button and browse to select a location to save your backup. It is recommended that you save your backup file to a location other than the location where the data is stored.

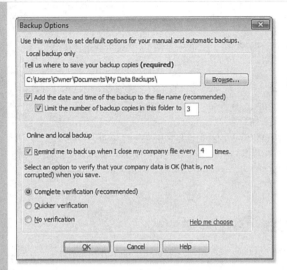

Figure 17.4
Create a backup of your QuickBooks file for safekeeping.

5. Optionally, choose to Add the Date and Time, and to Limit the Number of Backup Copies in the selected folder.

6. Select the Complete Verification (recommended) option. For more information, see the section in this chapter titled "Using the Verify Data Utility."

7. Click OK. If you have selected a location for the backup that is the same as the where the data is stored, a warning message might display recommending that you Change Location for the backup copy. Click Change Location (recommended) or Use This Location.

8. From the Create Backup dialog box, select Next.

9. Select Save It Now and click Next.

10. Type a filename for your backup, or accept the default filename.

11. Click Save.

> **⚠ caution**
> Complete Verification is only available when the file is in single-user mode when performing the backup.

Automating Your QuickBooks Backup

To create a schedule for automatically backing up your QuickBooks data file, follow these steps:

1. Follow steps 1–7 listed in the previous section titled "Creating a QuickBooks Backup."

2. Select one of the following options: Save It Now and Schedule Future Backups or Only Schedule Future Backups. The Where Do You Want to Backup Your Company File? message will display if you have not previously set your file to backup automatically.

3. Optionally, select the Save Backup Copy Automatically... and define the number of times.

4. To set a Backup on a schedule, click the New button to display schedule details as shown in Figure 17.5. Type a description for the backup, browse to the desired location, and define the number of Backup Copies to Keep.

Figure 17.5
Schedule an automatic backup of the QuickBooks file.

5. Select the Start Time, how often the task is run, and on what specific days.

6. Optionally, click Store Password if your computer is password protected. Click OK to return to the Schedule Backup dialog box.

7. Click OK to close the Schedule Backup dialog box.

8. Click Finish to save the schedule.

9. Click OK to close the confirmation message that a backup has been scheduled.

Restoring a Backup

If you find you need to restore your data from a backup, follow these steps:

1. From the menu bar, select File, Open or Restore Company.

2. Select Restore a Backup Copy. Click Next.

3. Select Local backup. Click Next.

4. Locate the backup file and click Open.

5. Click Next after reading the message about Where Do You Want to Restore the File.

6. Browse to select the location and type a name to be given to the restored file. Click Save.

7. QuickBooks provides a progress bar as the file is being restored. Click OK to the information window that the file was restored successfully.

Protecting the QuickBooks Operating Environment

To prevent an unexpected, or unattended shutdown an uninterruptable power supply (UPS) should be installed on each of your computers running QuickBooks, as well as all network components that connect those computers. An adequately sized UPS can prevent power blackouts, brownouts, and surges. A Smart-UPS that automatically begins closing open programs and powering down the computer prior to depletion of the UPS battery should be used when QuickBooks must be left running during unattended periods.

Power Protection

Even if a UPS protects your server and workstation, if the connecting network hardware (switches, hubs, or routers) are not protected, a sudden power event will produce a loss of connection between the QuickBooks client and QuickBooks server, which might result in data corruption. It is recommended that all network hardware also be UPS protected.

Keep your computer safe by preventing power-related corruptions to your QuickBooks and not overloading your UPS with any non-essential computing components.

 tip

Do not plug printers, or other appliances into any UPS protecting your computers and network components. Often when a printer or other appliance launches, it pulls a significant load of power that can actually produce a brownout condition within your UPS itself and compromise power protection.

Virus Protection

The Internet has changed our lives, but one unfortunate side effect has been the contagion of computer viruses sent via email (or other data transfers). Because of the Internet no computer, or network, is immune from attack. Malware programmers are looking for weaknesses in the computers of not just big corporations, but small businesses and individuals, in order to steal financial information or create havoc and destruction of our computer applications. Because QuickBooks is the leading financial software on the market, it is a favorite target of many who would seek to invade your Company files for their personal gain.

Good behavior on the part of computer users is not enough to protect your QuickBooks data from attacks. While surfing certain kinds of websites puts users at higher risks of infection, even legitimate websites can be compromised. Seemingly innocent results in a search engine can open hostile sites that immediately download a computer virus. Some of these viruses collect information from your computer (spyware) and some install malicious (malware) software, but they almost all disguise themselves just long enough to take down your data or your network. Even if you never surf the Web you are still vulnerable as long as you have an open Internet connection, or ever access a flash drive or CD.

A high-quality antivirus program is essential if you are running QuickBooks on your computer or over a network. There are effective programs that can run with a minimum of computer resources and will block the overwhelming majority of threats. Set your antivirus program to run in an always-on mode and to perform a regular (preferably daily) scan of your computer. Ensure these programs are up to date; you should update your antivirus software to the most current virus definitions prior to each complete scan. Do not turn your Antivirus software off unless you unplug your computer from the Internet and your network.

Windows Disk Defragmentation Utility

Fragmentation refers to any condition where data is not recorded in a logical continuous order. QuickBooks is subject to two different kinds of fragmentation—disk fragmentation and database fragmentation.

➡ *For more information on the latter, see "Database File Fragments," p. 569.*

An example of disk fragmentation would be when a QuickBooks invoice was recorded on your hard drive adjacent to a picture of your pets. Although it seems ridiculous to anyone who ever worked as a file clerk, this is the normal function of the Windows operating system.

Your QuickBooks company file can be fragmented on your computer's disk drive just like any of your other files. This occurs when the operating system cannot create, or insert new information into, the file in one logically contiguous space. Because the Windows operating system does not restrict the writing of data to only contiguous areas of your disk drive, as the total amount of data on your disk drive increases, fragmentation also increases.

Because of fragmentation, the hard drive's disk head must repeatedly move back and forth over the disk when reading and writing various parts of the file. The more the disk head must move from one area to another, the less efficient the disk drive is, lengthening the response time of QuickBooks trying to find your data.

To correct this type of fragmentation we must force our Windows computer to rewrite all of the parts of files to contiguous space on the hard drive. This is called defragmentation and QuickBooks users should routinely run the Disk Defragmentation tool included with Windows software. After running this tool, QuickBooks users should see an increase in the speed of file access and data retrieval.

If your disk drive is less than 10% full, run defragmentation three or four times per year. If your disk drive is running at 25% to 30% of capacity, perform a monthly defragmentation. If your disk drive is at 50% or more of capacity or you have a QuickBooks Company file in excess of 50MB, you might need to run defragmentation once a week.

CHAPTER

17

Defragmenting Your Windows 7 Computer

Choosing to defragment your computer can lead to a more responsive data file, providing quicker retrieval of data for reporting.

1. Click the Windows Orb or Start button in the lower-left corner of your screen.

2. Click All Programs.

3. Open the Accessories folder.

4. Open the Systems Tools folder.

5. Click Disk Defragmenter to open the utility displayed in Figure 17.6.

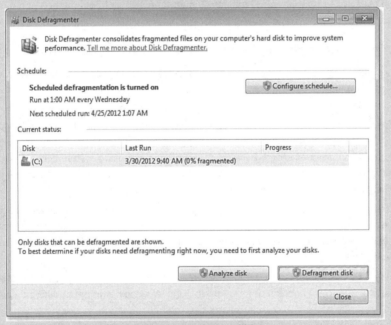

Figure 17.6
Run the defragmenter tool on your computer often.

6. Select the drive you want to defragment.

7. Click Analyze. A dialog box displays after the disk is analyzed, detailing if you need to perform the defragmentation.

8. To defragment the selected drive(s), click the Defragment Disk button. You can monitor the process in the Current status area (under the Progress column). After the process is complete, the results will be displayed.

9. To display more detailed information, click View Report.

10. To close the Disk Defragmenter, click Close.

Using Intuit Data Protect Online Backup Service

Intuit Data Protect is a subscription service that will automatically back up your company file(s) and optionally other important files from your computer. When you use Intuit Data Protect as your backup method all your data needed to restore your company file is saved to Intuit's secure server. The backup files created by Intuit Data Protect are stored for 45 days enabling you to not only restore the most recent backup but any prior backup during the last 45 days.

Once you have set up your Intuit Data Protect subscription you do not need to establish a backup schedule or perform manual backups. Intuit Data Protect will perform a once-a-day backup of every QuickBooks file you have configured for backup. This is unlike the manual backups, which should be done when no one is working in the file. The Intuit Data Protect backups run in the background enabling you to continue working normally in QuickBooks. If a scheduled backup is missed because your computer is off, or can't access the Internet, Intuit Data Protect will start a backup as soon as your computer is turned back on or Internet service becomes available.

To restore a backup made using the Intuit Data Protect Backup service, follow these steps:

1. From the QuickBooks Home page, open the Backup Status section in the lower-right corner and click View Details.

2. From the Backup Status dialog box, click Restore a Backup.

3. Select the Date and Time of the backup, and then select the File you want to restore, and click Continue.

4. Select the location where you want your file restored to, and click Restore.

5. Intuit Data Protect begins the process of restoring your file(s) to the designated location. This process can take a substantial period of time depending on the size and number of files you are restoring. Do not attempt to close either Intuit Data Protect or QuickBooks during the restore process.

Upon completion, Data Protect will display a message indicating that the restore completed.

Monitoring Your QuickBooks Database

Because QuickBooks is comprised of a series of tables that store your accounting records, it is important to monitor your data file from time to time to ensure your data has integrity and is of a proper size and configuration. There are a couple of methods in QuickBooks to monitor the database, including the Product Information dialog box and the Verify Data utility.

The Product Information Dialog Box

The Product Information dialog box provides valuable information about the health of your QuickBooks file. From an open QuickBooks file, press Ctrl+1 key or F2 on your keyboard. The Product Information dialog box provides a wealth of information including version, product license number, versions used, and much more. See Figure 17.7.

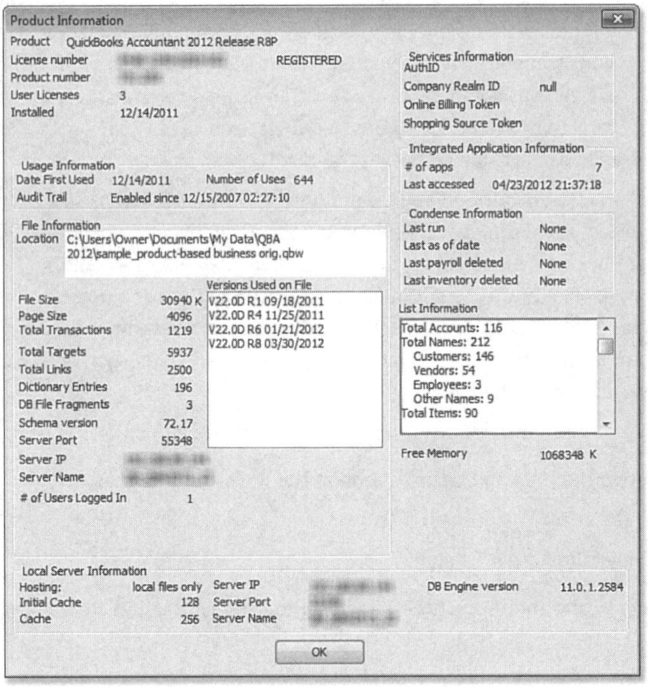

Figure 17.7
With QuickBooks open, press the F2 key on your keyboard to view useful information about the file.

File Size

In Figure 17.7, about halfway down the left side is a section that provides data about the File Size, Total Transactions, Total Targets, Total Links, and DB File Fragments. This information can help you judge if your data file is becoming too large for efficient processing of transactions and reports.

Many experts debate over the maximum file size of QuickBooks data and Intuit has not published any formal guidelines regarding file size limits. To calculate the anticipated growth of a data file:

1. Take the number of transactions each month times 2KB to get the monthly growth rate.

2. Take that amount times 12 for the annual KB growth per year.

3. Then divide that amount by 1024 for the number of MB per year.

Typically the file should grow by 30MB per year or less for Pro or Premier and 50MB per year or less for Enterprise to maintain reasonable performance. New condense features are available in the QuickBooks Accountant editions that can help in removing data from prior years, contact your

> **note**
>
> If you would like more information about QuickBooks file size restrictions, from the QuickBooks support site (http://support.quickbooks.intuit.com), search for Knowledge Base article INF12412.
>
> If you find your data file is becoming sluggish, you might consider starting a new data file or find companies listed on www.marketplace.intuit.com that will "shrink" your current file.

accounting professional for this service. Obviously, the age and processing speed of the computer with other factors might also affect the software's performance.

Factors such as the number of lines of detail for each transaction significantly increase the number of links per transaction—this factor alone can greatly impact the size of the database. Based on personal experience, QuickBooks Pro or Premier data file in excess of 200 MB or QuickBooks Enterprise files in excess of 450 MB might experience sluggish performance. QuickBooks file performance is impacted by so many variables; it is not possible to name specifics.

Database File Fragments

As mentioned earlier, file fragmentation can negatively affect the performance of QuickBooks. Because file fragmentation is a normal part of using Windows, we must assume some fragmentation is also normal. So the question becomes how many file fragments is too many? Some experts say more than 10 fragments is too many, others say 20, and still others say 50.

As a general rule, if the file is performing without issue and file fragments are fewer than 50 you need not be alarmed; however anytime your file exceeds 50 fragments it is time to reduce fragmentation.

 For more information, see "Reducing Database File Fragments," p. 575.

QuickBooks List Limitations

As shown previously in Figure 17.7, the Product Information dialog box includes the List Information section. This section includes the size of the various QuickBooks lists (both active and inactive entries), and is another important database statistic to monitor. QuickBooks lists have been preconfigured to limit the number of entries the database can support.

One of the most significant limitations deals with the number of names you can have in QuickBooks Pro or Premier—the combined limit of customers, employees, vendors, and other names is 14,500. QuickBooks does not permit you to delete any names that have been used in a transaction, and the list limits include both active and inactive entries. This list size restriction can be a serious limitation to a growing business. According to Intuit, QuickBooks Enterprise can support up to 1 million combined names although they note some performance degradation is likely as you approach this upper limit.

Similar list limits exist for the Items list—14,500 in Pro or Premier and 100,000 from a functional standpoint for Enterprise. Most other lists in QuickBooks Pro, Premier, or Enterprise are limited to 10,000 entries. One noted exception is the Price Levels list, which is limited to 100 entries in Pro and Premier and 750 entries in Enterprise.

Using the Verify Data Utility

Although the Verify Data utility can detect many forms of data corruption as well as test the integrity of the database, it also can be used to monitor the health of your Company file. Select this option when creating a backup of your QuickBooks Company file.

Additionally, if you use an external backup, or Intuit Data Protect, then run the Verify Data utility periodically to check the integrity of your Company file.

 caution

When running the Verify Data Utility, if QuickBooks shows the message Not Responding while the utility is running, do not attempt to close QuickBooks. Allow the utility to complete before closing.

To Run the Verify Data Utility

To check the health of your QuickBooks data file, follow these steps for using the Verify Data Utility:

1. Close all open windows within QuickBooks.

2. From the menu bar, select File, Switch to Single-User Mode. If this option is not displayed, then you are currently using the file in Single-user Mode.

3. From the menu bar, select File, Utilities, Verify Data.

QuickBooks will then begin to verify your data. The technical results are reported in the QBWin. log file. For more information, see "The QBWin.log File," p. 571. If no data integrity issues were detected, QuickBooks will display the prompt shown in Figure 17.8.

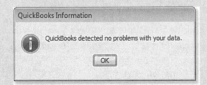

Figure 17.8
Message when the Verify Data utility detected no problems with the file.

The length of time the process will take will depend on the size of your Company file.

QuickBooks Database Corruption

On occasion, your QuickBooks Company file can become corrupted. Database corruption is any damage to a database that impacts its integrity or functionality.

Common Causes of Corruption

Database corruption can result from improper shut down of QuickBooks, as well as power issues (surges, spikes, and outages). It can also occur as a result of a fatal application (program) error. System hardware such as bad disk drives or raid controllers can corrupt data. Your operating system can produce QuickBooks data fragmentation.

In a multi-user environment, networking components (like wireless routers) might produce corruption because their failure can break the connection between the Application and Database Server.

A large QuickBooks file size does not necessarily cause data corruption, although there is more data in which corruptions can occur. Larger files will also have more fragmentation and performance issues if your hardware is not meeting the reported minimum requirements.

For more information, see the section in this chapter titled "System Requirements."

Signs of Data Corruption

QuickBooks might report data corruption by displaying specific problem messages or error codes.

Often the first sign of data corruption does not appear until a QuickBooks user sees an accounting transaction irregularity. For example—when an out-of-balance balance sheet or accounts receivables or payables sub-ledger report doesn't reconcile to the general ledger.

If you run the Verify Data utility and your Company file has lost integrity QuickBooks will display a warning such as the one shown in Figure 17.9, indicating you should run the Rebuild Data utility. In addition to the displayed message, additional information is provided in the QBWin.log file.

Figure 17.9
Some database corruption errors require using the Rebuild Data Utility.

The QBWin.log File

If the Verify Data utility detected an error in your data, you might want to get more information about the specific problem(s) within your data. QuickBooks records operational data, including information related to the Verify Data and Rebuild Data utilities within a log file called the QBWin.log.

To view the QBWin.log file, follow these steps:

1. With your QuickBooks Company file open, press the F2 key (or Ctrl+1) to display the Product Information dialog box.

2. Now press the F3 key (or Ctrl+2) to display the Tech Help dialog box.

3. Select the Open File tab.

4. Scroll down the list and click QBWIN.LOG file, and then click Open File. The file will open in Windows Notepad (see Figure 17.10).

5. The Verify Data section should be near the bottom of the log so scroll to the bottom and then scroll back up until you find the Verify portion of the log file, which will begin with:

   = = = = = = = = = = = * BEGIN VERIFY LOG * = = = = =

   The QBWIN.LOG file will end with:

   = = = = = = = = = == = = * END VERIFY LOG * = = = = = =

You can scroll through the log file to view errors detected with the file. I recommend you contact Intuit technical support or a local QuickBooks professional for reading and correcting any errors listed.

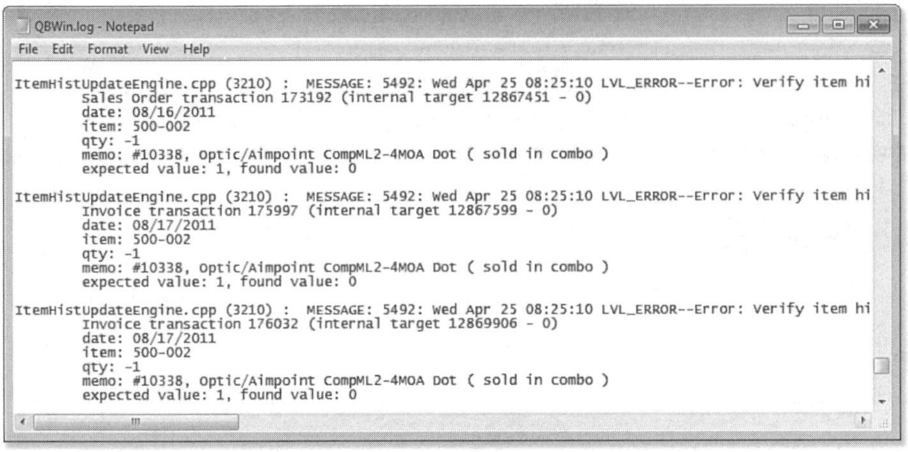

Figure 17.10
Review the QBWIN.log to determine errors that might be causing the error messages.

The QBWin.log is a snapshot of technical details during the current session of QuickBooks. It contains information about how the program performed when it was started, if it successfully connected with your Company file, and any errors experienced during operations or while performing the verify/rebuild utilities. There are many different messages that might be contained in your QBWin.log; some might represent minor errors and others might represent more severe forms of database corruption. The QuickBooks Support website contains many knowledge-based articles that correspond to the various errors. A few common error messages and possible solutions have been included in this section.

You might want to complete a rebuild of the company file after performing the suggested repairs.

➡ *For more information, see "Rebuilding Your Company File," p. 576.*

Error: Verify Memorized Report List...

A corrupted Memorized Report is usually associated with this error. QuickBooks will normally repair this problem if you re-sort the Memorized Report List followed by running the Rebuild Data Utility. To do so, follow these steps:

1. From the menu bar, select Reports, Memorized Reports, Memorized Report List.

2. From the Memorized Report drop-down list, select Re-sort list.

3. Click OK to the Re-sort prompt.

Error: Verify Names List (Such As Customers)...

This form of corruption occurs when one of the names lists has a database index error. Try resorting the Names List followed by running the Rebuild Data Utility to resolve this type of error.

To access the Names List, follow these steps while logged into the file in single-user mode:

1. From the menu bar, select Banking, Write Checks.

2. Place your cursor in the Pay to the Order of field.

3. On your keyboard, press Ctrl+L.

4. The Name List displays. From the Name drop-down list, select Re-sort List.

5. In the Re-sort List? message, click OK.

Error: Verify Name (Specific List): Duplicate Name Encountered...

QuickBooks might encounter a duplicate name. This might occur if you import data using the iif (Intuit Interchange Format) import file type or you use a third party application. Frequently one name might be marked as inactive or QuickBooks might have inserted an * (asterisk) in front of the duplicate name.

To locate the duplicate names and merge them together, follow these steps:

1. Find the names that are duplicated.

2. Edit one of the names to first change it to be unique; if QuickBooks has inserted an asterisk (*) remove that character from the name as part of this change. Save the new name.

3. Return to the name you just changed and edit it once again to change it to be identical to its duplicate, then click Save.

4. QuickBooks displays the Merge dialog box, as shown in Figure 17.11. Confirm the merge of both names by clicking Yes.

Figure 17.11
Certain lists in QuickBooks will let you merge duplicated names.

5. Run the Rebuild Data utility.

Error: Verify Target: Transaction Out of Balance...

This error usually results when the target record, (such as the check detail lines), do not equal the amount of the source record (such as the check total).

To correct this type of error, follow these steps:

1. Open the transaction identified in the QBWin.log report.

2. Verify if the amount in the header (such as check amount) is identical to the total of the amounts in the detail lines. If these amounts are different, you need to correct the erroneous amount(s).

3. Save the corrected transaction.

4. Run the Rebuild Data utility.

Error: Verify Target: Invalid Open Quantity...

This error can result when the link between an Estimate and Sales Order and its associated Invoice (for partial quantities) is broken.

To relink the transactions, follow these steps:

1. Open the transaction, reported in the QBWin.log.

2. Adding a "." (period) to an empty detail line of the transaction will not change any values for the transaction. However, doing so can help 're-link' the source and target transactions.

3. Save the transaction.

4. Run the Rebuild Data utility.

 *For more information, see "Rebuilding Your Company File," p. 576.*

Repairing List Corruptions

Several of the symptoms associated with data corruption, and QBWin.log messages detailed previously, involve problems with the various QuickBooks lists. For many lists you can resort the list simply by opening the list and clicking on the list's menu button located at the bottom of the list (such as Items). Prior to actually resorting the list, check the box labeled Include Inactive (if available) and select the option to change the list view from Hierarchical to Flat (not all lists offer a hierarchical view).

One of the major lists in QuickBooks is a hidden list called the Name List, which is a combined list of all the names (customers, employees, vendors, other names).

To sort all the name lists at once, follow these steps:

1. From the menu bar, select Banking, Write Checks.

2. Place your cursor in the Pay to the Order of field.

3. On your keyboard, press Ctrl+L.

4. The Name List displays. From the Name drop-down list, select Re-sort List.

5. In the Re-sort List? message, click OK.

Reducing Database File Fragments

The highly compressed QuickBooks Portable Company File can be useful in dealing with some forms of index corruption as well as fragmentation. When a Portable Company (*.QBM) File is restored QuickBooks re-creates all indexes associated with the database. In addition, the extreme level of compression applied when the file is produced eliminates file fragments. Therefore, creation and restoration of a Portable File might resolve many file-related issues.

To create and restore a Portable Company File:

1. From the menu bar, select File, Create Copy. The Save Copy or Backup dialog box displays as shown in Figure 17.12.

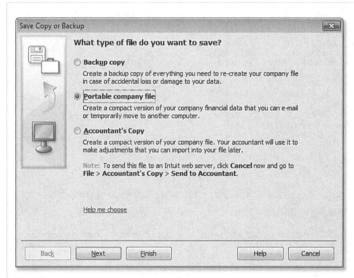

Figure 17.12
Create and restore a Portable Company File to help reduce database file fragments.

2. Choose Portable Company File and click Next.

3. Accept the default location and filename or select a location to save the file and type a desired name for the file.

🔺 **caution**
Always create a backup of your file before attempting this type of file restore.

4. A few individual progress messages will display; click OK on each of them.

5. Upon completion, QuickBooks displays an Information message indicating the file has been saved and details the designated location. Click OK.

6. To restore the Portable Company File, select File, Open or Restore Company from the menu bar.

7. Select Restore a Portable File and click Next.

8. Select the Portable Company File (ending in .QBM) you saved to the desktop (or your alternate location), and click Open.

9. In the Open or Restore Company dialog box, the Where Do You Want to Restore the File dialog displays. Review the message details regarding overwriting your current file and click Next as shown in Figure 17.13.

Figure 17.13
Review this information before restoring your Portable Company File.

10. Click Save and select a save location. Because you are intending to replace your current file, select your current file location and current filename.

11. Click Save. QuickBooks will replace your current file with the data restored from the QuickBooks Portable Company File.

Rebuilding Your Company File

The Rebuild Data utility can repair many QuickBooks Company file issues. The utility attempts to repair or update data found to be corrupted, which might include permanently deleting transactions or list entries that are damaged beyond repair or compromise overall integrity of the file.

Before running the rebuild utility, you should gather information for comparison after the rebuild is complete. This should include all summary reports including the Balance Sheet Standard and Profit & Loss Standard Report. You might also want to process additional reports such as those for payroll details or checkbook registers, and so on.

To use the QuickBooks Rebuild Data utility, follow these steps:

1. If you use your file in a multi-user install, you will need to log in to the file in single-user mode. From the menu bar, select File, Switch to Single User.

2. From the menu bar, select Utilities, Rebuild Data.

3. QuickBooks will display a warning message requiring a backup of the company file before actually starting the rebuild process. Follow the prompts to save a backup copy of your data.

4. When the backup is completed, the Rebuild Data utility will start. The time required to rebuild the database can vary depending on the size of your Company file. It is extremely important to permit the utility to finish completely.

5. QuickBooks will display a Rebuild Has Completed message. Click OK.

caution

Never rebuild a company file on a remote drive, or across a network. You should always copy the file to a local computer before running the Rebuild Data utility.

Close all unnecessary programs and turn off your windows screen saver and any power-saver functions before starting a rebuild.

After the Rebuild Data utility finishes, the data file might still have corrupted transactions, which the first pass of the rebuild did not correct. It might be necessary to rebuild your data more than once. As a general rule, if the utility will not resolve an issue in three or fewer passes, the database error cannot be fixed using the Rebuild Data utility.

Although severely damaged transactions are usually removed during the rebuild process, you might need to manually correct or delete other transactions that Rebuild Data could not correct, and then reenter them. Transactional data removed or corrected will be listed in the QBWin.log file along with corrupted transactions, which the Rebuild Data utility could not correct.

For severe cases of database integrity issues, you will want to contact Intuit's Technical Support.

Using the QuickBooks Company File Diagnostic Tool

The QuickBooks Company File tool helps to diagnose and repair several forms of damage that prevent company files from opening. The tool must be run on a corrupted QuickBooks file; you cannot run this tool across a network or a mapped drive.

Download this tool from the QuickBooks Technical Support website at http://support.quickbooks.intuit.com/support/Articles/HOW12723

To use the tool to diagnose and repair the type of file damage that prevents the file from opening normally, follow these steps:

1. Install the downloaded QuickBooks Company File Diagnostic Tool.

2. Click the installed icon to launch the tool. Figure 17.14 shows the dialog box that displays.

3. Click the Browse button to select the QuickBooks Company (*QBW) file that needs to be diagnosed and/or repaired.

4. Once you have located the corrupted company file, select it and click Open.

5. The main dialog box reopens; click the Diagnose/Repair button.

Click here for additional repair tools

Figure 17.14
Use this tool to Diagnose/Repair a QuickBooks Company file.

6. Enter the admin username and password for the company file and click Login.

7. Once you have logged into the file, the tool will begin the diagnosis and repair procedures. When the tool has finished the process, there are three possible outcomes:

   ■ The problem or error will be resolved and you should be able to open the QuickBooks file with full functionality restored.

   ■ Data damage continues to exist, which precludes QuickBooks from opening the file despite the diagnosis/repair procedures.

   ■ The tool detected no data damage that would preclude the file from opening.

8. If you receive a -6130, 0 error message, click the About link on the QuickBooks Company File Diagnostic Tool (see Figure 17.14).

9. In the About QuickBooks Company File Diagnostic Tool dialog box, select either the Force 6130 Fix or Force DataSync Fix check box, as shown in Figure 17.15.

10. Open the repaired Company (*QBW) file with QuickBooks and run the Verify Data and/or Rebuild Data utilities.

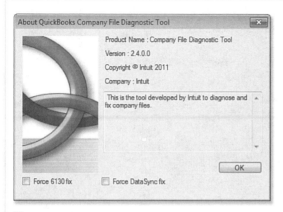

Figure 17.15
Additional tools available after selecting the Help link in the QuickBooks Company File Diagnostic Tool.

Resolving QuickBooks Program File Corruption Issues

Some corruption can be the result of problems with the QuickBooks program files. This can occur during installation if there is a conflict with some required component such as Microsoft .Net or even the Windows Registry. Generally, QuickBooks runs normally but at some point the program experiences fault errors or might not install an update properly. Usually, these problems can be resolved by repairing the QuickBooks installation.

To repair your QuickBooks program files, follow these steps:

1. From your Windows taskbar, click the Windows Orb or Start button, and select Control Panel.

2. In the Control Panel, double-click Programs.

3. In Programs select QuickBooks and choose Uninstall/Change.

4. Select Repair and click Next. QuickBooks will begin the repair, displaying a progress bar during the process.

5. When the repair is complete, click Finish.

The preceding procedure usually, not always, resolves file issues. In the event that it does not work, you will need to Uninstall QuickBooks and then reinstall it. Use the preceding steps to remove QuickBooks by selecting the uninstall options rather than repair.

USING OTHER PLANNING AND MANAGEMENT TOOLS

Planning and Budgeting

Like most business owners I have met, you probably know where your money will be spent each month yet you might not see the value in writing it down. There is an old saying that is very appropriate here: "When you fail to plan, you plan to fail." This saying couldn't be truer than when it comes to watching your business financials.

QuickBooks makes the task of creating and tracking a financial budget for your business easy. Just follow a few steps and in no time you can print useful reports that track actual financial performance and compare it to your original budget.

Create a Budget

The first step is to set up a budget. Follow these steps to begin using this feature in QuickBooks:

1. From the menu bar, select Company, Planning & Budgeting, Set Up Budgets. The Create a New Budget dialog box displays, as shown in Figure 18.1

 note

If you have previously created a budget, click the Create New Budget button in the Set Up Budgets dialog box (see Figure 18.4).

Figure 18.1
Create a Profit & Loss or Balance Sheet budget easily with QuickBooks.

2. Select the year you want to create the budget for.

3. Choose the budget type:

   ■ Profit and Loss

   ■ Balance Sheet

4. Click Next. Select from the following choices as shown in Figure 18.2:

   ■ **No Additional Criteria**—Simplest form of budgeting. I recommend you start with this choice.

   ■ **Customer:Job**—You can create a budget for your customers or jobs here, but a better method might be to use a QuickBooks estimate. For more information, see "Using QuickBooks Estimates," p. 290.

   ■ **Class**—If you are using classes (department tracking) then you might want to select the Class option. For more information on classes, see "Class," p. 86.

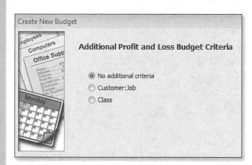

Figure 18.2
Choose the type of budget to create.

5. Click Next.

6. Choose how you want to create a budget from the choices displayed in Figure 18.3.

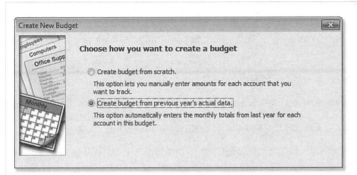

Figure 18.3
Choose from two methods for creating the new budget.

- **Create Budget from Scratch**—You will manually enter the estimated budget amounts. This method would take the most effort on your part.

- **Create a Budget from Previous Year's Actual Data**—I recommend starting with this option. The budget will be created using the prior year's data allowing you to modify the budgeted amounts as needed.

7. Click Finish. QuickBooks creates the new budget. In Figure 18.4, a new budget was created using actual revenue and expenses from the prior year.

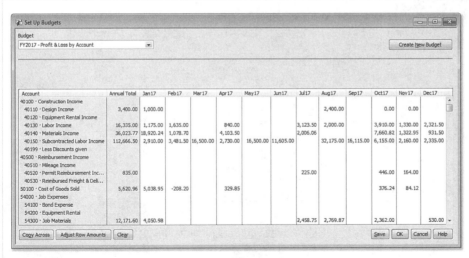

Figure 18.4
QuickBooks can create the budget quickly using actual information from the prior year.

Edit a Budget

Budgets can be edited at any time to accommodate changes in your business. Additionally, if you created the budget using last year's actual numbers, you can follow these steps to revise the budget information:

1. From the menu bar, select Company, Planning & Budgeting, Set Up Budgets. Your previously saved budget will display.

2. Optionally, click the drop-down list to select a different budget.

3. Optionally, click the Create New Budget and follow the steps listed in the previous section.

4. With your cursor, click in any cell to change the amount budgeted for that category and month.

5. Optionally, with your cursor in a specific cell, click Copy Across and QuickBooks will copy that amount to all the columns to the right of your current cursor position.

6. Optionally, with your cursor in a specific cell, click Adjust Row Amounts. You can choose to increase or decrease by a specific percentage or dollar amount. See Figure 18.5. Choose to update:

   - **1st Month**—Update budget amounts beginning with the first month in the year.

   - **Currently Selected Month**—Update budget amounts beginning with the currently selected month.

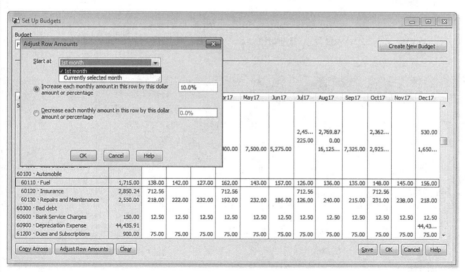

Figure 18.5
Use the Adjust Row Amounts dialog box to quickly change your budget amounts.

7. Click OK to close the Adjust Row Amounts dialog box. QuickBooks calculates new budget amounts depending on your selections in step 6.

8. Optionally, click Clear and answer Yes or No to the warning message about clearing this page of the budget.

9. Click Save to save your changes as you work.

10. To close the budget, click the X in the top right corner. You might be asked if you want to record your budget. Select Yes, No, or Cancel.

> ⚠ **caution**
>
> If you select Clear and then choose Yes, QuickBooks will remove all the budgeted amounts for the currently displayed budget.

Print Budget Reports

You now have a budget prepared. So let's see how your current year is progressing by viewing the budget reports included with QuickBooks. From the menu bar, select Reports, Budgets & Forecasts where you will find these reports:

- Budget Overview

- Budget vs. Actual

- Profit & Loss Budget Performance

- Budget vs. Actual Graph

- Forecast Overview

- Forecast vs. Actual

Figure 18.6 shows a Profit & Loss Budget vs. Actual report.

To display a budget report:

1. From the menu bar, select Reports, Budgets & Forecasts, and choose a report.

2. From the drop-down list, select the year's budget you want to review.

3. Click Next.

4. If the report offers multiple layout options, select the layout of your choice and click Next.

5. Click Finish to prepare the report.

You can also modify the information displayed on this report. Click Customize Report to modify these settings:

- Report Date Range

- Report Basis

- Columns and Rows

Optionally, click the Advanced button and choose to Display only Non-zero rows or columns. Also select the Show Only Rows and Columns with Budgets check box. See Figure 18.7.

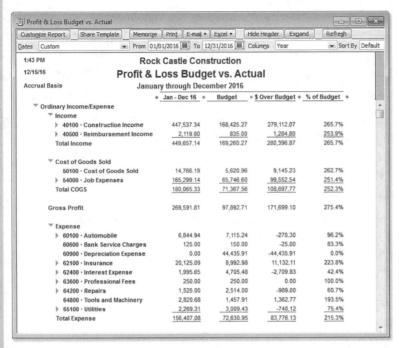

Figure 18.6
This report can be displayed for many different time periods, including day, month, and year.

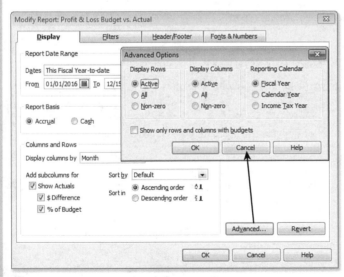

Figure 18.7
Modify the information displayed in the Budget vs. Actual report.

Delete a Budget

If you find it necessary to delete a budget and start over, follow these steps:

1. From the menu bar, select Company, Planning & Budgeting, Set Up Budgets. Your previously saved budget will display in the Set Up Budgets dialog box.

2. From the menu bar, select Edit, Delete Budget.

QuickBooks Loan Manager

Use the Loan Manager in QuickBooks to track loans you have created in QuickBooks. The Loan Manager helps you track all of your loans in one convenient location.

With the Loan Manager you can:

- View payment schedules

- Set up loan payments

- Analyze different loan payoff scenarios

Information to Collect

Before adding a loan to the Loan Manager you should have the following information about your loans available. This information is usually included on your original finance documents:

- Origination Date

- Payment Amount

- Payment Term

- Escrow Amount (if any)

- Interest Rate

Getting QuickBooks Ready

Before setting up a loan in the Loan Manger in QuickBooks, you will want to setup the following:

- **Create a Loan Payable Account**—Usually a long-term liability account. This account will display the balance owed on the loan.

- **Create an Expense Account**—To record the interest paid on the loan.

- **Optionally, Create an Escrow Account**—If required for your specific loan-tracking needs.

- **Create a Vendor Record**—This is for the loan payee.

If you have previously been using these QuickBooks accounts, make sure the balances in these accounts are up to date and agree with your lending institutions balances for the loan. Most businesses use a single interest expense account for all loans.

Setting Up a New Loan

To use QuickBooks to track your loan payment, follow these steps:

1. From the menu bar, select Banking, Loan Manager.

2. Click Add A Loan and complete the information as displayed in Figure 18.8.

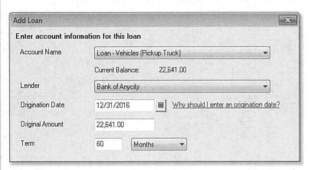

Figure 18.8
Complete the account information for the loan.

3. From the Account Name drop-down list, select the long-term liability account for the loan.

4. From the Lender drop-down list, select the payee.

5. Enter the loan Origination Date.

6. From the Terms drop-down list, select Weeks, Months, or Years. Click Next.

7. Enter the dates for Due Date of Next Payment, Payment Amount and optionally, Next Payment.

8. Select the Payment Period.

9. Optionally, select Yes or No to making an escrow payment and complete the fields for Escrow Payment Amount and Escrow Payment Account.

10. Optionally, select the box to be alerted 10 days before the payment is due. Click Next.

11. Enter the Interest Rate and select a Compounding Period.

12. Select a bank account from the Payment Account drop-down list.

13. Select the Interest Expense Account and the account for Fees and Charges.

 caution

As of the publication of this book, QuickBooks Loan Manager is not compatible with Internet Explorer 9. If that is your preferred browser, QuickBooks will display details about how to use Loan Manager with this browser.

14. Click Finish. QuickBooks displays information in the Loan Manager about the newly created loan. See Figure 18.9.

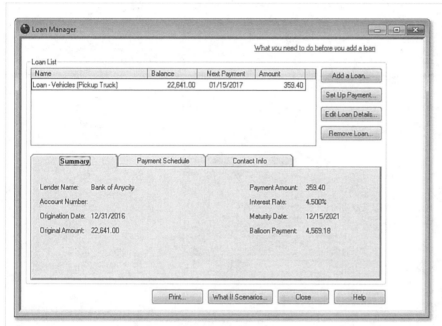

Figure 18.9
Use the Loan Manager to track long-term loan details.

Setting Up a Loan Payment

To set up a payment for the loan, follow these steps:

1. Select the loan from the list and click the Set Up Payment button. The Set Up Payment dialog box displays as shown in Figure 18.10.

2. From the This Payment Is drop-down list, select one of the following options: A Regular Payment or An Extra Payment.

3. View the Account Information and Payment Information. Modify the Payment Information if necessary.

4. Select a Payment Method of Write a Check or Enter a Bill.

5. Click OK and QuickBooks prepares a check or bill with the correct payment information.

CHAPTER

590 | Using Other Planning and Management Tools

18

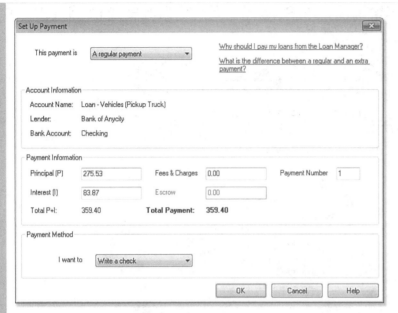

Figure 18.10
The Loan Manager can create the payment for the loan.

Additionally from the Loan Manager you can do the following:

- Edit the loan details or remove the loan

- View summary information about the loan

- View the payment schedule by payment number

- Access contact information for the vendor, as set up with the original vendor record

- Print the details of the loan

- View multiple What If Scenarios as shown in Figure 18.11

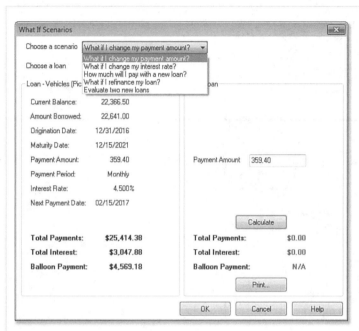

Figure 18.11
Use the QuickBooks Loan Manager to analyze different loan payoff scenarios.

Using the Year-End Guide

QuickBooks offers a ready-made Year End-Guide and checklist to help with your year-end tasks, as shown in Figure 18.12. Keep track of your progress as you get your file ready for your accountant or for tax time.

From the menu bar, select Help, Year-End Guide. Each task offers a link to more detailed help information. Optionally, click the Save Checkmarks button so you can keep track of completed tasks.

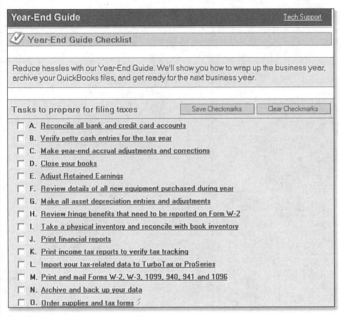

Figure 18.12
Use the Year-End Guide to help prepare your file for tax time.

Synchronizing QuickBooks Lists with Microsoft Outlook

If you use Microsoft Outlook to manage contact information, you can synchronize your contact data with QuickBooks. The information that can be synchronized includes:

- Customer and Job contact information

- Vendor contact information

- Other Names list contact information

To begin synchronizing your QuickBooks lists with Microsoft Outlook, follow these steps:

1. Before proceeding with this task, make sure you have a backup of your QuickBooks data and your Outlook contacts.

2. If you have not previously installed the free Contact Sync tool, from the menu bar, select File, Utilities, Synchronize Contacts. The Synchronize Contacts message displays. Select OK to be directed to the website (Internet connection required) to download the tool. Follow the download instructions.

note

If you delete a contact in Outlook, that name will not be deleted in QuickBooks.

note

If you need help backing up your Outlook Contacts, from the QuickBooks Help search box on the icon bar, type **"backing up Outlook data"** and select to search Help. Follow the appropriate links for more detailed information.

3. If you have previously installed the Contact Sync tool, you will be prompted to synchronize your contacts.

4. Click the file that was downloaded and follow the instructions to install. You will need to close Outlook before proceeding with the install.

5. After installing, open Outlook. The Contact Sync Setup Assistant displays. See Figure 18.13.

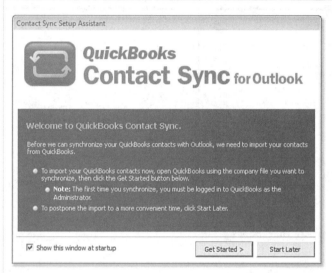

Figure 18.13
Setup of the QuickBooks Contact Sync is easy with step-by-step instructions.

6. Click Get Started and review the Begin Setup information. Click Setup.

7. QuickBooks Contact Sync displays the available Outlook folder. If more than one is detected, select the appropriate folder. Click Next.

8. Select from Customer, Jobs, and Vendors to Synchronize. Click Next.

9. Optionally, select to exclude from synchronization Outlook contacts marked as "Personal" or "Private" in Outlook. Click Next.

10. Review the defaults in the Mapping Fields window, as shown in Figure 18.14. Modify as needed or select Restore Defaults. Click Next.

11. If you selected to import Jobs and Vendors, complete the same information as detailed in step 10. Click Next.

 tip

If you want to have your QuickBooks contacts in a unique folder separate from your other contacts, create the new contact folder in Outlook and select the folder in step 7.

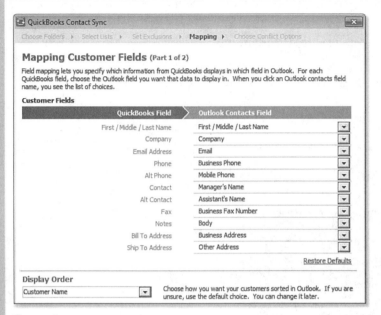

Figure 18.14
Modify the default mapping of fields from Outlook to QuickBooks.

12. Set an option for resolving any conflicts. Choices include:

- Let Me Decide Each Case

- Outlook Data Wins

- QuickBooks Data Wins

13. Click Save. Click Sync Now.

14. QuickBooks displays a Contact Overview Complete. If you selected the Let Me Decide Each Case in step 12, click Next to review the list of contacts to be imported.

15. Click to Accept the changes (see Figure 18.15) and import the contacts. QuickBooks displays a progress bar.

16. Click Accept. QuickBooks displays a Synchronization Complete Message, click OK to close.

17. You can now view your contacts in Outlook, or your Outlook contacts in QuickBooks. See Figure 18.16.

In Outlook you now have a QuickBooks Add-Ins (Outlook 2010) or a QuickBooks Toolbar (Outlook 2007 and earlier). From the Add-Ins you can change your synchronizing settings or Synchronize Contacts.

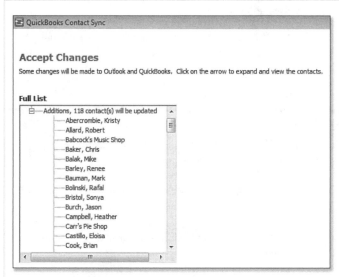

Figure 18.15
Review the contacts to be imported, if you selected the option in step 12 to Let Me Decide Each Case.

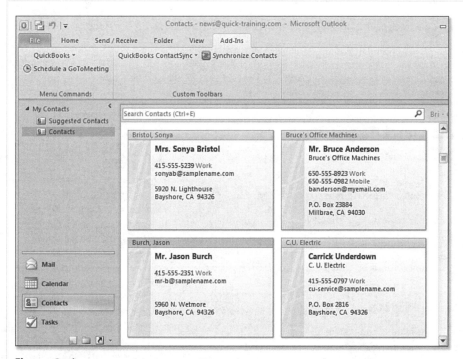

Figure 18.16
QuickBooks and Outlook will update with changes to contact details.

Using the QuickBooks Timer

The QuickBooks Timer is a separate program that can run on its own without QuickBooks. Time recorded with the QuickBooks Timer can be added to customer invoices when you do Timer and Expense billing.

➡ *For more information, see "Time and Expense Invoicing," p. 303.*

Features of the QuickBooks Timer include:

■ Track time spent on a task using a clock timer, or enter the time after you have done the work.

■ Track time without having access to the QuickBooks data.

■ Give a copy of the QuickBooks Timer program to people whom you want to track time such as employees or subcontractors.

The basic workflow for using the QuickBooks Timer requires some manual processes so be sure it is the right solution for you. The process includes the following four steps:

1. Once installed, the administrator of the QuickBooks file exports the current list of Service Items, Customers and Jobs, Vendors, and Employees.

2. The time keepers receive this file via email or on a removable storage device like a USB. The lists are imported into each individual QuickBooks timer file.

3. The time keepers track their time and then when completed export the time to a file.

4. The QuickBooks file administrator receives the file(s) and imports the time.

Each time the customers, jobs, vendor, employees, or service list items change a new export file must be sent and imported by each time keeper.

Installing the QuickBooks Timer

The QuickBooks Timer install file is located on the program CD-ROM. To install it, follow these steps:

1. Insert the QuickBooks CD-ROM into the computer.

2. Exit the QuickBooks startup if it displays.

3. Click the Microsoft Windows Start button and select Run.

4. Enter **D:\QBTimer** (where D:\ is your CD-ROM drive). Click OK.

5. Double-click the Setup file.

6. Follow the Timer installation instructions.

You can create a CD-ROM with the same install file and provide this CD to other time keepers who might or might not have access to QuickBooks.

 note

You can also download the program from the Intuit support website (http://support.quick-books.intuit.com) if you did not install your QuickBooks software from a CD-ROM. On the support website type **"QuickBooks Timer"** in the search box. Scroll and click the link for Install the QuickBooks Timer instructions. Included in the instructions is a link to download the file. Click the setup.exe file to being installing.

Preparing the Timer for Activities

Before time keepers can track their time you need to import the QuickBooks Timer Lists. To do so, follow these steps:

1. Launch the QuickBooks Timer. If you just recently installed the timer, you can launch it by clicking the Start button in Windows, All Programs, QuickBooks Timer, QuickBooks Pro Timer.

2. The No Timer File Is Open dialog box opens. Click Create New Timer File and click OK.

3. Type a name for the file (I use the QuickBooks company name) and select the proposed location for the file, or browse to a location of your choice. Click Save.

4. Click Yes, after reading the message about importing lists from QuickBooks.

5. The QuickBooks Timer help instructions display. Read the information or click the X in the top-right corner to close.

6. From your open QuickBooks file, select File, Utilities, Export, Timer Lists from the menu bar.

7. The Export Lists for Timer displays. Click OK.

8. QuickBooks opens a default location for the Timer Lists to be stored. This file will need to be updated as new customers, jobs, time keepers, an so on. are added to the file.

9. Provide a name for the file. Click Save. Click OK to the message that the data was exported successfully.

10. Launch the QuickBooks Timer as instructed in step 1.

11. From the File menu in QuickBooks Timer, select Import QuickBooks Lists.

12. Click Continue. Select the .IIF file to import, or browse to the location you stored the file in step 9. Click Open.

13. Click OK to close the Data Imported Successfully message.

You are now ready to begin tracking time with the QuickBooks Timer.

Tracking Time with the Timer

Time keepers can track time using the QuickBooks Timer even if they do not have access to the QuickBooks data file. However, to be current with the list of customers, jobs, or service items, the QuickBooks Administrator should frequently export the lists as detailed in the previous section.

To begin tracking time using the QuickBooks Timer, follow these steps:

1. Launch the QuickBooks Timer. If you just recently installed the timer, you can launch it by clicking the Start button in Windows, All Programs, QuickBooks Timer, QuickBooks Pro Timer.

 tip

Time format can be in decimal (10.20) or minutes (10:12). Log into the QuickBooks data as the Admin user and then from the menu bar, select Edit, Preferences, General, Company Preferences tab.

2. Click New Activity on the QuickBooks Pro Timer window.

3. Select the Date, Your Name (time keeper), Customer:Job, Service Item, optionally Class, and enter an optional Note as displayed in Figure 18.17.

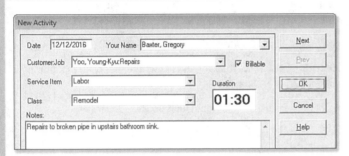

Figure 18.17
Enter your time after the service is performed, or click OK to start a "stop-watch" type of timer for the activity.

4. Optionally, select Billable if this item will be included on a customer's invoice.

5. Click OK. The Timer shows the current activity. Click Start.

6. The QuickBooks Timer now begins a "stop-watch" type of timer (see Figure 18.18). If instead you are entering your time after the service is performed, enter the time in the Duration field discussed in step 3.

Figure 18.18
You can choose to use a stop-watch timer to track activities.

7. Click Edit at any time you need to change the time recorded.

8. Click Stop to stop the timer and Resume to begin timing again.

9. Click Stop when you are done with the selected task.

Exporting Timer Activities

If you are not entering your time directly into the QuickBooks file, the file administrator will need you to export your timer activities so that they can be imported into the QuickBooks file. When you are instructed by the QuickBooks administrator to export the Timer activities, follow these steps:

1. From the QuickBooks Timer file menu, select Export Time Activities. Click Continue.

2. Select the date you will be exporting activities through. Click OK.

3. Accept the default location for storing the exported lists, or browse to select a location of your choosing. The file will have the extension of .IIF (Intuit Interchange Format). Remember this location, you will need to attach this file to an email or copy to a removable storage device such as a USB flash drive. Click Save.

4. Click OK to close the Data Exported Successfully message.

Each time keeper will need to provide this saved file to the QuickBooks administrator for importing into the QuickBooks file.

Importing Timer Activities into QuickBooks

One of the features of using this free timer program is that the user does not need to have QuickBooks installed.

When you want the timer activities included in your QuickBooks data file, you need to import the Exported Timer Activities. Ask each of your time keepers to follow the instructions listed previously for exporting their timer activities.

To import the Timer Activities received from your time keepers, follow these steps:

1. Receive your time keepers' individual QuickBooks Timer Exported Lists files. They will have an extension of .IIF (Intuit Interchange Format).

2. Launch QuickBooks. From the menu bar, select File, Utilities, Import, Timer Activities.

3. Click OK to the Import Activities from Timer message.

4. Browse to the location where you stored the Exported Timer Activities from your time keepers.

5. Select the file. Click Open. QuickBooks displays the QB Pro Timer Import Summary. Click View Report (see Figure 18.19) to see a listing of the time activities imported. See Figure 18.20.

 note

The next time you import timer activities, QuickBooks will remember where the lists were stored.

Figure 18.19
View a summary of the imported timer activities.

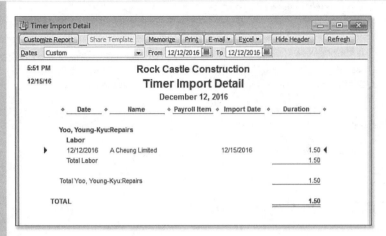

Figure 18.20
Details of the imported activities.

You can now include these imported timer activities on customer invoices, or issue vendor checks or employee checks using the timer activity totals. For more information on each these tasks, see the respective chapters in this book.

CLIENT DATA REVIEW

Introduction: Features and Benefits

Available with QuickBooks Accountant 2012 is the Client Data Review (CDR) feature, shown in Figure A.1. Accessing CDR tools and features is easier than ever with the new, customizable Accountant's Center. CDR is a collection of tools and reports used primarily by accounting professionals to streamline the many tasks involved in reviewing, troubleshooting, and correcting a client's QuickBooks data.

The CDR feature is available with QuickBooks Accountant 2012 and QuickBooks Enterprise Solutions Accountant 12.0. The CDR feature is not available for use with QuickBooks Online or QuickBooks for Mac.

With QuickBooks Accountant software, all of the features of CDR will work with a QuickBooks Accountant's Copy of your client's file. See Chapter 16, "Sharing Data with Your Accountant."

CDR can be used when working with a client's Accountant's Copy file type (.QBX file extension). Some feature limitations apply when working in an Accountant's Copy file-sharing type. Refer to Chapter 16 for more details on the benefits of working with this file type.

Typically, a best practice workflow using CDR tools is as follows:

1. Review with the client open Accounts Receivable, Accounts Payable, and other balances for which the client has current information.

2. Review your client's data file using the CDR-specific tasks and reports.

3. Make data corrections using CDR tools and set a QuickBooks closing date.

4. If completing a formal review, click Mark Review Complete, letting CDR "store" your period reviewed balances. (The client cannot change these reviewed balances!)

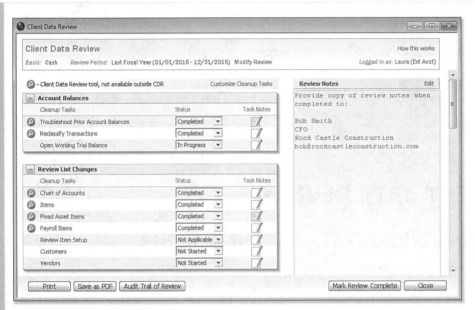

Figure A.1
Client Data Review (CDR) is helpful for finding and fixing your client's QuickBooks data entry errors.

5. Click Save as PDF to save the details of the review.

6. Print the details from the Client Data Review dialog box, Save the details as a PDF. You can also print an Audit Trail of Review, listing those transactions that were added or modified.

7. Begin your next review and let QuickBooks detail for you any and all changes to balances, transactions, and lists since your last completed review!

Your steps might differ slightly if you are working in a client's Accountants Copy file type. For more information on sharing data with your accountant using the Accountant's Copy, see Chapter 16.

There are specific tasks and reports that are available only with CDR. These tasks are indicated with the CDR icon. For example, see the icon next to the Troubleshoot Prior Account Balances task, as shown in Figure A.1. Other tasks listed without the icon indicate a feature or report that is available within and outside of the CDR functionality.

CDR offers robust tracking of the changes your client makes to the data between your reviews. CDR also offers the following:

> **tip**
>
> In QuickBooks 2012, CDR features can be used when QuickBooks is in multi-user mode. This means other users in the QuickBooks file can continue with their daily tasks while the accounting professional uses the CDR tools or features to review or make changes to the client's file.
>
> However, only one user can access Client Data Review at a time.

- Powerful time-saving tools for finding and fixing client entry errors: Reclassify Transactions, Write-Off Invoices, Fix Incorrectly Recorded Sales Tax, Inventory Troubleshooting, Identify Changes to Lists, Troubleshoot Beginning Balance Differences, Match Unapplied Vendor and Customer Credits, and Clear Up Undeposited Funds.

- Troubleshooting beginning balances "saves" the previously reviewed debit and credit balances; the tool then compares this stored balance to the same prior-dated balances in QuickBooks as of today. Your previously reviewed and stored QuickBooks balances cannot be modified by the client!

- QuickBooks suggests an adjusting journal entry to make so your prior-period reviewed balances agree with the current QuickBooks data for that period. You remain in control, deciding if you want to modify the detail in the journal entry.

- Identify what chart of accounts balances differ and the amount of the difference when compared to your prior period of reviewed financials.

- Track changes to the items lists, such as additions, name changes, and even tracking accounts or list items that were merged.

- Track changes made to list items, accounts assigned, or for payroll items when a change to a payroll tax rate is made.

- Working with the Open Windows dialog box? CDR displays in the Open Windows dialog box enabling you to move efficiently between activities in QuickBooks and the CDR activities.

- Conveniently work on CDR in QuickBooks and modify or add transactions as normal with an immediate refresh of the data in your review.

- Access the CDR while working in a client's Accountant's Copy file-sharing format. All CDR tools and features work with an Accountant's Copy. There are other restrictions when working with an Accountant's Copy and these are detailed in Chapter 16.

If you are an accounting professional and want to work most efficiently with your client's file, use QuickBooks Accountant 2012 or QuickBooks Enterprise Solutions Accountant 12.0.

 tip

As an accounting professional, would you like to "try" CDR even if you don't have the Accountant's edition of QuickBooks? Simply have your client create a user for you in her file and assign the External Accountant user type. For more information, see "Creating an External Accountant User Type," p. 538.

When you log into the client's Pro or Premier 2012 or Enterprise 12.0 data file as an External Accountant user, you will have access to the Accountant Center (which either opens automatically or you can access it from the Company menu). Although this Accountant Center is not customizable, you will have *limited* access to some of the features found only in QuickBooks Accountant software and selected CDR tools including:

- Create a Working Trial Balance
- Reclassify Transactions
- Fix Unapplied Payments and Credits
- Write Off Invoices

In addition, your Accountant Center provides easy access to other common QuickBooks tasks, memorized reports, reconciliation details, and updates especially for the accounting professional.

Accessing Client Data Review Tools and Features

New for QuickBooks Accountant 2012, accounting professionals can access common CDR tools and features in the software multiple ways including:

- **Accountant Center**—*New* for QuickBooks 2012, can be customized to include the tools you use most with your client's files

- **Accountant Menu**—Individual CDR tools and features without starting a review

- **Accountant Menu**—Launching a review with CDR

Before beginning to use CDR, determine if you need to do a formal review or just efficiently work on troubleshooting and fixing client data entry errors.

> **tip**
>
> You can use many of the CDR tools without opening a review. The date range that will default when using CDR tools is your last fiscal year. However, with most of the tools you can change the date range manually if needed.

Most of the CDR tools or reports can be accessed from the Accountant menu or Accountant Center without starting a review. If your client has engaged you simply to clean up data entry errors, then you might not need to open a review to complete these common tasks:

- Reclassify Transactions

- Fix Unapplied Customer and Vendor Credits

- Clear Up Undeposited Funds Account

- Write Off Invoices

- Fix Incorrectly Recorded Sales Tax

- Compare Balance Sheet and Inventory Valuation

- Troubleshoot Inventory

- Find Incorrectly Paid Payroll Liabilities

However, if part of your engagement with the client includes using the following CDR tools (detailed later in this chapter), you will need to "Start Review" formally using CDR:

- Troubleshoot Prior Account Balances

- Review List Changes

If your client sends you an Accountant's Copy file for her data, you will be able to access the features available with CDR. The benefit of using the Accountant's Copy file is that your client can continue her day-to-day operations while you make changes to her data. The file is then sent back to the client to import your changes.

Chapter 16 discusses the benefits of using the Accountant's Copy file, a preferred data-sharing method if you need to use the CDR while your client continues day-to-day work in the file.

If your client sends you a QuickBooks 2012 backup file (.QBB extension) or portable company file (.QBM file extension), both of these files when restored will enable you to use the CDR, but your changes will not be able to be merged into the client's data file.

Customizing the *New* Accountant Center

For the accounting professional a great benefit of using the Accountant versions of QuickBooks 2012 or Enterprise 12.0 is the *new* Accountant Center as displayed in Figure A.2. The Accountant Center offers easy access to Client Data Review tools and other accountant features.

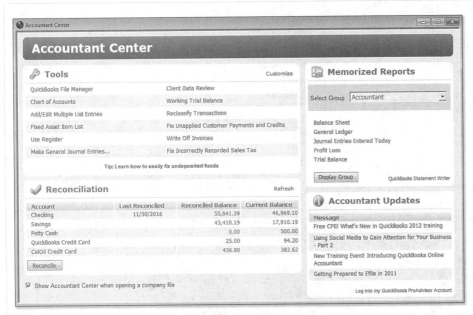

Figure A.2
Customize the Accountant Center to include those tools and features you use most when working with your client's data.

The Accountant Center can also be accessed from a client's 2012 Pro or Premier (non-accountant) and Enterprise 12.0 file when you, the accounting professional, log into the file as an External Accountant user.

By default a preference is set to have the Accountant Center open automatically. The Accountant Center can also be accessed from the Accountant menu. In a non-accountant edition of QuickBooks, you can log in as the External Accountant user type and access the Accountant Center from the Company menu.

tip

You only need to customize the Accountant Center once, and your customized view will display with each unique client file opened with your Accountant 2012 software. However, a shortcut won't appear on the Accountant Center if the feature it points to is not enabled in a particular client's file.

If you are using QuickBooks Accountant 2012 or Enterprise Accountant 12.0, practice customizing the Accountant Center with these instructions.

Customize the Accountant Center

Open the Accountant Center from the Accountant menu to customize the Tools section:

1. From the menu bar, select Accountant, Accountant Center.
2. Click the Customize link in the Tools panel of the Accountant Center. The Customize Your List of Tools dialog box displays. See Figure A.3.

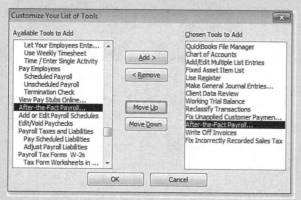

Figure A.3
Customize the New Accountant Center to include those tools you use most often.

3. From the Available Tools To Add list, select an action you want to add to the Chosen Tools to Add section and click the Add button.
4. Rearrange the order of the selected tools by selecting one in the Chosen Tools to Add list and then clicking the Move Up or Move Down button.
5. Optionally, to remove a tool, click the tool in the Chosen Tools to Add and then click the Remove button.
6. Click OK to close the Customize Your List of Tools dialog box and your changes will now be displayed in your very own Accountant Center.

The Accountant Center also provides easy access to Memorized Report Groups. You can learn about working with reporting in QuickBooks in Chapter 14, "Reporting in QuickBooks."

For accounting professionals, create your own memorized report group and access it from the Accountant Center when working with each client's file.

The Reconciliation panel includes timely information about your client's last reconciliation date—reconciled balance and current balance for all bank and credit card type accounts. Click Refresh to reflect recent changes to the client's data. More information about working with banking activities is included in Chapter 13, "Working with Bank and Credit Card Accounts."

The Accountant's Update section helps accounting professionals stay informed with important alerts, development tips, and links to training opportunities.

Customizing the Client Data Review Center

You can customize the list of displayed clean-up tasks in CDR. However, the changes you make to the list of displayed CDR tasks affects only the QuickBooks file currently opened. Additionally, some CDR tasks will display only if the related feature in QuickBooks is enabled (Sales Tax, for example).

To gain access to the customizing feature, you need to launch the CDR. To do so, follow these steps:

1. From the menu bar, select Accountant, Client Data Review, Client Data Review. You can also launch CDR from the QuickBooks icon bar if you are using QuickBooks Accountant 2012 or Enterprise Solutions Accountant 12.0.

2. If this is your first review for this client, the Client Data Review—Start Review dialog box displays, as shown in Figure A.4. From this dialog box, select the default Review Date Range shown, or select a date range from the following options in the drop-down list:

   - Last Fiscal Year (your default fiscal year is defined in the QuickBooks Company, Company Information menu)

   - Last Fiscal Quarter

   - Last Month

   - Custom (you will choose the From and To dates)

Figure A.4
After launching the CDR for the first time, you will select your review period and reporting basis.

3. Select the appropriate Review Basis—Accrual or Cash. This basis defaults from the preference setting in the QuickBooks file for reports.

4. Optionally, click to select to have Task Notes from previous reviews follow to the new review.

5. Click Start Review and the Client Data Review tasks display as previously shown in Figure A.1.

Modifying the Review Date and Basis

The Basis shown in the CDR defaulted from the QuickBooks data file preferences when the CDR was first launched, or the basis was manually selected on the Client Data Review—Start Review or Modify Review dialog box.

If after beginning a review, you need to change either the review period or basis, simply click the Modify Review link in the CDR, top center, to be returned to the dialog box (refer to Figure A.1).

 tip

If you find you need to change your default reporting basis after opening a review, you can do so on the Reports and Graphs tab of the Preferences dialog box (select Edit, Preferences from the menu bar). You will need to be logged in as the Admin or External Accountant user in single-user mode to change the global preference for reporting basis.

Customize Cleanup Tasks

You might have some clients who do not need a review of some of the task groups in their QuickBooks data. For example, you are working in a client's file who does not have to track or pay sales tax.

With CDR, you can remove those tasks that are not needed for the specifically open client file. The changes made in one client's file will not be made to another client's file CDR tasks.

With Client Data Review open, follow these steps to remove the sales tax task group (or any of the other tasks) from the CDR:

1. Click the Customize Cleanup Tasks link in the center of the CDR dialog box (refer to Figure A.1).

   The Client Data Review—Customize dialog box displays as shown in Figure A.5.

Figure A.5
Customize the tasks that are displayed for the currently opened client file.

2. Place your mouse pointer on any list item and click once to unselect that specific task or group of tasks. Clicking again will reselect the list item.

3. Click the Restore Defaults button to return to the original settings.

4. Click Help to open the help topic specific for CDR.

5. Click Save Changes or Cancel if you do not want to make the changes.

 tip

If the desired Categories/Task is not displayed in the Client Data Review—Customize dialog box, it is because for the currently opened QuickBooks file that feature is not currently enabled.

You have successfully changed the lists of tasks that displays for this client's data file only.

Minimize or Expand Task Groups

You might not want to remove a task completely, but instead you want to minimize it.

With Client Data Review open, follow these steps:

1. Click the (−) before a task group name to minimize the task group details.

2. Click the (+) before a task group name to maximize the task group details.

In the example shown in Figure A.6, you will select the (−) before the Review List Changes task group header. The result, as shown in Figure A.7, is to minimize a task. The Hide and Show Task state for each task group on the CDR is company file-dependent. The changes you make in one company file will not be made in other QuickBooks client files.

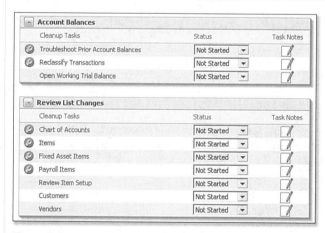

Figure A.6
View before minimizing the Review List Changes task.

Click to collapse

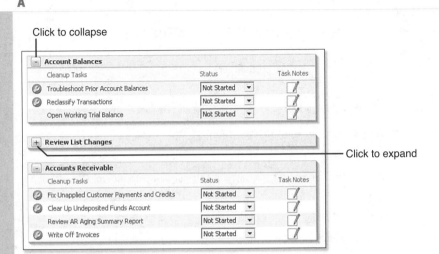

Click to expand

Figure A.7
View after minimizing the Review List Changes task.

Assigning Status and Notes to Review Tasks

To help in managing the review of a client's file, you have an associated status you can optionally assign to each task. This feature is useful for your own reference or if several accounting professionals are reviewing the same file.

To assign a new status or change an existing status, click the Status drop-down list and choose from one of the available choices:

- Not Started (which is the default status assigned to all tasks when a review is started)

- In Progress

- Completed

- Not Applicable

Optionally, you can record a note about a particular task. Click the task note icon to the right of a task. The Task Notes dialog box will display where you can document specific review notes for that task (see Figure A.8). These notes are included in the CDR notes when Save as PDF is selected.

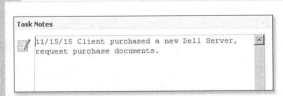

Figure A.8
Conveniently store task notes as you review the file.

When you return to a CDR in progress, or if you share the review with other accounting professionals at your firm, each individual can see the progress of a particular task in review.

After customizing the CDR to show or hide specific task groups, you should take one more precaution.

Before beginning the review and making changes to a client's file, make sure you are logged in with as an External Accountant type user. This will ensure your changes can be tracked separately from those made by the client and will also give you complete access to the Admin activities available in the CDR. For more information, read the "Creating an External Accountant User" section later in this chapter.

To see the currently logged in user, look to the top-right corner of the CDR. CDR identifies the username and whether she is an External Accountant as displayed in Figure A.1.

You are now ready to begin the review process. The following sections provide more details about the unique features and results you can expect when reviewing and correcting your client's data file using this innovative feature. You will never want to do a review the "old fashioned" way again!

Account Balances

Although you do not have to do the review task groups in any particular order, I do recommend you begin with the Account Balances task group. A reliable client data file review depends on accurate balance sheet reporting, which includes financial numbers from prior periods.

If a closing date was not set previously, or if the user was granted access to adding, modifying, or deleting prior year transactions, your ending balances that QuickBooks reports now might be different from those you used to prepare financials or tax return documents. Setting a closing date and password can help control changes to prior period transactions. More information about setting a closing date can be found in Chapter 16.

Troubleshoot Prior Account Balances

The first task included in Account Balances Review, Troubleshoot Prior Account Balances, displays the trial balance in debit and credit format, as shown in Figure A.9.

The Troubleshoot Account Balances tool displays these columns:

- **Accounts**—grouped by account type:
  - Assets
  - Liabilities
  - Equity
  - Income
  - Cost of Goods Sold
  - Expenses
  - Other Income
  - Other Expense

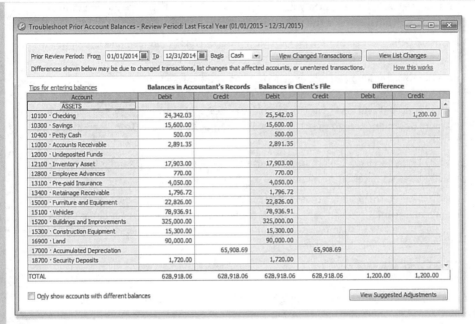

Figure A.9
Use Troubleshoot Prior Account Balances to correct any changes to prior period balances efficiently.

- **Balances in Accountant's Records**—debit and credit columns

- **Balances in Client's File**—debit and credit columns

- **Difference**—debit and credit columns

The primary purpose of this task is to provide a window where QuickBooks can compare the prior year's ending balances (as you used to prepare financials, tax returns, or monthly and quarterly reviews) with what QuickBooks currently shows for that same prior date range.

Your work will be complete in this window when there are no amounts left in the difference columns—indicating that the Balances in Accountant's Records agree with the Balances in Client's File for that same prior period date.

Entering Balances in Accountant's Records

If this is your first time using CDR with your client's data, you will need to enter the Balances in Accountant's Records columns in debit and credit spreadsheet format. You have two options for completing this task:

- Select Yes to the message that displays when you begin your first CDR of this file. CDR will now copy the columns of data from the Balances in Client's File to the Balances in Accountant's Records columns. Simply change any of the values copied to agree with your prior financials. If you select No to this message, a Copy Balances button is available on the top left for you to click to complete the task automatically.

- Or, manually enter the amounts in the Balances in Accountant's Records columns to agree with your last reported financials or filed tax return.

This is the only time you will be required to enter the balances. For future reviews, QuickBooks will populate the Balances in Accountant's Records columns with the reviewed balances as recorded when you selected the Mark Review as Complete at the bottom-right of the CDR Center.

The Troubleshoot Prior Account Balances task compares these prior balances to the current balances QuickBooks has for each account for the same prior date range. QuickBooks is determining for you which accounts have a discrepancy from the last review! Spend less time on clean-up tasks with CDR.

Any reported balance differences might have been less likely to occur if a closing date and password had been entered in your client's data file.

In Figure A.9 a difference is shown for the account Checking (and there is also a difference for the account Rent, not shown). The next section will detail how these CDR-dependent tasks will help you locate these differences.

tip

When working with the Troubleshoot Prior Account Balances task, if a chart of account was marked as inactive in QuickBooks but has a balance in the account as of the date range in the review, the CDR will include that account listing.

Select the Only Show Accounts with Different Balances checkbox if you want to view fewer rows of detail in the Troubleshoot Prior Account Balances task in CDR.

View Changed Transactions

If this is your first time using the CDR for a client's data file, QuickBooks will not be able to detail the specific changed transactions in the Differences columns. However, after you Mark Review as Complete for the first CDR, QuickBooks will begin tracking specific changed transactions from that time forward.

To determine what transactions dated on or before your last completed review date have been modified, double-click any amount displayed in the Differences column. A transaction listing report is displayed as shown in Figure A.10. The report identifies for you the specific transactions dated on or before the end of the last review period that have been added, modified, or deleted.

8:48 AM 12/15/16	Rock Castle Construction - Account: 63900 · Rent Transactions on/before 12/31/2014 - Changed on/after 01/01/2015								
	No list changes affect this account.								
Num ◦ Entered/Last Modified ◦	Last modified by ◦	State ◦	Date ◦	Name ◦	Account ◦	Split ◦	Debit ◦	Credit ◦
Transactions entered or modified by Admin								
Check 93								
93	12/15/2016 08:46:07	Laura (External Accountant)	*Deleted*					0.00	
93	12/15/2015 08:38:17	Admin	Prior	*12/01/2014*	Reyes Properties Overhead	10100 · Checking 63900 · Rent	63900 · Rent 10100 · Checking	1,200.00	1,200.00

Figure A.10
Using CDR can help you easily identify changes to transactions that affect the beginning balances.

If you double-clicked a difference amount on a specific line, the resulting report is filtered for transactions modified after your last review. You can limit what you see on the report by selecting the Customize Report button on the displayed report. You can filter for Entered/Last Modified dates to see only those transactions that were changed after you finished your review.

This one feature alone is why accountants should use QuickBooks Accountant 2012. Think of all the time you will save on future reviews of your client's data! Indeed, who will want to do a review the "old-fashioned" way?

 tip

Select the Only Show Accounts with Different Balances checkbox if you want to view fewer rows of detail in the Troubleshoot Prior Account Balances task in CDR.

View Suggested Adjustments

When QuickBooks detects any difference between the Balances in Accountant's Records and the Balances in Client's file, CDR suggests an adjusting journal entry for you to review.

To have QuickBooks assist in the preparation of this adjusting journal entry, follow these steps:

1. If there are differences detected, click the View Suggested Adjustments button. QuickBooks opens the Make General Journal Entries dialog box marked as an adjusting entry and dated as of the last date of the period under review (see Figure A.11). If your debits and credits are equal in the Review Last Balances columns, this journal entry should also have debits equal to credits for any differences that were detected.

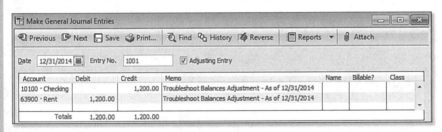

Figure A.11
QuickBooks prepares an adjusting journal entry to agree with your reviewed balances for the prior period.

2. If you are working in an Accountant's Copy file, you might also get a notice that any changes made to shaded fields in the journal entry will transfer back to the client. Select OK to close this message.

3. Click OK to close the message about automatically numbering your journal entries.

4. Click Save & Close to close the Make General Journal Entries dialog box.

 note

You will not be able to save the journal entry unless the totals of the debits and credits are equal.

5. Click View Suggested Reversing Entries if after these adjustments are made you need to reverse them; it is useful if the client corrected the error in a future accounting period. Or, click the Don't Reverse button to close the Reversing Entries dialog box.

6. Click the X in the top-right corner to close the Troubleshoot Prior Account Balances dialog box.

The Troubleshoot Prior Account Balances task is complete when there are no amounts in the Differences column. Optionally, enter a task note for the Troubleshooting Prior Account Balances task to document your work or note other necessary actions.

When the Mark Review Complete button is selected on the CDR dialog box, CDR will take the Balances in Client's File columns and transfer them to the Balances in Accountant's Records columns in the Troubleshoot Prior Account Balances dialog box. The Balances in Accountant's Records amounts *will not* change when clients add, modify, or delete transactions dated in your completed review period.

> **caution**
>
> If you selected View Suggested Adjustments and you had adjustments to an Accounts Receivable and Accounts Payable account, you will receive a warning message that you cannot adjust accounts receivable and accounts payable in the same journal entry. Instructions are given to remove one of the lines and the corresponding balancing line and enter it in a separate journal entry.

Reclassify Transactions

How often have you reviewed your client's QuickBooks data to see multiple transactions posted to the incorrect general ledger account? As an accountant, you will probably not want to spend the time needed to correct each individual transaction. A preferred method might be to create a journal entry transaction, which in effect "reclassifies" the amount out of the incorrect account and into the correct account.

With CDR in QuickBooks Accountant 2012 or Enterprise Solutions Accountant 12.0, there is the Reclassify Transactions feature. For 2012, you can access this tool from the Accountant Center, Accountant menu, or from an opened review using CDR.

From the Accounts panel on the left side of the Reclassify Transactions dialog box, you can:

- Accept or change the defaulted date range. These dates control the transactions that will display for reclassifying.

- Accept or change the defaulted Basis. This basis defaults from the setting found on the Company Information dialog box (select Company, Company Information from the menu bar).

- From the View drop-down list, choose to view Expense, Profit & Loss, or Balance Sheet accounts.

After selecting a chart of account listing on the left in the Accounts panel, you can filter the transactions displayed on the right in the Transactions panel with these options:

- From the Name drop-down list, leave the default of All which is all active list items. Or, select a specific list item from Customers, Employees, Vendor, or Other Names list.

> **💿 tip**
>
> When you select "Include Inactive Names" from the Name drop-down list in the Reclassify Transactions task, you will not affect the transactions displayed. Instead, the list will now include any inactive list items for you to select from.
>
> If you select an inactive name from the list, you will get a message from QuickBooks asking if you would like to use it once, make it active, or cancel.
>
> More information about working with lists can be found in Chapter 4, "Understanding QuickBooks Lists."

- From the Show Transactions drop-down list, the default of Non-Item-Based (can be reclassified) is selected. Other options include Item-Based (can only change the class) or All to show all transactions.

After reviewing the detailed transactions, you might find that a certain vendor had all transactions assigned to the wrong expense account. As an example, in Figure A.12 vendor Cal Gas & Electric had the transactions assigned to the Utilities:Water expense account. This was a mistake made on each of the checks all year. The proper account should have been the Utilities:Gas and Electric expense account.

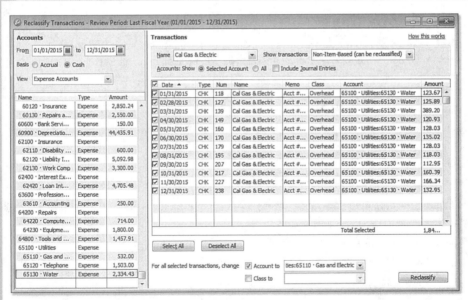

Figure A.12
Use the Reclassify Transactions dialog box to correct the account assigned to multiple transactions.

Prior to using CDR, accounting professionals would have created a journal entry reducing expenses recorded to the Utilities:Water account and increasing expenses for Utilities:Gas and Electric account. With this CDR feature, reclassifying the transactions is made easy by following these steps:

1. With the Reclassify Transactions dialog box displayed as shown in Figure A.12, select a date range for which you want to review and possibly reclassify transactions.

2. Accept the default Basis or change if needed.

3. From the View drop-down list, select the account types you want to review for reclassification.

   With a chart of accounts item selected in the Accounts panel on the left, you will see displayed to the right transactions assigned to that account for the date range and basis selected.

4. Optionally, from the Name drop-down list, select a specific vendor, customer, employee, or other name for which you want to filter the displayed transactions.

5. The Show Transactions drop-down list, will default to display only those transactions you can reclassify with this feature. Optionally, select to show Item-Based transactions. For item-based transactions, you can only reclassify the Class assigned. Or, select All to see both.

6. Optionally, select the Include Journal Entries checkbox.

7. If in step 5 you selected a specific name from the drop-down list, you might want to select in the Accounts: Show All. CDR will display all transactions for the Name selected for All accounts (not just the account selected on the left).

> **⚠ caution**
>
> Only non–item-based transactions can be reclassified with the CDR tool. If you need to edit the account assigned on item-based transactions, you will need to edit the individual item in the original transaction. For more information about working with QuickBooks Items, refer to Chapter 4.

8. As you make changes to the filters in Reclassify Transactions, the displayed transactions refresh automatically.

9. Optionally, choose Select All or Deselect All when choosing which transactions to reclassify.

10. For all selected transactions, select the proper general ledger account from the Account To drop-down list and optionally assign a new Class if desired.

11. Review your selections and click the Reclassify button. The window will refresh displaying the changes made to the transactions.

12. Continue reviewing all of the accounts until your review is complete.

13. Press the Escape key on your keyboard or click the X on the top right of the Reclassify Transactions dialog box when you are ready to close.

Open Working Trial Balance

The Working Trial Balance is a tool that has been available for years in the Premier Accountant and Enterprise Solutions Accountant versions of QuickBooks.

The Working Trial Balance, as shown in Figure A.13, displays the following details:

- Account
- Beginning Balance

- Transactions (for the selected date range)

- Adjustments (total of adjusting journal entries)

- Ending Balance

- Workpaper Reference (where you can record specific notes)

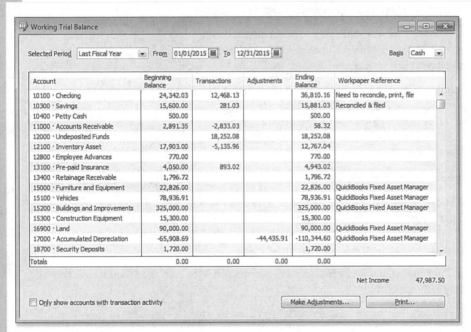

Figure A.13
Use the Working Trial Balance to make and review adjustments to the client's file in preparation for tax filings.

The Working Trial Balance provides a window to manage changes to a client's ending balances. You normally use this tool after you have matched the prior year balances in the Troubleshoot Prior Account Balances task with your records and you need to review and correct the next accounting period.

Click the Make Adjustments button to create an adjusting journal entry and watch the net impact to your client's Net Income with each saved journal entry change. When you are finished, click the Print button to prepare a report of your work.

Review List Changes

The Review List Changes feature is available only with your QuickBooks Accountant software and is only available when you launch a review using the Client Data Review feature. The type of changes tracked are specific to each task as detailed in the next several sections. Remember, if a task has the CDR icon in front of it, it indicates that the task can only be accessed using your

QuickBooks Accountant software. If any other tasks are listed, they simply link to the respective menu in QuickBooks for that activity.

Chart of Accounts

Reviewing the Chart of Accounts, correcting setup errors, making an account inactive, and merging like accounts were covered in detail in Chapter 4. When a CDR is marked as Completed, these list changes are also marked with an "R" for reviewed so that in future reviews, you can conveniently hide those changes.

Click the Chart of Accounts task in the Review List Changes task group. QuickBooks displays the Review List Changes dialog box as shown in Figure A.14.

Review List Changes				
Chart of Accounts	Items	Fixed Asset Items	Payroll Items	

After reviewing, click Mark All as Reviewed to hide reviewed items. To redisplay them, check Include Reviewed Items. How this works
(View Chart of Accounts)

Added

Reviewed	Account Name		Account Type
	Miscellaneous Expense		Expense
	Money Market CD		Bank

Changed -->   **-->Details of** Repairs

Reviewed	Account Name	Account Type		Data that Changed	Original Value	New Value
	Repairs	Expense		Account Name	Repairs	Repairs & Maintenance

Deleted

Reviewed	Account Name		Account Type
	Taxes:Property		Expense

Merged

Reviewed	Original Account Name	Destination Account Name	Account Type
	Miscellaneous	Miscellaneous Expense	Expense

☐ Include Reviewed Items   Mark All as Reviewed

Figure A.14
Easily track your client's changes to the chart of accounts.

The Chart of Accounts tab on the Review List Changes dialog box tracks the following types of changes:

- **Added**—Account Name and Account Type

- **Changed**—Marked Inactive, Name or Account Number changed, Account Type changed, Parent:Subaccount relationship changed, or Tax-Line Mapping changed

- **Deleted**—Account Name and Account Type

- **Merged**—Original Account Name, Destination Account Name, and Account Type

For changes your client has made that you want to indicate as "Reviewed," click the Mark All as Reviewed button. Changes you make to the lists while logged in as the new External Accountant user are automatically marked as reviewed.

The tabs at the top enable easy access to the remaining tracked list changes. Press the Escape key on your keyboard or click the X on the top right of the Review List Changes dialog box when you have completed this task.

Items

Chapter 4 details methods to find and troubleshoot item setup errors. This feature tracks changes made to items. When the review is completed, an "R" is placed next to each line item change to indicate it has been reviewed. In future Client Data Reviews, you can conveniently hide these previously reviewed changes.

Click the Items task in the Review List Changes task group. QuickBooks displays the Review List Changes dialog box, as shown in Figure A.15.

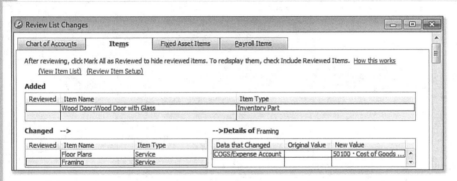

Figure A.15
Items affect accounting and reviewing changes to these will help in a client's file review.

The Items tab on the Review List Changes dialog box tracks the following:

- **Added**—Item Name and Item Type

- **Changed**—Displays the data that Changed with Original Value and New Value

- **Deleted**—Item Name and Item Type

- **Merged**—Original Item Name, Destination Item Name, and Item Type

When the Mark All as Reviewed button is selected, CDR feature will place an "R" in the Reviewed column for each item list change your client made. Changes you make to the list while logged in as the External Accountant user are automatically marked as reviewed.

Tabs at the top enable easy access to the remaining tracked list changes. Press the Escape key on your keyboard or click the X on the top right of the Review List Changes dialog box when you have completed this task.

Fixed Asset Items

The business owner using QuickBooks can create a Fixed Asset item type from the Fixed Asset Item List (select Lists, Fixed Asset Item List from the menu bar). Then when a purchase is made for the asset the respective Fixed Asset item can be recorded on a purchase order, or on the Items tab of the Enter Bills dialog box or the Write Checks dialog box. This tab tracks changes made to the list of fixed assets.

Click the Fixed Asset Items task in the Review List Changes task group. QuickBooks displays the Review List Changes dialog box, as shown in Figure A.16.

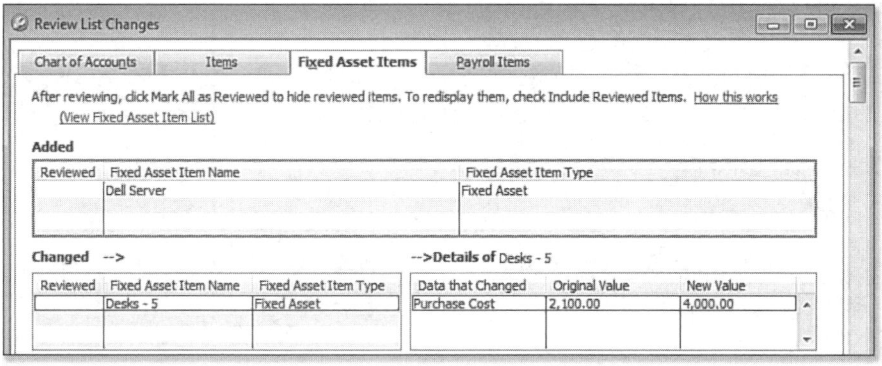

Figure A.16
Easily track additions, deletions, and changes to the client's Fixed Assets.

The Fixed Asset Items tab on the Review List Changes dialog box tracks the following fixed assets:

- **Added**—Fixed Asset Item Name and Fixed Asset Item Type

- **Changed**—Displays the data that Changed with Original Value and New Value

- **Deleted**—Fixed Asset Item Name and Fixed Asset Item Type

When the Mark All as Reviewed button is selected, the Client Data Review will place an "R" in the Reviewed column for each fixed asset item list change your client made. If you are logged into the file as an External Accountant user type, as you make list changes, they are automatically marked as Reviewed.

Tabs along the top of the Review List Changes dialog box enable easy access to the remaining tracked list changes. Press the Escape key on your keyboard or click the X on the top right of the Review List Changes dialog box when you have completed this task.

Payroll Items

Reviewing the purpose of Payroll Items was covered in detail in Chapter 11, "Setting Up Payroll." Details were also provided in Chapter 12, "Managing Payroll" to correct payroll setup errors. This feature tracks changes made to payroll items. When the review is completed, an "R" is placed next to each payroll item change to indicate that it has been reviewed. In future client data reviews, you can conveniently hide these.

This task will only display in a file that has the payroll preference enabled.

Click the Payroll Items task in the Review List Changes task group. QuickBooks displays the Review List Changes dialog box, as shown in Figure A.17.

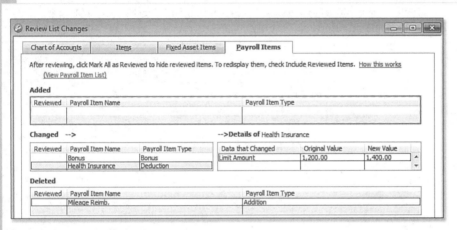

Figure A.17
See the changes the client made to payroll items throughout the year.

The Payroll Items tab on the Review List Changes dialog box tracks the following payroll items:

- **Added**—Payroll Item Name and Payroll Item Type

- **Changed**—Displays the data that Changed with Original Value and New Value

- **Deleted**—Payroll Item Name and Payroll Item Type

- **Merged**—Original Payroll Item Name, Destination Payroll Item Name, and Payroll Item Type

When the Mark All as Reviewed button is selected, the CDR will place an "R" in the Reviewed column for each item list change your client made. If you are logged into the file as an External Accountant user type, as you make list changes, they are automatically marked as Reviewed.

Tabs at the top enable easy access to the remaining tracked list changes. Press the Escape key on your keyboard or click the X on the top right to close the Review list Changes dialog box when you have completed this task.

Review Item Setup

Click the Review Item Setup in the Review List Changes task group. The Add/Edit Multiple List Entries dialog box displays.

From this dialog box, you can make changes to selected item types. More detail about working with the Add/Edit Multiple List Entries feature was included in Chapters 4 and 5.

Customers

In Figure A.18, note that the Customers task in the Review List Changes pane does not have a Client Data Review icon in front of the name, indicating that CDR is simply linking you back to the original Customer Center.

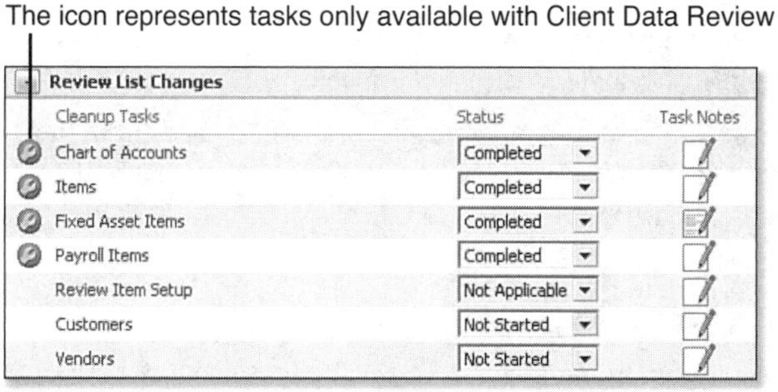

The icon represents tasks only available with Client Data Review

Review List Changes		
Cleanup Tasks	Status	Task Notes
Chart of Accounts	Completed	
Items	Completed	
Fixed Asset Items	Completed	
Payroll Items	Completed	
Review Item Setup	Not Applicable	
Customers	Not Started	
Vendors	Not Started	

Figure A.18
Tasks without the CDR icon provide quick access to the same menu in QuickBooks.

Refer to Chapter 9 for more details on how to use the Customer Center to gather information and easily find specific transactions.

Vendors

The Vendors task in the Review List Changes task group also does not have a CDR icon in front of the name, indicating that CDR is simply linking you back to the original Vendor Center.

Refer to Chapter 7, "Setting Up Vendors," for more details on how to use the Vendor Center to gather information and easily find specific transactions.

Accounts Receivable

Reviewing with your client her open Accounts Receivable is an important part of a successful review of a client's file. When there are errors in Accounts Receivable, the balance sheet and income statement accounts could be misstated.

A complete review of Accounts Receivable, including the proper process to use in QuickBooks for potentially avoiding the corrections detailed in this section, can be found in Chapter 9, "Setting Up Customers" and Chapter 10, "Managing Customers."

The tasks listed in the Accounts Receivable task group of the CDR will help you easily correct client mistakes made when the client recorded a customer payment or completed a deposit, but *did not* properly complete the transaction.

Recent versions of QuickBooks help discourage this error with messaging that warns the user not to use a Make Deposits transaction to record a customer payment. When recording a customer payment without assigning the payment to an open invoice, QuickBooks will provide a message that a credit will be left in the customer's account.

You might want to review the AR Aging Summary report first and then begin the process of using the CDR tools. Properly reviewing your client's data will help you make the most informed decisions about the corrections that might be needed.

Fix Unapplied Customer Payments and Credits

If your client entered a customer payment, but did not apply the payment to an invoice, this tool will help simplify the task of assigning the unapplied payment to the proper invoice.

Review the Open Invoices report (select Reports, Customers & Receivables, Open Invoices from the menu bar) before beginning to make corrections. This is especially important if you have more than one Accounts Receivable account in your chart of accounts.

To fix unapplied payments and credits, follow these steps:

1. If you are completing these changes as part of a dated review, from the menu bar, select Accountant, Client Data Review and launch Client Data Review. You will then select the Fix Unapplied Customer Payments and Credits task in the Accounts Receivable group.

2. If you are not completing these changes as part of a dated review, from the menu bar, select Accountant, Client Data Review and launch the Fix Unapplied Customer Payments and Credits task.

3. If you have more than one Accounts Receivable account, review the details for each by selecting the appropriate Accounts.

4. Select any of the customers on the list, as shown in Figure A.19. With a customer selected on the left, the Invoices and Charges tab will display any unapplied payments and credits (left side) and open invoices (right side) for that specific customer.

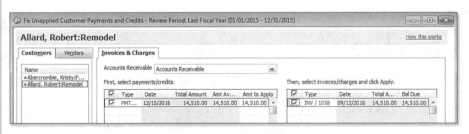

Figure A.19
Assign unapplied customer payments or credits to an open customer invoice.

5. On the Invoices and Charges tab, place a checkmark next to the payment or credit on the left pane and checkmark next to the associated open invoice on the right pane to which you want to apply the payment.

6. If you would like to only apply part of the credit or payment, enter the partial amount in the Amt to Apply column.

7. Click the Apply button to assign the payments or credits selected on the left to the selected open invoices on the right. The items are then grayed out to indicate that you have already assigned them.

8. Optionally, click the Auto Apply All button to apply all of the unapplied payments and credits to the invoices on the right.

9. Click Save to begin working on another customer record or Save & Close to complete the task.

 caution

Cash basis reporting taxpayers should proceed with caution when using this tool. In cash basis reporting, the date of the Receive Payments transaction is the date that revenue is recorded. If a customer payment was dated in the prior filed tax year and was *not* applied to the customer's open invoice, the income from the invoice would not have been included in cash basis reporting.

When you use CDR to assign the payment to the open invoice, QuickBooks will report the revenue associated with that invoice as of the *date* of the customer payment. This transaction will affect prior year cash basis financials.

This correction will change prior period financials. The CDR *does not* recognize the controls associated with setting a closing date. Additionally, QuickBooks *does not* provide any warnings that you are modifying a transaction dated on or before the closing date.

Recent editions of QuickBooks make recording unapplied credits and payments less likely to occur due to the many warnings that are provided when the transactions are entered.

Clear Up Undeposited Funds Account

Have you ever worked with a client's data file that had an incorrect undeposited funds balance? Did your client create a separate deposit transaction without assigning the receive payment to the deposit?

The undeposited funds account is a current asset type on the Balance Sheet. Like using a safe to store checks prior to taking them to the bank. Customer payments are recorded in QuickBooks increasing the amount in Undeposited Funds on the Balance Sheet. Later the checks are gathered and as a single deposit to the bank account (more details are provided in Chapter 9).

The Clear Up Undeposited Funds Account task can help you assign those undeposited funds to the deposit transaction that was created incorrectly.

Recent releases of QuickBooks make this error less likely to occur with the many warnings that are provided when the transactions are entered.

It is important to know that this feature will work when any of the following conditions apply:

- Receive Payments transaction was recorded and assigned to the Undeposited Funds account without including the payment in a Make Deposits transaction.

- Make Deposits transaction was recorded, the Received From column included the Customer or Customer:Job name, and the Account From column has an account assigned, which is typically an income account. See Figure A.20.

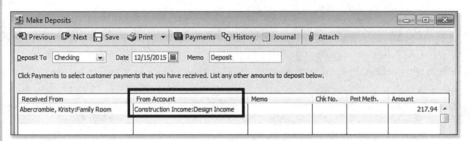

Figure A.20
Example of a customer payment recorded improperly on the Make Deposits transaction.

- If the Make Deposits transaction did not include a name in the Received From column, CDR will report that deposit transaction in the Clear Up Undeposited Funds Account CDR task assigned to a customer named "No Name in Deposit."

To clear up the Undeposited Funds account, follow these steps:

1. If you are completing these changes as part of a dated review, from the menu bar, select Accountant, Client Data Review and launch Client Data Review. You will then select the Clear Up Undeposited Funds task in the Accounts Receivable group.

2. If you are not completing these changes as part of a dated review, from the menu bar, select Accountant, Client Data Review and launch the Clear Up Undeposited Funds task.

3. The Show Deposits From field defaults to the review period selected when you started a client data review, or if you did not start a formal review the dates default to your last fiscal year. If needed, change the selected dates and click Refresh to display the changes.

4. The Payers pane on the left will display any customers with transactions meeting the criteria listed above. With a customer selected, review the payment transaction types on the right.

5. With a customer selected, place a checkmark next to the DEP transaction and also to the PMT transaction on the right with which you want to associate the payment as shown in Figure A.21.

6. Click the Apply button to assign. The list items are grayed out, indicating they have been applied to each other.

7. Click Save to begin correcting records for the next customer or Save & Close to complete the task.

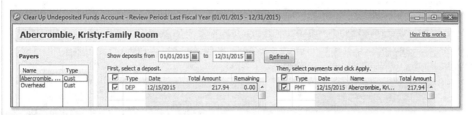

Figure A.21
Associate the customer payment in Clear Up Undeposited Funds Account to the incorrectly recorded Make Deposits transaction.

You are now ready to move on with your review or continue with additional clean-up tasks. I recommend reviewing the AR Summary Report first to get a general idea of the types of corrections you might need to make with the remaining accounts receivable CDR tasks.

 tip

Need to return to the original transaction in QuickBooks during your review? Simply double-click the selected transaction.

Reviewing the AR Aging Summary Report

Check the AR Aging Summary Report before fixing transactions. An individual transaction can be deceiving if you don't see its relationship with other related transactions.

When you select the Review AR Aging Summary Report link, QuickBooks opens the same titled report.

What exactly are you looking for on the aging report? You might be looking for customer credits that are aged and have not been applied to current open customer invoices. Or, perhaps as explained later in Chapter 10, you might want to remove an open balance from a customer's invoice.

I suggest you use the Open Invoices report instead of the Aging reports. The Open Invoices report shows the transactions listed separately instead of in summary form. The Open Invoices Report is not part of the CDR tool set. It is, however, a regularly used QuickBooks report. Because the Open Invoices Report shows the current A/R status, if you are reviewing it for a previous date, you will need to modify the report to show the open balances as of that prior date. To do this, follow these steps:

1. From the menu bar, select Reports, Customers & Receivables, Open Invoices. This report includes all open invoices, credits, and payments for your customers as of today's computer system date.

2. Review the report with today's date first. This will help you identify what corrections you might want to make using the tasks defined in this section. Reviewing it with today's date will also show if the correction you might have needed on a previous date has already been entered.

3. If you are reviewing for some date in the past, you can adjust the report to that date by clicking Customize Report at the top-left corner of the report window.

4. From the Display tab, click the Advanced button. In the Open Balance/Aging pane of the Advanced Options dialog box, change the selection to the Report Date option (see Figure A.22). This modification to the report enables you to see each customer's balance detail (see Figure A.23) as of the report date.

caution

If you do not modify this report as instructed here, QuickBooks will display the date you selected on the report, but will also reduce the balances owed for payments made after the report date.

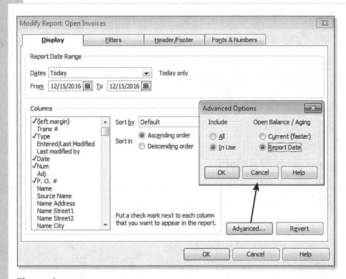

Figure A.22
The Open Invoices report, when modified, can be compared to the totals on your Balance Sheet report for some time in the past.

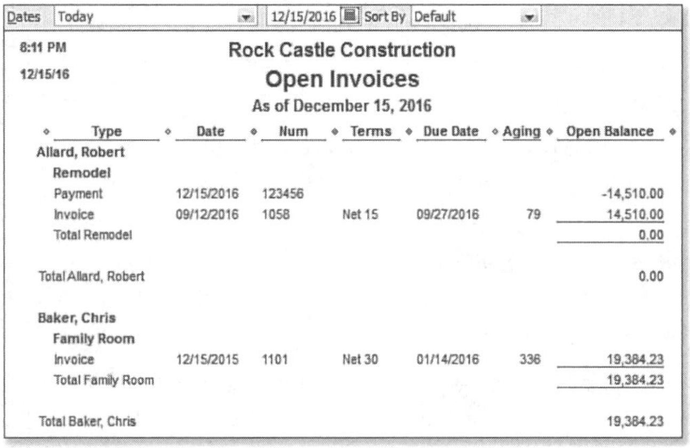

Figure A.23
The Open Invoices report easily shows unpaid balances and any unapplied customer credits or payments.

Write Off Invoices

Often, as accounting professionals, we need to adjust our client's Accounts Receivable balances. Perhaps there were several small unpaid finance charge invoices, or over the year our client's customers paid their invoices short of what was due.

Creating a customer credit memo and assigning the credit memo to the original open invoice was time-consuming for the accounting professional. Often a journal entry was created, correcting the accounts receivable balance on the Balance Sheet but leaving the QuickBooks user with extra line details in the A/R Aging Summary or Detail reports.

The Write Off Invoices feature shown in Figure A.24 is one convenient window where you can write off balances, review the suggested transaction, and print the details for your customer.

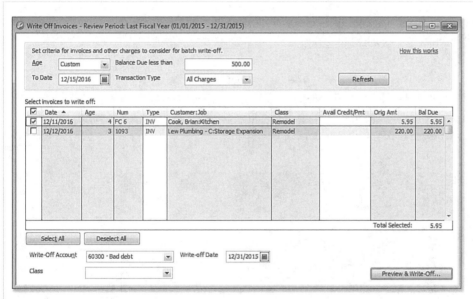

Figure A.24
Using CDR's Write Off Invoices makes removing open A/R uncollected balances easy!

To write off invoices, follow these steps:

1. If Client Data Review isn't already open, select Accountant, Accountant Center from the menu bar.

2. Select the Write Off Invoices task in the Accounts Receivable task group.

3. If presented with the warning that one or more customers in the list have available credits, click OK to close the message. Make sure you have done a thorough review of your client's Open Invoices reports as previously recommended.

4. From the Age drop-down list, select between showing receivables aged over 120 days, aged over 180 days, Review Period, or a custom date.

5. Optionally, enter an amount in the Balances Due Less Than box to limit the transactions that are displayed, which is particularly useful when writing off small balances only.

6. Select a To Date.

7. From the Transaction Type drop-down list, select All Charges, Invoices, Finance Charges, or Statement Charges.

8. Click Refresh if changing the filters.

9. Place a checkmark next to each transaction for which you want to write off the open balance. Optionally, click the Select All button or Deselect All button at the bottom of the screen to simplify the process.

10. From the drop-down lists, select the Write-Off Account and Write-Off Date. Optionally, select a Class.

11. Click the Preview & Write-Off button. CDR displays the Confirm Write-Off dialog box as shown in Figure A.25.

 tip

Earlier in this chapter, I recommended you review the AR Aging Summary report before using the Accounts Receivable CDR tools. However, even if you do not review the report, the Write Off Invoices dialog box will show the word "CREDITS" in the Avail Credit/Pmt column if the customer with the open invoice balance also has unapplied credits.

Click the CREDITS link to open the Fix Unapplied Customer Payments and Credits dialog box. Here you can apply the payment to the open invoice as instructed previously.

It might be more appropriate to assign the available credit rather than to write off the open balance.

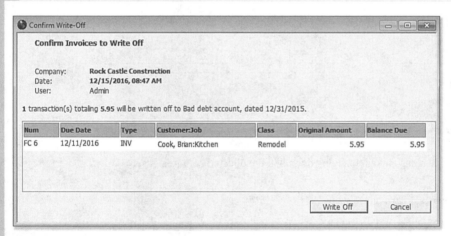

Figure A.25
You stay in control of the write-off, confirming the balances to be removed.

12. Click Write Off when you are done reviewing the invoices or click Cancel.

13. CDR returns you to the Write Off Invoices dialog box. Press the Escape key on your keyboard to view the Write-Off Completed details.

14. Click Save as PDF to print for your records.

You are now complete with the Accounts Receivable tasks. There are many QuickBooks preferences that will guide your clients as they manage undeposited funds and accounts receivable transactions. Review Chapters 9 and 10 for more details and other Accounts Receivable troubleshooting suggestions.

Accounts Payable

A complete review of Accounts Payable, including the proper process to use in QuickBooks, which potentially avoids the corrections detailed in this section, can be found in Chapter 7.

The tasks listed in the Accounts Payable section of the CDR feature can help you easily correct client mistakes made when the client has created a vendor credit or bill payment and did not assign it to the open vendor bill.

The Review Unpaid Bills Report is listed last in the Accounts Payable task group. I recommend reviewing this report as well as other reports prior to making corrections with the CDR. Properly reviewing your data will help you make the most informed decision on the corrections that might be needed.

 caution

Item receipts do not display in the CDR tools, but these transaction types are included in your client's open Accounts Payable balances. Review the Unpaid Vendor Bills report (select Reports, Vendors & Payables from the menu bar) for any aged item receipts.

Chapter 6 offers more specific details for correcting aged item receipts.

Fix Unapplied Vendor Payments and Credits

Chapter 7 detailed the proper accounts payable process, which is to use the Pay Bills dialog box to pay vendor bills. Some QuickBooks users might have used the Enter Bills transaction type and later paid that vendor bill using the Write Checks transaction instead of properly using the Pay Bills dialog box.

To fix unapplied vendor payments and credits, follow these steps:

1. If you are completing these changes as part of a dated review, from the menu bar, select Accountant, Client Data Review and launch Client Data Review. You will then select the Fix Unapplied Vendor Payments and Credits task in the Accounts Payable group.

2. If you are not completing these changes as part of a dated review, from the menu bar, select Accountant, Client Data Review and launch the Fix Unapplied Vendor Payments and Credits task.

3. The Vendors tab on the top left and the Bills tab on the right will be selected by default. Select any of the vendors on the list to the left. The Bills pane will display all unapplied vendor credits for the vendor selected on the left. The right of the Bills pane will display any open vendor bills for that specifically selected vendor.

 caution

If any of the checks listed in the left side of the Bills detail have an (*) asterisk in front of the word CHK this indicates that the expense is marked as billable to the customer. CDR will warn you that when you assign the check to an open vendor bill the expense will no longer be marked as billable.

More details about working with billable expenses are included in Chapter 9, in the section titled "Time and Expense Invoicing."

4. Place a checkmark next to the credit on the left and the open vendor bill on the right to which you want to apply the payment (see Figure A.26).

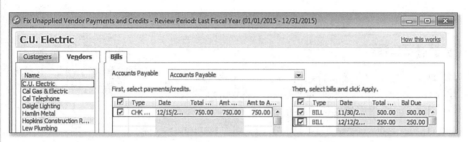

Figure A.26
Using CDR to assign a check written to a vendor with open bills saves time!

5. Click the Apply button to assign that specific vendor credit form with that specific vendor bill. The items selected will be grayed out, indicating that you have assigned them properly.

6. You must click Save to begin correcting transactions for another vendor or Save and Close to complete the task.

Evaluate and Correct 1099 Account Mapping

Setting up your vendors for proper 1099 status is important. However, be assured that if after reviewing this information you determine the original setup was incorrect, any changes made here will correct prior- and future-dated reports and forms.

When you select the link in the Accounts Payable task group for Evaluate and Correct 1099 Mapping, the Preferences dialog box for 1099s is displayed.

In the preference setting for Tax:1099, you can click the Yes button to select the Do You File option to let QuickBooks know you will be providing 1099 forms to your vendors at the end of the year. A new QuickBooks file will default with the preference set to Yes for filing 1099-MISC forms.

If this is your first time setting up 1099s in your file, click the link next to "if you're ready to prepare..." and the QuickBooks 1099 Wizard displays as shown in Figure A.27.

More detailed information about setting up your 1099s in QuickBooks is included in Chapter 7.

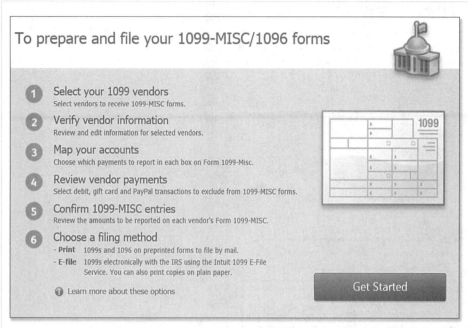

Figure A.27
Improved for QuickBooks 2012 is the QuickBooks 1099 Wizard.

Reviewing the Unpaid Bills Report

One of the first tasks you should do with your client is review the Unpaid Bills Report, primarily because the client will know best if the bills that are open are still due and payable to the vendor.

What exactly are you looking for on the aging report? You might be looking for vendor credits that are aged and have not been applied to current open vendor bills. Or, as Chapters 7 and 8 documented, you might see several aged item receipts for vendors you know your client has paid.

Use the information collected from this report to help determine the corrections that should be made with the tasks listed in the Accounts Payable task group of the CDR.

Sales Tax

This CDR feature not only identifies errors with using the incorrect payment form, but also fixes the transaction automatically for you!

More information about properly setting up and using sales tax is included in Chapter 9.

Before beginning the tasks listed in this section, you should review the client's settings (preferences) for sales tax as shown in Figure A.28. Additionally, the Sales Tax task group will not display in the CDR if the Sales Tax feature has not been enabled.

After reviewing and correcting your client's sales tax preference settings, you are prepared to begin the following CDR tasks.

⊘ Fix Incorrectly Recorded Sales Tax

QuickBooks uses a special Pay Sales Tax dialog box (as shown in Figure A.29) to record the sales tax liability payments properly. When payments are made using other transaction types, such as Write Checks, Pay Bills, or Make General Journal Entries, the Pay Sales Tax dialog box might not reflect the payments accurately.

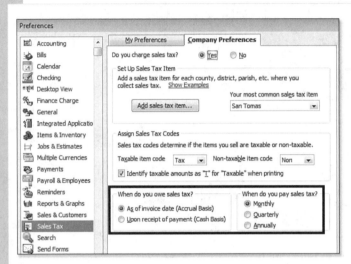

Figure A.28
Review Sales Tax preferences before making any corrections.

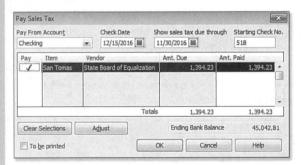

Figure A.29
Create properly paid sales tax in this dialog box.

The Fix Incorrectly Recorded Sales Tax task will help you identify and correct the transaction when a client paid her sales tax liability outside of the Pay Sales Tax dialog box. Figure A.30 shows the negative line entry that will be included in the Pay Sales Tax dialog box when a Write Checks transaction was created, assigned to the sales tax payable liability account, and payable to the sales tax vendor. Properly recorded sales tax payments will have a transaction type of TAXPMT in the checkbook register.

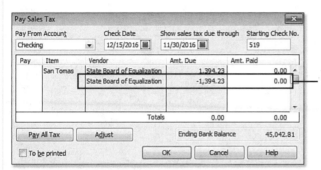

Figure A.30
Pay Sales Tax dialog box when an improperly recorded sales tax payment was made.

What exactly is this tool fixing? The tool will identify and fix non sales-tax-payable type transactions used to pay sales tax liability using Void and Replace functionality.

The tool will identify any Write Checks transactions where the payee is the same as an assigned payee for any sales tax item.

This tool *will not* identify any vendor bills, vendor bill payment checks, or journal entries recording payment for the Sales Tax Liability.

If this is your first incorrectly recorded sales tax transaction fix, you might want to change the "to" date to include today's date. This ensures you are seeing all sales tax payable transactions that were improperly recorded using the wrong–transaction in QuickBooks.

To fix incorrectly recorded sales tax, follow these steps:

1. If you are completing these changes as part of a dated review, from the menu bar, select Accountant, Client Data Review and launch Client Data Review. You will then select the Fix Incorrectly Recorded Sales Tax task in the Sales Tax group.

2. If you are not completing these changes as part of a dated review, from the menu bar, select Accountant, Client Data Review and launch the Fix Incorrectly Recorded Sales Tax task as shown in Figure A.31.

3. Double-click any transaction to see the originally created non-sales tax payment form to make sure it should be changed to a Sales Tax Payment. Make note of the check number or check date.

 caution

This might be a good time to review with your client the vendor names associated with different types of tax payments. Some states might have the same vendor name for multiple agency tax payments.

Suggest to your client that she use a unique vendor name for each different type of tax being paid. This will avoid CDR possibly correcting a non-sales tax type of payment made to vendor.

 caution

If your client has multiple lines recorded on her sales tax payable checks, such as including an additional fee for late payment penalty or other adjustment lines, you might want to use the link for making a manual Sales Tax Adjustment.

The Fix Incorrectly Recorded Sales Tax tool assumes all lines of the incorrect transaction belong in the Sales Tax Payable account.

Figure A.31
Automatically find and fix incorrectly recorded sales tax payment transactions.

4. Place a checkmark in each transaction to be fixed. Optionally, use the Select All button or Deselect All button to streamline the process.

5. Click Void & Replace (no shown in Figure A.31). CDR then creates a new Sales Tax Payment transaction and voids the original Write Checks transaction or Make General Journal Entries transaction.

6. Click Proceed to the Fix Sales Tax message that displays to continue with the change, or click Cancel to return to the CDR tool.

7. Click OK to close the message indicating that the transaction(s) have been fixed.

8. Click the X in the top-right corner to return to the CDR Center.

9. Return to your checkbook register (icon on the Home page) and look for the check number or date (or both) to view the original transaction voided and the new transaction created as a Sales Tax Payment type.

 tip

With the Void and Replace functionality included in the Fix Incorrectly Recorded Sales Tax tool, you can rest assured that if your original transaction was marked as cleared in a bank reconciliation, the newly created Sales Tax Payment transaction will also be marked as cleared.

Adjust Sales Tax Payable

If the Fix Incorrectly Recorded Sales Tax tool was not used to correct the client's sales tax records, you might instead want to use this manual Adjust Sales Tax Payable link.

In addition to reviewing fixing transactions, I recommend you review the Sales Tax Liability reports and your Balance Sheet balance for Sales Tax Payable before and after making corrections to your sales tax payable balances in QuickBooks.

When comparing these reports and the Pay Sales Tax dialog box, make sure each report is using the same basis —Accrual or Cash— and is prepared with the same reporting date. More information on working with the sales tax payable reports in QuickBooks can be found in Chapter 10.

Compare the following reports to each other for sales tax payable balances:

- **Balance Sheet**—Sales Tax Payable balance. Select Reports, Company & Financial, Balance Sheet Standard from the menu bar. Optionally, click the Modify button to change the report basis and date.

- **Sales Tax Liability Report**—Sales Tax Payable as of <date> column total. Select Vendors, Sales Tax, Sales Tax Liability from the menu bar.

- **Pay Sales Tax**—Amt. Due column total. Select Vendors, Sales Tax, Pay Sales Tax from the menu bar.

The end result of a properly made sales tax correcting entries or adjustment is that the totals listed in the above mentioned reports agree with each other.

To adjust sales tax payable, follow these steps:

1. If you are completing these changes as part of a dated review, from the menu bar, select Accountant, Client Data Review and launch Client Data Review. You will then select the Adjust Sales Tax Payable task in the Sales Tax group.

2. If you are not completing these changes as part of a dated review, from the menu bar, select Vendors, Sales Tax, Adjust Sales Tax Due.

   The Sales Tax Payable dialog displays as shown in Figure A.32.

Figure A.32
Use the Sales Tax Adjustment dialog box to adjust QuickBooks Sales Tax Payable properly.

3. Select the Adjustment Date.

4. Type in an Entry No if desired.

5. Select your Sales Tax Vendor from the drop-down list. Make sure the vendor selected is the same vendor assigned to your sales tax items.

6. Select the Adjustment Account from the drop-down list.

7. In the Adjustment pane, select the Increase Sales Tax By or Decrease the Sales Tax By option button. Enter an amount for the adjustment.

8. Enter a Memo or select the default memo.

9. Click OK to save the transaction.

QuickBooks will create a Make General Journal Entries transaction with a decrease (debit) or increase (credit) to the Sales Tax Payable account with the resulting debit or credit in the account that was selected in step 6.

The adjustments created remain unapplied in the Pay Sales Tax dialog box until you assign them to your next Sales Tax Payment.

Manage Sales Tax

Click the Manage Sales Tax task to properly set up and work with Sales Tax in your QuickBooks data file. Manage Sales Tax is also available from a shortcut on the Home page. For more information, see Chapters 9 and 10.

Pay Sales Tax

Click the Pay Sales Tax task to pay your sales tax properly in QuickBooks. For more information, see Chapter 9.

Sales Tax Preferences

Click the Sales Tax Preferences task to define sales tax-specific preferences affecting your QuickBooks data file. For more information, see Chapter 9.

Inventory

For the accounting professional, inventory is commonly one area of QuickBooks that is the least understood. Often when working with a client's file with inventory tracking, I will see a journal entry used to adjust inventory. Although this does make the adjustment to the inventory account balance on the Balance Sheet report, it does not reflect the adjustment in the Inventory Valuation Summary or Detail report.

Why is it that a journal entry shouldn't be used to adjust inventory? Consider that the inventory value on a balance sheet is the quantity of an item multiplied by a cost. When you create a journal entry, you can enter an amount for the adjustment, but you cannot associate it with an actual inventory item.

The following sections detail several inventory troubleshooting tools.

Review Inventory Setup

Chapter 6, "Managing Inventory," discusses several topics about the proper processes needed when your clients track inventory in their business.

When you click the Review Inventory Setup link in the CDR Inventory pane, the Add/Edit Multiple List Entries dialog box opens. From here, you can easily add or edit individual or multiple inventory or non-inventory items on the inventory list, as well as other lists.

The Review Inventory Setup is not a CDR-dependent task, but the link in the CDR center makes it easy to correct your client's inventory items.

Compare Balance Sheet and Inventory Valuation

This Compare Balance Sheet and Inventory Valuation CDR task is an inventory troubleshooting tool that will help you "diagnose" transaction errors involving the inventory asset account. In Chapter 6, you were introduced to the importance of comparing your client's Inventory Asset on the Balance Sheet report to the asset total on the Inventory Valuation Summary report.

When transactions are recorded to the inventory asset account without assigning an inventory item (such as a Make General Journal Entries transaction, or on the Expenses tab of a Write Checks transaction or an Enter Bills transaction by assigning the inventory asset account), the Inventory Valuation Summary report will no longer match the value of the Inventory Asset on the Balance Sheet report.

Another result of improperly recording inventory transactions is the potential for a misstatement of the value of the Cost of Goods Sold, or the cost of the inventory sold to a customer which would affect job costing reports.

To compare the balance sheet and inventory valuation, follow these steps:

1. From the menu bar, select Accountant, Client Data Review and launch Client Data Review.

2. Select the Compare Balance Sheet and Inventory Valuation task in the Inventory group.

3. The CDR tool displays the Inventory Asset account balance from the Balance Sheet for the selected As of date. Optionally, click the Balance Sheet link to review the report.

4. The CDR tool displays the total asset value from the Inventory Valuation Summary report for the selected As of date. Optionally, click the Inventory Valuation Summary link to review the report.

   A warning message is displayed (See Figure A.33) if there is a difference between the asset value reported on the two reports.

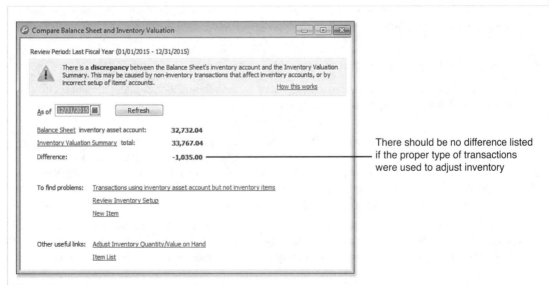

Figure A.33
Comparing Balance Sheet and Inventory Valuation is useful when troubleshooting inventory asset discrepancies.

5. Optionally, click the Transactions Using Inventory Asset Account But Not Inventory Items link, and the report in Figure A.34 displays. The report displays transactions that affect the Inventory Asset balance on the Balance Sheet, but are not properly affecting an inventory item.

| Dates | Custom | ▼ | From | | | To | 12/31/2015 | | Total By | Total only | ▼ | Sort By | Default | ▼ |

9:31 PM
12/15/16

Rock Castle Construction
Transactions using Inventory Asset Account but not Inventory Items
Cash Basis As of December 31, 2015

◦	Type	◦	Date	◦	Num	◦	Memo	◦	Account	◦	Split	◦	Debit	◦	Credit	◦
	General Journal		12/15/2015		1002		To agree wi...		Inventory Asset		Cost of Good...				1,035.00	
Total													0.00		1,035.00	

└─ General Journals should not be used to adjust inventory balances

Figure A.34
CDR makes it easy to locate transactions that are affecting the Inventory Asset but not using the proper form.

6. Optionally, click Review Inventory Setup to open Add/Edit Multiple List Entries.

7. Optionally, click New Item to create a new inventory item.

8. Optionally, click Adjust Inventory Quantity/Value on Hand to properly adjust inventory.

9. Optionally, click Item List to modify an item.

10. To close, press the Escape key on your keyboard or click the X in the top-right corner.

If you find these types of errors in your accounting for inventory, you will instead want to create an inventory adjustment to replace them with. QuickBooks will continue to report a difference between the reports if journal entries are recorded to the Inventory Asset account.

Troubleshoot Inventory

Chapter 6 provides useful content on troubleshooting issues surrounding inventory. One of the issues discussed in that chapter is the effect on the company's financials when inventory goes negative.

Negative inventory is caused when QuickBooks has recorded a higher quantity of inventory sold than is available to sell. This process might seem acceptable for some clients if they are waiting on back-ordered product but want to collect the payment from the customer in advance. Chapter 5 details better methods for handling back orders and other issues, which can result in negative inventory values and the misstated financials that can result.

Also, Chapter 6 explained that if an inventory item is marked as "inactive" the resulting inventory value will not appear on the Inventory Valuation Summary report. If a client truly has inventory in stock, although she is not selling it, the Inventory Valuation Summary report would be misstated.

With the Troubleshoot Inventory feature (see Figure A.35) in QuickBooks Accountant, many of the reports and processes that had to be reviewed for diagnosing inventory valuation errors can be replaced by using the new Troubleshoot Inventory CDR task. In fact, this tool is so valuable in detecting errors such as negative inventory and finding inactive items with a quantity on hand (to name just a couple), that as accounting professionals we should encourage our clients to upgrade to QuickBooks 2012.

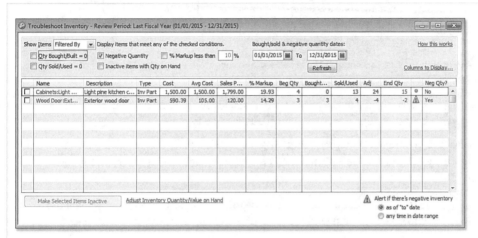

Figure A.35
Easily identify inventory with a negative quantity, and help your client better manage her inventory processes.

All users in QuickBooks Premier and QuickBooks Enterprise Solutions 2012 have a new Inventory Center, which offers the ability to list any items that have negative inventory.

To review your client's inventory using the Troubleshoot Inventory CDR task, follow these steps:

1. If you are completing these changes as part of a dated review, from the menu bar, select Accountant, Client Data Review and launch Client Data Review. You will then select the Troubleshoot Inventory task in the Inventory group.

2. If you are not completing these changes as part of a dated review, from the menu bar, select Accountant, Client Data Review and launch the Troubleshoot Inventory task.

3. From the Show Items drop-down list, select Filtered By, All, or All Active. This will help to display specific data for your review of your client's inventory.

4. Place a checkmark in any combination or all of the following:

   ■ Qty Bought/Built = 0

   ■ Qty Sold/Used = 0

   ■ Negative Quantity

   ■ Inactive Items with Qty on Hand

   ■ % Markup less than <enter the %>

5. The default date range is the same as the selected Review Period. Optionally, you can change the dates.

6. Click Refresh if you are changing the filters or dates to show current data.

7. Optionally, click Columns to Display to modify the content that is displayed.

   Inventory items that match your selected filter criteria are displayed. The column End Qty displays the number of units in stock as of the To date selected. Next to the End Qty column a green circle symbol displays if there is no negative inventory. A yellow caution symbol displays if inventory items have a negative inventory quantity.

8. Select the option for Alert to show if there is negative inventory As of the "to" Date or Any Time in Date Range.

9. Optionally, place a checkmark in the box in front of any inventory item and then click the Make Selected Items Inactive button to mark the inventory item as inactive.

10. Optionally, click the Adjust Inventory Quantity/Value on Hand to adjust the ending inventory balances to the client's physical inventory counted totals. More information is provided in the next section.

If your review using the CDR tools and features has identified inventory errors, you will want to read Chapter 6, in which you will find sections on troubleshooting inventory in QuickBooks.

Adjust Inventory Quantity/Value on Hand

Before you perform this task, you need to know what the actual ending quantity and value for each inventory item is currently. This is determined by completing a physical inventory count. Without this important step, you might make an adjustment that might not be supported by the actual count. To create a list used by the warehouse personnel to count inventory, select Vendors, Inventory Activities, Physical Inventory Worksheet from the menu bar.

Quantity Inventory Adjustment

The most common type of inventory adjustment is the Quantity Inventory Adjustment.

The Adjust Quantity/Value on Hand is not a CDR tool, but is accessible from the Vendors, Inventory Activities menu or from an opened Client Data Review. Optionally, if you use this feature often, you can also add this to your Accountant Center.

More details about properly using the Quantity Inventory Adjustment transaction can be found in Chapter 6.

The next section discusses a different type of inventory adjustment called a value adjustment.

Value Inventory Adjustment

When deciding whether to use a Quantity on Hand or Value Adjustment only, be sure of the net result you want to obtain. A value adjustment will not change the quantity on hand, but it will assign a new average cost by dividing the units in inventory by the new value.

Timing is important when doing a valuation adjustment. Value adjustments, if appropriate, should be carefully considered for their impact on the company's resulting financials.

The value inventory adjustment is a less common type of inventory adjustment. The Adjust Quantity/Value on Hand is not a CDR tool, but is accessible from the Vendors, Inventory Activities menu or from an opened CDR. Optionally, if you use this feature often, you can also add this to your Accountant Center.

Payroll

To have QuickBooks automatically calculate payroll, you or your client will need to purchase a payroll subscription from Intuit. When payroll is not prepared properly, many of the QuickBooks payroll transactions and calculations will not work correctly or at all.

➥ *For more detailed information on the payroll subscriptions offered as well as details of the proper payroll process, see Chapter 11, "Setting Up Payroll."*

The CDR tasks for payroll will help you find payroll errors and set defaults in your client's file, which will help to avoid future mistakes.

---

tip

Your ability as the accountant to make changes in a client's payroll setup as well as adjust payroll transactions is only possible when:

- You are working in a client's working data file (.QBW file extension). You cannot make changes to payroll transactions when working in an Accountant's Copy file copy.

- You are working onsite or remotely logged into the client's file (via the Internet) and your client has a current paid payroll subscription. The payroll features available will be limited by the payroll subscription the client owns.

- You are working with the client's file at your place of business and you have a paid payroll subscription from Intuit. Accounting professionals providing payroll services for their clients will benefit from using the QuickBooks Enhanced Payroll for Accountants subscription. See Chapter 11 for more details.

Find Incorrectly Paid Payroll Liabilities

Details about the proper methods to prepare payroll and how to pay the accrued liabilities are provided in Chapter 11. Some QuickBooks users might choose to use the Write Checks transaction when preparing their payroll liability payments. Incorrectly prepared payments will adjust the balance sheet balances, but will not be reflected accurately in the Payroll Center. However, over the last several years, payroll liability payment errors are less likely to occur due to improved error messaging that encourages the QuickBooks user to prepare these liability payments properly.

This CDR task delivers another timesaving tool—helping the accounting professional easily and quickly find payroll liability payments that were recorded incorrectly.

When you select the menu or link in CDR to Find Incorrectly Paid Payroll Liabilities (Payroll group), QuickBooks prepares a report titled Payroll Liabilities Paid by Regular Check. See Figure A.36, which displays the results in true debit and credit format for each item found. This report will find a Write Checks transaction that was payable to a payroll item vendor.

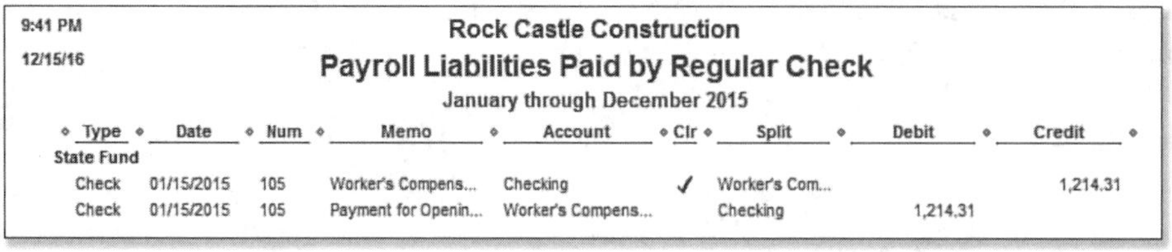

Figure A.36
This CDR report will find incorrectly paid payroll liability payment transaction types.

Use the details from this report to determine to which account your client has recorded these payroll liability payments. Did she record them to the payroll liabilities account or did she select an expense account by mistake? More details about troubleshooting payroll can be found in Chapter 12.

After you determine what account the original entries were posted to, you can complete a Payroll Liability Adjustment by following these steps:

1. From the menu bar, select Employees, Payroll Taxes and Liabilities, Adjust Payroll Liabilities to open the Liability Adjustment dialog box shown in Figure A.37.

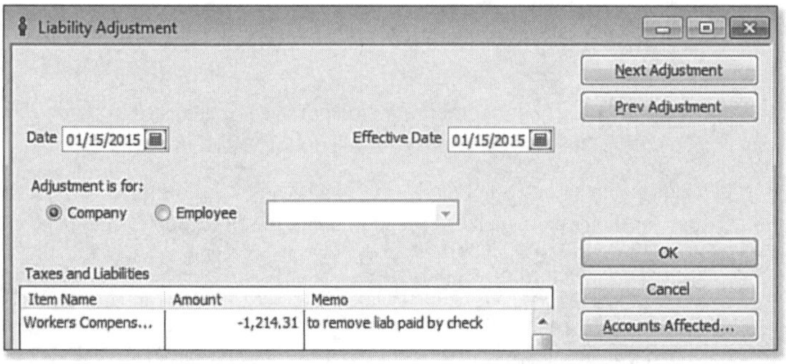

Figure A.37
Correct payroll liabilities paid incorrectly with a Liability Adjustment.

2. Enter the Date and Effective Date. Both should be dated in the quarter you want to effect the change.

3. Select Company for the adjustment. You would not select Employee here because the amounts calculated and paid were correct, just the type of transaction used to make the payment is incorrect.

4. Optionally, assign a Class if your business tracks different profit centers.

5. Click the Accounts Affected button. When determining which option button to select in the Affect Accounts? dialog box, take these suggestions into consideration:

- **Do Not Affect Accounts**—select if the original transaction was assigned to the correct payroll liability account on the balance sheet.

- **Affect Liability and Expense Accounts**—select if the original transaction was assigned to the expense account that is assigned to the payroll item used.

- **Select Affect Liability and Expense Accounts**—select if the original transaction was assigned to any other account other than those stated earlier. You will want to review your financials after making this adjustment and might need to create an adjusting journal entry to correct the balance in the account that was originally used.

6. Click OK.

7. QuickBooks might open another dialog box with the default account that is going to be affected. You can specify the account used on the original tax payment transaction being corrected.

8. Click OK to save the transaction.

9. Review the balances in the affected accounts to make sure the adjusting transactions have been entered correctly.

You can check this and other details of your client's payroll setup by completing the Run Payroll Checkup as discussed in Chapter 11.

Review Payroll Liabilities

Conveniently, from within CDR you have access to the Employee Center: Payroll Center. From the displayed dialog box, you can view multiple month calendars; your upcoming scheduled payroll processing dates; due dates and amounts for paying your payroll liabilities in a timely fashion; and even links to processing the quarterly and annual forms for federal filings and most state filings.

➥ *To learn more about using the Payroll Center, read Chapter 11.*

Review Employee Default Settings

QuickBooks CDR provides easy access to another feature that has been well hidden! Reviewing employee defaults will help your client process payroll with fewer mistakes, making future payroll reviews less time consuming.

➥ *You can learn more about setting these employee defaults in Chapter 11.*

Enter After-the-Fact Payroll

No longer is entering after-the-fact payroll time consuming! From within CDR, the accounting professional has access to this important feature. You or your client must have an active payroll subscription. If you or your client does not have an active payroll subscription, the After-the-Fact Payroll task will not display in the Payroll task group. Keep this in mind if you are working at the client's site or remotely logged into the client's data file.

Payroll entered through the After-the-Fact Payroll processing will also be included in all of the federal and state forms QuickBooks payroll subscriptions prepare.

Bank Reconciliation

There are many ways to troubleshoot bank reconciliation issues with your client's data. With QuickBooks Accountant 2012 you have access to the Accountant Center (see Figure A.2), which displays timely information about your client's bank and credit card reconciliations.

 Learn more about completing and troubleshooting your client's bank reconciliations in Chapter 13.

Reconcile Accounts

You can use the Reconcile Accounts link in the Bank Reconciliation task group of the CDR feature to troubleshoot or complete your client's monthly bank reconciliation. If you are working with a client's Accountants, Copy file, you will be able to reconcile the bank account and these reconciliations will be incorporated into your client's data.

 More details about this topic can be found in Chapter 16, "Sharing Data with Your Accountant."

In my years of working with clients QuickBooks files, the bank reconciliation is the task I most frequently see not completed at all, or not done correctly, yet it is one of the most important tasks for viewing trusted financials. The CDR feature helps you, the accountant, work with your client's data file when reviewing or completing the bank reconciliation.

Locate Discrepancies in Bank Reconciliation

After reviewing the client's previous bank reconciliations, you might determine that the beginning balance, which was once correct, is no longer correct. Perhaps your client modified, voided, or deleted a previously cleared transaction.

The Locate Discrepancies in Bank Reconciliation report will help you to easily find these. The report is added to the CDR, Bank Reconciliation group:

1. From the menu bar, select Accountant, Client Data Review and launch the Client Data Review feature.

2. In the Bank Reconciliation group, select the Locate Discrepancies in Bank Reconciliation task.

3. The Previous Reconciliation Discrepancy report displays. For each transaction on this report, you will see the modified date, reconciled amount, type of change (amount added or deleted), and the financial effect of the change (see Figure A.38) grouped by bank statement date.

Figure A.38
View details of previously cleared transactions that have been modified or deleted.

You can add the username to the report details to help in identifying who made the change to the transaction:

1. From the open Previous Reconciliation Discrepancy report, click Customize Report.

2. On the Display tab, place a checkmark on Last Modified By in the Columns box.

3. Click OK.

After reviewing the Previous Reconciliation Discrepancy report, you can prepare the Voided/Deleted report to help determine how to correct the transaction(s). To prepare this report, select Reports, Accountant & Taxes, Voided/Deleted Transactions Summary (or Detail) from the menu bar.

The Voided/Deleted report will not track discrepancies caused by changing the bank account associated with a transaction or changing a transaction amount. However, now with the Client Data Review, Review List Changes task will track changes made from adding, deleting, or even merging charts of accounts and other list items in QuickBooks.

 caution

Troubleshoot your beginning balance differences with the Previous Reconciliation Discrepancy report before completing the next month's reconciliation. Doing so is important because QuickBooks removes all details from the discrepancy report when you complete a new reconciliation. This is due to QuickBooks determining that you have solved the issue or you would not have completed the next month's bank reconciliation.

Reviewing Missing Checks

The Missing Checks report is useful when reviewing the accuracy of your client's bank account data. This report can help you determine whether any check transactions are missing or duplicated.

The Review Missing Checks link is conveniently included in the Bank Reconciliation cleanup tasks. In the Specify Account dialog box select the appropriate bank account from the drop-down list.

The resulting Missing Checks report shows all transactions that are withdrawals from (that is, credits to) the bank account and that have a reference number. Transaction types include check, bill payment, sales tax payment, liability payment, paycheck, and general journal entry type transactions, presented in order by their reference number (see Figure A.39).

You will look for any breaks in the detail with a ***Missing or ***Duplicate warning.

9:49 PM
12/15/16

Rock Castle Construction
Missing Checks
All Transactions

Type	Date	Num	Name	Memo	Account	Split	Amount
Liability Check	11/07/2016	447	State Fund		Checking	Worker's Com...	-804.16
*** Duplicate document numbers ***							
Check	11/07/2016	447	State Fund		Checking	Worker's Com...	-804.16
Check	11/12/2016	448	Patton Hardware S...		Checking	Job Materials	-48.10
Bill Pmt -Check	11/14/2016	449	McClain Appliances	85-93117	Checking	Accounts Pa...	-800.00
Bill Pmt -Check	11/14/2016	450	C.U. Electric		Checking	Accounts Pa...	-440.00
Bill Pmt -Check	11/14/2016	451	Larson Flooring		Checking	Accounts Pa...	-3,200.00
Bill Pmt -Check	11/14/2016	452	Middlefield Drywall	ROCK-0921	Checking	Accounts Pa...	-850.00
Bill Pmt -Check	11/14/2016	453	East Bayshore Au...	Monthly Truc...	Checking	Accounts Pa...	-532.97
Check	11/15/2016	454	Sergeant Insurance		Checking	-SPLIT-	-675.00
*** Missing numbers here ***							
Check	11/15/2016	456	QuickBooks Maste...		Checking	QuickBooks C...	-1,050.00
Check	11/15/2016	457	CalOil Company		Checking	CalOil Credit C...	-48.28
Sales Tax Paym...	11/15/2016	458	State Board of Equ...	ABCD 11-23...	Checking	-SPLIT-	-1,983.01

Figure A.39
The Missing Checks report can help you determine whether you need to enter any missing transactions before you reconcile.

Miscellaneous

This section of the CDR can be one of the most useful to you because it shows you how to set preferences to make your client's work more accurate and how to set a closing date, which will prevent or discourage a user from making changes to your reviewed data. If you are working with a client's Accountant's Copy, you will be able to set the Closing Date and optional Closing Date Password, which will be incorporated into the client's file.

Setting the Closing Date and Password

QuickBooks offers flexibility for accounting professionals who want to protect prior period data and those who need or want to make changes to prior period accounting records.

What exactly is a "closed" accounting period? Well, a business can decide to close a month when a task such as a bank reconciliation is done or a sales tax return is filed, or a business can simply close once a year when the data is finalized for tax preparation. Because QuickBooks does not require you to close the books, it is a decision of the accounting professional and business owner (see Chapter 16).

The option of setting a closing date and password makes it easy to protect prior period transactions from unwanted modifications. With additional user-specific security settings, the business owner and accountant can also manage who has the privilege to make changes to transactions dated on or before a specific closing date.

Step One—Setting the Date and Assigning the Password

The first step in controlling changes to closed accounting periods is to set a closing date and optionally (although recommended) a closing date password the user must provide when adding, deleting, or modifying a transaction dated on or before the closing date.

Another important reason for setting a closing date is to track additions, modifications, or deletions to transactions dated on or before a closing date. The Closing Date Exceptions report will not track these changes when a closing date is not set.

To set the closing date and optionally a password (different from the Admin or External Accountant password) from an open Client Data Review, follow these steps:

1. Click the Set Closing Date and Password link in the Miscellaneous group of the CDR center. The Accounting—Company Preferences tab of the Preferences dialog box opens.

2. Click the Set Date/Password button. The Set Closing Date and Password dialog box displays.

3. Optionally, select the following checkbox: Exclude Estimates, Sales Orders, and Purchase Orders from Closing Date Restrictions. These transactions are non-posting and changes made will not affect your financials.

4. Enter a closing date and optional password. Consider using your phone number as the password or "Call Accountant" to encourage your client to call you before making changes to closed period transactions.

5. Click OK to close the Set Closing Date and Password dialog box.

6. If the No Password Entered warning displays, select Yes to add or edit users or No to close the warning.

7. Click OK to close the Preferences dialog box.

Setting a closing date is only step one. Next, you must set user-specific privileges for users to whom you want to allow access to adding, deleting, or modifying a transaction dated on or before the closing date.

Step Two—Setting User-Specific Security

To be certain the closing date control is managed properly, review all users for their specific rights to change transactions up to and including a closing date. To view the following menu, you need to be logged into the file as the Admin user (External Accountant user type does not have the capability to create new users or change permissions for existing users):

1. From the menu bar, select Company, Set Up Users and Passwords, Set Up Users. The User List dialog box opens.

2. To view a user's existing security privileges (other than the Admin or External Accountant user) from the User List dialog box, select the user and click the View User button. You will be able to view in summary form the security settings for that user, as shown in Figure A.40.

3. Any user who should not have rights to changing closed period transactions should have an "N" placed in the last setting of Changing Closed Transactions.

4. If after reviewing a user's existing security privileges, you need to edit the setting referenced earlier, click Leave to close the View User Access dialog box.

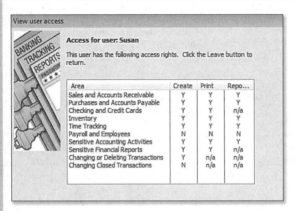

Figure A.40
Review in summary form the user's security privileges.

5. QuickBooks returns you to the User List dialog box. Select the username and click the Edit User button.

6. On the Change User Password and Access dialog box, optionally modify the username or password. Click Next to continue.

7. The User Access dialog box for the specific user displays. Choose Selected Areas and click Next to continue through each of the security selections until you reach the selections on Page 9 of the dialog box as shown in Figure A.41.

Figure A.41
With QuickBooks you set controls not to allow users to change transactions on or before a set closing date.

With the ease of doing client reviews, and now the security of knowing your hard work is documented and protected with a closing date, your future reviews should take even less time to complete, giving you more time to help your client with important management decisions!

Review QuickBooks Preferences

Don't forget during your review to manage properly the many useful preferences that will help you and your client work more efficiently and accurately in the QuickBooks data file.

QuickBooks offers two types of preferences:

- **My Preferences**—Choices selected on this tab are being defined only for the currently logged-in user. If you are setting preferences for your client, you should log in with her username, and then set the My Preferences. These settings can be changed while in a multi-user environment (when others are in the date file).

- **Company Preferences**—Preferences set on these tabs are global for all users in the QuickBooks data file. Often, these preferences can be set only when you are in single-user mode, meaning other users cannot be working in the file when you set Company Preferences. Both the Admin and the new External Accountant type user can modify Company Preferences.

There are preferences specific for accounting you will want to review. As the trusted accounting professional for your client, you will benefit by reviewing each of the available preferences, including:

- Accounting

- Bills

- Calendar

- Checking

- Desktop View

- Finance Charge

- General

- Integrated Applications

- Items & Inventory

- Jobs & Estimates

- Multiple Currencies

- Payments

- Payroll & Employees

- Reminders

- Reports & Graphs

- Sales & Customers

- Sales Tax

- Search

- Send Forms

- Service Connection

- Spelling

- Tax: 1099

- Time and Expenses

Of the preferences, those that can enhance the accounting accuracy of a QuickBooks file are discussed in more depth in the related chapter. For example, the Sales & Customer preferences that improve the client's accuracy in QuickBooks are detailed in Chapter 9.

With a password set and preferences reviewed, your next review of your client's data should take even less time using the CDR.

Finishing a Client Data Review

You can leave a CDR open for as long as it takes you to finish. When you close out of a task, your work is saved. Additionally, as you are working, you can conveniently select a QuickBooks menu outside of the Client Data Review and CDR will refresh automatically, including transactions created and modified.

Optionally, as you work through the many tasks, you can record an overall note for the review or individual notes assigned to specific tasks.

Saving the Review as a PDF

You can print the details of your CDR to paper or save as a PDF file. The information included with this document is shown in Figure A.42:

- Company Name

- Review Period (Last Fiscal Year, Quarter, Month, or Custom)

- Date Printed

- Dates included in this review

- Basis: Accrual or Cash

- Client Data Review Notes

- Cleanup Tasks and subtasks

- Status

- Task note

- Filename and path where the report is stored if prepared in PDF format

Client Data Review for Rock Castle Construction — Page 1 of 2

Rock Castle Construction

Review Period: **Last Fiscal Year** — Date Printed: **12/15/2016**

Dates: **01/01/2015 - 12/31/2015** — Basis: **Cash**

Review Notes:

```
Provide copy of review notes when completed to:

Bob Smith
CFO
Rock Castle Construction
bob@rockcastleconstruction.com
```

Cleanup Tasks	Status	Task Notes
Account Balances		
Troubleshoot Prior Account Balances	Completed	
Reclassify Transactions	Completed	
Open Working Trial Balance	In Progress	
Review List Changes		
Chart of Accounts	Completed	
Items	Completed	
Fixed Asset Items	Completed	11/15/15 Client purchased a new Dell Server, request purchase documents.
Payroll Items	Completed	
Review Item Setup	Not Started	
Customers	Not Started	
Vendors	Not Started	
Accounts Receivable		
Fix Unapplied Customer Payments and Credits	Not Started	
Clear Up Undeposited Funds Account	Not Started	
Review AR Aging Summary Report	Not Started	
Write Off Invoices	Not Started	
Accounts Payable		
Fix Unapplied Vendor Payments and Credits	Not Started	
Evaluate and Correct 1099 Account Mapping	Not Started	
Review Unpaid Bills Report	Not Started	
Sales Tax		
Fix Incorrectly Recorded Sales Tax	Not Started	
Adjust Sales Tax Payable	Not Started	
Manage Sales Tax	Not Started	
Pay Sales Tax	Not Started	
Sales Tax Preferences	Not Started	
Inventory		
Review Inventory Setup	Not Started	
Compare Balance Sheet and Inventory Valuation	Not Started	
Troubleshoot Inventory	Not Started	
Adjust Inventory Quantity/Value On Hand	Not Started	

Figure A.42
Print or Save to PDF the details of the review for your paper files.

Marking Review Complete

When you have completed all tasks in the CDR and you select the Mark Review Complete button, QuickBooks will:

- Provide the option to set a closing date and password.
- Change the Prior Review Period Dates in the Troubleshoot Account Balances task.
- In the Troubleshoot Account Balances tasks, transfer your final reviewed balances to the Last Review Balances column. (These amounts will not change even if a customer makes a change to a transaction dated in that review period!)
- Provide the option to carry over task notes to the next review.

Specific to the Troubleshoot Account Balances task, you do not have to Mark the Review as Complete for each review. However, your ending balances will be recorded only in the Last Review

Balances column when you mark the review as completed. Marking a review as completed still gives you the option to reopen a previously closed review.

Reopening a Client Data Review

After marking a review as complete and before you start the next review, you will have the option to reopen the previously marked completed review as shown in Figure A.43. After you start a new review, you will no longer have the option to reopen the previously completed review.

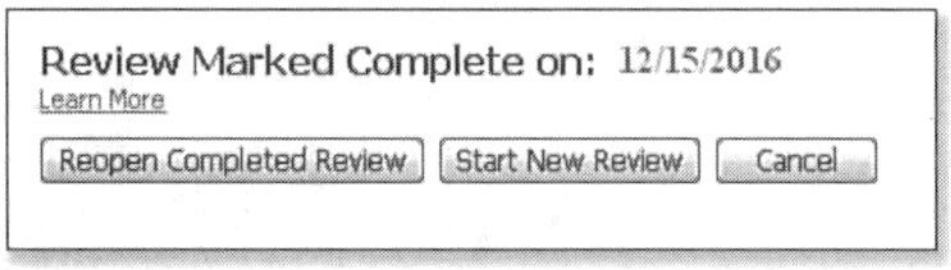

Figure A.43
Before starting a new review, you will have the option to open a previously closed review.

Reporting on Review Activity

Also available on the CDR Center is a link to the Audit Trail of Review report (see Figure A.44). You can use this report to detail the transactions you have added, modified, or deleted during your review. The Audit Trail report will not report on changes made to list items.

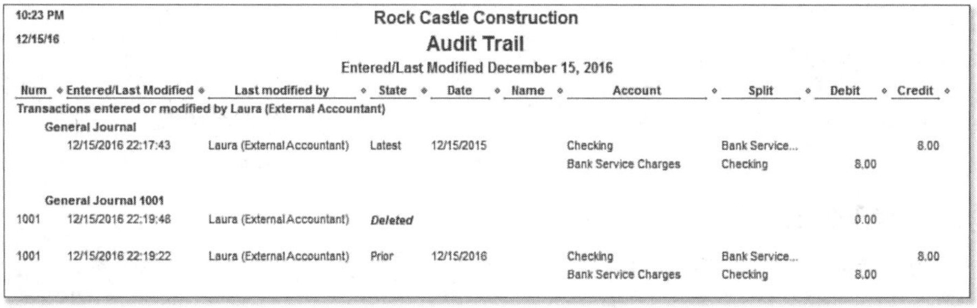

10:23 PM
12/15/16

Rock Castle Construction
Audit Trail
Entered/Last Modified December 15, 2016

Num	Entered/Last Modified	Last modified by	State	Date	Name	Account	Split	Debit	Credit
Transactions entered or modified by Laura (External Accountant)									
General Journal									
	12/15/2016 22:17:43	Laura (External Accountant)	Latest	12/15/2015		Checking	Bank Service...		8.00
						Bank Service Charges	Checking	8.00	
General Journal 1001									
1001	12/15/2016 22:19:48	Laura (External Accountant)	*Deleted*					0.00	
1001	12/15/2016 22:19:22	Laura (External Accountant)	Prior	12/15/2016		Checking	Bank Service...		8.00
						Bank Service Charges	Checking	8.00	

Figure A.44
The QuickBooks Audit Trail report helps identify what changes were made to transactions and by which user.

Additionally, if you used the new External Accountant type of login access, you were given all the rights of the Admin user (except adding or modifying users and viewing sensitive customer credit card information) and you can see your changes separate from the Admin or other users on this report.

The Audit Trail report provides details of additions and changes made to transactions, grouping the changes by username. The detail on this report shows the prior versions of the transaction and the latest version of the transaction, if it was edited. The Audit Trail report defaults to changes made as of today's date. This filter date can be modified for your needs.

The audit trail report can be lengthy to review. However, if as an accountant you try to track down specific user activity with transactions, this can be a useful report to review because the changes are grouped by username.

If you find undesired transaction changes, consider setting a closing date password and setting specific user security privileges as detailed earlier in this chapter.

Creating an External Accountant User

Setting up a QuickBooks user for each person who enters data provides a level of control over the sensitive data to be viewed by this user and gives access to specific areas in QuickBooks. For additional control, a user-specific password can also be assigned.

When you create a new user (or edit an existing user) in QuickBooks, you can assign that user as an External Accountant.

As an accounting professional using the CDR, you will want to request that your client create a username for you and assign the new External Accountant Type. If you then log into the client file with this new user type, you will benefit from:

- Complete Admin access, except you cannot create or edit users, or view sensitive customer credit card numbers.

- Reports such as the Audit Trail can be filtered in Excel for a specific username, enabling you to see your transactions separate from the client's transactions.

- Client Data Review distinguishes in the dialog box if your login is the new External Accountant type (see Figure A.1).

- Access to the Accountant Center, plus limited accountant and CDR tools when logging into a client's QuickBooks Pro, Premier, or Enterprise 2012 non-accountant edition file.

If you are reviewing your client's data using the Accountant's Copy file type or if you are not given the Admin login, this new External Accountant will have to be created before your client creates the Accountant's Copy or has you review her data file.

To create an External Accountant, follow these steps:

1. Open the QuickBooks data file using the Admin user (the default user QuickBooks creates with a new QuickBooks file) and enter the appropriate password if one was created.

2. From the menu bar, select Company, Set Up Users and Passwords, Set Up Users.

3. Enter the Admin user password if one was originally assigned. Click OK.

   The User List dialog box opens; it lists the current users set up for this file.

4. Click the Add User button to create a new user, or select an existing username and click the Edit User button.

5. The Set up (or Change) User Password and Access dialog box opens.

6. In the User Name field, type the name you want the user to be identified by in the file.

7. In the Password field, enter an optional password, and in the Confirm Password field, retype the password for accuracy.

8. Optionally, click the box to Add This User to My QuickBooks License. (See the explain link for more details.)

9. Click Next. You might receive a No Password Entered message, click Yes or No to creating a password. If you select Yes, you will be taken back to step 7. Optionally, select Do Not Display This Message in the Future.

10. The Access for User:<username> dialog box opens.

11. Select the option for External Accountant, as shown in Figure A.45.

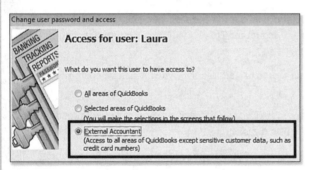

Figure A.45
Ask your client to create an External Accountant type user for your login.

12. Click Next.

13. QuickBooks provides a warning message, confirming that you want to give this new user access to all areas of QuickBooks except customer credit card numbers. Select Yes to assign the new External Accountant type privileges to this new or existing user.

14. The Access for User:<username> dialog box opens. The message restates that the new External Accountant user will have access to all areas of QuickBooks except sensitive customer credit card data. Click Finish to complete the process.

QUICKBOOKS STATEMENT WRITER

Overview

QuickBooks Statement Writer, formerly known as Intuit Statement Writer, is an extremely powerful and flexible reporting tool available for no additional fee with QuickBooks Accountant 2012 and all QuickBooks Enterprise Solutions 12.0 suites. Accounting professionals can use QuickBooks Statement Writer to prepare professional Generally Accepted Accounting Principles (GAAP)–compliant financials from QuickBooks data.

QuickBooks Statement Writer uses Microsoft Excel as the platform for creating customized financial reports from QuickBooks data. Additionally, QuickBooks Statement Writer keeps the statements synchronized with changes in the QuickBooks data. You can also add supporting documents created in Word and include them in your customized financials.

QuickBooks Statement Writer works with Excel 2003 or newer. (Note: It will *not* work with Microsoft Office 2003 Standard, 2003 Student Edition, or 2003 Small Business Edition.) QuickBooks Statement Writer currently only works with the 32-bit (not 64-bit) install of Excel 2010.

> **note**
>
> The QuickBooks Statement Writer feature replaces the Intuit Statement Writer (ISW) and Financial Statement Designer (FSD) reporting tools used in earlier versions of QuickBooks.
>
> If you are migrating from ISW or FSD to QuickBooks Statement Writer before preparing statements, visit http://accountant.intuit.com/ISW. Go to "Product Support" for details and tools to help with the conversion.

Terms

The following terms will help you when working with the QuickBooks Statement Writer:

- **QSW**—Refers to QuickBooks Statement Writer.
- **Statement**—Specific financial statement, such as a Balance Sheet or Income Statement.
- **Documents**—Created with Word, such as a cover sheet or letter.
- **Statement Writer Report**—Collection of statements and documents.

Workflow

There are three main steps when working with the QSW tool:

1. Open the QuickBooks file that contains the data using your QuickBooks Accountant 2012 or QuickBooks Enterprise Solutions 12.0 software (all editions).

2. Use the Report Designer for a step-by-step approach to creating a Statement Writer report.

3. Output the customized financial to Microsoft Excel, and use common Excel features or functions to add additional customization.

Benefits

Benefits of using QSW include the ability to

- Create customized, professional financial statements from your client's QuickBooks data without manually typing data into Excel.
- Include multiple financial statements and supporting documents in a single QSW report.
- Use one of the many templates provided to create your own statements. Templates come in a variety of formats for the Balance Sheet, Income Statement, Cash Flow Statement, Retained Earnings Statement, and Budget to Actual Statements.
- Use Microsoft Excel (2003 or newer) as the platform for customizing and utilizing all the additional features and reporting flexibility available in Excel.
- Refresh customized financials with current QuickBooks data without leaving the Excel QSW report.
- Combine multiple QuickBooks account lines into one line on financial statements without changing your client's QuickBooks data.
- Add your own rows or columns of detail.
- Drill down to QuickBooks data and make changes to transactions within the QSW tool.
- Easily view and add any missing accounts not included in the current statement.
- Create charts and graphs using Excel functionality.

- Add supporting documents, such as a cover sheet or compilation letter, created in Microsoft Word, so you have a complete set of financials ready to print.

- Share your customized reports with clients as an Excel spreadsheet or PDF-formatted document.

Getting Started

To launch QSW from your QuickBooks Accountant 2012 or QuickBooks Enterprise Solutions 12.0 software, follow these steps:

1. From the menu bar, select Reports, QuickBooks Statement Writer. If you are using QuickBooks Accountant or QuickBooks Enterprise Accountant software you can also launch QSW from the Accountant menu or the Accountant Center.

   ➡ *For more information, see "Customizing the New Accountant Center," p. 605.*

2. If prompted, select Download Update and then Install Update. If you are not prompted, skip to step 5 below.

3. Some computer systems require additional setup. If prompted with the User Account Control or other messages, follow the prompts to run QSW. You will only have to do these additional setup steps once.

4. Select Yes to the Install Shield Wizard and follow all prompts to install the update. Click Close to the QSW Update Manager message that you have the most current version.

5. The main QSW screen displays as shown in Figure B.1.

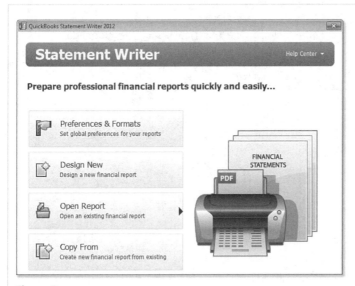

Figure B.1
The QuickBooks Statement Writer main screen offers easy access to all the features.

The following sections detail the different global preferences that can be set in QSW.

Preferences & Formats

From the Preferences & Formats menu you will set global preferences and settings for customized reports prepared from all of your client's files.

General Preferences

The General Preference settings dialog box opens when you launch the Preferences & Formats from the main QSW screen. These settings permit you to:

- Accept the default location for your stored reports or browse to a location of your choice.

- Accept the default location for storing QSW templates or browse to a location of your choice.

- Use advanced settings for choosing to manually configure net-work permissions.

- Run Diagnostics Now, which will check that your system, QuickBooks, and QSW are configured correctly.

- Reset all warnings.

- Reset defaults.

 note

Selecting OK on the General Preferences dialog box closes Preferences and returns you to the main QSW screen.

Optionally select Apply as you make changes. Next, select the Your Details menu tab to the left.

Your Details

Complete your Firm Name, Address, and other fields on the Your Details tab. The information entered here appears for all client files you open with this registered copy of QuickBooks. See Figure B.2.

Click the blue colored text to access help content about the currently displayed window.

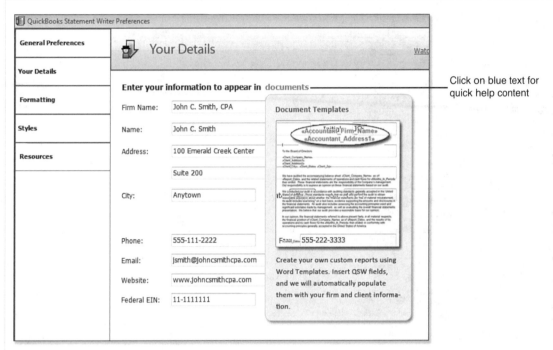

Click on blue text for quick help content

Figure B.2
Enter your firm information once and it will be included with each client's customized financial reports.

Formatting

On the Formatting tab, you can define the following global settings (see Figure B.3) for formatting all QSW statements. You can override these settings on individual statements when needed.

- **Automatic Underlines**—When total or subtotal rows are added to a statement, upon refresh underlines will be added.

- **Show**—Set defaults for displaying or not displaying decimals, column headers, inactive accounts, and zero-balance accounts.

- **Show Zero Balances As**—Default the format for displaying any cell with a zero balance.

- **Show Negative Numbers As**—Choose from several options.

- **Divide All Data By**—Option to round (or not) the displayed amount.

> ⚠ **caution**
> Data formatting preferences will be displayed in Excel, but not while working in the QSW Report Designer.

Select the Reset Defaults button to return to the original formatting settings. Select Apply to save your changes. Select OK to close and save changes.

Styles

Styles are used for formatting the font, font size, bold, italic, and justification of the text as shown in Figure B.4.

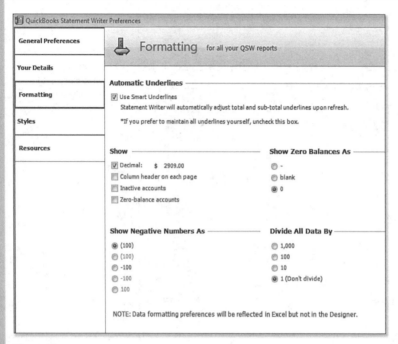

Figure B.3
Set default format settings for all QSW statements.

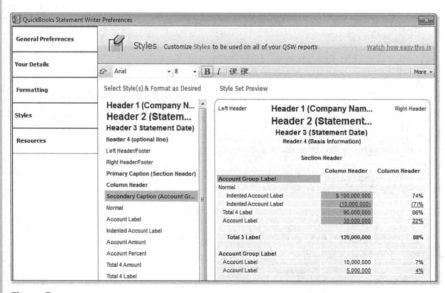

Figure B.4
Styles are used to set default font type and size. Style settings can be saved for reuse with other statements.

On the Styles tab, select any style(s) and change the format as desired.

To change the style for multiple headers, labels, or cells all at once, right-click with your mouse after selecting the content and choose the desired style.

After customizing your style, from the More drop-down list select Save as New Style Set. Enter a Style Set Name and this customized Style will be available the next time you create a new QSW statement.

 tip

To assign a style for multiple rows, hold down the Ctrl key on your keyboard when selecting multiple headers, labels, or cells.

Resources

Select the Resources tab for a listing of QSW resources and contact information. Additionally use this menu to download Intuit-provided statement and document templates.

Using the Report Designer

With the global preferences set, you are now prepared to create customized financials for your clients using QSW.

To begin using QSW, open your client's file in your QuickBooks Accountant 2012 or QuickBooks Enterprise 12.0 software (all suites) and launch QSW (as previously instructed).

You can use the ease of the QSW Report Designer to customize the financial report before creating it in Excel. You can further customize the report once you've exported it to Excel from the QSW.

Report Content

The Report Content tab displays when you launch QSW and select Design New. From this dialog box, you select your Report Date from pre-defined periods or choose a Custom Date range. This date range can be changed later without your returning to this dialog box.

Select from Accrual or Cash Basis. From the Statement and Document Templates panel select the desired template. With the template selected, click the arrows in the center to add or remove statements and documents as well as arrange their order in the Financial Report Contents pane. See Figure B.5.

Lastly, you will be required to provide a name for the report. These reports will be stored in the default location defined in preferences.

 For more information, see "General Preferences," p. 606.

Click Next to advance to the next task of customizing the columns of data to be included in the report.

 note

Each template in the Financial Report Contents column will become a worksheet within a single Excel workbook.

You do not need to worry about the order the statements or documents are added to the Financial Report Contents. When you are ready to print the financials, you specify the print order within Excel.

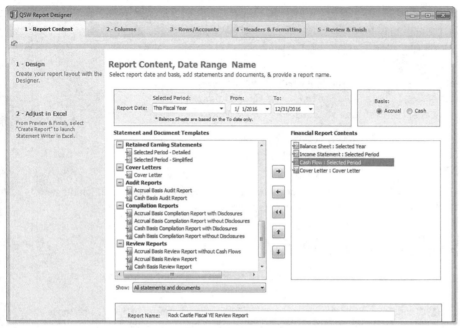

Figure B.5
The Report Date and Basis defined here can be modified later in the Statement Writer report.

Columns

Figure B.6 shows the Columns tab. A separate tab is created for each included statement or document. Click a specific statement to display data from the currently opened QuickBooks file (if a document is selected, instructions for modifying documents is provided).

Features of customizing columns include the ability to:

tip

A short-cut menu containing many of the functions will appear when you right-click a column within a report.

- Drag to insert columns, choosing from several types of columns including Blank, QuickBooks Data, Variance, and Total columns to mention just a few.

- Refresh the data displayed in the QSW Report Designer, change the position of columns, remove columns, and modify the column header or dates from the toolbar.

Click the Undo icon on the toolbar (see Figure B.6) to undo the last action. Click Next to advance to the Rows/Accounts tab. Alternatively, click the Rows/Accounts tab at the top the QSW Report Designer dialog box to access this tab directly.

Rows/Accounts

Figure B.7 shows the Rows/Accounts tab. A separate tab (worksheet) is created in Excel for each included statement or document. Click a specific statement to display data from the currently opened QuickBooks file (if a document is selected, instructions for modifying documents are provided).

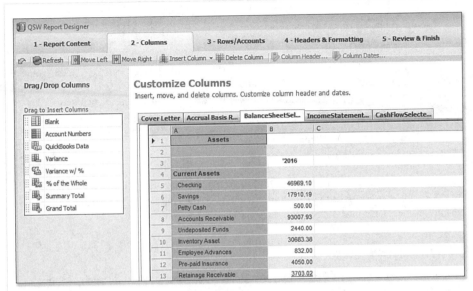

Figure B.6
Use the QSW Report Designer to customize the column properties in the selected statement.

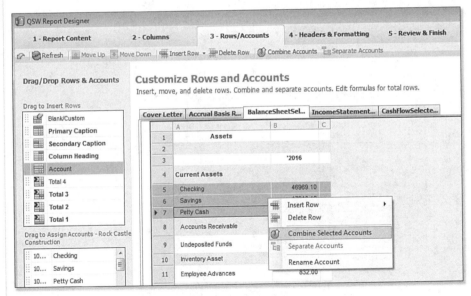

Figure B.7
Right-click to modify the currently selected row(s).

Features of this tab include the ability to:

- Drag to insert rows, choosing from several types of rows including Blank/Custom, Account, and a variety of Total row options.

- Use the following toolbar buttons to modify rows and accounts: Refresh, Move Up, Move Down, Insert Row, Delete Row, Combine Accounts, or Separate Accounts.

- Easily identify missing or new rows by selecting the Show: Missing/New option button in the lower-left corner.

tip

Combine rows together by selecting multiple rows with the Ctrl key on your keyboard. From the Rows/Accounts toolbar, select Combine Accounts.

Click the Undo icon on the left side of the toolbar to undo the last action. See Figure B.6. Click Next to advance to the Headers & Formatting tab. Alternatively, click the Headers & Formatting tab at the top of the QSW Report Designer dialog box to access this tab directly.

Headers & Formatting

Figure B.8 shows the Headers/Footers Formatting tab. A separate tab is created for each included statement or document. Click a specific statement (tab) to display data from the currently opened QuickBooks file (if a document (tab) is selected, instructions for modifying documents are provided).

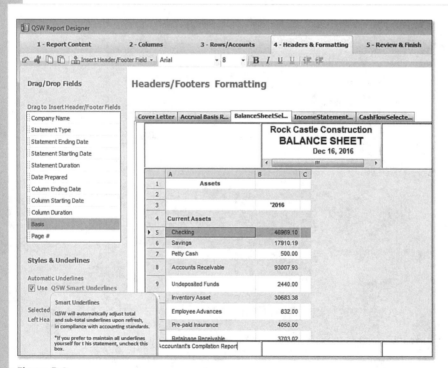

Figure B.8
Hover your cursor over blue text to view help content for that feature.

Features of this tab include the ability to:

- Drag to insert header and footer fields, choosing from several types of fields including Statement Ending Date, Date Prepared, Basis, and Page # to name just a few.

- Use the Header & Formatting toolbar buttons to cut, copy, and paste fields and change the font, size, and properties of a field.

- Use QSW Smart Underlines. For more information, click the blue text to display help content.

Click the Undo icon on the toolbar to undo the last action as shown in figure B.6. Click Next to advance to the Review & Finish tab. Alternatively, click the Review & Finish tab at the top of the QSW Report Designer to access this tab directly.

Review & Finish

If this is your first time creating the report using Report Designer, on the Review & Finish tab a separate tab is created for each included statement or document for review. Click a specific statement to display the customized formatting (if a document is selected, instructions for modifying documents are provided).

Select a specific statement and from the toolbar choose the Memorize Current Statement. You can then reuse this customized statement with new financial reports.

Choose Memorize Report Group from the toolbar to save the group of selected statements for use with a newly created financial report from another client's data.

Click Create Report to send your customization into Excel. QuickBooks will launch Excel and add the customized formatting you created in the Designer. Each statement will be an individual worksheet tab in a single Excel workbook. See Figure B.9.

 note

If you are returning to the Report Designer from a previously prepared QSW report you will not see the individual statement tabs at the top. Instead, you will have to select the desired statement in the Excel QSW then select the Report Designer icon from the QSW Document Actions pane toolbar to modify.

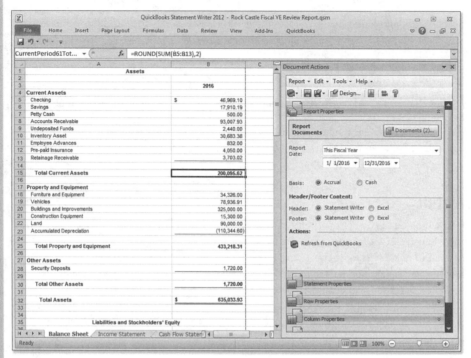

Figure B.9
QSW uses Excel for the completed report.

Opening a Previously Created Report

When a user clicks Open Report from the main QSW dialog box, the five most recently accessed reports for the currently opened company file display. Optionally, a user can select Browse to Open, which by default looks to the same folder where the current reports are stored.

After you select a report from the list or browsing to a report, QSW will launch the report in Excel. If prompted by your system, select Yes to any prompts to trust the source of the file. (Your version of Excel might have security settings that will not recognize the .QSM extension of the QSW stored report without your granting permission to trust the file type.)

Creating a New Report from a Memorized Report

Click the Copy From button on the main QSW dialog box to reuse a previously memorized statement or report group.

Click Browse, and QSW will default to the location where the most recent QSW report was stored. If necessary, browse to another location to find the report with the .QSM extension.

With the Source Report selected, click Open. The Copy From dialog box displays the Source Report location and the Destination folder. Provide a New Report Name and click Copy.

Select or deselect the option to Open New Report.

Modifying a Statement Writer Report in Excel

Now that you have created a Statement Writer report, you might find the need to customize the content for future reports or for use with other client's data files.

There are several methods you can use to edit an existing Statement Writer report, which include:

- Returning to the Report Designer

- Using the Document Actions pane

- Using the QSW icons on the Excel Add-Ins Ribbon (or Excel 2003 toolbar)

- Right-clicking a report column, row, or cell in Excel.

You might use one or all of these methods. The next sections provide additional details on working with each of these methods.

Method 1: Using the Report Designer

When creating the original Statement Writer report, you most likely used the Report Designer. You can return to this familiar tool to make edits to your existing Statement Writer report.

From a displayed Statement Writer report in Excel, click the Design icon on the Document Actions pane toolbar, as shown in Figure B.10.

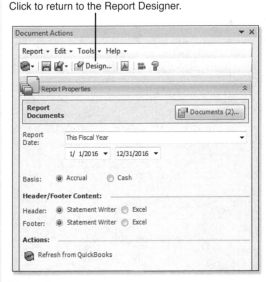

Click to return to the Report Designer.

Figure B.10
Access the Report Designer from the toolbar in the Document Actions pane.

If you have made formatting edits while in Excel, answer Yes or No to the warning message that displays. If you select Yes, the Report Designer for the current Statement Writer report opens.

 For more information, see "Using the Report Designer," p. 663.

For more information, see "Using the Report Designer," p. 663.

> **note**
>
> If you have multiple statements in your report, you will need to select the desired statement in Excel that you want to modify in Report Designer. Only the first time you create your QSW report will each statement display as an individual tab on the Report Designer, Review & Finish tab.

Method 2: Using the Document Actions Pane

There are several methods for editing an existing Statement Writer report; one method is accessing the many edit tools from the Document Actions pane.

The Document Actions pane, shown in Figure B.11, will only display when launch QuickBooks and then open a Statement Writer report from within the QSW. The file extension of .QSM is assigned to these reports by QSW and cannot be opened directly with Excel.

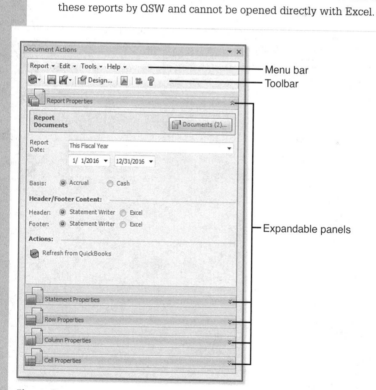

Figure B.11
Use the Document Actions pane to add or edit the Statement Writer report.

note

Are you having trouble viewing the Statement Writer pane in Microsoft Excel as shown in Figure B.11? First, be sure you have opened the QSW report after launching QSW from within the QuickBooks file. If you still do not see the Statement Writer pane you might have inadvertently closed it.

Depending on which version of Excel you have, reopening the Statement Writer pane requires different steps. In Excel 2010, select the Add-Ins ribbon and click the QSW Toolbar: Show Statement Writer Pane icon. In Excel 2007 and 2003, select the Add-Ins tab, select View, Toolbars, and place a checkmark next to QuickBooks Statement Writer. With Excel 2003, you might have to make the toolbar visible. Hover your mouse over the icons to find the icon that will reinstate your Statement Writer pane as shown later in Figure B.19.

Most, if not all, of the functionality detailed to this point in the chapter can be found by selecting one of the drop-down menus from the menu bar in the Document Actions pane.

Frequently used actions are included on the Documents Action toolbar, as shown previously in Figure B.11.

More detailed edits can be made by selecting one of the expandable panes for Report, Statement, Row, Column, and Cell Properties depending on the change you need to make.

Find Missing Accounts

Identifying new accounts created by your client since the last time you prepared a Statement Writer report used to be a daunting task. Now, it is easier than ever.

From the toolbar in the Document Actions pane, select Edit, Show All Accounts. The All Accounts dialog box displays as shown in Figure B.12. Any missing accounts from the customized financials will be displayed in red. Optionally, select to show only the Missing accounts.

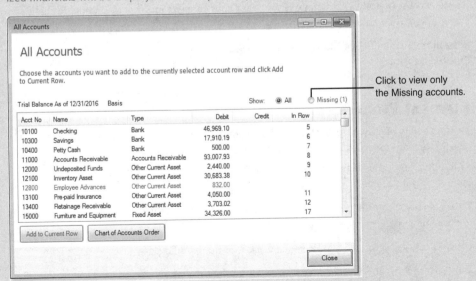

Click to view only the Missing accounts.

Figure B.12
Has your client added new accounts since preparing your last report? Locate them efficiently with the All Accounts dialog box.

To review or add the missing account(s), follow these steps:

1. After reviewing the missing accounts, click Close on the All Accounts dialog box.

2. From the Row Properties, choose to add a new account row or highlight with your cursor an existing row you want to add the missing account(s) to.

3. With your cursor on the row you want to add the account(s) to, from the toolbar in the Document Actions pane, select Edit, Show All Accounts.

4. Select the missing account(s).

5. Select the Add to Current Row button. As you complete this for each missing account(s) there will no longer be any accounts in red.

6. Click Close to return to the modified Statement Writer report.

Report Properties

The term used by QSW for a collection of statements is a Statement Writer report. When you need to make global changes to all statements within a report, use the Report Properties. With report properties (previously shown in Figure B.10) you can manage the following:

- **Documents**—Add or modify supporting documents. See, "Adding or Modifying a Supporting Document," p. 680.

- **Report Date**—Select from predetermined dates or choose a custom date.

- **Basis**—Specify whether you want to use accrual basis or cash basis reporting.

- **Header/Footer Content**—Designate if you want your changes in Excel to supersede changes you made in Report Designer.

- **Refresh from QuickBooks**—Restate the entire QSW Report (multiple statements) with updated QuickBooks data.

Statement Properties

When you need to modify properties that affect a single statement, not just a specific row or cell, use the Statement Properties task from the QSW Document Actions pane.

The Statement Properties task (shown in Figure B.13), controls changes made to the currently selected financial statement:

- **Title**—Modify the currently selected title in the Statement Properties pane or optionally modify the title directly in the appropriate Excel data cell.

- **Class Filter**—Filter for all classes, specific class, or for multiple classes.

- **Jobs Filter**—Filter for all jobs, specific jobs, or for multiple jobs.

- **Zero-Balance Accounts**—When selected, this option shows accounts with a zero balance; when not selected, accounts with a zero balance are hidden.

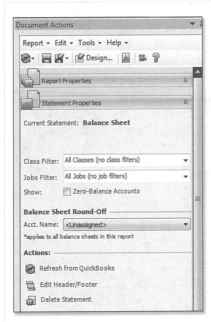

Figure B.13
Modify a selected statement from the Statement Properties panel.

- **Balance Sheet Round-Off**—Assign the account you will use for any rounding differences.

- **Refresh from QuickBooks**—Restate the currently selected statement with updated QuickBooks data.

- **Edit Header/Footer**—Change to the Header/Footer.

- **Delete Statement**—Remove a statement from a QSW Report.

Row Properties

To make a change to a specific row, and not affect other rows, review the features of the Row Properties task of the QSW Document Actions.

The Row Properties, shown in Figure B.14, affect formatting for the selected row and offer the following functionality when selecting a blank row:

- **Type**—Change the type of data that is represented in the cell, including Blank, Captions, Headings, Account (QuickBooks data), or Total types. For more information see the Table B.1 "Row Total Specifications" in this chapter.

- **Name**—Change the label of the cell (with the cell selected); the default is the account name.

Figure B.14
Use the Row Properties options to control the data you view in a particular row.

- **Manage Accounts**—Select from the following:

    - Combine accounts from selected rows

    - Add accounts by number, type, or name

    - Separate accounts that were previously combined

    - Remove accounts

    - Override zero-balance settings (from Statement Properties)

    - Reverse all the positive and negative numbers in the row.

- **Insert Rows**—Choose from Blank, Captions, Headings, Account (QuickBooks data), or Total types.

- **Delete**—Delete currently selected row. You have to use the QSW Delete Column function because the Excel worksheet is protected from using the Excel Delete command.

 tip

Did you know that to change the text in a row label, you can make the change directly in the Row Properties pane with the row selected, or simply type the new text directly into the appropriate cell of the spreadsheet? Entering new text using either of these options updates the Row Properties pane and the row label viewed for the statement.

Combine Account Rows

QuickBooks offers users a lot of flexibility for working with a chart of accounts. Often, several chart of account list items might have been created since your last review of the data. The QSW tool enables you to create customized financials grouping accounts together without affecting the client's original chart of accounts.

To combine account rows, follow these steps:

1. With the QSW statement open, click to highlight any two or more cells you want to combine into a single row. In the example shown in Figure B.15, the cells for Checking, Savings, and Petty Cash are selected.

Use the Control key on your keyboard to select multiple rows.

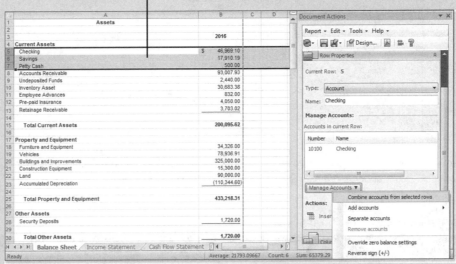

Figure B.15
Combine multiple QuickBooks account rows into one in the customized financials. No change is made to the QuickBooks file.

2. With multiple cells selected that you want to "roll up," select Combine Accounts from Selected Rows from the Manage Accounts drop-down list. Optionally select the Combine Accounts icon from the Excel Add-Ins ribbon.

3. Rename the label either in the Row Properties task or directly in the Excel cell. Figure B.16 shows that the row was renamed to Cash and Cash Equivalents.

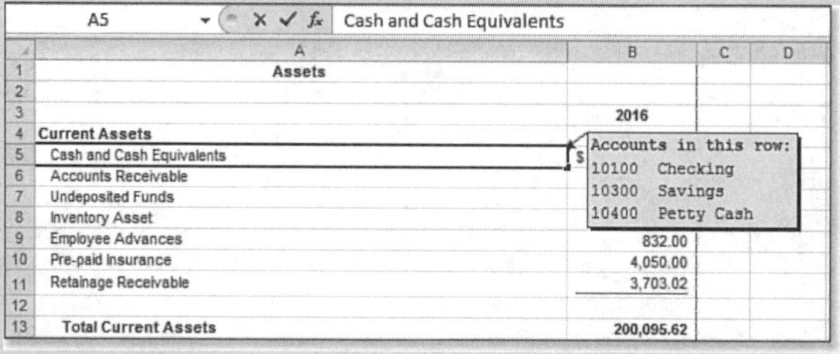

Figure B.16
Multiple cash rows are now included in a single row. Mouse over the row to see the accounts included.

4. Hover your mouse over the row to see a note of the accounts that are included in the new cell total.

To separate the accounts, in step 2 choose the Separate Accounts menu choice.

One of the most efficient uses in customizing your client's financials is the capability to combine "like" rows of data into a single row. Your financials will be more professional in appearance, while not affecting the client's chart of accounts.

New for QuickBooks Statement Writer 2012 is improved row Total types. Table B.1 provides some technical information on the characteristics of the different Total types:

Table Appendix B.1   Row Total Specifications

Total Row Type	Behavior
Total 4	Inserts a Total 4 row
	The row is inserted and the total is the sum of all accounts above this line and after the previous total.
	An underscore appears below the last value in the Total 4 group of accounts.
	The Row takes on the Total 4 Style.
Total 3	Inserts a Total 3 row
	All accounts and Total 4s above the current row and below the previous secondary caption or Total 3 row are included.
	An underscore appears below the last value in the Total 3 group of accounts.
	A blank row is inserted above the Total 3 row.
	The Row takes on the Total 3 Style.

Total Row Type	Behavior
Total 2	Inserts a Total 2 row
	All Total 3s above the current row and below the previous secondary caption are included.
	An underscore appears below the last account and Total 3 value in the secondary group.
	A blank row is inserted above the Total 3 row.
	The Row takes on the Total 2 Style.
Total 1	Inserts a Total 1 row
	All accounts and Total 2s, 3s, and 4s within the group above the new row and below the previous Total 1 or primary caption are included.
	A double underscore appears below the last value in the Total 1.
	A blank row is inserted above the Total 1 row.
	The Row takes on the Total 1 Style.

Column Properties

Use the Column Properties task (see Figure B.17) to change the properties of the selected column in the QSW statement. The options available in the Column Properties pane change depending on the type of column that is current when the pane is selected.

- **Type**—Choose the type of data in the column: Blank, Accounts (the column or statement header), Variance, % of the Whole, Summary Total, and Grand Total. Each type has its own unique column property options.

- **Heading**—Control the heading title of the currently selected column.

Depending on what type of column you have selected, the following menu options change:

- **Period**—Change the accounting period for the currently selected column.

- **Show Data**—Select to display past years for the same accounting period; used for side-by-side analysis.

- **Filter for Class**—If you are using class tracking, select all classes, combination of classes, or a single class.

- **Filter for Job**—Filter for all jobs, combination of jobs, or a single job.

- **Insert Column(s)**—Use to add columns from the specified allowed types. Types include Blank, Account Numbers, QuickBooks Data, Variance, % of the Whole, Summary Total, and Grand Total.

- **Delete**—Click to select the column you want to delete and then click the Delete Column button on the Column Properties pane. You have to use the QSW Delete Column function because the Excel worksheet is protected from using the Excel Delete command.

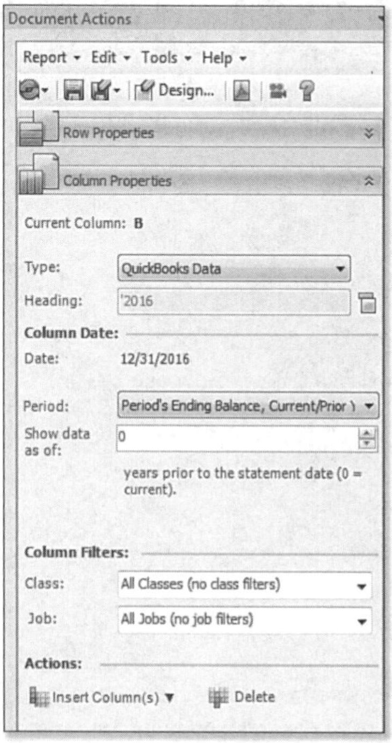

Figure B.17
Place your cursor in a column and then from the Column Properties panel control the contents of that column.

Cell Properties

The Cell QSW actions will vary by the type of cell selected. In Figure B.18 an account amount cell is selected. Cell Properties include:

- **Current Cell**—Indicate the cell reference for the currently selected cell.

- **Cell Type**—Determined and set by either row or column properties.

- **Temporary Balance Override**—Define a manual amount for an account cell.

- **Override Date**—Override the selected date for a specific cell, so the date range differs from the rest of the statement data.

- **Reset Date**—Return the cell date to match the date assigned to the entire statement.

- **Insert Field(s)**—Add any of the following information to a selected blank cell:

    - Accountant Information

    - Client Information

    - Basis

- Statement "From" Date

- Statement "To" Date

- Formatted Statement Date

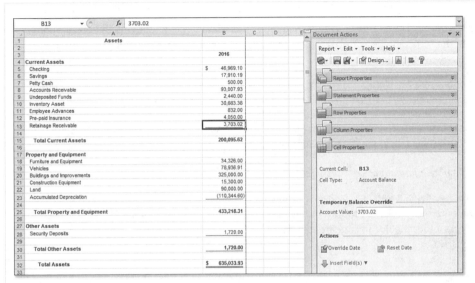

Figure B.18
Use the Cell Properties to manage the information displayed in a specific data cell.

Method 3: Using the Excel Add-Ins Ribbon Icons

You can also access selected editing functions from the Excel Add-Ins ribbon icon shown in Figure B.19.

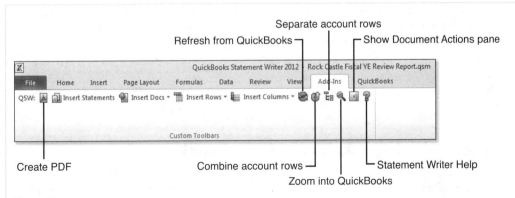

Figure B.19
Reinstate the QSW Document Actions pane and other activities available from the QSW toolbar.

Working with Supporting Documents

Another feature of the QuickBooks Statement Writer 2012 tool is the capability to create supporting documents to the customized statements.

There are two types of supporting documents you can add to your QSW statement:

- **Documents From Templates**—Created from templates that merge accountant and client information from the company file with boilerplate text. These documents are created with Word and have a file extension .dot.

- **Documents From My Computer**—Word documents you have already created and do not contain merged information. There are no limitations to the content of these documents.

You can add documents from templates or documents stored on your computer. Templates are both those that are shipped with the QSW product and those you can download directly from Intuit.

 For more information, see "Resources," p. 663.

The following sections detail how to create or modify existing document templates and then attach them to your Statement Writer report. When you complete your client's customized financials, you can specify the order the documents are to print in.

Overview

You can add or modify the provided supporting document templates or you can create them on your own using Microsoft Word. Supporting documents can be a combination of both text (your own manually typed content) or dynamic data fields from the QuickBooks file, which are selected from a predefined list. For example:

"We have audited the accompanying statement of assets, liabilities, and equity—(cash, income tax basis) of «Client Company Name»."

In the preceding text, the first part of the sentence is manually typed text. The field name is Client Company Name. The chevrons («») are required and are added automatically by Microsoft Word. When the final report is printed, the data from QuickBooks (in this example, the Client Company Name) is replaced where the field name is listed in the template.

When you are creating a template with merged fields, you use a Microsoft Word .dot file. The only time you open the .dot file is when you need to modify the template details. When the final report is prepared, the field names will look for current data from the QuickBooks file you are using with QSW.

Adding or Modifying a Supporting Document

You might have added a supporting document when you created the Statement Report using the Report Designer. In Figure B.5 a Cover Letter document was added to the Financial Report Contents in Report Designer. If you did not add documents during the Report Designer setup, you can add them from the Document button in the Report Properties panel as shown in Figure B.20.

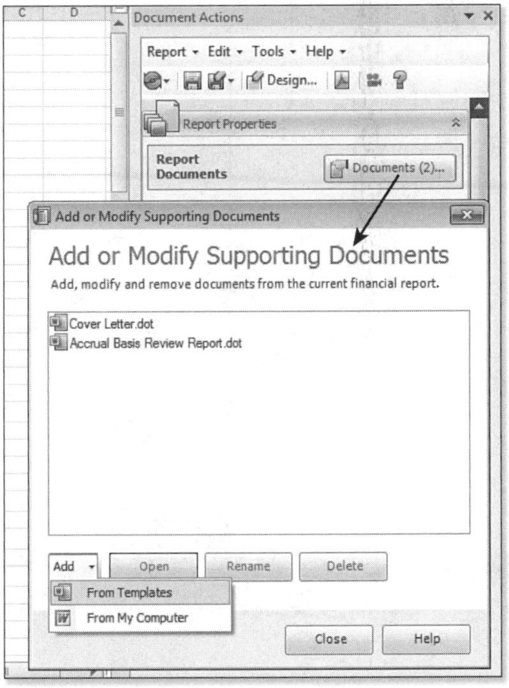

Figure B.20
View, add, open, rename, and delete supporting documents.

To add or modify a supporting document, follow these steps:

1. Open a Statement Writer report. From the Document Actions pane, expand the Report Properties panel.

2. Click the Documents button. The Add or Modify Supporting Documents dialog box displays any documents currently included in the Statement Report.

3. Click Add, to choose to add From Templates or From My Computer.

4. If you select From Templates, the Insert Documents dialog box displays as shown in Figure B.21.

5. Select the desired document template on the left and click the arrow pointing to the right to include the document in the Financial Report Contents.

6. Click OK. The new document displays in the Add or Modify Supporting Documents dialog box.

7. Optionally, with a document selected, click Rename or Delete.

8. To modify a selected document, click the Open button. QSW automatically launches Word.

Using templates saves you time by creating customized financial templates you can use with multiple clients Statement Writer reports.

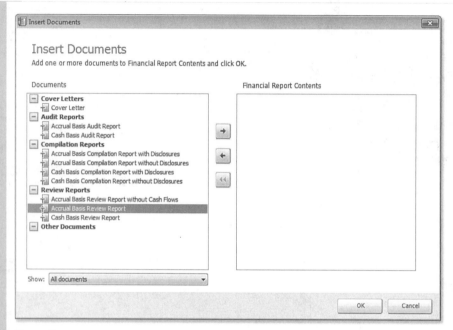

Figure B.21
Insert ready-made supporting documents or those you created.

Using the QSW Toolbar in Word

QSW adds a toolbar to Word to help you properly create supporting documents.

To access the toolbars in Word 2003, select View, choose Toolbars, and place a checkmark next to QuickBooks Statement Writer. In Word 2007 select the Add-Ins ribbon and QSW toolbar displays as shown in Figure B.22.

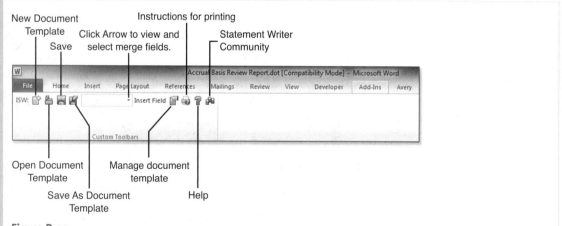

Figure B.22
Use the QSW toolbar in Word to create supporting documents with merged fields from the client's data.

Editing an Existing QSW Supporting Document

You might find it necessary to edit the text or fields in an existing QSW supporting document. You can access the Microsoft Word .dot templates directly from a QSW Report or you can browse to the stored templates directly from within Word.

To edit an existing QSW supporting document, follow these steps:

1. Launch the QSW tool from within QuickBooks.

2. From the Document Actions pane, Statement Properties, click the Documents button.

3. A list displays any supporting documents currently assigned to this QSW Report (refer to Figure B.20). Select a supporting document then click the Open button and skip to step 8. If no supporting documents are listed, go to step 4.

4. Click the Add button, and select From Templates.

5. The Insert Documents dialog box displays as shown in Figure B.21. Select a specific document and in the center of the window, click the arrow pointing to the right to add the selected document to the Financial Report Contents pane.

6. Optionally, select Show, All Documents, Intuit Documents, Custom Documents, or Custom Template Groups to filter for specific documents to choose from.

7. Repeat step 5 until you have added the necessary documents to your QSW report. Click OK to close the Insert Documents dialog box.

   The Add or Modify Supporting Documents dialog box displays with a list of added documents.

8. Click the Rename button if you want to give the document a new name for this QSW report.

9. Click the Open button. QSW opens the .dot template in Microsoft Word.

10. Edit the text as needed using Word's editing functions.

11. To add or edit merged data fields in Word 2003, select the QSW Toolbar. For Word 2007 and 2010 users, click the Add-Ins ribbon.

12. With your mouse in the location on the document where you want to add the merged field, select the desired field from the Insert Field drop-down menu as shown in Figure B.23.

13. When you are finished with your edits on the QSW Toolbar, click the Save button to save over the original document. Click the Save As button to save the document with a different name.

14. When you click Save As, the Save As—Document Template dialog box displays. Provide a Name for the template and choose a Type from the drop-down list as shown in Figure B.24.

15. Click OK to close the Save As—Document Template dialog box.

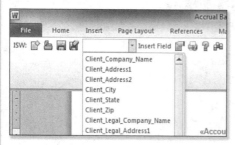

Figure B.23
Add QuickBooks data fields to customized document templates.

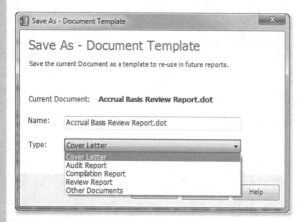

Figure B.24
Save your new supporting document as a template to be used with other client files.

Creating a New QSW Supporting Document

You can optionally create your own supporting document templates and store them on your computer.

To create a new QSW supporting document, follow these steps:

1. Open Microsoft Word.

2. Add the text or images as needed using Word editing functions.

3. To add or edit merged data fields in Word 2003, select the QSW toolbar. For Word 2007 or 2010 users, click the Add-Ins ribbon.

4. With your mouse in the location on the document where you want to add the merged field, select the desired field from the drop-down list items.

5. Click the Insert Field link (refer to Figure B.23) on the QSW toolbar.

6. When you are finished with your edits on the QSW toolbar, click the Save button to save over the original document. Click the Save As button to save the document with a different name.

7. When you click Save As, the Save As—Document Template dialog box displays (refer to Figure B.24). Provide a Name for the template and choose a Type from the drop-down list.

Now that you have created a new supporting document, you can attach the document to your QSW report so you can print a complete set of customized financials for your clients. Read on to the next section to learn more about attaching supporting documents.

Printing or Exporting a Statement Writer Report

In the previous section you learned how to add or modify supporting documents to your QSW report, making it a complete set of custom financials ready to print. QSW creates a PDF of the complete report set so you can print, send via email, and store it for future reference.

To print or export a Statement Writer report, follow these steps:

1. Launch the QSW tool from within QuickBooks.

2. If you have just opened your QSW Report, the QuickBooks data has automatically refreshed. If you have been modifying the QSW report or QuickBooks data, refresh the data by clicking the Refresh button on the Document Actions pane.

3. From the Document Actions pane, select Save As, QSW Report, Excel Workbook, Template Group, or PDF.

   If you selected Save as PDF, the Create PDF dialog box displays as shown in Figure B.25. The Available Report Contents show each of the statements and supporting documents you have included in this QSW report.

4. On the left pane, select a statement or document to include in your PDF.

5. Use the arrow pointing to the right to include the selected statement or document in the PDF Contents pane.

6. Select an item in the PDF Contents pane, and use the up or down arrow to organize the print order for your financials.

7. Optionally, select Set as Default Order so you do not have to make these choices again.

8. Optionally, select Open PDF upon Save.

9. Click Create.

10. If you selected Save as Excel Workbook, QSW opens a Windows Explorer window.

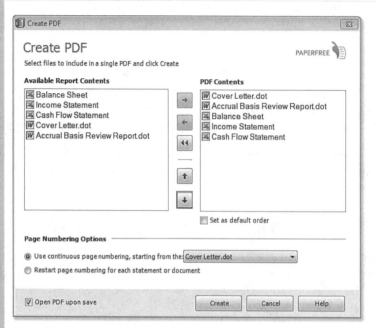

Figure B.25
You define the print order of the documents when creating a PDF.

11. Browse to the computer folder to which your Excel workbook should be saved and give the workbook a filename. Click Save.

Accounting professionals can use QSW to create financial reports that include statements and supporting documents. These reports can be saved as templates for use with other client files and for updating with future dated information.

 caution

When you export your QSW report to Excel, it is no longer linked to QuickBooks and therefore cannot be updated or refreshed.

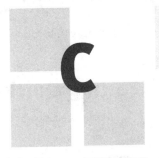

QUICKBOOKS SHORTCUTS

Introduction

These Windows keyboard shortcuts are provided to help you work efficiently in QuickBooks. With these shortcuts, you can keep your hands on the keyboard and minimize the time you might otherwise waste when using a computer mouse to activate a command or move to field on a transaction.

Editing QuickBooks Transactions and Lists

Use these shortcuts to save time editing a transaction or list in QuickBooks.

Key	Action
Ctrl+Del	Deletes the selected line in a transaction
Ctrl+Insert	Inserts a blank detail line in a transaction above your cursor
Ctrl+N	Creates a new transaction or list item
Ctrl+D	Deletes the current transaction or list item
Ctrl+E	Edits the selected item
Alt+S	Saves the selected transaction
Alt+N	Saves the selected transaction and advances to the next same type transaction
Alt+P	Saves the selected transaction and advances to the previous same type transaction
+	When in a field the Plus key advances to the next date or next number
-	When in a field the Minus key retreats to the previous date or previous number
Ctrl+Right Arrow	Advances to the next word in a text string
Ctrl+Left Arrow	Returns to the previous word in a text string

Opening QuickBooks Dialog Boxes and Lists

With an open QuickBooks file, use these shortcuts to open a variety of dialog boxes and lists.

Key	Action
F1	Opens QuickBooks Help
F2	Opens QuickBooks diagnostic information
F3	Opens the Search dialog box for company file information
F4	Opens the QuickBooks Technical Support Helper, where you can provide technical information to an Intuit QuickBooks support agent when troubleshooting a database issue
Ctrl+W	Opens the Write Checks dialog box
Ctrl+Q	Opens a QuickReport for the selected or related list item
Ctrl+Y	Opens a Transaction Journal report for the selected transaction

Key	Action
Ctrl+L	Opens the appropriate list on an open transaction in a field with a drop-down list
Ctrl+J	Opens the Customer Center
Ctrl+A	Opens the Chart of Accounts list
Ctrl+I	Opens the Create Invoices dialog box
Ctrl+R	Opens the Use Register dialog box
Ctrl+P	On an open transaction, report, or list, displays print options
Ctrl+D	Deletes the selected transaction or list item
Ctrl+F	Launches the Find dialog box, or with an open transaction displays Find filtered for that specific transaction type
Ctrl+H	On an open transaction, opens the Transaction History dialog box

Memorized Transactions

Use these keyboard shortcuts to save repeating transactions or to open the Memorized Transaction list.

Key	Action
Ctrl+M	From a displayed transaction, opens the Memorize Transaction dialog box
Ctrl+T	Opens the Memorized Transaction list

Standard Text Editing

These shortcuts make adding or modifying text more efficient.

Key	Action
Ctrl+Z	Undo typing or changes made in a field
Ctrl+X	Cut (delete) selected text
Ctrl+C	Copy selected text
Ctrl+V	Paste selected text
Del	Delete a character to the right
Backspace	Delete a character to the left

Opening QuickBooks Data Files

These shortcuts change how QuickBooks starts.

Key	Action
Ctrl	Before launching QuickBooks, press the Ctrl key on your keyboard. The No Company Open dialog box displays, where you can select from other listed data files. This shortcut is useful if you have trouble opening the last company file you accessed.
Alt	Before launching QuickBooks, press the Alt key on your keyboard. QuickBooks will launch without opening the dialog boxes that were open when you exited QuickBooks. This can be useful if your file takes a long time to open.

QuickBooks Date Shortcuts

Use these shortcuts to efficiently change dates on transactions or reports.

Key	Action
+	Plus key, advance to the next day
-	Minus key, previous day
T	Today
W	First day of the week
K	Last day of the week
M	First day of the month
H	Last day of the month
Y	First day of the year
R	Last day of the year
Alt+Down Arrow	In a date field, opens the calendar
[	For same date in previous week
]	For same date in next week
;	For same date last month
'	For same date next month

Miscellaneous Shortcuts

Be sure to test these out, they are sure to save you time as you work with QuickBooks transactions.

Key	Action
Shift+Tab	Returns to the prior field
Alt+F4	Closes QuickBooks and displays the No Company Open dialog box
Home	Returns to the first character in a field
End	Advances to the last character in a field
Tab	Advances to the next field
Ctrl+Page Up	Returns to the top of a long dialog box
Ctrl+Page Down	Advances to the bottom of a long dialog box
Ctrl+F6	Toggles between open dialog boxes (moves between items on the Open Windows list)

INDEX

Home Page

Company Snapshot, setting as default page, 476

customer activities, customizing, 254

customizing, 46-50

for vendor activities, 185

data display, customizing, 49-50

icons, customizing, 46-49

I

icon bar, 45-47

Calc icon, adding, 47

icons, customizing on Home page, 46-49

identifying uncleared transactions, 464-465

IIF (Intuit Interchange Format) files

importing, 92-94, 127-128

importing

accountants' changes, 530-533

IIF files, 92-94, 127-128

report templates, 490

timer activities, 599-600

income, in chart of accounts list, 79

income statements, 61

installing

maintenance releases, 560-561

QuickBooks

for multi-user mode, 554-555

required Windows permissions, 557-558

for single-user mode, 554

QuickBooks Timer, 596

Intuit Data Protect, 567

Intuit Online Payroll subscription, 381

inventory

accounting, overview, 111-112

aged accounts payable, reviewing, 176

aged item receipts, reviewing, 173-176

average cost valuation, reviewing, 170-173

backorders, handling, 152-155

features of different QuickBooks versions, 111-115

items

adding, 121-137

assemblies, 119-120, 131-133, 150-152

group items, 119-120, 133-134, 149-150

inventory part, 119

non-inventory part, 119

prices, changing, 128-130

receiving, 143-145

Multiple Unit of Measure feature, 134-137

negative inventory, 178-183

average cost from prior purchase transactions, handling, 179-183

paying for, 146-148

physical inventory count, performing, 160

quantity adjustments, 161-162

returns, handling, 155-158

selling, 148-149

value adjustments, performing, 162-165

vendor bill, entering, 145-146

vendor returns, handling, 158

Inventory Center, 165-166

Inventory feature

preferences, 115-118

purchase orders, creating, 142-143

transactions, types of, 139

inventory part item, 119

adding, 121-123

J-K

L

Q

R

How can we make this index more useful? Email us at indexes@quepublishing.com

W

X-Y-Z